PETERSON'S

GRADUATE SCHOOLS IN THE U.S.
1999

PETERSON'S
Princeton, New Jersey

About Peterson's

Peterson's is the country's largest educational information/communications company, providing the academic, consumer, and professional communities with books, software, and online services in support of lifelong education access and career choice. Well-known references include Peterson's annual guides to private schools, summer programs, colleges and universities, graduate and professional programs, financial aid, international study, adult learning, and career guidance. Peterson's Web site at petersons.com is the only comprehensive—and most heavily traveled—education resource on the Internet. The site carries all of Peterson's fully searchable major databases and includes financial aid sources, test-prep help, job postings, direct inquiry and application features, and specially created Virtual Campuses for every accredited academic institution and summer program in the U.S. and Canada that offers in-depth narratives, announcements, and multimedia features.

The colleges and universities represented in this book recognize that federal laws, where applicable, require compliance with Title IX (Education Amendments of 1972), Title VII (Civil Rights Act of 1964), and Section 504 of the Rehabilitation Act of 1973 as amended, prohibiting discrimination on the basis of sex, race, color, handicap, or national or ethnic origin in their educational programs and activities, including admissions and employment.

Editorial inquiries concerning this book should be addressed to:
Editor, Peterson's, P.O. Box 2123, Princeton, New Jersey 08543-2123

ISSN 1522-5623
ISBN 0-7689-0207-X

Composition and design by Peterson's

Printed in the United States of America

10 9 8 7 6 5 4 3 2 1

Contents

Introduction

About University Wire

University Wire was founded on the principle that college news is important. We believe that college students deserve the best news and information available, written by their peers and relevant to their lives. To gather that information, we tap into the hub of student life at any university—the campus paper. U-Wire is the premier source for campus news in the United States, with a finger on the pulse of more than 400 colleges and universities in fifty states. Every day, more than 2 million people nationwide gain a greater understanding of what it means be a college student today by reading U-Wire stories. Linking college students and faculty members across the country and keeping them informed, U-Wire and our parent company, Student Advantage, strive to make college life easier, more interesting, and more fun.

Now, by teaming up with Peterson's, U-Wire enters the higher education guide market with that same commitment to providing accurate, comprehensive information. The result is the Peterson's/U-Wire Graduate Studies Series. Whether you're currently an undergraduate student or you're working and contemplating going back to school, these guides have the information you need to help you make sound decisions as you plan your graduate school career.

Is Graduate School Right for You?

Recent data from the U.S. Census Bureau confirms that annual income is strongly related to degree attainment. Average annual earnings in America range from $13,697 for those without a high school diploma to $82,749 for those with professional degrees. However, an increase in salary shouldn't be your only consideration when deciding to pursue a graduate degree. You should carefully evaluate your strengths, personal preferences, and career objectives before you commit the time and money it takes to get your degree.

Motivation and persistence are good indicators of success in graduate school. You'll most likely spend a lot more time studying for your advanced degree than you did for your bachelor's, so check your motivation level. Are you ready to commit to more coffee-fueled nights in the library? Study sessions? Labs and problem sets? No matter what your field, going to grad school requires a serious commitment to academic life.

Your grad school experience will be more fun and rewarding if you work well with others. The intellectual interchange between students can be very stimulating, and you'll have more contact with faculty than you had as an undergraduate. It is crucial to establish a good rapport with your faculty mentors because they can have a huge impact on your future career.

Quality of life is an important consideration when deciding to pursue a graduate degree. You need to think about how graduate school will affect your personal life. Can you afford tuition and expenses if you're going to school full-time and earning no income? Can you afford to incur student loans and credit card debt? Can you find a program that will allow you to attend school part-time while you work or employ you as a teaching or residential assistant? Do you have family or relationship commitments that will be affected by your decision to attend grad school? Will you eventually get a good return on your grad school investment through an increased salary?

Finally, evaluate your career objectives to determine where an advanced degree fits in. A professional degree will rapidly advance your career in a specific area. If you already have some work experience related to that profession, even better. Earning a professional degree can be a relatively short-term investment of time and money that generates great rewards. The benefits of a professional degree include greater career mobility and flexibility, a higher salary, more responsibility, and greater job security. Expect similar benefits from a master's degree in a research area. Earning your Ph.D. is a more significant time commitment that requires initiative, independence, and self-discipline. Ultimately, however, a Ph.D will offer the greatest freedom to determine your own career path and the flexibility to take advantage of opportunities that arise as you travel it.

Maximize Your Career Potential

In some fields, an advanced degree is required. In others, graduate credentials will help you obtain better employment opportunities and a higher salary. Either way, a graduate education will have a profound effect on your career, but only if you pursue the right program.

Unlike your bachelor's degree, graduate degrees are very focused. Professional degrees in fields such as law, medicine, and business give you the tools needed to perform at a high level within a very specific field, such as pediatric medicine or patent law. A master's degree in an academic area will open doors in education, business, or government. The Ph.D. is a teaching and research degree but by no means restricts you to the world of academia. A Ph.D. can also be very useful in research and development work for corporations or the government.

Finding the Perfect Fit

With more than 1,700 institutions around the country offering graduate degrees, you have to do your homework. When researching schools, size and location are important criteria to consider. According to the Council of Graduate Schools, other significant areas to research are:

• availability of programs in your field of interest
• admissions criteria
• prerequisites for enrollment
• financial aid policies and programs
• degree requirements
• potential for employment after graduation

Be sure to look at the strengths and weaknesses of the individual department where you will be studying, as well as at those of the entire school. From the application process, when the department faculty reviews your application, to your professional life, when you carry the reputation of that department with you, the quality of the department should be your first concern. Make sure you also match your interests against each program. If you don't think you'll be happy at a school, it may not matter how good its reputation is.

There are many good sources for this information. You should investigate as many as possible. Consider this guide the launching pad and framework of your graduate school search. We have all the contact and program information that you need to do your own informed investigation. To find the graduate school that's perfect for you, however, you'll have to go beyond the pages of a book. Ask trusted faculty members at your undergraduate institution where they obtained their advanced degrees. Talk to current students at the schools you are researching to learn what it's like to be a student at those institutions. Get on line and check out institutional and individual Web sites. Make some campus visits to see if you can picture yourself living and studying there happily.

Your grad school career will be very different from your undergraduate one, and, we hope, it will be rewarding in many ways. With a little effort, you'll find the school that exactly suits your needs and preferences. Good luck!

_____

Kelly Bare Executive Editor, U-Wire Books

How to Use This Book

Overview

Peterson's/U-Wire: Graduate Schools in the U.S. 1999 provides general information on the graduate and professional programs offered by accredited colleges and universities in the United States and U.S. territories that are accredited by U.S. accrediting bodies recognized by the Department of Education or the Council on Higher Education Accreditation. A total of 771 institutions are profiled.

This book serves as an excellent starting point for individuals who are thinking of attending graduate school and who would like to begin researching their options. Whether you are certain of the field in which you'd like to do graduate work or whether you are considering several possible areas of study, this book will help you to target the schools that might best be suited to your needs and interests. You may already have one or more schools in mind, or for geographical or financial reasons, you may be interested in attending a particular institution and will want to know what it has to offer. Once again, this book is your best bet to help you begin narrowing the field and, hopefully, find the right school and program where you'll spend your days as a grad student.

This book gives the essential information on everything from applying to school to paying for it. The Introduction outlines some important issues for those considering graduate school, while The Insider's Guide to Graduate School, written by Kevin Boyer, Executive Director of the National Association of Graduate-Professional Students, contains information on what every graduate student needs to know. The Application Process addresses researching different graduate programs to choose the one that's right for you, setting a timetable for the various aspects of applying to graduate school, and finding out how to meet your chosen school's requirements, including advice on writing an application essay and succeeding in an interview. Paying for Graduate School describes the many sources of financial aid available to students and gives advice on managing your debt. Graduate Admissions Tests gives descriptions of and contact information for such standardized tests as the Graduate Record Examinations, Miller Analogies Test, Graduate Management Admission Test, Test of English as a Foreign Language, and the Praxis Series Tests for prospective teachers, as well as the admissions tests for medical, dental, law, and veterinary schools. Accreditation and Accrediting Agencies explains how institutions and programs become accredited and lists the different regional and specialized accrediting bodies. Abbreviations Used in This Book includes abbreviations of degree names, tests, and organizations and agencies used in the profiles. The Directory of Graduate Programs by Field lists the fields of study that are covered in the profiles, with an alphabetical listing of each of the institutions offering graduate or professional work in that field. Organized alphabetically by subject area, the Directory of Combined-Degree Programs lists the specific combined degrees available at each institution. Following the Profiles of Institutions Offering Graduate and Professional Work is an appendix, which lists the city, state, zip code, and the general application contact for every institution that is not Carnegie-classified as described below.

Profiles of Institutions Offering Graduate and Professional Work

HOW PROGRAMS ARE CLASSIFIED

This book uses the Carnegie Classification system to help you better identify which graduate schools and programs might be suited to your particular interests. Briefly, each institution profiled is classified as one of the following types of institutions:

- **Research Universities I**—These institutions award graduate degrees through the doctorate and give high priority to research. They award fifty or more doctoral degrees each year. In addition, they receive $40 million or more annually in federal support.
- **Research Universities II**—These institutions award graduate degrees through the doctorate and give high priority to research. They award fifty or more doctoral degrees each year and receive between $15.5 million and $40 million annually in federal support.
- **Doctoral Universities I**—These institutions award graduate degrees through the doctorate. They award at least forty doctoral degrees annually in five or more disciplines.
- **Doctoral Universities II**—These institutions award graduate degrees through the doctorate. They award annually at least ten doctoral degrees in three or more disciplines or twenty or more doctoral degrees in one or more disciplines.
- **Master's (Comprehensive) Universities and Colleges I**—These institutions, committed to graduate education through the master's degree, award forty or more master's degrees annually in three or more disciplines.
- **Master's (Comprehensive) Universities and Colleges II**—These institutions, committed to graduate education through the master's degree, award twenty or more master's degrees annually in one or more disciplines.

SCHOOL AND PROGRAM INFORMATION

In this book information is presented in profile form. Each profile serves as a capsule summary of basic information about

each institution. The format of the profiles is constant, making it easy to compare one institution with another and one program with another.

The following outline describes the profile information found in this guide and explains how best to use that information. Any item that does not apply to or was not provided by a graduate unit is omitted from its listing.

Identifying Information. The institution's name and address are followed by the institution's World Wide Web address, all in boldface type.

Enrollment. Figures for the number of students enrolled in graduate and professional programs pertain to the semester of highest enrollment from the 1997–98 academic year.

Graduate Faculty. Figures on the number of faculty members actively involved with graduate students through teaching or research are given.

Computer Facilities. A brief description of the computer facilities (campuswide network, Internet access, etc.) available at the institution is given.

Library Facilities. The resources of the institution's library or libraries are briefly described here.

Graduate Expenses. The cost of study for the 1998–99 academic year is given in two basic categories, tuition and fees. It is not possible to represent the complete tuition and fees schedule for each graduate unit, so a simplified version of the cost of studying in that unit is provided. Cost of study may be quite complex at a graduate institution, and prospective students are encouraged to contact the academic department administering the program of study for applicable tuition and fee information.

General Application Contact. The name listed is the person you should contact with general questions about applying to the institution, such as the Dean or Coordinator of Graduate Studies. The person's phone number is included.

Offerings. Each school of the highest academic or administrative units of the institution is listed, with the name of the unit head and his or her title following. Each field of study offered by the unit is listed with all postbaccalaureate degrees awarded in that area of study. To obtain information about a specific school or program at the institution, contact the name of the school or college head listed. If no unit head is given, you should contact the overall institution's general application contact for information on graduate admissions.

DATA COLLECTION AND EDITORIAL PROCEDURES

The information published in this book is collected through Peterson's Annual Survey of Graduate Institutions. Each spring and summer we send the survey to more than 1,700 institutions offering postbaccalaureate degree programs, including accredited institutions in the United States and U.S. territories. Deans and other administrators complete these surveys, providing information on specific programs as well as overall institutional information. Peterson's editorial staff then goes over each returned survey carefully and verifies or revises responses after further research and discussion with administrators at the institutions. Extensive files on past responses are kept from year to year.

While every effort is made to ensure the accuracy and completeness of the data, information is sometimes unavailable or changes occur after publication deadlines. All usable information received in time for publication has been included. The omission of any particular item from a directory or profile signifies either that the item is not applicable to the institution or program or that information was not available. Profiles of programs scheduled to begin during the 1998–99 academic year cannot, of course, include statistics on enrollment or, in many cases, the number of faculty members. If no usable information was submitted by an institution, its name, address, and program name are still included in order to indicate the existence of graduate work.

FOR MORE INFORMATION . . .

In addition to information about financial aid for graduate students and the GRE, the CD-ROM included in the back of this book contains in-depth descriptions of 308 of the schools profiled and listed in the appendix. These in-depth descriptions have been submitted by institutions that chose to prepare detailed program descriptions.

Additional information on institutions that do not have an in-depth description on the CD-ROM may be obtained by writing directly to the dean of the graduate school.

 Schools that have in-depth descriptions on the CD-ROM are marked next to their profile or appendix listing by the CD-ROM icon shown here. In addition to listing the degree programs available, each in-depth description provides detailed information on the school's research facilities, tuition and living and housing costs, financial aid, general school location, student profile, and institution history, application procedures, and faculty members—in short, facts that all prospective graduate students need to know about an institution when selecting a graduate program.

The Insider's Guide to Graduate School

Presumably, by picking up this book, you are close to making the decision to attend graduate school. If so, you will be one of America's 2.5 million students pursuing a postbaccalaureate degree. As you plan your degree program, please consider the issues below. If you're just thinking about graduate school, incorporate some of these issues in your decision-making process.

Will graduate work advance your career? Many people pursue graduate degrees as a career-enhancing move. Graduate degrees are increasingly important in the business world and in the nonprofit and public sectors. Graduate degrees have always been a key to success in academic employment. However, a graduate degree will not automatically enhance your career opportunities unless it is the right degree. Take the time to research the degree requirements of the career you are considering. Talk with people already in that field. Question personnel managers or career placement professionals.

Will your graduate work "net" you back enough to cover your debt? Whether you go to school full- or part-time, you will probably end up incurring student loan or credit card debt. Is it worth it? Graduate student loan debt is rising much faster than the cost of living and faster than tuition increases. Why? Few grants and scholarships are being offered, and more students have to choose student loans to pay for tuition, books, fees, and room and board.

The university you select will have a financial aid office that can help you choose the appropriate financial aid package for you. But they might ask you a basic question—"Will you get enough back to make this debt worth it?" A $50,000 student loan debt (which ends up costing you $75,000 or more if you take several years to repay the note) may not be worth the increase in salary you get as a result.

Remember that you will lose wages if you quit work to go back to school full-time, so plan your budget accordingly. Graduate and professional programs are great mind-expanding experiences. Get your graduate degree, but keep you eyes on your wallet so that the costs don't become mind-numbing.

Are you being swayed by marketing strategies when selecting your program? This book offers a great way to get basic information about university graduate programs. Universities also spend a lot of time and money marketing themselves so that you choose one over another. Differences in campuses can be striking. Even programs and departments on one campus can be very different from others.

You wouldn't select a university on the basis of its football team if you were a baseball player, so be sure to select your university *and* department based upon information from *that* department. You'd be surprised at how a small college or a state university can have a particular program that is much better than a private university or that a large public or private university program can have the same intimate feel you would expect from a smaller university.

Are you relying on "official" sources of information too strongly? Everyone knows that the best way to get a job is not through the help wanted ads but through "networking" with those who are in a position to make referrals and hires. The same is true of graduate programs. The best way to find out about a program is to talk with graduate students already in the program.

Sure, the "official" university and department information needs to be gathered first, but, as you close in on your decision, take the time to talk with graduate students in the programs you are considering. Ask the program or department chair to recommend 2 or 3 students with whom you can speak. Ask them questions about everything: How are grad students treated by faculty members? What are the "unwritten" expectations of those who serve as research or teaching assistants? What are the on-campus facilities like? Do graduate students socialize together?

Be sure to contact the university's Graduate Student Association (GSA). This organization can tell you about interdepartmental social events, campus parking, health facilities, and benefits for graduate student employees. If the university doesn't have a university-wide or departmental GSA, find out why not. A campus without an organization designed to represent graduate students and their interests might have a climate that makes being a graduate student difficult.

If you'll be a graduate student employee, what trade-offs will you have to make? Serving as a teaching assistant (TA) or research assistant (RA) or teaching an undergraduate course can be one of the most fulfilling parts of your graduate education. Most campuses pay a stipend and waive tuition for graduate teaching and research assistants. Being a TA or RA can provide real financial and educational benefits.

However, there are trade-offs, and sometimes these trade-offs vary greatly by department. Some departments have "official" work requirements that are very different from what you expected when put into practice. Some questions you might want to ask are: How many hours will you have to work per week? What kind of benefits are offered? Some universities offer excellent benefits to graduate student employees, while many other universities offer none. How will your stipend be eroded because you have to pay your own health insurance and parking permit fees?

Often there is a contractual relationship between you and your department. Does this contract offer you any protection? You may enter program with no previous teaching experience. Does the university or department offer TA training and resources? Is there a collective bargaining unit for graduate student employees?

Being a TA or an RA is usually a great value. Take the position, but keep your eyes and ears open, and know the procedures for pursuing a grievance should problems arise.

Once you've entered graduate school, remember to remain a whole person. Don't throw yourself into your studies to the detriment of your mental or physical health. Maintain your family relationships. Keep old friends—and make lots of new ones. Use the many resources on your new campus that are designed to keep you healthy and sane. Swim. Bike. Play tennis. Go to a GSA social hour. Visit campus cultural institutions. And, most importantly, enjoy graduate school. It can be the most rewarding experience of your life.

Kevin Boyer, Executive Director, National Association of Graduate-Professional Students (NAGPS)

NAGPS is a nonprofit organization designed to provide a mechanism for exchange of information among graduate/professional students, foster the development of graduate/professional student organizations, and improve the quality of graduate/professional education and student life in general. NAGPS offers many resources to students at member campuses and to student members. Student memberships are available for $22.50 per year and include a subscription to the NAGPS bimonthly news publication, a student discount card, and access to NAGPS' endorsed health insurance and dental plan, as well as many other benefits. To learn more about NAGPS, contact: NAGPS, 825 Green Bay Road, Suite 270, Wilmette, IL 60091; telephone: 888-88-NAGPS; fax: 847-256-8954; e-mail: nagps@netcom.com; World Wide Web: http://www.nagps.org/NAGPS/.

The Application Process

The decision to attend graduate school and the choice of an institution and degree program require serious consideration. The time, money, and energy you will expend doing graduate work are significant, and you will want to analyze your options carefully. Before you begin filing applications, you should evaluate your interests and goals, know what programs are available, and be clear about your reasons for pursuing a particular degree.

There are two excellent reasons for attending graduate school, and if your decision is based on one of these, you probably have made the right choice. There are careers such as medicine, law, and college and university teaching that require specialized training and, therefore, necessitate advanced education. Another motivation is to specialize in a subject that you have decided is of great importance, either for career goals or for personal satisfaction.

Degrees

Traditionally, graduate education has involved acquiring and communicating knowledge gained through original research in a particular academic field. The highest earned academic degree, which requires the pursuit of original research, is the Doctor of Philosophy (Ph.D.). In contrast, professional training stresses the practical application of knowledge and skills; this is true, for example, in the fields of business, law, and medicine. At the doctoral level, degrees in these areas include the Doctor of Business Administration (D.B.A.), Juris Doctor (J.D.), and the Doctor of Medicine (M.D.).

Master's degrees are offered in most fields and may also be academic or professional in orientation. In many fields, the master's degree may be the only professional degree needed for employment. This is the case, for example, in fine arts (M.F.A.), library science (M.L.S.), and social work (M.S.W.). (For a list of the graduate and professional degrees currently being offered in the United States and Canada, readers may refer to the appendix of degree abbreviations.)

Some people decide to earn a master's degree at one institution and then select a different university or a somewhat different program of study for doctoral work. This can be a way of acquiring a broad background: you can choose a master's program with one emphasis or orientation and a doctoral program with another. The total period of graduate study may be somewhat lengthened by proceeding this way, but probably not by much.

In recent years, the distinctions between traditional academic programs and professional programs have become blurred. The course of graduate education has changed direction in the last thirty years, and many programs have redefined their shape and focus. There are centers and institutes for research, many graduate programs are now interdepartmental and interdisciplinary, off-campus graduate programs have multiplied, and part-time graduate programs have increased. Colleges and universities have also established combined-degree programs, in many cases in order to enable students to combine academic and professional studies. As a result of such changes, you now have considerable freedom in determining the program best suited to your current needs as well as your long-term goals.

Choosing a Specialization and Researching Programs

There are several sources of information you should make use of in choosing a specialization and a program. A good way to begin is to consult the appropriate directories in these guides, which will tell you what programs exist in the field or fields you are interested in and, for each one, will give you information on degrees, research facilities, the faculty, financial aid resources, tuition and other costs, application requirements, and so on.

Talk with your college adviser and professors about your areas of interest and ask for their advice about the best programs to research. Besides being very well informed themselves, these faculty members may have colleagues at institutions you are investigating, and they can give you inside information about individual programs and the kind of background they seek in candidates for admission.

The valuable perspective of educators should not be overlooked. If the faculty members you know through your courses are not involved in your field of interest, do not hesitate to contact other appropriate professors at your institution or neighboring institutions to ask for advice on programs that might suit your goals. In addition, talk to graduate students studying in your field of interest; their advice can be valuable also.

Your decision about a field of study may be determined by your research interests or, if you choose to enter a professional school, by the appeal of a particular career. In either case, as you attempt to limit the number of institutions you will apply to, you will want to familiarize yourself with publications describing current research in your discipline. Find related professional journals and note who is publishing in the areas of specialization that interest you, as well as where they are teaching. Take note of the institutions represented on the publications' editorial boards (they are usually listed on the inside cover); such representation usually reflects strength in the discipline.

Being aware of who the top people are and where they are will pay off in a number of ways. A graduate department's reputation rests heavily on the reputation of its faculty, and in some disciplines it is more important to study under someone of note than it is to study at a college or university with a prestigious name. In addition, in certain fields graduate funds are often tied to a particular research project and, as a result, to the faculty member directing that project. Finally, most Ph.D. candidates (and nonprofessional master's degree candidates) must pick an adviser and one or more other faculty members who form a committee that directs and approves their work. Many times this choice must be made during the first semester, so it is important to learn as much as you can about faculty members before you begin your studies. As you research the faculties of various departments, keep in mind the following questions: What is their academic training? What are their research activities? What kind of concern do they have for teaching and student development?

There are other important factors to consider in judging the educational quality of a program. First, what kind of students enroll in the program? What are their academic abilities, achievements, skills, geographic representation, and level of professional success upon completion of the program? Second, what are the program's resources? What kind of financial support does it have? How complete is the library? What laboratory equipment and computer facilities are available? And third, what does the program have to offer in terms of both curriculum and services? What are its purposes, its course offerings, and its job placement and student advisement services? What is the student-faculty ratio, and what kind of interaction is there between students and professors? What internships, assistantships, and other experiential education opportunities are available?

When evaluating a particular institution's reputation in a given field, you may also want to look at published graduate program ratings. There is no single rating that is universally accepted, so you would be well advised to read several and not place too much importance on any one. Most consist of what are known as "peer ratings"; that is, they are the results of polls of respected scholars who are asked to rate graduate departments in their field of expertise. Many academicians feel that these ratings are too heavily based upon traditional concepts of what constitutes quality—such as the publications of the faculty—and that they perpetuate the notion of a research-oriented department as the only model of excellence in graduate education. Depending on whether your own goals are research-oriented, you may want to attribute more or less importance to this type of rating.

If possible, visit the institutions that interest you and talk with faculty members and currently enrolled students. Be sure, however, to write or call the admissions office a week in advance to give the person in charge a chance to set up appointments for you with faculty members and students.

Another invaluable tool for researching programs is the Internet. In addition to an institution's Web site, dig deeper to find the "unofficial" information, such as student reviews of faculty, editori-

als in the student newspaper, crime statistics, and alumni home pages. E-mail, listservs, newsgroups, bulletin boards, and chat rooms are all effective tools you should employ in your search for a graduate school program.

The Application Process

TIMETABLE

It is important to start gathering information early to be able to complete your applications on time. Most people should start the process a full year and a half before their anticipated date of matriculation. There are, however, some exceptions to this rule. The time frame will be different if you are applying for national scholarships or if your undergraduate institution has an evaluation committee through which you are applying, for example, to a health-care program. In such a situation, you may have to begin the process two years before your date of matriculation in order to take your graduate admission test and arrange for letters of recommendation early enough to meet deadlines.

Application deadlines may range from August (a year prior to matriculation) for early decision programs at medical schools using the American Medical College Application Service (AMCAS) to late spring or summer (when beginning graduate school in the fall) for a few programs with rolling admissions. Most deadlines for entry in the fall are between January and March. You should in all cases plan to meet formal deadlines; beyond this, you should be aware of the fact that many schools with rolling admissions encourage and act upon early applications. Applying early to a school with rolling admissions is usually advantageous, as it shows your enthusiasm for the program and gives admissions committees more time to evaluate the subjective components of your application, rather than just the "numbers." Applicants are not rejected early unless they are clearly below an institution's standards.

The timetable that appears below represents the ideal for most applicants.

Six months prior to applying
- Research areas of interest, institutions, and programs.
- Talk to advisers about application requirements.
- Register and prepare for appropriate graduate admission tests.
- Investigate national scholarships.
- If appropriate, obtain letters of recommendation.

Three months prior to applying
- Take required graduate admission tests.
- Write for application materials.
- Write your application essay.
- Check on application deadlines and rolling admissions policies.
- For medical, dental, osteopathy, podiatry, or law school, you may need to register for the national application or data assembly service most programs use.

Fall, a year before matriculating

• Obtain letters of recommendation.

• Take graduate admission tests if you haven't already.

• Send in completed applications.

Winter, before matriculating in the fall

• Complete the Free Application for Federal Student Aid (FAFSA) and Financial Aid PROFILE, if required.

Spring, before matriculating in the fall

• Check with all institutions before their deadlines to make sure your file is complete.

• Visit institutions that accept you.

• Send a deposit to your institution of choice.

• Notify other colleges and universities that accepted you of your decision so that they can admit students on their waiting list.

• Send thank-you notes to people who wrote your recommendation letters, informing them of your success.

You may not be able to adhere to this timetable if your application deadlines are very early, as is the case with medical schools, or if you decide to attend graduate school at the last minute. In any case, keep in mind the various application requirements and be sure to meet all deadlines. If deadlines are impossible to meet, call the institution to see if a late application will be considered.

OBTAINING APPLICATION FORMS AND INFORMATION

To obtain the materials you need, send a neatly typed or handwritten postcard requesting an application, a bulletin, and financial aid information to the address provided in this Guide. However, you may want to request an application by writing a formal letter directly to the department chair in which you briefly describe your training, experience, and specialized research interests. If you want to write to a particular faculty member about your background and interests in order to explore the possibility of an assistantship, you should also feel free to do so. However, do not ask a faculty member for an application, as this may cause a significant delay in your receipt of the forms.

NATIONAL APPLICATION SERVICES

In a few professional fields, there are national services that provide assistance with some part of the application process. These services are the Law School Data Assembly Service (LSDAS), American Medical College Application Service (AMCAS), American Association of Colleges of Osteopathic Medicine Application Service (AACOMAS), American Association of Colleges of Podiatric Medicine Application Service (AACPMAS), and American Association of Dental Schools Application Service (AADSAS). Many programs require applicants to use these services because they simplify the application process for both the professional programs' admissions committees and the applicant. The role these services play varies from one field to another. The LSDAS, for example, analyzes your transcript(s) and submits the analysis to the law schools to which you are applying, while the other

services provide a more complete application service. More information and applications for these services can be obtained from your undergraduate institution.

Going to Business School? Use GradAdvantage.

GradAdvantage is a new service developed by Educational Testing Service and Peterson's, and sponsored by the Graduate Management Admission Council (GMAC). GradAdvantage allows you to apply on line to as many business schools as you wish, enter most of your personal data only once, and have your application arrive at the admissions office with your secure Graduate Management Admission Test (GMAT) score attached. The GradAdvantage Web site, gradadvantage.org, also has a wealth of information about business schools, financing options, and GMAT registration and preparation.

With GradAdvantage, you can complete your applications online, save your work, and make revisions any time you are on the Web. You save time and avoid the headaches of conventional applications, like typing or printing onto pre-set paper forms, and sending your application by express mail services. The advantages for business schools include speed, security, and cost-effectiveness. The cost to you is $12 per application, and you can pay on line by credit card. The platform- and browser-independent service requires no substantial upgrades in hardware or software. All you have to do is remember the URL: gradadvantage.org.

MEETING APPLICATION REQUIREMENTS

Requirements vary from one field to another and from one institution to another. Read each program's requirements carefully; the importance of this cannot be overemphasized.

GRADUATE ADMISSION TESTS

Colleges and universities usually require a specific graduate admission test, and departments sometimes have their own requirements as well. Scores are used in evaluating the likelihood of your success in a particular program (based upon the success rate of past students with similar scores). Most programs will not accept scores more than three to five years old. The various tests are described a little later in this book.

TRANSCRIPTS

Admissions committees require official transcripts of your grades to evaluate your academic preparation for graduate study. Grade point averages are important but are not examined in isolation; the rigor of the courses you have taken, your course load, and the reputation of the undergraduate institution you have attended are also scrutinized. To have your college transcript sent to graduate institutions, contact your college registrar.

LETTERS OF RECOMMENDATION

Choosing people to write recommendations can be difficult, and most graduate schools require two or three letters. While recommendations from faculty members are essential for academically oriented programs, professional programs may seriously consider nonacademic recommendations from professionals in the field. Indeed, often these nonacademic recommendations are as respected as those from faculty members.

To begin the process of choosing references, identify likely candidates from among those you know through your classes, extracurricular activities, and jobs. A good reference will meet several of the following criteria: he or she has a high opinion of you, knows you well in more than one area of your life, is familiar with the institutions to which you are applying as well as the kind of study you are pursuing, has taught or worked with a large number of students and can make a favorable comparison of you with your peers, is known by the admissions committee and is regarded as someone whose judgment should be given weight, and has good written communication skills. No one person is likely to satisfy all these criteria, so choose those people who come closest to the ideal.

Once you have decided whom to ask for letters, you may wonder how to approach them. Ask them if they think they know you well enough to write a meaningful letter. Be aware that the later in the semester you ask, the more likely they are to hesitate because of time constraints; ask early in the fall semester of your senior year. Once those you ask to write letters agree in a suitably enthusiastic manner, make an appointment to talk with them. Go to the appointment with recommendation forms in hand, being sure to include addressed, stamped envelopes for their convenience. In addition, give them other supporting materials that will assist them in writing a good, detailed letter on your behalf. Such documents as transcripts, a resume, a copy of your application essay, and a copy of a research paper can help them write a thorough recommendation.

On the recommendation form, you will be asked to indicate whether you wish to waive or retain the right to see the recommendation. Before you decide, discuss the confidentiality of the letter with each writer. Many faculty members will not write a letter unless it is confidential. This does not necessarily mean that they will write a negative letter but, rather, that they believe it will carry more weight as part of your application if it is confidential. Waiving the right to see a letter does, in fact, usually increase its validity.

If you will not be applying to graduate school as a senior but you plan to pursue further education in the future, open a credentials file if your college or university offers this service. Letters of recommendation can be kept on file for you until you begin the application process. If you are returning to school after working for several years and did not establish a credentials file, it may be difficult to obtain letters of recommendation from professors at your undergraduate institution. In this case, contact the graduate schools you are applying to and ask what their policies are regarding your situation. They may waive the requirement of recommendation letters, allow you to substitute letters from employment supervisors, or suggest you enroll in relevant courses at a nearby institution and obtain letters from professors upon completion of the course work. Program policies vary considerably, so it is best to check with each school.

APPLICATION ESSAYS

Writing an essay, or personal statement, is often the most difficult part of the application process. Requirements vary widely in this regard. Some programs request only one or two paragraphs about why you want to pursue graduate study, while others require five or six separate essays in which you are expected to write at length about your motivation for graduate study, your strengths and weaknesses, your greatest achievements, and solutions to hypothetical problems. Business schools are notorious for requiring several time-consuming essays.

An essay or personal statement for an application should be essentially a statement of your ideas and goals. Usually it includes a certain amount of personal history, but, unless an institution specifically requests autobiographical information, you do not have to supply any. Even when the requirement is a "personal statement," the possibilities are almost unlimited. There is no set formula to follow, and, if you do write an autobiographical piece, it does not have to be arranged chronologically. Your aim should be a clear, succinct statement showing that you have a definite sense of what you want to do and enthusiasm for the field of study you have chosen. Your essay should reflect your writing abilities; more important, it should reveal the clarity, the focus, and the depth of your thinking.

Before writing anything, stop and consider what your reader might be looking for; the general directions or other parts of the application may give you an indication of this. Admissions committees may be trying to evaluate a number of things from your statement, including the following things about you:

• Motivation and commitment to a field of study

• Expectations with regard to the program and career opportunities

• Writing ability

• Major areas of interest

• Research or work experience

• Educational background

• Immediate and long-term goals

• Reasons for deciding to pursue graduate education in a particular field and at a particular institution

• Maturity

• Personal uniqueness—what you would add to the diversity of the entering class

There are two main approaches to organizing an essay. You can outline the points you want to cover and then expand on them, or you can put your ideas down on paper as they come to you, going over them, eliminating certain sentences, and moving others around until you achieve a logical sequence. Making an outline will probably lead to a well-organized essay, whereas writing spontaneously may yield a more inspired piece of writing. Use the approach you feel most comfortable with. Whichever approach you use, you will want someone to critique your essay. Your adviser and those who write your letters of recommendation may be very helpful to you in this regard. If they are in the field you plan to pursue, they will be able to tell you what things to stress and what things to keep brief. Do not be surprised, however, if you get differing opinions on the content of your essay. In the end, only you can decide on the best way of presenting yourself.

If there is information in your application that might reflect badly on you, such as poor grades or a low admission test score, it is better not to deal with it in your essay unless you are asked to. Keep your essay positive. You will need to explain anything that could be construed as negative in your application, however, as failure to do so may eliminate you from consideration. You can do this on a separate sheet entitled "Addendum," which you attach to the application, or in a cover letter that you enclose. In either form, your explanation should be short and to the point, avoiding long, tedious excuses. In addition to supplying your own explanation, you may find it appropriate to ask one or more of your recommenders to address the issue in their recommendation letter. Ask them to do this only if they are already familiar with your problem and could talk about it from a positive perspective.

In every case, essays should be word processed or typed. It is usually acceptable to attach pages to your application if the space provided is insufficient. Neatness, spelling, and grammar are important.

INTERVIEWS, PORTFOLIOS, AND AUDITIONS

Some graduate programs will require you to appear for an interview. In certain fields, you will have to submit a portfolio of your work or schedule an audition.

Interviews.

Interviews are usually required by medical schools and are often required or suggested by business schools and other programs. An interview can be a very important opportunity for you to persuade an institution's admissions officer or committee that you would be an excellent doctor, dentist, manager, etc.

Interviewers will be interested in the way you think and approach problems and will probably concentrate on questions that enable them to assess your thinking skills, rather than questions that call upon your grasp of technical knowledge. Some interviewers will ask controversial questions, such as "What is your viewpoint on abortion?" or give you a hypothetical situation and ask how you would handle it. Bear in mind that the interviewer is more interested in how you think than in what you think. As in your essay, you may be asked to address such topics as your motivation for graduate study, personal philosophy, career goals, related research and work experience, and areas of interest.

You should prepare for a graduate school interview as you would for a job interview. Think about the questions you are likely to be asked and practice verbalizing your answers. Think too about what you want interviewers to know about you so that you can present this information when the opportunity is given. Dress as you would for an employment interview.

Portfolios.

Many graduate programs in art, architecture, journalism, environmental design, and other fields involving visual creativity may require a portfolio as part of the application. The function of the portfolio is to show your skills and ability to do further work in a particular field, and it should reflect the scope of your cumulative training and experience. If you are applying to a program in graphic design, you may be required to submit a portfolio showing advertisements, posters, pamphlets, and illustra-

tions you have prepared. In fine arts, applicants must submit a portfolio with pieces related to their proposed major.

Individual programs have very specific requirements regarding what your portfolio should contain and how it should be arranged and labeled. Many programs request an interview and ask you to present your portfolio at that time. They may not want you to send the portfolio in advance or leave it with them after the interview, as they are not insured against its loss. If you do send it, you usually do so at your own risk, and you should label all pieces with your name and address.

Auditions.

Like a portfolio, the audition is a demonstration of your skills and talent, and it is often required by programs in music, theater, and dance. Although all programs require a reasonable level of proficiency, standards vary according to the field of study. In a nonperformance area like music education, you need only show that you have attained the level of proficiency normally acquired through an undergraduate program in that field. For a performance major, however, the audition is the most important element of the graduate application. Programs set specific requirements as to what material is appropriate, how long the performance should be, whether it should be memorized, and so on. The audition may be live or taped, but a live performance is usually preferred. In the case of performance students, a committee of professional musicians will view the audition and evaluate it according to prescribed standards.

SUBMITTING COMPLETED APPLICATIONS

Graduate schools have established a wide variety of procedures for filing applications, so read each institution's instructions carefully. Some may request that you send all application materials in one package (including letters of recommendation). Others—medical schools, for example—may have a two-step application process. This system requires the applicant to file a preliminary application; if this is reviewed favorably, he or she submits a second set of documents and a second application fee. Pay close attention to each school's instructions.

Graduate schools generally require an application fee. Sometimes this fee may be waived if you meet certain financial criteria. Check with your undergraduate financial aid office and the graduate schools to which you are applying to see if you qualify.

ADMISSION DECISIONS

At most institutions, once the graduate school office has received all of your application materials, your file is sent directly to the academic department. A faculty committee (or the department chairperson) then makes a recommendation to the chief graduate school officer (usually a graduate dean or vice president), who is responsible for the final admission decision. Professional schools at most institutions act independently of the graduate school office; applications are submitted to them directly, and they make their own admission decisions.

Usually a student's grade point average, letters of recommendation, and graduate admission test scores are the primary factors considered by admissions committees. The appropriateness of the undergraduate degree, an interview, and evidence of creative tal-

ent may also be taken into account. Normally the student's total record is examined closely, and the weight assigned to specific factors fluctuates from program to program. Few, if any, institutions base their decisions purely on numbers, that is, admission test scores and grade point average. A study by the Graduate Record Examinations Board found that grades and recommendations by known faculty members were considered to be somewhat more important than GRE General Test scores and that GRE Subject Test scores were rated as relatively unimportant (Oltman and Hartnett, 1984). This indicates that some graduate admission test scores may be of less importance than is commonly believed, but this will of course differ from program to program.

Some of the common reasons applicants are rejected for admission to graduate schools are inappropriate undergraduate curriculum; poor grades or lack of academic prerequisites; low admission test scores; weak or ineffective recommendation letters; a poor interview, portfolio, or audition; and lack of extracurricular activities, volunteer experience, or research activities. To give yourself the best chances of being admitted where you apply, try to make a realistic assessment of an institution's admission standards and your own qualifications. Remember, too, that missing deadlines and filing an incomplete application can also be a cause for rejection; be sure that your transcripts and recommendation letters are received on time.

Returning Students

Many graduate programs not only accept the older, returning student but actually prefer these "seasoned" candidates. Programs in business administration, social work, and other professional fields value mature applicants with work experience, for they have found that these students often show a higher level of motivation and commitment and work harder than 21-year-olds. Many programs also seek the diversity older students bring to the student body, as differences in perspective and experience make for interesting—and often intense—class discussions. Nonprofessional programs also view older students favorably if their academic and experiential preparation is recent enough and sufficient for the proposed fields of study.

Many institutions have programs designed to make the transition to academic life easier for the returning student. Such programs include low-cost child-care centers, emotional support programs for both the returning student and his or her spouse, and review courses of various kinds.

Other than making the necessary changes in their life-style, older students report that the most difficult aspect of returning to school is recovering, or developing, appropriate study habits. Initially, older students often feel at a disadvantage compared to students fresh out of an undergraduate program who are accustomed to preparing research papers and taking tests. This feeling can be overcome by taking advantage of noncredit courses in study skills and time management and review courses in math and writing, as well as by taking a tour of the library and becoming thoroughly familiar with it. By the end of the graduate program, most return-

ing students feel that their life experience gave them an edge, because they could use concrete experiences to help them understand academic theory.

If you choose to go back to school, you are not alone. A significant number of adults are currently enrolled in some kind of educational program in order to make their lives or careers more rewarding.

Part-Time Students

As graduate education has changed over the past thirty years, the number of part-time graduate programs has increased. Traditionally, graduate programs were completed by full-time students. Graduate schools instituted residence requirements, demanding that students take a full course load for a certain number of consecutive semesters. It was felt that total immersion in the field of study and extensive interaction with the faculty were necessary to achieve mastery of an academic area.

In most academic Ph.D. programs as well as many health-care fields, this is still the only approach. However, many other programs now admit part-time students or allow a portion of the requirements to be completed on a part-time basis. Professional schools are more likely to allow part-time study because many students work full-time in the field and pursue their degree in order to enhance their career credentials. Other applicants choose part-time study because of financial considerations. By continuing to work full-time while attending school, they take fewer economic risks.

Part-time programs vary considerably in quality and admissions standards. When evaluating a part-time program, use the same criteria you would use in judging the reputation of any graduate program. Some schools use more adjunct faculty members with weaker academic training for their night and weekend courses, and this could lower the quality of the program; however, adjunct lecturers often have excellent experiential knowledge. Admissions standards may be lower for a part-time program than for an equivalent full-time program at the same school, but, again, your fellow students in the part-time program may be practicing in the field and may have much to add to class discussions. Another concern is placement opportunities upon completion of the program. Some schools may not offer placement services to part-time students, and many employers do not value part-time training as highly as a full-time education. However, if a part-time program is the best option for you, do not hesitate to enroll after carefully researching available programs.

International Students

If you are an international student, you will follow the same application procedures as other graduate school applicants. However, you will have to meet additional requirements.

Since your success as a graduate student will depend on your ability to understand, write, read, and speak English, if English is not your native language, you will be required to take the Test of English as a Foreign Language (TOEFL), or a similar test. Some schools will waive the language test requirement, however, if you have a degree from a college or university in a country where the native language is English or if you have studied two or more

years in an undergraduate or graduate program in a country where the native language is English. As for all other tests, score requirements vary, but some schools admit students with lower scores on the condition that they enroll in an intensive English program before or during their graduate study. You should ask each school or department about its policies.

In addition to scores on your English test, or proof of competence in English, your formal application must be accompanied by a certified English translation of your academic transcripts. You may also be required to submit records of immunization and certain health certificates as well as documented evidence of financial support at the time of application. However, since you may apply for financial assistance from graduate schools as well as other sources, some institutions require evidence of financial support only as the last step in your formal admittance and may grant you conditional acceptance first.

Once you have been formally admitted into a graduate program and have submitted evidence of your source or sources of financial support, the school will send you Form I-20 or Form IAP-66, Certificate of Eligibility for Non-Immigrant Status. You must present this document, along with a passport from your own government, and evidence of financial support (some schools will require evidence of support for the entire course of study, while others require evidence of support only for the first year of study, if there is also documentation to show reasonable expectation of continued support) to a U.S. embassy or consulate to obtain an international student visa (F-1 with the Form I-20 or J-1 with the Form IAP-66).

Your own government may have other requirements you must meet to study in the United States. Be sure to investigate those requirements as well.

Once all the paperwork has been completed and approved, you are ready to make your travel arrangements. If your port of entry into the United States will be New York's Kennedy Airport, you can arrange, for a fee, to be met and assisted by a representative of the YMCA Arrivals Program. This person will help you through customs and assist you in making travel connections. He or she can also help you find temporary overnight accommodations, if needed. To inquire about fees for this service, contact the Arrivals Program by phone (212-727-8800 Ext. 130), fax (212-727-8814), or e-mail (jholt@ymcanyc.org). If you decide to take advantage of this assistance, you must provide the Arrivals Program with the following information: your name, age, sex, date and time of arrival, airline and flight number, college or university you will be attending, sponsoring agency (if any), and connecting flight information. Include a photo to help identify you, and note if you need overnight accommodations in New York. This information should be sent well in advance to YMCA Arrivals Program, 71 West 23rd Street, Suite 1904, New York, New York 10010.

When you arrive on your American college campus, you will want to contact the international student adviser. This person's job is to help international students in their academic and social adjustment. The adviser often coordinates special orientation programs for new students, which may consist of lectures on American culture, intensive language instruction, campus tours, academic placement examinations, and visits to places of cultural interest in the community. This adviser will also help you with travel and employment questions as well as financial concerns and will keep copies of your visa documents on file, which is required by U.S. immigration law.

A number of nonprofit educational organizations are available throughout the world to assist international students in planning graduate study in the United States. To learn how to get in touch with these organizations for detailed information, contact the U.S. embassy in your country.

Jane E. Levy
Senior Associate Director
University Career Center
Cornell University
and
Elinor R. Workman
Director of Career Services
Graduate School of Business
University of Chicago

Paying for Graduate School

If you're considering attending graduate school but fear you don't have enough money, don't despair. Financial support for graduate study does exist, although, admittedly, the information about support sources can be difficult to find.

Support for graduate study can take many forms, depending upon the field of study and program you pursue. For example, some 60 percent of doctoral students receive support in the form of either grants/fellowships or assistantships, whereas most students in master's programs rely on loans to pay for their graduate study. In addition, doctoral candidates are more likely to receive grants/fellowships and assistantships than master's degree students, and students in the sciences are more likely to receive aid than those in the arts and humanities.

For those of you who have experience with financial aid as an undergraduate, there are some differences for graduate students you'll notice right away. For one, aid to undergraduates is based primarily on need (although the number of colleges that now offer undergraduate merit-based aid is increasing). But graduate aid is often based on academic merit, especially in the arts and sciences. Second, as a graduate student, you are automatically "independent" for federal financial aid purposes, meaning your parents' income and assest information is not required in assessing your need for federal aid. And third, at some graduate schools, the awarding of aid may be administered by the academic departments or the graduate school itself, not the financial aid office. This means that at some schools, you may be involved with as many as three offices: a central financial aid office, the graduate school, *and* your academic department.

Financial Aid Myths
- Financial aid is just for poor people.
- Financial aid is just for smart people.
- Financial aid is mainly for minority students.
- I have a job, so I must not be eligible for aid.
- If I apply for aid, it will affect whether or not I'm admitted.
- Loans are not financial aid.

BE PREPARED

Being prepared for graduate school means you should put together a financial plan. So, before you enter graduate school, you should have answers to these questions:

- What should I be doing now to prepare for the cost of my graduate education?
- What can I do to minimize my costs once I arrive on campus?
- What financial aid programs are available at each of the schools to which I am applying?
- What financial aid programs are available outside the university, at the federal, state, or private level?
- What financing options do I have if I cannot pay the full cost from my own resources and those of my family?
- What should I know about the loans I am being offered?
- What impact will these loans have on me when I complete my program?

You'll find your answers in three guiding principles: think ahead, live within your means, and keep your head above water.

THINK AHEAD

The first step to putting together your financial plan comes from thinking about the future: the loss of your income while you're attending school, your projected income after you graduate, the annual rate of inflation, additional expenses you will incur as a student and after you graduate, and any loss of income you may experience later on from unintentional periods of unemployment, pregnancy, or disability. The cornerstone of thinking ahead is following a step-by-step process.

1. *Set your goals.* Decide what and where you want to study, whether you will attend full- or part-time, whether you'll work while attending, and what an appropriate level of debt would be. Consider whether you would attend full-time if you had enough financial aid or whether keeping your full-time job is an important priority in your life. Keep in mind that some employers have tuition reimbursement plans for full-time employees.
2. *Take inventory.* Collect your financial information and add up your assets—bank accounts, stocks, bonds, real estate, business and personal property. Then subtract your liabilities—money owed on your assets including credit card debt and car loans—to yield your net worth.
3. *Calculate your need.* Compare your net worth with the costs at the schools you are considering to get a rough estimate of how much of your assets you can use for your schooling.
4. *Create an action plan.* Determine how much you'll earn while in school, how much you think you will receive in grants and scholarships, and how much you plan to borrow. Don't forget to consider inflation and possible life changes that could affect your overall financial plan.
5. *Review your plan regularly.* Measure the progress of your plan every year and make adjustments for such things as increases in salary or other changes in your goals or circumstances.

LIVE WITHIN YOUR MEANS

The second step in being prepared is knowing how much you spend now so you can determine how much you'll spend when you're in school. Use the standard cost of attendance budget published by your school as a guide. But don't be surprised if your estimated budget is higher than the one the school provides, especially if you've been out of school for a while. Once you've figured out your budget, see if you can pare down your current costs and financial obligations so the lean years of graduate school don't come as too large a shock.

KEEP YOUR HEAD ABOVE WATER

Finally, the third step is managing the debt you'll accrue as a graduate student. Debt is manageable only when considered in terms of five things:

1. Your future income
2. The amount of time it takes to repay the loan
3. The interest rate you are being charged
4. Your personal lifestyle and expenses after graduation
5. Unexpected circumstances that change your income or your ability to repay what you owe

To make sure your educational debt is manageable, you should borrow an amount that requires payments of between 8 and 15 percent of your starting salary.

The approximate monthly installments for repaying borrowed principal at 5, 8–10, and 12 percent are indicated below.

Estimated Loan Repayment Schedule

Monthly Payments for Every $1000 Borrowed

Rate	5 years	10 years	15 years	20 years	25 years
5%	$18.87	$10.61	$ 7.91	$ 6.60	$ 5.85
8%	20.28	12.13	9.56	8.36	7.72
9%	20.76	12.67	10.14	9.00	8.39
10%	21.74	13.77	10.75	9.65	9.09
12%	22.24	14.35	12.00	11.01	10.53

You can use this table to estimate your monthly payments on a loan for any of the five repayment periods (5, 10, 15, 20, and 25 years). The amounts listed are the monthly payments for a $1000 loan for each of the interest rates. To estimate your monthly payment, choose the closest interest rate and multiply the amount of the payment listed by the total amount of your loan and then divide by 1,000. For example, for a total loan of $15,000 at 9 percent to be paid back over ten years, multiply $12.67 times 15,000 (190,050) divided by 1,000. This yields $190.05 per month.

If you're wondering just how much of a loan payment you can afford monthly without running into payment problems, consult the following chart.

HOW MUCH CAN YOU AFFORD TO REPAY?

This graph shows the monthly cash-flow outlook based on your total monthly loan payments in comparison with your monthly income earned after taxes. Ideally, to eliminate likely payment problems, your monthly loan payment should be less than 15 percent of your monthly income.

Of course, the best way to manage your debt is to borrow less. While cutting your personal budget may be one option, there are a few others you may want to consider:

- *Ask Your Family for Help:* Although the federal government considers you "independent," your parents and family may still be willing and able to help pay for your graduate education. If your family is not open to just giving you money, they may be open to making a low-interest (or deferred-interest) loan. Family loans usually have more attractive interest rates and repayment terms than commercial loans. They may also have tax consequences, so you may want to check with a tax adviser.
- *Push to Graduate Early:* It's possible to reduce your total indebtedness by completing your program ahead of schedule. You can either take more courses per semester or during the summer. Keep in mind, though, that these options reduce the time you have available to work.
- *Work More, Attend Less:* Another alternative is to enroll part-time, leaving more time to work. Remember, though, to qualify for aid, you must be enrolled at least half-time, which is usually considered six credits per term. And if you're enrolled less than half-time, you'll have to start repaying your loans once the grace period has expired.

Roll Your Loans into One

There's a good chance that as a graduate student you will have two or more loans included in your aid package, plus any money you borrowed as an undergraduate. That means when you start repaying, you could be making loan payments to several different lenders. Not only can the recordkeeping be a nightmare, but with each loan having a minimum payment, your total monthly payments may be more than you can handle. If that is the case, you may want to consider consolidating your federal loans.

There is no minimum or maximum on the amount of loans you must have in order to consolidate. Also, there is no consolidation fee. The interest rate varies annually, is adjusted every July 1, and

is capped at 8.25 percent. Your repayment can also be extended to up to thirty years, depending on the total amount you borrow, which will make your monthly payments lower (of course, you'll also be paying more total interest). With a consolidated loan, some lenders offer graduated or income-sensitive repayment options. Consult with your lender or the U.S. Department of Education about the types of consolidation provisions offered.

Plastic Mania

Any section on managing debt would be incomplete if it didn't mention the responsible use of credit cards. Most graduate students hold one or more credit cards, and many students find themselves in financial difficulties because of them. Here are two suggestions: use credit cards only for convenience, never for extended credit; and, if you have more than one credit card, keep only the one that has the lowest finance charge and the lowest limit.

Credit: Don't Let Your Past Haunt You

Many schools will check your credit history before they process any private educational loans for you. To make sure your credit rating is accurate, you may want to request a copy of your credit report before you start graduate school. You can get a copy of your report by sending a signed, written request to one of the four national credit reporting agencies at the address listed below. Include your full name, social security number, current address, any previous addresses for the past five years, date of birth, and daytime phone number. Call the agency before you request your report so you know whether there is a fee for this report. Note that you are entitled to a free copy of your credit report if you have been denied credit within the last sixty days. In addition, Experian currently provides complimentary credit reports once every twelve months.

Credit criteria used to review and approve student loans can include the following:

- Absence of negative credit
- No bankruptcies, foreclosures, repossessions, charge-offs, or open judgments
- No prior educational loan defaults, unless paid in full or making satisfactory repayments
- Absence of excessive past due accounts; that is, no 30-, 60-, or 90-day delinquencies on consumer loans or revolving charge accounts within the past two years

Credit Reporting Agencies

Experian
P.O. Box 9530
Allen, Texas 75013
888-397-3742

Equifax
P.O. Box 105873
Atlanta, Georgia 30348
800-685-1111

CSC Credit Services
Consumer Assistance Center
P.O. Box 674402
Houston, Texas 77267-4402
800-759-5979

Trans Union Corporation
P.O. Box 390
Springfield, Pennsylvania 19064-0390
800-888-4213

Types of Aid Available

There are three types of aid: money given to you (grants, scholarships, and fellowships), money you earn through work, and loans.

GRANTS, SCHOLARSHIPS, AND FELLOWSHIPS

Most grants, scholarships, and fellowships are outright awards that require no service in return. Often they provide the cost of tuition and fees plus a stipend to cover living expenses. Some are based exclusively on financial need, some exclusively on academic merit, and some on a combination of need and merit. As a rule, grants are awarded to those with financial need, although they may require the recipient to have expertise in a certain field. Fellowships and scholarships often connote selectivity based on ability—financial need is usually not a factor.

Federal Support

Several federal agencies fund fellowship and trainee programs for graduate and professional students. The amounts and types of assistance offered vary considerably by field of study.

National Institutes of Health (NIH). NIH sponsors many different fellowship opportunities. For example, it offers training grants administered through schools' research departments. Training grants provide tuition plus a twelve-month stipend of $11,496. For more information, call 301-435-0714.

National Science Foundation. Graduate Research Program Fellowships include tuition and fees plus a $15,000 stipend for three years of graduate study in engineering, mathematics, the natural sciences, the social sciences, and the history and philosophy of science. The application deadline is in early November. For more information, write to the National Science Foundation at Oak Ridge Associated Universities, P.O. Box 3010, Oak Ridge, Tennessee 37831-3010, or call 423-241-4300.

Graduate Assistantships in Areas of National Need. This program was designed to offer fellowships to oustanding doctoral candidates of superior ability. It is designed to offer financial assistance to students enrolled in specific programs for which there is both a national need and lack of qualified personnel. The definition of national need is determined by the Secretary of Education. Current areas include chemistry, engineering, mathematics, physics, and area studies. Funds are awarded to schools who then select their recipients, based on academic merit. Awardees must also demonstrate financial need. Awards include tuition plus a living

expense stipend of up to $14,000. Awards are not to exceed four years. Contact the graduate dean's office or academic department to see whether it participates in this program.

Foreign Language and Area Studies Fellowships (FLAS). FLAS fellowships are designed to finance graduate training in foreign languages and related area studies. Administered by the U.S. Department of Education, this program was developed to promote a wider knowledge and understanding of certain cultures and countries. Universities apply directly to the Department of Education for these funds and schools themselves select the recipients based on academic merit. Few fellowships are awarded to first-year students. Application deadlines vary by school.

Veterans' Benefits. Veterans may use their educational benefits for training at the graduate and professional levels. Contact your regional office of the Veterans Administration for more details.

State Support

Some states offer grants for graduate study, with California, Michigan, New York, North Carolina, Texas, and Virginia offering the largest programs. States grant approximately $2.9 million per year to graduate students. Due to fiscal constraints, however, some states have had to reduce or eliminate their financial aid programs for graduate study. To qualify for a particular state's aid you must be a resident of that state. Residency is established in most states after you have lived there for at least twelve consecutive months prior to enrolling in school. Many states provide funds for in-state students only; that is, funds are not transferable out of state. Contact your state scholarship office to determine what aid it offers.

Institutional Aid

Educational institutions using their own funds provide more than $3 billion in graduate assistance in the form of fellowships, tuition waivers, and assistantships. Consult each school's catalog for information about aid programs.

Corporate Aid

Some corporations provide graduate student support as part of the employee benefits package. Most employees who receive aid study at the master's level or take courses without enrolling in a particular degree program.

Aid from Foundations

Most foundations provide support in areas of interest to them. For example, for those studying for the Ph.D., the Howard Hughes Institute funds students in the biomedical sciences, while the Spencer Foundation funds dissertation research in the field of education.

The Foundation Center of New York City publishes several reference books on foundation support for graduate study. For more information, call 212-620-4230 or access their Web site at http://fdncenter.org.

Mellon Fellowships in the Humanities. Eighty entry-level, one-year, portable merit fellowships are awarded each year. Fellowships are for one year only and you should plan to seek support elsewhere for subsequent years. The stipend for Mellon fellows entering graduate school in 1998 is $14,000 plus tuition and mandated fees. Awards are highly competitive. Any college senior or graduate of the last five years who is a citizen or permanent resident of the United States and is applying to a Ph.D. program in a humanities field is encouraged to compete. The application deadline is in December. Contact Woodrow Wilson Fellowship Foundation, Mellon Fellowships CN5329, Princeton, New Jersey 08543-5329, 609-452-7007, e-mail mellon@woodrow.org, Web site: http://www.woodrow.org.

Financial Aid for Minorities and Women

Bureau of Indian Affairs. The Bureau of Indian Affairs (BIA) offers aid to students who are at least one quarter American Indian or native Alaskan and from a federally recognized tribe. Contact your tribal education officer, BIA area office, or call the Bureau of Indian Affairs at 202-208-3710.

The Ford Foundation Doctoral Fellowship for Minorities. Provides three-year doctoral fellowships and one-year dissertation fellowships. Predoctoral fellowships include an annual stipend of $14,000 to the fellow and an annual institutional grant of $7500 to the fellowship institution in lieu of tuition and fees. Dissertation fellows receive a stipend of $18,000 for a twelve-month period. Applications are due in early November. For more information, contact the Fellowship Office, National Research Council at 202-334-2872.

National Consortium for Graduate Degrees in Engineering and Science (GEM). GEM was founded in 1976 to help minority men and women pursue graduate study in engineering by helping them obtain practical experience through summer internships at consortium work-sites and finance graduate study toward a master's or Ph.D. degree. GEM administers the following programs:

Engineering Fellowship Program. Each fellow receives a GEM-sponsored summer internship and a portable fellowship tenable at one of seventy-seven GEM universities. The fellowship consists of tuition, fees, and a $6000 stipend per academic year.

Ph.D. Fellowship Program. The Ph.D. Science Fellowship and the Engineering Fellowship programs provide opportunities for minority students to obtain a Ph.D. in the natural sciences or in engineering through a program of paid summer research internships and financial support. Open to U.S. citizens who belong to one of the ethnic groups underrepresented in the natural sciences and engineering, GEM fellowships are awarded for a twelve-month period. Fellowships are tenable at universities participating in the GEM science or engineering Ph.D. programs. Awards include tuition, fees, and a $12,000 stipend. After the first year of study fellows are supported completely by their respective universities and support may include teaching or research assistantships. Forty fellowships are awarded annually in each program. The application deadline is December. For more information, contact GEM, Box 537, Notre Dame, Indiana 46556, call 219-287-1097, or visit their Web site at http://www.nd.edu/~gem/.

National Physical Sciences Consortium. Graduate fellowships are available in astronomy, chemistry, computer science, geology, materials science, mathematics, and physics for women and Black, Hispanic, and Native American students. These fellowships are

available only at member universities. Awards may vary by year in school and the application deadline is November 5. Fellows receive tuition plus a stipend of between $10,000 and $15,000. For more information, contact National Physical Sciences Consortium, Department 3NPS, c/o New Mexico State University, P.O. Box 30001, Las Cruces, New Mexico 88033-8003, call 505-646-6037, or visit their Web site at http://www.npsc.org.

In addition, below are some books available that describe financial aid opportunities for women and minorities.

The Directory of Financial Aids for Women by Gail Ann Schlachter (Reference Service Press, 1997) lists sources of support and identifies foundations and other organizations interested in helping women secure funding for graduate study.

The Association for Women in Science publishes *Grants-at-a-Glance,* a booklet highlighting fellowships for women in science. It can be ordered by calling 202-326-8940 or by visiting their Web site at http://www.awis.org.

Books such as *Financial Aid for Minorities* (Garrett Park, Md.: Garrett Park Press, 1998) describe financial aid opportunities for minority students. For more information, call 301-946-2553.

Reference Service Press also publishes four directories specifically for minorities: *Financial Aid for African Americans, Financial Aid for Asian Americans, Financial Aid for Hispanic Americans,* and *Financial Aid for Native Americans.*

For more information on financial aid for minorities, see the Minority On-Line Information Service (MOLIS) Web site at http://web.fie.com/web/mol/.

Disabled students are eligible to receive aid from a number of organizations. *Financial Aid for the Disabled and Their Families, 1996–98* by Gail Ann Schlachter and David R. Weber (Reference Service Press) lists aid opportunities for disabled students. The Vocational Rehabilitation Services in your home state can also provide information.

RESEARCHING GRANTS AND FELLOWSHIPS

The books listed below are good sources of information on grant and fellowship support for graduate education and should be consulted before you resort to borrowing. Keep in mind that grant support varies dramatically from field to field.

Annual Register of Grant Support: A Directory of Funding Sources, Wilmette, Illinois: National Register Publishing Co. This is a comprehensive guide to grants and awards from government agencies, foundations, and business and professional organizations.

Corporate Foundation Profiles, 10th ed. New York: Foundation Center, 1998. This is an in-depth, analytical profile of 250 of the largest company-sponsored foundations in the United States. Brief descriptions of all 700 company-sponsored foundations are also included. There is an index of subjects, types of support, and geographical locations.

The Foundation Directory, edited by Stan Olsen. New York: Foundation Center, 1998. This directory, with a supplement, gives detailed information on U.S. foundations, with brief descriptions of the purpose and activities of each.

The Grants Register 1998, 16th ed. Edited by Lisa Williams. New York: St. Martin's, 1998. This lists grant agencies alphabetically and gives information on awards available to graduate students, young professionals, and scholars for study and research.

Peterson's Grants for Graduate & Postdoctoral Study, 5th ed. Princeton: Peterson's, 1998. This book includes information on 1,400 grants, scholarships, awards, fellowships, and prizes. Originally compiled by the Office of Research Affairs at the Graduate School of the University of Massachusetts at Amherst, this guide is updated periodically by Peterson's.

Graduate schools sometimes publish listings of support sources in their catalogs, and some provide separate publications, such as the *Graduate Guide to Grants,* compiled by the Harvard Graduate School of Arts and Sciences. For more information, call 617-495-1814.

THE INTERNET AS A SOURCE OF FUNDING INFORMATION

If you have not explored the financial resources on the World Wide Web (the Web, for short), your research is not complete. Now available on the Web is a wealth of information ranging from loan and entrance applications to minority grants and scholarships.

University-Specific Information on the Web

Many universities have Web financial aid directories. Florida, Virginia Tech, Massachusetts, Emory, and Georgetown are just a few. Applications of admission can now be downloaded from the Web to start the graduate process. After that, detailed information can be obtained on financial aid processes, forms, and deadlines. University-specific grant and scholarship information can also be found, and more may be learned about financing information by using the Web than by an actual visit. Questions can be answered on line.

Scholarships on the Web

Many benefactors and other scholarship donors have pages on the Web listing pertinent information with regard to their specific scholarship. You can reach this information through a variety of methods. For example, you can find a directory listing minority scholarships, quickly look at the information on line, decide if it applies to you, and then move on. New scholarship pages are being added to the Web daily. Library and Web resources are productive—and free.

The Web also lists many services that will look for scholarships for you. Some of these services cost money and advertise more scholarships per dollar than any other service. While some of these might be helpful, beware. Check references to make sure a bona fide service is being offered. Your best bet initially is to surf the Web and use the traditional library resources on available scholarships.

Bank and Loan Information on the Web

Banks and loan servicing centers have pages on the Web, making it easier to access loan information. Having the information on screen in front of you instantaneously is more convenient than being put on hold on the phone. Any loan information such as interest rate variations, descriptions of loans, loan consolidation programs, and repayment charts can all be found on the Web.

WORK PROGRAMS

Certain types of support, such as teaching, research, and administrative assistantships, require recipients to provide service to the university in exchange for a salary or stipend; sometimes tuition is also provided or waived.

Teaching Assistantships

Because science and engineering classes are taught at the undergraduate level, you stand a good chance of securing a teaching assistantship. These positions usually involve conducting small classes, delivering lectures, correcting class work, grading papers, counseling students, and supervising laboratory groups. Usually about 20 hours of work is required each week.

Teaching assistantships provide excellent educational experience as well as financial support. TAs generally receive a salary (now considered taxable income). Sometimes tuition is provided or waived as well. In addition, at some schools, TAs can be declared state residents, qualifying them for the in-state tuition rates. Appointments are based on academic qualifications and are subject to the availability of funds within a department. If you are interested in a teaching assistantship, contact the academic department. Ordinarily you are not considered for such positions until you have been admitted to the graduate school.

Research Assistantships

Research Assistantships usually require that you assist in the research activities of a faculty member. Appointments are ordinarily made for the academic year. They are rarely offered to first-year students. Contact the academic department, describing your particular research interests. As is the case with teaching assistantships, research assistantships provide excellent academic training as well as practical experience and financial support.

Administrative Assistantships

These positions usually require 10 to 20 hours of work each week in an administrative office of the university. For example, those seeking a graduate degree in education may work in the admissions, financial aid, student affairs, or placement office of the school they are attending. Some administrative assistantships provide a tuition waiver, others a salary. Details concerning these positions can be found in the school catalog or by contacting the academic department directly.

Federal Work-Study Program (FWS)

This federally funded program provides eligible students with employment opportunities, usually in public and private nonprofit organizations. Federal funds pay up to 75 percent of the wages, with the remainder paid by the employing agency. FWS is available to graduate students who demonstrate financial need. Not all schools have these funds, and some only award undergraduates. Each school sets its application deadline and work-study earnings limits. Wages vary and are related to the type of work done.

Additional Employment Opportunities

Many schools provide on-campus employment opportunities that do not require demonstrated financial need. The student employment office on most campuses assists students in securing jobs both on and off the campus.

LOANS

Most needy graduate students, except those pursuing Ph.D.'s in certain fields, borrow to finance their graduate programs. There are basically two sources of student loans—the federal government and private loan programs. You should read and understand the terms of these loan programs before submitting your loan application.

Federal Loans

Federal Stafford Loans. The Federal Stafford Loan Program offers government-sponsored, low-interest loans to students through a private lender such as a bank, credit union, or savings and loan association.

There are two components of the Federal Stafford Loan program. Under the *subsidized* component of the program, the federal government pays the interest accruing on the loan while you are enrolled in graduate school on at least a half-time basis. Under the *unsubsidized* component of the program, you pay the interest on the loan from the day proceeds are issued. Eligibility for the federal subsidy is based on demonstrated financial need as determined by the financial aid office from the information you provide on the Free Application for Federal Student Aid (FAFSA). A cosigner is not required, since the loan is not based on creditworthiness.

Although Unsubsidized Federal Stafford Loans may not be as desirable as Subsidized Federal Stafford Loans from the consumer's perspective, they are a useful source of support for those who may not qualify for the subsidized loans or who need additional financial assistance.

Graduate students may borrow up to $18,500 per year through the Stafford Loan Program, up to a maximum of $138,500, including undergraduate borrowing. This may include up to $8500 in Subsidized Stafford Loans, depending on eligibility, up to a maximum of $65,000, including undergraduate borrowing. The amount of the loan borrowed through the Unsubsidized Stafford Program equals the total amount of the loan (as much $18,500) minus your eligibility for a Subsidized Stafford Loan (as much as $8500). You may borrow up to the cost of the school in which you are enrolled or will attend, minus estimated financial assistance from other federal, state, and private sources, up to a maximum of $18,500.

The interest rate for the Federal Stafford Loans varies annually and is set every July. The rate during in-school, grace, and deferment periods is based on the 91-Day U.S. Treasury Bill rate plus 2.5 percent, capped at 8.25 percent. The rate in repayment is based on the 91-Day U.S. Treasury Bill rate plus 3.1 percent, capped at 8.25 percent. However, the interest rate may soon be based on the ten-year Treasury Bill, pending current legislation.

Two fees are deducted from the loan proceeds upon disbursement: a guarantee fee of up to 1 percent, which is deposited in an insurance pool to ensure repayment to the lender if the borrower defaults, and a federally mandated 3 percent origination fee, which is used to offset the administrative cost of the Federal Stafford Loan Program.

Under the *subsidized* Federal Loan Program, repayment begins six months after your last enrollment on at least a half-time basis. Under the *unsubsidized* program, repayment of interest begins within thirty days from disbursement of the loan proceeds, and repayment of the principal begins six months after your last enrollment on at least a half-time basis. Some lenders may require that some payments may be made even while you are in school, although most lenders will allow you to defer payments and will add the accrued interest to the loan balance. Under both components of the program repayment may extend over a maximum of ten years with no prepayment penalty.

Federal Direct Loans. Some schools are participating in the Department of Education's Direct Lending Program instead of offering Federal Stafford Loans. The two programs are essentially the same except with the Direct Loans, schools themselves originate the loans with funds provided from the federal government. Terms and interest rates are virtually the same except that there are a few more repayment options with Federal Direct Loans.

Federal Perkins Loans. The Federal Perkins Loan is a long-term loan available to students demonstrating financial need and is administered directly by the school. Not all schools have these funds, and some may award them to undergraduates only. Eligibility is determined from the information you provide on the FAFSA. The school will notify you of your eligibility.

Eligible graduate students may borrow up to $5000 per year, up to a maximum of $30,000, including undergraduate borrowing (even if your previous Perkins Loans have been repaid.) The interest rate for Federal Perkins Loans is 5 percent, and no interest accrues while you remain in school at least half-time. There are no guarantee, loan, or disbursement fees. Repayment begins nine months after your last enrollment on at least a half-time basis and may extend over a maximum of ten years with no prepayment penalty.

Deferring Your Federal Loan Repayments. If you borrowed under the Federal Stafford Loan Program or the Federal Perkins Loan Program for previous undergraduate or graduate study, some of your repayments may be deferred (i.e., suspended) when you return to graduate school, depending on when you borrowed and under which program.

There are other deferment options available if you are temporarily unable to repay your loan. Information about these deferments is provided at your entrance and exit interviews. If you believe you are eligible for a deferment of your loan repayments, you must contact your lender to complete a deferment form. The deferment must be filed prior to the time your repayment is due, and it must be refiled when it expires if you remain eligible for deferment at that time.

Supplemental Loans

Many lending institutions offer supplemental loan programs and other financing plans, such as the ones described below, to students seeking assistance in meeting their expected contribution toward educational expenses.

If you are considering borrowing through a supplemental loan program, you should carefully consider the terms of the program and be sure to "read the fine print." Check with the program sponsor for the most current terms that will be applicable to the amounts you intend to borrow for graduate study. Most supplemental loan programs for graduate study offer unsubsidized, credit-based loans. In general, a credit-ready borrower is one who has a satisfactory credit history or no credit history at all. A creditworthy borrower generally must pass a credit test to be eligible to borrow or act as a cosigner for the loan funds.

Many supplemental loan programs have a minimum annual loan limit and a maximum annual loan limit. Some offer amounts equal to the cost of attendance minus any other aid you will receive for graduate study. If you are planning to borrow for several years of graduate study, consider whether there is a cumulative or aggregate limit on the amount you may borrow. Often this cumulative or aggregate limit will include any amounts you borrowed and have not repaid for undergraduate or previous graduate study.

The combination of the annual interest rate, loan fees, and the repayment terms you choose will determine how much the amount is that you will repay over time. Compare these features in combination before you decide which loan program to use. Some loans offer interest rates that are adjusted monthly, some quarterly, some annually. Some offer interest rates that are lower during the in-school, grace, and deferment periods, and then increase when you begin repayment. Most programs include a loan "origination" fee, which is usually deducted from the principal amount you receive when the loan is disbursed, and must be repaid along with the interest and other principal when you graduate, withdraw from school, or drop below half-time study. Sometimes the loan fees are reduced if you borrow with a qualified cosigner. Some programs allow you to defer interest and/or principal payments while you are enrolled in graduate school. Many programs allow you to capitalize your interest payments; the interest due on your loan is added to the outstanding balance of your loan, so you don't have to repay immediately, but this increases the amount you owe. Other programs allow you to pay the interest as you go, which will reduce the amount you later have to repay.

For more information about supplemental loan programs or to obtain applications, call the customer service phone numbers of the organizations listed below, access the sponsor's site on the World Wide Web, or visit your school's financial aid office.

American Express Alternative Loan. An unsubsidized, credit-based loan for credit-ready graduate students enrolled at least half-time, sponsored by American Express/California Higher Education Loan Authority (800-255-8374).

CitiAssist Graduate Loan. An unsubsidized, credit-based loan for graduate students in all disciplines, sponsored by Citibank (800-745-5473 or 800-946-4019; World Wide Web: http://www.citibank.com/student).

CollegeReserve Loan. An unsubsidized, credit-based loan for credit-worthy graduate students enrolled at least half-time, sponsored by USA Group (800-538-8492; World Wide Web: http://www.usagroup.com).

EXCEL Loan. An unsubsidized, credit-based loan for borrowers who are not credit-ready or who would prefer to borrow with a creditworthy cosigner to obtain a more attractive interest rate, sponsored by Nellie Mae (888-2TUITION).

GradAchiever Loan. An unsubsidized, credit-based loan for graduate students enrolled at least half-time, sponsored by Key Education Resources (800-KEY-LEND; World Wide Web: http://www.key.com/education/grad.html).

GradEXCEL Loan. An unsubsidized, credit-based loan for credit-ready graduate students enrolled at least half-time, sponsored by Nellie Mae (888-2TUITION).

Graduate Access Loan. An unsubsidized, credit-based loan for creditworthy graduate students enrolled at least half-time, sponsored by the Access Group (800-282-1550; World Wide Web: http://www.accessgroup.org).

Signature Student Loan. An unsubsidized, credit-based loan for graduate students enrolled at least half-time, sponsored by Sallie Mae (888-272-5543; World Wide Web: http://www.salliemae.com).

International Education and Study Abroad

A variety of funding sources are offered for study abroad and for foreign nationals studying in the United States. The Institute of International Education in New York assists students in locating such aid. It publishes *Funding for U.S. Study—A Guide for International Students and Professionals* and *Financial Resources for International Study,* a guide to organizations offering awards for overseas study. To learn more, visit the institute's Web site at http://www.iiebooks.org.

The Council on International Educational Exchange in New York publishes the *Student Travel Catalogue,* which lists fellowship sources and explains the council's services both for United States students traveling abroad and for foreign students coming to the United States. For more information, see the council's Web site at http://www.ciee.org.

The U.S. Department of Education administers programs that support fellowships related to international education. Foreign Language and Area Studies Fellowships and Fulbright-Hays Doctoral Dissertation Awards were established to promote knowledge and understanding of other countries and cultures. They offer support to graduate students interested in foreign languages and international relations. Discuss these and other foreign study opportunities with the financial aid officer or someone in the graduate school dean's office at the school you will attend.

How to Apply

All applicants for federal aid must complete the Free Application for Federal Student Aid (FAFSA). This application must be submitted *after* January 1 preceding enrollment in the fall. It is a good idea to submit the FAFSA as soon as possible after this date. On this form you report your income and asset information for the preceding calendar year and specify which schools will receive the data. Two to four weeks later you'll receive an acknowledg-

ment, the Student Aid Report (SAR), on which you can make any corrections. The schools you've designated will also receive the information and may begin asking you to send them documents, usually your U.S. income tax return, verifying what you reported.

In addition to the FAFSA, some graduate schools want additional information and will ask you to complete the CSS Financial Aid PROFILE. If your school requires this form, it will be listed in the PROFILE registration form available in college financial aid offices. Other schools use their own supplemental application. Check with your financial aid office to confirm which forms they require.

If you have already filed your federal income tax for the year, it will be much easier for you to complete these forms. If not, use estimates, but be certain to notify the financial aid office if your estimated figures differ from the actual ones once you have calculated them.

APPLICATION DEADLINES

Application deadlines vary. Some schools require you to apply for aid when applying for admission; others require that you be admitted before applying for aid. Aid application instructions and deadlines should be clearly stated in each school's application material. The FAFSA must be filed after January 1 of the year you are applying for aid but the Financial Aid PROFILE should be completed earlier, in October or November.

Determining Financial Need

Eligibility for need-based financial aid is based on your income during the calendar year prior to the academic year in which you apply for aid. Prior-year income is used because it is a good predictor of current-year income and is verifiable. If you have a significant reduction in income or assets after your aid application is completed, consult a financial aid counselor. If, for example, you are returning to school after working, you should let the financial aid counselor know your projected income for the year you will be in school. Aid counselors may use their "professional judgment" to revise your financial need, based on the actual income you will earn while you are in graduate school.

Need is determined by examining the difference between the cost of attendance at a given institution and the financial resources you bring to the table. Eligibility for aid is calculated by subtracting your resources from the total cost of attendance budget. These standard student budgets are generally on the low side of the norm. So if your expenses are higher because of medical bills, higher research travel, or more costly books, for example, a financial aid counselor can make an adjustment. Of course, you'll have to document any unusual expenses. Also, keep in mind that with limited grant and scholarship aid, a higher budget will probably mean either more loan or more working hours for you.

Tax Issues

Since the passage of the Tax Reform Act of 1986, grants, scholarships, and fellowships may be considered taxable income. That portion of the grant used for payment of tuition and course-required fees, books, supplies, and equipment is excludable from

taxable income. Grant support for living expenses is taxable. A good rule of thumb for determining the tax liability for grants and scholarships is to view anything that exceeds the actual cost of tuition, required fees, books, supplies related to courses, and required equipment as taxable.

- If you are employed by an educational institution or other organization that gives tuition reimbursement, you must pay tax on the value that exceeds $5250.
- If your tuition is waived in exchange for working at the institution, the tuition waiver is taxable. This includes waivers that come with teaching or research assistantships.
- Other student support, such as stipends and wages paid to research assistants and teaching assistants, is also taxable income. Student loans, however, are not taxable.
- If you are an international student you may or may not owe taxes depending upon the agreement the U.S. has negotiated with your home country. The United States has tax treaties with more than forty countries. You are responsible for making sure that the

school you attend follows the terms of the tax treaty. If your country does not have a tax treaty with the U.S., you may have as much as 30 percent withheld from your paycheck.

A Final Note

While amounts and eligibility criteria vary from field to field as well as from year to year, with thorough researh you can uncover many opportunities for graduate financial assistance. If you are interested in graduate study, discuss your plans with faculty members and advisers. Explore all options. Plan ahead, complete forms on time, and be tenacious in your search for support. No matter what your financial situation, if you are academically qualified and knowledgeable about the different sources of aid, you should be able to attend the graduate school of your choice.

Patricia McWade
Dean of Student Financial Services
Georgetown University

Graduate Admissions Tests

Standardized tests. The mere phrase is enough to elicit groans and grimaces from the most well-prepared grad school hopeful. However, like them or not, standardized tests (more specifically, the scores you receive on them) remain the ticket to admission for nearly all would-be grad students. So it's to your advantage to know as much as you can about them.

Many grad schools require applicants to submit scores on one or more general standardized tests, usually the Graduate Record Examinations (GRE) or the Miller Analogies Test (MAT). Here's a brief look at each of the tests, plus information on how to obtain registration materials.

Dental Admission Testing

The DAT consists of four exams covering natural sciences (biology, general chemistry, and organic chemistry), reading comprehension, quantitative reasoning, and perceptual ability. The entire test requires a half day. In 1999, the DAT will be given at Sylvan Technology Centers in each of the fifty states, the District of Columbia, and Puerto Rico. The DAT will be administered on regular business days. The exam fee is $150. The fee for each official report of scores, requested after the time of application, is $5. All fees must be paid with a certified check or money order.

FOR MORE INFORMATION

Department of Testing Services, American Dental Association, 211 East Chicago Avenue, Suite 1840, Chicago, Illinois 60611-2678. Telephone: 312-440-2689.

Graduate Management Admission Test

The GMAT, which is now administered as a computerized-adaptive test (CAT), is designed to help graduate management schools assess the qualifications of applicants for graduate-level programs in business and management.

The GMAT measures general verbal, mathematical, and analytical writing skills. The quantitative sections of the test measure basic math skills and understanding of elementary concepts and the ability to reason quantitatively, solve quantitative problems, and interpret graphic data. The verbal sections of the test measure the ability to understand and evaluate written English. The analytical writing sections of the test measure the ability to think critically and communicate ideas through writing.

FOR MORE INFORMATION

Information about how to register and prepare for the GMAT, as well as a list of testing centers, is available on the Web at http://www.gmat.org.

Peterson's offers *GMAT Success*, a complete guide to the GMAT. Visit your local bookstore or contact Peterson's at 800-225-0261.

Graduate Record Examinations

The GRE General Test and Subject Tests are designed to assess academic knowledge and skills relevant to graduate study. The General Test measures verbal, quantitative, and analytical reasoning skills, and the Subject Tests measure achievement in particular fields of study. The GRE tests are administered worldwide by Educational Testing Service (ETS) of Princeton, New Jersey, under policies established by the Graduate Record Examinations Board, an independent board affiliated with the Association of Graduate Schools and the Council of Graduate Schools.

Currently, the General Test is offered both as a computer-based test (CBT) and a paper-based test. However, GRE plans to phase out the paper-based General Test after April 1999 and introduce a Writing Test. Subject Tests, offered only as paper-based tests, are available in fourteen areas: biochemistry, cell and molecular biology; biology; chemistry; computer science; economics; engineering; geology; history; literature in English; mathematics; music; physics; psychology; and sociology.

While the paper-based General Test is not offered in many international locations, the CBT General Test is offered year-round at more than 600 test centers around the world. The CBT offers convenient scheduling, immediate viewing of unofficial scores, and faster score reporting. To schedule an appointment in the U.S., U.S. territories, or Canada, call 800-GRE-CALL. For international testing, refer to the 1998–99 *GRE Information and Registration Bulletin* or the GRE Web site (http://www.gre.org) for a list of the regional registration centers. The *GRE Bulletin* contains registration and program services information for both CBT and paper-based testing.

Fees for the CBT General Test and the paper-based General Test and Subject Tests are $96 for testing in the U.S. and U.S. Territories and $120 in all other locations. Fees are subject to change.

Nonstandard testing accommodations are available for test takers with disabilities through both the CBT and paper-based testing programs. Students who cannot test on Saturdays for religious reasons may request a Monday paper-based administration immediately following a regular Saturday test date. Refer to the *GRE Bulletin* for more information.

Test takers can register by phone or fax for computer-based testing, by mail for both computer-based and paper-based testing,

or on line for paper-based testing. Test takers should consider admission deadlines and register early to get their preferred test dates.

FOR MORE INFORMATION

GRE-ETS, P.O. Box 6000, Princeton, New Jersey 08541-6000. Telephone: 609-771-7670. World Wide Web: http://www.gre.org.

Peterson's offers *GRE Success*, a complete guide to the GRE. Visit your local bookstore or contact Peterson's at 800-225-0261.

Law School Admission Test

The Law School Admission Test is a half-day standardized test required for admission to all 195 Law School Admission-Council-member law schools. It consists of five 35-minute sections of multiple-choice questions, four of which contribute to the test taker's score. These sections include one reading comprehension section, one analytical reasoning section, and two logical reasoning sections. (The fifth section is used to pretest new test items and to preequate new test forms.) A 30-minute writing sample is administered at the end of the test. The writing sample is not scored by the Council; however, copies of the writing sample are sent to all law schools to which you apply. Scores on the LSAT range from 120 to 180; 120 is the lowest possible score and 180 is the highest.

The LSAT is administered at test centers in each of the fifty states, the District of Columbia, Puerto Rico, and Canada and many other countries. The 1999 test dates for the LSAT are June 14 and Ocotober 2 and 4. Members of recognized religious groups observing the Sabbath on Saturday may arrange to take the test on the Monday following a Saturday administration (except in June). Special accomodations are available for disabled students.

The LSAT is offered by the Law School Admission Council. The LSAT fee is $86 (subject to change) and must be paid each time you register to take the test.

FOR MORE INFORMATION

Peterson's offers LSAT Success, a complete guide to the LSAT. Visit your local bookstore or contact Peterson's at 800-225-0261.

Medical College Admission Test

The MCAT assesses knowledge of basic biology, chemistry, and physics concepts; ability to solve scientific problems and critical thinking; and writing skills. Four separate scores are reported. The Verbal Reasoning, Physical Sciences, and Biological Sciences sections of the test are composed of multiple-choice items; scores are reported on a scale ranging from 1 (lowest) to 15 (highest). The Writing Sample section consists of two 30-minute essays; the score is reported on a scale of J (lowest) to T (highest).

The Verbal Reasoning section assesses students' abilities to comprehend, reason, and think critically. The two science sections—Biological Sciences and Physical Sciences—consist entirely of science problems and assess knowledge of basic, introductory-level science concepts through their application to the solution of science problems. Essay questions on the Writing Sample are designed to assess skill in the development of a central idea, synthesis of concepts and ideas, cohesive and logical presentation of ideas, and clear writing.

The MCAT is offered twice a year; the 1999 test dates are April 17 and August 21. The exam is given at test centers in all fifty states, the District of Columbia, Puerto Rico, the Virgin Islands, and selected countries. Students who, for religious reasons, can't take the exam on Saturday can arrange for Sunday test dates.

FOR MORE INFORMATION

Additional information may be found on the AAMC Web site at http://www.aamc.org.

Peterson's offers *MCAT Success*, a complete guide to the MCAT. Visit your local bookstore or contact Peterson's at 800-225-0261.

Miller Analogies Test

The MAT, accepted by more than 2,300 grad school programs, is a mental ability test that requires the solution of 100 problems stated in the form of analogies. The test uses different types of analogies to sample general information and a variety of fields, such as fine arts, literature, mathematics, natural science, and social science. Examinees are allowed 50 minutes to complete the test.

The MAT is offered at more than 600 test centers in the United States and Canada and is given on an as-needed basis at most test centers. Fees are determined by each test center.

FOR MORE INFORMATION

The Psychological Corporation, 555 Academic Court, San Antonio, Texas 78204. Telephone: 210-299-1061 or 800-622-3231 (7 a.m. to 7 p.m., Monday through Friday, Central time).

Optometry Admission Test

Given two times each year at established testing centers in the United States and Canada, the OAT is designed to measure general academic ability and scientific knowledge of applicants to schools and colleges of optometry. The test includes sections on a survey of the natural sciences (biology, general chemistry, and organic chemistry), reading comprehension, quantitative reasoning, and physics.

In 1999, the test will be administered on October 23. The examination fee for applicants taking the test at centers in the United States and Canada is $80; applicants requesting special arrangements must pay a total of $170. There is a late fee charge of $15. The fee for individuals registering at regular test centers on the day of the test is $160. The fee for each official report of scores, requested after the time of application, is $5. All fees must be paid with a certified check or money order.

FOR MORE INFORMATION

Optometry Admission Testing Program, 211 East Chicago Avenue, Suite 1846, Chicago, Illinois 60611-2678. Telephone: 312-440-2693.

Pharmacy College Admission Test

Designed to measure general academic ability and scientific knowledge, the PCAT includes sections on verbal ability, quantitative ability, reading comprehension, and knowledge of biology and chemistry. The test is given three times each year—January, April, and October—at established testing centers in the United States and Canada. Sunday testing may be arranged for applicants

who, for religious reasons, can't take the test on Saturday. The examination fee is $40; additional fees are charged for standby registration.

FOR MORE INFORMATION

Contact a college of pharmacy or: The Psychological Corporation, 555 Academic Court, San Antonio, Texas 78204. Telephone: 210-299-1061 or 800-622-3231 (7 a.m. to 7 p.m., Monday through Friday, Central time).

The Praxis Series Tests

The Praxis Series tests include the continuing NTE Programs Core Battery tests, the Specialty Area tests, and the Pre-Professional Skills Tests (PPST) of reading, mathematics, and writing. In addition, The Praxis Series offers Subject Assessments and the computer-based Academic Skills Assessments.

The tests are standardized, secure examinations that provide objective measures of academic achievement for college students entering or completing teacher education programs and for advanced candidates who have received additional training in specific fields.

ETS conducts the program, but it is assisted and advised by professional educators from all sections of the country. The tests themselves are developed and revised periodically with the assistance of committees of recognized authorities in specific subject fields. These committees are usually appointed from nominations made by appropriate national professional associations.

The Core Battery includes three 2-hour tests of communication skills, general knowledge, and professional knowledge. During 1999, the tests are administered on March 13, April 24, and June 12. The registration fee is $35. Please refer to the 1998–99 Praxis registration bulletin for the test fees.

Specialty Area and Subject Assessment tests measure understanding of content and methods applicable to the separate subject areas. More than 140 Specialty Area and Subject Assessment tests are administered on March 13, April 24, and June 12. The fees for the 1-hour and 2-hour multiple choice tests are $45 and $60, respectively. The fees for the 1-hour and 2-hour constructed response tests are $50 and $65, respectively.

The Pre-Professional Skills Tests consist of three separate 1-hour tests of basic proficiency in communication and computation skills—reading, mathematics, and writing (including an essay). Four Pre-Professional Skills Tests are scheduled for 1999: March 13, April 24, and June 12. Test fees are $18 for each test.

The computer-based Academic Skills Assessments are available at selected institutional sites and at Sylvan Learning Centers by appointment. Test fees are $70, $90, and $110 for one, two, or three tests, respectively, taken on the same test date.

FOR MORE INFORMATION

Additional information is available from The Praxis Series, P.O. Box 6051, Educational Testing Service, Princeton, New Jersey 08541-6051. Telephone: 609-771-7395. World Wide Web: http//www.ets.org/praxis/.

Test of English as a Foreign Language

The purpose of the TOEFL test is to evaluate the English proficiency of people whose native language is not English.

TOEFL is now administered as a computer-based test throughout most of the world. The computer-based TOEFL test is available year-round by appointment only. It is not necessary to have previous computer experience to take the test. Examinees will be given all the instructions and practice needed to perform the necessary computer tasks before the actual test begins. The test consists of four sections—listening, reading, structure, and writing. Total testing time is approximately 4 hours. The fee for the computer-based TOEFL test is $100, which must be paid in U.S. dollars. The *Information Bulletin for Computer-Based Testing* contains information about the new testing format, registration procedures, and testing sites.

The TOEFL test is given at many test centers throughout the world and is administered by Educational Testing Service (ETS) under the general direction of a policy council established by the College Board and the Graduate Record Examinations Board.

FOR MORE INFORMATION

TOEFL, P.O. Box 6151, Princeton, New Jersey 08541-6151. Telephone: 609-771-7100. E-mail: toefl@ets.org. World Wide Web: http://www.toefl.org.

Test of Spoken English

The TSE evaluates the spoken English proficiency of people whose native language is not English. The test, which takes about 30 minutes, requires examinees to demonstrate their ability to speak English by answering a variety of questions presented in printed and recorded form. All the answers to test questions are recorded on tape; no writing is required. TSE is given at selected TOEFL test centers worldwide. The test is administered by Educational Testing Service.

The 1999 test dates are March 19, April 17, May 15, and June 11. The registration fee is $125, payable in U.S. dollars.

FOR MORE INFORMATION

Registration material is found in the *Information Bulletin for the Test of Spoken English* available from: TOEFL, P.O. Box 6151, Princeton, New Jersey 08541-6151. Telephone: 609-771-7100.

Veterinary College Admission Test

The VCAT is published and administered by The Psychological Corporation, a division of Harcourt Brace & Company, for applicants seeking admission to schools and colleges of veterinary medicine. The test contains sections on verbal ability, biology, chemistry, quantitative ability, and reading comprehension.

The VCAT is offered in January, October, and November at testing centers in the United States and Canada. Sunday testing may be arranged for applicants who, for religious reasons, can't take the test on Saturday. The exam fee is $60; additional fees are charged for standby registration.

FOR MORE INFORMATION

Contact a college of veterinary medicine or: The Psychological Corporation, 555 Academic Court, San Antonio, Texas 78204. Telephone: 210-299-1061 or 800-622-3231 (7 a.m. to 7 p.m., Monday through Friday, Central time).

Accreditation and Accrediting Agencies

Colleges and universities in the United States, as well as their individual academic and professional programs, are accredited by nongovernmental agencies concerned with monitoring the quality of education in this country. Agencies with both regional and national jurisdictions grant accreditation to institutions as a whole, while specialized bodies acting on a nationwide basis—often national professional associations—grant accreditation to departments and programs in specific fields.

Institutional and specialized accrediting agencies share the same basic concerns:
• The purpose a school, department, or program has set for itself and how well it fulfills that purpose
• The adequacy of its financial and other resources
• The quality of its academic offerings
• The level of services it provides

Agencies that grant institutional accreditation take a broader view, of course, and examine university-wide or college-wide services that a specialized agency may not.

When applying for accreditation, a school or program prepares a self-evaluation, focusing on the concerns mentioned above and usually including an assessment of both its strengths and weaknesses. A team of representatives of the accrediting body reviews this evaluation, visits the campus, and makes its own report. Then the accrediting body makes a decision on the application. Even when accreditation is granted, the agency often makes a recommendation regarding how the institution or program can improve. All institutions and programs are also reviewed every few years to determine whether they continue to meet established standards; if they do not, they may lose their accreditation.

Accrediting agencies themselves are reviewed and evaluated periodically by the U.S. Department of Education and the Council for Higher Education Accreditation (CHEA). Agencies recognized adhere to certain standards and practices, and their authority in matters of accreditation is widely accepted.

Accreditation is not a simple matter, either for schools seeking accreditation or for students deciding where to apply. In fact, in certain fields the very meaning and methods of accreditation are the subject of debate. Graduate school applicants should be aware of the safeguards provided by regional accreditation, especially in terms of degree acceptance and institutional longevity. Applicants should also understand the role that specialized accreditation plays in their field, as this varies from one discipline to another. In certain professional fields, it is necessary to have graduated from a program that is accredited in order to be eligible for a license to practice, and in some fields the federal government also makes this a hiring requirement. In other disciplines, accreditation is not as essential, and there can be excellent programs that are not accredited. In fact, some programs choose not to seek accreditation, although most do.

Institutions and programs that apply for accreditation are sometimes granted the status of candidate for accreditation, or what is known as "preaccreditation." This may happen, for example, when an academic unit is too new to have met all the requirements for accreditation. Such status signifies initial recognition and indicates that the school or program in question is working to fulfill all requirements; it does not, however, guarantee that accreditation will be granted.

You should contact agencies directly for answers to your questions about accreditation. The names and addresses of agencies recognized by the U.S. Department of Education and the Council for Higher Education Accreditation are listed below.

Institutional Accrediting Agencies—Regional

MIDDLE STATES ASSOCIATION OF COLLEGES AND SCHOOLS
Accredits institutions in Delaware, District of Columbia, Maryland, New Jersey, New York, Pennsylvania, Puerto Rico, and the Virgin Islands.
Jean Avnet Morse, Executive Director
Commission on Higher Education
3624 Market Street
Philadelphia, Pennsylvania 19104-2680
Telephone: 215-662-5606
Fax: 215-662-5950
E-mail: jamorse@msache.org

NEW ENGLAND ASSOCIATION OF SCHOOLS AND COLLEGES
Accredits institutions in Connecticut, Maine, Massachusetts, New Hampshire, Rhode Island, and Vermont.
Charles M. Cook, Director
Commission on Institutions of Higher Education
209 Burlington Road
Bedford, Massachusetts 01730-1433
Telephone: 781-271-0022
Fax: 781-271-0950
E-mail: ccook@neasc.org

NORTH CENTRAL ASSOCIATION OF COLLEGES AND SCHOOLS

Accredits institutions in Arizona, Arkansas, Colorado, Illinois, Indiana, Iowa, Kansas, Michigan, Minnesota, Missouri, Nebraska, New Mexico, North Dakota, Ohio, Oklahoma, South Dakota, West Virginia, Wisconsin, and Wyoming.

Steve Crow, Executive Director
Commission on Institutions of Higher Education
30 North LaSalle, Suite 2400
Chicago, Illinois 60602-2504
Telephone: 312-263-0456
Fax: 312-263-7462
E-mail: crow@ncacihe.org

NORTHWEST ASSOCIATION OF SCHOOLS AND COLLEGES

Accredits institutions in Alaska, Idaho, Montana, Nevada, Oregon, Utah, and Washington.

Sandra E. Elman, Executive Director
Commission on Colleges
11130 Northeast 33rd Place, Suite 120
Seattle, Washington 98004
Telephone: 425-827-2005
Fax: 425-827-3395
E-mail: selman@u.washington.edu

SOUTHERN ASSOCIATION OF COLLEGES AND SCHOOLS

Accredits institutions in Alabama, Florida, Georgia, Kentucky, Louisiana, Mississippi, North Carolina, South Carolina, Tennessee, Texas, and Virginia.

James T. Rogers, Executive Director
Commission on Colleges
1866 Southern Lane
Decatur, Georgia 30033-4097
Telephone: 404-679-4500
Fax: 404-679-4558
E-mail: jrogers@sacscoc.org

WESTERN ASSOCIATION OF SCHOOLS AND COLLEGES

Accredits institutions in California, Guam, and Hawaii.

Ralph A. Wolff, Executive Director
Accrediting Commission for Senior Colleges and Universities
Mills College
P.O. Box 9990
Oakland, California 94613-0990
Telephone: 510-632-5000
Fax: 510-632-8361
E-mail: rwolff@wasc.mills.edu

Institutional Accrediting Agencies—Other

ACCREDITING COUNCIL FOR INDEPENDENT COLLEGES AND SCHOOLS

Stephen D. Parker, Executive Director
750 First Street, NE, Suite 980
Washington, D.C. 20002-4241
Telephone: 202-336-6780
Fax: 202-842-2593
E-mail: acics@digex.net
World Wide Web: http://www.acics.org

DISTANCE EDUCATION AND TRAINING COUNCIL

Michael P. Lambert, Executive Secretary
1601 Eighteenth Street, NW
Washington, D.C. 20009-2529
Telephone: 202-234-5100
Fax: 202-332-1386
E-mail: detc@detc.org
World Wide Web: http://www.detc.org

Specialized Accrediting Agencies

ACUPUNCTURE

Dort S. Bigg, Executive Director
Accreditation Commission for Acupuncture and Oriental Medicine
1010 Wayne Avenue, Suite 1270
Silver Spring, Maryland 20910
Telephone: 301-608-9680
Fax: 301-608-9576
E-mail: 73352.2467@compuserve.com

ART AND DESIGN

Samuel Hope, Executive Director
National Association of Schools of Art and Design
11250 Roger Bacon Drive, Suite 21
Reston, Virginia 20190
Telephone: 703-437-0700
Fax: 703-437-6312
E-mail: kpmnasm@aol.com

CHIROPRACTIC

Paul D. Walker, Executive Director
The Council on Chiropractic Education
7975 North Hayden Road, Suite A-210
Scottsdale, Arizona 85258
Telephone: 602-443-8877
Fax: 602-483-7333
E-mail: cceoffice@aol.com

CLINICAL LABORATORY SCIENCE

Cynthia Wells, Chairman
National Accrediting Agency for Clinical Laboratory Sciences
8410 West Bryn Mawr Avenue, Suite 670
Chicago, Illinois 60631
Telephone: 312-714-8880
Fax: 312-714-8886
E-mail: naacls@msc.net

DANCE

Samuel Hope, Executive Director
National Association of Schools of Dance
11250 Roger Bacon Drive, Suite 21
Reston, Virginia 20190
Telephone: 703-437-0700
Fax: 703-437-6312
E-mail: kpmnasm@aol.com

DENTISTRY

James J. Koelbl, Associate Executive Director, Education
American Dental Association
211 East Chicago Avenue, 18th Floor
Chicago, Illinois 60611
Telephone: 312-440-2500

Fax: 312-440-2915
World Wide Web: http://www.ada.org

EDUCATION

Arthur Wise, President
National Council for Accreditation of Teacher Education
2010 Massachusetts Avenue, NW
Washington, D.C. 20036-1023
Telephone: 202-466-7496
Fax: 202-296-6620
E-mail: ncate@ncate.org

ENGINEERING

George D. Peterson, Executive Director
Accreditation Board for Engineering and Technology, Inc.
111 Market Place, Suite 1050
Baltimore, Maryland 21202
Telephone: 410-347-7700
Fax: 410-625-2238
E-mail: kaberle@abet.ba.md.us

ENVIRONMENT

Gary Silverman
National Environmental Health Science and Protection
Accreditation Council
102 Health Center
College of Health and Human Services
Bowling Green State University
Bowling Green, Ohio 43403-0280
Telephone: 419-372-7774
Fax: 419-372-2897
E-mail: silverma@bgnet.bgsu.edu

FORESTRY

P. Gregory Smith, Director, Science and Education
Committee on Education
Society of American Foresters
5400 Grosvenor Lane
Bethesda, Maryland 20814-2198
Telephone: 301-897-8720 Ext. 119
Fax: 301-897-3690
E-mail: smithg@safnet.org
World Wide Web: http://www.safnet.org

HEALTH SERVICES ADMINISTRATION

Patrick M. Sobczak, President
Accrediting Commission on Education for Health Services
Administration
1911 North Fort Myer Drive, Suite 503
Arlington, Virginia 22209-1603
Telephone: 703-524-0511
Fax: 703-525-4791
E-mail: accredcom@aol.com

INTERIOR DESIGN

Kayem Dunn, Director
Foundation for Interior Design Education Research
60 Monroe Center, NW, Suite 300
Grand Rapids, Michigan 49503-2920
Telephone: 616-458-0400
Fax: 616-458-0460

JOURNALISM AND MASS COMMUNICATIONS

Susanne Shaw, Executive Director
Accrediting Council on Education in Journalism and Mass
Communications
School of Journalism
Stauffer-Flint Hall
University of Kansas
Lawrence, Kansas 66045
Telephone: 913-864-3986
Fax: 913-864-5225
E-mail: sshaw@ukans.edu
World Wide Web: http://www.ukans.edu/~acejmc

LANDSCAPE ARCHITECTURE

Ronald C. Leighton, Accreditation Manager
Landscape Architectural Accreditation Board
American Society of Landscape Architects
4401 Connecticut Avenue, NW, Fifth Floor
Washington, D.C. 20008-2369
Telephone: 202-686-2752
Fax: 202-686-1001
E-mail: rleighton@asla.org
World Wide Web: http://www.asla.org/asla/

LAW

Carl Monk, Executive Vice President
Accreditation Committee
Association of American Law Schools
1201 Connecticut Avenue, NW, Suite 800
Washington, D.C. 20036-2605
Telephone: 202-296-8851
Fax: 202-296-8869
E-mail: cmonk@aals.org
World Wide Web: http://www.aals.org

James P. White, Consultant on Legal Education
American Bar Association
Indiana University
550 West North Street
Indianapolis, Indiana 46202
Telephone: 317-264-8340
Fax: 317-264-8355
E-mail: jwhite@iupui.edu

LIBRARY

Mary Taylor, Acting Director
Committee on Accreditation
American Library Association
50 East Huron Street
Chicago, Illinois 60611
Telephone: 800-545-2433 Ext. 2436
Fax: 312-280-2433
E-mail: mtaylor@ala.org

MARRIAGE AND FAMILY THERAPY

Colleen Peterson, Executive Director
American Association for Marriage and Family Therapy
1133 15th Street, NW, Suite 300
Washington, D.C. 20005-2710
Telephone: 202-452-0109
Fax: 202-232-2329
E-mail: cpeterson@aamft.org

MEDICAL ILLUSTRATION
Alice Katz, Chair
Accreditation Review Committee for the Medical Illustrator
University of Illinois at Chicago
1919 West Taylor, Room 213
Chicago, Illinois 60612-7249
Telephone: 312-996-1303
Fax: 312-996-8342
E-mail: aakatz@uic.edu

MEDICINE
Liaison Committee on Medical Education
The LCME is administered in even-numbered years, beginning
   each July 1, by:
Donald G. Kassebaum, M.D., Secretary
Association of American Medical Colleges
2450 N Street, NW
Washington, D.C. 20037
Telephone: 202-828-0596
Fax: 202-828-1125
E-mail: dgkassebaum@aamc.org
World Wide Web: http://www.aamc.org
The LCME is administered in odd-numbered years, beginning
   each July 1, by:
Harry S. Jonas, M.D., Secretary
American Medical Association
515 North State Street
Chicago, Illinois 60610
Telephone: 312-464-4657
Fax: 312-464-5830
E-mail: harry_jonas@ama-assn.org
World Wide Web: http://www.ama-assn.org

MUSIC
Samuel Hope, Executive Director
National Association of Schools of Music
11250 Roger Bacon Drive, Suite 21
Reston, Virginia 20190
Telephone: 703-437-0700
Fax: 703-437-6312
E-mail: kpmnasm@aol.com

NATUROPATHIC MEDICINE
Robert Lofft, Executive Director
Council on Naturopathic Medical Education
P.O. Box 11426
Eugene, Oregon 97440-3626
Telephone: 541-484-6028
E-mail: crest@clipper.net

NURSE ANESTHESIA
Betty J. Horton, Director of Accreditation
Council on Accreditation of Nurse Anesthetists Educational
   Programs
222 South Prospect Avenue, Suite 304
Park Ridge, Illinois 60068-4010
Telephone: 847-692-7050
Fax: 847-693-7137
E-mail: 75777.1576@compuserve.com

NURSE MIDWIFERY
Helen Varney Burst, Chair
Division of Accreditation

American College of Nurse-Midwives
818 Connecticut Avenue, NW, Suite 900
Washington, D.C. 20006
Telephone: 202-728-9877
Fax: 202-728-9897
E-mail: lslatter@acnm.org

NURSING
Geraldene Felton, Executive Director
National League for Nursing
350 Hudson Street
New York, New York 10014
Telephone: 800-669-1656
Fax: 212-989-3710
E-mail: gfelton@nln.org

OCCUPATIONAL THERAPY
Doris Gordon, Director
American Occupational Therapy Association
4720 Montgomery Lane
P.O. Box 31220
Bethesda, Maryland 20824-1220
Telephone: 301-652-2682
Fax: 301-652-7711
E-mail: DORISG@AOTA.ORG

OPTOMETRY
Joyce Urbeck, Administrative Director
Council on Optometric Education
American Optometric Association
243 North Lindbergh Boulevard
St. Louis, Missouri 63141
Telephone: 314-991-4100
Fax: 314-991-4101
E-mail: urbeckcoe@aol.com

OSTEOPATHIC MEDICINE
Konrad Retz, Executive Director
Bureau of Professional Education, Council on Predoctoral
   Education
American Osteopathic Association
142 East Ontario Street
Chicago, Illinois 60611
Telephone: 312-280-5840
Fax: 312-280-3860

PASTORAL EDUCATION
Russell H. Davis, Executive Director
Accreditation Commission
Association for Clinical Pastoral Education, Inc.
1549 Claremont Road, Suite 103
Decatur, Georgia 30033-4611
Telephone: 404-320-1472
Fax: 404-320-0849
E-mail: 71210.2243@compuserve.com

PHARMACY
Daniel A. Nona, Executive Director
American Council on Pharmaceutical Education
311 West Superior Street
Chicago, Illinois 60610
Telephone: 312-664-3575
Fax: 312-664-4652
E-mail: acpe@compuserve.com

PHYSICAL THERAPY

Virginia Nieland, Director
Department of Accreditation
American Physical Therapy Association
Trans Potomac Plaza
1111 North Fairfax Street
Alexandria, Virginia 22314
Telephone: 703-684-3245
Fax: 703-684-7343
E-mail: vnieland@apta.org

PLANNING

Beatrice Clupper, Director
American Institute of Certified Planners/Association of
    Collegiate Schools of Planning
Merle Hay Tower, Suite 302
3800 Merle Hay Road
Des Moines, Iowa 50310
Telephone: 515-252-0729 or 0733
Fax: 515-252-7404
E-mail: fi_pab@netins.net

PODIATRIC MEDICINE

Alan R. Tinkleman, Director
Council on Podiatric Medical Education
American Podiatric Medical Association
9312 Old Georgetown Road
Bethesda, Maryland 20814-2752
Telephone: 301-571-9200
Fax: 301-581-9299
E-mail: artinkleman@apma.org

PSYCHOLOGY AND COUNSELING

Susan F. Zlotlow, Director
American Psychological Association
750 First Street, NE
Washington, D.C. 20002-4242
Telephone: 202-336-5979
Fax: 202-336-5978
E-mail: pdn.apa@email.apa.org
World Wide Web: http://www.apa.org/ed/accred.html

Carol L. Bobby, Executive Director
Council for Accreditation of Counseling and Related
    Educational Programs
American Counseling Association
5999 Stevenson Avenue
Alexandria, Virginia 22304
Telephone: 703-823-9800 Ext. 301
Fax: 703-823-0252
E-mail: cacrep@aol.com

PUBLIC AFFAIRS AND ADMINISTRATION

Michael A. Brintnall, Executive Director
Commission on Peer Review and Accreditation
National Association of Schools of Public Affairs and
    Administration
1120 G Street, NW, Suite 730
Washington, D.C. 20005
Telephone: 202-628-8965
Fax: 202-626-4978
E-mail: naspaa@naspaa.org
World Wide Web: http://cwis.unomaha.edu/~wwwpa/nashome.
    html

PUBLIC HEALTH

Patricia Evans, Executive Director
Council on Education for Public Health
1015 Fifteenth Street, NW, Suite 403
Washington, D.C. 20005
Telephone: 202-789-1050
Fax: 202-789-1895
E-mail: evan0015@cdc.gov

RABBINICAL AND TALMUDIC EDUCATION

Bernard Fryshman, Executive Vice President
Association of Advanced Rabbinical and Talmudic Schools
175 Fifth Avenue, Suite 711
New York, New York 10010
Telephone: 212-477-0950
Fax: 212-533-5335

REHABILITATION EDUCATION

Jeanne Patterson, Executive Director
Council on Rehabilitation Education
Commission on Standards and Accreditation
1835 Rohlwing Road, Suite E
Rolling Meadows, Illinois 60008
Telephone: 847-394-1785
Fax: 847-394-2108
E-mail: patters@polaris.net

SOCIAL WORK

Nancy Randolph, Director
Council on Social Work Education
1600 Duke Street, Suite 300
Alexandria, Virginia 22314
Telephone: 703-683-8080
Fax: 703-683-8099
E-mail: accred@cswe.org
World Wide Web: http://www.cswe.org

SPEECH-LANGUAGE PATHOLOGY AND AUDIOLOGY

Sharon Goldsmith, Director
American Speech-Language-Hearing Association
10801 Rockville Pike
Rockville, Maryland 20852
Telephone: 301-897-5700
Fax: 301-571-0457
E-mail: sgoldsmith@asha.org
World Wide Web: http://www.asha.org/

THEATER

Samuel Hope, Executive Director
National Association of Schools of Theatre
11250 Roger Bacon Drive, Suite 21
Reston, Virginia 20190
Telephone: 703-437-0700
Fax: 703-437-6312
E-mail: kpmnasm@aol.com

THEOLOGY

James L. Waits, Executive Director
Association of Theological Schools in the United States and
    Canada
10 Summit Park Drive
Pittsburgh, Pennsylvania 15275-1103
Telephone: 412-788-6505

Fax: 412-788-6510
E-mail: ats@ats.edu

VETERINARY MEDICINE

Donald G. Simmons, Director of Education and
    Research Division
American Veterinary Medical Association
1931 North Meacham Road, Suite 100
Schaumburg, Illinois 60173
Telephone: 847-925-8070
Fax: 847-925-1329
E-mail: dsimmons@avma.org

Abbreviations Used in this Book

The following list includes abbreviations of degree names used in the profiles. Because some degrees (e.g., Doctor of Education) can be abbreviated in more than one way (e.g., D Ed or Ed D) and because the abbreviations used reflect the preferences of the individual colleges and universities, the list may include two or more abbreviations for a single degree.

Degrees

AC	Advanced Certificate
AD	Artist's Diploma Doctor of Arts
ADP	Artist's Diploma
Adv C	Advanced Certificate
Adv M	Advanced Master
AE	Aerospace Engineer Agricultural Engineer
AEMBA	Advanced Executive Master of Business Administration
Aerospace E	Aerospace Engineer
AGC	Advanced Graduate Certificate
AGSC	Advanced Graduate Specialist Certificate
ALM	Master of Liberal Arts
AM	Master of Arts
AMPC	Advanced Management Program for Clinician
AMRS	Master of Arts in Religious Studies
A Mus D	Doctor of Musical Arts
APC	Advanced Professional Certificate
App ME	Applied Mechanics
App Sc	Applied Scientist
Au D	Doctor of Audiology
B Th	Bachelor of Theology
CAES	Certificate of Advanced Educational Specialization
CAGS	Certificate of Advanced Graduate Studies
CAL	Certificate of Advanced Librarianship Certificate in Applied Linguistics
CAMS	Certificate of Advanced Management Studies
CAPS	Certificate of Advanced Professional Studies
CAS	Certificate of Advanced Studies
CASPA	Certificate of Advanced Study in Public Administration
CASR	Certificate in Advanced Social Research
CBHS	Certificate in Basic Health Sciences
CCJA	Certificate in Criminal Justice Administration
CE	Civil Engineer
CG	Certificate in Gerontology
CGS	Certificate of Graduate Studies

Ch E	Chemical Engineer
Chem E	Chemical Engineer
CHSS	Counseling and Human Services Specialist
CIF	Certificate in International Finance
CITS	Certificate of Individual Theological Studies
CLIS	Certificate of Library and Information Science
CMH	Certificate in Medical Humanities
CMS	Certificate in Ministerial Studies Certificate in Music Studies
CNM	Certificate in Nonprofit Management
CP	Certificate in Performance
CPC	Certificate in Professional Counseling Certificate in Publications and Communications
CPH	Certificate in Public Health
C Phil	Candidate in Philosophy Certificate in Philosophy
CPI	Certificate in Planning Information
CPM	Certificate in Public Management
CPS	Certificate of Professional Studies
CSD	Certificate in Spiritual Direction
CSE	Computer Systems Engineer
CSS	Certificate of Special Studies
CTS	Certificate of Theological Studies Certified Tax Specialist
CURP	Certificate in Urban and Regional Planning
DA	Doctor of Accounting Doctor of Arts
DA Ed	Doctor of Arts in Education
D Arch	Doctor of Architecture
DAST	Diploma of Advanced Studies in Teaching
DBA	Doctor of Business Administration
DC	Doctor of Chiropractic
DCC	Doctor of Computer Science
D Chem	Doctor of Chemistry
DCL	Doctor of Canon Law Doctor of Civil Law
DCM	Doctor of Church Music
DCS	Doctor of Computer Science
DDS	Doctor of Dental Surgery
DE	Doctor of Engineering
D Ed	Doctor of Education
DEM	Doctor of Educational Ministry
D Eng	Doctor of Engineering
D Env	Doctor of Environment

DES	Doctor of Engineering Science		DSW	Doctor of Social Work
DF	Doctor of Forestry		D Th	Doctor of Theology
DFA	Doctor of Fine Arts		DVM	Doctor of Veterinary Medicine
DFES	Doctor of Forestry and Environmental Studies		DV Sc	Doctor of Veterinary Science
DGP	Diploma in Graduate and Professional Studies		EAA	Engineer in Aeronautics and Astronautics
DHA	Doctor of Health Administration		EAS	Education Administration Specialist
DHCE	Doctor of Health Care Ethics		Ed D	Doctor of Education
DHL	Doctor of Hebrew Letters Doctor of Hebrew Literature		Ed DCT	Doctor of Education in College Teaching
DHS	Doctor of Human Services		EDM	Executive Doctorate in Management
DIBA	Doctor of International Business Administration		Ed M	Master of Education
Dip CS	Diploma in Christian Studies		Ed S	Specialist in Education
DIT	Doctor of Industrial Technology		EE	Electrical Engineer
DJ Ed	Doctor of Jewish Education		EM	Mining Engineer
DJS	Doctor of Jewish Studies		EMBA	Executive Master of Business Administration
D Jur	Doctor of Jurisprudence		EMIB	Executive Master of International Business
D Law	Doctor of Law		EMPA	Executive Master of Public Affairs
D Litt	Doctor of Letters		EMRA	Executive Master of Rehabilitation Administration
DM	Doctor of Management Doctor of Music		EMS	Executive Master of Science
DMA	Doctor of Musical Arts		EMSF	Executive Master of Science in Finance
DMD	Doctor of Dental Medicine		EMSILR	Executive Master of Science in Industrial and Labor Relations
DME	Doctor of Music Education		Eng	Engineer
D Med Sc	Doctor of Medical Science		Engr	Engineer
D Min	Doctor of Ministry		Eng Sc D	Doctor of Engineering Science
D Min PCC	Doctor of Ministry, Pastoral Care, and Counseling		Exec Ed D	Executive Doctor of Education
D Miss	Doctor of Missiology		Exec MBA	Executive Master of Business Administration
DML	Doctor of Modern Languages		Exec MGA	Executive Master of General Administration
DMM	Doctor of Music Ministry		Exec MIM	Executive Master of International Management
D Mus	Doctor of Music		Exec MPA	Executive Master of Public Administration
D Mus A	Doctor of Musical Arts		Exec MPH	Executive Master of Public Health
D Mus Ed	Doctor of Music Education		Exec MS	Executive Master of Science
DNS	Doctor of Nursing Science		GDPA	Graduate Diploma in Public Administration
DN Sc	Doctor of Nursing Science		GDRE	Graduate Diploma in Religious Education
DO	Doctor of Osteopathy		Geol E	Geological Engineer
DPA	Diploma in Public Administration Doctor of Public Administration		GMBA	Global Master of Business Administration
DPC	Doctor of Pastoral Counseling		GPD	Graduate Performance Diploma
DPE	Doctor of Physical Education		GPMBA	Global Professional Master of Business Administration
DPH	Doctor of Public Health		HSD	Doctor of Health and Safety
D Phil	Doctor of Philosophy		HS Dir	Director of Health and Safety
DPM	Doctor of Podiatric Medicine		IEMBA	International Executive Master of Business Administration
DPS	Doctor of Professional Studies		IMA	Interdisciplinary Master of Arts
D Ps	Diploma of Psychology Doctor of Psychology		IMBA	Integrative Master of Business Administration International Master of Business Administration
DPT	Doctor of Physical Therapy		IOE	Industrial and Operations Engineer
Dr DES	Doctor of Design		JCD	Doctor of Canon Law
Dr OT	Doctor of Occupational Therapy		JCL	Licentiate in Canon Law
Dr PH	Doctor of Public Health		JD	Juris Doctor
D Sc	Doctor of Science		JSD	Doctor of Juridical Science Doctor of Jurisprudence
D Sc D	Doctor of Science in Dentistry		JSM	Master of Science of Law
DSM	Doctor of Sacred Music		LL B	Bachelor of Laws
DSN	Doctor of Science in Nursing		LL D	Doctor of Laws
DS Sc	Doctor of Social Science			

LL M	Master of Laws
LL M CL	Master of Laws in Comparative Law
LL M T	Master of Laws in Taxation
L Th	Licenciate in Theology
MA	Master of Arts
MAA	Master of Administrative Arts Master of Aeronautics and Astronautics Master of Applied Arts
MAAA	Master of Arts in Arts Administration
MAABS	Master of Arts in Applied Behavioral Sciences
MAADAM	Master of Arts in Alcoholism and Drug Abuse Ministry
MAAE	Master of Aeronautical and Astronautical Engineering Master of Arts in Applied Economics Master of Arts in Art Education
MAAT	Master of Arts in Applied Theology Master of Arts in Art Therapy
MAB	Master of Agribusiness Master of Arts in Business
MABC	Master of Arts in Biblical Counseling
MABM	Master of Agribusiness Management
MABS	Master of Arts in Behavioral Science Master of Arts in Biblical Studies
M Ac	Master of Accountancy Master of Accounting Master of Acupuncture
MAC	Master of Arts in Communication Master of Arts in Counseling
MACAT	Master of Arts in Counseling Psychology: Art Therapy
M Acc	Master of Accountancy
MACCM	Master of Arts in Church and Community Ministry
M Acct	Master of Accountancy Master of Accounting
M Accy	Master of Accountancy
MACE	Master of Arts in Christian Education Master of Arts in Computer Education
MACH	Master of Arts in Church History
MACL	Master of Arts in Classroom Psychology
MACM	Master of Arts in Christian Ministries Master of Arts in Church Music
MACO	Master of Arts in Counseling
M Ac OM	Master of Acupuncture and Oriental Medicine
MA Comm	Master of Arts in Communication
MACP	Master of Arts in Community Psychology Master of Arts in Counseling Psychology
MACT	Master of Arts in College Teaching
MACTM	Master of Applied Communication Theory and Methodology
M Acy	Master of Accountancy
MACY	Master of Arts in Accountancy
M Ad	Master of Administration
M Ad Ed	Master of Adult Education
MADH	Master of Applied Development and Health
M Adm	Master of Administration
M Admin	Master of Administration
M Adm Mgt	Master of Administrative Management
MADR	Master of Arts in Dispute Resolution

MAE	Master of Aerospace Engineering Master of Agricultural Economics Master of Agricultural Education Master of Agricultural Engineering Master of Art Education Master of Arts in Education Master of Arts in English Master of Automotive Engineering
MA Ed	Master of Arts in Education
MA Ed U	Master of Arts in Education
M Aero E	Master of Aerospace Engineering
MAES	Master of Arts in Environmental Sciences
MAF	Master of Arts in Finance
MAFIS	Master of Accountancy and Financial Information Systems
MAFLL	Master of Arts in Foreign Language and Literature
MAFM	Master of Accounting and Financial Management
M Ag	Master of Agriculture
MAG	Master of Applied Geography
M Ag Ed	Master of Agricultural Education
MAGP	Master of Arts in Gerontological Psychology
M Agr	Master of Agriculture
MAGU	Master of Urban Analysis and Management
MAH	Master of Arts in Humanities
MAHCD	Master of Applied Human and Community Development
MAHL	Master of Arts in Hebrew Letters Master of Arts in Hebrew Literature
MAHRM	Master of Arts in Human Resources Management
MAICS	Master of Arts in Intercultural Studies
MAIDM	Master of Arts in Interior Design and Merchandising
MAIND	Master of Arts in Interior Design
MAIR	Master of Arts in Industrial Relations
MAIS	Master of Accounting and Information Systems Master of Accounting Information Systems Master of Arts in Interdisciplinary Studies Master of Arts in International Studies
MAJ	Master of Arts in Journalism
MAJC	Master of Arts in Journalism and Communication
MAJCS	Master of Arts in Jewish Communal Service
MAJE	Master of Arts in Jewish Education
MAJ Ed	Master of Arts in Jewish Education
MAJS	Master of Arts in Jewish Studies
MALA	Master of Arts in Liberal Arts Master of Arts in Liturgical Arts
MALAS	Master of Arts in Latin American Studies
MALD	Master of Arts in Law and Diplomacy
MALER	Master of Arts in Labor and Employment Relations
MALIS	Master of Arts in Library and Information Science
MALL	Master of Arts in Liberal Learning
MALS	Master of Arts in Liberal Studies Master of Arts in Library Science
MAM	Master of Agriculture and Management Master of Animal Medicine Master of Applied Mechanics Master of Arts in Management Master of Arts Management Master of Arts—Ministry Master of Association Management Master of Avian Medicine Master of Aviation Management
MAMB	Master of Applied Molecular Biology

MAMC	Master of Arts in Mass Communication
MAME	Master of Arts in Missions/Evangelism
MAMFC	Master of Arts in Marriage and Family Counseling
MAMFCC	Master of Arts in Marriage, Family, and Child Counseling
MAMFT	Master of Arts in Marriage and Family Therapy
MA Min	Master of Arts in Ministry
MA Missions	Master of Arts in Missions
MAML	Master of Arts in School Media Librarianship
MAMM	Master of Arts in Ministry Management Master of Arts in Music Ministry
MAMS	Master of Applied Mathematical Sciences Master of Associated Medical Sciences
MAM Sc	Master of Applied Mathematical Science
MAMT	Master of Arts in Mathematics Teaching
M Anesth Ed	Master of Anesthesiology Education
MANM	Master of Arts in Nonprofit Management
MANT	Master of Arts in New Testament
MAO	Master of Arts in Organizational Psychology
MAOE	Master of Adult and Occupational Education
MAOM	Master of Arts in Organizational Management
MAOT	Master of Arts in Old Testament
MAP	Master of Applied Psychology Master of Arts in Planning
MAPA	Master of Arts in Public Administration Master of Arts in Public Affairs
MA Past St	Master of Arts in Pastoral Studies
MAPC	Master of Arts in Pastoral Counseling
MAPE	Master of Arts in Physical Education Master of Arts in Political Economy
MAPM	Master of Arts in Pastoral Ministry Master of Arts in Pastoral Music
M Ap Ma	Master of Applied Mathematics
MAP Min	Master of Arts in Pastoral Ministry
MAPP	Master of Arts in Public Policy
M Appl Stat	Master of Applied Statistics
M App St	Master of Applied Statistics
MA Ps	Master of Arts in Psychology
MAPS	Master of Arts in Pastoral Studies
MA Psych	Master of Arts in Psychology
MAPW	Master of Arts in Professional Writing
M Aq	Master of Aquaculture
MA (R)	Master of Arts (Research)
MAR	Master of Arts in Religion Master of Arts in Research
MA(R)	Master of Arts (Research)
M Arc	Master of Architecture
MARC	Master of Arts in Religious Communication
M Arch	Master of Architecture
M Arch E	Master of Architectural Engineering
M Arch H	Master of Architectural History
M Arch UD	Master of Architecture in Urban Design
MARE	Master of Arts in Religious Education
Mar Eng	Marine Engineer
MARL	Master of Arts in Religious Leadership
MARS	Master of Arts in Religious Studies

MART	Master of Arts in Religion and Theology
MAS	Master of Accounting Science Master of Administrative Science Master of Aeronautical Science Master of American Studies Master of Applied Science Master of Applied Spirituality Master of Applied Statistics Master of Archival Studies
MASA	Master of Advanced Studies in Architecture
MASAC	Master of Arts in Substance Abuse Counseling
MA Sc	Master of Applied Science
MASD	Master of Arts in Spiritual Direction
MASLA	Master of Advanced Studies in Landscape Architecture
MASM	Master of Arts in Specialized Ministries Master of Arts in Special Ministries
MASP	Master of Arts in School Psychology
MASPAA	Master of Arts in Sports and Athletic Administration
MASS	Master of Arts in Social Science Master of Arts in Special Studies
MA(T)	Master of Arts in Teaching
MAT	Master of Arts in Teaching Master of Arts in Theology
MATCM	Master of Acupuncture and Traditional Chinese Medicine
MATE	Master of Arts for the Teaching of English
Mat E	Materials Engineer
MATESL	Master of Arts in Teaching English as a Second Language
MATESOL	Master of Arts in Teaching English to Speakers of Other Languages
MATEX	Master of Arts in Textiles
MATFL	Master of Arts in Teaching Foreign Language
MA Th	Master of Arts in Theology
MATH	Master of Arts in Therapy
MATI	Master of Administration of Information Technology
MATL	Master of Arts in Teaching of Languages
MATM	Master of Arts in Teaching of Mathematics
MATS	Master of Arts in Teaching of Science Master of Arts in Theological Studies Master of Arts in Transforming Spirituality
MAUA	Master of Arts in Urban Affairs
MAUD	Master of Arts in Urban Design
MAURP	Master of Arts in Urban and Regional Planning
MAV Ed	Master of Administration in Vocational Education
MAW	Master of Arts in Worship Master of Arts in Writing
MBA	Master of Business Administration
MBAA	Master of Business Administration in Aviation
MBA Arts	Master of Business Administration in Arts
MBAE	Master of Biological and Agricultural Engineering Master of Biosystems and Agricultural Engineering
MBA-EP	Master of Business Administration–Experienced Professionals
MBAi	Master of Business Administration–International
MBAIB	Master of Business Administration in International Business
MBAPA	Master of Business Administration–Physician Assistant
MBA-PE	Master of Business Administration–Physician's Executive
MBATM	Master of Business in Telecommunication Management
MBC	Master of Building Construction

ABBREVIATIONS USED IN THIS BOOK

MBE	Master of Bilingual Education Master of Business Economics Master of Business Education	M Cp E	Master of Computer Engineering
		MCRP	Master of City and Regional Planning
MBHCM	Master of Behavioral Health Care Management	MCS	Master of Clinical Science Master of Communication Studies Master of Computer Science
M Bio E	Master of Bioengineering		
M Biomath	Master of Biomathematics	MC Sc	Master of Computer Science
MBMSE	Master of Business Management and Software Engineering	MCSM	Master of Construction Science/Management
MBOL	Master of Business and Organizational Leadership	MCT	Master of Christian Theology
MBS	Master of Basic Science Master of Behavioral Science Master of Biblical Studies Master of Biological Science Master of Biomedical Sciences Master of Building Science Master of Business Studies	MD	Doctor of Medicine
		MDA	Master of Development Administration
		MDE	Master of Developmental Economics Master of Distance Education
		M Dec S	Master of Decision Sciences
MBSI	Master of Business Information Science	M Dent Sc	Master of Dental Sciences
MBT	Master of Business Taxation	M Des	Master of Design
M Bus Ed	Master of Business Education	M Des S	Master of Design Studies
MC	Master of Communication Master of Counseling	M Div	Master of Divinity
		M Div CM	Master of Divinity in Church Music
MCA	Master of Commercial Aviation Master of Communication Arts	MDR	Master of Dispute Resolution
		MDS	Master of Decision Sciences Master of Dental Surgery
MCC	Master of Computer Science		
MCD	Master of Communications Disorders	ME	Master of Education Master of Engineering
MCDCC	Master of Career Development and Community Counseling		
MCE	Master of Christian Education Master of Civil Engineering Master of Control Engineering	MEA	Master of Engineering Administration Master of Engineering Architecture
		M Ec	Master of Economics
MC Ed	Master of Continuing Education	MECE	Master of Electrical and Computer Engineering
MCED	Master of Community Economic Development	Mech E	Mechanical Engineer
MCEM	Master of Construction Engineering Management	M Econ	Master of Economics
MCG	Master of Clinical Gerontology	MED	Master of Education of the Deaf
MCH	Master of Community Health	M Ed	Master of Education
M Ch E	Master of Chemical Engineering	MEDS	Master of Environmental Design Studies
M Chem E	Master of Chemical Engineering	M Ed T	Master of Education in Teaching
MCIS	Master of Computer and Information Science Master of Computer Information Systems	MEE	Master of Electrical Engineering Master of Environmental Engineering
M Civil E	Master of Civil Engineering	ME Ed	Master of Agriculture and Extension Education
MCJ	Master of Comparative Jurisprudence Master of Criminal Justice	MEEM	Master of Environmental Engineering and Management
		MEENE	Master of Engineering in Environmental Engineering
MCJA	Master of Criminal Justice Administration	MEERM	Master of Earth and Environmental Resource Management
MCL	Master of Canon Law Master of Civil Law Master of Comparative Law	MEL	Master of Educational Leadership
		M Elec E	Master of Electrical Engineering
M Cl D	Master of Clinical Dentistry	MEM	Master of Ecosystem Management Master of Educational Ministry Master of Engineering Management Master of Environmental Management
M Cl Sc	Master of Clinical Science		
MCM	Master of Christian Ministry Master of Church Management Master of Church Ministry Master of Church Music Master of Clinical Microbiology Master of Construction Management		
		MEMS	Master of Emergency Medical Service Master of Engineering in Manufacturing Systems
		M Eng	Master of Engineering
MCMS	Master of Clinical Medical Science	M Eng Mgt	Master of Engineering Management
M Co E	Master of Computer Engineering	M Engr	Master of Engineering
M Comp E	Master of Computer Engineering	M En S	Master of Environmental Sciences
M Coun	Master of Counseling	M Env	Master of Environment
MCP	Master of City Planning Master of Community Planning Master of Community Psychology Master of Counseling Psychology	M Env Des	Master of Environmental Design
		M Env E	Master of Environmental Engineering
		MENVEGR	Master of Environmental Engineering
		M Envir E	Master of Environmental Engineering
MCPD	Master of Community Planning and Development	M Env Sc	Master of Environmental Science

MEP	Master of Engineering Physics Master of Environmental Planning
MEPC	Master of Environmental Pollution Control
MEPD	Master of Education–Professional Development
MEPM	Master of Environmental Policy and Management
MER	Master of Energy Resources
MES	Master of Engineering Science Master of Environmental Studies Master of Special Education
ME Sc	Master of Engineering Science
MESM	Master of Environmental Science and Management
MESS	Master of Exercise and Sport Sciences
MET	Master of Education in Teaching
Met E	Metallurgical Engineer
METM	Master of Engineering and Technology Management
MEVE	Master of Environmental Engineering
M Ext Ed	Master of Extension Education
MF	Master of Finance Master of Forestry
MFA	Master of Fine Arts
MFAS	Master of Fisheries and Aquatic Science
MFAW	Master of Fine Arts in Writing
MFC	Master of Forest Conservation
MFCC	Marriage and Family Counseling Certificate Marriage, Family, and Child Counseling
MFCS	Master of Family and Consumer Sciences
MFE	Master of Financial Economics Master of Forest Engineering
M Fin	Master of Finance
MFR	Master of Forest Resources
M Fr	Master of French
MFRC	Master of Forest Resources and Conservation
MFS	Master of Family Studies Master of Food Science Master of Forensic Studies Master of Forest Studies Master of French Studies
MFT	Master of Family Therapy
MGA	Master of Government Administration
MGCOD	Master of Group Counseling and Organizational Dynamics
MGD	Master of Graphic Design
M Gen E	Master of General Engineering
M Geo E	Master of Geological Engineering
M Geoenv E	Master of Geoenvironmental Engineering
M Geotech E	Master of Geotechnical Engineering
MGIS	Master of Geographic Information Science
MGP	Master of Gestion de Projet
MGPGP	Master of Group Process and Group Psychotherapy
MGS	Master of General Studies Master of Gerontological Studies
MH	Master of Health Master of Humanities
MHA	Master of Health Administration Master of Hospital Administration
MHAMS	Master of Historical Administration and Museum Studies
MHCA	Master of Health Care Administration
MHCI	Master of Human-Computer Interaction

MHD	Master of Human Development
MHE	Master of Health Education Master of Higher Education Master of Home Economics Master of Human Ecology
MHE Ed	Master of Home Economics Education
MHHS	Master of Health and Human Services
MHK	Master of Human Kinetics
MHL	Master of Hebrew Literature
MHM	Master of Hotel Management
MHMS	Master of Health Management Systems
MHP	Master of Health Professions Master of Heritage Preservation Master of Historic Preservation Master of Humanities in Philosophy
MHPE	Master of Health and Physical Education Master of Health Professions Education Master of Health Promotion and Education
MHR	Master of Human Resources
MHRD	Master in Human Resource Development
MHRDOD	Master of Human Resource Development/Organizational Development
MHRIM	Master of Hotel, Restaurant, and Institutional Management
MHRIR	Master of Human Resources and Industrial Relations
MHRLR	Master of Human Resources and Labor Relations
MHRM	Master of Human Resources Management
MHROD	Master of Human Resources and Organization Development
MHRTA	Master in Hotel, Restaurant, Tourism, and Administration
MHS	Master of Healthcare Systems Master of Health Sciences Master of Hispanic Studies Master of Humane Studies Master of Human Services
MHSA	Master of Health Services Administration Master of Human Services Administration
MH Sc	Master of Health Sciences
MHSE	Master of Health Science Education
M Hum	Master of Humanities
M Hum Svcs	Master of Human Services
MI	Master of Instruction Master of Insurance
MIA	Master of Intercultural Administration Master of Interior Architecture Master of International Administration Master of International Affairs
MI Arch	Master of Interior Architecture
MIB	Master of International Business
MIBA	Master of International Business Administration
MIBS	Master of International Business Studies
MICS	Master of Arts in Intercultural Studies
MID	Master of Industrial Design Master of Interior Design
MIE	Master of Industrial Engineering
MIE Mgmt	Master of Industrial Engineering Management
MIHM	Master of International Health Management
MIIM	Master of International and Intercultural Management
MIJ	Master of International Journalism
MILR	Master of Industrial and Labor Relations

MIM	Master of Industrial Management Master of Information Management Master of International Management
MIMLA	Master of International Management for Latin America
MIMOT	Master of International Management of Technology
MIMS	Master of Information Management and Systems Master of Integrated Manufacturing Systems
M In Ed	Master of Industrial Education
Minl E	Mineral Engineer
MIP	Master of Infrastructure Planning Master of Intellectual Property
MIPP	Master of International Public Policy
MIR	Master of Industrial Relations
MIS	Master of Individualized Studies Master of Industrial Statistics Master of Information Science Master of Information Systems Master of Interdisciplinary Studies Master of International Studies
MISM	Master of Information Systems Management
MI St	Master of Information Studies
MIT	Master in Teaching Master of Information Technology Master of Industrial Technology Master of Initial Teaching
MITA	Master of Information Technology Administration
MITM	Master of International Technology Management
MJ	Master of Journalism Master of Jurisprudence
MJA	Master of Justice Administration
MJ Ed	Master of Jewish Education
MJPM	Master of Justice Policy and Management
MJS	Master of Judaic Studies Master of Juridical Science
M Kin	Master of Kinesiology
MLA	Master of Landscape Architecture Master of Liberal Arts
M Land Arch	Master of Landscape Architecture
ML Arch	Master of Landscape Architecture
MLAS	Master of Laboratory Animal Science
MLAUD	Master of Landscape Architecture in Urban Development
MLD	Master of Leadership Studies
MLE	Master of Applied Linguistics and Exegesis
MLHR	Master of Labor and Human Resources
MLI	Master of Legal Institutions
MLIR	Master of Labor and Industrial Relations
MLIS	Master of Library and Information Science Master of Library and Information Services
M Lit M	Master of Liturgical Music
M Litt	Master of Letters
MLM	Master of Library Media
MLOG	Master of Engineering Logistics
MLRHR	Master of Labor Relations and Human Resources
MLS	Master of Legal Studies Master of Liberal Studies Master of Library Science Master of Library Services Master of Life Sciences Master of Medical Laboratory Sciences
MLSP	Master of Law and Social Policy

MM	Master of Management Master of Ministry Master of Modern Studies Master of Music
MMA	Master of Manpower Administration Master of Marine Affairs Master of Media Arts Master of Musical Arts
MMAE	Master of Mechanical and Aerospace Engineering
MMAS	Master of Military Art and Science
M Math	Master of Mathematics
M Mat SE	Master of Material Science and Engineering
MMC	Master of Managerial Communication Master of Mass Communications
MMCM	Master of Music in Church Music
MME	Master of Manufacturing Engineering Master of Mathematics for Educators Master of Mechanical Engineering Master of Mining Engineering Master of Music Education
M Mech E	Master of Mechanical Engineering
MM Ed	Master of Music Education
M Med Sc	Master of Medical Science
MMF	Master of Mathematical Finance
MMFT	Master of Marriage and Family Therapy
M Mgmt	Master of Management
M Mgt	Master of Management
MMH	Master of Management in Hospitality Master of Medical History Master of Medical Humanities
M Min	Master of Ministries
MMIS	Master of Management Information Systems
M Miss	Master of Missiology
MMM	Master of Management in Manufacturing Master of Manufacturing Management Master of Medical Management Master of Ministry Management
MMME	Master of Metallurgical and Materials Engineering
MMP	Master of Marine Policy Master of Music Performance
MMPA	Master of Management and Professional Accounting
MMR	Master of Marketing Research
MMS	Master of Management Science Master of Management Studies Master of Marine Science Master of Marketing Science Master of Materials Science Master of Medical Science Master of Modern Studies
MM Sc	Master of Medical Science
MMSE	Master of Manufacturing Systems Engineering
MM St	Master of Museum Studies
MMT	Master of Movement Therapy Master of Music Teaching Master of Music Therapy
M Mtl E	Master of Materials Engineering Master of Metal Engineering
M Mu	Master of Music
M Mu Ed	Master of Music Education
M Mus	Master of Music
M Mus Ed	Master of Music Education
MN	Master of Nursing

MNA	Master of Nonprofit Administration
	Master of Nurse Anesthesia
	Master of Nursing Administration
MNAS	Master of Natural and Applied Science
M Nat Sci	Master of Natural Science
MNE	Master of Nuclear Engineering
MNM	Master of Nonprofit Management
MNO	Master of Nonprofit Organization
MNPL	Master of Not-for-Profit Leadership
MNR	Master of Natural Resources
MNRM	Master of Natural Resource Management
MNS	Master of Natural Science
	Master of Nursing Science
	Master of Nutritional Sciences
MN Sc	Master of Nursing Science
M Nurs	Master of Nursing
MOA	Maître d'Orthophonie et d'Audiologie
MOB	Master of Organizational Behavior
M Oc E	Master of Oceanographic Engineering
MOD	Master of Organizational Development
MOH	Master of Occupational Health
MOL	Master of Organizational Leadership
MOM	Master of Manufacturing
MOR	Master of Operations Research
MOT	Master of Occupational Therapy
MoTM	Master of Technology Management
MP	Master of Planning
MPA	Master of Physician Assistant
	Master of Professional Accountancy
	Master of Public Administration
	Master of Public Affairs
MPA-URP	Master of Public Affairs and Urban and Regional Planning
MP Acc	Master of Professional Accountancy
	Master of Professional Accounting
MP Acct	Master of Professional Accounting
MP Aff	Master of Public Affairs
MPAS	Master of Physical Activity Studies
	Master of Physician Assistant Science
	Master of Physician Assistant Studies
MPC	Master of Pastoral Counseling
	Master of Professional Communication
	Master of Professional Counseling
	Master of Public Communication
MPE	Master of Physical Education
MPEM	Master of Project Engineering and Management
MPH	Master of Public Health
M Pharm	Master of Pharmacy
MPHE	Master of Public Health Education
M Phil	Master of Philosophy
M Phil F	Master of Philosophical Foundations
MPHTM	Master of Public Health and Tropical Medicine
MPIA	Master of Public and International Affairs
M Pl	Master of Planning
MPM	Master of Personnel Management
	Master of Pest Management
	Master of Professional Management
	Master of Project Management
	Master of Public Management
M Pol	Master of Political Science

MPP	Master of Public Policy
MPPA	Master of Public Policy Administration
MPPM	Master of Public and Private Management
	Master of Public Policy and Management
MPPPM	Master of Plant Protection and Pest Management
MPPUP	Master of Public Policy and Urban Planning
M Pr A	Master of Professional Accountancy
M Pr Met	Master of Professional Meteorology
M Prob S	Master of Probability and Statistics
M Prof Past	Master of Professional Pastoral
MPRTM	Master of Parks, Recreation, and Tourism Management
MPS	Master of Pastoral Studies
	Master of Policy Sciences
	Master of Political Science
	Master of Preservation Studies
	Master of Professional Studies
	Master of Public Service
M Ps	Master of Psychology
MPSA	Master of Public Service Administration
MPSRE	Master of Professional Studies in Real Estate
M Psych	Master of Psychology
MPT	Master of Pastoral Theology
	Master of Physical Therapy
MP Th	Master of Pastoral Theology
M Pub	Master of Publishing
MPVM	Master of Preventive Veterinary Medicine
MPW	Master of Public Works
MQM	Master of Quality Management
MQS	Master of Quality Systems
MRC	Master of Rehabilitation Counseling
MRCP	Master of Regional and City Planning
	Master of Regional and Community Planning
MRE	Master of Religious Education
MRECM	Master of Real Estate and Construction Management
MRED	Master of Real Estate Development
M Rel	Master of Religion
M Rel Ed	Master of Religious Education
MRLS	Master of Resources Law Studies
MRM	Master of Resources Management
MRP	Master of Regional Planning
MRRA	Master of Recreation Resources Administration
MRS	Master of Religious Studies
MRTP	Master of Rural and Town Planning
MS	Master of Science
MSA	Master of School Administration
	Master of Science Administration
	Master of Science in Accounting
	Master of Science in Administration
	Master of Science in Anesthesia
	Master of Science in Anthropology
	Master of Science in Architecture
	Master of Science in Aviation
	Master of Sports Administration
MSAA	Master of Science in Astronautics and Aeronautics
MSAAE	Master of Science in Aeronautical and Astronautical Engineering
MSABE	Master of Science in Agricultural and Biological Engineering
MSACC	Master of Science in Accounting
MS Acct	Master of Science in Accounting

MS Accy	Master of Science in Accountancy		MSCJA	Master of Science in Criminal Justice Administration
MS Admin	Master of Science in Administration		MSCLS	Master of Science in Clinical Laboratory Science
MSAE	Master of Science in Aerospace Engineering			Master of Science in Clinical Laboratory Studies
	Master of Science in Agricultural Engineering		M Sc N	Master of Science in Nursing
	Master of Science in Architectural Engineering		MSCNU	Master of Science in Clinical Nutrition
	Master of Science in Art Education		MS Coun	Master of Science in Counseling
MSAER	Master of Science in Aerospace Engineering		M Sc P	Master of Science in Planning
MS Ag	Master of Science in Agriculture		MSCP	Master of Science in Clinical Psychology
MSAIS	Master of Science in Accounting Information Systems			Master of Science in Counseling Psychology
MSAM	Master of Science in Applied Mathematics		MS Cp E	Master of Science in Computer Engineering
MSAP	Master of Science in Applied Psychology		M Sc Pl	Master of Science in Planning
MSA Phy	Master of Science in Applied Physics		M Sc PT	Master of Science in Physical Therapy
MS Arch	Master of Science in Architecture		MSCRP	Master of Science in City and Regional Planning
MS Arch St	Master of Science in Architectural Studies			Master of Science in Community and Regional Planning
MSAS	Master of Science in Architectural Studies		MSCS	Master of Science in Computer Science
MSAT	Master of Science in Advanced Technology			Master of Science in Construction Science
MSB	Master of Science in Business		MSCSD	Master of Science in Communication Sciences and Disorders
MSBA	Master of Science in Business Administration		MSCSE	Master of Science in Computer and Systems Engineering
MSBAE	Master of Science in Biological and Agricultural Engineering			Master of Science in Computer Science and Engineering
	Master of Science in Biosystems and Agricultural Engineering		M Sc T	Master of Science in Teaching
MSBE	Master of Science in Biomedical Engineering		MSD	Master of Science in Dentistry
	Master of Science in Business Education			Master of Science in Design
MSBENG	Master of Science in Bioengineering			Master of Science in Dietetics
MS Bio E	Master of Science in Bioengineering		MSDD	Master of Science in Design and Development
	Master of Science in Biomedical Engineering			Master of Software Design and Development
MS Biol	Master of Science in Biology		MSE	Master of Science in Education
MS Bm E	Master of Science in Biomedical Engineering			Master of Science in Engineering
MSBMS	Master of Science in Basic Medical Science			Master of Science Education
MSBS	Master of Science in Biomedical Sciences			Master of Secondary Education
MSC	Master of Science in Commerce			Master of Software Engineering
	Master of Science in Communication			Master of Special Education
	Master of Science in Computers		MSEAS	Master of Science in Earth and Atmospheric Sciences
	Master of Science in Counseling		MSEC	Master of Science in Economic Aspects of Chemistry
	Master of Speech and Communication		MSECE	Master of Science in Electrical and Computer Engineering
M Sc	Master of Science		MS Eco	Master of Science in Economics
M Sc A	Master of Science (Applied)		MS Econ	Master of Science in Economics
M Sc BMC	Master of Science in Biomedical Communications		MS Ed	Master of Science in Education
M Sc CS	Master of Science in Computer Science		MSED	Master of Sustainable Economic Development
MSCD	Master of Science in Communication Disorders		MS Ed U	Master of Science in Education
	Master of Science in Community Development		MSEE	Master of Science in Electrical Engineering
MSCDIS	Master of Science in Communication Disorders			Master of Science in Electronic Engineering
MSCE	Master of Science in Civil Engineering			Master of Science in Environmental Engineering
	Master of Science in Clinical Engineering		MSEH	Master of Science in Environmental Health
	Master of Science in Clinical Epidemiology		MSEL	Master of Science in Environmental Law
	Master of Science in Computer Engineering			Master of Studies in Environmental Law
	Master of Science in Continuing Education		MSEM	Master of Science in Engineering and Management
M Sc E	Master of Science in Engineering			Master of Science in Engineering Management
MSCEE	Master of Science in Civil and Environmental Engineering			Master of Science in Engineering Mechanics
M Sc Eng	Master of Science in Engineering			Master of Science in Engineering of Mines
M Sc Engr	Master of Science in Engineering			Master of Science in Environmental Management
M Sc F	Master of Science in Forestry		MSE Mgt	Master of Science in Engineering Management
MSCF	Master of Science in Computational Finance		MS En E	Master of Science in Environmental Engineering
M Sc FE	Master of Science in Forest Engineering		MSENE	Master of Science in Environmental Engineering
MS Ch E	Master of Science in Chemical Engineering		MS Eng	Master of Science in Engineering
MS Chem	Master of Science in Chemistry		MS Engr	Master of Science in Engineering
MSCIS	Master of Science in Computer and Information Systems		MS Env E	Master of Science in Environmental Engineering
	Master of Science in Computer Information Science		MSER	Master of Science in Energy Resources
MSCJ	Master of Science in Criminal Justice		MSES	Master of Science in Engineering Science
				Master of Science in Environmental Studies

MSESM	Master of Science in Engineering Science and Mechanics Master of Science in Environmental Systems Management	MSIT	Master of Science in Industrial Technology Master of Science in Instructional Technology
MSESS	Master of Science in Exercise and Sport Studies	MSITM	Master of Science in Information Technology Management
MSET	Master of Science in Engineering Technology	MSJ	Master of Science in Journalism Master of Science in Jurisprudence
MSETM	Master of Science in Environmental Technology Management	MSJBS	Master of Science in Japanese Business Studies
MSEV	Master of Science in Environmental Engineering	MSJPS	Master of Science in Justice and Public Safety
MSF	Master of Science in Finance Master of Science in Forestry	MSJS	Master of Science in Jewish Studies
MSFAM	Master of Science in Family Studies	MSK	Master of Science in Kinesiology
MSFM	Master of Financial Management	MSL	Master of School Leadership Master of Science in Librarianship Master of Science in Limnology Master of Studies in Law
MSFOR	Master of Science in Forestry		
MSFS	Master of Science in Family Studies Master of Science in Financial Services Master of Science in Foreign Service Master of Science in Forensic Science	MSLA	Master of Science in Legal Administration
		MSLP	Master of Speech-Language Pathology
MSG	Master of Science in Gerontology	MSLS	Master of Science in Library Science Master of Science in Logistics Systems
MSGC	Master of Science in Genetic Counseling	MSM	Master of Sacred Ministry Master of Sacred Music Master of Science in Management Master of Service Management
MS Geo E	Master of Science in Geological Engineering		
MSH	Master of Science in Hospice		
MSHA	Master of Science in Health Administration		
MSHCI	Master of Science in Human Computer Interaction	MSMAE	Master of Science in Materials Engineering
MSHCPM	Master of Science in Health Care Policy and Management	MS Mat	Master of Science in Materials Engineering
MSHCS	Master of Science in Human and Consumer Science	MS Mat E	Master of Science in Materials Engineering
MSH Ed	Master of Science in Health Education	MS Math	Master of Science in Mathematics
MSHES	Master of Science in Human Environmental Sciences	MS Mat SE	Master of Science in Material Science and Engineering
MSHP	Master of Science in Health Professions	MSMC	Master of Science in Marketing Communications Master of Science in Mass Communications
MSHR	Master of Science in Human Resources		
MSHRM	Master of Science in Human Resource Management	MSMCS	Master of Science in Management and Computer Science
MSHROD	Master of Science in Human Resources and Organizational Development	MSME	Master of Science in Mathematics Education Master of Science in Mechanical Engineering
MSHS	Master of Science in Health and Safety Master of Science in Health Science Master of Science in Health Systems	MS Met E	Master of Science in Metallurgical Engineering
		MS Metr	Master of Science in Meteorology
		MSMFE	Master of Science in Manufacturing Engineering
MSHSA	Master of Science in Human Service Administration	MS Mfg E	Master of Science in Manufacturing Engineering
MSHSE	Master of Science in Health Science Education	MSMfSE	Master of Science in Manufacturing Systems Engineering
MSHT	Master of Science in History of Technology	MSMGEN	Master of Science in Management and General Engineering
MSI	Master of Science in Instruction Master of Science in Insurance	MS Mgt	Master of Science in Management
		MSMI	Master of Science in Medical Illustration
MSIA	Master of Science in Industrial Administration Master of Science in International Administration Master of Science in International Affairs	MS Min	Master of Science in Mining
		MS Min E	Master of Science in Mining Engineering
MSIB	Master of Science in International Business	MSMIS	Master of Science in Management Information Systems
MSIBK	Master of Science in International Banking	MSMM	Master of Science in Manufacturing Management
MSIDM	Master of Science in Interior Design and Merchandising	MSMOT	Master of Science in Management of Technology
MSIDT	Master of Science in Information Design and Technology	MSMS	Master of Science in Management Science Master of Science in Medical Sciences
MSIE	Master of Science in Industrial Engineering Master of Science in International Economics	MSMSA	Master of Science in Management Systems Analysis
MSIL	Master of Science in International Logistics	MSMSE	Master of Science in Manufacturing Systems Engineering Master of Science in Material Science and Engineering Master of Science in Material Science Engineering
MSIMC	Master of Science in Information Management and Communication Master of Science in Integrated Marketing Communications		
		MSMT	Master of Science in Medical Technology
MS Int A	Master of Science in International Affairs	MS Mt E	Master of Science in Materials Engineering
MSIO	Master of Science in Industrial Optimization	MSN	Master of Science in Nursing
MSIPC	Master of Science in Information Processing and Communications	MSNA	Master of Science in Nurse Anesthesia
		MSNE	Master of Science in Nuclear Engineering
MSIR	Master of Science in Industrial Relations	MSN(R)	Master of Science in Nursing (Research)
MSIS	Master of Science in Information Science Master of Science in Information Systems Master of Science in Interdisciplinary Studies	MSNS	Master of Science in Natural Science
		MS Nsg	Master of Science in Nursing

MSOB	Master of Science in Organizational Behavior
M Soc	Master of Sociology
MSOD	Master of Science in Organizational Development
MSOM	Master of Science in Organization and Management
MSOR	Master of Science in Operations Research
MSOT	Master of Science in Occupational Technology Master of Science in Occupational Therapy
MSP	Master of School Psychology Master of Science in Pharmacy Master of Science in Planning Master of Social Psychology Master of Speech Pathology
MSPA	Master of Science in Professional Accountancy Master of Science in Public Administration Master of Speech Pathology and Audiology
MSPAS	Master of Science in Physician Assistant Studies
MSPC	Master of Science in Professional Communications
MSPE	Master of Science in Petroleum Engineering Master of Science in Physical Education
M Sp Ed	Master of Special Education
MS Pet E	Master of Science in Petroleum Engineering
MSP Ex	Master of Science in Exercise Physiology
MSPFP	Master of Science in Personal Financial Planning
MSPG	Master of Science in Psychology
MSPH	Master of Science in Public Health
MS Phr	Master of Science in Pharmacy
MSPHR	Master of Science in Pharmacy
MS Phys	Master of Science in Physics
MS Phys Op	Master of Science in Physiological Optics
MSPNGE	Master of Science in Petroleum and Natural Gas Engineering
MS Poly	Master of Science in Polymers
MSPS	Master of Science in Planning Studies Master of Science in Psychological Services
MS Psy	Master of Science in Psychology
MSPT	Master of Science in Physical Therapy
MS Pub P	Master of Science in Public Policy
MSQSM	Master of Science in Quality Systems Management
MSR	Master of Science in Rehabilitation Sciences
MS(R)	Master of Science (Research)
MSRA	Master of Science in Recreation Administration
MSRC	Master of Science in Resource Conservation
MSRE	Master of Science in Religious Education
MSRMP	Master of Science in Radiological Medical Physics
MS(R)PT	Master of Science (Research) in Physical Therapy
MSRS	Master of Science in Radiological Sciences Master of Science in Recreational Studies
MSRTM	Master of Science in Resort and Tourism Management
MSS	Master of Science in Safety Master of Science in Software Master of Selected Studies Master of Social Science Master of Social Services Master of Special Studies Master of Sports Science
MSSA	Master of Science in Social Administration
MSSE	Master of Science in Software Engineering
MSSI	Master of Science in Strategic Intelligence
MSSL	Master of Science in Speech and Language

MSSM	Master of Science in Science Management Master of Science in Systems Management
MSSPA	Master of Science in Student Personnel Administration
MS Sp Ed	Master of Science in Special Education
MSSS	Master of Science in Systems Science
MS Stat	Master of Science in Statistics
MSSW	Master of Science in Social Work
MST	Master of Science in Taxation Master of Science in Teaching Master of Science in Telecommunications Master of Science in Transportation Master of Science Teaching Master of Science Technology Master of Secondary Teaching Master of Speech Therapy Master of Systems Technology
MSTA	Master of Science in Statistics
M Stat	Master of Statistics
MSTC	Master of Science in Telecommunications
MST Ch	Master of Science in Textile Chemistry
MSTD	Master of Science in Training and Development
MSTE	Master of Science in Technical Education Master of Science in Textile Engineering Master of Science in Transportation Engineering
MS Text	Master of Science in Textiles
MSTM	Master of Science in Teaching Mathematics Master of Science in Technology Management Master of Science in Tropical Medicine
M Struct E	Master of Structural Engineering
MSUD	Master of Science in Urban Design
MSUESM	Master of Science in Urban Environmental Systems Management
MSVE	Master of Science in Vocational Education
MSW	Master of Social Work
M Sw E	Master of Software Engineering
MSWE	Master of Software Engineering
M Sw En	Master of Software Engineering
MSWREE	Master of Science in Water Resources and Environmental Engineering
MT	Master of Taxation Master of Teaching Master of Technology Master of Textiles
MTA	Master of Tax Accounting Master of Teaching Art Master of Theater Arts
M Tax	Master of Taxation
MTC	Master of Technical Communications
MTCM	Master of Traditional Chinese Medicine
MTE	Master of Teacher Education
M Tech	Master of Technology
MTEL	Master of Telecommunications
MTESL	Master in Teaching English as a Second Language
M Th	Master of Theology
MTHM	Master of Tourism and Hospitality Management
M Th Past	Master of Pastoral Theology
MTI	Master of Information Technology
MTLM	Master of Transportation and Logistics Management

MTM	Master of Telecommunications Management Master of the Teaching of Mathematics Master of Theology and Ministry		PE Dir	Director of Physical Education
			PGC	Post-Graduate Certificate
MTMH	Master of Tropical Medicine and Hygiene		Pharm D	Doctor of Pharmacy
MTOM	Master of Traditional Oriental Medicine		PhD	Doctor of Philosophy
M Tox	Master of Toxicology		Ph L	Licentiate of Philosophy
MTP	Master of Transpersonal Psychology		PMBA	Professional Master of Business Administration
MTPW	Master of Technical and Professional Writing		PMC	Post Master's Certificate
M Trans E	Master of Transportation Engineering		PMSA	Professional Master of Science in Accounting
MTS	Master of Teaching Science Master of Theological Studies		Psy D	Doctor of Psychology
			Psy M	Master of Psychology
MTSC	Master of Technical and Scientific Communication Master of Theological Studies Counseling		Psy S	Specialist in Psychology
			Re D	Doctor of Recreation
MTX	Master of Taxation		Re Dir	Director of Recreation
MUA	Master of Urban Affairs Master of Urban Architecture		Rh D	Doctor of Rehabilitation
			SAS	School Administrator and Supervisor
MUD	Master of Urban Design		SCCT	Specialist in Community College Teaching
MUP	Master of Urban Planning		Sc D	Doctor of Science
MUPDD	Master of Urban Planning, Design, and Development		Sc M	Master of Science
MUPP	Master of Urban Planning and Policy		SD	Doctor of Science Specialist Degree
MURP	Master of Urban and Regional Planning Master of Urban and Rural Planning		SJD	Doctor of Juridical Science
			SLPD	Doctor of Speech-Language Pathology
MURPL	Master of Urban and Regional Planning		SLS	Specialist in Library Science
MUS	Master of Urban Studies		SM	Master of Science
Mus AD	Doctor of Musical Arts		SM Arch S	Master of Science in Architectural Studies
Mus Doc	Doctor of Music		SMBT	Master of Science in Building Technology
Mus M	Master of Music		SM Vis S	Master of Science in Visual Studies
MVE	Master of Vocational Education		SP	Specialist Degree
M Vet Sc	Master of Veterinary Science		SPA	Specialist in Public Administration
MVTE	Master of Vocational-Technical Education		Sp C	Specialist in Counseling
MVT Ed	Master of Vocational and Technical Education		Sp Ed	Specialist in Education
MWC	Master of Wildlife Conservation		Sp Ed S	Special Education Specialist
MWPS	Master of Wood and Paper Science		SPS	School Psychology Specialist Special Education Specialist
MWRA	Master of Water Resources Administration		S Psy S	Specialist in Psychological Services
MWS	Master of Women's Studies			
MZS	Master of Zoological Science		Spt	Specialist Degree
Naval E	Naval Engineer		SSP	Specialist in School Psychology
Nav Arch	Naval Architecture		STB	Bachelor of Sacred Theology
ND	Doctor of Naturopathic Medicine Doctor of Nursing		STD	Doctor of Sacred Theology
			STL	Licentiate of Sacred Theology
NE	Nuclear Engineer		STM	Master of Sacred Theology
NPMC	Nonprofit Management Certificate		Th D	Doctor of Theology
Nuc E	Nuclear Engineer		Th M	Master of Theology
Ocean E	Ocean Engineer		TMBA	Transnational Master of Business Administration
OD	Doctor of Optometry		V Ed S	Vocational Education Specialist
OTD	Doctor of Occupational Therapy		VMD	Doctor of Veterinary Medicine
PD	Doctor of Pharmacy Performer Diploma Professional Diploma		WEMBA	Weekend Executive Master of Business Administration
			XMA	Executive Master of Arts
PDD	Professional Development Degree		XMBA	Executive Master of Business Administration
PED	Doctor of Physical Education			

Directory of Graduate and Professional Programs by Field

This directory lists 396 fields of study, with an alphabetical listing of each of the Carnegie classified institutions offering graduate or professional work in that field. The directory enables readers who are interested in a particular academic area to quickly identify the colleges and universities that they might wish to attend. In each field, degree levels are given if an institution provided the information in response to Peterson's Annual Survey of Graduate Institutions. An *M* indicates that a master's degree program is offered; a *D* indicates that a doctoral program is offered; a *P* indicates that the first professional degree is offered; and an *O* signifies that other advanced degrees (e.g., certificates and specialist degrees) are offered. If no degree is listed, the school offers a degree in a subdiscipline of the field, not in the field itself.

All of the programs listed in this directory are profiled. For the page number of the profile, the reader should refer to the index in the back of this book.

ACCOUNTING

Institution	Degree
Abilene Christian University	M
Adelphi University	M
Alabama State University	M
American University	M
Angelo State University	M
Appalachian State University	M
Arizona State University	M,D
Arizona State University West	O
Auburn University	M
Ball State University	M
Baruch College of the City University of New York	M,D
Baylor University	M
Bloomsburg University of Pennsylvania	M
Boise State University	M
Boston College	M
Boston University	D
Bowling Green State University	M
Bradley University	M
Brigham Young University	M
Brooklyn College of the City University of New York	M
California State University, Chico	M
California State University, Fullerton	M
California State University, Hayward	M
California State University, Los Angeles	M
California State University, Northridge	M
California State University, Sacramento	M
Canisius College	M
Carnegie Mellon University	D
Case Western Reserve University	M,D
The Catholic University of America	M
Central Michigan University	M
Central Missouri State University	M
Charleston Southern University	M
Claremont Graduate University	M
Clemson University	M
Cleveland State University	M
The College of Saint Rose	M
Colorado State University	M
Columbia University	M,D
Cornell University	D
Dallas Baptist University	M
Delta State University	M
DePaul University	P,M
Dominican University	M
Drexel University	M,D
East Carolina University	M
Eastern College	M
Eastern Michigan University	M
East Tennessee State University	M
Fairfield University	M,O
Fairleigh Dickinson University, Florham–Madison Campus	M
Fairleigh Dickinson University, Teaneck–Hackensack Campus	M
Florida Agricultural and Mechanical University	M
Florida Atlantic University	M
Florida International University	M,D
Florida State University	M
Fordham University	M
Fort Hays State University	M
Gannon University	O
George Mason University	M
The George Washington University	M,D
Georgia Southern University	M
Georgia State University	M,D
Golden Gate University	M
Gonzaga University	M
Governors State University	M
Graduate School and University Center of the City University of New York	D
Hawaii Pacific University	M
Hofstra University	M
Houston Baptist University	M
Illinois State University	M
Indiana University Bloomington	D
Indiana University Northwest	M,O
Indiana University South Bend	M
Inter American University of Puerto Rico, Metropolitan Campus	M
Inter American University of Puerto Rico, San Germán Campus	M
Iona College (New Rochelle)	M,D
Jackson State University	M,D
James Madison University	M
Kansas State University	M
Kennesaw State University	M
Kent State University	M,D
Lehman College of the City University of New York	M
Long Island University, Brooklyn Campus	M
Long Island University, C.W. Post Campus	M,O
Louisiana State University and Agricultural and Mechanical College	M,D
Louisiana Tech University	M,D
Loyola University Chicago	M
Manhattan College	M
Miami University	M
Michigan State University	M,D
Middle Tennessee State University	M
Mississippi College	M
Mississippi State University	M
Montana State University–Bozeman	M
Montclair State University	M
New Mexico State University	M
New York University	M,D,O
North Carolina State University	M
Northeastern Illinois University	M
Northeastern University	M,O
Northern Illinois University	M
Northwestern University	D
Northwest Missouri State University	M
Nova Southeastern University	M
Oakland University	M
The Ohio State University	M,D
Ohio University	M
Oklahoma City University	M
Oklahoma State University	M,D
Old Dominion University	M
Oral Roberts University	M
Pace University	M
Pennsylvania State University University Park Campus	M,D
Philadelphia College of Textiles and Science	M
Pittsburg State University	M
Purdue University	M,D
Quinnipiac College	M
Rensselaer Polytechnic Institute	M,D
Rochester Institute of Technology	M
Roosevelt University	M
Rutgers, The State University of New Jersey, Newark	M,D
St. Ambrose University	M
St. Bonaventure University	M
St. Cloud State University	M
St. Edward's University	O
St. John's University (NY)	M,O
Saint Joseph's University	M
Saint Louis University	M,D
Saint Peter's College (Jersey City)	M,O
St. Thomas University	M
Salve Regina University	M
San Diego State University	M
San Jose State University	M
Seton Hall University	M,O
Slippery Rock University of Pennsylvania	M
Southern Illinois University at Carbondale	M,D
Southern Illinois University at Edwardsville	M
Southern University and Agricultural and Mechanical College	M
Southern Utah University	M
Southwest Baptist University	M
Southwest Missouri State University	M
Southwest Texas State University	M
State University of New York at Albany	M
State University of New York at Binghamton	M,D
State University of New York Institute of Technology at Utica/Rome	M
State University of West Georgia	M
Stephen F. Austin State University	M
Stetson University	M
Suffolk University	M,O
Syracuse University	M,D
Temple University (Philadelphia)	M,D
Texas A&M International University	M
Texas A&M University (College Station)	M,D
Texas A&M University–Corpus Christi	M
Texas Christian University	M
Texas Tech University	M,D
Towson University	M
Trinity University	M
Troy State University Dothan	M
Truman State University	M
Universidad del Turabo	M
Universidad Metropolitana	M
The University of Akron	M
The University of Alabama (Tuscaloosa)	M,D
The University of Alabama in Huntsville	M
The University of Arizona	M
University of Arkansas (Fayetteville)	M
University of Baltimore	M

University of California, Berkeley D
University of Central Florida M
University of Chicago M
University of Cincinnati M,D
University of Colorado at Boulder M
University of Colorado at Colorado Springs M
University of Colorado at Denver M
University of Connecticut M,D
University of Delaware M
University of Denver M
University of Florida M,D
University of Georgia M
University of Hartford M
University of Hawaii at Manoa M
University of Houston M,D
University of Houston–Clear Lake M
University of Idaho M
University of Illinois at Chicago M
University of Illinois at Springfield M
University of Illinois at Urbana–Champaign M,D
University of Indianapolis M
The University of Iowa M,D
University of Kansas M,D
University of Kentucky M
The University of Memphis M,D
University of Miami M
University of Minnesota, Twin Cities Campus M,D
University of Mississippi M,D
University of Missouri–Columbia M,D
University of Missouri–Kansas City M
University of Missouri–St. Louis M
The University of Montana–Missoula M
University of Nebraska at Omaha M
University of Nebraska–Lincoln M,D
University of Nevada, Las Vegas M
University of Nevada, Reno M
University of New Haven M
University of New Mexico M
University of New Orleans M
The University of North Carolina at Chapel Hill M,D
University of North Carolina at Charlotte M
University of North Carolina at Greensboro M
University of North Carolina at Wilmington M
University of North Florida M
University of North Texas M,D
University of Notre Dame M
University of Oklahoma M
University of Oregon D
University of Pennsylvania M,D
University of Rhode Island M
University of St. Thomas (MN) M,O
University of Scranton M
University of South Alabama M
University of South Carolina (Columbia) M
University of South Dakota M
University of Southern California M
University of Southern Indiana M
University of Southern Mississippi M
University of South Florida M
University of Tennessee at Chattanooga M
The University of Tennessee at Martin M
University of Tennessee, Knoxville M,D
The University of Texas at Arlington M
The University of Texas at Austin M,D
The University of Texas at El Paso M
The University of Texas at San Antonio M
The University of Texas of the Permian Basin M
University of Toledo M
University of Tulsa M
University of Utah M,D
University of Virginia M
University of West Florida M
University of Wisconsin–Madison M,D
University of Wisconsin–Whitewater M
Utah State University M
Virginia Commonwealth University D
Virginia Polytechnic Institute and State University M,D
Wake Forest University M
Washington State University M
Weber State University M
Western Carolina University M
Western Illinois University M
Western Kentucky University M
Western Michigan University M
Western New England College M
West Texas A&M University M
West Virginia University M
Wheeling Jesuit University M
Wichita State University M
Widener University M
Wilkes University M
Wright State University M
Yale University D
Youngstown State University M

ACOUSTICS

The Catholic University of America M,D
Pennsylvania State University University Park Campus M,D

ACTUARIAL SCIENCE

Ball State University M
Boston University M
Georgia State University M
Roosevelt University M
Temple University (Philadelphia) M
University of Nebraska–Lincoln M
University of Wisconsin–Madison M,D

ADULT EDUCATION

Appalachian State University M,O
Auburn University M,D,O
Ball State University M,D
Boston University M,D,O
California State University, Los Angeles M
Central Missouri State University M
Cheyney University of Pennsylvania M
Cleveland State University M
Coppin State College M
Cornell University M,D
Curry College M,O
Drake University M,D,O
East Carolina University M
Eastern Washington University M
Elmira College M
Florida Agricultural and Mechanical University M
Florida Atlantic University M,D,O
Florida International University M
Florida State University M,D,O
Fordham University M
Georgia Southern University M
Harvard University D
Indiana University of Pennsylvania M
Iowa State University of Science and Technology M,D
Kansas State University M,D
Marshall University M
Michigan State University M,D
Morehead State University M,O
National–Louis University M,D,O
National University M
North Carolina Agricultural and Technical State University M
North Carolina State University M,D
Northern Illinois University M,D
Nova Southeastern University D
Oregon State University M
Pennsylvania State University Harrisburg Campus of the Capital College D
Pennsylvania State University University Park Campus M,D
Portland State University D
Rutgers, The State University of New Jersey, New Brunswick M,D
Saint Joseph's University M
San Francisco State University M,O
Seattle University M
Suffolk University M,O
Teachers College, Columbia University M,D
Tennessee State University M
Texas A&M University (College Station) M,D
Texas A&M University–Kingsville M
Troy State University Montgomery M
Tusculum College M
University of Alaska Anchorage M
University of Arkansas (Fayetteville) M,D,O
University of Arkansas at Little Rock M
University of Central Oklahoma M
University of Connecticut M,D
University of Denver M,D
University of Georgia M,D,O
University of Idaho M,D
The University of Memphis D
University of Michigan–Dearborn M
University of Minnesota, Twin Cities Campus M
University of Missouri–Columbia M,D,O
University of Nebraska–Lincoln M
University of Oklahoma M,D
University of Rhode Island M
University of Southern Maine M,O
University of Southern Mississippi M,D,O
University of South Florida M,D,O
University of Tennessee, Knoxville M,D
University of the Incarnate Word M
The University of West Alabama M
University of Wisconsin–Madison M,D
University of Wisconsin–Platteville M
University of Wyoming M,D,O
Valdosta State University D
Virginia Commonwealth University M
Virginia Polytechnic Institute and State University M,D,O
Western Washington University M

ADVANCED PRACTICE NURSING

Barry University M
Baylor University M
Bowie State University M
Brenau University M
California State University, Fresno M
Case Western Reserve University M
The Catholic University of America M
Columbia University M,O
DePaul University M
Duke University M
Duquesne University M
D'Youville College M
Eastern Kentucky University M
East Tennessee State University O
Edinboro University of Pennsylvania M
Emory University M
Fairfield University M,O
Florida Atlantic University M,O
Florida State University M
Gannon University M,O
George Mason University M
Georgia Southern University M,O
Gwynedd–Mercy College M
Hawaii Pacific University M
Holy Names College M
Houston Baptist University M
Howard University O
Hunter College of the City University of New York M,O
Johns Hopkins University M,O
Kennesaw State University M
La Roche College M
La Salle University M
Long Island University, Brooklyn Campus M
Long Island University, C.W. Post Campus M,O
Loyola University Chicago M
Loyola University New Orleans M
Mankato State University M
Marquette University M
Marymount University M
Midwestern State University M
Mount Saint Mary College M
New York University M,O
Niagara University M
Northeastern University M,O
North Georgia College & State University M
Pacific Lutheran University M
Quinnipiac College M
Rutgers, The State University of New Jersey, Newark M
Sage Graduate School M
Saginaw Valley State University M
St. John Fisher College O
Saint Louis University M,O
Saint Martin's College M
Saint Xavier University M,O
San Francisco State University M
San Jose State University M
Seattle Pacific University M
Seton Hall University M
Simmons College M,O
Sonoma State University M
Southern Illinois University at Edwardsville M
Spalding University M
State University of New York at Stony Brook O
State University of New York Institute of Technology at Utica/Rome M,O
Texas Woman's University M,D
University of Cincinnati M
University of Colorado at Colorado Springs M
University of Delaware M,O
University of Hawaii at Manoa M
University of Mary M
University of Miami M
University of Michigan M
University of Minnesota, Twin Cities Campus M
University of Missouri–Kansas City M
University of Nevada, Las Vegas M
University of New Mexico M,O
University of Northern Colorado M
University of North Florida M
University of Pennsylvania M,O
University of Pittsburgh M
University of Portland O
University of San Diego M
University of San Francisco M
University of Scranton M
University of South Carolina (Columbia) O
The University of Tampa M
University of Tennessee at Chattanooga M
The University of Texas at El Paso M
University of Wisconsin–Oshkosh M
Vanderbilt University M
Villanova University O
Virginia Commonwealth University O
Wagner College O
Wayne State University M,O
West Virginia University O
Wilmington College (DE) M
Wright State University M

ADVERTISING AND PUBLIC RELATIONS

Austin Peay State University M
Ball State University M
Barry University M
Boston University M
California State University, Fullerton M
Colorado State University M
Emerson College M
Golden Gate University M,O
Iona College (New Rochelle) M
Marquette University M
Michigan State University M
Monmouth University O
Northwestern University M
Oklahoma City University M
Rowan University M
San Diego State University M
Syracuse University M
The University of Alabama (Tuscaloosa) M,D
University of Denver M
University of Florida M,D
University of Houston M
University of Illinois at Urbana–Champaign M
University of Maryland, College Park M,D
University of Miami M
University of New Haven M
University of Oklahoma M
University of St. Thomas (MN) O
University of Southern California M
University of Southern Mississippi M
University of Tennessee, Knoxville M,D
The University of Texas at Austin M,D
University of the Sacred Heart M
University of Wisconsin–Stevens Point M
Virginia Commonwealth University M
Wayne State University M

AEROSPACE/AERONAUTICAL ENGINEERING

Arizona State University M,D
Auburn University M,D
Boston University M,D
Brown University M,D
California Institute of Technology M,D,O
California Polytechnic State University, San Luis Obispo M
California State University, Long Beach M
California State University, Northridge M
Cornell University M,D
Embry–Riddle Aeronautical University (FL) M
Embry–Riddle Aeronautical University, Extended Campus M
Florida Institute of Technology M,D
Georgia Institute of Technology M,D
Howard University M,D
Illinois Institute of Technology M,D
Iowa State University of Science and Technology M,D
Massachusetts Institute of Technology M,D,O
Middle Tennessee State University M
Mississippi State University M,D
North Carolina State University M,D

P—first professional degree; M—master's degree; D—doctorate; O—other advanced degree.

Aerospace/Aeronautical Engineering (continued)

- The Ohio State University M,D
- Old Dominion University M,D
- Pennsylvania State University University Park Campus M,D
- Polytechnic University, Brooklyn Campus M
- Polytechnic University, Farmingdale Campus M
- Princeton University M,D
- Purdue University M,D
- Rensselaer Polytechnic Institute M,D
- Rutgers, The State University of New Jersey, New Brunswick M,D
- Saint Louis University M
- San Diego State University M,D
- San Jose State University M
- Stanford University M,D,O
- State University of New York at Buffalo M,D
- Syracuse University M,D
- Texas A&M University (College Station) M,D
- The University of Alabama (Tuscaloosa) M,D
- The University of Alabama in Huntsville M
- The University of Arizona M,D
- University of California, Davis M,D,O
- University of California, Irvine M,D
- University of California, Los Angeles M,D
- University of California, San Diego M,D
- University of Central Florida M,D
- University of Cincinnati M,D
- University of Colorado at Boulder M,D
- University of Colorado at Colorado Springs M
- University of Connecticut M,D
- University of Dayton M,D
- University of Florida M,D,O
- University of Houston M,D
- University of Illinois at Urbana–Champaign M,D
- University of Kansas M,D
- University of Maryland, College Park M,D
- University of Michigan M,D,O
- University of Minnesota, Twin Cities Campus M,D
- University of Missouri–Columbia M,D
- University of Missouri–Rolla M,D
- University of Notre Dame M,D
- University of Oklahoma M,D
- University of Southern California M,D,O
- University of Tennessee, Knoxville M,D
- The University of Texas at Arlington M,D
- The University of Texas at Austin M,D
- University of Virginia M,D
- University of Washington M,D
- Utah State University M,D
- Virginia Polytechnic Institute and State University M,D
- Webster University M
- West Virginia University M,D
- Wichita State University M,D

AFRICAN-AMERICAN STUDIES

- Ashland University M
- Boston University M
- Clark Atlanta University M,D
- Cornell University M
- Morgan State University M
- North Carolina Agricultural and Technical State University M
- The Ohio State University M
- Princeton University D
- State University of New York at Albany M
- Temple University (Philadelphia) M,D
- University of California, Berkeley D
- University of California, Los Angeles M
- The University of Iowa M
- University of Maryland, Baltimore County M
- University of Massachusetts Amherst M,D
- University of Wisconsin–Madison M
- Yale University M,D

AFRICAN STUDIES

- Boston University O
- Columbia University O
- Cornell University M
- Howard University M,D
- Johns Hopkins University M,D
- New York University M
- The Ohio State University M
- Ohio University M
- State University of New York at Albany M
- University of California, Los Angeles M
- University of Connecticut M
- University of Florida O
- University of Illinois at Urbana–Champaign M
- University of Wisconsin–Madison M,D
- Yale University M

AGRICULTURAL ECONOMICS AND AGRIBUSINESS

- Alabama Agricultural and Mechanical University M
- Alcorn State University M
- Auburn University M,D
- California Polytechnic State University, San Luis Obispo M
- Clemson University M
- Colorado State University M,D
- Cornell University M,D
- Illinois State University M
- Iowa State University of Science and Technology M,D
- Kansas State University M,D
- Louisiana State University and Agricultural and Mechanical College M,D
- Michigan State University M,D
- Mississippi State University M,D
- New Mexico State University M
- North Carolina Agricultural and Technical State University M
- North Carolina State University M,D
- North Dakota State University M
- Northwest Missouri State University M
- The Ohio State University M,D
- Oklahoma State University M,D
- Oregon State University M,D
- Pennsylvania State University University Park Campus M,D
- Prairie View A&M University M
- Purdue University M,D
- Rutgers, The State University of New Jersey, New Brunswick M
- Sam Houston State University M
- Santa Clara University M
- South Carolina State University M
- Southern Illinois University at Carbondale M
- Stanford University M,D
- Texas A&M University (College Station) M,D
- Texas A&M University–Kingsville M
- Texas Tech University M,D
- Tuskegee University M
- The University of Arizona M
- University of Arkansas (Fayetteville) M
- University of California, Berkeley D
- University of California, Davis M,D
- University of Connecticut M,D
- University of Delaware M
- University of Florida M,D
- University of Georgia M,D
- University of Hawaii at Manoa M,D
- University of Idaho M
- University of Illinois at Urbana–Champaign M,D
- University of Kentucky M,D
- University of Maine (Orono) M
- University of Maryland, College Park M,D
- University of Massachusetts Amherst M,D
- University of Minnesota, Twin Cities Campus M,D
- University of Missouri–Columbia M,D
- University of Nebraska–Lincoln M,D
- University of Nevada, Reno M
- University of Puerto Rico, Mayagüez Campus M
- University of Tennessee, Knoxville M,D
- University of Vermont M
- University of Wisconsin–Madison M,D
- University of Wyoming M
- Utah State University M
- Virginia Polytechnic Institute and State University M,D
- Washington State University M,D
- West Texas A&M University M
- West Virginia University M

AGRICULTURAL EDUCATION

- Alcorn State University M
- Clemson University M
- Cornell University M,D
- Eastern Kentucky University M
- Florida Agricultural and Mechanical University M
- Iowa State University of Science and Technology M,D
- Louisiana State University and Agricultural and Mechanical College M,D
- Michigan State University M,D
- Mississippi State University M,D,O
- New Mexico State University M
- North Carolina Agricultural and Technical State University M
- North Carolina State University M,O
- North Dakota State University M
- Northwest Missouri State University M
- The Ohio State University M,D
- Oklahoma State University M,D
- Oregon State University M
- Pennsylvania State University University Park Campus M,D
- Purdue University M,D,O
- Sam Houston State University M
- Southwest Texas State University M
- Stephen F. Austin State University M
- Texas A&M University (College Station) M,D
- Texas A&M University–Commerce M
- Texas A&M University–Kingsville M
- Texas Tech University M
- The University of Arizona M
- University of Arkansas (Fayetteville) M
- University of Florida M
- University of Georgia M
- University of Idaho M
- University of Illinois at Urbana–Champaign M
- University of Maryland, College Park M,D,O
- University of Maryland Eastern Shore M
- University of Minnesota, Twin Cities Campus M
- University of Nebraska–Lincoln M
- University of Puerto Rico, Mayagüez Campus M
- University of Tennessee, Knoxville M
- University of Wisconsin–River Falls M
- Utah State University M
- West Virginia University M

AGRICULTURAL ENGINEERING

- Auburn University M,D
- Clemson University M,D
- Colorado State University M,D
- Cornell University M,D
- Iowa State University of Science and Technology M,D
- Kansas State University M,D
- Louisiana State University and Agricultural and Mechanical College M,D
- Michigan State University M,D
- Mississippi State University D
- North Carolina State University M,D
- North Dakota State University M
- The Ohio State University M,D
- Oklahoma State University M,D
- Pennsylvania State University University Park Campus M,D
- Purdue University M,D
- Rutgers, The State University of New Jersey, New Brunswick M
- South Dakota State University M,D
- Texas A&M University (College Station) M,D
- The University of Arizona M,D
- University of Arkansas (Fayetteville) M
- University of California, Davis M,D
- University of Dayton M
- University of Florida M,D,O
- University of Georgia M,D
- University of Hawaii at Manoa M
- University of Idaho M,D
- University of Illinois at Urbana–Champaign M,D
- University of Kentucky M,D
- University of Maine (Orono) M
- University of Maryland, College Park M,D
- University of Minnesota, Twin Cities Campus M,D
- University of Missouri–Columbia M,D
- University of Nebraska–Lincoln M,D
- University of Tennessee, Knoxville M,D
- University of Wisconsin–Madison M,D
- Utah State University M,D
- Virginia Polytechnic Institute and State University M,D

AGRICULTURAL SCIENCES

- Alabama Agricultural and Mechanical University M,D,O
- Alcorn State University M
- Arkansas State University M,O
- Auburn University M,D
- Brigham Young University M,D
- California Polytechnic State University, San Luis Obispo M
- California State Polytechnic University, Pomona M
- California State University, Chico M
- California State University, Fresno M
- Central Missouri State University M
- Clemson University M,D
- Colorado State University M,D
- Illinois State University M
- Iowa State University of Science and Technology M,D
- Kansas State University M,D
- Louisiana State University and Agricultural and Mechanical College M,D
- Michigan State University M,D
- Mississippi State University M,D,O
- Montana State University–Bozeman M,D
- Murray State University M
- New Mexico State University M,D
- North Carolina Agricultural and Technical State University M
- North Carolina State University M,D
- North Dakota State University M,D
- Northwest Missouri State University M
- The Ohio State University M,D
- Oklahoma State University M,D
- Oregon State University M,D
- Pennsylvania State University University Park Campus M,D
- Prairie View A&M University M
- Purdue University M,D
- Sam Houston State University M
- South Dakota State University M,D
- Southern Illinois University at Carbondale M
- Southern University and Agricultural and Mechanical College M
- Tarleton State University M
- Tennessee State University M
- Texas A&M University (College Station) M,D
- Texas A&M University–Commerce M
- Texas A&M University–Kingsville M,D
- Texas Tech University M,D
- Tuskegee University M
- The University of Arizona M,D
- University of Arkansas (Fayetteville) M,D
- University of California, Davis M
- University of Connecticut M,D
- University of Delaware M,D
- University of Florida M,D,O
- University of Georgia M,D
- University of Hawaii at Manoa M,D
- University of Idaho M,D
- University of Illinois at Urbana–Champaign M,D
- University of Kentucky M,D
- University of Maine (Orono) M,D
- University of Maryland, College Park M,D,O
- University of Maryland Eastern Shore M
- University of Minnesota, Twin Cities Campus M,D
- University of Missouri–Columbia M,D
- University of Nebraska–Lincoln M,D
- University of Nevada, Reno M,D
- University of New Hampshire M,D
- University of Puerto Rico, Mayagüez Campus M
- University of Tennessee, Knoxville M,D
- University of Vermont M,D
- University of Wisconsin–Madison M,D
- University of Wisconsin–Platteville M
- University of Wisconsin–River Falls M
- University of Wyoming M,D
- Utah State University M,D
- Virginia Polytechnic Institute and State University M,D
- Washington State University M,D
- Western Kentucky University M
- West Texas A&M University M
- West Virginia University M,D

AGRONOMY AND SOIL SCIENCES

- Alabama Agricultural and Mechanical University M,D
- Alcorn State University M
- Auburn University M,D
- Brigham Young University M
- Clemson University M,D
- Colorado State University M,D
- Cornell University M,D
- Iowa State University of Science and Technology M,D

Kansas State University M,D
Louisiana State University and Agricultural and Mechanical College M,D
Michigan State University M,D
Mississippi State University M,D
Montana State University–Bozeman M,D
New Mexico State University M,D
North Carolina State University M,D
North Dakota State University M,D
The Ohio State University M,D
Oklahoma State University M,D
Oregon State University M,D
Pennsylvania State University University Park Campus M,D
Purdue University M,D
South Dakota State University M,D
Southern Illinois University at Carbondale M
Texas A&M University (College Station) M,D
Texas A&M University–Kingsville M
Texas Tech University M,D
Tuskegee University M
The University of Arizona M,D
University of Arkansas (Fayetteville) M,D
University of California, Davis M,D
University of California, Riverside M,D
University of Connecticut M,D
University of Delaware M,D
University of Florida M,D
University of Georgia M,D
University of Hawaii at Manoa M,D
University of Idaho M,D
University of Illinois at Urbana–Champaign M,D
University of Kentucky M,D
University of Maine (Orono) M
University of Maryland, College Park M,D
University of Massachusetts Amherst M,D
University of Minnesota, Twin Cities Campus M,D
University of Missouri–Columbia M,D
University of Nebraska–Lincoln M,D
University of New Hampshire M
University of Puerto Rico, Mayagüez Campus M
University of Tennessee, Knoxville M,D
University of Vermont M,D
University of Wisconsin–Madison M,D
University of Wyoming M,D
Utah State University M,D
Virginia Polytechnic Institute and State University M,D
Washington State University M,D
West Virginia University M,D

ALLIED HEALTH

Alabama State University M
Allegheny University of the Health Sciences M,D
Andrews University M
Baylor University M
Boston University M,D,O
Creighton University P,D
Duquesne University M
East Carolina University M,D
Eastern Kentucky University M
East Tennessee State University M
Emory University M
Florida Atlantic University M
Georgia Southern University M,O
Georgia State University M,D
Governors State University M
Grand Valley State University M
Idaho State University M,D,O
Ithaca College M
Loma Linda University M,D
Long Island University, C.W. Post Campus M,O
Mankato State University M,O
Marymount University M
Northern Arizona University M
Northern Michigan University M
Nova Southeastern University M,D
Oakland University M
The Ohio State University M
Old Dominion University M,D,O
Quinnipiac College M
Regis University M
Saint Louis University M
Seton Hall University M,D
Slippery Rock University of Pennsylvania M
Southwest Texas State University M
State University of New York at Buffalo M,D
Temple University (Philadelphia) M,D
Tennessee State University M
Towson University M
The University of Alabama at Birmingham M,D,O
University of Connecticut M
University of Detroit Mercy M
University of Florida M,D
University of Illinois at Chicago M,D
University of Kansas M,D
University of Kentucky M
University of Louisville M
University of Massachusetts Lowell M,D
The University of North Carolina at Chapel Hill M
University of North Florida M,O
University of South Alabama M,D
University of South Dakota M
University of Southern California M,D,O
The University of Texas at El Paso M
University of Vermont M
University of Wisconsin–Eau Claire M
University of Wisconsin–Milwaukee M
Virginia Commonwealth University M,D,O
Washington University in St. Louis M,D
Wayne State University M
Wichita State University M

ALLOPATHIC MEDICINE

Allegheny University of the Health Sciences P
Boston University P
Brown University P
Case Western Reserve University P
Columbia University P
Creighton University P
Dartmouth College P
Duke University P
East Carolina University P
East Tennessee State University P
Emory University P
Georgetown University P
The George Washington University P
Harvard University P
Howard University P
Indiana University–Purdue University Indianapolis P
Johns Hopkins University P
Loma Linda University P
Loyola University Chicago P
Marshall University P
Mercer University (Macon) P,M
Michigan State University P
New York University P
Northwestern University P
The Ohio State University P
Saint Louis University P
Southern Illinois University at Carbondale P
Stanford University P
State University of New York at Buffalo P
State University of New York at Stony Brook P
Temple University (Philadelphia) P
Texas A&M University (College Station) P
Tufts University P
Tulane University P,M,D,O
The University of Alabama at Birmingham P,M,D
The University of Arizona P
University of California, Davis P
University of California, Irvine P
University of California, Los Angeles P
University of California, San Diego P
University of California, San Francisco P,D
University of Chicago P
University of Cincinnati P
University of Florida P
University of Hawaii at Manoa P
University of Illinois at Chicago P
University of Illinois at Urbana–Champaign P
The University of Iowa P
University of Kansas P
University of Kentucky P
University of Louisville P
University of Miami P
University of Michigan P
University of Minnesota, Duluth P
University of Minnesota, Twin Cities Campus P
University of Missouri–Columbia P
University of Missouri–Kansas City P
University of Nevada, Reno P
University of New Mexico P
The University of North Carolina at Chapel Hill P
University of North Dakota P
University of Pennsylvania P
University of Pittsburgh P
University of Rochester P
University of South Alabama P
University of South Carolina (Columbia) P
University of South Dakota P
University of Southern California P
University of South Florida P
University of Utah P
University of Vermont P
University of Virginia P,M
University of Washington P
University of Wisconsin–Madison P
Vanderbilt University P,M
Virginia Commonwealth University P
Wake Forest University P
Washington University in St. Louis P
Wayne State University P
West Virginia University P
Wright State University P
Yale University P
Yeshiva University P

AMERICAN STUDIES

Appalachian State University M
Baylor University M
Boston University M,D
Bowling Green State University M,D
Brandeis University M,D
Brigham Young University M
Brown University M,D
California State University, Fullerton M
Case Western Reserve University M,D
Claremont Graduate University M,D
College of William and Mary M,D
Columbia University M
Cornell University M
East Carolina University M
Eastern Michigan University M
Fairfield University M
Florida State University M
The George Washington University M,D
Harvard University D
Indiana University Bloomington D
Michigan State University M,D
New Mexico Highlands University M
New York University M,D
Northeastern State University M
Pennsylvania State University Harrisburg Campus of the Capital College M
Pepperdine University (Malibu) M
Purdue University M,D
Saint Louis University M,D
Seton Hall University M
State University of New York at Buffalo M,D
State University of New York College at Cortland O
The University of Alabama (Tuscaloosa) M
The University of Arizona M
University of California, Los Angeles M
University of Central Oklahoma M
University of Delaware M,D
University of Hawaii at Manoa M,D
The University of Iowa M,D
University of Kansas M,D
University of Maryland, College Park M,D
University of Massachusetts Boston M
University of Michigan M,D
University of Michigan–Flint M
University of Minnesota, Twin Cities Campus M,D
University of Mississippi M
University of New Mexico M,D
University of Pennsylvania M,D
University of Southern Maine M
University of South Florida M
University of Southwestern Louisiana D
The University of Texas at Austin M,D
University of Wyoming M
Utah State University M
Washington State University M,D
Western Carolina University M
Yale University M,D

ANALYTICAL CHEMISTRY

Boston College M,D
Brigham Young University M,D
California State University, Fullerton M
California State University, Los Angeles M
Case Western Reserve University M,D
Clarkson University M,D
Cleveland State University M,D
Cornell University D
Florida State University M,D
Georgetown University M,D
The George Washington University M,D
Georgia State University D
Governors State University M
Howard University M,D
Illinois Institute of Technology M,D
Kansas State University M
Kent State University M,D
Lehigh University M,D
Marquette University M,D
Michigan State University M,D
Mississippi State University M,D
Northeastern University D
Old Dominion University M
Oregon State University M,D
Purdue University M,D
Rutgers, The State University of New Jersey, Newark M,D
Rutgers, The State University of New Jersey, New Brunswick M,D
San Jose State University M
Seton Hall University M,D
South Dakota State University M,D
Southern University and Agricultural and Mechanical College M
State University of New York at Binghamton D
Stevens Institute of Technology M,D,O
Tufts University M,D
The University of Akron M,D
University of Cincinnati M,D
University of Georgia M,D
University of Louisville M,D
University of Maryland, College Park M,D
University of Michigan D
University of Missouri–Columbia M,D
University of Missouri–Kansas City M,D
University of Nebraska–Lincoln D
University of Nevada, Las Vegas M
University of Southern Mississippi M,D
University of South Florida M,D
University of Tennessee, Knoxville M,D
The University of Texas at Austin M,D
University of Toledo M,D
University of Wisconsin–Madison M
Wake Forest University M,D
Washington State University M,D

ANATOMY

Allegheny University of the Health Sciences M,D
Auburn University M
Boston University M,D
Case Western Reserve University M
Colorado State University M,D
Columbia University M,D
Cornell University M,D
Duke University D
East Carolina University D
East Tennessee State University M,D
Howard University M,D
Indiana University–Purdue University Indianapolis M,D
Iowa State University of Science and Technology M,D
Johns Hopkins University D
Kansas State University M,D
Loma Linda University M,D
Loyola University Chicago M,D
Michigan State University M,D
New York University M,D
The Ohio State University M,D
Purdue University M,D
Saint Louis University M,D
State University of New York at Buffalo M,D
State University of New York at Stony Brook D
Temple University (Philadelphia) D
Texas A&M University (College Station) M,D
Tulane University M,D
The University of Alabama at Birmingham D
The University of Arizona D
University of California, Irvine M,D
University of California, Los Angeles D
University of California, San Francisco D
University of Chicago D
University of Cincinnati D
University of Delaware M,D
University of Florida D
University of Georgia M
University of Illinois at Chicago M,D

P—first professional degree; M—master's degree; D—doctorate; O—other advanced degree.

Peterson's/U-Wire: Graduate Schools in the U.S. 1999 47

Anatomy (continued)

The University of Iowa	D
University of Kansas	M,D
University of Kentucky	D
University of Louisville	M,D
University of Michigan	D
University of Minnesota, Duluth	M,D
University of Missouri–Columbia	M,D
The University of North Carolina at Chapel Hill	D
University of North Dakota	M,D
University of Rochester	M,D
University of South Carolina (Columbia)	D
University of South Dakota	M,D
University of Southern California	M,D
University of South Florida	D
University of Tennessee, Knoxville	D
University of Utah	M,D
University of Vermont	D
University of Wisconsin–Madison	M,D
Virginia Commonwealth University	M,D,O
Wake Forest University	D
Wayne State University	M,D
West Virginia University	M,D
Wright State University	M
Yeshiva University	D

ANIMAL BEHAVIOR

Arizona State University	M,D
University of California, Davis	D
University of Colorado at Boulder	M,D
University of Minnesota, Twin Cities Campus	M,D
University of Tennessee, Knoxville	M,D

ANIMAL SCIENCES

Alabama Agricultural and Mechanical University	M
Alcorn State University	M
Angelo State University	M
Auburn University	M,D
Brigham Young University	M
California State Polytechnic University, Pomona	M
California State University, Fresno	M
Clemson University	M,D
Colorado State University	M,D
Cornell University	M,D
Iowa State University of Science and Technology	M,D
Kansas State University	M,D
Louisiana State University and Agricultural and Mechanical College	M,D
Michigan State University	M,D
Mississippi State University	M
Montana State University–Bozeman	M
New Mexico State University	M,D
North Carolina State University	M,D
North Dakota State University	M,D
The Ohio State University	M,D
Oklahoma State University	M,D
Oregon State University	M,D
Pennsylvania State University University Park Campus	M,D
Purdue University	M,D
Rutgers, The State University of New Jersey, New Brunswick	M,D
South Dakota State University	M,D
Southern Illinois University at Carbondale	M
Sul Ross State University	M
Texas A&M University (College Station)	M,D
Texas A&M University–Kingsville	M
Texas Tech University	M,D
Tuskegee University	M
The University of Arizona	M,D
University of Arkansas (Fayetteville)	M,D
University of California, Davis	M
University of Connecticut	M,D
University of Florida	M,D
University of Georgia	M,D
University of Hawaii at Manoa	M
University of Idaho	M,D
University of Illinois at Urbana–Champaign	M,D
University of Kentucky	M,D
University of Maine (Orono)	M
University of Maryland, College Park	M,D
University of Massachusetts Amherst	M,D
University of Minnesota, Twin Cities Campus	M,D
University of Missouri–Columbia	M,D
University of Nebraska–Lincoln	M,D
University of Nevada, Reno	M
University of New Hampshire	M,D
University of Puerto Rico, Mayagüez Campus	M
University of Rhode Island	M
University of Tennessee, Knoxville	M,D
University of Vermont	M,D
University of Wisconsin–Madison	M,D
University of Wyoming	M,D
Utah State University	M,D
Virginia Polytechnic Institute and State University	M,D
Washington State University	M,D
West Texas A&M University	M
West Virginia University	M,D

ANTHROPOLOGY

American University	M,D
Arizona State University	M,D
Ball State University	M
Baylor University	M
Boston University	M,D
Brandeis University	M,D
Brigham Young University	M
Brown University	M,D
California State University, Bakersfield	M
California State University, Fullerton	M
California State University, Hayward	M
California State University, Long Beach	M
California State University, Los Angeles	M
California State University, Northridge	M
California State University, Sacramento	M
Case Western Reserve University	M,D
The Catholic University of America	M,D
City College of the City University of New York	M
College of William and Mary	M
Colorado State University	M
Columbia University	M,D
Cornell University	M,D
Duke University	D
East Carolina University	M
Eastern New Mexico University	M
Emory University	D
Florida Atlantic University	M
Florida State University	M
The George Washington University	M
Georgia State University	M
Graduate School and University Center of the City University of New York	D
Harvard University	M,D
Hunter College of the City University of New York	M
Idaho State University	M
Indiana University Bloomington	M,D
Iowa State University of Science and Technology	M
Johns Hopkins University	M,D
Kent State University	M,D
Lehigh University	M
Louisiana State University and Agricultural and Mechanical College	M,D
Michigan State University	M,D
Montclair State University	M
New Mexico Highlands University	M
New Mexico State University	M
New School University	M,D
New York University	M,D
Northern Arizona University	M
Northern Illinois University	M
Northwestern University	D
The Ohio State University	M,D
Oregon State University	M
Pennsylvania State University University Park Campus	M,D
Portland State University	M,D
Princeton University	D
Purdue University	M,D
Rice University	M,D
Rutgers, The State University of New Jersey, New Brunswick	M,D
San Diego State University	M
San Francisco State University	M
Southern Illinois University at Carbondale	M,D
Southern Methodist University	M,D
Stanford University	M,D
State University of New York at Albany	M,D
State University of New York at Binghamton	M,D
State University of New York at Buffalo	M,D
State University of New York at Stony Brook	M,D
Syracuse University	M,D
Teachers College, Columbia University	M,D
Temple University (Philadelphia)	M,D
Texas A&M University (College Station)	M,D
Texas Tech University	M
Tulane University	M,D
The University of Alabama (Tuscaloosa)	M
The University of Alabama at Birmingham	M
University of Alaska Fairbanks	M,D
The University of Arizona	M,D
University of Arkansas (Fayetteville)	M,D
University of California, Berkeley	D
University of California, Davis	M,D
University of California, Irvine	M,D
University of California, Los Angeles	M,D
University of California, Riverside	M,D
University of California, San Diego	D
University of California, San Francisco	D
University of California, Santa Barbara	M,D
University of California, Santa Cruz	M,D
University of Chicago	D
University of Cincinnati	M
University of Colorado at Boulder	M,D
University of Colorado at Denver	M
University of Connecticut	M,D
University of Denver	M
University of Florida	M,D
University of Georgia	M,D
University of Hawaii at Manoa	M,D
University of Houston	M
University of Idaho	M
University of Illinois at Chicago	M,D
University of Illinois at Urbana–Champaign	M,D
The University of Iowa	M,D
University of Kansas	M,D
University of Kentucky	M,D
University of Maryland, College Park	M
University of Massachusetts Amherst	M,D
The University of Memphis	M
University of Michigan	M,D
University of Minnesota, Duluth	M
University of Minnesota, Twin Cities Campus	M,D
University of Mississippi	M
University of Missouri–Columbia	M,D
The University of Montana–Missoula	M
University of Nebraska–Lincoln	M
University of Nevada, Las Vegas	M
University of Nevada, Reno	M,D
University of New Mexico	M,D
The University of North Carolina at Chapel Hill	M,D
University of Oklahoma	M,D
University of Oregon	M,D
University of Pennsylvania	M,D
University of Pittsburgh	M,D
University of Rochester	M,D
University of South Carolina (Columbia)	M
University of Southern California	M,D
University of Southern Mississippi	M
University of South Florida	M,D
University of Tennessee, Knoxville	M,D
The University of Texas at Arlington	M
The University of Texas at Austin	M,D
The University of Texas at San Antonio	M
University of Toledo	M
University of Tulsa	M
University of Utah	M,D
University of Virginia	M,D
University of Washington	M,D
University of Wisconsin–Madison	M,D
University of Wisconsin–Milwaukee	M,D
University of Wyoming	M
Valdosta State University	M
Vanderbilt University	M,D
Wake Forest University	M
Washington State University	M,D
Washington University in St. Louis	M,D
Wayne State University	M,D
Western Michigan University	M
Western Washington University	M
West Virginia University	M
Wichita State University	M
Yale University	M,D

APPLIED ARTS AND DESIGN

Alfred University	M
Arizona State University	M
California State University, Fullerton	M
California State University, Los Angeles	M
Clemson University	M
Drexel University	M
The George Washington University	M
Howard University	M
Illinois Institute of Technology	M,D
Indiana University Bloomington	M,D
Iowa State University of Science and Technology	M
Lamar University	M
Louisiana State University and Agricultural and Mechanical College	M
Louisiana Tech University	M
New School University	M
New York University	M
North Carolina State University	M
The Ohio State University	M
Purdue University	M
Rochester Institute of Technology	M
San Diego State University	M
San Jose State University	M
Southern Illinois University at Carbondale	M
State University of New York at Buffalo	M
Stephen F. Austin State University	M
Sul Ross State University	M
Syracuse University	M
University of California, Berkeley	M
University of California, Los Angeles	M
University of Cincinnati	M
University of Illinois at Chicago	M
University of Illinois at Urbana–Champaign	M,D
University of Kansas	M
University of Massachusetts Dartmouth	M
University of Michigan	M
University of Minnesota, Twin Cities Campus	M,D
University of Notre Dame	M
Virginia Commonwealth University	M
Wayne State University	M
Western Michigan University	M
Yale University	M

APPLIED MATHEMATICS

American University	M
Arizona State University	M,D
Auburn University	M,D
Brown University	M,D
California Institute of Technology	D
California State Polytechnic University, Pomona	M
California State University, Fullerton	M
California State University, Long Beach	M
California State University, Los Angeles	M
Case Western Reserve University	M,D
Claremont Graduate University	M
Clark Atlanta University	M
Clemson University	M,D
Cleveland State University	M
Cornell University	M,D
DePaul University	M
East Carolina University	M
Florida Institute of Technology	M,D
Florida State University	M,D
The George Washington University	M
Georgia Institute of Technology	M
Hampton University	M
Harvard University	M,D
Hofstra University	M
Howard University	M,D
Hunter College of the City University of New York	M
Illinois Institute of Technology	M,D
Indiana University Bloomington	M,D
Indiana University of Pennsylvania	M
Indiana University–Purdue University Fort Wayne	M
Indiana University–Purdue University Indianapolis	M,D
Iowa State University of Science and Technology	M,D
Kent State University	M,D
Lehigh University	M,D
Long Island University, C.W. Post Campus	M
Massachusetts Institute of Technology	D
Michigan State University	M,D
Montclair State University	M

New Jersey Institute of Technology	M
Nicholls State University	M
North Carolina State University	M,D
North Dakota State University	M,D
Northwestern University	M,D
Oakland University	M
Oklahoma State University	M
Old Dominion University	M,D
Pennsylvania State University University Park Campus	M,D
Princeton University	D
Purdue University Calumet	M
Rensselaer Polytechnic Institute	M
Rice University	M,D
Rochester Institute of Technology	M
Rutgers, The State University of New Jersey, New Brunswick	M,D
St. John's University (NY)	M
San Diego State University	M
Santa Clara University	M
Southern Methodist University	M
State University of New York at Stony Brook	M,D
Stevens Institute of Technology	M,D
Temple University (Philadelphia)	M,D
Towson University	M
Tulane University	M
The University of Akron	M,D
The University of Alabama (Tuscaloosa)	D
The University of Alabama at Birmingham	D
The University of Alabama in Huntsville	D
The University of Arizona	M,D
University of Arkansas at Little Rock	M
University of California, Berkeley	D
University of California, Davis	M,D
University of California, San Diego	M
University of California, Santa Barbara	M
University of California, Santa Cruz	M,D
University of Central Oklahoma	M
University of Chicago	M,D
University of Cincinnati	M,D
University of Colorado at Boulder	M,D
University of Colorado at Colorado Springs	M
University of Colorado at Denver	M,D
University of Dayton	M
University of Delaware	M,D
University of Denver	M
University of Florida	M,D
University of Georgia	M
University of Houston	M
University of Illinois at Chicago	M,D
University of Illinois at Urbana–Champaign	M
The University of Iowa	D
University of Kansas	M,D
University of Maryland, Baltimore County	M,D
University of Maryland, College Park	M,D
University of Massachusetts Amherst	M
University of Massachusetts Lowell	M
The University of Memphis	M
University of Minnesota, Duluth	M
University of Missouri–Columbia	M
University of Missouri–Rolla	M
The University of Montana–Missoula	M,D
University of Nevada, Las Vegas	M
University of New Hampshire	M
University of North Carolina at Charlotte	M,D
University of Pittsburgh	M
University of Puerto Rico, Mayagüez Campus	M
University of Rhode Island	D
University of Southern California	M,D
University of South Florida	D
University of Tennessee, Knoxville	M
The University of Texas at Austin	M,D
The University of Texas at Dallas	M,D
University of Toledo	M
University of Washington	M,D
Virginia Commonwealth University	M
Virginia Polytechnic Institute and State University	M,D
Washington State University	M,D
Wayne State University	M,D
Western Michigan University	M
Wichita State University	D
Worcester Polytechnic Institute	M
Wright State University	M
Yale University	M,D

APPLIED PHYSICS

Alabama Agricultural and Mechanical University	D
Appalachian State University	M
Brooklyn College of the City University of New York	M
California Institute of Technology	M,D
Carnegie Mellon University	D
Case Western Reserve University	M,D
Colorado School of Mines	D
Columbia University	M,D
Cornell University	M,D
DePaul University	M
George Mason University	M
Georgia Institute of Technology	M
Harvard University	M,D
Michigan Technological University	D
New Jersey Institute of Technology	M,D
Pittsburg State University	M
Princeton University	M,D
Rensselaer Polytechnic Institute	M,D
Rice University	M,D
Stanford University	M,D
State University of New York at Binghamton	M
State University of New York at Buffalo	M,D
Texas Tech University	M,D
University of California, San Diego	M,D
University of Central Oklahoma	M
University of Maryland, Baltimore County	M,D
University of Massachusetts Boston	M
University of Massachusetts Lowell	M,D
University of Michigan	D
University of New Orleans	M
University of North Carolina at Charlotte	M
University of Puerto Rico, Río Piedras	M
University of South Florida	M
University of Southwestern Louisiana	M
University of Washington	M,D
Virginia Commonwealth University	M
Yale University	M,D

AQUACULTURE

Auburn University	M,D
Clemson University	M
University of Florida	M,D
University of Rhode Island	M
Virginia Polytechnic Institute and State University	M,D

ARCHAEOLOGY

Boston University	M,D
Brown University	M,D
Columbia University	M,D
Cornell University	M,D
Florida State University	M
George Mason University	M
Graduate School and University Center of the City University of New York	D
Harvard University	M,D
Indiana University Bloomington	M,D
Michigan Technological University	M
New York University	M,D
Northern Arizona University	M
Princeton University	D
Southern Methodist University	M,D
Tufts University	M
University of California, Berkeley	M,D
University of California, Los Angeles	M,D,O
University of Chicago	M,D
The University of Memphis	M
University of Michigan	D
University of Minnesota, Duluth	M,D
University of Minnesota, Twin Cities Campus	M,D
University of Missouri–Columbia	M,D
The University of North Carolina at Chapel Hill	M,D
University of Pennsylvania	M,D
University of Tennessee, Knoxville	M,D
The University of Texas at Austin	M,D
University of Virginia	M,D
Washington University in St. Louis	M,D
Yale University	M

ARCHITECTURAL ENGINEERING

Illinois Institute of Technology	M,D
Kansas State University	M
North Carolina Agricultural and Technical State University	M
Oklahoma State University	M
Pennsylvania State University University Park Campus	M,D
Rensselaer Polytechnic Institute	M
University of Colorado at Boulder	M,D
University of Kansas	M
The University of Memphis	M
University of Miami	M,D
The University of Texas at Austin	M

ARCHITECTURAL HISTORY

Arizona State University	D
Cornell University	M,D
Graduate School and University Center of the City University of New York	D
Texas A&M University (College Station)	M
University of California, Berkeley	M,D
University of Pittsburgh	M,D
University of Virginia	M,D

ARCHITECTURE

Arizona State University	M
Auburn University	M
Ball State University	M
California Polytechnic State University, San Luis Obispo	M
California State Polytechnic University, Pomona	M
Carnegie Mellon University	M,D
The Catholic University of America	M
City College of the City University of New York	M,O
Clemson University	M
Columbia College (IL)	M
Columbia University	M
Cornell University	M,D
Florida Agricultural and Mechanical University	M
Florida International University	M
Georgia Institute of Technology	M,D
Harvard University	M,D
Howard University	M
Illinois Institute of Technology	M,D
Iowa State University of Science and Technology	M
Kansas State University	M
Kent State University	M
Louisiana State University and Agricultural and Mechanical College	M
Massachusetts Institute of Technology	M,D
Miami University	M
Mississippi State University	M
Montana State University–Bozeman	M
Morgan State University	M
New Jersey Institute of Technology	M
New School University	M
New York Institute of Technology	M
North Carolina State University	M
The Ohio State University	M
Oklahoma State University	M
Pennsylvania State University University Park Campus	M
Princeton University	M,D
Rensselaer Polytechnic Institute	M
Rice University	M,D
State University of New York at Buffalo	M
Syracuse University	M
Texas A&M University (College Station)	M,D
Texas Tech University	M
Tulane University	M
The University of Arizona	M
University of California, Berkeley	M,D
University of California, Los Angeles	M,D
University of Cincinnati	M
University of Colorado at Denver	M,D
University of Florida	M,D
University of Hawaii at Manoa	M
University of Houston	M
University of Idaho	M
University of Illinois at Chicago	M
University of Illinois at Urbana–Champaign	M
University of Kansas	M
University of Kentucky	M
University of Maryland, College Park	M
University of Miami	M
University of Michigan	M,D
University of Minnesota, Twin Cities Campus	M
University of Nebraska–Lincoln	M
University of Nevada, Las Vegas	M
University of New Mexico	M
University of North Carolina at Charlotte	M
University of Notre Dame	M
University of Oklahoma	M
University of Oregon	M
University of Pennsylvania	M,D,O
University of Puerto Rico, Río Piedras	M
University of Southern California	M
University of South Florida	M
University of Tennessee, Knoxville	M
The University of Texas at Arlington	M
The University of Texas at Austin	M,D
The University of Texas at San Antonio	M
University of Utah	M
University of Virginia	M
University of Washington	M,O
University of Wisconsin–Milwaukee	M,D
Virginia Polytechnic Institute and State University	M
Washington State University	M
Washington University in St. Louis	M
Yale University	M

ART EDUCATION

Adelphi University	M
Alabama Agricultural and Mechanical University	M
Ball State University	M
Beaver College	M
Boise State University	M
Boston University	M
Bridgewater State College	M
Brigham Young University	M
Brooklyn College of the City University of New York	M
California State University, Long Beach	M
California State University, Los Angeles	M
Carthage College	M
Case Western Reserve University	M
Central Connecticut State University	M
Central Missouri State University	M
City College of the City University of New York	M
College of Mount St. Joseph	M
College of New Rochelle	M
College of Notre Dame	M
The College of Saint Rose	M
Columbus State University	M
Eastern Kentucky University	M
Eastern Michigan University	M
Eastern Washington University	M
Fitchburg State College	M
Florida Atlantic University	M
Florida International University	M
Florida State University	M,D,O
Georgia Southern University	M,O
Georgia State University	M,O
Gonzaga University	M
Harvard University	M
Henderson State University	M
Hofstra University	M
Illinois State University	D
Indiana University Bloomington	M
Indiana University–Purdue University Indianapolis	M
Jacksonville University	M
James Madison University	M
Kean University	M
Kent State University	M
Kutztown University of Pennsylvania	M
Lander University	M
Lesley College	M,O
Long Island University, C.W. Post Campus	M
Mankato State University	M
Mansfield University of Pennsylvania	M
Maryville University of Saint Louis	M
Marywood University	M
Miami University	M
Millersville University of Pennsylvania	M
Mississippi College	M
Moorhead State University	M
Morehead State University	M
Nazareth College of Rochester	M
New Jersey City University	M
New York University	M,D
North Carolina Agricultural and Technical State University	M
North Georgia College & State University	M
Northwest Missouri State University	M
The Ohio State University	M,D

P—first professional degree; M—master's degree; D—doctorate; O—other advanced degree.

Art Education (continued)

Ohio University	M
Pennsylvania State University University Park Campus	M,D
Plymouth State College of the University System of New Hampshire	M
Purdue University	D
Queens College of the City University of New York	M
Radford University	M
Rhode Island College	M
Rochester Institute of Technology	M
Rockford College	M
Rowan University	M
St. Cloud State University	M
Sam Houston State University	M
San Jose State University	M
Southern Connecticut State University	M
State University of New York at New Paltz	M
State University of New York at Oswego	M
State University of New York College at Buffalo	M
State University of West Georgia	M
Sul Ross State University	M
Syracuse University	M,O
Teachers College, Columbia University	M,D
Temple University (Philadelphia)	M
Texas Tech University	M,O
Texas Woman's University	M
Towson University	M
The University of Alabama (Tuscaloosa)	M
The University of Alabama at Birmingham	M,O
The University of Arizona	M
University of Arkansas at Little Rock	M
University of Central Florida	M
University of Cincinnati	M
University of Florida	M
University of Georgia	M,D,O
University of Houston	M
University of Idaho	M
University of Illinois at Urbana–Champaign	M,D
University of Indianapolis	M
The University of Iowa	M,D
University of Kansas	M
University of Kentucky	M
University of Louisville	M
University of Massachusetts Dartmouth	M
University of Minnesota, Twin Cities Campus	M,D
University of Mississippi	M
University of Nebraska at Kearney	M
University of New Mexico	M
University of North Carolina at Greensboro	M
University of Northern Iowa	M
University of North Texas	M,D
University of South Alabama	M
University of South Carolina (Columbia)	M
University of Southern Mississippi	M
University of South Florida	M
University of Tennessee, Knoxville	M
The University of Texas at Austin	M
University of Toledo	M
University of Utah	M
University of Wisconsin–Madison	M
University of Wisconsin–Milwaukee	M
University of Wisconsin–Superior	M
Valdosta State University	M
Virginia Commonwealth University	M
Wayne State College	M
Western Carolina University	M
Western Kentucky University	M
Western Washington University	M
West Virginia University	M
Wichita State University	M
Winthrop University	M
Xavier University	M

ART/FINE ARTS

Adams State College	M
Adelphi University	M
Alfred University	M
American University	M
Arizona State University	M
Arkansas State University	M
Auburn University	M
Ball State University	M
Barry University	M
Bloomsburg University of Pennsylvania	M
Boise State University	M
Boston University	M
Bowling Green State University	M
Bradley University	M
Brandeis University	O
Brigham Young University	M
Brooklyn College of the City University of New York	M
California State University, Chico	M
California State University, Fresno	M
California State University, Fullerton	M,O
California State University, Long Beach	M
California State University, Los Angeles	M
California State University, Northridge	M
California State University, Sacramento	M
Carnegie Mellon University	M
Central Michigan University	M
Central Missouri State University	M
Central Washington University	M
City College of the City University of New York	M
Claremont Graduate University	M
Clemson University	M
College of New Rochelle	M
Colorado State University	M
Columbia University	M
Cornell University	M
Drake University	M
East Carolina University	M
Eastern Illinois University	M
Eastern Michigan University	M
East Tennessee State University	M
Edinboro University of Pennsylvania	M
Florida Atlantic University	M
Florida State University	M
Fontbonne College	M
Fort Hays State University	M
The George Washington University	M
Georgia Southern University	M
Georgia State University	M
Governors State University	M
Howard University	M
Humboldt State University	M
Hunter College of the City University of New York	M
Idaho State University	M
Illinois State University	M,D
Indiana State University	M
Indiana University Bloomington	M,D
Indiana University of Pennsylvania	M
James Madison University	M
John F. Kennedy University	M
Johnson State College	M
Kansas State University	M
Kent State University	M
Lamar University	M
Lehman College of the City University of New York	M
Long Island University, C.W. Post Campus	M
Louisiana State University and Agricultural and Mechanical College	M
Louisiana Tech University	M
Maharishi University of Management	M
Mankato State University	M
Marshall University	M
Marywood University	M
Miami University	M
Michigan State University	M
Mississippi College	M
Mississippi State University	M
Montana State University–Bozeman	M
Montclair State University	M
Moorhead State University	M
Morehead State University	M
Murray State University	M
New Jersey City University	M
New Mexico State University	M
New School University	M
New York University	M,D,O
Norfolk State University	M
Northern Illinois University	M
Northwestern State University of Louisiana	M
Northwestern University	M
Norwich University	M
The Ohio State University	M
Ohio University	M
Old Dominion University	M
Pennsylvania State University University Park Campus	M
Pittsburg State University	M
Portland State University	M
Purdue University	M
Queens College of the City University of New York	M
Radford University	M
Rensselaer Polytechnic Institute	M
Rhode Island College	M
Rochester Institute of Technology	M
Rutgers, The State University of New Jersey, New Brunswick	M
St. Cloud State University	M
Sam Houston State University	M
San Diego State University	M
San Francisco State University	M
San Jose State University	M
Southern Illinois University at Carbondale	M
Southern Illinois University at Edwardsville	M
Southern Methodist University	M
Stanford University	M,D
State University of New York at Albany	M
State University of New York at Buffalo	M
State University of New York at New Paltz	M
State University of New York at Oswego	M
State University of New York at Stony Brook	M
State University of New York College at Brockport	M
Stephen F. Austin State University	M
Sul Ross State University	M
Syracuse University	M
Temple University (Philadelphia)	M
Texas A&M University–Commerce	M
Texas A&M University–Kingsville	M
Texas Christian University	M
Texas Tech University	M,D
Texas Woman's University	M
Towson University	M
Tufts University	M
Tulane University	M
The University of Alabama (Tuscaloosa)	M
The University of Arizona	M
University of Arkansas (Fayetteville)	M
University of Arkansas at Little Rock	M
University of California, Berkeley	M
University of California, Davis	M
University of California, Irvine	M
University of California, Los Angeles	M
University of California, San Diego	M
University of California, Santa Barbara	M
University of California, Santa Cruz	O
University of Chicago	M,D
University of Cincinnati	M
University of Colorado at Boulder	M
University of Connecticut	M
University of Delaware	M
University of Denver	M
University of Florida	M
University of Georgia	M,D
University of Guam	M
University of Hartford	M
University of Hawaii at Manoa	M
University of Houston	M
University of Idaho	M
University of Illinois at Chicago	M
University of Indianapolis	M
The University of Iowa	M
University of Kansas	M
University of Kentucky	M
University of Louisville	M
University of Maryland, Baltimore County	M
University of Maryland, College Park	M
University of Massachusetts Amherst	M
University of Massachusetts Dartmouth	M
The University of Memphis	M
University of Miami	M
University of Michigan	M
University of Minnesota, Duluth	M
University of Minnesota, Twin Cities Campus	M
University of Mississippi	M
University of Missouri–Columbia	M
University of Missouri–Kansas City	M
The University of Montana–Missoula	M
University of Nebraska–Lincoln	M
University of Nevada, Las Vegas	M
University of New Mexico	M
University of New Orleans	M
The University of North Carolina at Chapel Hill	M
University of North Carolina at Greensboro	M
University of North Dakota	M
University of Northern Colorado	M
University of Northern Iowa	M
University of North Texas	M,D
University of Notre Dame	M
University of Oklahoma	M
University of Oregon	M
University of Pennsylvania	M
University of Rochester	M,D
University of Saint Francis (IN)	M
University of South Carolina (Columbia)	M
University of South Dakota	M
University of Southern California	M
University of South Florida	M
University of Tennessee, Knoxville	M
The University of Texas at Austin	M
The University of Texas at El Paso	M
The University of Texas at San Antonio	M
The University of Texas at Tyler	M
University of Tulsa	M
University of Utah	M
University of Washington	M
University of Wisconsin–Madison	M
University of Wisconsin–Milwaukee	M
University of Wisconsin–Superior	M
University of Wyoming	M
Utah State University	M
Valdosta State University	M
Vanderbilt University	M
Virginia Commonwealth University	M
Washington State University	M
Washington University in St. Louis	M
Wayne State University	M
Webster University	M
Western Carolina University	M
West Texas A&M University	M
West Virginia University	M
Wichita State University	M
William Paterson University of New Jersey	M
Winthrop University	M
Yale University	M

ART HISTORY

American University	M
Bloomsburg University of Pennsylvania	M
Boston University	M,D,O
Bowling Green State University	M
Brigham Young University	M
Brooklyn College of the City University of New York	M
Brown University	M,D
California State University, Fullerton	M
California State University, Long Beach	M
California State University, Los Angeles	M
California State University, Northridge	M
Case Western Reserve University	M,D
City College of the City University of New York	M
Cleveland State University	M
Columbia University	M,D
Cornell University	D
Duke University	D
Emory University	D
Florida State University	M,D
The George Washington University	M,D
Georgia State University	M
Graduate School and University Center of the City University of New York	D
Harvard University	D
Howard University	M
Hunter College of the City University of New York	M
Illinois State University	M
Indiana State University	M
Indiana University Bloomington	M,D
James Madison University	M
Johns Hopkins University	M,D
Lamar University	M
Louisiana State University and Agricultural and Mechanical College	M
Michigan State University	M
Montclair State University	M
New York University	M,D
Northwestern University	D
The Ohio State University	M,D
Ohio University	M
Pennsylvania State University University Park Campus	M,D
Queens College of the City University of New York	M
Rice University	M

Rutgers, The State University of
New Jersey, New Brunswick — M,D
San Diego State University — M
San Francisco State University — M
San Jose State University — M
Southern Methodist University — M
State University of New York at
Binghamton — M,D
State University of New York at
Buffalo — M
State University of New York at
Stony Brook — M,D
Sul Ross State University — M
Syracuse University — M
Temple University (Philadelphia) — M,D
Texas Woman's University — M
Tufts University — M
Tulane University — M
The University of Alabama
(Tuscaloosa) — M
The University of Alabama at
Birmingham — M
The University of Arizona — M
University of Arkansas at Little
Rock — M
University of California, Berkeley — D
University of California, Davis — M
University of California, Irvine — D
University of California, Los
Angeles — M,D
University of California, Riverside — M
University of California, Santa
Barbara — M,D
University of Chicago — M,D
University of Cincinnati — M
University of Colorado at Boulder — M
University of Connecticut — M
University of Delaware — M,D
University of Denver — M
University of Florida — M
University of Georgia — M
University of Hawaii at Manoa — M
University of Illinois at Chicago — M
University of Illinois at Urbana–
Champaign — M,D
The University of Iowa — M,D
University of Kansas — M,D
University of Kentucky — M
University of Louisville — M,D
University of Maryland, College
Park — M,D
University of Massachusetts
Amherst — M
The University of Memphis — M
University of Miami — M
University of Michigan — D
University of Minnesota, Duluth — M
University of Minnesota, Twin
Cities Campus — M,D
University of Mississippi — M
University of Missouri–Columbia — M,D
University of Missouri–Kansas
City — M
University of Nebraska–Lincoln — M
University of New Mexico — M,D
The University of North Carolina
at Chapel Hill — M,D
University of North Texas — M
University of Notre Dame — M
University of Oklahoma — M
University of Oregon — M,D
University of Pennsylvania — M,D
University of Pittsburgh — M,D
University of Rochester — M,D
University of St. Thomas (MN) — M
University of South Carolina
(Columbia) — M
University of Southern California — M,D,O
University of South Florida — M
The University of Texas at Austin — M,D
The University of Texas at San
Antonio — M
University of Utah — M
University of Virginia — M,D
University of Washington — M,D
University of Wisconsin–Madison — M,D
University of
Wisconsin–Milwaukee — M,O
University of Wisconsin–Superior — M
Virginia Commonwealth
University — M,D
Washington University in St.
Louis — M,D
Wayne State University — M
West Virginia University — M
Yale University — D

ARTIFICIAL INTELLIGENCE/ROBOTICS

Carnegie Mellon University — D
The Catholic University of
America — M,D
Cornell University — M,D
Howard University — M,D
Ohio University — D
San Jose State University — M
University of California, San
Diego — M,D

University of Georgia — M
University of Southern California — M

ARTS ADMINISTRATION

American University — M,O
Boston University — M
Carnegie Mellon University — M
Columbia College (IL) — M
Drexel University — M
Eastern Michigan University — M
Florida State University — M
Golden Gate University — M,O
Illinois State University — D
Indiana University Bloomington — M
New York University — M
The Ohio State University — M
Oklahoma City University — M
Saint Mary's University of
Minnesota — M
Shenandoah University — M
Southern Methodist University — M
State University of New York at
Binghamton — M
Teachers College, Columbia
University — M
Temple University (Philadelphia) — M,D
Texas Tech University — M,D
The University of Akron — M
University of Cincinnati — M
University of Illinois at Springfield — M
University of New Orleans — M
University of Oregon — M
University of Southern California — M
University of Wisconsin–Madison — M
Webster University — M

ART THERAPY

Allegheny University of the
Health Sciences — M
Barry University — M
California State University, Los
Angeles — M
College of New Rochelle — M
College of Notre Dame — M
Emporia State University — M
The George Washington
University — M
Hofstra University — M
John F. Kennedy University — O
Lesley College — M,O
Long Island University, C.W. Post
Campus — M
Marylhurst University — M
Marywood University — M
Nazareth College of Rochester — M
New York University — M
Norwich University — M
Sage Graduate School — M
Southern Illinois University at
Edwardsville — M
Springfield College (MA) — M,O
University of Illinois at Chicago — M
University of Louisville — M
University of Wisconsin–Superior — M

ASIAN LANGUAGES

Brigham Young University — M
Columbia University — M,D
Cornell University — M,D
Harvard University — M,D
Indiana University Bloomington — M,D
The Ohio State University — M,D
San Francisco State University — M
Stanford University — M,D
University of California, Berkeley — M,D
University of California, Irvine — M,D
University of California, Los
Angeles — M,D
University of Chicago — M,D
University of Colorado at Boulder — M
University of Hawaii at Manoa — M,D
University of Illinois at Urbana–
Champaign — M,D
University of Kansas — M
University of Massachusetts
Amherst — M
University of Michigan — M,D
University of Minnesota, Twin
Cities Campus — M,D
University of Oregon — M,D
University of Southern California — M,D
The University of Texas at Austin — M,D
University of Washington — M,D
University of Wisconsin–Madison — M,D
Washington University in St.
Louis — M,D
Yale University — D

ASIAN STUDIES

Brigham Young University — M
California State University, Long
Beach — M,O
Columbia University — M,D,O
Cornell University — M,D
Duke University — M

Florida State University — M
The George Washington
University — M
Harvard University — M,D,O
Indiana University Bloomington — M,D,O
Johns Hopkins University — M,D
Ohio University — M
Princeton University — D
St. John's University (NY) — M
San Diego State University — M
Seton Hall University — M
Stanford University — M
The University of Arizona — M,D
University of California, Berkeley — M,D
University of California, Los
Angeles — M,D
University of California, Santa
Barbara — M
University of Chicago — M,D
University of Hawaii at Manoa — M
University of Illinois at Urbana–
Champaign — M,D
The University of Iowa — M
University of Kansas — M
University of Michigan — M,D
University of Minnesota, Twin
Cities Campus — M
University of Oregon — M
University of Pennsylvania — M,D
University of Pittsburgh — M
University of San Francisco — M
University of Southern California — M,D
The University of Texas at Austin — M,D
University of Virginia — M
University of Washington — M
University of Wisconsin–Madison — M
Washington University in St.
Louis — M,D
Yale University — M

ASTRONOMY

Arizona State University — M,D
Boston University — M,D
Bowling Green State University — M
Brigham Young University — M,D
California Institute of Technology — D
Case Western Reserve
University — M,D
Clemson University — M,D
Columbia University — M,D
Cornell University — D
Dartmouth College — D
Georgia State University — M
Harvard University — M,D
Indiana University Bloomington — M,D
Iowa State University of Science
and Technology — M,D
Johns Hopkins University — D
Louisiana State University and
Agricultural and Mechanical
College — M,D
Mankato State University — M
New Mexico State University — M,D
Northwestern University — D
The Ohio State University — M,D
Pennsylvania State University
University Park Campus — M,D
Rice University — M,D
San Diego State University — M
The University of Arizona — M,D
University of California, Los
Angeles — D
University of California, Santa
Cruz — D
University of Chicago — M,D
University of Delaware — M,D
University of Florida — M,D
University of Hawaii at Manoa — M,D
University of Illinois at Urbana–
Champaign — M,D
The University of Iowa — M
University of Kansas — M,D
University of Kentucky — M,D
University of Maryland, College
Park — M,D
University of Massachusetts
Amherst — M,D
University of Michigan — M,D
University of Minnesota, Twin
Cities Campus — M,D
University of Nebraska–Lincoln — M,D
The University of North Carolina
at Chapel Hill — M,D
University of Pittsburgh — M,D
University of Rochester — M,D
University of South Carolina
(Columbia) — M,D
University of Southern
Mississippi — M
The University of Texas at Austin — M,D
University of Virginia — M,D
University of Washington — M,D
University of Wisconsin–Madison — M,D
University of Wyoming — M,D
Vanderbilt University — M
West Chester University of
Pennsylvania — M

Yale University — M,D

ASTROPHYSICS

Bowling Green State University — M
Clemson University — M,D
Cornell University — D
Harvard University — M,D
Indiana University Bloomington — D
Louisiana State University and
Agricultural and Mechanical
College — D
Michigan State University — D
Northwestern University — D
Pennsylvania State University
University Park Campus — M,D
Princeton University — D
Rensselaer Polytechnic Institute — M,D
Rice University — M,D
San Francisco State University — M
University of Alaska Fairbanks — M,D
University of California, Berkeley — D
University of California, Los
Angeles — M,D
University of California, Santa
Cruz — D
University of Chicago — M,D
University of Colorado at Boulder — M,D
University of Minnesota, Twin
Cities Campus — M,D
The University of North Carolina
at Chapel Hill — M,D
University of Oklahoma — M,D
University of Pennsylvania — D

ATMOSPHERIC SCIENCES

City College of the City
University of New York — M,D
Clemson University — M,D
Colorado State University — M,D
Columbia University — M,D
Cornell University — M,D
Creighton University — M
Drexel University — M,D
Georgia Institute of Technology — M,D
Howard University — M,D
Massachusetts Institute of
Technology — M,D
North Carolina State University — M,D
The Ohio State University — M,D
Oregon State University — M,D
Princeton University — D
Purdue University — M,D
Saint Louis University — M,D
South Dakota State University — D
State University of New York at
Albany — M,D
State University of New York at
Stony Brook — D
Texas Tech University — M,D
The University of Alabama in
Huntsville — M,D
University of Alaska Fairbanks — M,D
The University of Arizona — M,D
University of California, Davis — M,D
University of California, Los
Angeles — M,D,O
University of Chicago — M,D
University of Colorado at Boulder — M,D
University of Delaware — D
University of Illinois at Urbana–
Champaign — M,D
University of Miami — M,D
University of Michigan — M,D
University of Missouri–Columbia — M,D
University of Nevada, Reno — M,D
University of North Dakota — M
University of Washington — M,D
University of Wisconsin–Madison — M,D
University of Wyoming — M,D

BACTERIOLOGY

Purdue University — M,D
Texas Woman's University — M
The University of Iowa — M,D
University of Virginia — M,D
University of Wisconsin–Madison — M,D
Wagner College — M

BIOCHEMICAL ENGINEERING

California Polytechnic State
University, San Luis Obispo — M
Cornell University — M,D
Dartmouth College — M,D
Drexel University — M
Rutgers, The State University of
New Jersey, New Brunswick — M,D
University of California, Irvine — M,D
The University of Iowa — M,D
University of Maryland, Baltimore
County — M,D

BIOCHEMISTRY

Adelphi University — M

P—first professional degree; M—master's degree; D—doctorate; O—other advanced degree.

Biochemistry (continued)

Allegheny University of the Health Sciences	M,D
Arizona State University	M,D
Boston College	M,D
Boston University	M,D
Brandeis University	M,D
Brigham Young University	M,D
Brown University	M,D
California Institute of Technology	D
California State University, Fullerton	M
California State University, Hayward	M
California State University, Long Beach	M
California State University, Los Angeles	M
Carnegie Mellon University	D
Case Western Reserve University	M,D
City College of the City University of New York	M,D
Clark University	M,D
Clemson University	M,D
Colorado State University	M,D
Columbia University	M,D
Cornell University	D
Dartmouth College	D
Duke University	D,O
Duquesne University	M,D
East Carolina University	D
East Tennessee State University	M,D
Emory University	D
Florida Atlantic University	M
Florida State University	M,D
Georgetown University	M,D
The George Washington University	M,D
Georgia Institute of Technology	M,D
Graduate School and University Center of the City University of New York	D
Harvard University	M,D
Howard University	M,D
Hunter College of the City University of New York	M
Illinois Institute of Technology	M
Indiana University Bloomington	M,D
Indiana University–Purdue University Indianapolis	M,D
Iowa State University of Science and Technology	M,D
Johns Hopkins University	D
Kansas State University	M,D
Kent State University	D
Lehigh University	M,D
Loma Linda University	M,D
Louisiana State University and Agricultural and Mechanical College	M,D
Loyola University Chicago	M,D
Massachusetts Institute of Technology	M,D
Miami University	M,D
Michigan State University	M,D
Mississippi State University	M,D
Montana State University–Bozeman	M,D
New Mexico State University	M,D
New York University	M,D
North Carolina State University	M,D
North Dakota State University	M,D
Northern Illinois University	M,D
Northwestern University	D
The Ohio State University	M,D
Oklahoma State University	M,D
Old Dominion University	M,D
Oregon State University	M,D
Pennsylvania State University University Park Campus	M,D
Purdue University	M,D
Queens College of the City University of New York	M
Rensselaer Polytechnic Institute	M,D
Rice University	M,D
Rutgers, The State University of New Jersey, Newark	M,D
Rutgers, The State University of New Jersey, New Brunswick	M,D
Saint Joseph College (CT)	M
Saint Louis University	D
San Jose State University	M
Seton Hall University	M,D
South Dakota State University	M,D
Southern Illinois University at Carbondale	M,D
Southern University and Agricultural and Mechanical College	M
Stanford University	D
State University of New York at Albany	M,D
State University of New York at Buffalo	M,D
State University of New York at Stony Brook	D
Stevens Institute of Technology	M,D,O
Temple University (Philadelphia)	M,D
Texas A&M University (College Station)	M,D
Tufts University	D
Tulane University	M,D
The University of Akron	M,D
The University of Alabama at Birmingham	D
University of Alaska Fairbanks	M,D
The University of Arizona	M,D
University of Arkansas (Fayetteville)	M,D
University of California, Berkeley	D
University of California, Davis	M,D
University of California, Irvine	D
University of California, Los Angeles	M,D,O
University of California, Riverside	M,D
University of California, San Diego	D
University of California, San Francisco	D
University of California, Santa Barbara	D
University of Chicago	D
University of Cincinnati	M,D
University of Colorado at Boulder	M,D
University of Connecticut	M,D
University of Delaware	M,D
University of Detroit Mercy	M,D
University of Florida	D
University of Georgia	M,D
University of Hawaii at Manoa	M,D
University of Houston	M,D
University of Idaho	M,D
University of Illinois at Chicago	M,D
University of Illinois at Urbana–Champaign	M,D
The University of Iowa	M,D
University of Kansas	M,D
University of Kentucky	D
University of Louisville	M,D
University of Maine (Orono)	M,D
University of Maryland, Baltimore County	M,D
University of Maryland, College Park	M,D
University of Massachusetts Amherst	M,D
University of Massachusetts Lowell	D
University of Miami	D
University of Michigan	D
University of Minnesota, Duluth	M,D
University of Minnesota, Twin Cities Campus	D
University of Missouri–Columbia	M,D
University of Missouri–Kansas City	D
The University of Montana–Missoula	M,D
University of Nebraska–Lincoln	M,D
University of Nevada, Reno	M,D
University of New Hampshire	M,D
University of New Mexico	M,D
The University of North Carolina at Chapel Hill	M,D
University of North Dakota	M,D
University of North Texas	M,D
University of Notre Dame	M,D
University of Oklahoma	M,D
University of Oregon	M,D
University of Pennsylvania	D
University of Pittsburgh	M,D
University of Rhode Island	M,D
University of Rochester	M,D
University of Scranton	M
University of South Alabama	D
University of South Carolina (Columbia)	M,D
University of South Dakota	M,D
University of Southern California	M,D
University of Southern Mississippi	M,D
University of South Florida	M,D
University of Tennessee, Knoxville	M,D
The University of Texas at Austin	M,D
University of the Pacific	M,D
University of Toledo	M,D
University of Utah	M,D
University of Vermont	M,D
University of Virginia	D
University of Washington	D
University of Wisconsin–Madison	M,D
Utah State University	M,D
Vanderbilt University	M,D
Virginia Commonwealth University	M,D,O
Virginia Polytechnic Institute and State University	M,D
Wake Forest University	D
Washington State University	M,D
Washington University in St. Louis	D
Wayne State University	M,D
West Virginia University	M,D
Worcester Polytechnic Institute	M,D
Wright State University	M
Yale University	M,D
Yeshiva University	D

BIOENGINEERING

Allegheny University of the Health Sciences	D
Arizona State University	M,D
Carnegie Mellon University	D
Case Western Reserve University	D
Clemson University	M,D
Colorado State University	M,D
Cornell University	M,D
Georgia Institute of Technology	M,D,O
Kansas State University	M,D
Louisiana State University and Agricultural and Mechanical College	M,D
Mississippi State University	M,D
North Carolina State University	M,D
The Ohio State University	M,D
Oklahoma State University	M,D
Oregon State University	M,D
Pennsylvania State University University Park Campus	M,D
Purdue University	M,D
Rice University	M,D
Rutgers, The State University of New Jersey, New Brunswick	M
Syracuse University	M
Texas A&M University (College Station)	M,D
University of Arkansas (Fayetteville)	M
University of California, Berkeley	D
University of California, San Diego	M,D
University of California, San Francisco	D
University of Connecticut	M
University of Georgia	M,D
University of Hawaii at Manoa	M
University of Illinois at Chicago	M,D
University of Illinois at Urbana–Champaign	
University of Maryland, College Park	M,D
University of Missouri–Columbia	M,D
University of Nebraska–Lincoln	M,D
University of Notre Dame	M
University of Pennsylvania	M,D
University of Pittsburgh	M,D
University of Toledo	M,D
University of Utah	M,D
University of Washington	M,D
Virginia Polytechnic Institute and State University	M,D

BIOETHICS

Case Western Reserve University	M
Duquesne University	M,D
Loma Linda University	M
Saint Louis University	D
University of Pittsburgh	M
University of Tennessee, Knoxville	M,D
University of Virginia	M
University of Washington	M,D

BIOLOGICAL AND BIOMEDICAL SCIENCES

Adelphi University	M
Alabama Agricultural and Mechanical University	M
Alabama State University	M,O
Alcorn State University	M
Allegheny University of the Health Sciences	M,D
American University	M
Andrews University	M
Angelo State University	M
Anna Maria College	M
Appalachian State University	M
Arizona State University	M,D
Arkansas State University	M,D,O
Auburn University	D
Austin Peay State University	M
Ball State University	M,D
Barry University	M
Baylor University	M,D
Bemidji State University	M
Bloomsburg University of Pennsylvania	M
Boise State University	M
Boston College	M,D
Boston University	M,D
Bowling Green State University	M,D,O
Bradley University	M
Brandeis University	M,D,O
Bridgewater State College	M
Brigham Young University	M,D
Brooklyn College of the City University of New York	M,D
Brown University	M,D
California Institute of Technology	D
California Polytechnic State University, San Luis Obispo	M
California State Polytechnic University, Pomona	M
California State University, Chico	M
California State University, Dominguez Hills	M,O
California State University, Fresno	M
California State University, Fullerton	M
California State University, Hayward	M
California State University, Long Beach	M
California State University, Los Angeles	M
California State University, Northridge	M
California State University, Sacramento	M
California State University, San Bernardino	M
California University of Pennsylvania	M
Carnegie Mellon University	D
Case Western Reserve University	M,D
The Catholic University of America	M,D
Central Connecticut State University	M
Central Michigan University	M
Central Missouri State University	M
Central Washington University	M
Chicago State University	M
City College of the City University of New York	M,D
Clarion University of Pennsylvania	M
Clark Atlanta University	M,D
Clark University	M,D
Clemson University	M,D
Cleveland State University	M,D
College of William and Mary	M
Colorado State University	M,D
Columbia University	M,D
Cornell University	M,D
Creighton University	M,D
Dartmouth College	M,D
Delaware State University	M
Delta State University	M
DePaul University	M
Drake University	M
Drexel University	M,D
Duquesne University	M
East Carolina University	M,D
Eastern Illinois University	M
Eastern Kentucky University	M
Eastern Michigan University	M
Eastern New Mexico University	M
Eastern Washington University	M
East Stroudsburg University of Pennsylvania	M
East Tennessee State University	M,D
Edinboro University of Pennsylvania	M
Emory University	D
Emporia State University	M
Fairleigh Dickinson University, Florham–Madison Campus	M
Fairleigh Dickinson University, Teaneck–Hackensack Campus	M
Fayetteville State University	M
Florida Agricultural and Mechanical University	M
Florida Atlantic University	M
Florida Institute of Technology	M,D
Florida International University	M,D
Florida State University	M,D
Fordham University	M,D
Fort Hays State University	M
Frostburg State University	M
George Mason University	M
Georgetown University	M,D
The George Washington University	M,D
Georgia College and State University	M
Georgia Institute of Technology	M,D
Georgian Court College	M
Georgia Southern University	M
Georgia State University	M,D
Graduate School and University Center of the City University of New York	D
Hampton University	M
Harvard University	D,O
Hofstra University	M
Hood College	M
Howard University	M,D
Humboldt State University	M
Hunter College of the City University of New York	M,D
Idaho State University	M,D
Illinois Institute of Technology	M,D

Illinois State University	M,D
Indiana State University	M,D
Indiana University Bloomington	M,D
Indiana University of Pennsylvania	M
Indiana University–Purdue University Fort Wayne	M
Indiana University–Purdue University Indianapolis	M,D
Jackson State University	M,D
Jacksonville State University	M
James Madison University	M
John Carroll University	M
Johns Hopkins University	M,D
Kansas State University	M,D
Kent State University	M,D
Lamar University	M
Lehigh University	M,D
Lehman College of the City University of New York	M,D
Loma Linda University	M,D
Long Island University, Brooklyn Campus	M
Long Island University, C.W. Post Campus	M
Louisiana State University and Agricultural and Mechanical College	M,D
Louisiana State University in Shreveport	M
Louisiana Tech University	M
Loyola University Chicago	M
Mankato State University	M
Marquette University	M,D
Marshall University	M,D
Massachusetts Institute of Technology	P,D
McNeese State University	M
Michigan State University	M,D
Michigan Technological University	M,D
Middle Tennessee State University	M
Midwestern State University	M
Millersville University of Pennsylvania	M
Mississippi College	M
Mississippi State University	M,D
Montana State University–Bozeman	M,D
Montclair State University	M
Morehead State University	M
Murray State University	M,D
New Mexico Highlands University	M
New Mexico State University	M,D
New York University	M,D
North Carolina Agricultural and Technical State University	M
North Carolina Central University	M
North Carolina State University	M,D
Northeastern Illinois University	M
Northeastern University	M,D
Northeast Louisiana University	M
Northern Arizona University	M,D
Northern Illinois University	M,D
Northern Michigan University	M
Northwestern University	D
Northwest Missouri State University	M
Nova Southeastern University	M
Oakland University	M
The Ohio State University	M,D
Ohio University	M,D
Old Dominion University	M,D
Pennsylvania State University University Park Campus	M,D
Pittsburg State University	M
Portland State University	M,D
Prairie View A&M University	M
Princeton University	D
Purdue University	M,D
Purdue University Calumet	M
Queens College of the City University of New York	M
Quinnipiac College	M
Rensselaer Polytechnic Institute	M,D
Rhode Island College	M
Rockefeller University	D
Rutgers, The State University of New Jersey, Camden	M
Rutgers, The State University of New Jersey, Newark	M,D
St. Cloud State University	M
Saint Francis College (PA)	M
St. John's University (NY)	M,D
Saint Joseph College (CT)	M,O
Saint Joseph's University	M
Saint Louis University	M,D
Sam Houston State University	M
San Diego State University	M,D
San Francisco State University	M
San Jose State University	M
Seton Hall University	M
Shippensburg University of Pennsylvania	M
Sonoma State University	M
South Dakota State University	M,D
Southeastern Louisiana University	M
Southeast Missouri State University	M
Southern Connecticut State University	M
Southern Illinois University at Carbondale	M,D
Southern Illinois University at Edwardsville	M
Southern Methodist University	M,D
Southern University and Agricultural and Mechanical College	M
Southwest Missouri State University	M
Southwest Texas State University	M
Stanford University	M,D
State University of New York at Albany	M,D
State University of New York at Binghamton	M,D
State University of New York at Buffalo	M,D
State University of New York at New Paltz	M
State University of New York at Stony Brook	D
State University of New York College at Brockport	M
State University of New York College at Buffalo	M
State University of New York College at Cortland	M
State University of New York College at Fredonia	M
State University of New York College at Oneonta	M
State University of West Georgia	M
Stephen F. Austin State University	M
Sul Ross State University	M
Syracuse University	M,D
Tarleton State University	M
Temple University (Philadelphia)	M,D
Tennessee State University	M,D
Tennessee Technological University	M
Texas A&M University (College Station)	M,D
Texas A&M University–Commerce	M
Texas A&M University–Corpus Christi	M
Texas A&M University–Kingsville	M
Texas Christian University	M
Texas Southern University	M
Texas Tech University	M,D
Texas Woman's University	M,D
Towson University	M
Truman State University	M
Tufts University	M,D,O
Tulane University	M,D
Tuskegee University	M
The University of Akron	M
The University of Alabama (Tuscaloosa)	M,D
The University of Alabama at Birmingham	M,D
The University of Alabama in Huntsville	M
University of Alaska Anchorage	M
University of Alaska Fairbanks	M,D
The University of Arizona	M,D
University of Arkansas (Fayetteville)	M,D
University of California, Berkeley	D
University of California, Davis	M,D
University of California, Irvine	M,D
University of California, Los Angeles	M,D,O
University of California, Riverside	M,D
University of California, San Diego	D
University of California, San Francisco	D
University of California, Santa Cruz	D
University of Central Arkansas	M
University of Central Florida	M
University of Central Oklahoma	M
University of Chicago	M,D
University of Cincinnati	M,D
University of Colorado at Denver	M
University of Connecticut	M,D
University of Dayton	M,D
University of Delaware	M,D
University of Denver	M,D
University of Detroit Mercy	M
University of Florida	M,D
University of Guam	M
University of Hartford	M
University of Hawaii at Manoa	M,D
University of Houston	M,D
University of Houston–Clear Lake	M
University of Idaho	M,D
University of Illinois at Chicago	M,D
University of Illinois at Springfield	M
University of Illinois at Urbana–Champaign	M,D
University of Indianapolis	M
The University of Iowa	M,D
University of Kansas	M,D
University of Kentucky	M,D
University of Louisville	M,D
University of Maine (Orono)	M,D
University of Maryland, Baltimore County	M,D
University of Massachusetts Amherst	M,D
University of Massachusetts Boston	M
University of Massachusetts Dartmouth	M
University of Massachusetts Lowell	M,D
The University of Memphis	M,D
University of Miami	M,D
University of Michigan	M,D
University of Minnesota, Duluth	M
University of Minnesota, Twin Cities Campus	M,D
University of Mississippi	M,D
University of Missouri–Columbia	M,D
University of Missouri–Kansas City	M,D
University of Missouri–St. Louis	M,D,O
The University of Montana–Missoula	M,D
University of Nebraska at Kearney	M
University of Nebraska at Omaha	M
University of Nebraska–Lincoln	M,D
University of Nevada, Las Vegas	M,D
University of Nevada, Reno	M,D
University of New Hampshire	M,D
University of New Mexico	M,D
University of New Orleans	M
The University of North Carolina at Chapel Hill	M,D
University of North Carolina at Charlotte	M
University of North Carolina at Greensboro	M
University of North Carolina at Wilmington	M
University of North Dakota	M,D
University of Northern Colorado	M,D
University of Northern Iowa	M
University of North Texas	M,D
University of Notre Dame	M,D
University of Oregon	M,D
University of Pennsylvania	M,D
University of Pittsburgh	M,D
University of Puerto Rico, Mayagüez Campus	M
University of Puerto Rico, Río Piedras	M,D
University of Richmond	M
University of Rochester	M,D,O
University of San Francisco	M
University of South Alabama	M,D
University of South Carolina (Columbia)	M,D
University of South Dakota	M,D
University of Southern California	M,D
University of Southern Mississippi	M,D
University of South Florida	M,D
University of Southwestern Louisiana	M,D
University of Tennessee, Knoxville	M,D
The University of Texas at Arlington	M,D
The University of Texas at Austin	M,D
The University of Texas at Brownsville	M
The University of Texas at El Paso	M
The University of Texas at San Antonio	M,D
The University of Texas at Tyler	M
The University of Texas of the Permian Basin	M
The University of Texas–Pan American	M
University of the Incarnate Word	M
University of the Pacific	M
University of Toledo	M,D
University of Tulsa	M,D
University of Utah	M,D
University of Vermont	M,D
University of Virginia	M,D
University of Washington	M,D
University of West Florida	M
University of Wisconsin–Eau Claire	M
University of Wisconsin–La Crosse	M
University of Wisconsin–Madison	M,D
University of Wisconsin–Milwaukee	M,D
University of Wisconsin–Oshkosh	M
Utah State University	M,D
Vanderbilt University	M,D
Villanova University	M
Virginia Commonwealth University	M,D,O
Virginia Polytechnic Institute and State University	M,D
Virginia State University	M
Wake Forest University	M,D
Walla Walla College	M
Washington State University	M
Washington University in St. Louis	D
Wayne State University	M,D,O
West Chester University of Pennsylvania	M
Western Carolina University	M
Western Connecticut State University	M
Western Illinois University	M
Western Kentucky University	M
Western Michigan University	M,D
Western Washington University	M
West Texas A&M University	M
West Virginia University	M,D
Wichita State University	M
William Paterson University of New Jersey	M
Winthrop University	M
Worcester Polytechnic Institute	M,D
Wright State University	M,D
Yale University	D
Yeshiva University	D
Youngstown State University	M

BIOMEDICAL ENGINEERING

Allegheny University of the Health Sciences	D
Arizona State University	M,D
Boston University	M,D
Brown University	M,D
California State University, Northridge	M
California State University, Sacramento	M
Carnegie Mellon University	M,D
Case Western Reserve University	M,D
The Catholic University of America	M,D
Clemson University	M,D
Colorado State University	M,D
Columbia University	M,D
Cornell University	D
Dartmouth College	M,D
Drexel University	M,D
Duke University	M,D
Georgia Institute of Technology	M,D,O
Harvard University	D
Indiana University–Purdue University Indianapolis	M,D
Iowa State University of Science and Technology	M,D
Johns Hopkins University	M,D
Louisiana Tech University	M,D
Marquette University	M,D
Massachusetts Institute of Technology	D
Mercer University (Macon)	M
New Jersey Institute of Technology	M
Northwestern University	M,D
The Ohio State University	M,D
Pennsylvania State University University Park Campus	M,D
Purdue University	M,D
Rensselaer Polytechnic Institute	M,D
Rice University	M,D
Rutgers, The State University of New Jersey, New Brunswick	M,D
Stanford University	M
State University of New York at Stony Brook	O
Syracuse University	M
Texas A&M University (College Station)	M,D
Tulane University	M,D
The University of Akron	M,D
The University of Alabama at Birmingham	M,D
University of California, Berkeley	D
University of California, Davis	M,D
University of California, Irvine	D
University of California, Los Angeles	M,D
University of California, San Diego	M,D
University of California, San Francisco	D
University of Connecticut	M,D
University of Florida	M,D
University of Houston	M
University of Illinois at Chicago	M,D
University of Illinois at Urbana–Champaign	
The University of Iowa	M,D
University of Kentucky	M,D
The University of Memphis	M,D

P—first professional degree; M—master's degree; D—doctorate; O—other advanced degree.

Biomedical Engineering (continued)

University of Miami	M,D
University of Michigan	M,D
University of Minnesota, Twin Cities Campus	M,D
University of Nevada, Reno	M,D
The University of North Carolina at Chapel Hill	M,D
University of Pennsylvania	M,D
University of Pittsburgh	M,D
University of Rochester	M,D
University of Southern California	M,D
University of Tennessee, Knoxville	M,D
The University of Texas at Arlington	M,D
The University of Texas at Austin	M,D
University of Utah	M,D
University of Vermont	M
University of Virginia	M,D
University of Washington	M,D
Vanderbilt University	M,D
Virginia Commonwealth University	M,D
Wake Forest University	D
Washington University in St. Louis	M,D
Wayne State University	M,D
Worcester Polytechnic Institute	M,D
Wright State University	M

BIOMETRICS

Cornell University	M,D
North Carolina State University	M,D
Oregon State University	M,D
State University of New York at Albany	M,D
State University of New York at Buffalo	M
The University of Alabama at Birmingham	M,D
University of California, Los Angeles	M,D
University of Nebraska–Lincoln	M
University of Southern California	M,D
University of Wisconsin–Madison	M

BIOPHYSICS

Boston University	M,D
Brandeis University	D
California Institute of Technology	D
Carnegie Mellon University	D
Case Western Reserve University	D
Clemson University	M,D
Columbia University	M,D
Cornell University	D
Duke University	O
East Carolina University	M
Emory University	M,D
Florida State University	D
Georgetown University	M,D
Harvard University	D
Howard University	D
Indiana University–Purdue University Indianapolis	M,D
Iowa State University of Science and Technology	M,D
Johns Hopkins University	M,D
Massachusetts Institute of Technology	D
New York University	D
Northwestern University	D
The Ohio State University	M,D
Oregon State University	M,D
Princeton University	D
Purdue University	D
Rensselaer Polytechnic Institute	M,D
Stanford University	D
State University of New York at Buffalo	M,D
State University of New York at Stony Brook	D
Syracuse University	D
Texas A&M University (College Station)	M,D
The University of Alabama at Birmingham	D
University of California, Berkeley	M,D
University of California, Davis	M,D
University of California, Irvine	D
University of California, San Diego	M,D
University of California, San Francisco	D
University of Cincinnati	M,D
University of Connecticut	M,D
University of Hawaii at Manoa	M,D
University of Illinois at Chicago	M,D
University of Illinois at Urbana–Champaign	D
The University of Iowa	M,D
University of Louisville	M,D
University of Miami	D
University of Michigan	D
University of Minnesota, Twin Cities Campus	M,D
University of Missouri–Kansas City	D
The University of North Carolina at Chapel Hill	M,D
University of Pennsylvania	D
University of Rochester	M,D
University of Southern California	M,D
University of South Florida	D
University of Vermont	M,D
University of Virginia	D
University of Washington	D
University of Wisconsin–Madison	D
Vanderbilt University	D
Virginia Commonwealth University	M,D,O
Washington State University	M,D
Washington University in St. Louis	D
Wright State University	M
Yale University	M,D
Yeshiva University	D

BIOPSYCHOLOGY

American University	M
Carnegie Mellon University	D
Columbia University	M,D
Cornell University	D
Drexel University	M,D
Duke University	D
Emory University	D
Florida State University	D
Graduate School and University Center of the City University of New York	D
Harvard University	M,D
Howard University	D
Hunter College of the City University of New York	M
Louisiana State University and Agricultural and Mechanical College	M,D
Northwestern University	D
The Ohio State University	D
Pennsylvania State University University Park Campus	M,D
Rutgers, The State University of New Jersey, Newark	D
Rutgers, The State University of New Jersey, New Brunswick	D
State University of New York at Albany	D
State University of New York at Binghamton	M,D
State University of New York at Stony Brook	D
University of California, Irvine	D
University of Chicago	D
University of Colorado at Boulder	M,D
University of Connecticut	M,D
University of Delaware	D
University of Hartford	M
University of Illinois at Urbana–Champaign	M,D
University of Michigan	D
University of Minnesota, Twin Cities Campus	D
University of New Orleans	D
University of Oregon	M,D
University of Wisconsin–Madison	D

BIOSTATISTICS

Boston University	M,D
Brown University	M,D
Case Western Reserve University	M,D
Columbia University	M,D
Drexel University	M
Emory University	M,D
Georgetown University	M
The George Washington University	M,D
Harvard University	M,D
Johns Hopkins University	M,D
Loma Linda University	M
New York University	D
The Ohio State University	D
San Diego State University	M
Tulane University	M,D
The University of Alabama at Birmingham	M,D
University of California, Berkeley	M,D
University of California, Los Angeles	M,D
University of Cincinnati	M
University of Hawaii at Manoa	M,D
University of Illinois at Chicago	M,D
The University of Iowa	M,D
University of Michigan	M,D
University of Minnesota, Twin Cities Campus	M,D
The University of North Carolina at Chapel Hill	M,D
University of Pittsburgh	M,D
University of Rochester	M,D
University of South Carolina (Columbia)	M,D
University of South Florida	M,D
University of Utah	M
University of Vermont	M
University of Washington	M,D
Virginia Commonwealth University	M,D
Western Michigan University	M
Yale University	M,D

BIOTECHNOLOGY

Brown University	M,D
Dartmouth College	M,D
East Carolina University	M
Florida Institute of Technology	M
Howard University	M
Illinois Institute of Technology	M
Manhattan College	M
North Carolina State University	M
Northwestern University	M,D
Stephen F. Austin State University	M
Tufts University	O
University of Connecticut	M
University of Massachusetts Boston	M
University of Minnesota, Twin Cities Campus	M
University of Missouri–St. Louis	O
University of Pennsylvania	M
University of Tennessee, Knoxville	M
The University of Texas at Dallas	M,D
The University of Texas at San Antonio	M
University of Washington	D
William Paterson University of New Jersey	M
Worcester Polytechnic Institute	M,D
Worcester State College	M

BOTANY AND PLANT SCIENCES

Alabama Agricultural and Mechanical University	D
Arizona State University	M,D
Auburn University	M,D
Boston University	M,D
Brigham Young University	M,D
California State University, Chico	M
California State University, Fresno	M
California State University, Fullerton	M
Claremont Graduate University	M,D
Clemson University	M
Colorado State University	M,D
Cornell University	M,D
Duke University	D
Eastern Illinois University	M
Emporia State University	M
Florida State University	M,D
The George Washington University	M,D
Illinois State University	D
Indiana University Bloomington	M,D
Iowa State University of Science and Technology	M,D
Kent State University	M,D
Lehman College of the City University of New York	D
Louisiana State University and Agricultural and Mechanical College	M,D
Miami University	M,D
Michigan State University	M,D
Mississippi State University	M,D
Montana State University–Bozeman	D
North Carolina Agricultural and Technical State University	M
North Carolina State University	M,D
North Dakota State University	M,D
The Ohio State University	M,D
Ohio University	M,D
Oklahoma State University	M,D
Oregon State University	M,D
Purdue University	M,D
Rensselaer Polytechnic Institute	M,D
Rutgers, The State University of New Jersey, New Brunswick	M,D
South Dakota State University	M,D
Southern Illinois University at Carbondale	M,D
State University of New York at Buffalo	M,D
Texas A&M University (College Station)	M,D
Texas A&M University–Kingsville	M
Texas Tech University	M,D
University of Alaska Fairbanks	M,D
The University of Arizona	M,D
University of Arkansas (Fayetteville)	D
University of California, Berkeley	D
University of California, Davis	M,D
University of California, Riverside	M,D
University of Colorado at Boulder	M,D
University of Connecticut	M,D
University of Delaware	M,D
University of Florida	M,D
University of Georgia	M,D
University of Hawaii at Manoa	M,D
University of Idaho	M,D
University of Illinois at Chicago	M,D
University of Illinois at Urbana–Champaign	M,D
The University of Iowa	M,D
University of Kansas	M,D
University of Kentucky	M
University of Maine (Orono)	M,D
University of Maryland, College Park	M,D
University of Massachusetts Amherst	M,D
The University of Memphis	M,D
University of Michigan	M,D
University of Minnesota, Twin Cities Campus	M,D
University of New Hampshire	M,D
University of New Mexico	M,D
The University of North Carolina at Chapel Hill	M,D
University of North Dakota	M,D
University of Oklahoma	M,D
University of Pennsylvania	D
University of Rhode Island	M,D
University of South Florida	M
University of Tennessee, Knoxville	M,D
The University of Texas at Austin	M,D
University of Vermont	M,D
University of Washington	M,D
University of Wisconsin–Madison	M,D
University of Wisconsin–Oshkosh	M
University of Wyoming	M,D
Utah State University	M,D
Virginia Polytechnic Institute and State University	M,D
Washington State University	M,D
Washington University in St. Louis	D
West Texas A&M University	M
West Virginia University	M,D
Yale University	D

BUSINESS ADMINISTRATION AND MANAGEMENT

Abilene Christian University	M
Adelphi University	M,O
Alabama Agricultural and Mechanical University	M
Alabama State University	M
Alaska Pacific University	M
Albany State University	M
Alfred University	M
Amber University	M
American International College	M
American University	M
Andrews University	M
Angelo State University	M
Anna Maria College	M
Appalachian State University	M
Aquinas College (MI)	M
Arizona State University	M,D
Arizona State University West	M
Arkansas State University	M
Ashland University	M
Assumption College	M,O
Auburn University	M,D
Auburn University Montgomery	M
Augusta State University	M
Aurora University	M
Averett College	M
Avila College	M
Azusa Pacific University	M
Baker University	M
Baldwin-Wallace College	M
Ball State University	M
Barry University	M
Baruch College of the City University of New York	M,D,O
Baylor University	M
Bellarmine College	M
Bellevue University	M
Belmont University	M
Benedictine University	M
Bloomsburg University of Pennsylvania	M
Boise State University	M
Boston College	M,D
Boston University	M,D
Bowie State University	M
Bowling Green State University	M
Bradley University	M
Brandeis University	M
Brenau University	M
Brigham Young University	M
Butler University	M
California Lutheran University	M
California Polytechnic State University, San Luis Obispo	M

California State Polytechnic University, Pomona	M
California State University, Bakersfield	M
California State University, Chico	M
California State University, Dominguez Hills	M
California State University, Fresno	M
California State University, Fullerton	M
California State University, Hayward	M
California State University, Long Beach	M
California State University, Los Angeles	M
California State University, Northridge	M
California State University, Sacramento	M
California State University, San Bernardino	M
California State University, San Marcos	M
California State University, Stanislaus	M
California University of Pennsylvania	M
Campbell University	M
Canisius College	M
Capital University	M
Cardinal Stritch University	M
Carnegie Mellon University	M
Case Western Reserve University	M,D,O
The Catholic University of America	M,D
Centenary College of Louisiana	M
Central Connecticut State University	M
Central Michigan University	M
Central Missouri State University	M
Chadron State College	M
Chaminade University of Honolulu	M
Chapman University	M
Charleston Southern University	M
Christian Brothers University	M
The Citadel, The Military College of South Carolina	M
City University	M,O
Claremont Graduate University	M,D,O
Clarion University of Pennsylvania	M
Clark Atlanta University	M
Clarkson University	M
Clark University	M
Clemson University	M,D
Cleveland State University	M,D
College Misericordia	M
College of Notre Dame	M
College of Notre Dame of Maryland	M
The College of Saint Rose	M
College of St. Scholastica	M
College of William and Mary	M
Colorado Christian University	M
Colorado State University	M
Columbia University	M,D
Columbus State University	M
Cornell University	M,D
Creighton University	M
Dallas Baptist University	M
Dartmouth College	M
Delaware State University	M
Delta State University	M
DePaul University	P,M
Dominican College of San Rafael	M
Dominican University	M
Dowling College	M,O
Drake University	M
Drexel University	M,D,O
Drury College	M
Duke University	M,D
Duquesne University	M
D'Youville College	M
East Carolina University	M
Eastern College	M
Eastern Illinois University	M
Eastern Kentucky University	M
Eastern Michigan University	M
Eastern New Mexico University	M
Eastern Washington University	M
East Tennessee State University	M
Edgewood College	M
Elon College	M
Embry-Riddle Aeronautical University (FL)	M
Embry-Riddle Aeronautical University, Extended Campus	M
Emmanuel College (MA)	M
Emory University	M
Emporia State University	M
Fairfield University	M,O
Fairleigh Dickinson University, Florham-Madison Campus	M
Fairleigh Dickinson University, Teaneck–Hackensack Campus	M
Fayetteville State University	M
Ferris State University	M
Fitchburg State College	M
Florida Agricultural and Mechanical University	M
Florida Atlantic University	M,D
Florida Institute of Technology	M
Florida International University	M,D
Florida State University	M,D
Fontbonne College	M
Fordham University	M,O
Fort Hays State University	M
Framingham State College	M
Franciscan University of Steubenville	M
Francis Marion University	M
Fresno Pacific University	M
Friends University	M
Frostburg State University	M
Gannon University	M,O
Gardner–Webb University	M
George Mason University	M
Georgetown University	M
The George Washington University	M,D
Georgia College and State University	M
Georgia Institute of Technology	M,D
Georgian Court College	M
Georgia Southern University	M
Georgia Southwestern State University	M
Georgia State University	M,D
Golden Gate University	M,D,O
Gonzaga University	M
Governors State University	M
Graduate School and University Center of the City University of New York	D
Grambling State University	M
Grand Valley State University	M
Hampton University	M
Hardin–Simmons University	M
Harvard University	M,D,O
Hawaii Pacific University	M
Henderson State University	M
Hofstra University	M
Holy Names College	M
Hood College	M
Hope International University	M
Houston Baptist University	M
Howard University	M
Humboldt State University	M
Idaho State University	M
Illinois Institute of Technology	M,D
Illinois State University	M
Indiana State University	M,D,O
Indiana University Bloomington	M,D
Indiana University Kokomo	M
Indiana University Northwest	M,O
Indiana University of Pennsylvania	M
Indiana University–Purdue University Fort Wayne	M
Indiana University–Purdue University Indianapolis	M
Indiana University South Bend	M
Indiana Wesleyan University	M
Inter American University of Puerto Rico, Metropolitan Campus	M
Inter American University of Puerto Rico, San Germán Campus	M
Iona College (New Rochelle)	M,O
Iowa State University of Science and Technology	M
Jackson State University	M,D
Jacksonville State University	M
Jacksonville University	M
James Madison University	M
John Carroll University	M
John F. Kennedy University	M,O
Johns Hopkins University	M,O
Kansas State University	M
Kennesaw State University	M
Kent State University	M
Kutztown University of Pennsylvania	M
Lake Erie College	M
Lake Superior State University	M
Lamar University	M
La Salle University	M,O
La Sierra University	M
Lehigh University	M,D
Lenoir–Rhyne College	M
Lesley College	M
Lewis University	M
Lincoln Memorial University	M
Lincoln University (MO)	M
Lindenwood University	M
Long Island University, Brooklyn Campus	M
Long Island University, C.W. Post Campus	M,O
Louisiana State University and Agricultural and Mechanical College	M,D
Louisiana State University in Shreveport	M
Louisiana Tech University	M,D
Loyola College	M
Loyola Marymount University	M
Loyola University Chicago	M
Loyola University New Orleans	M
Lynchburg College	M
Madonna University	M
Maharishi University of Management	M,D
Manhattan College	M
Mankato State University	M
Marian College of Fond du Lac	M
Marist College	M,O
Marquette University	M
Marshall University	M
Marylhurst University	M
Marymount University	M
Maryville University of Saint Louis	M
Marywood University	M
Massachusetts Institute of Technology	M,D
McNeese State University	M
Mercer University (Macon)	M
Mercer University, Cecil B. Day Campus	M
Meredith College	M
Metropolitan State University	M
Miami University	M
Michigan State University	M,D
Michigan Technological University	M
MidAmerica Nazarene University	M
Middle Tennessee State University	M
Midwestern State University	M
Minot State University	M
Mississippi College	M
Mississippi State University	M,D
Monmouth University	M
Montclair State University	M
Moorhead State University	M
Morehead State University	M
Morgan State University	M
Mount Saint Mary College	M
Mount Saint Mary's College and Seminary	M
Murray State University	M
National–Louis University	M
National University	M
Nazareth College of Rochester	M
New Mexico Highlands University	M
New Mexico State University	M,D
New School University	M,D,O
New York Institute of Technology	M
New York University	M,D,O
Niagara University	M
Nicholls State University	M
North Carolina Central University	M
North Carolina State University	M,D
North Central College	M
North Dakota State University	M
Northeastern Illinois University	M
Northeastern State University	M
Northeastern University	M,O
Northeast Louisiana University	M
Northern Arizona University	M
Northern Illinois University	M
Northern Kentucky University	M
Northwestern University	M
Northwest Missouri State University	M
Nova Southeastern University	M,D
Oakland University	M
The Ohio State University	M,D
Ohio University	M
Oklahoma City University	M
Oklahoma State University	M,D
Old Dominion University	M,D
Olivet Nazarene University	M
Oral Roberts University	M
Oregon State University	M,O
Our Lady of the Lake University of San Antonio	M
Pace University	M,D,O
Pacific Lutheran University	M
Park College	M
Pennsylvania State University at Erie, The Behrend College	M
Pennsylvania State University Harrisburg Campus of the Capital College	M
Pennsylvania State University University Park Campus	M,D
Pepperdine University (Culver City)	M
Pepperdine University (Malibu)	M
Pfeiffer University	M
Philadelphia College of Textiles and Science	M
Phillips University	M
Pittsburg State University	M
Plymouth State College of the University System of New Hampshire	M
Polytechnic University, Brooklyn Campus	M
Polytechnic University, Farmingdale Campus	M
Polytechnic University, Westchester Graduate Center	M
Pontifical Catholic University of Puerto Rico	M
Portland State University	M,D
Prairie View A&M University	M
Providence College	M
Purdue University	M,D
Purdue University Calumet	M
Queens College	M
Quinnipiac College	M
Radford University	M
Regis University	M
Rensselaer Polytechnic Institute	M,D
Rice University	M
Rider University	M
Rivier College	M
Rochester Institute of Technology	M
Rockford College	M
Rockhurst College	M
Rollins College	M
Roosevelt University	M
Rowan University	M
Rutgers, The State University of New Jersey, Camden	M
Rutgers, The State University of New Jersey, Newark	M,D
Sacred Heart University	M
Sage Graduate School	M
Saginaw Valley State University	M
St. Ambrose University	M
St. Bonaventure University	M,O
St. Cloud State University	M
St. Edward's University	M,O
Saint Francis College (PA)	M
St. John Fisher College	M
St. John's University (NY)	M,O
Saint Joseph's University	M
Saint Louis University	M,D
Saint Martin's College	M
Saint Mary's College of California	M
Saint Mary's University of Minnesota	M
St. Mary's University of San Antonio	M
Saint Michael's College	M,O
Saint Peter's College (Jersey City)	M
St. Thomas University	M,O
Saint Xavier University	M,O
Salem State College	M
Salisbury State University	M
Salve Regina University	M
Samford University	M
Sam Houston State University	M
San Diego State University	M
San Francisco State University	M
San Jose State University	M
Santa Clara University	M
Seattle Pacific University	M
Seattle University	M,O
Seton Hall University	M,O
Shenandoah University	M
Shippensburg University of Pennsylvania	M
Simmons College	M
Slippery Rock University of Pennsylvania	M
Sonoma State University	M
South Carolina State University	M
Southeastern Louisiana University	M
Southeastern Oklahoma State University	M
Southeast Missouri State University	M
Southern Arkansas University–Magnolia	M
Southern Connecticut State University	M
Southern Illinois University at Carbondale	M,D
Southern Illinois University at Edwardsville	M
Southern Methodist University	M
Southern Nazarene University	M
Southern Oregon University	M
Southern University and Agricultural and Mechanical College	M
Southwest Baptist University	M
Southwestern Oklahoma State University	M
Southwest Missouri State University	M
Southwest Texas State University	M
Spring Hill College	M
Stanford University	M,D
State University of New York at Albany	M,D

P—first professional degree; M—master's degree; D—doctorate; O—other advanced degree.

Business Administration and Management (continued)

State University of New York at Binghamton	M,D
State University of New York at Buffalo	M,D
State University of New York at New Paltz	M
State University of New York at Oswego	M
State University of New York at Stony Brook	M
State University of New York College at Fredonia	M
State University of New York College at Oneonta	M
State University of New York Institute of Technology at Utica/Rome	M
State University of West Georgia	M
Stephen F. Austin State University	M
Stetson University	M
Stevens Institute of Technology	M,D,O
Suffolk University	M,O
Sul Ross State University	M
Syracuse University	M,D
Tarleton State University	M
Temple University (Philadelphia)	M,D
Tennessee State University	M
Tennessee Technological University	M
Texas A&M International University	M
Texas A&M University (College Station)	M,D
Texas A&M University–Commerce	M
Texas A&M University–Corpus Christi	M
Texas A&M University–Kingsville	M
Texas A&M University–Texarkana	M
Texas Christian University	M
Texas Southern University	M
Texas Tech University	M,D,O
Texas Wesleyan University	M
Texas Woman's University	M
Trinity College (DC)	M
Troy State University (Troy)	M
Troy State University Dothan	M
Troy State University Montgomery	M
Tulane University	M,D
Tusculum College	M
United States International University	M,D
Universidad del Turabo	M
Universidad Metropolitana	M
The University of Akron	M
The University of Alabama (Tuscaloosa)	M,D
The University of Alabama at Birmingham	M,D
The University of Alabama in Huntsville	M
University of Alaska Anchorage	M
University of Alaska Fairbanks	M
University of Alaska Southeast	M
The University of Arizona	M,D
University of Arkansas (Fayetteville)	M,D
University of Arkansas at Little Rock	M
University of Baltimore	M
University of Bridgeport	M
University of California, Berkeley	M,D
University of California, Davis	M
University of California, Irvine	M,D
University of California, Los Angeles	M,D
University of California, Riverside	M
University of Central Arkansas	M
University of Central Florida	M,D
University of Central Oklahoma	M
University of Central Texas	M
University of Charleston	M
University of Chicago	M,D
University of Cincinnati	M,D
University of Colorado at Boulder	M,D
University of Colorado at Colorado Springs	M
University of Colorado at Denver	M
University of Connecticut	M,D
University of Dayton	M
University of Delaware	M
University of Denver	M
University of Detroit Mercy	M
University of Dubuque	M
University of Florida	M,D
University of Georgia	M,D
University of Guam	M
University of Hartford	M
University of Hawaii at Manoa	M
University of Houston	M,D
University of Houston–Clear Lake	M
University of Houston–Victoria	M
University of Idaho	M

University of Illinois at Chicago	M
University of Illinois at Springfield	M
University of Illinois at Urbana–Champaign	M,D
University of Indianapolis	M
The University of Iowa	M,D
University of Kansas	M
University of Kentucky	M,D
University of La Verne	M
University of Louisville	M
University of Maine (Orono)	M
University of Mary	M
University of Mary Hardin–Baylor	M
University of Maryland, College Park	M,D
University of Maryland University College	M
University of Massachusetts Amherst	M,D
University of Massachusetts Boston	M
University of Massachusetts Dartmouth	M
University of Massachusetts Lowell	M
The University of Memphis	M,D
University of Miami	M,D,O
University of Michigan	M,D
University of Michigan–Dearborn	M
University of Michigan–Flint	M
University of Minnesota, Duluth	M
University of Minnesota, Twin Cities Campus	M,D
University of Mississippi	M
University of Missouri–Columbia	M,D
University of Missouri–Kansas City	M
University of Missouri–St. Louis	M
University of Mobile	M
The University of Montana–Missoula	M
University of Nebraska at Kearney	M
University of Nebraska at Omaha	M
University of Nebraska–Lincoln	M,D
University of Nevada, Las Vegas	M
University of Nevada, Reno	M
University of New Hampshire	M
University of New Haven	M
University of New Mexico	M
University of New Orleans	M
University of North Alabama	M
The University of North Carolina at Chapel Hill	M,D
University of North Carolina at Charlotte	M
University of North Carolina at Greensboro	M,O
University of North Carolina at Pembroke	M
University of North Carolina at Wilmington	M
University of North Dakota	M
University of Northern Iowa	M
University of North Florida	M
University of North Texas	M,D
University of Notre Dame	M
University of Oklahoma	M,D
University of Oregon	M,D
University of Pennsylvania	M,D
University of Pittsburgh	M,D
University of Portland	M
University of Puerto Rico, Mayagüez Campus	M
University of Puerto Rico, Río Piedras	M
University of Redlands	M
University of Rhode Island	M,D
University of Richmond	M
University of Rochester	M,D
University of St. Francis (IL)	M
University of Saint Francis (IN)	M
University of St. Thomas (MN)	M,O
University of St. Thomas (TX)	M
University of San Diego	M
University of San Francisco	M
University of Scranton	M
University of South Alabama	M
University of South Carolina (Columbia)	M,D
University of South Dakota	M
University of Southern California	M,D
University of Southern Indiana	M
University of Southern Maine	M
University of Southern Mississippi	M
University of South Florida	M,D
University of Southwestern Louisiana	M
The University of Tampa	M
University of Tennessee at Chattanooga	M
The University of Tennessee at Martin	M
University of Tennessee, Knoxville	M,D
The University of Texas at Arlington	M,D

The University of Texas at Austin	M,D
The University of Texas at Brownsville	M
The University of Texas at Dallas	M,D
The University of Texas at El Paso	M
The University of Texas at San Antonio	M
The University of Texas at Tyler	M
The University of Texas of the Permian Basin	M
The University of Texas–Pan American	M,D
University of the District of Columbia	M
University of the Incarnate Word	M
University of the Pacific	M
University of the Sacred Heart	M
University of the Virgin Islands	M
University of Toledo	M
University of Tulsa	M
University of Utah	M,D
University of Vermont	M
University of Virginia	M,D
University of Washington	M,D
University of West Florida	M
University of Wisconsin–Eau Claire	M
University of Wisconsin–Green Bay	M
University of Wisconsin–La Crosse	M
University of Wisconsin–Madison	M,D
University of Wisconsin–Milwaukee	M,D
University of Wisconsin–Oshkosh	M
University of Wisconsin–Parkside	M
University of Wisconsin–Stevens Point	M
University of Wisconsin–Whitewater	M
University of Wyoming	M
Utah State University	M
Valdosta State University	M
Vanderbilt University	M,D
Villanova University	M
Virginia Commonwealth University	M,D,O
Virginia Polytechnic Institute and State University	M,D
Virginia State University	M
Wagner College	M
Wake Forest University	M
Walsh University	M
Washburn University of Topeka	M
Washington State University	M,D
Washington University in St. Louis	M,D
Wayne State College	M
Wayne State University	M
Weber State University	M
Webster University	M,D
West Chester University of Pennsylvania	M
Western Carolina University	M
Western Connecticut State University	M
Western Illinois University	M
Western Kentucky University	M
Western Michigan University	M
Western New England College	M
Western New Mexico University	M
Western Washington University	M
Westminster College of Salt Lake City	M
West Texas A&M University	M
West Virginia University	M
West Virginia Wesleyan College	M
Wheeling Jesuit University	M
Whitworth College	M
Wichita State University	M
Widener University	M
Wilkes University	M
William Carey College	M
William Paterson University of New Jersey	M
Wilmington College (DE)	M
Winona State University	M
Winthrop University	M
Woodbury University	M
Worcester Polytechnic Institute	M
Wright State University	M
Xavier University	M
Yale University	M,D
Youngstown State University	M

BUSINESS EDUCATION

Albany State University	M
Alfred University	M
Arkansas State University	M,O
Ashland University	M
Ball State University	M
Bloomsburg University of Pennsylvania	M
Bowling Green State University	M
California State University, Northridge	M

Central Connecticut State University	M
Central Michigan University	M
Central Washington University	M
Chadron State College	M
College of Mount St. Joseph	M
Eastern Illinois University	M
Eastern Kentucky University	M
Eastern Michigan University	M
Eastern Washington University	M
Emporia State University	M
Florida Agricultural and Mechanical University	M
Georgia Southern University	M
Georgia Southwestern State University	M
Georgia State University	M
Indiana State University	M,D,O
Indiana University of Pennsylvania	M
Inter American University of Puerto Rico, Metropolitan Campus	M
Inter American University of Puerto Rico, San Germán Campus	M
Iona College (New Rochelle)	M
Jackson State University	M
Lehman College of the City University of New York	M
Louisiana State University and Agricultural and Mechanical College	M
Louisiana Tech University	M
Mankato State University	M
McNeese State University	M
Middle Tennessee State University	M
Mississippi College	M
Mississippi State University	M
Montana State University–Bozeman	M
Montclair State University	M
Nazareth College of Rochester	M
New York University	M,D,O
Northwestern State University of Louisiana	M
Northwest Missouri State University	M
Old Dominion University	M
Rider University	M
Shippensburg University of Pennsylvania	M
South Carolina State University	M
Southeast Missouri State University	M
Southern Illinois University at Edwardsville	M
State University of New York College at Buffalo	M
State University of West Georgia	M,O
Texas A&M International University	M
Texas Southern University	M
Troy State University Dothan	M
University of Central Arkansas	M
University of Central Florida	M
University of Georgia	M
University of Idaho	M
University of Louisville	M
University of Maryland, College Park	M,D,O
University of Minnesota, Twin Cities Campus	M
University of Nebraska at Kearney	M
University of North Carolina at Greensboro	M
University of North Dakota	M
University of South Alabama	M
University of South Florida	M
University of Toledo	M
University of Wisconsin–Whitewater	M
Utah State University	M,D
Valdosta State University	M,D,O
Wayne State College	M
Western Kentucky University	M
Winona State University	M
Winthrop University	M
Wright State University	M

CANADIAN STUDIES

Johns Hopkins University	M,D

CARDIOVASCULAR SCIENCES

Allegheny University of the Health Sciences	M,D
Northeastern University	M
University of Virginia	

CELL BIOLOGY

Allegheny University of the Health Sciences	M,D
Arizona State University	M,D
Boston University	M,D

Brandeis University	D
Brown University	M,D
California Institute of Technology	D
Carnegie Mellon University	D
Case Western Reserve University	M,D
The Catholic University of America	M,D
Colorado State University	M,D
Columbia University	M,D
Cornell University	D
Dartmouth College	
Duke University	D,O
East Carolina University	D
East Tennessee State University	M,D
Emory University	D
Emporia State University	M
Florida Institute of Technology	M,D
Florida State University	M,D
Fordham University	M,D
George Mason University	M
Georgetown University	D
Harvard University	D
Illinois Institute of Technology	M
Indiana University Bloomington	D
Iowa State University of Science and Technology	M,D
Johns Hopkins University	D
Kansas State University	M,D
Kent State University	M,D
Loyola University Chicago	M,D
Maharishi University of Management	M,D
Marquette University	M,D
Massachusetts Institute of Technology	D
Michigan State University	D
New York University	M,D
North Carolina State University	M,D
North Dakota State University	D
Northwestern University	D
Oakland University	M
The Ohio State University	M,D
Ohio University	M,D
Oregon State University	D
Princeton University	D
Purdue University	D
Quinnipiac College	M
Rensselaer Polytechnic Institute	M,D
Rice University	M,D
Rutgers, The State University of New Jersey, New Brunswick	M,D
Saint Louis University	D
San Diego State University	D
San Francisco State University	M
State University of New York at Albany	M,D
State University of New York at Buffalo	M,D
State University of New York at Stony Brook	M,D
Temple University (Philadelphia)	D
Texas A&M University (College Station)	D
Tufts University	D
Tulane University	M,D
The University of Alabama at Birmingham	D
The University of Arizona	M,D
University of California, Berkeley	D
University of California, Davis	D
University of California, Irvine	M,D
University of California, Los Angeles	D
University of California, San Diego	D
University of California, San Francisco	D
University of California, Santa Barbara	M,D
University of California, Santa Cruz	D
University of Chicago	D
University of Cincinnati	D
University of Colorado at Boulder	M,D
University of Connecticut	M,D
University of Florida	M,D
University of Georgia	M,D
University of Hawaii at Manoa	M,D
University of Illinois at Chicago	M,D
University of Illinois at Urbana–Champaign	D
The University of Iowa	D
University of Kansas	M,D
University of Maryland, Baltimore County	D
University of Maryland, College Park	D
University of Massachusetts Amherst	M,D
The University of Memphis	M,D
University of Miami	D
University of Michigan	D
University of Minnesota, Duluth	M,D
University of Minnesota, Twin Cities Campus	M,D
University of Missouri–Kansas City	M,D
University of Nevada, Reno	M,D
University of New Haven	M
University of New Mexico	M,D
The University of North Carolina at Chapel Hill	M,D
University of Notre Dame	M,D
University of Pennsylvania	D
University of Pittsburgh	M,D
University of Rochester	M,D
University of South Alabama	D
University of South Carolina (Columbia)	M,D
University of Southern California	M,D
University of South Florida	D
The University of Texas at Dallas	M,D
University of Utah	D
University of Vermont	M,D
University of Virginia	D
University of Washington	D
University of Wisconsin–Madison	M,D
Vanderbilt University	M,D
Virginia Polytechnic Institute and State University	D
Washington State University	M,D
Washington University in St. Louis	D
Wayne State University	M,D
West Virginia University	M,D
Yale University	D
Yeshiva University	D

CELTIC LANGUAGES

Harvard University	M,D

CERAMIC SCIENCES AND ENGINEERING

Alfred University	M,D
Clemson University	M,D
Georgia Institute of Technology	M,D
Massachusetts Institute of Technology	D
The Ohio State University	M,D
Pennsylvania State University University Park Campus	M,D
Rensselaer Polytechnic Institute	M,D
Rutgers, The State University of New Jersey, New Brunswick	M,D
University of California, Berkeley	M,D
University of California, Los Angeles	M,D
University of Cincinnati	M,D
University of Florida	M,D,O
University of Missouri–Rolla	M,D
University of Washington	M

CHEMICAL ENGINEERING

Arizona State University	M,D
Auburn University	M,D
Brigham Young University	M,D
Brown University	M,D
California Institute of Technology	M,D
Carnegie Mellon University	M,D
Case Western Reserve University	M,D
City College of the City University of New York	M,D
Clarkson University	M,D
Clemson University	M,D
Cleveland State University	M,D
Colorado School of Mines	M,D
Colorado State University	M,D
Columbia University	M,D,O
Cornell University	M,D
Drexel University	M,D
Florida Agricultural and Mechanical University	M,D
Florida Institute of Technology	M,D
Florida State University	M,D
Georgia Institute of Technology	M,D,O
Graduate School and University Center of the City University of New York	D
Howard University	M
Illinois Institute of Technology	M,D
Iowa State University of Science and Technology	M,D
Johns Hopkins University	M,D
Kansas State University	M,D
Lamar University	M,D
Lehigh University	M,D
Louisiana State University and Agricultural and Mechanical College	M,D
Louisiana Tech University	M,D
Manhattan College	M
Marshall University	M
Massachusetts Institute of Technology	M,D,O
McNeese State University	M
Michigan State University	M,D
Michigan Technological University	M,D
Mississippi State University	M,D
Montana State University–Bozeman	M,D
New Jersey Institute of Technology	M,D,O
New Mexico State University	M,D
North Carolina Agricultural and Technical State University	M
North Carolina State University	M,D
Northeastern University	M,D
Northwestern University	M,D
The Ohio State University	M,D
Ohio University	M,D
Oklahoma State University	M,D
Oregon State University	M,D
Pennsylvania State University University Park Campus	M,D
Polytechnic University, Brooklyn Campus	M,D
Princeton University	M,D
Purdue University	M,D
Rensselaer Polytechnic Institute	M,D
Rice University	M,D
Rutgers, The State University of New Jersey, New Brunswick	M,D
San Jose State University	M
Stanford University	M,D,O
State University of New York at Buffalo	M,D
Stevens Institute of Technology	M,D,O
Syracuse University	M,D
Tennessee Technological University	M,D
Texas A&M University (College Station)	M,D
Texas A&M University–Kingsville	M
Texas Tech University	M,D
Tufts University	M,D
Tulane University	M,D
The University of Akron	M,D
The University of Alabama (Tuscaloosa)	M,D
The University of Alabama in Huntsville	M
The University of Arizona	M,D
University of Arkansas (Fayetteville)	M
University of California, Berkeley	M,D
University of California, Davis	M,D,O
University of California, Irvine	M,D
University of California, Los Angeles	M,D
University of California, San Diego	M,D
University of California, Santa Barbara	M,D
University of Cincinnati	M,D
University of Colorado at Boulder	M,D
University of Connecticut	M,D
University of Dayton	M
University of Delaware	M,D
University of Detroit Mercy	M,D
University of Florida	M,D,O
University of Houston	M,D
University of Idaho	M,D
University of Illinois at Chicago	M,D
University of Illinois at Urbana–Champaign	M,D
The University of Iowa	M,D
University of Kansas	M,D
University of Kentucky	M,D
University of Louisville	M,D
University of Maine (Orono)	M,D
University of Maryland, Baltimore County	M,D
University of Maryland, College Park	M,D
University of Massachusetts Amherst	M,D
University of Massachusetts Lowell	M
University of Michigan	M,D,O
University of Minnesota, Twin Cities Campus	M,D
University of Missouri–Columbia	M,D
University of Missouri–Rolla	M,D
University of Nebraska–Lincoln	M,D
University of Nevada, Reno	M,D
University of New Hampshire	M,D
University of New Mexico	M,D
University of North Dakota	M
University of Notre Dame	M,D
University of Oklahoma	M,D
University of Pennsylvania	M,D
University of Pittsburgh	M,D
University of Puerto Rico, Mayagüez Campus	M
University of Rhode Island	M,D
University of Rochester	M,D
University of South Alabama	M
University of South Carolina (Columbia)	M,D
University of Southern California	M,D,O
University of South Florida	M,D
University of Southwestern Louisiana	M
University of Tennessee, Knoxville	M,D
The University of Texas at Austin	M,D
University of Toledo	M,D
University of Tulsa	M,D
University of Utah	M,D
University of Virginia	M,D
University of Washington	M,D
University of Wisconsin–Madison	M,D
University of Wyoming	M,D
Vanderbilt University	M,D
Villanova University	M
Virginia Polytechnic Institute and State University	M,D
Washington State University	M,D
Washington University in St. Louis	M,D
Wayne State University	M,D
Western Michigan University	M
West Virginia University	M,D
Widener University	M
Worcester Polytechnic Institute	M,D
Yale University	M,D
Youngstown State University	M

CHEMISTRY

Adelphi University	M
American University	M,D
Arizona State University	M,D
Arkansas State University	M,O
Auburn University	M,D
Ball State University	M
Baylor University	M,D
Boston College	M,D
Boston University	M,D
Bowling Green State University	M,D
Bradley University	M
Brandeis University	M,D
Bridgewater State College	M
Brigham Young University	M,D
Brooklyn College of the City University of New York	M,D
Brown University	M,D
Butler University	M
California Institute of Technology	D
California State Polytechnic University, Pomona	M
California State University, Fresno	M
California State University, Fullerton	M
California State University, Hayward	M
California State University, Long Beach	M
California State University, Los Angeles	M
California State University, Northridge	M
California State University, Sacramento	M
Carnegie Mellon University	M,D
Case Western Reserve University	M,D
The Catholic University of America	M,D
Central Connecticut State University	M
Central Michigan University	M
Central Washington University	M
City College of the City University of New York	M,D
Clark Atlanta University	M,D
Clarkson University	M,D
Clark University	M,D
Clemson University	M,D
Cleveland State University	M,D
College of Staten Island of the City University of New York	D
College of William and Mary	M
Colorado School of Mines	M,D
Colorado State University	M,D
Columbia University	M,D
Cornell University	D
Dartmouth College	D
Delaware State University	M
DePaul University	M
Drexel University	M,D
Duke University	D
Duquesne University	M,D
East Carolina University	M
Eastern Illinois University	M
Eastern Kentucky University	M
Eastern Michigan University	M
Eastern New Mexico University	M
East Tennessee State University	M
Emory University	M,D
Emporia State University	M
Fairleigh Dickinson University, Florham–Madison Campus	M
Fairleigh Dickinson University, Teaneck–Hackensack Campus	M
Florida Agricultural and Mechanical University	M
Florida Atlantic University	M
Florida Institute of Technology	M,D
Florida International University	M
Florida State University	M,D
George Mason University	M
Georgetown University	M,D
The George Washington University	M,D

P—first professional degree; M—master's degree; D—doctorate; O—other advanced degree.

Chemistry (continued)

Georgia Institute of Technology	M,D
Georgia State University	M,D
Graduate School and University Center of the City University of New York	D
Hampton University	M
Harvard University	M,D
Howard University	M,D
Idaho State University	M
Illinois Institute of Technology	M,D
Illinois State University	M
Indiana State University	M
Indiana University Bloomington	M,D
Indiana University of Pennsylvania	M
Indiana University–Purdue University Fort Wayne	M
Indiana University–Purdue University Indianapolis	M,D
Iowa State University of Science and Technology	M,D
Jackson State University	M
John Carroll University	M
Johns Hopkins University	M,D
Kansas State University	M,D
Kent State University	M,D
Lamar University	M
Lehigh University	M,D
Long Island University, Brooklyn Campus	M
Louisiana State University and Agricultural and Mechanical College	M,D
Louisiana Tech University	M
Loyola University Chicago	M,D
Mankato State University	M
Marquette University	M,D
Marshall University	M
Massachusetts Institute of Technology	M,D
McNeese State University	M
Miami University	M,D
Michigan State University	M,D
Michigan Technological University	M,D
Middle Tennessee State University	M,D
Mississippi State University	M,D
Montana State University–Bozeman	M,D
Montclair State University	M
Murray State University	M
New Jersey Institute of Technology	M,D
New Mexico Highlands University	M
New Mexico State University	M,D
New York University	M,D
North Carolina Agricultural and Technical State University	M
North Carolina Central University	M
North Carolina State University	M,D
North Dakota State University	M,D
Northeastern Illinois University	M
Northeastern University	M,D
Northeast Louisiana University	M
Northern Arizona University	M
Northern Illinois University	M,D
Northern Michigan University	M
Northwestern University	D
Oakland University	M,D
The Ohio State University	M,D
Ohio University	M,D
Oklahoma State University	M,D
Old Dominion University	M,D
Oregon State University	M,D
Pennsylvania State University University Park Campus	M,D
Pittsburg State University	M
Polytechnic University, Brooklyn Campus	M,D
Polytechnic University, Farmingdale Campus	M,D
Polytechnic University, Westchester Graduate Center	M
Pontifical Catholic University of Puerto Rico	M
Portland State University	M,D
Prairie View A&M University	M
Princeton University	M,D
Purdue University	M,D
Queens College of the City University of New York	M
Rensselaer Polytechnic Institute	M,D
Rice University	M,D
Rochester Institute of Technology	M
Roosevelt University	M
Rutgers, The State University of New Jersey, Newark	M,D
Rutgers, The State University of New Jersey, New Brunswick	M,D
Sacred Heart University	M
St. John's University (NY)	M
Saint Joseph College (CT)	M,O
Saint Joseph's University	M
Saint Louis University	M
Sam Houston State University	M
San Diego State University	M,D
San Francisco State University	M
San Jose State University	M
Seton Hall University	M,D
South Dakota State University	M,D
Southeast Missouri State University	M
Southern Connecticut State University	M
Southern Illinois University at Carbondale	M,D
Southern Illinois University at Edwardsville	M
Southern Methodist University	M
Southern University and Agricultural and Mechanical College	M
Southwest Missouri State University	M
Southwest Texas State University	M
Stanford University	D
State University of New York at Albany	M,D
State University of New York at Binghamton	M,D
State University of New York at Buffalo	M,D
State University of New York at New Paltz	M
State University of New York at Oswego	M
State University of New York at Stony Brook	M,D
State University of New York College at Buffalo	M
State University of New York College at Fredonia	M
State University of New York College of Environmental Science and Forestry	M,D
Stephen F. Austin State University	M
Stevens Institute of Technology	M,D,O
Sul Ross State University	M
Syracuse University	M,D
Temple University (Philadelphia)	M,D
Tennessee State University	M
Tennessee Technological University	M
Texas A&M University (College Station)	M,D
Texas A&M University–Commerce	M
Texas A&M University–Kingsville	M
Texas Christian University	M,D
Texas Southern University	M
Texas Tech University	M,D
Texas Woman's University	M
Tufts University	M,D
Tulane University	M,D
Tuskegee University	M
The University of Akron	M,D
The University of Alabama (Tuscaloosa)	M,D
The University of Alabama at Birmingham	M,D
The University of Alabama in Huntsville	M
University of Alaska Fairbanks	M,D
The University of Arizona	M,D
University of Arkansas (Fayetteville)	M,D
University of Arkansas at Little Rock	M
University of California, Berkeley	M,D
University of California, Davis	M,D
University of California, Irvine	M,D
University of California, Los Angeles	M,D,O
University of California, Riverside	M,D
University of California, San Diego	D
University of California, Santa Barbara	M,D
University of California, Santa Cruz	M,D
University of Central Florida	M
University of Chicago	M,D
University of Cincinnati	M,D
University of Colorado at Boulder	M,D
University of Colorado at Denver	M
University of Connecticut	M,D
University of Delaware	M,D
University of Denver	M,D
University of Detroit Mercy	M,D
University of Florida	M,D
University of Georgia	M,D
University of Hawaii at Manoa	M,D
University of Houston	M,D
University of Houston–Clear Lake	M
University of Idaho	M,D
University of Illinois at Chicago	M,D
University of Illinois at Urbana–Champaign	M,D
The University of Iowa	M,D
University of Kansas	M,D
University of Kentucky	M,D
University of Louisville	M,D
University of Maine (Orono)	M,D
University of Maryland, Baltimore County	M,D
University of Maryland, College Park	M,D
University of Massachusetts Amherst	M,D
University of Massachusetts Boston	M
University of Massachusetts Dartmouth	M
University of Massachusetts Lowell	M,D
The University of Memphis	M,D
University of Miami	M,D
University of Michigan	D
University of Minnesota, Duluth	M
University of Minnesota, Twin Cities Campus	M,D
University of Mississippi	M,D
University of Missouri–Columbia	M,D
University of Missouri–Kansas City	M,D
University of Missouri–Rolla	M,D
University of Missouri–St. Louis	M,D
The University of Montana–Missoula	M,D
University of Nebraska–Lincoln	M,D
University of Nevada, Las Vegas	M
University of Nevada, Reno	M,D
University of New Hampshire	M,D
University of New Mexico	M,D
University of New Orleans	M,D
The University of North Carolina at Chapel Hill	M,D
University of North Carolina at Charlotte	M
University of North Carolina at Greensboro	M
University of North Carolina at Wilmington	M
University of North Dakota	M,D
University of Northern Colorado	M,D
University of Northern Iowa	M
University of North Texas	M,D
University of Notre Dame	M,D
University of Oklahoma	M,D
University of Oregon	M,D
University of Pennsylvania	M,D
University of Pittsburgh	M,D
University of Puerto Rico, Mayagüez Campus	M
University of Puerto Rico, Río Piedras	M,D
University of Rhode Island	M,D
University of Rochester	M,D
University of San Francisco	M
University of Scranton	M
University of South Carolina (Columbia)	M,D
University of South Dakota	M
University of Southern California	M,D
University of Southern Mississippi	M,D
University of South Florida	M,D
University of Tennessee, Knoxville	M,D
The University of Texas at Arlington	M,D
The University of Texas at Austin	M,D
The University of Texas at Dallas	M,D
The University of Texas at El Paso	M
The University of Texas at San Antonio	M
The University of Texas at Tyler	M
University of the Pacific	M,D
University of Toledo	M,D
University of Utah	M,D
University of Vermont	M,D
University of Virginia	M,D
University of Washington	M,D
University of Wisconsin–Madison	M,D
University of Wisconsin–Milwaukee	M,D
University of Wyoming	M,D
Utah State University	M,D
Vanderbilt University	M,D
Villanova University	M,D
Virginia Commonwealth University	M,D
Virginia Polytechnic Institute and State University	M,D
Wake Forest University	M,D
Washington State University	M,D
Washington University in St. Louis	M,D
Wayne State University	M,D
West Chester University of Pennsylvania	M
Western Carolina University	M
Western Illinois University	M
Western Kentucky University	M,D
Western Michigan University	M
Western Washington University	M
West Texas A&M University	M
West Virginia University	M,D
Wichita State University	M,D
Worcester Polytechnic Institute	M,D
Wright State University	M
Yale University	D
Youngstown State University	M

CHILD AND FAMILY STUDIES

Abilene Christian University	M
Auburn University	M,D
Bowling Green State University	M
Brandeis University	M
Brigham Young University	M,D
California State University, Fresno	M
California State University, Los Angeles	M
Central Washington University	M
Colorado State University	M
Cornell University	D
East Carolina University	M
Fitchburg State College	O
Florida State University	M,D
Friends University	M
Harvard University	M
Indiana State University	M
Indiana University Bloomington	M
Iowa State University of Science and Technology	M,D
Kansas State University	M,D
Kent State University	M
Loma Linda University	M,O
Loyola University Chicago	M
Miami University	M
Michigan State University	M,D
Middle Tennessee State University	M
Montclair State University	M
North Dakota State University	M
Northern Illinois University	M
Nova Southeastern University	M,D
The Ohio State University	M,D
Ohio University	M
Oklahoma State University	M,D
Oregon State University	M,D
Pennsylvania State University University Park Campus	M,D
Purdue University	M,D
Sage Graduate School	M
St. Cloud State University	M
San Jose State University	M
South Carolina State University	M
Stanford University	D
Syracuse University	M,D
Tennessee State University	M
Texas Tech University	M,D
Texas Woman's University	M,D
Tufts University	M,D,O
The University of Akron	M
The University of Alabama (Tuscaloosa)	M
University of California, Davis	M
University of Connecticut	M,D
University of Delaware	M,D
University of Denver	M,D
University of Georgia	M,D
University of Illinois at Springfield	M
University of Kentucky	M
University of La Verne	M
University of Maryland, College Park	M
University of Minnesota, Twin Cities Campus	M,D
University of Missouri–Columbia	M
University of Nebraska–Lincoln	M,D
University of Nevada, Reno	M
University of New Hampshire	M
University of New Mexico	M,D
University of North Carolina at Greensboro	M,D
University of North Texas	M
University of Pittsburgh	M
University of Rhode Island	M
The University of Tennessee at Martin	M
University of Tennessee, Knoxville	M,D
The University of Texas at Austin	M,D
The University of Texas at Dallas	M
University of Utah	M
University of Wisconsin–Madison	M,D
Utah State University	M,D
Virginia Polytechnic Institute and State University	M,D
Wayne State University	O
West Virginia University	M

CHIROPRACTIC

University of Bridgeport	P

CITY AND REGIONAL PLANNING

Alabama Agricultural and Mechanical University	M
Arizona State University	M
Auburn University	M
Ball State University	M
Boston University	M

California Polytechnic State University, San Luis Obispo	M
California State Polytechnic University, Pomona	M
California State University, Chico	M
California State University, San Bernardino	M
Carnegie Mellon University	M
The Catholic University of America	M
Clemson University	M
Cleveland State University	M
Columbia University	M,D
Cornell University	M,D
Delta State University	M
DePaul University	O
Eastern Kentucky University	M
Eastern Washington University	M
Florida Atlantic University	M
Florida International University	M
Florida State University	M,D
Georgia Institute of Technology	M
Georgia State University	M
Harvard University	M,D
Hunter College of the City University of New York	M
Indiana University Bloomington	D
Indiana University–Purdue University Indianapolis	M
Iowa State University of Science and Technology	M
Jackson State University	M
Kansas State University	M
Massachusetts Institute of Technology	M,D
Michigan State University	M,D
Morgan State University	M
Murray State University	M
New York University	M,O
The Ohio State University	M,D
Old Dominion University	M
Portland State University	M
Princeton University	M,D
Rutgers, The State University of New Jersey, New Brunswick	M,D
San Diego State University	M
San Jose State University	M
Southwest Missouri State University	M
State University of New York at Albany	M
State University of New York at Buffalo	M
Texas A&M University (College Station)	M,D
Texas Southern University	M
Texas Tech University	D
Tufts University	M
The University of Akron	D
The University of Arizona	M
University of California, Berkeley	M,D
University of California, Davis	M
University of California, Irvine	M,D
University of California, Los Angeles	M,D
University of Cincinnati	M
University of Colorado at Denver	M
University of Florida	M,D
University of Hawaii at Manoa	M
University of Illinois at Chicago	M,D
University of Illinois at Urbana–Champaign	M,D
The University of Iowa	M
University of Kansas	M
University of Louisville	M
University of Maryland, College Park	M
University of Massachusetts Amherst	M,D
The University of Memphis	M
University of Michigan	M,D,O
University of Minnesota, Twin Cities Campus	M
The University of Montana–Missoula	M
University of Nebraska–Lincoln	M
University of New Mexico	M
University of New Orleans	M
The University of North Carolina at Chapel Hill	M,D
University of Oklahoma	M
University of Oregon	M
University of Pennsylvania	M,D,O
University of Pittsburgh	M,O
University of Puerto Rico, Río Piedras	M
University of Rhode Island	M
University of Southern California	M,D
University of Southern Maine	M
University of Tennessee, Knoxville	M
The University of Texas at Arlington	M
The University of Texas at Austin	M,D
University of Toledo	M
University of Virginia	M
University of Washington	M,D
University of Wisconsin–Madison	M,D
University of Wisconsin–Milwaukee	M
Utah State University	M
Virginia Commonwealth University	M,O
Virginia Polytechnic Institute and State University	M
Washington State University	M
Wayne State University	M
West Chester University of Pennsylvania	M
Western Kentucky University	M

CIVIL ENGINEERING

Arizona State University	M,D
Auburn University	M,D
Bradley University	M
Brigham Young University	M,D
California Institute of Technology	M,D,O
California Polytechnic State University, San Luis Obispo	M
California State University, Fresno	M
California State University, Fullerton	M
California State University, Long Beach	M,O
California State University, Los Angeles	M
California State University, Northridge	M
California State University, Sacramento	M
Carnegie Mellon University	M,D
Case Western Reserve University	M,D
The Catholic University of America	M
City College of the City University of New York	M,D
Clarkson University	M,D
Clemson University	M,D
Cleveland State University	M,D
Colorado State University	M,D
Columbia University	M,D,O
Cornell University	M,D
Drexel University	M,D
Duke University	M,D
Florida Agricultural and Mechanical University	M
Florida Atlantic University	M
Florida Institute of Technology	M,D
Florida International University	M
Florida State University	M,D
The George Washington University	M,D,O
Georgia Institute of Technology	M,D
Graduate School and University Center of the City University of New York	D
Howard University	M
Illinois Institute of Technology	M,D
Iowa State University of Science and Technology	M,D
Johns Hopkins University	M,D
Kansas State University	M,D
Lamar University	M,D
Lehigh University	M,D
Louisiana State University and Agricultural and Mechanical College	M,D
Louisiana Tech University	M,D
Loyola Marymount University	M
Manhattan College	M
Marquette University	M,D
Massachusetts Institute of Technology	M,D,O
McNeese State University	M
Michigan State University	M,D
Michigan Technological University	M,D
Mississippi State University	D
Montana State University–Bozeman	M,D
New Jersey Institute of Technology	M,D,O
New Mexico State University	M,D
North Carolina Agricultural and Technical State University	M
North Carolina State University	M,D
North Dakota State University	M
Northeastern University	M,D
Northwestern University	M,D
The Ohio State University	M,D
Ohio University	M
Oklahoma State University	M,D
Old Dominion University	M,D
Oregon State University	M,D
Pennsylvania State University University Park Campus	M,D
Polytechnic University, Brooklyn Campus	M,D
Polytechnic University, Farmingdale Campus	M,D
Polytechnic University, Westchester Graduate Center	M,D
Portland State University	M,D
Princeton University	M,D
Purdue University	M,D
Rensselaer Polytechnic Institute	M,D
Rice University	M,D
Rutgers, The State University of New Jersey, New Brunswick	M,D
San Diego State University	M
San Jose State University	M
Santa Clara University	M
South Dakota State University	M
Southern Illinois University at Carbondale	M
Southern Illinois University at Edwardsville	M
Stanford University	M,D,O
State University of New York at Buffalo	M,D
Stevens Institute of Technology	M,D,O
Syracuse University	M,D
Temple University (Philadelphia)	M
Tennessee Technological University	M,D
Texas A&M University (College Station)	M,D
Texas A&M University–Kingsville	M
Texas Tech University	M,D
Tufts University	M,D
Tulane University	M,D
The University of Akron	M,D
The University of Alabama (Tuscaloosa)	M,D
The University of Alabama at Birmingham	M
The University of Alabama in Huntsville	M
University of Alaska Anchorage	M
University of Alaska Fairbanks	M
The University of Arizona	M,D
University of Arkansas (Fayetteville)	M
University of California, Berkeley	M,D
University of California, Davis	M,D,O
University of California, Irvine	M,D
University of California, Los Angeles	M,D
University of Central Florida	M,D
University of Cincinnati	M,D
University of Colorado at Boulder	M,D
University of Colorado at Denver	M,D
University of Connecticut	M,D
University of Dayton	M
University of Delaware	M,D
University of Detroit Mercy	M,D
University of Florida	M,D,O
University of Hawaii at Manoa	M,D
University of Houston	M,D
University of Idaho	M,D
University of Illinois at Chicago	M,D
University of Illinois at Urbana–Champaign	M,D
The University of Iowa	M,D
University of Kansas	M,D
University of Kentucky	M,D
University of Louisville	M,D
University of Maine (Orono)	M,D
University of Maryland, College Park	M,D
University of Massachusetts Amherst	M,D
University of Massachusetts Lowell	M
The University of Memphis	M,D
University of Miami	M,D
University of Michigan	M,D,O
University of Minnesota, Twin Cities Campus	M,D
University of Missouri–Columbia	M,D
University of Missouri–Rolla	M,D
University of Nebraska–Lincoln	M,D
University of Nevada, Las Vegas	M,D
University of Nevada, Reno	M,D
University of New Hampshire	M,D
University of New Mexico	M,D
University of New Orleans	M
University of North Carolina at Charlotte	M
University of North Dakota	M
University of Notre Dame	M,D
University of Oklahoma	M,D
University of Pittsburgh	M,D
University of Portland	M
University of Puerto Rico, Mayagüez Campus	M,D
University of Rhode Island	M,D
University of South Carolina (Columbia)	M,D
University of Southern California	M,D,O
University of South Florida	M,D
University of Southwestern Louisiana	M
University of Tennessee, Knoxville	M,D
The University of Texas at Arlington	M,D
The University of Texas at Austin	M,D
The University of Texas at El Paso	M
The University of Texas at San Antonio	M
University of Toledo	M,D
University of Utah	M,D
University of Vermont	M,D
University of Virginia	M,D
University of Washington	M,D
University of Wisconsin–Madison	M,D
University of Wyoming	M,D
Utah State University	M,D,O
Vanderbilt University	M,D
Villanova University	M
Virginia Polytechnic Institute and State University	M,D
Washington State University	M,D
Washington University in St. Louis	M,D
Wayne State University	M,D
West Virginia University	M,D
Widener University	M
Worcester Polytechnic Institute	M,D
Youngstown State University	M

CLASSICS

Boston College	M
Boston University	M,D
Brown University	M,D
The Catholic University of America	M,D
Columbia University	M,D
Cornell University	D
Duke University	D
Florida State University	M,D
Fordham University	M,D
Georgia State University	M,O
Graduate School and University Center of the City University of New York	M,D
Harvard University	M,D
Hunter College of the City University of New York	M
Indiana State University	M
Indiana University Bloomington	M,D
Johns Hopkins University	M,D
Kent State University	M
Loyola University Chicago	M,D
New York University	M,D
Northwestern University	M,D
The Ohio State University	M,D
Princeton University	D
Rutgers, The State University of New Jersey, New Brunswick	M,D
San Francisco State University	M
Stanford University	M,D
State University of New York at Albany	M
State University of New York at Buffalo	M,D
Syracuse University	M,D
Tufts University	M
Tulane University	M
The University of Arizona	M
University of California, Berkeley	M,D
University of California, Irvine	M,D
University of California, Los Angeles	M,D,O
University of California, Santa Barbara	M,D
University of Chicago	M,D
University of Cincinnati	M,D
University of Colorado at Boulder	M,D
University of Florida	M
University of Georgia	M
University of Hawaii at Manoa	M
University of Illinois at Urbana–Champaign	M,D
The University of Iowa	M,D
University of Kansas	M
University of Kentucky	M
University of Maryland, College Park	M
University of Massachusetts Amherst	M
University of Michigan	M,D
University of Minnesota, Twin Cities Campus	M,D
University of Mississippi	M
University of Missouri–Columbia	M,D
University of Nebraska–Lincoln	M
The University of North Carolina at Chapel Hill	M,D
University of North Carolina at Greensboro	M
University of Oregon	M
University of Pennsylvania	M,D
University of Pittsburgh	M,D
University of Southern California	M,D
The University of Texas at Austin	M,D
University of Vermont	M
University of Virginia	M,D
University of Washington	M,D
University of Wisconsin–Madison	M,D
University of Wisconsin–Milwaukee	M
Vanderbilt University	M,D
Villanova University	M

P—first professional degree; M—master's degree; D—doctorate; O—other advanced degree.

Classics (continued)
Washington University in St. Louis M
Wayne State University M
Yale University D

CLINICAL LABORATORY SCIENCES
California State University, Dominguez Hills M,O
The Catholic University of America M,D
Duke University M
Indiana State University M
Johns Hopkins University M,D
Long Island University, C.W. Post Campus M
Michigan State University M
Quinnipiac College M
San Francisco State University M
State University of New York at Buffalo M
The University of Alabama at Birmingham M
University of Illinois at Chicago M
University of Massachusetts Lowell M
University of Minnesota, Twin Cities Campus M
University of Pittsburgh M
University of Rhode Island M
University of Washington M
University of Wisconsin–Milwaukee M
Virginia Commonwealth University M
Wayne State University M

CLINICAL PSYCHOLOGY
Abilene Christian University M
Adelphi University D,O
Alabama Agricultural and Mechanical University M
Allegheny University of the Health Sciences M,D
American International College M
American University D
Appalachian State University M
Arizona State University D
Austin Peay State University M
Azusa Pacific University M,D
Ball State University M
Barry University M
Baylor University M,D
Boston University D
Bowling Green State University M,D
Brigham Young University D
California Lutheran University M
California State University, Dominguez Hills M
California State University, Fullerton M
California State University, San Bernardino M
Case Western Reserve University D
The Catholic University of America D
Central Michigan University D
City College of the City University of New York D
Clark University D
Cleveland State University M
College of William and Mary D
DePaul University M,D
Drexel University M,D
Duke University D
Duquesne University D
East Carolina University M
Eastern Illinois University M
Eastern Kentucky University M
Eastern Michigan University M
East Tennessee State University M
Edinboro University of Pennsylvania M
Emory University D
Emporia State University M
Fairleigh Dickinson University, Florham–Madison Campus M
Fairleigh Dickinson University, Teaneck–Hackensack Campus D
Florida Institute of Technology D
Florida State University D
Fordham University D
Francis Marion University M
Gallaudet University D
George Mason University D
The George Washington University D
Georgia State University D
Graduate School and University Center of the City University of New York D
Hofstra University M,D
Howard University D
Hunter College of the City University of New York M
Idaho State University D
Illinois Institute of Technology D
Illinois State University M
Immaculata College D
Indiana State University D
Indiana University Bloomington D
Indiana University–Purdue University Indianapolis M,D
Jackson State University D
Kent State University M,D
La Salle University M,D
Lesley College M
Loma Linda University D
Long Island University, Brooklyn Campus D
Long Island University, C.W. Post Campus D
Louisiana State University and Agricultural and Mechanical College M,D
Loyola College M,D,O
Loyola University Chicago D
Mankato State University M
Mansfield University of Pennsylvania M
Marquette University M
Marshall University M
Miami University D
Millersville University of Pennsylvania M
Montclair State University M
Morehead State University M
Murray State University M
New School University D
New York University D
Norfolk State University M
North Dakota State University M
Northwestern State University of Louisiana M
Northwestern University D
Nova Southeastern University D
The Ohio State University D
Ohio University D
Oklahoma State University D
Old Dominion University D
Pace University D
Pennsylvania State University University Park Campus M,D
Pepperdine University (Culver City) M
Pontifical Catholic University of Puerto Rico M
Queens College of the City University of New York M
Radford University M
Roosevelt University M,D
Rutgers, The State University of New Jersey, New Brunswick M,D
St. John's University (NY) D
Saint Louis University M,D
St. Mary's University of San Antonio M
Saint Michael's College M
Sam Houston State University M
San Diego State University M,D
San Jose State University M
Seattle Pacific University D
Seton Hall University D
Southern Illinois University at Carbondale M,D
Southern Methodist University M
State University of New York at Albany D
State University of New York at Binghamton M,D
State University of New York at Buffalo D
State University of New York at Stony Brook D
Suffolk University D
Syracuse University M,D
Teachers College, Columbia University D
Temple University (Philadelphia) D
Texas A&M University (College Station) M,D
Towson University M
The Union Institute D
United States International University D
The University of Alabama (Tuscaloosa) D
University of Alaska Anchorage M
University of California, San Diego D
University of California, Santa Barbara M,D
University of Central Florida M,D
University of Cincinnati D
University of Connecticut D
University of Dayton M
University of Delaware D
University of Denver D
University of Detroit Mercy M,D
University of Florida D
University of Georgia M,D
University of Hartford M,D
University of Hawaii at Manoa D
University of Houston D
University of Houston–Clear Lake M
University of Illinois at Springfield M
University of Illinois at Urbana–Champaign M,D
University of Kansas M,D
University of Louisville D
University of Maine (Orono) D
University of Maryland, College Park D
University of Massachusetts Amherst M,D
University of Massachusetts Boston D
University of Massachusetts Dartmouth M
The University of Memphis D
University of Miami D
University of Michigan D
University of Minnesota, Twin Cities Campus D
University of Mississippi D
University of Missouri–St. Louis D,O
The University of Montana–Missoula D
University of New Mexico M,D
The University of North Carolina at Chapel Hill M,D
University of North Carolina at Charlotte M
University of North Carolina at Greensboro M,D
University of North Dakota D
University of North Texas D
University of Oregon D
University of Pennsylvania D
University of Pittsburgh D
University of Rhode Island D
University of Rochester D
University of South Carolina (Columbia) D
University of South Dakota M,D
University of Southern California D
University of South Florida D
University of Tennessee, Knoxville D
The University of Texas at El Paso M
The University of Texas of the Permian Basin M
The University of Texas–Pan American M
University of Toledo D
University of Tulsa M,D
University of Vermont D
University of Virginia D
University of Washington D
University of Wisconsin–Madison D
University of Wisconsin–Milwaukee M,D
Valparaiso University M
Virginia Commonwealth University D
Virginia Polytechnic Institute and State University D
Washburn University of Topeka M
Washington State University D
Washington University in St. Louis D
Wayne State University D
Western Carolina University M
Western Illinois University M
Western Michigan University M,D
Westfield State College M
Wichita State University D
Widener University D
Xavier University D
Yeshiva University D

CLOTHING AND TEXTILES
Auburn University M
Colorado State University M
Cornell University M,D
Florida State University M,D
Indiana State University M
Indiana University Bloomington M
Iowa State University of Science and Technology M,D
Kansas State University M,D
Michigan State University M
North Carolina State University M,D
North Dakota State University M
The Ohio State University M,D
Oklahoma State University M,D
Oregon State University M,D
Philadelphia College of Textiles and Science M
Purdue University M,D
Texas Tech University M,D
Texas Woman's University M,D
The University of Akron M
The University of Alabama (Tuscaloosa) M
University of California, Davis M
University of Central Oklahoma M
University of Georgia M,D
University of Kentucky M
University of Maryland, College Park M,D
University of Missouri–Columbia M
University of Nebraska–Lincoln M,D
University of North Texas M
University of Rhode Island M
University of Tennessee, Knoxville M,D
University of Wisconsin–Madison M
Virginia Polytechnic Institute and State University M,D
Washington State University M
Western Kentucky University M

COGNITIVE SCIENCES
Boston University M,D
Brandeis University D
Brown University M,D
Carnegie Mellon University D
Claremont Graduate University M,D
Dartmouth College D
Duke University D
Emory University D
Florida State University D
The George Washington University D
Georgia Institute of Technology M
Graduate School and University Center of the City University of New York D
Harvard University M,D
Johns Hopkins University M,D
Louisiana State University and Agricultural and Mechanical College M,D
Massachusetts Institute of Technology D
New York University D
Northwestern University D
The Ohio State University D
Rutgers, The State University of New Jersey, Newark D
Rutgers, The State University of New Jersey, New Brunswick D
State University of New York at Binghamton M,D
State University of New York at Buffalo D
Temple University (Philadelphia) D
The University of Akron M,D
The University of Alabama (Tuscaloosa) D
University of California, San Diego D
University of Connecticut D
University of Delaware D
University of Illinois at Urbana–Champaign M,D
University of Maryland, College Park D
University of Minnesota, Twin Cities Campus D
University of Notre Dame D
University of Oregon M,D
University of Pittsburgh D
University of Rochester M,D
The University of Texas at Dallas M
University of Wisconsin–Madison D
Wayne State University D

COMMUNICATION
Abilene Christian University M
American University M
Andrews University M
Arizona State University M,D
Arkansas State University M
Auburn University M
Austin Peay State University M
Ball State University M
Barry University M
Baylor University M
Bloomsburg University of Pennsylvania M
Boise State University M
Boston University M
Bowling Green State University M,D
Brigham Young University M
California State University, Chico M
California State University, Fullerton M
California State University, Los Angeles M
California State University, Northridge M
California State University, Sacramento M
California University of Pennsylvania M
Carnegie Mellon University M
Central Connecticut State University M
Central Michigan University M
Central Missouri State University M
Clarion University of Pennsylvania M

Clark University	M
Clemson University	M
Cleveland State University	M
College of New Rochelle	M,O
Colorado State University	M
Cornell University	M,D
DePaul University	M
Drake University	M
Drexel University	M
Drury College	M
Duquesne University	M
Eastern Michigan University	M
Eastern New Mexico University	M
Eastern Washington University	M
Edinboro University of Pennsylvania	M
Emerson College	M
Fairleigh Dickinson University, Teaneck–Hackensack Campus	M
Fitchburg State College	M
Florida Atlantic University	M
Florida Institute of Technology	M
Florida State University	M,D
Fordham University	M
Fort Hays State University	M
Georgetown University	M
Georgia State University	M
Governors State University	M
Grand Valley State University	M
Harvard University	O
Howard University	M,D
Hunter College of the City University of New York	M
Illinois Institute of Technology	M
Illinois State University	M
Indiana State University	M
Indiana University Bloomington	M,D
Indiana University–Purdue University Fort Wayne	M
Iona College (New Rochelle)	M,O
Ithaca College	M
John Carroll University	M
Kent State University	M,D
Loyola Marymount University	M
Loyola University New Orleans	M
Marquette University	M
Marshall University	M
Marywood University	M
Miami University	M
Michigan State University	M,D
Michigan Technological University	M,D
Mississippi College	M
Monmouth University	M,O
Morehead State University	M
New Jersey Institute of Technology	M
New Mexico State University	M
New School University	M
New York Institute of Technology	M
New York University	M,D,O
Norfolk State University	M
North Dakota State University	M
Northeastern State University	M
Northeast Louisiana University	M
Northern Illinois University	M
Northwestern University	M,D
The Ohio State University	M,D
Ohio University	M,D
Pennsylvania State University University Park Campus	M,D
Pepperdine University (Malibu)	M
Pittsburg State University	M
Purdue University	M,D
Purdue University Calumet	M
Queens College of the City University of New York	M
Rensselaer Polytechnic Institute	M,D
Rochester Institute of Technology	M
Roosevelt University	M
Rutgers, The State University of New Jersey, New Brunswick	M,D
Saint Louis University	M
San Diego State University	M
San Jose State University	M
Seton Hall University	M
Shippensburg University of Pennsylvania	M
South Dakota State University	M
Southern Illinois University at Carbondale	M,D
Southern Methodist University	M
Southwest Missouri State University	M
Southwest Texas State University	M
Stanford University	M,D
State University of New York at Albany	M,D
State University of New York at Buffalo	M,D
State University of New York College at Brockport	M
Stephen F. Austin State University	M
Suffolk University	M
Syracuse University	M,D
Teachers College, Columbia University	M,D
Temple University (Philadelphia)	M,D
Texas Southern University	M
Texas Tech University	M
The University of Akron	M
The University of Alabama (Tuscaloosa)	M,D,O
The University of Arizona	M,D
University of Arkansas (Fayetteville)	M
University of California, San Diego	M,D
University of California, Santa Barbara	D
University of California, Santa Cruz	O
University of Central Florida	M
University of Cincinnati	M
University of Colorado at Boulder	M,D
University of Colorado at Colorado Springs	M
University of Colorado at Denver	M
University of Connecticut	M
University of Dayton	M
University of Delaware	M
University of Denver	M,D
University of Dubuque	M
University of Florida	M,D
University of Georgia	M,D
University of Hartford	M
University of Hawaii at Manoa	M,D
University of Houston	M
University of Illinois at Chicago	M
University of Illinois at Springfield	M
University of Illinois at Urbana–Champaign	D
The University of Iowa	M,D
University of Kansas	M,D
University of Kentucky	M,D
University of Maine (Orono)	M
University of Maryland, Baltimore County	M
University of Maryland, College Park	M,D
University of Massachusetts Amherst	M,D
The University of Memphis	M,D
University of Miami	M
University of Missouri–Columbia	M,D
University of Missouri–Kansas City	M
The University of Montana–Missoula	M
University of Montevallo	M
University of Nebraska at Omaha	M
University of Nebraska–Lincoln	M,D
University of Nevada, Las Vegas	M
University of New Mexico	M,D
The University of North Carolina at Chapel Hill	M
University of North Carolina at Greensboro	M
University of North Dakota	M
University of Northern Colorado	M
University of Northern Iowa	M
University of North Texas	M
University of Oklahoma	M,D
University of Oregon	M,D
University of Pennsylvania	M,D
University of Portland	M
University of St. Thomas (MN)	O
University of South Alabama	M
University of Southern California	M,D,O
University of Southern Mississippi	M,D
University of South Florida	M,D
University of Southwestern Louisiana	M
University of Tennessee, Knoxville	M,D
The University of Texas at Austin	M,D
The University of Texas at Dallas	D
The University of Texas at El Paso	M
The University of Texas at Tyler	M
The University of Texas–Pan American	M
University of the Incarnate Word	M
University of the Pacific	M
University of Utah	M,D
University of Vermont	M
University of Washington	M,D
University of West Florida	M
University of Wisconsin–Madison	M,D
University of Wisconsin–Milwaukee	M
University of Wisconsin–Stevens Point	M
University of Wisconsin–Superior	M
University of Wisconsin–Whitewater	M
University of Wyoming	M
Utah State University	M
Wake Forest University	M
Washington State University	M
Wayne State College	M
Wayne State University	M,D
Webster University	M
West Chester University of Pennsylvania	M
Western Illinois University	M
Western Kentucky University	M
Western Michigan University	M
Westminster College of Salt Lake City	M
West Texas A&M University	M
West Virginia University	M
Wichita State University	M
William Paterson University of New Jersey	M

COMMUNICATION DISORDERS

Adelphi University	M,D
Alabama Agricultural and Mechanical University	M
Appalachian State University	M
Arizona State University	M,D
Arkansas State University	M
Auburn University	M
Ball State University	M,O
Baylor University	M
Bloomsburg University of Pennsylvania	M
Boston University	M,D,O
Bowling Green State University	M,D
Brigham Young University	M
Brooklyn College of the City University of New York	M
California State University, Chico	M
California State University, Fresno	M
California State University, Fullerton	M
California State University, Hayward	M
California State University, Long Beach	M
California State University, Los Angeles	M
California State University, Northridge	M
California State University, Sacramento	M
California University of Pennsylvania	M
Case Western Reserve University	M,D,O
Central Michigan University	M,D
Central Missouri State University	M
Clarion University of Pennsylvania	M
Cleveland State University	M
The College of New Jersey	M
The College of Saint Rose	M
Duquesne University	M
East Carolina University	M,D
Eastern Illinois University	M
Eastern Kentucky University	M
Eastern Michigan University	M
Eastern New Mexico University	M
Eastern Washington University	M
East Stroudsburg University of Pennsylvania	M
East Tennessee State University	M
Edinboro University of Pennsylvania	M
Emerson College	M,D
Florida Atlantic University	M
Florida State University	M,D
Fontbonne College	M
Fort Hays State University	M
Gallaudet University	M,D
The George Washington University	M
Georgia State University	M
Governors State University	M
Graduate School and University Center of the City University of New York	D
Hampton University	M
Harvard University	D
Hofstra University	M
Howard University	M,D
Hunter College of the City University of New York	M
Idaho State University	M
Illinois State University	M
Indiana State University	M,D,O
Indiana University Bloomington	M,D
Indiana University of Pennsylvania	M
Ithaca College	M
Jackson State University	M
James Madison University	M
Kean University	M
Kent State University	M,D
Lamar University	M
Lehman College of the City University of New York	M
Loma Linda University	M
Long Island University, Brooklyn Campus	M
Long Island University, C.W. Post Campus	M
Louisiana State University and Agricultural and Mechanical College	M,D
Louisiana Tech University	M
Loyola College	M,O
Mankato State University	M
Marquette University	M
Marshall University	M
Marywood University	M
Massachusetts Institute of Technology	D
Miami University	M
Michigan State University	M,D
Minot State University	M
Montclair State University	M
Moorhead State University	M
Murray State University	M
Nazareth College of Rochester	M
New Mexico State University	M
New York University	M,D
North Carolina Central University	M
Northeastern University	M
Northeast Louisiana University	M
Northern Arizona University	M
Northern Illinois University	M
Northern Michigan University	M
Northwestern University	M,D
Nova Southeastern University	M,D
The Ohio State University	M,D
Ohio University	M,D
Oklahoma State University	M
Old Dominion University	M
Our Lady of the Lake University of San Antonio	M
Pennsylvania State University University Park Campus	M,D
Plattsburgh State University of New York	M
Portland State University	M
Purdue University	M,D
Queens College of the City University of New York	M
Radford University	M
St. Cloud State University	M
St. John's University (NY)	M
Saint Louis University	M
Saint Xavier University	M
San Diego State University	M,D
San Francisco State University	M
San Jose State University	M
Seton Hall University	M
South Carolina State University	M
Southeast Missouri State University	M
Southern Connecticut State University	M
Southern Illinois University at Carbondale	M
Southern Illinois University at Edwardsville	M
Southwest Missouri State University	M
Southwest Texas State University	M
State University of New York at Buffalo	M,D
State University of New York at New Paltz	M
State University of New York College at Buffalo	M
State University of New York College at Fredonia	M
State University of New York College at Geneseo	M
Stephen F. Austin State University	M
Syracuse University	M,D
Teachers College, Columbia University	M,D
Temple University (Philadelphia)	M
Texas A&M University–Kingsville	M
Texas Christian University	M
Texas Woman's University	M
Towson University	M
Truman State University	M
The University of Akron	M
The University of Alabama (Tuscaloosa)	M
The University of Arizona	M,D
University of Arkansas (Fayetteville)	M
University of California, San Diego	D
University of California, Santa Barbara	M,D
University of Central Arkansas	M
University of Central Florida	M
University of Central Oklahoma	M
University of Cincinnati	M,D
University of Colorado at Boulder	M,D
University of Connecticut	M,D
University of Florida	M,D
University of Georgia	M,D,O
University of Hawaii at Manoa	M
University of Houston	M
University of Illinois at Urbana–Champaign	M,D
The University of Iowa	M,D
University of Kansas	M,D

P—first professional degree; M—master's degree; D—doctorate; O—other advanced degree.

Communication Disorders (continued)

University of Kentucky	M
University of Louisville	M
University of Maine (Orono)	M
University of Maryland, College Park	M,D
University of Massachusetts Amherst	M,D
The University of Memphis	M,D
University of Minnesota, Duluth	M
University of Minnesota, Twin Cities Campus	M,D
University of Mississippi	M
University of Missouri–Columbia	M
University of Montevallo	M
University of Nebraska at Kearney	M
University of Nebraska at Omaha	M
University of Nebraska–Lincoln	M
University of Nevada, Reno	M,D
University of New Hampshire	M
University of New Mexico	M
The University of North Carolina at Chapel Hill	M
University of North Carolina at Greensboro	M
University of North Dakota	M
University of Northern Colorado	M
University of Northern Iowa	M
University of North Texas	M
University of Oregon	M,D
University of Pittsburgh	M,D
University of Redlands	M
University of Rhode Island	M
University of South Alabama	M,D
University of South Carolina (Columbia)	M,D
University of South Dakota	M
University of Southern Mississippi	M,D
University of South Florida	M
University of Southwestern Louisiana	M
University of Tennessee, Knoxville	M,D
The University of Texas at Austin	M,D
The University of Texas at Dallas	M
The University of Texas at El Paso	M
The University of Texas–Pan American	M
University of the District of Columbia	M
University of the Pacific	M
University of Toledo	M
University of Tulsa	M
University of Utah	M,D
University of Virginia	M
University of Washington	M,D
University of Wisconsin–Eau Claire	M
University of Wisconsin–Madison	M,D
University of Wisconsin–Milwaukee	M
University of Wisconsin–Oshkosh	M
University of Wisconsin–River Falls	M
University of Wisconsin–Stevens Point	M
University of Wisconsin–Whitewater	M
University of Wyoming	M
Utah State University	M,O
Valdosta State University	M
Vanderbilt University	M,D
Washington State University	M
Washington University in St. Louis	M,D
Wayne State University	M,D
West Chester University of Pennsylvania	M
Western Carolina University	M
Western Illinois University	M
Western Kentucky University	M
Western Michigan University	M
Western Washington University	M
West Virginia University	M
Wichita State University	M,D
William Paterson University of New Jersey	M
Worcester State College	M

COMMUNITY COLLEGE EDUCATION

Eastern Washington University	M
Florida International University	D
George Mason University	D
Michigan State University	M
North Carolina State University	M,D
Pittsburg State University	O
Princeton University	D
University of South Florida	M
Western Carolina University	M

COMMUNITY HEALTH

Brooklyn College of the City University of New York	M
Brown University	M,D
Columbia University	M,D
Emory University	M
The George Washington University	M
Harvard University	M
Long Island University, Brooklyn Campus	M
Mankato State University	M
Old Dominion University	M
Sage Graduate School	M
Saint Louis University	M
State University of New York at Buffalo	D
Temple University (Philadelphia)	M
Trinity College (DC)	M
University of California, Los Angeles	M,D
University of Hawaii at Manoa	M
University of Illinois at Chicago	M,D
University of Illinois at Urbana–Champaign	M,D
The University of Iowa	M
University of Minnesota, Twin Cities Campus	M
University of Missouri–Columbia	M
University of North Carolina at Greensboro	M
University of Northern Colorado	M
University of North Texas	M
University of Pittsburgh	M
University of South Florida	M,D
University of Tennessee, Knoxville	M,D
University of Wisconsin–La Crosse	M
Wayne State University	M,O
West Virginia University	M

COMPARATIVE AND INTERDISCIPLINARY ARTS

Columbia College (IL)	M
Goddard College	M
John F. Kennedy University	M
Ohio University	D
San Francisco State University	M

COMPARATIVE LITERATURE

Arizona State University	M
Brandeis University	M,D
Brigham Young University	M
Brown University	M,D
California State University, Fullerton	M
Carnegie Mellon University	M,D
Case Western Reserve University	M
The Catholic University of America	M,D
Columbia University	M,D
Cornell University	D
Dartmouth College	M
Duke University	D
Emory University	M,D,O
Florida Atlantic University	M
Graduate School and University Center of the City University of New York	M,D
Harvard University	D
Hofstra University	M
Indiana University Bloomington	M,D
Johns Hopkins University	D
Louisiana State University and Agricultural and Mechanical College	M,D
Michigan State University	M
Montclair State University	M
New York University	M,D
Northwestern University	D
Pennsylvania State University University Park Campus	M,D
Princeton University	D
Purdue University	M,D
Rutgers, The State University of New Jersey, New Brunswick	D
San Francisco State University	M
Stanford University	D
State University of New York at Binghamton	M,D
State University of New York at Buffalo	M,D
State University of New York at Stony Brook	M,D
The University of Arizona	M,D
University of Arkansas (Fayetteville)	M,D
University of California, Berkeley	M,D
University of California, Davis	M,D
University of California, Irvine	M,D
University of California, Los Angeles	M,D,O
University of California, Riverside	M,D
University of California, San Diego	M,D
University of California, Santa Barbara	M,D
University of California, Santa Cruz	M,D
University of Chicago	M,D
University of Colorado at Boulder	M,D
University of Connecticut	M,D
University of Georgia	M,D
University of Illinois at Urbana–Champaign	M,D
The University of Iowa	M,D
University of Maryland, College Park	M,D
University of Massachusetts Amherst	M,D
University of Michigan	D
University of Minnesota, Twin Cities Campus	M,D
University of Missouri–Columbia	M
University of New Mexico	M
The University of North Carolina at Chapel Hill	M,D
University of Oregon	M,D
University of Pennsylvania	M,D
University of Puerto Rico, Río Piedras	M
University of Rochester	M,D
University of South Carolina (Columbia)	M,D
University of Southern California	M,D
The University of Texas at Austin	M,D
The University of Texas at Dallas	M,D
University of Utah	M,D
University of Washington	M,D
University of Wisconsin–Madison	M,D
University of Wisconsin–Milwaukee	M,D
Utah State University	M
Vanderbilt University	M,D
Washington University in St. Louis	M,D
Wayne State University	M
Western Kentucky University	M
West Virginia University	M
Yale University	D

COMPUTATIONAL SCIENCES

California Institute of Technology	M,D
Carnegie Mellon University	D
Clemson University	M,D
College of William and Mary	M
Cornell University	M,D
Embry-Riddle Aeronautical University (FL)	M
George Mason University	D
The George Washington University	M
Louisiana Tech University	D
Massachusetts Institute of Technology	D
Michigan State University	M
Michigan Technological University	D
Mississippi State University	M,D
Princeton University	D
Radford University	M
Rice University	M,D
Stanford University	M,D
Temple University (Philadelphia)	M,D
The University of Iowa	D
University of Minnesota, Duluth	M
University of Minnesota, Twin Cities Campus	M,D
University of Mississippi	M,D
University of Puerto Rico, Mayagüez Campus	M
The University of Texas at Austin	M,D
Western Michigan University	M

COMPUTER ART AND DESIGN

Carnegie Mellon University	M
Columbia University	M
Florida Atlantic University	M
Mississippi State University	M
New Mexico Highlands University	M
New School University	M
Rensselaer Polytechnic Institute	M
Rochester Institute of Technology	M
Syracuse University	M

COMPUTER EDUCATION

Ashland University	M
Beaver College	M,O
Bemidji State University	M
California State University, Dominguez Hills	M,O
California State University, Los Angeles	M
California University of Pennsylvania	M
Cardinal Stritch University	M
Cleveland State University	M
Concordia University (IL)	M,O
Eastern Washington University	M
Florida Institute of Technology	M,D,O
Fontbonne College	M
Fort Hays State University	M
Gonzaga University	M
Jacksonville University	M
Lesley College	M,O
Long Island University, C.W. Post Campus	M,O
Mississippi College	M
Nazareth College of Rochester	M
Northwest Missouri State University	M
Nova Southeastern University	M,D,O
Ohio University	M
Oklahoma State University	D
Philadelphia College of Textiles and Science	M
Plymouth State College of the University System of New Hampshire	M
Rivier College	M
Rowan University	O
Saint Martin's College	M
Shenandoah University	M
Shippensburg University of Pennsylvania	M
State University of New York College at Buffalo	M
Teachers College, Columbia University	M
University of Bridgeport	M,O
University of Central Oklahoma	M
University of Florida	M,D,O
University of Georgia	M
University of Michigan	M,D
University of Northern Iowa	M
University of North Texas	M
Webster University	M
Wilkes University	M

COMPUTER ENGINEERING

Auburn University	M,D
Boston University	M,D
California State University, Long Beach	M
California State University, Northridge	M
Carnegie Mellon University	M,D
Case Western Reserve University	M,D
Clarkson University	M,D
Clemson University	M,D
Cleveland State University	M,D
Cornell University	M,D
Dartmouth College	M,D
Drexel University	M,D
Duke University	M,D
Fairleigh Dickinson University, Teaneck–Hackensack Campus	M
Florida Atlantic University	M,D
Florida Institute of Technology	M,D
Florida International University	M
Georgia Institute of Technology	M,D
Illinois Institute of Technology	M,D
Indiana State University	M
Iowa State University of Science and Technology	M,D
Johns Hopkins University	M,D
Kansas State University	M,D
Lehigh University	M
Louisiana State University and Agricultural and Mechanical College	M,D
Manhattan College	M
Marquette University	M,D
Mississippi State University	M,D
Montana State University–Bozeman	M,D
New Jersey Institute of Technology	M,D,O
New Mexico State University	M,D
North Carolina State University	M,D
Northeastern University	M,D
Northwestern University	M,D
Oakland University	M
Oklahoma State University	M,D
Old Dominion University	M,D
Oregon State University	M,D
Pennsylvania State University University Park Campus	M,D
Portland State University	M,D
Princeton University	M,D
Purdue University	M,D
Rensselaer Polytechnic Institute	M,D
Rice University	M,D
Rochester Institute of Technology	M
Rutgers, The State University of New Jersey, New Brunswick	M,D
St. Mary's University of San Antonio	M
San Jose State University	M
Santa Clara University	M,D,O
Southern Methodist University	M,D
State University of New York at Buffalo	M,D
Stevens Institute of Technology	M,D,O
Syracuse University	M,D,O

Temple University (Philadelphia)	M
Texas A&M University (College Station)	M,D
The University of Alabama at Birmingham	M,D
The University of Alabama in Huntsville	M,D
The University of Arizona	M,D
University of Arkansas (Fayetteville)	M
University of Bridgeport	M
University of California, Davis	M,D
University of California, Irvine	M,D
University of California, San Diego	M,D
University of California, Santa Barbara	M,D
University of California, Santa Cruz	M,D
University of Central Florida	M,D
University of Cincinnati	M,D
University of Colorado at Boulder	M,D
University of Colorado at Colorado Springs	M,D
University of Denver	M
University of Florida	M,D,O
University of Houston	M,D
University of Houston–Clear Lake	M
University of Idaho	M
University of Illinois at Chicago	M,D
University of Illinois at Urbana–Champaign	M,D
The University of Iowa	M,D
University of Louisville	D
University of Maine (Orono)	M
University of Maryland, Baltimore County	M,D
University of Massachusetts Amherst	M,D
University of Massachusetts Lowell	M,D
The University of Memphis	M
University of Miami	M,D
University of Michigan	M,D
University of Michigan–Dearborn	M
University of Minnesota, Twin Cities Campus	M,D
University of Missouri–Columbia	M
University of Nebraska–Lincoln	M,D
University of Nevada, Las Vegas	M,D
University of New Mexico	M,D
University of Notre Dame	M,D
University of Puerto Rico, Mayagüez Campus	M
University of Rhode Island	M,D
University of South Carolina (Columbia)	M,D
University of Southern California	M,D
University of South Florida	M
University of Southwestern Louisiana	M,D
The University of Texas at Arlington	M,D
The University of Texas at Austin	M,D
The University of Texas at El Paso	M,D
Villanova University	M
Virginia Polytechnic Institute and State University	M,D
Wayne State University	M,D
Western Michigan University	M
West Virginia University	D
Widener University	M
Worcester Polytechnic Institute	M,D
Wright State University	M,D

COMPUTER SCIENCE

Alabama Agricultural and Mechanical University	M
Alcorn State University	M
American University	M
Angelo State University	M
Appalachian State University	M
Arizona State University	M,D
Arkansas State University	M
Auburn University	M,D
Azusa Pacific University	M,O
Ball State University	M
Baylor University	M
Boise State University	M
Boston University	M,D
Bowie State University	M
Bowling Green State University	M
Bradley University	M
Brandeis University	M,D
Bridgewater State College	M
Brigham Young University	M,D
Brooklyn College of the City University of New York	M,D
Brown University	M,D
California Institute of Technology	M,D
California Polytechnic State University, San Luis Obispo	M
California State Polytechnic University, Pomona	M
California State University, Chico	M

California State University, Fresno	M
California State University, Fullerton	M
California State University, Hayward	M
California State University, Long Beach	M
California State University, Northridge	M
California State University, Sacramento	M
California State University, San Bernardino	M
California State University, San Marcos	M
Carnegie Mellon University	M,D
Case Western Reserve University	M,D
The Catholic University of America	M,D
Central Michigan University	M
City College of the City University of New York	M,D
Clark Atlanta University	M
Clarkson University	M,D
Clemson University	M,D
College of Staten Island of the City University of New York	M,D
College of William and Mary	M,D
Colorado School of Mines	M,D
Colorado State University	M,D
Columbia University	M,D,O
Columbus State University	M
Cornell University	M,D
Creighton University	M
Dartmouth College	M,D
DePaul University	M,D
Drexel University	M
Duke University	M,D
East Carolina University	M
Eastern Michigan University	M
Eastern Washington University	M
East Stroudsburg University of Pennsylvania	M
East Tennessee State University	M
Emory University	M,D
Fairleigh Dickinson University, Florham–Madison Campus	M
Fairleigh Dickinson University, Teaneck–Hackensack Campus	M
Fitchburg State College	M
Florida Atlantic University	M,D
Florida Institute of Technology	M,D
Florida International University	M,D
Florida State University	M,D
Fordham University	M
George Mason University	M
The George Washington University	M,D,O
Georgia Institute of Technology	M,D
Georgia Southwestern State University	M
Governors State University	M
Graduate School and University Center of the City University of New York	D
Hampton University	M
Harvard University	M,D
Hofstra University	M
Hood College	M
Howard University	M
Hunter College of the City University of New York	M,D
Illinois Institute of Technology	M,D
Illinois State University	M
Indiana University Bloomington	M,D
Indiana University–Purdue University Fort Wayne	M
Indiana University–Purdue University Indianapolis	M
Iona College (New Rochelle)	M
Iowa State University of Science and Technology	M,D
Jackson State University	M
James Madison University	M
Johns Hopkins University	M,D
Kansas State University	M,D
Kent State University	M,D
Kutztown University of Pennsylvania	M
Lamar University	M
La Salle University	M
Lehigh University	M,D
Lehman College of the City University of New York	M
Long Island University, Brooklyn Campus	M
Louisiana State University and Agricultural and Mechanical College	M,D
Louisiana Tech University	M
Loyola Marymount University	M
Loyola University Chicago	M
Loyola University New Orleans	M
Maharishi University of Management	M
Mankato State University	M

Marist College	M
Marycrest International University	M
Marymount University	M
Massachusetts Institute of Technology	M,D,O
McNeese State University	M
Miami University	M
Michigan State University	M,D
Michigan Technological University	M,D
Middle Tennessee State University	M
Midwestern State University	M
Mississippi College	M
Mississippi State University	M,D
Monmouth University	M
Montana State University–Bozeman	M,D
Montclair State University	M
New Jersey Institute of Technology	M,D
New Mexico Highlands University	M
New Mexico State University	M,D
New York Institute of Technology	M
New York University	M,D
North Carolina Agricultural and Technical State University	M
North Carolina State University	M,D
North Central College	M
North Dakota State University	M,D
Northeastern Illinois University	M
Northeastern University	M,D
Northern Illinois University	M
Northwestern University	D
Northwest Missouri State University	M
Nova Southeastern University	M,D
Oakland University	M
The Ohio State University	M,D
Oklahoma City University	M
Oklahoma State University	M,D
Old Dominion University	M,D
Oregon State University	M,D
Pace University	M,O
Pennsylvania State University Harrisburg Campus of the Capital College	M
Pennsylvania State University University Park Campus	M,D
Polytechnic University, Brooklyn Campus	M,D
Polytechnic University, Farmingdale Campus	M,D
Polytechnic University, Westchester Graduate Center	M,D
Portland State University	M
Princeton University	M,D
Purdue University	M,D
Queens College of the City University of New York	M
Rensselaer Polytechnic Institute	M,D
Rice University	M,D
Rivier College	M
Rochester Institute of Technology	M,O
Roosevelt University	M
Rutgers, The State University of New Jersey, New Brunswick	M,D
Sacred Heart University	M
St. Cloud State University	M
St. John's University (NY)	M
Saint Joseph's University	M
St. Mary's University of San Antonio	M
Sam Houston State University	M
San Diego State University	M
San Francisco State University	M
San Jose State University	M
Santa Clara University	M,D,O
Shippensburg University of Pennsylvania	M
South Dakota State University	M
Southern Illinois University at Carbondale	M
Southern Illinois University at Edwardsville	M
Southern Methodist University	M,D
Southern Oregon University	M
Southern University and Agricultural and Mechanical College	M
Southwest Texas State University	M
Stanford University	M,D
State University of New York at Albany	M,D
State University of New York at Binghamton	M,D
State University of New York at Buffalo	M,D
State University of New York at New Paltz	M
State University of New York at Stony Brook	M,D,O
State University of New York Institute of Technology at Utica/Rome	M
Stephen F. Austin State University	M
Stevens Institute of Technology	M,D,O

Suffolk University	M
Syracuse University	M,D
Temple University (Philadelphia)	M,D
Texas A&M University (College Station)	M,D
Texas A&M University–Commerce	M
Texas A&M University–Corpus Christi	M
Texas A&M University–Kingsville	M
Texas Tech University	M,D
Towson University	M
Tufts University	M,D
Tulane University	M,D
The University of Akron	M
The University of Alabama (Tuscaloosa)	M,D
The University of Alabama at Birmingham	M,D
The University of Alabama in Huntsville	M,D
University of Alaska Fairbanks	M
The University of Arizona	M,D
University of Arkansas (Fayetteville)	M
University of Arkansas at Little Rock	M
University of Bridgeport	M
University of California, Berkeley	M,D
University of California, Davis	M,D
University of California, Irvine	M,D
University of California, Los Angeles	M,D
University of California, Riverside	M,D
University of California, San Diego	M,D
University of California, Santa Barbara	M,D
University of California, Santa Cruz	M,D
University of Central Florida	M,D
University of Central Oklahoma	M
University of Chicago	M,D
University of Cincinnati	M,D
University of Colorado at Boulder	M,D
University of Colorado at Colorado Springs	M
University of Colorado at Denver	M
University of Connecticut	M,D
University of Dayton	M
University of Delaware	M,D
University of Denver	M,D
University of Detroit Mercy	M
University of Florida	M,D,O
University of Georgia	M,D
University of Hawaii at Manoa	D
University of Houston	M,D
University of Houston–Clear Lake	M
University of Idaho	M,D
University of Illinois at Chicago	M,D
University of Illinois at Springfield	M
University of Illinois at Urbana–Champaign	M,D
The University of Iowa	M,D
University of Kansas	M,D
University of Kentucky	M,D
University of Louisville	M,D
University of Maine (Orono)	M
University of Maryland, Baltimore County	M,D
University of Maryland, College Park	M,D
University of Maryland Eastern Shore	M
University of Massachusetts Amherst	M,D
University of Massachusetts Boston	M,D
University of Massachusetts Dartmouth	M
University of Massachusetts Lowell	M,D
The University of Memphis	M,D
University of Miami	M,D
University of Michigan	M,D
University of Michigan–Dearborn	M
University of Minnesota, Duluth	M
University of Minnesota, Twin Cities Campus	M,D
University of Missouri–Columbia	M
University of Missouri–Kansas City	M,D
University of Missouri–Rolla	M,D
The University of Montana–Missoula	M
University of Nebraska at Omaha	M
University of Nebraska–Lincoln	M,D
University of Nevada, Las Vegas	M,D
University of Nevada, Reno	M
University of New Hampshire	M,D
University of New Haven	M
University of New Mexico	M,D
University of New Orleans	M
The University of North Carolina at Chapel Hill	M,D
University of North Carolina at Charlotte	M

P—first professional degree; M—master's degree; D—doctorate; O—other advanced degree.

Computer Science (continued)

University of North Dakota	M
University of Northern Iowa	M
University of North Florida	M
University of North Texas	M,D
University of Notre Dame	M,D
University of Oklahoma	M,D
University of Oregon	M,D
University of Pennsylvania	M,D
University of Pittsburgh	M,D
University of Rhode Island	M,D
University of Rochester	M,D
University of San Francisco	M
University of South Alabama	M
University of South Carolina (Columbia)	M,D
University of South Dakota	M
University of Southern California	M,D
University of Southern Maine	M
University of Southern Mississippi	M,D
University of South Florida	M
University of Southwestern Louisiana	M,D
University of Tennessee at Chattanooga	M
University of Tennessee, Knoxville	M,D
The University of Texas at Arlington	M,D
The University of Texas at Austin	M,D
The University of Texas at Dallas	M,D
The University of Texas at El Paso	M
The University of Texas at San Antonio	M,D
The University of Texas at Tyler	M
The University of Texas–Pan American	M
University of Toledo	M,D
University of Tulsa	M,D
University of Utah	M,D
University of Vermont	M
University of Virginia	M,D
University of Washington	M,D
University of West Florida	M
University of Wisconsin–Madison	M,D
University of Wisconsin–Milwaukee	M,D
University of Wyoming	M,D
Utah State University	M
Vanderbilt University	M,D
Villanova University	M
Virginia Commonwealth University	M
Virginia Polytechnic Institute and State University	M,D
Wake Forest University	M
Washington State University	M,D
Washington University in St. Louis	M,D
Wayne State University	M,D
Webster University	M,O
West Chester University of Pennsylvania	M
Western Carolina University	M
Western Connecticut State University	M
Western Illinois University	M
Western Kentucky University	M
Western Michigan University	M,D
Western Washington University	M
West Virginia University	M,D
Wichita State University	M
Worcester Polytechnic Institute	M,D
Wright State University	M,D
Yale University	D

CONFLICT RESOLUTION AND MEDIATION/PEACE STUDIES

American University	M
Beaver College	M
California State University, Dominguez Hills	M,O
Chaminade University of Honolulu	M
Cornell University	M,D
Dallas Baptist University	M
Duquesne University	O
Fresno Pacific University	M
George Mason University	M,D
John F. Kennedy University	O
Lesley College	M
Montclair State University	M
Nova Southeastern University	M,D,O
Pepperdine University (Malibu)	M
United States International University	M
University of Massachusetts Boston	M,O
University of Notre Dame	M
University of Pennsylvania	M,D
Wayne State University	M,O

CONSERVATION BIOLOGY

Columbia University	O

Florida Institute of Technology	M
Frostburg State University	M
San Francisco State University	M
State University of New York at Albany	M
University of Arkansas (Fayetteville)	D
University of Hawaii at Manoa	M,D
University of Maryland, College Park	M
University of Minnesota, Twin Cities Campus	M,D
University of Missouri–St. Louis	O
University of Nevada, Reno	D
University of New Mexico	M,D
University of Wisconsin–Madison	M
Virginia Polytechnic Institute and State University	M,D

CONSTRUCTION ENGINEERING AND MANAGEMENT

Arizona State University	M
Auburn University	M,D
Bradley University	M
Brigham Young University	M
The Catholic University of America	M
Clemson University	M
Colorado State University	M
Columbia University	M
Florida Institute of Technology	M
Florida International University	M
Georgia Institute of Technology	M,D
Iowa State University of Science and Technology	M,D
Marquette University	M,D
Michigan State University	M
Montana State University– Bozeman	M
State University of New York at Buffalo	M,D
Stevens Institute of Technology	M
Texas A&M University (College Station)	M,D
University of California, Berkeley	M,D
University of Colorado at Boulder	M,D
University of Denver	M
University of Florida	M,D
University of Houston	M
University of Michigan	M
University of Missouri–Rolla	M,D
University of Southern California	M
University of Washington	M,D
Washington University in St. Louis	M
Western Michigan University	M

CONSUMER ECONOMICS

California State University, Fresno	M
California State University, Long Beach	M
Colorado State University	M
Cornell University	M,D
Florida State University	M,D
Iowa State University of Science and Technology	M,D
Mankato State University	M
Michigan State University	M
Montclair State University	M
The Ohio State University	M,D
Oregon State University	M,D
Purdue University	M,D
Syracuse University	M
Texas Tech University	M,D
The University of Alabama (Tuscaloosa)	M
The University of Arizona	M,D
University of Georgia	M,D
University of Illinois at Urbana– Champaign	M,D
University of Maryland, College Park	M,D
University of Massachusetts Amherst	M
The University of Memphis	M
University of Missouri–Columbia	M
University of Nebraska–Lincoln	M,D
University of Tennessee, Knoxville	M,D
University of Utah	M
University of Wisconsin–Madison	M
University of Wyoming	M
Virginia Polytechnic Institute and State University	M,D

CORPORATE AND ORGANIZATIONAL COMMUNICATION

Austin Peay State University	M
Barry University	M
Bowie State University	M,O
Canisius College	M
Carnegie Mellon University	M
Columbia University	M
Emerson College	M

Fairleigh Dickinson University, Florham–Madison Campus	M
Fairleigh Dickinson University, Teaneck–Hackensack Campus	M
Florida Institute of Technology	M
Fordham University	M
Howard University	M,D
Illinois Institute of Technology	M
Iona College (New Rochelle)	M
John Carroll University	M
La Salle University	M
Lindenwood University	M
Marquette University	M
Monmouth University	M
Northwestern University	M
Radford University	M
Rollins College	M
Roosevelt University	M
St. Cloud State University	M
San Diego State University	M
Seton Hall University	M
Simmons College	M
Syracuse University	M
University of Alaska Fairbanks	M
University of Arkansas at Little Rock	M
University of Colorado at Boulder	M
University of Connecticut	M,D
University of Denver	M
University of Portland	M
University of St. Thomas (MN)	M,O
University of Southern California	M,D
University of Wisconsin–Stevens Point	M
University of Wisconsin–Whitewater	M
Wayne State University	M
Western Kentucky University	M
Western Michigan University	M

COUNSELING PSYCHOLOGY

Abilene Christian University	M
Alabama Agricultural and Mechanical University	M
Alaska Pacific University	M
Allegheny University of the Health Sciences	M
Amber University	M
Andrews University	M,D
Anna Maria College	M,O
Arizona State University	D
Assumption College	M,O
Auburn University	M,D,O
Ball State University	M,D
Beaver College	M
Benedictine University	M
Boston College	M,D
Boston University	D
Bowie State University	M
Brigham Young University	D
Butler University	O
California State University, Bakersfield	M
California State University, Chico	M
California State University, Sacramento	M
California State University, San Bernardino	M
California State University, Stanislaus	M
Central Washington University	M
Chaminade University of Honolulu	M
Chapman University	M
Chestnut Hill College	M,D
Cleveland State University	M
College of New Rochelle	M
College of Notre Dame	M
Colorado State University	D
Columbus State University	M
Concordia University (IL)	M,O
Dominican College of San Rafael	M
Eastern College	M
Eastern Nazarene College	M
Eastern Washington University	M
Fitchburg State College	M,O
Florida State University	D
Fordham University	D
Fort Valley State University	M
Framingham State College	M
Franciscan University of Steubenville	M
Frostburg State University	M
Gallaudet University	M
Gannon University	M
Gardner–Webb University	M
Georgian Court College	M
Georgia State University	M,D,O
Goddard College	M
Golden Gate University	M
Gonzaga University	M
Holy Names College	M
Howard University	M,D,O
Idaho State University	M,D,O
Illinois State University	M
Immaculata College	M,O
Indiana State University	D

Indiana University Bloomington	M,D,O
James Madison University	M,O
John F. Kennedy University	M
Kutztown University of Pennsylvania	M
La Salle University	M
Lehigh University	M,D,O
Lesley College	M,O
Lewis University	M
Liberty University	M
Lindenwood University	M
Louisiana Tech University	D
Loyola College	M,O
Loyola Marymount University	M
Loyola University Chicago	D
Marist College	M
Marymount University	M
Marywood University	M
Michigan State University	D
Mississippi College	M
Monmouth University	M,O
Morehead State University	M
Mount St. Mary's College	M
National University	M
New Jersey City University	M
New Mexico State University	M,D,O
New York University	D
Nicholls State University	M
Northeastern State University	M
Northeastern University	M,D,O
Northwestern University	M
Northwest Missouri State University	M
Notre Dame College	M
Nova Southeastern University	M
The Ohio State University	D
Oklahoma City University	M
Our Lady of the Lake University of San Antonio	M,D
Pennsylvania State University University Park Campus	D
Radford University	M
Rivier College	M
Rutgers, The State University of New Jersey, New Brunswick	M,D
Saint Martin's College	M
Saint Mary's University of Minnesota	M
St. Mary's University of San Antonio	D,O
St. Thomas University	M
Saint Xavier University	M,O
Salve Regina University	M,O
San Jose State University	M
Santa Clara University	M
Seton Hall University	D
Slippery Rock University of Pennsylvania	M
Southeast Missouri State University	M
Southern Illinois University at Carbondale	M,D
Southern Methodist University	M
Southern Nazarene University	M
Springfield College (MA)	M,O
Stanford University	D
State University of New York at Albany	M,D,O
State University of New York at Buffalo	D
State University of New York at Oswego	M,O
Teachers College, Columbia University	M,D
Temple University (Philadelphia)	M,D
Tennessee State University	D
Texas A&M University (College Station)	D
Texas A&M University–Texarkana	M
Texas Woman's University	M,D
Towson University	M
Trevecca Nazarene University	M
Truman State University	M
United States International University	M
The University of Akron	M,D
University of Alaska Anchorage	M
University of Baltimore	M
University of California, Santa Barbara	M,D
University of Central Arkansas	M
University of Colorado at Denver	M
University of Connecticut	M,D
University of Denver	M,D
University of Georgia	D
University of Houston	M,D
University of Kansas	M,D
University of Kentucky	M,D,O
University of La Verne	M
University of Mary Hardin–Baylor	M
University of Maryland, College Park	D
The University of Memphis	D
University of Miami	M,D
University of Minnesota, Twin Cities Campus	D
University of Missouri–Columbia	M,D,O

University of Missouri–Kansas City	D
University of Nevada, Las Vegas	M
University of New Mexico	M,D,O
University of North Dakota	M,D
University of Northern Colorado	M,D
University of North Florida	M
University of North Texas	M,D
University of Notre Dame	D
University of Oklahoma	M,D
University of Oregon	M,D
University of Pennsylvania	M
University of Rhode Island	M
University of Saint Francis (IN)	M
University of San Francisco	M,D
University of Southern California	M,D,O
University of Tennessee, Knoxville	D
University of the Pacific	M,D
University of Wisconsin–Madison	D
Valparaiso University	M
Virginia Commonwealth University	D
Walla Walla College	M
Washington State University	M,D
Webster University	M
Western Michigan University	M,D
Western Washington University	M
Westfield State College	M
West Virginia University	M,D

COUNSELOR EDUCATION

Abilene Christian University	M
Adams State College	M
Alabama Agricultural and Mechanical University	M,O
Alabama State University	M,O
Alcorn State University	M
Alfred University	M
Angelo State University	M
Appalachian State University	M,O
Arizona State University	M
Arkansas State University	M,O
Auburn University	M,D,O
Auburn University Montgomery	M,O
Augusta State University	M,O
Austin Peay State University	M,O
Barry University	M,D,O
Boise State University	M
Boston University	M,O
Bowie State University	M
Bowling Green State University	M
Bradley University	M
Bridgewater State College	M
Brigham Young University	M,D
Brooklyn College of the City University of New York	M,O
Butler University	M,O
California Lutheran University	M
California Polytechnic State University, San Luis Obispo	M
California State University, Bakersfield	M
California State University, Dominguez Hills	M
California State University, Fresno	M
California State University, Fullerton	M
California State University, Hayward	M
California State University, Long Beach	M,O
California State University, Los Angeles	M
California State University, Northridge	M,O
California State University, Sacramento	M
California State University, San Bernardino	M
California State University, Stanislaus	M
California University of Pennsylvania	M
Campbell University	M
Canisius College	M,O
Carthage College	M
The Catholic University of America	M
Central Connecticut State University	M
Central Michigan University	M,O
Central Missouri State University	M,O
Central Washington University	M
Chadron State College	M,O
Chapman University	M
Chicago State University	M
The Citadel, The Military College of South Carolina	M
City College of the City University of New York	M
Clark Atlanta University	M,D
Clemson University	M
Cleveland State University	M,O
The College of New Jersey	M
The College of Saint Rose	M
College of William and Mary	M,D
Columbus State University	M,O
Concordia University (IL)	M,O
Creighton University	M
Dallas Baptist University	M
Delta State University	M
DePaul University	M
Drake University	M,D
Duquesne University	M
East Carolina University	M,O
East Central University	M
Eastern College	M
Eastern Illinois University	M,O
Eastern Kentucky University	M,O
Eastern Michigan University	M,O
Eastern New Mexico University	M
Eastern Washington University	M
East Tennessee State University	M
Edinboro University of Pennsylvania	M
Emporia State University	M
Fairfield University	M,O
Fitchburg State College	M,O
Florida Agricultural and Mechanical University	M
Florida Atlantic University	M,O
Florida International University	M
Florida State University	M,O
Fordham University	M,O
Fort Hays State University	M
Fort Valley State University	M,O
Fresno Pacific University	M
Frostburg State University	M
Gallaudet University	M
George Mason University	M
The George Washington University	M,D,O
Georgia Southern University	M,O
Georgia State University	M,D,O
Governors State University	M
Gwynedd-Mercy College	M
Hampton University	M
Hardin–Simmons University	M
Henderson State University	M
Heritage College	M
Hofstra University	M,O
Houston Baptist University	M
Howard University	M,D,O
Hunter College of the City University of New York	M
Idaho State University	M,D,O
Illinois State University	M
Immaculata College	O
Indiana State University	M,D,O
Indiana University Bloomington	M,O
Indiana University of Pennsylvania	M
Indiana University–Purdue University Fort Wayne	M
Indiana University–Purdue University Indianapolis	M
Indiana University South Bend	M
Indiana University Southeast	M
Indiana Wesleyan University	M
Inter American University of Puerto Rico, Metropolitan Campus	M
Inter American University of Puerto Rico, San Germán Campus	M
Iowa State University of Science and Technology	M
Jackson State University	M,O
Jacksonville State University	M
John Carroll University	M,O
Johns Hopkins University	M,D,O
Johnson State College	M
Kansas State University	M,D
Kean University	M,O
Keene State College	M
Kent State University	M,D,O
Kutztown University of Pennsylvania	M
Lamar University	M
La Sierra University	M,O
Lehigh University	M,O
Lehman College of the City University of New York	M
Lenoir–Rhyne College	M,O
Lincoln University (MO)	M
Long Island University, Brooklyn Campus	M,O
Long Island University, C.W. Post Campus	M
Longwood College	M
Louisiana State University and Agricultural and Mechanical College	M,O
Louisiana Tech University	M,O
Loyola College	M,O
Loyola Marymount University	M
Loyola University Chicago	M
Loyola University New Orleans	M
Lynchburg College	M
Manhattan College	M,O
Mankato State University	M
Marshall University	M,O
Marymount University	M
Marywood University	M
McNeese State University	M
Michigan State University	M,D
Middle Tennessee State University	M,O
Midwestern State University	M
Millersville University of Pennsylvania	M
Mississippi College	M,O
Mississippi State University	M,D
Montana State University–Billings	M
Montana State University–Northern	M
Montclair State University	M
Moorhead State University	M
Morehead State University	M,O
Murray State University	M,O
National University	M
New Mexico Highlands University	M
New Mexico State University	M,D,O
New York University	M,D,O
Niagara University	M,O
Nicholls State University	M,O
North Carolina Agricultural and Technical State University	M
North Carolina Central University	M
North Carolina State University	M,D,O
North Dakota State University	M
Northeastern Illinois University	M
Northeastern State University	M
Northeastern University	M
Northeast Louisiana University	M,O
Northern Arizona University	M,D
Northern Illinois University	M,D
Northern State University	M
Northwestern Oklahoma State University	M
Northwestern State University of Louisiana	M,O
Northwest Missouri State University	M
Notre Dame College	M
Oakland University	M,O
Ohio University	M,D
Oklahoma State University	M
Old Dominion University	M,O
Oregon State University	M,D
Our Lady of the Lake University of San Antonio	M
Pennsylvania State University University Park Campus	M,D
Pittsburg State University	M
Plattsburgh State University of New York	M,O
Plymouth State College of the University System of New Hampshire	M
Portland State University	M
Prairie View A&M University	M
Providence College	M
Purdue University	M,D,O
Purdue University Calumet	M
Queens College of the City University of New York	M
Radford University	M
Rhode Island College	M,O
Rider University	M,O
Rivier College	M
Rollins College	M
Roosevelt University	M
Sage Graduate School	M,O
St. Bonaventure University	M,O
St. Cloud State University	M
St. John's University (NY)	M
Saint Joseph College (CT)	M,O
Saint Louis University	M,D
Saint Martin's College	M
Saint Mary's College of California	M
St. Thomas University	M,O
Salem State College	M
Sam Houston State University	M
San Diego State University	M
San Francisco State University	M
San Jose State University	M
Santa Clara University	M
Seattle Pacific University	M
Seattle University	M
Seton Hall University	M
Shippensburg University of Pennsylvania	M
Slippery Rock University of Pennsylvania	M
Sonoma State University	M
South Carolina State University	M
South Dakota State University	M
Southeastern Louisiana University	M,O
Southeastern Oklahoma State University	M
Southeast Missouri State University	M
Southern Arkansas University–Magnolia	M
Southern Connecticut State University	M,O
Southern Illinois University at Carbondale	M,D
Southern Oregon University	M
Southern University and Agricultural and Mechanical College	M
Southwestern Oklahoma State University	M
Southwest Missouri State University	M
Southwest Texas State University	M
Spalding University	M
Springfield College (MA)	M,O
State University of New York at Albany	O
State University of New York at Buffalo	M,D,O
State University of New York College at Brockport	M,O
State University of New York College at Oneonta	M,O
State University of West Georgia	M,O
Stephen F. Austin State University	M
Stetson University	M
Suffolk University	M,O
Sul Ross State University	M
Syracuse University	M,D,O
Tarleton State University	M
Temple University (Philadelphia)	M
Tennessee State University	M
Texas A&M International University	M
Texas A&M University–Commerce	M,D
Texas A&M University–Corpus Christi	M
Texas A&M University–Kingsville	M
Texas Southern University	M,D
Texas Tech University	M,D,O
Texas Woman's University	M
Trevecca Nazarene University	M
Trinity College (DC)	M
Troy State University (Troy)	M
Troy State University Dothan	M,O
Troy State University Montgomery	M,O
Tuskegee University	M
The University of Akron	M
The University of Alabama (Tuscaloosa)	D,O
The University of Alabama at Birmingham	M
University of Alaska Anchorage	M
University of Alaska Fairbanks	M
University of Arkansas (Fayetteville)	M,D,O
University of Arkansas at Little Rock	M
University of Central Arkansas	M
University of Central Florida	M
University of Central Oklahoma	M
University of Cincinnati	M,D,O
University of Colorado at Colorado Springs	M
University of Colorado at Denver	M
University of Dayton	M
University of Delaware	M
University of Detroit Mercy	M
University of Evansville	M
University of Florida	M,D,O
University of Georgia	M,D
University of Guam	M
University of Hartford	M,O
University of Hawaii at Manoa	M
University of Houston–Clear Lake	M
University of Idaho	M,D,O
The University of Iowa	M,D,O
University of La Verne	M
University of Louisville	M,D,O
University of Maine (Orono)	M,O
University of Maryland, College Park	M,D,O
University of Maryland Eastern Shore	M
University of Massachusetts Amherst	M,D,O
University of Massachusetts Boston	M,O
The University of Memphis	M,D
University of Missouri–Kansas City	M,D,O
University of Missouri–St. Louis	M
The University of Montana–Missoula	M,D,O
University of Montevallo	M
University of Nebraska at Kearney	M,O
University of Nebraska at Omaha	M
University of Nevada, Reno	M,D,O
University of New Hampshire	M
University of New Orleans	M,D,O
University of North Alabama	M
The University of North Carolina at Chapel Hill	M
University of North Carolina at Charlotte	M
University of North Carolina at Greensboro	M,D,O

P—first professional degree; M—master's degree; D—doctorate; O—other advanced degree.

Counselor Education (continued)

University of North Carolina at Pembroke	M
University of Northern Colorado	M,D
University of Northern Iowa	M,D
University of North Florida	M
University of North Texas	M,D
University of Oklahoma	M
University of Pittsburgh	M
University of Puerto Rico, Río Piedras	M,D
University of Saint Francis (IN)	M
University of San Diego	M
University of San Francisco	M
University of Scranton	M
University of South Alabama	M,O
University of South Carolina (Columbia)	M,D,O
University of South Dakota	M,D,O
University of Southern Maine	M,O
University of South Florida	M
University of Southwestern Louisiana	M
University of Tennessee at Chattanooga	M
The University of Tennessee at Martin	M
University of Tennessee, Knoxville	M,O
The University of Texas at Brownsville	M
The University of Texas of the Permian Basin	M
The University of Texas–Pan American	M
University of the District of Columbia	M
University of the Pacific	M
University of Toledo	M,D,O
University of Vermont	M
University of Virginia	M,D,O
University of Washington	M,D
The University of West Alabama	M
University of Wisconsin–Madison	M
University of Wisconsin–Oshkosh	M
University of Wisconsin–Platteville	M
University of Wisconsin–River Falls	M
University of Wisconsin–Stevens Point	M
University of Wisconsin–Stout	M,O
University of Wisconsin–Superior	M
University of Wisconsin–Whitewater	M
Valdosta State University	M,O
Vanderbilt University	M
Villanova University	M
Virginia Commonwealth University	M
Virginia State University	M
Wake Forest University	M
Walla Walla College	M
Walsh University	M
Wayne State College	M
Wayne State University	M,D,O
West Chester University of Pennsylvania	M
Western Carolina University	M
Western Connecticut State University	M
Western Illinois University	M
Western Kentucky University	M,O
Western Michigan University	M,D
Western New Mexico University	M
Western Washington University	M
West Texas A&M University	M
Whitworth College	M
Wichita State University	M
William Paterson University of New Jersey	M
Wilmington College (DE)	M
Winona State University	M
Winthrop University	M
Wright State University	M
Xavier University	M
Xavier University of Louisiana	M
Youngstown State University	M

CRIMINAL JUSTICE AND CRIMINOLOGY

Alabama State University	M
Albany State University	M
American International College	M
American University	M,D
Anna Maria College	M
Armstrong Atlantic State University	M
Auburn University Montgomery	M
Boston University	M
California State University, Fresno	M
California State University, Long Beach	M
California State University, Los Angeles	M
California State University, Sacramento	M
California State University, San Bernardino	M
Central Connecticut State University	M
Central Michigan University	M
Central Missouri State University	M,O
Chaminade University of Honolulu	M
Chapman University	M
Chicago State University	M
Clark Atlanta University	M
Coppin State College	M
Delta State University	M
Drury College	M
East Central University	M
Eastern Kentucky University	M
Eastern Michigan University	M
East Tennessee State University	M
Ferris State University	M
Fitchburg State College	M
Florida Atlantic University	M
Florida International University	M
Florida State University	M,D
The George Washington University	M
Georgia State University	M
Graduate School and University Center of the City University of New York	D
Grambling State University	M
Illinois State University	M
Indiana State University	M
Indiana University Bloomington	M,D
Indiana University Northwest	M
Indiana University of Pennsylvania	M,D
Inter American University of Puerto Rico, Metropolitan Campus	M
Iona College (New Rochelle)	M
Jackson State University	M
Jacksonville State University	M
Kent State University	M
Lewis University	M
Long Island University, C.W. Post Campus	M
Longwood College	M
Loyola University Chicago	M
Marshall University	M
Metropolitan State University	M
Michigan State University	M,D
Middle Tennessee State University	M
Minot State University	M
Monmouth University	M
National University	M
New Jersey City University	M
New Mexico State University	M
Niagara University	M
North Carolina Central University	M
Northeastern State University	M
Northeastern University	M
Northeast Louisiana University	M
Northern Arizona University	M
Oklahoma City University	M
Oklahoma State University	M
Pennsylvania State University University Park Campus	M,D
Pontifical Catholic University of Puerto Rico	M
Portland State University	M,D
Radford University	M
Rutgers, The State University of New Jersey, Newark	M,D
Saginaw Valley State University	M
St. Ambrose University	M
St. Cloud State University	M
Saint Joseph's University	M
St. Mary's University of San Antonio	M
St. Thomas University	M,O
Salve Regina University	M
Sam Houston State University	M,D
San Diego State University	M
San Jose State University	M
Seton Hall University	M
Shippensburg University of Pennsylvania	M
Southeast Missouri State University	M
Southern Illinois University at Carbondale	M
Southwest Texas State University	M
State University of New York at Albany	M,D
State University of New York College at Buffalo	M
Suffolk University	M
Sul Ross State University	M
Temple University (Philadelphia)	M,D
Tennessee State University	M
Texas A&M International University	M
Troy State University (Troy)	M
Universidad del Turabo	M
The University of Alabama (Tuscaloosa)	M
The University of Alabama at Birmingham	M
University of Arkansas at Little Rock	M
University of Baltimore	M
University of California, Irvine	M,D
University of Central Florida	M
University of Central Oklahoma	M
University of Central Texas	M
University of Cincinnati	M,D
University of Colorado at Colorado Springs	M
University of Colorado at Denver	M
University of Delaware	M,D
University of Detroit Mercy	M
University of Illinois at Chicago	M
The University of Iowa	M
University of Louisville	M
University of Maryland, College Park	M,D
University of Massachusetts Lowell	M
The University of Memphis	M
University of Missouri–Kansas City	M
University of Missouri–St. Louis	M,D
University of Nebraska at Omaha	M,D
University of Nevada, Las Vegas	M
University of New Haven	M
University of North Alabama	M
University of North Carolina at Charlotte	M
University of North Florida	M
University of South Carolina (Columbia)	M
University of Southern Mississippi	M
University of South Florida	M,D
University of Tennessee at Chattanooga	M
University of Tennessee, Knoxville	M,D
The University of Texas at Arlington	M
The University of Texas of the Permian Basin	M
The University of Texas–Pan American	M
University of Wisconsin–Milwaukee	M
Valdosta State University	M
Villanova University	M
Virginia Commonwealth University	M,O
Washington State University	M
Wayne State University	M
Webster University	M
West Chester University of Pennsylvania	M
Western Illinois University	M
Western New England College	M
Western Oregon University	M
Westfield State College	M
Wichita State University	M
Widener University	M
Wilmington College (DE)	M
Xavier University	M
Youngstown State University	M

CURRICULUM AND INSTRUCTION

Andrews University	M,D,O
Angelo State University	M
Arizona State University	M,D
Arkansas State University	M,O
Arkansas Tech University	M
Ashland University	M
Auburn University	M,D,O
Austin Peay State University	M
Averett College	M
Azusa Pacific University	M
Ball State University	M,O
Baylor University	M,D,O
Beaver College	O
Bemidji State University	M
Benedictine University	M
Bloomsburg University of Pennsylvania	M
Boise State University	M,D
Boston College	M,D,O
Boston University	D
Bradley University	M
California Polytechnic State University, San Luis Obispo	M
California State University, Bakersfield	M
California State University, Chico	M
California State University, Dominguez Hills	M
California State University, Fresno	M
California State University, Sacramento	M
California State University, Stanislaus	M
Calvin College	M
Castleton State College	M
The Catholic University of America	M
Centenary College of Louisiana	M
Central Connecticut State University	M
Central Missouri State University	M,O
Central Washington University	M
Chapman University	M
Chicago State University	M
The Citadel, The Military College of South Carolina	M
City University	M
Claremont Graduate University	M,D
Clark Atlanta University	M,O
Clemson University	D
Cleveland State University	M
College Misericordia	M
College of William and Mary	M
Colorado Christian University	M
Concordia University (IL)	M,O
Converse College	O
Coppin State College	M
Cornell University	M,D
Delaware State University	M
DePaul University	M
Dominican College of San Rafael	M
Drake University	M,D,O
Drexel University	M
Duquesne University	D
Eastern Michigan University	M
Eastern Washington University	M
Emporia State University	M
Fairleigh Dickinson University, Teaneck–Hackensack Campus	M
Florida Atlantic University	D,O
Florida International University	D,O
Fordham University	M,D
Fresno Pacific University	M
Frostburg State University	M
Gannon University	M
The George Washington University	M,D,O
Georgia Southern University	D
Georgia State University	D
Gonzaga University	M
Grambling State University	D
Harvard University	M,D,O
Hood College	M
Idaho State University	M
Illinois State University	M,D
Indiana State University	M,D,O
Indiana University Bloomington	M,D,O
Indiana Wesleyan University	M
Inter American University of Puerto Rico, San Germán Campus	M
Iowa State University of Science and Technology	M,D
Johnson State College	M
Kansas State University	D
Kean University	M,O
Keene State College	M
Kent State University	M,D,O
Kutztown University of Pennsylvania	M
La Sierra University	M,D,O
Lehigh University	D
Lesley College	M,O
Louisiana State University and Agricultural and Mechanical College	M,D,O
Louisiana Tech University	M,D
Loyola College	M,O
Loyola University Chicago	M,D
Lynchburg College	M
Mankato State University	M,O
Miami University	M
Michigan State University	M,D,O
MidAmerica Nazarene University	M
Middle Tennessee State University	M,O
Montana State University–Billings	M
Moorhead State University	M
Morehead State University	D,O
National–Louis University	M,D,O
National University	M
New Mexico Highlands University	M
New Mexico State University	M,D,O
Nicholls State University	M
North Carolina State University	M,D
Northeastern State University	M
Northeastern University	M
Northeast Louisiana University	D
Northern Arizona University	D
Northern Illinois University	M,D
Notre Dame College	M
Oakland University	M,O
The Ohio State University	M,D
Oklahoma State University	M,D,O
Olivet Nazarene University	M
Oral Roberts University	M
Our Lady of the Lake University of San Antonio	M
Pace University	M
Pacific Lutheran University	M

Pennsylvania State University Harrisburg Campus of the Capital College	M
Pennsylvania State University University Park Campus	M,D
Portland State University	M,D
Prairie View A&M University	M
Purdue University	M,D,O
Purdue University Calumet	M
Radford University	M
Rhode Island College	O
Rider University	M
Rowan University	M,O
St. Bonaventure University	M
Saint Louis University	M,D
Saint Martin's College	M
Saint Michael's College	M,O
Saint Peter's College (Jersey City)	M,O
Saint Xavier University	M
Sam Houston State University	D
Seattle Pacific University	M
Seattle University	M
Sonoma State University	M
South Dakota State University	M
Southern Illinois University at Carbondale	M,D
Southern Illinois University at Edwardsville	D
Stanford University	M,D
State University of New York at Albany	M,D,O
Syracuse University	M,D,O
Teachers College, Columbia University	M,D
Tennessee State University	D
Tennessee Technological University	M,O
Texas A&M University (College Station)	M,D
Texas A&M University–Corpus Christi	M
Texas Southern University	M,D
Texas Tech University	M,D,O
Trevecca Nazarene University	M
Trinity College (DC)	M
The University of Alabama (Tuscaloosa)	D
University of Alaska Fairbanks	M
University of Arkansas (Fayetteville)	D
University of California, Davis	D
University of Central Florida	D,O
University of Cincinnati	M,D
University of Colorado at Boulder	M,D
University of Colorado at Colorado Springs	M
University of Colorado at Denver	M
University of Connecticut	M,D
University of Delaware	M,D
University of Denver	M,D
University of Detroit Mercy	M
University of Hawaii at Manoa	D
University of Houston	M,D
University of Houston–Clear Lake	M
University of Illinois at Chicago	M,D
University of Illinois at Urbana–Champaign	M,D,O
The University of Iowa	O
University of Kentucky	M,D
University of Massachusetts Amherst	M,D,O
University of Massachusetts Boston	M
University of Massachusetts Lowell	M,D,O
The University of Memphis	M,D
University of Michigan	M
University of Minnesota, Twin Cities Campus	M,D
University of Mississippi	M,D,O
University of Missouri–Columbia	M,D,O
University of Missouri–Kansas City	M,D,O
The University of Montana–Missoula	M,O
University of Nebraska at Kearney	M
University of Nebraska–Lincoln	M,D,O
University of Nevada, Las Vegas	M,D,O
University of Nevada, Reno	M,D,O
University of New Mexico	O
University of New Orleans	M,D,O
The University of North Carolina at Chapel Hill	M,D
University of North Carolina at Greensboro	D
University of Northern Iowa	M,D
University of North Texas	D
University of Oklahoma	M,D
University of Puerto Rico, Río Piedras	M,D
University of Redlands	M
University of St. Thomas (MN)	M,O
University of San Diego	M
University of San Francisco	M,D
University of South Carolina (Columbia)	D
University of South Dakota	M,D,O
University of Southern California	M,D
University of Southern Mississippi	M,D,O
University of Southwestern Louisiana	M
University of Tennessee at Chattanooga	M
University of Tennessee, Knoxville	M,D,O
The University of Texas at Austin	M,D
The University of Texas at Brownsville	M
University of the Pacific	M,D
University of Toledo	M,D,O
University of Vermont	M
University of Virginia	M,D,O
University of Washington	M,D
University of West Florida	D,O
University of Wisconsin–Madison	M,D
University of Wisconsin–Milwaukee	M
University of Wisconsin–Oshkosh	M
University of Wisconsin–Superior	M
University of Wisconsin–Whitewater	M
Utah State University	D
Valdosta State University	D
Valparaiso University	M
Vanderbilt University	M
Virginia Commonwealth University	M
Virginia Polytechnic Institute and State University	M,D,O
Walla Walla College	M
Washburn University of Topeka	M
Washington State University	D
Wayne State College	M
Wayne State University	D,O
Weber State University	M
West Texas A&M University	M
West Virginia University	M,D
Wichita State University	M
Winthrop University	O
Xavier University of Louisiana	M

DANCE

American University	M
Arizona State University	M
Brigham Young University	M
California State University, Fullerton	M
California State University, Long Beach	M
Case Western Reserve University	M
Florida State University	M
George Mason University	M
Indiana University Bloomington	M
New York University	M,D
The Ohio State University	M
Sam Houston State University	M
San Diego State University	M
Shenandoah University	M
Southern Methodist University	M
State University of New York College at Brockport	M
Teachers College, Columbia University	M
Temple University (Philadelphia)	M,D
Texas Christian University	M
Texas Woman's University	M,D
Tufts University	M,D
University of California, Irvine	M
University of California, Los Angeles	M
University of California, Riverside	M,D
University of Colorado at Boulder	M,D
University of Hawaii at Manoa	M,D
University of Illinois at Urbana–Champaign	M
The University of Iowa	M
University of Michigan	M
University of Minnesota, Twin Cities Campus	M,D
University of Nebraska–Lincoln	M
University of Nevada, Las Vegas	M
University of New Mexico	M
University of North Carolina at Greensboro	M
University of Oklahoma	M
University of Oregon	M
University of Utah	M
University of Washington	M
University of Wisconsin–Milwaukee	M

DECORATIVE ARTS

New School University	M

DEMOGRAPHY AND POPULATION STUDIES

Arizona State University	M,D
Brown University	D
Cornell University	M,D
Duke University	D
Florida State University	M,O
Fordham University	M,D
Georgetown University	M
Harvard University	M,D
Johns Hopkins University	M,D
Pennsylvania State University University Park Campus	M,D
Princeton University	D,O
State University of New York at Albany	O
Tulane University	M
University of California, Berkeley	M,D
University of Illinois at Urbana–Champaign	M,D
University of Pennsylvania	M,D
University of Southern California	M

DENTAL HYGIENE

Boston University	M,D,O
Old Dominion University	M
University of Missouri–Kansas City	M
The University of North Carolina at Chapel Hill	M

DENTISTRY

Boston University	P
Case Western Reserve University	P
Columbia University	P
Creighton University	P
Harvard University	P
Howard University	P,O
Indiana University–Purdue University Indianapolis	P
Loma Linda University	P
Marquette University	P
New York University	P
Nova Southeastern University	P
The Ohio State University	P
Southern Illinois University at Edwardsville	P
State University of New York at Buffalo	P
State University of New York at Stony Brook	P,O
Temple University (Philadelphia)	P
Tufts University	P
The University of Alabama at Birmingham	P,M,D
University of California, Los Angeles	P,O
University of California, San Francisco	P
University of Detroit Mercy	P,M,O
University of Florida	P
University of Illinois at Chicago	P
The University of Iowa	P
University of Kentucky	P,M
University of Louisville	P
University of Michigan	P
University of Minnesota, Twin Cities Campus	P
University of Missouri–Kansas City	P
The University of North Carolina at Chapel Hill	P
University of Pennsylvania	P
University of Pittsburgh	P
University of Southern California	P,O
University of the Pacific	P
University of Washington	P
Virginia Commonwealth University	P
West Virginia University	P

DEVELOPMENTAL BIOLOGY

Arizona State University	M,D
Brandeis University	D
Brown University	M,D
California Institute of Technology	D
Carnegie Mellon University	D
Case Western Reserve University	D
Columbia University	M,D
Cornell University	D
Emory University	D
Florida State University	M,D
Indiana University Bloomington	D
Iowa State University of Science and Technology	M,D
Johns Hopkins University	D
Kansas State University	M,D
Marquette University	M,D
Massachusetts Institute of Technology	D
New York University	D
Northwestern University	D
The Ohio State University	M,D
Pennsylvania State University University Park Campus	M,D
Princeton University	D
Purdue University	D
Rensselaer Polytechnic Institute	M,D
Rutgers, The State University of New Jersey, New Brunswick	M,D
Stanford University	D
State University of New York at Albany	M,D
State University of New York at Buffalo	M,D
State University of New York at Stony Brook	M,D
Tufts University	D
The University of Alabama at Birmingham	M,D
University of California, Berkeley	D
University of California, Davis	D
University of California, Irvine	M,D
University of California, Los Angeles	D
University of California, San Diego	D
University of California, Santa Barbara	M,D
University of Chicago	D
University of Cincinnati	M,D
University of Colorado at Boulder	M,D
University of Connecticut	M,D
University of Illinois at Chicago	D
University of Miami	D
University of Michigan	D
University of Minnesota, Twin Cities Campus	M,D
The University of North Carolina at Chapel Hill	M,D
University of Notre Dame	M,D
University of Pennsylvania	D
University of Pittsburgh	D
University of Rochester	M,D
University of Wisconsin–Madison	D
Washington University in St. Louis	D
West Virginia University	M,D
Yale University	D
Yeshiva University	D

DEVELOPMENTAL PSYCHOLOGY

Andrews University	M
Arizona State University	D
Boston College	M,D
Bowling Green State University	M,D
Brandeis University	D
California State University, San Bernardino	M
Carnegie Mellon University	D
Claremont Graduate University	M,D
Clark University	D
Cornell University	D
Duke University	D
Eastern Washington University	M
Emory University	D
Florida International University	D
Fordham University	D
Gallaudet University	M
George Mason University	M,D
The George Washington University	M,D
Graduate School and University Center of the City University of New York	D
Harvard University	M,D
Howard University	D
Hunter College of the City University of New York	M
Illinois State University	M
Louisiana State University and Agricultural and Mechanical College	M,D
Loyola University Chicago	D
Michigan State University	M,D
New York University	D
The Ohio State University	D
Pennsylvania State University University Park Campus	M,D
Rutgers, The State University of New Jersey, New Brunswick	D
Suffolk University	D
Teachers College, Columbia University	M,D
Temple University (Philadelphia)	D
Tufts University	D
The University of Alabama at Birmingham	D
University of California, Santa Cruz	D
University of Connecticut	D
University of Houston	D
University of Illinois at Urbana–Champaign	M,D
University of Kansas	M,D
University of Maine (Orono)	M
University of Maryland, Baltimore County	D
University of Maryland, College Park	D
University of Miami	D
University of Michigan	D
University of Nebraska at Omaha	D
University of New Orleans	D

P—first professional degree; M—master's degree; D—doctorate; O—other advanced degree.

Developmental Psychology (continued)

The University of North Carolina at Chapel Hill	M,D
University of Notre Dame	D
University of Oregon	M,D
University of Pittsburgh	D
University of Rochester	D
University of Wisconsin–Madison	D
Virginia Polytechnic Institute and State University	M,D
Wayne State University	D
Yeshiva University	D

DRUG AND ALCOHOL ABUSE COUNSELING

The College of New Jersey	O
Fairleigh Dickinson University, Florham–Madison Campus	M
Francis Marion University	M
Governors State University	M
John F. Kennedy University	O
Johns Hopkins University	O
Kean University	M
Long Island University, Brooklyn Campus	O
Loyola College	O
National–Louis University	M,O
New York University	M
Northeast Louisiana University	M
Nova Southeastern University	M
Pace University	M
Sage Graduate School	M
St. Mary's University of San Antonio	M,O
Slippery Rock University of Pennsylvania	M
Springfield College (MA)	M,O
University of Alaska Anchorage	O
University of Detroit Mercy	O
University of North Florida	M
Villanova University	M
Virginia Commonwealth University	M,O
Wayne State University	O

EARLY CHILDHOOD EDUCATION

Adelphi University	M
Alabama Agricultural and Mechanical University	M,O
Alabama State University	M,O
Albany State University	M
Appalachian State University	M
Arkansas State University	M
Ashland University	M
Auburn University	M,D,O
Auburn University Montgomery	M,O
Augusta State University	M,O
Ball State University	M,D
Barry University	M
Baruch College of the City University of New York	M
Beaver College	M,O
Bellarmine College	M
Bloomsburg University of Pennsylvania	M
Boise State University	M
Boston College	M
Boston University	M,D,O
Brenau University	M,O
Bridgewater State College	M
Brooklyn College of the City University of New York	M
California State University, Bakersfield	M
California State University, Fresno	M
California State University, Northridge	M
California State University, Sacramento	M
California University of Pennsylvania	M
Central Connecticut State University	M
Central Michigan University	M
Chestnut Hill College	M
Chicago State University	M
City College of the City University of New York	M
Cleveland State University	M
College of Mount St. Joseph	M
College of New Rochelle	M
College of Notre Dame	M
The College of Saint Rose	M
Columbus State University	M,O
Concordia University (IL)	M,O
Cumberland College	M
Dallas Baptist University	M
Dominican University	M
Eastern Connecticut State University	M
Eastern Michigan University	M
Eastern Nazarene College	M,O
Eastern Washington University	M
East Tennessee State University	M
Edinboro University of Pennsylvania	M
Emory University	M
Emporia State University	M
Fairfield University	M,O
Fitchburg State College	M
Florida Agricultural and Mechanical University	M
Florida Atlantic University	M
Florida International University	M
Florida State University	M,D,O
Fordham University	M
Fort Valley State University	M
Francis Marion University	M
Gallaudet University	M,O
Gannon University	M,O
George Mason University	M
The George Washington University	M
Georgia College and State University	M,O
Georgia Southern University	M,O
Georgia Southwestern State University	M,O
Georgia State University	M,D,O
Grambling State University	M
Grand Valley State University	M
Henderson State University	M
Heritage College	M
Hofstra University	M
Hood College	M
Howard University	M,O
Hunter College of the City University of New York	M
Idaho State University	M
Indiana State University	M,D,O
Indiana University Bloomington	M,O
Indiana University of Pennsylvania	M
Jackson State University	M,D,O
Jacksonville State University	M
Jacksonville University	O
James Madison University	M
Johns Hopkins University	M
Johnson State College	M
Kean University	M
Kennesaw State University	M
Kent State University	M
Lehman College of the City University of New York	M
Lenoir–Rhyne College	M
Lesley College	M
Loyola University Chicago	M,D
Lynchburg College	M
Mankato State University	M
Marshall University	M
Marycrest International University	M
Marygrove College	M
Maryville University of Saint Louis	M
Marywood University	M
McNeese State University	M
Mercer University (Macon)	M,O
Mercer University, Cecil B. Day Campus	M,O
Middle Tennessee State University	M
Montana State University–Billings	M
Murray State University	M
National–Louis University	M,O
Nazareth College of Rochester	M
New Jersey City University	M
New York University	M,D,O
Norfolk State University	M
North Carolina Agricultural and Technical State University	M
Northeastern State University	M
Northern Arizona University	M
Northern Illinois University	M
North Georgia College & State University	M
Northwestern State University of Louisiana	M
Northwest Missouri State University	M
Nova Southeastern University	M,D,O
Oakland University	M,O
Ohio University	M
Oklahoma City University	M
Old Dominion University	M
Oral Roberts University	M
Pacific University	M
Pennsylvania State University University Park Campus	M,D
Portland State University	M
Rhode Island College	M
Rivier College	M
Roosevelt University	M
Rutgers, The State University of New Jersey, New Brunswick	M,D,O
Saginaw Valley State University	M
Saint Joseph College (CT)	M
Saint Mary's College of California	M
Salem State College	M
Salisbury State University	M
Samford University	M,O
Sam Houston State University	M
San Francisco State University	M
Slippery Rock University of Pennsylvania	M
Sonoma State University	M
South Carolina State University	M
Southern Connecticut State University	M
Southern Oregon University	M
Southwestern Oklahoma State University	M
Spring Hill College	M
State University of New York at Binghamton	M
State University of New York at Buffalo	M,D
State University of New York at New Paltz	M
State University of West Georgia	M,O
Stephen F. Austin State University	M
Syracuse University	M
Teachers College, Columbia University	M,D
Temple University (Philadelphia)	M,O
Tennessee Technological University	M,O
Texas A&M International University	M
Texas A&M University–Commerce	M
Texas A&M University–Kingsville	M
Texas Southern University	M
Texas Tech University	M,O
Texas Woman's University	M,D
Towson University	M,O
Trinity College (DC)	M
Troy State University (Troy)	M,O
Troy State University Dothan	M,O
Tufts University	M
The University of Alabama (Tuscaloosa)	M,O
The University of Alabama at Birmingham	M,D,O
University of Alaska Southeast	M
University of Arkansas (Fayetteville)	M
University of Arkansas at Little Rock	M,O
University of Bridgeport	M,O
University of Central Arkansas	M
University of Central Oklahoma	M
University of Cincinnati	M
University of Colorado at Denver	M
University of Detroit Mercy	M
University of Florida	M,D,O
University of Georgia	M,D,O
University of Hartford	M
University of Houston	M
University of Houston–Clear Lake	M
The University of Iowa	M,D,O
University of Kansas	M,D
University of Louisville	M
University of Maryland, College Park	M,D,O
University of Massachusetts Amherst	M,D,O
The University of Memphis	M,D
University of Miami	M,O
University of Michigan	M,D
University of Minnesota, Twin Cities Campus	M,D
University of Montevallo	M,O
University of Nebraska at Kearney	M
University of New Hampshire	M
University of North Alabama	M
The University of North Carolina at Chapel Hill	D
University of North Dakota	M
University of Northern Colorado	M
University of Northern Iowa	M
University of North Texas	M,D
University of Oklahoma	M,D
University of Pennsylvania	M
University of Pittsburgh	M
University of Portland	M
University of Puerto Rico, Río Piedras	M
University of Richmond	M
University of South Alabama	M,O
University of South Carolina (Columbia)	M,D
University of Southern Mississippi	M,O
University of South Florida	M,D
University of Tennessee at Chattanooga	M
University of Tennessee, Knoxville	M,D
The University of Texas at Brownsville	M
The University of Texas at Tyler	M
The University of Texas of the Permian Basin	M
The University of Texas–Pan American	M
University of the District of Columbia	M
University of the Incarnate Word	M
University of Toledo	M
The University of West Alabama	M
University of West Florida	M
University of Wisconsin–Milwaukee	M
University of Wisconsin–Oshkosh	M
Valdosta State University	M,O
Vanderbilt University	M,D
Virginia Commonwealth University	M
Washington University in St. Louis	M,O
Webster University	M
Western Kentucky University	M
Western Michigan University	M
Western Oregon University	M
Westfield State College	M
Winona State University	M
Worcester State College	M
Wright State University	M
Xavier University	M
Youngstown State University	M

EAST EUROPEAN AND RUSSIAN STUDIES

Boston College	M
Columbia University	O
Florida State University	M
Georgetown University	M
The George Washington University	M
Harvard University	M
Hunter College of the City University of New York	M
Indiana University Bloomington	M,O
Johns Hopkins University	M,D
La Salle University	M
The Ohio State University	M,O
Stanford University	M
University of Connecticut	M
University of Illinois at Chicago	M,D
University of Illinois at Urbana–Champaign	M
University of Kansas	M
University of Michigan	M
University of Minnesota, Twin Cities Campus	M
The University of Texas at Austin	M
University of Washington	M
Yale University	M

ECOLOGY

Arizona State University	M,D
Boston University	M,D
Brown University	M,D
Colorado State University	M,D
Columbia University	D,O
Cornell University	D
Duke University	M,D
Eastern Kentucky University	M
Emory University	D
Florida Institute of Technology	M,D
Florida State University	M,D
Fordham University	M,D
Frostburg State University	M
George Mason University	M
Goddard College	M
Illinois State University	D
Indiana State University	M,D
Indiana University Bloomington	M,D
Iowa State University of Science and Technology	M,D
Kansas State University	M,D
Kent State University	M,D
Lesley College	M
Mankato State University	M
Marquette University	M,D
Michigan State University	
North Carolina State University	M,D
Oklahoma State University	M,D
Old Dominion University	D
Pennsylvania State University University Park Campus	M,D
Princeton University	D
Purdue University	M,D
Rice University	M,D
Rutgers, The State University of New Jersey, New Brunswick	M,D
San Diego State University	D
San Francisco State University	M
State University of New York at Albany	M,D
State University of New York at Buffalo	M,D
State University of New York at Stony Brook	D
The University of Alabama at Birmingham	M,D
The University of Arizona	M,D
University of California, Davis	M,D
University of California, Irvine	M,D
University of California, San Diego	D
University of California, Santa Barbara	M,D

University of Chicago	D
University of Colorado at Boulder	M,D
University of Connecticut	M,D
University of Delaware	M,D
University of Florida	M,D
University of Georgia	M,D
University of Hawaii at Manoa	M,D
University of Illinois at Chicago	M,D
University of Illinois at Urbana–Champaign	D
University of Kansas	M,D
University of Maine (Orono)	M,D
University of Miami	M,D
University of Minnesota, Twin Cities Campus	M,D
The University of Montana–Missoula	M,D
University of Nevada, Reno	D
University of New Mexico	M,D
The University of North Carolina at Chapel Hill	M,D
University of North Dakota	M,D
University of Notre Dame	M,D
University of Oregon	M,D
University of Pennsylvania	D
University of Pittsburgh	M,D
University of Rochester	M,D
University of South Carolina (Columbia)	M,D
University of South Florida	D
University of Tennessee, Knoxville	M,D
University of Utah	M,D
University of Wisconsin–Madison	M,D
Utah State University	M,D
Virginia Polytechnic Institute and State University	M,D
Washington University in St. Louis	D
West Virginia University	M,D
William Paterson University of New Jersey	M

ECONOMICS

Alabama Agricultural and Mechanical University	M
American University	M,D
Arizona State University	M,D
Auburn University	M,D
Ball State University	M
Baruch College of the City University of New York	M
Baylor University	M
Boston College	M,D
Boston University	M,D
Bowling Green State University	M
Brandeis University	M,D
Brooklyn College of the City University of New York	M
Brown University	M,D
California Institute of Technology	D
California State Polytechnic University, Pomona	M
California State University, Fullerton	M
California State University, Hayward	M
California State University, Long Beach	M
California State University, Los Angeles	M
California State University, Sacramento	M
Carnegie Mellon University	D
Case Western Reserve University	M
The Catholic University of America	M,D
Central Michigan University	M
Central Missouri State University	M
City College of the City University of New York	M
Claremont Graduate University	M,D
Clark Atlanta University	M
Clark University	D
Clemson University	M,D
Cleveland State University	M
Colorado State University	M,D
Columbia University	M,D
Cornell University	D
DePaul University	M
Drexel University	M,D
Duke University	M,D
East Carolina University	M
Eastern College	M
Eastern Illinois University	M
Eastern Michigan University	M
Emory University	M,D
Emporia State University	M
Fairleigh Dickinson University, Florham–Madison Campus	M
Fairleigh Dickinson University, Teaneck–Hackensack Campus	M
Florida Atlantic University	M
Florida International University	M,D
Florida State University	M,D
Fordham University	M,D,O

Fort Hays State University	M
George Mason University	M,D
Georgetown University	D
The George Washington University	M,D
Georgia Institute of Technology	M
Georgia State University	M,D
Golden Gate University	M
Graduate School and University Center of the City University of New York	D
Harvard University	M,D
Howard University	M,D
Hunter College of the City University of New York	M
Illinois State University	M
Indiana State University	M
Indiana University Bloomington	M,D
Iowa State University of Science and Technology	M,D
Johns Hopkins University	M,D
Kansas State University	M,D
Kent State University	M,D
Lehigh University	M,D
Long Island University, Brooklyn Campus	M
Louisiana State University and Agricultural and Mechanical College	M,D
Louisiana Tech University	M,D
Loyola College	M
Mankato State University	M
Marquette University	M
Massachusetts Institute of Technology	D
Miami University	M
Michigan State University	M,D
Middle Tennessee State University	M,D
Montana State University–Bozeman	M
Montclair State University	M
Murray State University	M
New Mexico State University	M
New School University	M,D
New York University	M,D,O
North Carolina State University	M,D
Northeastern University	M,D
Northern Illinois University	M,D
Northwestern University	M,D
The Ohio State University	M,D
Ohio University	M
Oklahoma State University	M,D
Old Dominion University	M
Oregon State University	M,D
Pace University	M
Pennsylvania State University University Park Campus	M,D
Portland State University	M,D
Princeton University	D
Purdue University	D
Queens College of the City University of New York	M
Quinnipiac College	M
Radford University	M
Rensselaer Polytechnic Institute	M,D
Rice University	M,D
Roosevelt University	M
Rutgers, The State University of New Jersey, Newark	M
Rutgers, The State University of New Jersey, New Brunswick	M,D
St. Cloud State University	M
St. John's University (NY)	M,O
Saint Louis University	M,D
Saint Martin's College	M
St. Mary's University of San Antonio	M
San Diego State University	M
San Francisco State University	M
San Jose State University	M
Seattle University	M,O
Seton Hall University	M
South Dakota State University	M
Southern Illinois University at Carbondale	M,D
Southern Illinois University at Edwardsville	M
Southern Methodist University	M,D
Stanford University	D
State University of New York at Albany	M,D,O
State University of New York at Binghamton	M,D
State University of New York at Buffalo	M,D
State University of New York at Stony Brook	M,D
Suffolk University	M
Syracuse University	M,D
Teachers College, Columbia University	M,D
Temple University (Philadelphia)	M,D
Texas A&M University (College Station)	M,D
Texas A&M University–Commerce	M
Texas Christian University	M

Texas Tech University	M,D
Tufts University	M
Tulane University	M,D
The University of Akron	M
The University of Alabama (Tuscaloosa)	M,D
University of Alaska Fairbanks	M
The University of Arizona	M,D
University of Arkansas (Fayetteville)	M,D
University of California, Berkeley	D
University of California, Davis	M,D
University of California, Irvine	M,D
University of California, Los Angeles	D
University of California, Riverside	M,D
University of California, San Diego	D
University of California, Santa Barbara	M,D
University of California, Santa Cruz	M,D
University of Central Florida	M
University of Chicago	D
University of Cincinnati	M,D
University of Colorado at Boulder	M,D
University of Colorado at Denver	M
University of Connecticut	M,D
University of Delaware	M,D
University of Denver	M
University of Detroit Mercy	M
University of Florida	M,D
University of Georgia	M,D
University of Hawaii at Manoa	M,D
University of Houston	M,D
University of Idaho	M
University of Illinois at Chicago	M,D
University of Illinois at Springfield	M
University of Illinois at Urbana–Champaign	M,D
The University of Iowa	D
University of Kansas	M,D
University of Kentucky	M,D
University of Maine (Orono)	M
University of Maryland, College Park	M,D
University of Massachusetts Amherst	M,D
The University of Memphis	M,D
University of Miami	M,D
University of Michigan	M,D
University of Minnesota, Twin Cities Campus	M,D
University of Mississippi	M,D
University of Missouri–Columbia	M,D
University of Missouri–Kansas City	M,D
University of Missouri–St. Louis	M,O
The University of Montana–Missoula	M
University of Nebraska at Omaha	M
University of Nebraska–Lincoln	M,D
University of Nevada, Las Vegas	M
University of Nevada, Reno	M
University of New Hampshire	M,D
University of New Mexico	M,D
University of New Orleans	M,D
The University of North Carolina at Chapel Hill	M,D
University of North Carolina at Charlotte	M
University of North Carolina at Greensboro	M
University of North Texas	M
University of Notre Dame	M,D
University of Oklahoma	M,D
University of Oregon	M,D
University of Pennsylvania	D
University of Pittsburgh	M,D
University of Puerto Rico, Rio Piedras	M
University of Rhode Island	M,D
University of Rochester	M,D
University of San Francisco	M
University of South Carolina (Columbia)	M,D
University of Southern California	M,D
University of Southern Mississippi	M
University of South Florida	M
University of Tennessee at Chattanooga	M
University of Tennessee, Knoxville	M,D
The University of Texas at Arlington	M
The University of Texas at Austin	M,D
The University of Texas at Dallas	D
The University of Texas at El Paso	M
The University of Texas at Tyler	M
University of Toledo	M
University of Utah	M,D
University of Virginia	M,D
University of Washington	M,D
University of Wisconsin–Madison	D
University of Wisconsin–Milwaukee	M,D

University of Wyoming	M,D
Utah State University	M,D
Vanderbilt University	M,D
Virginia Commonwealth University	M,D
Virginia Polytechnic Institute and State University	M,D
Virginia State University	M
Washington State University	M,D
Washington University in St. Louis	M,D
Wayne State University	M,D,O
West Chester University of Pennsylvania	M
Western Illinois University	M
Western Kentucky University	M
Western Michigan University	M,D
West Texas A&M University	M
West Virginia University	M,D
Wichita State University	M
Wright State University	M
Yale University	M,D
Youngstown State University	M

EDUCATION

Abilene Christian University	M
Adams State College	M
Adelphi University	M,D,O
Alabama Agricultural and Mechanical University	M,O
Alabama State University	M,O
Alaska Pacific University	M
Albany State University	M,O
Alcorn State University	M,O
Alfred University	M
American International College	M,D,O
American University	M,D
Andrews University	M,D,O
Angelo State University	M
Anna Maria College	M
Appalachian State University	M,D,O
Aquinas College (MI)	M
Arizona State University	M,D
Arizona State University West	M
Arkansas State University	M,D,O
Arkansas Tech University	M,D
Armstrong Atlantic State University	M
Ashland University	M
Assumption College	M
Auburn University	M,D,O
Auburn University Montgomery	M,O
Augusta State University	M,O
Aurora University	M,O
Austin Peay State University	M,O
Averett College	M
Avila College	M
Azusa Pacific University	M,D
Baker University	M
Baldwin-Wallace College	M
Ball State University	M,D,O
Barry University	M,D,O
Baruch College of the City University of New York	M
Baylor University	M,D,O
Beaver College	M,O
Bellarmine College	M
Belmont University	M
Bemidji State University	M
Benedictine University	M
Biola University	M
Bloomsburg University of Pennsylvania	M
Boise State University	M,D
Boston College	M,D,O
Boston University	M,D,O
Bowie State University	M
Bowling Green State University	M,D,O
Bradley University	M
Brenau University	M,O
Bridgewater State College	M,O
Brigham Young University	M,D,O
Brooklyn College of the City University of New York	M,O
Brown University	M
Butler University	M,O
Cabrini College	M
California Lutheran University	M
California Polytechnic State University, San Luis Obispo	M
California State Polytechnic University, Pomona	M
California State University, Bakersfield	M
California State University, Chico	M
California State University, Dominguez Hills	M,O
California State University, Fresno	M
California State University, Fullerton	M
California State University, Hayward	M
California State University, Long Beach	M,O
California State University, Los Angeles	M,D

P—first professional degree; M—master's degree; D—doctorate; O—other advanced degree.

Education (continued)

California State University, Northridge	M,O
California State University, Sacramento	M
California State University, San Bernardino	M
California State University, San Marcos	M
California State University, Stanislaus	M
California University of Pennsylvania	M
Calvin College	M
Campbell University	M
Canisius College	M,O
Cardinal Stritch University	M,D
Carnegie Mellon University	D
Carthage College	M,O
Castleton State College	M,O
The Catholic University of America	M,D
Centenary College of Louisiana	M
Central Connecticut State University	M,O
Central Michigan University	M,O
Central Missouri State University	M,D,O
Central Washington University	M
Chadron State College	M,O
Chaminade University of Honolulu	M
Chapman University	M
Charleston Southern University	M
Cheyney University of Pennsylvania	M
Chicago State University	M
The Citadel, The Military College of South Carolina	M,O
City College of the City University of New York	M,O
City University	M,O
Claremont Graduate University	M,D
Clarion University of Pennsylvania	M
Clark Atlanta University	M,D,O
Clark University	M
Clemson University	M,D,O
Cleveland State University	M,D,O
College Misericordia	M
College of Mount St. Joseph	M
The College of New Jersey	M,O
College of New Rochelle	M,O
College of Notre Dame	M,O
College of Notre Dame of Maryland	M
College of St. Catherine	M
The College of Saint Rose	M,O
College of St. Scholastica	M
College of Staten Island of the City University of New York	M,O
College of William and Mary	M,D
Columbia College (IL)	M
Columbus State University	M,O
Converse College	M,O
Coppin State College	M
Cornell University	M,D
Creighton University	M
Cumberland College	M,O
Curry College	M,O
Dallas Baptist University	M
Delaware State University	M
Delta State University	M,D,O
DePaul University	M
Dominican College of San Rafael	M,O
Dominican University	M
Dowling College	M,O
Drake University	M,D,O
Drexel University	M
Drury College	M
Duke University	M
Duquesne University	M,D,O
D'Youville College	M
East Carolina University	M,D,O
East Central University	M
Eastern College	M,O
Eastern Connecticut State University	M
Eastern Illinois University	M,O
Eastern Kentucky University	M,O
Eastern Michigan University	M,D,O
Eastern Nazarene College	M,O
Eastern New Mexico University	M
Eastern Washington University	M
East Stroudsburg University of Pennsylvania	M
East Tennessee State University	M,D,O
Edgewood College	M,O
Edinboro University of Pennsylvania	M,O
Elmira College	M
Elon College	M
Emmanuel College (MA)	M
Emory University	M,D,O
Emporia State University	M,O
Fairfield University	M,O
Fairleigh Dickinson University, Florham–Madison Campus	M
Fairleigh Dickinson University, Teaneck–Hackensack Campus	M
Fayetteville State University	D
Ferris State University	M
Fitchburg State College	M,O
Florida Agricultural and Mechanical University	M
Florida Atlantic University	M,D,O
Florida International University	M,D,O
Florida State University	M,D,O
Fontbonne College	M
Fordham University	M,D,O
Fort Hays State University	M,O
Framingham State College	M
Franciscan University of Steubenville	M
Francis Marion University	M
Fresno Pacific University	M
Frostburg State University	M
Gallaudet University	M,D,O
Gannon University	M,O
Gardner–Webb University	M
George Mason University	M,D
The George Washington University	M,D,O
Georgia College and State University	M,O
Georgian Court College	M
Georgia Southern University	M,D,O
Georgia Southwestern State University	M,O
Georgia State University	M,D,O
Goddard College	M
Gonzaga University	M,D
Governors State University	M
Grambling State University	M,D
Grand Valley State University	M
Gwynedd–Mercy College	M
Hampton University	M
Harding University	M
Hardin–Simmons University	M
Harvard University	M,D,O
Henderson State University	M
Heritage College	M
Hofstra University	M,D,O
Holy Names College	M,O
Hood College	M
Hope International University	M
Houston Baptist University	M
Howard University	M,D,O
Hunter College of the City University of New York	M,O
Idaho State University	M,D,O
Illinois State University	M,D
Indiana State University	M,D,O
Indiana University Bloomington	M,D,O
Indiana University Kokomo	M
Indiana University Northwest	M
Indiana University of Pennsylvania	M,D,O
Indiana University–Purdue University Fort Wayne	M
Indiana University–Purdue University Indianapolis	M
Indiana University South Bend	M
Indiana University Southeast	M
Indiana Wesleyan University	M
Inter American University of Puerto Rico, Metropolitan Campus	M,D
Inter American University of Puerto Rico, San Germán Campus	M
Iowa State University of Science and Technology	M,D
Jackson State University	M,D,O
Jacksonville State University	M,O
Jacksonville University	M,O
James Madison University	M
John Carroll University	M
John F. Kennedy University	M
Johns Hopkins University	M,D,O
Johnson State College	M
Kansas State University	M,D
Kean University	M,O
Keene State College	M
Kennesaw State University	M
Kent State University	M,D,O
Kutztown University of Pennsylvania	M
Lake Erie College	M
Lamar University	M,O
Lander University	M
La Salle University	M
La Sierra University	M,D,O
Lehigh University	M,D,O
Lehman College of the City University of New York	M
Lenoir–Rhyne College	M,O
Lesley College	M,D,O
Lewis University	M,O
Liberty University	M
Lincoln Memorial University	M,O
Lincoln University (MO)	M
Lindenwood University	M
Long Island University, Brooklyn Campus	M,O
Long Island University, C.W. Post Campus	M,O
Long Island University, Southampton College	M
Longwood College	M
Louisiana State University and Agricultural and Mechanical College	M,D,O
Louisiana State University in Shreveport	M,O
Louisiana Tech University	M,D,O
Loyola College	M,O
Loyola Marymount University	M
Loyola University Chicago	M,D
Loyola University New Orleans	M
Lynchburg College	M
Madonna University	M
Maharishi University of Management	M
Manhattan College	M,O
Mankato State University	M,O
Mansfield University of Pennsylvania	M
Marian College of Fond du Lac	M
Marquette University	M,D,O
Marshall University	M,D,O
Marycrest International University	M
Marygrove College	M
Marymount University	M
Maryville University of Saint Louis	M
Marywood University	M
McNeese State University	M,O
Mercer University (Macon)	M,O
Mercer University, Cecil B. Day Campus	M,O
Meredith College	M
Miami University	M,D,O
Michigan State University	M,D,O
MidAmerica Nazarene University	M
Middle Tennessee State University	M,D,O
Midwestern State University	M
Millersville University of Pennsylvania	M,O
Mississippi College	M,O
Mississippi State University	M,D,O
Monmouth University	M,O
Montana State University–Billings	M
Montana State University–Bozeman	M,D,O
Montana State University–Northern	M
Montclair State University	M
Moorhead State University	M,O
Morehead State University	M,D,O
Morgan State University	M,D
Mount Saint Mary College	M
Mount St. Mary's College	M
Mount Saint Mary's College and Seminary	M
Murray State University	M,D,O
National–Louis University	M,D,O
National University	M
Nazareth College of Rochester	M
New Jersey City University	M,O
New Mexico Highlands University	M
New Mexico State University	M,D,O
New School University	M
New York Institute of Technology	M,O
New York University	M,D,O
Niagara University	M,O
Nicholls State University	M
Norfolk State University	M
North Carolina Agricultural and Technical State University	M
North Carolina Central University	M
North Carolina State University	M,D,O
North Central College	M
North Dakota State University	M,O
Northeastern Illinois University	M
Northeastern State University	M
Northeastern University	M
Northeast Louisiana University	M,D,O
Northern Arizona University	M,D
Northern Illinois University	M,D,O
Northern Kentucky University	M
Northern Michigan University	M
Northern State University	M
North Georgia College & State University	M
Northwestern Oklahoma State University	M
Northwestern State University of Louisiana	M,O
Northwestern University	M,D
Northwest Missouri State University	M,O
Notre Dame College	M
Nova Southeastern University	M,D,O
Oakland University	M,D,O
The Ohio State University	M,D,O
Ohio University	M,D,O
Oklahoma City University	M
Oklahoma State University	M,D,O
Old Dominion University	M,D,O
Olivet Nazarene University	M
Oral Roberts University	M
Oregon State University	M,D
Our Lady of the Lake University of San Antonio	M,D
Pace University	M,O
Pacific Lutheran University	M
Pacific University	M
Park College	M
Pennsylvania State University Harrisburg Campus of the Capital College	M,D
Pennsylvania State University University Park Campus	M,D
Pepperdine University (Culver City)	M,D
Phillips University	M
Pittsburg State University	M,O
Plattsburgh State University of New York	M,O
Plymouth State College of the University System of New Hampshire	M
Point Loma Nazarene University	M,D,O
Pontifical Catholic University of Puerto Rico	M
Portland State University	M,D
Prairie View A&M University	M
Providence College	M
Purdue University	M,D,O
Purdue University Calumet	M
Queens College	M
Queens College of the City University of New York	M,O
Quinnipiac College	M
Radford University	M
Regis University	M
Rhode Island College	D
Rice University	M
Rider University	M,O
Rivier College	M
Rockford College	M
Rollins College	M
Roosevelt University	M,D
Rowan University	M,D,O
Rutgers, The State University of New Jersey, New Brunswick	M,D,O
Sacred Heart University	M,O
Sage Graduate School	M,O
Saginaw Valley State University	M,O
St. Bonaventure University	M,O
St. Cloud State University	M,O
St. Edward's University	M
Saint Francis College (PA)	M
St. John's University (NY)	M,D,O
Saint Joseph College (CT)	M,O
Saint Joseph's University	M,O
Saint Louis University	M,D,O
Saint Martin's College	M
Saint Mary's College of California	M
Saint Mary's University of Minnesota	M
St. Mary's University of San Antonio	M
Saint Michael's College	M,O
Saint Peter's College (Jersey City)	M,O
St. Thomas University	M,O
Saint Xavier University	M,O
Salem State College	M
Salisbury State University	M
Salve Regina University	M
Samford University	M,O
Sam Houston State University	M,D,O
San Diego State University	M,D
San Francisco State University	M,D,O
San Jose State University	M,O
Santa Clara University	M,O
Seattle Pacific University	M,D
Seattle University	M,D,O
Seton Hall University	M,D,O
Shenandoah University	M
Shippensburg University of Pennsylvania	M
Simmons College	M
Slippery Rock University of Pennsylvania	M
Sonoma State University	M
South Carolina State University	M,D,O
South Dakota State University	M
Southeastern Louisiana University	M,O
Southeastern Oklahoma State University	M
Southern Arkansas University–Magnolia	M
Southern Connecticut State University	M,O
Southern Illinois University at Carbondale	M,D
Southern Illinois University at Edwardsville	M,D,O
Southern Nazarene University	M
Southern Oregon University	M
Southern University and Agricultural and Mechanical College	M
Southern Utah University	M
Southwest Baptist University	M

Southwestern Oklahoma State University	M
Southwest Missouri State University	M,O
Southwest Texas State University	M
Spalding University	M,D
Springfield College (MA)	M
Spring Hill College	M
Stanford University	M,D
State University of New York at Albany	M,D,O
State University of New York at Binghamton	M,D
State University of New York at Buffalo	M,D,O
State University of New York at New Paltz	M,O
State University of New York at Oswego	M,D,O
State University of New York College at Brockport	M
State University of New York College at Cortland	M,O
State University of New York College at Fredonia	M,O
State University of New York College at Geneseo	M
State University of New York College at Oneonta	M,O
State University of New York College at Potsdam	M
State University of West Georgia	M,D,O
Stephen F. Austin State University	M,D
Stetson University	M,O
Suffolk University	M,O
Sul Ross State University	M
Syracuse University	M,D,O
Tarleton State University	M,O
Teachers College, Columbia University	M,D
Temple University (Philadelphia)	M,D,O
Tennessee State University	M,D
Tennessee Technological University	M,O
Texas A&M International University	M
Texas A&M University (College Station)	M,D
Texas A&M University–Commerce	M,D
Texas A&M University–Corpus Christi	M,D
Texas A&M University–Kingsville	M,D
Texas A&M University–Texarkana	M
Texas Christian University	M
Texas Southern University	M,D
Texas Tech University	M,D,O
Texas Wesleyan University	M
Texas Woman's University	M,D
Towson University	M
Trevecca Nazarene University	M
Trinity College (DC)	M
Trinity University	M
Troy State University (Troy)	M,O
Troy State University Dothan	M,O
Troy State University Montgomery	M,O
Truman State University	M
Tufts University	M,O
Tulane University	O
Tusculum College	M
Tuskegee University	M
Union College (KY)	M
United States International University	M,D
Universidad del Turabo	M
Universidad Metropolitana	M
The University of Akron	M,D
The University of Alabama (Tuscaloosa)	M,D,O
The University of Alabama at Birmingham	M,D,O
University of Alaska Anchorage	M
University of Alaska Fairbanks	M,O
University of Alaska Southeast	M
The University of Arizona	M,D,O
University of Arkansas (Fayetteville)	M,D,O
University of Arkansas at Little Rock	M,D,O
University of Bridgeport	M,D,O
University of California, Berkeley	M,D,O
University of California, Davis	M,D
University of California, Irvine	D
University of California, Los Angeles	M,D
University of California, Riverside	M,D
University of California, San Diego	M
University of California, Santa Barbara	M,D
University of California, Santa Cruz	M,O
University of Central Arkansas	M,O
University of Central Florida	M,D,O
University of Central Oklahoma	M
University of Chicago	M,O
University of Cincinnati	M,D,O
University of Colorado at Boulder	M,D
University of Colorado at Colorado Springs	M
University of Colorado at Denver	M,D,O
University of Connecticut	M,D
University of Dayton	M,D,O
University of Delaware	M,D
University of Denver	M,D,O
University of Detroit Mercy	M,O
University of Dubuque	M
University of Evansville	M
University of Florida	M,D,O
University of Georgia	M,D,O
University of Guam	M
University of Hartford	M,D,O
University of Hawaii at Manoa	M,D
University of Houston	M,D
University of Houston–Clear Lake	M
University of Houston–Victoria	M
University of Idaho	M,D,O
University of Illinois at Chicago	M,D
University of Illinois at Urbana–Champaign	M,D,O
University of Indianapolis	M
The University of Iowa	M,D,O
University of Kansas	M,D,O
University of Kentucky	M,D,O
University of La Verne	M,O
University of Louisville	M,D,O
University of Maine (Orono)	M,D,O
University of Mary	M
University of Mary Hardin–Baylor	M
University of Maryland, Baltimore County	M
University of Maryland, College Park	M,D,O
University of Maryland Eastern Shore	M
University of Massachusetts Amherst	M,D,O
University of Massachusetts Boston	M,D,O
University of Massachusetts Dartmouth	M
University of Massachusetts Lowell	M,D,O
The University of Memphis	M,D,O
University of Miami	M,D,O
University of Michigan	M,D
University of Michigan–Dearborn	M
University of Minnesota, Twin Cities Campus	M,D,O
University of Mississippi	M,D,O
University of Missouri–Columbia	M,D,O
University of Missouri–Kansas City	M,D,O
University of Missouri–St. Louis	M,D
University of Mobile	M
The University of Montana–Missoula	M,D,O
University of Montevallo	M,O
University of Nebraska at Kearney	M,O
University of Nebraska at Omaha	M,D,O
University of Nebraska–Lincoln	M,D,O
University of Nevada, Las Vegas	M,D,O
University of Nevada, Reno	M,D,O
University of New England	M
University of New Hampshire	M,D,O
University of New Haven	M,O
University of New Mexico	M,D,O
University of New Orleans	M,D,O
University of North Alabama	M,O
The University of North Carolina at Chapel Hill	M,D
University of North Carolina at Charlotte	M,D,O
University of North Carolina at Greensboro	M,D,O
University of North Carolina at Pembroke	M
University of North Carolina at Wilmington	M
University of North Dakota	M,D,O
University of Northern Colorado	M,D,O
University of Northern Iowa	M,D,O
University of North Florida	M,D
University of North Texas	M,D,O
University of Oklahoma	M,D
University of Oregon	M,D
University of Pennsylvania	M,D
University of Pittsburgh	M,D
University of Portland	M
University of Puerto Rico, Río Piedras	M,D
University of Redlands	M
University of Rhode Island	M
University of Richmond	M
University of Rochester	M,D
University of St. Francis (IL)	M
University of Saint Francis (IN)	M
University of St. Thomas (MN)	M,D,O
University of St. Thomas (TX)	M
University of San Diego	M,D
University of San Francisco	M,D
University of Scranton	M
University of South Alabama	M,D,O
University of South Carolina (Columbia)	M,D,O
University of South Dakota	M,D,O
University of Southern California	M,D,O
University of Southern Indiana	M
University of Southern Maine	M,O
University of Southern Mississippi	M,D,O
University of South Florida	M,D,O
University of Southwestern Louisiana	M
University of Tennessee at Chattanooga	M
The University of Tennessee at Martin	M
University of Tennessee, Knoxville	M,D,O
The University of Texas at Arlington	M
The University of Texas at Austin	M,D
The University of Texas at Brownsville	M,D
The University of Texas at El Paso	M,D
The University of Texas at San Antonio	M
The University of Texas at Tyler	M,O
The University of Texas of the Permian Basin	M
The University of Texas–Pan American	M,D
University of the District of Columbia	M
University of the Incarnate Word	M
University of the Pacific	M,D
University of the Sacred Heart	M
University of the Virgin Islands	M
University of Toledo	M,D,O
University of Tulsa	M
University of Utah	M,D
University of Vermont	M,D
University of Virginia	M,D,O
University of Washington	M,D
The University of West Alabama	M
University of West Florida	M,D,O
University of Wisconsin–Eau Claire	M
University of Wisconsin–La Crosse	M
University of Wisconsin–Madison	M,D
University of Wisconsin–Milwaukee	M,D
University of Wisconsin–Oshkosh	M
University of Wisconsin–Platteville	M
University of Wisconsin–River Falls	M
University of Wisconsin–Stevens Point	M
University of Wisconsin–Stout	M
University of Wisconsin–Superior	M
University of Wisconsin–Whitewater	M
University of Wyoming	M,D,O
Utah State University	M,D,O
Valdosta State University	M,D,O
Valparaiso University	M
Vanderbilt University	M,D,O
Villanova University	M
Virginia Commonwealth University	M,D,O
Virginia Polytechnic Institute and State University	M,D,O
Virginia State University	M
Viterbo College	M
Wagner College	M
Wake Forest University	M
Walla Walla College	M
Walsh University	M
Washburn University of Topeka	M
Washington State University	M,D
Washington University in St. Louis	M,D,O
Wayne State College	M,O
Wayne State University	M,D,O
Weber State University	M
Webster University	M
West Chester University of Pennsylvania	M
Western Carolina University	M,D,O
Western Connecticut State University	M
Western Illinois University	M,O
Western Kentucky University	M,D,O
Western Michigan University	M,D,O
Western New Mexico University	M
Western Oregon University	M
Western Washington University	M
Westfield State College	M,O
Westminster College of Salt Lake City	M
West Texas A&M University	M
West Virginia University	M,D
Whitworth College	M
Wichita State University	M,D,O
Widener University	M,D
Wilkes University	M
William Carey College	M
William Paterson University of New Jersey	M
Wilmington College (DE)	M,D
Winona State University	M,O
Winthrop University	M,O
Worcester State College	M,O
Wright State University	M,D,O
Xavier University	M
Xavier University of Louisiana	M
Youngstown State University	M,D

EDUCATIONAL ADMINISTRATION

Abilene Christian University	M
Alabama Agricultural and Mechanical University	M
Alabama State University	M,O
Albany State University	M,O
Alcorn State University	M
American International College	M,O
American University	M
Andrews University	M,D,O
Angelo State University	M
Appalachian State University	M,D
Arizona State University	M,D
Arizona State University West	M
Arkansas State University	M,D,O
Arkansas Tech University	M
Ashland University	M
Auburn University	M,D,O
Auburn University Montgomery	M,O
Augusta State University	M,O
Aurora University	M
Austin Peay State University	M,O
Azusa Pacific University	M,D
Baldwin-Wallace College	M
Ball State University	M,D,O
Barry University	M,D,O
Baruch College of the City University of New York	M
Baylor University	M,D,O
Beaver College	M,O
Belmont University	M
Bemidji State University	M
Boston College	M,D,O
Boston University	M,D,O
Bowie State University	M
Bowling Green State University	M,D,O
Bradley University	M
Bridgewater State College	M,O
Brigham Young University	M,D
Brooklyn College of the City University of New York	O
Butler University	M,O
California Lutheran University	M
California Polytechnic State University, San Luis Obispo	M
California State University, Bakersfield	M
California State University, Dominguez Hills	M
California State University, Fresno	M,D
California State University, Fullerton	M
California State University, Hayward	M
California State University, Long Beach	M
California State University, Los Angeles	M
California State University, Northridge	M
California State University, Sacramento	M
California State University, San Bernardino	M
California State University, Stanislaus	M
California University of Pennsylvania	M
Calvin College	M
Campbell University	M
Canisius College	M,O
Cardinal Stritch University	M,O
Castleton State College	M,O
The Catholic University of America	M,D
Centenary College of Louisiana	M
Central Connecticut State University	M,O
Central Michigan University	M,O
Central Missouri State University	M,D,O
Central Washington University	M
Chadron State College	M,O
Chapman University	M
Charleston Southern University	M
Cheyney University of Pennsylvania	M
Chicago State University	M
The Citadel, The Military College of South Carolina	M,O
City College of the City University of New York	M,O
City University	M,O
Claremont Graduate University	M,D
Clark Atlanta University	M,D,O

P—first professional degree; M—master's degree; D—doctorate; O—other advanced degree.

Educational Administration (continued)

Clemson University	M,D,O
Cleveland State University	M,O
The College of New Jersey	M
College of New Rochelle	M,O
College of Notre Dame of Maryland	M
The College of Saint Rose	M,O
College of Staten Island of the City University of New York	O
College of William and Mary	M,D
Columbus State University	M,O
Concordia University (IL)	M,O
Converse College	O
Cornell University	M,D
Creighton University	M
Cumberland College	O
Dallas Baptist University	M
Delta State University	M,O
DePaul University	M
Dominican University	M
Dowling College	O
Drake University	M,D,O
Duquesne University	M,D
East Carolina University	M,D,O
Eastern Illinois University	M,O
Eastern Kentucky University	M,O
Eastern Michigan University	M,D,O
Eastern Nazarene College	M,O
Eastern Washington University	M
East Tennessee State University	M,D,O
Edgewood College	M,O
Edinboro University of Pennsylvania	M,O
Emporia State University	M
Fayetteville State University	M
Fitchburg State College	M,O
Florida Agricultural and Mechanical University	M
Florida Atlantic University	M,D,O
Florida International University	D,O
Florida State University	M,D,O
Fordham University	M,D,O
Fort Hays State University	M,O
Framingham State College	M
Franciscan University of Steubenville	M
Fresno Pacific University	M
Friends University	M
Frostburg State University	M
Gallaudet University	M,D,O
Gardner–Webb University	M
George Mason University	M
The George Washington University	M,D,O
Georgia College and State University	M,O
Georgian Court College	M
Georgia Southern University	M,D,O
Georgia State University	M,D,O
Gonzaga University	M,D
Governors State University	M
Grambling State University	D
Grand Valley State University	M
Gwynedd–Mercy College	M
Harding University	M
Harvard University	M,D,O
Henderson State University	M
Heritage College	M
Hofstra University	M,D,O
Hood College	M
Houston Baptist University	M
Howard University	M,O
Hunter College of the City University of New York	O
Idaho State University	M,D,O
Illinois State University	M,D
Immaculata College	M,D,O
Indiana State University	M,D,O
Indiana University Bloomington	M,D,O
Indiana University of Pennsylvania	M,D,O
Indiana University–Purdue University Fort Wayne	M
Indiana University–Purdue University Indianapolis	M
Inter American University of Puerto Rico, Metropolitan Campus	M
Inter American University of Puerto Rico, San Germán Campus	M
Iona College (New Rochelle)	M,O
Iowa State University of Science and Technology	M,D
Jackson State University	M,D,O
Jacksonville State University	M,O
Jacksonville University	M
James Madison University	M
John Carroll University	M
Johns Hopkins University	M,D,O
Johnson State College	M
Kansas State University	M,D
Kean University	M,O
Keene State College	M
Kent State University	M,D,O
Kutztown University of Pennsylvania	M
Lamar University	M
La Sierra University	M,D,O
Lehigh University	M,D,O
Lesley College	M,O
Lewis University	O
Liberty University	M
Lincoln University (MO)	M
Long Island University, Brooklyn Campus	M,O
Long Island University, C.W. Post Campus	M,O
Longwood College	M
Louisiana State University and Agricultural and Mechanical College	M,D,O
Louisiana Tech University	D
Loyola College	M,O
Loyola Marymount University	M
Loyola University Chicago	M,D
Lynchburg College	M
Madonna University	M
Manhattan College	M,O
Mankato State University	M,O
Marian College of Fond du Lac	M
Marshall University	M,D,O
Marygrove College	M
Marywood University	M
McNeese State University	M,O
Miami University	M,D
Michigan State University	M,D,O
Middle Tennessee State University	M,O
Midwestern State University	M
Mississippi College	M
Mississippi State University	M,D,O
Monmouth University	M,O
Montclair State University	M
Moorhead State University	M,O
Morehead State University	O
Morgan State University	M,D
Mount St. Mary's College	M
Murray State University	O
National–Louis University	M,D,O
National University	M
New Jersey City University	M
New Mexico Highlands University	M
New Mexico State University	M,D,O
New York University	M,D,O
Niagara University	M,O
Nicholls State University	M
Norfolk State University	M
North Carolina Agricultural and Technical State University	M
North Carolina Central University	M
North Dakota State University	M,O
Northeastern Illinois University	M
Northeastern State University	M
Northeast Louisiana University	M,D,O
Northern Arizona University	M,D
Northern Illinois University	M,D,O
Northern Michigan University	M
Northern State University	M
Northwestern State University of Louisiana	M,O
Northwestern University	M
Northwest Missouri State University	M,O
Notre Dame College	M
Nova Southeastern University	M,D,O
Oakland University	M,O
The Ohio State University	M,D,O
Ohio University	M,D,O
Oklahoma State University	M,D,O
Old Dominion University	M,O
Oral Roberts University	M
Oregon State University	M
Our Lady of the Lake University of San Antonio	M
Pace University	M,O
Pacific Lutheran University	M
Pennsylvania State University University Park Campus	M,D
Pepperdine University (Culver City)	M,D
Pittsburg State University	M,O
Plattsburgh State University of New York	M,O
Plymouth State College of the University System of New Hampshire	M
Portland State University	M,D
Prairie View A&M University	M
Providence College	M
Purdue University	M,D,O
Purdue University Calumet	M
Queens College of the City University of New York	O
Radford University	M
Rhode Island College	M,O
Rider University	M
Rivier College	M
Roosevelt University	M,D
Rowan University	M,D,O
Rutgers, The State University of New Jersey, New Brunswick	M,D,O
Sacred Heart University	O
Saginaw Valley State University	M,O
St. Bonaventure University	M,O
St. Cloud State University	M,O
Saint Francis College (PA)	M
St. John's University (NY)	M,D,O
Saint Louis University	M,D,O
Saint Mary's College of California	M
Saint Mary's University of Minnesota	M,D
St. Mary's University of San Antonio	M
Saint Michael's College	M,O
Saint Peter's College (Jersey City)	M,O
Saint Xavier University	M
Salem State College	M
Salisbury State University	M
Samford University	M,O
Sam Houston State University	M
San Diego State University	M
San Francisco State University	M,O
San Jose State University	M,O
Santa Clara University	M
Seattle Pacific University	M,D
Seattle University	M,D,O
Seton Hall University	M,D,O
Shippensburg University of Pennsylvania	M
Sonoma State University	M
South Carolina State University	D,O
South Dakota State University	M
Southeastern Louisiana University	M,O
Southeastern Oklahoma State University	M
Southeast Missouri State University	M,D,O
Southern Connecticut State University	O
Southern Illinois University at Carbondale	M,D
Southern Illinois University at Edwardsville	M,O
Southern Oregon University	M
Southern University and Agricultural and Mechanical College	M
Southwest Baptist University	M
Southwestern Oklahoma State University	M
Southwest Missouri State University	M,O
Southwest Texas State University	M
Spalding University	M,D
Springfield College (MA)	M,O
Stanford University	M,D
State University of New York at Albany	M,D,O
State University of New York at Buffalo	M,D,O
State University of New York at New Paltz	M,O
State University of New York at Oswego	M,D,O
State University of New York at Stony Brook	O
State University of New York College at Brockport	M,O
State University of New York College at Buffalo	M,O
State University of New York College at Cortland	O
State University of New York College at Fredonia	O
State University of West Georgia	M,D,O
Stephen F. Austin State University	M,D
Stetson University	M,O
Suffolk University	M,O
Sul Ross State University	M
Syracuse University	M,D,O
Tarleton State University	M,O
Teachers College, Columbia University	M,D
Temple University (Philadelphia)	M,D
Tennessee State University	M,D
Tennessee Technological University	M,O
Texas A&M International University	M
Texas A&M University (College Station)	M,D
Texas A&M University–Commerce	M,D
Texas A&M University–Corpus Christi	M,D
Texas A&M University–Kingsville	M,D
Texas Christian University	M
Texas Southern University	M,D
Texas Tech University	M,D,O
Texas Woman's University	M
Trevecca Nazarene University	M
Trinity College (DC)	M
Trinity University	M
Troy State University (Troy)	M
Troy State University Dothan	M,O
Troy State University Montgomery	O
Tuskegee University	M
Union College (KY)	O
United States International University	M,D
Universidad del Turabo	M
Universidad Metropolitana	M
The University of Akron	M,D
The University of Alabama (Tuscaloosa)	M,D,O
The University of Alabama at Birmingham	M,D,O
University of Alaska Anchorage	M
University of Alaska Fairbanks	M
The University of Arizona	M,D,O
University of Arkansas (Fayetteville)	M,D,O
University of Arkansas at Little Rock	M,D,O
University of Bridgeport	D,O
University of California, Berkeley	M,D
University of California, Irvine	D
University of California, Los Angeles	D
University of Central Arkansas	M,O
University of Central Florida	M,D,O
University of Central Oklahoma	M
University of Cincinnati	M,D,O
University of Colorado at Denver	M,D,O
University of Connecticut	M,D
University of Dayton	M,D,O
University of Delaware	M,D
University of Denver	M,D
University of Detroit Mercy	M,O
University of Florida	M,D,O
University of Georgia	M,D,O
University of Guam	M
University of Hartford	M,D,O
University of Hawaii at Manoa	M,D
University of Houston	M,D
University of Houston–Clear Lake	M
University of Idaho	M,D,O
University of Illinois at Chicago	M,D
University of Illinois at Springfield	M
University of Illinois at Urbana–Champaign	M,D,O
The University of Iowa	M,D,O
University of Kansas	M,D,O
University of Kentucky	D,O
University of La Verne	M,D,O
University of Louisville	M,D,O
University of Maine (Orono)	M,D,O
University of Mary	M
University of Mary Hardin–Baylor	M
University of Maryland, College Park	M,D
University of Massachusetts Amherst	M,D,O
University of Massachusetts Boston	M,D,O
University of Massachusetts Lowell	M,D,O
The University of Memphis	M,D,O
University of Miami	M,D,O
University of Michigan	M,D
University of Minnesota, Twin Cities Campus	M,D,O
University of Mississippi	M,D,O
University of Missouri–Columbia	M,D,O
University of Missouri–Kansas City	M,D,O
University of Missouri–St. Louis	M
The University of Montana–Missoula	M,O
University of Montevallo	O
University of Nebraska at Kearney	M,O
University of Nebraska at Omaha	M,D,O
University of Nebraska–Lincoln	M,D,O
University of Nevada, Las Vegas	M,D,O
University of Nevada, Reno	M,D,O
University of New Hampshire	M,O
University of New Mexico	M,D,O
University of New Orleans	M,D,O
University of North Alabama	M,O
The University of North Carolina at Chapel Hill	M,D
University of North Carolina at Charlotte	M,D,O
University of North Carolina at Greensboro	M,D,O
University of North Carolina at Pembroke	M
University of North Carolina at Wilmington	M
University of North Dakota	M,D,O
University of Northern Colorado	M,D,O
University of Northern Iowa	M,D
University of North Florida	M,D
University of North Texas	M,D
University of Oklahoma	M,D
University of Oregon	M,D
University of Pennsylvania	M,D
University of Pittsburgh	M,D
University of Puerto Rico, Río Piedras	M,D
University of Redlands	M
University of St. Thomas (MN)	M,D,O

University of San Diego	M,D
University of San Francisco	M,D
University of Scranton	M
University of South Alabama	M,O
University of South Carolina (Columbia)	M,D,O
University of South Dakota	M,D,O
University of Southern California	M,D
University of Southern Maine	M,O
University of Southern Mississippi	M,D,O
University of South Florida	M,D,O
University of Southwestern Louisiana	M
University of Tennessee at Chattanooga	M
University of Tennessee, Knoxville	M,D,O
The University of Texas at Austin	M,D
The University of Texas at Brownsville	M
The University of Texas at El Paso	D
The University of Texas at Tyler	M,O
The University of Texas of the Permian Basin	M
The University of Texas–Pan American	M
University of the Pacific	M,D
University of Toledo	M,D,O
University of Utah	M,D
University of Vermont	M,D
University of Virginia	M,D,O
University of Washington	M,D
The University of West Alabama	M
University of West Florida	M,O
University of Wisconsin–Green Bay	M
University of Wisconsin–La Crosse	M
University of Wisconsin–Madison	M,D
University of Wisconsin–Milwaukee	M
University of Wisconsin–Oshkosh	M
University of Wisconsin–Stevens Point	M
University of Wisconsin–Superior	M,O
University of Wisconsin–Whitewater	M
University of Wyoming	M,D,O
Valdosta State University	M,D,O
Vanderbilt University	M,D,O
Villanova University	M
Virginia Commonwealth University	M
Virginia Polytechnic Institute and State University	M,D,O
Virginia State University	M
Walla Walla College	M
Washburn University of Topeka	M
Washington State University	M,D
Wayne State College	M,O
Wayne State University	M,D,O
Western Carolina University	M,D,O
Western Illinois University	M,O
Western Kentucky University	M,D,O
Western Michigan University	M,D,O
Western New Mexico University	M
Western Washington University	M
Westfield State College	M,O
West Texas A&M University	M
West Virginia University	M,D
Whitworth College	M
Wichita State University	M,D
Wilkes University	M
William Carey College	M
Wilmington College (DE)	M,D
Winona State University	M,O
Winthrop University	M,O
Worcester State College	M
Wright State University	M,O
Xavier University	M
Xavier University of Louisiana	M
Yeshiva University	M,D,O
Youngstown State University	M,D

EDUCATIONAL MEASUREMENT AND EVALUATION

Abilene Christian University	M
Adelphi University	O
Angelo State University	M
Boston College	M,D,O
Claremont Graduate University	M,D
Cleveland State University	M
Cornell University	M,D
Florida State University	M,D,O
Gallaudet University	M
Georgia State University	M,D
Hofstra University	M
Houston Baptist University	M
Iowa State University of Science and Technology	M
Kent State University	M,D
Louisiana State University and Agricultural and Mechanical College	D
Loyola University Chicago	M,D
Michigan State University	D
Mississippi State University	M
Morehead State University	D
New York University	M
Northeastern University	M
Northwestern Oklahoma State University	M
Ohio University	M,D
Rutgers, The State University of New Jersey, New Brunswick	M,D
Seattle University	O
Southern Connecticut State University	M
Southern Illinois University at Carbondale	D
Southwestern Oklahoma State University	M
State University of New York at Albany	D
Sul Ross State University	M
Syracuse University	M,D,O
Teachers College, Columbia University	M,D
Texas A&M University (College Station)	M,D
Texas Christian University	M
The University of Alabama (Tuscaloosa)	D
University of California, Berkeley	M,D
University of Colorado at Boulder	D
University of Connecticut	M,D
University of Delaware	M,D
University of Denver	M,D
University of Florida	M,D,O
University of Hawaii at Manoa	D
The University of Iowa	M,D,O
University of Kentucky	M,D
University of Louisville	D
University of Maryland, College Park	M,D
University of Massachusetts Amherst	M,D,O
The University of Memphis	M,D
University of Miami	M,D
University of Michigan	D
University of Minnesota, Twin Cities Campus	M,D
University of Missouri–Kansas City	M
University of Nevada, Las Vegas	D
University of North Carolina at Greensboro	M,D
University of North Dakota	D
University of North Texas	D
University of Pennsylvania	M,D
University of Pittsburgh	M,D
University of Puerto Rico, Río Piedras	M
University of South Carolina (Columbia)	M,D
University of South Florida	M,D,O
University of Tennessee, Knoxville	D
The University of Texas–Pan American	M
University of the Incarnate Word	M
University of the Pacific	M
University of Toledo	M,D
University of Virginia	M,D
University of Washington	M,D
Utah State University	D
Vanderbilt University	M,D
Virginia Polytechnic Institute and State University	D
Washington University in St. Louis	D
Wayne State University	M,D
West Chester University of Pennsylvania	M
West Texas A&M University	M
Wilkes University	M

EDUCATIONAL MEDIA/INSTRUCTIONAL TECHNOLOGY

Alabama State University	M,O
Appalachian State University	M
Arizona State University	M,D
Arkansas Tech University	M
Auburn University	M
Azusa Pacific University	M
Barry University	M,D,O
Beaver College	M
Bloomsburg University of Pennsylvania	M
Boise State University	M
Boston University	M,D,O
Bridgewater State College	M
Brigham Young University	M,D
California State University, Chico	M
California State University, Los Angeles	M
California State University, San Bernardino	M
California State University, Stanislaus	M
Central Connecticut State University	M
Central Michigan University	M
Chestnut Hill College	M
Chicago State University	M
City University	M
The College of New Jersey	O
College of Notre Dame	M
Dowling College	O
East Carolina University	M,O
Eastern Washington University	M
East Tennessee State University	M
Emmanuel College (MA)	M
Emporia State University	M
Fairfield University	M,O
Florida Atlantic University	M
Florida State University	M,D,O
Fort Hays State University	M
Fresno Pacific University	M
Gannon University	M
George Mason University	M
The George Washington University	M
Georgia College and State University	M
Georgia Southern University	M,O
Georgia State University	M,D,O
Governors State University	M
Grand Valley State University	M
Harvard University	M
Indiana State University	M,D,O
Indiana University Bloomington	M,D,O
Inter American University of Puerto Rico, Metropolitan Campus	M
Iona College (New Rochelle)	M,O
Iowa State University of Science and Technology	M,D
Jackson State University	M
Jacksonville State University	M
Jacksonville University	M
James Madison University	M
Johns Hopkins University	M,O
Kent State University	M,D
Lehigh University	M,D
Long Island University, Brooklyn Campus	M,O
Longwood College	M
Mankato State University	M,O
Marshall University	M
Marywood University	M
McNeese State University	M
Mississippi State University	M
Montana State University–Billings	M
National-Louis University	M,O
National University	M
New York Institute of Technology	M,O
New York University	M,D,O
North Carolina Agricultural and Technical State University	M
North Carolina Central University	M
Northern Illinois University	M,D
Northwestern Oklahoma State University	M
Northwestern University	M,D
Nova Southeastern University	M,D,O
Oakland University	O
Ohio University	M
Old Dominion University	M
Our Lady of the Lake University of San Antonio	M
Pacific Lutheran University	M
Pennsylvania State University University Park Campus	M,D
Pepperdine University (Culver City)	M,D
Portland State University	M
Prairie View A&M University	M
Purdue University	M,D,O
Purdue University Calumet	M
Radford University	M
Rochester Institute of Technology	M
Rowan University	M,O
St. Cloud State University	M
Saint Michael's College	M
Salem State College	M
Salisbury State University	M
San Diego State University	M
San Francisco State University	M,O
San Jose State University	M,O
Seton Hall University	M,O
Southern Arkansas University–Magnolia	M
Southern Connecticut State University	M
Southern Illinois University at Edwardsville	M
Southern University and Agricultural and Mechanical College	M
Southwestern Oklahoma State University	M
State University of New York at Albany	M,O
State University of New York at Stony Brook	O
State University of New York College at Potsdam	M
State University of West Georgia	M,O
Teachers College, Columbia University	M,D
Tennessee State University	M
Texas A&M University (College Station)	M
Texas A&M University–Commerce	M
Texas Southern University	M
Texas Tech University	M,D
Towson University	M
United States International University	M,D
University of Arkansas (Fayetteville)	M
University of Arkansas at Little Rock	M
University of Central Arkansas	M
University of Central Florida	M,D
University of Central Oklahoma	M
University of Colorado at Denver	M
University of Connecticut	M,D
University of Florida	M,D,O
University of Georgia	M,D,O
University of Hartford	M
University of Hawaii at Manoa	M
University of Houston–Clear Lake	M
The University of Iowa	M,D,O
University of Maryland, Baltimore County	M
University of Maryland, College Park	M,D
University of Massachusetts Amherst	M,D,O
The University of Memphis	M,D
University of Nebraska at Kearney	M
University of Nevada, Las Vegas	M
University of New Mexico	M,D,O
University of North Carolina at Charlotte	M
University of Northern Colorado	M
University of Northern Iowa	M
University of Oregon	D
University of St. Thomas (MN)	M,O
University of South Alabama	M,D,O
University of South Carolina (Columbia)	M
University of Southern California	M
University of South Florida	M,D
University of Tennessee, Knoxville	M,D,O
The University of Texas at Brownsville	M
University of the Sacred Heart	M
University of Toledo	M
The University of West Alabama	M
University of Wisconsin–Stout	M
Utah State University	M,D,O
Valdosta State University	M
Virginia State University	M
Wayne State University	M,D,O
West Chester University of Pennsylvania	M
Western Illinois University	M
Western Kentucky University	M
Western Oregon University	M
Western Washington University	M
Westfield State College	M
West Texas A&M University	M
Winthrop University	M

EDUCATIONAL PSYCHOLOGY

American International College	M,D
Andrews University	M,D
Arizona State University	M,D
Auburn University	D
Austin Peay State University	O
Ball State University	M,D,O
Baylor University	M,D,O
Beaver College	O
Boston College	M,D
Brigham Young University	M,D
California State University, Long Beach	M
California State University, Northridge	M
The Catholic University of America	D
Chapman University	M
Clark Atlanta University	M,D
The College of Saint Rose	M
Cornell University	M,D
Eastern College	M
Eastern Illinois University	M,O
Eastern Michigan University	M
Edinboro University of Pennsylvania	M
Florida State University	M,D,O
Fordham University	M,D,O
Georgia State University	M,D
Graduate School and University Center of the City University of New York	D
Harvard University	M,D,O
Howard University	M,D,O
Illinois State University	M

P—first professional degree; M—master's degree; D—doctorate; O—other advanced degree.

Educational Psychology (continued)

Indiana State University	M,D,O
Indiana University Bloomington	M,D,O
Indiana University of Pennsylvania	M,O
John Carroll University	M
Kansas State University	M,D
Kean University	M
Kent State University	M
La Sierra University	M,O
Loyola Marymount University	M
Loyola University Chicago	M,D
Marist College	M
Miami University	M,O
Michigan State University	M,D
Minot State University	O
Mississippi State University	M,D
Montclair State University	M
Morehead State University	D
National–Louis University	M,D,O
New Jersey City University	M,O
Northeastern University	M
Northern Arizona University	D
Northern Illinois University	M,D
Oklahoma State University	M,D
Pennsylvania State University University Park Campus	M,D
Purdue University	M,D
Rhode Island College	M
Rutgers, The State University of New Jersey, New Brunswick	M,D
Southern Illinois University at Carbondale	M,D
Stanford University	M,D
State University of New York at Albany	M,D,O
State University of New York at Buffalo	M,D,O
Teachers College, Columbia University	M,D
Temple University (Philadelphia)	M,D
Tennessee Technological University	M,O
Texas A&M University (College Station)	M,D
Texas A&M University–Commerce	D
Texas Tech University	M,D,O
The University of Alabama (Tuscaloosa)	M,D,O
The University of Arizona	M,D
University of California, Davis	D
University of Colorado at Boulder	M,D
University of Colorado at Denver	M
University of Connecticut	M,D
University of Denver	M,D,O
University of Florida	M,D,O
University of Georgia	M,D,O
University of Hawaii at Manoa	M,D
University of Houston	M,D
University of Illinois at Urbana–Champaign	M,D,O
The University of Iowa	M,D,O
University of Kentucky	M,D,O
University of Mary Hardin–Baylor	M
University of Maryland, College Park	M,D,O
The University of Memphis	M,D
University of Minnesota, Duluth	M
University of Minnesota, Twin Cities Campus	M,D,O
University of Mississippi	M,D,O
University of Missouri–Columbia	M,D,O
University of Missouri–Kansas City	M
University of Nebraska at Omaha	M
University of Nebraska–Lincoln	M,O
University of Nevada, Las Vegas	M
University of Nevada, Reno	M,D,O
University of New Mexico	M,D
The University of North Carolina at Chapel Hill	M,D
University of Northern Colorado	M,D
University of Northern Iowa	M,O
University of Oklahoma	M,D
University of Pittsburgh	D
University of South Dakota	M,D,O
University of Southern California	M,D
University of Tennessee, Knoxville	M,D
The University of Texas at Austin	M,D
The University of Texas at El Paso	M
The University of Texas–Pan American	M
University of the Pacific	M,D
University of Toledo	M,D
University of Utah	M,D
University of Virginia	M,D,O
University of Wisconsin–Madison	M,D
University of Wisconsin–Milwaukee	M
Washington State University	M,D
Wayne State University	M,D,O
West Virginia University	M,D
Wichita State University	M

EDUCATION OF THE GIFTED

Arkansas State University	M
Arkansas Tech University	M
Ashland University	M
Barry University	M,D,O
California State University, Los Angeles	M
California State University, Northridge	M
Carthage College	M
Clark Atlanta University	M,O
Cleveland State University	M
College of New Rochelle	M,O
College of William and Mary	M
Converse College	M
Drury College	M
Emporia State University	M
Grand Valley State University	M
Hardin–Simmons University	M
Indiana State University	M,O
Jacksonville University	O
Johns Hopkins University	M,O
Johnson State College	M
Kent State University	M
Lenoir–Rhyne College	M
Mankato State University	M
Maryville University of Saint Louis	M
Millersville University of Pennsylvania	M
Norfolk State University	M
Northeastern Illinois University	M
Ohio University	M
Oklahoma City University	M
Purdue University	M
St. Cloud State University	M
Southern Arkansas University–Magnolia	M
Teachers College, Columbia University	M,D
Texas A&M International University	M
Texas A&M University (College Station)	M
University of Arkansas at Little Rock	M
University of Connecticut	M,D
University of Georgia	D
University of Houston	M
University of Kansas	M,D,O
University of Nebraska at Kearney	M
University of Northern Iowa	M
University of St. Thomas (MN)	M
University of South Alabama	M
University of Southern Mississippi	M,D,O
University of South Florida	M
University of Southwestern Louisiana	M
The University of Texas–Pan American	M
Whitworth College	M
William Carey College	M
Wright State University	M
Xavier University	M
Youngstown State University	M

EDUCATION OF THE MULTIPLY HANDICAPPED

Boston College	M
Cleveland State University	M
Fresno Pacific University	M
Gallaudet University	M,O
Georgia State University	M
Kent State University	M
Mankato State University	M
Minot State University	M
Montana State University–Billings	M
Norfolk State University	M
University of Arkansas at Little Rock	M
University of South Alabama	M
Valdosta State University	M,O
Western Oregon University	M
Wright State University	M
Xavier University	M

ELECTRICAL ENGINEERING

Alfred University	M
Arizona State University	M,D
Auburn University	M,D
Boston University	M,D
Bradley University	M
Brigham Young University	M,D
Brown University	M,D
California Institute of Technology	M,D,O
California Polytechnic State University, San Luis Obispo	M
California State Polytechnic University, Pomona	M
California State University, Chico	M
California State University, Fresno	M
California State University, Fullerton	M
California State University, Long Beach	M
California State University, Los Angeles	M
California State University, Northridge	M
California State University, Sacramento	M
Carnegie Mellon University	M,D
Case Western Reserve University	M,D
The Catholic University of America	M,D
City College of the City University of New York	M,D
Clarkson University	M,D
Clemson University	M,D
Cleveland State University	M,D
Colorado State University	M,D
Columbia University	M,D,O
Cornell University	M,D
Dartmouth College	M,D
Drexel University	M,D
Duke University	M,D
Fairleigh Dickinson University, Teaneck–Hackensack Campus	M
Florida Agricultural and Mechanical University	M,D
Florida Atlantic University	M,D
Florida Institute of Technology	M,D
Florida International University	M,D
Florida State University	M,D
Gannon University	M
George Mason University	M
The George Washington University	M,D,O
Georgia Institute of Technology	M,D
Gonzaga University	M
Graduate School and University Center of the City University of New York	D
Howard University	M,D
Illinois Institute of Technology	M,D
Indiana University–Purdue University Indianapolis	M,D
Iowa State University of Science and Technology	M,D
Johns Hopkins University	M,D
Kansas State University	M,D
Lamar University	M,D
Lehigh University	M,D
Louisiana State University and Agricultural and Mechanical College	M,D
Louisiana Tech University	M,D
Loyola Marymount University	M
Manhattan College	M
Mankato State University	M
Marquette University	M,D
Massachusetts Institute of Technology	M,D,O
McNeese State University	M
Mercer University (Macon)	M
Mercer University, Cecil B. Day Campus	M
Michigan State University	M,D
Michigan Technological University	M,D
Mississippi State University	M,D
Monmouth University	M
Montana State University–Bozeman	M,D
New Jersey Institute of Technology	M,D,O
New Mexico State University	M,D
New York Institute of Technology	M
North Carolina Agricultural and Technical State University	M,D
North Carolina State University	M,D
North Dakota State University	M
Northeastern University	M,D
Northern Illinois University	M
Northwestern University	M,D
Oakland University	M
The Ohio State University	M,D
Ohio University	M,D
Oklahoma State University	M,D
Old Dominion University	M,D
Oregon State University	M,D
Pennsylvania State University Harrisburg Campus of the Capital College	M
Pennsylvania State University University Park Campus	M,D
Polytechnic University, Brooklyn Campus	M,D
Polytechnic University, Farmingdale Campus	M,D
Polytechnic University, Westchester Graduate Center	M,D
Portland State University	M,D
Princeton University	M,D
Purdue University	M,D
Rensselaer Polytechnic Institute	M,D
Rice University	M,D
Rochester Institute of Technology	M
Rutgers, The State University of New Jersey, New Brunswick	M,D
St. Mary's University of San Antonio	M
San Diego State University	M
San Jose State University	M
Santa Clara University	M,D,O
South Dakota State University	M
Southern Illinois University at Carbondale	M,D
Southern Illinois University at Edwardsville	M
Southern Methodist University	M,D
Stanford University	M,D,O
State University of New York at Binghamton	M,D
State University of New York at Buffalo	M,D
State University of New York at Stony Brook	M,D,O
Stevens Institute of Technology	M,D,O
Syracuse University	M,D,O
Temple University (Philadelphia)	M
Tennessee Technological University	M,D
Texas A&M University (College Station)	M,D
Texas A&M University–Kingsville	M
Texas Tech University	M,D
Tufts University	M,D,O
Tulane University	M,D
Tuskegee University	M
The University of Akron	M,D
The University of Alabama (Tuscaloosa)	M,D
The University of Alabama at Birmingham	M,D
The University of Alabama in Huntsville	M,D
University of Alaska Fairbanks	M
The University of Arizona	M,D
University of Arkansas (Fayetteville)	M
University of Bridgeport	M
University of California, Berkeley	M,D
University of California, Davis	M,D
University of California, Irvine	M,D
University of California, Los Angeles	M,D
University of California, Riverside	M,D
University of California, San Diego	M,D
University of California, Santa Barbara	M,D
University of Central Florida	M,D
University of Cincinnati	M,D
University of Colorado at Boulder	M,D
University of Colorado at Colorado Springs	M,D
University of Colorado at Denver	M
University of Connecticut	M,D
University of Dayton	M,D
University of Delaware	M,D
University of Denver	M
University of Detroit Mercy	M,D
University of Florida	M,D,O
University of Hawaii at Manoa	M,D
University of Houston	M,D
University of Idaho	M,D
University of Illinois at Chicago	M,D
University of Illinois at Urbana–Champaign	M,D
The University of Iowa	M,D
University of Kansas	M,D
University of Kentucky	M,D
University of Louisville	M
University of Maine (Orono)	M
University of Maryland, Baltimore County	M,D
University of Maryland, College Park	M,D
University of Massachusetts Amherst	M,D
University of Massachusetts Dartmouth	M,D
University of Massachusetts Lowell	M,D
The University of Memphis	M,D
University of Miami	M,D
University of Michigan	M,D,O
University of Michigan–Dearborn	M
University of Minnesota, Twin Cities Campus	M,D
University of Missouri–Columbia	M,D
University of Missouri–Rolla	M,D
University of Nebraska–Lincoln	M,D
University of Nevada, Las Vegas	M,D
University of Nevada, Reno	M,D
University of New Hampshire	M,D
University of New Haven	M
University of New Mexico	M,D
University of New Orleans	M
University of North Carolina at Charlotte	M,D
University of North Dakota	M
University of Notre Dame	M,D
University of Oklahoma	M,D
University of Pennsylvania	M,D
University of Pittsburgh	M,D
University of Portland	M

University of Puerto Rico, Mayagüez Campus — M
University of Rhode Island — M,D
University of Rochester — M,D
University of South Alabama — M
University of South Carolina (Columbia) — M,D
University of Southern California — M,D,O
University of South Florida — M,D
University of Tennessee, Knoxville — M,D
The University of Texas at Arlington — M,D
The University of Texas at Austin — M,D
The University of Texas at Dallas — M,D
The University of Texas at El Paso — M,D
The University of Texas at San Antonio — M
University of Toledo — M,D
University of Tulsa — M
University of Utah — M,D,O
University of Vermont — M,D
University of Virginia — M,D
University of Washington — M,D
University of Wisconsin–Madison — M,D
University of Wyoming — M,D
Utah State University — M,D,O
Vanderbilt University — M,D
Villanova University — M
Virginia Polytechnic Institute and State University — M,D
Washington State University — M,D
Washington University in St. Louis — M,D
Wayne State University — M,D
Western Michigan University — M
Western New England College — M
West Virginia University — M,D
Wichita State University — M,D
Widener University — M
Wilkes University — M
Worcester Polytechnic Institute — M,D
Wright State University — M
Yale University — M,D
Youngstown State University — M

ELECTRONIC MATERIALS

Massachusetts Institute of Technology — D
Princeton University — M,D

ELEMENTARY EDUCATION

Abilene Christian University — M
Adams State College — M
Adelphi University — M
Alabama Agricultural and Mechanical University — M,O
Alabama State University — M,O
Alaska Pacific University — M
Alcorn State University — M,O
Alfred University — M
American International College — M,O
American University — M
Andrews University — M
Appalachian State University — M
Arizona State University West — M
Arkansas State University — M,O
Arkansas Tech University — M
Armstrong Atlantic State University — M,D,O
Auburn University — M,D,O
Auburn University Montgomery — M,O
Austin Peay State University — M,O
Ball State University — M,D
Barry University — M
Baruch College of the City University of New York — M
Beaver College — M,O
Bellarmine College — M
Belmont University — M
Benedictine University — M
Bloomsburg University of Pennsylvania — M
Boston College — M
Boston University — M
Bowie State University — M
Bowling Green State University — M
Bridgewater State College — M
Brigham Young University — M
Brooklyn College of the City University of New York — M
Brown University — M
Butler University — M
California State University, Fullerton — M
California State University, Long Beach — M
California State University, Los Angeles — M
California State University, Northridge — M
California State University, San Bernardino — M
California State University, Stanislaus — M

California University of Pennsylvania — M
Campbell University — M
Centenary College of Louisiana — M
Central Connecticut State University — M
Central Michigan University — M
Central Missouri State University — M
Central Washington University — M
Chadron State College — M
Charleston Southern University — M
Chestnut Hill College — M
Cheyney University of Pennsylvania — M
Chicago State University — M
City College of the City University of New York — M
Clarion University of Pennsylvania — M
Clemson University — M
Cleveland State University — M
College of Mount St. Joseph — M
The College of New Jersey — M
College of New Rochelle — M
College of Notre Dame — M,O
The College of Saint Rose — M
College of Staten Island of the City University of New York — M
Columbia College (IL) — M
Converse College — M
Cumberland College — M,O
Dallas Baptist University — M
Delta State University — M,O
DePaul University — M
Dowling College — M
Drake University — M
Drury College — M
Duquesne University — M
D'Youville College — M
East Carolina University — M
Eastern Connecticut State University — M
Eastern Illinois University — M
Eastern Kentucky University — M
Eastern Michigan University — M
Eastern Nazarene College — M,O
Eastern Washington University — M
East Stroudsburg University of Pennsylvania — M
East Tennessee State University — M
Edinboro University of Pennsylvania — M
Elmira College — M
Elon College — M
Emporia State University — M
Fairfield University — M
Fairleigh Dickinson University, Teaneck–Hackensack Campus — M
Fayetteville State University — M
Fitchburg State College — M
Florida Agricultural and Mechanical University — M
Florida Atlantic University — M,D
Florida International University — M
Florida State University — M,D,O
Fordham University — M
Fort Hays State University — M
Francis Marion University — M
Friends University — M
Frostburg State University — M
Gallaudet University — M,O
Gardner–Webb University — M
The George Washington University — M
Grambling State University — M
Grand Valley State University — M
Hampton University — M
Harding University — M
Hardin–Simmons University — M
Harvard University — D
Henderson State University — M
Hofstra University — M
Hood College — M
Houston Baptist University — M
Howard University — M
Hunter College of the City University of New York — M
Immaculata College — O
Indiana State University — M,D,O
Indiana University Bloomington — M,O
Indiana University Kokomo — M
Indiana University Northwest — M
Indiana University of Pennsylvania — D
Indiana University–Purdue University Fort Wayne — M
Indiana University–Purdue University Indianapolis — M
Indiana University South Bend — M
Indiana University Southeast — M
Inter American University of Puerto Rico, Metropolitan Campus — M
Iona College (New Rochelle) — M
Iowa State University of Science and Technology — M
Jackson State University — M,D,O
Jacksonville State University — M

Jacksonville University — M
John Carroll University — M
Johns Hopkins University — M
Kansas State University — M
Kennesaw State University — M
Kent State University — M
Kutztown University of Pennsylvania — M
Lamar University — M,O
Lander University — M
Lehigh University — M,D,O
Lehman College of the City University of New York — M
Lenoir–Rhyne College — M
Lesley College — M
Liberty University — M
Lincoln University (MO) — M
Long Island University, Brooklyn Campus — M
Long Island University, C.W. Post Campus — M
Long Island University, Southampton College — M
Longwood College — M
Louisiana State University and Agricultural and Mechanical College — M
Loyola Marymount University — M
Loyola University New Orleans — M
Maharishi University of Management — M
Mankato State University — M,O
Mansfield University of Pennsylvania — M
Marshall University — M
Marymount University — M
Maryville University of Saint Louis — M
Marywood University — M
McNeese State University — M
Miami University — M
Middle Tennessee State University — M,O
Midwestern State University — M
Millersville University of Pennsylvania — M
Minot State University — M
Mississippi College — M
Mississippi State University — M,D,O
Monmouth University — M
Montana State University–Northern — M
Moorhead State University — M
Morehead State University — M
Morgan State University — M
Mount Saint Mary College — M
Mount St. Mary's College — M
Murray State University — M,O
National–Louis University — M
Nazareth College of Rochester — M
New York Institute of Technology — M
New York University — M,D,O
Niagara University — M
North Carolina Agricultural and Technical State University — M
North Carolina Central University — M
Northeastern State University — M
Northeast Louisiana University — M,O
Northern Arizona University — M
Northern Illinois University — M
Northern Kentucky University — M
Northern Michigan University — M
Northern State University — M
Northwestern Oklahoma State University — M
Northwestern State University of Louisiana — M,O
Northwestern University — M
Northwest Missouri State University — M
Notre Dame College — M
Nova Southeastern University — M,O
Ohio University — M
Oklahoma City University — M
Old Dominion University — M
Olivet Nazarene University — M
Oregon State University — M
Pacific Lutheran University — M
Pacific University — M
Pennsylvania State University University Park Campus — M,D
Phillips University — M
Pittsburg State University — M,O
Plattsburgh State University of New York — M
Plymouth State College of the University System of New Hampshire — M
Portland State University — M
Purdue University — M
Purdue University Calumet — M
Queens College — M
Queens College of the City University of New York — M,O
Rhode Island College — M
Rivier College — M
Rockford College — M
Rollins College — M

Roosevelt University — M
Rowan University — M,O
Rutgers, The State University of New Jersey, New Brunswick — M,D,O
Sacred Heart University — M
Sage Graduate School — M
Saginaw Valley State University — M
St. Cloud State University — M
St. John's University (NY) — M
Saint Joseph College (CT) — M
Saint Peter's College (Jersey City) — O
St. Thomas University — M
Salem State College — M
Salisbury State University — M
Samford University — M,O
Sam Houston State University — M,O
San Diego State University — M
San Francisco State University — M
San Jose State University — M
Seton Hall University — M
Shippensburg University of Pennsylvania — M
Simmons College — M
Slippery Rock University of Pennsylvania — M
South Carolina State University — M
Southeastern Louisiana University — M,O
Southeastern Oklahoma State University — M
Southeast Missouri State University — M
Southern Arkansas University–Magnolia — M
Southern Connecticut State University — M
Southern Illinois University at Edwardsville — M
Southern Oregon University — M
Southern University and Agricultural and Mechanical College — M
Southern Utah University — M
Southwestern Oklahoma State University — M
Southwest Missouri State University — M
Southwest Texas State University — M
Spalding University — M
Spring Hill College — M
State University of New York at Binghamton — M
State University of New York at Buffalo — M,D
State University of New York at New Paltz — M
State University of New York at Oswego — M
State University of New York College at Brockport — M
State University of New York College at Buffalo — M
State University of New York College at Cortland — M
State University of New York College at Fredonia — M
State University of New York College at Geneseo — M
State University of New York College at Oneonta — M
State University of New York College at Potsdam — M
Stephen F. Austin State University — M
Stetson University — M
Sul Ross State University — M
Syracuse University — M,O
Tarleton State University — M,O
Teachers College, Columbia University — M
Temple University (Philadelphia) — M,O
Tennessee State University — M,D
Tennessee Technological University — M,O
Texas A&M International University — M
Texas A&M University–Commerce — M,D
Texas A&M University–Corpus Christi — M
Texas A&M University–Kingsville — M
Texas A&M University–Texarkana — M
Texas Christian University — M
Texas Southern University — M
Texas Tech University — M,D,O
Texas Woman's University — M
Towson University — M,O
Trevecca Nazarene University — M
Trinity College (DC) — M
Troy State University (Troy) — M,O
Troy State University Dothan — M,O
Troy State University Montgomery — M
Tufts University — M
Union College (KY) — M
The University of Akron — M,D

P—first professional degree; M—master's degree; D—doctorate; O—other advanced degree.

Elementary Education (continued)

The University of Alabama (Tuscaloosa)	M,D,O
The University of Alabama at Birmingham	M,O
University of Alaska Southeast	M
The University of Arizona	M,D
University of Arkansas (Fayetteville)	M
University of Arkansas at Little Rock	M,O
University of Bridgeport	M,O
University of Central Arkansas	M
University of Central Florida	M
University of Central Oklahoma	M
University of Cincinnati	M,D
University of Connecticut	M,D
University of Florida	M,D,O
University of Georgia	M,D,O
University of Hartford	M
University of Hawaii at Manoa	M
University of Houston	M
University of Idaho	M
University of Illinois at Chicago	M
University of Indianapolis	M
The University of Iowa	M,D,O
University of Louisville	M,O
University of Maine (Orono)	M,O
University of Mary	M
University of Massachusetts Amherst	M,D,O
University of Massachusetts Boston	M
The University of Memphis	M
University of Miami	M,O
University of Minnesota, Twin Cities Campus	M,D
University of Missouri–Kansas City	M
University of Missouri–St. Louis	M
University of Montevallo	M,O
University of Nebraska at Kearney	M
University of Nebraska at Omaha	M
University of Nevada, Las Vegas	M
University of Nevada, Reno	M
University of New Hampshire	M
University of New Mexico	M
University of North Alabama	M
The University of North Carolina at Chapel Hill	M
University of North Carolina at Charlotte	M
University of North Carolina at Greensboro	M
University of North Carolina at Pembroke	M
University of North Carolina at Wilmington	M
University of North Dakota	M,D
University of Northern Colorado	M,D
University of North Florida	M
University of North Texas	M
University of Oklahoma	M,D
University of Pennsylvania	M
University of Pittsburgh	M
University of Puerto Rico, Río Piedras	M
University of Rhode Island	M
University of Richmond	M
University of Scranton	M
University of South Alabama	M,O
University of South Carolina (Columbia)	M,D
University of South Dakota	M
University of Southern Indiana	M
University of Southern Mississippi	M,D,O
University of South Florida	M,D,O
University of Tennessee, Knoxville	M,D,O
The University of Texas at Brownsville	M
The University of Texas at Tyler	M,O
The University of Texas of the Permian Basin	M
The University of Texas–Pan American	M
University of the Incarnate Word	M
University of Toledo	M
University of Utah	M
The University of West Alabama	M
University of West Florida	M
University of Wisconsin–Eau Claire	M
University of Wisconsin–La Crosse	M
University of Wisconsin–Milwaukee	M
University of Wisconsin–Platteville	M
University of Wisconsin–River Falls	M
University of Wisconsin–Stevens Point	M
Utah State University	M
Vanderbilt University	M,D
Villanova University	M
Virginia State University	M
Wagner College	M
Washington State University	M,D
Washington University in St. Louis	M,O
Wayne State College	M
Wayne State University	M
West Chester University of Pennsylvania	M
Western Carolina University	M
Western Connecticut State University	M
Western Illinois University	M
Western Kentucky University	M,O
Western Michigan University	M
Western New Mexico University	M
Western Oregon University	M
Western Washington University	M
Westfield State College	M
West Texas A&M University	M
West Virginia University	M
Wilkes University	M
William Carey College	M
William Paterson University of New Jersey	M
Wilmington College (DE)	M
Winona State University	M
Winthrop University	M,O
Worcester State College	M
Wright State University	M
Xavier University	M
Youngstown State University	M

EMERGENCY MEDICAL SERVICES

Allegheny University of the Health Sciences	M

ENERGY AND POWER ENGINEERING

New Jersey Institute of Technology	M
Rensselaer Polytechnic Institute	M,D
Southern Illinois University at Carbondale	D
University of Massachusetts Lowell	M,D
The University of Memphis	M
University of North Dakota	D
Worcester Polytechnic Institute	M,D

ENERGY MANAGEMENT AND POLICY

Boston University	M
Colorado School of Mines	M,O
New York Institute of Technology	M
University of California, Berkeley	M,D
University of Maryland, Baltimore County	M,D
University of Pittsburgh	M

ENGINEERING AND APPLIED SCIENCES

Alabama Agricultural and Mechanical University	M
Arizona State University	M,D
Auburn University	M,D
Boston University	M,D
Bradley University	M
Brigham Young University	M,D
Brown University	M,D
California Institute of Technology	M,D,O
California Polytechnic State University, San Luis Obispo	M
California State Polytechnic University, Pomona	M
California State University, Chico	M
California State University, Fresno	M
California State University, Fullerton	M
California State University, Long Beach	M,D,O
California State University, Los Angeles	M
California State University, Northridge	M
California State University, Sacramento	M
Carnegie Mellon University	M,D
Case Western Reserve University	M,D
The Catholic University of America	M,D
Central Missouri State University	D
Christian Brothers University	M
City College of the City University of New York	M,D
Clarkson University	M,D
Clemson University	M,D
Cleveland State University	M,D
College of William and Mary	M,D
Colorado School of Mines	M,D,O
Colorado State University	M,D
Columbia University	M,D,O
Cornell University	M,D
Dartmouth College	M,D
Drexel University	M,D
Duke University	M,D
East Carolina University	M
Eastern Illinois University	M
East Tennessee State University	M
Fairleigh Dickinson University, Teaneck–Hackensack Campus	M
Florida Agricultural and Mechanical University	M,D
Florida Atlantic University	M,D
Florida Institute of Technology	M,D
Florida International University	M,D
Florida State University	M,D
Gannon University	M
George Mason University	M,D
The George Washington University	M,D,O
Georgia Institute of Technology	M,D,O
Golden Gate University	M,O
Gonzaga University	M
Graduate School and University Center of the City University of New York	D
Harvard University	M,D,O
Howard University	M,D
Idaho State University	M,D
Illinois Institute of Technology	M,D
Indiana State University	M,D
Indiana University–Purdue University Fort Wayne	M
Indiana University–Purdue University Indianapolis	M,D
Iowa State University of Science and Technology	M,D
Johns Hopkins University	M,D
Kansas State University	M,D
Lamar University	M,D
Lehigh University	M,D
Louisiana State University and Agricultural and Mechanical College	M,D
Louisiana Tech University	M,D
Loyola College	M
Loyola Marymount University	M
Manhattan College	M
Marquette University	M,D
Marshall University	M
Massachusetts Institute of Technology	M,D,O
McNeese State University	M
Mercer University (Macon)	M
Mercer University, Cecil B. Day Campus	M
Miami University	M
Michigan State University	M,D
Michigan Technological University	M,D
Mississippi State University	M,D
Montana State University–Bozeman	M,D
Montana Tech of The University of Montana	M
Morgan State University	M,D
Murray State University	M
National University	M
New Jersey Institute of Technology	M,D,O
New Mexico State University	M,D
New York Institute of Technology	M,O
North Carolina Agricultural and Technical State University	M,D
North Carolina State University	M,D,O
North Dakota State University	M,D
Northeastern University	M,D
Northern Illinois University	M
Northwestern University	M,D
Oakland University	M,D
The Ohio State University	M,D
Ohio University	M,D
Oklahoma State University	M,D
Old Dominion University	M,D
Oregon State University	M,D
Pennsylvania State University at Erie, The Behrend College	M
Pennsylvania State University Harrisburg Campus of the Capital College	M
Pennsylvania State University University Park Campus	M,D
Pittsburg State University	M
Portland State University	M,D
Prairie View A&M University	M
Princeton University	M,D
Purdue University	M,D
Purdue University Calumet	M
Rensselaer Polytechnic Institute	M,D
Rice University	M,D
Rochester Institute of Technology	M,O
Rowan University	M
Rutgers, The State University of New Jersey, New Brunswick	M,D
Saginaw Valley State University	M
St. Cloud State University	M
St. Mary's University of San Antonio	M
San Diego State University	M,D
San Francisco State University	M
San Jose State University	M
Santa Clara University	M,D,O
Seattle University	M
South Dakota State University	M,D
Southern Illinois University at Carbondale	M,D
Southern Illinois University at Edwardsville	M
Southern Methodist University	M,D
Stanford University	M,D,O
State University of New York at Binghamton	M,D
State University of New York at Buffalo	M,D
State University of New York at New Paltz	M
State University of New York at Stony Brook	M,D,O
State University of New York Institute of Technology at Utica/Rome	M
Stevens Institute of Technology	M,D,O
Syracuse University	M,D,O
Temple University (Philadelphia)	M,D
Tennessee State University	M
Tennessee Technological University	M,D
Texas A&M University (College Station)	M,D
Texas A&M University–Kingsville	M
Texas Tech University	M,D
Tufts University	M,D
Tulane University	M,D
Tuskegee University	M
The University of Akron	M,D
The University of Alabama (Tuscaloosa)	M,D
The University of Alabama at Birmingham	M,D
The University of Alabama in Huntsville	M,D
University of Alaska Anchorage	M
The University of Arizona	M,D
University of Arkansas (Fayetteville)	M,D
University of Arkansas at Little Rock	M,D
University of Bridgeport	M
University of California, Berkeley	M,D
University of California, Davis	M,D,O
University of California, Irvine	M,D
University of California, Los Angeles	M,D
University of California, Riverside	M,D
University of California, San Diego	M,D
University of California, Santa Barbara	M,D
University of Central Florida	M,D
University of Cincinnati	M,D
University of Colorado at Boulder	M,D
University of Colorado at Colorado Springs	M,D
University of Colorado at Denver	M,D
University of Connecticut	M,D
University of Dayton	M,D
University of Delaware	M,D
University of Denver	M,D
University of Detroit Mercy	M,D
University of Florida	M,D,O
University of Hartford	M
University of Hawaii at Manoa	M,D
University of Houston	M,D
University of Idaho	M,D
University of Illinois at Chicago	M,D
University of Illinois at Urbana–Champaign	M,D
The University of Iowa	M,D
University of Kansas	M,D
University of Kentucky	M,D
University of Louisville	M,D
University of Maine (Orono)	M,D
University of Maryland, Baltimore County	M,D
University of Maryland, College Park	M,D
University of Massachusetts Amherst	M,D
University of Massachusetts Dartmouth	M,D
University of Massachusetts Lowell	M,D
The University of Memphis	M,D
University of Miami	M,D
University of Michigan	M,D,O
University of Michigan–Dearborn	M,D
University of Minnesota, Twin Cities Campus	M,D
University of Mississippi	M,D
University of Missouri–Columbia	M,D
University of Missouri–Rolla	M,D
University of Nebraska–Lincoln	M,D
University of Nevada, Las Vegas	M,D
University of Nevada, Reno	M,D
University of New Hampshire	M,D
University of New Haven	M,O
University of New Mexico	M,D
University of New Orleans	M,D,O
University of North Carolina at Charlotte	M,D

University of North Dakota	M,D
University of North Texas	M
University of Notre Dame	M,D
University of Oklahoma	M,D
University of Pennsylvania	M,D
University of Pittsburgh	M,D,O
University of Portland	M
University of Puerto Rico, Mayagüez Campus	M,D
University of Rhode Island	M,D
University of Rochester	M,D
University of St. Thomas (MN)	M,O
University of South Alabama	M
University of South Carolina (Columbia)	M,D
University of Southern California	M,D,O
University of Southern Indiana	M
University of Southern Mississippi	M
University of South Florida	M,D
University of Southwestern Louisiana	M,D
University of Tennessee at Chattanooga	M
University of Tennessee, Knoxville	M,D
The University of Texas at Arlington	M,D
The University of Texas at Austin	M,D
The University of Texas at Dallas	M,D
The University of Texas at El Paso	M,D
The University of Texas at San Antonio	M
The University of Texas at Tyler	M
University of Toledo	M,D
University of Tulsa	M,D
University of Utah	M,D,O
University of Vermont	M,D
University of Virginia	M,D
University of Washington	M,D
University of Wisconsin–Madison	M,D,O
University of Wisconsin–Milwaukee	M,D
University of Wyoming	M,D
Utah State University	M,D,O
Vanderbilt University	M,D
Villanova University	M,O
Virginia Commonwealth University	M,D
Virginia Polytechnic Institute and State University	M,D
Washington State University	M,D
Washington University in St. Louis	M,D
Wayne State University	M,D,O
Western Michigan University	M,D
Western New England College	M
West Texas A&M University	M
West Virginia University	M,D
Wichita State University	M,D
Widener University	M
Wilkes University	M
Worcester Polytechnic Institute	M,D
Wright State University	M,D
Yale University	M,D
Youngstown State University	M

ENGINEERING DESIGN

The Catholic University of America	D
Stanford University	M
Stevens Institute of Technology	M
University of Illinois at Urbana–Champaign	M
University of New Haven	O

ENGINEERING MANAGEMENT

Brigham Young University	M
California Polytechnic State University, San Luis Obispo	
California State University, Northridge	M
The Catholic University of America	M
Clarkson University	M
Colorado State University	M
Dartmouth College	M
Drexel University	M,D
Duke University	M
Florida Institute of Technology	M
The George Washington University	M,D,O
Lamar University	M
Long Island University, C.W. Post Campus	M
Loyola Marymount University	M
Marquette University	M
Marshall University	M
Massachusetts Institute of Technology	M,O
Mercer University (Macon)	M
Mercer University, Cecil B. Day Campus	M
New Jersey Institute of Technology	M

Northeastern University	M
Northwestern University	M,D
Oakland University	M
Ohio University	M
Old Dominion University	M,D
Pennsylvania State University University Park Campus	M
Portland State University	M,D
Rensselaer Polytechnic Institute	M,D
Rochester Institute of Technology	M
Saint Martin's College	M
St. Mary's University of San Antonio	M
Santa Clara University	M
Southern Methodist University	M,D
Stanford University	M,D,O
Syracuse University	M
Tufts University	M
The University of Akron	M
The University of Alabama in Huntsville	M,D
University of Alaska Anchorage	M
University of Alaska Fairbanks	M
University of Central Florida	M
University of Colorado at Boulder	M
University of Dayton	M
University of Denver	M
University of Detroit Mercy	M
University of Florida	M,D
University of Kansas	M
University of Maryland, Baltimore County	M
University of Maryland University College	M
University of Massachusetts Amherst	M
University of Michigan–Dearborn	M
University of Missouri–Rolla	M,D
University of New Orleans	M,O
University of Southern California	M
University of South Florida	M,D
University of Southwestern Louisiana	M
University of Tennessee at Chattanooga	M
University of Tennessee, Knoxville	M
University of Tulsa	M
University of Utah	M
Virginia Polytechnic Institute and State University	M
Wayne State University	M
Western Michigan University	M
Widener University	M
Worcester Polytechnic Institute	M

ENGINEERING PHYSICS

Cornell University	M,D
George Mason University	M
Mississippi State University	D
Polytechnic University, Farmingdale Campus	M
Polytechnic University, Westchester Graduate Center	M
Rensselaer Polytechnic Institute	M,D
Stevens Institute of Technology	M,D,O
University of California, San Diego	M,D
University of Florida	M,D,O
University of Maine (Orono)	M
University of Oklahoma	M,D
University of South Florida	D
University of Vermont	M
University of Virginia	M,D
University of Wisconsin–Madison	M,D
Yale University	M,D

ENGLISH

Abilene Christian University	M
Adelphi University	M
American University	M
Andrews University	M
Angelo State University	M
Appalachian State University	M
Arizona State University	M,D
Arkansas State University	M,O
Auburn University	M,D
Austin Peay State University	M
Ball State University	M,D
Baylor University	M,D
Beaver College	M
Bemidji State University	M
Boise State University	M
Boston College	M,D,O
Boston University	M,D
Bowling Green State University	M,D
Bradley University	M
Brandeis University	M,D
Bridgewater State College	M
Brigham Young University	M
Brooklyn College of the City University of New York	M
Brown University	M,D
Butler University	M
California Polytechnic State University, San Luis Obispo	M

California State Polytechnic University, Pomona	M
California State University, Bakersfield	M
California State University, Chico	M
California State University, Dominguez Hills	M,O
California State University, Fresno	M
California State University, Fullerton	M
California State University, Hayward	M
California State University, Long Beach	M
California State University, Los Angeles	M
California State University, Northridge	M
California State University, Sacramento	M
California State University, San Bernardino	M
California State University, San Marcos	M
California State University, Stanislaus	M
California University of Pennsylvania	M
Carnegie Mellon University	M,D
Case Western Reserve University	M,D
The Catholic University of America	M,D
Central Connecticut State University	M
Central Michigan University	M
Central Missouri State University	M
Central Washington University	M
Chapman University	M
Chicago State University	M
The Citadel, The Military College of South Carolina	M
City College of the City University of New York	M
Claremont Graduate University	M,D
Clarion University of Pennsylvania	M
Clark Atlanta University	M
Clark University	M
Clemson University	M
Cleveland State University	M
The College of New Jersey	M
College of Notre Dame	M
The College of Saint Rose	M
College of Staten Island of the City University of New York	M
College of William and Mary	M
Colorado State University	M
Columbia University	M,D
Cornell University	M,D
DePaul University	M
Duke University	D
Duquesne University	M,D
East Carolina University	M
Eastern Illinois University	M
Eastern Kentucky University	M
Eastern Michigan University	M
Eastern New Mexico University	M
Eastern Washington University	M
East Tennessee State University	M
Emory University	M,D
Emporia State University	M
Fairleigh Dickinson University, Teaneck–Hackensack Campus	M
Fayetteville State University	M
Florida Atlantic University	M
Florida International University	M
Florida State University	M,D
Fordham University	M,D
Fort Hays State University	M
Gannon University	M
George Mason University	M
Georgetown University	M
The George Washington University	M,D
Georgia College and State University	M
Georgia Southern University	M
Georgia State University	M,D
Gonzaga University	M
Governors State University	M
Graduate School and University Center of the City University of New York	D
Hardin–Simmons University	M
Harvard University	M,D,O
Henderson State University	M
Hofstra University	M
Holy Names College	M
Howard University	M,D
Humboldt State University	M
Hunter College of the City University of New York	M
Idaho State University	M,D
Illinois State University	M
Indiana State University	M,O
Indiana University Bloomington	M,D

Indiana University of Pennsylvania	M,D
Indiana University–Purdue University Fort Wayne	M
Iona College (New Rochelle)	M
Iowa State University of Science and Technology	M,D
Jackson State University	M
Jacksonville State University	M
James Madison University	M
John Carroll University	M
Johns Hopkins University	D
Kansas State University	M
Kent State University	M,D
Kutztown University of Pennsylvania	M
Lamar University	M
La Sierra University	M
Lehigh University	M,D
Lehman College of the City University of New York	M
Long Island University, Brooklyn Campus	M
Long Island University, C.W. Post Campus	M
Long Island University, Southampton College	M
Longwood College	M
Louisiana State University and Agricultural and Mechanical College	M,D
Louisiana Tech University	M
Loyola Marymount University	M
Loyola University Chicago	M,D
Maharishi University of Management	M
Mankato State University	M
Marquette University	M,D
Marshall University	M
McNeese State University	M
Miami University	M,D
Michigan State University	M,D
Middle Tennessee State University	M,D
Midwestern State University	M
Millersville University of Pennsylvania	M
Mississippi College	M
Mississippi State University	M
Montclair State University	M
Morehead State University	M
Morgan State University	M
Murray State University	M
New Mexico Highlands University	M
New Mexico State University	M,D
New York University	M,D
North Carolina Agricultural and Technical State University	M
North Carolina Central University	M
North Carolina State University	M
North Dakota State University	M
Northeastern Illinois University	M
Northeastern University	M,D,O
Northeast Louisiana University	M
Northern Arizona University	M
Northern Illinois University	M,D
Northern Michigan University	M
Northwestern State University of Louisiana	M
Northwestern University	M,D
Northwest Missouri State University	M
Oakland University	M
The Ohio State University	M,D
Ohio University	M,D
Oklahoma State University	M,D
Old Dominion University	M
Oregon State University	M
Our Lady of the Lake University of San Antonio	M
Pennsylvania State University University Park Campus	M,D
Pittsburg State University	M
Portland State University	M
Prairie View A&M University	M
Princeton University	D
Purdue University	M,D
Purdue University Calumet	M
Queens College of the City University of New York	M
Radford University	M
Rhode Island College	M
Rice University	M,D
Rivier College	M
Roosevelt University	M
Rutgers, The State University of New Jersey, Camden	M
Rutgers, The State University of New Jersey, Newark	M
Rutgers, The State University of New Jersey, New Brunswick	D
St. Bonaventure University	M
St. Cloud State University	M
St. John's University (NY)	M,D
Saint Louis University	M,D
Saint Xavier University	M,O
Salem State College	M
Salisbury State University	M

P—first professional degree; M—master's degree; D—doctorate; O—other advanced degree.

English (continued)

Sam Houston State University	M
San Diego State University	M
San Francisco State University	M,O
San Jose State University	M
Seton Hall University	M
Shippensburg University of Pennsylvania	M
Simmons College	M
Slippery Rock University of Pennsylvania	M
Sonoma State University	M
South Dakota State University	M
Southeastern Louisiana University	M
Southeast Missouri State University	M
Southern Connecticut State University	M
Southern Illinois University at Carbondale	M,D
Southern Illinois University at Edwardsville	M
Southern Methodist University	M
Southern Oregon University	M
Southwest Missouri State University	M
Southwest Texas State University	M
Stanford University	M,D
State University of New York at Albany	M,D
State University of New York at Binghamton	M,D
State University of New York at Buffalo	M,D
State University of New York at New Paltz	M
State University of New York at Oswego	M
State University of New York at Stony Brook	M,D
State University of New York College at Brockport	M
State University of New York College at Buffalo	M
State University of New York College at Cortland	M
State University of New York College at Fredonia	M
State University of New York College at Oneonta	M
State University of New York College at Potsdam	M
State University of West Georgia	M
Stephen F. Austin State University	M
Stetson University	M
Sul Ross State University	M
Syracuse University	M,D
Tarleton State University	M
Temple University (Philadelphia)	M,D
Tennessee State University	M
Tennessee Technological University	M
Texas A&M International University	M
Texas A&M University (College Station)	M,D
Texas A&M University–Commerce	M
Texas A&M University–Corpus Christi	M
Texas A&M University–Kingsville	M
Texas Christian University	M,D
Texas Southern University	M
Texas Tech University	M,D
Texas Woman's University	M,D
Truman State University	M
Tufts University	M,D
Tulane University	M,D
The University of Akron	M
The University of Alabama (Tuscaloosa)	M,D
The University of Alabama at Birmingham	M
The University of Alabama in Huntsville	M
University of Alaska Anchorage	M
University of Alaska Fairbanks	M
The University of Arizona	M,D
University of Arkansas (Fayetteville)	M,D
University of California, Berkeley	D
University of California, Davis	M,D
University of California, Irvine	M,D
University of California, Los Angeles	D,O
University of California, Riverside	M,D
University of California, San Diego	M,D
University of California, Santa Barbara	M,D
University of Central Arkansas	M
University of Central Florida	M
University of Central Oklahoma	M
University of Chicago	M,D
University of Cincinnati	M,D
University of Colorado at Boulder	M,D
University of Colorado at Denver	M
University of Connecticut	M,D
University of Delaware	M,D
University of Denver	M,D
University of Florida	M,D
University of Georgia	M,D
University of Hawaii at Manoa	M,D
University of Houston	M,D
University of Houston–Clear Lake	M
University of Idaho	M
University of Illinois at Chicago	M,D
University of Illinois at Springfield	M
University of Illinois at Urbana–Champaign	M,D
University of Indianapolis	M
The University of Iowa	M,D
University of Kansas	M,D
University of Kentucky	M,D
University of Louisville	M,D
University of Maine (Orono)	M
University of Maryland, College Park	M,D
University of Massachusetts Amherst	M,D
University of Massachusetts Boston	M
The University of Memphis	M
University of Miami	M,D
University of Michigan	M,D
University of Minnesota, Duluth	M
University of Minnesota, Twin Cities Campus	M,D
University of Mississippi	M,D
University of Missouri–Columbia	M,D
University of Missouri–Kansas City	M,D
University of Missouri–St. Louis	M
The University of Montana–Missoula	M
University of Montevallo	M
University of Nebraska at Kearney	M
University of Nebraska at Omaha	M
University of Nebraska–Lincoln	M,D
University of Nevada, Las Vegas	M,D
University of Nevada, Reno	M,D
University of New Hampshire	M,D
University of New Mexico	M,D
University of New Orleans	M
The University of North Carolina at Chapel Hill	M,D
University of North Carolina at Charlotte	M
University of North Carolina at Greensboro	M,D
University of North Carolina at Wilmington	M
University of North Dakota	M,D
University of Northern Colorado	M
University of Northern Iowa	M
University of North Florida	M
University of North Texas	M,D
University of Notre Dame	M,D
University of Oklahoma	M,D
University of Oregon	M,D
University of Pennsylvania	M,D
University of Pittsburgh	M,D
University of Puerto Rico, Mayagüez Campus	M
University of Puerto Rico, Río Piedras	M
University of Rhode Island	M,D
University of Richmond	M
University of Rochester	M,D
University of St. Thomas (MN)	M
University of Scranton	M
University of South Alabama	M
University of South Carolina (Columbia)	M,D
University of South Dakota	M,D
University of Southern California	M,D
University of Southern Mississippi	M,D
University of South Florida	M,D
University of Southwestern Louisiana	M,D
University of Tennessee at Chattanooga	M
University of Tennessee, Knoxville	M,D
The University of Texas at Arlington	M,D
The University of Texas at Austin	M,D
The University of Texas at Brownsville	M
The University of Texas at El Paso	M
The University of Texas at San Antonio	M
The University of Texas at Tyler	M
The University of Texas of the Permian Basin	M
The University of Texas–Pan American	M
University of the Incarnate Word	M
University of the Pacific	M
University of Toledo	M,D
University of Tulsa	M,D
University of Utah	M,D
University of Vermont	M
University of Virginia	M,D
University of Washington	M,D
University of West Florida	M
University of Wisconsin–Eau Claire	M
University of Wisconsin–Madison	M,D
University of Wisconsin–Milwaukee	M,D
University of Wisconsin–Stevens Point	M
University of Wyoming	M
Utah State University	M
Valdosta State University	M
Valparaiso University	M
Vanderbilt University	M,D
Villanova University	M
Virginia Commonwealth University	M
Virginia Polytechnic Institute and State University	M
Virginia State University	M
Wake Forest University	M
Washington State University	M,D
Washington University in St. Louis	M,D
Wayne State University	M,D
West Chester University of Pennsylvania	M
Western Carolina University	M
Western Connecticut State University	M
Western Illinois University	M
Western Kentucky University	M
Western Michigan University	M,D
Western Washington University	M
Westfield State College	M
West Texas A&M University	M
West Virginia University	M,D
Wichita State University	M
William Paterson University of New Jersey	M
Winona State University	M
Winthrop University	M
Wright State University	M
Xavier University	M
Yale University	M,D
Youngstown State University	M

ENGLISH AS A SECOND LANGUAGE

Adelphi University	M,O
American University	M,O
Andrews University	M
Arizona State University	M
Azusa Pacific University	M,O
Biola University	M,O
Boston University	M,O
Bowling Green State University	M
Brigham Young University	M,O
California State University, Dominguez Hills	O
California State University, Fresno	M
California State University, Fullerton	M
California State University, Los Angeles	M
California State University, Sacramento	M
California State University, San Bernardino	M
California State University, Stanislaus	M
Cardinal Stritch University	M
The Catholic University of America	M
Central Connecticut State University	M
Central Michigan University	M
Central Missouri State University	M
Central Washington University	M
Chapman University	M
City University	M,O
Cleveland State University	M
The College of New Jersey	M,O
College of New Rochelle	M
Eastern College	O
Eastern Michigan University	M
Eastern Nazarene College	M,O
Fairfield University	M,O
Fairleigh Dickinson University, Teaneck–Hackensack Campus	M
Florida International University	M
Fordham University	M
Fresno Pacific University	M
George Mason University	M
Georgetown University	M,O
Georgia State University	M
Heritage College	M
Hofstra University	M
Holy Names College	O
Hunter College of the City University of New York	M
Indiana University Bloomington	M,D,O
Indiana University of Pennsylvania	M
Inter American University of Puerto Rico, Metropolitan Campus	M
Inter American University of Puerto Rico, San Germán Campus	M
Kean University	M,O
Lehman College of the City University of New York	M
Long Island University, Brooklyn Campus	M
Long Island University, C.W. Post Campus	M
Loyola Marymount University	M
Marymount University	M
Michigan State University	M
Murray State University	M
Nazareth College of Rochester	M
New Jersey City University	M
New York University	M,D,O
Northern Arizona University	M,D
Notre Dame College	M
Nova Southeastern University	M,O
Oklahoma City University	M
Oral Roberts University	M
Pennsylvania State University University Park Campus	M
Portland State University	M
Queens College of the City University of New York	M
Rhode Island College	M
Rowan University	O
Rutgers, The State University of New Jersey, New Brunswick	M,D
St. Cloud State University	M
St. John's University (NY)	M
Saint Michael's College	M
Salem State College	M
Salisbury State University	M
Sam Houston State University	O
San Francisco State University	M
San Jose State University	M
Seattle Pacific University	M
Seattle University	M
Seton Hall University	M,O
Simmons College	M
Southeast Missouri State University	M
Southern Connecticut State University	M
Southern Illinois University at Carbondale	M
Southern Illinois University at Edwardsville	M
State University of New York at Buffalo	M,D
State University of New York at New Paltz	M
State University of New York at Stony Brook	M,D
Teachers College, Columbia University	M,D
Texas A&M University–Kingsville	M
United States International University	M,D
Universidad del Turabo	M
The University of Alabama (Tuscaloosa)	M
The University of Arizona	M,D
University of California, Los Angeles	M,O
University of Central Florida	M
University of Colorado at Denver	M
University of Delaware	M
University of Florida	O
University of Guam	M
University of Hawaii at Manoa	M,D
University of Houston	M
University of Idaho	M
University of Illinois at Chicago	M
University of Illinois at Urbana–Champaign	M
University of Kansas	M,D
University of Maryland, College Park	M
University of Massachusetts Boston	M
University of Miami	M,O
University of Nevada, Las Vegas	M
University of Nevada, Reno	M
University of North Carolina at Charlotte	M
University of Northern Iowa	M
University of Pennsylvania	M,D
University of Puerto Rico, Río Piedras	M
University of San Francisco	M
University of South Carolina (Columbia)	O
University of Southern California	M
University of Southern Maine	M,O
University of South Florida	M
University of Tennessee, Knoxville	M,D,O
The University of Texas at Brownsville	M

The University of Texas at San Antonio — M
The University of Texas–Pan American — M
University of Toledo — M
University of Washington — M
Wayne State College — M
West Chester University of Pennsylvania — M
Western Kentucky University — M
Western Oregon University — M
West Virginia University — M
Whitworth College — M
Wright State University — M

ENGLISH EDUCATION

Adelphi University — M
Alabama State University — M
Albany State University — M
Alfred University — M
American International College — M
Andrews University — M
Arkansas State University — M,O
Arkansas Tech University — M
Auburn University — M,D,O
Beaver College — M,O
Belmont University — M
Boston College — M
Boston University — M,D,O
Brooklyn College of the City University of New York — M
Brown University — M
California State University, San Bernardino — M
Campbell University — M
Carthage College — M
Central Missouri State University — M
Central Washington University — M
Chadron State College — M
Chapman University — M
Charleston Southern University — M
City College of the City University of New York — M
Clemson University — M
College of Notre Dame — M
Colorado State University — M
Columbia College (IL) — M,O
Columbus State University — M
Delta State University — M
Eastern Kentucky University — M
Edinboro University of Pennsylvania — M
Fairleigh Dickinson University, Teaneck–Hackensack Campus — M
Fitchburg State College — M
Florida International University — M
Florida State University — M,D,O
Framingham State College — M
Gardner–Webb University — M
Georgia Southern University — M,O
Georgia State University — M,D,O
Grand Valley State University — M
Henderson State University — M
Hofstra University — M,O
Hunter College of the City University of New York — M
Indiana University Bloomington — M
Indiana University of Pennsylvania — M
Iona College (New Rochelle) — M
Jackson State University — M
Jacksonville University — M
Kutztown University of Pennsylvania — M
Lander University — M
Lehman College of the City University of New York — M
Long Island University, Brooklyn Campus — M
Long Island University, C.W. Post Campus — M
Longwood College — M
Louisiana Tech University — M
Loyola Marymount University — M
Lynchburg College — M
Mankato State University — M
McNeese State University — M
Mercer University (Macon) — M
Miami University — M
Michigan State University — M
Millersville University of Pennsylvania — M
Minot State University — M
National–Louis University — M,O
New York University — M,D,O
North Carolina Agricultural and Technical State University — M
Northeastern Illinois University — M
Northeast Louisiana University — M
Northern State University — M
North Georgia College & State University — M
Northwestern State University of Louisiana — M
Northwest Missouri State University — M
Nova Southeastern University — M,O

Oregon State University — M
Plattsburgh State University of New York — M
Purdue University — M,D,O
Queens College of the City University of New York — M,O
Quinnipiac College — M
Rockford College — M
Rollins College — M
Rutgers, The State University of New Jersey, New Brunswick — M
Salem State College — M
Salisbury State University — M
San Francisco State University — O
South Carolina State University — M
Southern Illinois University at Edwardsville — M
Stanford University — M
State University of New York at Binghamton — M
State University of New York at Buffalo — D
State University of New York at Stony Brook — M
State University of New York College at Brockport — M
State University of New York College at Buffalo — M
State University of New York College at Cortland — M
State University of New York College at Oneonta — M
Syracuse University — M,D,O
Teachers College, Columbia University — M,D
Texas A&M University–Commerce — D
University of Alaska Fairbanks — M
The University of Arizona — D
University of California, Berkeley — O
University of Central Florida — M
University of Colorado at Denver — M
University of Connecticut — M,D
University of Delaware — M
University of Florida — M,D,O
University of Georgia — M,O
University of Idaho — M
University of Illinois at Chicago — M
University of Indianapolis — M
The University of Iowa — D
University of Michigan — M,D
University of Minnesota, Twin Cities Campus — M
The University of Montana–Missoula — M
University of Nebraska at Kearney — M
University of Nevada, Las Vegas — M
University of New Hampshire — M
The University of North Carolina at Chapel Hill — M
University of North Carolina at Greensboro — M,D
University of North Carolina at Pembroke — M
University of Oklahoma — M,D
University of Pittsburgh — M,D
University of Puerto Rico, Río Piedras — M
University of South Carolina (Columbia) — M
University of South Florida — M,D,O
University of Tennessee, Knoxville — M,D,O
The University of Texas at Tyler — M,O
University of the District of Columbia — M
University of Vermont — M
The University of West Alabama — M
University of Wisconsin–Eau Claire — M
University of Wisconsin–Madison — M
University of Wisconsin–River Falls — M
Vanderbilt University — M,D
Washington State University — M
Wayne State College — M
Western Carolina University — M
Western Kentucky University — M
Wilkes University — M
Worcester State College — M
Xavier University — M

ENTOMOLOGY

Auburn University — M,D
Clemson University — M,D
Colorado State University — M,D
Cornell University — M,D
Iowa State University of Science and Technology — M,D
Kansas State University — M,D
Louisiana State University and Agricultural and Mechanical College — M,D
Michigan State University — M,D
Mississippi State University — M,D

Montana State University–Bozeman — M
New Mexico State University — M
North Carolina State University — M,D
North Dakota State University — M,D
The Ohio State University — M,D
Oklahoma State University — M,D
Oregon State University — M,D
Pennsylvania State University, University Park Campus — M,D
Purdue University — M,D
Rutgers, The State University of New Jersey, New Brunswick — M,D
South Dakota State University — M
Texas A&M University (College Station) — M,D
Texas Tech University — M
The University of Arizona — M,D
University of Arkansas (Fayetteville) — M,D
University of California, Davis — M,D
University of California, Riverside — M,D
University of Connecticut — M,D
University of Delaware — M,D
University of Florida — M,D
University of Georgia — M,D
University of Hawaii at Manoa — M,D
University of Idaho — M,D
University of Illinois at Urbana–Champaign — M,D
University of Kansas — M,D
University of Kentucky — M,D
University of Maine (Orono) — M
University of Maryland, College Park — M,D
University of Massachusetts Amherst — M,D
University of Minnesota, Twin Cities Campus — M,D
University of Missouri–Columbia — M,D
University of Nebraska–Lincoln — M,D
University of North Dakota — M,D
University of Rhode Island — M,D
University of Tennessee, Knoxville — M
University of Wisconsin–Madison — M,D
University of Wyoming — M,D
Virginia Polytechnic Institute and State University — M,D
Washington State University — M,D

ENTREPRENEURSHIP

American University — M
California Lutheran University — M
California State University, Hayward — M
Columbia University — M
DePaul University — M
Golden Gate University — M
Indiana University Bloomington — M
Kennesaw State University — M
Rensselaer Polytechnic Institute — M
Suffolk University — M
Trinity College (DC) — M
University of Colorado at Boulder — M
University of Houston — M,D
University of Tennessee, Knoxville — M

ENVIRONMENTAL AND OCCUPATIONAL HEALTH

Anna Maria College — M
Boston University — M,D
California State University, Fresno — M
California State University, Northridge — M
Central Missouri State University — M,O
Colorado State University — M,D
Columbia University — M,D
East Carolina University — M
East Tennessee State University — M
Emory University — M
The George Washington University — M
Harvard University — M,D
Hunter College of the City University of New York — M
Indiana University of Pennsylvania — M
Johns Hopkins University — M,D
Loma Linda University — M
Montclair State University — M
Murray State University — M
New York University — M,D
Northwestern University — M,D
Old Dominion University — M
Oregon State University — M
Polytechnic University, Brooklyn Campus — M
Purdue University — M,D
Saint Joseph's University — M
San Diego State University — M
State University of New York at Albany — M,D

State University of New York at Stony Brook — O
Temple University (Philadelphia) — M
Tufts University — M,D
Tulane University — M,D
The University of Alabama at Birmingham — M,D
University of California, Berkeley — M,D
University of California, Irvine — M,D
University of California, Los Angeles — M,D
University of Cincinnati — M,D
University of Georgia — M
University of Hawaii at Manoa — M
University of Illinois at Chicago — M,D
The University of Iowa — M,D
University of Miami — M
University of Michigan — M,D
University of Minnesota, Twin Cities Campus — M,D
University of Nevada, Reno — M,D
University of New Haven — M
University of Oklahoma — M
University of Pittsburgh — M,D
University of Rochester — M
University of South Carolina (Columbia) — M,D
University of Southern Mississippi — M
University of South Florida — M,D
University of Washington — M,D
University of Wisconsin–Eau Claire — M
Virginia Commonwealth University — M
Wayne State University — M
Western Kentucky University — M
Western Washington University — M
Yale University — M,D

ENVIRONMENTAL BIOLOGY

Baylor University — M
Eastern Illinois University — M
Emporia State University — M
Governors State University — M
Hood College — M
New York University — D
Ohio University — M,D
Rutgers, The State University of New Jersey, New Brunswick — M,D
Sonoma State University — M
State University of New York College of Environmental Science and Forestry — M,D
Tennessee Technological University — M
University of Colorado at Boulder — M,D
University of Louisville — D
University of Massachusetts Amherst — M,D
University of Massachusetts Boston — D
University of Nevada, Las Vegas — D
University of North Dakota — M,D
University of Notre Dame — M,D
University of Southern Mississippi — M,D
University of Southwestern Louisiana — D
University of Wisconsin–Madison — M,D
Utah State University — M,D
Washington University in St. Louis — D
West Virginia University — D

ENVIRONMENTAL DESIGN

Arizona State University — D
Cornell University — M
Michigan State University — D
San Diego State University — M
San Jose State University — M
Texas Tech University — M,D
University of California, Berkeley — M,D
University of California, Irvine — M,D
University of Missouri–Columbia — M
Virginia Polytechnic Institute and State University — D
Yale University — M

ENVIRONMENTAL ENGINEERING

Auburn University — M,D
California Institute of Technology — M,D
California Polytechnic State University, San Luis Obispo — M
Carnegie Mellon University — M,D
Case Western Reserve University — M,D
The Catholic University of America — M
Clarkson University — M,D
Clemson University — M,D
Colorado School of Mines — M,D
Colorado State University — M,D
Columbia University — M
Cornell University — M,D
Dartmouth College — M,D

Environmental Engineering (continued)

Drexel University	M,D
Duke University	M,D
Florida Institute of Technology	M
Florida International University	M
The George Washington University	M,D,O
Georgia Institute of Technology	M,D
Harvard University	M,D
Idaho State University	M
Illinois Institute of Technology	M,D
Iowa State University of Science and Technology	M,D
Johns Hopkins University	M,D
Lamar University	M
Lehigh University	M,D
Louisiana State University and Agricultural and Mechanical College	M,D
Loyola Marymount University	M
Manhattan College	M
Marquette University	M,D
Marshall University	M
Massachusetts Institute of Technology	M,D,O
Michigan State University	M,D
Michigan Technological University	M,D
Mississippi State University	M
Montana State University–Bozeman	M,D
Montana Tech of The University of Montana	M
Murray State University	M
New Jersey Institute of Technology	M,D
New Mexico State University	M
New York Institute of Technology	M,O
North Dakota State University	M
Northeastern University	M,D
Northwestern University	M,D
Ohio University	M,D
Oklahoma State University	M,D
Old Dominion University	M,D
Oregon State University	M,D
Pennsylvania State University Harrisburg Campus of the Capital College	M
Pennsylvania State University University Park Campus	M,D
Polytechnic University, Brooklyn Campus	M
Polytechnic University, Farmingdale Campus	M
Polytechnic University, Westchester Graduate Center	M
Princeton University	D
Rensselaer Polytechnic Institute	M,D
Rice University	M,D
Rutgers, The State University of New Jersey, New Brunswick	M,D
South Dakota State University	M
Stanford University	M,D,O
State University of New York at Buffalo	M,D
State University of New York College of Environmental Science and Forestry	M,D
Stevens Institute of Technology	M,D,O
Syracuse University	M,D
Temple University (Philadelphia)	M
Texas A&M University (College Station)	M,D
Texas A&M University–Kingsville	M
Texas Tech University	M
Tufts University	M,D
Tulane University	M,D
The University of Alabama (Tuscaloosa)	M
The University of Alabama at Birmingham	M
The University of Alabama in Huntsville	M
University of Alaska Anchorage	M
University of Alaska Fairbanks	M
The University of Arizona	M,D
University of Arkansas (Fayetteville)	M
University of California, Berkeley	M,D
University of California, Davis	M,D,O
University of California, Irvine	M,D
University of California, Los Angeles	M,D
University of California, Santa Barbara	M,D
University of Central Florida	M,D
University of Cincinnati	M,D
University of Colorado at Boulder	M,D
University of Connecticut	M,D
University of Dayton	M
University of Delaware	M,D
University of Detroit Mercy	M,D
University of Florida	M,D,O
University of Houston	M,D
University of Illinois at Urbana–Champaign	M,D
The University of Iowa	M,D
University of Kansas	M,D
University of Maine (Orono)	M,D
University of Maryland, College Park	M,D
University of Massachusetts Amherst	M
University of Massachusetts Lowell	M
The University of Memphis	M
University of Michigan	M,D,O
University of Missouri–Columbia	M,D
University of Missouri–Rolla	M,D
University of Nebraska–Lincoln	M,D
University of Nevada, Las Vegas	M,D
University of Nevada, Reno	M,D
University of New Haven	M,O
The University of North Carolina at Chapel Hill	M,D
University of Notre Dame	M
University of Oklahoma	M
University of Pittsburgh	M,D
University of Rhode Island	M,D
University of Southern California	M,D
University of South Florida	M,D
University of Tennessee, Knoxville	M
The University of Texas at Arlington	M,D
The University of Texas at Austin	M
The University of Texas at El Paso	D
University of Virginia	M,D
University of Washington	M,D
University of Wisconsin–Madison	M,D
University of Wyoming	M
Utah State University	M,D,O
Vanderbilt University	M,D
Villanova University	M
Virginia Polytechnic Institute and State University	M,D
Washington State University	M
Washington University in St. Louis	M,D
West Virginia University	M,D
Worcester Polytechnic Institute	M,D
Youngstown State University	M

ENVIRONMENTAL POLICY AND RESOURCE MANAGEMENT

Adelphi University	O
American University	M
Arizona State University	M
Baylor University	M
Bemidji State University	M
Boise State University	M
Boston University	M
Brown University	M
California State University, Fullerton	M
Central Washington University	M
Clark University	M
Colorado State University	M,D
Cornell University	M,D
Duke University	M,D
Duquesne University	M,O
Fairleigh Dickinson University, Teaneck–Hackensack Campus	M
Florida Institute of Technology	M
Florida International University	M
Friends University	M
George Mason University	M,D
The George Washington University	M
Hardin–Simmons University	M
Illinois Institute of Technology	M
Lamar University	M
Lesley College	M
Long Island University, C.W. Post Campus	M
Longwood College	M
Louisiana State University and Agricultural and Mechanical College	M
Michigan State University	M,D
Michigan Technological University	M
Montclair State University	M
National University	M
New Jersey Institute of Technology	M
North Carolina State University	M
North Dakota State University	M
Northeastern Illinois University	M
Northwestern University	M
Oregon State University	M
Pennsylvania State University University Park Campus	M,D
Portland State University	M
Princeton University	M,D
Rensselaer Polytechnic Institute	M,D
St. Cloud State University	M
Saint Joseph's University	M
Samford University	M
San Francisco State University	M
San Jose State University	M
Shippensburg University of Pennsylvania	M
Slippery Rock University of Pennsylvania	M
Southern Illinois University at Edwardsville	M
Southwest Missouri State University	M
Southwest Texas State University	M
Stanford University	M
State University of New York at Albany	M
State University of New York College of Environmental Science and Forestry	M,D
Texas Tech University	D
Troy State University (Troy)	M
Tufts University	M,D,O
Universidad del Turabo	M
Universidad Metropolitana	M
University of Alaska Fairbanks	M
The University of Arizona	M
University of California, Berkeley	M,D
University of California, Irvine	M,D
University of California, Santa Barbara	M
University of California, Santa Cruz	D
University of Connecticut	M
University of Delaware	M,D
University of Denver	M
University of Hawaii at Manoa	M
University of Houston–Clear Lake	M
University of Idaho	M,D
University of Illinois at Springfield	M
University of Maine (Orono)	M
University of Maryland, College Park	M
University of Maryland University College	M
University of Michigan	M,D
The University of Montana–Missoula	M
University of Nevada, Reno	M
University of New Hampshire	M
University of New Mexico	M
University of Oregon	M
University of Rhode Island	M,D
University of St. Thomas (MN)	M
University of San Francisco	M
University of South Carolina (Columbia)	M
University of Tennessee, Knoxville	M,D
University of Vermont	M,D
University of Washington	M,D
University of West Florida	M
University of Wisconsin–Green Bay	M
University of Wisconsin–Madison	M,D
Virginia Commonwealth University	M
Webster University	M
West Virginia University	D

ENVIRONMENTAL SCIENCES

Alabama Agricultural and Mechanical University	M
Alaska Pacific University	M
American University	M
Arkansas State University	D
California State University, Fullerton	M
City College of the City University of New York	D
Cleveland State University	M,D
College of Staten Island of the City University of New York	M
Colorado School of Mines	M,D
Columbus State University	M
Drexel University	M,D
Duke University	M,D
Duquesne University	M,O
Florida Atlantic University	M
Florida Institute of Technology	M,D
Florida International University	M
George Mason University	M,D
The George Washington University	M
Graduate School and University Center of the City University of New York	D
Harvard University	M,D
Humboldt State University	M
Indiana University Bloomington	M,D
Inter American University of Puerto Rico, San Germán Campus	M
Jackson State University	M,D
Lehigh University	M,D
Long Island University, C.W. Post Campus	M
Louisiana State University and Agricultural and Mechanical College	D
Louisiana State University in Shreveport	M
Loyola Marymount University	M
Mankato State University	M
Marshall University	M
McNeese State University	M
Miami University	M
Michigan State University	M,D
Montana State University–Bozeman	M
Montclair State University	M
New Jersey Institute of Technology	M,D
Nova Southeastern University	M
Oakland University	D
The Ohio State University	M,D
Ohio University	M
Oklahoma State University	M,D
Pace University	M
Pennsylvania State University Harrisburg Campus of the Capital College	M
Pennsylvania State University University Park Campus	M
Polytechnic University, Brooklyn Campus	M
Portland State University	M,D
Rensselaer Polytechnic Institute	M,D
Rice University	M,D
Rutgers, The State University of New Jersey, New Brunswick	M,D
South Dakota State University	D
Southern University and Agricultural and Mechanical College	M
Stanford University	M,D,O
State University of New York at Stony Brook	M
State University of New York College of Environmental Science and Forestry	M,D
Stephen F. Austin State University	M
Tarleton State University	M
Tennessee Technological University	D
Texas A&M University–Corpus Christi	M
Texas Christian University	M
Tufts University	M,D
Tuskegee University	M
The University of Akron	M
The University of Alabama in Huntsville	M,D
University of Alaska Anchorage	M
University of Alaska Fairbanks	M
The University of Arizona	M,D
University of California, Berkeley	M,D
University of California, Davis	M,D
University of California, Los Angeles	D
University of California, Riverside	M,D
University of California, Santa Barbara	M
University of Cincinnati	M,D
University of Colorado at Denver	M
University of Guam	M
University of Houston–Clear Lake	M
University of Idaho	M
University of Illinois at Urbana–Champaign	M,D
University of Kansas	M,D
University of Maine (Orono)	M,D
University of Maryland, Baltimore County	M,D
University of Maryland, College Park	M,D
University of Maryland Eastern Shore	M,D
University of Massachusetts Boston	M,D
University of Massachusetts Lowell	M,D
The University of Montana–Missoula	M
University of Nevada, Las Vegas	M
University of Nevada, Reno	M,D
University of New Haven	M
The University of North Carolina at Chapel Hill	M,D
University of Northern Iowa	M
University of North Texas	M,D
University of Oklahoma	M,D
University of Rochester	M
University of Tennessee at Chattanooga	M
The University of Texas at Arlington	M
The University of Texas at El Paso	D
The University of Texas at San Antonio	M
University of Virginia	M,D
University of Wisconsin–Green Bay	M
University of Wisconsin–Madison	M,D
Virginia Commonwealth University	M
Virginia Polytechnic Institute and State University	M,D

- Washington State University M,D
- Washington University in St. Louis M
- Western Connecticut State University M
- Western Washington University M
- West Texas A&M University M
- Wichita State University M
- Wright State University M
- Yale University M,D

EPIDEMIOLOGY

- Boston University M,D
- Brown University M,D
- California State University, Long Beach M
- Case Western Reserve University M,D
- Columbia University M,D
- Cornell University M
- Emory University M,D
- Georgetown University M
- The George Washington University M,D
- Harvard University M,D
- Johns Hopkins University M,D
- Loma Linda University M,D
- Michigan State University M
- New York University D
- North Carolina State University M,D
- Purdue University M,D
- San Diego State University M,D
- Stanford University M,D
- State University of New York at Albany M,D
- State University of New York at Buffalo M,D
- Texas A&M University (College Station) M
- Tulane University M,D
- The University of Alabama at Birmingham M,D
- The University of Arizona M,D
- University of California, Berkeley M,D
- University of California, Davis M,D
- University of California, Los Angeles M,D
- University of California, San Diego D
- University of Cincinnati M
- University of Hawaii at Manoa M,D
- University of Illinois at Chicago M,D
- The University of Iowa M,D
- University of Maryland, Baltimore County M
- University of Miami D
- University of Michigan M,D
- University of Minnesota, Twin Cities Campus M,D
- The University of North Carolina at Chapel Hill M,D
- University of Pennsylvania M,D
- University of Pittsburgh M,D
- University of South Carolina (Columbia) M,D
- University of Southern California M,D
- University of South Florida M,D
- University of Virginia M
- University of Washington M,D
- University of Wisconsin–Madison M,D
- Wake Forest University M
- Yale University M,D

ERGONOMICS AND HUMAN FACTORS

- Cornell University M
- Embry-Riddle Aeronautical University (FL) M
- Florida Institute of Technology M
- Purdue University M,D
- Rensselaer Polytechnic Institute M
- San Jose State University M
- Tufts University M
- The University of Iowa M,D
- University of Miami D
- Wright State University M

ETHICS

- Claremont Graduate University M,D
- Marquette University M,D
- University of Baltimore M
- University of Nevada, Las Vegas M

EVOLUTIONARY BIOLOGY

- Arizona State University M,D
- Boston University M,D
- Brown University M,D
- Columbia University D,O
- Cornell University D
- Emory University D
- Florida State University M,D
- George Mason University M
- Harvard University D
- Indiana University Bloomington M,D
- Iowa State University of Science and Technology M,D
- Lehigh University M,D
- Michigan State University
- New York University D
- Northwestern University D
- Pennsylvania State University University Park Campus M,D
- Princeton University D
- Purdue University M,D
- Rice University M,D
- Rutgers, The State University of New Jersey, New Brunswick M,D
- State University of New York at Albany M,D
- State University of New York at Stony Brook D
- The University of Arizona M,D
- University of California, Davis D
- University of California, Irvine M,D
- University of California, Riverside D
- University of California, San Diego D
- University of California, Santa Barbara M,D
- University of Chicago D
- University of Colorado at Boulder M,D
- University of Hawaii at Manoa M,D
- University of Illinois at Chicago M,D
- University of Illinois at Urbana–Champaign D
- University of Massachusetts Amherst M,D
- University of Miami M,D
- University of Minnesota, Twin Cities Campus M,D
- University of Nevada, Reno D
- University of New Mexico M,D
- The University of North Carolina at Chapel Hill M,D
- University of Notre Dame M,D
- University of Oregon M,D
- University of Pittsburgh M,D
- University of Rochester M,D
- University of Southwestern Louisiana D
- University of Tennessee, Knoxville M,D
- University of Utah M,D
- Washington University in St. Louis D

EXERCISE AND SPORTS SCIENCE

- Adelphi University O
- American University M
- Appalachian State University M
- Arizona State University M,D
- Ashland University M
- Ball State University D
- Barry University M
- Benedictine University M
- Bloomsburg University of Pennsylvania M
- Boise State University M
- Brigham Young University M,D
- Brooklyn College of the City University of New York M
- California State University, Fresno M
- California University of Pennsylvania M
- Central Connecticut State University M
- Central Michigan University M,O
- Central Missouri State University M
- Cleveland State University M
- College of St. Scholastica M
- Colorado State University M
- East Carolina University M
- East Stroudsburg University of Pennsylvania M
- Florida Atlantic University M
- Florida State University M
- George Mason University M
- The George Washington University M
- Georgia State University M,D
- Howard University M
- Indiana State University M
- Indiana University Bloomington M,D
- Indiana University of Pennsylvania M
- Ithaca College M
- Kent State University M,D
- Long Island University, Brooklyn Campus M
- Marshall University M
- Miami University M
- Michigan State University M,D
- Mississippi State University M
- Montclair State University M
- New Mexico Highlands University M
- Northeastern Illinois University M
- Northeastern University M
- Northern Michigan University M
- Oakland University M
- Ohio University M
- Oregon State University M,D
- Purdue University M,D
- Queens College of the City University of New York M
- St. Cloud State University M
- San Diego State University M
- Springfield College (MA) M,O
- State University of New York at Buffalo M,D
- Syracuse University M,O
- Texas Tech University M
- Texas Woman's University M,D
- The University of Akron M
- The University of Arizona M
- University of California, Davis M
- University of Connecticut M,D
- University of Delaware M
- University of Florida M,D
- University of Georgia M,D,O
- University of Houston M
- University of Houston–Clear Lake M
- The University of Iowa M,D
- University of Louisville M
- University of Massachusetts Amherst M,D
- The University of Memphis M
- University of Miami M,D
- University of Mississippi M,D
- University of Missouri–Columbia M,D
- University of Nebraska at Kearney M
- University of Nevada, Las Vegas M
- University of New Orleans M
- The University of North Carolina at Chapel Hill M
- University of North Carolina at Greensboro M,D
- University of North Florida M
- University of Oklahoma M
- University of Oregon M,D
- University of Pittsburgh M,D
- University of South Alabama M
- University of South Carolina (Columbia) M,D
- University of Southern California M,D
- University of Tennessee, Knoxville M,D
- The University of Texas at El Paso M
- The University of Texas at Tyler M
- University of the Pacific M
- University of Toledo M
- University of Utah M,D
- University of Wisconsin–La Crosse M
- Virginia Polytechnic Institute and State University M,D
- Wake Forest University M
- West Chester University of Pennsylvania M
- Western Michigan University M
- West Texas A&M University M
- West Virginia University M
- Wichita State University M

EXPERIMENTAL PSYCHOLOGY

- Adelphi University D
- American University M,D
- Bowling Green State University M,D
- Brooklyn College of the City University of New York M
- California State University, San Bernardino M
- Case Western Reserve University D
- The Catholic University of America D
- Central Michigan University M,D
- Central Washington University M
- City College of the City University of New York D
- Clark University D
- Cleveland State University M
- College of William and Mary M
- Colorado State University D
- Columbia University M,D
- Cornell University D
- DePaul University M,D
- Duke University D
- Fairleigh Dickinson University, Florham-Madison Campus M
- George Mason University M
- Graduate School and University Center of the City University of New York D
- Harvard University M,D
- Howard University D
- Hunter College of the City University of New York M
- Illinois State University M
- Johns Hopkins University D
- Kent State University M,D
- Lehigh University M,D
- Long Island University, C.W. Post Campus M
- Miami University D
- Morehead State University M
- Northeast Louisiana University M
- The Ohio State University D
- Ohio University D
- Oklahoma State University D
- Pennsylvania State University University Park Campus M,D
- St. John's University (NY) M
- Saint Louis University M,D
- Southern Illinois University at Carbondale M,D
- State University of New York at Albany D
- State University of New York at Stony Brook D
- Syracuse University M,D
- Temple University (Philadelphia) D
- Towson University M
- The University of Alabama (Tuscaloosa) D
- University of California, Santa Cruz D
- University of Cincinnati M,D
- University of Connecticut D
- University of Dayton M
- University of Hartford M
- University of Kansas D
- University of Louisville D
- University of Maine (Orono) M,D
- University of Maryland, College Park D
- The University of Memphis D
- University of Mississippi D
- University of Missouri–St. Louis D
- The University of Montana–Missoula D
- University of Nebraska at Omaha D
- University of New Mexico M,D
- The University of North Carolina at Chapel Hill M,D
- University of North Texas M,D
- University of Rhode Island D
- University of South Carolina (Columbia) M,D
- University of South Florida D
- University of Tennessee at Chattanooga M
- University of Tennessee, Knoxville M,D
- The University of Texas at El Paso M
- The University of Texas–Pan American M
- University of Toledo M,D
- University of Wisconsin–Oshkosh M
- Virginia Polytechnic Institute and State University D
- Washington University in St. Louis M,D
- Western Michigan University M,D
- Xavier University M

FACILITIES MANAGEMENT

- Cornell University M
- Indiana State University M
- Indiana University of Pennsylvania M
- Michigan State University M
- University of North Texas M

FILM, TELEVISION, AND VIDEO

- American University M
- Boston University M
- Brooklyn College of the City University of New York M
- California State University, Fullerton M
- Central Michigan University M
- Chapman University M
- Claremont Graduate University M
- Columbia College (IL) M
- Columbia University M
- Emerson College M
- Florida State University M
- George Mason University M
- Howard University M
- Loyola Marymount University M
- New Mexico Highlands University M
- New York University M
- Northwestern University M,D
- Ohio University M
- Rochester Institute of Technology M
- San Diego State University M
- San Francisco State University M
- Southern Illinois University at Carbondale M
- Southern Methodist University M
- Stanford University M
- Syracuse University M
- Temple University (Philadelphia) M
- The University of Alabama (Tuscaloosa) M,D
- University of California, Los Angeles M,D
- University of Denver M
- The University of Iowa M
- The University of Memphis M
- University of Miami M

P—first professional degree; M—master's degree; D—doctorate; O—other advanced degree.

Film, Television, and Video (continued)

University of New Orleans	M
University of North Carolina at Greensboro	M
University of North Texas	M
University of Oklahoma	M
University of Southern California	M,D
The University of Texas at Austin	M
University of Utah	M
University of Wisconsin–Milwaukee	M
Virginia Commonwealth University	M

FINANCE AND BANKING

Adelphi University	M,O
Alabama Agricultural and Mechanical University	M
American University	M
Arizona State University	D
Baruch College of the City University of New York	M,D
Boston College	M,D
Boston University	M,D
Brandeis University	M,D
California Lutheran University	M
California State University, Fullerton	M
California State University, Hayward	M
California State University, Los Angeles	M
California State University, Northridge	M
Carnegie Mellon University	D
Case Western Reserve University	M,D
The Catholic University of America	M
Central Michigan University	M
Charleston Southern University	M
City University	M,O
Claremont Graduate University	M
Clark Atlanta University	M
Clark University	M
Colorado State University	M
Columbia University	M,D
Cornell University	D
Dallas Baptist University	M
DePaul University	M,O
Dowling College	M,O
Drexel University	M,D
East Carolina University	M
Eastern College	M
Eastern Michigan University	M
Emporia State University	M
Fairfield University	M,O
Fairleigh Dickinson University, Florham–Madison Campus	M
Fairleigh Dickinson University, Teaneck–Hackensack Campus	M
Florida Agricultural and Mechanical University	M
Florida International University	M,D
Fordham University	M
Fort Hays State University	M
Gannon University	O
The George Washington University	M,D
Georgia State University	M,D
Golden Gate University	M,O
Graduate School and University Center of the City University of New York	D
Hawaii Pacific University	M
Hofstra University	M
Houston Baptist University	M
Illinois Institute of Technology	M
Indiana University Bloomington	M,D
Inter American University of Puerto Rico, Metropolitan Campus	M
Inter American University of Puerto Rico, San Germán Campus	M
Iona College (New Rochelle)	M,O
Johns Hopkins University	O
Kennesaw State University	M
Kent State University	D
Long Island University, C.W. Post Campus	M,O
Louisiana State University and Agricultural and Mechanical College	M,D
Louisiana Tech University	M,D
Loyola College	M
Manhattan College	M
Marywood University	M
Metropolitan State University	M
Miami University	M
Michigan State University	M,D
Middle Tennessee State University	M,D
Montclair State University	M
New York University	M,D,O
Northeastern Illinois University	M
Northeastern University	M
Northern Illinois University	M
Northwestern University	D
Oklahoma City University	M
Oklahoma State University	M,D
Oral Roberts University	M
Our Lady of the Lake University of San Antonio	M
Pace University	M
Pennsylvania State University University Park Campus	M,D
Philadelphia College of Textiles and Science	M
Polytechnic University, Brooklyn Campus	M
Polytechnic University, Farmingdale Campus	M
Polytechnic University, Westchester Graduate Center	M
Purdue University	M,D
Quinnipiac College	M
Rensselaer Polytechnic Institute	M,D
Rochester Institute of Technology	M
Rutgers, The State University of New Jersey, Newark	M,D
Sage Graduate School	M
St. Bonaventure University	M
St. Cloud State University	M
St. John's University (NY)	M,O
Saint Joseph's University	M
Saint Louis University	M,D
Saint Xavier University	M,O
San Diego State University	M
Seattle University	M,O
Seton Hall University	M
State University of New York at Albany	M
State University of New York at Binghamton	M,D
Suffolk University	M
Syracuse University	M,D
Temple University (Philadelphia)	M,D
Texas A&M International University	M
Texas A&M University (College Station)	M,D
Texas Tech University	M,D
Troy State University Dothan	M
United States International University	D
The University of Akron	M
The University of Alabama (Tuscaloosa)	M,D
The University of Arizona	M
University of Baltimore	M
University of California, Berkeley	D
University of Central Florida	D
University of Chicago	M
University of Cincinnati	M,D
University of Colorado at Boulder	M,D
University of Colorado at Colorado Springs	M
University of Colorado at Denver	M
University of Connecticut	D
University of Denver	M
University of Florida	M,D
University of Hartford	M
University of Houston	M,D
University of Houston–Clear Lake	M
University of Illinois at Chicago	D
University of Illinois at Urbana–Champaign	M,D
The University of Iowa	D
University of Kansas	D
The University of Memphis	M,D
University of Michigan	M
University of Minnesota, Twin Cities Campus	M,D
University of Missouri–St. Louis	M
University of Nebraska–Lincoln	M,D
University of New Haven	M
University of New Mexico	M
The University of North Carolina at Chapel Hill	D
University of North Texas	M,D
University of Oregon	M,D
University of Pennsylvania	D
University of Rhode Island	M
University of St. Thomas (MN)	M,O
University of San Francisco	M
University of Scranton	M
University of Southern California	M
University of Tennessee at Chattanooga	M
University of Tennessee, Knoxville	M,D
The University of Texas at Arlington	M
The University of Texas at Austin	D
University of Toledo	M
University of Utah	M,D
University of Wisconsin–Madison	M,D
University of Wyoming	M
Vanderbilt University	D
Virginia Commonwealth University	M,D
Virginia Polytechnic Institute and State University	D
Virginia State University	M
Wagner College	M
Webster University	M
West Chester University of Pennsylvania	M
Western New England College	M
West Texas A&M University	M
Wilkes University	M
Wright State University	M
Yale University	D
Youngstown State University	M

FIRE PROTECTION ENGINEERING

University of Maryland, College Park	M
University of New Haven	M
Worcester Polytechnic Institute	M,D

FISH, GAME, AND WILDLIFE MANAGEMENT

Auburn University	M,D
Brigham Young University	M,D
Clemson University	M
Colorado State University	M,D
Cornell University	M,D
Frostburg State University	M
Iowa State University of Science and Technology	M,D
Louisiana State University and Agricultural and Mechanical College	M,D
Michigan State University	M,D
Mississippi State University	M,D
Montana State University–Bozeman	M,D
New Mexico State University	M
North Carolina State University	M
Oregon State University	M,D
Pennsylvania State University University Park Campus	M,D
South Dakota State University	M,D
Sul Ross State University	M
Tennessee Technological University	M
Texas A&M University (College Station)	M,D
Texas A&M University–Kingsville	M,D
Texas Tech University	M,D
University of Alaska Fairbanks	M,D
The University of Arizona	M,D
University of Florida	M,D
University of Idaho	M,D
University of Maine (Orono)	M,D
University of Massachusetts Amherst	M,D
University of Miami	M,D
University of Minnesota, Twin Cities Campus	M,D
University of Missouri–Columbia	M,D
University of Nebraska–Lincoln	M
University of New Hampshire	M
University of North Dakota	M,D
University of Rhode Island	M
University of Tennessee, Knoxville	M
University of Vermont	M
University of Washington	M,D
Utah State University	M,D
Virginia Polytechnic Institute and State University	M,D
West Virginia University	M

FOLKLORE

The George Washington University	M
University of California, Berkeley	M
University of California, Los Angeles	M,D
The University of North Carolina at Chapel Hill	M
University of Oregon	M
University of Pennsylvania	M,D
University of Southwestern Louisiana	M
The University of Texas at Austin	M,D
Utah State University	M
Western Kentucky University	M

FOOD SCIENCE AND TECHNOLOGY

Alabama Agricultural and Mechanical University	M,D
Auburn University	M,D
Brigham Young University	M
California State Polytechnic University, Pomona	M
California State University, Fresno	M
Chapman University	M
Clemson University	D
Colorado State University	M,D
Cornell University	M,D
Drexel University	M,D
Florida State University	M,D
Framingham State College	M
Illinois Institute of Technology	M
Iowa State University of Science and Technology	M,D
Kansas State University	M,D
Louisiana State University and Agricultural and Mechanical College	M,D
Michigan State University	M,D
Mississippi State University	M,D
North Carolina State University	M,D
North Dakota State University	M,D
The Ohio State University	M,D
Oklahoma State University	M,D
Oregon State University	M,D
Pennsylvania State University University Park Campus	M,D
Purdue University	M,D
Rutgers, The State University of New Jersey, New Brunswick	M,D
Texas A&M University (College Station)	M,D
Texas Tech University	M,D
Texas Woman's University	M,D
Tuskegee University	M
The University of Akron	M
University of Arkansas (Fayetteville)	M,D
University of California, Davis	M,D
University of Delaware	M,D
University of Florida	M,D
University of Georgia	M,D
University of Hawaii at Manoa	M
University of Idaho	M
University of Illinois at Urbana–Champaign	M,D
University of Kentucky	M
University of Maine (Orono)	M,D
University of Maryland, College Park	M,D
University of Maryland Eastern Shore	M
University of Massachusetts Amherst	M,D
University of Minnesota, Twin Cities Campus	M,D
University of Missouri–Columbia	M,D
University of Nebraska–Lincoln	M,D
University of Puerto Rico, Mayagüez Campus	M
University of Rhode Island	M,D
The University of Tennessee at Martin	M
University of Tennessee, Knoxville	M,D
University of Wisconsin–Madison	M,D
University of Wisconsin–Stout	M
University of Wyoming	M
Utah State University	M,D
Virginia Polytechnic Institute and State University	M,D
Washington State University	M,D
Wayne State University	M,D
West Virginia University	D

FOREIGN LANGUAGES EDUCATION

Adelphi University	M
Andrews University	M
Auburn University	M
Boston College	M
Boston University	M
Bowling Green State University	M
Brigham Young University	M
Brooklyn College of the City University of New York	M
College of Notre Dame	M
Eastern Washington University	M
Florida Atlantic University	M
Florida International University	M
Georgia Southern University	M
Hardin–Simmons University	M
Hunter College of the City University of New York	M
Indiana University Bloomington	M
Indiana University–Purdue University Indianapolis	M
Iona College (New Rochelle)	M
Jacksonville University	M
Long Island University, C.W. Post Campus	M
Louisiana Tech University	M
Loyola Marymount University	M
Marygrove College	M
Michigan State University	M
Middle Tennessee State University	M
Millersville University of Pennsylvania	M
New York University	M,O
North Georgia College & State University	M
Plattsburgh State University of New York	M
Purdue University	M,D,O
Queens College of the City University of New York	M,O
Quinnipiac College	M

Rhode Island College — M
Rivier College — M
Rutgers, The State University of New Jersey, New Brunswick — M,D,O
Southwest Texas State University — M
Stanford University — M,D
State University of New York at Binghamton — M
State University of New York at Buffalo — D
State University of New York at Stony Brook — M
State University of New York College at Cortland — M
Teachers College, Columbia University — M,D
University of Central Florida — M
University of Connecticut — M,D
University of Delaware — M
University of Florida — M,D,O
University of Georgia — M,D,O
University of Hawaii at Manoa — D
University of Idaho — M
University of Illinois at Urbana–Champaign — M
University of Louisville — M
University of Maine (Orono) — M
University of Massachusetts Amherst — M
University of Michigan — M
University of Missouri–Columbia — M
University of Nebraska at Kearney — M
The University of North Carolina at Chapel Hill — M
University of Pittsburgh — M,D
University of Puerto Rico, Río Piedras — M
University of South Carolina (Columbia) — M
University of Southern Mississippi — M
University of South Florida — M
University of Tennessee, Knoxville — M,D,O
The University of Texas at Austin — M,D
University of Utah — M
University of Vermont — M
University of Virginia — M
University of Wisconsin–Madison — M
West Chester University of Pennsylvania — M
Western Kentucky University — M

FORENSIC SCIENCES

Castleton State College — M
Fitchburg State College — M,O
The George Washington University — M
Marshall University — M
National University — M
The University of Alabama at Birmingham — M
University of Illinois at Chicago — M
University of New Haven — M
Virginia Commonwealth University — M

FORESTRY

Auburn University — M,D
Clemson University — M,D
Colorado State University — M,D
Cornell University — M,D
Duke University — M
Harvard University — M
Iowa State University of Science and Technology — M,D
Louisiana State University and Agricultural and Mechanical College — M,D
Michigan State University — M,D
Michigan Technological University — M,D
Mississippi State University — M,D
North Carolina State University — M,D
Northern Arizona University — M,D
Oklahoma State University — M
Oregon State University — M,D
Pennsylvania State University University Park Campus — M,D
Purdue University — M,D
Southern Illinois University at Carbondale — M
Southern University and Agricultural and Mechanical College — M
State University of New York College of Environmental Science and Forestry — M,D
Stephen F. Austin State University — M,D
Texas A&M University (College Station) — M,D
The University of Arizona — M,D
University of California, Berkeley — M,D
University of Florida — M,D

University of Georgia — M,D
University of Idaho — M,D
University of Kentucky — M
University of Maine (Orono) — M,D
University of Massachusetts Amherst — M,D
University of Michigan — M,D
University of Minnesota, Twin Cities Campus — M,D
University of Missouri–Columbia — M,D
The University of Montana–Missoula — D
University of Nebraska–Lincoln — M,D
University of New Hampshire — M
University of Tennessee, Knoxville — M
University of Vermont — M
University of Washington — M,D
University of Wisconsin–Madison — M,D
Utah State University — M,D
Virginia Polytechnic Institute and State University — M,D
West Virginia University — M,D
Yale University — M,D

FOUNDATIONS AND PHILOSOPHY OF EDUCATION

Appalachian State University — M
Arizona State University — M
Brigham Young University — M,D
California State University, Long Beach — M
California State University, Los Angeles — M
California State University, Northridge — M
Central Connecticut State University — M
Clemson University — M
College of Mount St. Joseph — M
Duquesne University — M
Eastern Michigan University — M
Eastern Washington University — M
Fairfield University — M,O
Florida Atlantic University — M
Florida State University — M,D,O
The George Washington University — M
Georgia College and State University — M,O
Georgia State University — M,D
Harvard University — M,D,O
Hofstra University — M,O
Indiana University Bloomington — M,D
Iowa State University of Science and Technology — M
Kansas State University — M,D
Kent State University — M,D
Loyola College — M,O
Loyola University Chicago — M,D
Maharishi University of Management — M
New York University — M,D
Niagara University — M
Northern Illinois University — M
The Ohio State University — M,D
Pennsylvania State University University Park Campus — M,D
Purdue University — M
Rutgers, The State University of New Jersey, New Brunswick — M,D,O
Saint Louis University — M,D
Southern Connecticut State University — O
Stanford University — D
State University of New York at Binghamton — D
State University of New York at Buffalo — M,D,O
Syracuse University — M,D
Teachers College, Columbia University — M,D
Texas A&M University (College Station) — M,D
Troy State University (Troy) — M
Troy State University Dothan — M
University of California, Berkeley — M,D
University of Cincinnati — M,D
University of Connecticut — M,D
University of Florida — M,D,O
University of Hawaii at Manoa — M,D
University of Houston — M,D
University of Illinois at Urbana–Champaign — M,D,O
The University of Iowa — M,D
University of Kansas — M,D
University of Kentucky — M,D
University of Maryland, College Park — M,D,O
University of Michigan — M,D
University of New Mexico — M,D
University of New Orleans — M,D,O
University of Oklahoma — M,D
University of Oregon — M,D
University of Pennsylvania — M,D
University of Pittsburgh — M,D
University of South Alabama — M,O

University of South Carolina (Columbia) — D
University of Tennessee, Knoxville — M
The University of Texas at El Paso — D
University of the Pacific — M,D
University of Toledo — M,D
University of Utah — M,D
The University of West Alabama — M
University of Wisconsin–Madison — M,D
University of Wisconsin–Milwaukee — M
Wayne State University — D
Western Illinois University — M

FRENCH

American University — M,O
Arizona State University — M
Auburn University — M
Boston College — M,D
Boston University — M,D
Bowling Green State University — M
Brigham Young University — M
Brown University — M,D
California State University, Fullerton — M
California State University, Long Beach — M
California State University, Los Angeles — M
Case Western Reserve University — M,D
The Catholic University of America — M,D
Central Connecticut State University — M
Colorado State University — M
Columbia University — M,D
Duke University — D
Eastern Michigan University — M
Emory University — M,D
Florida Atlantic University — M
Florida State University — M,D
Georgia State University — M,O
Graduate School and University Center of the City University of New York — D
Harvard University — M,D
Howard University — M
Hunter College of the City University of New York — M
Illinois State University — M
Indiana State University — M
Indiana University Bloomington — M,D
Johns Hopkins University — D
Kansas State University — M
Kent State University — M
Louisiana State University and Agricultural and Mechanical College — M,D
Mankato State University — M
Miami University — M
Michigan State University — M,D
Millersville University of Pennsylvania — M
Mississippi State University — M
Montclair State University — M
New York University — M,D,O
North Carolina Central University — M
Northern Illinois University — M
Northwestern University — D
The Ohio State University — M,D
Ohio University — M
Pennsylvania State University University Park Campus — M,D
Portland State University — M
Princeton University — D
Purdue University — M,D
Queens College of the City University of New York — M
Rhode Island College — M
Rice University — M,D
Rutgers, The State University of New Jersey, New Brunswick — M,D
Saint Louis University — M
San Diego State University — M
San Francisco State University — M
San Jose State University — M
Seton Hall University — M
Simmons College — M
Southern Connecticut State University — M
Stanford University — M,D
State University of New York at Albany — M,D
State University of New York at Binghamton — M
State University of New York at Buffalo — M,D
State University of New York at Stony Brook — M,D
Syracuse University — M,D
Texas A&M University–Commerce — M
Tufts University — M
Tulane University — M,D

The University of Alabama (Tuscaloosa) — M,D
The University of Arizona — M,D
University of Arkansas (Fayetteville) — M
University of California, Berkeley — M,D
University of California, Davis — M,D
University of California, Irvine — M,D
University of California, Los Angeles — M,D,O
University of California, Riverside — M
University of California, San Diego — M,D
University of California, Santa Barbara — M,D
University of Chicago — M,D
University of Cincinnati — M,D
University of Colorado at Boulder — M,D
University of Connecticut — M,D
University of Delaware — M
University of Denver — M
University of Florida — M,D
University of Georgia — M
University of Hawaii at Manoa — M
University of Houston — M
University of Idaho — M
University of Illinois at Chicago — M
University of Illinois at Urbana–Champaign — M,D
The University of Iowa — M,D
University of Kansas — M,D
University of Kentucky — M
University of Louisville — M
University of Maine (Orono) — M
University of Maryland, College Park — M,D
University of Massachusetts Amherst — M,D
The University of Memphis — M
University of Miami — M,D
University of Michigan — D
University of Minnesota, Twin Cities Campus — M,D
University of Mississippi — M
University of Missouri–Columbia — M,D
The University of Montana–Missoula — M
University of Nebraska–Lincoln — M,D
University of Nevada, Las Vegas — M
University of Nevada, Reno — M
University of New Mexico — M,D
The University of North Carolina at Chapel Hill — M,D
University of North Carolina at Greensboro — M
University of Northern Iowa — M
University of North Texas — M
University of Notre Dame — M
University of Oklahoma — M,D
University of Oregon — M
University of Pennsylvania — M,D
University of Pittsburgh — M,D
University of Rhode Island — M
University of Rochester — M
University of South Carolina (Columbia) — M,D
University of Southern California — M,D
University of South Florida — M
University of Southwestern Louisiana — M,D
University of Tennessee, Knoxville — M,D
The University of Texas at Arlington — M
The University of Texas at Austin — M,D
University of Toledo — M
University of Utah — M,D
University of Vermont — M
University of Virginia — M,D
University of Washington — M,D
University of Wisconsin–Madison — M,D
University of Wisconsin–Milwaukee — M
University of Wyoming — M
Vanderbilt University — M,D
Washington University in St. Louis — M,D
Wayne State University — M
West Chester University of Pennsylvania — M
West Virginia University — M
Yale University — M,D

GENETIC COUNSELING

Beaver College — M
Brandeis University — M
California State University, Northridge — M
Case Western Reserve University — M
Northwestern University — M
Tulane University — M,D
University of California, Berkeley — M
University of California, Irvine — M
University of Cincinnati — M
University of Minnesota, Twin Cities Campus — M

P—first professional degree; M—master's degree; D—doctorate; O—other advanced degree.

Genetic Counseling (continued)

University of Pittsburgh	M
University of South Carolina (Columbia)	M
Virginia Commonwealth University	M

GENETICS

Allegheny University of the Health Sciences	M,D
Arizona State University	M,D
Brandeis University	D
California Institute of Technology	D
Carnegie Mellon University	D
Case Western Reserve University	D
Clemson University	M,D
Colorado State University	M,D
Columbia University	M,D
Cornell University	D
Duke University	D
Emory University	D
Florida State University	M,D
The George Washington University	M,D
Harvard University	D
Howard University	M,D
Illinois State University	D
Indiana University Bloomington	D
Indiana University–Purdue University Indianapolis	M,D
Iowa State University of Science and Technology	M,D
Johns Hopkins University	M,D
Kansas State University	M,D
Marquette University	M,D
Massachusetts Institute of Technology	D
Michigan State University	D
Mississippi State University	M
New York University	M
North Carolina State University	M,D
Northwestern University	D
The Ohio State University	M,D
Oklahoma State University	M,D
Oregon State University	M,D
Pennsylvania State University University Park Campus	M,D
Purdue University	M,D
Rutgers, The State University of New Jersey, New Brunswick	M,D
Stanford University	D
State University of New York at Albany	M,D
State University of New York at Buffalo	M,D
State University of New York at Stony Brook	D
Temple University (Philadelphia)	D
Texas A&M University (College Station)	M,D
Tufts University	D
The University of Alabama at Birmingham	D
The University of Arizona	M,D
University of California, Berkeley	D
University of California, Davis	M,D
University of California, Irvine	D
University of California, Los Angeles	D
University of California, Riverside	D
University of California, San Diego	D
University of California, San Francisco	D
University of Chicago	D
University of Cincinnati	D
University of Colorado at Boulder	M,D
University of Connecticut	M,D
University of Delaware	M,D
University of Florida	M,D
University of Georgia	M,D
University of Hawaii at Manoa	M,D
University of Illinois at Chicago	D
The University of Iowa	M,D
University of Kansas	M,D
University of Miami	M,D
University of Michigan	
University of Minnesota, Twin Cities Campus	M,D
University of Missouri–Columbia	M,D
University of New Hampshire	M,D
University of New Mexico	M,D
The University of North Carolina at Chapel Hill	M,D
University of North Dakota	M,D
University of Notre Dame	M,D
University of Oregon	D
University of Pennsylvania	D
University of Pittsburgh	M,D
University of Rhode Island	M,D
University of Rochester	M,D
University of Tennessee, Knoxville	M,D
University of Utah	M,D
University of Vermont	M,D
University of Virginia	D
University of Washington	D
University of Wisconsin–Madison	M,D
Virginia Polytechnic Institute and State University	D
Wake Forest University	M
Washington State University	M,D
Washington University in St. Louis	D
Wayne State University	M,D
West Virginia University	M,D
Yale University	D
Yeshiva University	D

GEOCHEMISTRY

California Institute of Technology	M,D
California State University, Fullerton	M
Colorado School of Mines	M,D
Columbia University	M,D
Cornell University	M,D
The George Washington University	M,D
Indiana University Bloomington	M,D
Johns Hopkins University	M,D
Massachusetts Institute of Technology	M,D
Montana Tech of The University of Montana	M
Pennsylvania State University University Park Campus	M,D
Rensselaer Polytechnic Institute	M,D
University of California, Los Angeles	M,D,O
University of Georgia	M,D
University of Hawaii at Manoa	M,D
University of Illinois at Chicago	M,D
University of Illinois at Urbana–Champaign	M,D
University of Michigan	M,D
University of Missouri–Rolla	M,D
University of Nevada, Reno	M,D
University of New Hampshire	M
The University of Texas at Dallas	M,D
Washington University in St. Louis	D
Yale University	D

GEODETIC SCIENCES

Columbia University	M,D
The Ohio State University	M,D

GEOGRAPHY

Appalachian State University	M
Arizona State University	M,D
Boston University	M,D
Brigham Young University	M
California State University, Chico	M
California State University, Fresno	M
California State University, Fullerton	M
California State University, Hayward	M
California State University, Long Beach	M
California State University, Los Angeles	M
California State University, Northridge	M
California University of Pennsylvania	M
Central Connecticut State University	M
Chicago State University	M
Clark University	D
East Carolina University	M
Eastern Michigan University	M
East Tennessee State University	M
Florida Atlantic University	M
Florida State University	M,D
George Mason University	M
The George Washington University	M
Georgia State University	M
Hunter College of the City University of New York	M
Indiana State University	M,D
Indiana University Bloomington	M,D
Indiana University of Pennsylvania	M
Johns Hopkins University	M,D
Kansas State University	M,D
Kent State University	M,D
Louisiana State University and Agricultural and Mechanical College	M,D
Mankato State University	M
Marshall University	M
Miami University	M
Michigan State University	M,D
Montclair State University	M
Murray State University	M
New Mexico State University	M
North Carolina State University	M
Northeastern Illinois University	M
Northern Arizona University	M
Northern Illinois University	M
The Ohio State University	M,D
Ohio University	M
Oklahoma State University	M
Oregon State University	M,D
Pennsylvania State University University Park Campus	M,D
Portland State University	M,D
Rutgers, The State University of New Jersey, New Brunswick	M,D
St. Cloud State University	M
Salem State College	M
San Diego State University	M,D
San Francisco State University	M
San Jose State University	M
South Dakota State University	M
Southern Illinois University at Carbondale	M,D
Southern Illinois University at Edwardsville	M
Southwest Texas State University	M,D
State University of New York at Albany	M,O
State University of New York at Binghamton	M
State University of New York at Buffalo	M,D
Syracuse University	M,D
Temple University (Philadelphia)	M
Texas A&M University (College Station)	M,D
Towson University	M
The University of Akron	M,D
The University of Alabama (Tuscaloosa)	M
The University of Arizona	M,D
University of Arkansas (Fayetteville)	M,D
University of California, Berkeley	D
University of California, Davis	M,D
University of California, Los Angeles	M,D,O
University of California, Riverside	M,D
University of California, Santa Barbara	M,D
University of Cincinnati	M,D
University of Colorado at Boulder	M,D
University of Connecticut	M,D
University of Delaware	M,D
University of Denver	M,D
University of Florida	M,D
University of Georgia	M,D
University of Hawaii at Manoa	M,D
University of Idaho	M,D
University of Illinois at Chicago	M
University of Illinois at Urbana–Champaign	M,D
The University of Iowa	M,D
University of Kansas	M,D
University of Kentucky	M,D
University of Maryland, College Park	M,D
University of Massachusetts Amherst	M
The University of Memphis	M
University of Minnesota, Twin Cities Campus	M,D
University of Missouri–Columbia	M
The University of Montana–Missoula	M
University of Nebraska at Omaha	M
University of Nebraska–Lincoln	M,D
University of Nevada, Reno	M
University of New Mexico	M
University of New Orleans	M
The University of North Carolina at Chapel Hill	M,D
University of North Carolina at Charlotte	M
University of North Carolina at Greensboro	M
University of North Dakota	M
University of Northern Iowa	M
University of Oklahoma	M,D
University of Oregon	M,D
University of South Carolina (Columbia)	M,D
University of Southern California	M,D
University of Southern Mississippi	M
University of South Florida	M
University of Tennessee, Knoxville	M,D
The University of Texas at Austin	M,D
University of Toledo	M
University of Utah	M,D
University of Vermont	M
University of Washington	M,D
University of Wisconsin–Madison	M,D,O
University of Wisconsin–Milwaukee	M,D
University of Wyoming	M
Utah State University	M
Valparaiso University	M
Virginia Polytechnic Institute and State University	M
Wayne State University	M
West Chester University of Pennsylvania	M
Western Illinois University	M
Western Kentucky University	M
Western Michigan University	M
Western Washington University	M
West Virginia University	M,D

GEOLOGICAL ENGINEERING

Arizona State University	M,D
Colorado School of Mines	M,D,O
Columbia University	M
Drexel University	M
Michigan Technological University	M
Montana Tech of The University of Montana	M
The University of Akron	M
University of Alaska Fairbanks	M,O
The University of Arizona	M,D
University of California, Berkeley	M,D
University of Idaho	M
University of Minnesota, Twin Cities Campus	M,D
University of Missouri–Rolla	M,D
University of Nevada, Reno	M,O
University of Oklahoma	M,D
University of Utah	M,D
University of Wisconsin–Madison	M,D

GEOLOGY

Auburn University	M
Ball State University	M
Baylor University	M,D
Boise State University	M
Boston College	M
Bowling Green State University	M
Brigham Young University	M
Brooklyn College of the City University of New York	M
California Institute of Technology	M,D
California State University, Bakersfield	M
California State University, Fresno	M
California State University, Hayward	M
California State University, Long Beach	M
California State University, Los Angeles	M
California State University, Northridge	M
Case Western Reserve University	M,D
Central Washington University	M
Cleveland State University	M,D
Colorado School of Mines	M,D,O
Colorado State University	M
Cornell University	M,D
Duke University	M,D
East Carolina University	M
Eastern Kentucky University	M,D
Eastern Washington University	M
Florida Atlantic University	M
Florida International University	M,D
Florida State University	M,D
Fort Hays State University	M
The George Washington University	M,D
Georgia State University	M,O
Idaho State University	M
Indiana State University	M
Indiana University Bloomington	M,D
Indiana University–Purdue University Indianapolis	M
Iowa State University of Science and Technology	M,D
Johns Hopkins University	M,D
Kansas State University	M,D
Kent State University	M,D
Lehigh University	M,D
Loma Linda University	M
Louisiana State University and Agricultural and Mechanical College	M,D
Massachusetts Institute of Technology	M,D
Miami University	M,D
Michigan State University	M,D
Michigan Technological University	M,D
Montana Tech of The University of Montana	M
New Mexico State University	M
North Carolina State University	M,D
Northern Arizona University	M
Northern Illinois University	M,D
Northwestern University	M,D
The Ohio State University	M,D
Ohio University	M
Oklahoma State University	M
Old Dominion University	M
Oregon State University	M,D
Pennsylvania State University University Park Campus	M,D

Portland State University	M,D
Princeton University	D
Queens College of the City University of New York	M
Rice University	M,D
Rutgers, The State University of New Jersey, Newark	M
Rutgers, The State University of New Jersey, New Brunswick	M,D
San Diego State University	M
San Jose State University	M
Southern Illinois University at Carbondale	M,D
Southern Methodist University	M,D
State University of New York at Albany	M,D
State University of New York at Binghamton	M,D
State University of New York at Buffalo	M,D
State University of New York at New Paltz	M
Stephen F. Austin State University	M
Sul Ross State University	M
Syracuse University	M,D
Temple University (Philadelphia)	M
Texas A&M University (College Station)	M,D
Texas A&M University–Kingsville	M
Texas Christian University	M
Tulane University	M,D
The University of Akron	M
The University of Alabama (Tuscaloosa)	M,D
University of Alaska Fairbanks	M,D
University of Arkansas (Fayetteville)	M
University of California, Berkeley	M,D
University of California, Davis	M,D
University of California, Los Angeles	M,D,O
University of California, Riverside	M,D
University of California, San Diego	M,D
University of California, Santa Barbara	M,D
University of Cincinnati	M,D
University of Colorado at Boulder	M,D
University of Connecticut	M,D
University of Delaware	M,D
University of Florida	M,D
University of Hawaii at Manoa	M,D
University of Houston	M,D
University of Idaho	M,D
University of Illinois at Chicago	M,D
University of Illinois at Urbana–Champaign	M,D
The University of Iowa	M,D
University of Kansas	M,D
University of Kentucky	M,D
University of Maine (Orono)	M,D
University of Maryland, College Park	M,D
University of Massachusetts Amherst	M
The University of Memphis	M,D
University of Miami	M,D
University of Michigan	M,D
University of Minnesota, Duluth	M,D
University of Minnesota, Twin Cities Campus	M,D
University of Missouri–Columbia	M,D
University of Missouri–Kansas City	M
University of Missouri–Rolla	M,D
The University of Montana–Missoula	M,D
University of Nevada, Reno	M,D,O
University of New Hampshire	M,D
University of New Orleans	M
The University of North Carolina at Chapel Hill	M,D
University of North Carolina at Wilmington	M
University of North Dakota	M,D
University of Oklahoma	M,D
University of Oregon	M,D
University of Pennsylvania	M,D
University of Pittsburgh	M,D
University of Puerto Rico, Mayagüez Campus	M
University of Rhode Island	M
University of Rochester	M,D
University of South Carolina (Columbia)	M,D
University of Southern Mississippi	M
University of South Florida	M,D,O
University of Southwestern Louisiana	M
University of Tennessee, Knoxville	M,D
The University of Texas at Arlington	M
The University of Texas at Austin	M,D
The University of Texas at Dallas	M,D
The University of Texas at El Paso	M,D
The University of Texas at San Antonio	M
The University of Texas of the Permian Basin	M
University of Toledo	M
University of Tulsa	M
University of Utah	M,D
University of Vermont	M
University of Washington	M,D
University of Wisconsin–Madison	M,D
University of Wisconsin–Milwaukee	M,D
University of Wyoming	M,D
Utah State University	M
Vanderbilt University	M
Virginia Polytechnic Institute and State University	M,D
Washington State University	M,D
Washington University in St. Louis	M,D
Wayne State University	M
West Chester University of Pennsylvania	M
Western Michigan University	M,D
Western Washington University	M
West Virginia University	M,D
Wichita State University	M
Wright State University	M
Yale University	D

GEOPHYSICS

Boise State University	M
Boston College	M
California Institute of Technology	M,D
Colorado School of Mines	M,D,O
Columbia University	M,D
Cornell University	M,D
Florida State University	D
Idaho State University	M
Indiana University Bloomington	M,D
Johns Hopkins University	M,D
Louisiana State University and Agricultural and Mechanical College	M,D
Massachusetts Institute of Technology	M,D
Michigan Technological University	M
North Carolina State University	M,D
Oregon State University	M,D
Pennsylvania State University University Park Campus	M,D
Princeton University	D
Rensselaer Polytechnic Institute	M,D
Rice University	M,D
Southern Methodist University	M,D
Stanford University	M,D
Texas A&M University (College Station)	M,D
The University of Akron	M
University of Alaska Fairbanks	M,D
University of California, Berkeley	M,D
University of California, Los Angeles	M,D
University of California, Santa Barbara	M
University of Chicago	M,D
University of Colorado at Boulder	D
University of Connecticut	M,D
University of Georgia	M,D
University of Hawaii at Manoa	M,D
University of Houston	M,D
University of Idaho	M
University of Illinois at Chicago	M,D
University of Illinois at Urbana–Champaign	M,D
The University of Memphis	M,D
University of Miami	M,D
University of Minnesota, Twin Cities Campus	M,D
University of Missouri–Rolla	M,D
University of Nevada, Reno	M,D
University of New Orleans	M
University of Oklahoma	M
The University of Texas at Dallas	M,D
The University of Texas at El Paso	M
University of Utah	M,D
University of Washington	M,D
University of Wisconsin–Madison	M,D
University of Wyoming	M,D
Virginia Polytechnic Institute and State University	M,D
Washington University in St. Louis	D
Wright State University	M
Yale University	D

GEOSCIENCES

Adelphi University	M,O
Ball State University	M
Baylor University	M
Boston University	M,D
Brown University	M,D
California State University, Chico	M
California University of Pennsylvania	M
Case Western Reserve University	M,D
Central Connecticut State University	M
City College of the City University of New York	M,D
Colorado School of Mines	O
Colorado State University	M,D
Columbia University	M,D
Cornell University	M,D
Dartmouth College	M,D
Emporia State University	M
Georgia Institute of Technology	M,D
Graduate School and University Center of the City University of New York	D
Harvard University	M,D
Indiana State University	M
Indiana University Bloomington	M,D
Iowa State University of Science and Technology	M,D
Lehigh University	M,D
Massachusetts Institute of Technology	M,D
Michigan State University	M,D
Mississippi State University	M
Montana State University–Bozeman	M
Montana Tech of The University of Montana	M
Montclair State University	M
North Carolina Central University	M
North Carolina State University	M,D
Northeastern Illinois University	M
Northeast Louisiana University	M
Northern Arizona University	M
Northwestern University	M,D
Pennsylvania State University University Park Campus	M,D
Princeton University	D
Purdue University	M,D
Radford University	M
Rensselaer Polytechnic Institute	M,D
Saint Louis University	M,D
Southeast Missouri State University	M
Stanford University	M,D,O
State University of New York at Albany	M,D
State University of New York at Stony Brook	M,D
State University of New York College at Oneonta	M
Texas A&M University–Commerce	M
Texas Tech University	M,D
The University of Akron	M
The University of Arizona	M,D
University of California, Irvine	D
University of California, Los Angeles	M,D,O
University of California, Riverside	M,D
University of California, Santa Cruz	M,D
University of Chicago	M,D
University of Illinois at Urbana–Champaign	M,D
University of Maine (Orono)	M,D
University of Massachusetts Amherst	D
University of Michigan	M,D
University of Missouri–Kansas City	M,D
University of Nebraska–Lincoln	M,D
University of Nevada, Las Vegas	M
University of New Hampshire	M,D
University of New Mexico	M,D
University of North Carolina at Charlotte	M
University of Northern Colorado	M
University of Notre Dame	M,D
University of South Carolina (Columbia)	M,D
University of Southern California	M,D
The University of Texas at Austin	M,D
The University of Texas at Dallas	M,D
University of Tulsa	M,D
Washington University in St. Louis	M,D
Western Michigan University	M
Yale University	D

GEOTECHNICAL ENGINEERING

Auburn University	M,D
Case Western Reserve University	M,D
The Catholic University of America	M
Colorado State University	M,D
Cornell University	M,D
Florida Institute of Technology	M
Iowa State University of Science and Technology	M,D
Louisiana State University and Agricultural and Mechanical College	M,D
Marquette University	M,D
Michigan Technological University	D
Northwestern University	M,D
Ohio University	M,D
Rensselaer Polytechnic Institute	M,D
State University of New York at Buffalo	M,D
Texas A&M University (College Station)	M,D
Tufts University	M,D
University of California, Berkeley	M,D
University of California, Los Angeles	M,D
University of Colorado at Boulder	M,D
University of Delaware	M,D
University of Illinois at Chicago	D
University of Maine (Orono)	M,D
University of Missouri–Columbia	M,D
University of Missouri–Rolla	M,D
University of Oklahoma	M
University of Rhode Island	M,D
University of Southern California	M
The University of Texas at Austin	M,D
University of Washington	M,D

GERMAN

Arizona State University	M
Bowling Green State University	M
Brigham Young University	M
Brown University	M,D
California State University, Fullerton	M
California State University, Long Beach	M
The Catholic University of America	M
Colorado State University	M
Columbia University	M,D
Cornell University	M,D
Duke University	D
Eastern Michigan University	M
Florida Atlantic University	M
Florida State University	M
Georgetown University	M,D
Georgia State University	M,O
Graduate School and University Center of the City University of New York	M,D
Harvard University	M,D
Illinois State University	M
Indiana University Bloomington	M,D
Johns Hopkins University	M,D
Kansas State University	M
Kent State University	M
Mankato State University	M
Michigan State University	M,D
Millersville University of Pennsylvania	M
New York University	M,D
Northwestern University	D
The Ohio State University	M,D
Pennsylvania State University University Park Campus	M,D
Portland State University	M
Princeton University	D
Purdue University	M,D
Rice University	M,D
Rutgers, The State University of New Jersey, New Brunswick	M,D
San Francisco State University	M
Stanford University	M,D
State University of New York at Buffalo	M,D
State University of New York at Stony Brook	M,D
Syracuse University	M,D
Texas Tech University	M
Tufts University	M
Tulane University	M,D
The University of Alabama (Tuscaloosa)	M
The University of Arizona	M
University of Arkansas (Fayetteville)	M
University of California, Berkeley	M,D
University of California, Davis	M,D
University of California, Irvine	M,D
University of California, Los Angeles	M,D,O
University of California, San Diego	M,D
University of California, Santa Barbara	M,D
University of Chicago	M,D
University of Cincinnati	M,D
University of Colorado at Boulder	M
University of Connecticut	M,D
University of Delaware	M
University of Denver	M
University of Florida	M,D
University of Georgia	M
University of Hawaii at Manoa	M
University of Illinois at Chicago	M,D

P—first professional degree; M—master's degree; D—doctorate; O—other advanced degree.

German (continued)

University of Illinois at Urbana–Champaign M,D
The University of Iowa M,D
University of Kansas M,D
University of Kentucky M
University of Louisville M
University of Maryland, College Park M,D
University of Massachusetts Amherst M,D
University of Michigan M,D
University of Minnesota, Twin Cities Campus M,D
University of Mississippi M
University of Missouri–Columbia M
The University of Montana–Missoula M
University of Nebraska–Lincoln M,D
University of Nevada, Reno M
University of New Mexico M
The University of North Carolina at Chapel Hill M,D
University of Northern Iowa M
University of Notre Dame M
University of Oklahoma M
University of Oregon M,D
University of Pennsylvania M,D
University of Pittsburgh M,D
University of Rochester M
University of South Carolina (Columbia) M
University of Southern California M,D
University of Tennessee, Knoxville M,D
The University of Texas at Arlington M
The University of Texas at Austin M,D
University of Toledo M
University of Utah M,D
University of Vermont M
University of Virginia M,D
University of Washington M,D
University of Wisconsin–Madison M,D
University of Wisconsin–Milwaukee M
University of Wyoming M
Vanderbilt University M,D
Washington University in St. Louis M,D
Wayne State University M,D
West Virginia University M
Yale University M,D

GERONTOLOGICAL NURSING

Boston College M
Case Western Reserve University M
The Catholic University of America M
Columbia University M,O
Duke University M,O
Emory University M
Gannon University M
Georgia State University M
Gwynedd-Mercy College M
Hunter College of the City University of New York M
La Roche College M
Lehman College of the City University of New York M
Loma Linda University M
Marquette University O
Nazareth College of Rochester M
New York University M,O
Pacific Lutheran University M
Rutgers, The State University of New Jersey, Newark M
Saint Louis University M,O
San Jose State University M
Seton Hall University M
State University of New York at New Paltz M
State University of New York at Stony Brook M
University of Delaware M,O
University of Massachusetts Lowell M
University of Michigan M
University of Minnesota, Twin Cities Campus M
University of New Mexico M
University of North Carolina at Greensboro O
University of Pennsylvania M
University of Utah M,O
Vanderbilt University M

GERONTOLOGY

Abilene Christian University M
Appalachian State University M
Arizona State University O
Arizona State University West O
Ball State University M
Baylor University M
Brown University M,D
California State University, Dominguez Hills M
California State University, Long Beach M
Case Western Reserve University O
Central Missouri State University M
Clark University O
College of New Rochelle M,O
College of Notre Dame M
College of Notre Dame of Maryland M
Concordia University (IL) M,O
Eastern Illinois University M
Gannon University O
George Mason University M
Georgia State University M
Hofstra University M
Lindenwood University M
Long Island University, Brooklyn Campus O
Long Island University, C.W. Post Campus M,O
Mankato State University M
Miami University M
National-Louis University M,O
Northeastern Illinois University M
Northeast Louisiana University M,O
Nova Southeastern University M
Oregon State University M
Portland State University O
Roosevelt University M
Sage Graduate School M
St. Cloud State University M
Saint Joseph College (CT) M
Saint Joseph's University M
San Francisco State University M
San Jose State University M
State University of West Georgia M
Syracuse University M
Texas A&M University–Kingsville M
The University of Akron M,D
The University of Arizona M,O
University of Arkansas at Little Rock M,O
University of Central Oklahoma M
University of Illinois at Springfield M
University of Kentucky D
University of Massachusetts Boston D
University of Missouri–St. Louis M,O
University of Nebraska at Omaha M,O
University of New Orleans O
University of North Carolina at Charlotte M
University of North Carolina at Greensboro O
University of Northern Colorado M
University of North Florida O
University of North Texas M,O
University of Pittsburgh O
University of South Alabama O
University of South Carolina (Columbia) O
University of Southern California M,D,O
University of South Florida M,D
University of Tennessee, Knoxville M
University of the Incarnate Word M
University of Utah M,O
Virginia Commonwealth University M,O
Virginia Polytechnic Institute and State University M,D
Wayne State University O
Webster University M
Western Illinois University M
Western Kentucky University M
Wichita State University M

GRAPHIC DESIGN

Boston University M
California State University, Los Angeles M
City College of the City University of New York M
College of New Rochelle M
Colorado State University M
Florida Atlantic University M
George Mason University M
Illinois Institute of Technology M,D
Illinois State University M
Indiana State University M
Indiana University Bloomington M
Iowa State University of Science and Technology M
Kent State University M
Louisiana Tech University M
Michigan State University M
North Carolina State University M
Pennsylvania State University University Park Campus M
Rochester Institute of Technology M
San Diego State University M
San Jose State University M
Syracuse University M
Temple University (Philadelphia) M
Texas Woman's University M
University of Baltimore M
University of Cincinnati M
University of Guam M
University of Houston M
University of Illinois at Chicago M
University of Illinois at Urbana–Champaign M
University of Massachusetts Dartmouth M
The University of Memphis M
University of Miami M
University of Minnesota, Duluth M
University of New Orleans M
University of North Texas M
University of Notre Dame M
University of Tennessee, Knoxville M
University of Utah M
Virginia Commonwealth University M
Western Michigan University M
Yale University M

HEALTH EDUCATION

Adams State College M
Adelphi University M,O
Albany State University M
Alcorn State University M
Allegheny University of the Health Sciences M
Arkansas Tech University M,D
Auburn University M,D,O
Austin Peay State University M
Ball State University M
Baylor University M
Beaver College M
Boston University M,O
Brigham Young University M
Brooklyn College of the City University of New York M
California State University, Long Beach M
California State University, Los Angeles M
California State University, Northridge M
Central Washington University M
The Citadel, The Military College of South Carolina M
Cleveland State University M
The College of New Jersey M
East Carolina University M
Eastern College M
Eastern Kentucky University M
East Stroudsburg University of Pennsylvania M
Edinboro University of Pennsylvania O
Florida Agricultural and Mechanical University M
Florida International University M
Florida State University M
Fort Hays State University M
Frostburg State University M
Georgia College and State University M,O
Georgia Southern University M,O
Georgia Southwestern State University M
Hofstra University M
Howard University M
Illinois State University M
Indiana State University M
Indiana University Bloomington M,O
Indiana University of Pennsylvania M
Inter American University of Puerto Rico, Metropolitan Campus M
Iowa State University of Science and Technology M
Jackson State University M
Jacksonville State University M
James Madison University M
John F. Kennedy University M
Kent State University M
Lehman College of the City University of New York M
Lesley College M
Loma Linda University M,D
Long Island University, Brooklyn Campus M
Louisiana Tech University M
Mankato State University M
Marshall University M
McNeese State University M
Middle Tennessee State University M,D
Mississippi State University M
Montclair State University M
Morehead State University M,D
New Jersey City University M
New York University M,D,O
North Carolina Agricultural and Technical State University M
Northeast Louisiana University M
Northern Arizona University M
Northern State University M
Northwest Missouri State University M
Nova Southeastern University D
The Ohio State University M,D
Oklahoma State University M,D
Oregon State University M
Pennsylvania State University Harrisburg Campus of the Capital College M
Plymouth State College of the University System of New Hampshire M
Portland State University M
Prairie View A&M University M
Rhode Island College M
Rowan University M,O
Sage Graduate School M
Saint Joseph's University M
Saint Mary's College of California M
Sam Houston State University M
San Francisco State University M
South Dakota State University M
Southeastern Louisiana University M
Southern Arkansas University–Magnolia M
Southern Connecticut State University M
Southern Illinois University at Carbondale M,D
Southern Illinois University at Edwardsville M
Southwestern Oklahoma State University M
Southwest Texas State University M
Springfield College (MA) M
State University of New York College at Brockport M
State University of New York College at Cortland M
Stephen F. Austin State University M
Syracuse University M,O
Tarleton State University M,O
Teachers College, Columbia University M,D
Temple University (Philadelphia) M,D
Tennessee State University M
Tennessee Technological University M
Texas A&M University (College Station) M,D
Texas A&M University–Commerce M
Texas A&M University–Kingsville M
Texas Southern University M
Texas Woman's University M,D
Tulane University M
Union College (KY) M
The University of Alabama (Tuscaloosa) M,D,O
The University of Alabama at Birmingham M,D,O
The University of Arizona M
University of Arkansas (Fayetteville) M,D
University of California, Berkeley M
University of Central Arkansas M
University of Central Oklahoma M
University of Cincinnati M
University of Colorado at Denver D
University of Detroit Mercy M
University of Florida M,D
University of Georgia M,D,O
University of Hawaii at Manoa M
University of Houston M,D
University of Illinois at Chicago M
University of Kansas M,D
University of Maryland, Baltimore County M
University of Maryland, College Park M,D
University of Michigan–Flint M
The University of Montana–Missoula M
University of Montevallo M,O
University of Nebraska at Omaha M
University of Nebraska–Lincoln M
University of New Mexico M,D
University of New Orleans M,O
The University of North Carolina at Chapel Hill M,D
University of North Carolina at Charlotte M
University of Northern Iowa M
University of Pittsburgh M
University of Rhode Island M
University of South Alabama M
University of South Carolina (Columbia) M,D,O
University of South Dakota M
University of Southern Mississippi M
University of Tennessee, Knoxville M,D
The University of Texas at Austin M,D

- The University of Texas at Tyler M
- University of Toledo M,D
- University of Utah M,D
- University of Virginia M,D
- University of West Florida M
- University of Wisconsin–La Crosse M
- University of Wyoming M
- Utah State University M
- Valdosta State University M
- Vanderbilt University M
- Virginia Polytechnic Institute and State University M
- Wayne State College M
- Wayne State University M
- West Chester University of Pennsylvania M
- Western Illinois University M
- Western Kentucky University M
- Worcester State College M
- Wright State University M

HEALTH PHYSICS/RADIOLOGICAL HEALTH

- Allegheny University of the Health Sciences M,D
- Colorado State University M,D
- Emory University M,D
- Georgetown University M
- Georgia Institute of Technology M,D
- Johns Hopkins University M,D
- Massachusetts Institute of Technology M,D
- Midwestern State University M
- New York University D
- Northwestern University M,D
- Oregon State University M
- Purdue University M,D
- San Diego State University M
- Texas A&M University (College Station) M
- University of Cincinnati M,D
- University of Florida M,D
- University of Illinois at Urbana–Champaign M,D
- University of Kentucky M
- University of Massachusetts Lowell M,D
- University of Miami M
- University of Michigan M
- University of Missouri–Columbia M
- University of Nevada, Las Vegas M
- University of Pittsburgh O
- The University of Texas at Arlington M
- Wayne State University M,D

HEALTH PROMOTION

- Ball State University M
- Boston University M
- Bridgewater State College M
- Brigham Young University M
- California State University, Fresno M
- Central Michigan University M
- The George Washington University M
- Harvard University M,D
- Idaho State University M
- Indiana University Bloomington M
- Lehman College of the City University of New York M
- Loma Linda University M,D
- Marymount University M
- Mississippi State University M
- Northern Arizona University M
- Northwestern State University of Louisiana M
- Portland State University M
- Purdue University M,D
- San Diego State University M
- Simmons College M
- Southwest Missouri State University M
- Springfield College (MA) M,O
- Trinity College (DC) M
- The University of Alabama (Tuscaloosa) M,D
- The University of Alabama at Birmingham D,O
- University of Delaware M
- University of Georgia M,D,O
- University of Hawaii at Manoa D
- University of Kentucky M,D
- University of Massachusetts Lowell D
- The University of Memphis M
- University of Michigan M,D
- University of North Texas M
- University of Pittsburgh M
- University of South Carolina (Columbia) M,D,O
- University of Southern California M
- University of Tennessee, Knoxville M
- University of Utah M,D
- Western Illinois University M
- West Virginia University M

HEALTH PSYCHOLOGY

- Allegheny University of the Health Sciences
- Duke University D
- Rutgers, The State University of New Jersey, New Brunswick D
- Santa Clara University M
- Springfield College (MA) M,D,O
- State University of New York at Stony Brook D
- University of California, Irvine D
- University of Florida D
- University of Hartford M
- University of Miami D
- University of North Texas D
- University of Pittsburgh D
- Yeshiva University D

HEALTH SERVICES MANAGEMENT AND HOSPITAL ADMINISTRATION

- Arizona State University M
- Armstrong Atlantic State University M
- Baldwin-Wallace College M
- Barry University M
- Baruch College of the City University of New York M
- Baylor University M
- Bellevue University M
- Boston University M
- Brandeis University M
- Brooklyn College of the City University of New York M
- California Lutheran University M
- California State University, Bakersfield M
- California State University, Chico M
- California State University, Fresno M
- California State University, Long Beach M,O
- California State University, Los Angeles M
- California State University, Northridge M
- California State University, San Bernardino M
- Cardinal Stritch University M
- Carnegie Mellon University M
- Central Michigan University M,O
- Chapman University M
- Charleston Southern University M
- Clark University M
- Clemson University M
- Columbia University M,D
- Cornell University M
- DePaul University M
- Duke University M
- Duquesne University M
- D'Youville College M
- Eastern Kentucky University M
- Emory University M
- Florida Institute of Technology M
- Florida International University M
- Framingham State College M
- Gannon University M,O
- The George Washington University M,O
- Georgia Institute of Technology M
- Georgia State University M
- Golden Gate University M,O
- Governors State University M
- Harvard University M,D
- Hofstra University M
- Houston Baptist University M
- Howard University M
- Idaho State University M,D
- Indiana State University M
- Indiana University Northwest M
- Indiana University–Purdue University Indianapolis M
- Iona College (New Rochelle) M,O
- Johns Hopkins University M,D,O
- Kean University M
- Lesley College M
- Lindenwood University M
- Loma Linda University M
- Long Island University, Brooklyn Campus M
- Long Island University, C.W. Post Campus M,O
- Madonna University M
- Marshall University M
- Marymount University M
- Marywood University M
- Mercer University, Cecil B. Day Campus M
- Mississippi College M
- Montana State University–Billings M
- Montana State University–Bozeman M
- National University M
- New Jersey City University M
- New School University M,O
- New York University M,D,O
- Northeastern University M
- Northwestern University M
- Nova Southeastern University M
- The Ohio State University M,D
- Ohio University M
- Oklahoma City University M
- Old Dominion University D,O
- Oregon State University M
- Our Lady of the Lake University of San Antonio M
- Pace University M
- Pennsylvania State University Harrisburg Campus of the Capital College M
- Pennsylvania State University University Park Campus M,D
- Philadelphia College of Textiles and Science M
- Portland State University M
- Quinnipiac College M
- Rochester Institute of Technology M,O
- Rutgers, The State University of New Jersey, Camden M
- Rutgers, The State University of New Jersey, Newark M
- Sacred Heart University M
- Sage Graduate School M
- St. Ambrose University M
- St. John's University (NY) M
- Saint Joseph's University M
- Saint Louis University M
- Saint Mary's College of California M
- Saint Mary's University of Minnesota M
- St. Thomas University M,O
- Saint Xavier University M,O
- Salve Regina University M
- San Diego State University M
- San Jose State University O
- Seton Hall University M
- Simmons College M,O
- Southeast Missouri State University M
- Southwest Baptist University M
- Southwest Texas State University M
- Springfield College (MA) M
- State University of New York at Albany M
- State University of New York at Binghamton M
- State University of New York at Stony Brook M,O
- Suffolk University M
- Temple University (Philadelphia) M
- Texas Tech University M,O
- Texas Woman's University M
- Trinity University M
- Tulane University M,D
- The University of Alabama at Birmingham M,D
- University of Arkansas at Little Rock M
- University of California, Berkeley M,D
- University of California, Los Angeles M,D
- University of Central Florida M
- University of Chicago M,O
- University of Cincinnati M
- University of Colorado at Denver M
- University of Connecticut M
- University of Denver M
- University of Detroit Mercy M
- University of Evansville M
- University of Florida M,D
- University of Georgia M,D
- University of Hawaii at Manoa M
- University of Houston M
- University of Houston–Clear Lake M
- University of Illinois at Chicago M,D
- The University of Iowa M,D
- University of Kansas M
- University of Kentucky M
- University of La Verne M
- University of Mary Hardin–Baylor M
- University of Maryland, Baltimore County M
- University of Massachusetts Lowell M
- The University of Memphis M
- University of Miami O
- University of Michigan M,D
- University of Minnesota, Twin Cities Campus M,D
- University of Missouri–Columbia M
- University of New Hampshire M
- University of New Haven M
- The University of North Carolina at Chapel Hill M,D
- University of North Carolina at Charlotte M
- University of North Florida M
- University of North Texas M
- University of Pennsylvania M,D
- University of Pittsburgh M,D,O
- University of St. Francis (IL) M,O
- University of St. Thomas (MN) M,O
- University of San Francisco M
- University of Scranton M
- University of South Carolina (Columbia) M,D
- University of Southern California M
- University of Southern Maine M
- University of Southern Mississippi M
- University of South Florida M,D
- University of Southwestern Louisiana M
- The University of Texas at Tyler M
- University of Virginia M
- University of Washington M
- University of Wisconsin–Madison M,D
- University of Wisconsin–Oshkosh M
- Villanova University M
- Virginia Commonwealth University M,D
- Washington University in St. Louis M
- Webster University M
- West Chester University of Pennsylvania M
- Western Carolina University M
- Western Kentucky University M
- Western New England College M
- Widener University M
- Wilkes University M
- Wright State University M
- Xavier University M
- Yale University M,D
- Youngstown State University M

HEALTH SERVICES RESEARCH

- Arizona State University D
- Brown University M,D
- Case Western Reserve University M,D
- Cornell University M
- Dartmouth College M,D
- Johns Hopkins University M,D
- Saint Louis University D
- Southwest Texas State University M
- Stanford University M
- University of Michigan M
- University of Minnesota, Twin Cities Campus M,D
- University of Rochester D
- University of Southern California D
- University of Virginia M
- University of Wisconsin–Madison M,D
- Virginia Commonwealth University D
- Wake Forest University M

HIGHER EDUCATION

- Appalachian State University M,O
- Arizona State University M,D
- Auburn University M,D,O
- Azusa Pacific University M
- Barry University M,D
- Baruch College of the City University of New York M
- Boston College M,D
- Boston University M
- Bowling Green State University D
- Claremont Graduate University M,D
- Dallas Baptist University M
- DePaul University M
- Drake University M,D,O
- Eastern Kentucky University M
- Eastern Washington University M
- Florida State University M,D,O
- The George Washington University M,D,O
- Georgia State University D
- Harvard University D
- Illinois State University D
- Indiana State University M
- Indiana University Bloomington M,D
- Indiana University of Pennsylvania M
- Inter American University of Puerto Rico, Metropolitan Campus M
- Inter American University of Puerto Rico, San Germán Campus M
- Iowa State University of Science and Technology M,D
- Kent State University M,D,O
- Loyola University Chicago D
- Mankato State University M
- Morehead State University M,O
- New York University M,D
- Northeastern State University M
- Northwestern University M
- Nova Southeastern University D
- Ohio University M,D
- Oklahoma State University M,D,O
- Pennsylvania State University University Park Campus M,D
- Portland State University D
- Rowan University M

P—first professional degree; M—master's degree; D—doctorate; O—other advanced degree.

Higher Education (continued)

St. John's University (NY)	M
Saint Louis University	M,D,O
San Jose State University	M,O
Seton Hall University	D,O
Southern Illinois University at Carbondale	M
Spalding University	M
Stanford University	M,D
Syracuse University	M,D,O
Teachers College, Columbia University	M,D
Texas A&M University–Commerce	M,D
Texas A&M University–Kingsville	D
Texas Southern University	M
Texas Tech University	M,D
The University of Akron	M
The University of Alabama (Tuscaloosa)	M,D,O
The University of Arizona	M,D
University of Arkansas (Fayetteville)	M,D,O
University of Arkansas at Little Rock	D
University of Central Oklahoma	M
University of Connecticut	M,D
University of Delaware	M
University of Denver	M,D
University of Florida	D,O
University of Georgia	D
University of Houston	M
The University of Iowa	M,D,O
University of Kansas	M,D
University of Kentucky	M
University of Louisville	M
University of Maine (Orono)	M,O
University of Mary	M
University of Massachusetts Amherst	M,D,O
University of Massachusetts Boston	D
The University of Memphis	D
University of Miami	M,D
University of Michigan	M
University of Minnesota, Twin Cities Campus	M,D
University of Mississippi	M
University of Missouri–Columbia	M,D,O
University of Nevada, Las Vegas	M
University of North Carolina at Greensboro	M
University of North Texas	D
University of Oklahoma	M,D
University of Oregon	M
University of Pennsylvania	M,D
University of South Carolina (Columbia)	M
University of South Florida	M,D,O
University of Tennessee, Knoxville	M,D
University of Toledo	M,D
University of Virginia	D,O
Vanderbilt University	M,D,O
Wayne State University	D

HISPANIC STUDIES

Brown University	M,D
California State University, Los Angeles	M
California State University, Northridge	M
New Mexico Highlands University	M
Northwestern University	D
Pontifical Catholic University of Puerto Rico	M
San Jose State University	M
University of California, Los Angeles	D
University of California, Santa Barbara	D
University of Illinois at Chicago	M,D
University of New Mexico	D
University of Pittsburgh	M,D
University of Puerto Rico, Mayagüez Campus	M
University of Puerto Rico, Río Piedras	M,D

HISTORIC PRESERVATION

Ball State University	M
Boston University	M
Colorado State University	M
Columbia University	M
Cornell University	M
Eastern Michigan University	M
The George Washington University	M
Georgia State University	M
Middle Tennessee State University	D
New York University	O
State University of New York College at Buffalo	M,O
Texas A&M University (College Station)	M

Texas Tech University	D
University of Delaware	M,D
University of Georgia	M
University of Kentucky	M
University of Oregon	M
University of Pennsylvania	M,O
University of South Carolina (Columbia)	M,O
University of Vermont	M,O
University of Washington	M
Western Kentucky University	M

HISTORY

Abilene Christian University	M
Alabama State University	M
American University	M,D
Andrews University	M
Angelo State University	M
Appalachian State University	M
Arizona State University	M,D
Arkansas State University	M,O
Armstrong Atlantic State University	M
Auburn University	M,D
Ball State University	M
Baylor University	M
Boise State University	M
Boston College	M,D
Boston University	M,D
Bowling Green State University	M,D
Brandeis University	M,D
Bridgewater State College	M
Brigham Young University	M,D
Brooklyn College of the City University of New York	M
Brown University	M,D
Butler University	M
California State University, Bakersfield	M
California State University, Chico	M
California State University, Fresno	M
California State University, Fullerton	M
California State University, Hayward	M
California State University, Long Beach	M
California State University, Los Angeles	M
California State University, Northridge	M
California State University, Stanislaus	M
Carnegie Mellon University	M,D
Case Western Reserve University	M,D
The Catholic University of America	M,D
Central Connecticut State University	M
Central Michigan University	M,D
Central Missouri State University	M
Central Washington University	M
Chicago State University	M
The Citadel, The Military College of South Carolina	M
City College of the City University of New York	M
Claremont Graduate University	M,D
Clark Atlanta University	M
Clark University	M,D,O
Clemson University	M
Cleveland State University	M
The College of Saint Rose	M
College of William and Mary	M,D
Colorado State University	M
Columbia University	M,D
Cornell University	M,D
DePaul University	M
Duke University	D
Duquesne University	M
East Carolina University	M
Eastern Illinois University	M
Eastern Kentucky University	M
Eastern Michigan University	M
Eastern Washington University	M
East Stroudsburg University of Pennsylvania	M
East Tennessee State University	M
Emory University	M,D
Emporia State University	M
Fairleigh Dickinson University, Teaneck-Hackensack Campus	M
Fayetteville State University	M
Florida Atlantic University	M
Florida International University	M,D
Florida State University	M,D
Fordham University	M,D
Fort Hays State University	M
George Mason University	M
Georgetown University	M,D
The George Washington University	M,D
Georgia College and State University	M
Georgia Southern University	M

Georgia State University	M,D
Graduate School and University Center of the City University of New York	D
Hardin–Simmons University	M
Harvard University	D
Howard University	M,D
Hunter College of the City University of New York	M
Illinois State University	M
Indiana State University	M
Indiana University Bloomington	M,D
Indiana University of Pennsylvania	M
Iona College (New Rochelle)	M
Iowa State University of Science and Technology	M,D
Jackson State University	M
Jacksonville State University	M
James Madison University	M
John Carroll University	M
Johns Hopkins University	M,D
Kansas State University	M,D
Kent State University	M,D
Lamar University	M
Lehigh University	M,D
Lehman College of the City University of New York	M
Lincoln University (MO)	M
Long Island University, Brooklyn Campus	M
Long Island University, C.W. Post Campus	M
Louisiana State University and Agricultural and Mechanical College	M,D
Louisiana Tech University	M
Loyola University Chicago	M,D
Mankato State University	M
Marquette University	M,D
Marshall University	M
Miami University	M
Michigan State University	M,D
Middle Tennessee State University	M,D
Midwestern State University	M
Millersville University of Pennsylvania	M
Mississippi College	M
Mississippi State University	M,D
Monmouth University	M
Montana State University–Bozeman	M
Montclair State University	M
Morgan State University	M,D
Murray State University	M
New Jersey Institute of Technology	M
New Mexico Highlands University	M
New Mexico State University	M
New School University	M,D
New York University	M,D,O
North Carolina Central University	M
North Carolina State University	M
North Dakota State University	M
Northeastern Illinois University	M
Northeastern University	M,D
Northeast Louisiana University	M
Northern Arizona University	M,D
Northern Illinois University	M,D
Northwestern State University of Louisiana	M
Northwestern University	D
Northwest Missouri State University	M
Oakland University	M
The Ohio State University	M,D,O
Ohio University	M,D
Oklahoma State University	M,D
Old Dominion University	M
Pennsylvania State University University Park Campus	M,D
Pepperdine University (Malibu)	M
Pittsburg State University	M
Pontifical Catholic University of Puerto Rico	M
Portland State University	M
Princeton University	D
Providence College	M,D
Purdue University	M,D
Purdue University Calumet	M
Queens College of the City University of New York	M
Rhode Island College	M
Rice University	M,D
Roosevelt University	M
Rutgers, The State University of New Jersey, Camden	M
Rutgers, The State University of New Jersey, Newark	M
Rutgers, The State University of New Jersey, New Brunswick	D
St. Bonaventure University	M
St. Cloud State University	M
St. John's University (NY)	M,D
Saint Louis University	M,D
St. Mary's University of San Antonio	M

Salem State College	M
Sam Houston State University	M
San Diego State University	M
San Francisco State University	M
San Jose State University	M
Seton Hall University	M
Shippensburg University of Pennsylvania	M
Slippery Rock University of Pennsylvania	M
Sonoma State University	M
Southeastern Louisiana University	M
Southeast Missouri State University	M
Southern Connecticut State University	M
Southern Illinois University at Carbondale	M,D
Southern Illinois University at Edwardsville	M
Southern Methodist University	M
Southern University and Agricultural and Mechanical College	M
Southwest Missouri State University	M
Southwest Texas State University	M
Stanford University	M,D
State University of New York at Albany	M,D,O
State University of New York at Binghamton	M,D
State University of New York at Buffalo	M,D
State University of New York at Oswego	M
State University of New York at Stony Brook	M,D
State University of New York College at Brockport	M
State University of New York College at Buffalo	M
State University of New York College at Cortland	M
State University of New York College at Oneonta	M
State University of West Georgia	M
Stephen F. Austin State University	M
Sul Ross State University	M
Syracuse University	M,D
Tarleton State University	M
Temple University (Philadelphia)	M,D
Texas A&M International University	M
Texas A&M University (College Station)	M,D
Texas A&M University–Commerce	M
Texas A&M University–Kingsville	M
Texas Christian University	M
Texas Southern University	M
Texas Tech University	M,D
Texas Woman's University	M
Troy State University Dothan	M
Truman State University	M
Tufts University	M,D
Tulane University	M,D
The University of Akron	M,D
The University of Alabama (Tuscaloosa)	M,D
The University of Alabama at Birmingham	M
The University of Alabama in Huntsville	M
The University of Arizona	M,D
University of Arkansas (Fayetteville)	M,D
University of California, Berkeley	M,D,O
University of California, Davis	M,D
University of California, Irvine	M,D
University of California, Los Angeles	M,D,O
University of California, Riverside	M,D
University of California, San Diego	M,D
University of California, Santa Barbara	M,D
University of California, Santa Cruz	D
University of Central Arkansas	M
University of Central Florida	M
University of Central Oklahoma	M
University of Chicago	M,D
University of Cincinnati	M,D
University of Colorado at Boulder	M,D
University of Colorado at Colorado Springs	M
University of Colorado at Denver	M
University of Connecticut	M,D
University of Delaware	M,D
University of Denver	M
University of Florida	M,D
University of Georgia	M,D
University of Hawaii at Manoa	M,D
University of Houston	M,D

University of Houston–Clear Lake M
University of Idaho M,D
University of Illinois at Chicago M,D
University of Illinois at Urbana–Champaign M,D
University of Indianapolis M
The University of Iowa M,D
University of Kansas M,D
University of Kentucky M,D
University of Louisville M
University of Maine (Orono) M,D
University of Maryland, Baltimore County M
University of Maryland, College Park M,D
University of Massachusetts Amherst M,D
University of Massachusetts Boston M
The University of Memphis M,D
University of Miami M,D
University of Michigan M,D
University of Minnesota, Twin Cities Campus M,D
University of Mississippi M,D
University of Missouri–Columbia M,D
University of Missouri–Kansas City M,D
University of Missouri–St. Louis M
The University of Montana–Missoula M
University of Montevallo M
University of Nebraska at Kearney M
University of Nebraska at Omaha M
University of Nebraska–Lincoln M,D
University of Nevada, Las Vegas M,D
University of Nevada, Reno M,D
University of New Hampshire M,D
University of New Mexico M,D
University of New Orleans M
The University of North Carolina at Chapel Hill M,D
University of North Carolina at Charlotte M
University of North Carolina at Greensboro M
University of North Carolina at Wilmington M
University of North Dakota M,D
University of Northern Colorado M
University of Northern Iowa M
University of North Florida M
University of North Texas M,D
University of Notre Dame M,D
University of Oklahoma M,D
University of Oregon M,D
University of Pennsylvania M,D
University of Pittsburgh M,D
University of Puerto Rico, Río Piedras M,D
University of Rhode Island M
University of Richmond M
University of Rochester M,D
University of San Diego M
University of Scranton M
University of South Alabama M
University of South Carolina (Columbia) M,D,O
University of South Dakota M
University of Southern California M,D
University of Southern Mississippi M,D
University of South Florida M
University of Southwestern Louisiana M
University of Tennessee, Knoxville M,D
The University of Texas at Arlington M
The University of Texas at Austin M,D
The University of Texas at El Paso M
The University of Texas at San Antonio M
The University of Texas at Tyler M,O
The University of Texas of the Permian Basin M
The University of Texas–Pan American M
University of the Pacific M
University of Toledo M,D
University of Tulsa M
University of Utah M,D
University of Vermont M
University of Virginia M,D
University of Washington M,D
University of West Florida M
University of Wisconsin–Eau Claire M
University of Wisconsin–Madison M,D
University of Wisconsin–Milwaukee M
University of Wisconsin–Stevens Point M
University of Wyoming M
Utah State University M
Valdosta State University M
Valparaiso University M
Vanderbilt University M,D
Villanova University M
Virginia Commonwealth University M
Virginia Polytechnic Institute and State University M
Virginia State University M
Wake Forest University M
Washington State University M,D
Washington University in St. Louis M,D
Wayne State University M,D,O
West Chester University of Pennsylvania M
Western Carolina University M
Western Connecticut State University M
Western Illinois University M
Western Kentucky University M
Western Michigan University M,D
Western Washington University M
Westfield State College M
West Texas A&M University M
West Virginia University M,D
Wichita State University M
William Paterson University of New Jersey M
Winthrop University M
Wright State University M
Xavier University M
Yale University M,D
Youngstown State University M

HISTORY OF MEDICINE

Duke University
New Jersey Institute of Technology M
Rutgers, The State University of New Jersey, New Brunswick D
University of Minnesota, Twin Cities Campus M,D
Yale University M,D

HISTORY OF SCIENCE

Brown University M,D
Cornell University M,D
Georgia Institute of Technology M,D
Harvard University M,D
Indiana University Bloomington M,D
Iowa State University of Science and Technology M,D
Johns Hopkins University M,D
Massachusetts Institute of Technology D
New Jersey Institute of Technology M
Polytechnic University, Brooklyn Campus M
Princeton University D
Rensselaer Polytechnic Institute M,D
Rutgers, The State University of New Jersey, New Brunswick D
University of California, Berkeley D
University of California, San Francisco M,D
University of California, Santa Barbara D
University of Chicago M,D
University of Massachusetts Amherst M
University of Minnesota, Twin Cities Campus M,D
University of Notre Dame M,D
University of Oklahoma M,D
University of Pennsylvania M,D
University of Pittsburgh M,D
University of Wisconsin–Madison M,D
Virginia Polytechnic Institute and State University M,D
Yale University M,D

HOME ECONOMICS

Alabama Agricultural and Mechanical University M
Appalachian State University M
Ball State University M
Bowling Green State University M
California State University, Fresno M
California State University, Long Beach M
California State University, Los Angeles M
Central Michigan University M
Central Washington University M
Cornell University M,D
East Carolina University M
Eastern Illinois University M
Eastern Michigan University M
Florida State University M,D
Illinois State University M
Indiana State University M
Iowa State University of Science and Technology M,D
Kansas State University M,D
Kent State University M
Lamar University M
Louisiana State University and Agricultural and Mechanical College M,D
Louisiana Tech University M
Marshall University M
Michigan State University M,D
Montclair State University M
New Mexico State University M
North Carolina Central University M
Northern Illinois University M
The Ohio State University M,D
Oklahoma State University M,D
Oregon State University M,D
Prairie View A&M University M
Purdue University M,D
Sam Houston State University M
San Francisco State University M
South Dakota State University M
Southeast Missouri State University M
Stephen F. Austin State University M
Texas A&M University–Kingsville M
Texas Southern University M
Texas Tech University M,D
Tuskegee University M
The University of Akron M
The University of Alabama (Tuscaloosa) M
The University of Arizona M,D
University of Arkansas (Fayetteville) M
University of Central Arkansas M
University of Central Oklahoma M
University of Georgia M,D
University of Idaho M
University of Kentucky M
University of Minnesota, Twin Cities Campus M,D
University of Missouri–Columbia M,D
University of Nebraska–Lincoln M,D
University of North Carolina at Greensboro M,D
University of North Florida M
University of Southern Mississippi M
University of Southwestern Louisiana M
The University of Tennessee at Martin M
University of Tennessee, Knoxville M,D
The University of Texas at Austin M,D
University of Wisconsin–Madison M,D
University of Wisconsin–Stevens Point M
University of Wisconsin–Stout M
Utah State University M
Virginia Polytechnic Institute and State University M,D,O
Western Carolina University M
Western Kentucky University M

HOME ECONOMICS EDUCATION

Brooklyn College of the City University of New York M
Central Washington University M
Eastern Kentucky University M
Florida International University M
Framingham State College M
Idaho State University M
Iowa State University of Science and Technology M,D
Louisiana State University and Agricultural and Mechanical College M
Michigan State University M
Montclair State University M
North Dakota State University M
Northwestern State University of Louisiana M
The Ohio State University M,D
Oregon State University M
Purdue University M,D,O
Queens College of the City University of New York M
South Carolina State University M
State University of New York College at Oneonta M
Texas Southern University M
Texas Tech University M,D
The University of Arizona M
University of Georgia M
University of Montevallo M
University of North Carolina at Greensboro M,D
University of Puerto Rico, Río Piedras M
University of Rhode Island M
Western Carolina University M
Western Kentucky University M
Western Michigan University M
Winthrop University M

HORTICULTURE

Alabama Agricultural and Mechanical University M
Auburn University M,D
Brigham Young University M
Clemson University M,D
Colorado State University M,D
Cornell University M,D
Iowa State University of Science and Technology M,D
Kansas State University M,D
Louisiana State University and Agricultural and Mechanical College M,D
Michigan State University M,D
New Mexico State University M,D
North Carolina State University M,D
North Dakota State University M
The Ohio State University M,D
Oklahoma State University M
Oregon State University M,D
Pennsylvania State University University Park Campus M,D
Purdue University M,D
Rutgers, The State University of New Jersey, New Brunswick M,D
Southern Illinois University at Carbondale M
Texas A&M University (College Station) M,D
Texas Tech University M
University of Arkansas (Fayetteville) M
University of California, Davis M
University of Delaware M
University of Florida M,D
University of Georgia M,D
University of Hawaii at Manoa M,D
University of Maryland, College Park M,D
University of Minnesota, Twin Cities Campus M,D
University of Missouri–Columbia M,D
University of Nebraska–Lincoln M,D
University of Puerto Rico, Mayagüez Campus M
University of Tennessee, Knoxville M
University of Washington M,D
University of Wisconsin–Madison M,D
Virginia Polytechnic Institute and State University M,D
Washington State University M,D

HOSPITALITY MANAGEMENT

Central Michigan University M
Cornell University M,D
Florida International University M
The George Washington University M
Golden Gate University M
Iowa State University of Science and Technology M,D
Kansas State University M,D
Michigan State University M
New York University M,D
The Ohio State University M,D
Oklahoma State University M,D
Pennsylvania State University University Park Campus M
Purdue University M
Rochester Institute of Technology M
Roosevelt University M
Temple University (Philadelphia) M
Texas Tech University M
Texas Woman's University M
The University of Alabama (Tuscaloosa) M
University of Denver M
University of Hawaii at Manoa M
University of Houston M
University of Massachusetts Amherst M
University of Missouri–Columbia M
University of Nevada, Las Vegas M,D
University of New Haven M
University of North Carolina at Greensboro M,D
University of North Texas M
University of South Carolina (Columbia) M
University of Tennessee, Knoxville M
University of Wisconsin–Stout M
Virginia Polytechnic Institute and State University M,D

HUMAN DEVELOPMENT

Arizona State University M,D
Auburn University M,D
Boston University M,D,O
Bowling Green State University M
Bradley University M
Brigham Young University M,D
California State University, San Bernardino M

P—first professional degree; M—master's degree; D—doctorate; O—other advanced degree.

Human Development (continued)

The Catholic University of America D
Claremont Graduate University M,D
Colorado State University M
Cornell University D
DePaul University M
Duke University D
The George Washington University M,D,O
Harvard University M,D,O
Howard University M
Indiana University Bloomington M
Iowa State University of Science and Technology M,D
Kent State University D,O
Loyola University Chicago M,D
Marywood University D
Montana State University–Bozeman M
National–Louis University M,D,O
New York Institute of Technology M
Northeastern University M
Northwestern University D
The Ohio State University M,D
Oregon State University M,D
Our Lady of the Lake University of San Antonio M
Pennsylvania State University University Park Campus M,D
Purdue University M,D
Saint Joseph College (CT) M
Saint Louis University M
Saint Mary's University of Minnesota M
Southern Illinois University at Carbondale M
Texas A&M University (College Station) D
Texas Southern University M
Texas Tech University M,D
Troy State University (Troy) M
Troy State University Montgomery M,O
The University of Alabama (Tuscaloosa) M
University of California, Berkeley M,D
University of California, Davis D
University of California, Irvine D
University of Central Oklahoma M
University of Chicago D
University of Connecticut M,D
University of Delaware M
University of Illinois at Chicago M,D
University of Illinois at Springfield M
University of Illinois at Urbana–Champaign M,D
University of Kansas M
University of Maine (Orono) M
University of Maryland, College Park M,D,O
University of Missouri–Columbia M
University of Nevada, Reno M
University of North Carolina at Greensboro M,D
University of North Texas M
University of Pennsylvania M,D
University of Tennessee, Knoxville D
The University of Texas at Dallas M,D
University of Washington M,D
Utah State University M
Vanderbilt University M,D
Virginia Polytechnic Institute and State University M,D
Walsh University M
Washington State University M
Wayne State University M

HUMAN GENETICS

Allegheny University of the Health Sciences M,D
Case Western Reserve University D
Hofstra University M
Howard University M,D
Johns Hopkins University D
Tulane University M,D
University of California, Los Angeles M,D
University of Michigan M,D
University of Minnesota, Twin Cities Campus M,D
University of Pittsburgh M,D
Virginia Commonwealth University M,D,O

HUMANITIES

Andrews University M
Arizona State University M
Beaver College M
Brigham Young University M
California State University, Dominguez Hills M
Central Michigan University M
Claremont Graduate University M,D
Clark Atlanta University D
Dominican College of San Rafael M
Duke University M
Florida State University M,D
Frostburg State University M
George Mason University D
Grambling State University M
Hofstra University M
Indiana State University M
John Carroll University M
Marshall University M
Marymount University M
Michigan State University M
New York University M,O
Old Dominion University M
Pennsylvania State University Harrisburg Campus of the Capital College M
Salve Regina University M,D,O
San Francisco State University M
Simmons College M
Stanford University M
State University of New York at Albany D
State University of New York at Buffalo M
Syracuse University M,D
Texas Tech University M
University of California, Santa Cruz D
University of Chicago M
University of Colorado at Denver M
University of Houston–Clear Lake M
University of Louisville M
The University of Texas at Arlington M,D
The University of Texas at Dallas M,D
University of West Florida M
Western Kentucky University M
Wright State University M
Xavier University M

HUMAN RESOURCES DEVELOPMENT

Abilene Christian University M
Amber University M
American International College M,O
Azusa Pacific University M
Barry University M,D
Bowie State University M
California State University, Sacramento M
Chapman University M
City University M
Clemson University M
College of New Rochelle M,O
Florida International University M
Friends University M
The George Washington University M,D,O
Georgia State University M,D
Heritage College M
Illinois Institute of Technology M
Indiana State University M
Indiana University Bloomington M
Inter American University of Puerto Rico, Metropolitan Campus M
Inter American University of Puerto Rico, San Germán Campus M
John F. Kennedy University M,O
Johns Hopkins University M
Kennesaw State University M
Lesley College M
Loyola University Chicago M
Marquette University M
National–Louis University M
New School University O
North Carolina Agricultural and Technical State University M
Northeastern Illinois University M
Oakland University M
Pennsylvania State University University Park Campus M
Pittsburg State University M
Rensselaer Polytechnic Institute D
Rochester Institute of Technology M
Rollins College M
St. John Fisher College M
Suffolk University M,O
Texas A&M University (College Station) M,D
Towson University M
Trinity College (DC) M
Universidad del Turabo M
University of Bridgeport M
University of Georgia M
University of Oregon M
University of San Francisco M
University of Scranton M
University of Tennessee, Knoxville M,D
University of Wisconsin–Stout M
Vanderbilt University M,D
Villanova University M
Virginia Polytechnic Institute and State University M,D
Webster University M
Western Carolina University M
Western New England College M
Xavier University M

HUMAN RESOURCES MANAGEMENT

Adelphi University O
Alabama Agricultural and Mechanical University M
Albany State University M
Amber University M
American University M
Appalachian State University M
Auburn University D
Baruch College of the City University of New York M
Boston College M,D
Boston University M,D,O
California State University, Hayward M
California State University, Sacramento M
Case Western Reserve University M,D
The Catholic University of America M
Central Michigan University M,O
Chapman University M
Claremont Graduate University M
Clarkson University M
Cleveland State University M
Columbia University M
Cornell University M,D
Dallas Baptist University M
DePaul University M
East Central University M
Eastern Michigan University M
Emmanuel College (MA) M
Fairfield University M,O
Fairleigh Dickinson University, Florham–Madison Campus M
Fairleigh Dickinson University, Teaneck–Hackensack Campus M
Florida Institute of Technology M
Fordham University M
Framingham State College M
Gannon University O
George Mason University M
The George Washington University M
Georgia State University M,D
Golden Gate University M,O
Hawaii Pacific University M
Houston Baptist University M
Indiana University Bloomington M
Inter American University of Puerto Rico, Metropolitan Campus M
Inter American University of Puerto Rico, San Germán Campus M
Iona College (New Rochelle) M,O
Kennesaw State University M
La Roche College M
Lesley College M
Lindenwood University M
Long Island University, C.W. Post Campus M
Loyola University Chicago M
Lynchburg College M
Marquette University M
Marshall University M
Marygrove College M
Marymount University M
Metropolitan State University M
Michigan State University M,D
National–Louis University M
National University M
New School University M,O
New York Institute of Technology M,O
New York University M,O
North Carolina Agricultural and Technical State University M
Nova Southeastern University M
The Ohio State University M,D
Purdue University M,D
Rensselaer Polytechnic Institute M,D
Rivier College M
Rollins College M
Rutgers, The State University of New Jersey, Newark M
Rutgers, The State University of New Jersey, New Brunswick M,D
Sage Graduate School M
Saint Francis College (PA) M
St. Thomas University M,O
Salve Regina University M
Seton Hall University M
Southeast Missouri State University M
State University of New York at Albany M
Suffolk University M
Syracuse University M
Temple University (Philadelphia) M,D
Trinity College (DC) M
Troy State University (Troy) M
Troy State University Dothan M
Troy State University Montgomery M
Universidad del Turabo M
The University of Akron M
University of Charleston M
University of Connecticut M
University of Florida D
University of Hartford M
University of Houston–Clear Lake M
University of Illinois at Chicago D
University of Illinois at Urbana–Champaign M,D
The University of Iowa D
The University of Memphis M
University of Minnesota, Twin Cities Campus M,D
University of Missouri–St. Louis O
University of New Haven M
University of New Mexico M
University of North Florida M
University of Oregon M
University of St. Thomas (MN) M,O
University of Scranton M
University of South Carolina (Columbia) M
The University of Texas at Arlington M
University of the Sacred Heart M
University of Utah M
University of Wisconsin–Madison M
Utah State University M
Virginia Commonwealth University M
Webster University M
Western New England College M
Widener University M
Wilkes University M
Wilmington College (DE) M

HUMAN SERVICES

Abilene Christian University M
Bellevue University M
Brandeis University M
California State University, Sacramento M
Concordia University (IL) M,O
Cornell University M,D
DePaul University M
Drury College M
Florida State University M,D,O
Indiana University Northwest M
Kansas State University M,D
Lehigh University M
Lesley College M
Lincoln University (PA) M
Lindenwood University M
Mankato State University M
Moorhead State University M
Murray State University M
National–Louis University M,O
National University M
Rider University M
Sage Graduate School M
St. Edward's University M
St. Mary's University of San Antonio M,D,O
Springfield College (MA) M
State University of New York at Oswego M
Syracuse University M
Universidad del Turabo M
University of Bridgeport M
University of Colorado at Colorado Springs M
University of Massachusetts Boston M
University of Oklahoma M
Valdosta State University M
Villanova University M
Wayne State University O
Youngstown State University M

HYDRAULICS

Auburn University M,D
Colorado State University M,D
Cornell University M,D
Texas A&M University (College Station) M,D
University of Missouri–Rolla M,D
University of Washington M,D

HYDROLOGY

Auburn University M,D
California State University, Bakersfield M
California State University, Chico M
Clemson University M
Colorado School of Mines O
Colorado State University M,D
Cornell University M,D
Georgia State University O
Idaho State University M

Illinois State University | M
Montana Tech of The University of Montana | M
Rensselaer Polytechnic Institute | M
Syracuse University | M
Texas A&M University (College Station) | M,D
The University of Arizona | M,D
University of California, Davis | M,D
University of Hawaii at Manoa | M,D
University of Idaho | M
University of Missouri–Rolla | M,D
University of Nevada, Reno | M,D
University of New Hampshire | M
University of South Florida | M,O
University of Washington | M,D
Utah State University | M
Wright State University | M

ILLUSTRATION

California State University, Long Beach | M
Kent State University | M
State University of New York at Buffalo | M
Syracuse University | M
University of Miami | M
University of Utah | M

IMMUNOLOGY

Allegheny University of the Health Sciences | M,D
Boston University | D
Brown University | M,D
California Institute of Technology | D
Case Western Reserve University | M,D
Colorado State University | M,D
Cornell University | M,D
Creighton University | M,D
Dartmouth College | D
Duke University | D
East Carolina University | D
Emory University | D
Florida State University | M,D
Georgetown University | D
Harvard University | M,D
Indiana University–Purdue University Indianapolis | M,D
Iowa State University of Science and Technology | M,D
Johns Hopkins University | M,D
Kansas State University | M,D
Long Island University, C.W. Post Campus | M
Loyola University Chicago | M,D
Massachusetts Institute of Technology | D
New York University | D
North Carolina State University | M,D
Northwestern University | D
The Ohio State University | M,D
Purdue University | M,D
Rutgers, The State University of New Jersey, New Brunswick | M,D
Saint Louis University | D
Stanford University | D
State University of New York at Albany | M,D
State University of New York at Buffalo | M,D
State University of New York at Stony Brook | D
Temple University (Philadelphia) | M,D
Texas A&M University (College Station) | D
Tufts University | D
Tulane University | M,D
The University of Arizona | M,D
University of California, Berkeley | D
University of California, Davis | M,D
University of California, Los Angeles | D
University of California, San Diego | D
University of California, San Francisco | D
University of Chicago | D
University of Florida | D
University of Illinois at Chicago | D
The University of Iowa | M,D
University of Kansas | D
University of Kentucky | D
University of Louisville | M,D
University of Miami | D
University of Michigan | D
University of Minnesota, Duluth | M,D
University of Minnesota, Twin Cities Campus | D
University of Missouri–Columbia | M,D
University of New Mexico | M,D
The University of North Carolina at Chapel Hill | M,D
University of North Dakota | M,D
University of Pennsylvania | D
University of Pittsburgh | M,D

University of Rochester | M,D
University of South Alabama | D
University of South Carolina (Columbia) | D
University of Southern California | M,D
University of Southern Maine | M
University of South Florida | D
University of Utah | D
University of Virginia | M,D
University of Washington | D
University of Wisconsin–Madison | M,D
Vanderbilt University | M,D
Virginia Commonwealth University | M,D,O
Wake Forest University | D
Washington University in St. Louis | D
Wayne State University | M,D
West Virginia University | M,D
Wright State University | M
Yale University | D
Yeshiva University | D

INDUSTRIAL AND LABOR RELATIONS

Baruch College of the City University of New York | M
Case Western Reserve University | M,D
Cleveland State University | M
Cornell University | M,D
Georgia State University | M,D
Indiana University of Pennsylvania | M
Inter American University of Puerto Rico, Metropolitan Campus | M
Inter American University of Puerto Rico, San Germán Campus | M
Iowa State University of Science and Technology | M
Loyola University Chicago | M
Marshall University | M
Michigan State University | M,D
Middle Tennessee State University | M
New School University | O
New York Institute of Technology | M,O
The Ohio State University | M,D
Pennsylvania State University University Park Campus | M
Rutgers, The State University of New Jersey, New Brunswick | M,D
Saint Francis College (PA) | M
State University of New York at Stony Brook | M,O
The University of Akron | M
University of California, Berkeley | D
University of Cincinnati | M
University of Illinois at Urbana–Champaign | M,D
University of Louisville | M
University of Massachusetts Amherst | M
University of Minnesota, Twin Cities Campus | M,D
University of New Haven | M
University of North Texas | M,D
University of Oregon | M
University of Pittsburgh | O
University of Rhode Island | M
University of Wisconsin–Madison | M,D
University of Wisconsin–Milwaukee | M
Virginia Commonwealth University | M
Wayne State University | M
West Virginia University | M

INDUSTRIAL AND MANUFACTURING MANAGEMENT

Baruch College of the City University of New York | M
Boston University | D
California Polytechnic State University, San Luis Obispo | M
Carnegie Mellon University | M,D
The Catholic University of America | D
Central Connecticut State University | M
Central Michigan University | M
Central Missouri State University | M
Clarkson University | M
Clemson University | M,D
DePaul University | M
Eastern Michigan University | M
Fairleigh Dickinson University, Florham–Madison Campus | M
Fairleigh Dickinson University, Teaneck–Hackensack Campus | M
The George Washington University | M
Golden Gate University | M,O
Illinois Institute of Technology | M

Inter American University of Puerto Rico, Metropolitan Campus | M
Iona College (New Rochelle) | M,O
Lynchburg College | M
Massachusetts Institute of Technology | M
Michigan State University | M,D
Michigan Technological University | M
New Jersey Institute of Technology | M,D
New York University | M
Northeastern State University | M
Northern Illinois University | M
Northwestern University | M
Pennsylvania State University University Park Campus | M,D
Polytechnic University, Brooklyn Campus | M
Polytechnic University, Farmingdale Campus | M
Polytechnic University, Westchester Graduate Center | M
Purdue University | M
Rensselaer Polytechnic Institute | M,D
Rochester Institute of Technology | M
Southeastern Oklahoma State University | M
Stevens Institute of Technology | M,O
Syracuse University | M,D
Texas Tech University | D
Towson University | M
The University of Alabama (Tuscaloosa) | M,D
University of Cincinnati | M,D
University of Colorado at Colorado Springs | M
University of Hartford | M
University of Houston | M,D
University of La Verne | M
University of Massachusetts Lowell | M
University of Minnesota, Twin Cities Campus | M,D
University of North Dakota | M
University of North Texas | M,D
University of Rhode Island | M
University of St. Thomas (MN) | M
University of Southern Indiana | M
University of Southern Maine | M
University of Tennessee at Chattanooga | M
University of Tennessee, Knoxville | M
University of Toledo | M,D
University of Wisconsin–Madison | M,D
University of Wisconsin–Platteville | M
Vanderbilt University | D
Worcester Polytechnic Institute | M
Wright State University | M

INDUSTRIAL AND ORGANIZATIONAL PSYCHOLOGY

Appalachian State University | M
Baruch College of the City University of New York | M,D,O
Bowling Green State University | M,D
Brooklyn College of the City University of New York | M
California State University, San Bernardino | M
Central Michigan University | M,D
Central Washington University | M
Claremont Graduate University | M,D
Clemson University | D
Cleveland State University | M
Colorado State University | D
DePaul University | M,D
Emporia State University | M
Fairleigh Dickinson University, Florham–Madison Campus | M
Florida Institute of Technology | M
George Mason University | M,D
The George Washington University | D
Golden Gate University | M
Graduate School and University Center of the City University of New York | D
Hofstra University | M
Hunter College of the City University of New York | M
Illinois Institute of Technology | D
Illinois State University | M
Indiana University–Purdue University Indianapolis | M
John F. Kennedy University | M,O
Kean University | M
Louisiana State University and Agricultural and Mechanical College | M,D
Louisiana Tech University | M
Mankato State University | M
Middle Tennessee State University | M

Montclair State University | M
New York University | D
The Ohio State University | D
Ohio University | D
Old Dominion University | D
Pennsylvania State University University Park Campus | M,D
Pontifical Catholic University of Puerto Rico | M
Radford University | M
Rensselaer Polytechnic Institute | M
Rice University | M,D
Roosevelt University | M
Rutgers, The State University of New Jersey, New Brunswick | M,D
Saint Mary's College of California | M
St. Mary's University of San Antonio | M
San Diego State University | M
San Jose State University | M
Springfield College (MA) | M,O
State University of New York at Albany | D
Teachers College, Columbia University | M,D
Temple University (Philadelphia) | M,D
Texas A&M University (College Station) | M,D
United States International University | M,D
The University of Akron | M,D
University of Baltimore | M
University of Central Florida | M,D
University of Connecticut | D
University of Detroit Mercy | M
University of Hartford | M
University of Houston | D
University of Maryland, College Park | M,D
University of Michigan | D
University of Minnesota, Twin Cities Campus | D
University of Nebraska at Omaha | M,D
University of New Haven | M,O
University of North Carolina at Charlotte | M
University of North Texas | M
University of South Florida | D
University of Tennessee at Chattanooga | M
University of Tennessee, Knoxville | M,D
University of Tulsa | M,D
University of Wisconsin–Oshkosh | M
Virginia Polytechnic Institute and State University | M,D
Wayne State University | D
Western Michigan University | M
Wright State University | M,D
Xavier University | M

INDUSTRIAL DESIGN

Auburn University | M
Illinois Institute of Technology | M,D
North Carolina State University | M
The Ohio State University | M
Rochester Institute of Technology | M
San Francisco State University | M
San Jose State University | M
Syracuse University | M
University of Cincinnati | M
University of Illinois at Chicago | M
University of Illinois at Urbana–Champaign | M
University of Notre Dame | M

INDUSTRIAL HYGIENE

Central Missouri State University | M
Harvard University | M,D
Montana Tech of The University of Montana | M
Purdue University | M,D
San Diego State University | M
Texas A&M University (College Station) | M
The University of Alabama at Birmingham | M,D
University of Cincinnati | M
The University of Iowa | M
University of Michigan | M,D
University of Minnesota, Twin Cities Campus | M,D
University of New Haven | M
University of South Carolina (Columbia) | M,D
University of Washington | M,D
Wayne State University | M

INDUSTRIAL/MANAGEMENT ENGINEERING

Alfred University | M
Arizona State University | M,D
Auburn University | M,D
Bradley University | M

Industrial/Management Engineering (continued)

California Polytechnic State University, San Luis Obispo M
California State University, Fresno M
California State University, Northridge M
Case Western Reserve University M,D
Central Missouri State University M
Clemson University M,D
Cleveland State University M,D
Colorado State University M,D
Columbia University M,D,O
Cornell University M,D
Eastern Michigan University M
Florida Agricultural and Mechanical University M
Florida International University M
Florida State University M,D
Georgia Institute of Technology M,D
Georgia Southern University M
Illinois State University M
Indiana State University M
Iowa State University of Science and Technology M,D
Kansas State University M,D
Lamar University M,D
Lehigh University M,D
Louisiana State University and Agricultural and Mechanical College M,D
Louisiana Tech University M,D
Loyola Marymount University M
Mississippi State University M,D
Montana State University–Bozeman M,D
Montana Tech of The University of Montana M
New Jersey Institute of Technology M,D
New Mexico State University M,D
North Carolina Agricultural and Technical State University M,D
North Carolina State University M,D
North Dakota State University M
Northeastern University M,D
Northern Illinois University M
Northwestern University M,D
The Ohio State University M,D
Ohio University M
Oklahoma State University M,D
Oregon State University M,D
Pennsylvania State University University Park Campus M,D
Polytechnic University, Brooklyn Campus M
Purdue University M,D
Rensselaer Polytechnic Institute M
Rochester Institute of Technology M
Rutgers, The State University of New Jersey, New Brunswick M,D
St. Mary's University of San Antonio M
South Dakota State University M
Southwest Texas State University M
Stanford University M,D,O
State University of New York at Binghamton M,D
State University of New York at Buffalo M,D
State University of New York College at Buffalo M
Tennessee Technological University M,D
Texas A&M University (College Station) M,D
Texas A&M University–Kingsville M
Texas Tech University M,D
The University of Alabama (Tuscaloosa) M
The University of Alabama in Huntsville M,D
The University of Arizona M,D
University of Arkansas (Fayetteville) M
University of Bridgeport M
University of California, Berkeley M,D
University of Central Florida M,D
University of Cincinnati M,D
University of Dayton M
University of Florida M,D,O
University of Houston M,D
University of Illinois at Chicago M,D
University of Illinois at Urbana–Champaign M,D
The University of Iowa M,D
University of Louisville M,D
University of Massachusetts Amherst M,D
University of Massachusetts Lowell M,D
The University of Memphis M
University of Miami M,D
University of Michigan M,D,O
University of Michigan–Dearborn M
University of Minnesota, Twin Cities Campus M,D
University of Missouri–Columbia M,D
University of Nebraska–Lincoln M,D
University of New Haven M,O
University of Oklahoma M,D
University of Pittsburgh M,D
University of Puerto Rico, Mayagüez Campus M
University of Rhode Island M
University of Southern California M,D,O
University of South Florida M,D
University of Tennessee, Knoxville M,D
The University of Texas at Arlington M,D
The University of Texas at Austin M,D
The University of Texas at El Paso M
University of Toledo M,D
University of Wisconsin–Madison M,D
Virginia Polytechnic Institute and State University M,D
Wayne State University M,D
Western Carolina University M
Western Illinois University M
Western Michigan University M
Western New England College M
West Virginia University M,D
Wichita State University M,D
Youngstown State University M

INFORMATION SCIENCE

Alcorn State University M
American University M,O
Ball State University M
Barry University M
Bradley University M
Brooklyn College of the City University of New York M,D
California State University, Fullerton M
Carnegie Mellon University M,D
Claremont Graduate University M,D
Clark Atlanta University M
DePaul University M
Drexel University M,D,O
East Tennessee State University M
Fairfield University M,O
Florida Institute of Technology M
George Mason University M,D
Grand Valley State University M
Hood College M
Kansas State University M,D
Kutztown University of Pennsylvania M
Long Island University, C.W. Post Campus M
Marist College M
Marshall University M
New Jersey Institute of Technology M,D
New York University M
Northeastern University M
Northwestern University M
Nova Southeastern University M,D
The Ohio State University M,D
Pace University M
Polytechnic University, Brooklyn Campus M
Polytechnic University, Farmingdale Campus M
Polytechnic University, Westchester Graduate Center M
Princeton University M,D
Rivier College M
Rochester Institute of Technology M
Sacred Heart University M
St. Mary's University of San Antonio M
San Jose State University M
Shippensburg University of Pennsylvania M
State University of New York at Albany M,D
State University of New York at Stony Brook O
State University of New York Institute of Technology at Utica/Rome M
Stevens Institute of Technology M,O
Syracuse University M,D
Temple University (Philadelphia) M,D
The University of Alabama at Birmingham M,D
University of Arkansas at Little Rock M
University of California, Irvine M,D
University of Delaware M,D
University of Florida M,D,O
University of Hawaii at Manoa D
University of Houston–Clear Lake M
University of Maryland, Baltimore County M,D
University of Michigan–Dearborn M
University of Minnesota, Twin Cities Campus M,D
University of New Haven M
University of North Carolina at Charlotte D
University of North Florida M
University of North Texas D
University of Oregon M,D
University of Pennsylvania M,D
University of Pittsburgh M,D,O
University of South Alabama M
University of Tennessee, Knoxville D
Virginia Polytechnic Institute and State University M

INFORMATION STUDIES

The Catholic University of America M
Central Missouri State University M
Clark Atlanta University M,O
College of St. Catherine M
Dominican University M,O
Drexel University M,D,O
Emporia State University M,D
Florida State University M,D
Indiana University Bloomington M,D,O
Long Island University, C.W. Post Campus M,D,O
Louisiana State University and Agricultural and Mechanical College M,O
Montana State University–Billings M
North Carolina Central University M
Queens College of the City University of New York M,O
Rutgers, The State University of New Jersey, New Brunswick M,D
St. John's University (NY) M,O
San Jose State University M
Simmons College M,D
Southern Connecticut State University O
State University of New York at Albany M,O
State University of New York at Buffalo M,O
Syracuse University M,D
Texas Woman's University M,D
The University of Alabama (Tuscaloosa) M,O
The University of Arizona M,D
University of California, Berkeley M,D
University of California, Los Angeles M,D,O
University of Denver M
University of Hawaii at Manoa M,D,O
University of Illinois at Urbana–Champaign M,D,O
The University of Iowa M
University of Maryland, College Park M,D
University of Michigan M,D
University of Missouri–Columbia M
The University of North Carolina at Chapel Hill M,D,O
University of North Carolina at Greensboro M
University of North Texas M,D
University of Oklahoma M,O
University of Pittsburgh M,D,O
University of Rhode Island M
University of South Carolina (Columbia) M,O
University of South Florida M
University of Tennessee, Knoxville M
The University of Texas at Austin M,D
University of Wisconsin–Madison M,D,O
University of Wisconsin–Milwaukee M,O
Wayne State University M,O

INORGANIC CHEMISTRY

Boston College M,D
Boston University M,D
Brandeis University M,D
Brigham Young University M,D
California State University, Fullerton M
California State University, Los Angeles M
Case Western Reserve University M,D
Clark Atlanta University M,D
Clarkson University M,D
Cleveland State University M
Columbia University M,D
Cornell University D
Florida State University M,D
Georgetown University M,D
The George Washington University M,D
Harvard University M,D
Howard University M,D
Illinois Institute of Technology M,D
Kansas State University M
Kent State University M,D
Lehigh University M,D
Marquette University M,D
Massachusetts Institute of Technology M,D
Michigan State University M,D
Mississippi State University M,D
Northeastern University D
Oregon State University M,D
Purdue University M,D
Rensselaer Polytechnic Institute M,D
Rutgers, The State University of New Jersey, Newark M,D
Rutgers, The State University of New Jersey, New Brunswick M,D
San Jose State University M
Seton Hall University M,D
South Dakota State University M,D
Southern University and Agricultural and Mechanical College M
State University of New York at Binghamton D
Tufts University M,D
The University of Akron M,D
University of Cincinnati M,D
University of Georgia M,D
University of Louisville M,D
University of Maryland, College Park M,D
University of Miami D
University of Michigan D
University of Missouri–Columbia M,D
University of Missouri–Kansas City M,D
The University of Montana–Missoula D
University of Nebraska–Lincoln D
University of Notre Dame M,D
University of Southern Mississippi M,D
University of South Florida M,D
University of Tennessee, Knoxville M,D
The University of Texas at Austin M,D
University of Toledo M,D
Wake Forest University M,D
Washington State University M,D
Yale University D

INSURANCE

California State University, Northridge M
Georgia State University M,D
Pennsylvania State University University Park Campus M,D
Temple University (Philadelphia) M
University of Hartford M
University of North Texas M,D
University of Pennsylvania M,D
University of St. Thomas (MN) M
University of Wisconsin–Madison M,D
Virginia Commonwealth University M

INTERDISCIPLINARY STUDIES

Angelo State University M
Baylor University M,D
Boise State University M
Boston University M,D
Bowling Green State University M,D
California State University, Chico M
California State University, Fullerton M
California State University, Hayward M,O
California State University, Long Beach M
California State University, Los Angeles M
California State University, Northridge M
California State University, Sacramento M
California State University, San Bernardino M
California State University, Stanislaus M
Central Washington University M
Claremont Graduate University M
DePaul University M
Eastern Washington University M
Emory University D
Fitchburg State College O
Fresno Pacific University M
George Mason University M
Goddard College M
Graduate School and University Center of the City University of New York M,D
Hofstra University M
Idaho State University M
Iowa State University of Science and Technology M
John F. Kennedy University M

Lesley College — M
Long Island University, C.W. Post Campus — M
Loyola College — M
Mankato State University — M
Marquette University — D
Marylhurst University — M
New Mexico State University — M,D
New York University — M
Norwich University — M
The Ohio State University — M,D
Ohio University — M
Rochester Institute of Technology — M
St. Cloud State University — M
San Diego State University — M
San Jose State University — M
Sonoma State University — M
Southern Methodist University — M
Southwest Texas State University — M
State University of New York College at Buffalo — M
Stephen F. Austin State University — M
Teachers College, Columbia University — M,D
Texas A&M International University — M
Texas A&M University–Corpus Christi — M
Texas A&M University–Texarkana — M
Texas Tech University — M,D
The Union Institute — D
United States International University — M
University of Alaska Anchorage — M
University of Alaska Fairbanks — M,D
The University of Arizona — M,D,O
University of Cincinnati — D
University of Houston–Victoria — M
University of Idaho — M
University of Illinois at Springfield — M
University of Louisville — M
University of Minnesota, Twin Cities Campus — M,D
University of Missouri–Kansas City — D
The University of Montana–Missoula — M
University of Northern Colorado — M,D,O
University of North Texas — M,D
University of South Dakota — M
The University of Texas at Arlington — M
The University of Texas at Brownsville — M
The University of Texas at Dallas — M
The University of Texas at El Paso — M
The University of Texas–Pan American — M
University of the Incarnate Word — M
University of Wisconsin–Milwaukee — D
Virginia Commonwealth University — M
Virginia State University — M
Wayne State University — M,D
West Texas A&M University — M
Wright State University — M

INTERIOR DESIGN

Colorado State University — M
Columbia College (IL) — M
Cornell University — M
Drexel University — M
Florida State University — M
Indiana University Bloomington — M
Iowa State University of Science and Technology — M
Louisiana Tech University — M
Mankato State University — M
Marymount University — M
Michigan State University — M
New School University — M
Rochester Institute of Technology — M
San Diego State University — M
San Jose State University — M
Syracuse University — M
The University of Alabama (Tuscaloosa) — M
University of Central Oklahoma — M
University of Cincinnati — M
University of Georgia — M,D
University of Houston — M
University of Kentucky — M
University of Massachusetts Amherst — M
The University of Memphis — M
University of Minnesota, Twin Cities Campus — M,D
University of North Carolina at Greensboro — M
University of North Texas — M
University of Oregon — M
University of Tennessee, Knoxville — M
University of Wisconsin–Madison — M

Virginia Commonwealth University — M
Virginia Polytechnic Institute and State University — M,D
Washington State University — M
Western Kentucky University — M

INTERNATIONAL AFFAIRS

American University — M,D,O
Andrews University — M
Angelo State University — M
Baylor University — M
Boston University — M,O
Brandeis University — M,D
Brigham Young University — M
California State University, Fresno — M
California State University, Sacramento — M
California State University, Stanislaus — M
The Catholic University of America — M
Central Connecticut State University — M
Central Michigan University — M,O
City College of the City University of New York — M
Claremont Graduate University — M
Clark Atlanta University — M,D
Clark University — M
Columbia University — M
Cornell University — M,D
Creighton University — M
DePaul University — M
Dominican College of San Rafael — M
Duke University — M
East Carolina University — M
Fairleigh Dickinson University, Teaneck–Hackensack Campus — M
Florida International University — M,D
Florida State University — M
Fordham University — M,O
George Mason University — M
Georgetown University — M,D
The George Washington University — M
Georgia Institute of Technology — M
Golden Gate University — M,O
Harvard University — M,D
Indiana University of Pennsylvania — M
Johns Hopkins University — M,D,O
Kent State University — M,D
Lesley College — M,O
Long Island University, Brooklyn Campus — O
Long Island University, C.W. Post Campus — M
Loyola University Chicago — M,D
Marquette University — M
Morgan State University — M
New York University — M,O
North Carolina State University — M
Northeastern University — M,D
Ohio University — M
Old Dominion University — M,D
Princeton University — M,D
Rutgers, The State University of New Jersey, Camden — M
Rutgers, The State University of New Jersey, Newark — M
Rutgers, The State University of New Jersey, New Brunswick — D
St. John Fisher College — M
St. Mary's University of San Antonio — M
Salve Regina University — M
San Francisco State University — M
Seton Hall University — M
Stanford University — M
Syracuse University — M,D
Troy State University (Troy) — M
Tufts University — M,D
Tulane University — M
United States International University — M
University of California, Berkeley — M
University of California, San Diego — M,D
University of California, Santa Cruz — D
University of Central Oklahoma — M
University of Chicago — M
University of Colorado at Boulder — M
University of Connecticut — M
University of Delaware — M,D
University of Denver — M,D
University of Detroit Mercy — M
University of Florida — M,D
University of Kentucky — M
University of Miami — M,D
University of Missouri–St. Louis — O
University of New Orleans — M
University of Notre Dame — M,D
University of Oregon — M
University of Pennsylvania — M

University of Pittsburgh — M,D,O
University of Rhode Island — M,O
University of San Diego — M
University of South Carolina (Columbia) — M,D
University of Southern California — M,D
University of Virginia — M,D
University of Washington — M
University of Wyoming — M
Webster University — M
Yale University — M

INTERNATIONAL AND COMPARATIVE EDUCATION

American University — M
Boston University — M
Claremont Graduate University — M,D
Florida International University — M
Florida State University — M,D,O
The George Washington University — M
Harvard University — M,D
Howard University — M,O
Indiana University Bloomington — M
Iowa State University of Science and Technology — M
Lesley College — M
Louisiana State University and Agricultural and Mechanical College — M,D
Loyola University Chicago — M,D
New York University — M,D
Stanford University — M,D
Teachers College, Columbia University — M,D
University of Bridgeport — M,O
University of Florida — M,D,O
University of Massachusetts Amherst — M,D,O
University of Minnesota, Twin Cities Campus — M,D
University of Pittsburgh — M,D
University of San Francisco — M,D
University of Southern California — M

INTERNATIONAL BUSINESS

American University — M
Azusa Pacific University — M
Baldwin-Wallace College — M
Baruch College of the City University of New York — M
Baylor University — M
Boston University — M
Brandeis University — M,D
California Lutheran University — M
California State University, Fullerton — M
California State University, Hayward — M
California State University, Los Angeles — M
Cardinal Stritch University — M
Central Connecticut State University — M
Chaminade University of Honolulu — M
Claremont Graduate University — M
Clark Atlanta University — M
Columbia University — M
Dallas Baptist University — M
DePaul University — M
Dominican College of San Rafael — M
Drury University — M
D'Youville College — M
Eastern Michigan University — M
Fairfield University — M,O
Fairleigh Dickinson University, Florham–Madison Campus — M
Fairleigh Dickinson University, Teaneck–Hackensack Campus — M
Florida Institute of Technology — M
Florida International University — M,D
The George Washington University — M,D
Georgia State University — M
Golden Gate University — M,O
Hawaii Pacific University — M
Hofstra University — M
Hope International University — M
Indiana University Bloomington — M
Iona College (New Rochelle) — M,O
Long Island University, C.W. Post Campus — M
Loyola College — M
Madonna University — M
Manhattan College — M
Metropolitan State University — M
Montclair State University — M
National University — M
New York University — M,D,O
Nova Southeastern University — M,D
Oklahoma City University — M
Oral Roberts University — M
Our Lady of the Lake University of San Antonio — M
Pace University — M

Pepperdine University (Culver City) — M
Pepperdine University (Malibu) — M
Philadelphia College of Textiles and Science — M
Portland State University — M
Quinnipiac College — M
Rochester Institute of Technology — M
Roosevelt University — M
Rutgers, The State University of New Jersey, Newark — M,D
Saint Joseph's University — M
Saint Louis University — M,D
Saint Mary's College of California — M
Saint Peter's College (Jersey City) — M
St. Thomas University — M,O
San Diego State University — M
Seattle University — M,O
Seton Hall University — M,O
Suffolk University — M
Sul Ross State University — M
Syracuse University — M
Temple University (Philadelphia) — M
Texas A&M International University — M
United States International University — M,D
The University of Akron — M
University of Chicago — M
University of Cincinnati — M
University of Colorado at Denver — M
University of Connecticut — M
University of Hartford — M
University of Hawaii at Manoa — D
University of Houston — M
University of Kentucky — M
University of Maryland University College — M
The University of Memphis — M
University of Miami — M
University of New Haven — M
University of New Mexico — M
University of North Carolina at Greensboro — O
University of Pennsylvania — M
University of Pittsburgh — M
University of Rhode Island — M
University of St. Thomas (MN) — M,O
University of San Francisco — M
University of Scranton — M
University of South Carolina (Columbia) — M
University of Southern California — M
University of Tennessee, Knoxville — M
The University of Texas at Dallas — M,D
University of the Incarnate Word — M
University of Toledo — M
University of Wisconsin–Madison — M
Vanderbilt University — M
Virginia Commonwealth University — D
Wagner College — M
Webster University — M
Western New England College — M
Whitworth College — M
Wilkes University — M
Wright State University — M

INTERNATIONAL HEALTH

Boston University — M,O
Emory University — M
The George Washington University — M
Harvard University — M,D
Johns Hopkins University — M,D
Loma Linda University — M
Tulane University — M,D
The University of Alabama at Birmingham — M,D
University of Hawaii at Manoa — M
University of Michigan — M
Yale University — M

ITALIAN

Boston College — M
Brown University — M,D
The Catholic University of America — M
Columbia University — M,D
Graduate School and University Center of the City University of New York — D
Harvard University — M,D
Hunter College of the City University of New York — M
Indiana University Bloomington — M,D
Johns Hopkins University — M,D
New York University — M,D
Northwestern University — D
The Ohio State University — M,D
Queens College of the City University of New York — M
Rutgers, The State University of New Jersey, New Brunswick — M,D

P—first professional degree; M—master's degree; D—doctorate; O—other advanced degree.

Italian (continued)

San Francisco State University	M
Stanford University	M,D
State University of New York at Albany	M
State University of New York at Binghamton	M
State University of New York at Stony Brook	M,D
University of California, Berkeley	M,D
University of California, Los Angeles	M,D,O
University of Chicago	M,D
University of Connecticut	M,D
University of Illinois at Urbana–Champaign	M,D
University of Minnesota, Twin Cities Campus	M,D
The University of North Carolina at Chapel Hill	M,D
University of Notre Dame	M
University of Oregon	M
University of Pennsylvania	M,D
University of Pittsburgh	M
University of Tennessee, Knoxville	D
University of Virginia	M
University of Washington	M
University of Wisconsin–Madison	M,D
University of Wisconsin–Milwaukee	M
Wayne State University	M
Yale University	D

JEWISH STUDIES

Brandeis University	M,D
Brooklyn College of the City University of New York	M
Brown University	M,D
Clark University	D
Columbia University	M,D
Cornell University	M,D
Emory University	M
Harvard University	M,D
New York University	M,D
Seton Hall University	M
University of Chicago	M,D
University of Denver	M
University of Pennsylvania	M,D
University of Wisconsin–Madison	M,D
University of Wisconsin–Milwaukee	M
Washington University in St. Louis	M
Yeshiva University	M,D

JOURNALISM

Abilene Christian University	M
American University	M
Arizona State University	M
Arkansas State University	M
Austin Peay State University	M
Ball State University	M
Baylor University	M
Boston University	M
California State University, Fullerton	M
California State University, Northridge	M
Columbia College (IL)	M
Columbia University	M
Emerson College	M
Florida Agricultural and Mechanical University	M
Georgia College and State University	M
Georgia State University	M
Indiana University Bloomington	M,D
Indiana University of Pennsylvania	M
Iona College (New Rochelle)	M
Iowa State University of Science and Technology	M
Kent State University	M
Marquette University	M
Marshall University	M
Michigan State University	M
New York University	M,O
Norfolk State University	M
Northeastern University	M
Northwestern University	M
The Ohio State University	M
Ohio University	M,D
Polytechnic University, Brooklyn Campus	M
Quinnipiac College	M
Roosevelt University	M
South Dakota State University	M
Southern Illinois University at Carbondale	M,D
Stanford University	M
Syracuse University	M
Temple University (Philadelphia)	M
Texas A&M University–Commerce	M
Texas Southern University	M
The University of Alabama (Tuscaloosa)	M,D
The University of Arizona	M
University of Arkansas (Fayetteville)	M
University of Arkansas at Little Rock	M
University of California, Berkeley	M
University of Colorado at Boulder	M,D
University of Florida	M,D
University of Georgia	M,D
University of Illinois at Springfield	M
University of Illinois at Urbana–Champaign	M
The University of Iowa	M
University of Kansas	M
University of Maryland, College Park	M,D
The University of Memphis	M
University of Miami	M
University of Mississippi	M
University of Missouri–Columbia	M,D
The University of Montana–Missoula	M
University of Nebraska–Lincoln	M
University of Nevada, Reno	M
University of North Texas	M
University of Oklahoma	M
University of Oregon	M,D
University of South Carolina (Columbia)	M,D
University of Southern California	M,O
University of Tennessee, Knoxville	M,D
The University of Texas at Austin	M,D
University of Wisconsin–Madison	M,D
West Virginia University	M

KINESIOLOGY AND MOVEMENT STUDIES

Angelo State University	M
Boston University	M,D,O
Bowling Green State University	M
California Polytechnic State University, San Luis Obispo	M
California State Polytechnic University, Pomona	M
California State University, Fresno	M
California State University, Long Beach	M
California State University, Northridge	M
Florida State University	M,D
Georgia Southern University	M
Indiana University Bloomington	M,D,O
Inter American University of Puerto Rico, San Germán Campus	M
James Madison University	M
Kansas State University	M
Lamar University	M
Louisiana State University and Agricultural and Mechanical College	M,D
New York University	M
Oregon State University	M
Pennsylvania State University University Park Campus	M,D
Sam Houston State University	M
Sonoma State University	M
Southeastern Louisiana University	M
Southern Arkansas University–Magnolia	M
Springfield College (MA)	M
Teachers College, Columbia University	M,D
Temple University (Philadelphia)	D
Texas A&M University (College Station)	M,D
Texas A&M University–Kingsville	M
Texas Christian University	M
Texas Woman's University	M,D
University of Arkansas (Fayetteville)	M,D
University of Central Arkansas	M
University of Colorado at Boulder	M,D
University of Delaware	M,D
University of Illinois at Chicago	M
University of Illinois at Urbana–Champaign	M,D
University of Kentucky	M,D
University of Maine (Orono)	M,O
University of Maryland, College Park	M,D
University of Michigan	M,D,O
University of Minnesota, Twin Cities Campus	M,D
University of Nevada, Las Vegas	M
University of New Hampshire	M
The University of North Carolina at Chapel Hill	M
University of North Dakota	M
University of Northern Colorado	M,D
University of North Texas	M
University of Oregon	M,D
University of Pittsburgh	M,D
University of Southern California	M,D
The University of Texas at Austin	M,D
The University of Texas at El Paso	M
The University of Texas at Tyler	M
The University of Texas–Pan American	M
University of Wisconsin–Madison	M,D
University of Wisconsin–Milwaukee	M
Virginia Polytechnic Institute and State University	M,D
Washington State University	M
Washington University in St. Louis	D
West Chester University of Pennsylvania	M,O

LANDSCAPE ARCHITECTURE

Ball State University	M
California State Polytechnic University, Pomona	M
Colorado State University	M,D
Cornell University	M
Florida International University	M
Harvard University	M,D
Iowa State University of Science and Technology	M
Kansas State University	M
Louisiana State University and Agricultural and Mechanical College	M
Morgan State University	M
North Carolina State University	M
The Ohio State University	M
Oklahoma State University	M
Pennsylvania State University University Park Campus	M
State University of New York College of Environmental Science and Forestry	M
Texas A&M University (College Station)	M,D
Texas Tech University	M
The University of Arizona	M
University of California, Berkeley	M
University of Colorado at Denver	M
University of Florida	M
University of Georgia	M
University of Illinois at Urbana–Champaign	M
University of Massachusetts Amherst	M
University of Michigan	M,D
University of Minnesota, Twin Cities Campus	M
University of Oklahoma	M
University of Oregon	M
University of Pennsylvania	M,O
University of Southern California	M
The University of Texas at Arlington	M
University of Virginia	M
University of Washington	M
University of Wisconsin–Madison	M
Utah State University	M
Virginia Polytechnic Institute and State University	M

LATIN AMERICAN STUDIES

American University	M,O
Arizona State University	M,D
Brown University	M,D
California State University, Los Angeles	M
Columbia University	O
Duke University	D,O
Florida International University	M
Georgetown University	M
The George Washington University	M
Indiana University Bloomington	M
Johns Hopkins University	M,D
La Salle University	M
New York University	M
The Ohio State University	O
Ohio University	M
Princeton University	D
San Diego State University	M
Southern Methodist University	M
Stanford University	M
State University of New York at Albany	M,O
Tulane University	M,D
The University of Alabama (Tuscaloosa)	M
The University of Arizona	M
University of California, Berkeley	M,D
University of California, Los Angeles	M
University of California, San Diego	M
University of California, Santa Barbara	M,D
University of Chicago	M
University of Connecticut	M
University of Florida	M,O
University of Illinois at Urbana–Champaign	M
University of Kansas	M
University of New Mexico	M,D
The University of North Carolina at Chapel Hill	O
University of Pittsburgh	O
The University of Texas at Austin	M,D
University of Wisconsin–Madison	M
Vanderbilt University	M

LAW

American University	P,M
Arizona State University	P
Baylor University	P
Boston College	P
Boston University	P,M
Brigham Young University	P,M
Campbell University	P
Capital University	P,M
Case Western Reserve University	P,M
The Catholic University of America	P
Chapman University	P
Cleveland State University	P,M
College of William and Mary	P,M
Columbia University	P,M,D
Cornell University	P,M,D
Creighton University	P
DePaul University	P,M
Drake University	P
Duke University	P,M,D
Duquesne University	P
Emory University	P,M
Florida State University	P
Fordham University	P,M
George Mason University	P
Georgetown University	P,M,D
The George Washington University	P,M,D
Georgia State University	P
Golden Gate University	P,M,D
Gonzaga University	P
Harvard University	P,M,D
Hofstra University	P
Howard University	P,M
Illinois Institute of Technology	P,M
Indiana University Bloomington	P,M,D
Indiana University–Purdue University Indianapolis	P
Inter American University of Puerto Rico, Metropolitan Campus	P
John F. Kennedy University	P
Louisiana State University and Agricultural and Mechanical College	P,M
Loyola Marymount University	P
Loyola University Chicago	P,M,D
Loyola University New Orleans	P
Marquette University	P
Mercer University (Macon)	P
Mississippi College	P
New York University	P,M,D
North Carolina Central University	P
Northeastern University	P
Northern Illinois University	P
Northern Kentucky University	P
Northwestern University	P,M,D
Nova Southeastern University	P
The Ohio State University	P
Oklahoma City University	P
Pace University	P,M,D
Pepperdine University (Malibu)	P
Pontifical Catholic University of Puerto Rico	P,M
Quinnipiac College	P
Rutgers, The State University of New Jersey, Camden	P
Rutgers, The State University of New Jersey, Newark	P
St. John's University (NY)	P
Saint Louis University	P,M
St. Mary's University of San Antonio	P
St. Thomas University	P
Samford University	P
Santa Clara University	P,M,O
Seattle University	P
Seton Hall University	P,M
Southern Illinois University at Carbondale	P
Southern Methodist University	P,M,D
Southern University and Agricultural and Mechanical College	P
Stanford University	P,M,D
State University of New York at Buffalo	P
Stetson University	P
Suffolk University	P
Syracuse University	P
Temple University (Philadelphia)	P,M
Texas Southern University	P

Texas Tech University | P
Texas Wesleyan University | P
Tulane University | P,M,D
The University of Akron | P
The University of Alabama (Tuscaloosa) | P,M
The University of Arizona | P,M
University of Arkansas (Fayetteville) | P,M
University of Arkansas at Little Rock | P
University of Baltimore | P,M
University of California, Berkeley | P,M,D
University of California, Davis | P,M
University of California, Los Angeles | P,M
University of Chicago | P,M,D
University of Cincinnati | P
University of Colorado at Boulder | P
University of Connecticut | P
University of Dayton | P
University of Denver | P,M
University of Detroit Mercy | P
University of Florida | P,M
University of Georgia | P,M
University of Hawaii at Manoa | P
University of Houston | P,M
University of Idaho | P
University of Illinois at Urbana–Champaign | P,M,D
The University of Iowa | P,M
University of Kansas | P
University of Kentucky | P
University of La Verne | P
University of Louisville | P
University of Maryland, College Park | P
The University of Memphis | P
University of Miami | P,M
University of Michigan | P,M,D
University of Minnesota, Twin Cities Campus | P,M
University of Mississippi | P
University of Missouri–Columbia | P
University of Missouri–Kansas City | P,M
The University of Montana–Missoula | P
University of Nebraska–Lincoln | P
University of New Mexico | P
The University of North Carolina at Chapel Hill | P
University of North Dakota | P
University of Notre Dame | P,M,D
University of Oklahoma | P
University of Oregon | P
University of Pennsylvania | P,M,D
University of Pittsburgh | P,M
University of Puerto Rico, Río Piedras | P
University of Richmond | P
University of San Diego | P,M,O
University of San Francisco | P
University of South Carolina (Columbia) | P
University of South Dakota | P
University of Southern California | P
University of Southern Maine | P
University of Tennessee, Knoxville | P
The University of Texas at Austin | P,M
University of the District of Columbia | P
University of the Pacific | P,M
University of Toledo | P
University of Tulsa | P
University of Utah | P,M
University of Virginia | P,M,D
University of Washington | P,M,D
University of Wisconsin–Madison | P,M,D
University of Wyoming | P
Valparaiso University | P,M
Vanderbilt University | P
Villanova University | P,M
Wake Forest University | P,M
Washburn University of Topeka | P
Washington University in St. Louis | P,M,D
Wayne State University | P,M
Western New England College | P
West Virginia University | P
Widener University | P,M
Yale University | P,M,D
Yeshiva University | P

LEGAL AND JUSTICE STUDIES

American University | M
Arizona State University | M,D
Boston University | M
Case Western Reserve University | M
The Catholic University of America | D,O
DePaul University | M
Golden Gate University | M,D
Governors State University | M
Marymount University | M

Montclair State University | M
New York University | D
Northeastern University | M,D
Rutgers, The State University of New Jersey, New Brunswick | D
Temple University (Philadelphia) | M
University of Baltimore | M
University of California, Berkeley | D
University of Denver | M
University of Illinois at Springfield | M
University of Nebraska–Lincoln | M
University of Nevada, Reno | M
University of Pennsylvania | M
University of Pittsburgh | O
University of San Diego | M
University of the Pacific | M
University of Wisconsin–Madison | M,O
Webster University | M,O

LEISURE STUDIES

Aurora University | M
Boston University | M,O
Bowling Green State University | M
California State University, Long Beach | M
California State University, Northridge | M
Central Michigan University | M
Howard University | M
Indiana University Bloomington | D
New York University | M,D,O
Oklahoma State University | M,D
Pennsylvania State University University Park Campus | M,D
Radford University | M
San Francisco State University | M
San Jose State University | M
Southern Connecticut State University | M
State University of New York College at Brockport | M
Temple University (Philadelphia) | M
University of Connecticut | M,D
University of Georgia | M,D
University of Illinois at Urbana–Champaign | M,D
The University of Iowa | M
The University of Memphis | M
University of Minnesota, Twin Cities Campus | M,D
University of Mississippi | M,D
University of Nevada, Las Vegas | M
The University of North Carolina at Chapel Hill | M
University of Northern Iowa | M
University of North Texas | M,O
University of South Alabama | M
University of Toledo | M
University of Utah | M,D
University of West Florida | M
Washington State University | M

LIBERAL STUDIES

Abilene Christian University | M
Arkansas Tech University | M
Auburn University Montgomery | M
Baker University | M
Bellarmine College | M
Boston University | M
Bradley University | M
Brooklyn College of the City University of New York | M
Christian Brothers University | M
Clark University | M
College of Notre Dame of Maryland | M
College of Staten Island of the City University of New York | M
Columbia University | M
Creighton University | M
Dallas Baptist University | M
Dartmouth College | M
DePaul University | M
Duke University | M
Duquesne University | M
Fordham University | M
Fort Hays State University | M
George Mason University | M
Georgetown University | M
Golden Gate University | M
Graduate School and University Center of the City University of New York | M
Harvard University | M
Houston Baptist University | M
Indiana University–Purdue University Fort Wayne | M
Indiana University South Bend | M
Jacksonville State University | M
Johns Hopkins University | M,O
Kean University | M
Kent State University | M
Louisiana State University and Agricultural and Mechanical College | M

Louisiana State University in Shreveport | M
Mary Washington College | M
Monmouth University | M
Moorhead State University | M
New School University | M
North Carolina State University | M
North Central College | M
Northern Arizona University | M
Northwestern University | M
Oklahoma City University | M
Plattsburgh State University of New York | M
Queens College of the City University of New York | M
Regis University | M
Rollins College | M
Roosevelt University | M
Rutgers, The State University of New Jersey, Camden | M
Rutgers, The State University of New Jersey, Newark | M
St. John's University (NY) | M
San Diego State University | M
Spring Hill College | M
State University of New York at Albany | M
State University of New York at Stony Brook | M
State University of New York College at Brockport | M
Temple University (Philadelphia) | M
Texas Christian University | M
Towson University | M
Tulane University | M
University of Arkansas at Little Rock | M
University of Delaware | M
University of Denver | M
University of Detroit Mercy | M
University of Maine (Orono) | M
University of Miami | M
University of Michigan–Dearborn | M
University of New Hampshire | M
University of North Carolina at Charlotte | M
University of North Carolina at Greensboro | M
University of Oklahoma | M
University of Richmond | M
University of St. Thomas (TX) | M
University of Southern Indiana | M
University of South Florida | M
University of Toledo | M
Valparaiso University | M
Vanderbilt University | M
Villanova University | M
Wake Forest University | M
West Virginia University | M
Wichita State University | M
Widener University | M
Winthrop University | M

LIBRARY SCIENCE

Appalachian State University | M,O
The Catholic University of America | M
Central Missouri State University | M,O
Chicago State University | M
Clarion University of Pennsylvania | M
Clark Atlanta University | M,O
College of St. Catherine | M
Dominican University | M,O
Drexel University | M,D,O
East Carolina University | M,O
Emporia State University | M,D
Florida State University | M,D
Indiana University Bloomington | M,D,O
Inter American University of Puerto Rico, San Germán Campus | M
Kent State University | M
Kutztown University of Pennsylvania | M
Long Island University, C.W. Post Campus | M,D,O
Louisiana State University and Agricultural and Mechanical College | M,O
North Carolina Central University | M
Queens College of the City University of New York | M,O
Rutgers, The State University of New Jersey, New Brunswick | M,D
St. John's University (NY) | M,O
Sam Houston State University | M
San Jose State University | M
Simmons College | M,D
Southern Connecticut State University | M,O
Spalding University | M
State University of New York at Albany | M,O
State University of New York at Buffalo | M,O
Syracuse University | M,O

Texas Woman's University | M,D
The University of Alabama (Tuscaloosa) | M,O
The University of Arizona | M,D
University of California, Los Angeles | M,D,O
University of Central Arkansas | M
University of Denver | M
University of Hawaii at Manoa | M,D,O
University of Illinois at Urbana–Champaign | M,D,O
The University of Iowa | M
University of Kentucky | M
University of Maryland, College Park | M,D
University of Michigan | M,D
University of Missouri–Columbia | M
The University of North Carolina at Chapel Hill | M,D,O
University of North Carolina at Greensboro | M
University of North Texas | M,D
University of Oklahoma | M,O
University of Pittsburgh | M,D,O
University of Puerto Rico, Río Piedras | M
University of Rhode Island | M
University of South Carolina (Columbia) | M,O
University of Southern Mississippi | M,O
University of South Florida | M
University of Tennessee, Knoxville | M
The University of Texas at Austin | M,D
University of Washington | M
University of Wisconsin–Madison | M,D,O
University of Wisconsin–Milwaukee | M,O
Wayne State University | M,O

LIMNOLOGY

Baylor University | M
Cornell University | D
University of Alaska Fairbanks | M,D
University of Florida | M,D
University of Wisconsin–Madison | M,D
Western Connecticut State University | M
William Paterson University of New Jersey | M

LINGUISTICS

Arizona State University | M,D
Ball State University | M
Biola University | M
Boston College | M
Boston University | M,D
Brigham Young University | M,O
Brown University | M,D
California State University, Fresno | M
California State University, Fullerton | M
California State University, Long Beach | M
California State University, Northridge | M
California State University, San Bernardino | M
Carnegie Mellon University | D
Cornell University | M,D
Eastern Michigan University | M
Florida International University | M
Gallaudet University | M
George Mason University | M
Georgetown University | M,D,O
Georgia State University | M
Graduate School and University Center of the City University of New York | M,D
Harvard University | M,D
Hofstra University | M
Indiana State University | M
Indiana University Bloomington | M,D,O
Indiana University of Pennsylvania | M,D
Louisiana State University and Agricultural and Mechanical College | M,D
Massachusetts Institute of Technology | D
Miami University | M
Michigan State University | M,D
Montclair State University | M
New York University | M,D
Northeastern Illinois University | M
Northeastern University | M
Northern Arizona University | M,D
Northwestern University | M,D
Oakland University | M
The Ohio State University | M,D
Ohio University | M
Old Dominion University | M
Purdue University | M,D

P—first professional degree; M—master's degree; D—doctorate; O—other advanced degree.

Linguistics (continued)

Queens College of the City University of New York	M
Rice University	M,D
Rutgers, The State University of New Jersey, New Brunswick	D
San Diego State University	M,O
San Francisco State University	M
San Jose State University	M,O
Southern Illinois University at Carbondale	M
Stanford University	M,D
State University of New York at Buffalo	M,D
State University of New York at Stony Brook	M,D
Syracuse University	M
Teachers College, Columbia University	M,D
Temple University (Philadelphia)	M
The University of Arizona	M,D
University of California, Berkeley	M,D
University of California, Davis	M
University of California, Irvine	M,D
University of California, Los Angeles	M,D,O
University of California, San Diego	D
University of California, Santa Barbara	M,D
University of California, Santa Cruz	M,D
University of Chicago	M,D
University of Colorado at Boulder	M,D
University of Connecticut	M,D
University of Delaware	M,D
University of Florida	M,D,O
University of Georgia	M,D
University of Hawaii at Manoa	M,D
University of Houston	M
University of Illinois at Chicago	M
University of Illinois at Urbana–Champaign	M,D
The University of Iowa	M,D
University of Kansas	M,D
University of Louisville	M
University of Maryland, College Park	M,D
University of Massachusetts Amherst	M,D
University of Michigan	D
University of Minnesota, Twin Cities Campus	M,D
The University of Montana–Missoula	M
University of New Mexico	M,D
The University of North Carolina at Chapel Hill	M,D
University of North Dakota	M
University of Oregon	M,D
University of Pennsylvania	M,D
University of Pittsburgh	M,D
University of Puerto Rico, Río Piedras	M
University of Rochester	M,D
University of South Carolina (Columbia)	M,D,O
University of Southern California	M,D
University of South Florida	M
University of Tennessee, Knoxville	D
The University of Texas at Arlington	M
The University of Texas at Austin	M,D
The University of Texas at El Paso	M
University of Utah	M
University of Virginia	M
University of Washington	M,D
University of Wisconsin–Madison	M,D
Wayne State University	M
West Virginia University	M
Yale University	D

LOGISTICS

Arizona State University	D
Florida Institute of Technology	M
The George Washington University	M
Georgia College and State University	M
Golden Gate University	M,O
Massachusetts Institute of Technology	M
Michigan State University	M
Northwestern University	M
Pennsylvania State University University Park Campus	M,D
Syracuse University	M
Texas A&M International University	M
Universidad del Turabo	M
University of Arkansas (Fayetteville)	M
University of Minnesota, Twin Cities Campus	M,D
University of New Haven	M,O
University of Tennessee, Knoxville	M,D
University of Wisconsin–Madison	M
Wright State University	M

MANAGEMENT INFORMATION SYSTEMS

American University	M
Andrews University	M
Arizona State University	M,D
Auburn University	M,D
Baruch College of the City University of New York	M
Baylor University	M
Bellevue University	M
Benedictine University	M
Boise State University	M
Boston College	M
Boston University	M,D
Bowie State University	M,O
Brigham Young University	M
California Lutheran University	M
California State University, Dominguez Hills	M
California State University, Fullerton	M
California State University, Hayward	M
California State University, Los Angeles	M
California State University, Sacramento	M
Case Western Reserve University	M,D
Central Michigan University	M,O
Christian Brothers University	M
City University	M,O
Claremont Graduate University	M,D
Clarkson University	M
Cleveland State University	M,D
College of Notre Dame	M
Colorado State University	M
Cornell University	D
Dallas Baptist University	M
DePaul University	M
Dominican University	M
Duquesne University	M
Eastern Michigan University	M
Fairleigh Dickinson University, Teaneck–Hackensack Campus	M
Ferris State University	M
Florida Agricultural and Mechanical University	M
Florida Institute of Technology	M
Florida International University	M
Fordham University	M
Fort Hays State University	M
Friends University	M
The George Washington University	M
Georgia Southwestern State University	M
Georgia State University	M,D
Golden Gate University	M,O
Graduate School and University Center of the City University of New York	D
Hawaii Pacific University	M
Hofstra University	M
Houston Baptist University	M
Indiana University Bloomington	M,D
Iona College (New Rochelle)	M,O
Jackson State University	M
Johns Hopkins University	M,O
Kean University	M
Kennesaw State University	M
Kent State University	D
Lesley College	M
Long Island University, C.W. Post Campus	M
Louisiana State University and Agricultural and Mechanical College	M,D
Loyola University Chicago	M
Manhattan College	M
Marymount University	M
Marywood University	M
Metropolitan State University	M
Miami University	M
Middle Tennessee State University	M
Mississippi State University	M
New York University	M,D,O
North Carolina State University	M
North Central College	M
Northern Arizona University	M
Northern Illinois University	M
Northwestern University	M
Nova Southeastern University	M,D
The Ohio State University	M,D
Oklahoma City University	M
Pace University	M
Pennsylvania State University Harrisburg Campus of the Capital College	M
Pennsylvania State University University Park Campus	M
Philadelphia College of Textiles and Science	M
Purdue University	M,D
Quinnipiac College	M
Regis University	M
Rensselaer Polytechnic Institute	M,D
Roosevelt University	M
Rutgers, The State University of New Jersey, Newark	M,D
St. John's University (NY)	M,O
Saint Joseph's University	M
Saint Louis University	M,D
St. Mary's University of San Antonio	M
Saint Peter's College (Jersey City)	M
San Diego State University	M
Seattle Pacific University	M
Seton Hall University	M
Southern Illinois University at Edwardsville	M
Southwest Missouri State University	M
State University of New York at Albany	M
Stevens Institute of Technology	M,D,O
Syracuse University	M,D
Temple University (Philadelphia)	M
Texas A&M International University	M
Texas A&M University (College Station)	M,D
Texas Tech University	M,D
Towson University	M
Troy State University Dothan	M
Troy State University Montgomery	M
The University of Akron	M
The University of Arizona	M
University of Arkansas (Fayetteville)	M
University of Baltimore	M
University of Cincinnati	M,D
University of Colorado at Colorado Springs	M
University of Colorado at Denver	M
University of Denver	M
University of Detroit Mercy	M
University of Florida	M,D
University of Hartford	M
University of Houston	M,D
University of Illinois at Chicago	M,D
University of Illinois at Springfield	M
The University of Iowa	M
University of Maryland University College	M
The University of Memphis	M,D
University of Miami	M,O
University of Minnesota, Twin Cities Campus	M,D
University of Mississippi	M
University of Missouri–St. Louis	M
University of New Haven	M,D
University of New Mexico	M
The University of North Carolina at Chapel Hill	D
University of North Carolina at Greensboro	M
University of North Texas	M,D
University of Oregon	M
University of Pennsylvania	M,D
University of Pittsburgh	M,O
University of Redlands	M
University of Rhode Island	M
University of St. Thomas (MN)	M
University of Southern California	M
University of South Florida	M
The University of Texas at Arlington	M,D
The University of Texas at Austin	D
University of the Sacred Heart	M
University of Toledo	M,D
University of Tulsa	M
University of Virginia	M
University of Wisconsin–Madison	M,D
Utah State University	M,D
Virginia Commonwealth University	M,D,O
Webster University	M
Western New England College	M
Wilkes University	M
Worcester Polytechnic Institute	M
Wright State University	M

MANAGEMENT OF TECHNOLOGY

Boston University	M
Embry–Riddle Aeronautical University, Extended Campus	M
The George Washington University	M
Georgia Institute of Technology	M
Illinois Institute of Technology	M
Lehigh University	M
Marshall University	M
Mercer University (Macon)	M
Mercer University, Cecil B. Day Campus	M
National University	M
North Carolina Agricultural and Technical State University	M
Northern Kentucky University	M
Pacific Lutheran University	M
Pepperdine University (Culver City)	M
Polytechnic University, Brooklyn Campus	M
Polytechnic University, Westchester Graduate Center	M
Rensselaer Polytechnic Institute	M
Rhode Island College	M
St. Ambrose University	M
Southwest Texas State University	M
State University of New York at Stony Brook	M
Stevens Institute of Technology	M,D,O
Texas A&M University–Commerce	M
University of California, San Diego	M
University of Colorado at Boulder	M
University of Denver	M
University of Maryland University College	M
University of Miami	M
University of Minnesota, Twin Cities Campus	M
University of New Mexico	M
University of Pennsylvania	M
The University of Texas at San Antonio	M
University of Tulsa	M
University of Wisconsin–Stout	M
Vanderbilt University	M,D

MANAGEMENT STRATEGY AND POLICY

Azusa Pacific University	M
Baruch College of the City University of New York	M,D
Boston College	M
Boston University	M
Case Western Reserve University	M,D
Claremont Graduate University	M
DePaul University	M
Dominican College of San Rafael	M
Drexel University	D
The George Washington University	M,D
Michigan State University	D
Northwestern University	D
Purdue University	M,D
Rensselaer Polytechnic Institute	D
Stevens Institute of Technology	M
Syracuse University	D
Temple University (Philadelphia)	M,D
United States International University	D
The University of Arizona	M
University of Florida	D
University of Hartford	M
University of Minnesota, Twin Cities Campus	M,D
University of New Haven	M
The University of North Carolina at Chapel Hill	D

MANUFACTURING ENGINEERING

Auburn University	M
Boston University	M,D
Bowling Green State University	M
Bradley University	M
Brigham Young University	M
Colorado State University	M,D
Cornell University	D
Drexel University	M,D
Eastern Kentucky University	M
East Tennessee State University	M
Florida Atlantic University	M
Illinois Institute of Technology	M
Iowa State University of Science and Technology	M,D
Kansas State University	M,D
Lehigh University	M
Louisiana Tech University	M
Mankato State University	M
Marquette University	M,D
Massachusetts Institute of Technology	M
Michigan State University	M,D
Murray State University	M
New Jersey Institute of Technology	M
North Carolina State University	M
Northeastern University	M,D
Northwestern University	M
Ohio University	M
Oklahoma State University	M
Old Dominion University	M
Oregon State University	M
Polytechnic University, Brooklyn Campus	M

Polytechnic University, Westchester Graduate Center	M
Portland State University	M
Purdue University	M,D
Rensselaer Polytechnic Institute	M
Rochester Institute of Technology	M
Southern Illinois University at Carbondale	M
Southern Methodist University	M
Stanford University	M
Syracuse University	M
Tufts University	O
University of California, Los Angeles	M
University of Central Florida	M
University of Detroit Mercy	M,D
University of Florida	M,D,O
University of Houston	M
The University of Iowa	M,D
University of Kentucky	M
University of Maryland, College Park	M,D
University of Massachusetts Amherst	M
The University of Memphis	M
University of Michigan	M,D
University of Michigan–Dearborn	M,D
University of Minnesota, Twin Cities Campus	M
University of Nebraska–Lincoln	M,D
University of New Mexico	M
University of Pittsburgh	M
University of Rhode Island	M
University of St. Thomas (MN)	M,O
University of Southern California	M
University of Tennessee, Knoxville	M
The University of Texas at Austin	M
The University of Texas at El Paso	M
University of Wisconsin–Madison	M
Villanova University	O
Wayne State University	M
Western Michigan University	M
Western New England College	M
Wichita State University	M,D
Worcester Polytechnic Institute	M,D

MARINE BIOLOGY

Boston University	M,D
California State University, Stanislaus	M
Florida Institute of Technology	M,D
Florida State University	M,D
Massachusetts Institute of Technology	D
Nova Southeastern University	M
Rutgers, The State University of New Jersey, New Brunswick	M,D
San Francisco State University	M
Southwest Texas State University	M
The University of Alabama at Birmingham	M,D
University of Alaska Fairbanks	M
University of California, San Diego	M,D
University of California, Santa Barbara	M,D
University of Colorado at Boulder	M,D
University of Guam	M
University of Hawaii at Manoa	M,D
University of Maine (Orono)	M,D
University of Massachusetts Dartmouth	M
University of Miami	M,D
University of North Carolina at Wilmington	M
University of Oregon	M,D
University of Southern California	M,D
University of Southern Mississippi	M,D
University of South Florida	M,D

MARINE SCIENCES

California State University, Fresno	M
California State University, Hayward	M
California State University, Sacramento	M
College of William and Mary	M,D
Duke University	M,D
Florida Institute of Technology	M
North Carolina State University	M,D
Nova Southeastern University	M
Oregon State University	M
San Jose State University	M
State University of New York at Stony Brook	M
University of Alaska Fairbanks	M,D
University of California, San Diego	M,D
University of California, Santa Barbara	M,D
University of California, Santa Cruz	M
University of Connecticut	M,D
University of Delaware	M,D
University of Florida	M,D
University of Georgia	M,D
University of Maine (Orono)	M
University of Maryland, Baltimore County	M,D
University of Maryland, College Park	M,D
University of Maryland Eastern Shore	M,D
University of Massachusetts Boston	D
University of Miami	M,D
The University of North Carolina at Chapel Hill	M,D
University of Puerto Rico, Mayagüez Campus	M,D
University of San Diego	M
University of South Alabama	M,D
University of South Carolina (Columbia)	M,D
University of Southern California	M,D
University of Southern Mississippi	M,D
University of South Florida	M,D
The University of Texas at Austin	M,D
University of Washington	M
University of Wisconsin–Madison	M,D

MARKETING

Alabama Agricultural and Mechanical University	M
American University	M
Andrews University	M
Arizona State University	D
Baruch College of the City University of New York	M,D
Boston College	M
Boston University	D
California Lutheran University	M
California State University, Fullerton	M
California State University, Hayward	M
California State University, Los Angeles	M
California State University, Northridge	M
Carnegie Mellon University	D
Case Western Reserve University	M,D
Central Michigan University	M
Charleston Southern University	M
City University	M,O
Claremont Graduate University	M
Clark Atlanta University	M
Colorado State University	M
Columbia University	M,D
Cornell University	D
Dallas Baptist University	M
Delta State University	M
DePaul University	M
Drexel University	M,D
East Carolina University	M
Eastern College	M
Eastern Michigan University	M
Emporia State University	M
Fairfield University	M,O
Fairleigh Dickinson University, Florham–Madison Campus	M
Fairleigh Dickinson University, Teaneck–Hackensack Campus	M
Florida Agricultural and Mechanical University	M
Florida International University	M,D
Fordham University	M
The George Washington University	M,D
Georgia State University	M,D
Golden Gate University	M
Hawaii Pacific University	M
Hofstra University	M
Houston Baptist University	M
Illinois Institute of Technology	M
Indiana University Bloomington	M,D
Inter American University of Puerto Rico, Metropolitan Campus	M
Inter American University of Puerto Rico, San Germán Campus	M
Iona College (New Rochelle)	M,O
Johns Hopkins University	M
Kennesaw State University	M
Kent State University	D
Lindenwood University	M
Long Island University, C.W. Post Campus	M
Louisiana State University and Agricultural and Mechanical College	M,D
Louisiana Tech University	M,D
Loyola College	M
Manhattan College	M
Metropolitan State University	M
Miami University	M
Michigan State University	M,D
Montclair State University	M
New York University	M,D,O
Northeastern Illinois University	M
Northwestern University	M,D
Oklahoma City University	M
Oklahoma State University	M,D
Oral Roberts University	M
Pace University	M
Pennsylvania State University University Park Campus	M,D
Philadelphia College of Textiles and Science	M
Purdue University	M,D
Quinnipiac College	M
Rensselaer Polytechnic Institute	M
Rutgers, The State University of New Jersey, Newark	M,D
Sage Graduate School	M
St. Bonaventure University	M
St. Cloud State University	M
St. John's University (NY)	M,O
Saint Joseph's University	M
Saint Louis University	M,D
Saint Xavier University	M
San Diego State University	M
Seton Hall University	M
State University of New York at Albany	M
Stephen F. Austin State University	M
Syracuse University	M,D
Temple University (Philadelphia)	M,D
Texas A&M University (College Station)	M,D
Texas Tech University	M,D
United States International University	D
Universidad del Turabo	M
Universidad Metropolitana	M
The University of Akron	M
The University of Alabama (Tuscaloosa)	M,D
The University of Arizona	M
University of California, Berkeley	D
University of Cincinnati	M,D
University of Colorado at Boulder	M,D
University of Colorado at Colorado Springs	M
University of Colorado at Denver	M
University of Connecticut	M,D
University of Denver	M
University of Florida	M,D
University of Hartford	M
University of Houston	M,D
University of Illinois at Chicago	D
The University of Iowa	D
University of Kansas	D
The University of Memphis	M,D
University of Minnesota, Twin Cities Campus	M,D
University of Missouri–St. Louis	M,O
University of Nebraska–Lincoln	M,D
University of New Haven	M
University of New Mexico	M
The University of North Carolina at Chapel Hill	D
University of North Carolina at Greensboro	M,D
University of North Texas	M,D
University of Oregon	M,D
University of Pennsylvania	D
University of Rhode Island	M
University of St. Thomas (MN)	M,O
University of San Francisco	M
University of Scranton	M
University of Tennessee at Chattanooga	M
University of Tennessee, Knoxville	M,D
The University of Texas at Arlington	M
The University of Texas at Austin	D
University of the Sacred Heart	M
University of Toledo	M
University of Utah	M,D
University of Wisconsin–Madison	M
Vanderbilt University	D
Virginia Commonwealth University	M,D
Virginia Polytechnic Institute and State University	D
Wagner College	M
Webster University	M
Western Kentucky University	M
Western New England College	M
Wilkes University	M
Worcester Polytechnic Institute	M
Wright State University	M
Yale University	D
Youngstown State University	M

MARKETING RESEARCH

Pace University	M
Southern Illinois University at Edwardsville	M
University of Georgia	M
The University of Texas at Arlington	M
University of Wisconsin–Madison	M

MARRIAGE AND FAMILY THERAPY

Abilene Christian University	M
Allegheny University of the Health Sciences	M,D
Appalachian State University	M
Arizona State University	D
Barry University	M,O
Brigham Young University	M,D
California Lutheran University	M
California State University, Bakersfield	
California State University, Dominguez Hills	M
California State University, Fresno	M
California State University, Northridge	O
Chapman University	M
City University	M
Converse College	O
East Carolina University	M
Eastern Nazarene College	M
Edgewood College	M
Fairfield University	M
Fitchburg State College	O
Florida State University	D
Friends University	M
Golden Gate University	M
Harding University	M
Hardin–Simmons University	M
Hofstra University	M,O
Idaho State University	O
Indiana State University	M
Iona College (New Rochelle)	M,O
Iowa State University of Science and Technology	D
Kutztown University of Pennsylvania	M
La Salle University	D
Loma Linda University	M
Long Island University, Brooklyn Campus	M
Loyola Marymount University	M
Michigan State University	M
Mississippi College	M
Northeast Louisiana University	M,D
Northwestern University	M
Nova Southeastern University	M,D,O
Pacific Lutheran University	M
Purdue University	M,D
Purdue University Calumet	M
Saint Joseph College (CT)	M
Saint Louis University	M,D
Saint Mary's College of California	M
St. Mary's University of San Antonio	M,O
St. Thomas University	M
San Francisco State University	M
Santa Clara University	M
Seattle Pacific University	M
Seton Hall University	M,D,O
Sonoma State University	M
Southern Connecticut State University	M
Springfield College (MA)	M,O
Stetson University	M
Syracuse University	M,D
Texas Tech University	D
Texas Woman's University	M,D
Trevecca Nazarene University	M
United States International University	M,D
The University of Akron	M
The University of Alabama at Birmingham	M
University of Florida	M,D,O
University of Houston–Clear Lake	M
University of Miami	M
University of Nevada, Las Vegas	M
University of New Hampshire	M
University of North Carolina at Greensboro	O
University of Pittsburgh	O
University of Rochester	M
University of San Diego	M
University of San Francisco	M
University of Southern California	D,O
University of Southern Mississippi	M
University of Wisconsin–Stout	M
Virginia Polytechnic Institute and State University	M,D
Wayne State University	M

MASS COMMUNICATION

Abilene Christian University	M
American University	M
Auburn University	M
Boston University	M
Bowling Green State University	M,D
California State University, Chico	M

P—first professional degree; M—master's degree; D—doctorate; O—other advanced degree.

Mass Communication (continued)

California State University, Fresno — M
California State University, Northridge — M
The College of Saint Rose — M
Drake University — M
Eastern New Mexico University — M
Emerson College — M
Florida International University — M
Florida State University — M,D
Fordham University — M
Grambling State University — M
Howard University — M,D
Hunter College of the City University of New York — M
Indiana University Bloomington — D
Iowa State University of Science and Technology — M
Jackson State University — M
Kansas State University — M
Kent State University — M
Lindenwood University — M
Louisiana State University and Agricultural and Mechanical College — M
Loyola University New Orleans — M
Marquette University — M
Miami University — M
Middle Tennessee State University — M
Monmouth University — M
Murray State University — M
Norfolk State University — M
North Dakota State University — M
Oklahoma State University — M,D
Pennsylvania State University University Park Campus — D
San Diego State University — M
San Jose State University — M
Seton Hall University — M
Southern Illinois University at Edwardsville — M
Southern University and Agricultural and Mechanical College — M
Southwest Texas State University — M
Stephen F. Austin State University — M
Syracuse University — D
Temple University (Philadelphia) — D
Texas Tech University — M
Towson University — M
University of Colorado at Boulder — M,D
University of Connecticut — M
University of Denver — M
University of Georgia — M,D
University of Houston — M
University of Illinois at Chicago — M
The University of Iowa — M,D
University of Maryland, College Park — M,D
University of Michigan — D
University of Minnesota, Twin Cities Campus — M,D
University of Nebraska–Lincoln — M
University of Nevada, Las Vegas — M
The University of North Carolina at Chapel Hill — M,D
University of Oklahoma — M
University of Puerto Rico, Río Piedras — M
University of South Dakota — M
University of Southern California — D
University of South Florida — M
University of Southwestern Louisiana — M
University of Wisconsin–Madison — M,D
University of Wisconsin–Milwaukee — M
University of Wisconsin–Stevens Point — M
University of Wisconsin–Superior — M
University of Wisconsin–Whitewater — M
Virginia Commonwealth University — M
Western Illinois University — M

MATERIALS ENGINEERING

Arizona State University — M,D
Auburn University — M,D
California State University, Northridge — M
Carnegie Mellon University — M,D
Case Western Reserve University — M,D
Clemson University — M,D
Colorado School of Mines — M,D
Colorado State University — M,D
Columbia University — M,D,O
Cornell University — M,D
Dartmouth College — M,D
Drexel University — M,D
Georgia Institute of Technology — M,D
Howard University — M,D
Illinois Institute of Technology — M,D

Iowa State University of Science and Technology — M,D
Johns Hopkins University — M,D
Lehigh University — M,D
Marquette University — M,D
Massachusetts Institute of Technology — M,D,O
Michigan Technological University — M,D
New Jersey Institute of Technology — M,D
North Carolina State University — M,D
Northwestern University — M,D
Pennsylvania State University University Park Campus — M,D
Purdue University — M,D
Rensselaer Polytechnic Institute — M,D
Rochester Institute of Technology — M
San Jose State University — M
Southern Methodist University — M
Stanford University — M,D,O
State University of New York at Stony Brook — M,D
Stevens Institute of Technology — M,D,O
Texas A&M University (College Station) — M,D
The University of Alabama (Tuscaloosa) — M,D
The University of Alabama at Birmingham — M,D
The University of Alabama in Huntsville — M
The University of Arizona — M,D
University of California, Berkeley — M,D
University of California, Irvine — M,D
University of California, Los Angeles — M,D
University of California, Santa Barbara — M,D
University of Central Florida — M,D
University of Cincinnati — M,D
University of Dayton — M,D
University of Delaware — M,D
University of Florida — M,D,O
University of Houston — M,D
University of Illinois at Chicago — M,D
University of Illinois at Urbana–Champaign — M,D
University of Maryland, College Park — M,D
University of Michigan — M,D
University of Minnesota, Twin Cities Campus — M,D
University of Nebraska–Lincoln — M
University of Pennsylvania — M,D
University of Pittsburgh — M,D
University of Southern California — M
The University of Texas at Arlington — M,D
The University of Texas at Austin — M,D
The University of Texas at El Paso — D
University of Utah — M,D
University of Washington — M,D
Vanderbilt University — M,D
Virginia Polytechnic Institute and State University — M,D
Washington State University — M,D
Washington University in St. Louis — M,D
Wayne State University — M,D,O
Western Michigan University — M
Worcester Polytechnic Institute — M,D
Wright State University — M

MATERIALS SCIENCES

Alabama Agricultural and Mechanical University — D
Arizona State University — M,D
Brown University — M,D
California Institute of Technology — M,D
California Polytechnic State University, San Luis Obispo — M
Carnegie Mellon University — M,D
Case Western Reserve University — M,D
Clemson University — M,D
Colorado School of Mines — M,D
Columbia University — M,D,O
Cornell University — M,D
Dartmouth College — M,D
Duke University — M,D
The George Washington University — M,D
Howard University — M,D
Iowa State University of Science and Technology — M,D
Jackson State University — M
Johns Hopkins University — M,D
Lehigh University — M,D
Marquette University — M,D
Massachusetts Institute of Technology — M,D,O
Michigan State University — M,D
New Jersey Institute of Technology — M,D
Norfolk State University — M

North Carolina State University — M,D
Northwestern University — M,D
Ohio University — D
Oregon State University — M
Pennsylvania State University University Park Campus — M,D
Polytechnic University, Brooklyn Campus — M,D
Rensselaer Polytechnic Institute — M,D
Rice University — M,D
Rochester Institute of Technology — M
Rutgers, The State University of New Jersey, New Brunswick — M,D
Southern Methodist University — M
Southwest Missouri State University — M
Stanford University — M,D,O
State University of New York at Buffalo — M
State University of New York at Stony Brook — M,D
Stevens Institute of Technology — M,D,O
Syracuse University — M,D
The University of Alabama (Tuscaloosa) — D
The University of Alabama at Birmingham — D
The University of Alabama in Huntsville — M,D
The University of Arizona — M,D
University of California, Berkeley — M,D
University of California, Davis — M,D,O
University of California, Irvine — M,D
University of California, Los Angeles — M,D
University of California, San Diego — M,D
University of California, Santa Barbara — M,D
University of Central Florida — M,D
University of Cincinnati — M,D
University of Connecticut — M,D
University of Delaware — M,D
University of Denver — D
University of Florida — M,D,O
University of Illinois at Urbana–Champaign — M,D
University of Kentucky — M,D
University of Maryland, College Park — M,D
University of Michigan — M,D
University of Minnesota, Twin Cities Campus — M,D
The University of North Carolina at Chapel Hill — M,D
University of North Texas — M,D
University of Pennsylvania — M,D
University of Pittsburgh — M,D
University of Rochester — M,D
University of Southern California — M,D,O
University of Tennessee, Knoxville — M,D
The University of Texas at Arlington — M,D
The University of Texas at Austin — M,D
The University of Texas at El Paso — D
University of Utah — M,D
University of Vermont — M,D
University of Virginia — M,D
University of Washington — M,D
University of Wisconsin–Madison — M,D
Vanderbilt University — M,D
Virginia Polytechnic Institute and State University — M,D
Washington State University — M,D
Washington University in St. Louis — M,D
Wayne State University — M,D,O
Western Michigan University — M
Worcester Polytechnic Institute — M,D
Wright State University — M
Youngstown State University — M

MATERNAL AND CHILD HEALTH

Boston University — M,O
Columbia University — M
The George Washington University — M
Harvard University — M,D
Johns Hopkins University — M,D
Tulane University — M,D
The University of Alabama at Birmingham — M
University of California, Berkeley — M
University of Hawaii at Manoa — M
University of Minnesota, Twin Cities Campus — M
The University of North Carolina at Chapel Hill — M,D

MATERNAL/CHILD-CARE NURSING

Adelphi University — M,O
Baylor University — M
Boston College — M

Case Western Reserve University — M
The Catholic University of America — M
Columbia University — M,O
Duke University — M,O
Emory University — M
Florida Atlantic University — M,O
Georgia State University — M
Gwynedd–Mercy College — M
Hunter College of the City University of New York — M,O
Johns Hopkins University — M,O
Kent State University — M
Lehman College of the City University of New York — M
Loma Linda University — M
Loyola University Chicago — M
Marquette University — M,O
New York University — M,O
Northeastern University — M,O
Rutgers, The State University of New Jersey, Newark — M
Saint Joseph College (CT) — M
Saint Louis University — M,O
Seton Hall University — M
State University of New York at Buffalo — M
State University of New York at Stony Brook — M,O
Texas Woman's University — M
University of Cincinnati — M
University of Colorado at Colorado Springs — M
University of Delaware — M,O
University of Illinois at Chicago — M
University of Michigan — M
University of Minnesota, Twin Cities Campus — M
University of Missouri–Kansas City — M
University of New Mexico — M
University of Pennsylvania — M,O
University of Pittsburgh — M
University of South Alabama — M
The University of Texas at El Paso — M
Vanderbilt University — M
Villanova University — M
Virginia Commonwealth University — M
Wayne State University — M,O
Wichita State University — M
Wright State University — M

MATHEMATICAL PHYSICS

Princeton University — D
University of Colorado at Boulder — D
Virginia Polytechnic Institute and State University — M,D

MATHEMATICS

Adelphi University — M,D
Alabama State University — M,O
American University — M
Andrews University — M
Angelo State University — M
Appalachian State University — M
Arizona State University — M,D
Arkansas State University — M
Auburn University — M,D
Ball State University — M
Baylor University — M
Boston College — M
Boston University — M,D
Bowling Green State University — M,D,O
Brandeis University — D
Brigham Young University — M,D
Brooklyn College of the City University of New York — M
Brown University — M,D
California Institute of Technology — D
California Polytechnic State University, San Luis Obispo — M
California State Polytechnic University, Pomona — M
California State University, Fresno — M
California State University, Fullerton — M
California State University, Hayward — M
California State University, Long Beach — M
California State University, Los Angeles — M
California State University, Northridge — M
California State University, Sacramento — M
California State University, San Bernardino — M
California State University, San Marcos — M
Carnegie Mellon University — M,D

Case Western Reserve University	M,D
Central Connecticut State University	M
Central Michigan University	M,D
Central Missouri State University	M
Central Washington University	M
Chicago State University	M
City College of the City University of New York	M
Claremont Graduate University	M,D
Clarkson University	M,D
Clemson University	M,D
Cleveland State University	M
Colorado School of Mines	M,D
Colorado State University	M,D
Columbia University	M,D
Cornell University	D
Creighton University	M
Dartmouth College	D
Drexel University	M,D
Duke University	D
East Carolina University	M
Eastern Illinois University	M
Eastern Kentucky University	M
Eastern Michigan University	M
Eastern New Mexico University	M
Eastern Washington University	M
East Tennessee State University	M
Emory University	M,D
Emporia State University	M
Fairleigh Dickinson University, Florham–Madison Campus	M
Fairleigh Dickinson University, Teaneck–Hackensack Campus	M
Fayetteville State University	M
Florida Atlantic University	M,D
Florida International University	M
Florida State University	M,D
George Mason University	M
The George Washington University	M,D
Georgia Institute of Technology	M,D
Georgian Court College	M
Georgia Southern University	M
Georgia State University	M
Graduate School and University Center of the City University of New York	D
Harvard University	M,D
Howard University	M,D
Hunter College of the City University of New York	M
Idaho State University	M,D
Illinois State University	M
Indiana State University	M
Indiana University Bloomington	M,D
Indiana University of Pennsylvania	M
Indiana University–Purdue University Fort Wayne	M
Indiana University–Purdue University Indianapolis	M,D
Iowa State University of Science and Technology	M,D
Jackson State University	M
Jacksonville State University	M
John Carroll University	M
Johns Hopkins University	M,D
Kansas State University	M,D
Kent State University	M,D
Kutztown University of Pennsylvania	M
Lamar University	M
Lehigh University	M,D
Lehman College of the City University of New York	M
Long Island University, C.W. Post Campus	M
Louisiana State University and Agricultural and Mechanical College	M,D
Louisiana Tech University	M
Loyola University Chicago	M
Loyola University New Orleans	M
Maharishi University of Management	M
Mankato State University	M
Marquette University	M,D
Marshall University	M
Massachusetts Institute of Technology	D
McNeese State University	M
Miami University	M
Michigan State University	M,D
Michigan Technological University	M,D
Middle Tennessee State University	M
Mississippi College	M
Mississippi State University	M,D
Montana State University–Bozeman	M,D
Montclair State University	M
Morgan State University	M
Murray State University	M
New Jersey Institute of Technology	M,D
New Mexico State University	M,D
New York University	M,D
Nicholls State University	M
North Carolina Central University	M
North Carolina State University	M,D
North Dakota State University	M,D
Northeastern Illinois University	M
Northeastern University	M,D
Northern Arizona University	M
Northern Illinois University	M,D
Northwestern University	D
Oakland University	M,O
The Ohio State University	M,D
Ohio University	M,D
Oklahoma State University	M,D
Old Dominion University	M,D
Oregon State University	M,D
Pennsylvania State University University Park Campus	M,D
Pittsburg State University	M
Polytechnic University, Brooklyn Campus	M,D
Polytechnic University, Farmingdale Campus	M,D
Portland State University	M,D
Prairie View A&M University	M
Princeton University	D
Purdue University	M,D
Queens College of the City University of New York	M
Rensselaer Polytechnic Institute	M,D
Rhode Island College	M,O
Rice University	M,D
Rivier College	M
Roosevelt University	M
Rowan University	M
Rutgers, The State University of New Jersey, Camden	M
Rutgers, The State University of New Jersey, Newark	D
Rutgers, The State University of New Jersey, New Brunswick	M,D
St. Cloud State University	M
St. John's University (NY)	M
Saint Louis University	M,D
Salem State College	M
Sam Houston State University	M
San Diego State University	M,D
San Francisco State University	M
San Jose State University	M
Shippensburg University of Pennsylvania	M
South Dakota State University	M
Southeast Missouri State University	M
Southern Illinois University at Carbondale	M,D
Southern Illinois University at Edwardsville	M
Southern Methodist University	M,D
Southern Oregon University	M
Southern University and Agricultural and Mechanical College	M
Southwest Missouri State University	M
Southwest Texas State University	M
Stanford University	M,D
State University of New York at Albany	M,D
State University of New York at Binghamton	M,D
State University of New York at Buffalo	M,D
State University of New York at New Paltz	M
State University of New York at Stony Brook	M,D
State University of New York College at Brockport	M
State University of New York College at Fredonia	M
State University of New York College at Potsdam	M
Stephen F. Austin State University	M
Stevens Institute of Technology	M,D
Syracuse University	M,D
Tarleton State University	M
Temple University (Philadelphia)	M,D
Tennessee State University	M
Tennessee Technological University	M
Texas A&M International University	M
Texas A&M University (College Station)	M,D
Texas A&M University–Commerce	M
Texas A&M University–Corpus Christi	M
Texas A&M University–Kingsville	M
Texas Christian University	M
Texas Southern University	M
Texas Tech University	M,D
Texas Woman's University	M
Truman State University	M
Tufts University	M,D
Tulane University	M,D
The University of Akron	M
The University of Alabama (Tuscaloosa)	M,D
The University of Alabama at Birmingham	M,D
The University of Alabama in Huntsville	M,D
University of Alaska Fairbanks	M,D
The University of Arizona	M,D
University of Arkansas (Fayetteville)	M,D
University of California, Berkeley	M,D,O
University of California, Davis	M,D
University of California, Irvine	M,D
University of California, Los Angeles	M,D,O
University of California, Riverside	M,D
University of California, San Diego	M,D
University of California, Santa Barbara	M,D
University of California, Santa Cruz	M,D
University of Central Arkansas	M
University of Central Florida	M,D
University of Central Oklahoma	M
University of Chicago	M,D
University of Cincinnati	M,D
University of Colorado at Boulder	M,D
University of Connecticut	M,D
University of Delaware	M,D
University of Denver	M,D
University of Detroit Mercy	M
University of Florida	M,D
University of Georgia	M,D
University of Hawaii at Manoa	M,D
University of Houston	M,D
University of Houston–Clear Lake	M
University of Idaho	M,D
University of Illinois at Chicago	M,D
University of Illinois at Springfield	M
University of Illinois at Urbana–Champaign	M,D
The University of Iowa	M,D
University of Kansas	M,D
University of Kentucky	M,D
University of Louisville	M
University of Maine (Orono)	M
University of Maryland, College Park	M,D
University of Massachusetts Amherst	M,D
University of Massachusetts Lowell	M
The University of Memphis	M,D
University of Miami	M,D
University of Michigan	M,D
University of Minnesota, Twin Cities Campus	M,D
University of Mississippi	M,D
University of Missouri–Columbia	M,D
University of Missouri–Kansas City	M,D
University of Missouri–Rolla	M,D
University of Missouri–St. Louis	M,D
The University of Montana–Missoula	M,D
University of Nebraska at Omaha	M
University of Nebraska–Lincoln	M,D
University of Nevada, Las Vegas	M
University of Nevada, Reno	M
University of New Hampshire	M,D
University of New Mexico	M,D
University of New Orleans	M
The University of North Carolina at Chapel Hill	M,D
University of North Carolina at Charlotte	M,D
University of North Carolina at Greensboro	M
University of North Carolina at Wilmington	M
University of North Dakota	M
University of Northern Colorado	M,D
University of Northern Iowa	M
University of North Florida	M
University of North Texas	M,D
University of Notre Dame	M,D
University of Oklahoma	M,D
University of Oregon	M,D
University of Pennsylvania	M,D
University of Pittsburgh	M,D
University of Puerto Rico, Mayagüez Campus	M
University of Puerto Rico, Río Piedras	M
University of Rhode Island	M,D
University of Rochester	M,D
University of South Alabama	M
University of South Carolina (Columbia)	M,D
University of South Dakota	M
University of Southern California	M,D
University of Southern Mississippi	M
University of South Florida	M,D
University of Southwestern Louisiana	M,D
University of Tennessee, Knoxville	M,D
The University of Texas at Arlington	M,D
The University of Texas at Austin	M,D
The University of Texas at Dallas	M,D
The University of Texas at El Paso	M
The University of Texas at San Antonio	M
The University of Texas at Tyler	M
The University of Texas–Pan American	M
University of the District of Columbia	M
University of the Incarnate Word	M
University of Toledo	M,D
University of Tulsa	M
University of Utah	M,D
University of Vermont	M,D
University of Virginia	M,D
University of Washington	M,D
University of West Florida	M
University of Wisconsin–Madison	M,D
University of Wisconsin–Milwaukee	M,D
University of Wyoming	M,D
Utah State University	M,D
Vanderbilt University	M,D
Villanova University	M
Virginia Commonwealth University	M,O
Virginia Polytechnic Institute and State University	M,D
Virginia State University	M
Wake Forest University	M
Washington State University	M,D
Washington University in St. Louis	M,D
Wayne State University	M,D
West Chester University of Pennsylvania	M
Western Carolina University	M
Western Connecticut State University	M
Western Illinois University	M
Western Kentucky University	M
Western Michigan University	M,D
Western Washington University	M
West Texas A&M University	M
West Virginia University	M,D
Wichita State University	M,D
Wilkes University	M
Winthrop University	M
Worcester Polytechnic Institute	M,D
Wright State University	M
Yale University	M,D
Youngstown State University	M

MATHEMATICS EDUCATION

Adelphi University	M
Alabama State University	M
Albany State University	M
Alfred University	M
American International College	M
American University	D
Arkansas Tech University	M
Auburn University	M,D,O
Ball State University	M
Beaver College	M,O
Bemidji State University	M
Boise State University	M
Boston College	M
Boston University	M,D,O
Bowling Green State University	O
Bridgewater State College	M
Brooklyn College of the City University of New York	M
California State University, Fullerton	M
California University of Pennsylvania	M
Campbell University	M
Central Missouri State University	M
The Citadel, The Military College of South Carolina	M
City College of the City University of New York	M
Claremont Graduate University	M
Clarion University of Pennsylvania	M
Clemson University	M
Columbus State University	M,O
Concordia University (IL)	M,O
Cornell University	M
Delta State University	M
DePaul University	M
Eastern Connecticut State University	M
Eastern Illinois University	M
Eastern Kentucky University	M
Eastern Washington University	M
Edinboro University of Pennsylvania	M

P—first professional degree; M—master's degree; D—doctorate; O—other advanced degree.

Mathematics Education (continued)

Fairleigh Dickinson University, Teaneck–Hackensack Campus	M
Fayetteville State University	M
Fitchburg State College	M
Florida Institute of Technology	M,D,O
Florida International University	M
Florida State University	M,D,O
Fort Hays State University	M
Framingham State College	M
Fresno Pacific University	M
Georgia Southern University	M,O
Georgia State University	M,D,O
Grand Valley State University	M
Harvard University	M,O
Henderson State University	M
Hofstra University	M
Hood College	M
Hunter College of the City University of New York	M
Illinois State University	D
Indiana University Bloomington	M
Indiana University of Pennsylvania	M
Iona College (New Rochelle)	M
Iowa State University of Science and Technology	M
Jacksonville University	M
Kean University	M
Kutztown University of Pennsylvania	M
Lehman College of the City University of New York	M
Long Island University, Brooklyn Campus	M
Long Island University, C.W. Post Campus	M
Louisiana Tech University	M
Loyola Marymount University	M
Mankato State University	M
Marquette University	M
McNeese State University	M
Mercer University (Macon)	M
Michigan State University	M,D
Middle Tennessee State University	M
Millersville University of Pennsylvania	M
Minot State University	M
Mississippi College	M
Montclair State University	M
National-Louis University	M,O
New Jersey City University	M
New York University	M,D
North Carolina Agricultural and Technical State University	M
North Carolina State University	M,D
Northeastern Illinois University	M
Northern Michigan University	M
North Georgia College & State University	M
Northwestern State University of Louisiana	M
Northwest Missouri State University	M
Nova Southeastern University	M,O
Ohio University	M,D
Oregon State University	M,D
Plattsburgh State University of New York	M
Plymouth State College of the University System of New Hampshire	M
Portland State University	D
Providence College	M
Purdue University	M,D,O
Queens College of the City University of New York	M,O
Quinnipiac College	M
Rollins College	M
Rowan University	M,O
Rutgers, The State University of New Jersey, New Brunswick	M,D,O
St. John Fisher College	M
Saint Joseph's University	M
Salem State College	M
Salisbury State University	M
San Diego State University	D
San Francisco State University	M
Shippensburg University of Pennsylvania	M
Slippery Rock University of Pennsylvania	M
South Carolina State University	M
Southern Arkansas University–Magnolia	M
Southern Connecticut State University	M
Stanford University	M
State University of New York at Albany	M
State University of New York at Binghamton	M
State University of New York at Buffalo	D
State University of New York College at Brockport	M
State University of New York College at Buffalo	M
State University of New York College at Cortland	M
State University of New York College at Oneonta	M
Stephen F. Austin State University	M
Syracuse University	M,D,O
Teachers College, Columbia University	M,D
Temple University (Philadelphia)	M,D
Texas A&M University (College Station)	M,D
University of Alaska Fairbanks	M,D
University of Arkansas (Fayetteville)	M
University of California, Berkeley	M,D
University of Central Florida	M
University of Central Oklahoma	M
University of Cincinnati	M
University of Connecticut	M,D
University of Detroit Mercy	M
University of Florida	M,D,O
University of Georgia	M,D,O
University of Houston	M
University of Idaho	M
University of Illinois at Chicago	M
University of Illinois at Urbana–Champaign	M
University of Massachusetts Lowell	D
University of Michigan	M,D
University of Minnesota, Twin Cities Campus	M,D
University of Missouri–Rolla	M
The University of Montana–Missoula	M,D
University of Nebraska at Kearney	M
University of Nevada, Las Vegas	M
University of Nevada, Reno	M
University of New Hampshire	D
The University of North Carolina at Chapel Hill	M
University of North Carolina at Charlotte	M
University of North Carolina at Pembroke	M
University of Northern Colorado	M,D
University of Northern Iowa	M
University of North Florida	M
University of Oklahoma	M,D
University of Pittsburgh	M,D
University of Puerto Rico, Río Piedras	M
University of South Carolina (Columbia)	M
University of South Florida	M,D,O
University of Tennessee, Knoxville	M,D,O
The University of Texas at Austin	M,D
The University of Texas at Dallas	M
The University of Texas at San Antonio	M
The University of Texas at Tyler	M,O
University of Tulsa	M
University of Vermont	M
The University of West Alabama	M
University of West Florida	M
University of Wisconsin–Eau Claire	M
University of Wisconsin–Madison	M
University of Wisconsin–Oshkosh	M
University of Wisconsin–River Falls	M
Vanderbilt University	M,D
Villanova University	M
Virginia Commonwealth University	M
Virginia State University	M
Washington University in St. Louis	M
Wayne State College	M
Webster University	M
Western Carolina University	M
Western Kentucky University	M
Western Michigan University	M,D
Western Oregon University	M
Wheeling Jesuit University	M
Wilkes University	M
Xavier University	M

MECHANICAL ENGINEERING

Alfred University	M
Arizona State University	M,D
Auburn University	M,D
Boston University	M,D
Bradley University	M
Brigham Young University	M,D
Brown University	M,D
California Institute of Technology	M,D,O
California Polytechnic State University, San Luis Obispo	M
California State University, Chico	M
California State University, Fresno	M
California State University, Fullerton	M
California State University, Long Beach	M
California State University, Los Angeles	M
California State University, Northridge	M
California State University, Sacramento	M
Carnegie Mellon University	M,D
Case Western Reserve University	M,D
The Catholic University of America	M
City College of the City University of New York	M,D
Clarkson University	M,D
Clemson University	M,D
Cleveland State University	M,D
Colorado State University	M,D
Columbia University	M,D
Cornell University	M,D
Dartmouth College	M,D
Drexel University	M,D
Duke University	M,D
Florida Agricultural and Mechanical University	M,D
Florida Atlantic University	M,D
Florida Institute of Technology	M,D
Florida International University	M,D
Florida State University	M,D
Gannon University	M
The George Washington University	M,D,O
Georgia Institute of Technology	M,D
Graduate School and University Center of the City University of New York	D
Howard University	M,D
Illinois Institute of Technology	M,D
Indiana University–Purdue University Indianapolis	M
Iowa State University of Science and Technology	M,D
Johns Hopkins University	M,D
Kansas State University	M,D
Lamar University	M,D
Lehigh University	M,D
Louisiana State University and Agricultural and Mechanical College	M,D
Louisiana Tech University	M,D
Loyola Marymount University	M
Manhattan College	M
Marquette University	M,D
Massachusetts Institute of Technology	M,D,O
McNeese State University	M
Mercer University (Macon)	M
Michigan State University	M,D
Michigan Technological University	M,D
Mississippi State University	M,D
Montana State University–Bozeman	M,D
New Jersey Institute of Technology	M,D,O
New Mexico State University	M,D
New York Institute of Technology	M
North Carolina Agricultural and Technical State University	M,D
North Carolina State University	M,D
North Dakota State University	M
Northeastern University	M,D
Northern Illinois University	M
Northwestern University	M,D
Oakland University	M
The Ohio State University	M,D
Ohio University	M,D
Oklahoma State University	M,D
Old Dominion University	M,D
Oregon State University	M,D
Pennsylvania State University University Park Campus	M,D
Polytechnic University, Brooklyn Campus	M,D
Polytechnic University, Farmingdale Campus	M,D
Portland State University	M,D
Princeton University	M,D
Purdue University	M,D
Rensselaer Polytechnic Institute	M,D
Rice University	M,D
Rochester Institute of Technology	M
Rutgers, The State University of New Jersey, New Brunswick	M,D
San Diego State University	M,D
San Jose State University	M
Santa Clara University	M,D,O
South Dakota State University	M
Southern Illinois University at Carbondale	M
Southern Methodist University	M,D
Stanford University	M,D,O
State University of New York at Binghamton	M,D
State University of New York at Buffalo	M,D
State University of New York at Stony Brook	M,D
Stevens Institute of Technology	M,D,O
Syracuse University	M,D
Temple University (Philadelphia)	M
Tennessee Technological University	M,D
Texas A&M University (College Station)	M,D
Texas A&M University–Kingsville	M
Texas Tech University	M,D
Tufts University	M,D
Tulane University	M,D
Tuskegee University	M
The University of Akron	M,D
The University of Alabama (Tuscaloosa)	M,D
The University of Alabama at Birmingham	M,D
The University of Alabama in Huntsville	M,D
University of Alaska Fairbanks	M
The University of Arizona	M,D
University of Arkansas (Fayetteville)	M
University of Bridgeport	M
University of California, Berkeley	M,D
University of California, Davis	M,D,O
University of California, Irvine	M,D
University of California, Los Angeles	M,D
University of California, San Diego	M,D
University of California, Santa Barbara	M,D
University of Central Florida	M,D
University of Cincinnati	M,D
University of Colorado at Boulder	M,D
University of Colorado at Denver	M
University of Connecticut	M,D
University of Dayton	M,D
University of Delaware	M,D
University of Denver	M
University of Detroit Mercy	M,D
University of Florida	M,D,O
University of Hawaii at Manoa	M,D
University of Houston	M,D
University of Idaho	M,D
University of Illinois at Chicago	M,D
University of Illinois at Urbana–Champaign	M,D
The University of Iowa	M,D
University of Kansas	M,D
University of Kentucky	M,D
University of Louisville	M
University of Maine (Orono)	M
University of Maryland, Baltimore County	M,D
University of Maryland, College Park	M,D
University of Massachusetts Amherst	M,D
University of Massachusetts Dartmouth	M
University of Massachusetts Lowell	M,D
The University of Memphis	M,D
University of Miami	M,D
University of Michigan	M,D
University of Michigan–Dearborn	M
University of Minnesota, Twin Cities Campus	M,D
University of Missouri–Columbia	M,D
University of Missouri–Rolla	M,D
University of Nebraska–Lincoln	M,D
University of Nevada, Las Vegas	M,D
University of Nevada, Reno	M,D
University of New Hampshire	M,D
University of New Haven	M
University of New Mexico	M,D
University of New Orleans	M
University of North Carolina at Charlotte	M,D
University of North Dakota	M
University of Notre Dame	M,D
University of Oklahoma	M,D
University of Pennsylvania	M,D
University of Pittsburgh	M,D
University of Portland	M
University of Puerto Rico, Mayagüez Campus	M
University of Rhode Island	M,D
University of Rochester	M,D
University of South Alabama	M
University of South Carolina (Columbia)	M,D
University of Southern California	M,D,O
University of South Florida	M,D
University of Southwestern Louisiana	M
University of Tennessee, Knoxville	M,D
The University of Texas at Arlington	M,D
The University of Texas at Austin	M,D

The University of Texas at El Paso	M
The University of Texas at San Antonio	M
University of Toledo	M,D
University of Tulsa	M,D
University of Utah	M,D
University of Vermont	M,D
University of Virginia	M,D
University of Washington	M,D
University of Wisconsin–Madison	M,D
University of Wyoming	M,D
Utah State University	M,D
Vanderbilt University	M,D
Villanova University	M,O
Virginia Polytechnic Institute and State University	M,D
Washington State University	M,D
Washington University in St. Louis	M,D
Wayne State University	M,D
Western Michigan University	M,D
Western New England College	M
West Virginia University	M,D
Wichita State University	M,D
Widener University	M
Worcester Polytechnic Institute	M,D
Wright State University	M
Yale University	M,D
Youngstown State University	M

MECHANICS

Brown University	M,D
California Institute of Technology	M,D
California State University, Fullerton	M
California State University, Northridge	M
The Catholic University of America	M,D
Clemson University	M,D
Colorado State University	M,D
Columbia University	M,D,O
Cornell University	M,D
Drexel University	M,D
Georgia Institute of Technology	M,D
Howard University	M,D
Iowa State University of Science and Technology	M,D
Johns Hopkins University	M,D
Lehigh University	M,D
Louisiana State University and Agricultural and Mechanical College	M,D
Michigan State University	M,D
Michigan Technological University	M
Mississippi State University	M
North Dakota State University	M
Northwestern University	M,D
The Ohio State University	M,D
Old Dominion University	M,D
Pennsylvania State University University Park Campus	M,D
Rensselaer Polytechnic Institute	M,D
Rutgers, The State University of New Jersey, New Brunswick	M,D
San Diego State University	M,D
San Jose State University	M
Southern Illinois University at Carbondale	M,D
State University of New York at Buffalo	M,D
The University of Alabama (Tuscaloosa)	M,D
The University of Arizona	M,D
University of California, Berkeley	M,D
University of California, San Diego	M,D
University of Cincinnati	M,D
University of Connecticut	D
University of Dayton	M
University of Florida	M,D,O
University of Illinois at Urbana–Champaign	M,D
University of Kentucky	M,D
University of Maryland, Baltimore County	M,D
University of Maryland, College Park	M,D
University of Massachusetts Lowell	D
University of Michigan	M,D,O
University of Minnesota, Twin Cities Campus	M,D
University of Missouri–Rolla	M,D
University of Nebraska–Lincoln	M,D
University of Pennsylvania	M,D
University of Rhode Island	M,D
University of Southern California	M
University of Tennessee, Knoxville	M,D
The University of Texas at Arlington	M
The University of Texas at Austin	M,D
University of Utah	M
University of Virginia	M
University of Washington	M,D
University of Wisconsin–Madison	M,D
Virginia Polytechnic Institute and State University	M,D
Yale University	M,D

MEDIA STUDIES

American University	M
Arkansas State University	M
Austin Peay State University	M
Ball State University	M
Barry University	M
Boston University	M
California State University, Fullerton	M
Central Michigan University	M
Columbia College (IL)	M
Duquesne University	M
Emerson College	M
Georgia Institute of Technology	M
Georgia State University	M
Governors State University	M
Hunter College of the City University of New York	M
Indiana State University	M
Kutztown University of Pennsylvania	M
Marquette University	M
Massachusetts Institute of Technology	M,D
Michigan State University	M,D
Monmouth University	O
New Mexico Highlands University	M
New School University	M
New York University	M,D
Norfolk State University	M
Northwestern University	M,D
Ohio University	M,D
Pennsylvania State University University Park Campus	M
Queens College of the City University of New York	M
San Diego State University	M
San Francisco State University	M
Southern Illinois University at Carbondale	M
Southern Methodist University	M
Stanford University	M
Syracuse University	M
Temple University (Philadelphia)	M,D
Texas Christian University	M
Texas Southern University	M
The University of Alabama (Tuscaloosa)	M,D
The University of Arizona	M
University of Colorado at Boulder	D
University of Denver	M
University of Florida	M,D
The University of Iowa	M,D
University of Oklahoma	M
University of South Carolina (Columbia)	M
University of Southern California	M
University of Tennessee, Knoxville	M,D
The University of Texas at Austin	M,D
Wayne State University	M,D
Webster University	M

MEDICAL ILLUSTRATION

Johns Hopkins University	M
Rochester Institute of Technology	M
University of Michigan	M

MEDICAL INFORMATICS

College of St. Scholastica	M
Columbia University	M,D
Duke University	O
Massachusetts Institute of Technology	M
New Jersey Institute of Technology	M,D
Stanford University	M,D
The University of Alabama at Birmingham	M
University of California, San Francisco	M,D
University of Minnesota, Twin Cities Campus	M,D
University of Pittsburgh	M
University of Utah	M,D
University of Virginia	M

MEDICAL MICROBIOLOGY

Allegheny University of the Health Sciences	M
Creighton University	M,D
The Ohio State University	M,D
Rutgers, The State University of New Jersey, New Brunswick	M,D
Texas A&M University (College Station)	D
University of Georgia	M,D
University of Hawaii at Manoa	M,D
University of Minnesota, Duluth	M,D
University of South Florida	D
University of Wisconsin–Madison	M

MEDICAL PHYSICS

Allegheny University of the Health Sciences	M,D
Columbia University	M,D
East Carolina University	M
Harvard University	D
Illinois Institute of Technology	M,D
Massachusetts Institute of Technology	D
Oakland University	D
Purdue University	M,D
University of California, Los Angeles	M,D
University of Chicago	M,D
University of Colorado at Boulder	D
University of Florida	M,D
University of Kentucky	M
University of Minnesota, Twin Cities Campus	M,D
University of Missouri–Columbia	M
University of Wisconsin–Madison	M,D
Wayne State University	D
Wright State University	M

MEDICAL/SURGICAL NURSING

Adelphi University	M,O
Boston College	M
Case Western Reserve University	M
The Catholic University of America	M
Columbia University	M,O
Duke University	M,O
Emory University	M
Florida Atlantic University	M,O
Gannon University	M
George Mason University	M
Gwynedd–Mercy College	M
Hunter College of the City University of New York	M
Johns Hopkins University	M,O
Kent State University	M
La Roche College	M
La Salle University	M
Lehman College of the City University of New York	M
Loyola University Chicago	M
Madonna University	M
Marquette University	M,O
Marymount University	M
Mount Saint Mary College	M
New York University	M,O
Oakland University	M
Pontifical Catholic University of Puerto Rico	M
Rutgers, The State University of New Jersey, Newark	M
Sage Graduate School	M
Saint Louis University	M,O
Saint Xavier University	M
Seton Hall University	M
Southern Illinois University at Edwardsville	M
State University of New York at Buffalo	M
State University of New York at Stony Brook	M,O
Texas Woman's University	M,D
University of Cincinnati	M
University of Colorado at Colorado Springs	M
University of Hawaii at Manoa	M
University of Illinois at Chicago	M
University of Miami	M
University of Michigan	M
University of Minnesota, Twin Cities Campus	M
University of Missouri–Kansas City	M
University of New Mexico	M
University of Pennsylvania	M
University of San Francisco	M
University of South Alabama	M
University of Southern Maine	M,O
University of Tennessee at Chattanooga	M
The University of Texas at El Paso	M
Vanderbilt University	M
Villanova University	M
Virginia Commonwealth University	M
Wayne State University	M
Wichita State University	M
Wright State University	M

MEDICAL TECHNOLOGY

California State University, Long Beach	M
Eastern Washington University	M
Florida International University	M
Georgia State University	M
Inter American University of Puerto Rico, Metropolitan Campus	M
Inter American University of Puerto Rico, San Germán Campus	O
Michigan State University	M
Northeastern University	M,D
Old Dominion University	M
St. John's University (NY)	M
Salve Regina University	M
University of North Dakota	M
University of Southern Mississippi	M
University of the Sacred Heart	O
University of Utah	M
University of Vermont	M
Wayne State University	M
West Virginia University	M

MEDIEVAL AND RENAISSANCE STUDIES

Arizona State University	O
The Catholic University of America	M,D,O
Columbia University	M
Cornell University	D
Duke University	O
Fordham University	M,D
Graduate School and University Center of the City University of New York	D
Harvard University	M,D
Indiana University Bloomington	D
Marquette University	M
Rutgers, The State University of New Jersey, New Brunswick	D
Southern Methodist University	M
University of Connecticut	M,D
University of Notre Dame	M,D
Western Michigan University	M
Yale University	M,D

METALLURGICAL ENGINEERING AND METALLURGY

Colorado School of Mines	M,D
Columbia University	O
Georgia Institute of Technology	M,D
Illinois Institute of Technology	M,D
Massachusetts Institute of Technology	D,O
Michigan Technological University	M,D
Montana Tech of The University of Montana	M
The Ohio State University	M,D
Pennsylvania State University University Park Campus	M,D
Purdue University	M
Rensselaer Polytechnic Institute	M,D
Rutgers, The State University of New Jersey, New Brunswick	M,D
The University of Alabama (Tuscaloosa)	M,D
The University of Alabama at Birmingham	D
University of California, Berkeley	M,D
University of California, Los Angeles	M,D
University of Cincinnati	M,D
University of Connecticut	M,D
University of Florida	M,D,O
University of Idaho	M,D
University of Missouri–Rolla	M,D
University of Nevada, Reno	M,D,O
University of Pittsburgh	M,D
University of Tennessee, Knoxville	M,D
The University of Texas at El Paso	M
University of Utah	M,D
University of Washington	M
University of Wisconsin–Madison	M,D

METEOROLOGY

Florida State University	M,D
Massachusetts Institute of Technology	M,D
North Carolina State University	M,D
Pennsylvania State University University Park Campus	M,D
San Jose State University	M
Texas A&M University (College Station)	M,D
University of Hawaii at Manoa	M,D
University of Maryland, College Park	M,D
University of Miami	M,D
University of Oklahoma	M,D
University of Utah	M,D
Yale University	D

MICROBIOLOGY

Allegheny University of the Health Sciences	M,D

P—first professional degree; M—master's degree; D—doctorate; O—other advanced degree.

Microbiology (continued)

Arizona State University	M,D
Auburn University	M,D
Boston University	M,D
Brandeis University	D
Brigham Young University	M,D
Brown University	M,D
California State University, Fullerton	M
California State University, Long Beach	M
California State University, Los Angeles	M
Case Western Reserve University	D
The Catholic University of America	M,D
Clemson University	M,D
Colorado State University	M,D
Columbia University	M,D
Cornell University	D
Dartmouth College	
Duke University	D
East Carolina University	D
East Tennessee State University	M,D
Emory University	D
Emporia State University	M
Florida State University	M,D
Georgetown University	D
The George Washington University	M,D
Harvard University	D
Howard University	D
Idaho State University	M
Illinois Institute of Technology	M
Illinois State University	D
Indiana State University	M,D
Indiana University Bloomington	M,D
Indiana University–Purdue University Indianapolis	M,D
Iowa State University of Science and Technology	M,D
Johns Hopkins University	M,D
Kansas State University	M,D
Loma Linda University	M,D
Long Island University, C.W. Post Campus	M
Louisiana State University and Agricultural and Mechanical College	M,D
Loyola University Chicago	M,D
Marquette University	M,D
Massachusetts Institute of Technology	D
Miami University	M,D
Michigan State University	D
Montana State University–Bozeman	M,D
New York University	M,D
North Carolina State University	M,D
North Dakota State University	M,D
Northwestern University	D
The Ohio State University	M,D
Ohio University	M,D
Oklahoma State University	M,D
Oregon State University	M,D
Pennsylvania State University University Park Campus	M,D
Purdue University	D
Quinnipiac College	M
Rensselaer Polytechnic Institute	M,D
Rutgers, The State University of New Jersey, New Brunswick	M,D
Saint Louis University	D
San Diego State University	M
San Francisco State University	M
Seton Hall University	M
South Dakota State University	M
Southern Illinois University at Carbondale	M,D
Stanford University	D
State University of New York at Buffalo	M,D
State University of New York at Stony Brook	D
Temple University (Philadelphia)	M,D
Texas A&M University (College Station)	M,D
Texas Tech University	M
Tufts University	D
Tulane University	M,D
The University of Alabama at Birmingham	D
The University of Arizona	M,D
University of California, Berkeley	D
University of California, Davis	M,D
University of California, Irvine	D
University of California, Los Angeles	D
University of California, Riverside	M,D
University of California, San Francisco	D
University of Central Florida	M
University of Cincinnati	D
University of Colorado at Boulder	M,D
University of Connecticut	M,D
University of Delaware	M,D
University of Florida	M,D

University of Georgia	M,D
University of Hawaii at Manoa	M,D
University of Idaho	M,D
University of Illinois at Chicago	D
University of Illinois at Urbana–Champaign	M,D
The University of Iowa	M,D
University of Kansas	M,D
University of Kentucky	D
University of Louisville	M,D
University of Maine (Orono)	M,D
University of Maryland, College Park	M,D
University of Massachusetts Amherst	M,D
The University of Memphis	M,D
University of Miami	D
University of Michigan	D
University of Minnesota, Twin Cities Campus	M,D
University of Missouri–Columbia	M,D
The University of Montana–Missoula	M,D
University of New Hampshire	M,D
University of New Mexico	M,D
The University of North Carolina at Chapel Hill	M,D
University of North Dakota	M,D
University of Oklahoma	M,D
University of Pennsylvania	D
University of Pittsburgh	M,D
University of Rhode Island	M,D
University of Rochester	M,D
University of South Alabama	D
University of South Carolina (Columbia)	D
University of South Dakota	M,D
University of Southern California	M,D
University of Southern Mississippi	M,D
University of South Florida	M
University of Tennessee, Knoxville	M,D
The University of Texas at Austin	M,D
University of Utah	D
University of Vermont	M,D
University of Virginia	D
University of Washington	D
University of Wisconsin–La Crosse	M
University of Wisconsin–Madison	M,D
University of Wisconsin–Oshkosh	M
Vanderbilt University	M,D
Virginia Commonwealth University	M,D,O
Virginia Polytechnic Institute and State University	M,D
Wake Forest University	D
Washington State University	M,D
Washington University in St. Louis	D
Wayne State University	M,D
West Virginia University	M,D
Wright State University	M
Yale University	D
Yeshiva University	D

MIDDLE SCHOOL EDUCATION

Alaska Pacific University	M
Albany State University	M
Armstrong Atlantic State University	M
Augusta State University	M,O
Ball State University	M
Bellarmine College	M
Brenau University	M,O
Campbell University	M
Central Michigan University	M
Cleveland State University	M
Columbus State University	M,O
Cumberland College	M
Drury College	M
East Carolina University	M
Eastern Illinois University	M
Eastern Michigan University	M
Eastern Nazarene College	M,O
Edinboro University of Pennsylvania	M
Emory University	M
Fayetteville State University	M
Fitchburg State College	M
Fort Valley State University	M
Gardner–Webb University	M
George Mason University	M
Georgia College and State University	M,O
Georgia Southern University	M,O
Georgia Southwestern State University	M,O
Georgia State University	M,O
James Madison University	M
Kennesaw State University	M
Lenoir–Rhyne College	M
Lesley College	M
Long Island University, C.W. Post Campus	M
Lynchburg College	M

Maryville University of Saint Louis	M
Mercer University (Macon)	M,O
Mercer University, Cecil B. Day Campus	M,O
Middle Tennessee State University	M
Morehead State University	M
Morgan State University	M
Murray State University	M,O
North Carolina Agricultural and Technical State University	M
North Carolina State University	M
North Georgia College & State University	M
Northwest Missouri State University	M
Nova Southeastern University	D
Ohio University	M
Pacific University	M
Quinnipiac College	M
Saginaw Valley State University	M
St. Cloud State University	M
Simmons College	M
Southeast Missouri State University	M
Spalding University	M
State University of West Georgia	M,O
Tufts University	M
Union College (KY)	M
University of Arkansas (Fayetteville)	M
University of Florida	M,D,O
University of Georgia	M,D,O
University of Louisville	M
University of Nebraska at Kearney	M
University of Nevada, Las Vegas	M
University of North Carolina at Charlotte	M
University of North Carolina at Greensboro	M
University of North Carolina at Pembroke	M
University of Northern Iowa	M
University of St. Francis (IL)	M
University of South Florida	M
University of West Florida	M
University of Wisconsin–Milwaukee	M
University of Wisconsin–Platteville	M
Valdosta State University	M,O
Virginia Commonwealth University	M
Western Carolina University	M
Western Kentucky University	M
Western Michigan University	M
Western Oregon University	M
Westfield State College	M
Worcester State College	M,O
Youngstown State University	M

MILITARY AND DEFENSE STUDIES

California State University, San Bernardino	M
Georgetown University	M
The George Washington University	M
Norwich University	M
Southwest Missouri State University	M

MINERAL ECONOMICS

Colorado School of Mines	M,D
Michigan Technological University	M
Montana Tech of The University of Montana	M
Pennsylvania State University University Park Campus	M,D
The University of Arizona	M,D

MINERAL/MINING ENGINEERING

Colorado School of Mines	M,D
Columbia University	D,O
Michigan Technological University	M,D
Montana Tech of The University of Montana	M
Pennsylvania State University University Park Campus	M,D
Southern Illinois University at Carbondale	M
The University of Alabama (Tuscaloosa)	M
University of Alaska Fairbanks	M,O
The University of Arizona	M,D
University of California, Berkeley	M,D
University of Idaho	M,D
University of Kentucky	M,D
University of Missouri–Rolla	M,D
University of Nevada, Reno	M,O
University of North Dakota	M
University of Utah	M,D

Virginia Polytechnic Institute and State University	M,D
West Virginia University	M,D

MISSIONS AND MISSIOLOGY

Abilene Christian University	M
Ashland University	M
Biola University	D
Grand Rapids Baptist Seminary	P,M,D
Hope International University	M
Oral Roberts University	M

MOLECULAR BIOLOGY

Allegheny University of the Health Sciences	M,D
Arizona State University	M,D
Boston University	M,D
Brandeis University	D
Brigham Young University	M,D
Brown University	M,D
California Institute of Technology	D
Carnegie Mellon University	D
Case Western Reserve University	D
Clark University	M,D
Colorado State University	M,D
Columbia University	M,D
Cornell University	M,D
Dartmouth College	
Duke University	D,O
East Carolina University	M
Emory University	D
Florida Institute of Technology	M,D
Florida State University	M,D
Fordham University	M,D
George Mason University	M
Georgetown University	D
The George Washington University	M,D
Harvard University	D
Howard University	M,D
Indiana University Bloomington	M,D
Indiana University–Purdue University Indianapolis	M,D
Iowa State University of Science and Technology	M,D
Johns Hopkins University	D
Kansas State University	M,D
Kent State University	M,D
Lehigh University	M,D
Loyola University Chicago	D
Maharishi University of Management	M,D
Marquette University	M,D
Michigan State University	D
Mississippi State University	M,D
Montana State University–Bozeman	M,D
New Mexico State University	M,D
New York University	D
North Dakota State University	D
Northwestern University	D
The Ohio State University	M,D
Ohio University	M,D
Oklahoma State University	M,D
Oregon State University	D
Pennsylvania State University University Park Campus	M,D
Princeton University	D
Purdue University	D
Quinnipiac College	M
Rensselaer Polytechnic Institute	M,D
Rutgers, The State University of New Jersey, New Brunswick	M,D
Saint Louis University	D
San Diego State University	M,D
San Francisco State University	M
Southern Illinois University at Carbondale	M,D
State University of New York at Albany	M,D
State University of New York at Buffalo	M,D
State University of New York at Stony Brook	D
Temple University (Philadelphia)	D
Texas A&M University (College Station)	D
Texas Woman's University	D
Tufts University	D
Tulane University	M,D
The University of Alabama at Birmingham	
The University of Arizona	M,D
University of California, Berkeley	D
University of California, Davis	M,D
University of California, Irvine	D
University of California, Los Angeles	M,D,O
University of California, San Diego	D
University of California, San Francisco	D
University of California, Santa Barbara	M,D

University of California, Santa Cruz	D
University of Central Florida	M
University of Chicago	D
University of Cincinnati	M,D
University of Colorado at Boulder	M,D
University of Delaware	M,D
University of Florida	D
University of Georgia	M,D
University of Hawaii at Manoa	M,D
University of Idaho	M,D
University of Illinois at Chicago	M,D
University of Illinois at Urbana–Champaign	[illegible]
The University of Iowa	D
University of Kansas	M,D
University of Maine (Orono)	M,D
University of Maryland, Baltimore County	M,D
University of Maryland, College Park	D
University of Massachusetts Amherst	M,D
The University of Memphis	M,D
University of Miami	D
University of Michigan	D
University of Minnesota, Duluth	M,D
University of Minnesota, Twin Cities Campus	M,D
University of Missouri–Kansas City	M,D
University of Nevada, Reno	M,D
University of New Hampshire	M,D
University of New Haven	M
University of New Mexico	M,D
The University of North Carolina at Chapel Hill	M,D
University of North Texas	M,D
University of Notre Dame	M,D
University of Oregon	D
University of Pennsylvania	D
University of Pittsburgh	D
University of Rochester	M,D
University of South Carolina (Columbia)	M,D
University of South Dakota	M,D
University of Southern California	M,D
University of Southern Mississippi	M,D
University of South Florida	D
The University of Texas at Austin	M,D
The University of Texas at Dallas	M,D
University of Utah	D
University of Vermont	M,D
University of Virginia	
University of Washington	D
University of Wisconsin–Madison	M,D
University of Wisconsin–Parkside	M
University of Wyoming	M,D
Utah State University	M,D
Vanderbilt University	M,D
Virginia Polytechnic Institute and State University	D
Wake Forest University	D
Washington University in St. Louis	D
Wayne State University	M,D
West Virginia University	M,D
William Paterson University of New Jersey	M
Wright State University	M
Yale University	D
Yeshiva University	D

MOLECULAR MEDICINE

Cornell University	D
Johns Hopkins University	D
University of Cincinnati	D
University of Virginia	D
Yale University	D

MULTILINGUAL AND MULTICULTURAL EDUCATION

Adelphi University	M
Azusa Pacific University	M
Boston University	M,D,O
Brooklyn College of the City University of New York	M
Brown University	M
California State University, Bakersfield	M
California State University, Chico	M
California State University, Dominguez Hills	M
California State University, Fullerton	M
California State University, Los Angeles	M
California State University, Sacramento	M
California State University, San Bernardino	M
California State University, Stanislaus	M
Chicago State University	M
City College of the City University of New York	M
Cleveland State University	M
College of Notre Dame	M
Columbia College (IL)	M
DePaul University	M
Eastern College	M
Eastern Michigan University	M
Eastern Nazarene College	M,O
Fairfield University	M,O
Fairleigh Dickinson University, Teaneck–Hackensack Campus	M
Florida State University	M,D,O
Fordham University	M
Fresno Pacific University	M
George Mason University	M
Georgetown University	O
Heritage College	M
Hofstra University	M
Houston Baptist University	M
Hunter College of the City University of New York	M
Immaculata College	M
Iona College (New Rochelle)	M
Kean University	M,O
Lehigh University	M
Lehman College of the City University of New York	M
Lesley College	M
Long Island University, Brooklyn Campus	M
Long Island University, C.W. Post Campus	M
Loyola Marymount University	M
Mankato State University	M
Maryville University of Saint Louis	M
National University	M
New Jersey City University	M
New York University	M,D,O
Northeastern Illinois University	M
Northern Arizona University	M
Pennsylvania State University University Park Campus	M,D
Queens College of the City University of New York	M
Rhode Island College	M
St. John's University (NY)	M
Sam Houston State University	O
San Diego State University	M
Seton Hall University	M,O
Southern Connecticut State University	M
Stanford University	M,D
State University of New York at Buffalo	M
State University of New York College at Brockport	M
State University of New York College at Buffalo	M
Sul Ross State University	M
Teachers College, Columbia University	M
Texas A&M International University	M
Texas A&M University (College Station)	M,D
Texas A&M University–Kingsville	M,D
Texas Southern University	M
Texas Tech University	M,D
Universidad del Turabo	M
University of Alaska Fairbanks	M,O
The University of Arizona	M,D,O
University of California, Berkeley	M,D,O
University of Colorado at Boulder	M,D
University of Connecticut	M,D
University of Delaware	M
University of Florida	M,D,O
University of Houston	M
University of Houston–Clear Lake	M
University of Massachusetts Amherst	M,D,O
University of Massachusetts Boston	M
University of Minnesota, Twin Cities Campus	M,D
University of New Mexico	D,O
University of Pennsylvania	M
University of San Francisco	M,D
University of Tennessee, Knoxville	M,D
The University of Texas at San Antonio	M
The University of Texas–Pan American	M
Xavier University	M

MUSEUM STUDIES

Baylor University	M
Boston University	O
California State University, Chico	M
California State University, Fullerton	O
Case Western Reserve University	M,D
City College of the City University of New York	M
College of New Rochelle	O
Colorado State University	M
Duquesne University	M
Framingham State College	M
The George Washington University	M,O
Hampton University	M
Harvard University	O
John F. Kennedy University	M,O
New York University	M,D,O
Rutgers, The State University of New Jersey, New Brunswick	M
San Francisco State University	M
Seton Hall University	M
State University of New York College at Oneonta	M
Syracuse University	M
Texas Tech University	M
Tufts University	O
University of Central Oklahoma	M
University of Colorado at Boulder	M
University of Delaware	O
University of Denver	M
University of Kansas	M
University of Michigan	O
University of Nebraska–Lincoln	M
University of South Carolina (Columbia)	M,O
University of Washington	M
University of Wisconsin–Milwaukee	O
Wayne State University	O

MUSIC

Alabama Agricultural and Mechanical University	M
Alabama State University	M
Andrews University	M
Appalachian State University	M
Arizona State University	M,D
Arkansas State University	M,O
Ashland University	M
Auburn University	M
Austin Peay State University	M
Azusa Pacific University	M
Baylor University	M
Boise State University	M
Boston University	M,D,O
Bowling Green State University	M
Brandeis University	M,D
Brigham Young University	M,D
Brooklyn College of the City University of New York	M
Brown University	M,D
Butler University	M
California State University, Chico	M
California State University, Fresno	M
California State University, Fullerton	M
California State University, Hayward	M
California State University, Long Beach	M
California State University, Los Angeles	M
California State University, Northridge	M
California State University, Sacramento	M
Carnegie Mellon University	M
Case Western Reserve University	M,D
The Catholic University of America	M,D
Central Michigan University	M
Central Missouri State University	M
Central Washington University	M
City College of the City University of New York	M
Claremont Graduate University	M,D
Cleveland State University	M
The College of New Jersey	M
College of Notre Dame	M
The College of Saint Rose	M
Colorado State University	M
Columbia University	M,D
Concordia University (IL)	M,O
Converse College	M
Cornell University	M,D
Dartmouth College	M
DePaul University	M,O
Drake University	M
Duke University	M,D
Duquesne University	M,O
East Carolina University	M
Eastern Illinois University	M
Eastern Kentucky University	M
Eastern Michigan University	M
Eastern New Mexico University	M
Eastern Washington University	M
Emory University	M
Emporia State University	M
Florida Atlantic University	M
Florida International University	M
Florida State University	M,D
George Mason University	M
Georgia Southern University	M
Georgia State University	M
Graduate School and University Center of the City University of New York	D
Hardin–Simmons University	M
Harvard University	M,D
Holy Names College	M,O
Hope International University	M
Howard University	M
Hunter College of the City University of New York	M
Illinois State University	M
Indiana State University	M
Indiana University Bloomington	M,D,O
Indiana University of Pennsylvania	M
Indiana University South Bend	M
Ithaca College	M
Jacksonville State University	M
James Madison University	M
Johns Hopkins University	M,D,O
Kansas State University	M
Kent State University	M,D
Lamar University	M
Lehman College of the City University of New York	M
Long Island University, C.W. Post Campus	M
Louisiana State University and Agricultural and Mechanical College	M,D
Loyola University New Orleans	M
Mankato State University	M
Mannes College of Music, New School University	M,O
Marshall University	M
Marywood University	M
McNeese State University	M
Meredith College	M
Miami University	M
Michigan State University	M,D
Middle Tennessee State University	M
Mississippi College	M
Montclair State University	M
Moorhead State University	M
Morehead State University	M
Morgan State University	M
Murray State University	M
New Mexico State University	M
New York University	M,D,O
Norfolk State University	M
North Carolina Central University	M
Northeastern Illinois University	M
Northeast Louisiana University	M
Northern Arizona University	M
Northern Illinois University	M,O
Northwestern State University of Louisiana	M
Northwestern University	M,D,O
Oakland University	M
The Ohio State University	M,D
Ohio University	M
Oklahoma City University	M
Oklahoma State University	M
Pennsylvania State University University Park Campus	M
Pittsburg State University	M
Portland State University	M
Prairie View A&M University	M
Princeton University	D
Queens College of the City University of New York	M
Radford University	M
Rensselaer Polytechnic Institute	M
Rhode Island College	M
Rice University	M,D
Rider University	M
Roosevelt University	M,O
Rutgers, The State University of New Jersey, Newark	M
Rutgers, The State University of New Jersey, New Brunswick	M,D,O
St. Cloud State University	M
Samford University	M
Sam Houston State University	M
San Diego State University	M
San Francisco State University	M
San Jose State University	M
Santa Clara University	M
Shenandoah University	M,D
Southeastern Louisiana University	M
Southern Illinois University at Carbondale	M
Southern Illinois University at Edwardsville	M
Southern Methodist University	M
Southern Oregon University	M
Southwestern Oklahoma State University	M
Southwest Missouri State University	M
Southwest Texas State University	M
Stanford University	M,D

P—first professional degree; M—master's degree; D—doctorate; O—other advanced degree.

Music (continued)

State University of New York at Binghamton	M
State University of New York at Buffalo	M,D,O
State University of New York at New Paltz	M
State University of New York at Stony Brook	M,D
State University of New York College at Fredonia	M
State University of New York College at Potsdam	M
State University of West Georgia	M
Stephen F. Austin State University	M
Syracuse University	M
Temple University (Philadelphia)	M,D
Texas A&M University–Commerce	M
Texas Christian University	M
Texas Southern University	M
Texas Tech University	M,D
Texas Woman's University	M
Towson University	M
Truman State University	M
Tufts University	M
Tulane University	M
The University of Akron	M
The University of Alabama (Tuscaloosa)	M,D,O
University of Alaska Fairbanks	M
The University of Arizona	M,D
University of Arkansas (Fayetteville)	M
University of California, Berkeley	M,D
University of California, Davis	M,D
University of California, Irvine	M
University of California, Los Angeles	M,D
University of California, Riverside	M
University of California, San Diego	M,D
University of California, Santa Barbara	M,D
University of California, Santa Cruz	M
University of Central Arkansas	M
University of Central Oklahoma	M
University of Chicago	M,D
University of Cincinnati	M,D,O
University of Colorado at Boulder	M,D
University of Connecticut	M,D
University of Denver	M
University of Florida	M,D
University of Georgia	M,D
University of Hartford	M,D,O
University of Hawaii at Manoa	M,D
University of Houston	M,D
University of Idaho	M
University of Illinois at Urbana–Champaign	M,D
The University of Iowa	M,D
University of Kansas	M,D
University of Kentucky	M,D
University of Louisville	M,D
University of Maine (Orono)	M
University of Maryland, Baltimore County	M,D
University of Maryland, College Park	M,D
University of Massachusetts Amherst	M,D
University of Massachusetts Lowell	M
The University of Memphis	M,D
University of Miami	M,D,O
University of Michigan	M,D
University of Minnesota, Twin Cities Campus	M,D
University of Mississippi	M,D
University of Missouri–Columbia	M
University of Missouri–Kansas City	M,D
The University of Montana–Missoula	M
University of Montevallo	M
University of Nebraska at Omaha	M
University of Nebraska–Lincoln	M,D
University of Nevada, Las Vegas	M
University of Nevada, Reno	M
University of New Hampshire	M
University of New Mexico	M
University of New Orleans	M
The University of North Carolina at Chapel Hill	M,D
University of North Carolina at Greensboro	M,D
University of North Dakota	M
University of Northern Colorado	M,D
University of Northern Iowa	M
University of North Texas	M,D
University of Notre Dame	M
University of Oklahoma	M,D
University of Oregon	M,D
University of Pennsylvania	M,D
University of Pittsburgh	M,D
University of Portland	M

University of Redlands	M
University of Rhode Island	M
University of Rochester	M,D
University of St. Thomas (MN)	M
University of South Carolina (Columbia)	M,D,O
University of South Dakota	M
University of Southern California	M,D
University of Southern Mississippi	M,D
University of South Florida	M,D
University of Southwestern Louisiana	M
University of Tennessee at Chattanooga	M
University of Tennessee, Knoxville	M
The University of Texas at Austin	M,D
The University of Texas at El Paso	M
The University of Texas at San Antonio	M
The University of Texas at Tyler	M
University of the Pacific	M
University of Toledo	M
University of Tulsa	M
University of Utah	M,D
University of Virginia	M
University of Washington	M,D
University of Wisconsin–Madison	M,D
University of Wisconsin–Milwaukee	M
University of Wisconsin–Whitewater	M
University of Wyoming	M
Valparaiso University	M
Virginia Commonwealth University	M
Washington State University	M
Washington University in St. Louis	M,D
Wayne State University	M,O
Webster University	M
West Chester University of Pennsylvania	M
Western Carolina University	M
Western Illinois University	M
Western Michigan University	M
Western Washington University	M
West Texas A&M University	M
West Virginia University	M,D
Wichita State University	M
Winthrop University	M
Yale University	M,D,O
Youngstown State University	M

MUSIC EDUCATION

Adelphi University	M
Alabama Agricultural and Mechanical University	M
Alabama State University	M
Albany State University	M
Angelo State University	M
Appalachian State University	M
Arkansas State University	M,O
Auburn University	M,D,O
Austin Peay State University	M
Azusa Pacific University	M
Ball State University	M,D
Baylor University	M
Beaver College	M
Belmont University	M
Boise State University	M
Boston University	M,D
Bowling Green State University	M
Brigham Young University	M
Brooklyn College of the City University of New York	M
Butler University	M
California State University, Fresno	M
California State University, Fullerton	M
California State University, Los Angeles	M
California State University, Northridge	M
Case Western Reserve University	M,D
The Catholic University of America	M,D
Central Connecticut State University	M
Central Michigan University	M
Claremont Graduate University	M
Cleveland State University	M
College of Notre Dame	M
The College of Saint Rose	M
Colorado State University	M
Columbus State University	M
Converse College	M
Delta State University	M
DePaul University	M
Drake University	M
Duquesne University	M
East Carolina University	M
Eastern Kentucky University	M

Eastern Nazarene College	M,O
Eastern Washington University	M
East Tennessee State University	M
Emporia State University	M
Florida International University	M
Florida State University	M,D
George Mason University	M
Georgia Southern University	M,O
Georgia State University	M,O
Hardin–Simmons University	M
Hofstra University	M
Holy Names College	M,O
Howard University	M
Hunter College of the City University of New York	M
Indiana State University	M
Indiana University of Pennsylvania	M
Indiana University South Bend	M
Ithaca College	M
Jackson State University	M
Jacksonville State University	M
Jacksonville University	M
James Madison University	M
Kent State University	M,D
Lamar University	M
Long Island University, C.W. Post Campus	M
Louisiana State University and Agricultural and Mechanical College	D
Mansfield University of Pennsylvania	M
Marywood University	M
McNeese State University	M
Miami University	M
Michigan State University	M,D
Minot State University	M
Mississippi College	M
Mississippi State University	M
Montclair State University	M
Moorhead State University	M
Morehead State University	M
Murray State University	M
Nazareth College of Rochester	M
New Jersey City University	M
New York University	M,D,O
Norfolk State University	M
Northwestern University	M,D
Northwest Missouri State University	M
Oregon State University	M
Pennsylvania State University University Park Campus	M,D
Pittsburg State University	M
Portland State University	M
Queens College of the City University of New York	M,O
Radford University	M
Rhode Island College	M
Rollins College	M
Roosevelt University	M,O
Rowan University	M
St. Cloud State University	M
Salisbury State University	M
Samford University	M
Sam Houston State University	M
Shenandoah University	M,D
Southeast Missouri State University	M
Southern Illinois University at Carbondale	M
Southwest Texas State University	M
State University of New York at Buffalo	M,O
State University of New York at New Paltz	M
State University of New York College at Fredonia	M
State University of New York College at Potsdam	M
State University of West Georgia	M
Syracuse University	M
Teachers College, Columbia University	M,D
Temple University (Philadelphia)	M,D
Tennessee State University	M
Texas A&M University–Commerce	M
Texas A&M University–Kingsville	M
Texas Christian University	M
Texas Tech University	M,O
Texas Woman's University	M
Towson University	M,O
Union College (KY)	M
The University of Akron	M
The University of Alabama (Tuscaloosa)	M,D,O
The University of Alabama at Birmingham	M
University of Alaska Fairbanks	M
The University of Arizona	M,D
University of Arkansas (Fayetteville)	M
University of Central Arkansas	M
University of Central Florida	M
University of Central Oklahoma	M
University of Cincinnati	M,D

University of Colorado at Boulder	M,D
University of Connecticut	M,D
University of Denver	M
University of Florida	M,D
University of Georgia	M,D,O
University of Hartford	M,D
University of Houston	M,D
The University of Iowa	M,D
University of Kansas	M,D
University of Louisville	M
University of Maryland, College Park	M,D
University of Massachusetts Lowell	M
The University of Memphis	M,D
University of Miami	M,D,O
University of Michigan	D
University of Minnesota, Duluth	M
University of Missouri–Kansas City	M,D
University of Missouri–St. Louis	M
The University of Montana–Missoula	M
University of Nebraska at Kearney	M
University of Nevada, Las Vegas	M
University of New Hampshire	M
The University of North Carolina at Chapel Hill	M
University of North Carolina at Greensboro	M,D
University of North Dakota	M
University of Northern Colorado	M,D
University of Northern Iowa	M
University of North Florida	M
University of North Texas	M,D
University of Oklahoma	M,D
University of Oregon	M,D
University of Portland	M
University of Rochester	M,D
University of St. Thomas (MN)	M
University of South Alabama	M
University of South Carolina (Columbia)	M,D
University of Southern California	M,D
University of Southern Mississippi	M,D
University of South Florida	M,D
University of Southwestern Louisiana	M
University of Tennessee, Knoxville	M
The University of Texas at El Paso	M
University of Toledo	M
University of Tulsa	M
University of Washington	M,D
University of Wisconsin–Madison	M,D
University of Wisconsin–Stevens Point	M
University of Wyoming	M
Valdosta State University	M
Virginia Commonwealth University	M
Wayne State College	M
Wayne State University	M
Webster University	M
West Chester University of Pennsylvania	M
Western Connecticut State University	M
Western Kentucky University	M
Wichita State University	M
Winthrop University	M
Wright State University	M
Xavier University	M
Youngstown State University	M

NATURAL RESOURCES

Ball State University	M
Cornell University	M,D
Duke University	M,D
Humboldt State University	M
Mississippi State University	D
North Carolina State University	M,D
The Ohio State University	M
Purdue University	M,D
Slippery Rock University of Pennsylvania	M
Texas A&M University (College Station)	M
The University of Arizona	M,D
University of Connecticut	M
University of Georgia	M,D
University of Illinois at Urbana–Champaign	M,D
University of Maine (Orono)	D
University of Michigan	M,D
The University of Montana–Missoula	M
University of New Hampshire	D
University of Rhode Island	M,D
University of Wisconsin–Stevens Point	M
University of Wyoming	M
Utah State University	M

Virginia Polytechnic Institute and State University — M,D
Washington State University — M,D
West Virginia University — D

NATUROPATHIC MEDICINE
University of Bridgeport — D

NEAR AND MIDDLE EASTERN LANGUAGES
Brigham Young University — M
The Catholic University of America — M,D
Columbia University — M,D
Georgetown University — M,D
Harvard University — M,D
Indiana University Bloomington — M,D
The Ohio State University — M
University of California, Los Angeles — M,D,O
University of Chicago — M,D
University of Michigan — M,D
The University of Texas at Austin — M,D
University of Wisconsin–Madison — M,D
Yale University — M,D

NEAR AND MIDDLE EASTERN STUDIES
Brandeis University — M,D
Brigham Young University — M
Columbia University — M,D,O
Cornell University — M,D
Georgetown University — M,O
Harvard University — M,D
Johns Hopkins University — M,D
New York University — M,D
Princeton University — M,D
The University of Arizona — M,D
University of California, Berkeley — M,D,O
University of California, Los Angeles — M,D,O
University of Chicago — M,D
University of Michigan — M,D
University of Pennsylvania — M,D
The University of Texas at Austin — M,D
University of Utah — M,D
University of Virginia — M
University of Washington — M,D
Washington University in St. Louis — M
Wayne State University — M

NEUROSCIENCE
Allegheny University of the Health Sciences — M,D
Arizona State University — D
Baylor University — M,D
Boston University — M,D
Brandeis University — M,D
Brown University — M,D
California Institute of Technology — M,D
Case Western Reserve University — D
College of Staten Island of the City University of New York — D
Colorado State University — M,D
Columbia University — M,D
Cornell University — D
Dartmouth College — D
Duke University — D
Emory University — D
Florida State University — D
Georgetown University — D
The George Washington University — D
Graduate School and University Center of the City University of New York — D
Harvard University — D
Indiana University Bloomington — D
Indiana University–Purdue University Indianapolis — M,D
Iowa State University of Science and Technology — M,D
Johns Hopkins University — D
Kent State University — M,D
Lehigh University — M,D
Loyola University Chicago — M,D
Maharishi University of Management — M,D
Marquette University — M,D
Massachusetts Institute of Technology — D
Michigan State University — D
New York University — D
Northwestern University — M,D
The Ohio State University — M,D
Pennsylvania State University University Park Campus — M,D
Princeton University — D
Purdue University — M,D
Rutgers, The State University of New Jersey, Newark — D
Rutgers, The State University of New Jersey, New Brunswick — D

Saint Louis University — M,D
Stanford University — D
State University of New York at Albany — M,D
State University of New York at Buffalo — D
State University of New York at Stony Brook — D
Syracuse University — M,D
Teachers College, Columbia University — M
Texas A&M University (College Station) — D
Texas Woman's University — D
Tufts University — D
Tulane University — M,D
The University of Alabama at Birmingham — D
The University of Arizona — D
University of California, Berkeley — D
University of California, Davis — D
University of California, Irvine — M,D
University of California, Los Angeles — D
University of California, San Diego — D
University of California, San Francisco — D
University of Chicago — D
University of Cincinnati — D
University of Colorado at Boulder — M,D
University of Connecticut — M,D
University of Delaware — M,D
University of Florida — M,D
University of Hawaii at Manoa — M,D
University of Illinois at Chicago — M,D
University of Illinois at Urbana–Champaign — D
The University of Iowa — D
University of Kentucky — D
University of Louisville — M,D
University of Maryland, Baltimore County — M,D
University of Maryland, College Park — D
University of Massachusetts Amherst — M,D
University of Miami — D
University of Michigan — D
University of Minnesota, Twin Cities Campus — M,D
University of New Mexico — D
The University of North Carolina at Chapel Hill — D
University of Oregon — D
University of Pennsylvania — M,D
University of Pittsburgh — M,D
University of Rochester — M,D
University of Southern California — M,D
The University of Texas at Austin — M
The University of Texas at Dallas — M
The University of Texas at San Antonio — D
University of Utah — M,D
University of Vermont — D
University of Virginia — D
University of Washington — D
University of Wisconsin–Madison — M,D
Vanderbilt University — D
Virginia Commonwealth University — M
Wake Forest University — D
Washington State University — M,D
Washington University in St. Louis — D
Wayne State University — D
Yale University — D
Yeshiva University — D

NONPROFIT MANAGEMENT
Boston University — M
Case Western Reserve University — M,O
DePaul University — M,O
Eastern College — M
Georgia State University — M
Hope International University — M
Indiana University Northwest — O
Lesley College — M
New School University — M
New York University — M,O
Northwestern University — M
Pace University — M
Regis University — M,O
San Francisco State University — M
Seattle University — M
Seton Hall University — M
Suffolk University — M
Trinity College (DC) — O
Tufts University — M
The University of Memphis — M
University of Notre Dame — M
University of St. Thomas (MN) — M,O
University of San Francisco — M
Worcester State College — M

NORTHERN STUDIES
University of Alaska Fairbanks — M,D

NUCLEAR ENGINEERING
Cornell University — M,D
Georgia Institute of Technology — M,D
Idaho State University — M
Kansas State University — M,D
Louisiana State University and Agricultural and Mechanical College — M
Massachusetts Institute of Technology — M,D,O
Mississippi State University — D
North Carolina State University — M,D
The Ohio State University — M,D
Oregon State University — M,D
Pennsylvania State University University Park Campus — M,D
Purdue University — M,D
Rensselaer Polytechnic Institute — M,D
Texas A&M University (College Station) — M,D
The University of Arizona — M,D
University of California, Berkeley — M,D
University of Cincinnati — M,D
University of Florida — M,D,O
University of Idaho — M,D
University of Illinois at Urbana–Champaign — M,D
University of Maryland, College Park — M,D
University of Michigan — M,D,O
University of Missouri–Columbia — M,D
University of Missouri–Rolla — M,D
University of New Mexico — M,D
University of Tennessee, Knoxville — M,D
University of Utah — M,D
University of Virginia — M,D
University of Wisconsin–Madison — M,D

NURSE ANESTHESIA
Barry University — M
California State University, Long Beach — M
Case Western Reserve University — M
Columbia University — M
DePaul University — M
Emory University — M
Gannon University — M
Gonzaga University — M
La Roche College — M
Murray State University — M
Northeastern University — M
Oakland University — M
Saint Joseph's University — M
Saint Mary's University of Minnesota — M
Southern Illinois University at Edwardsville — M
Southwest Missouri State University — M
State University of New York at Buffalo — M
Texas Wesleyan University — M
The University of Alabama at Birmingham — M
University of Cincinnati — M
University of Detroit Mercy — M
University of Kansas — M
University of Michigan–Flint — M
University of New England — M
University of North Carolina at Greensboro — M,O
University of Pittsburgh — M
University of South Carolina (Columbia) — M
University of Tennessee at Chattanooga — M
University of Wisconsin–La Crosse — M
Villanova University — M,O
Virginia Commonwealth University — M
Wayne State University — M
Webster University — M
Xavier University of Louisiana — M

NURSE MIDWIFERY
Boston University — O
Case Western Reserve University — M
Columbia University — M
Emory University — M
Marquette University — M,O
New York University — M,O
Philadelphia College of Textiles and Science — M
State University of New York at Stony Brook — M,O
University of Cincinnati — M
University of Illinois at Chicago — M
University of Miami — M

University of Michigan — M
University of Minnesota, Twin Cities Campus — M
University of New Mexico — M
University of Pennsylvania — M
The University of Texas at El Paso — M
Vanderbilt University — M
Virginia Commonwealth University — M

NURSING
Abilene Christian University — M
Adelphi University — M,D,O
Albany State University — M
Alcorn State University — M
Allegheny University of the Health Sciences — M,O
Andrews University — M
Angelo State University — M
Arizona State University — M
Arkansas State University — M
Armstrong Atlantic State University — M
Azusa Pacific University — M
Ball State University — M
Barry University — D
Baylor University — M
Bellarmine College — M
Belmont University — M
Bloomsburg University of Pennsylvania — M
Boston College — M,D
Bowie State University — M
Bradley University — M
Brenau University — M
Brigham Young University — M
California State University, Bakersfield — M
California State University, Chico — M
California State University, Dominguez Hills — M
California State University, Fresno — M
California State University, Long Beach — M
California State University, Los Angeles — M
California State University, Sacramento — M
Capital University — M
Case Western Reserve University — M,D
The Catholic University of America — M,D
Clarion University of Pennsylvania — M
Clemson University — M
College Misericordia — M
The College of New Jersey — M
College of New Rochelle — M,O
College of St. Catherine — M
College of St. Scholastica — M
Columbia University — M,D,O
Creighton University — M
Delta State University — M
DePaul University — M
Drake University — M
Duke University — M,O
Duquesne University — M,D
D'Youville College — M
East Carolina University — M
Eastern Kentucky University — M
Eastern Washington University — M
East Tennessee State University — M,O
Edgewood College — M
Edinboro University of Pennsylvania — M
Emory University — M
Fairfield University — M,O
Fairleigh Dickinson University, Teaneck–Hackensack Campus — M
Fitchburg State College — M
Florida Atlantic University — M,O
Florida International University — M
Florida State University — M
Fort Hays State University — M
Gannon University — M,O
George Mason University — M,D
Georgetown University — M
Georgia College and State University — M
Georgia Southern University — M,O
Georgia State University — M,D
Gonzaga University — M
Governors State University — M
Grambling State University — M
Grand Valley State University — M
Gwynedd–Mercy College — M
Hampton University — M
Hardin–Simmons University — M
Hawaii Pacific University — M
Holy Names College — M
Houston Baptist University — M
Howard University — M,O
Hunter College of the City University of New York — M,O

Nursing (continued)

Idaho State University	M,O
Indiana State University	M
Indiana University of Pennsylvania	M
Indiana University–Purdue University Indianapolis	M,D
Indiana Wesleyan University	M
Johns Hopkins University	M,D,O
Kean University	M
Kennesaw State University	M
Kent State University	M
La Roche College	M
La Salle University	M
Lehman College of the City University of New York	M
Lewis University	M,O
Loma Linda University	M,O
Long Island University, Brooklyn Campus	M
Long Island University, C.W. Post Campus	M,O
Loyola University Chicago	M,D
Loyola University New Orleans	M
Madonna University	M
Mankato State University	M
Marquette University	M,O
Marshall University	M
Marymount University	M
McNeese State University	M
Metropolitan State University	M
Michigan State University	M
Midwestern State University	M
Millersville University of Pennsylvania	M
Monmouth University	M
Montana State University–Bozeman	M
Mount Saint Mary College	M
Murray State University	M
Nazareth College of Rochester	M
New Mexico State University	M
New York University	M,D,O
Niagara University	M
Northeastern University	M,O
Northern Arizona University	M
Northern Illinois University	M
Northern Kentucky University	M
Northern Michigan University	M
North Georgia College & State University	M
Northwestern State University of Louisiana	M
Oakland University	M
The Ohio State University	M,D
Old Dominion University	M,O
Pace University	M,O
Pacific Lutheran University	M
Pennsylvania State University University Park Campus	M
Pittsburg State University	M
Pontifical Catholic University of Puerto Rico	M
Purdue University Calumet	M
Queens College	M
Quinnipiac College	M
Radford University	M
Regis University	M
Rivier College	M
Rutgers, The State University of New Jersey, Newark	M,D
Sacred Heart University	M
Sage Graduate School	M,O
Saginaw Valley State University	M
St. John Fisher College	M,O
Saint Joseph College (CT)	M
Saint Louis University	D
Saint Martin's College	M
Saint Peter's College (Jersey City)	M
Saint Xavier University	M,O
Salem State College	M
Salisbury State University	M
Samford University	M
San Diego State University	M
San Francisco State University	M
San Jose State University	M
Seattle Pacific University	M
Seattle University	M,O
Seton Hall University	M
Shenandoah University	M
Simmons College	M,O
Slippery Rock University of Pennsylvania	M
South Dakota State University	M
Southeastern Louisiana University	M
Southeast Missouri State University	M
Southern Connecticut State University	M
Southern Illinois University at Edwardsville	M
Southern University and Agricultural and Mechanical College	M
Southwest Missouri State University	M
Spalding University	M
State University of New York at Binghamton	M,D,O
State University of New York at Buffalo	M,D
State University of New York at New Paltz	M
State University of New York at Stony Brook	M,O
State University of New York Institute of Technology at Utica/Rome	M,O
Syracuse University	M
Temple University (Philadelphia)	M
Tennessee State University	M
Texas A&M University–Corpus Christi	M
Texas Woman's University	M,D
Troy State University (Troy)	M
The University of Akron	M
The University of Alabama at Birmingham	M,D
The University of Alabama in Huntsville	M
University of Alaska Anchorage	M
The University of Arizona	M,D
University of California, Los Angeles	M,D
University of California, San Francisco	M,D
University of Central Arkansas	M
University of Central Florida	M
University of Cincinnati	M,D
University of Colorado at Colorado Springs	M
University of Connecticut	M,D
University of Delaware	M,O
University of Evansville	M
University of Florida	M,D
University of Hartford	M
University of Hawaii at Manoa	M,O
University of Illinois at Chicago	M,D
The University of Iowa	M,D
University of Kansas	M,D
University of Kentucky	M,D
University of Louisville	M
University of Maine (Orono)	M,O
University of Mary	M
University of Massachusetts Amherst	M,D
University of Massachusetts Boston	M,D
University of Massachusetts Dartmouth	M
University of Massachusetts Lowell	M,D
University of Miami	M,D
University of Michigan	M,D,O
University of Minnesota, Twin Cities Campus	M,D
University of Missouri–Columbia	M,D
University of Missouri–Kansas City	M,D
University of Missouri–St. Louis	M,D
University of Mobile	M
University of Nevada, Las Vegas	M
University of Nevada, Reno	M
University of New Hampshire	M
University of New Mexico	M,O
The University of North Carolina at Chapel Hill	M,D
University of North Carolina at Charlotte	M
University of North Carolina at Greensboro	M,O
University of North Dakota	M
University of Northern Colorado	M
University of Pennsylvania	M,D,O
University of Pittsburgh	M,D
University of Portland	M,O
University of Rhode Island	M,D
University of Rochester	M,D
University of Saint Francis (IN)	M
University of San Diego	M,D
University of San Francisco	M
University of Scranton	M
University of South Alabama	M
University of South Carolina (Columbia)	M,D
University of Southern California	M,O
University of Southern Indiana	M
University of Southern Maine	M,O
University of Southern Mississippi	M
University of South Florida	M,D
University of Southwestern Louisiana	M
The University of Tampa	M
University of Tennessee at Chattanooga	M
University of Tennessee, Knoxville	M,D
The University of Texas at Arlington	M
The University of Texas at Austin	M,D
The University of Texas at El Paso	M
The University of Texas at Tyler	M
The University of Texas–Pan American	M
University of the Incarnate Word	M
University of Utah	M,D
University of Vermont	M
University of Virginia	M,D
University of Washington	M,D
University of Wisconsin–Eau Claire	M
University of Wisconsin–Madison	M,D
University of Wisconsin–Milwaukee	M,D
University of Wisconsin–Oshkosh	M
University of Wyoming	M
Valdosta State University	M
Valparaiso University	M
Vanderbilt University	M,D
Villanova University	M,O
Virginia Commonwealth University	M,D,O
Viterbo College	M
Wagner College	M
Washington State University	M
Wayne State University	M,D,O
Webster University	M
West Chester University of Pennsylvania	M
Western Connecticut State University	M
Western Kentucky University	M
Westminster College of Salt Lake City	M
West Texas A&M University	M
West Virginia University	M,O
Wheeling Jesuit University	M
Wichita State University	M
Widener University	M,D,O
Wilkes University	M
William Paterson University of New Jersey	M
Wilmington College (DE)	M
Winona State University	M
Wright State University	M
Xavier University	M
Yale University	M,D,O
Youngstown State University	M

NURSING ADMINISTRATION

Adelphi University	M,O
Barry University	M
Baylor University	M
Bellarmine College	M
Bowie State University	M
Capital University	M
The Catholic University of America	M
Duke University	M,O
Duquesne University	M
Florida Atlantic University	M
Gannon University	M
George Mason University	M
Hunter College of the City University of New York	M
Indiana University–Purdue University Fort Wayne	M
Johns Hopkins University	M
Kent State University	M
La Roche College	M
La Salle University	M
Lewis University	M,O
Loma Linda University	M,O
Loyola University Chicago	M
Madonna University	M
Mankato State University	M
Marymount University	M
Mount Saint Mary College	M
Northeastern University	M
Oakland University	M
Pacific Lutheran University	M
Queens College	M
Sacred Heart University	M
Saginaw Valley State University	M
Saint Louis University	M,O
Saint Martin's College	M
Saint Xavier University	M
San Francisco State University	M
San Jose State University	M
Seton Hall University	M
Spalding University	M
State University of New York Institute of Technology at Utica/Rome	M
Texas A&M University–Corpus Christi	M
The University of Akron	M
University of Cincinnati	M
University of Connecticut	M
University of Delaware	M,O
University of Hawaii at Manoa	M
University of Illinois at Chicago	M
University of Mary	M
University of Massachusetts Lowell	D
University of Michigan	M
University of Minnesota, Twin Cities Campus	M
University of New Mexico	M,O
University of North Carolina at Greensboro	M
University of Pennsylvania	M,D
University of Pittsburgh	M
University of Portland	O
University of Rhode Island	M
University of San Diego	M
University of San Francisco	M
University of South Carolina (Columbia)	M,O
University of Southern Maine	M
University of Southern Mississippi	M
The University of Tampa	M
University of Tennessee at Chattanooga	M
The University of Texas at Arlington	M
The University of Texas at El Paso	M
University of Tulsa	M
Valdosta State University	M
Villanova University	M,O
Virginia Commonwealth University	M
Wayne State University	M
Wichita State University	M
Wright State University	M
Xavier University	M

NURSING EDUCATION

Adelphi University	M,O
Barry University	M
Bellarmine College	M
Bowie State University	M
The Catholic University of America	M
Duquesne University	M
Eastern Michigan University	M
Eastern Washington University	M
Florida State University	M
Georgia State University	D
Indiana Wesleyan University	M
Kent State University	M
La Salle University	M
Lewis University	M
Mankato State University	M
Marymount University	M
Midwestern State University	M
Mount Saint Mary College	M
New York University	M
Saginaw Valley State University	M
San Francisco State University	M
San Jose State University	M
Seton Hall University	M
State University of New York College at Oneonta	M
Teachers College, Columbia University	M,D
The University of Akron	M
University of Connecticut	M
University of Mary	M
University of Minnesota, Twin Cities Campus	M
University of Northern Colorado	M
University of Pittsburgh	M
University of Rhode Island	M
University of Tennessee at Chattanooga	M
The University of Texas at Arlington	M
Villanova University	M
Wayne State University	O
Wichita State University	M
Wright State University	M

NUTRITION

Allegheny University of the Health Sciences	D
Andrews University	M
Auburn University	M,D
Boston University	M,D
Bowling Green State University	M
Brigham Young University	M
Brooklyn College of the City University of New York	M
California State Polytechnic University, Pomona	M
California State University, Chico	M
California State University, Fresno	M
California State University, Long Beach	M
California State University, Los Angeles	M
Case Western Reserve University	M,D
Central Washington University	M
Chapman University	M
Clemson University	M,D
Colorado State University	M,D
Columbia University	M,D
Cornell University	M,D
Drexel University	M,D
East Carolina University	M
Eastern Illinois University	M

Eastern Kentucky University	M
East Tennessee State University	M
Emory University	D
Florida International University	M,D
Florida State University	M,D
Framingham State College	M
Georgia State University	M
Harvard University	D
Howard University	M,D
Hunter College of the City University of New York	M
Immaculata College	M
Indiana State University	M
Indiana University Bloomington	M
Indiana University of Pennsylvania	M
Indiana University–Purdue University Indianapolis	M
Iowa State University of Science and Technology	M,D
Johns Hopkins University	M,D
Kansas State University	M,D
Kent State University	M
Lehman College of the City University of New York	M
Loma Linda University	M,D
Long Island University, C.W. Post Campus	M,O
Louisiana Tech University	M
Marywood University	M
Michigan State University	M,D
Middle Tennessee State University	M
Mississippi State University	M,D
New York Institute of Technology	M
New York University	M,D
North Carolina Agricultural and Technical State University	M
North Carolina State University	M,D
North Dakota State University	M,D
Northern Illinois University	M
The Ohio State University	M,D
Ohio University	M
Oklahoma State University	M,D
Oregon State University	M,D
Pennsylvania State University University Park Campus	M,D
Purdue University	M,D
Rutgers, The State University of New Jersey, New Brunswick	M,D
Sage Graduate School	M
Saint Joseph College (CT)	M
Saint Louis University	M
San Diego State University	M
San Jose State University	M
Simmons College	M
South Carolina State University	M
Southern Illinois University at Carbondale	M
State University of New York at Buffalo	M
Syracuse University	M,D
Texas A&M University (College Station)	M,D
Texas Southern University	M
Texas Tech University	M,D
Texas Woman's University	M,D
Tufts University	M,D
Tulane University	M
Tuskegee University	M
The University of Akron	M
The University of Alabama (Tuscaloosa)	M
The University of Alabama at Birmingham	M,D,O
The University of Arizona	M,D
University of Bridgeport	M
University of California, Berkeley	M,D
University of California, Davis	M,D
University of Central Oklahoma	M
University of Chicago	M,D
University of Cincinnati	M
University of Connecticut	M,D
University of Delaware	M
University of Florida	M,D
University of Georgia	M,D
University of Hawaii at Manoa	M
University of Illinois at Chicago	M,D
University of Illinois at Urbana–Champaign	M,D
University of Kansas	M
University of Kentucky	M,D
University of Maine (Orono)	M,D
University of Maryland, College Park	M,D
University of Massachusetts Amherst	M,D
The University of Memphis	M
University of Michigan	M
University of Minnesota, Twin Cities Campus	M,D
University of Missouri–Columbia	M,D
University of Nebraska–Lincoln	M,D
University of Nevada, Reno	M
University of New Hampshire	M,D
University of New Haven	M
University of New Mexico	M
The University of North Carolina at Chapel Hill	M,D
University of North Carolina at Greensboro	M,D
University of North Florida	M
University of Rhode Island	M,D
University of Southern California	M,D
University of Southern Mississippi	M
The University of Tennessee at Martin	M
University of Tennessee, Knoxville	M
The University of Texas at Austin	M,D
University of the Incarnate Word	M
University of Utah	M
University of Vermont	M
University of Washington	M,D
University of Wisconsin–Madison	M,D
University of Wisconsin–Stevens Point	M
University of Wisconsin–Stout	M
University of Wyoming	M
Utah State University	M,D
Virginia Polytechnic Institute and State University	M,D
Washington State University	M,D
Wayne State University	M,D
Western Kentucky University	M
Winthrop University	M

OCCUPATIONAL THERAPY

Belmont University	M
Boston University	M,D,O
College Misericordia	M
College of St. Catherine	M
College of St. Scholastica	M
Colorado State University	M
Columbia University	M
Creighton University	D
Duquesne University	M
East Carolina University	M
Eastern Kentucky University	M
Eastern Michigan University	M
Florida International University	M
Governors State University	M
Grand Valley State University	M
Idaho State University	M
Ithaca College	M
New York University	M,D
Nova Southeastern University	M,D
Pacific University	M
Philadelphia College of Textiles and Science	M
Rockhurst College	M
Saint Francis College (PA)	M
San Jose State University	M
Seton Hall University	M
Shenandoah University	M
Springfield College (MA)	M,O
State University of New York at Buffalo	M,D
Temple University (Philadelphia)	M
Texas Woman's University	M,D
Towson University	M
Tufts University	M,O
The University of Alabama at Birmingham	M
University of Central Arkansas	M
University of Florida	M
University of Illinois at Chicago	M
University of Indianapolis	M
University of Kansas	M
University of New Hampshire	M
The University of North Carolina at Chapel Hill	M
University of Pittsburgh	M
University of South Dakota	M
University of Southern California	M,D
University of Washington	M
University of Wisconsin–Milwaukee	M
Virginia Commonwealth University	M
Washington University in St. Louis	M
Wayne State University	M
Western Michigan University	M
West Virginia University	M
Worcester State College	M
Xavier University	O

OCEAN ENGINEERING

Florida Atlantic University	M,D
Florida Institute of Technology	M,D
Massachusetts Institute of Technology	M,D,O
Oregon State University	M
Stevens Institute of Technology	M,D
Texas A&M University (College Station)	M,D
University of California, Berkeley	M,D
University of California, San Diego	M,D
University of Connecticut	M,D
University of Delaware	M,D
University of Florida	M,D,O
University of Hawaii at Manoa	M,D
University of Miami	M
University of Michigan	M,D,O
University of New Hampshire	M
University of Rhode Island	M,D
University of Southern California	M
Virginia Polytechnic Institute and State University	M

OCEANOGRAPHY

Columbia University	M,D
Cornell University	D
Florida Institute of Technology	M,D
Florida State University	M,D
Johns Hopkins University	M,D
Louisiana State University and Agricultural and Mechanical College	M,D
Massachusetts Institute of Technology	M,D,O
North Carolina State University	M,D
Nova Southeastern University	M,D
Old Dominion University	M,D
Oregon State University	M,D
Princeton University	D
Rutgers, The State University of New Jersey, New Brunswick	M,D
State University of New York at Stony Brook	D
Texas A&M University (College Station)	M,D
University of Alaska Fairbanks	M,D
University of California, San Diego	M,D
University of Connecticut	M,D
University of Georgia	M,D
University of Hawaii at Manoa	M,D
University of Maine (Orono)	M,D
University of Miami	M,D
University of Michigan	M,D
University of New Hampshire	M,D
University of Puerto Rico, Mayagüez Campus	M,D
University of Rhode Island	M,D
University of Southern California	M,D
University of South Florida	M,D
University of Washington	M,D
University of Wisconsin–Madison	M,D
Western Connecticut State University	M
Yale University	D

ONCOLOGY

Allegheny University of the Health Sciences	M,D
Brown University	D
Cornell University	M,D
Duke University	D
Emory University	M
Georgetown University	
The George Washington University	D
Harvard University	D
Kansas State University	M,D
New York University	D
Northwestern University	D
Stanford University	D
State University of New York at Buffalo	D
The University of Arizona	D
University of California, San Diego	D
University of Chicago	D
University of Pennsylvania	D
University of Utah	M,D
University of Wisconsin–Madison	M,D
Vanderbilt University	
Wake Forest University	D
Wayne State University	M,D

ONCOLOGY NURSING

Case Western Reserve University	M
Columbia University	M,O
Duke University	M,O
Emory University	M
Gwynedd–Mercy College	M
Johns Hopkins University	M
Loyola University Chicago	M
University of Delaware	M,O
University of Minnesota, Twin Cities Campus	M
University of Pennsylvania	M

OPERATIONS RESEARCH

Baruch College of the City University of New York	M
California State University, Fullerton	M
California State University, Hayward	M
Carnegie Mellon University	D
Case Western Reserve University	M,D
Claremont Graduate University	M
Clemson University	M,D
College of William and Mary	M
Columbia University	M,D,O
Cornell University	M,D
Embry–Riddle Aeronautical University (FL)	M
Florida Institute of Technology	M,D
George Mason University	M
The George Washington University	M,D,O
Georgia Institute of Technology	M
Georgia State University	M,D
Idaho State University	M
Indiana University–Purdue University Fort Wayne	M
Iowa State University of Science and Technology	M
Louisiana Tech University	M
Massachusetts Institute of Technology	M,D
Miami University	M
Michigan State University	M
New York University	M,D,O
North Carolina State University	M,D
North Dakota State University	M
Northeastern University	M
Old Dominion University	M
Oregon State University	M
Princeton University	M,D
Purdue University	M,D
Rensselaer Polytechnic Institute	M
Rutgers, The State University of New Jersey, New Brunswick	D
St. Mary's University of San Antonio	M
Seton Hall University	M
Southern Methodist University	M,D
Stanford University	M,D,O
The University of Alabama in Huntsville	M
University of Arkansas (Fayetteville)	M
University of California, Berkeley	M,D
University of California, Los Angeles	M,D
University of Central Florida	M
University of Delaware	M,D
University of Florida	M,D,O
University of Houston	M,D
University of Illinois at Chicago	D
The University of Iowa	M,D
University of Massachusetts Amherst	M,D
University of Michigan	M,D,O
University of Minnesota, Twin Cities Campus	M,D
The University of Montana–Missoula	M,D
University of New Haven	M
The University of North Carolina at Chapel Hill	M,D
University of Southern California	M
The University of Texas at Austin	M,D
Virginia Commonwealth University	M
Virginia Polytechnic Institute and State University	M,D
Wayne State University	M
Western Michigan University	M
Yale University	D

OPTICAL SCIENCES

Alabama Agricultural and Mechanical University	D
Cleveland State University	M
Indiana University Bloomington	M,D
The Ohio State University	M,D
Rochester Institute of Technology	M,D
Tufts University	O
The University of Alabama in Huntsville	D
The University of Arizona	M,D
University of Central Florida	M,D
University of Dayton	M,D
University of Maryland, Baltimore County	M,D
University of Massachusetts Lowell	M
University of New Mexico	D
University of Rochester	M,D

OPTOMETRY

Ferris State University	P
Indiana University Bloomington	P
Inter American University of Puerto Rico, Metropolitan Campus	P
Northeastern State University	P
Nova Southeastern University	P
The Ohio State University	P
Pacific University	P
The University of Alabama at Birmingham	P,M,D
University of California, Berkeley	P
University of Houston	P

P—first professional degree; M—master's degree; D—doctorate; O—other advanced degree.

Optometry (continued)

University of Missouri–St. Louis	P

ORAL AND DENTAL SCIENCES

Boston University	M,D,O
Case Western Reserve University	M,O
Columbia University	M
Emory University	O
Harvard University	M,D,O
Indiana University–Purdue University Indianapolis	M,D
Loma Linda University	M,O
Marquette University	M
New York University	M,O
The Ohio State University	M,D
Saint Louis University	M
State University of New York at Buffalo	M,D,O
State University of New York at Stony Brook	D,O
Temple University (Philadelphia)	M,O
Tufts University	M,O
The University of Alabama at Birmingham	M
University of California, Los Angeles	M,D
University of California, San Francisco	M,D
University of Connecticut	M
University of Detroit Mercy	M,O
University of Florida	M,D
University of Illinois at Chicago	M
The University of Iowa	M,D,O
University of Kentucky	M
University of Louisville	M
University of Michigan	M,D,O
University of Minnesota, Twin Cities Campus	M,D
University of Missouri–Kansas City	M,D,O
The University of North Carolina at Chapel Hill	M,D
University of Pittsburgh	M,O
University of Rochester	M
University of Southern California	M,D
University of the Pacific	M
University of Washington	M,D
West Virginia University	M

ORGANIC CHEMISTRY

Boston College	M,D
Boston University	M,D
Brandeis University	M,D
Brigham Young University	M,D
California State University, Fullerton	M
California State University, Los Angeles	M
Case Western Reserve University	M,D
Clark Atlanta University	M,D
Clarkson University	M,D
Cleveland State University	M
Columbia University	M,D
Cornell University	D
Florida State University	M,D
Georgetown University	M,D
The George Washington University	M,D
Georgia State University	D
Harvard University	M,D
Howard University	M,D
Illinois Institute of Technology	M,D
Kansas State University	M
Kent State University	M,D
Lehigh University	M,D
Marquette University	M,D
Massachusetts Institute of Technology	M,D
Michigan State University	M,D
Mississippi State University	M,D
Northeastern University	D
Old Dominion University	M
Oregon State University	M,D
Purdue University	M,D
Rensselaer Polytechnic Institute	M,D
Rutgers, The State University of New Jersey, Newark	M,D
Rutgers, The State University of New Jersey, New Brunswick	M,D
San Jose State University	M
Seton Hall University	M,D
South Dakota State University	M,D
Southern University and Agricultural and Mechanical College	M
State University of New York at Binghamton	D
Stevens Institute of Technology	M,D
Tufts University	M,D
The University of Akron	M,D
University of Cincinnati	M,D
University of Georgia	M,D
University of Louisville	M,D
University of Maryland, College Park	M,D
University of Miami	D
University of Michigan	D
University of Missouri–Columbia	M,D
University of Missouri–Kansas City	M,D
The University of Montana–Missoula	D
University of Nebraska–Lincoln	D
University of Notre Dame	M,D
University of Southern Mississippi	M,D
University of South Florida	M,D
University of Tennessee, Knoxville	M,D
The University of Texas at Austin	M,D
University of Toledo	M,D
Wake Forest University	M,D
Washington State University	M,D
Washington University in St. Louis	D
Western Kentucky University	D
Yale University	D

ORGANIZATIONAL BEHAVIOR

American International College	M
American University	M
Baruch College of the City University of New York	M,D
Benedictine University	M,D
Boston College	M,D
Boston University	D
Bowling Green State University	M
Brigham Young University	M
California Lutheran University	M
Carnegie Mellon University	M,D
Case Western Reserve University	M,D
Chapman University	M
Charleston Southern University	M
Claremont Graduate University	M
College of St. Catherine	M
Cornell University	M,D
Dallas Baptist University	M
Dominican University	M
Drexel University	D
Eastern Connecticut State University	M
Eastern Michigan University	M
Fairleigh Dickinson University, Florham-Madison Campus	M
George Mason University	M
The George Washington University	M
Golden Gate University	M
Gonzaga University	M
Graduate School and University Center of the City University of New York	D
Harvard University	D
Hawaii Pacific University	M
Indiana University Bloomington	D
John F. Kennedy University	O
Loyola University Chicago	M
Marian College of Fond du Lac	M
Marymount University	M
Metropolitan State University	M
Michigan State University	D
Northwestern University	D
Pepperdine University (Culver City)	M
Pfeiffer University	M
Polytechnic University, Brooklyn Campus	M
Polytechnic University, Westchester Graduate Center	M
Purdue University	M,D
Rensselaer Polytechnic Institute	M
Rutgers, The State University of New Jersey, Newark	M
Saginaw Valley State University	M
State University of New York at Albany	D
Syracuse University	M,D
Trevecca Nazarene University	M
University of California, Berkeley	D
University of Colorado at Boulder	M,D
University of Colorado at Colorado Springs	M
University of Hartford	M
The University of Iowa	D
University of La Verne	M
University of Missouri–St. Louis	M
University of New Haven	M
The University of North Carolina at Chapel Hill	D
University of North Carolina at Pembroke	M
University of North Texas	D
University of Pennsylvania	M
University of San Francisco	M
University of Scranton	M
University of Tennessee at Chattanooga	M
Vanderbilt University	D

OSTEOPATHIC MEDICINE

Michigan State University	P
New York Institute of Technology	P
Nova Southeastern University	P
Ohio University	P
University of New England	P

PAPER AND PULP ENGINEERING

Georgia Institute of Technology	O
Miami University	M
North Carolina State University	M,D
Oregon State University	M,D
University of Washington	M,D
Western Michigan University	M

PARASITOLOGY

New York University	D
Purdue University	M,D
Tulane University	M,D
University of Georgia	M,D
University of New Mexico	M,D
University of Notre Dame	M,D
University of Pennsylvania	D
Yale University	D

PASTORAL MINISTRY AND COUNSELING

Abilene Christian University	M,D
Ashland University	M,D
Assumption College	M
Azusa Pacific University	M
Barry University	M,D
Boston College	M,D
Cardinal Stritch University	M
Emmanuel College (MA)	O
Gannon University	M,O
Georgia State University	O
Gonzaga University	M
Grand Rapids Baptist Seminary	P,M,D
Harding University	M
Hardin–Simmons University	M
Holy Names College	M,O
Hope International University	M
Iona College (New Rochelle)	M,O
La Salle University	M
Loyola College	M,D,O
Loyola Marymount University	M
Loyola University Chicago	M
Marygrove College	M
Olivet Nazarene University	M
Oral Roberts University	M
Providence College	M
Regis University	M
St. Ambrose University	M
Saint Francis College (PA)	M
St. John's University (NY)	O
Saint Mary's University of Minnesota	M,O
St. Mary's University of San Antonio	M
St. Thomas University	M,O
Santa Clara University	M
Seattle University	M
Seton Hall University	P,M
Spalding University	M
University of Dayton	M
University of St. Thomas (MN)	M,D
University of San Diego	M
University of San Francisco	M,O
Wake Forest University	M

PATHOLOGY

Allegheny University of the Health Sciences	D
Auburn University	M
Boston University	D
Brown University	M,D
Case Western Reserve University	M,D
Colorado State University	M,D
Columbia University	M,D
Duke University	M,D
East Carolina University	D
Georgetown University	M,D
Harvard University	D
Indiana University–Purdue University Indianapolis	M,D
Iowa State University of Science and Technology	M,D
Kansas State University	M,D
Michigan State University	M,D
New York University	D
North Carolina State University	M,D
The Ohio State University	M,D
Oregon State University	M
Pennsylvania State University University Park Campus	M,D
Purdue University	M,D
Quinnipiac College	M
Saint Louis University	M,D
State University of New York at Albany	M,D
State University of New York at Buffalo	M,D
State University of New York at Stony Brook	D
Temple University (Philadelphia)	D
Texas A&M University (College Station)	M,D
The University of Alabama at Birmingham	D
The University of Arizona	M,D
University of California, Davis	M,D
University of California, Los Angeles	M,D
University of California, San Diego	D
University of California, San Francisco	D
University of Chicago	D
University of Cincinnati	D
University of Connecticut	M,D
University of Florida	M,D
University of Georgia	M,D
University of Illinois at Chicago	M,D
The University of Iowa	M
University of Kansas	M,D
University of Michigan	D
University of Minnesota, Twin Cities Campus	D
University of Missouri–Columbia	M,D
University of New Mexico	M,D
The University of North Carolina at Chapel Hill	M,D
University of Pennsylvania	D
University of Pittsburgh	M,D
University of Rochester	M,D
University of South Carolina (Columbia)	D
University of Southern California	M,D
University of South Florida	D
University of Utah	D
University of Vermont	M
University of Washington	M,D
University of Wisconsin–Madison	D
University of Wyoming	M
Vanderbilt University	D
Virginia Commonwealth University	M,D
Wake Forest University	M,D
Washington State University	M,D
Wayne State University	D
Yale University	D
Yeshiva University	D

PETROLEUM ENGINEERING

Colorado School of Mines	M,D
Louisiana State University and Agricultural and Mechanical College	M,D
Mississippi State University	D
Montana Tech of The University of Montana	M
Pennsylvania State University University Park Campus	M,D
Stanford University	M,D,O
Texas A&M University (College Station)	M,D
Texas A&M University–Kingsville	M
Texas Tech University	M
University of Alaska Fairbanks	M
University of California, Berkeley	M,D
University of Houston	M
University of Kansas	M,D
University of Missouri–Rolla	M,D
University of Oklahoma	M,D
University of Pittsburgh	M,D
University of Southern California	M,D,O
University of Southwestern Louisiana	M
The University of Texas at Austin	M,D
University of Tulsa	M,D
University of Utah	M,D
University of Wyoming	M,D
West Virginia University	M

PHARMACEUTICAL SCIENCES

Auburn University	M,D
Butler University	P,M
Creighton University	M
Duquesne University	M,D
Florida Agricultural and Mechanical University	M,D
Idaho State University	M,D
Long Island University, Brooklyn Campus	M,D
Long Island University, C.W. Post Campus	M
Mercer University, Cecil B. Day Campus	D
North Dakota State University	M,D
Northeastern University	M,D
Northeast Louisiana University	M,D
The Ohio State University	M,D
Oregon State University	P,M,D
Purdue University	M,D
Rutgers, The State University of New Jersey, New Brunswick	M,D
St. John's University (NY)	M,D
South Dakota State University	M

- State University of New York at Buffalo M,D
- Temple University (Philadelphia) M,D
- The University of Arizona M,D
- University of California, San Francisco D
- University of Cincinnati M,D
- University of Connecticut M,D
- University of Florida M,D
- University of Georgia M,D
- University of Houston M,D
- University of Illinois at Chicago M,D
- The University of Iowa M,D
- University of Kansas M,D
- University of Kentucky M,D
- University of Michigan M,D
- University of Minnesota, Twin Cities Campus M,D
- University of Mississippi M,D
- University of Missouri–Kansas City M
- The University of Montana–Missoula M,D
- University of New Mexico M,D
- The University of North Carolina at Chapel Hill M,D
- University of Pittsburgh M,D
- University of Rhode Island M,D
- University of South Carolina (Columbia) M,D
- University of Southern California M,D
- The University of Texas at Austin M,D
- University of the Pacific M,D
- University of Toledo M,D
- University of Utah M,D
- University of Washington M,D
- University of Wisconsin–Madison D
- Virginia Commonwealth University M,D
- Wayne State University M,D
- West Virginia University M,D

PHARMACOLOGY

- Allegheny University of the Health Sciences M,D
- Auburn University M
- Boston University M,D
- Brown University M,D
- Case Western Reserve University D
- Columbia University M,D
- Cornell University M,D
- Creighton University M,D
- Dartmouth College D
- Duke University D
- Duquesne University M,D
- East Carolina University D
- East Tennessee State University M,D
- Emory University D
- Florida Agricultural and Mechanical University M,D
- Georgetown University D
- The George Washington University M,D
- Harvard University D
- Howard University M,D
- Idaho State University M,D
- Indiana University–Purdue University Indianapolis M,D
- Johns Hopkins University D
- Kent State University M,D
- Loma Linda University M,D
- Long Island University, Brooklyn Campus M
- Loyola University Chicago M,D
- Michigan State University M,D
- New York University D
- North Carolina State University M,D
- North Dakota State University M
- Northeastern University M,D
- Northwestern University D
- The Ohio State University M,D
- Purdue University M,D
- Rutgers, The State University of New Jersey, New Brunswick D
- St. John's University (NY) M,D
- Saint Louis University M,D
- Southern Illinois University at Carbondale M,D
- Stanford University D
- State University of New York at Buffalo M,D
- State University of New York at Stony Brook D
- Temple University (Philadelphia) M,D
- Texas A&M University (College Station) D
- Tufts University D
- Tulane University M,D
- The University of Alabama at Birmingham D
- The University of Arizona M,D
- University of California, Davis M,D
- University of California, Irvine M,D
- University of California, Los Angeles D
- University of California, San Diego D
- University of Chicago D
- University of Cincinnati D
- University of Connecticut M,D
- University of Florida M,D
- University of Georgia M,D
- University of Hawaii at Manoa M,D
- University of Houston M,D
- University of Illinois at Chicago D
- The University of Iowa D
- University of Kansas M,D
- University of Kentucky M,D
- University of Louisville M,D
- University of Miami D
- University of Michigan D
- University of Minnesota, Duluth M,D
- University of Minnesota, Twin Cities Campus M,D
- University of Mississippi M,D
- University of Missouri–Columbia M,D
- The University of Montana–Missoula D
- University of Nevada, Reno M,D
- The University of North Carolina at Chapel Hill D
- University of North Dakota M,D
- University of Pennsylvania D
- University of Pittsburgh M,D
- University of Rhode Island M,D
- University of Rochester M,D
- University of South Alabama D
- University of South Carolina (Columbia) D
- University of South Dakota M,D
- University of Southern California M,D
- University of South Florida D
- University of the Pacific M,D
- University of Toledo M
- University of Utah M,D
- University of Vermont M,D
- University of Virginia D
- University of Washington M,D
- University of Wisconsin–Madison M,D
- Vanderbilt University D
- Virginia Commonwealth University M,D,O
- Wake Forest University D
- Washington State University M,D
- Wayne State University M,D
- West Virginia University M,D
- Yale University D
- Yeshiva University D

PHARMACY

- Auburn University P
- Butler University P,M
- Campbell University P
- Creighton University P
- Drake University P
- Duquesne University P
- Ferris State University P
- Florida Agricultural and Mechanical University P
- Howard University P
- Idaho State University P,M,D
- Long Island University, Brooklyn Campus P
- Mercer University, Cecil B. Day Campus P
- Northeastern University P
- Nova Southeastern University P
- The Ohio State University P
- Purdue University P
- Rutgers, The State University of New Jersey, New Brunswick P
- St. John's University (NY) P
- Samford University P
- Shenandoah University P
- South Dakota State University P
- State University of New York at Buffalo P
- Temple University (Philadelphia) P
- Texas Southern University P
- The University of Arizona P,M,D
- University of California, San Francisco P
- University of Cincinnati P
- University of Florida P
- University of Georgia P
- University of Houston P,M
- University of Illinois at Chicago P
- The University of Iowa P
- University of Kentucky P
- University of Michigan P
- University of Minnesota, Twin Cities Campus P
- University of Mississippi P
- University of Missouri–Kansas City P
- University of New Mexico P
- University of Pittsburgh P
- University of Rhode Island P
- University of South Carolina (Columbia) P
- University of Southern California P
- The University of Texas at Austin P
- University of the Pacific P
- University of Toledo P
- University of Utah P,M
- University of Washington P
- University of Wisconsin–Madison P,M,D
- Virginia Commonwealth University P
- Washington State University P
- Wayne State University P,M
- West Virginia University P
- Wilkes University P
- Xavier University of Louisiana P

PHILANTHROPIC STUDIES

- Indiana University–Purdue University Indianapolis M
- Saint Mary's University of Minnesota M

PHILOSOPHY

- American University M
- Arizona State University M
- Ashland University M
- Baylor University M
- Boston College M,D
- Boston University M,D
- Bowling Green State University M,D
- Brown University M,D
- California State University, Long Beach M
- California State University, Los Angeles M
- Carnegie Mellon University M,D
- The Catholic University of America M,D,O
- Claremont Graduate University M,D
- Cleveland State University M
- Colorado State University M
- Columbia University M,D
- Cornell University D
- DePaul University M,D
- Duke University D
- Duquesne University M,D
- Emory University M,D
- Florida State University M,D
- Fordham University M,D
- Franciscan University of Steubenville M
- Georgetown University M,D
- The George Washington University M
- Georgia State University M
- Gonzaga University M
- Graduate School and University Center of the City University of New York M,D
- Harvard University M,D
- Howard University M
- Indiana University Bloomington M,D
- Johns Hopkins University M,D
- Kent State University M
- Lewis University M
- Louisiana State University and Agricultural and Mechanical College M
- Loyola University Chicago M,D
- Marquette University M,D
- Massachusetts Institute of Technology D
- Miami University M
- Michigan State University M,D
- New School University M,D
- New York University M,D
- Northern Illinois University M
- Northwestern University D
- The Ohio State University M,D
- Ohio University M
- Oklahoma State University M
- Pennsylvania State University University Park Campus M,D
- Princeton University D
- Purdue University M,D
- Rensselaer Polytechnic Institute M
- Rice University M,D
- Rutgers, The State University of New Jersey, New Brunswick D
- Saint Louis University M,D
- San Diego State University M
- San Francisco State University M,O
- San Jose State University M,O
- Shippensburg University of Pennsylvania M
- Southern Illinois University at Carbondale M,D
- Stanford University M,D
- State University of New York at Albany M,D
- State University of New York at Binghamton M,D
- State University of New York at Buffalo M,D
- State University of New York at Stony Brook M,D
- Syracuse University M,D
- Temple University (Philadelphia) M,D
- Texas A&M University (College Station) M
- Texas Tech University M
- Tufts University M
- Tulane University M,D
- The University of Arizona M,D
- University of Arkansas (Fayetteville) M,D
- University of California, Berkeley D
- University of California, Davis M,D
- University of California, Irvine M,D
- University of California, Los Angeles D,O
- University of California, Riverside M,D
- University of California, San Diego D
- University of California, Santa Barbara D
- University of Chicago M,D
- University of Cincinnati M,D
- University of Colorado at Boulder M,D
- University of Connecticut M,D
- University of Denver M
- University of Florida M,D
- University of Georgia M,D
- University of Hawaii at Manoa M,D
- University of Houston M
- University of Illinois at Chicago M,D
- University of Illinois at Urbana–Champaign M,D
- The University of Iowa M,D
- University of Kansas M,D
- University of Kentucky M,D
- University of Louisville M
- University of Maryland, College Park M,D
- University of Massachusetts Amherst M,D
- The University of Memphis M,D
- University of Miami M,D
- University of Michigan M,D
- University of Minnesota, Twin Cities Campus M,D
- University of Mississippi M
- University of Missouri–Columbia M,D
- The University of Montana–Missoula M
- University of Nebraska–Lincoln M,D
- University of Nevada, Reno M
- University of New Mexico M,D
- The University of North Carolina at Chapel Hill M,D
- University of Notre Dame M,D
- University of Oklahoma M,D
- University of Oregon M,D
- University of Pennsylvania M,D
- University of Pittsburgh M,D
- University of Puerto Rico, Río Piedras M
- University of Rhode Island M
- University of Rochester M,D
- University of St. Thomas (TX) M,D
- University of South Carolina (Columbia) M,D
- University of Southern California M,D
- University of Southern Mississippi M
- University of South Florida M,D
- University of Tennessee, Knoxville M,D
- The University of Texas at Austin M,D
- University of Toledo M
- University of Utah M,D
- University of Virginia M,D
- University of Washington M,D
- University of Wisconsin–Madison M,D
- University of Wisconsin–Milwaukee M
- University of Wyoming M
- Vanderbilt University M,D
- Villanova University M,D
- Virginia Polytechnic Institute and State University M
- Washington University in St. Louis M,D
- Wayne State University M,D
- West Chester University of Pennsylvania M
- Western Kentucky University M
- Western Michigan University M
- Yale University D

PHOTOGRAPHY

- Barry University M
- Bradley University M
- Brooklyn College of the City University of New York M
- California State University, Fullerton M
- California State University, Los Angeles M
- Claremont Graduate University M
- Columbia College (IL) M
- Columbia University M
- Cornell University M
- The George Washington University M

P—first professional degree; M—master's degree; D—doctorate; O—other advanced degree.

Photography (continued)

Howard University	M
Illinois Institute of Technology	M
Illinois State University	M
Indiana State University	M
Indiana University Bloomington	M
James Madison University	M
Lamar University	M
Louisiana State University and Agricultural and Mechanical College	M
Louisiana Tech University	M
Ohio University	M
Rochester Institute of Technology	M
San Jose State University	M
Southern Illinois University at Carbondale	M
Southern Methodist University	M
State University of New York at Buffalo	M
State University of New York at New Paltz	M
Syracuse University	M
Temple University (Philadelphia)	M
Texas Woman's University	M
The University of Alabama (Tuscaloosa)	M
University of Colorado at Boulder	M
University of Houston	M
The University of Memphis	M
University of Miami	M
University of New Mexico	M
University of New Orleans	M
University of North Texas	M
University of Notre Dame	M
University of Oklahoma	M
University of Tennessee, Knoxville	M
University of Utah	M
Virginia Commonwealth University	M
Washington University in St. Louis	M
Yale University	M

PHYSICAL CHEMISTRY

Boston College	M,D
Boston University	M,D
Brandeis University	M,D
Brigham Young University	M,D
California State University, Fullerton	M
California State University, Los Angeles	M
Case Western Reserve University	M,D
Clark Atlanta University	M,D
Clarkson University	M,D
Cleveland State University	M,D
Columbia University	M,D
Cornell University	D
Florida State University	M,D
Georgetown University	M,D
The George Washington University	M,D
Harvard University	M,D
Howard University	M,D
Illinois Institute of Technology	M,D
Kansas State University	M
Kent State University	M,D
Lehigh University	M,D
Marquette University	M,D
Massachusetts Institute of Technology	M,D
Michigan State University	D
Mississippi State University	M,D
Northeastern University	D
The Ohio State University	M,D
Oklahoma State University	M
Old Dominion University	M
Oregon State University	M,D
Polytechnic University, Brooklyn Campus	D
Princeton University	D
Purdue University	M,D
Rensselaer Polytechnic Institute	M,D
Rutgers, The State University of New Jersey, Newark	M,D
Rutgers, The State University of New Jersey, New Brunswick	M,D
San Jose State University	M
Seton Hall University	M,D
South Dakota State University	M,D
Southern University and Agricultural and Mechanical College	M
State University of New York at Binghamton	D
Stevens Institute of Technology	M,D
Tufts University	M,D
The University of Akron	M,D
University of Cincinnati	M,D
University of Georgia	M,D
University of Louisville	M,D
University of Maryland, College Park	M,D
University of Miami	D

University of Michigan	D
University of Missouri–Columbia	M,D
University of Missouri–Kansas City	M,D
The University of Montana–Missoula	D
University of Nebraska–Lincoln	D
University of Notre Dame	M,D
University of Puerto Rico, Río Piedras	D
University of Southern California	D
University of Southern Mississippi	M,D
University of South Florida	M,D
University of Tennessee, Knoxville	M,D
The University of Texas at Austin	M,D
University of Toledo	M,D
University of Utah	D
Wake Forest University	M,D
Washington State University	M,D
Yale University	D

PHYSICAL EDUCATION

Adams State College	M
Adelphi University	M,O
Alabama Agricultural and Mechanical University	M
Alabama State University	M,O
Albany State University	M
Alcorn State University	M
Angelo State University	M
Appalachian State University	M
Arizona State University	M
Arkansas State University	M,O
Arkansas Tech University	M,D
Auburn University	M,D,O
Auburn University Montgomery	M,O
Austin Peay State University	M
Azusa Pacific University	M
Ball State University	M,D
Baylor University	M
Bemidji State University	M
Boston University	M,D,O
Bridgewater State College	M
Brigham Young University	M,D
Brooklyn College of the City University of New York	M
California Polytechnic State University, San Luis Obispo	M
California State University, Chico	M
California State University, Dominguez Hills	M
California State University, Fullerton	M
California State University, Hayward	M
California State University, Long Beach	M
California State University, Los Angeles	M
California State University, Sacramento	M
California State University, Stanislaus	M
Campbell University	M
Canisius College	M
Central Connecticut State University	M
Central Michigan University	M,O
Central Missouri State University	M,O
Central Washington University	M
Chicago State University	M
The Citadel, The Military College of South Carolina	M
Cleveland State University	M
The College of New Jersey	M
Columbus State University	M
Delta State University	M
DePaul University	M
Drury College	M
Eastern Illinois University	M
Eastern Kentucky University	M
Eastern Michigan University	M
Eastern Nazarene College	M,O
Eastern New Mexico University	M
Eastern Washington University	M
East Stroudsburg University of Pennsylvania	M
East Tennessee State University	M
Edinboro University of Pennsylvania	O
Emporia State University	M
Fairleigh Dickinson University, Teaneck–Hackensack Campus	M
Florida Agricultural and Mechanical University	M
Florida International University	M
Florida State University	M,D,O
Fort Hays State University	M
Frostburg State University	M
Gardner–Webb University	M
Georgia College and State University	M,O
Georgia Southern University	M,O
Georgia Southwestern State University	M

Georgia State University	M,O
Hardin–Simmons University	M
Henderson State University	M
Hofstra University	M
Humboldt State University	M
Illinois State University	M
Indiana State University	M
Indiana University Bloomington	M,D,O
Indiana University of Pennsylvania	M
Inter American University of Puerto Rico, Metropolitan Campus	M
Inter American University of Puerto Rico, San Germán Campus	M
Iowa State University of Science and Technology	M
Jackson State University	M
Jacksonville State University	M
Kent State University	M,D
Long Island University, Brooklyn Campus	M
Longwood College	M
Louisiana Tech University	M
Lynchburg College	M
Mankato State University	M,O
Marshall University	M
McNeese State University	M
Michigan State University	M,D
Middle Tennessee State University	M,D
Midwestern State University	M
Mississippi State University	M
Montclair State University	M
Morehead State University	M,D
Murray State University	M
New Mexico Highlands University	M
North Carolina Agricultural and Technical State University	M
North Carolina Central University	M
North Dakota State University	M
Northeast Louisiana University	M
Northern Arizona University	M
Northern Illinois University	M
Northern State University	M
North Georgia College & State University	M
Northwest Missouri State University	M
The Ohio State University	M,D
Ohio University	M
Oklahoma State University	M,D
Old Dominion University	M
Oregon State University	M
Pittsburg State University	M
Prairie View A&M University	M
Purdue University	M
Queens College of the City University of New York	M
Radford University	M
Rowan University	M,O
St. Cloud State University	M
Saint Mary's College of California	M
San Francisco State University	M
San Jose State University	M
Slippery Rock University of Pennsylvania	M
South Dakota State University	M
Southeast Missouri State University	M
Southern Connecticut State University	M
Southern Illinois University at Carbondale	M
Southern Illinois University at Edwardsville	M
Southwestern Oklahoma State University	M
Southwest Texas State University	M
Springfield College (MA)	M,D,O
State University of New York at Stony Brook	O
State University of New York College at Brockport	M
State University of New York College at Cortland	M
State University of West Georgia	M,O
Stephen F. Austin State University	M
Sul Ross State University	M
Syracuse University	M,O
Tarleton State University	M,O
Teachers College, Columbia University	M,D
Temple University (Philadelphia)	M,D
Tennessee State University	M
Tennessee Technological University	M
Texas A&M University (College Station)	M,D
Texas A&M University–Commerce	M
Texas Christian University	M
Texas Southern University	M
Texas Tech University	M,O
Texas Woman's University	M,D
The University of Akron	M

The University of Alabama at Birmingham	M,O
University of Arkansas (Fayetteville)	M
University of Central Florida	M
University of Colorado at Boulder	M
University of Dayton	M
University of Delaware	M
University of Florida	D
University of Georgia	M,D,O
University of Houston	M,D
University of Idaho	M,D
The University of Iowa	M,D
University of Kansas	M,D
University of Louisville	M
University of Maine (Orono)	M,O
University of Massachusetts Amherst	M,D,O
The University of Montana–Missoula	M
University of Montevallo	M,O
University of Nebraska at Kearney	M
University of Nebraska at Omaha	M
University of Nebraska–Lincoln	M
University of Nevada, Reno	M
University of New Mexico	M,D,O
University of New Orleans	M,O
The University of North Carolina at Chapel Hill	M
University of Northern Colorado	M,D
University of Northern Iowa	M
University of Rhode Island	M
University of South Alabama	M,O
University of South Carolina (Columbia)	M,D
University of South Dakota	M
University of Southern Mississippi	M,D
University of South Florida	M
University of Tennessee at Chattanooga	M
The University of Texas of the Permian Basin	M
University of the Incarnate Word	M
University of Toledo	M,D
University of Virginia	M,D
The University of West Alabama	M
University of West Florida	M
University of Wisconsin–La Crosse	M
University of Wyoming	M
Utah State University	M
Valdosta State University	M
Virginia Commonwealth University	M
Virginia Polytechnic Institute and State University	M
Wayne State College	M
Wayne State University	M
West Chester University of Pennsylvania	M,O
Western Carolina University	M
Western Illinois University	M
Western Kentucky University	M
Western Michigan University	M
Western Washington University	M
West Virginia University	M,D
Whitworth College	M
Wichita State University	M
Winona State University	M
Winthrop University	M
Wright State University	M

PHYSICAL THERAPY

Alabama State University	M
Allegheny University of the Health Sciences	M,D
American International College	M
Andrews University	M
Armstrong Atlantic State University	M
Azusa Pacific University	M
Baylor University	M
Beaver College	M,D
Belmont University	M
Boston University	M,D
California State University, Fresno	M
California State University, Northridge	M
Central Michigan University	M
Chapman University	M
College Misericordia	M
College of St. Catherine	M
College of St. Scholastica	M
Columbia University	M
Creighton University	D
Duke University	M
Duquesne University	M
D'Youville College	M
East Carolina University	M
Eastern Washington University	M
Elon College	M
Emory University	M
Florida Atlantic University	M
Florida International University	M

Gannon University	M
Georgia State University	M
Governors State University	M
Grand Valley State University	M
Hardin–Simmons University	M
Idaho State University	M
Ithaca College	M
Loma Linda University	M,D
Long Island University, Brooklyn Campus	M
Marquette University	M
Marymount University	M
Mount St. Mary's College	M
New York University	M,D
Northern Arizona University	M
North Georgia College & State University	M
Northwestern University	M
Nova Southeastern University	M
Oakland University	M
Ohio University	M
Old Dominion University	M
Pacific University	M
Quinnipiac College	M
Regis University	M
Rockhurst College	M
Rutgers, The State University of New Jersey, Camden	M
Sacred Heart University	M
St. Ambrose University	M
Saint Francis College (PA)	M
Saint Louis University	M
San Francisco State University	M
Shenandoah University	M
Simmons College	M
Slippery Rock University of Pennsylvania	D
Southwest Baptist University	M
Southwest Texas State University	M
Springfield College (MA)	M
Temple University (Philadelphia)	M,D
Texas Woman's University	M,D
The University of Alabama at Birmingham	M
University of California, San Francisco	M
University of Central Arkansas	M,D
University of Delaware	M
University of Florida	M
University of Illinois at Chicago	M
University of Indianapolis	M
The University of Iowa	M,D
University of Kansas	M
University of Kentucky	M
University of Mary	M
University of Maryland Eastern Shore	M
University of Massachusetts Lowell	M
University of Miami	M,D
University of Michigan–Flint	M
University of Minnesota, Twin Cities Campus	M,D
University of Missouri–Columbia	M
University of Mobile	M
The University of Montana–Missoula	M
The University of North Carolina at Chapel Hill	M
University of North Dakota	M
University of Pittsburgh	M
University of Rhode Island	M
University of South Dakota	M
University of Southern California	M,D
University of Tennessee at Chattanooga	M
University of the Pacific	M
University of Utah	M
University of Vermont	M
University of Washington	M
University of Wisconsin–La Crosse	M
Virginia Commonwealth University	M,D
Walsh University	M
Washington University in St. Louis	M,D
Wayne State University	M
Western Carolina University	M
West Virginia University	M
Wheeling Jesuit University	M
Wichita State University	M
Widener University	M
Worcester State College	M

PHYSICIAN ASSISTANT STUDIES

Barry University	M
Beaver College	M
Central Michigan University	M
Duke University	M
Duquesne University	M
Emory University	M
Grand Valley State University	M
Marquette University	M
Northeastern University	M
Pacific University	M
Quinnipiac College	M
Saint Francis College (PA)	M
Seton Hall University	M
Trevecca Nazarene University	M
University of Detroit Mercy	M
University of Florida	M
The University of Iowa	M
University of New England	M
University of South Alabama	M
Wayne State University	M
Yale University	O

PHYSICS

Adelphi University	M
Alabama Agricultural and Mechanical University	M,D
American University	M,D
Andrews University	M
Arizona State University	M,D
Auburn University	M,D
Ball State University	M
Baylor University	M,D
Boston College	M,D
Boston University	M,D
Bowling Green State University	M
Brandeis University	M,D
Brigham Young University	M,D
Brooklyn College of the City University of New York	M,D
Brown University	M,D
California Institute of Technology	D
California State University, Fresno	M
California State University, Fullerton	M
California State University, Long Beach	M
California State University, Los Angeles	M
California State University, Northridge	M
Carnegie Mellon University	M,D
Case Western Reserve University	M,D
The Catholic University of America	M,D
Central Connecticut State University	M
Central Michigan University	M
City College of the City University of New York	M,D
Clark Atlanta University	M
Clarkson University	M,D
Clark University	M,D
Clemson University	M,D
Cleveland State University	M
College of William and Mary	M,D
Colorado School of Mines	M,D
Colorado State University	M,D
Columbia University	M,D
Cornell University	M,D
Creighton University	M
Dartmouth College	D
Delaware State University	M
DePaul University	M
Drexel University	M,D
Duke University	D
East Carolina University	M
Eastern Michigan University	M
Emory University	M,D
Emporia State University	M
Fairleigh Dickinson University, Teaneck–Hackensack Campus	M
Florida Agricultural and Mechanical University	M
Florida Atlantic University	M,D
Florida Institute of Technology	M,D
Florida International University	M
Florida State University	M,D
The George Washington University	M,D
Georgia Institute of Technology	M,D
Georgia State University	M,D
Graduate School and University Center of the City University of New York	D
Hampton University	M,D
Harvard University	M,D
Howard University	M,D
Hunter College of the City University of New York	M,D
Idaho State University	M
Illinois Institute of Technology	M,D
Indiana State University	M
Indiana University Bloomington	M,D
Indiana University of Pennsylvania	M
Indiana University–Purdue University Indianapolis	M,D
Iowa State University of Science and Technology	M,D
John Carroll University	M
Johns Hopkins University	D
Kansas State University	M,D
Kent State University	M,D
Lehigh University	M,D
Louisiana State University and Agricultural and Mechanical College	M,D
Louisiana Tech University	M,D
Maharishi University of Management	M,D
Mankato State University	M
Marshall University	M
Massachusetts Institute of Technology	M,D
Miami University	M
Michigan State University	M,D
Michigan Technological University	M,D
Mississippi State University	M,D
Montana State University–Bozeman	M,D
Murray State University	M
New Mexico State University	M,D
New York University	M,D
North Carolina State University	M,D
North Dakota State University	M,D
Northeastern University	M,D
Northern Illinois University	M
Northwestern University	D
Oakland University	M,D
The Ohio State University	M,D
Ohio University	M,D
Oklahoma State University	M,D
Old Dominion University	M,D
Oregon State University	M,D
Pennsylvania State University University Park Campus	M,D
Pittsburg State University	M
Polytechnic University, Brooklyn Campus	M,D
Polytechnic University, Farmingdale Campus	M,D
Portland State University	M,D
Princeton University	D
Purdue University	M,D
Queens College of the City University of New York	M
Rensselaer Polytechnic Institute	M,D
Rice University	M,D
Rutgers, The State University of New Jersey, New Brunswick	M,D
Sam Houston State University	M
San Diego State University	M
San Francisco State University	M
San Jose State University	M
South Dakota State University	M
Southern Illinois University at Carbondale	M
Southern Illinois University at Edwardsville	M
Southern Methodist University	M,D
Southern University and Agricultural and Mechanical College	M
Southwest Texas State University	M
Stanford University	M,D
State University of New York at Albany	M,D
State University of New York at Binghamton	M
State University of New York at Buffalo	M,D
State University of New York at New Paltz	M
State University of New York at Stony Brook	M,D
Stephen F. Austin State University	M
Stevens Institute of Technology	M,D,O
Syracuse University	M,D
Temple University (Philadelphia)	M,D
Texas A&M University (College Station)	M,D
Texas A&M University–Commerce	M
Texas Christian University	M,D
Texas Tech University	M,D
Tufts University	M,D
Tulane University	M,D
The University of Akron	M
The University of Alabama (Tuscaloosa)	M,D
The University of Alabama at Birmingham	M,D
The University of Alabama in Huntsville	M,D
University of Alaska Fairbanks	M,D
The University of Arizona	M,D
University of Arkansas (Fayetteville)	M,D
University of California, Berkeley	D
University of California, Davis	M,D
University of California, Irvine	M,D
University of California, Los Angeles	M,D
University of California, Riverside	M,D
University of California, San Diego	M,D
University of California, Santa Barbara	D
University of California, Santa Cruz	M,D
University of Central Florida	M,D
University of Chicago	M,D
University of Cincinnati	M,D
University of Colorado at Boulder	M,D
University of Colorado at Colorado Springs	M
University of Connecticut	M,D
University of Delaware	M,D
University of Denver	M,D
University of Florida	M,D
University of Georgia	M,D
University of Hawaii at Manoa	M,D
University of Houston	M,D
University of Idaho	M,D
University of Illinois at Chicago	M,D
University of Illinois at Urbana–Champaign	M,D
The University of Iowa	M,D
University of Kansas	M,D
University of Kentucky	M,D
University of Louisville	M
University of Maine (Orono)	M,D
University of Maryland, Baltimore County	M,D
University of Maryland, College Park	M,D
University of Massachusetts Amherst	M,D
University of Massachusetts Dartmouth	M,D
University of Massachusetts Lowell	M,D
The University of Memphis	M
University of Miami	M,D
University of Michigan	M,D
University of Minnesota, Duluth	M
University of Minnesota, Twin Cities Campus	M,D
University of Mississippi	M,D
University of Missouri–Columbia	M,D
University of Missouri–Kansas City	M,D
University of Missouri–Rolla	M,D
University of Missouri–St. Louis	M,D
University of Nebraska–Lincoln	M,D
University of Nevada, Las Vegas	M,D
University of Nevada, Reno	M,D
University of New Hampshire	M,D
University of New Mexico	M,D
University of New Orleans	M
University of North Dakota	M,D
University of North Texas	M,D
University of Notre Dame	M,D
University of Oklahoma	M,D
University of Oregon	M,D
University of Pennsylvania	D
University of Pittsburgh	M,D
University of Puerto Rico, Mayagüez Campus	M
University of Puerto Rico, Río Piedras	M,D
University of Rhode Island	M,D
University of Rochester	M,D
University of South Carolina (Columbia)	M,D
University of Southern California	M,D
University of Southern Mississippi	M
University of South Florida	M,D
University of Southwestern Louisiana	M
University of Tennessee, Knoxville	M,D
The University of Texas at Arlington	M,D
The University of Texas at Austin	M,D
The University of Texas at Dallas	M,D
The University of Texas at El Paso	M
The University of Texas at Tyler	M
University of Toledo	M,D
University of Utah	M,D
University of Vermont	M
University of Virginia	M,D
University of Washington	M,D
University of Wisconsin–Madison	M,D
University of Wisconsin–Milwaukee	M,D
University of Wisconsin–Oshkosh	M
University of Wyoming	M,D
Utah State University	M,D
Vanderbilt University	M,D
Virginia Commonwealth University	M
Virginia Polytechnic Institute and State University	M,D
Virginia State University	M
Wake Forest University	M,D
Washington State University	M,D
Washington University in St. Louis	M,D
Wayne State University	M,D
Western Carolina University	M
Western Illinois University	M
Western Michigan University	M,D
West Virginia University	M,D
Wichita State University	M
Wilkes University	M
Worcester Polytechnic Institute	M,D
Wright State University	M
Yale University	D

P—first professional degree; M—master's degree; D—doctorate; O—other advanced degree.

PHYSIOLOGY

Allegheny University of the Health Sciences	D
Arizona State University	M,D
Auburn University	M
Ball State University	M
Boston University	M,D
Brown University	M,D
Case Western Reserve University	D
Clemson University	M,D
Colorado State University	M,D
Columbia University	M,D
Cornell University	M,D
Dartmouth College	D
Duke University	D
East Carolina University	D
East Tennessee State University	M,D
Emory University	D
Florida State University	M,D
Georgetown University	M,D
Howard University	D
Illinois State University	D
Indiana State University	M,D
Indiana University–Purdue University Indianapolis	M,D
Iowa State University of Science and Technology	M,D
Johns Hopkins University	M,D
Kansas State University	M,D
Kent State University	M,D
Loma Linda University	M,D
Loyola University Chicago	M,D
Maharishi University of Management	M,D
Marquette University	M,D
Massachusetts Institute of Technology	D
Michigan State University	M,D
Mississippi State University	M,D
New York University	M,D
North Carolina State University	M,D
Northwestern University	M,D
The Ohio State University	M,D
Pennsylvania State University University Park Campus	M,D
Purdue University	M,D
Rutgers, The State University of New Jersey, New Brunswick	D
Saint Louis University	M,D
San Francisco State University	M
Southern Illinois University at Carbondale	M,D
Stanford University	D
State University of New York at Buffalo	M,D
State University of New York at Stony Brook	D
Teachers College, Columbia University	M,D
Temple University (Philadelphia)	M,D
Texas A&M University (College Station)	M,D
Tufts University	D
Tulane University	M,D
The University of Alabama at Birmingham	M,D
The University of Arizona	D
University of California, Berkeley	M,D
University of California, Davis	M,D
University of California, Irvine	D
University of California, Los Angeles	M,D
University of California, San Diego	D
University of California, San Francisco	D
University of Chicago	D
University of Cincinnati	M,D
University of Colorado at Boulder	M,D
University of Connecticut	M,D
University of Delaware	M,D
University of Florida	D
University of Georgia	M,D
University of Hawaii at Manoa	M,D
University of Illinois at Chicago	M,D
University of Illinois at Urbana–Champaign	M,D
The University of Iowa	M,D
University of Kansas	M,D
University of Kentucky	D
University of Louisville	M,D
University of Miami	D
University of Michigan	D
University of Minnesota, Duluth	M,D
University of Minnesota, Twin Cities Campus	M,D
University of Missouri–Columbia	M,D
University of Nevada, Reno	M,D
University of New Mexico	M,D
The University of North Carolina at Chapel Hill	D
University of North Dakota	M,D
University of Notre Dame	M,D
University of Pennsylvania	D
University of Pittsburgh	M,D
University of Rochester	M,D
University of South Alabama	D
University of South Carolina (Columbia)	D
University of South Dakota	M,D
University of Southern California	M,D
University of South Florida	D
University of Tennessee, Knoxville	M,D
University of the Pacific	M,D
University of Utah	D
University of Vermont	M,D
University of Virginia	D
University of Washington	D
University of Wisconsin–Madison	M,D
University of Wyoming	M,D
Vanderbilt University	D
Virginia Commonwealth University	M,D,O
Wake Forest University	D
Washington State University	D
Wayne State University	M,D
West Virginia University	M,D
William Paterson University of New Jersey	M
Wright State University	M
Yale University	D
Yeshiva University	D

PLANETARY AND SPACE SCIENCES

California Institute of Technology	M,D
Columbia University	M,D
Cornell University	D
Florida Institute of Technology	M,D
Harvard University	M,D
Johns Hopkins University	M,D
Massachusetts Institute of Technology	M,D
Rensselaer Polytechnic Institute	M,D
State University of New York at Stony Brook	M,D
The University of Arizona	M,D
University of California, Los Angeles	M,D,O
University of Chicago	M,D
University of Hawaii at Manoa	M,D
University of Michigan	M,D
University of New Mexico	M,D
University of North Dakota	M
University of Pittsburgh	M,D
Washington University in St. Louis	M,D

PLANT MOLECULAR BIOLOGY

Cornell University	D
University of California, Los Angeles	D
University of California, San Diego	D
University of Connecticut	M,D
University of Florida	M,D
University of Washington	D

PLANT PATHOLOGY

Auburn University	M,D
Clemson University	M,D
Colorado State University	M,D
Cornell University	M,D
Iowa State University of Science and Technology	M,D
Kansas State University	M,D
Louisiana State University and Agricultural and Mechanical College	M,D
Michigan State University	M,D
Mississippi State University	M,D
Montana State University–Bozeman	M,D
New Mexico State University	M
North Carolina State University	M,D
North Dakota State University	M,D
The Ohio State University	M,D
Oklahoma State University	M,D
Oregon State University	M,D
Pennsylvania State University University Park Campus	M,D
Purdue University	M,D
Rutgers, The State University of New Jersey, New Brunswick	M,D
South Dakota State University	M
Texas A&M University (College Station)	M,D
The University of Arizona	M,D
University of Arkansas (Fayetteville)	M
University of California, Davis	M,D
University of California, Riverside	M,D
University of Florida	M,D
University of Georgia	M,D
University of Hawaii at Manoa	M,D
University of Idaho	M,D
University of Kentucky	M,D
University of Maine (Orono)	M
University of Minnesota, Twin Cities Campus	M,D
University of Missouri–Columbia	M,D
University of Rhode Island	M,D
University of Tennessee, Knoxville	M
University of Wisconsin–Madison	M,D
University of Wyoming	M
Virginia Polytechnic Institute and State University	M,D
Washington State University	M,D

PLANT PHYSIOLOGY

Auburn University	M,D
Clemson University	D
Colorado State University	M,D
Cornell University	D
Iowa State University of Science and Technology	M,D
Oregon State University	M,D
Pennsylvania State University University Park Campus	M,D
Purdue University	D
Rutgers, The State University of New Jersey, New Brunswick	M,D
Texas A&M University (College Station)	M,D
University of Colorado at Boulder	M,D
University of Hawaii at Manoa	M,D
University of Kentucky	D
University of Tennessee, Knoxville	M,D
Virginia Polytechnic Institute and State University	M,D
Washington State University	M,D

PLASMA PHYSICS

California Institute of Technology	M,D
Massachusetts Institute of Technology	M
Princeton University	D
Rensselaer Polytechnic Institute	M,D
University of Colorado at Boulder	M,D

PODIATRIC MEDICINE

Barry University	P
Temple University (Philadelphia)	P

POLITICAL SCIENCE

American University	M,D
Appalachian State University	M
Arizona State University	M,D
Arkansas State University	M,O
Auburn University	M,D
Auburn University Montgomery	M
Ball State University	M
Baylor University	M
Boston College	M,D
Boston University	M,D
Bowling Green State University	
Brandeis University	M,D
Brooklyn College of the City University of New York	M
Brown University	M,D
California Institute of Technology	D
California State University, Chico	M
California State University, Fullerton	M
California State University, Long Beach	M
California State University, Los Angeles	M
California State University, Northridge	M
California State University, Sacramento	M
Case Western Reserve University	M,D
The Catholic University of America	M,D
Central Michigan University	M
Claremont Graduate University	M,D
Clark Atlanta University	M,D
The College of Saint Rose	M
Colorado State University	M,D
Columbia University	M,D
Cornell University	D
Duke University	M,D
Eastern Illinois University	M
Eastern Kentucky University	M
East Stroudsburg University of Pennsylvania	M
Emory University	D
Fairleigh Dickinson University, Teaneck–Hackensack Campus	M
Fayetteville State University	M
Florida Atlantic University	M
Florida International University	M,D
Florida State University	M,D
Fordham University	M,D
Georgetown University	M,D
The George Washington University	M,D
Georgia Southern University	M
Georgia State University	M,D
Governors State University	M
Graduate School and University Center of the City University of New York	M,D
Harvard University	M,D
Howard University	M,D
Idaho State University	M,D
Illinois State University	M
Indiana State University	M
Indiana University Bloomington	M,D
Indiana University of Pennsylvania	M
Iowa State University of Science and Technology	M
Jackson State University	M
Jacksonville State University	M
Johns Hopkins University	M,D
Kansas State University	M
Kent State University	M,D
Lamar University	M
Lehigh University	M
Long Island University, Brooklyn Campus	M
Long Island University, C.W. Post Campus	M
Louisiana State University and Agricultural and Mechanical College	M,D
Loyola University Chicago	M,D
Mankato State University	M
Marquette University	M
Marshall University	M
Massachusetts Institute of Technology	M,D
Miami University	M,D
Michigan State University	M,D
Midwestern State University	M
Mississippi State University	M,D
Montclair State University	M
New Mexico Highlands University	M
New Mexico State University	M
New School University	M,D
New York University	M,D
North Carolina State University	M
North Dakota State University	M
Northeastern Illinois University	M
Northeastern University	M,D
Northern Arizona University	M,D
Northern Illinois University	M,D
Northwestern University	M,D
The Ohio State University	M,D,O
Ohio University	M
Oklahoma State University	M
Pennsylvania State University University Park Campus	M,D
Portland State University	M,D
Prairie View A&M University	M
Princeton University	D
Purdue University	M,D
Purdue University Calumet	M
Queens College of the City University of New York	M
Rice University	M,D
Roosevelt University	M
Rutgers, The State University of New Jersey, Newark	M
Rutgers, The State University of New Jersey, New Brunswick	M,D
Saginaw Valley State University	M
St. John's University (NY)	M
St. Mary's University of San Antonio	M
Sam Houston State University	M
San Diego State University	M
San Francisco State University	M
Sonoma State University	M
Southern Connecticut State University	M
Southern Illinois University at Carbondale	M,D
Southern University and Agricultural and Mechanical College	M
Southwest Texas State University	M
Stanford University	M,D
State University of New York at Albany	M,D
State University of New York at Binghamton	M,D
State University of New York at Buffalo	M,D
State University of New York at Stony Brook	M,D
Suffolk University	M
Sul Ross State University	M
Syracuse University	M,D
Tarleton State University	M
Teachers College, Columbia University	M,D
Temple University (Philadelphia)	M,D
Texas A&M International University	M
Texas A&M University (College Station)	M,D
Texas A&M University–Kingsville	M
Texas Tech University	M,D
Texas Woman's University	M
Tulane University	M,D
The University of Akron	M
The University of Alabama (Tuscaloosa)	M,D
The University of Arizona	M,D

University of Arkansas (Fayetteville)	M
University of California, Berkeley	D
University of California, Davis	M,D
University of California, Irvine	M,D
University of California, Los Angeles	M,D,O
University of California, Riverside	M,D
University of California, San Diego	D
University of California, Santa Barbara	M,D
University of Central Florida	M
University of Central Oklahoma	M
University of Chicago	D
University of Cincinnati	M,D
University of Colorado at Boulder	M,D
University of Colorado at Denver	M
University of Connecticut	M,D
University of Delaware	M,D
University of Detroit Mercy	M
University of Florida	M,D,O
University of Georgia	M,D
University of Hawaii at Manoa	M,D
University of Houston	M,D
University of Idaho	M,D
University of Illinois at Chicago	M,D
University of Illinois at Springfield	M
University of Illinois at Urbana–Champaign	M,D
The University of Iowa	M,D
University of Kansas	M,D
University of Kentucky	M,D
University of Louisville	M
University of Maryland, College Park	M,D
University of Massachusetts Amherst	M,D
University of Massachusetts Boston	O
The University of Memphis	M
University of Miami	M
University of Michigan	M,D
University of Minnesota, Twin Cities Campus	M,D
University of Mississippi	M,D
University of Missouri–Columbia	M,D
University of Missouri–Kansas City	M,D
University of Missouri–St. Louis	M,D
The University of Montana–Missoula	M
University of Nebraska at Omaha	M
University of Nebraska–Lincoln	M,D
University of Nevada, Las Vegas	M
University of Nevada, Reno	M,D
University of New Hampshire	M
University of New Mexico	M,D
University of New Orleans	M,D
The University of North Carolina at Chapel Hill	M,D
University of North Carolina at Greensboro	M
University of North Dakota	M
University of Northern Iowa	M
University of North Texas	M,D
University of Notre Dame	M,D
University of Oklahoma	M,D
University of Oregon	M,D
University of Pennsylvania	M,D
University of Pittsburgh	M,D
University of Rhode Island	M,O
University of Richmond	M
University of Rochester	M,D
University of South Carolina (Columbia)	M,D
University of South Dakota	M
University of Southern California	M,D
University of Southern Mississippi	M
University of South Florida	M
University of Tennessee, Knoxville	M,D
The University of Texas at Arlington	M
The University of Texas at Austin	M,D
The University of Texas at El Paso	M
The University of Texas at San Antonio	M
University of Toledo	M
University of Utah	M,D
University of Vermont	M
University of Virginia	M,D
University of Washington	M,D
University of West Florida	M
University of Wisconsin–Madison	M,D
University of Wisconsin–Milwaukee	M,D
University of Wyoming	M
Utah State University	M
Vanderbilt University	M,D
Villanova University	M
Virginia Polytechnic Institute and State University	M
Washington State University	M,D
Washington University in St. Louis	M,D
Wayne State University	M,D
Western Illinois University	M
Western Michigan University	M,D
Western Washington University	M
West Texas A&M University	M
West Virginia University	M,D
Wichita State University	M
Yale University	D

POLYMER SCIENCE AND ENGINEERING

Carnegie Mellon University	M
Case Western Reserve University	M,D
Clemson University	M,D
Cornell University	M,D
Eastern Michigan University	M
Georgia Institute of Technology	M
Lehigh University	M,D
Massachusetts Institute of Technology	D
North Dakota State University	M,D
Pennsylvania State University University Park Campus	M,D
Polytechnic University, Brooklyn Campus	M,D
Princeton University	M,D
Rensselaer Polytechnic Institute	M,D
Rutgers, The State University of New Jersey, New Brunswick	M,D
San Jose State University	M
The University of Akron	M,D
University of Cincinnati	M,D
University of Connecticut	M,D
University of Detroit Mercy	M
University of Florida	M,D,O
University of Massachusetts Amherst	M,D
University of Massachusetts Lowell	M,D
University of Missouri–Kansas City	M,D
University of Southern Mississippi	M,D
University of Tennessee, Knoxville	M,D
Wayne State University	O

PORTUGUESE

Brigham Young University	M
Harvard University	M,D
Indiana University Bloomington	M,D
New York University	M,D
The Ohio State University	M,D
Tulane University	M,D
University of California, Los Angeles	M
University of California, Santa Barbara	M,D
University of Minnesota, Twin Cities Campus	M,D
University of New Mexico	M,D
The University of North Carolina at Chapel Hill	M,D
University of Tennessee, Knoxville	D
The University of Texas at Austin	M,D
University of Wisconsin–Madison	M,D
Vanderbilt University	M,D
Yale University	M,D

PROJECT MANAGEMENT

City University	M,O
The George Washington University	M
Golden Gate University	M,O
Lesley College	M
Montana State University–Bozeman	M
Montana Tech of The University of Montana	M
Northwestern University	M
Stevens Institute of Technology	M,O
Texas A&M University (College Station)	M,D
Towson University	M
Western Carolina University	M
Wright State University	M

PSYCHIATRIC NURSING

Adelphi University	M,O
Boston College	M
Case Western Reserve University	M
The Catholic University of America	M
Columbia University	M,O
Emory University	M
Georgia State University	M
Hunter College of the City University of New York	M
Kent State University	M
New York University	M,O
Northeastern University	M,O
Pontifical Catholic University of Puerto Rico	M
Rutgers, The State University of New Jersey, Newark	M
Sage Graduate School	M
Saint Joseph College (CT)	M
Saint Louis University	M,O
Saint Xavier University	M
Southern Illinois University at Edwardsville	M
State University of New York at Stony Brook	M,O
Texas Woman's University	M
University of Cincinnati	M
University of Illinois at Chicago	M
University of Massachusetts Lowell	M
University of Michigan	M
University of New Mexico	M
University of Pennsylvania	M
University of Pittsburgh	M
University of South Alabama	M
University of South Carolina (Columbia)	M
University of Southern Maine	M,O
University of Southern Mississippi	M
The University of Texas at El Paso	M
Vanderbilt University	M
Virginia Commonwealth University	M
Wayne State University	M
Wichita State University	M

PSYCHOLOGY

Abilene Christian University	M
Adelphi University	M,D,O
Alabama Agricultural and Mechanical University	M,O
Allegheny University of the Health Sciences	M,D
American International College	M,D,O
American University	M,D
Andrews University	M,D,O
Angelo State University	M
Anna Maria College	M,O
Appalachian State University	M,O
Arizona State University	D
Assumption College	M,O
Auburn University	M,D
Auburn University Montgomery	M
Augusta State University	M
Austin Peay State University	M
Avila College	M
Ball State University	M
Barry University	M,O
Baylor University	M,D
Beaver College	M
Biola University	D
Boston College	D
Boston University	M,D
Bowling Green State University	M,D
Brandeis University	M,D
Bridgewater State College	M
Brigham Young University	M,D
Brooklyn College of the City University of New York	M,D
Brown University	M,D
California Lutheran University	M
California Polytechnic State University, San Luis Obispo	M
California State Polytechnic University, Pomona	M
California State University, Bakersfield	M
California State University, Chico	M
California State University, Dominguez Hills	M
California State University, Fresno	M
California State University, Fullerton	M
California State University, Long Beach	M
California State University, Los Angeles	M
California State University, Northridge	M
California State University, Sacramento	M
California State University, San Bernardino	M
California State University, San Marcos	M
California State University, Stanislaus	M
Carnegie Mellon University	D
Case Western Reserve University	D
Castleton State College	M
The Catholic University of America	M,D
Central Connecticut State University	M
Central Michigan University	M,D,O
Central Missouri State University	M,O
Central Washington University	M
Chapman University	M
The Citadel, The Military College of South Carolina	M,O
City College of the City University of New York	M,D
City University	M
Claremont Graduate University	M,D
Clark University	D
Clemson University	M,D
Cleveland State University	M
College of Notre Dame	M
College of Staten Island of the City University of New York	D
College of William and Mary	M,D
Colorado State University	D
Columbia University	M,D
Concordia University (IL)	M,O
Coppin State College	M
Cornell University	D
Dartmouth College	D
DePaul University	M,D
Drake University	M
Drexel University	M,D
Duke University	D
Duquesne University	M,D
East Carolina University	M,O
East Central University	M
Eastern Illinois University	M,O
Eastern Kentucky University	M,O
Eastern Michigan University	M
Eastern New Mexico University	M
Eastern Washington University	M
East Tennessee State University	M
Edinboro University of Pennsylvania	M
Emory University	D
Emporia State University	M
Fairfield University	M,O
Fairleigh Dickinson University, Florham–Madison Campus	M
Fairleigh Dickinson University, Teaneck–Hackensack Campus	M,D
Fayetteville State University	M
Florida Agricultural and Mechanical University	M
Florida Atlantic University	M,D
Florida Institute of Technology	M,D
Florida International University	M,D
Florida State University	D
Fordham University	D
Fort Hays State University	M
Framingham State College	M
Francis Marion University	M
Frostburg State University	M
Gallaudet University	M,D,O
Gardner–Webb University	M
George Mason University	M,D
Georgetown University	D
The George Washington University	M,D
Georgia College and State University	M
Georgia Institute of Technology	M,D
Georgia Southern University	M
Georgia Southwestern State University	M
Georgia State University	D
Golden Gate University	M,O
Governors State University	M
Graduate School and University Center of the City University of New York	D
Hardin–Simmons University	M
Harvard University	M,D
Hofstra University	M,D
Hood College	M
Houston Baptist University	M
Howard University	M,D
Humboldt State University	M
Hunter College of the City University of New York	M
Idaho State University	M,D
Illinois Institute of Technology	M,D
Illinois State University	M,D,O
Immaculata College	M,D,O
Indiana State University	M,D
Indiana University Bloomington	D
Indiana University of Pennsylvania	M,D
Indiana University–Purdue University Indianapolis	M,D
Indiana University South Bend	M
Inter American University of Puerto Rico, Metropolitan Campus	M
Inter American University of Puerto Rico, San Germán Campus	M
Iona College (New Rochelle)	M
Iowa State University of Science and Technology	M,D,O
Jackson State University	D
Jacksonville State University	M
James Madison University	M,D,O
John F. Kennedy University	M,D,O
Johns Hopkins University	D
Kansas State University	M,D

P—first professional degree; M—master's degree; D—doctorate; O—other advanced degree.

Psychology (continued)

Kean University	M,O
Kent State University	M,D
Lamar University	M
La Salle University	D
Lehigh University	M,D
Lesley College	M,O
Lewis University	M
Long Island University, Brooklyn Campus	M,D
Long Island University, C.W. Post Campus	M,D
Louisiana State University and Agricultural and Mechanical College	M,D
Louisiana Tech University	M,D,O
Loyola College	M,D,O
Loyola Marymount University	M
Loyola University Chicago	M,D
Maharishi University of Management	M,D
Mankato State University	M
Mansfield University of Pennsylvania	M
Marist College	M,O
Marquette University	M,D
Marshall University	M
Marymount University	M
Marywood University	M
Massachusetts Institute of Technology	D
McNeese State University	M
Miami University	D
Michigan State University	M,D
Middle Tennessee State University	M,O
Midwestern State University	M
Millersville University of Pennsylvania	M,O
Mississippi State University	M
Monmouth University	M,O
Montana State University–Bozeman	M
Montclair State University	M
Moorhead State University	M,O
Morehead State University	M
Murray State University	M
National–Louis University	M,O
National University	M
New Jersey City University	M,O
New Mexico Highlands University	M
New Mexico State University	M,D
New School University	M,D
New York University	M,D,O
Norfolk State University	M,D
North Carolina Central University	M
North Carolina State University	M,D
North Dakota State University	M
Northeastern State University	M
Northeastern University	M,D,O
Northeast Louisiana University	M,O
Northern Arizona University	M
Northern Illinois University	M,D
Northwestern Oklahoma State University	M
Northwestern State University of Louisiana	M,O
Northwestern University	D
Northwest Missouri State University	M
Nova Southeastern University	M,D
The Ohio State University	M,D
Ohio University	D
Oklahoma State University	M,D
Old Dominion University	M,D
Our Lady of the Lake University of San Antonio	M,D
Pace University	M,D
Pacific University	M,D
Pennsylvania State University Harrisburg Campus of the Capital College	M
Pennsylvania State University University Park Campus	M,D
Pepperdine University (Culver City)	M,D
Pittsburg State University	M
Plattsburgh State University of New York	M,O
Pontifical Catholic University of Puerto Rico	M
Portland State University	M,D
Princeton University	D
Purdue University	D
Queens College of the City University of New York	M
Radford University	M,O
Rensselaer Polytechnic Institute	M
Rhode Island College	M
Rice University	M,D
Roosevelt University	M,D
Rowan University	M
Rutgers, The State University of New Jersey, Newark	D
Rutgers, The State University of New Jersey, New Brunswick	M,D
Sage Graduate School	M
St. Bonaventure University	M
St. Cloud State University	M
St. John's University (NY)	M,D
Saint Joseph's University	M
Saint Louis University	M,D
Saint Mary's College of California	M
St. Mary's University of San Antonio	M
Saint Xavier University	M,O
Salem State College	M
Salisbury State University	M
Sam Houston State University	M
San Diego State University	M,D
San Francisco State University	M
San Jose State University	M
Seattle University	M
Seton Hall University	M,D,O
Shippensburg University of Pennsylvania	M
Sonoma State University	M
Southeastern Louisiana University	M
Southern Connecticut State University	M
Southern Illinois University at Carbondale	M,D
Southern Illinois University at Edwardsville	M
Southern Methodist University	M,D
Southern Nazarene University	M
Southern Oregon University	M
Southern University and Agricultural and Mechanical College	M
Southwestern Oklahoma State University	M
Southwest Missouri State University	M
Spalding University	M,D
Stanford University	D
State University of New York at Albany	M,D
State University of New York at Binghamton	M,D
State University of New York at Buffalo	M,D
State University of New York at New Paltz	M
State University of New York at Stony Brook	M,D
State University of New York College at Brockport	M
State University of West Georgia	M
Stephen F. Austin State University	M
Suffolk University	D
Sul Ross State University	M
Syracuse University	M,D
Temple University (Philadelphia)	D
Tennessee State University	M,D
Texas A&M International University	M
Texas A&M University (College Station)	M,D
Texas A&M University–Commerce	M,D
Texas A&M University–Corpus Christi	M
Texas A&M University–Kingsville	M
Texas Christian University	M,D
Texas Tech University	M,D
Texas Woman's University	M,D
Towson University	M,O
Tufts University	M,D
Tulane University	M,D
United States International University	M,D
The University of Akron	M,D
The University of Alabama (Tuscaloosa)	M,D
The University of Alabama at Birmingham	M,D
The University of Alabama in Huntsville	M
University of Alaska Anchorage	M
University of Alaska Fairbanks	M
The University of Arizona	M,D
University of Arkansas (Fayetteville)	M,D
University of Arkansas at Little Rock	M
University of Baltimore	M
University of California, Berkeley	D
University of California, Davis	D
University of California, Irvine	M,D
University of California, Los Angeles	D,O
University of California, Riverside	M,D
University of California, San Diego	D
University of California, Santa Barbara	M,D
University of California, Santa Cruz	D
University of Central Arkansas	M
University of Central Florida	M,D
University of Central Oklahoma	M
University of Chicago	D
University of Cincinnati	M,D
University of Colorado at Boulder	M,D
University of Colorado at Colorado Springs	M
University of Colorado at Denver	M
University of Connecticut	M,D
University of Dayton	M
University of Delaware	D
University of Denver	D
University of Detroit Mercy	M,D,O
University of Florida	M,D
University of Georgia	M,D
University of Hartford	M
University of Hawaii at Manoa	M,D
University of Houston	D
University of Houston–Clear Lake	M
University of Houston–Victoria	M
University of Idaho	M
University of Illinois at Chicago	D
University of Illinois at Springfield	M
University of Illinois at Urbana–Champaign	M,D
The University of Iowa	M,D
University of Kansas	M,D
University of Kentucky	M,D
University of Louisville	M,D
University of Maine (Orono)	M,D
University of Mary Hardin–Baylor	M
University of Maryland, Baltimore County	D
University of Maryland, College Park	M,D
University of Massachusetts Amherst	M,D
University of Massachusetts Dartmouth	M
University of Massachusetts Lowell	M
The University of Memphis	M,D
University of Miami	D
University of Michigan	D
University of Minnesota, Twin Cities Campus	M,D
University of Mississippi	M,D
University of Missouri–Columbia	M,D
University of Missouri–Kansas City	M,D
University of Missouri–St. Louis	M,D,O
The University of Montana–Missoula	M,D,O
University of Nebraska at Omaha	M,D,O
University of Nebraska–Lincoln	M,D
University of Nevada, Las Vegas	M
University of Nevada, Reno	M,D
University of New Hampshire	D
University of New Mexico	M,D
University of New Orleans	M,D
The University of North Carolina at Chapel Hill	M,D
University of North Carolina at Charlotte	M
University of North Carolina at Greensboro	M,D
University of North Carolina at Wilmington	M
University of North Dakota	M,D
University of Northern Colorado	M
University of Northern Iowa	M
University of North Florida	M
University of North Texas	M,D
University of Notre Dame	D
University of Oklahoma	M,D
University of Oregon	M,D
University of Pennsylvania	D
University of Pittsburgh	M,D
University of Puerto Rico, Río Piedras	M,D
University of Rhode Island	M,D
University of Richmond	M
University of Rochester	M,D
University of Saint Francis (IN)	M
University of St. Thomas (MN)	M,D
University of South Alabama	M
University of South Carolina (Columbia)	M,D
University of South Dakota	M,D
University of Southern California	D
University of Southern Mississippi	M,D,O
University of South Florida	D
University of Southwestern Louisiana	M
University of Tennessee at Chattanooga	M
University of Tennessee, Knoxville	M,D
The University of Texas at Arlington	M,D
The University of Texas at Austin	D
The University of Texas at Brownsville	M
The University of Texas at El Paso	M,D
The University of Texas at San Antonio	M
The University of Texas at Tyler	M,O
The University of Texas of the Permian Basin	M
The University of Texas–Pan American	M
University of the Pacific	M
University of Toledo	M,D
University of Tulsa	M,D
University of Utah	M,D
University of Vermont	D
University of Virginia	M,D
University of Washington	D
University of West Florida	M
University of Wisconsin–Eau Claire	M
University of Wisconsin–La Crosse	M,O
University of Wisconsin–Madison	D
University of Wisconsin–Milwaukee	M,D
University of Wisconsin–Oshkosh	M
University of Wisconsin–Stout	M
University of Wisconsin–Whitewater	M
University of Wyoming	M,D
Utah State University	M,D
Valdosta State University	M,O
Valparaiso University	M
Vanderbilt University	M,D
Villanova University	M
Virginia Commonwealth University	D
Virginia Polytechnic Institute and State University	M,D
Virginia State University	M
Wake Forest University	M
Washburn University of Topeka	M
Washington State University	M,D
Washington University in St. Louis	M,D
Wayne State University	M,D
West Chester University of Pennsylvania	M
Western Carolina University	M
Western Illinois University	M,O
Western Kentucky University	M,O
Western Michigan University	M,D,O
Western Washington University	M
Westfield State College	M
West Texas A&M University	M
West Virginia University	M,D
Wichita State University	D
Widener University	
Wilmington College (DE)	M
Winthrop University	M,O
Wright State University	M,D
Xavier University	M,D
Yale University	M,D
Yeshiva University	M,D

PUBLIC HEALTH

Allegheny University of the Health Sciences	M
Armstrong Atlantic State University	M
Benedictine University	M
Boise State University	M
Boston University	M,D,O
Bowling Green State University	M
Brooklyn College of the City University of New York	M
California State University, Fresno	M
California State University, Northridge	M
Columbia University	M,D
East Stroudsburg University of Pennsylvania	M
East Tennessee State University	M
Emerson College	M
Emory University	M,D
Florida International University	M
The George Washington University	M,D
Harvard University	M,D,O
Hunter College of the City University of New York	M
Idaho State University	M
Indiana University Bloomington	M,D,O
Johns Hopkins University	M,D
Loma Linda University	M,D
New Mexico State University	M
New York University	M,D,O
Northern Arizona University	M
Northern Illinois University	M
Northwestern University	M
The Ohio State University	M,D
Old Dominion University	M,O
Oregon State University	M
Portland State University	M
Rutgers, The State University of New Jersey, New Brunswick	M,D
Saint Louis University	M,D
San Diego State University	M,D
San Jose State University	M,O
Southern Connecticut State University	M
State University of New York at Albany	M,D
Temple University (Philadelphia)	M

Tufts University	M
Tulane University	M,D,O
The University of Alabama at Birmingham	M,D
The University of Arizona	M
University of California, Berkeley	M,D
University of California, Los Angeles	M,D
University of California, San Diego	D
University of Connecticut	M
University of Denver	M
University of Hawaii at Manoa	M,D
University of Illinois at Chicago	M,D
University of Illinois at Springfield	M
The University of Iowa	M
University of Kansas	M
University of Kentucky	M
University of Massachusetts Amherst	M,D
University of Miami	M
University of Michigan	M,D
University of Minnesota, Twin Cities Campus	M,D
University of New Mexico	M
The University of North Carolina at Chapel Hill	M,D
University of Northern Colorado	M
University of Pittsburgh	M,D,O
University of Rochester	M
University of South Carolina (Columbia)	M
University of Southern California	M
University of Southern Mississippi	M
University of South Florida	M,D
University of Tennessee, Knoxville	M
University of Toledo	M
University of Utah	M
University of Washington	M,D
University of Wisconsin–Eau Claire	M
University of Wisconsin–La Crosse	M
Vanderbilt University	M
Virginia Commonwealth University	M
Western Kentucky University	M
West Virginia University	M
Wichita State University	M
Yale University	M,D

PUBLIC HEALTH NURSING

Bellarmine College	M
Boston College	M
Case Western Reserve University	M
Georgia Southern University	M
Georgia State University	D
Hawaii Pacific University	M
Holy Names College	M
Hunter College of the City University of New York	M
Indiana Wesleyan University	M
Johns Hopkins University	M
La Roche College	M
La Salle University	M
Lewis University	M
Northeastern University	M,O
Rutgers, The State University of New Jersey, Newark	M
Sage Graduate School	M
Saint Louis University	M,O
Saint Xavier University	M
San Jose State University	M
Southern Illinois University at Edwardsville	M
Texas Woman's University	M
University of Cincinnati	M
University of Hawaii at Manoa	M
University of Illinois at Chicago	M
University of Massachusetts Lowell	M
University of Michigan	M
University of Minnesota, Twin Cities Campus	M,D
University of New Mexico	M
The University of North Carolina at Chapel Hill	M
University of San Diego	M
University of South Carolina (Columbia)	M
University of Southern Mississippi	M
The University of Texas at El Paso	M
Valdosta State University	M
Wayne State University	M
West Chester University of Pennsylvania	M
Wright State University	M

PUBLIC HISTORY

Arizona State University	M
California State University, Sacramento	M
Eastern Illinois University	M
Florida State University	M
New York University	M,O
North Carolina State University	M
Northeastern University	M
Rutgers, The State University of New Jersey, Camden	M
Simmons College	
Sonoma State University	M
State University of New York at Albany	O
University of Arkansas at Little Rock	M
University of Houston	M
University of Illinois at Springfield	M
University of Kansas	M
University of Massachusetts Amherst	M
University of Michigan	M
University of New Orleans	M
Wayne State University	O

PUBLIC POLICY AND ADMINISTRATION

Albany State University	M
Alfred University	M
American International College	M
American University	M,D
Andrews University	M
Angelo State University	M
Appalachian State University	M
Arizona State University	M,D
Arkansas State University	M
Auburn University	M,D
Auburn University Montgomery	M,D
Augusta State University	M
Ball State University	M
Baruch College of the City University of New York	M
Baylor University	M
Boise State University	M
Boston University	M
Bowie State University	M
Bowling Green State University	M
Brandeis University	M,D
Bridgewater State College	M
Brigham Young University	M
Brooklyn College of the City University of New York	M
California Lutheran University	M
California State University, Bakersfield	M
California State University, Chico	M
California State University, Dominguez Hills	M
California State University, Fresno	M
California State University, Fullerton	M
California State University, Hayward	M
California State University, Long Beach	M,O
California State University, Los Angeles	M
California State University, Northridge	M
California State University, Sacramento	M
California State University, San Bernardino	M
California State University, Stanislaus	M
Carnegie Mellon University	M,D
Central Michigan University	M,O
Chaminade University of Honolulu	M
City University	M,O
Claremont Graduate University	M,D
Clark Atlanta University	M
Clark University	M,O
Clemson University	M
Cleveland State University	M
College of Notre Dame	M
College of William and Mary	M
Columbia University	M
Columbus State University	M
Cornell University	M
DePaul University	M,O
Drake University	M
Duke University	M
Duquesne University	M,O
East Carolina University	M
Eastern Kentucky University	M
Eastern Michigan University	M
Eastern Washington University	M
East Tennessee State University	M
Fairleigh Dickinson University, Teaneck–Hackensack Campus	M
Florida Atlantic University	M,D
Florida Institute of Technology	M
Florida International University	M,D
Florida State University	M,D,O
Framingham State College	M
Gannon University	M,O
George Mason University	M,D
Georgetown University	M
The George Washington University	M,D
Georgia College and State University	M
Georgia Institute of Technology	M,D
Georgia Southern University	M
Georgia State University	M
Golden Gate University	M,D
Governors State University	M
Graduate School and University Center of the City University of New York	M,D
Grambling State University	M
Grand Valley State University	M
Harvard University	M,D
Howard University	M
Idaho State University	M
Illinois Institute of Technology	M
Indiana State University	M
Indiana University Bloomington	M,D
Indiana University Northwest	M,O
Indiana University of Pennsylvania	M
Indiana University–Purdue University Fort Wayne	M,O
Indiana University–Purdue University Indianapolis	M,O
Indiana University South Bend	M
Jackson State University	M,D
Jacksonville State University	M
James Madison University	M
Johns Hopkins University	M
Kansas State University	M
Kean University	M
Kennesaw State University	M
Kent State University	M
Kentucky State University	M
Kutztown University of Pennsylvania	M
Lake Superior State University	M
Lamar University	M
Long Island University, Brooklyn Campus	M
Long Island University, C.W. Post Campus	M,O
Louisiana State University and Agricultural and Mechanical College	M
Mankato State University	M
Marist College	M,O
Marshall University	M
Marywood University	M
Michigan State University	M
Midwestern State University	M
Mississippi State University	M,D
Montana State University–Bozeman	M
Moorhead State University	M
Murray State University	M
National University	M
New Mexico Highlands University	M
New School University	D
New York University	M,D,O
North Carolina Central University	M
North Carolina State University	M,D
Northeastern University	M,D
Northern Arizona University	M,D
Northern Illinois University	M
Northern Kentucky University	M
Northern Michigan University	M
North Georgia College & State University	M
Northwestern University	D
Nova Southeastern University	M,D
Oakland University	M
The Ohio State University	M,D
Ohio University	M
Oklahoma City University	M
Oklahoma State University	M
Old Dominion University	M
Pace University	M
Park College	M
Pennsylvania State University Harrisburg Campus of the Capital College	M,D
Pepperdine University (Malibu)	M
Pontifical Catholic University of Puerto Rico	M
Portland State University	M,D
Princeton University	M,D
Roosevelt University	M
Rutgers, The State University of New Jersey, Camden	M
Rutgers, The State University of New Jersey, Newark	M,D
Rutgers, The State University of New Jersey, New Brunswick	M
Sage Graduate School	M
St. John's University (NY)	M
Saint Louis University	M,D
St. Mary's University of San Antonio	M
St. Thomas University	M,O
San Diego State University	M
San Francisco State University	M
San Jose State University	M
Seattle University	M
Seton Hall University	M
Shippensburg University of Pennsylvania	M
Slippery Rock University of Pennsylvania	M
Sonoma State University	M
Southeast Missouri State University	M
Southern Illinois University at Carbondale	M
Southern Illinois University at Edwardsville	M
Southern University and Agricultural and Mechanical College	M,D
Southwest Missouri State University	M
Southwest Texas State University	M
State University of New York at Albany	M,D,O
State University of New York at Binghamton	M,D
State University of New York at Stony Brook	M
State University of New York College at Brockport	M
State University of West Georgia	M
Suffolk University	M,O
Sul Ross State University	M
Syracuse University	M,D
Tennessee State University	M,D
Texas A&M University (College Station)	M
Texas A&M University–Corpus Christi	M
Texas Southern University	M
Texas Tech University	M,D
Troy State University (Troy)	M
Tufts University	M
Tulane University	M
The University of Akron	M,D
The University of Alabama (Tuscaloosa)	M
The University of Alabama at Birmingham	M
The University of Alabama in Huntsville	M
University of Alaska Anchorage	M
University of Alaska Southeast	M
The University of Arizona	M,D
University of Arkansas (Fayetteville)	M
University of Arkansas at Little Rock	M
University of Baltimore	M
University of California, Berkeley	M,D
University of California, Los Angeles	M
University of Central Florida	M,D
University of Central Texas	M
University of Chicago	M,D
University of Cincinnati	M
University of Colorado at Boulder	M
University of Colorado at Colorado Springs	M
University of Colorado at Denver	M,D
University of Connecticut	M
University of Dayton	M
University of Delaware	M,D
University of Detroit Mercy	M
University of Florida	M,O
University of Georgia	M,D
University of Guam	M
University of Hawaii at Manoa	M,O
University of Houston	M
University of Houston–Clear Lake	M
University of Idaho	M
University of Illinois at Chicago	M,D
University of Illinois at Springfield	M
University of Kansas	M
University of Kentucky	M,D
University of La Verne	M,D
University of Louisville	M
University of Maine (Orono)	M
University of Maryland, Baltimore County	M,D
University of Maryland, College Park	M,D
University of Massachusetts Amherst	M
University of Massachusetts Boston	M,D
The University of Memphis	M
University of Michigan	M,D
University of Michigan–Dearborn	M
University of Michigan–Flint	M
University of Minnesota, Twin Cities Campus	M
University of Missouri–Columbia	M
University of Missouri–Kansas City	M,D
University of Missouri–St. Louis	M
The University of Montana–Missoula	M
University of Nebraska at Omaha	M,D
University of Nevada, Las Vegas	M
University of Nevada, Reno	M

P—first professional degree; M—master's degree; D—doctorate; O—other advanced degree.

Public Policy and Administration (continued)

- University of New Hampshire M
- University of New Haven M
- University of New Mexico M
- University of New Orleans M
- The University of North Carolina at Chapel Hill M,D
- University of North Carolina at Charlotte M
- University of North Carolina at Greensboro M
- University of North Dakota M
- University of Northern Iowa M
- University of North Florida M
- University of North Texas M
- University of Oklahoma M
- University of Oregon M
- University of Pennsylvania M,D
- University of Pittsburgh M,D,O
- University of Puerto Rico, Río Piedras M
- University of Rhode Island M
- University of Rochester M
- University of San Francisco M
- University of South Alabama M
- University of South Carolina (Columbia) M
- University of South Dakota M
- University of Southern California M,D,O
- University of Southern Maine M
- University of South Florida M
- University of Tennessee at Chattanooga M
- University of Tennessee, Knoxville M
- The University of Texas at Arlington M,D
- The University of Texas at Austin M,D
- The University of Texas at Dallas M
- The University of Texas at San Antonio M
- The University of Texas at Tyler M
- The University of Texas–Pan American M
- University of the District of Columbia M
- University of the Virgin Islands M
- University of Toledo M
- University of Utah M,O
- University of Vermont M
- University of Washington M
- University of West Florida M
- University of Wisconsin–Madison M
- University of Wisconsin–Milwaukee M
- University of Wisconsin–Oshkosh M
- University of Wyoming M
- Valdosta State University M
- Villanova University M
- Virginia Commonwealth University M,D,O
- Virginia Polytechnic Institute and State University M,D,O
- Washington State University M
- Washington University in St. Louis M
- Wayne State University M
- Webster University M
- West Chester University of Pennsylvania M
- Western Carolina University M
- Western Connecticut State University M
- Western Kentucky University M
- Western Michigan University M,D
- West Virginia University M
- Wichita State University M
- Widener University M
- Wilmington College (DE) M

PUBLISHING

- Drexel University M
- Emerson College M
- New York University M
- Northwestern University M
- Pace University M
- Rochester Institute of Technology M
- University of Baltimore M

QUALITY MANAGEMENT

- California State University, Dominguez Hills M
- Case Western Reserve University M
- Dowling College M,O
- Eastern Michigan University M
- Fordham University O
- Friends University M
- Hawaii Pacific University M
- Loyola University New Orleans M
- Madonna University M
- Marian College of Fond du Lac M
- North Carolina State University M
- Pennsylvania State University University Park Campus M
- Rutgers, The State University of New Jersey, New Brunswick M
- San Jose State University M
- The University of Iowa M

QUANTITATIVE ANALYSIS

- California State University, Hayward M
- Clark Atlanta University M
- Cornell University D
- Drexel University M,D
- Fairleigh Dickinson University, Florham–Madison Campus M
- Fairleigh Dickinson University, Teaneck–Hackensack Campus M
- Hofstra University M
- Louisiana Tech University M,D
- Loyola College M
- Montclair State University M
- New York University O
- Purdue University M,D
- Rensselaer Polytechnic Institute M
- St. John's University (NY) M,O
- Saint Louis University M,D
- Seton Hall University M
- Texas Tech University M,D
- Troy State University Dothan M
- University of Cincinnati M,D
- University of Hartford M
- University of Minnesota, Twin Cities Campus M,D
- University of Missouri–St. Louis M
- The University of North Carolina at Chapel Hill D
- University of Oregon M,D
- University of Rhode Island D
- Virginia Commonwealth University M,D

RADIATION BIOLOGY

- Auburn University M
- Colorado State University M,D
- Florida State University M,D
- Georgetown University M
- The George Washington University D
- Harvard University D
- New York University D
- University of California, Irvine M,D
- The University of Iowa M,D

RANGE SCIENCE

- Brigham Young University M,D
- Colorado State University M,D
- Kansas State University M,D
- Montana State University–Bozeman M
- New Mexico State University M,D
- North Dakota State University M,D
- Oregon State University M,D
- Sul Ross State University M
- Texas A&M University (College Station) M,D
- Texas A&M University–Kingsville M
- Texas Tech University M,D
- The University of Arizona M,D
- University of California, Berkeley M
- University of Idaho M,D
- University of Wyoming M,D
- Utah State University M,D

READING EDUCATION

- Abilene Christian University M
- Adelphi University M,O
- Albany State University M
- Alfred University M
- American International College M,O
- Andrews University M
- Angelo State University M
- Appalachian State University M,O
- Arkansas State University M,O
- Ashland University M
- Auburn University D,O
- Auburn University Montgomery M,O
- Austin Peay State University M
- Averett College M
- Baldwin-Wallace College M
- Ball State University M,D
- Barry University M,O
- Beaver College M,O
- Bloomsburg University of Pennsylvania M
- Boise State University M
- Boston College M,O
- Boston University M,D,O
- Bowie State University M
- Bowling Green State University M,O
- Bridgewater State College M
- Brigham Young University D
- Brooklyn College of the City University of New York M
- Butler University M
- California Lutheran University M
- California Polytechnic State University, San Luis Obispo M
- California State University, Bakersfield M
- California State University, Chico M
- California State University, Fresno M
- California State University, Fullerton M
- California State University, Los Angeles M
- California State University, Sacramento M
- California State University, San Bernardino M
- California State University, Stanislaus M
- California University of Pennsylvania M
- Calvin College M
- Canisius College M
- Cardinal Stritch University M
- Carthage College M,O
- Castleton State College M,O
- Central Connecticut State University M,O
- Central Missouri State University M
- Central Washington University M
- Chapman University M
- Chicago State University M
- The Citadel, The Military College of South Carolina M
- City College of the City University of New York M,O
- Claremont Graduate University M,D
- Clarion University of Pennsylvania M
- Clemson University M
- Cleveland State University M
- College of Mount St. Joseph M
- The College of New Jersey M
- College of New Rochelle M
- The College of Saint Rose M
- Columbus State University M,O
- Concordia University (IL) M,O
- Cumberland College M
- Curry College M,O
- Dallas Baptist University M
- DePaul University M
- Dowling College M
- Duquesne University M
- East Carolina University M
- Eastern Connecticut State University M
- Eastern Kentucky University M
- Eastern Michigan University M
- Eastern Nazarene College M,O
- Eastern Washington University M
- East Stroudsburg University of Pennsylvania M
- East Tennessee State University M
- Edinboro University of Pennsylvania M,O
- Elmira College M
- Emporia State University M
- Florida Atlantic University M
- Florida International University M
- Florida State University M,D,O
- Fordham University M,O
- Framingham State College M
- Fresno Pacific University M
- Frostburg State University M
- Gannon University M,O
- George Mason University M
- Georgian Court College M
- Georgia Southern University M,O
- Georgia Southwestern State University M
- Georgia State University M,O
- Grand Valley State University M
- Gwynedd–Mercy College M
- Hardin–Simmons University M
- Harvard University M,D,O
- Hofstra University M,D,O
- Hood College M
- Houston Baptist University M
- Howard University M,O
- Hunter College of the City University of New York M
- Idaho State University M
- Illinois State University M
- Indiana State University M,D,O
- Indiana University Bloomington M,D,O
- Indiana University of Pennsylvania M,O
- Jacksonville University M
- James Madison University M
- Johns Hopkins University M,O
- Johnson State College M
- Kean University M,O
- Kent State University M
- Kutztown University of Pennsylvania M
- Lake Erie College M
- Lehman College of the City University of New York M
- Lenoir–Rhyne College M
- Lesley College M,O
- Liberty University M
- Long Island University, Brooklyn Campus M
- Long Island University, C.W. Post Campus M
- Long Island University, Southampton College M
- Longwood College M
- Louisiana Tech University O
- Loyola College M,O
- Loyola Marymount University M
- Loyola University New Orleans M
- Lynchburg College M
- Madonna University M
- Mankato State University M
- Marshall University M,O
- Marycrest International University M
- Marygrove College M
- Marywood University M
- McNeese State University M
- Mercer University (Macon) M
- Miami University M
- Michigan State University M
- Middle Tennessee State University M
- Midwestern State University M
- Millersville University of Pennsylvania M
- Monmouth University M,O
- Montana State University–Billings M
- Montclair State University M
- Moorhead State University M
- Morehead State University M
- Murray State University M
- National–Louis University M,D,O
- Nazareth College of Rochester M
- New Jersey City University M
- New Mexico State University O
- New York University M,D
- North Carolina Agricultural and Technical State University M
- Northeastern Illinois University M
- Northeastern State University M
- Northeastern University M
- Northeast Louisiana University M
- Northern Arizona University M
- Northern Illinois University M,D
- Northern State University M
- Northwestern Oklahoma State University M
- Northwestern State University of Louisiana M,O
- Northwest Missouri State University M
- Notre Dame College M
- Nova Southeastern University M,O
- Oakland University M,D,O
- Ohio University M,D
- Old Dominion University M
- Pacific Lutheran University M
- Pennsylvania State University University Park Campus M,D
- Pittsburg State University O
- Plattsburgh State University of New York M
- Plymouth State College of the University System of New Hampshire M
- Portland State University M
- Purdue University M,D,O
- Queens College of the City University of New York M
- Radford University M
- Rhode Island College M,O
- Rider University M
- Rivier College M
- Rockford College M
- Roosevelt University M
- Rowan University M
- Rutgers, The State University of New Jersey, New Brunswick M,D,O
- Sage Graduate School M
- Saginaw Valley State University M
- St. Bonaventure University M
- St. Cloud State University M
- St. John's University (NY) M,O
- Saint Joseph's University M
- Saint Martin's College M
- Saint Mary's College of California M
- St. Mary's University of San Antonio M
- Saint Michael's College M
- Saint Peter's College (Jersey City) M
- Saint Xavier University M
- Salem State College M
- Salisbury State University M
- Sam Houston State University M
- San Diego State University M
- San Francisco State University O
- Seattle Pacific University M
- Shippensburg University of Pennsylvania M
- Slippery Rock University of Pennsylvania M
- Sonoma State University M
- Southeastern Louisiana University M

Southern Arkansas University–Magnolia	M
Southern Connecticut State University	M,O
Southern Oregon University	M
Southwest Missouri State University	M
Southwest Texas State University	M
Spalding University	M
Spring Hill College	M
State University of New York at Albany	M,D,O
State University of New York at Binghamton	M
State University of New York at Buffalo	M,D
State University of New York at New Paltz	M
State University of New York at Oswego	M
State University of New York College at Brockport	M
State University of New York College at Buffalo	M
State University of New York College at Cortland	M
State University of New York College at Fredonia	M
State University of New York College at Geneseo	M
State University of New York College at Oneonta	M
State University of New York College at Potsdam	M
State University of West Georgia	M,O
Sul Ross State University	M
Syracuse University	M,D,O
Tarleton State University	O
Teachers College, Columbia University	M
Temple University (Philadelphia)	M,D
Tennessee State University	M
Tennessee Technological University	M,O
Texas A&M International University	M
Texas A&M University (College Station)	M,D
Texas A&M University–Commerce	M
Texas A&M University–Kingsville	M
Texas Southern University	M
Texas Tech University	M,D,O
Texas Woman's University	M,D
Towson University	M,O
Trinity College (DC)	M
Union College (KY)	M
The University of Arizona	M,D,O
University of Arkansas at Little Rock	M,O
University of Bridgeport	M,O
University of California, Berkeley	M,D,O
University of Central Arkansas	M
University of Central Florida	M
University of Central Oklahoma	M
University of Cincinnati	M,D
University of Connecticut	M,D
University of Florida	M,D,O
University of Georgia	M,D,O
University of Guam	M
University of Houston	M
University of Houston–Clear Lake	M
University of Illinois at Chicago	M
University of Kansas	M,D,O
University of La Verne	M
University of Louisville	M
University of Maine (Orono)	M,D,O
University of Mary Hardin–Baylor	M
University of Maryland, College Park	M,D,O
University of Massachusetts Amherst	M,D,O
University of Massachusetts Lowell	M,D,O
The University of Memphis	M,D
University of Miami	M,D,O
University of Michigan	M,D
University of Minnesota, Twin Cities Campus	M
University of Missouri–Kansas City	M,O
University of Nebraska at Kearney	M
University of Nebraska at Omaha	M
University of New Hampshire	M,D
University of North Alabama	M
The University of North Carolina at Chapel Hill	D
University of North Carolina at Charlotte	M
University of North Carolina at Pembroke	M
University of North Carolina at Wilmington	M
University of North Dakota	M
University of Northern Colorado	M
University of Northern Iowa	M
University of North Texas	M,D
University of Oklahoma	M,D
University of Pennsylvania	M,D
University of Pittsburgh	M,D
University of Rhode Island	M
University of Richmond	M
University of Saint Francis (IN)	M
University of Scranton	M
University of South Alabama	M
University of South Carolina (Columbia)	M,D
University of Southern California	D
University of Southern Maine	M,O
University of Southern Mississippi	M,O
University of South Florida	M,D,O
University of Tennessee at Chattanooga	M
University of Tennessee, Knoxville	M,D,O
The University of Texas at Brownsville	M
The University of Texas at Tyler	M,O
The University of Texas of the Permian Basin	M
The University of Texas–Pan American	M
University of the Incarnate Word	M
University of Vermont	M
University of West Florida	M
University of Wisconsin–Eau Claire	M
University of Wisconsin–La Crosse	M
University of Wisconsin–Milwaukee	M
University of Wisconsin–Oshkosh	M
University of Wisconsin–River Falls	M
University of Wisconsin–Stevens Point	M
University of Wisconsin–Superior	M
University of Wisconsin–Whitewater	M
Valdosta State University	M,O
Vanderbilt University	M,D
Virginia Commonwealth University	M
Walla Walla College	M
Washburn University of Topeka	M
Wayne State University	D,O
West Chester University of Pennsylvania	M
Western Carolina University	M
Western Connecticut State University	M
Western Illinois University	M
Western Kentucky University	M
Western Michigan University	M
Western New Mexico University	M
Western Oregon University	M
Western Washington University	M
Westfield State College	M
West Texas A&M University	M
West Virginia University	M
Whitworth College	M
William Paterson University of New Jersey	M
Winthrop University	M
Worcester State College	M,O
Xavier University	M
Youngstown State University	M

REAL ESTATE

American University	M
California State University, Northridge	M
California State University, Sacramento	M
Columbia University	M
Cornell University	M
The George Washington University	M
Georgia State University	M,D
Johns Hopkins University	M
Massachusetts Institute of Technology	M
New York University	M
Northwestern University	M
Pennsylvania State University University Park Campus	M,D
Temple University (Philadelphia)	M
University of Cincinnati	M
University of Denver	M
University of Florida	M,D
The University of Memphis	M
University of North Texas	M,D
University of Pennsylvania	M
University of St. Thomas (MN)	M
University of Southern California	M
The University of Texas at Arlington	M
University of Wisconsin–Madison	M,D
Virginia Commonwealth University	M,O
Webster University	M

RECREATION AND PARK MANAGEMENT

Adams State College	M
Arizona State University	M
Aurora University	M
Baylor University	M
Bowling Green State University	M
Brigham Young University	M
California State University, Chico	M
California State University, Long Beach	M
California State University, Northridge	M
California State University, Sacramento	M
Central Michigan University	M
Central Washington University	M
Clemson University	M,D
Cleveland State University	M
Colorado State University	M,D
Delta State University	M
Eastern Kentucky University	M
Florida Agricultural and Mechanical University	M
Florida International University	M
Florida State University	M
Fort Hays State University	M
Frostburg State University	M
Georgia Southern University	M
Hardin–Simmons University	M
Howard University	M
Indiana University Bloomington	M,D,O
Lehman College of the City University of New York	M
Michigan State University	M,D
Middle Tennessee State University	M,D
Morehead State University	M,D
New York University	M,D,O
North Carolina Central University	M
North Carolina State University	M
The Ohio State University	M,D
Old Dominion University	M
San Francisco State University	M
San Jose State University	M
Slippery Rock University of Pennsylvania	M
South Dakota State University	M
Southern Connecticut State University	M
Southern Illinois University at Carbondale	M
Southern Illinois University at Edwardsville	M
Southern University and Agricultural and Mechanical College	M
Southwestern Oklahoma State University	M
Springfield College (MA)	M
State University of New York College at Brockport	M
State University of New York College at Cortland	M
Temple University (Philadelphia)	M
Tennessee State University	M
Texas A&M University (College Station)	M,D
University of Arkansas (Fayetteville)	M
University of Florida	M,D
University of Georgia	M,D
University of Idaho	M
University of Maryland, College Park	M,D
University of Minnesota, Twin Cities Campus	M,D
University of Missouri–Columbia	M
The University of Montana–Missoula	M
University of Montevallo	M,O
University of Nebraska at Omaha	M
University of Nebraska–Lincoln	M
University of New Mexico	M,D,O
The University of North Carolina at Chapel Hill	M
University of North Carolina at Greensboro	M
University of North Texas	M,O
University of Rhode Island	M
University of South Alabama	M
University of Southern Mississippi	M,D
University of Tennessee, Knoxville	M
University of Toledo	M
University of Utah	M,D
University of Wisconsin–La Crosse	M
University of Wyoming	M
Utah State University	M,D
Virginia Commonwealth University	M
Virginia Polytechnic Institute and State University	M,D
Washington State University	M
Wayne State University	M
Western Illinois University	M
Western Kentucky University	M
West Virginia University	M
Wright State University	M

REHABILITATION COUNSELING

Appalachian State University	M
Arkansas State University	M
Assumption College	M,O
Barry University	M,O
Boston University	M,D,O
Bowling Green State University	M
California State University, Fresno	M
California State University, Los Angeles	M
California State University, San Bernardino	M
City University	M,O
Coppin State College	M
DePaul University	M,O
East Central University	M
Edinboro University of Pennsylvania	M
Emporia State University	M
Florida State University	M,D,O
Fort Valley State University	M
The George Washington University	M,D
Georgia State University	M,O
Hofstra University	M
Hunter College of the City University of New York	M
Illinois Institute of Technology	M
Indiana University–Purdue University Indianapolis	M,D
Jackson State University	M
Kent State University	M,O
La Salle University	D
Mankato State University	M
Michigan State University	M,D
Mississippi State University	M
Montana State University–Billings	M
New York University	M,D
Northeastern University	M
Ohio University	M
St. Cloud State University	M
St. John's University (NY)	M
San Diego State University	M
San Francisco State University	M
South Carolina State University	M
Southern Illinois University at Carbondale	M,D
Southern University and Agricultural and Mechanical College	M
Springfield College (MA)	M,O
State University of New York at Albany	M
State University of New York at Buffalo	M
Syracuse University	M,D
The University of Alabama at Birmingham	M
The University of Arizona	M,D,O
University of Arkansas (Fayetteville)	M,D
University of Cincinnati	M,O
University of Florida	M
University of Georgia	M
University of Illinois at Urbana–Champaign	M
The University of Iowa	M,D
University of Kentucky	M
University of Maryland, College Park	M
The University of Memphis	M
University of Nevada, Las Vegas	M
The University of North Carolina at Chapel Hill	M
University of Northern Colorado	M,D
University of North Texas	M
University of Puerto Rico, Río Piedras	M
University of Scranton	M
University of South Carolina (Columbia)	M
University of South Florida	M
University of Southwestern Louisiana	M
University of Tennessee, Knoxville	M
University of Wisconsin–Madison	M,D
University of Wisconsin–Milwaukee	M
University of Wisconsin–Stout	M
Villanova University	M
Virginia Commonwealth University	M,O
Wayne State University	M,O
Western Michigan University	M
Western Oregon University	M
West Virginia University	M
Wilmington College (DE)	M
Wright State University	M

REHABILITATION NURSING

Loyola University Chicago	M

P—first professional degree; M—master's degree; D—doctorate; O—other advanced degree.

REHABILITATION SCIENCES

East Carolina University	M
East Stroudsburg University of Pennsylvania	M
Northeastern Illinois University	M
State University of New York at Buffalo	D
University of Delaware	M
University of Florida	D
University of Illinois at Urbana–Champaign	M
University of Minnesota, Twin Cities Campus	M,D
University of North Texas	M
University of Pittsburgh	M,D,O
University of Washington	M
University of Wisconsin–La Crosse	M
University of Wisconsin–Madison	M
Wayne State University	M

RELIABILITY ENGINEERING

The University of Arizona	M
University of Maryland, College Park	M,D

RELIGION

Abilene Christian University	M
Arizona State University	M
Ashland University	M
Azusa Pacific University	M
Baylor University	M,D
Biola University	M
Boston University	M,D
Brown University	M,D
Cardinal Stritch University	M
The Catholic University of America	M,D,O
Chestnut Hill College	M
Claremont Graduate University	M,D
College of Mount St. Joseph	M
Colorado Christian University	M
Columbia University	M,D
Concordia University (IL)	M,O
Duke University	D
Edgewood College	M
Emory University	D
Florida International University	M
Florida State University	M,D
Fordham University	M,O
The George Washington University	M
Gonzaga University	P,M
Grand Rapids Baptist Seminary	M
Hardin–Simmons University	M
Harvard University	M,D
Holy Names College	M,O
Indiana State University	M
Indiana University Bloomington	M,D
John Carroll University	M
La Salle University	M
La Sierra University	M
Liberty University	M
Loyola University New Orleans	M
Miami University	M
Mount St. Mary's College	M
New York University	M,O
Northwestern University	M,D
Oklahoma City University	M
Olivet Nazarene University	M
Park College	M
Pepperdine University (Malibu)	P,M
Point Loma Nazarene University	M
Princeton University	D
Providence College	M
Rice University	M,D
Sacred Heart University	M
Saint Joseph College (CT)	M,O
Santa Clara University	M
Seton Hall University	M
Southern Methodist University	M,D
Southern Nazarene University	M
Southwest Missouri State University	M
Spalding University	M
Stanford University	M,D
Syracuse University	M,D
Temple University (Philadelphia)	M,D
Trevecca Nazarene University	M
University of California, Berkeley	D
University of California, Santa Barbara	M,D
University of Chicago	P,M,D
University of Colorado at Boulder	M
University of Denver	M,D
University of Detroit Mercy	M
University of Florida	M
University of Georgia	M
University of Hawaii at Manoa	M
The University of Iowa	M,D
University of Kansas	M
University of Missouri–Columbia	M
University of Mobile	M
The University of North Carolina at Chapel Hill	M,D
University of Pennsylvania	D
University of Pittsburgh	M,D
University of South Carolina (Columbia)	M
University of Southern California	M,D
University of South Florida	M
University of Tennessee, Knoxville	M
University of the Incarnate Word	M
University of Virginia	M,D
University of Washington	M
University of Wisconsin–Madison	D
Vanderbilt University	M,D
Villanova University	M
Wake Forest University	M
Washington University in St. Louis	M
Western Kentucky University	M
Western Michigan University	M,D
Yale University	D

RELIGIOUS EDUCATION

Abilene Christian University	M
Andrews University	M,D,O
Ashland University	M
Assumption College	M
Biola University	M,D
Boston College	M,D
Campbell University	M
Cardinal Stritch University	M
The Catholic University of America	M,D
College of Notre Dame	M
Fordham University	M,O
Grand Rapids Baptist Seminary	P,M,D
La Sierra University	M
Loyola University Chicago	M
Oklahoma City University	M
Oral Roberts University	M
Pfeiffer University	M
Providence College	M
Stanford University	D
Teachers College, Columbia University	M,D
University of Portland	M
University of St. Thomas (MN)	M
University of San Diego	M
University of San Francisco	O
Xavier University	M
Yeshiva University	M,D,O

REPRODUCTIVE BIOLOGY

Johns Hopkins University	M,D
Northwestern University	D
University of Hawaii at Manoa	D
University of Wyoming	M,D

ROMANCE LANGUAGES

Appalachian State University	M
The Catholic University of America	M,D
Clark Atlanta University	M
Columbia University	M,D
Cornell University	D
New York University	M,D
Southern Connecticut State University	M
State University of New York at Stony Brook	M
Syracuse University	M,D
Texas Tech University	M
The University of Alabama (Tuscaloosa)	M,D
University of California, Berkeley	D
University of California, Los Angeles	M,D,O
University of Georgia	M,D
University of Miami	D
University of Missouri–Columbia	M,D
University of Missouri–Kansas City	M
University of New Mexico	D
University of New Orleans	M
The University of North Carolina at Chapel Hill	M,D
University of Notre Dame	M
University of Oregon	M,D
University of Pennsylvania	M,D
University of Washington	M,D
Washington University in St. Louis	M,D

RURAL PLANNING AND STUDIES

California State University, Chico	M
Cornell University	M
Iowa State University of Science and Technology	D
Mississippi State University	D
State University of West Georgia	M
The University of Montana–Missoula	M
University of Wyoming	M

RURAL SOCIOLOGY

Auburn University	M,D
Cornell University	M,D
Iowa State University of Science and Technology	M,D
North Carolina State University	M
The Ohio State University	M,D
Pennsylvania State University University Park Campus	M,D
South Dakota State University	M,D
University of Missouri–Columbia	M,D
University of Tennessee, Knoxville	M,D
University of Wisconsin–Madison	M

RUSSIAN

American University	M,O
Boston College	M
Brigham Young University	M
Brown University	M,D
Columbia University	M,D
Cornell University	M,D
Harvard University	M,D
Michigan State University	M,D
New York University	M
Pennsylvania State University University Park Campus	M
San Francisco State University	M
Stanford University	M
State University of New York at Albany	M,O
State University of New York at Stony Brook	D
Syracuse University	M
The University of Arizona	M
University of California, Berkeley	M,D
University of Illinois at Urbana–Champaign	M,D
The University of Iowa	M
University of Maryland, College Park	M
The University of North Carolina at Chapel Hill	M,D
University of Oregon	M
University of Tennessee, Knoxville	D
University of Washington	M,D

SAFETY ENGINEERING

Murray State University	M
New Jersey Institute of Technology	M
Texas A&M University (College Station)	M
University of Wisconsin–Stout	M
West Virginia University	M

SCANDINAVIAN LANGUAGES

Brigham Young University	M
Harvard University	M,D
University of California, Berkeley	M,D
University of California, Los Angeles	M,D
University of Minnesota, Twin Cities Campus	M,D
University of Washington	M,D
University of Wisconsin–Madison	M,D

SCHOOL PSYCHOLOGY

Abilene Christian University	M
Alabama Agricultural and Mechanical University	M
Alfred University	M,D,O
American International College	M,O
Andrews University	O
Appalachian State University	M,O
Auburn University	M,D,O
Austin Peay State University	M
Ball State University	M,D,O
Barry University	M,O
Beaver College	M
Bowling Green State University	M
Brigham Young University	M
Brooklyn College of the City University of New York	M,O
Butler University	M,O
California State University, Los Angeles	M
California State University, Sacramento	M
California University of Pennsylvania	M
Central Michigan University	D,O
Central Washington University	M
The Citadel, The Military College of South Carolina	O
City College of the City University of New York	M,O
City University	M
College of New Rochelle	M
The College of Saint Rose	M,O
College of William and Mary	M,D
Duquesne University	M,O
East Carolina University	O
Eastern Illinois University	O
Eastern Kentucky University	O
Eastern Washington University	M
Edinboro University of Pennsylvania	O
Emporia State University	M,O
Fairfield University	M,O
Fairleigh Dickinson University, Teaneck–Hackensack Campus	M,D
Florida Agricultural and Mechanical University	M
Florida International University	O
Florida State University	M,O
Fordham University	D,O
Fort Hays State University	O
Francis Marion University	M
Fresno Pacific University	M
Gallaudet University	M,O
Gardner–Webb University	M
George Mason University	M
Georgia Southern University	M,O
Georgia State University	M,D,O
Hofstra University	M,D
Howard University	M,D,O
Idaho State University	M,O
Illinois State University	M,D,O
Immaculata College	O
Indiana State University	M,D,O
Indiana University Bloomington	O
Indiana University of Pennsylvania	D
Iowa State University of Science and Technology	O
James Madison University	M,O
Kean University	O
Kent State University	M,D,O
La Sierra University	O
Lehigh University	D,O
Lesley College	M
Long Island University, Brooklyn Campus	M
Louisiana State University and Agricultural and Mechanical College	M,D
Louisiana State University in Shreveport	O
Loyola Marymount University	M
Loyola University Chicago	M,D
Marist College	M,O
Marshall University	M,O
Miami University	M,O
Michigan State University	D,O
Middle Tennessee State University	O
Millersville University of Pennsylvania	M,O
Mississippi State University	D
Moorhead State University	M,O
National–Louis University	M,D,O
National University	M
New Jersey City University	O
New York University	D,O
Nicholls State University	M,O
Northeastern University	M,D,O
Northeast Louisiana University	M,O
Northern Arizona University	M
Northwestern State University of Louisiana	O
Pace University	M,D
Pennsylvania State University University Park Campus	M,D
Pittsburg State University	O
Plattsburgh State University of New York	O
Queens College of the City University of New York	M,O
Radford University	O
Rhode Island College	O
Rochester Institute of Technology	M,O
Rowan University	M,O
Rutgers, The State University of New Jersey, New Brunswick	M,D
St. John's University (NY)	M
Sam Houston State University	M
San Diego State University	M
Seattle University	O
Seton Hall University	O
Southern Connecticut State University	M,O
Southern Illinois University at Edwardsville	O
Southwest Texas State University	M
State University of New York at Albany	D,O
State University of New York at Buffalo	M
State University of New York at Oswego	M,O
Stephen F. Austin State University	M
Syracuse University	D
Teachers College, Columbia University	M,D
Temple University (Philadelphia)	M,D
Tennessee State University	M,D
Texas A&M University (College Station)	D
Texas Woman's University	M,D
Towson University	M,O
Trinity University	M
Troy State University Dothan	M

Tufts University	M,O
The University of Akron	M,D
The University of Alabama (Tuscaloosa)	M,D,O
The University of Alabama at Birmingham	M
University of California, Berkeley	D
University of California, Santa Barbara	M,D
University of Central Arkansas	M
University of Central Florida	O
University of Cincinnati	M,D
University of Connecticut	M,D
University of Dayton	M
University	
University	
University	
University	
University	
University	
University	
Lake	
University	
University	
University	
Park	
University	
Amherst	
University of Boston	
The Universi	
University of Cities Cam	
The Universi Missoula	
University of Kearney	
University of I	
University of I	
The University at Chapel H	
University of N Greensboro	
University of N	
University of N	
University of N	
University of O	
University of Pe	
University of Rh	
University of Sc (Columbia)	
University of So	
University of So	
University of Ter Chattanooga	
University of Ten Knoxville	
The University of American	
University of the I	
University of Tole	
University of Was	
University of Wisc Claire	
University of Wisc Crosse	
University of Wisc Falls	
University of Wisc	M
University of Wisconsin–Superior	M
University of Wisconsin–Whitewater	M
Valdosta State University	M,O
Valparaiso University	M
Virginia Polytechnic Institute and State University	D
Wayne State University	M
Western Carolina University	M
Western Illinois University	M,O
Western Kentucky University	O
Western Michigan University	D,O
Wichita State University	O
Yeshiva University	D

(handwritten note overlaid: P.O # 21899 Date 8/99 Vendor # 000748 Price: 23.94)

SCIENCE EDUCATION

Adelphi University	M
Alabama State University	M,O
Albany State University	M
Alfred University	M
Andrews University	M
Arkansas State University	M,O
Auburn University	M,D,O
Ball State University	M
Beaver College	M,O
Bemidji State University	M
Bloomsburg University of Pennsylvania	M
Boise State University	M
Boston College	M
Boston University	M,D,O
Bowling Green State University	M,D
Bridgewater State College	M
Brigham Young University	M
Brooklyn College of the City University of New York	M
Brown University	M

California State University, Fullerton	M
California State University, San Bernardino	M
California University of Pennsylvania	M
Carthage College	M
Central Michigan University	M
Charleston Southern University	M
The Citadel, The Military College of South Carolina	M
City College of the City University of New York	M
	M
	D
	M
	M
	M,O
	M
	M
	M
	M
	M
	M
	M
	M
	M
	M
La Roche College	
Lehman College of the City University of New York	M
Long Island University, C.W. Post Campus	M
Louisiana State University in Shreveport	M
Louisiana Tech University	M
Loyola Marymount University	M
Maryville University of Saint Louis	M
McNeese State University	M
Mercer University (Macon)	M
Michigan State University	M,D
Middle Tennessee State University	M
Minot State University	M
Mississippi College	M
Montana State University–Northern	M
Montclair State University	M
National–Louis University	M,O
New York University	M
Niagara University	M
North Carolina Agricultural and Technical State University	M
North Carolina State University	M,D
Northeastern University	M,D
Northern Arizona University	M
Northern Michigan University	M
North Georgia College & State University	M
Northwestern State University of Louisiana	M
Northwest Missouri State University	M
Nova Southeastern University	M,O
Oregon State University	M,D
Pennsylvania State University University Park Campus	M,D

Plattsburgh State University of New York	M
Plymouth State College of the University System of New Hampshire	M
Portland State University	M
Purdue University	M,D,O
Queens College of the City University of New York	M,O
Quinnipiac College	M
Rhode Island College	M
Rowan University	M
Rutgers, The State University of New Jersey, New Brunswick	M,D,O
Saginaw Valley State University	M
St. John Fisher College	M
Saint Joseph College (CT)	M
Saint Joseph's University	M
Salem State College	M,O
Salisbury State University	M
San Diego State University	D
Slippery Rock University of Pennsylvania	M
South Carolina State University	M
Southeast Missouri State University	M
Southern Arkansas University–Magnolia	M
Southern Connecticut State University	M,O
Southern Oregon University	M
Southwest Missouri State University	M
Stanford University	M
State University of New York at Binghamton	M
State University of New York at Buffalo	D
State University of New York at New Paltz	M
State University of New York at Stony Brook	M
State University of New York College at Brockport	M
State University of New York College at Buffalo	M
State University of New York College at Cortland	M
State University of New York College at Oneonta	M
Syracuse University	M,D,O
Teachers College, Columbia University	M,D
Temple University (Philadelphia)	M,D
Texas A&M University (College Station)	M,D
Texas Woman's University	M
Tuskegee University	M
Universidad Metropolitana	M
University of Alaska Fairbanks	M,D
University of California, Berkeley	M,D
University of California, Los Angeles	M
University of Central Florida	M
University of Connecticut	M,D
University of Florida	M,D,O
University of Georgia	M,D,O
University of Houston	M
University of Idaho	M
The University of Iowa	M,D
University of Maine (Orono)	M,O
University of Maryland, College Park	M,D,O
University of Massachusetts Lowell	D
University of Michigan	M,D
University of Minnesota, Twin Cities Campus	M,D
University of Missouri–Rolla	M
The University of Montana–Missoula	M
University of Nebraska at Kearney	M
University of New Orleans	M
The University of North Carolina at Chapel Hill	M
University of Northern Colorado	M,D
University of Northern Iowa	M,O
University of North Florida	M
University of Oklahoma	M,D
University of Pittsburgh	M,D
University of Puerto Rico, Río Piedras	M
University of South Alabama	M
University of South Carolina (Columbia)	M
University of Southern Mississippi	M,D
University of South Florida	M,D,O
University of Tennessee, Knoxville	M,D,O
The University of Texas at Austin	M,D
The University of Texas at Dallas	M
The University of Texas at Tyler	M,O
University of Tulsa	M
University of Utah	M
University of Vermont	M,D
University of Virginia	M

The University of West Alabama	M
University of West Florida	M
University of Wisconsin–Eau Claire	M
University of Wisconsin–Madison	M
University of Wisconsin–Oshkosh	M
University of Wisconsin–River Falls	M
University of Wyoming	M
Vanderbilt University	M,D
Wayne State College	M
Wayne State University	O
Webster University	M
Western Carolina University	M
Western Kentucky University	M
Western Michigan University	M,D
Western Oregon University	M
Western Washington University	M
Wheeling Jesuit University	M
Wilkes University	M
Wright State University	M

SECONDARY EDUCATION

Abilene Christian University	M
Adams State College	M
Adelphi University	M
Alabama Agricultural and Mechanical University	M,O
Alabama State University	M,O
Albany State University	M
Alcorn State University	M
Alfred University	M
American International College	M,O
American University	M
Andrews University	M
Appalachian State University	M
Arizona State University West	M
Arkansas State University	M,D,O
Armstrong Atlantic State University	M
Auburn University	M,D,O
Auburn University Montgomery	M,O
Augusta State University	M,O
Austin Peay State University	O
Ball State University	M
Beaver College	M,O
Boston College	M
Bowie State University	M
Bowling Green State University	M
Bridgewater State College	M
Brooklyn College of the City University of New York	M
Brown University	M
Butler University	M
California State University, Long Beach	M
California State University, Los Angeles	M
California State University, Northridge	M
California State University, San Bernardino	M
California State University, Stanislaus	M
Campbell University	M
Canisius College	M
Central Connecticut State University	M
Central Michigan University	M
Central Missouri State University	M
Chadron State College	M
Charleston Southern University	M
Chicago State University	M
The Citadel, The Military College of South Carolina	M
City College of the City University of New York	M
Clemson University	M
Cleveland State University	M
The College of New Jersey	M
College of Notre Dame	M,O
The College of Saint Rose	M
College of Staten Island of the City University of New York	M
Columbus State University	M,O
Converse College	M
Cumberland College	M,O
DePaul University	M
Dowling College	M
Drake University	M
Drury College	M
Duquesne University	M
D'Youville College	M
Eastern Kentucky University	M
Eastern Michigan University	M
Eastern Nazarene College	M,O
East Stroudsburg University of Pennsylvania	M
East Tennessee State University	M
Edinboro University of Pennsylvania	M
Elmira College	M
Emory University	M
Emporia State University	M
Fayetteville State University	M
Fitchburg State College	M

P—first professional degree; M—master's degree; D—doctorate; O—other advanced degree.

Secondary Education (continued)

Florida Agricultural and Mechanical University	M
Fordham University	M
Fort Hays State University	M
Francis Marion University	M
Friends University	M
Frostburg State University	M
Gallaudet University	M,O
Gannon University	M
George Mason University	M
The George Washington University	M
Georgia College and State University	M,O
Georgia Southwestern State University	M
Harding University	M
Hardin–Simmons University	M
Harvard University	D
Henderson State University	M
Hofstra University	M
Hood College	M
Houston Baptist University	M
Howard University	M,O
Hunter College of the City University of New York	M
Indiana State University	M,D,O
Indiana University Bloomington	M,O
Indiana University Northwest	M
Indiana University–Purdue University Fort Wayne	M
Indiana University–Purdue University Indianapolis	M
Indiana University South Bend	M
Indiana University Southeast	M
Iona College (New Rochelle)	M
Iowa State University of Science and Technology	M
Jackson State University	M,O
Jacksonville State University	M
Jacksonville University	O
James Madison University	M
John Carroll University	M
Johns Hopkins University	M
Kansas State University	M
Kent State University	M
Kutztown University of Pennsylvania	M
Lamar University	M,O
Lehigh University	M,O
Liberty University	M
Lincoln University (MO)	M
Long Island University, C.W. Post Campus	M
Louisiana State University and Agricultural and Mechanical College	M
Louisiana Tech University	M
Loyola Marymount University	M
Loyola University New Orleans	M
Lynchburg College	M
Maharishi University of Management	M
Mankato State University	M,O
Mansfield University of Pennsylvania	M
Marshall University	M
Marymount University	M
Maryville University of Saint Louis	M
McNeese State University	M
Miami University	M
Middle Tennessee State University	M,O
Midwestern State University	M
Mississippi College	M
Mississippi State University	M,D,O
Montana State University–Billings	M
Morehead State University	M
Mount Saint Mary College	M
Mount St. Mary's College	M
Murray State University	M,O
National-Louis University	M
Nazareth College of Rochester	M
New School University	M
Niagara University	M
Norfolk State University	M
Northeastern State University	M
Northeast Louisiana University	M,O
Northern Arizona University	M
Northern Kentucky University	M
Northern Michigan University	M
Northern State University	M
North Georgia College & State University	M
Northwestern Oklahoma State University	M
Northwestern State University of Louisiana	M,O
Northwestern University	M
Northwest Missouri State University	M
Notre Dame College	M
Ohio University	M
Oklahoma City University	M
Old Dominion University	M
Olivet Nazarene University	M
Pacific Lutheran University	M
Pacific University	M
Phillips University	M
Pittsburg State University	M,O
Plattsburgh State University of New York	M
Plymouth State College of the University System of New Hampshire	M
Portland State University	M
Purdue University Calumet	M
Queens College of the City University of New York	M,O
Quinnipiac College	M
Rhode Island College	M
Rivier College	M
Rochester Institute of Technology	M
Rockford College	M
Rollins College	M
Roosevelt University	M
Rowan University	M
Sacred Heart University	M
Sage Graduate School	M,O
Saginaw Valley State University	M
St. Bonaventure University	M
St. Cloud State University	M
St. John's University (NY)	M
Saint Joseph College (CT)	M
Saint Joseph's University	M
Salisbury State University	M
Sam Houston State University	M,O
San Diego State University	M
San Francisco State University	M,O
San Jose State University	M
Seattle Pacific University	M
Seton Hall University	M,O
Simmons College	M
Slippery Rock University of Pennsylvania	M
South Carolina State University	M
Southeastern Louisiana University	M
Southeastern Oklahoma State University	M
Southeast Missouri State University	M
Southern Connecticut State University	M
Southern Illinois University at Edwardsville	M
Southern Oregon University	M
Southern University and Agricultural and Mechanical College	M
Southern Utah University	M
Southwestern Oklahoma State University	M
Southwest Missouri State University	M
Southwest Texas State University	M
Springfield College (MA)	M
State University of New York at Albany	M
State University of New York at Binghamton	M
State University of New York at Buffalo	M,D
State University of New York at New Paltz	M
State University of New York at Oswego	M
State University of New York College at Brockport	M
State University of New York College at Cortland	M
State University of New York College at Fredonia	M
State University of New York College at Geneseo	M
State University of New York College at Oneonta	M
State University of New York College at Potsdam	M
State University of West Georgia	M,O
Stephen F. Austin State University	M,D
Suffolk University	M
Sul Ross State University	M
Tarleton State University	M,O
Temple University (Philadelphia)	M,O
Tennessee State University	M,D
Tennessee Technological University	M,O
Texas A&M International University	M
Texas A&M University–Commerce	M,D
Texas A&M University–Corpus Christi	M
Texas A&M University–Kingsville	M
Texas A&M University–Texarkana	M
Texas Christian University	M
Texas Southern University	M
Texas Tech University	M,D,O
Towson University	M,O
Trinity College (DC)	M
Troy State University (Troy)	M,O
Troy State University Dothan	M
Tufts University	M
Union College (KY)	M
The University of Akron	M,D
The University of Alabama (Tuscaloosa)	M,D,O
The University of Alabama at Birmingham	M,O
University of Alaska Southeast	M
The University of Arizona	M,D,O
University of Arkansas (Fayetteville)	M
University of Arkansas at Little Rock	M
University of Bridgeport	M,O
University of Central Arkansas	M
University of Central Florida	M
University of Central Oklahoma	M
University of Cincinnati	M
University of Connecticut	M,D
University of Delaware	M
University of Florida	M,D,O
University of Georgia	M,D,O
University of Guam	M
University of Hartford	M
University of Hawaii at Manoa	M
University of Houston	M
University of Houston–Clear Lake	M
University of Idaho	M
University of Illinois at Chicago	M
University of Indianapolis	M
The University of Iowa	M,D,O
University of Louisville	M,O
University of Maine (Orono)	M,O
University of Mary	M
University of Maryland, College Park	M,D,O
University of Massachusetts Amherst	M,D,O
University of Massachusetts Boston	M
The University of Memphis	M
University of Mississippi	M
University of Missouri–Kansas City	M
University of Missouri–St. Louis	M
University of Montevallo	M,O
University of Nebraska at Omaha	M
University of Nevada, Las Vegas	M
University of Nevada, Reno	M
University of New Hampshire	M
University of New Mexico	M
University of North Alabama	M
The University of North Carolina at Chapel Hill	M
University of North Carolina at Charlotte	M
University of North Carolina at Greensboro	M
University of North Dakota	D
University of North Florida	M
University of North Texas	M
University of Oklahoma	M,D
University of Pennsylvania	M
University of Pittsburgh	M,D
University of Portland	M
University of Puerto Rico, Río Piedras	M
University of Rhode Island	M
University of Richmond	M
University of Scranton	M
University of South Alabama	M,O
University of South Carolina (Columbia)	M,D
University of South Dakota	M
University of Southern Indiana	M
University of Southern Mississippi	M,D,O
University of South Florida	D
University of Tennessee at Chattanooga	M
The University of Texas at Tyler	M,O
The University of Texas of the Permian Basin	M
The University of Texas–Pan American	M
University of the Incarnate Word	M
University of Toledo	M
University of Utah	M
The University of West Alabama	M
University of Wisconsin–Eau Claire	M
University of Wisconsin–La Crosse	M
University of Wisconsin–Milwaukee	M
University of Wisconsin–Platteville	M
Utah State University	M
Valdosta State University	M,D,O
Vanderbilt University	M
Villanova University	M
Virginia Commonwealth University	M,O
Wagner College	M
Wake Forest University	M
Washington State University	M,D
Washington University in St. Louis	M
Wayne State University	M
West Chester University of Pennsylvania	M
Western Carolina University	M
Western Connecticut State University	M
Western Kentucky University	M,O
Western New Mexico University	M
Western Oregon University	M
Western Washington University	M
Westfield State College	M
West Texas A&M University	M
West Virginia University	M
Wilkes University	M
William Carey College	M
Winthrop University	M,O
Worcester State College	M,O
Wright State University	M
Xavier University	M
Youngstown State University	M

SLAVIC LANGUAGES

Boston College	M
Brown University	M,D
Columbia University	M,D
Cornell University	M,D
Duke University	M,D
Florida State University	M
Harvard University	M,D
Indiana University Bloomington	M,D
New York University	M
Northwestern University	D
The Ohio State University	M,D,O
Princeton University	D
Stanford University	M,D
State University of New York at Stony Brook	M
Syracuse University	M
University of California, Berkeley	M,D
University of California, Los Angeles	M,D,O
University of Chicago	M,D
University of Illinois at Chicago	M,D
University of Illinois at Urbana–Champaign	M,D
University of Kansas	M,D
University of Michigan	D
The University of North Carolina at Chapel Hill	M,D
University of Pittsburgh	M,D
University of Southern California	M,D
The University of Texas at Austin	M,D
University of Virginia	M,D
University of Washington	M,D
University of Wisconsin–Madison	M,D
University of Wisconsin–Milwaukee	M
Yale University	M,D

SOCIAL PSYCHOLOGY

American University	M
Arizona State University	D
Auburn University	M,D,O
Ball State University	M
Beaver College	M
Brandeis University	D
Brooklyn College of the City University of New York	M
California State University, Fullerton	M
Carnegie Mellon University	D
Claremont Graduate University	M,D
College of New Rochelle	M
Columbia University	M,D
Cornell University	M,D
DePaul University	M,D
Fairleigh Dickinson University, Florham–Madison Campus	M
Florida Agricultural and Mechanical University	M
Francis Marion University	M
The George Washington University	M,D
Georgia State University	D
Graduate School and University Center of the City University of New York	D
Harvard University	M,D
Henderson State University	M
Hofstra University	M,D
Howard University	D
Indiana State University	M
Indiana University Bloomington	D
Lesley College	M
Loyola University Chicago	M,D
Mansfield University of Pennsylvania	M
Marist College	M
Miami University	D
New York University	D
Norfolk State University	M
Northwestern State University of Louisiana	M
Northwestern University	D

The Ohio State University D
Pace University M,D
Pennsylvania State University Harrisburg Campus of the Capital College M
Pennsylvania State University University Park Campus M,D
Rutgers, The State University of New Jersey, Newark D
Rutgers, The State University of New Jersey, New Brunswick D
Sage Graduate School M
Saint Martin's College M
State University of New York at Albany D
State University of New York at Buffalo D
State University of New York at Stony Brook D
Syracuse University D
Teachers College, Columbia University M,D
Temple University (Philadelphia) D
University of Alaska Fairbanks M
University of California, Santa Cruz D
University of Central Arkansas M
University of Central Oklahoma M
University of Cincinnati D
University of Connecticut D
University of Delaware D
University of Houston D
University of Illinois at Urbana–Champaign M,D
University of Kansas D
University of Maine (Orono) M
University of Maryland, College Park D
University of Massachusetts Lowell M
University of Michigan D
University of Minnesota, Twin Cities Campus D
University of Missouri–Kansas City D
University of Nevada, Reno D
University of New Haven M,O
The University of North Carolina at Chapel Hill M,D
University of North Carolina at Charlotte M
University of Notre Dame D
University of Oregon M,D
University of Pennsylvania D
University of Pittsburgh D
University of Rochester D
University of Scranton M
University of South Carolina (Columbia) D
University of Tennessee, Knoxville M
University of Wisconsin–Madison D
Washington University in St. Louis M,D
Wayne State University D
Western Illinois University M
Wichita State University D
Wilmington College (DE) M

SOCIAL SCIENCES

Alabama State University M
Appalachian State University M
Arkansas State University M,O
Ball State University M
California Institute of Technology M,D
California State University, Chico M
California State University, Fullerton M
California State University, Sacramento M
California State University, San Bernardino M
California University of Pennsylvania M
Carnegie Mellon University M,D
Central Connecticut State University M
Claremont Graduate University M,D
Eastern Michigan University M
Edinboro University of Pennsylvania M
Florida Agricultural and Mechanical University M
Florida State University M
Gannon University M
George Mason University D
Henderson State University M
Humboldt State University M
Long Island University, Brooklyn Campus M,O
Mankato State University M
Massachusetts Institute of Technology D
Michigan State University M,D
Mississippi College M
Montclair State University M
New School University M,D
Ohio University M
Oklahoma City University M
Pittsburg State University M
Queens College of the City University of New York M
San Francisco State University M
San Jose State University M
Simmons College M
Southern Oregon University M
State University of New York at Binghamton M
State University of New York at Buffalo M
State University of New York at Stony Brook M
State University of New York College at Fredonia M
Syracuse University M,D
Troy State University Dothan M
University of California, Irvine M,D
University of California, Santa Cruz D
University of Chicago M,D
University of Colorado at Denver M
University of Northern Colorado M
The University of Texas at Brownsville M
The University of Texas at Tyler M

SOCIAL SCIENCES EDUCATION

Adelphi University M
Alabama State University M
Alfred University M
American International College M
Andrews University M
Arkansas Tech University M
Auburn University M,D,O
Beaver College M
Boston College M
Boston University M,D,O
Brooklyn College of the City University of New York M
Brown University M
California State University, San Bernardino M
California State University, Stanislaus M
Campbell University M
Carthage College M
Central Missouri State University M
Chadron State College M
Chaminade University of Honolulu M
Charleston Southern University M
The Citadel, The Military College of South Carolina M
City College of the City University of New York M
Claremont Graduate University M,D
Clemson University M
College of Notre Dame M
Columbus State University M,O
Delta State University M
DePaul University M
East Carolina University M
Eastern Kentucky University M
Eastern Washington University M
Edinboro University of Pennsylvania M
Emporia State University M
Fairleigh Dickinson University, Teaneck–Hackensack Campus M
Fayetteville State University M
Fitchburg State College M
Florida International University M
Florida State University M,D,O
Framingham State College M
Georgia Southern University M,O
Georgia State University M,D,O
Gonzaga University M
Grambling State University M
Grand Valley State University M
Hardin–Simmons University M
Henderson State University M
Hunter College of the City University of New York M
Indiana University Bloomington M
Iona College (New Rochelle) M
Kutztown University of Pennsylvania M
Lehman College of the City University of New York M
Long Island University, C.W. Post Campus M
Longwood College M
Louisiana Tech University M
Loyola Marymount University M
Mankato State University M
Marshall University M
McNeese State University M
Mercer University (Macon) M
Michigan State University M
Montclair State University M
New York University M,D
North Carolina Agricultural and Technical State University M
North Georgia College & State University M
Northwestern State University of Louisiana M
Northwest Missouri State University M
Nova Southeastern University M,O
Ohio University M,D
Pennsylvania State University University Park Campus M,D
Plattsburgh State University of New York M
Plymouth State College of the University System of New Hampshire M
Portland State University M
Princeton University D
Purdue University M,D,O
Queens College of the City University of New York M,O
Quinnipiac College M
Rockford College M
Rutgers, The State University of New Jersey, New Brunswick M,D,O
Salem State College M
Salisbury State University M
South Carolina State University M
Southwest Texas State University M,D
Stanford University M,D
State University of New York at Binghamton M
State University of New York at Stony Brook M
State University of New York College at Brockport M
State University of New York College at Buffalo M
State University of New York College at Cortland M
State University of New York College at Oneonta M
Syracuse University M,O
Teachers College, Columbia University M,D
Texas A&M University–Commerce M
University of Central Florida M
University of Connecticut M,D
University of Denver M
University of Florida M,D,O
University of Georgia M,D,O
University of Houston M
University of Idaho M
University of Indianapolis M
University of Maine (Orono) M,O
University of Michigan M
University of Minnesota, Twin Cities Campus M,D
University of Nebraska at Kearney M
The University of North Carolina at Chapel Hill M
University of Oklahoma M,D
University of Pittsburgh M,D
University of Puerto Rico, Río Piedras M
University of South Carolina (Columbia) M
University of South Florida M
University of Tennessee, Knoxville M,D,O
The University of Texas at Tyler M,O
University of Vermont M
The University of West Alabama M
University of Wisconsin–Eau Claire M
University of Wisconsin–Madison M
University of Wisconsin–River Falls M
Vanderbilt University M,D
Wayne State College M
Wayne State University O
Webster University M
Western Carolina University M
Western Kentucky University M
Western Oregon University M
Wilkes University M
Worcester State College M

SOCIAL WORK

Adelphi University M,D,O
Alabama Agricultural and Mechanical University M
Andrews University M
Arizona State University M,D
Aurora University M
Barry University M,D
Baylor University M
Boise State University M
Boston College M,D
Boston University M,D
Brigham Young University M
California State University, Bakersfield M
California State University, Fresno M
California State University, Long Beach M
California State University, Los Angeles M
California State University, Sacramento M
California State University, San Bernardino M
California State University, Stanislaus M
California University of Pennsylvania M
Case Western Reserve University M,D,O
The Catholic University of America M,D
Central Michigan University M
Clark Atlanta University M,D
Cleveland State University M
College of St. Catherine M
Colorado State University M
Columbia University M,D
Delaware State University M
Delta State University M
East Carolina University M
Eastern Michigan University M
Eastern Washington University M
Florida International University M,D
Florida State University M,D
Fordham University M,D
Gallaudet University M
Governors State University M
Graduate School and University Center of the City University of New York D
Grambling State University M
Grand Valley State University M
Howard University M,D
Hunter College of the City University of New York M,D
Indiana University Northwest M
Indiana University–Purdue University Indianapolis M,D
Indiana University South Bend M
Inter American University of Puerto Rico, Metropolitan Campus M
Jackson State University M,D
Kean University M
Loma Linda University M
Louisiana State University and Agricultural and Mechanical College M,D
Loyola University Chicago M,D
Marywood University M
Michigan State University M,D
New Mexico Highlands University M
New Mexico State University M
New York University M,D
Norfolk State University M,D
North Carolina Agricultural and Technical State University M
The Ohio State University M,D
Our Lady of the Lake University of San Antonio M
Pontifical Catholic University of Puerto Rico M
Portland State University M,D
Radford University M
Rhode Island College M
Rutgers, The State University of New Jersey, New Brunswick M,D
St. Ambrose University M
Saint Louis University M
Salem State College M
San Diego State University M
San Francisco State University M
San Jose State University M
Simmons College M,D
Southern Connecticut State University M
Southern Illinois University at Carbondale M
Southern Illinois University at Edwardsville M
Southern University at New Orleans M
Southwest Missouri State University M
Southwest Texas State University M
Spalding University M
Springfield College (MA) M
State University of New York at Albany M,D
State University of New York at Buffalo M,D
State University of New York at Stony Brook M,D
Stephen F. Austin State University M
Syracuse University M
Temple University (Philadelphia) M
Tulane University M,D,O
The University of Akron M
The University of Alabama (Tuscaloosa) M,D
University of Alaska Anchorage M

P—first professional degree; M—master's degree; D—doctorate; O—other advanced degree.

Social Work (continued)

University of Arkansas at Little Rock	M
University of California, Berkeley	M,D
University of California, Los Angeles	M,D
University of Central Florida	M
University of Chicago	M,D
University of Cincinnati	M
University of Connecticut	M
University of Dayton	M
University of Denver	M,D
University of Georgia	M,D
University of Hawaii at Manoa	M,D
University of Houston	M,D
University of Illinois at Chicago	M,D
University of Illinois at Urbana–Champaign	M,D
The University of Iowa	M,D
University of Kansas	M,D
University of Kentucky	M,D
University of Louisville	M,D
University of Maine (Orono)	M
University of Michigan	M,D
University of Minnesota, Duluth	M
University of Minnesota, Twin Cities Campus	M,D
University of Missouri–Columbia	M
University of Missouri–St. Louis	O
University of Nebraska at Omaha	M
University of Nevada, Las Vegas	M
University of Nevada, Reno	M
University of New England	M
University of New Hampshire	M
The University of North Carolina at Chapel Hill	M,O
University of North Carolina at Greensboro	M
University of North Dakota	M
University of Oklahoma	M
University of Pennsylvania	M,D
University of Pittsburgh	M,D
University of Puerto Rico, Río Piedras	M
University of St. Thomas (MN)	M
University of South Carolina (Columbia)	M,D
University of Southern California	M,D
University of Southern Indiana	M
University of Southern Mississippi	M
University of South Florida	M
University of Tennessee, Knoxville	M,D
The University of Texas at Arlington	M,D
The University of Texas at Austin	M,D
The University of Texas–Pan American	M
University of Utah	M,D
University of Vermont	M
University of Washington	M,D
University of Wisconsin–La Crosse	M
University of Wisconsin–Madison	M,D
University of Wisconsin–Milwaukee	M
University of Wyoming	M
Valdosta State University	M
Virginia Commonwealth University	M,D
Walla Walla College	M
Washington University in St. Louis	M,D
Wayne State University	M,O
West Chester University of Pennsylvania	M
Western Michigan University	M
West Virginia University	M
Widener University	M
Yeshiva University	M,D

SOCIOLOGY

Alabama State University	M
American University	M,D
Arizona State University	M,D
Arkansas State University	M,O
Auburn University	M
Ball State University	M
Baylor University	M,D
Boston College	M,D
Boston University	M,D
Bowling Green State University	M,D
Brandeis University	M,D
Brigham Young University	M,D
Brooklyn College of the City University of New York	M
Brown University	M,D
California State University, Bakersfield	M
California State University, Dominguez Hills	M,O
California State University, Fullerton	M
California State University, Hayward	M

California State University, Los Angeles	M
California State University, Northridge	M
California State University, Sacramento	M
California State University, San Marcos	M
Case Western Reserve University	D
The Catholic University of America	M,D
Central Michigan University	M
Central Missouri State University	M
City College of the City University of New York	M
Clark Atlanta University	M
Clemson University	M
Cleveland State University	M
Colorado State University	M,D
Columbia University	M,D
Cornell University	M,D
DePaul University	M
Duke University	M,D
East Carolina University	M
Eastern Michigan University	M
East Tennessee State University	M
Emory University	M,D
Fayetteville State University	M
Florida Atlantic University	M
Florida International University	M,D
Florida State University	M,D
Fordham University	M,D
George Mason University	M
The George Washington University	M
Georgia Southern University	M
Georgia Southwestern State University	M
Georgia State University	M,D
Graduate School and University Center of the City University of New York	D
Harvard University	M,D
Howard University	M,D
Humboldt State University	M
Hunter College of the City University of New York	M
Idaho State University	M
Illinois State University	M
Indiana State University	M
Indiana University Bloomington	M,D
Indiana University of Pennsylvania	M,D
Indiana University–Purdue University Fort Wayne	M
Iowa State University of Science and Technology	M,D
Jackson State University	M
Johns Hopkins University	M,D
Kansas State University	M,D
Kent State University	M,D
Lehigh University	M
Lincoln University (MO)	M
Long Island University, Brooklyn Campus	M
Louisiana State University and Agricultural and Mechanical College	M,D
Loyola University Chicago	M,D
Mankato State University	M
Marshall University	M
Michigan State University	M,D
Middle Tennessee State University	M
Mississippi College	M
Mississippi State University	M,D
Montclair State University	M
Morehead State University	M
Morgan State University	M
New Mexico State University	M
New School University	M,D
New York University	M,D
Norfolk State University	M
North Carolina Central University	M
North Carolina State University	M,D
North Dakota State University	M
Northeastern University	M,D
Northern Arizona University	M
Northern Illinois University	M
Northwestern University	D
The Ohio State University	M,D
Ohio University	M
Oklahoma State University	M,D
Old Dominion University	M
Our Lady of the Lake University of San Antonio	M
Pennsylvania State University University Park Campus	M,D
Portland State University	M,D
Prairie View A&M University	M
Princeton University	D
Purdue University	M,D
Queens College of the City University of New York	M
Roosevelt University	M
Rutgers, The State University of New Jersey, New Brunswick	M,D

St. John's University (NY)	M
Sam Houston State University	M
San Diego State University	M
Southern Connecticut State University	M
Southern Illinois University at Carbondale	M,D
Southern Illinois University at Edwardsville	M
Southern University and Agricultural and Mechanical College	M
Southwest Texas State University	M
Stanford University	D
State University of New York at Albany	M,D,O
State University of New York at Binghamton	M,D
State University of New York at Buffalo	M,D
State University of New York at New Paltz	M
State University of New York at Stony Brook	M,D
State University of West Georgia	M
Syracuse University	M,D
Teachers College, Columbia University	M,D
Temple University (Philadelphia)	M,D
Texas A&M International University	M
Texas A&M University (College Station)	M,D
Texas A&M University–Commerce	M
Texas A&M University–Kingsville	M
Texas Southern University	M
Texas Tech University	M
Texas Woman's University	M,D
Tulane University	M,D
The University of Akron	M,D
The University of Alabama at Birmingham	M,D
The University of Arizona	M,D
University of Arkansas (Fayetteville)	M
University of California, Berkeley	D
University of California, Davis	M,D
University of California, Irvine	M,D
University of California, Los Angeles	M,D,O
University of California, Riverside	M,D
University of California, San Diego	D
University of California, San Francisco	D
University of California, Santa Barbara	D
University of California, Santa Cruz	D
University of Central Florida	M
University of Chicago	M,D
University of Cincinnati	M,D
University of Colorado at Boulder	M,D
University of Colorado at Colorado Springs	M
University of Colorado at Denver	M
University of Connecticut	M,D
University of Delaware	M,D
University of Denver	M,D
University of Florida	M,D
University of Georgia	M,D
University of Hawaii at Manoa	M,D
University of Houston	M
University of Houston–Clear Lake	M
University of Illinois at Chicago	M,D
University of Illinois at Urbana–Champaign	M,D
University of Indianapolis	M
The University of Iowa	M,D
University of Kansas	M,D
University of Kentucky	M,D
University of Louisville	M
University of Maryland, Baltimore County	M
University of Maryland, College Park	M,D
University of Massachusetts Amherst	M,D
University of Massachusetts Boston	M
The University of Memphis	M
University of Miami	M,D
University of Michigan	M,D
University of Minnesota, Duluth	M
University of Minnesota, Twin Cities Campus	M,D
University of Mississippi	M
University of Missouri–Columbia	M,D
University of Missouri–Kansas City	M,D
University of Missouri–St. Louis	M
The University of Montana–Missoula	M
University of Nebraska at Omaha	M
University of Nebraska–Lincoln	M,D
University of Nevada, Las Vegas	M,D

University of Nevada, Reno	M
University of New Hampshire	M,D
University of New Mexico	M,D
University of New Orleans	M
The University of North Carolina at Chapel Hill	M,D
University of North Carolina at Charlotte	M
University of North Carolina at Greensboro	M
University of North Dakota	M
University of Northern Iowa	M
University of North Texas	M,D
University of Notre Dame	M,D
University of Oklahoma	M,D
University of Oregon	M,D
University of Pennsylvania	M,D
University of Pittsburgh	M,D
University of Puerto Rico, Río Piedras	M
University of South Alabama	M
University of South Carolina (Columbia)	M,D
University of South Dakota	M
University of Southern California	M,D
University of South Florida	M
University of Tennessee, Knoxville	M,D
The University of Texas at Arlington	M
The University of Texas at Austin	M,D
The University of Texas at El Paso	M
The University of Texas at San Antonio	M
The University of Texas–Pan American	M
University of the Pacific	M
University of Toledo	M
University of Utah	M,D
University of Virginia	M,D
University of Washington	M,D
University of Wisconsin–Madison	M,D
University of Wisconsin–Milwaukee	M
University of Wyoming	M
Utah State University	M,D
Vanderbilt University	M,D
Virginia Commonwealth University	M,O
Virginia Polytechnic Institute and State University	M,D
Washington State University	M,D
Wayne State University	M,D
Western Illinois University	M
Western Kentucky University	M
Western Michigan University	M,D
Western Washington University	M
West Virginia University	M
Wichita State University	M
William Paterson University of New Jersey	M
Yale University	D

SOFTWARE ENGINEERING

Azusa Pacific University	M,O
California State University, Sacramento	M
Carnegie Mellon University	M
Central Michigan University	M,O
DePaul University	M
Drexel University	M
Embry–Riddle Aeronautical University (FL)	M
Gannon University	M
George Mason University	M
Grand Valley State University	M
Kansas State University	M
Mercer University (Macon)	M
Mercer University, Cecil B. Day Campus	M
Monmouth University	M
National University	M
Oakland University	M
Rochester Institute of Technology	M,O
San Jose State University	M
Santa Clara University	O
Seattle University	M
Southern Methodist University	M
State University of New York at Stony Brook	O
Texas Christian University	M
University of Connecticut	M,D
University of Houston–Clear Lake	M
University of Maryland, College Park	M
University of Maryland University College	M
University of Minnesota, Twin Cities Campus	M
University of Missouri–Kansas City	M
University of New Haven	M
University of St. Thomas (MN)	M,O
University of Scranton	M
University of Southern California	M

The University of Texas at Arlington — M,D
Wayne State University — M
West Virginia University — M
Widener University — M

SPANISH

American University — M,O
Arizona State University — M,D
Auburn University — M
Baylor University — M
Boston College — M,D
Boston University — M,D
Bowling Green State University — M
Brigham Young University — M
Brooklyn College of the City University of New York — M
California State University, Fresno — M
California State University, Fullerton — M
California State University, Long Beach — M
California State University, Los Angeles — M
California State University, Northridge — M
California State University, Sacramento — M
The Catholic University of America — M,D
Central Connecticut State University — M
City College of the City University of New York — M
Cleveland State University — M
Colorado State University — M
Columbia University — M,D
Duke University — D
Eastern Michigan University — M
Emory University — M,D,O
Florida Atlantic University — M
Florida International University — M,D
Florida State University — M,D
Georgetown University — M,D
Georgia State University — M,O
Graduate School and University Center of the City University of New York — D
Harvard University — M,D
Howard University — M
Hunter College of the City University of New York — M
Illinois State University — M
Indiana State University — M
Indiana University Bloomington — M,D
Inter American University of Puerto Rico, Metropolitan Campus — M
Iona College (New Rochelle) — M
Johns Hopkins University — M,D
Kansas State University — M
Kent State University — M
Lehman College of the City University of New York — M
Long Island University, C.W. Post Campus — M
Louisiana State University and Agricultural and Mechanical College — M
Loyola University Chicago — M
Mankato State University — M
Marquette University — M
Miami University — M
Michigan State University — M,D
Millersville University of Pennsylvania — M
Mississippi State University — M
Montclair State University — M
New Mexico Highlands University — M
New Mexico State University — M
New York University — M,D
Northern Illinois University — M
The Ohio State University — M,D
Ohio University — M
Pennsylvania State University University Park Campus — M,D
Portland State University — M
Princeton University — D
Purdue University — M,D
Queens College of the City University of New York — M
Rice University — M
Roosevelt University — M
Rutgers, The State University of New Jersey, New Brunswick — M,D
St. John's University (NY) — M
Saint Louis University — M
San Diego State University — M
San Francisco State University — M
San Jose State University — M
Seton Hall University — M
Simmons College — M
Southern Connecticut State University — M
Southwest Texas State University — M
Stanford University — M,D

State University of New York at Albany — M,D
State University of New York at Binghamton — M,O
State University of New York at Buffalo — M,D
State University of New York at Stony Brook — M,D
Syracuse University — M,D
Temple University (Philadelphia) — M,D
Texas A&M International University — M
Texas A&M University (College Station) — M
Texas A&M University–Commerce — M
Texas A&M University–Kingsville — M
Texas Tech University — M,D
Tulane University — M,D
The University of Akron — M
The University of Alabama (Tuscaloosa) — M,D
The University of Arizona — M,D
University of Arkansas (Fayetteville) — M
University of California, Berkeley — M,D
University of California, Davis — M,D
University of California, Irvine — M,D
University of California, Los Angeles — M
University of California, Riverside — M,D
University of California, San Diego — M,D
University of California, Santa Barbara — M,D
University of Central Florida — M
University of Chicago — M,D
University of Cincinnati — M,D
University of Colorado at Boulder — M,D
University of Connecticut — M,D
University of Delaware — M
University of Denver — M
University of Florida — M,D
University of Georgia — M
University of Hawaii at Manoa — M
University of Houston — M,D
University of Idaho — M
The University of Iowa — M,D
University of Kansas — M,D
University of Kentucky — M,D
University of Louisville — M
University of Maryland, College Park — M,D
University of Massachusetts Amherst — M,D
The University of Memphis — M
University of Miami — M,D
University of Michigan — D
University of Minnesota, Twin Cities Campus — M,D
University of Mississippi — M
University of Missouri–Columbia — M,D
The University of Montana–Missoula — M
University of Nebraska–Lincoln — M,D
University of Nevada, Las Vegas — M
University of Nevada, Reno — M
University of New Hampshire — M
University of New Mexico — M,D
The University of North Carolina at Chapel Hill — M,D
University of North Carolina at Greensboro — M
University of Northern Colorado — M
University of Northern Iowa — M
University of North Texas — M
University of Notre Dame — M
University of Oklahoma — M,D
University of Oregon — M
University of Pennsylvania — M,D
University of Pittsburgh — M,D
University of Rhode Island — M
University of Rochester — M
University of South Carolina (Columbia) — M
University of Southern California — M,D
University of South Florida — M
University of Tennessee, Knoxville — M,D
The University of Texas at Arlington — M
The University of Texas at Austin — M,D
The University of Texas at Brownsville — M
The University of Texas at El Paso — M
The University of Texas at San Antonio — M
The University of Texas–Pan American — M
University of Toledo — M
University of Utah — M,D
University of Virginia — M,D
University of Washington — M,D
University of Wisconsin–Madison — M,D
University of Wisconsin–Milwaukee — M
University of Wyoming — M

Vanderbilt University — M,D
Villanova University — M
Washington State University — M
Washington University in St. Louis — M,D
Wayne State University — M
West Chester University of Pennsylvania — M
Western Michigan University — M
West Virginia University — M
Wichita State University — M
Winthrop University — M
Yale University — M,D

SPECIAL EDUCATION

Adams State College — M
Adelphi University — M,O
Alabama Agricultural and Mechanical University — M
Alabama State University — M
Albany State University — M
Alcorn State University — M
American International College — M,O
American University — M
Appalachian State University — M
Arizona State University — M
Arizona State University West — M
Arkansas State University — M
Armstrong Atlantic State University — M
Ashland University — M
Assumption College — M
Auburn University — M,D,O
Auburn University Montgomery — M,O
Augusta State University — M,O
Austin Peay State University — M
Azusa Pacific University — M
Baldwin-Wallace College — M
Ball State University — M,D,O
Barry University — M,D,O
Beaver College — M,O
Bellarmine College — M
Bemidji State University — M
Benedictine University — M
Bloomsburg University of Pennsylvania — M
Boise State University — M
Boston College — M,D,O
Boston University — M,D,O
Bowie State University — M
Bowling Green State University — M
Bradley University — M
Brenau University — M
Bridgewater State College — M
Brigham Young University — M,D
Brooklyn College of the City University of New York — M
Butler University — M
California Lutheran University — M
California Polytechnic State University, San Luis Obispo — M
California State University, Bakersfield — M
California State University, Chico — M
California State University, Dominguez Hills — M
California State University, Fresno — M
California State University, Fullerton — M
California State University, Hayward — M
California State University, Long Beach — M
California State University, Los Angeles — M,D
California State University, Northridge — M
California State University, Sacramento — M
California State University, San Bernardino — M
California State University, Stanislaus — M
California University of Pennsylvania — M
Calvin College — M
Canisius College — M
Cardinal Stritch University — M
Castleton State College — M
Central Connecticut State University — M
Central Michigan University — M
Central Missouri State University — M,O
Central Washington University — M
Chapman University — M
Cheyney University of Pennsylvania — M
Chicago State University — M
The Citadel, The Military College of South Carolina — M
City College of the City University of New York — M
City University — M
Clarion University of Pennsylvania — M
Clemson University — M

Cleveland State University — M
College of Mount St. Joseph — M
The College of New Jersey — M
College of New Rochelle — M
The College of Saint Rose — M
College of Staten Island of the City University of New York — M
College of William and Mary — M
Columbus State University — M,O
Converse College — M
Coppin State College — M
Cumberland College — M
Curry College — M,O
Delaware State University — M
Delta State University — M
DePaul University — M
Dominican University — M
Dowling College — M
Drake University — M
Duquesne University — M
D'Youville College — M
East Carolina University — M
Eastern Illinois University — M
Eastern Kentucky University — M,O
Eastern Michigan University — M,O
Eastern Nazarene College — M,O
Eastern New Mexico University — M
Eastern Washington University — M
East Stroudsburg University of Pennsylvania — M
East Tennessee State University — M
Edgewood College — M,O
Edinboro University of Pennsylvania — M
Elon College — M
Emporia State University — M
Fairfield University — M,O
Fairleigh Dickinson University, Teaneck–Hackensack Campus — M
Fayetteville State University — M
Fitchburg State College — M
Florida Atlantic University — M,D
Florida International University — M,D
Florida State University — M,D,O
Fordham University — M,O
Fort Hays State University — M
Framingham State College — M
Francis Marion University — M
Fresno Pacific University — M
Gallaudet University — M,D,O
George Mason University — M
The George Washington University — M,D,O
Georgia College and State University — M
Georgian Court College — M
Georgia Southern University — M,O
Georgia State University — M,D,O
Gonzaga University — M
Governors State University — M
Grand Valley State University — M
Hampton University — M
Henderson State University — M
Heritage College — M
Hofstra University — M,O
Hood College — M
Houston Baptist University — M
Howard University — M,O
Hunter College of the City University of New York — M
Idaho State University — M,O
Illinois State University — M,D
Indiana State University — M,D,O
Indiana University Bloomington — M,D,O
Indiana University of Pennsylvania — M
Indiana University–Purdue University Indianapolis — M
Indiana University South Bend — M
Inter American University of Puerto Rico, Metropolitan Campus — M
Inter American University of Puerto Rico, San Germán Campus — M
Iowa State University of Science and Technology — M
Jackson State University — M,O
Jacksonville State University — M
Jacksonville University — O
James Madison University — M
Johns Hopkins University — M,D,O
Johnson State College — M
Kansas State University — M,D
Kean University — M
Keene State College — M
Kennesaw State University — M
Kent State University — M,D,O
Lamar University — M,D,O
La Sierra University — M
Lehigh University — M,D,O
Lehman College of the City University of New York — M
Lesley College — M,O
Long Island University, Brooklyn Campus — M
Long Island University, C.W. Post Campus — M

P—first professional degree; M—master's degree; D—doctorate; O—other advanced degree.

Special Education (continued)

Longwood College	M
Louisiana Tech University	M
Loyola College	M,O
Loyola Marymount University	M
Loyola University Chicago	M
Lynchburg College	M
Madonna University	M
Manhattan College	M,O
Mankato State University	M
Mansfield University of Pennsylvania	M
Marshall University	M
Marygrove College	M
Marymount University	M
Marywood University	M
McNeese State University	M
Miami University	M
Michigan State University	M,D
Middle Tennessee State University	M
Midwestern State University	M
Millersville University of Pennsylvania	M
Minot State University	M
Mississippi State University	M,D,O
Monmouth University	M,O
Montana State University–Billings	M
Montclair State University	M
Moorhead State University	M
Morehead State University	M,D
Mount Saint Mary College	M
Mount St. Mary's College	M
Murray State University	M
National–Louis University	M,O
National University	M
Nazareth College of Rochester	M
New Jersey City University	M
New Mexico Highlands University	M
New Mexico State University	M
New York University	M,O
North Carolina Central University	M
North Carolina State University	M
Northeastern Illinois University	M
Northeastern State University	M
Northeastern University	M
Northeast Louisiana University	M
Northern Arizona University	M
Northern Illinois University	M,D
Northern Michigan University	M
Northern State University	M
North Georgia College & State University	M
Northwestern State University of Louisiana	M,O
Northwestern University	M,D
Northwest Missouri State University	M
Notre Dame College	M
Nova Southeastern University	M,O
Oakland University	M,O
Ohio University	M
Old Dominion University	M
Our Lady of the Lake University of San Antonio	M
Pacific Lutheran University	M
Pennsylvania State University University Park Campus	M,D
Pittsburg State University	M
Plattsburgh State University of New York	M
Portland State University	M
Prairie View A&M University	M
Providence College	M
Purdue University	M
Queens College of the City University of New York	M
Radford University	M
Rhode Island College	M,O
Rivier College	M
Rochester Institute of Technology	M,O
Rockford College	M
Rowan University	M,O
Rutgers, The State University of New Jersey, New Brunswick	M,D
Sage Graduate School	M
Saginaw Valley State University	M
St. Ambrose University	M
St. Bonaventure University	M
St. Cloud State University	M,O
St. John's University (NY)	M,O
Saint Joseph College (CT)	M
Saint Joseph's University	M
Saint Louis University	M
Saint Martin's College	M
Saint Mary's College of California	M
Saint Mary's University of Minnesota	M
Saint Michael's College	M,O
Saint Xavier University	M
Salem State College	M
Sam Houston State University	M
San Diego State University	M
San Francisco State University	M,D,O
San Jose State University	M
Santa Clara University	M
Shippensburg University of Pennsylvania	M

Simmons College	M
Slippery Rock University of Pennsylvania	M
Sonoma State University	M
South Carolina State University	M
Southeastern Louisiana University	M
Southeast Missouri State University	M
Southern Arkansas University–Magnolia	M
Southern Connecticut State University	M,O
Southern Illinois University at Carbondale	M
Southern Illinois University at Edwardsville	M
Southern Oregon University	M
Southern University and Agricultural and Mechanical College	M,D
Southwestern Oklahoma State University	M
Southwest Missouri State University	M
Southwest Texas State University	M
State University of New York at Albany	M
State University of New York at Binghamton	M
State University of New York at New Paltz	M
State University of New York at Oswego	M
State University of New York College at Buffalo	M
State University of New York College at Geneseo	M
State University of New York College at Potsdam	M
State University of West Georgia	M,O
Stephen F. Austin State University	M
Stetson University	M
Syracuse University	M,D
Tarleton State University	O
Teachers College, Columbia University	M,D
Temple University (Philadelphia)	M
Tennessee State University	M,D
Tennessee Technological University	M,O
Texas A&M University (College Station)	M,D
Texas A&M University–Commerce	M,D
Texas A&M University–Corpus Christi	M
Texas A&M University–Kingsville	M
Texas A&M University–Texarkana	M
Texas Christian University	M
Texas Southern University	M
Texas Tech University	M,D,O
Texas Woman's University	M,D
Trinity College (DC)	M
Troy State University (Troy)	M,O
Troy State University Dothan	M
Union College (KY)	M
Universidad del Turabo	M
The University of Akron	M
The University of Alabama (Tuscaloosa)	M,D,O
The University of Alabama at Birmingham	M,O
University of Alaska Anchorage	M
The University of Arizona	M,D,O
University of Arkansas (Fayetteville)	M
University of Arkansas at Little Rock	M
University of California, Berkeley	D
University of California, Los Angeles	D
University of Central Arkansas	M
University of Central Florida	M
University of Central Oklahoma	M
University of Cincinnati	M,D
University of Colorado at Colorado Springs	M
University of Colorado at Denver	M
University of Connecticut	M,D
University of Delaware	M
University of Detroit Mercy	M
University of Dubuque	M
University of Evansville	M
University of Florida	M,D,O
University of Georgia	M,D,O
University of Guam	M
University of Hartford	M
University of Hawaii at Manoa	M,D
University of Houston	M,D
University of Idaho	M,O
University of Illinois at Chicago	M,D
University of Illinois at Urbana–Champaign	M,D,O
The University of Iowa	M,D,O
University of Kansas	M,D,O
University of Kentucky	M,D,O

University of La Verne	M
University of Louisville	M,D,O
University of Maine (Orono)	M,O
University of Mary	M
University of Maryland, College Park	M,D,O
University of Maryland Eastern Shore	M
University of Massachusetts Amherst	M,D,O
University of Massachusetts Boston	M
The University of Memphis	M,D
University of Miami	M,D,O
University of Michigan	M
University of Michigan–Dearborn	M
University of Minnesota, Twin Cities Campus	M
University of Missouri–Columbia	M,D,O
University of Missouri–Kansas City	M
University of Missouri–St. Louis	M
University of Nebraska at Kearney	M
University of Nebraska at Omaha	M
University of Nebraska–Lincoln	M
University of Nevada, Las Vegas	M,D,O
University of Nevada, Reno	M
University of New Hampshire	M
University of New Mexico	M,D,O
University of New Orleans	M,D,O
University of North Alabama	M
The University of North Carolina at Chapel Hill	M
University of North Carolina at Charlotte	M
University of North Carolina at Greensboro	M
University of North Carolina at Wilmington	M
University of North Dakota	M,D
University of Northern Colorado	M,D
University of Northern Iowa	M
University of North Florida	M
University of North Texas	M,D
University of Oklahoma	M,D
University of Oregon	M,D
University of Pittsburgh	M,D
University of Portland	M
University of Puerto Rico, Río Piedras	M
University of Richmond	M
University of Saint Francis (IN)	M
University of St. Thomas (MN)	M
University of San Diego	M
University of South Alabama	M,O
University of South Carolina (Columbia)	M,D
University of South Dakota	M
University of Southern California	M
University of Southern Maine	M
University of Southern Mississippi	M,D,O
University of South Florida	M,D,O
University of Tennessee at Chattanooga	M
University of Tennessee, Knoxville	M,D
The University of Texas at Austin	M,D
The University of Texas at Brownsville	M
The University of Texas at Tyler	M,O
The University of Texas of the Permian Basin	M
The University of Texas–Pan American	M
University of the Incarnate Word	M
University of the Pacific	M,D
University of Toledo	M
University of Utah	M,D
University of Vermont	M
University of Virginia	M,D,O
University of Washington	M,D
The University of West Alabama	M
University of West Florida	M
University of Wisconsin–Eau Claire	M
University of Wisconsin–La Crosse	M
University of Wisconsin–Madison	M,D
University of Wisconsin–Milwaukee	M
University of Wisconsin–Oshkosh	M
University of Wisconsin–Superior	M
University of Wisconsin–Whitewater	M
Utah State University	M,D
Valdosta State University	M,O
Valparaiso University	M
Vanderbilt University	M,D,O
Virginia Commonwealth University	M
Virginia Polytechnic Institute and State University	D,O
Virginia State University	M
Wagner College	M
Walla Walla College	M
Washburn University of Topeka	M

Wayne State College	M
Wayne State University	M,D,O
Webster University	M
West Chester University of Pennsylvania	M
Western Carolina University	M
Western Illinois University	M
Western Kentucky University	M
Western Michigan University	M,D
Western New Mexico University	M
Western Oregon University	M
Western Washington University	M
Westfield State College	M
West Virginia University	M,D
Whitworth College	M
Wichita State University	M
William Carey College	M
William Paterson University of New Jersey	M
Wilmington College (DE)	M
Winona State University	M
Winthrop University	M,O
Wright State University	M
Xavier University	M
Youngstown State University	M

SPEECH AND INTERPERSONAL COMMUNICATION

Abilene Christian University	M
Arizona State University	M
Arkansas State University	M,O
Austin Peay State University	M
Ball State University	M
Bowling Green State University	M,D
Bridgewater State College	M
Brooklyn College of the City University of New York	M
California State University, Chico	M
California State University, Fresno	M
California State University, Fullerton	M
California State University, Hayward	M
California State University, Long Beach	M
California State University, Los Angeles	M
California State University, Northridge	M
Carnegie Mellon University	M,D
The Catholic University of America	M,D
Central Michigan University	M
Central Missouri State University	M
Colorado State University	M
Eastern Illinois University	M
Eastern Michigan University	M
Eastern New Mexico University	M
Emerson College	M
Florida State University	M,D
Georgia College and State University	M
Georgia State University	M
Idaho State University	M
Indiana University Bloomington	M,D
Kansas State University	M
Louisiana State University and Agricultural and Mechanical College	M,D
Louisiana Tech University	M
Mankato State University	M
Marquette University	M
Miami University	M
Montclair State University	M
Murray State University	M
New York University	M,O
Norfolk State University	M
North Dakota State University	M
Northeastern Illinois University	M
Northwestern University	M,D
Ohio University	M,D
Oklahoma State University	M
Pennsylvania State University University Park Campus	M,D
Portland State University	M
Rensselaer Polytechnic Institute	M,D
St. Mary's University of San Antonio	M
San Francisco State University	M
San Jose State University	M
Southern Illinois University at Carbondale	M,D
Southern Illinois University at Edwardsville	M
Southwest Texas State University	M
Syracuse University	M
Temple University (Philadelphia)	M
Texas A&M University (College Station)	M
Texas A&M University–Commerce	M
Texas Christian University	M
Texas Southern University	M
The University of Alabama (Tuscaloosa)	M,D

University of Arkansas at Little Rock — M
University of California, Berkeley — D
University of Connecticut — M
University of Denver — M,D
University of Georgia — M,D
University of Hawaii at Manoa — M
University of Houston — M
University of Illinois at Urbana–Champaign — M,D
The University of Iowa — M,D
University of Maryland, College Park — M,D
University of Minnesota, Twin Cities Campus — M,D
University of Nebraska at Kearney — M
University of Nevada, Reno — M
University of North Carolina at Greensboro — M
University of Pittsburgh — M,D
University of South Dakota — M
University of Southern California — D
University of Tennessee, Knoxville — D
The University of Texas–Pan American — M
University of Washington — M,D
University of Wisconsin–Stevens Point — M
University of Wisconsin–Superior — M
Wake Forest University — M
Wayne State University — M,D
Western Kentucky University — M

SPORTS ADMINISTRATION

Adelphi University — O
Appalachian State University — M
Barry University — M
Boise State University — M
Bowling Green State University — M
Brooklyn College of the City University of New York — M
Canisius College — M
Central Michigan University — M
Cleveland State University — M
Eastern Kentucky University — M
East Stroudsburg University of Pennsylvania — M
Florida State University — M,D,O
The George Washington University — M
Georgia Southern University — M
Georgia State University — M
Gonzaga University — M
Grambling State University — M
Hardin–Simmons University — M
Idaho State University — M
Indiana University Bloomington — M
Indiana University of Pennsylvania — M
Mississippi State University — M
Montclair State University — M
Morehead State University — M
North Carolina State University — M
North Dakota State University — M
Northwestern State University of Louisiana — M
Ohio University — M
Old Dominion University — M
St. Cloud State University — M
St. Thomas University — M
Seton Hall University — M
Springfield College (MA) — M,O
Temple University (Philadelphia) — M
University of Denver — M
University of Miami — M,D
University of New Orleans — M
The University of North Carolina at Chapel Hill — M
University of Oklahoma — M
University of Rhode Island — M
University of St. Thomas (MN) — M
University of San Francisco — M
University of Tennessee, Knoxville — M
University of the Incarnate Word — M
University of Wisconsin–La Crosse — M
Wayne State University — M
West Chester University of Pennsylvania — M
Western Illinois University — M
Western Michigan University — M
Whitworth College — M
Wichita State University — M
Xavier University — M

STATISTICS

American University — M,D,O
Arizona State University — M,D
Auburn University — M,D
Ball State University — M
Baruch College of the City University of New York — M
Baylor University — M,D

Boston University — M,D
Bowling Green State University — M,D,O
Brigham Young University — M
California State University, Fullerton — M
California State University, Hayward — M
California State University, Sacramento — M
Carnegie Mellon University — M,D
Case Western Reserve University — M,D
Claremont Graduate University — M,D
Clemson University — M,D
Colorado State University — M,D
Columbia University — M,D
Cornell University — M,D
Creighton University — M
Duke University — D
Florida State University — M,D
George Mason University — M
The George Washington University — M,D
Georgia Institute of Technology — M
Harvard University — M,D
Indiana University Bloomington — M,D
Indiana University–Purdue University Indianapolis — M
Iowa State University of Science and Technology — M,D
Kansas State University — M,D
Lehigh University — M
Louisiana State University and Agricultural and Mechanical College — M
Louisiana Tech University — M
Mankato State University — M
Marquette University — M
McNeese State University — M
Miami University — M
Michigan State University — M,D
Mississippi State University — M,D
Montana State University–Bozeman — M,D
Montclair State University — M
New Mexico State University — M
New York University — M,D,O
North Carolina State University — M,D
North Dakota State University — M
Northern Illinois University — M
Northwestern University — M,D
Oakland University — M,O
The Ohio State University — M,D
Oklahoma State University — M,D
Old Dominion University — M,D
Oregon State University — M,D
Pennsylvania State University University Park Campus — M,D
Princeton University — M,D
Purdue University — M,D
Rensselaer Polytechnic Institute — M
Rice University — M,D
Rochester Institute of Technology — M,O
Rutgers, The State University of New Jersey, New Brunswick — M,D
St. John's University (NY) — M
San Diego State University — M
Southern Illinois University at Carbondale — M
Southern Illinois University at Edwardsville — M
Southern Methodist University — M,D
Stanford University — M,D
State University of New York at Albany — M,D
State University of New York at Binghamton — M,D
State University of New York at Buffalo — M,D
State University of New York at Stony Brook — M,D
Stephen F. Austin State University — M
Stevens Institute of Technology — M,O
Syracuse University — M
Temple University (Philadelphia) — M,D
Texas A&M University (College Station) — M,D
Texas Tech University — M
Tulane University — M
The University of Akron — M
The University of Alabama (Tuscaloosa) — M,D
The University of Arizona — M,D
University of Arkansas (Fayetteville) — M
University of Arkansas at Little Rock — M
University of California, Berkeley — M,D
University of California, Davis — M,D
University of California, Riverside — M,D
University of California, San Diego — M
University of California, Santa Barbara — M,D
University of Central Florida — M
University of Central Oklahoma — M
University of Chicago — M,D

University of Cincinnati — M,D
University of Connecticut — M,D
University of Florida — M,D
University of Georgia — M,D
University of Houston — M,D
University of Houston–Clear Lake — M
University of Idaho — M
University of Illinois at Chicago — M,D
University of Illinois at Springfield — M
University of Illinois at Urbana–Champaign — M,D
The University of Iowa — M,D
University of Kansas — M,D
University of Kentucky — M,D
University of Maryland, Baltimore County — M,D
University of Maryland, College Park — M,D
University of Massachusetts Amherst — M,D
The University of Memphis — M,D
University of Michigan — M,D
University of Minnesota, Twin Cities Campus — M,D
University of Missouri–Columbia — M,D
University of Missouri–Kansas City — M,D
The University of Montana–Missoula — M,D
University of Nebraska–Lincoln — M,D
University of Nevada, Las Vegas — M
University of Nevada, Reno — M
University of New Mexico — M,D
The University of North Carolina at Chapel Hill — M,D
University of North Carolina at Charlotte — M
University of Northern Colorado — M,D
University of North Florida — M
University of Pennsylvania — M,D
University of Pittsburgh — M,D
University of Puerto Rico, Mayagüez Campus — M
University of Rhode Island — M,D
University of Rochester — M,D
University of South Carolina (Columbia) — M,D
University of Southern California — M
University of Southwestern Louisiana — M,D
University of Tennessee, Knoxville — M,D
The University of Texas at Austin — M
The University of Texas at Dallas — M,D
The University of Texas at El Paso — M
The University of Texas at San Antonio — M
University of Toledo — M
University of Utah — M,D
University of Vermont — M
University of Virginia — M,D
University of Washington — M,D
University of West Florida — M
University of Wisconsin–Madison — M,D
University of Wyoming — M,D
Utah State University — M
Villanova University — M
Virginia Commonwealth University — M,O
Virginia Polytechnic Institute and State University — M,D
Washington University in St. Louis — M,D
Wayne State University — M,D
Western Michigan University — M,D
West Virginia University — M
Wichita State University — M,D
Worcester Polytechnic Institute — M
Wright State University — M
Yale University — M,D

STRUCTURAL BIOLOGY

Boston University — M,D
Cornell University — D
Northwestern University — D
Stanford University — D
State University of New York at Albany — M,D
University of Illinois at Urbana–Champaign — D
University of Pennsylvania — D
University of South Alabama — D
University of Washington — D

STRUCTURAL ENGINEERING

Auburn University — M,D
California State University, Northridge — M
Case Western Reserve University — M,D
The Catholic University of America — M,D
Colorado State University — M,D
Cornell University — M,D

Florida Institute of Technology — M
Iowa State University of Science and Technology — M,D
Louisiana State University and Agricultural and Mechanical College — M,D
Marquette University — M,D
Mississippi State University — M
Northwestern University — M,D
Ohio University — M
Pennsylvania State University University Park Campus — M,D
Princeton University — M,D
Rensselaer Polytechnic Institute — M,D
Rice University — M,D
State University of New York at Buffalo — M,D
Texas A&M University (College Station) — M,D
Tufts University — M,D
University of California, Berkeley — M,D
University of California, Irvine — M,D
University of California, Los Angeles — M,D
University of California, San Diego — M,D
University of Colorado at Boulder — M,D
University of Dayton — M
University of Delaware — M,D
University of Maine (Orono) — M,D
The University of Memphis — M
University of Missouri–Columbia — M,D
University of Missouri–Rolla — M,D
University of North Dakota — M
University of Oklahoma — M
University of Rhode Island — M,D
University of Southern California — M
University of Virginia — M,D
University of Washington — M,D
Washington University in St. Louis — M,D

SURVEYING SCIENCE AND ENGINEERING

The Ohio State University — M,D

SYSTEMS ENGINEERING

Auburn University — M,D
Boston University — M,D
California Institute of Technology — D
California State University, Fullerton — M
Case Western Reserve University — M,D
Colorado School of Mines — M,D
Embry–Riddle Aeronautical University (FL) — M
Florida Atlantic University — M
George Mason University — M
Georgia Institute of Technology — M,D
Iowa State University of Science and Technology — M
Lehigh University — M
Marshall University — M
Massachusetts Institute of Technology — M,O
Murray State University — M
Northeastern University — M
Oakland University — M,D
The Ohio State University — M,D
Ohio University — M
Oklahoma State University — M
Polytechnic University, Brooklyn Campus — M
Polytechnic University, Westchester Graduate Center — M
Purdue University — M,D
Rensselaer Polytechnic Institute — M,D
Rochester Institute of Technology — M
Rutgers, The State University of New Jersey, New Brunswick — M,D
San Jose State University — M
Southern Methodist University — M
Stanford University — M,D,O
The University of Arizona — M,D
University of Connecticut — M,D
University of Florida — M,D,O
University of Houston — M,D
University of Illinois at Urbana–Champaign — M
University of Maryland, College Park — M
University of Massachusetts Lowell — M,D
The University of Memphis — M
University of Michigan — M,D
University of Michigan–Dearborn — M
University of New Hampshire — D
University of Pennsylvania — M,D
University of Pittsburgh — M
University of Rhode Island — M,D
University of St. Thomas (MN) — M
University of Southern California — M,D,O
University of Virginia — M,D
University of West Florida — M

Systems Engineering (continued)

Virginia Polytechnic Institute and State University	M
Washington University in St. Louis	D
Youngstown State University	M

SYSTEMS SCIENCE

Fairleigh Dickinson University, Teaneck–Hackensack Campus	M
Louisiana State University and Agricultural and Mechanical College	M
Portland State University	D
Salve Regina University	M
State University of New York at Binghamton	M,D
Syracuse University	M,D
Washington University in St. Louis	M,D

TAXATION

American University	M
Arizona State University	M
Baruch College of the City University of New York	M
Boston University	M
California State University, Fullerton	M
California State University, Hayward	M
California State University, Los Angeles	M
California State University, Northridge	M
Capital University	M
Case Western Reserve University	M
Colorado State University	M
DePaul University	M
Drexel University	M
Duquesne University	M
Fairfield University	M,O
Fairleigh Dickinson University, Florham–Madison Campus	M
Fairleigh Dickinson University, Teaneck–Hackensack Campus	M
Florida Atlantic University	M
Florida International University	M,D
Fontbonne College	M
Fordham University	M
George Mason University	M
Georgetown University	M
The George Washington University	M
Georgia State University	M
Golden Gate University	M,O
Grand Valley State University	M
Hofstra University	M
Long Island University, Brooklyn Campus	M
Long Island University, C.W. Post Campus	M
Mississippi State University	M
New York University	M,D,O
Northeastern University	M,O
Northern Illinois University	M
Old Dominion University	M
Pace University	M
Philadelphia College of Textiles and Science	M
Portland State University	M
St. John's University (NY)	M,O
Saint Xavier University	M,O
San Francisco State University	M
San Jose State University	M
Seton Hall University	M,O
Southern Methodist University	M
State University of New York at Albany	M
Suffolk University	M
Temple University (Philadelphia)	M
Texas Tech University	M
The University of Akron	M
The University of Alabama (Tuscaloosa)	M
University of Baltimore	M
University of Central Florida	M
University of Colorado at Boulder	M
University of Denver	M
University of Florida	M
University of Hartford	M
University of Houston	M,D
The University of Memphis	M
University of Miami	M
University of Minnesota, Twin Cities Campus	M
University of Mississippi	M
University of Missouri–Kansas City	M
University of Missouri–St. Louis	O
University of New Haven	M
University of New Mexico	M
University of New Orleans	M
University of San Diego	M,O

University of South Carolina (Columbia)	M
University of Southern California	M
The University of Texas at Arlington	M
The University of Texas at San Antonio	M
University of the Sacred Heart	M
University of Tulsa	M
University of Washington	M
Villanova University	M
Virginia Commonwealth University	M,D
Wayne State University	M
Widener University	M

TECHNICAL WRITING

Boise State University	M
Bowling Green State University	M
Carnegie Mellon University	M
Colorado State University	M
Drexel University	M
Florida Institute of Technology	M
Illinois Institute of Technology	M
James Madison University	M
Mercer University, Cecil B. Day Campus	M
Miami University	M
Michigan Technological University	M,D
Montana Tech of The University of Montana	M
New Jersey Institute of Technology	M
North Carolina State University	M
Northeastern University	M,O
Oregon State University	M
Polytechnic University, Brooklyn Campus	M
Rensselaer Polytechnic Institute	M
San Jose State University	M
Texas Tech University	M,D
University of Arkansas at Little Rock	M
University of Central Florida	M
University of Colorado at Denver	M
University of Michigan	M
University of Minnesota, Twin Cities Campus	M,D
University of Washington	M

TECHNOLOGY AND PUBLIC POLICY

California State University, Los Angeles	M
Carnegie Mellon University	M,D
Colorado State University	D
Eastern Michigan University	M
The George Washington University	M,D
Kent State University	M
Massachusetts Institute of Technology	M,D
Northwestern University	M,O
Rensselaer Polytechnic Institute	M,D
St. Cloud State University	M
Stanford University	M,D,O
University of Minnesota, Twin Cities Campus	M
The University of Texas at Austin	M
Washington University in St. Louis	M,D

TELECOMMUNICATIONS

Azusa Pacific University	M,O
Boston University	M
Columbia University	M
DePaul University	M
Drexel University	M
George Mason University	M
The George Washington University	M
Iona College (New Rochelle)	M,O
Michigan State University	M
New Jersey Institute of Technology	M
North Carolina State University	M
Northwestern University	M,O
Pace University	M,O
Pennsylvania State University University Park Campus	M
Polytechnic University, Brooklyn Campus	M
Polytechnic University, Farmingdale Campus	M
Polytechnic University, Westchester Graduate Center	M
Rochester Institute of Technology	M
Roosevelt University	M
Saint Mary's University of Minnesota	M
State University of New York Institute of Technology at Utica/Rome	M
Syracuse University	M
University of California, San Diego	M,D

University of Colorado at Boulder	M
University of Denver	M
University of Maryland, College Park	M
University of Missouri–Kansas City	M,D
University of New Haven	M
University of Pennsylvania	M
University of Pittsburgh	M,O
University of Southwestern Louisiana	M
The University of Texas at Dallas	M
Western Illinois University	M
Widener University	M

TELECOMMUNICATIONS MANAGEMENT

Alaska Pacific University	M
Golden Gate University	M,O
National University	M
Northwestern University	M,O
Oklahoma State University	M
Polytechnic University, Brooklyn Campus	M
Polytechnic University, Westchester Graduate Center	M
Stevens Institute of Technology	M,D,O
Syracuse University	M
University of Colorado at Boulder	M
University of Denver	M
University of Maryland University College	M
University of Miami	M,O
University of Pennsylvania	M
University of San Francisco	M
Webster University	M

TEXTILE DESIGN

California State University, Los Angeles	M
Central Washington University	M
Colorado State University	M
Cornell University	M,D
Drexel University	M
Illinois State University	M
Indiana University Bloomington	M
James Madison University	M
Kent State University	M
Miami University	M
New School University	M
Philadelphia College of Textiles and Science	M
Rochester Institute of Technology	M
San Jose State University	M
Southern Illinois University at Edwardsville	M
Sul Ross State University	M
Syracuse University	M
Temple University (Philadelphia)	M
Texas Woman's University	M
University of California, Davis	M
University of Cincinnati	M
University of Massachusetts Dartmouth	M
University of Minnesota, Twin Cities Campus	M,D
University of North Carolina at Greensboro	M,D
University of North Texas	M
University of Wisconsin–Madison	D
Western Michigan University	M

TEXTILE SCIENCES AND ENGINEERING

Auburn University	M
Clemson University	M,D
Cornell University	M,D
Georgia Institute of Technology	M,D
North Carolina State University	M,D
Philadelphia College of Textiles and Science	M
University of Massachusetts Dartmouth	M

THEATER

Arizona State University	M,D
Arkansas State University	M,O
Austin Peay State University	M
Baylor University	M
Boston University	M,O
Bowling Green State University	M,D
Brandeis University	M
Brigham Young University	M,D
Brooklyn College of the City University of New York	M
Brown University	M
California State University, Fullerton	M
California State University, Long Beach	M
California State University, Los Angeles	M
California State University, Northridge	M

California State University, Sacramento	M
Carnegie Mellon University	M
Case Western Reserve University	M,D
The Catholic University of America	M
Central Michigan University	M
Central Missouri State University	M
Central Washington University	M
Claremont Graduate University	M
Columbia University	M,D
Cornell University	D
DePaul University	M,O
Eastern Michigan University	M
Emerson College	M
Florida Atlantic University	M
Florida State University	M,D
The George Washington University	M
Georgia State University	M
Graduate School and University Center of the City University of New York	D
Humboldt State University	M
Hunter College of the City University of New York	M
Idaho State University	M
Illinois State University	M
Indiana State University	M
Indiana University Bloomington	M,D
Kent State University	M
Lamar University	M
Lesley College	M
Lindenwood University	M
Long Island University, C.W. Post Campus	M
Louisiana State University and Agricultural and Mechanical College	M,D
Mankato State University	M
Marquette University	M
Miami University	M
Michigan State University	M
Montclair State University	M
New School University	M
New York University	M,D,O
North Dakota State University	M
Northern Illinois University	M
Northwestern University	M,D
The Ohio State University	M,D
Ohio University	M
Oklahoma City University	M
Oklahoma State University	M
Pennsylvania State University University Park Campus	M
Pittsburg State University	M
Portland State University	M
Purdue University	M
Roosevelt University	M
Rutgers, The State University of New Jersey, New Brunswick	M
San Diego State University	M
San Francisco State University	M
San Jose State University	M
South Dakota State University	M
Southern Illinois University at Carbondale	M,D
Southern Methodist University	M
Southwest Missouri State University	M
Southwest Texas State University	M
Stanford University	D
State University of New York at Albany	M
State University of New York at Binghamton	M
State University of New York at Stony Brook	M
Stephen F. Austin State University	M
Syracuse University	M
Temple University (Philadelphia)	M
Texas A&M University–Commerce	M
Texas Tech University	M,D
Texas Woman's University	M
Towson University	M
Tufts University	M,D
Tulane University	M
The University of Akron	M
The University of Alabama (Tuscaloosa)	M
The University of Arizona	M
University of Arkansas (Fayetteville)	M
University of California, Berkeley	D,O
University of California, Davis	M,D
University of California, Irvine	M
University of California, Los Angeles	M,D
University of California, San Diego	M
University of California, Santa Barbara	M,D
University of California, Santa Cruz	O
University of Central Oklahoma	M

University of Cincinnati	M
University of Colorado at Boulder	M,D
University of Colorado at Denver	M
University of Connecticut	M
University of Delaware	M
University of Florida	M,D
University of Georgia	M,D
University of Hawaii at Manoa	M,D
University of Houston	M
University of Idaho	M
University of Illinois at Chicago	M
University of Illinois at Urbana–Champaign	M,D
The University of Iowa	M
University of Kansas	M,D
University of Kentucky	M
University of Louisville	M
University of Maine (Orono)	M
University of Maryland, College Park	M,D
University of Massachusetts Amherst	M
The University of Memphis	M
University of Minnesota, Twin Cities Campus	M,D
University of Mississippi	M
University of Missouri–Columbia	M,D
University of Missouri–Kansas City	M
The University of Montana–Missoula	M
University of Nebraska at Omaha	M
University of Nebraska–Lincoln	M,D
University of Nevada, Las Vegas	M
University of New Mexico	M
University of New Orleans	M
The University of North Carolina at Chapel Hill	M
University of North Carolina at Greensboro	M
University of North Dakota	M
University of Northern Iowa	M
University of North Texas	M
University of Oklahoma	M
University of Oregon	M,D
University of Pittsburgh	M,D
University of Portland	M
University of San Diego	M
University of South Carolina (Columbia)	M
University of South Dakota	M
University of Southern California	M
University of Southern Mississippi	M
University of South Florida	M
University of Tennessee, Knoxville	M
The University of Texas at Austin	M,D
The University of Texas at El Paso	M
The University of Texas at Tyler	M
The University of Texas–Pan American	M
University of Utah	M,D
University of Virginia	M
University of Washington	M,D
University of Wisconsin–Madison	M,D
University of Wisconsin–Milwaukee	M
University of Wisconsin–Superior	M
Utah State University	M
Villanova University	M,O
Virginia Commonwealth University	M
Virginia Polytechnic Institute and State University	M
Washington State University	M
Washington University in St. Louis	M
Wayne State University	M,D
Western Illinois University	M
Western Washington University	M
West Virginia University	M
Yale University	M,D,O

THEOLOGY

Abilene Christian University	P,M
Andrews University	P,M,D
Ashland University	P,M,D
Assumption College	M,O
Azusa Pacific University	P,M,D
Barry University	M,D
Baylor University	P,M
Biola University	P,M,D
Boston College	M,D
Boston University	P,M,D
Campbell University	P,M
The Catholic University of America	P,M,D,O
Claremont Graduate University	M,D
College of Mount St. Joseph	M
College of St. Catherine	M
Creighton University	M
Duke University	P,M
Duquesne University	M,D
Emory University	P,M,D
Fordham University	M,D
Franciscan University of Steubenville	M
Friends University	M
Gardner–Webb University	P
Georgian Court College	M
Gonzaga University	P,M
Grand Rapids Baptist Seminary	P,M,D
Hardin–Simmons University	P
Harvard University	P,M,D
Hope International University	M
Houston Baptist University	M
Howard University	P,M,D
Indiana Wesleyan University	M
La Salle University	M
Liberty University	P,M,D
Loyola Marymount University	M
Loyola University Chicago	P,M,D
Loyola University New Orleans	M
Marquette University	M,D
Marywood University	M
Mercer University, Cecil B. Day Campus	P
Mount St. Mary's College	M
Mount Saint Mary's College and Seminary	P,M
Notre Dame College	M
Olivet Nazarene University	M
Oral Roberts University	P,M,D
Pontifical Catholic University of Puerto Rico	M
St. Bonaventure University	M,O
St. John's University (NY)	P,M,O
Saint Louis University	M,D
St. Mary's University of San Antonio	M
Saint Michael's College	M,O
Samford University	P,M,D
Seattle University	P,M
Seton Hall University	P,M,O
Southern Methodist University	P,M,D
Southern Nazarene University	M
Spring Hill College	M
Texas Christian University	P,M,D,O
University of Chicago	P,M,D
University of Dayton	M
University of Dubuque	P,M,D
University of Notre Dame	P,M,D
University of St. Thomas (MN)	P,M,D
University of St. Thomas (TX)	P,M,O
University of San Diego	M
University of San Francisco	M,O
University of Scranton	M
Vanderbilt University	P,M
Villanova University	M
Wheeling Jesuit University	M
Xavier University	M
Xavier University of Louisiana	M
Yale University	P,M

THEORETICAL CHEMISTRY

Boston University	M,D
Cornell University	D
Georgetown University	M,D
Howard University	M,D
Illinois Institute of Technology	M,D
University of Tennessee, Knoxville	D

THEORETICAL PHYSICS

Cornell University	M,D
Harvard University	M,D
Rutgers, The State University of New Jersey, New Brunswick	M,D

THEORY AND CRITICISM OF FILM, TELEVISION, AND VIDEO

American University	M
Boston University	M
Brigham Young University	M,D
Chapman University	M
Claremont Graduate University	M
College of Staten Island of the City University of New York	M
Columbia University	M
Emory University	M
New York University	M,D
Ohio University	M
San Francisco State University	M
University of Kansas	M,D
University of Miami	M
University of Southern California	M,D

THERAPIES—DANCE, DRAMA, AND MUSIC

Allegheny University of the Health Sciences	M
Colorado State University	M
Columbia College (IL)	M
East Carolina University	M
Florida State University	M
Immaculata College	M
Lesley College	M,O
Michigan State University	M
New York University	M,D
Southern Methodist University	M
Temple University (Philadelphia)	M
Texas Woman's University	M
University of California, Los Angeles	M
University of Miami	M,D,O

TOXICOLOGY

American University	M,O
Brown University	D
Case Western Reserve University	M,D
Clemson University	M,D
Columbia University	M,D
Cornell University	M,D
Dartmouth College	D
Duke University	O
Duquesne University	M,D
Emory University	D
Florida Agricultural and Mechanical University	M,D
The George Washington University	M
Indiana University–Purdue University Indianapolis	M,D
Iowa State University of Science and Technology	M,D
Johns Hopkins University	D
Long Island University, Brooklyn Campus	M
Louisiana State University and Agricultural and Mechanical College	M
Massachusetts Institute of Technology	M,D
Michigan State University	M,D
New York University	M,D
North Carolina State University	M,D
North Dakota State University	M
Northeastern University	M,D
Northwestern University	D
The Ohio State University	M,D
Oregon State University	M,D
Purdue University	M,D
Rutgers, The State University of New Jersey, New Brunswick	M,D
St. John's University (NY)	M,D
San Diego State University	M
State University of New York at Albany	M,D
State University of New York at Buffalo	M,D
Texas A&M University (College Station)	M,D
The University of Alabama at Birmingham	
The University of Arizona	M,D
University of California, Davis	M,D
University of California, Irvine	M,D
University of California, Riverside	M,D
University of Cincinnati	M,D
University of Connecticut	M,D
University of Georgia	M,D
University of Illinois at Chicago	D
University of Kansas	M,D
University of Kentucky	M,D
University of Maryland, College Park	M,D
University of Maryland Eastern Shore	M,D
University of Michigan	M,D
University of Minnesota, Duluth	M,D
University of Minnesota, Twin Cities Campus	M,D
University of Mississippi	D
University of New Mexico	M,D
The University of North Carolina at Chapel Hill	M,D
University of North Dakota	M,D
University of Rhode Island	M,D
University of Rochester	M,D
University of Southern California	M,D
University of Utah	M,D
University of Washington	M,D
University of Wisconsin–Madison	M,D
Utah State University	M,D
Vanderbilt University	
Virginia Commonwealth University	M,D,O
Washington State University	M,D
Wayne State University	M,D
West Virginia University	M,D

TRANSLATION AND INTERPRETATION

American University	O
Gallaudet University	M
Rutgers, The State University of New Jersey, New Brunswick	M
State University of New York at Binghamton	O
University of Arkansas (Fayetteville)	M
The University of Iowa	M
University of Puerto Rico, Río Piedras	M,O

TRANSPORTATION AND HIGHWAY ENGINEERING

Auburn University	M,D
Central Missouri State University	M
Cornell University	M,D
Iowa State University of Science and Technology	M,D
Louisiana State University and Agricultural and Mechanical College	M,D
Marquette University	M,D
Massachusetts Institute of Technology	M,D
New Jersey Institute of Technology	M,D
Northwestern University	M,D
Pennsylvania State University University Park Campus	M,D
Polytechnic University, Brooklyn Campus	M
Polytechnic University, Farmingdale Campus	M
Princeton University	M,D
Rensselaer Polytechnic Institute	M,D
Texas A&M University (College Station)	M,D
Texas Southern University	M
University of Arkansas (Fayetteville)	M
University of California, Berkeley	M,D
University of California, Davis	M,D
University of California, Irvine	M,D
University of Dayton	M
University of Delaware	M,D
The University of Memphis	M
University of Michigan	O
University of Michigan–Dearborn	M
University of Missouri–Columbia	M
University of Oklahoma	M
University of Rhode Island	M,D
University of Southern California	M
University of Virginia	M,D
University of Washington	M,D
Villanova University	M
Washington University in St. Louis	D

TRANSPORTATION MANAGEMENT

Arizona State University	O
Delta State University	M
Dowling College	M,O
Embry–Riddle Aeronautical University (FL)	M
Embry–Riddle Aeronautical University, Extended Campus	M
Georgia State University	M
Iowa State University of Science and Technology	M
Massachusetts Institute of Technology	M,D
Michigan State University	D
Middle Tennessee State University	M
Morgan State University	M
New Jersey Institute of Technology	M,D
Northwestern University	M
Polytechnic University, Brooklyn Campus	M
Polytechnic University, Westchester Graduate Center	M
San Jose State University	M
Syracuse University	M
University of Arkansas (Fayetteville)	M
University of California, Davis	M,D
University of Dubuque	M
University of Tennessee, Knoxville	M,D
University of Virginia	M,D

TRAVEL AND TOURISM

Clemson University	M,D
The George Washington University	M
Golden Gate University	M
Michigan State University	M,D
New York University	M
North Carolina State University	M
Purdue University	M
Rochester Institute of Technology	M
Temple University (Philadelphia)	M
University of Denver	M
University of Hawaii at Manoa	M
University of Massachusetts Amherst	M
University of New Haven	M
University of South Carolina (Columbia)	M
University of Tennessee, Knoxville	M
University of Wisconsin–Stout	M
Western Illinois University	M

P—first professional degree; M—master's degree; D—doctorate; O—other advanced degree.

URBAN DESIGN

City College of the City University of New York	M
Columbia University	M
Harvard University	M
New York Institute of Technology	M
Rice University	M
State University of New York at Buffalo	M
University of California, Berkeley	M
University of Colorado at Denver	M
University of Miami	M
University of Washington	M,D,O
Washington University in St. Louis	M

URBAN EDUCATION

Cleveland State University	D
Columbia College (IL)	M
Concordia University (IL)	M
DePaul University	M
Florida International University	M
Harvard University	D
Morgan State University	D
New Jersey City University	M
Norfolk State University	M
Northeastern Illinois University	M
Old Dominion University	D
Saint Peter's College (Jersey City)	M
Temple University (Philadelphia)	M,D
Texas Southern University	D
Trinity College (DC)	M
University of Massachusetts Boston	D
University of Nebraska at Omaha	M
University of Wisconsin–Milwaukee	M,D
Virginia Commonwealth University	D

URBAN STUDIES

Alabama Agricultural and Mechanical University	M
Boston University	M
Brooklyn College of the City University of New York	M
Cleveland State University	M,D
East Tennessee State University	M
Georgia State University	M
Graduate School and University Center of the City University of New York	M,D
Hunter College of the City University of New York	M
Long Island University, Brooklyn Campus	M
Mankato State University	M
Massachusetts Institute of Technology	M,D
Michigan State University	M,D
Montclair State University	M
New Jersey City University	M
New School University	M
Norfolk State University	M
Old Dominion University	M,D
Portland State University	M,D
Queens College of the City University of New York	M
Rutgers, The State University of New Jersey, Newark	M
Saint Louis University	M
Southern Connecticut State University	M
State University of New York at Albany	O
State University of New York at Buffalo	M
Temple University (Philadelphia)	M
Trinity University	M
Tufts University	M
The University of Akron	M,D
University of Central Oklahoma	M
University of Delaware	M,D
University of Louisville	D
University of New Orleans	M,D
The University of Texas at Arlington	M
University of Wisconsin–Milwaukee	M,D
Virginia Polytechnic Institute and State University	M
Wright State University	M

VETERINARY MEDICINE

Auburn University	P
Colorado State University	P
Cornell University	P
Iowa State University of Science and Technology	P
Kansas State University	P
Louisiana State University and Agricultural and Mechanical College	P,M,D
Michigan State University	P
Mississippi State University	P
North Carolina State University	P
The Ohio State University	P
Oklahoma State University	P
Oregon State University	P
Purdue University	P
Texas A&M University (College Station)	P
Tufts University	P
Tuskegee University	P
University of California, Davis	P
University of Florida	P
University of Georgia	P
University of Illinois at Urbana–Champaign	P
University of Minnesota, Twin Cities Campus	P
University of Missouri–Columbia	P
University of Pennsylvania	P
University of Tennessee, Knoxville	P
University of Wisconsin–Madison	P
Virginia Polytechnic Institute and State University	P
Washington State University	P

VETERINARY SCIENCES

Allegheny University of the Health Sciences	M
Auburn University	M,D
Colorado State University	M,D
Cornell University	M,D
Iowa State University of Science and Technology	M,D
Kansas State University	M
Louisiana State University and Agricultural and Mechanical College	P,M,D
Michigan State University	M,D
Mississippi State University	M,D
North Carolina State University	M,D
North Dakota State University	M,D
The Ohio State University	M,D
Oklahoma State University	M,D
Oregon State University	M,D
Pennsylvania State University University Park Campus	M,D
Purdue University	M,D
Texas A&M University (College Station)	M,D
Tufts University	M
Tuskegee University	M
The University of Arizona	M,D
University of California, Davis	M,O
University of Florida	M,D
University of Georgia	M,D
University of Idaho	M,D
University of Illinois at Urbana–Champaign	M,D
University of Kentucky	M,D
University of Massachusetts Amherst	M,D
University of Minnesota, Twin Cities Campus	M,D
University of Missouri–Columbia	M,D
University of Nebraska–Lincoln	M,D
University of Wisconsin–Madison	M,D
Utah State University	M,D
Virginia Polytechnic Institute and State University	M,D
Washington State University	M,D
West Virginia University	M

VIROLOGY

Cornell University	M,D
Harvard University	D
Johns Hopkins University	D
Kansas State University	M,D
Loyola University Chicago	M,D
Purdue University	M,D
Rutgers, The State University of New Jersey, New Brunswick	M,D
Texas A&M University (College Station)	D
University of California, San Diego	D
University of Chicago	D
The University of Iowa	M,D
University of Pennsylvania	D
University of Pittsburgh	M,D
University of Virginia	M,D

VISION SCIENCES

Emory University	M
Indiana University Bloomington	M,D
Pacific University	M
The University of Alabama at Birmingham	M,D
The University of Alabama in Huntsville	D
University of California, Berkeley	M,D
University of Chicago	M,D
University of Houston	M,D
University of Louisville	D
University of Missouri–St. Louis	M,D

VOCATIONAL AND TECHNICAL EDUCATION

Alabama Agricultural and Mechanical University	M
Alcorn State University	M
Appalachian State University	M
Auburn University	M,D,O
Ball State University	M
Bemidji State University	M
Bowling Green State University	M
Brigham Young University	M
California State University, Long Beach	M
California State University, Los Angeles	M
California State University, San Bernardino	M
California University of Pennsylvania	M
Central Connecticut State University	M
Central Michigan University	M
Central Missouri State University	M,O
Chicago State University	M
City College of the City University of New York	M
Clemson University	M,D
Colorado State University	M,D
Drake University	M
East Carolina University	M
Eastern Kentucky University	M
Eastern Michigan University	M
Eastern Washington University	M
Ferris State University	M
Fitchburg State College	M
Florida Agricultural and Mechanical University	M
Florida International University	M
Florida State University	D,O
Georgia Southern University	M,O
Georgia State University	M,D,O
Idaho State University	M
Indiana State University	M,D
Inter American University of Puerto Rico, Metropolitan Campus	M
Iowa State University of Science and Technology	M,D
Jackson State University	M
James Madison University	M
Kent State University	M
Louisiana State University and Agricultural and Mechanical College	M,D
Mankato State University	M
Marshall University	M
Middle Tennessee State University	M
Millersville University of Pennsylvania	M
Mississippi State University	M
Montana State University–Northern	M
Montclair State University	M
Morehead State University	M,D
Murray State University	M
North Carolina Agricultural and Technical State University	M
North Carolina State University	M,D,O
Northern Arizona University	M
Northwest Missouri State University	M
Nova Southeastern University	D
The Ohio State University	D
Oklahoma State University	M,D,O
Old Dominion University	M
Oregon State University	M
Pennsylvania State University University Park Campus	M,D
Pittsburg State University	M,O
Purdue University	M,D,O
Rhode Island College	M
Rutgers, The State University of New Jersey, New Brunswick	M,D,O
Sam Houston State University	M
South Carolina State University	M
Southern Illinois University at Carbondale	M,D
Southwest Texas State University	M
State University of New York at Oswego	M
State University of New York College at Buffalo	M
Sul Ross State University	M
Temple University (Philadelphia)	M
Texas A&M University (College Station)	M,D
Texas A&M University–Commerce	M
Texas A&M University–Corpus Christi	M
Texas Woman's University	M,D
Tuskegee University	M
The University of Akron	M
University of Alaska Anchorage	M
University of Arkansas (Fayetteville)	M,D,O
University of Central Florida	M
University of Connecticut	M,D
University of Georgia	M,D,O
University of Idaho	M,D,O
University of Illinois at Urbana–Champaign	M,D,O
University of Kentucky	M,D,O
University of Louisville	M
University of Maryland, College Park	M,D,O
University of Minnesota, Twin Cities Campus	M
University of Missouri–Columbia	M,D,O
University of Nebraska–Lincoln	M
University of Nevada, Las Vegas	M
University of New Hampshire	M
University of North Dakota	M
University of Northern Iowa	M,D
University of North Texas	M,D,O
University of South Carolina (Columbia)	M
University of Southern Maine	M
University of Southern Mississippi	M
University of South Florida	M,D,O
The University of Texas at Tyler	M
University of Toledo	M
University of Vermont	M
University of West Florida	M
University of Wisconsin–Madison	M,D
University of Wisconsin–Platteville	M
University of Wisconsin–Stout	M,O
Utah State University	M
Valdosta State University	M,D,O
Virginia Polytechnic Institute and State University	M,D,O
Virginia State University	M,O
Wayne State College	M
Western Michigan University	M
Westfield State College	M
West Virginia University	M,D
Wright State University	M

WASTE MANAGEMENT

Colorado State University	M
Idaho State University	M
Rutgers, The State University of New Jersey, New Brunswick	M,D
Southern Methodist University	M
State University of New York at Stony Brook	M,O
University of Idaho	M
University of New Mexico	M
University of Oklahoma	M
University of South Carolina (Columbia)	M,D
Wayne State University	M,O

WATER RESOURCES

Colorado State University	M,D
Duke University	M,D
Iowa State University of Science and Technology	M,D
Johns Hopkins University	M,D
Rutgers, The State University of New Jersey, New Brunswick	M,D
South Dakota State University	D
The University of Arizona	M,D
University of Florida	M,D
University of Illinois at Chicago	M,D
University of Kansas	M
University of Minnesota, Twin Cities Campus	M,D
University of Missouri–Rolla	M,D
University of Nevada, Las Vegas	M
University of Oklahoma	M
University of Vermont	M
University of Wisconsin–Madison	M
Utah State University	M,D

WATER RESOURCES ENGINEERING

California Polytechnic State University, San Luis Obispo	M
Colorado State University	M,D
Cornell University	M,D
Florida Institute of Technology	M
Louisiana State University and Agricultural and Mechanical College	M,D
Marquette University	M,D
Ohio University	M
Oregon State University	M,D
Pennsylvania State University University Park Campus	M,D
Princeton University	D
State University of New York at Buffalo	M,D
Texas A&M University (College Station)	M,D
Tufts University	M,D
University of California, Berkeley	M,D
University of California, Irvine	M,D
University of California, Los Angeles	M,D
University of Colorado at Boulder	M,D
University of Delaware	M,D

University of Kansas	M
University of Maryland, College Park	M,D
The University of Memphis	M
University of Missouri–Columbia	M,D
University of Southern California	M
The University of Texas at Austin	M
University of Virginia	M,D
Utah State University	M,D
Villanova University	M

WESTERN EUROPEAN STUDIES

Boston College	M
Brown University	M,D
The Catholic University of America	M
Claremont Graduate University	M,D
Columbia University	M,O
East Carolina University	M
Georgetown University	M
The George Washington University	M
Indiana University Bloomington	M,D,O
Johns Hopkins University	M,D
New York University	M
University of California, Santa Barbara	M
University of Connecticut	M
University of Nevada, Reno	D
Washington University in St. Louis	M

WOMEN'S STUDIES

Brandeis University	M
Claremont Graduate University	M
Clark Atlanta University	M,D
Clark University	D
DePaul University	O
Duke University	O
Eastern Michigan University	M
Emory University	D,O
The George Washington University	M,D
Georgia State University	M
Graduate School and University Center of the City University of New York	M,D
Mankato State University	M
New School University	M
New York University	M
The Ohio State University	M
Roosevelt University	M
Rutgers, The State University of New Jersey, New Brunswick	M,D
San Diego State University	M
San Francisco State University	M
Southern Connecticut State University	M
State University of New York at Buffalo	M
The University of Alabama (Tuscaloosa)	M
The University of Arizona	M
University of Cincinnati	M,O
The University of Iowa	D
University of Massachusetts Boston	O
University of Michigan	D,O
University of Missouri–St. Louis	O
University of Northern Iowa	M
University of Oklahoma	M
University of Pittsburgh	O

University of South Carolina (Columbia)	O
University of South Florida	M

WRITING

Abilene Christian University	M
American University	M
Arizona State University	M
Boston University	M
Bowling Green State University	M,D
Brooklyn College of the City University of New York	M
Brown University	M
California State University, Fresno	M
California State University, Sacramento	M
California State University, San Marcos	M
Carnegie Mellon University	M
Chapman University	M
City College of the City University of New York	M
Claremont Graduate University	M
Clemson University	M
Colorado State University	M
Columbia College (IL)	M
Columbia University	M
Cornell University	M
DePaul University	M
Eastern Michigan University	M
Eastern Washington University	M
Emerson College	M
Florida International University	M
Florida State University	M,D
George Mason University	M
Georgia State University	M,D
Goddard College	M
Illinois State University	M
Indiana University Bloomington	M
Johns Hopkins University	M
Kennesaw State University	M
Long Island University, Brooklyn Campus	M
Long Island University, Southampton College	M
Louisiana State University and Agricultural and Mechanical College	M
Loyola Marymount University	M
Maharishi University of Management	M
Mankato State University	M
McNeese State University	M
Miami University	M
Michigan State University	M
Moorhead State University	M
National–Louis University	M
New Mexico Highlands University	M
New School University	M
New York University	M
Northeastern Illinois University	M
Northeastern University	M,D
Northwestern University	M
Norwich University	M
Old Dominion University	M
Pennsylvania State University University Park Campus	M,D
Purdue University	M
Queens College of the City University of New York	M
Rensselaer Polytechnic Institute	M,D

Rivier College	M
Roosevelt University	M
Saint Mary's College of California	M
Saint Xavier University	M,O
Salisbury State University	M
San Diego State University	M
San Francisco State University	M
Sonoma State University	M
Southern Illinois University at Carbondale	M
Southwest Texas State University	M
Syracuse University	M
Temple University (Philadelphia)	M
Towson University	M
The University of Akron	M
The University of Alabama (Tuscaloosa)	M
University of Alaska Anchorage	M
University of Alaska Fairbanks	M
The University of Arizona	M
University of Arkansas (Fayetteville)	M
University of Arkansas at Little Rock	M
University of Baltimore	M
University of California, Davis	M
University of California, Irvine	M
University of Central Florida	M
University of Central Oklahoma	M
University of Colorado at Boulder	M
University of Houston	M,D
University of Idaho	M
University of Illinois at Chicago	M,D
The University of Iowa	M,D
University of Maryland, College Park	M
University of Massachusetts Amherst	M
University of Massachusetts Dartmouth	M
The University of Memphis	M
University of Michigan	M
The University of Montana–Missoula	M
University of Nevada, Las Vegas	M
University of New Orleans	M
University of North Carolina at Greensboro	M
University of North Carolina at Wilmington	M
University of Notre Dame	M
University of Oregon	M
University of Pennsylvania	M,D
University of St. Thomas (MN)	O
University of San Francisco	M
University of South Carolina (Columbia)	M
University of Southern California	M
University of Southern Mississippi	M
University of Southwestern Louisiana	M,D
The University of Texas at Austin	M
The University of Texas at El Paso	M
University of Utah	M
University of Virginia	M
Utah State University	M
Virginia Commonwealth University	M
Washington University in St. Louis	M
Wayne State University	M,D

Western Illinois University	M
Western Kentucky University	M
Western Michigan University	M
Westminster College of Salt Lake City	M
Wichita State University	M

ZOOLOGY

Auburn University	M,D
Boston University	M,D
Brigham Young University	M,D
Clemson University	M,D
Colorado State University	M,D
Cornell University	D
Duke University	D
Eastern Illinois University	M
Emporia State University	M
Florida State University	M,D
The George Washington University	M,D
Illinois State University	D
Indiana University Bloomington	M,D
Iowa State University of Science and Technology	M,D
Kent State University	M,D
Louisiana State University and Agricultural and Mechanical College	M,D
Miami University	M,D
Michigan State University	M,D
North Carolina State University	M,D
North Dakota State University	M,D
The Ohio State University	M,D
Ohio University	M,D
Oklahoma State University	M,D
Oregon State University	M,D
Southern Illinois University at Carbondale	M,D
Texas A&M University (College Station)	M,D
Texas Tech University	M,D
Texas Woman's University	M
University of Alaska Fairbanks	M,D
University of California, Davis	M
University of Chicago	D
University of Colorado at Boulder	M,D
University of Connecticut	M,D
University of Florida	M,D
University of Hawaii at Manoa	M,D
University of Idaho	M,D
University of Maine (Orono)	M,D
University of Maryland, College Park	M,D
The University of Memphis	M,D
University of Minnesota, Twin Cities Campus	M,D
University of New Hampshire	M,D
University of New Mexico	M,D
University of North Dakota	M,D
University of Oklahoma	M,D
University of Rhode Island	M,D
University of South Carolina (Columbia)	M,D
University of South Florida	M
The University of Texas at Austin	M,D
University of Washington	D
University of Wisconsin–Madison	M,D
University of Wisconsin–Oshkosh	M
University of Wyoming	M,D
Virginia Polytechnic Institute and State University	M,D
Washington State University	M,D

P—first professional degree; M—master's degree; D—doctorate; O—other advanced degree.

Directory of Combined-Degree Programs

Over the past decade or so there has been a dramatic increase in both the number and variety of graduate-level combined-degree programs created to bridge the gap between different specialized fields. This directory will help you locate specific programs and learn about the variety of programs available.

The Combined-Degree Programs directory is organized alphabetically by field. Each combination field name is followed by the specific degrees available (in parentheses) and by a list of the institutions offering graduate degree programs in those combined fields. All programs are listed only once, so check under each possible field name. For example, those interested in combined-degree programs in the fields of law and business administration can find such programs under the heading "Law/Business Administration" but not under "Business Administration/Law," for which there is no listing.

Accounting/Taxation (MBA/MS)
Fordham University

Anthropology/Culture and Media (MA/Certificate, PhD/Certificate)
New York University

Anthropology/History (MA/Certificate)
New York University

Anthropology/Justice Studies (MA/MS)
Arizona State University

Arab Studies/Government (MA/PhD)
Georgetown University

Architecture/Business Administration (M Arch/MBA, M Arch/MS)
Arizona State University
Illinois Institute of Technology
Iowa State University of Science and Technology
New Jersey Institute of Technology
State University of New York at Buffalo
University of Illinois at Urbana–Champaign
University of Michigan
University of Nebraska–Lincoln
University of Utah
Washington University in St. Louis
Yale University

Architecture/Civil Engineering (M Arch/MS)
University of Illinois at Urbana–Champaign

Architecture/Construction Management (M Arch/MCM)
Washington University in St. Louis

Architecture/Engineering (M Arch/M Eng, M Arch/MS, M Arch/MSE)
University of California, Berkeley
University of Michigan
University of Pennsylvania

Architecture/Environmental Design (M Arch/M Env Des)
Yale University

Architecture/Historic Preservation (M Arch/MS)
Columbia University

Architecture/Infrastructure Planning (M Arch/MIP)
New Jersey Institute of Technology

Architecture/Landscape Architecture (M Arch/MLA)
University of California, Berkeley
University of Michigan
University of Pennsylvania

Architecture/Social Work (M Arch/MSW)
Washington University in St. Louis

Architecture/Urban Design (M Arch/Certificate, M Arch/MAUD)
University of Pennsylvania
Washington University in St. Louis

Architecture/Urban and Regional Planning (M Arch/MCP, M Arch/MCRP, M Arch/M Pl, M Arch/MRP, M Arch/MS, M Arch/MUP)
Columbia University
Cornell University
Georgia Institute of Technology
Iowa State University of Science and Technology
State University of New York at Buffalo
University of California, Berkeley
University of Illinois at Urbana–Champaign
University of Kansas
University of Maryland, College Park
University of Michigan
University of Nebraska–Lincoln
University of New Mexico
University of Southern California
The University of Texas at Arlington
University of Wisconsin–Milwaukee

Art History/Museum Studies (MA/Certificate, MA/Diploma)
New York University
Tufts University

Business Administration/Accounting (MBA/M Acc, MBA/MS)
Northeastern University
Saint Peter's College
Samford University
University of Colorado at Denver
University of Illinois at Chicago

Business Administration/Agricultural Economics (MBA/MS, MBA/M Sc)
Southern Illinois University at Carbondale
University of California, Davis

Business Administration/Agriculture (MBA/M Ag, MBA/M Agr)
Texas Tech University

Business Administration/American Studies (MBA/MA, MBA/PhD)
Claremont Graduate University

Business Administration/Arts Administration (MBA/MA)
Southern Methodist University
University of Cincinnati

Business Administration/Asian Studies (MBA/AM, MBA/Diploma, MBA/MA)
University of California, Berkeley
University of Michigan
University of Southern California
The University of Texas at Austin
University of Virginia
Washington University in St. Louis

Business Administration/Biomedical Sciences (MBA/MA, MBA/MS)
Boston College
Boston University
University of Rochester

Business Administration/Communications (MBA/MA, MBA/MS)
Boston University
The University of Texas at Austin

Business Administration/Computer Science (MBA/MS)
University of California, Los Angeles
University of Illinois at Urbana–Champaign

Business Administration/Construction Science (MBA/MS)
University of Oklahoma

Business Administration/Economics (MBA/MA, MBA/MS, MBA/PhD)
Boston University
Claremont Graduate University
University of Delaware
University of Illinois at Chicago
Wright State University

Business Administration/Education (MBA/Ed M, MBA/M Ed, MBA/PhD)
Claremont Graduate University
University of Illinois at Urbana–Champaign

Business Administration/English (MBA/MA, MBA/PhD)
Claremont Graduate University
St. Bonaventure University

Business Administration/Environmental Management (MBA/MEM, MBA/MS)
Duke University
Duquesne University
Illinois Institute of Technology

Business Administration/Environmental Studies (MBA/MES, MBA/MS)
Duquesne University
Yale University

Business Administration/European Studies (MBA/MA, MBA/PhD)
Claremont Graduate University

Business Administration/Exercise and Sport Science (MBA/MESS)
University of Florida

Business Administration/Finance (MBA/MS, MBA/MSF)
Boston College
Illinois Institute of Technology
University of Colorado at Denver

Business Administration/Fine Arts (MBA/MFA)
Yale University

Business Administration/Foreign Service (MBA/MS)
Georgetown University

Business Administration/Forestry (MBA/MF, MBA/MFS, MBA/MS)
Duke University
Michigan State University
University of Michigan
Yale University

Business Administration/French (MBA/MA)
New York University
University of Oklahoma

Business Administration/Geography (MBA/MA)
State University of New York at Buffalo

Business Administration/Geology and Geophysics (MBA/MS)
Boston College

Business Administration/German (MBA/MA)
University of Oklahoma

Business Administration/Gerontology (MBA/MS)
University of Southern California

Business Administration/Government (MBA/MA)
University of Virginia

Business Administration/Health Administration (MBA/MA, MBA/MHA, MBA/MHSA, MBA/MPH, MBA/MS, MBA/MSHMS, MS/AMPC)
Arizona State University
Duquesne University
Georgia State University
Indiana University–Purdue University Indianapolis
New York University
The Ohio State University
Pfeiffer University
Saint Louis University
Temple University
University of Colorado at Denver
University of Florida
University of Houston–Clear Lake
The University of Iowa
University of Michigan
The University of North Carolina at Chapel Hill
University of Oklahoma
University of Washington
Washington University in St. Louis
Xavier University

Business Administration/History (MBA/MA, MBA/PhD)
Claremont Graduate University
State University of New York at Binghamton
University of Houston

Business Administration/Industrial Engineering (MBA/MIE, MBA/MS, MBA/MSE, MBA/MSIE)
Columbia University
University of Cincinnati
University of Houston
University of Illinois at Urbana–Champaign
University of Miami
University of Michigan–Dearborn
University of New Haven
University of Southern California
University of Tennessee, Knoxville

Business Administration/Industrial and Labor Relations (MBA/MILR)
Cornell University

Business Administration/Information Science (DBA/MIS, PhD/MIS)
Indiana University Bloomington

Business Administration/Instructional Technology (MBA/MS)
Philadelphia College of Textiles and Science

Business Administration/International Business (MBA/MIB, MBA/MS)
Seton Hall University
University of Colorado at Denver
University of Pittsburgh
University of San Diego

Business Administration/International Management (MBA/MIM)
Arizona State University
Arizona State University West
Baylor University
Drury College
University of Colorado at Denver
University of Houston
Washington University in St. Louis

Business Administration/International Studies (MBA/AM, MBA/MA, MBA/MAIS, MBA/MIA)
American University
Boston University
Brigham Young University
Columbia University
The George Washington University
Johns Hopkins University
University of California, Berkeley
University of Chicago
University of Connecticut
University of Pennsylvania
University of Virginia
University of Washington
Yale University

Business Administration/Japanese Business Studies (MBA/MSJBS)
Chaminade University of Honolulu

Business Administration/Journalism (MBA/MA, MBA/MS)
Columbia University
New York University
University of Illinois at Urbana–Champaign

Business Administration/Landscape Architecture (MBA/MLA)
University of Michigan

Business Administration/Latin American Studies (MBA/AM, MBA/MA, MBA/MALAS)
San Diego State University
Tulane University
University of California, Los Angeles
University of Chicago
University of New Mexico
The University of Texas at Austin
Vanderbilt University

Business Administration/Liberal Studies (MBA/MALS)
Duquesne University

Business Administration/Linguistics (MBA/MA)
Boston College

Business Administration/Management (MBA/Certificate, MBA/MS)
Case Western Reserve University
New York University
Rutgers, The State University of New Jersey, Newark
University of Colorado at Denver

Business Administration/Management Information Systems (MBA/MS, MBA/MSMIS, MBA/PhD)
Benedictine University
Boston University
Claremont Graduate University
Duquesne University
University of Colorado at Denver
University of Pittsburgh

Business Administration/Management and Organizational Behavior (MBA/MS)
Benedictine University

Business Administration/Management of Technology (MBA/M Eng)
Vanderbilt University

Business Administration/Marketing (MBA/MS)
Philadelphia College of Textiles and Science
University of Colorado at Denver

Business Administration/Mathematics (MBA/MA, MBA/MS, MBA/PhD)
Boston College
Claremont Graduate University
University of Oklahoma

Business Administration/Middle Eastern Studies (MBA/AM, MBA/MA)
University of Chicago
The University of Texas at Austin
University of Virginia

Business Administration/Mining Engineering (MBA/MS)
Columbia University
University of Utah

Business Administration/Modern Middle Eastern and North African Studies (MBA/AM)
University of Michigan

Business Administration/Music (MBA/MM, MBA/PhD)
Claremont Graduate University
University of Michigan

Business Administration/Nursing (MBA/MS, MBA/MSN, MBA/PhD, MSBA/MSN, MS/MSN)
Barry University
Boston College
Capital University
Case Western Reserve University
Columbia University
Duke University
Duquesne University
Gannon University
Indiana State University
Johns Hopkins University
La Salle University
Loyola University Chicago
Madonna University
Northeastern University
The Ohio State University
Sacred Heart University
Sage Graduate School
Saint Louis University
Saint Xavier University
Salem State College

Samford University
Texas Tech University
The University of Alabama at Birmingham
University of Baltimore
University of California, Los Angeles
University of Cincinnati
University of Illinois at Chicago
The University of Iowa
University of Massachusetts Boston
University of Pennsylvania
University of Rochester
University of San Diego
University of San Francisco
University of Southern California
The University of Texas at Austin
The University of Texas at Tyler
University of the Incarnate Word
University of Virginia
Vanderbilt University
Wichita State University
Wright State University
Yale University

Business Administration/Nursing Administration (MBA/MNA, MBA/MS)
University of Colorado at Denver
University of Michigan
University of Tulsa

Business Administration/Operations Research (MBA/MS)
Columbia University

Business Administration/Pharmacy Administration (MBA/MS)
University of Oklahoma

Business Administration/Philosophy (MBA/MA, MBA/PhD)
Claremont Graduate University

Business Administration/Political Science (MBA/MA, MBA/PhD)
Claremont Graduate University
New York University

Business Administration/Psychology (MBA/PhD, MBA/Psy D)
Claremont Graduate University
Widener University

Business Administration/Public Affairs (MBA/MP Aff)
The University of Texas at Austin

Business Administration/Public Health (MBA/MPH, MBA/MSPH)
Benedictine University
Boston University
Columbia University
Emory University
Rutgers, The State University of New Jersey, New Brunswick
Tulane University
The University of Alabama at Birmingham
University of California, Berkeley
University of California, Los Angeles
University of Illinois at Chicago
University of Missouri–Columbia
The University of North Carolina at Chapel Hill
University of Oklahoma
University of Rochester
Yale University

Business Administration/Public and International Affairs (MBA/MPIA)
University of Pittsburgh

Business Administration/Real Estate Development (MBA/MRED)
University of Southern California

Business Administration/Religion (MBA/PhD)
Claremont Graduate University

Business Administration/Russian and East European Studies (MBA/AM, MBA/MA)
Boston College
University of Michigan
The University of Texas at Austin

Business Administration/Social Work (MBA/AM, MBA/MS, MBA/MSW)
Boston College
Columbia University
University of Chicago
University of Connecticut
University of Houston
University of Michigan
University of Pennsylvania
Washington University in St. Louis

Business Administration/Sociology (MBA/PhD)
Boston College

Business Administration/Spanish (MBA/MA)
University of Houston
University of Oklahoma

Business Administration/Sports Management (MBA/MS)
Barry University

Business Administration/Statistics (MBA/MS)
Iowa State University of Science and Technology

Business Administration/Systems Engineering (MBA/ME, MBA/MS)
University of Southern California
University of Virginia

Business Administration/Taxation (MBA/MS)
Duquesne University
Philadelphia College of Textiles and Science
Seton Hall University

Business Administration/Telecommunications (MBA/MA, MBA/MS)
Southern Illinois University at Carbondale
University of Colorado at Boulder

Business Administration/Urban Design (MBA/MAUD)
Washington University in St. Louis

Business Administration/Urban and Regional Planning (MBA/MA, MBA/MCRP, MBA/M Pl, MBA/MRP, MBA/MS)
Columbia University
Iowa State University of Science and Technology
University of California, Los Angeles
The University of North Carolina at Chapel Hill
University of Southern California

Chemical Engineering/Petroleum Engineering (MS Ch E/MSPE)
University of Pittsburgh

Civil Law/Latin American Studies (MCL/MA)
Tulane University

Communication Management/Jewish Communal Service (MA/MAJCS)
University of Southern California

Computational Finance/Industrial Administration (MSCF/MSIA)
Carnegie Mellon University

Counseling Psychology/Criminal Justice Administration (MSCP/MSCJA)
Chaminade University of Honolulu

Counseling Psychology/Religious Education and Pastoral Ministry (MA/MA)
Boston College

Counseling and Psychological Services/Developmental Disabilities (MA/MA)
Saint Mary's University of Minnesota

Creative Writing/Teaching of Writing (MFA/MA)
Columbia College

Dentistry/Biomedical Engineering (DMD/PhD)
The University of Alabama at Birmingham

Dentistry/Biomedical Sciences (DDS/MS, DDS/PhD, DMD/MS, DMD/PhD, MSD/PhD, MS/Certificate, PhD/Certificate)
Columbia University
Loma Linda University
The Ohio State University
Tufts University
The University of Alabama at Birmingham
University of California, Los Angeles
University of Illinois at Chicago
University of Washington
Virginia Commonwealth University

Dentistry/Business Administration (DDS/MBA, DMD/MBA)
Columbia University
Temple University
University of Southern California

Dentistry/Education (DMD/MS Ed)
University of Pennsylvania

Dentistry/Gerontology (DDS/MS)
University of Southern California

Dentistry/Public Health (DDS/MPH, DMD/MPH)
Columbia University
University of Illinois at Chicago
The University of North Carolina at Chapel Hill

Economics/Foreign Service (MA/MS)
Georgetown University

Education/Communications Management (MAT/MS)
Simmons College

Education/Counseling (M Ed/MA, MS/CAS)
State University of New York at Oswego

Education/Educational Administration (MAT/Certificate, MS Ed/CAS)
State University of New York at Oswego

Education/English (MAT/MA)
Simmons College

Education/Environmental Management (MAT/MEM)
Duke University

Education/French (MAT/MA)
Simmons College

Education/Latin American Studies (M Ed/MA)
University of California, Los Angeles

Education/School Psychology (MS/CAS)
State University of New York at Oswego

Education/Spanish (MAT/MA)
Simmons College

Electrical Engineering/Physics (MS/MS)
University of South Florida

Engineering Management/Business Administration (MEM/MBA)
Dartmouth College

Engineering Management/Electrical Engineering and Computer Science (MEM/MS)
The George Washington University

Engineering/Business Administration (ME/MBA, M Eng/MBA, M Eng/M Mgt, M Engr/MBA, MS/MBA, MSE/MBA)
Boston University
Brigham Young University
California Polytechnic State University, San Luis Obispo
Cornell University
Duke University
Rensselaer Polytechnic Institute
Rice University
University of California, Davis
University of Illinois at Urbana–Champaign
University of Michigan
University of Pennsylvania
The University of Texas at Austin
University of Washington
Widener University

Engineering/International Management of Technology (MSE/MIMOT)
Arizona State University

Engineering/Public Policy and Administration (MS/MPA, MS/MPP, MSE/MP Aff)
New York University
University of California, Berkeley
The University of Texas at Austin

Engineering/Urban and Regional Planning (MA Sc/MURP, M Eng/MURP, MS/MCP, MS/MCRP, MS/MUP, MSE/MCP)
California Polytechnic State University, San Luis Obispo
University of California, Berkeley
University of Pennsylvania
University of Wisconsin–Milwaukee

English Education/Literature (MA/PhD)
University of Delaware

English Literature/Literature (MA/PhD)
University of Delaware

Environmental Sciences/Biology (MSES/MA)
Indiana University Bloomington

Environmental Sciences/Geological Sciences (MSES/MS)
Indiana University Bloomington

Environmental Studies/International Relations (MES/MA)
Yale University

Family Studies/Family Studies (MA/Certificate)
Loma Linda University

Film and Television/African Area Studies (MFA/MA)
University of California, Los Angeles

Fine Arts/Art History (MFA/MA, MFA/MS)
Tufts University

Fine Arts/Museum Studies (MFA/Certificate, PhD/Certificate)
New York University
Tufts University

Fine Arts/Photography (MFA/MA)
Barry University

Forest Resources/International Studies (MFR/MAIS)
University of Washington

Forestry/International Relations (MF/MA, MFS/MA)
Yale University

German and European Studies/Economics (MA/PhD)
Georgetown University

German and European Studies/German (MA/PhD)
Georgetown University

German and European Studies/Government (MA/PhD)
Georgetown University

German/History (MA/MA)
Bowling Green State University

Gerontology/Jewish Communal Service (MA/MAJCS, MSG/MAJCS, MS/MAJCS)
University of Southern California

Health Administration/Economics (MHSA/AM)
University of Michigan

Health Administration/Gerontology (MHA/MS)
University of Southern California

Health Administration/Human Resource Management (MHA/MHRM)
Washington University in St. Louis

Health Sciences/International Studies (MHS/MA)
Johns Hopkins University

Health Services Administration/Industrial and Operations Engineering (MHSA/MS)
University of Michigan

Human Resources/Organizational Development (MSHR/MSOD)
Loyola University Chicago

Human Resources/Training and Development (MSHR/MSTD)
Loyola University Chicago

Human and Health Services Administration/Management (MA/MA)
Saint Mary's University of Minnesota

Industrial Relations/Organizational Development (MSIR/MSOD)
Loyola University Chicago

Industrial Relations/Training and Development (MSIR/MSTD)
Loyola University Chicago

International Studies/Public Services (MA/MS)
DePaul University

Journalism/Asian Studies (MJ/MA)
University of California, Berkeley

Journalism/International Studies (MJ/MA, MS/MIA)
Columbia University
University of California, Berkeley

Journalism/Latin American Studies (MJ/MA)
University of California, Berkeley

Landscape Architecture/Russian and East European Studies (MLA/AM)
University of Michigan

Latin American Studies/Government (MA/PhD)
Georgetown University

Law/Accounting (JD/MA, JD/M Ac, JD/M Acc, JD/M Acct, JD/MPA, JD/MP Acc, JD/MS, JD/MS/MBA)
The Catholic University of America
Gonzaga University
Northeastern University
Samford University
Southern Illinois University at Carbondale
Syracuse University
University of Florida
University of Georgia
The University of Iowa
University of Nebraska–Lincoln
University of South Carolina
University of South Dakota
University of Tulsa
University of Virginia

Law/African American World Studies (JD/MA)
The University of Iowa

Law/Agricultural Economics (JD/MS)
Drake University
Texas Tech University

Law/American Indian Studies (JD/MA)
The University of Arizona
University of California, Los Angeles

Law/American Studies (JD/AM, JD/MA, JD/PhD)
College of William and Mary
University of Pennsylvania

Law/Anthropology (JD/AM, JD/MA, JD/PhD)
Columbia University
State University of New York at Buffalo

Law/Applied Economics (JD/MA, JD/MAE, JD/MS)
Duke University
Seattle University
Southern Methodist University
Texas Tech University

Law/Arts Management (JD/MAM)
University of Pittsburgh

Law/Asian Studies (JD/AM, JD/MA, JD/PhD)
The George Washington University
University of California, Berkeley
University of Hawaii at Manoa
University of Pennsylvania
Washington University in St. Louis

Law/Bioethics (JD/MA)
Case Western Reserve University

Law/Biology (JD/MS)
University of Richmond
University of Tulsa

Law/Business Administration (JD/MA, JD/MBA, JD/MS, LL B/MBA, MALD/MBA)
American University
Arizona State University
Baruch College of the City University of New York
Baylor University
Boston College
Brigham Young University
Capital University
Case Western Reserve University
The Catholic University of America
Cleveland State University
The College of Saint Rose
College of William and Mary
Columbia University
Cornell University
Creighton University
Dartmouth College
DePaul University
Dominican University
Drake University
Duke University
Duquesne University
Emory University
Florida State University
Fordham University
Georgetown University
The George Washington University
Georgia State University
Golden Gate University
Gonzaga University
Harvard University
Hofstra University
Howard University
Illinois Institute of Technology

Indiana University Bloomington
Indiana University–Purdue University Indianapolis
Long Island University, C.W. Post Campus
Loyola Marymount University
Loyola University Chicago
Loyola University New Orleans
Marquette University
Mercer University
Mississippi College
New York University
North Carolina Central University
Northeastern University
Northern Kentucky University
Nova Southeastern University
The Ohio State University
Oklahoma City University
Pace University
Pepperdine University
Pontifical Catholic University of Puerto Rico
Quinnipiac College
Rensselaer Polytechnic Institute
Rutgers, The State University of New Jersey, Camden
Rutgers, The State University of New Jersey, Newark
Sage Graduate School
St. John's University
Saint Louis University
St. Mary's University of San Antonio
Samford University
Santa Clara University
Seattle University
Seton Hall University
Southern Illinois University at Carbondale
Southern Methodist University
Stanford University
State University of New York at Buffalo
Stetson University
Suffolk University
Syracuse University
Temple University
Texas Southern University
Texas Tech University
Tufts University
Tulane University
The University of Akron
The University of Alabama
The University of Arizona
University of Arkansas at Little Rock
University of Baltimore
University of California, Berkeley
University of California, Davis
University of California, Los Angeles
University of Chicago
University of Cincinnati
University of Colorado at Boulder
University of Connecticut
University of Dayton
University of Denver
University of Detroit Mercy
University of Florida
University of Georgia
University of Houston
University of Illinois at Urbana–Champaign
The University of Iowa
University of Kansas
University of Kentucky
University of Louisville
University of Maryland, College Park
The University of Memphis
University of Miami
University of Michigan

University of Mississippi
University of Missouri–Columbia
University of Missouri–Kansas City
University of Nebraska–Lincoln
University of New Mexico
The University of North Carolina at Chapel Hill
University of Oklahoma
University of Oregon
University of Pennsylvania
University of Pittsburgh
University of Richmond
University of San Diego
University of San Francisco
University of South Carolina
University of South Dakota
University of Southern California
University of Tennessee, Knoxville
The University of Texas at Austin
University of the Pacific
University of Toledo
University of Tulsa
University of Utah
University of Virginia
University of Washington
Vanderbilt University
Villanova University
Wake Forest University
Washington University in St. Louis
Wayne State University
West Virginia University
Widener University
Yale University

Law/Communications (JD/MA, JD/MS)
Syracuse University
University of Southern California

Law/Criminal Justice (JD/MA, JD/MCJ, JD/MS, LL B/MA)
Rutgers, The State University of New Jersey, Newark
University of Baltimore
University of Maryland, College Park
University of South Carolina

Law/Economics (JD/AM, JD/MA, JD/MS, JD/PhD, LL B/MA, LL B/PhD)
Arizona State University
The Catholic University of America
Columbia University
Duke University
Florida State University
Iowa State University of Science and Technology
New York University
St. Mary's University of San Antonio
State University of New York at Buffalo
Syracuse University
The University of Arizona
University of California, Berkeley
University of Chicago
The University of Iowa
University of Kansas
University of Michigan
University of Missouri–Columbia
University of Nebraska–Lincoln
University of Pennsylvania
University of South Carolina
University of Southern California
University of Virginia
Washington University in St. Louis

Law/Education (JD/Ed D, JD/MA, JD/MAE, JD/M Ed, JD/PhD)
Brigham Young University
Samford University

University of California, Los Angeles
University of Nebraska–Lincoln

Law/Educational Administration (JD/MA, JD/PhD)
Boston College
University of Florida
The University of Iowa
University of Nebraska–Lincoln
University of South Dakota

Law/Engineering Management (JD/MS)
Illinois Institute of Technology

Law/Engineering and Computer Science (JD/MS)
Syracuse University

Law/English (JD/AM, JD/MA)
Duke University
University of South Dakota
University of Tulsa

Law/Environmental Management (JD/MEM, JD/MS, JD/MSEM)
Duke University
Duquesne University
Samford University
University of Oklahoma

Law/Environmental Studies (JD/AM, JD/MES, JD/MPS, JD/MS, JD/MSEL, JD/MSES, LL B/MES)
Duke University
Duquesne University
Indiana University Bloomington
Syracuse University
The University of Montana–Missoula
University of Oregon
Yale University

Law/European Studies (JD/MA)
The George Washington University

Law/Exercise and Sport Science (JD/MESS)
University of Florida

Law/Finance (JD/MA, JD/MS, JD/MSF)
The Catholic University of America
Illinois Institute of Technology
Seattle University
Suffolk University

Law/Fine Arts (JD/MA)
Syracuse University

Law/Foreign Service (JD/MS)
Georgetown University

Law/Forestry (JD/MF, JD/MFS)
Duke University
Yale University

Law/French Studies (JD/MA)
New York University

Law/Geography (JD/MA)
The University of Iowa

Law/Gerontology (JD/MS)
University of Southern California

Law/Government Administration (JD/MGA)
University of Pennsylvania

Law/Health Administration (JD/MA, JD/MBA, JD/MHA, JD/MHSA, JD/MPH, JD/MS, LL B/MHSA)
Arizona State University
Boston University
The George Washington University
Indiana University–Purdue University Indianapolis
The Ohio State University

Quinnipiac College
Saint Louis University
Tulane University
University of Cincinnati
The University of Iowa
University of Kansas
University of Michigan
University of Oklahoma
University of Richmond
Virginia Commonwealth University
Washington University in St. Louis

Law/History (JD/AM, JD/MA, JD/PhD)
The Catholic University of America
Columbia University
Duke University
New York University
State University of New York at Buffalo
Syracuse University
Texas Southern University
University of Chicago
University of Florida
University of Houston
The University of Iowa
University of Richmond
University of South Dakota
University of Tulsa
University of Virginia
Wayne State University

Law/Human Development and Family Studies (JD/MA)
University of Missouri–Columbia

Law/Humanities (JD/AM)
Duke University

Law/Industrial Administration (JD/MSIA)
Carnegie Mellon University

Law/Industrial Engineering (JD/MS)
St. Mary's University of San Antonio

Law/Industrial and Labor Relations (JD/MILR, JD/MSIR, LL B/MIR)
Cornell University
Loyola University Chicago

Law/Information Resources Management (JD/MS)
Syracuse University

Law/International Business (JD/MIB, JD/MIBS)
Seattle University
University of San Diego
University of South Carolina

Law/International Economics (JD/MSIE)
Suffolk University

Law/International Management (JD/MIM)
University of Denver

Law/International Relations (JD/AM, JD/MA)
Boston University
Golden Gate University
St. Mary's University of San Antonio
Syracuse University
University of Chicago
University of San Diego
University of Southern California
Yale University

Law/International Studies (JD/MA, JD/MAIS, JD/MIA, JD/MS, JD/MSIA)
American University
Columbia University
Florida State University

The George Washington University
Johns Hopkins University
Marquette University
University of California, Berkeley
University of Denver
University of Pittsburgh
University of Virginia
University of Washington

Law/Journalism (JD/MA, JD/MJ, JD/MS, MALD/MSJ)
Columbia University
Tufts University
University of California, Berkeley
The University of Iowa

Law/Justice Studies (JD/MS, JD/PhD)
American University
Arizona State University

Law/Latin American Studies (JD/MA, JD/MALAS)
The George Washington University
New York University
University of New Mexico
The University of Texas at Austin

Law/Law (JD/CAGS, JD/Certificate, JD/JCL, JD/LL B, JD/LL M, JD/MA, JD/MALD, JD/MEL, JD/MIP, JD/PhD, MCL/LL M)
Capital University
The Catholic University of America
Cornell University
Duke University
Harvard University
Illinois Institute of Technology
New York University
Temple University
Tufts University
University of Baltimore
University of Detroit Mercy
University of Hawaii at Manoa
University of Missouri–Kansas City

Law/Legal Studies (JD/MA, JD/MS, JD/PhD)
Case Western Reserve University
Northeastern University

Law/Library Science (JD/MA, JD/MLIS, JD/MLS, JD/MS, JD/MSLS, LL B/MLIS)
The Catholic University of America
Indiana University Bloomington
North Carolina Central University
Southern Connecticut State University
Syracuse University
University of Connecticut
University of Hawaii at Manoa
The University of Iowa

Law/Management (JD/MA, JD/MAM, JD/MM, JD/PhD)
Northwestern University
Syracuse University

Law/Marine Science (JD/MS)
University of Miami

Law/Mass Communication (JD/MA, JD/MAMC, JD/MS)
Boston University
Drake University
Loyola University New Orleans
University of Florida

Law/Mechanical Engineering (JD/MS)
Duke University

Law/Medical Ethics (JD/MA)
University of Pittsburgh

Law/Medical Humanities (JD/PhD)
University of Houston

Law/Mental Health Counseling (JD/MS)
Nova Southeastern University

Law/Middle Eastern Studies (JD/AM, JD/MA, JD/PhD)
Harvard University
University of Pennsylvania
The University of Texas at Austin

Law/Modern Middle Eastern and North African Studies (JD/AM)
University of Michigan

Law/Natural Resources and Environment (JD/MS)
University of Michigan

Law/Nonprofit Organization (JD/MNO)
Case Western Reserve University

Law/Nursing (JD/MSN)
Capital University

Law/Occupational Health (JD/MPH, JD/MS)
University of Oklahoma

Law/Organizational Behavior (JD/MOB)
Brigham Young University

Law/Personnel and Employee Relations (JD/MPER)
University of South Carolina

Law/Pharmacy (JD/Pharm D)
Drake University

Law/Philosophy (JD/AM, JD/MA, JD/PhD, LL B/PhD)
The Catholic University of America
Columbia University
Duke University
Georgetown University
New York University
Rutgers, The State University of New Jersey, Newark
State University of New York at Buffalo
Syracuse University
The University of Arizona
The University of Iowa
University of Kansas
University of Pennsylvania
University of Southern California
University of Virginia

Law/Physics (JD/PhD)
The University of Iowa

Law/Policy Sciences (JD/MPS, JD/PhD)
University of Baltimore
University of Maryland, Baltimore County

Law/Political Science (JD/AM, JD/MA, JD/MS, JD/PhD, LL B/MA)
Brooklyn College of the City University of New York
The Catholic University of America
Columbia University
Drake University
Duke University
Georgetown University
Iowa State University of Science and Technology
Loyola University Chicago
Marquette University
New York University
Rutgers, The State University of New Jersey, Camden
Rutgers, The State University of New Jersey, Newark
Rutgers, The State University of New Jersey, New Brunswick
St. John's University
Southern Illinois University at Carbondale
State University of New York at Buffalo
Syracuse University
University of Michigan

University of Nebraska–Lincoln
University of South Dakota
University of Virginia
Washington University in St. Louis
Wayne State University

Law/Preservation Studies (JD/MA)
Boston University

Law/Psychology (JD/AM, JD/MA, JD/PhD, JD/Psy D)
Allegheny University of the Health Sciences
The Catholic University of America
Columbia University
Duke University
Golden Gate University
The University of Arizona
University of Denver
University of Florida
University of Maryland, Baltimore County
University of Nebraska–Lincoln
University of South Dakota
University of Tulsa
Villanova University
Widener University

Law/Public Affairs (JD/MPA, JD/MP Aff, JD/MS)
Columbia University
The University of Arizona
University of Pittsburgh
The University of Texas at Austin

Law/Public Health (JD/MPH, JD/MSPH, LL M/MPH, LL M/MSPH)
Boston University
Emory University
The George Washington University
Saint Louis University
Samford University
Tulane University
The University of Alabama at Birmingham
University of Connecticut
University of Houston
University of Miami
The University of North Carolina at Chapel Hill
University of Oklahoma
University of Pittsburgh

Law/Public Management (JD/MPM)
University of Maryland, College Park

Law/Public Policy and Administration (JD/AM, JD/MA, JD/MAPA, JD/MAPPS, JD/MPA, JD/MPP, JD/MS, LL B/MPA, LL M/MPA)
Brigham Young University
Carnegie Mellon University
Cleveland State University
College of William and Mary
Cornell University
Drake University
Duke University
Florida State University
The George Washington University
Georgia State University
Golden Gate University
Harvard University
Illinois Institute of Technology
Indiana University Bloomington
Indiana University–Purdue University Indianapolis
Long Island University, C.W. Post Campus
Louisiana State University and Agricultural and Mechanical College
New York University
The Ohio State University
Pace University

Princeton University
Rutgers, The State University of New Jersey, New Brunswick
Saint Louis University
St. Mary's University of San Antonio
Samford University
Southern Illinois University at Carbondale
State University of New York at Albany
Suffolk University
Syracuse University
Texas Southern University
Texas Tech University
The University of Akron
University of Baltimore
University of California, Berkeley
University of Colorado at Boulder
University of Connecticut
University of Florida
University of Kansas
University of Kentucky
University of Michigan
University of Minnesota, Twin Cities Campus
University of Missouri–Kansas City
The University of Montana–Missoula
University of New Mexico
The University of North Carolina at Chapel Hill
University of Pittsburgh
University of South Carolina
University of South Dakota
University of Southern California
University of Southern Maine
University of Tennessee, Knoxville
University of Utah
University of Washington
University of Wyoming
West Virginia University

Law/Public and International Affairs (JD/MPIA)
University of Pittsburgh

Law/Real Estate Development (JD/MRED)
University of Southern California

Law/Religion (JD/MA, JD/MAR)
Loyola University New Orleans
University of Southern California
Yale University

Law/Romance Studies (JD/AM)
Duke University

Law/Russian and East European Studies (JD/AM, JD/MA, LL B/MA)
The George Washington University
University of Michigan
The University of Texas at Austin

Law/Science, Technology, and Public Policy (JD/MA)
The George Washington University

Law/Security Policy Studies (JD/MA)
The George Washington University

Law/Social Administration (JD/MSSA)
Case Western Reserve University

Law/Social Foundations (JD/MA)
The University of Iowa

Law/Social Sciences (JD/PhD)
Northwestern University

Law/Social Work (JD/MS, JD/MSW, LL B/MSW)
Boston College
The Catholic University of America
Columbia University

Drake University
Florida State University
Fordham University
Loyola University Chicago
New York University
Rutgers, The State University of New Jersey, Camden
San Diego State University
Southern Illinois University at Carbondale
State University of New York at Buffalo
Syracuse University
Tulane University
University of California, Berkeley
University of Connecticut
University of Denver
The University of Iowa
University of Kansas
The University of North Carolina at Chapel Hill
University of Pennsylvania
University of Richmond
University of Southern California
Virginia Commonwealth University
Washington University in St. Louis

Law/Sociology (JD/MA, JD/PhD)
Columbia University
New York University
State University of New York at Buffalo
University of Denver
University of Florida
University of Virginia

Law/Sports Administration (JD/MSA)
Capital University

Law/Taxation (JD/MBT, JD/MT, JD/M Tax)
Baylor University
The University of Akron
University of Southern California
University of Tulsa

Law/Theater Studies (JD/MFA)
Columbia University

Law/Theology (JD/MA, JD/M Div, JD/MTS)
Duke University
Duquesne University
Emory University
St. Mary's University of San Antonio
Samford University
University of Louisville
Vanderbilt University
Yale University

Law/Urban and Environmental Policy (MALD/MA)
Tufts University

Law/Urban and Regional Planning (JD/MA, JD/MAUA, JD/MAURP, JD/MCP, JD/MCRP, JD/MP, JD/MRP, JD/MS, JD/MSCRP, JD/MSP, JD/MUP, JD/MURP)
Columbia University
Cornell University
Florida State University
Hunter College of the City University of New York
New York University
Rutgers, The State University of New Jersey, Camden
Rutgers, The State University of New Jersey, Newark
Rutgers, The State University of New Jersey, New Brunswick
Saint Louis University
Texas Southern University
University of California, Berkeley
University of California, Los Angeles
University of Cincinnati
University of Florida

University of Hawaii at Manoa
University of Illinois at Urbana–Champaign
The University of Iowa
University of Kansas
University of Nebraska–Lincoln
The University of North Carolina at Chapel Hill
University of Pennsylvania
University of Pittsburgh
University of Richmond
The University of Texas at Austin
University of Virginia
Virginia Commonwealth University

Law/Women's Studies (JD/MA)
University of Cincinnati

Library Science/American Studies (MLIS/MA)
University of Hawaii at Manoa

Library Science/Art History (MLS/MA, MS/MS)
Indiana University Bloomington

Library Science/Asian Studies (MLIS/MA)
University of Hawaii at Manoa

Library Science/Biology (MSLS/MS)
The Catholic University of America

Library Science/Business Administration (MA/MBA, MLIS/MBA)
Dominican University
University of California, Los Angeles
The University of Iowa
University of Oklahoma

Library Science/Chemistry (MLS/MS)
Southern Connecticut State University

Library Science/Comparative Literature (MLIS/MA, MLS/MA)
Indiana University Bloomington
University of Wisconsin–Milwaukee

Library Science/Education (MLIS/M Ed, MS/MS Ed)
Simmons College
University of Oklahoma

Library Science/English (MLIS/MA, MLS/MA, MLS/MS, MSLS/MA)
The Catholic University of America
Southern Connecticut State University
State University of New York at Albany
University of South Carolina
University of Wisconsin–Milwaukee

Library Science/Foreign Languages (MLS/MS)
Southern Connecticut State University

Library Science/Geography (MLIS/MA, MLS/MA)
University of Maryland, College Park
University of Wisconsin–Milwaukee

Library Science/Government (MLS/MA)
St. John's University

Library Science/Greek and Latin (MSLS/MA)
The Catholic University of America

Library Science/History (MLIS/MA, MLS/MA, MLS/MS, MS/MA, MSLS/MA)
The Catholic University of America
Dominican University
Indiana University Bloomington
Simmons College
Southern Connecticut State University
State University of New York at Albany
University of California, Los Angeles
University of Hawaii at Manoa

University of Maryland, College Park
University of South Carolina
University of Wisconsin–Milwaukee

Library Science/History and Philosophy of Science (MLS/MA)
Indiana University Bloomington

Library Science/Instructional Technology (MLS/MS)
Southern Connecticut State University

Library Science/Journalism (MLS/MA)
Indiana University Bloomington

Library Science/Latin American Studies (MLIS/MA)
University of California, Los Angeles

Library Science/Library Science (MLIS/MS)
University of Hawaii at Manoa

Library Science/Music (MLIS/MM, MLS/MA, MSLS/MA)
The Catholic University of America
Dominican University
Indiana University Bloomington
University of Wisconsin–Milwaukee

Library Science/Pacific Island Studies (MLIS/MA)
University of Hawaii at Manoa

Library Science/Pharmaceutical Sciences (MLS/MS)
St. John's University

Library Science/Religious Studies (MSLS/MA)
The Catholic University of America

Library Science/Spanish (MLS/MA)
Rutgers, The State University of New Jersey, New Brunswick

Library Science/Urban Studies (MLIS/MS)
University of Wisconsin–Milwaukee

Manufacturing/Industrial Administration (MOM/MSIA)
Carnegie Mellon University

Marine Affairs/International Studies (MMA/MAIS)
University of Washington

Medicine/Anthropology (MD/PhD)
University of Illinois at Urbana–Champaign

Medicine/Art and Design (MD/PhD)
University of Illinois at Urbana–Champaign

Medicine/Bioethics (MD/MA)
University of Pittsburgh

Medicine/Biomedical Engineering (MD/MS, MD/PhD)
Allegheny University of the Health Sciences
Case Western Reserve University
Dartmouth College
Drexel University
Georgia Institute of Technology
Johns Hopkins University
The University of Akron
The University of Alabama at Birmingham
University of Illinois at Chicago
University of Pennsylvania
Vanderbilt University

Medicine/Biomedical Sciences (MD/MA, MD/MM Sc, MD/MS, MD/PhD)
Allegheny University of the Health Sciences
Boston University
Brown University
Case Western Reserve University
Columbia University
Cornell University
Creighton University
Dartmouth College
East Carolina University

Emory University
Georgetown University
The George Washington University
Georgia State University
Graduate School and University Center of the City University of New York
Harvard University
Howard University
Indiana University Bloomington
Indiana University–Purdue University Indianapolis
Loma Linda University
Loyola University Chicago
Massachusetts Institute of Technology
Michigan State University
New York University
Northwestern University
The Ohio State University
Purdue University
Rockefeller University
Rutgers, The State University of New Jersey, New Brunswick
Saint Louis University
Stanford University
State University of New York at Buffalo
State University of New York at Stony Brook
Temple University
Texas A&M University
Tufts University
Tulane University
The University of Arizona
University of California, Berkeley
University of California, Davis
University of California, Irvine
University of California, Los Angeles
University of California, San Diego
University of California, San Francisco
University of Chicago
University of Cincinnati
University of Florida
University of Illinois at Chicago
University of Illinois at Urbana–Champaign
The University of Iowa
University of Kansas
University of Kentucky
University of Louisville
University of Maryland, Baltimore County
University of Miami
University of Michigan
University of Missouri–Columbia
University of Missouri–Kansas City
University of Nevada, Reno
The University of North Carolina at Chapel Hill
University of North Dakota
University of Pennsylvania
University of Rochester
University of Southern California
University of Utah
University of Vermont
University of Virginia
University of Washington
University of Wisconsin–Madison
Vanderbilt University
Virginia Commonwealth University
Wake Forest University
Washington University in St. Louis
Wayne State University
West Virginia University
Yale University
Yeshiva University

Medicine/Business Administration (MD/MBA, MD/MM, MD/PhD)
Dartmouth College
Duke University
Georgetown University
Northwestern University
University of California, Davis
University of Chicago
University of Illinois at Urbana–Champaign
University of Pennsylvania
Wake Forest University
Widener University

Medicine/Chemistry (MD/PhD)
Indiana University–Purdue University Indianapolis
University of Illinois at Urbana–Champaign
University of Maryland, Baltimore County
Yale University

Medicine/Communications Research (MD/PhD)
University of Illinois at Urbana–Champaign

Medicine/Computer Science (MD/PhD)
University of Illinois at Urbana–Champaign

Medicine/Dentistry (MD/DDS)
Columbia University

Medicine/Economics (MD/PhD)
New York University
University of Illinois at Urbana–Champaign

Medicine/Education (MD/PhD)
University of Illinois at Urbana–Champaign

Medicine/Engineering (MD/PhD)
Rice University
University of Illinois at Urbana–Champaign

Medicine/English (MD/PhD)
University of Illinois at Urbana–Champaign

Medicine/Environmental Health Sciences (MD/MS)
Case Western Reserve University

Medicine/Health Administration (MD/MHA)
The Ohio State University
Tulane University
Washington University in St. Louis
Widener University

Medicine/History (MD/PhD)
University of Illinois at Urbana–Champaign

Medicine/Kinesiology (MD/PhD)
University of Illinois at Urbana–Champaign

Medicine/Law (MD/JD)
Duke University
Rutgers, The State University of New Jersey, Camden
Southern Illinois University at Carbondale
University of Illinois at Urbana–Champaign
Yale University

Medicine/Mathematics (MD/PhD)
University of Illinois at Urbana–Champaign

Medicine/Medical History (MD/PhD)
Duke University

Medicine/Philosophy (MD/MA, MD/PhD)
The Catholic University of America
Georgetown University
New York University
University of Illinois at Urbana–Champaign

Medicine/Physics (MD/PhD)
University of Illinois at Urbana–Champaign

Medicine/Political Science (MD/PhD)
University of Illinois at Urbana–Champaign

Medicine/Psychology (MD/PhD)
University of Chicago
University of Illinois at Urbana–Champaign
Yale University

Medicine/Public Health (MD/Dr PH, MD/MPH, MD/MSPH, MD/PhD, MD/Sc D)
Boston University
Columbia University
Duke University
Emory University
The George Washington University
Harvard University
Johns Hopkins University
Northwestern University
The Ohio State University
Rutgers, The State University of New Jersey, New Brunswick
Saint Louis University
Tufts University
Tulane University
University of California, Berkeley
University of California, Davis
University of California, San Francisco
University of Illinois at Chicago
University of Illinois at Urbana–Champaign
University of Miami
University of Michigan
The University of North Carolina at Chapel Hill
University of Rochester
University of Utah
University of Washington
Yale University

Medicine/Public Policy and Administration (MD/AM, MD/MPA, MD/MPP)
Duke University
Harvard University
New York University

Medicine/Public Service (MD/PhD)
New York University

Medicine/Religion (MD/MAR)
Yale University

Medicine/Social Work (MD/PhD)
University of Illinois at Urbana–Champaign

Medicine/Sociology (MD/PhD)
University of Illinois at Urbana–Champaign

Medicine/Speech and Hearing Science (MD/PhD)
University of Illinois at Urbana–Champaign

Medicine/Statistics (MD/PhD)
University of Illinois at Urbana–Champaign

Medicine/Theology (MD/M Div)
Yale University

Medicine/Tropical Medicine (MD/MPHTM)
Tulane University

National Security Studies/Government (MA/PhD)
Georgetown University

Natural Resources and Environment/Russian and East European Studies (MS/AM)
University of Michigan

Near Eastern and Judaic Studies/Jewish Communal Service (MA/MA)
Brandeis University

Nursing/Anthropology (MSN/MA)
Case Western Reserve University

Nursing/Bioethics (MSN/MA)
Case Western Reserve University

Nursing/Health Administration (MN/MHSA, MS/MHA, MS/ MHSA, MSN/MHA)
Arizona State University
Indiana University–Purdue University Indianapolis
The Ohio State University
University of North Carolina at Charlotte

Nursing/International Business (MSN/MIB)
University of San Diego

Nursing/Latin American Studies (MSN/MALAS)
University of New Mexico

Nursing/Lay Ministry (MSN/MA)
Capital University

Nursing/Management (MA/MS)
New York University

Nursing/Nursing Education (MSN/MA)
Seton Hall University

Nursing/Organizational Behavior (MSN/MSOB)
University of Hartford

Nursing/Theology (MSN/MATS, MSN/M Div)
Loyola University Chicago

Optometry/Public Health (OD/MPH)
The University of Alabama at Birmingham

Optometry/Vision Sciences (OD/MS, OD/PhD)
The Ohio State University
The University of Alabama at Birmingham

Organizational Behavior/International Relations (MOB/MA)
Brigham Young University

Organizational Development/Training and Development (MSOD/MSTD)
Loyola University Chicago

Osteopathic Medicine/Biomedical Sciences (DO/MS, DO/PhD)
Michigan State University
Ohio University

Osteopathic Medicine/Business Administration (DO/MBA)
New York Institute of Technology
Saint Joseph's University

Osteopathic Medicine/Clinical Nutrition (DO/MS)
New York Institute of Technology

Pharmacy/Biomedical Sciences (Pharm D/PhD)
University of Southern California

Pharmacy/Business Administration (MS/MBA, Pharm D/MBA)
Drake University
Duquesne University
Mercer University, Cecil B. Day Campus
University of Florida
University of Southern California

Pharmacy/Chemistry (PhD/MS)
Eastern Michigan University

Pharmacy/Pharmaceutical Sciences (Pharm D/PhD)
Mercer University, Cecil B. Day Campus
University of California, San Francisco
University of Florida
University of Michigan
University of Southern California
University of the Pacific
Virginia Commonwealth University

Pharmacy/Pharmacy Health Care Administration (Pharm D/ PhD)
University of Florida

Pharmacy/Physician Assistant Studies (Pharm D/MPAS)
University of Florida

Philosophy/Philosophy of Religion and Theology (MA/PhD)
Claremont Graduate University

Podiatric Medicine/Bioengineering (DPM/PhD)
University of Pennsylvania

Podiatric Medicine/Biomedical Sciences (DPM/PhD)
Temple University

Political Science/German (MA/MA)
Bowling Green State University

Political Science/Government Administration (AM/MGA)
University of Pennsylvania

Psychology/Health Administration (Psy D/MHA, Psy D/MHSA)
Widener University

Public Affairs/Asian Studies (MP Aff/MA)
The University of Texas at Austin

Public Affairs/Communication (MP Aff/MA)
The University of Texas at Austin

Public Affairs/Latin American Studies (MP Aff/MA)
The University of Texas at Austin

Public Affairs/Middle Eastern Studies (MP Aff/MA)
The University of Texas at Austin

Public Affairs/Russian and East European Studies (MP Aff/ MA)
The University of Texas at Austin

Public Health/African Area Studies (MPH/MA)
University of California, Los Angeles

Public Health/Biomedical Sciences (MPH/MA)
Boston University

Public Health/Economics (MPH/MA)
Boston University

Public Health/Environmental Studies (MPH/MES)
Yale University

Public Health/Epidemiology (MPH/PhD)
The University of Alabama at Birmingham

Public Health/Forestry (MPH/MFS)
Yale University

Public Health/Health Administration (MPH/MHA)
University of Pittsburgh

Public Health/Health Services (MPH/MSHS, MPH/PhD)
The George Washington University
Saint Louis University
University of Rochester

Public Health/International Affairs (MPH/MA, MPH/MIA)
Columbia University
Yale University

Public Health/International Studies (MPH/MAIS)
University of Washington

Public Health/Islamic Studies (MPH/MA)
University of California, Los Angeles

Public Health/Latin American Studies (MPH/MA)
University of California, Los Angeles

Public Health/Management Information Systems (MPH/MS)
Benedictine University

Public Health/Management and Organizational Behavior (MPH/MS)
Benedictine University

Public Health/Modern Middle Eastern and North African Studies (MPH/AM)
University of Michigan

Public Health/Nursing (MPH/MN, MPH/MS, MPH/MSN)
California State University, Long Beach
Columbia University
Emory University
Hunter College of the City University of New York
Johns Hopkins University
Saint Louis University
University of Illinois at Chicago
University of Minnesota, Twin Cities Campus
University of South Carolina
University of Washington
Yale University

Public Health/Nutrition and Dietetics (MPH/MS)
Saint Louis University

Public Health/Occupational Therapy (MPH/MS)
Columbia University

Public Health/Psychology (Dr PH/Psy D, MPH/PhD)
Loma Linda University
The University of Alabama at Birmingham

Public Policy and Administration/Business Administration (AM/MBA, MA/MBA, MPA/MBA, MPM/MBA, MPP/MBA)
City University
College of William and Mary
Duke University
Eastern Washington University
Georgetown University
Illinois Institute of Technology
University of Chicago
University of Maryland, College Park
University of Michigan
University of New Haven

Public Policy and Administration/Counseling and Human Relations (MPA/MS)
Suffolk University

Public Policy and Administration/Criminology (MPA/MSC)
Florida State University

Public Policy and Administration/Economics (MPP/AM)
University of Michigan

Public Policy and Administration/Education (MPA/Certificate, MPA/Ed D, MPA/MAT, MPA/PhD, MS/PhD)
University of Rochester
University of Utah

Public Policy and Administration/Environmental Management (MPP/MEM)
Duke University

Public Policy and Administration/Environmental Sciences (MPA/MSES)
Indiana University Bloomington

Public Policy and Administration/Forestry (MPP/MF)
Duke University

Public Policy and Administration/Gerontology (MPA/MS)
University of Southern California

Public Policy and Administration/Health Administration (MPA/MHA, MPP/MHSA)
The Ohio State University
University of Michigan

Public Policy and Administration/Information Science (MPA/MSIS)
University of Pittsburgh

Public Policy and Administration/International Studies (MPA/MAIS, MPP/MA)
University of California, Berkeley
University of Washington

Public Policy and Administration/Jewish Studies (MA/MA, MPA/MAJCS)
University of Southern California

Public Policy and Administration/Latin American and Caribbean Studies (MPA/MA)
Indiana University Bloomington

Public Policy and Administration/Library Science (MPA/MLS)
Indiana University Bloomington

Public Policy and Administration/Middle East Studies (MPA/MA)
University of Utah

Public Policy and Administration/Natural Resources and Environment (MPP/MS)
University of Michigan

Public Policy and Administration/Nursing (MPA/MSN)
Indiana University–Purdue University Indianapolis

Public Policy and Administration/Policy Sciences (MPA/PhD)
University of Maryland, Baltimore County

Public Policy and Administration/Public Health (MPA/MPH, MPA/MSPH, MPP/MPH, MS/MPH)
Columbia University
The University of Alabama at Birmingham
University of California, Berkeley
University of Miami
University of Michigan
University of Missouri–Columbia
University of Rochester

Public Policy and Administration/Public and International Affairs (MPA/MPIA)
University of Pittsburgh

Public Policy and Administration/Russian and East European Studies (MPA/MA)
Indiana University Bloomington

Public Policy and Administration/Urban and Regional Planning (MAPA/MA, MPA/MCP, MPA/MCRP, MPA/M Pl, MPA/MRCP, MPA/MRP, MPA/MSP, MPA/MUP, MPA/MURP)
Auburn University
Eastern Washington University
Florida State University
Iowa State University of Science and Technology
Mankato State University
University of Kansas
University of New Mexico
The University of North Carolina at Chapel Hill
University of Oklahoma
University of Pittsburgh
University of Southern California
University of Wisconsin–Milwaukee

Public and International Affairs/Information Science (MPIA/MSIS)
University of Pittsburgh

Public and International Affairs/Urban and Regional Planning (MPIA/MURP)
University of Pittsburgh

Religion/Forestry (MAR/MF)
Yale University

Russian Area Studies/Government (MA/PhD)
Georgetown University

School Psychology/School Psychology (MA/CAGS)
American International College

Social Administration/Nonprofit Organization (MSSA/MNO)
Case Western Reserve University

Social Administration/Social Welfare (MSSA/PhD)
Case Western Reserve University

Social Work/Communication (MSW/MA)
University of Denver

Social Work/Criminal Justice (MSW/MA)
State University of New York at Albany

Social Work/Education (MS/MS Ed, MSW/Ed D, MSW/Ed M, MSW/M Ed, MSW/MS Ed)
Boston University
Columbia University
University of Pennsylvania

Social Work/Gerontology (MSW/MS)
University of Southern California

Social Work/International Studies (MSW/MA)
University of Denver

Social Work/Jewish Studies (MS/MA, MSW/Certificate, MSW/MA, MSW/MAJCS)
Columbia University
University of Denver
University of Pennsylvania
University of Pittsburgh
University of Southern California
Washington University in St. Louis
Yeshiva University

Social Work/Management (MSW/MS)
New York University

Social Work/Public Health (MS/MPH, MSW/MPH, PhD/MPH)
Boston University
Columbia University
Saint Louis University
San Diego State University
Tulane University
University of Michigan
University of Minnesota, Twin Cities Campus
The University of North Carolina at Chapel Hill
University of Pittsburgh
University of Washington

Social Work/Public Policy and Administration (MS/MPA, MSW/MPA, MSW/MPP, PhD/MPA)
Columbia University
Eastern Washington University
Florida State University
Marywood University
University of Connecticut
University of Michigan
University of Minnesota, Twin Cities Campus
University of Pittsburgh
University of South Carolina
University of Southern California
University of Utah
West Virginia University

Social Work/Public and International Affairs (MSW/MPIA)
University of Pittsburgh

Social Work/Religion (MSW/MA, MSW/MAR)
Yale University

Social Work/Religious Education (MSW/MA)
Virginia Commonwealth University

Social Work/Religious Education and Pastoral Ministry (MSW/MA)
Boston College

Social Work/Social Ministry (MSW/Certificate)
University of Pennsylvania

Social Work/Social Science (MSW/MACO)
State University of New York at Binghamton

Social Work/Social Welfare (MSW/PhD)
University of California, Berkeley

Social Work/Sociology (MSW/MA)
State University of New York at Albany
State University of New York at New Paltz

Social Work/Urban Design (MSW/MAUD)
Washington University in St. Louis

Social Work/Urban and Regional Planning (MS/MS, MSSW/MA, MSW/MA, MSW/MCP, MSW/M Pl, MSW/MS, MSW/MUP, MSW/MURP)
Columbia University
The University of Iowa
University of Michigan
University of Pennsylvania
University of Pittsburgh
University of Southern California
The University of Texas at Arlington

Telecommunications/Management (MS/MA)
Saint Mary's University of Minnesota

Theology/Business Administration (MA/MBA, MATS/MBA, M Div/MA, M Div/MBA)
Eastern College
Emory University
Samford University
University of Pittsburgh
Yale University

Theology/Economic Development (M Div/MS)
Eastern College

Theology/Education (MA/M Ed, M Div/M Ed, M Div/MS Ed)
Samford University

Theology/Forestry (M Div/MF)
Yale University

Theology/Library Science (M Div/MLIS, M Div/MLS)
Dominican University

Theology/Pastoral Counseling (M Div/MA, M Div/MAPC)
Loyola University Chicago

Theology/Public Health (M Div/MPH)
University of Pittsburgh

Theology/Public Policy and Administration (M Div/MA, M Div/MPP, M Div/MS)
Carnegie Mellon University
University of Chicago

Theology/Social Work (MA/MSW, M Div/AM, M Div/MA, M Div/MS, M Div/MSSW, M Div/MSW, M Div/MTS/MSW, MTS/MSW)
Boston University
Columbia University
Loyola University Chicago
Rutgers, The State University of New Jersey, New Brunswick
University of Chicago
University of Connecticut
University of Denver
University of Pittsburgh
Yale University

Theology/Theology (M Div/MA, M Div/MABS, M Div/MATS, M Div/MA Th, M Div/MSM, M Div/MTS, M Div/PhD, M Div/D Min, STM/Th D)
Boston University

Urban and Regional Planning/Agricultural Economics (MCRP/MS)
Rutgers, The State University of New Jersey, New Brunswick

Urban and Regional Planning/American Studies (MUP/MA)
University of Kansas

Urban and Regional Planning/Civil Engineering (MCP/MSCE)
Georgia Institute of Technology

Urban and Regional Planning/Economics (MA/MA, M Pl/MA, MS/MA)
The University of Iowa
University of Southern California

Urban and Regional Planning/Geography (MSCRP/PhD)
The University of Texas at Austin

Urban and Regional Planning/Gerontology (M Pl/MS)
University of Southern California

Urban and Regional Planning/Government Administration (MCP/MGA)
University of Pennsylvania

Urban and Regional Planning/Historic Preservation (MS/MS)
Columbia University

Urban and Regional Planning/Hospital and Health Administration (MA/MA, MS/MA)
The University of Iowa

Urban and Regional Planning/Information Science (MURP/MSIS)
University of Pittsburgh

Urban and Regional Planning/International Affairs (MS/MIA)
Columbia University

Urban and Regional Planning/Landscape Architecture (MCP/MLA, MCRP/MLA, M Pl/ML Arch, MRCP/MLA, MRP/MLA, MUP/MLA)
Cornell University
Iowa State University of Science and Technology

University of California, Berkeley
University of Massachusetts Amherst
University of Michigan
University of Oklahoma
University of Southern California

Urban and Regional Planning/Latin American Studies (MA/MA, MCRP/MALAS, MSCRP/MA)
University of California, Los Angeles
University of New Mexico
The University of Texas at Austin

Urban and Regional Planning/Preventive Medicine (MA/MS, MS/MS)
The University of Iowa

Urban and Regional Planning/Public Health (MCP/MPH, MS/MPH)
Columbia University
University of California, Berkeley

Veterinary Medicine/Animals and Public Policy (DVM/MS)
Tufts University

Veterinary Medicine/Bioengineering (VMD/PhD)
University of Pennsylvania

Veterinary Medicine/Biomedical Sciences (DVM/MPVM, DVM/MS, DVM/PhD, VMD/PhD)
Auburn University
North Carolina State University
The Ohio State University
Purdue University
Texas A&M University
Tufts University
University of California, Davis
University of Pennsylvania
Washington State University

Veterinary Medicine/Business Administration (VMD/MBA)
University of Pennsylvania

Veterinary Medicine/Legal Studies (DVM/MA)
Tufts University

Visual Studies/Visual Studies (MA/MFA)
Norfolk State University

Profiles of Institutions Offering Graduate and Professional Work

ALABAMA

ALABAMA AGRICULTURAL AND MECHANICAL UNIVERSITY
Normal, AL 35762-1357
http://www.aamu.edu/

Public coed university. *Enrollment: 5,094 graduate, professional, and undergraduate students. Graduate faculty: 138 full-time, 14 part-time. Computer facilities: Campuswide network is available with full Internet access. Total number of PCs/terminals supplied for student use: 155. Computer services are offered at no charge. Library facilities: J. F. Drake Memorial Learning Resources Center. Graduate expenses: Tuition of $2782 per year full-time, $565 per semester (minimum) part-time for state residents; $5164 per year full-time, $1015 per semester (minimum) part-time for nonresidents. Fees of $560 per year full-time, $390 per year part-time. General application contact: Dr. Robert H. Lehman, Dean, School of Graduate Studies, 205-851-5266.*

School of Graduate Studies
Dr. Robert H. Lehman, Dean

School of Agricultural and Environmental Sciences
Dr. James W. Shuford, Dean
Programs in:
    agribusiness • MS
    agricultural and environmental science • Ed S
    animal sciences • MS
    crop science • MS
    environmental science • MS
    food science • PhD
    food science and technology • MS
    home economics • MS
    horticulture • MS
    plant and soil science • PhD
    soil science • MS
    urban and regional planning • MURP
    urban studies • MS

School of Arts and Sciences
Dr. Jerry Shipman, Dean
Programs in:
    applied physics • PhD
    biology • MS
    computer science • MS
    materials science • PhD
    optics • PhD
    physics • MS
    social work • MSW

School of Business
Dr. Barbara A. P. Jones, Dean
Programs in:
    economics and finance • MS
    management and marketing • MBA

School of Education
Dr. Phillip Redrick, Interim Dean
Programs in:
    art and art education • M Ed
    clinical psychology • MS
    counseling and guidance • Ed S, MS
    counseling psychology • MS
    early childhood education • Ed S, M Ed, MS
    education • Ed S, M Ed
    elementary education • Ed S, M Ed, MS
    higher administration • MS
    music • MS
    music education • M Ed
    personnel management • MS
    physical education • M Ed, MS
    psychometry • MS
    school psychology • MS
    special education • M Ed, MS
    speech pathology • M Ed, MS

School of Engineering and Technology
Dr. Arthur Bond, Dean
Programs in:
    industry and education • MS
    trade and industrial education • M Ed

ALABAMA STATE UNIVERSITY
Montgomery, AL 36101-0271
http://www.alasu.edu/

Public coed comprehensive institution. *Enrollment: 5,274 graduate, professional, and undergraduate students. Graduate faculty: 33 full-time, 8 part-time. Computer facilities: Campuswide network is available with full Internet access. Computer service fees are included with tuition and fees. Library facilities: Levi Watkins Learning Center. Graduate expenses: Tuition of $85 per credit hour for state residents; $170 per credit hour for nonresidents. Fees of $486 per year. General application contact: Dr. Fred Dauser, Dean of Graduate Studies, 334-229-4276.*

School of Graduate Studies
Dr. Fred Dauser, Dean

College of Arts and Sciences
Dr. William Lawson, Dean
Programs in:
    biology • MS
    biology education • Ed S
    history and social science • MA, MS
    mathematics • Ed S, MS
    physical therapy • MS
    sociology and criminal justice • MA, MS

College of Business Administration
Dr. Percy Vaughn, Dean
Program in:
    accountancy • MS

College of Education
Dr. Daniel Vertrees, Dean
Programs in:
    biology education • M Ed
    early childhood education • Ed S, M Ed
    educational administration • Ed S, M Ed
    elementary education • Ed S, M Ed
    English education • M Ed
    guidance and counseling • Ed S, M Ed, MS
    history education • M Ed
    library educational media • Ed S, M Ed
    mathematics education • M Ed
    physical education • Ed S, M Ed
    secondary education • Ed S
    special education • M Ed

School of Music
Dr. Horace B. Lamar, Dean
Programs in:
    history/literature • MA
    music • MA
    music education • MME
    performance • MA
    theory/composition • MA

AUBURN UNIVERSITY
Auburn University, AL 36849-0001

http://www.auburn.edu/

Public coed university. *Enrollment: 21,505 graduate, professional, and undergraduate students. Graduate faculty: 1,153 full-time. Library facilities: Ralph B. Draughon Library plus 2 additional on-campus libraries. Graduate expenses: Tuition of $2760 per year full-time, $76 per credit hour part-time for state residents; $8280 per year full-time, $228 per credit hour part-time for nonresidents. Fees of $30 per year full-time, $160 per quarter part-time for state residents; $30 per year full-time, $480 per quarter part-time for nonresidents. General application contact: Dr. John F. Pritchett, Dean of the Graduate School, 334-844-4700.*

Graduate School
Dr. John F. Pritchett, Dean
Programs in:
    anatomy and histology • MS
    biomedical sciences • PhD
    large animal surgery and medicine • MS
    pathobiology • MS
    pharmacy • MS, PhD
    physiology and pharmacology • MS
    radiology • MS
    small animal surgery and medicine • MS

College of Agriculture
Dr. James E. Marion, Dean
Programs in:
    agricultural economics and rural sociology • M Ag, MS, PhD
    agricultural engineering • MS, PhD
    agronomy and soils • M Ag, MS, PhD
    animal and dairy sciences • M Ag, MS, PhD
    entomology • M Ag, MS, PhD
    fisheries and allied aquacultures • M Aq, MS, PhD
    horticulture • M Ag, MS, PhD
    plant pathology • M Ag, MS, PhD
    poultry science • M Ag, MS, PhD

College of Architecture, Design, and Construction
Dr. J. Thomas Regan, Dean
Programs in:
    building science • MBC
    community planning • MCP
    industrial design • MID

College of Business
Dr. C. Wayne Alderman, Dean
Programs in:
    accountancy • M Acc
    business administration • MBA
    economics • MS, PhD
    human relations management • PhD
    management • MS
    management information systems • MMIS, PhD

College of Education
Dr. Richard C. Kunkel, Dean
Programs in:
    college student development • Ed D, Ed S, M Ed, MS, PhD
    community agency counseling • Ed D, Ed S, M Ed, MS, PhD
    counseling psychology • PhD
    curriculum and instruction • Ed D, Ed S, M Ed, MS
    curriculum supervision • Ed D, Ed S, M Ed, MS
    early childhood education • Ed S, M Ed, MS, PhD
    educational psychology • PhD
    elementary education • Ed S, M Ed, MS, PhD
    English language arts • Ed S, M Ed, MS, PhD
    foreign languages • M Ed, MS
    health and human performance • Ed D, Ed S, M Ed, MS, PhD
    higher education administration • Ed D, Ed S, M Ed, MS
    mathematics • Ed S, M Ed, MS, PhD
    media instructional design • MS
    media specialist • M Ed
    music education • Ed S, M Ed, MS, PhD
    postsecondary education • PhD
    reading education • Ed S, PhD
    rehabilitation and special education • Ed S, M Ed, MS, PhD
    school administration • Ed D, Ed S, M Ed, MS
    school counseling • Ed D, Ed S, M Ed, MS, PhD
    school psychometry • Ed D, Ed S, M Ed, MS, PhD
    science • Ed S, M Ed, MS, PhD
    secondary education • Ed S, M Ed, MS, PhD
    social studies • Ed S, M Ed, MS, PhD
    vocational and adult education • Ed D, Ed S, M Ed, MS

College of Engineering
Dr. William F. Walker, Dean
Programs in:
    aerospace engineering • MAE, MS, PhD
    chemical engineering • M Ch E, MS, PhD

Auburn University (continued)

computer science and engineering • MCSE, MS, PhD
construction engineering and management • MCE, MS, PhD
electrical engineering • MEE, MS, PhD
environmental engineering • MCE, MS, PhD
geotechnical/materials engineering • MCE, MS, PhD
hydraulics/hydrology • MCE, MS, PhD
industrial and systems engineering • MIE, MS, PhD
manufacturing systems engineering • MMSE, MS
materials engineering • M Mtl E, MS, PhD
mechanical engineering • MME, MS, PhD
structural engineering • MCE, MS, PhD
transportation engineering • MCE, MS, PhD

College of Liberal Arts
John G. Heilman, Interim Co-Dean
Programs in:
art • MFA
audiology • MCD, MS
communication • MA, MACT, MSC
English • MA, MACT, PhD
French • MA, MACT, MFS
history • MA, PhD
mass communications • MA, MACT, MSC
music • MM
political science • MA
psychology • MS, PhD
public administration • MPA, PhD
Spanish • MA, MACT, MHS
speech pathology • MCD, MS

College of Sciences and Mathematics
Dr. Stewart W. Schneller, Dean
Programs in:
botany • MS, PhD
chemistry • MACT, MS, PhD
discrete and statistical sciences • M Prob S, MAM, MS, PhD
geology • MS
mathematics • MAM, MS, PhD
microbiology • MS, PhD
physics • MS, PhD
plant physiology • MS, PhD
wildlife science • MS, PhD
zoological science • MZS
zoology • MACT, MS, PhD

Interdepartmental Programs
Dr. John F. Pritchett, Dean, Graduate School
Programs in:
sociology • MA, MACT, MS
textile science • MS

School of Forestry
Dr. Emmett F. Thompson, Dean
Program in:
forestry • MF, MS, PhD

School of Human Sciences
Dr. June Henton, Dean
Programs in:
apparel and textiles • MS
college teaching • MACT

human development and family studies • MACT, MS, PhD
nutrition and food science • MACT, MS, PhD

College of Veterinary Medicine
Dr. Timothy R. Boosinger, Dean
Programs in:
anatomy and histology • MS
biomedical sciences • PhD
large animal surgery and medicine • MS
pathobiology • MS
physiology and pharmacology • MS
radiology • MS
small animal surgery and medicine • MS
veterinary medicine • DVM

School of Pharmacy
Dr. R. Lee Evans Jr., Dean
Program in:
pharmacy • MS, PhD, Pharm D

AUBURN UNIVERSITY MONTGOMERY
Montgomery, AL 36124-4023

http://www.aum.edu/

Public coed comprehensive institution. *Enrollment: 5,526 graduate, professional, and undergraduate students. Graduate faculty: 128 full-time, 31 part-time. Computer facilities: Campuswide network is available. Total number of PCs/terminals supplied for student use: 200. Computer services are offered at no charge. Library facilities: Library Tower. Graduate expenses: $2664 per year full-time, $85 per quarter hour part-time for state residents; $7080 per year full-time, $255 per quarter hour part-time for nonresidents. General application contact: Tina Higbe, Coordinator of Admissions, 334-244-3621.*

School of Business
Dr. Keith Lantz, Dean
Program in:
business • MBA

School of Education
Dr. Morgan Simpson, Interim Dean
Programs in:
counseling • Ed S, M Ed
early childhood education • Ed S, M Ed
education administration • Ed S, M Ed
elementary education • Ed S, M Ed
physical education • M Ed
reading education • Ed S, M Ed
secondary education • Ed S, M Ed
special education • Ed S, M Ed

School of Liberal Arts
Dr. Robbie Jean Walker, Dean
Program in:
    liberal arts • MLA

School of Sciences
Joe B. Hill, Dean
Programs in:
    justice and public safety • MSJPS
    political science • MPS
    psychology • MSPG
    public administration • MPA, PhD

JACKSONVILLE STATE UNIVERSITY
Jacksonville, AL 36265-9982

http://www.jsu.edu/

Public coed comprehensive institution. *Enrollment: 7,327 graduate, professional, and undergraduate students. Graduate faculty: 133 full-time.* Library facilities: *Houston Cole Library.* Graduate expenses: *Tuition of $2140 per year full-time, $107 per semester hour part-time for state residents; $4280 per year full-time, $214 per semester hour part-time for nonresidents. Fees of $30 per semester.* General application contact: *Dr. William D. Carr, Dean of the College of Graduate Studies and Continuing Education, 205-782-5329.*

College of Graduate Studies and Continuing Education
Dr. William D. Carr, Dean
Programs in:
    general studies • MA
    public administration • MPA

College of Arts and Sciences
Dr. William D. Carr, Dean, College of Graduate Studies and
    Continuing Education
Programs in:
    biology • MS
    criminal justice • MS
    English • MA
    history • MA
    mathematics • MS
    music • MA
    political science • MA
    psychology • MS

College of Commerce and Business Administration
Dr. William D. Carr, Dean, College of Graduate Studies and
    Continuing Education
Program in:
    commerce and business administration • MBA

College of Education
Dr. William D. Carr, Dean, College of Graduate Studies and
    Continuing Education
Programs in:
    early childhood education • MS Ed
    elementary education • MS Ed
    guidance and counseling • MS
    health and physical education • MS Ed
    instructional media • MS Ed
    music education • MM Ed
    school administration • Ed S, MS Ed
    secondary education • MS Ed
    special education • MS Ed

SAMFORD UNIVERSITY
Birmingham, AL 35229-0002

http://www.samford.edu/

Independent-religious coed university. *Enrollment: 4,485 graduate, professional, and undergraduate students. Graduate faculty: 175 full-time, 116 part-time.* Computer facilities: *Campuswide network is available with full Internet access. Total number of PCs/terminals supplied for student use: 300. Computer services are offered at no charge.* Library facilities: *Davis Library plus 3 additional on-campus libraries.* Graduate expenses: *$344 per credit hour.* General application contact: *Phil Kimrey, Dean of Admissions and Financial Aid, 205-870-2871.*

Beeson School of Divinity
Dr. Timothy George, Dean
Program in:
    theology • D Min, M Div, MTS

Cumberland School of Law
Dr. Barry A. Currier, Dean
Program in:
    law • JD

Howard College of Arts and Sciences
Dr. Rod Davis, Dean
Program in:
    environmental management • MSEM

Ida V. Moffett School of Nursing
Dr. Marian K. Baur, Dean
Program in:
    nursing • MSN

McWhorter School of Pharmacy
Dr. Joe Dean, Dean
Program in:
    pharmacy • Pharm D

School of Business
Dr. Carl Bellas, Dean
Program in:
    business • M Acc, MBA

Samford University (continued)
School of Education
Dr. Ruth Ash, Dean
Programs in:
   early childhood education • Ed S, MS Ed
   educational administration • Ed S, MS Ed
   elementary education • Ed S, MS Ed
   music education • MS Ed

School of Music
Dr. Milburn Price, Dean
Program in:
   music • MM, MME

SPRING HILL COLLEGE
Mobile, AL 36608-1791
http://www.shc.edu/

Independent-religious coed comprehensive institution. *Enrollment:* 1,400 graduate, professional, and undergraduate students. Graduate faculty: *19 full-time, 11 part-time.* Computer facilities: *Campuswide network is available with full Internet access. Total number of PCs/terminals supplied for student use: 100. Computer services are offered at no charge.* Library facilities: *Thomas Byrne Library plus 1 additional on-campus library.* Graduate expenses: *$245 per credit hour.* General application contact: *Joyce Genz, Director of Graduate Programs Administration, 334-380-3094.*

Graduate Programs
Joyce Genz, Director of Graduate Programs Administration
Programs in:
   business administration • MBA
   early childhood education • MAT, MS Ed
   elementary education • MAT, MS Ed
   liberal studies • MLA
   teaching of reading • MS Ed
   theological studies • MA, MTS

TROY STATE UNIVERSITY
Troy, AL 36082
http://www.troyst.edu/

Public coed comprehensive institution. *Enrollment: 11,556 graduate, professional, and undergraduate students. Graduate faculty: 283.* Computer facilities: *Campuswide network is available with full Internet access. Total number of PCs/terminals supplied for student use: 300. Computer service fees are included with tuition and fees.* Library facilities: *main library plus 3 additional on-campus libraries.* Graduate expenses: *Tuition of $2040 per year full-time, $68 per hour part-time for state residents; $4200 per year full-time, $140 per hour part-time for nonresidents. Fees of $240 per year full-time, $27 per quarter (minimum) part-time.* General application contact: *Teresa Rodgers, Director of Graduate Admissions, 334-670-3188.*

Graduate School
Dr. Rudolph M. Argenti, Dean

College of Arts and Sciences
Dr. Robert Pullen, Dean
Programs in:
   administration of criminal justice • MS
   corrections • MS
   environmental analysis and management • MS
   international relations • MS
   police administration • MS
   public administration • MS

College of Health and Human Services
Dr. Sandra Greniewicki, Dean
Program in:
   nursing • MS

School of Education
Dr. Anita Hardin, Dean
Programs in:
   counseling and human development • MS
   counselor education • MS
   early childhood education • Ed S, MS
   educational leadership/administration • MS
   elementary education • Ed S, MS
   emotional conflict • MS
   foundations of education • MS
   guidance services • MS
   learning disabilities • MS
   mental retardation • MS
   mild learning handicapped • Ed S, MS
   N–12 education • Ed S, MS
   secondary education • Ed S, MS

University College
Dr. Rodney Cox, Dean
Programs in:
   administration of criminal justice • MS
   business administration • MBA
   corrections • MS
   international relations • MS
   management • MS
   personnel management • MS
   police administration • MS
   public administration • MS

TROY STATE UNIVERSITY DOTHAN
Dothan, AL 36304-0368
http://www.tsud.edu/

Public coed comprehensive institution. *Enrollment: 2,112 graduate, professional, and undergraduate students. Graduate faculty: 120 full-time, 71 part-time.* Computer facilities: *Campuswide network is available with full Internet access. Total number of PCs/terminals supplied for student use: 150. Computer service fees are included with tuition and fees.* Library facilities: *main library.* Graduate expenses: *Tuition of $68 per credit hour for state residents; $140 per credit hour for nonresidents. Fees of $2 per credit hour.* General

application contact: *Reta Cordell, Director of Admissions and Records, 334-983-6556.*

Graduate School

Dr. Barbara Alford, Executive Vice President

College of Arts and Sciences

Dr. Barbara Alford, Executive Vice President, Graduate School
Program in:
　history and social sciences • MS

School of Business

Dr. Adair Gilbert, Interim Dean
Programs in:
　accounting • MBA, MS
　business education • MS
　business law • MS
　computer information systems • MS
　finance • MS
　general business • MBA
　human resource management • MBA, MS
　quantitative methods • MS

School of Education

Dr. Betty Anderson, Dean
Programs in:
　counseling and psychology • MS
　educational administration • MS Ed
　elementary education • Ed S, MS Ed
　foundations of education • MS
　pre-elementary education • Ed S, MS Ed
　school administration • Ed S
　school counseling • Ed S, MS Ed
　school psychology • MS Ed
　secondary education • MS Ed
　special education • MS Ed

TROY STATE UNIVERSITY MONTGOMERY

Montgomery, AL 36103-4419

http://www.tsum.edu/

Public coed comprehensive institution. *Enrollment: 3,349 graduate, professional, and undergraduate students. Graduate faculty: 29 full-time, 34 part-time. Computer facilities: Campuswide network is available with full Internet access. Computer service fees are included with tuition and fees. Library facilities: main library. Graduate expenses: Tuition of $52 per quarter hour for state residents; $104 per quarter hour for nonresidents. Fees of $30 per year. General application contact: Dr. James P. Sutton Jr., Dean of Graduate Studies, 334-241-9581.*

Graduate Programs

Dr. James P. Sutton Jr., Dean of Graduate Studies

Division of Business

Dr. Freda Hartman, Dean
Programs in:
　business administration • MBA
　computer and information science • MS
　human resources management • MS

Division of Counseling, Education, and Psychology

Dr. Donald Thompson, Dean
Programs in:
　adult education • MS
　counseling and human development • Ed S, MS
　elementary education • MS
　general education administration • Ed S
　teaching • MA

TUSKEGEE UNIVERSITY

Tuskegee, AL 36088

http://www.tusk.edu/

Independent coed comprehensive institution. *Enrollment: 3,023 graduate, professional, and undergraduate students. Graduate faculty: 112 full-time, 11 part-time. Library facilities: Hollis Burke Frissell Library plus 3 additional on-campus libraries. General application contact: Elva E. Bradley, Dean of Admissions and Records, 334-727-8580.*

Graduate Programs

Dr. William L. Lester, Provost

College of Agricultural, Environmental and Natural Sciences

Dr. Walter A. Hill, Dean
Programs in:
　agricultural economics • MS
　animal and poultry sciences • MS
　biology • MS
　chemistry • MS
　environmental sciences • MS
　food and nutrition science • MS
　home economics • MS
　soil sciences and management • MS

College of Engineering, Architecture and Physical Sciences

Dr. Ben Oni, Acting Dean
Programs in:
　electrical engineering • MSEE
　mechanical engineering • MSME

College of Liberal Arts and Education

Dr. Mary A. Jones, Acting Dean
Programs in:
　counseling and student development • M Ed, MS
　extension and technical education • M Ed, MS
　general science education • M Ed, MS
　personnel administration • M Ed, MS
　school counseling • M Ed, MS

Tuskegee University (continued)
College of Veterinary Medicine and Allied Health
Dr. Albert W. Dade, Dean
Program in:
   veterinary medicine • DVM, MS

THE UNIVERSITY OF ALABAMA
Tuscaloosa, AL 35487
http://www.ua.edu/

Public coed university. *Enrollment:* 17,810 graduate, professional, and undergraduate students. Graduate faculty: *523 full-time, 185 part-time.* Computer facilities: *Campuswide network is available with full Internet access. Total number of PCs/terminals supplied for student use: 160. Computer service fees are included with tuition and fees.* Library facilities: *Amelia Gayle Gorgas Library plus 8 additional on-campus libraries.* Graduate expenses: *$2684 per year full-time, $594 per semester (minimum) part-time for state residents; $7216 per year full-time, $1248 per semester (minimum) part-time for nonresidents.* General application contact: *Libby Williams, Admissions Supervisor, 205-348-5921.*

Graduate School
Ronald Rogers, Dean

College of Arts and Sciences
James D. Yarbrough, Dean
Programs in:
   acting • MFA
   administration • DMA
   American studies • MA
   anthropology • MA
   applied mathematics • PhD
   art education • MA
   art history • MA
   audiology • MS
   biological sciences • MS, PhD
   ceramics • MA, MFA
   chemistry • MS, PhD
   clinical psychology • PhD
   cognitive psychology • PhD
   composition • DMA
   costume design • MFA
   creative writing • MFA
   criminal justice • MSCJ
   directing • MFA
   experimental psychology • PhD
   fiction • MFA
   French • MA, PhD
   French and Spanish • PhD
   geography • MS
   geology • MS, PhD
   German • MA
   history • MA, PhD
   Latin American studies • MA
   literature • MA, PhD
   materials science • PhD
   mathematics • MA
   music education • Ed D, Ed S
   musicology • MM
   painting • MA, MFA
   performance • DMA, MM
   photography • MA, MFA
   physics • MS, PhD
   playwriting/dramaturgy • MFA
   poetry • MFA
   political science • MA, MPA, PhD
   printmaking • MA, MFA
   psychology • MA
   public administration • MPA
   pure mathematics • PhD
   rhetoric and composition • MA, PhD
   Romance languages • MA, PhD
   scene design/technical production • MFA
   sculpture • MA, MFA
   Spanish • MA, PhD
   speech-language pathology • MS
   stage management • MFA
   studio art • MA, MFA
   teaching English to speakers of other languages • MA
   theatre • MFA
   theatre management/administration • MFA
   theory and criticism • MA
   women's studies • MA

College of Communication
Dr. Dolf Zillmann, Senior Associate Dean for Graduate Studies and Research
Programs in:
   advertising and public relations • MA, PhD
   book arts • MFA
   journalism • MA, PhD
   library and information studies • Ed S, MLIS
   speech communication • MA, PhD
   telecommunication and film • MA, PhD

College of Education
Dr. John Dolly, Dean
Programs in:
   counselor education • Ed D, Ed S, PhD
   early childhood education • Ed S, MA
   educational administration • Ed D, MA, PhD
   educational leadership • Ed S, MA
   educational psychology • Ed D, Ed S, MA, PhD
   educational research • PhD
   elementary education • Ed D, Ed S, MA, PhD
   health education • Ed S, MA
   health education and promotion • MA, PhD
   higher education administration • Ed D, Ed S, MA, PhD
   human performance • Ed S, MA, PhD
   instructional leadership • Ed D, PhD
   music education • Ed D, MA
   school psychology • Ed D, Ed S, MA, PhD
   secondary education • Ed D, Ed S, MA, PhD
   special education • Ed D, Ed S, MA, PhD

College of Engineering
Raymond W. Flumerfelt, Dean
Programs in:
   aerospace engineering and mechanics • MSAE, MSESM, PhD
   chemical engineering • MS Ch E, PhD

civil engineering • MSCE, PhD
computer science • MSCS, PhD
electrical engineering • MSEE, PhD
environmental engineering • MSE
industrial engineering • MSE, MSIE
materials science • PhD
mechanical engineering • MSME, PhD
metallurgical and materials engineering • MS Met E, PhD
mineral engineering • MS Min E

College of Human Environmental Sciences

Dr. Judy L. Bonner, Dean
Programs in:
clothing, textiles, and interior design • MSHES
general home economics and consumer science • MSHES
human development and family life • MSHES
human nutrition and hospitality management • MSHES

School of Social Work

Dr. Lucinda L. Roff, Dean
Program in:
social work • MSW, PhD

The Manderson Graduate School of Business

J. Barry Mason, Dean
Programs in:
accounting • M Acc, PhD
applied statistics • MS, PhD
banking and finance • MA, MSC, PhD
business administration • Exec MBA, MBA
economics • MA, MSC, PhD
management science • MA, MBA, PhD
manufacturing management • MA, MBA, PhD
marketing and management • MA, MSC, PhD
production management • MA, MBA, PhD
tax accounting • MTA

School of Law

Kenneth C. Randall, Dean
Program in:
law • JD, LL M in Tax, MCL

THE UNIVERSITY OF ALABAMA AT BIRMINGHAM

Birmingham, AL 35294

http://www.uab.edu/

Public coed university. *Enrollment:* 14,933 graduate, professional, and undergraduate students. Graduate faculty: *783 full-time, 27 part-time.* Computer facilities: *Campuswide network is available. Total number of PCs/terminals supplied for student use: 400. Computer service fees are applied as a separate charge.* Library facilities: *Mervyn Sterne Library plus 1 additional on-campus library.* Graduate expenses: *Tuition of $99 per credit hour for state residents; $198 per credit hour for nonresidents. Fees of $516 per year (minimum) full-time, $73 per quarter (minimum) part-time for state residents; $516 per year (minimum) full-time, $73 per unit (minimum)*

part-time for nonresidents. General application contact: Julie Bryant, Director of Graduate Admissions, 205-934-8243.

Graduate School

Dr. Joan F. Lorden, Dean
Programs in:
anatomy • PhD
basic medical sciences • MSBMS
biochemistry • PhD
biophysical sciences • PhD
dental public health • MPH
dentistry • MS
medical genetics • PhD
oral biology • MS
pathology • PhD
pharmacology • PhD
physiology and biophysics • PhD
vision science • MS, PhD

Graduate School of Management

Dr. W. Jack Duncan, Interim Dean
Programs in:
administration-health services • PhD
management • M Acct, MBA

School of Arts and Humanities

Dr. Theodore M. Benditt, Dean
Programs in:
art history • MA
English • MA

School of Education

Dr. Clint E. Bruess, Dean
Programs in:
agency counseling • MA
allied health-education • Ed S, MA Ed
arts education • Ed S, MA Ed
early childhood education • Ed S, MA Ed, PhD
educational leadership • Ed D, Ed S, MA Ed, PhD
elementary education • Ed S, MA Ed
health education • Ed S, MA Ed
health education/health promotion • Ed S, PhD
high school education • Ed S, MA Ed
marriage and family counseling • MA
music education • MA Ed
physical education • Ed S, MA Ed
rehabilitation counseling • MA
school counseling • MA
school psychology • MA Ed
special education • Ed S, MA Ed

School of Engineering

Dr. Stephen Szygenda, Dean
Programs in:
biomedical engineering • MSBE, PhD
civil and environmental engineering • MSCE
electrical and computer engineering • MSEE, PhD
materials engineering • MS Mt E
materials/metallurgical engineering • PhD
materials science • PhD
mechanical engineering • MSME, PhD
metallurgical engineering • PhD

The University of Alabama at Birmingham (continued)

School of Health Related Professions

Dr. Charles L. Joiner, Dean

Programs in:
 administration-health services • PhD
 clinical laboratory sciences • MSCLS
 clinical nutrition and dietetics • Certificate, MS
 health administration • MSHA
 health informatics • MS
 nurse anesthesia • MNA
 nutrition sciences • PhD
 occupational therapy • MS
 physical therapy • MS

School of Natural Sciences and Mathematics

Dr. Michael Neilson, Acting Dean

Programs in:
 applied mathematics • PhD
 chemistry • MS, PhD
 comparative and cellular biology • PhD
 comparative and cellular physiology • MS
 computer and information sciences • MS, PhD
 marine science • MS, PhD
 mathematics • MS
 microbial ecology and physiology • MS, PhD
 physics • MS, PhD
 reproduction and development • MS, PhD

School of Nursing

Dr. Rachel Z. Booth, Dean

Program in:
 nursing • DSN, MSN

School of Public Health

Dr. Eli I. Capilouto, Dean

Programs in:
 biomathematics • MS, PhD
 biometry • MPH
 biostatistics • MS, PhD
 environmental health • Dr PH, MPH, MSPH, PhD
 environmental toxicology • MSPH, PhD
 epidemiology • Dr PH, MPH, MSPH, PhD
 health behavior • MPH
 health care organization and policy • MPH, MSPH
 health education/promotion • PhD
 industrial hygiene • Dr PH, MPH, MSPH, PhD
 international health • Dr PH, MPH
 maternal and child health • MSPH
 occupational health and safety • Dr PH, MPH, MSPH
 public health nutrition • Dr PH, MPH

School of Social and Behavioral Sciences

Dr. Tennant S. McWilliams, Dean

Programs in:
 anthropology • MA
 behavioral neuroscience • PhD
 criminal justice • MSCJ
 developmental psychology • PhD
 forensic science • MSFS
 government and public service • MA
 history • MA
 medical psychology • PhD
 medical sociology • PhD
 psychology • MS

 public administration • MPA
 sociology • MA

School of Dentistry

Dr. Mary Lynne Capilouto, Interim Dean

Programs in:
 anatomy • PhD
 basic medical sciences • MSBMS
 biochemistry • PhD
 biophysical sciences • PhD
 dental public health • MPH
 dentistry • DMD
 medical genetics • PhD
 oral biology • MS
 pathology • PhD
 pharmacology • PhD
 physiology and biophysics • PhD

School of Medicine

Dr. William B. Deal Jr., Interim Dean

Programs in:
 anatomy • PhD
 basic medical sciences • MSBMS
 biochemistry • PhD
 biophysical sciences • PhD
 medical genetics • PhD
 medicine • MD
 pathology • PhD
 pharmacology • PhD
 physiology and biophysics • PhD

School of Optometry

Dr. Arol Augsburger, Dean

Programs in:
 optometry • OD
 vision science • MS, PhD

THE UNIVERSITY OF ALABAMA IN HUNTSVILLE
Huntsville, AL 35899

http://www.uah.edu/

Public coed university. *Enrollment: 5,070 graduate, professional, and undergraduate students. Graduate faculty: 217 full-time, 27 part-time. Computer facilities: Campuswide network is available with full Internet access. Total number of PCs/terminals supplied for student use: 300. Computer service fees are included with tuition and fees. Library facilities: main library. Graduate expenses: $2886 per year full-time, $540 per semester (minimum) part-time for state residents; $5298 per year full-time, $1098 per semester (minimum) part-time for nonresidents. General application contact: Dr. James Johannes, Dean of Graduate Studies, 205-890-6002.*

School of Graduate Studies
Dr. James Johannes, Dean
Programs in:
 materials science • MS, PhD
 optical science and engineering • PhD

College of Administrative Science
Dr. C. David Billings, Dean
Programs in:
 accountancy • M Acc
 management • MSM

College of Engineering
Dr. Stephen Kowel, Dean
Programs in:
 aerospace engineering • MSE
 chemical and materials engineering • MSE
 civil and environmental engineering • MSE
 computer engineering • PhD
 electrical and computer engineering • MSE
 electrical engineering • PhD
 engineering management • MSE, PhD
 industrial engineering • MSE, PhD
 mechanical engineering • MSE, PhD
 operations research • MSOR
 optical science and engineering • PhD

College of Liberal Arts
Dr. Sue Kirkpatrick, Dean
Programs in:
 English • MA
 history • MA
 psychology • MA
 public affairs • MA

College of Nursing
Dr. Fay Raines, Dean
Program in:
 nursing • MSN

College of Science
Dr. Graeme Duthie, Dean
Programs in:
 applied mathematics • PhD
 atmospheric and environmental science • MS, PhD
 biological sciences • MS
 chemistry • MS
 computer science • MS, PhD
 mathematics • MA, MS
 physics • MS, PhD

UNIVERSITY OF MOBILE
Mobile, AL 36663-0220

http://www.umobile.edu/

Independent-religious coed comprehensive institution. *Enrollment:* 2,634 graduate, professional, and undergraduate students. Graduate faculty: *28 full-time, 36 part-time.* Library facilities: *J. L. Bedsole Library.* Graduate expenses: *$160 per semester hour.* General

application contact: *Kaye F. Brown, Dean, Graduate and Special Programs, 334-675-5990 Ext. 270.*

Graduate Programs
Kaye F. Brown, Dean, Graduate and Special Programs
Programs in:
 business administration • MBA
 nursing • MSN
 physical therapy • MSPT
 religious studies • MA
 teacher education • MA

UNIVERSITY OF MONTEVALLO
Montevallo, AL 35115

http://www.montevallo.edu/

Public coed comprehensive institution. Computer facilities: *Campuswide network is available with full Internet access. Total number of PCs/ terminals supplied for student use: 94. Computer services are offered at no charge.* Library facilities: *Carmichael Library.* General application contact: *Assistant Registrar for Graduate Studies, 205-665-6350.*

College of Arts and Sciences
Programs in:
 English • MA
 history • MA
 home economics • MAT
 speech pathology and audiology • MS

College of Education
Programs in:
 early childhood education • Ed S, M Ed
 educational administration • Ed S
 elementary education • Ed S, M Ed
 guidance and counseling • M Ed
 health, physical education, and recreation • Ed S, M Ed
 secondary education • Ed S, M Ed
 traffic education • Ed S, M Ed

College of Fine Arts
Programs in:
 communication arts • MA
 music • MM

UNIVERSITY OF NORTH ALABAMA
Florence, AL 35632-0001

http://www.una.edu/

Public coed comprehensive institution. *Enrollment: 5,575* graduate, professional, and undergraduate students. Graduate faculty: *0 full-time, 35 part-time.* Library facilities: *Collier Library plus 3 additional on-campus libraries.* Graduate expenses: *Tuition of $2448 per year*

University of North Alabama (continued)
full-time, $102 per credit hour part-time for state residents; $4896 per year full-time, $204 per credit hour part-time for nonresidents. Fees of $3 per semester. General application contact: Dr. G. Daniel Howard, Dean of Research and Assistant to the President, 205-765-4221.

College of Arts and Sciences
Dr. Jack Moore, Dean
Program in:
    criminal justice • MSCJ

College of Business
Dr. Michael Butler, Dean
Program in:
    business • MBA

College of Education
Dr. Fred L. Hattabaugh, Dean
Programs in:
    counseling • MA Ed
    early childhood education • MA Ed
    education leadership • Ed S
    elementary education • MA Ed
    learning disabilities • MA Ed
    mentally retarded • MA Ed
    mild learning handicapped • MA Ed
    non-school-based counseling • MA
    non-school-based teaching • MA
    principalship • MA Ed
    reading specialization • MA Ed
    secondary education • MA Ed
    superintendency • MA Ed
    supervision of instruction • MA Ed

 # UNIVERSITY OF SOUTH ALABAMA
Mobile, AL 36688-0002
http://www.usouthal.edu/

Public coed university. *Enrollment:* 11,999 graduate, professional, and undergraduate students. Graduate faculty: *455 full-time, 27 part-time.* Library facilities: *main library plus 2 additional on-campus libraries.* Graduate expenses: *Tuition of $107 per semester hour for state residents; $213 per semester hour for nonresidents. Fees of $201 per year full-time, $68 per semester part-time.* General application contact: *Dr. James L. Wolfe, Associate Vice President for Research and Dean of the Graduate School, 334-460-6310.*

Graduate School
Dr. James L. Wolfe, Associate Vice President for Research and Dean
Programs in:
    biochemistry • PhD
    microbiology and immunology • PhD
    pharmacology • PhD

    physiology • PhD
    structural and cellular biology • PhD

College of Allied Health Professions
Dr. Patsy Covey, Dean
Programs in:
    communication sciences and disorders • PhD
    physician assistant studies • MHS
    speech and hearing sciences • MS

College of Arts and Sciences
Dr. Lawrence Allen, Dean
Programs in:
    biological sciences • MS
    communication • MA
    English • MA
    gerontology • Certificate
    history • MA
    marine sciences • MS, PhD
    mathematics • MS
    psychology • MS
    public administration • MPA
    sociology • MA

College of Business and Management Studies
Dr. Carl Moore, Dean
Programs in:
    accounting • M Acct
    business management • MBA

College of Education
George E. Uhlig, Dean
Programs in:
    art/music education • M Ed
    business education • M Ed
    counseling • Ed S, M Ed, MS
    early childhood education • Ed S, M Ed
    educational leadership and foundations • Ed S, M Ed
    educational media • M Ed, MS
    education of the emotionally disturbed • M Ed
    education of the gifted • M Ed
    elementary education • Ed S, M Ed
    exercise technology • MS
    health education • M Ed
    instructional design • MS
    instructional design and development • PhD
    learning disability • M Ed
    leisure services • MS
    mentally retarded • M Ed
    multihandicapped education • M Ed
    natural science education • M Ed
    physical education • Ed S, M Ed
    reading • M Ed
    science education • M Ed
    secondary education • Ed S, M Ed
    special education • Ed S, M Ed
    therapeutic recreation • MS

College of Engineering
Dr. David T. Hayhurst, Dean
Programs in:
    chemical engineering • MS Ch E
    computer and electrical engineering • MSEE
    mechanical engineering • MSME

College of Nursing
Dr. Amanda Baker, Dean
Programs in:
　adult health nursing • MSN
　community mental health nursing • MSN
　maternal child nursing • MSN

Division of Computer and Information Sciences
Dr. David Feinstein, Chairman
Programs in:
　computer science • MS
　information science • MS

College of Medicine
Dr. William A. Gardner Jr., Interim Dean
Programs in:
　biochemistry • PhD
　medicine • MD
　microbiology and immunology • PhD
　pharmacology • PhD
　physiology • PhD
　structural and cellular biology • PhD

THE UNIVERSITY OF WEST ALABAMA
Livingston, AL 35470

http://www.westal.edu/

Public coed comprehensive institution. *Enrollment:* 2,153 graduate, professional, and undergraduate students. *Graduate faculty: 51 full-time, 2 part-time. Computer facilities: Campuswide network is available with full Internet access. Computer services are offered at no charge. Library facilities: Tutwiler Library plus 1 additional on-campus library. Graduate expenses: $70 per quarter hour.* General application contact: *Dr. Joe B. Wilkins, Dean of Graduate Studies, 205-652-3647.*

School of Graduate Studies

College of Education
Programs in:
　biology with certification • MAT
　continuing education • MSCE
　early childhood education • M Ed
　elementary education • M Ed
　environmental science with certification • MAT
　guidance and counseling • M Ed
　history with certification • MAT
　language arts with certification • MAT
　library media • M Ed
　library media with certification • MAT
　mathematics with certification • MAT
　physical education • M Ed, MAT
　school administration • M Ed
　secondary education • M Ed, MAT
　special education • M Ed

College of Liberal Arts
Programs in:
　history • MAT
　language arts • MAT
　library media • MAT
　social science • MAT

College of Natural Sciences and Mathematics
Programs in:
　biological sciences • MAT
　environmental science • MAT
　mathematics • MAT

ALASKA

ALASKA PACIFIC UNIVERSITY
Anchorage, AK 99508-4672

http://www.alaskapacific.edu/

Independent coed comprehensive institution. *Enrollment:* 563 graduate, professional, and undergraduate students. *Graduate faculty: 18 full-time, 6 part-time. Computer facilities: Total number of PCs/terminals supplied for student use: 40. Computer services are offered at no charge. Library facilities: Consortium Library. Graduate expenses: Tuition of $6600 per year full-time, $370 per credit hour part-time. Fees of $80 per year.* General application contact: *Kirsty Gladkoff, Associate Director of Admissions, 907-564-8248.*

Graduate Programs
Dr. Charles B. Fahl, Academic Dean
Programs in:
　business administration • MBA
　counseling psychology • MSCP
　environmental science • MSES
　K–8 • MAT
　teaching • MAT
　telecommunication management • MBATM

UNIVERSITY OF ALASKA ANCHORAGE
Anchorage, AK 99508-8060

http://www.uaa.alaska.edu/

Public coed comprehensive institution. *Enrollment:* 12,011 graduate, professional, and undergraduate students. *Graduate faculty: 356 full-time, 579 part-time. Computer facilities: Campuswide network is available with full Internet access. Computer service fees are included with tuition and fees. Library facilities: Consortium Library. Graduate expenses: Tuition of $2988 per year full-time, $1990 per year part-time for state residents; $5814 per year full-time, $3876 per year part-time for nonresidents. Fees of $298*

University of Alaska Anchorage (continued)
per year. General application contact: *Linda Berg Smith, Associate Vice Chancellor for Enrollment Services, 907-786-1529.*

College of Arts and Sciences
Dr. Ted Kassier, Dean
Programs in:
    biological sciences • MS
    clinical psychology • MS
    counseling psychology • MS
    creative writing • MFA
    interdisciplinary studies • MA, MS

College of Business and Public Policy
Dr. Hayden Green, Dean
Programs in:
    business administration • MBA
    public administration • MPA

College of Health, Education and Social Welfare
Dr. Alex McNeill, Dean
Program in:
    substance abuse disorders • Certificate

School of Education
Dr. Alex McNeill, Dean, College of Health, Education and Social Welfare
Programs in:
    adult education • M Ed
    counseling and guidance • M Ed
    educational leadership • M Ed
    master teacher • M Ed
    special education • M Ed
    teaching • MAT

School of Nursing and Health Science
Dr. Tina De Lapp, Interim Director
Program in:
    nursing and health science • MS

School of Social Welfare
Dr. Elizabeth Sirles, Coordinator
Program in:
    social work • MSW

Community and Technical College
Dr. Erie Johnson, Head
Program in:
    vocational education • MS

School of Engineering
Dr. Robert Miller, Director
Programs in:
    arctic engineering • MS
    civil engineering • MCE, MS
    engineering management • MS
    environmental quality engineering • MS
    environmental quality science • MS
    science management • MS

UNIVERSITY OF ALASKA FAIRBANKS
Fairbanks, AK 99775-7480
http://www.uaf.edu/

Public coed university. *Enrollment: 8,360 graduate, professional, and undergraduate students. Graduate faculty: 291 full-time, 59 part-time. Computer facilities: Campuswide network is available with full Internet access. Computer service fees are included with tuition and fees. Library facilities: Rasmuson Library plus 1 additional on-campus library. Graduate expenses: Tuition of $162 per credit for state residents; $316 per credit for nonresidents. Fees of $520 per year full-time, $45 per semester (minimum) part-time.* General application contact: *Ann Tremarello, Director, Admissions and Records, 907-474-7500.*

Graduate School
Dr. Joe Kan, Dean

College of Liberal Arts
Dr. Gorden Hedahl, Dean
Programs in:
    Alaskan ethnomusicology • MA
    anthropology • MA, PhD
    community psychology • MA
    creative writing • MFA
    English • MA
    music • MAT
    music education • MA
    music history • MA
    music theory • MA
    Northern studies • MA, PhD
    performance • MA
    professional communications • MA

College of Natural Resource Development and Management
Dr. Joe Kan, Dean, Graduate School
Programs in:
    business administration • MBA
    geological engineering • EM, MS
    mineral preparation engineering • MS
    mining engineering • EM, MS
    natural resources management • MS
    petroleum engineering • MS
    resource economics • MS

College of Science, Engineering and Mathematics
Dr. Paul Reichardt, Dean
Programs in:
    arctic engineering • MS
    atmospheric science • MS, PhD
    biochemistry • MS, PhD
    biology • MAT, MS, PhD
    botany • MS, PhD
    chemistry • MA, MAT, MS
    civil engineering • MCE, MS
    computer science • MS
    electrical engineering • MEE, MS
    engineering management • MS

environmental quality engineering • MS
environmental quality science • MS
geology • MS, PhD
geophysics • MS, PhD
geoscience • MAT
mathematics • MAT, MS, PhD
mechanical engineering • MS
physics • MS, PhD
science management • MS
space physics • MS, PhD
wildlife biology and management • MS, PhD
zoology • MS, PhD

Interdisciplinary Programs
Dr. Joe Kan, Dean, Graduate School
Program in:
    interdisciplinary studies • MA, MS, PhD

School of Education
Dr. Joe Kan, Director
Programs in:
    cross-cultural education • Ed S, M Ed
    curriculum and instruction • M Ed
    educational administration • M Ed
    guidance and counseling • M Ed
    language and literature • M Ed

School of Fisheries and Ocean Sciences
Dr. Vera Alexander, Dean
Programs in:
    biological oceanography • PhD
    chemical oceanography • PhD
    fisheries • MS, PhD
    marine biology • MS
    oceanography • MS, PhD
    physical oceanography • PhD

UNIVERSITY OF ALASKA SOUTHEAST
Juneau, AK 99801-8625

http://www.jun.alaska.edu/

Public coed comprehensive institution. Enrollment: 1,182 graduate, professional, and undergraduate students. Graduate faculty: 10 full-time. Computer facilities: Campuswide network is available with full Internet access. Total number of PCs/terminals supplied for student use: 60. Computer service fees are applied as a separate charge. Library facilities: Egan Library. Graduate expenses: $162 per credit for state residents; $316 per credit for nonresidents. General application contact: Greg Wagner, Recruiter, 907-465-6239.

Graduate Programs
Dr. Roberta Stell, Vice Chancellor for Academic Affairs
Programs in:
    business administration • MBA
    early childhood education • M Ed
    elementary education • M Ed, MAT

public administration • MPA
secondary education • M Ed, MAT

ARIZONA

 # ARIZONA STATE UNIVERSITY
Tempe, AZ 85287

http://www.asu.edu/graduate/

Public coed university. Enrollment: 42,189 graduate, professional, and undergraduate students. Graduate faculty: 1,779 full-time, 229 part-time. Computer facilities: Campuswide network is available with full Internet access. Computer services are offered at no charge. Library facilities: Charles Trumbull Hayden Library plus 6 additional on-campus libraries. Graduate expenses: Tuition of $2088 per year full-time, $110 per hour part-time for state residents; $9040 per year full-time, $377 per hour part-time for nonresidents. Fees of $72 per year full-time, $18 per semester (minimum) part-time. General application contact: Graduate Admissions, 602-965-6113.

Graduate College
Dr. Bianca L. Bernstein, Dean
Programs in:
    creative writing • MFA
    curriculum and instruction • PhD
    exercise science • PhD
    gerontology • Certificate
    justice studies • PhD
    public administration • DPA
    science and engineering of materials • PhD
    speech and hearing science • PhD
    statistics • MS
    transportation systems • Certificate

College of Architecture and Environmental Design
Dr. John Meunier, Dean
Programs in:
    architecture • M Arch
    building design • MS
    design • MSD, PhD
    environmental resources • MS
    history, theory, and criticism • PhD
    planning • MEP, PhD

College of Business
Dr. Larry E. Penley, Dean
Programs in:
    accountancy • M Accy, PhD
    business administration • MBA
    economics • MS, PhD
    finance • PhD
    health administration and policy • MHSA
    health services research • PhD
    information management • MS, PhD
    management • PhD
    marketing • PhD

Arizona State University (continued)
    supply chain management • PhD
    taxation • M Tax

College of Education
Dr. David Berliner, Dean
Programs in:
    counseling • M Ed, MC
    counseling psychology • PhD
    curriculum and instruction • Ed D, M Ed, MA
    educational administration and supervision • Ed D,
       M Ed
    educational leadership and policy studies • PhD
    educational media and computers • M Ed
    educational psychology • M Ed, MA, PhD
    higher and post-secondary education • Ed D, M Ed
    learning and instructional technology • M Ed, MA, PhD
    social and philosophical foundations of education • MA
    special education • M Ed, MA

College of Engineering and Applied Sciences
Dr. Peter E. Crouch, Dean
Programs in:
    aerospace engineering • MS, MSE, PhD
    bioengineering • MS, PhD
    chemical engineering • MS, MSE, PhD
    civil engineering • MS, MSE, PhD
    computer science • MCS, MS, PhD
    construction • MS
    electrical engineering • MS, MSE, PhD
    engineering and applied sciences • M Eng
    engineering science • MS, MSE, PhD
    industrial engineering • MS, MSE, PhD
    materials science and engineering • MS, MSE, PhD
    mechanical engineering • MS, MSE, PhD

College of Fine Arts
Dr. J. Robert Wills, Dean
Programs in:
    art • MA, MFA
    dance • MFA
    music • DMA, MA, MM
    theater • MA, MFA, PhD

College of Liberal Arts and Sciences
Dr. Gary S. Krahenbuhl, Dean
Programs in:
    anthropology • MA, PhD
    applied mathematics • MA, PhD
    Asian history • MA, PhD
    behavior • MS, PhD
    behavioral neuroscience • PhD
    biology • MNS
    British history • MA, PhD
    cell and developmental biology • MS, PhD
    chemistry and biochemistry • MNS, MS, PhD
    clinical psychology • PhD
    cognitive/behavioral systems • PhD
    communication disorders • MS
    comparative literature • MA
    demography and population studies • MA, PhD
    developmental psychology • PhD
    ecology • MS, PhD
    English • MA, PhD

    environmental psychology • PhD
    European history • MA, PhD
    evolution • MS, PhD
    family resources and human development • MS
    family science • PhD
    French • MA
    genetics • MS, PhD
    geography • MA, PhD
    geological engineering • MS, PhD
    German • MA
    humanities • MA
    Latin American studies • MA, PhD
    liberal arts and sciences • MFA, MPE
    linguistics • MA
    literature • PhD
    literature and language • MA
    mathematics • MA, MNS, PhD
    medieval studies • Certificate
    microbiology • MNS, MS, PhD
    molecular and cellular biology • MS, PhD
    natural science • MNS
    philosophy • MA
    physics and astronomy • MNS, MS, PhD
    physiology • MS, PhD
    plant biology • MNS, MS, PhD
    political science • MA, PhD
    public history • MA
    quantitative research methods • PhD
    religious studies • MA
    Renaissance studies • Certificate
    rhetoric and composition • MA
    rhetoric/composition and linguistics • PhD
    social psychology • PhD
    sociology • MA, PhD
    Spanish • MA, PhD
    statistics • MA, PhD
    teaching English as a second language • MTESL
    U.S. history • PhD
    U.S. western history • MA

College of Nursing
Dr. Barbara H. Durand, Dean
Program in:
    nursing • MS

College of Public Programs
Dr. Anne L. Schneider, Dean
Programs in:
    communication • PhD
    journalism and telecommunication • MMC
    justice studies • MS
    public affairs • DPA, MPA
    recreation • MS
    speech and interpersonal communication • MA

School of Social Work
Dr. Emilia E. Martinez-Brawley, Dean
Program in:
    social work • MSW, PhD

College of Law
Alan A. Matheson, Interim Dean
Program in:
    law • JD

ARIZONA STATE UNIVERSITY WEST

Phoenix, AZ 85069-7100

http://www.west.asu.edu/

Public coed upper-level institution. *Enrollment: 2,876 graduate, professional, and undergraduate students. Graduate faculty: 35 full-time, 13 part-time. Computer facilities: Campuswide network is available with full Internet access. Total number of PCs/terminals supplied for student use: 382. Computer services are offered at no charge.* Library facilities: *Fletcher Library.* Graduate expenses: *Tuition of $2088 per year full-time, $330 per course part-time for state residents; $9040 per year full-time, $1131 per course part-time for nonresidents. Fees of $10 per year (minimum).* General application contact: *Marge A. Runyan, Coordinator, Graduate College, 602-543-4567.*

College of Education

Dr. William S. Svoboda, Dean
Programs in:
    educational administration and supervision • M Ed
    elementary education • M Ed
    secondary education • M Ed
    special education • M Ed

College of Human Services

Dr. Jan Shirreffs, Director
Program in:
    gerontology • Certificate

School of Management

Dr. Abagail McWilliams, MBA Programs Director
Programs in:
    accountancy • Certificate
    business • MBA

NORTHERN ARIZONA UNIVERSITY

Flagstaff, AZ 86011

http://www.nau.edu/

Public coed university. *Enrollment: 19,618 graduate, professional, and undergraduate students. Graduate faculty: 503 full-time, 327 part-time. Computer facilities: Campuswide network is available with full Internet access. Total number of PCs/terminals supplied for student use: 1,200. Computer service fees are included with tuition and fees.* Library facilities: *Cline Library.* Graduate expenses: *Tuition of $2088 per year full-time, $330 per semester (minimum) part-time for state residents; $8004 per year full-time, $1002 per semester (minimum) part-time for nonresidents. Fees of $72 per year full-time, $18 per semester (minimum) part-time.* General application contact: *Dr. Patricia Baron, Director of Graduate Admissions, 520-523-4348.*

Graduate College

Dr. Kathryn Cruz-Uribe, Interim Associate Provost for Research and Graduate Studies and Graduate Dean

Center for Excellence in Education

Dr. Melvin E. Hall, Executive Director
Programs in:
    bilingual/multicultural education • M Ed
    counseling • Ed D, M Ed, MA
    curriculum and instruction • Ed D
    early childhood education • M Ed
    educational leadership • Ed D, M Ed
    educational psychology • Ed D
    elementary education • M Ed
    reading and learning disabilities • M Ed
    school psychology • MA
    secondary education • M Ed
    special education • M Ed
    vocational education • MVE

College of Arts and Sciences

Suzanne Shipley, Dean
Programs in:
    applied linguistics • PhD
    biology • MS, PhD
    biology education • MAT
    chemistry • MS
    earth science • MAT, MS
    English • MA
    geology • MS
    history • MA, PhD
    liberal studies • MLS
    mathematics • MAT, MS
    physical science • MAT
    quaternary studies • MS
    teaching English as a second language • MAT

College of Business Administration

Dr. Patricia Meyers, Dean
Programs in:
    general management • MBA
    management information systems • MBA

College of Ecosystem Science and Management

Dr. David Patton, Dean
Programs in:
    forestry • MSF, PhD
    rural geography • MA

College of Health Professions

Dr. Susan Peterson-Mansfield, Interim Dean
Programs in:
    health education and health promotion • MPH
    nursing • MSN
    physical education • MA
    physical therapy • MPT
    speech pathology • MS

College of Social and Behavioral Sciences

M. Susanna Maxwell, Dean
Programs in:
    anthropology • MA
    archaeology • MA
    criminal justice • MS
    political science • MA, PhD

Northern Arizona University (continued)
   psychology • MA
   public administration • MPA
   public policy • PhD
   sociology and social work • MA

School of Performing Arts
Garry Owens, Director
Program in:
   performing arts • MM

THE UNIVERSITY OF ARIZONA
Tucson, AZ 85721

http://www.arizona.edu/

Public coed university. *Enrollment: 33,737 graduate, professional, and undergraduate students. Graduate faculty: 1,392 full-time, 103 part-time. Computer facilities: Campuswide network is available with full Internet access. Computer services are offered at no charge. Library facilities: main library plus 3 additional on-campus libraries. Graduate expenses: $2162 per year full-time, $337 per semester (minimum) part-time for state residents; $6860 per year full-time, $1138 per semester (minimum) part-time for nonresidents. General application contact: Graduate Admissions Office, 520-621-3132.*

Graduate College
Programs in:
   biochemistry • MS, PhD
   optical sciences • MS, PhD
   public health • MPH

College of Agriculture
Programs in:
   agricultural and biosystems engineering • MS, PhD
   agricultural and resource economics • MS
   agricultural education • M Ag Ed, MS
   animal sciences • MS, PhD
   dietetics • MS
   entomology • MS, PhD
   family and consumer resources • MS, PhD
   forest-watershed management • MS, PhD
   home economics education • MHE Ed
   landscape architecture • ML Arch
   nutritional sciences • MS
   pathobiology • MS, PhD
   plant pathology • MS, PhD
   plant sciences • MS, PhD
   range management • MS, PhD
   renewable natural resources • MS, PhD
   soil, water and environmental science • MS, PhD
   wildlife and fisheries science • MS, PhD

College of Architecture
Program in:
   architecture • M Arch

College of Business and Public Administration
Programs in:
   accounting • M Ac, PhD
   business administration • MBA
   economics • MA, PhD
   finance • MS, PhD
   management • PhD
   management and policy • MS
   management information systems • MS, PhD
   marketing • MS, PhD
   public administration • MPA

College of Education
Programs in:
   bilingual education • M Ed
   bilingual/multicultural education • MA
   educational administration • Ed D, Ed S, M Ed, MA, PhD
   educational psychology • MA, PhD
   elementary education • Ed D, M Ed, MT
   higher education • Ed D, M Ed, MA, PhD
   language, reading and culture • Ed D, Ed S, MA, PhD
   reading • Ed D, Ed S, M Ed, MA, PhD
   secondary education • Ed D, Ed S, M Ed, MT
   special education and rehabilitation • Ed D, Ed S, M Ed, MA, MS, PhD
   teaching and teacher education • Ed D, Ed S, MA, PhD

College of Engineering and Mines
Programs in:
   aerospace engineering • MS, PhD
   chemical engineering • MS, PhD
   civil engineering • MS, PhD
   electrical and computer engineering • MS, PhD
   engineering mechanics • MS, PhD
   environmental engineering • MS, PhD
   geological and geophysical engineering • MS, PhD
   hydrology • MS, PhD
   industrial engineering • MS
   materials science and engineering • MS, PhD
   mechanical engineering • MS, PhD
   mineral economics • MS, PhD
   mining engineering • MS, PhD
   nuclear engineering • MS, PhD
   reliability and quality engineering • MS
   systems and industrial engineering • PhD
   systems engineering • MS
   water resource administration • MS, PhD

College of Fine Arts
Programs in:
   art education • MA
   art history • MA
   art (studio) • MFA
   composition • A Mus D, MM
   conducting • A Mus D, MM
   media arts • MA
   music education • MM, PhD
   musicology • MM
   music theory • MM, PhD
   performance • A Mus D, MM
   theatre arts • MA, MFA

College of Humanities
Programs in:
classics • MA
creative writing • MFA
East Asian studies • MA, PhD
English • M Ed, MA, PhD
English as a second language • MA
French • M Ed, MA, PhD
German • M Ed, MA
rhetoric, composition and teaching of English • PhD
Russian • M Ed, MA
Spanish • M Ed, MA, PhD

College of Nursing
Program in:
nursing • MS, PhD

College of Pharmacy
Programs in:
pharmaceutical sciences • MS, PhD
pharmacology • MS
pharmacy • MS, PhD, Pharm D
toxicology • MS

College of Science
Programs in:
astronomy • MS, PhD
atmospheric sciences • MS, PhD
botany • MS, PhD
chemistry • MA, MS, PhD
computer science • MS, PhD
ecology and evolutionary biology • MS, PhD
geosciences • MS, PhD
mathematics • M Ed, MA, MS, PhD
molecular and cellular biology • MS, PhD
physics • M Ed, MS, PhD
planetary sciences • MS, PhD
speech and hearing sciences • MS, PhD
statistics • MS, PhD

College of Social and Behavioral Sciences
Programs in:
anthropology • MA, PhD
communication • MA, PhD
geography • MA, PhD
history • M Ed, MA, PhD
journalism • MA
Latin American studies • MA
library science • MA, PhD
linguistics • MA, PhD
Near Eastern studies • MA, PhD
philosophy • MA, PhD
political science • MA, PhD
psychology • MA, PhD
sociology • MA, PhD
women's studies • MA

Graduate Interdisciplinary Programs
Programs in:
American Indian studies • MA
applied mathematics • MS, PhD
arid land resource sciences • PhD
cancer biology • PhD
comparative cultural and literary studies • MA, PhD

epidemiology • MS, PhD
genetics • MS, PhD
gerontological studies • Certificate, MS
insect science • PhD
neuroscience • PhD
nutritional sciences • PhD
pharmacology and toxicology • PhD
physiological sciences • PhD
planning • MS
second language acquisition and teaching • PhD

School of Health Related Professions
Programs in:
exercise and sport science • MA, MS
health education • M Ed

College of Law
Joel Seligman, Dean
Programs in:
international trade law • LL M
law • JD

College of Medicine
Programs in:
biochemistry • MS, PhD
cell biology and anatomy • PhD
medicine • MD
microbiology and immunology • MS, PhD
public health • MPH

ARKANSAS

 ARKANSAS STATE UNIVERSITY
State University, AR 72467
http://www.astate.edu/

Public coed comprehensive institution. *Enrollment: 10,012 graduate, professional, and undergraduate students. Graduate faculty: 258 full-time, 8 part-time. Computer facilities: Campuswide network is available with full Internet access. Total number of PCs/terminals supplied for student use: 421. Computer services are offered at no charge. Library facilities: Dean B. Ellis Library. Graduate expenses: Tuition of $2760 per year full-time, $115 per credit hour part-time for state residents; $6936 per year full-time, $289 per credit hour part-time for nonresidents. Fees of $506 per year full-time, $44 per semester (minimum) part-time. General application contact: Dr. George Foldesy, Interim Dean of the Graduate School, 870-972-3029.*

Arkansas State University (continued)
Graduate School
Dr. George Foldesy, Interim Dean

College of Agriculture
Dr. Keith Rogers, Dean
Program in:
  agriculture • MS, MSA, SCCT

College of Arts and Sciences
Dr. Richard D. McGhee, Dean
Programs in:
  biology • MS
  biology education • MSE, SCCT
  chemistry • MS
  chemistry education • MSE, SCCT
  computer science • MS
  English • MA
  English education • MSE, SCCT
  environmental sciences • PhD
  history • MA, SCCT
  mathematics • MS, MSE
  political science • MA, SCCT
  public administration • MPA
  social science • MSE, SCCT
  sociology • MA, SCCT

College of Business
Dr. Roger Roderick, Dean
Programs in:
  business administration • MBA
  business education • MSE, SCCT

College of Communications
Dr. Russell Shain, Dean
Programs in:
  journalism • MSMC
  radio-television • MSMC

College of Education
Dr. Evelyn Lynch, Dean
Programs in:
  counselor education • Ed S, MSE
  curriculum and instruction • Ed S, MSE
  early childhood education • MSE
  early childhood services • MS
  educational administration • Ed S, MSE
  educational leadership • Ed D
  elementary counselor education • MSE
  elementary education • MSE
  gifted and talented education • MSE
  physical education • MS, MSE, SCCT
  reading • MSE, SCCT
  rehabilitation counseling • MRC
  secondary counselor education • MSE
  secondary education teaching • MSE
  special education • MSE

College of Fine Arts
Dr. Russell Shain, Dean
Programs in:
  art • MA
  music education • MME, SCCT
  performance • MM
  speech communication and theater arts • MA, SCCT

College of Nursing and Health Professions
Dr. Susan Hanrahan, Dean
Programs in:
  communication disorders • MCD
  nursing • MSN

ARKANSAS TECH UNIVERSITY
Russellville, AR 72801-2222
http://www.atu.edu/

Public coed comprehensive institution. *Enrollment: 4,490 graduate, professional, and undergraduate students. Graduate faculty: 99 full-time. Library facilities: Tomlinson Library. Graduate expenses: Tuition of $98 per credit hour for state residents; $196 per credit hour for nonresidents. Fees of $30 per semester. General application contact: Dr. Eldon G. Clary, Dean of Graduate Studies, 501-968-0398.*

Graduate Studies
Dr. Eldon G. Clary, Dean

School of Education
Dr. Dennis W. Fleniken, Dean
Programs in:
  educational leadership • M Ed
  elementary education • M Ed
  English • M Ed
  gifted education • MSE
  health and physical education • M Ed, PhD
  instructional improvement • M Ed
  instructional technology • M Ed
  mathematics • M Ed
  social studies • M Ed

School of Liberal Arts
Dr. Georgena Duncan, Dean
Program in:
  liberal arts • MLA

HARDING UNIVERSITY
Searcy, AR 72149-0001
http://www.harding.edu/

Independent-religious coed comprehensive institution. *Enrollment: 3,899 graduate, professional, and undergraduate students. Graduate faculty: 0 full-time, 39 part-time. Computer facilities: Campuswide network is available with full Internet access. Total number of PCs/terminals supplied for student use: 140. Computer services are offered at no charge. Library facilities: Brackett Library. Graduate expenses: Tuition of $212 per credit hour. Fees of $39 per credit hour. General application contact: Dr. Dee Carson, Director of Graduate Studies in Education, 501-279-4315.*

College of Bible and Religion
Dr. Tom Alexander, Dean
Programs in:
    marriage and family therapy • MS
    ministry • MA

School of Education
Dr. Dee Carson, Director
Programs in:
    elementary education • M Ed
    elementary school administration • M Ed
    secondary education • M Ed, MSE

HENDERSON STATE UNIVERSITY
Arkadelphia, AR 71999-0001

http://www.hsu.edu/

Public coed comprehensive institution. *Enrollment: 3,555 graduate, professional, and undergraduate students. Graduate faculty: 120 full-time, 15 part-time. Computer facilities: Campuswide network is available with full Internet access. Total number of PCs/terminals supplied for student use: 165. Computer services are offered at no charge. Library facilities: Huie Library. Graduate expenses: Tuition of $120 per credit hour for state residents; $240 per credit hour for nonresidents. Fees of $105 per semester (minimum) full-time, $52 per semester (minimum) part-time. General application contact: Dr. Johnnie Roebuck, Graduate Dean, 870-230-5126.*

Graduate Studies
Dr. Johnnie Roebuck, Dean

Ellis College of Arts and Sciences
Dr. Joe Wright, Dean
Programs in:
    English • MLA
    social studies • MLA

School of Business Administration
Dr. Louis Dawkins, Dean
Program in:
    business administration • MBA

School of Education
Dr. Joye Norris, Dean
Programs in:
    art education • MSE
    biology education • MSE
    community counseling • MS
    early childhood/special education • MSE
    education of the mildly handicapped • MSE
    elementary school administration • MSE
    elementary school counseling • MSE
    English education • MSE
    general elementary education • MSE
    mathematics education • MSE
    physical education • MSE
    secondary school administration • MSE
    secondary school counseling • MSE
    social sciences education • MSE

SOUTHERN ARKANSAS UNIVERSITY–MAGNOLIA
Magnolia, AR 71753

http://www.saumag.edu/hompg1.html

Public coed comprehensive institution. *Enrollment: 2,564 graduate, professional, and undergraduate students. Graduate faculty: 32 full-time, 10 part-time. Computer facilities: Campuswide network is available with full Internet access. Total number of PCs/terminals supplied for student use: 150. Computer service fees are included with tuition and fees. Library facilities: Magale Library. Graduate expenses: Tuition of $95 per hour for state residents; $138 per hour for nonresidents. Fees of $2 per hour. General application contact: Dr. Daniel L. Bernard, Dean, Graduate Studies, 870-235-4055.*

Graduate Program in Education
Dr. Danield L. Bernard, Dean, Graduate Studies
Programs in:
    agency counseling • M Ed
    elementary counseling • M Ed
    elementary education • M Ed
    gifted and talented education • M Ed
    health, kinesiology and recreation • M Ed
    library media • M Ed
    mathematics and general science education • M Ed
    reading education • M Ed
    secondary counseling • M Ed
    special education • M Ed

Program in Business Administration
Program in:
    business administration • MBA

UNIVERSITY OF ARKANSAS
Fayetteville, AR 72701-1201

http://www.uark.edu/

Public coed university. *Enrollment: 14,692 graduate, professional, and undergraduate students. Graduate faculty: 837 full-time, 69 part-time. Computer facilities: Campuswide network is available with full Internet access. Total number of PCs/terminals supplied for student use: 800. Computer services are offered at no charge. Library facilities: Mullins Library plus 5 additional on-campus libraries. Graduate expenses: $3144 per year full-time, $173 per credit hour part-time for state residents; $7140 per year full-time, $395 per credit hour part-time for nonresidents. General application contact: Gail G. Piha, Assistant to the Dean of the Graduate School, 501-575-4401.*

University of Arkansas (continued)
Graduate School
Dr. Collis R. Geren, Associate Vice Chancellor and Dean

College of Business Administration
Dr. Doyle Williams, Dean
Programs in:
   accounting • M Acc
   business administration • MBA, PhD
   computer information systems and quantitative analysis •
      MIS
   economics • MA, PhD
   transportation and logistics management • MTLM

College of Education
Charles Stegman, Dean
Programs in:
   adult education • Ed D, Ed S, M Ed
   childhood education • MAT
   communication disorders • MS
   counseling education • Ed S, MS, PhD
   curriculum and instruction • PhD
   education • Ed D, Ed S, M Ed
   educational administration • Ed D, Ed S, M Ed
   educational technology • M Ed
   elementary education • M Ed
   health, physical education, and recreation • Ed D
   health science • MS, PhD
   higher education • Ed D, Ed S, M Ed
   kinesiology • MS, PhD
   middle-level education • MAT
   physical education • M Ed, MAT
   recreation • M Ed
   rehabilitation • MS, PhD
   secondary education • M Ed, MAT
   special education • M Ed, MAT
   vocational education • Ed D, Ed S, M Ed, MAT

College of Engineering
Dr. Otto Loewer, Dean
Programs in:
   biological and agricultural engineering • MSBAE
   chemical engineering • MS Ch E
   civil engineering • MSCE
   computer systems engineering • MSCSE
   electrical engineering • MSEE
   engineering • MSE, PhD
   environmental engineering • MS En E
   industrial engineering • MSIE
   mechanical engineering • MSME
   operations research • MSOR
   transportation engineering • MSTE

Dale Bumpers College of Agricultural, Food and Life Sciences
Dr. C. J. Scifres, Dean
Programs in:
   agricultural and extension education • MAT, MS
   agricultural economics • MS
   agronomy • MS, PhD
   animal science • MS, PhD
   biological and agricultural engineering • MSBAE
   entomology • MS, PhD
   food science • MS, PhD

   general agriculture • MS
   horticulture • MS
   human environmental sciences • MS
   plant pathology • MS
   plant science • PhD
   poultry science • MS, PhD

J. William Fulbright College of Arts and Sciences
Dr. Bernard Madison, Dean
Programs in:
   anthropology • MA
   applied music • MM
   art • MFA
   arts and sciences • M Ed
   biology • MA, MS, PhD
   chemistry and biochemistry • MS, PhD
   communication • MA
   comparative literature • MA, PhD
   composition • MM
   computer science • MS
   creative writing • MFA
   drama • MA, MFA
   English • MA, PhD
   environmental dynamics • PhD
   French • MA
   geography • MA
   geology • MS
   German • MA
   history • MA, PhD
   journalism • MA
   mathematics • MS, PhD
   music education • MM
   music history • MM
   music theory • MM
   philosophy • MA, PhD
   physics • MA, MS, PhD
   political science • MA
   psychology • MA, PhD
   public administration • MPA
   secondary mathematics • MA
   sociology • MA
   Spanish • MA
   statistics • MS
   translation • MFA

School of Law
Leonard P. Strickman, Dean
Programs in:
   agricultural law • LL M
   law • JD

UNIVERSITY OF ARKANSAS AT LITTLE ROCK
Little Rock, AR 72204-1099

http://www.ualr.edu/

Public coed university. *Enrollment:* 10,959 graduate, professional, and undergraduate students. *Computer facilities: Campuswide network is available with full Internet access. Total number of PCs/*

terminals supplied for student use: 750. Computer service fees are included with tuition and fees. Library facilities: *Ottenheimer Library plus 1 additional on-campus library.* Graduate expenses: *Tuition of $2466 per year full-time, $137 per credit hour part-time for state residents; $5256 per year full-time, $292 per credit hour part-time for nonresidents. Fees of $216 per year full-time, $36 per semester (minimum) part-time.* General application contact: *Dr. Richard Hanson, Dean of the Graduate School, 501-569-8661.*

Graduate School
Dr. Richard Hanson, Dean

College of Arts, Humanities, and Social Science
Dr. Deborah Baldwin, Dean
Programs in:
    applied psychology • MAP
    art education • MA
    art history • MA
    expository writing • MA
    liberal studies • MALS
    public history • MA
    studio art • MA
    technical writing • MA

College of Business Administration
Dr. William C. Goolsby, Dean
Program in:
    business administration • MBA

College of Education
Dr. Angela Sewall, Dean
Programs in:
    adult education • M Ed
    early childhood education • Ed S, M Ed
    early childhood special education • M Ed
    educational administration and supervision • Ed D, Ed S, M Ed
    education of hearing impaired children • M Ed
    elementary education • Ed S, M Ed
    higher education administration • Ed D
    instructional resources • M Ed
    orientation and mobility • MA
    reading • Ed S, M Ed
    rehabilitation for the blind • MA
    rehabilitation teaching • MA
    school counseling • M Ed
    secondary education • M Ed
    teaching of the mildly disabled student • M Ed
    teaching persons with severe disabilities • M Ed
    teaching the gifted and talented • M Ed
    teaching the visually impaired child • M Ed

College of Professional Studies
Dr. John Gray, Dean
Programs in:
    applied gerontology • CG
    clinical social work • MSW
    criminal justice • MA
    gerontology • MA
    health services administration • MHSA
    interpersonal communications • MA
    journalism • MA
    organizational communications • MA

    public administration • MPA
    social program administration • MSW

College of Sciences and Engineering Technology
Dr. Jesse O. Snowden Jr., Dean
Programs in:
    applied analysis • MS
    applied mathematics • MS
    chemistry • MA, MS
    computer and information science • MS
    instrumental sciences • MS, PhD
    mathematical statistics • MS

School of Law
Rodney K. Smith, Dean
Program in:
    law • JD

UNIVERSITY OF CENTRAL ARKANSAS
Conway, AR 72035-0001

http://www.uca.edu/

Public coed comprehensive institution. *Enrollment: 8,938 graduate, professional, and undergraduate students. Graduate faculty: 199 full-time, 49 part-time. Computer facilities: Campuswide network is available with full Internet access. Total number of PCs/terminals supplied for student use: 475. Computer service fees are included with tuition and fees. Library facilities: Torreyson Library plus 1 additional on-campus library.* Graduate expenses: *Tuition of $161 per credit hour for state residents; $298 per credit hour for nonresidents. Fees of $50 per year full-time, $30 per year part-time.* General application contact: *Dr. Elaine McNiece, Dean of the Graduate School, 501-450-3124.*

Graduate School
Dr. Elaine McNiece, Graduate Dean

College of Business Administration
Dr. Joe Horton, Dean
Program in:
    business administration • MBA

College of Education
Dr. Fred Litton, Interim Dean
Programs in:
    business education • MSE
    community service counseling • MS
    counseling psychology • MS
    early childhood education • MSE
    early childhood special education • MSE
    education • Ed S
    education media and library science • MS
    elementary education • MSE
    elementary school counseling • MS
    elementary school leadership • MSE
    mildly handicapped • MSE
    moderately/profoundly handicapped • MSE

University of Central Arkansas (continued)
   reading education • MSE
   school psychology • MS
   secondary school counseling • MS
   secondary school leadership • MSE
   seriously emotionally disturbed • MSE
   student personnel services in higher education • MS

College of Fine Arts and Communication
Dr. Robert G. Everding, Dean
Programs in:
   choral conducting • MM
   instrumental conducting • MM
   music education • MM
   music theory • MM
   performance • MM

College of Health and Applied Sciences
Dr. Neil Hattlestad, Dean
Programs in:
   family and consumer sciences • MS
   health sciences • MS
   kinesiology • MS
   nursing • MSN
   occupational therapy • MS
   physical therapy • MS, PhD
   speech-language pathology • MS

College of Liberal Arts
Dr. Gary Stark, Dean
Programs in:
   English • MA
   history • MA
   liberal arts • MS, MSE

College of Natural Sciences and Math
Dr. Stephen Addison, Interim Dean
Programs in:
   biological science • MS
   mathematics • MA

CALIFORNIA

 AZUSA PACIFIC UNIVERSITY
Azusa, CA 91702-7000

http://www.apu.edu/

Independent-religious coed comprehensive institution. *Enrollment:* 5,000 graduate, professional, and undergraduate students. *Graduate faculty: 97 full-time, 99 part-time. Computer facilities: Campuswide network is available with full Internet access. Computer services are offered at no charge. Library facilities: Marshburn Memorial Library plus 2 additional on-campus libraries. Graduate expenses: Tuition of $350 per unit. Fees of $57 per year. General application contact: Margaret Albertson, Director of Institutional Research, 626-815-5405.*

Graduate Studies
Margaret Albertson, Director of Institutional Research

College of Liberal Arts and Sciences
Dr. David Weeks, Dean
Programs in:
   applied computer science and technology • MS
   client/server technology • Certificate, MS
   computer information systems • Certificate, MS
   computer science • Certificate
   end-user support • MS
   end-user training and support • Certificate
   inter-emphasis • MS
   physical therapy • MPT
   software engineering • Certificate, MS, MSE
   teaching English to speakers of other languages •
      Certificate, MA
   technical programming • Certificate, MS
   telecommunications • Certificate, MS

Graduate School of Theology
Dr. Les Blank, Dean
Programs in:
   pastoral studies • MAPS
   religion • MA
   theology • D Min, M Div

School of Business and Management
Dr. Phillip Lewis, Dean
Programs in:
   business administration • MBA
   human resource development • MHRD
   international business • MBA
   organizational management • MAOM
   strategic management • MBA

School of Education and Behavioral Studies
Dr. Alice Watkins, Dean
Programs in:
   clinical psychology • MA, Psy D
   college student affairs • M Ed
   curriculum and instruction • MA
   educational leadership and administration • Ed D
   educational technology • M Ed
   language development • MA
   physical education • M Ed
   pupil personnel services • MA
   school administration • MA
   social science leadership studies • MA
   special education • MA

School of Music
Dr. Don Neufeld, Professor
Programs in:
   conducting • M Mus
   education • M Mus

School of Nursing
Dr. Rose Liegler, Dean
Program in:
   nursing • MSN

BIOLA UNIVERSITY
La Mirada, CA 90639-0001

http://www.biola.edu/

Independent-religious coed university. *Enrollment:* 3,273 graduate, professional, and undergraduate students. Graduate faculty: *133 full-time.* Computer facilities: *Campuswide network is available with full Internet access. Total number of PCs/terminals supplied for student use: 55. Computer service fees are included with tuition and fees.* Library facilities: *Rose Memorial Library.* Graduate expenses: *Tuition of $9810 per year full-time, $327 per unit part-time. Fees of $40 per year full-time.* General application contact: *Roy Allinson, Director of Graduate Admissions, 562-903-4752.*

Rosemead School of Psychology
Dr. Patricia Pike, Administrative Dean
Program in:
    psychology • PhD, Psy D

School of Arts and Sciences
Dr. Lucille Richardson, Chair of Education Department
Program in:
    arts and sciences • MA Ed

School of Continuing Studies
Dr. Craig Hazen, Director
Program in:
    Christian apologetics • MA

School of Intercultural Studies
Dr. Donald Douglas, Dean
Programs in:
    applied linguistics • MA
    intercultural studies • MAICS, PhD
    missiology • D Miss
    teaching English to speakers of other languages •
      Certificate, MA

Talbot School of Theology
Dr. Dennis Dirks, Dean
Programs in:
    Christian education • MACE
    divinity • M Div
    education • Ed D
    ministry • MAMIN
    practical theology • MA
    theology • D Min, MA, Th M

CALIFORNIA INSTITUTE OF TECHNOLOGY
Pasadena, CA 91125-0001

http://www.cco.caltech.edu/

Independent coed university. *Enrollment:* 995 matriculated graduate/professional students. Graduate faculty: *432 full-time, 56 part-time.* Computer facilities: *Campuswide network is available with full Internet access. Total number of PCs/terminals supplied for student use: 60. Computer service fees are included with tuition and fees.* Library facilities: *Caltech Library Systems plus 6 additional on-campus libraries.* Graduate expenses: *Tuition of $18,950 per year. Fees of $24 per year.* General application contact: *Natalie Gilmore, Graduate Office, 626-395-6346.*

Division of Biology
Dr. Melvin Simon, Chairman
Programs in:
    biochemistry • PhD
    cell biology and biophysics • PhD
    developmental biology • PhD
    genetics • PhD
    immunology • PhD
    molecular biology • PhD
    neurobiology • PhD

Division of Chemistry and Chemical Engineering
Peter B. Dervan, Chairman
Programs in:
    chemical engineering • MS, PhD
    chemistry • PhD

Division of Engineering and Applied Science
Dr. John H. Seinfeld, Chairman
Programs in:
    aeronautics • Engr, MS, PhD
    applied mathematics • PhD
    applied mechanics • MS, PhD
    applied physics • MS, PhD
    civil engineering • Engr, MS, PhD
    computation and neural systems • MS, PhD
    computer science • MS, PhD
    control and dynamical systems • PhD
    electrical engineering • Engr, MS, PhD
    engineering science • MS, PhD
    environmental engineering science • MS, PhD
    materials science • MS, PhD
    mechanical engineering • Engr, MS, PhD
    plasma physics • MS, PhD

Division of Geological and Planetary Sciences
Dr. Edward M. Stolper, Chair
Programs in:
    cosmochemistry • PhD
    geobiology • PhD
    geochemistry • MS, PhD
    geology • MS, PhD
    geophysics • MS, PhD
    planetary science • MS, PhD

California Institute of Technology (continued)

Division of Physics, Mathematics and Astronomy

Charles Peck, Chairman
Programs in:
astronomy • PhD
computation and neural systems • MS, PhD
mathematics • PhD
physics • PhD

Division of the Humanities and Social Sciences

John O. Ledyard, Chairman
Programs in:
economics • PhD
political science • PhD
social science • MS

CALIFORNIA LUTHERAN UNIVERSITY

Thousand Oaks, CA 91360-2787

http://www.clunet.edu/

Independent-religious coed comprehensive institution. *Enrollment:* 2,674 graduate, professional, and undergraduate students. *Graduate faculty: 31 full-time, 73 part-time. Computer facilities: Campuswide network is available with full Internet access. Computer services are offered at no charge. Library facilities: Pearson Library.* Graduate expenses: *$335 per unit.* General application contact: *DeAnne Taylor, Director of Graduate Enrollment Services, 805-493-3127.*

Graduate Studies

Programs in:
clinical psychology • MS
marital and family therapy • MS
public administration • MPA

School of Business Administration

Dr. Ronald Hagler, Director
Programs in:
finance • MBA
healthcare management • MBA
international business • MBA
management information systems • MBA
marketing • MBA
organizational behavior • MBA
small business/entrepreneurship • MBA

School of Education

Dr. Carol Bartell, Dean
Programs in:
counseling and guidance • MS
education • M Ed
educational administration • MA
reading education • MA
special education • MS

 # CALIFORNIA POLYTECHNIC STATE UNIVERSITY, SAN LUIS OBISPO

San Luis Obispo, CA 93407

http://www.calpoly.edu/

Public coed comprehensive institution. *Enrollment:* 16,735 graduate, professional, and undergraduate students. Computer facilities: *Campuswide network is available with full Internet access. Total number of PCs/terminals supplied for student use: 1,600. Computer services are offered at no charge. Library facilities: Robert F. Kennedy Library.* Graduate expenses: *Tuition of $0 for state residents; $164 per unit for nonresidents. Fees of $2102 per year full-time, $1632 per year part-time.* General application contact: *Jim Maraviglia, Admissions Office, 805-756-2311.*

Center for Teacher Education

Dr. Susan Roper, Director
Programs in:
curriculum and instruction • MA
education • MA
educational administration • MA
reading • MA
special education • MA

College of Agriculture

Glen Casey, Graduate Coordinator
Program in:
agriculture • MS

College of Architecture and Environmental Design

Martin Harms, Dean
Programs in:
architecture • MS Arch
city and regional planning • MCRP

College of Business

Dr. William Boynton, Dean
Programs in:
agribusiness management • MBA
industrial and technical studies • MA

College of Engineering

Dr. Peter Y. Lee, Dean
Programs in:
aeronautical engineering • MSAE
biochemical engineering • MS
computer science • MSCS
industrial engineering • MS
materials engineering • MS
mechanical engineering • MS
water engineering • MS

College of Liberal Arts

Harry Sharp Jr., Interim Dean
Programs in:
English • MA
psychology • MS

College of Science and Mathematics
Philip S. Bailey, Dean
Programs in:
    biological sciences • MS
    mathematics • MS
    physical education and kinesiology • MS

CALIFORNIA STATE POLYTECHNIC UNIVERSITY, POMONA
Pomona, CA 91768-2557

http://www.csupomona.edu/

Public coed comprehensive institution. *Enrollment:* 17,246 graduate, professional, and undergraduate students. Library facilities: *University Library.* Graduate expenses: *Tuition of $0 for state residents; $164 per unit for nonresidents. Fees of $1953 per year full-time, $1287 per year part-time.* General application contact: *Rose M. Smith, Director, 909-869-3423.*

Graduate Studies
Dr. Patricia M. Hopkins, Associate Vice President for
    Academic Affairs

College of Agriculture
Dr. Wayne R. Bidlack, Dean
Programs in:
    agricultural science • MS
    animal science • MS
    foods and nutrition • MS

College of Business Administration
Dr. Eric J. McLaughlin, Director
Program in:
    business administration • MBA, MSBA

College of Engineering
Dr. Carl E. Rathmann, Interim Dean
Programs in:
    electrical engineering • MSEE
    engineering • MSE

College of Environmental Design
Linda Sanders, Dean
Programs in:
    architecture • M Arch
    landscape architecture • M Land Arch
    urban and regional planning • MURP

College of Letters, Arts, and Social Sciences
Dr. Barbara J. Way, Interim Dean
Programs in:
    economics • MS
    English • MA
    kinesiology • MS
    psychology • MS

College of Science
Dr. Simon J. Bernau, Dean
Programs in:
    applied mathematics • MS
    biological sciences • MS
    chemistry • MS
    computer science • MS
    pure mathematics • MS

School of Education and Integrative Studies
Dr. Richard A. Navarro, Dean
Program in:
    education and integrative studies • MA

CALIFORNIA STATE UNIVERSITY, BAKERSFIELD
Bakersfield, CA 93311-1099

http://www.csubak.edu/

Public coed comprehensive institution. *Enrollment:* 5,717 graduate, professional, and undergraduate students. *Graduate faculty:* 315. Library facilities: *Walter Stiern Library.* Graduate expenses: *Tuition of $0 for state residents; $246 per unit full-time, $164 per unit part-time for nonresidents. Fees of $1584 per year full-time, $918 per year part-time.* General application contact: *Kathy Smith, Office of Graduate Studies and Research, 805-664-2231.*

Graduate Studies and Research
Dr. Selina Ganopole, Dean

School of Arts and Sciences
Dr. Ray Giegle, Dean
Programs in:
    anthropology • MA
    counseling psychology • MS
    English • MA
    family and child counseling • MFCC
    geology • MS
    history • MA
    hydrology • MS
    nursing • MS
    psychology • MS
    social work • MSW
    sociology • MA

School of Business and Public Administration
Ron Eaves, Interim Dean
Programs in:
    business administration • MBA
    health care management • MSA
    public administration • MPA

School of Education
Dr. Lon Kellenberger, Interim Dean
Programs in:
    bilingual/bicultural education • MA
    counseling • MS
    counseling and personnel services • MA

California State University, Bakersfield (continued)
early childhood education • MA
educational administration • MA
elementary curriculum and instruction • MA
reading education • MA
secondary curriculum and instruction • MA
special education • MA

CALIFORNIA STATE UNIVERSITY, CHICO
Chico, CA 95929-0722

http://www.csuchico.edu/

Public coed comprehensive institution. *Enrollment: 14,247 graduate, professional, and undergraduate students. Graduate faculty: 589 full-time, 227 part-time. Computer facilities: Campuswide network is available with full Internet access. Computer services are offered at no charge. Library facilities: Meriam Library plus 2 additional on-campus libraries. Graduate expenses: Tuition of $0 for state residents; $246 per unit for nonresidents. Fees of $2108 per year full-time, $1442 per year part-time. General application contact: Dr. Robert M. Jackson, Dean, Graduate and International Programs, 530-898-6880.*

Graduate School
Dr. Robert M. Jackson, Dean, Graduate and International Programs
Programs in:
applied mechanical engineering • MS
interdisciplinary studies • MA, MS
simulation science • MS

College of Behavioral and Social Sciences
Dr. James E. Jacob, Dean
Programs in:
counseling • MS
geography • MA
health administration • MPA
museum studies • MA
political science • MA
psychology • MA
public administration • MPA
rural and town planning • MRTP
social science • MA

College of Business
Dr. Arno J. Rethans, Dean
Programs in:
accountancy • MSA
business administration • MBA

College of Communication and Education
Dr. Stephen King, Dean
Programs in:
curriculum and instruction • MA
education • MA
human communication • MA
information and communication studies • MA

instructional technology • MA
linguistically and culturally diverse learners • MA
physical education • MA
public communication • MA
reading and language arts • MA
recreation administration • MA
special education • MA
speech pathology and audiology • MA

College of Engineering, Computer Science, and Technology
Dr. Kenneth Derucher, Dean
Programs in:
computer science • MS
electrical engineering • MS

College of Humanities and Fine Arts
Dr. Donald J. Heinz, Dean
Programs in:
art • MA
English • MA
history • MA
music • MA

College of Natural Sciences
Dr. Roger Lederer, Dean
Programs in:
biological sciences • MS
botany • MS
earth sciences • MS
hydrology and hydrogeology • MS
nursing • MS
nutrition education • MS

School of Agriculture
Annette Levi, Acting Dean
Program in:
agriculture • MS

CALIFORNIA STATE UNIVERSITY, DOMINGUEZ HILLS
Carson, CA 90747-0001

http://www.csudh.edu/

Public coed comprehensive institution. *Enrollment: 12,378 graduate, professional, and undergraduate students. Graduate faculty: 292 full-time, 243 part-time. Library facilities: Educational Resources Center. Graduate expenses: Tuition of $0 for state residents; $246 per unit for nonresidents. Fees of $1896 per year full-time, $1230 per year part-time. General application contact: Alonzo Rodriguez, Director of Admissions, 310-243-3613.*

College of Arts and Sciences
Dr. Selase Williams, Dean
Programs in:
applied behavioral science • MA
biology • MA
clinical psychology • MA
English • MA

general psychology • MA
gerontology • MA
human cytogenic technology • Certificate
humanities • MA
marriage, family, and child counseling • MS
negotiation and conflict resolution • Certificate, MA
quality assurance • MS
rhetoric and composition • Certificate
social research • Certificate
sociology • MA
teaching English as a second language • Certificate

School of Education
Dr. Joseph Braun, Dean
Programs in:
computer-based education • Certificate, MA
counseling • MA
educational administration • MA
individualized education • MA
learning handicapped • MA
multicultural education • MA
physical education • MA
severely handicapped • MA
teaching/curriculum • MA

School of Health
Diane Vines, Dean
Programs in:
clinical sciences • Certificate, MS
nursing • MSN

School of Management
Dr. Yoram Neumann, Dean
Programs in:
computer information systems • MBA
public administration • MPA

CALIFORNIA STATE UNIVERSITY, FRESNO
Fresno, CA 93740

http://www.csufresno.edu/

Public coed comprehensive institution. *Enrollment:* 18,113 graduate, professional, and undergraduate students. Graduate faculty: *404 full-time, 42 part-time.* Computer facilities: *Campuswide network is available with full Internet access. Total number of PCs/terminals supplied for student use: 1,500. Computer services are offered at no charge.* Library facilities: *Henry Madden Library.* Graduate expenses: *Tuition of $0 for state residents; $246 per unit for nonresidents. Fees of $1872 per year full-time, $1206 per year part-time.* General application contact: *Dr. Vivian A. Vidoli, Dean, Division of Graduate Studies, 209-278-2448.*

Division of Graduate Studies
Dr. Vivian A. Vidoli, Dean
Program in:
educational leadership • Ed D

School of Agricultural Sciences and Technology
Dr. Daniel P. Bartell, Dean
Programs in:
agricultural chemistry • MS
agriculture • MS
animal science • MS
family and consumer sciences • MS
food science and nutrition • MS
industrial technology • MS

School of Arts and Humanities
Dr. Luis F. Costa, Dean
Programs in:
art • MA
composition theory • MA
creative writing • MFA
English as a second language • MA
general linguistics • MA
linguistics • MA
literature • MA
mass communication • MA
music • MA
music education • MA
nonfiction prose • MA
performance • MA
Spanish • MA
speech • MA
speech communication • MA

School of Education and Human Development
Dr. Paul Shaker, Dean
Programs in:
administration and supervision • MA
curriculum and instruction • MA
early childhood education • MA
education • MA
marriage, family and child counseling • MS
reading/language arts • MA
rehabilitation counseling • MS
special education • MA

School of Engineering
Dr. Karl Longley, Dean
Programs in:
civil engineering • MS
computer science • MS
electrical engineering • MS
mechanical engineering • MS

School of Health and Social Work
Benjamin Cuellar, Dean
Programs in:
clinical specialty • MS
communicative disorders • MA
education of the deaf • MA
environmental/occupational health • MPH
exercise science • MA
health administration • MPH
health promotion • MPH
nursing • MS
physical therapy • MPT
primary care nurse practitioner • MS
social work education • MSW
speech/language pathology • MA

California State University, Fresno (continued)

School of Natural Sciences
Dr. Kin-Ping Wong, Dean
Programs in:
   biology • MA
   chemistry • MS
   geology • MS
   marine sciences • MS
   mathematics • MA
   physics • MS
   psychology • MA, MS

School of Social Sciences
Dr. Ellen Gruenbaum, Dean
Programs in:
   geography • MA
   history • MA
   international relations • MA
   public administration • MPA
   social sciences • MS

Sid Craig School of Business
Dr. Fred Evans, Dean
Program in:
   business administration • MBA

CALIFORNIA STATE UNIVERSITY, FULLERTON
Fullerton, CA 92834-9480

http://www.fullerton.edu/

Public coed comprehensive institution. *Enrollment:* 24,906 graduate, professional, and undergraduate students. Graduate faculty: 526 full-time, 710 part-time. Graduate expenses: Tuition of $0 for state residents; $246 per unit for nonresidents. Fees of $1947 per year full-time, $1281 per year part-time. General application contact: Gladys M. Fleckles, Director, Graduate Studies, 714-278-2618.

Graduate Studies
Dr. Thomas Klammer, Associate Vice President, Academic Programs
Program in:
   interdisciplinary studies • MA

School of Business Administration and Economics
Dr. Ephraim Smith, Dean
Programs in:
   accounting • MBA, MS
   business administration • MBA
   business economics • MBA
   economics • MA
   finance • MBA
   international business • MBA
   management • MBA
   management information systems • MS
   management science • MBA, MS
   marketing • MBA
   operations research • MS
   statistics • MS
   taxation • MS

School of Communications
Dr. Rick Pullen, Dean
Programs in:
   advertising • MA
   communications • MA
   communicative disorders • MA
   journalism education • MA
   news editorial • MA
   photo communication • MA
   public relations • MA
   radio, television and film • MA
   speech communication • MA
   technical communication • MA
   theory and process • MA

School of Engineering and Computer Science
Dr. Richard Rolke, Acting Dean
Programs in:
   applications administrative information systems • MS
   applications mathematical methods • MS
   civil engineering and engineering mechanics • MS
   computer science • MS
   electrical engineering • MS
   engineering science • MS
   information processing systems • MS
   mechanical engineering • MS
   systems engineering • MS

School of Human Development and Community Service
Dr. Soraya Coley, Dean
Programs in:
   bilingual/bicultural education • MS
   counseling • MS
   educational leadership • MS
   elementary curriculum and instruction • MS
   physical education • MS
   reading • MS
   special education • MS

School of Humanities and Social Sciences
Dr. Donald Castro, Dean
Programs in:
   American studies • MA
   analysis of specific language structures • MA
   anthropological linguistics • MA
   anthropology • MA
   applied linguistics • MA
   clinical/community psychology • MS
   communication and semantics • MA
   comparative literature • MA
   disorders of communication • MA
   English • MA
   environmental education and communication • MS
   environmental policy and planning • MS
   environmental sciences • MS
   experimental phonetics • MA
   French • MA
   geography • MA
   German • MA
   history • MA
   political science • MA

psychology • MA
public administration • MPA
social sciences • MA
sociology • MA
Spanish • MA
teaching English to speakers of other languages • MS
technological studies • MS

School of Natural Science and Mathematics
Dr. Kolf Jayaweera, Dean
Programs in:
    analytical chemistry • MS
    applied mathematics • MA
    biochemistry • MS
    biological science • MA
    botany • MA
    geochemistry • MS
    inorganic chemistry • MS
    mathematics • MA
    mathematics for secondary school teachers • MA
    microbiology • MA
    organic chemistry • MS
    physical chemistry • MS
    physics • MA
    teaching science • MA

School of the Arts
Jerry Samuelson, Dean
Programs in:
    acting • MFA
    acting and directing • MA
    art • MA, MFA
    art history • MA
    ceramics • MFA
    crafts • MA, MFA
    creative photography • MFA
    dance • MA
    design • MA, MFA
    directing • MFA
    dramatic literature/criticism • MA
    drawing and painting • MA, MFA
    museum studies • Certificate
    music education • MA
    music history and literature • MA
    oral interpretation • MA
    performance • MM
    playwriting • MA
    printmaking • MFA
    sculpture • MA, MFA
    technical theater • MA
    technical theater and design • MFA
    television • MA
    theatre for children • MA
    theatre history • MA
    theory-composition • MM

CALIFORNIA STATE UNIVERSITY, HAYWARD
Hayward, CA 94542-3000
http://www.csuhayward.edu/

Public coed comprehensive institution. Enrollment: 12,650 graduate, professional, and undergraduate students. Graduate faculty: 368 full-time. Computer facilities: Campuswide network is available with full Internet access. Total number of PCs/terminals supplied for student use: 400. Computer service fees are included with tuition and fees. Library facilities: University Library. Graduate expenses: Tuition of $0 for state residents; $164 per unit for nonresidents. Fees of $1827 per year full-time, $1161 per year part-time. General application contact: Dr. Maria De Anda-Ramos, Executive Director, Admissions and Outreach, 510-885-2624.

Graduate Programs
Dr. Carl Bellone, Dean
Program in:
    interdisciplinary studies • Certificate, MA, MS

School of Arts, Letters, and Social Sciences
Dr. Carlos Navarro, Dean
Programs in:
    anthropology • MA
    English • MA
    geography • MA
    history • MA
    music • MA
    public administration • MPA
    sociology • MA
    speech communication • MA
    speech pathology • MS

School of Business and Economics
Dr. Jay Tontz, Dean
Programs in:
    accounting • MBA
    administration • MBA
    computer information systems • MBA
    economics • MA, MBA
    finance • MBA
    human resources management • MBA
    international business • MBA
    management sciences • MBA
    marketing management • MBA
    new ventures/small business management • MBA
    operations research • MBA
    quantitative business methods • MS
    taxation • MBA, MS

School of Education
Dr. Arthurlene Towner, Dean
Programs in:
    counseling • MS
    educational leadership • MS
    physical education • MS
    special education • MS
    teacher education • MS

California State University, Hayward (continued)
School of Science
Dr. William Leung, Dean
Programs in:
  biochemistry • MS
  biological sciences • MS
  chemistry • MS
  computer science • MS
  geology • MS
  marine sciences • MS
  mathematics • MS
  statistics • MS

CALIFORNIA STATE UNIVERSITY, LONG BEACH
Long Beach, CA 90840-0119

http://www.csulb.edu/

Public coed comprehensive institution. *Enrollment: 27,810 graduate, professional, and undergraduate students. Graduate faculty: 833 full-time, 634 part-time. Computer facilities: Campuswide network is available with full Internet access. Total number of PCs/terminals supplied for student use: 1,483. Computer service fees are included with tuition and fees. Library facilities: University Library. Graduate expenses: Tuition of $0 for state residents; $246 per unit for nonresidents. Fees of $1846 per year full-time, $1180 per year part-time. General application contact: Dr. Keith I. Polakoff, Associate Vice President for Academic Affairs, 562-985-4128.*

Graduate Studies
Dr. Keith I. Polakoff, Associate Vice President for Academic Affairs

College of Business Administration
Dr. C. J. Walter, Dean
Program in:
  business administration • MBA

College of Education
Dr. Jean Houck, Acting Dean
Programs in:
  educational administration • MA
  educational psychology • MA
  elementary education • MA
  guidance and counseling • Certificate, MS
  secondary education • MA
  social and philosophical foundations of education • MA
  special education • MS

College of Engineering
Dr. J. Richard Williams, Dean
Programs in:
  aerospace engineering • MSAE
  civil engineering • CE, MSCE, MSE
  computer engineering • MS
  computer science • MS
  electrical engineering • MSE, MSEE
  engineering • PhD
  mechanical engineering • MSE, MSME

College of Health and Human Services
Dr. Donald Lauda, Dean
Programs in:
  audiology • MA
  community health education • MPH
  criminal justice • MS
  gerontology • MS
  health care administration • Certificate, MS
  health science • MS
  home economics • MA
  kinesiology and physical education • MA
  nurse anesthesiology • MS
  nursing • MS
  nutritional sciences • MS
  occupational studies • MA
  public policy and administration • Certificate, MPA
  recreation and leisure studies • MS
  social work • MSW
  speech pathology • MA

College of Liberal Arts
Dr. Dorothy Abrahamse, Dean
Programs in:
  anthropology • MA
  Asian American studies • Certificate
  Asian studies • MA
  communication studies • MA
  economics • MA
  English • MA
  French • MA
  geography • MA
  German • MA
  history • MA
  linguistics • MA
  philosophy • MA
  political science • MA
  psychology • MA, MS
  Spanish • MA

College of Natural Sciences
Dr. Glenn Nagel, Dean
Programs in:
  applied mathematics • MA
  biochemistry • MS
  biological sciences • MS
  chemistry • MS
  geological sciences • MS
  mathematics • MA
  medical technology • MPH
  metals physics • MS
  microbiology • MS
  natural sciences • Certificate
  nurse epidemiology • MPH
  physics • MS

College of the Arts
Dr. Wade Hobgood, Dean
Programs in:
  art education • MA
  art history • MA
  crafts • MA, MFA
  dance • MFA
  illustration • MA, MFA
  music • MA, MM

pictorial arts • MA, MFA
theatre arts • MA, MFA

Interdisciplinary Studies Program
Dr. Margaret Toohey-Costa, Director
Program in:
interdisciplinary studies • MA, MS

CALIFORNIA STATE UNIVERSITY, LOS ANGELES
Los Angeles, CA 90032-8530
http://www.calstatela.edu/

Public coed comprehensive institution. *Enrollment: 19,160 gradu-ate, professional, and undergraduate students. Graduate faculty: 513 full-time, 622 part-time. Computer facilities: Campuswide network is available with full Internet access. Total number of PCs/terminals supplied for student use: 1,200. Computer services are offered at no charge. Library facilities: John F. Kennedy Memorial Library. Graduate expenses: Tuition of $0 for state residents; $164 per unit for nonresidents. Fees of $1763 per year full-time, $1097 per year part-time. General application contact: Dr. Theodore Crovello, Dean of Graduate Studies, 213-343-3820.*

Graduate Studies
Dr. Theodore Crovello, Dean

School of Arts and Letters
Carl Selkin, Dean
Programs in:
art • MA
art education • MA
art history • MA
art therapy • MA
ceramics, metals, and textiles • MA
crafts • MFA
design • MA, MFA
English • MA
fine arts • MFA
French • MA
music composition • MM
music education • MA
musicology • MA
painting, sculpture, and graphic arts • MA
performance • MM
philosophy • MA
photography • MA
Spanish • MA
speech communication • MA
studio arts • MFA
theater arts • MA

School of Business and Economics
Dr. Hugh Warren, Acting Dean
Programs in:
accountancy • MS
accounting • MBA
analytical quantitative economics • MA

business economics • MA, MBA, MS
business information systems • MBA
business taxation • MS
economics • MA
finance and banking • MBA, MS
financial accounting • MS
health care management • MS
information systems • MS
international business • MBA, MS
management • MBA, MS
management accounting • MS
management information systems • MS
marketing • MBA, MS
office management • MBA

School of Education
Dr. Allen Mori, Dean
Programs in:
adult and continuing education • MA
applied behavior analysis • MS
community college counseling • MS
computer education • MA
early childhood education for the handicapped • MA
educational administration • MA
education of handicapped adolescents and young adults • MA
education of the communication handicapped • MA
education of the learning handicapped • MA
education of the physically handicapped • MA
education of the severely handicapped • MA
education of the visually handicapped • MA
elementary teaching • MA
gifted education • MA
instructional technology • MA
multicultural and multilingual special education • MA
orientation and mobility specialist for the blind • MA
psychological foundations • MA
reading • MA
rehabilitation counseling • MS
resource specialist • MA
school counseling and school psychology • MS
secondary teaching • MA
social foundations • MA
special education • PhD
special interests • MA
teaching English to speakers of other languages • MA

School of Engineering and Technology
Dr. Raymond Landis, Dean
Programs in:
civil engineering • MS
electrical engineering • MS
industrial and technical studies • MA
mechanical engineering • MS
vocational education • MA

School of Health and Human Services
Dr. Jo Ann Johnson, Acting Dean
Programs in:
child development • MA
communicative disorders • MA
criminalistics • MS
criminal justice • MS
health science • MA

California State University, Los Angeles (continued)
  hearing • MA
  home economics • MA
  nursing • MS
  nutritional science • MS
  physical education • MA
  social work • MSW
  speech • MA

School of Natural and Social Sciences
Dr. David Soltz, Dean
Programs in:
  analytical chemistry • MS
  anthropology • MA
  applied mathematics • MS
  biochemistry • MS
  biology • MS
  chemistry • MS
  geography • MA
  geology • MS
  history • MA
  inorganic chemistry • MS
  Latin American studies • MA
  mathematics • MS
  Mexican-American studies • MA
  microbiology • MS
  organic chemistry • MS
  physical chemistry • MS
  physics • MS
  political science • MA
  psychology • MA, MS
  public administration • MS
  sociology • MA

CALIFORNIA STATE UNIVERSITY, NORTHRIDGE
Northridge, CA 91330

http://www.csun.edu/

Public coed comprehensive institution. *Enrollment: 27,653 graduate, professional, and undergraduate students. Graduate faculty: 801 full-time, 679 part-time. Library facilities: Oviatt Library plus 1 additional on-campus library. Graduate expenses: Tuition of $0 for state residents; $246 per unit for nonresidents. Fees of $1970 per year full-time, $1304 per year part-time. General application contact: Dr. Mack Johnson, Associate Vice President, 818-677-2138.*

Graduate Studies
Dr. Mack Johnson, Associate Vice President
Program in:
  interdisciplinary studies • MA, MS

College of Business Administration and Economics
Dr. William Hosek, Dean
Programs in:
  accounting • MS
  administrative/office management • MBA
  business administration • MBA

  business education • MBA, MS
  finance, real estate and insurance • MBA
  management • MBA
  management science • MBA
  marketing • MBA
  production and management systems analysis • MS
  taxation • MS

College of Education
Dr. Carolyn L. Ellner, Dean
Programs in:
  administration and supervision • MA
  counseling • MS
  early childhood education • MA
  early childhood special education • MA
  education • MA, MS
  educational foundations • MA
  educational psychology and counseling • MA
  educational therapy • MA
  education of the deaf and hard of hearing • MA
  education of the gifted • MA
  education of the learning handicapped • MA
  education of the severely handicapped • MA
  elementary education • MA
  genetic counseling • MS
  marriage, family and child counseling • MFCC
  secondary education • MA

College of Engineering and Computer Science
Dr. Dorothy Miller, Interim Dean
Programs in:
  aerospace engineering • MS
  applied engineering • MS
  applied mechanics • MSE
  biomedical engineering • MS
  civil engineering • MS
  communications/radar engineering • MS
  computer science • MS
  control engineering • MS
  digital/computer engineering • MS
  electronics engineering • MS
  engineering • MS
  engineering management • MS
  industrial engineering • MS
  machine design • MS
  materials engineering • MS
  mechanical engineering • MS
  mechanics • MS
  microwave/antenna engineering • MS
  structural engineering • MS
  thermofluids • MS

College of Health and Human Development
Dr. Ann Stutts, Dean
Programs in:
  communicative disorders and sciences • MA
  environmental health • MS
  family environmental sciences • MS
  health administration • MS
  health education • MS
  health science • MS
  kinesiology • MA
  leisure studies and recreation • MS
  physical therapy • MS
  public health • MPH

College of Humanities
Dr. Jorge Garcia, Dean
Programs in:
Chicano studies • MA
English • MA
linguistics • MA
Spanish • MA

College of Science and Mathematics
Dr. Edward J. Carroll, Interim Dean
Programs in:
biology • MS
chemistry • MS
genetic counseling • MS
geological sciences • MS
mathematics • MS
physics • MS

College of Social and Behavioral Sciences
Dr. William Flores, Dean
Programs in:
anthropology • MA
geography • MA
history • MA
political science • MA
psychology • MA
public administration • MPA
sociology • MA

College of the Arts, Media, and Communications
Dr. Philip Handler, Dean
Programs in:
art history • MA
arts • MA
composition • MM
mass communication • MA
music education • MA
musicology • MA
music theory • MA
news communication • MA
performance • MM
speech communication • MA
theater • MA

CALIFORNIA STATE UNIVERSITY, SACRAMENTO
Sacramento, CA 95819-6048

http://www.csus.edu/

Public coed comprehensive institution. *Enrollment:* 18,100 graduate, professional, and undergraduate students. Library facilities: *main library.* Graduate expenses: *Tuition of $0 for state residents; $246 per unit for nonresidents. Fees of $2012 per year full-time, $1346 per year part-time.* General application contact: *Bonnie Pesely, Coordinator of Graduate Admissions, 916-278-6470.*

Graduate Studies
Dr. Ric Brown, Associate Vice President, Research and Graduate Studies
Program in:
special majors • MA, MS

School of Arts and Letters
Dr. William J. Sullivan, Dean
Programs in:
communication studies • MA
creative writing • MA
drama • MA
music • MM
public history • MA
Spanish • MA
studio art • MA
teaching English to speakers of other languages • MA

School of Business Administration
Dr. Fel Ramey, Dean
Programs in:
accountancy • MS
business administration • MBA
human resources • MBA
management information science • MS
urban land development • MBA

School of Education
Dr. Diane Cordero De Noriega, Dean
Programs in:
bilingual/cross-cultural education • MA
career counseling • MS
curriculum and instruction • MA
early childhood education • MA
educational administration • MA
generic counseling • MS
guidance • MA
reading education • MA
school counseling • MS
school psychology • MS
special education • MA

School of Engineering and Computer Science
Dr. Braja Das, Dean
Programs in:
biomedical engineering • MS
civil engineering • MS
computer systems • MS
electrical engineering • MS
mechanical engineering • MS
software engineering • MS

School of Health and Human Services
Dr. M. Harter, Dean
Programs in:
audiology • MS
criminal justice • MS
family and children's services • MSW
health care • MSW
mental health • MSW
nursing • MS
physical education • MS
recreation administration • MS
social justice and corrections • MSW
speech pathology • MS

California State University, Sacramento (continued)

School of Natural Sciences and Mathematics
Marion O'Leary, Dean
Programs in:
biological sciences • MA, MS
chemistry • MS
counseling psychology • MA
immunohematology • MS
marine science • MS
mathematics and statistics • MA

School of Social Sciences
Joseph F. Sheley, Dean
Programs in:
anthropology • MA
economics • MA
government • MA
international affairs • MA
public policy and administration • MPPA
social sciences • MA
sociology • MA

CALIFORNIA STATE UNIVERSITY, SAN BERNARDINO

San Bernardino, CA 92407-2397

http://www.csusb.edu/

Public coed comprehensive institution. *Enrollment:* 13,280 graduate, professional, and undergraduate students. Library facilities: *Pfau Library.* Graduate expenses: *Tuition of $0 for state residents; $164 per unit for nonresidents. Fees of $1922 per year full-time, $1256 per year part-time.* General application contact: *Lydia Ortega, Director of Admissions, 909-880-5200.*

Graduate Studies
Julius D. Kaplan, Dean
Program in:
interdisciplinary studies • MA

School of Business and Public Administration
Dr. Steven Mintz, Dean
Programs in:
business administration • MBA
public administration • MPA

School of Education
Patricia Arlin, Dean
Programs in:
bilingual/cross-cultural education • MA
counseling/guidance • MS
counselor education • MA
elementary education • MA
English as a second language • MA
environmental education • MA
history and English for secondary teachers • MA
instructional technology • MA
reading • MA
rehabilitation counseling • MA

school administration • MA
secondary education • MA
special education • MA
vocational education • MA

School of Humanities
Dr. Beverly Hendricks, Dean
Programs in:
English as a second language/linguistics • MA
English composition • MA

School of Natural Sciences
Paul Vicknair, Acting Dean
Programs in:
biology • MS
computer science • MS
health services administration • MS
mathematics • MA

School of Social and Behavioral Sciences
John Conley, Dean
Programs in:
clinical/counseling psychology • MS
criminal justice • MA
general/experimental psychology • MA
human development • MA
industrial organizational psychology • MS
life span developmental psychology • MA
national security studies • MA
psychology • MS
social sciences • MA
social work • MSW
urban planning • MUP

CALIFORNIA STATE UNIVERSITY, SAN MARCOS

San Marcos, CA 92096

http://www.csusm.edu/

Public coed comprehensive institution. *Enrollment:* 4,409 graduate, professional, and undergraduate students. Computer facilities: *Campuswide network is available with full Internet access. Computer services are offered at no charge.* Library facilities: *main library plus 1 additional on-campus library.* Graduate expenses: *Tuition of $0 for state residents; $246 per unit for nonresidents. Fees of $1790 per year full-time, $1104 per year part-time.* General application contact: *Ellen Villalobos, Support Staff, 760-750-4800.*

College of Education
Dr. Steve Lilly, Dean
Program in:
education • MA

Graduate Program in Business Administration
Newton Marqulies, Dean, College of Business Administration
Programs in:
business management • MBA
government management • MBA

Graduate Program in Literature and Writing Studies

Renee Curry, Director
Program in:
 literature and writing studies • MA

Graduate Program in Psychology

Sheri O'Boyle, Director
Program in:
 psychology • MA

Graduate Program in Sociological Practice

Therese Baker, Director
Program in:
 sociological practice • MA

Program in Computer Science

Rika Yoshii, Director
Program in:
 computer science • MS

Program in Mathematical Sciences

David Barsky, Director
Program in:
 mathematical sciences • MS

CALIFORNIA STATE UNIVERSITY, STANISLAUS

Turlock, CA 95382

http://lead.csustan.edu/

Public coed comprehensive institution. *Enrollment: 6,100 graduate, professional, and undergraduate students. Computer facilities: Campuswide network is available with full Internet access. Total number of PCs/terminals supplied for student use: 200. Computer services are offered at no charge. Library facilities: Vasche Library. Graduate expenses: Tuition of $0 for state residents; $246 per unit for nonresidents. Fees of $1779 per year full-time, $1113 per year part-time. General application contact: Mary Coker, Coordinator, Graduate Studies, 209-667-3129.*

Graduate Programs

Dr. Diana Mayer Demetrulias, Dean of Graduate Studies
Program in:
 interdisciplinary studies • MA, MS

College of Arts, Letters, and Sciences

Dr. Mary P. Cullinan, Dean
Programs in:
 behavior analysis psychology • MS
 counseling psychology • MS
 English • MA
 general psychology • MA
 history • MA
 international relations • MA
 marine science • MS

public administration • MPA
secondary school history teaching • MA
social work • MSW
teaching English to speakers of other languages • MA

School of Business Administration

Dr. Gordon L. Patzer, Dean
Program in:
 business administration • MBA

School of Education

Dr. Irma Guzman Wagner, Dean
Programs in:
 educational administration • MA Ed
 educational technology • MA Ed
 elementary education • MA Ed
 multilingual education • MA Ed
 physical education • MA Ed
 reading education • MA Ed
 school counseling • MA Ed
 secondary education • MA Ed
 special education • MA Ed

CHAPMAN UNIVERSITY

Orange, CA 92866

http://www.chapman.edu/

Independent-religious coed comprehensive institution. *Enrollment: 3,673 graduate, professional, and undergraduate students. Graduate faculty: 188 full-time, 45 part-time. Computer facilities: Campuswide network is available with full Internet access. Total number of PCs/terminals supplied for student use: 170. Computer service fees are included with tuition and fees. Library facilities: Thurmond Clarke Memorial Library. Graduate expenses: $460 per credit. General application contact: Saundra R. Hoover, Director of Graduate Admissions, 714-997-6786.*

Graduate Studies

Dr. Barbara E. G. Mulch, Vice Provost and Dean
Programs in:
 counseling psychology • MA
 criminal justice • MA
 food science and nutrition • MS
 health administration • MHA
 human resources • MS, MSHR
 marriage, family, and child counseling • MA
 organizational leadership • MA

School of Business and Economics

Dr. Richard McDowell, Dean
Program in:
 business and economics • Exec MBA, MBA

School of Communication Arts

Ron Thronson, Dean
Programs in:
 creative writing • MFA
 English education • MA
 literature • MA

Chapman University (continued)
    teaching English as a second language • MA
    teaching literature and composition • MA

School of Education
Dr. Jim Brown, Dean
Programs in:
    career counseling • MA
    curriculum and instruction • MA
    educational administration • MA
    educational psychology • MA
    learning handicapped • MA
    reading education • MA
    school counseling • MA
    severely handicapped • MA
    special education • MA

School of Film and Television
Robert Bassett, Dean
Programs in:
    film studies • MA
    producing • MFA
    production • MFA
    screenwriting • MFA

School of Law
Parham Williams, Dean
Program in:
    law • JD

School of Physical Therapy
Marcia Greenberg, Director
Program in:
    physical therapy • MPT

CLAREMONT GRADUATE UNIVERSITY

Claremont, CA 91711-6163

http://www.cgu.edu/

Independent coed graduate-only institution. *Enrollment:* 2,088 matriculated graduate/professional students. Graduate faculty: *86 full-time, 85 part-time.* Computer facilities: *Campuswide network is available with full Internet access. Total number of PCs/terminals supplied for student use: 90. Computer service fees are included with tuition and fees.* Library facilities: *Honnold Library plus 3 additional on-campus libraries.* Graduate expenses: *Tuition of $20,250 per year full-time, $913 per unit part-time. Fees of $130 per year.* General application contact: *Diane J. Guido, Associate Dean, 909-621-8263.*

Graduate Programs
Thomas R. Rochon, Provost and Dean
Programs in:
    church music • DCM, MA
    cognitive psychology • MA, PhD
    comparative and intercultural studies • MA, PhD
    composition • DMA, MA
    cross-cultural studies • MA, PhD
    curriculum and teaching • MA, PhD
    developmental psychology • MA, PhD
    drawing • MA, MFA
    engineering mathematics • PhD
    evaluation and quantitative analysis • MA, PhD
    filmmaking • MA, MFA
    financial engineering • MS
    growth and development • MA, PhD
    higher education • MA, PhD
    history • MA
    human resources design • MS
    information systems • MIS
    interdisciplinary studies • MA
    management of information systems • MSMIS, PhD
    mathematics education • MA
    music education • MA
    musicology • MA, PhD
    operations research and statistics • MA, MS
    organizational behavior • MA, PhD
    organization and administration • MA, PhD
    painting • MA, MFA
    performance • DMA, MA
    performance/installation • MA, MFA
    photography • MA, MFA
    physical applied mathematics • MA, MS
    printmaking • MA, MFA
    program design, management, and evaluation • MA
    pure mathematics • MA, MS, PhD
    reading and language development • MA, PhD
    scientific computing • MA, MS
    sculpture • MA, MFA
    social environmental psychology • PhD
    social psychology • MA
    systematics and evolution of higher plants • MA, PhD
    systems and control theory • MA, MS
    teaching/learning process • MA, PhD

Graduate Humanities Center
Janet Brodie, Chair
Programs in:
    American studies • MA, PhD
    cultural studies • MA, PhD
    English • M Phil, MA, PhD
    European studies • MA, PhD
    Hebrew Bible • MA, PhD
    history • MA, PhD
    history of Christianity • MA, PhD
    literature and creative writing • MA
    literature and film • MA
    literature and theatre • MA
    New Testament • MA, PhD
    philosophy and education • MA, PhD
    philosophy and social theory • MA, PhD
    philosophy of religion • MA, PhD
    philosophy of religion and theology • MA, PhD
    theology, ethics and culture • MA, PhD
    Western philosophy • MA, PhD
    women's studies in religion • MA

Peter F. Drucker Graduate Management Center
John Shaw, Dean
Programs in:
    accounting control • MBA
    applied economics • MBA
    business administration • MBA
    executive management • AEMBA, Certificate, EMBA,
      MA, PhD
    finance • MBA
    information systems • MBA
    international business • MBA
    marketing • MBA
    organizational behavior • MBA
    public policy • MBA
    strategic management • MBA

School of Politics and Economics
Thomas R. Rochon, Provost and Dean, Graduate Programs
Programs in:
    business and financial economics • MA, PhD
    economics • PhD
    international economic policy and management • MA,
      PhD
    international studies • MA, MAIS
    political economy • MA, MAPE
    political economy and public policy • MA, PhD
    political science • PhD
    politics • MA, MAP
    public policy • MA, MAPP

COLLEGE OF NOTRE DAME
Belmont, CA 94002-1997

http://www.cnd.edu/

Independent-religious coed comprehensive institution. *Enrollment:* 1,754 graduate, professional, and undergraduate students. *Graduate faculty: 18 full-time, 82 part-time. Library facilities: main library. Graduate expenses: $460 per unit. General application contact: Barbara Sterner, Assistant to the Graduate Dean for Admissions, 650-508-3527.*

Graduate School
Dr. Elaine L. Cohen, Dean
Programs in:
    art therapy • MAAT, MAMFT
    business administration • MBA
    counseling psychology • MACP
    educational technology • M Ed
    elementary education • Certificate
    English • MA
    gerontology • MA
    Montessori teaching • M Ed
    multicultural education • M Ed
    music • MM
    pedagogy • MM
    performance • MM
    public administration • MPA
    secondary education • Certificate, MAT

    systems management • MSSM
    teaching art • MAT
    teaching biology • MAT
    teaching English • MAT
    teaching French • MAT
    teaching music • MAT
    teaching religious studies • MAT
    teaching social sciences • MAT

DOMINICAN COLLEGE OF SAN RAFAEL
San Rafael, CA 94901-2298

http://www.dominican.edu/

Independent coed comprehensive institution. *Enrollment:* 1,453 graduate, professional, and undergraduate students. *Graduate faculty: 14 full-time, 38 part-time. Computer facilities: Campuswide network is available with full Internet access. Total number of PCs/ terminals supplied for student use: 29. Computer service fees are included with tuition and fees. Library facilities: Archbishop Alemany Library. Graduate expenses: Tuition of $12,816 per year full-time, $534 per unit part-time. Fees of $320 per year full-time. General application contact: Sr. Mary Aquinas Nimitz, OP, Vice President for Institutional Research, 415-485-3271.*

Graduate Programs
Dr. Denise Lucy, Vice President for Academic Affairs

School of Arts and Sciences
Dr. James Boitano, Dean
Programs in:
    counseling psychology • MS
    humanities • MA

School of Business and International Studies
Dr. Françoise O. Lepage, Dean
Programs in:
    international business, Pacific basin • MBA
    international economic and political assessment, Pacific
      basin • MA

School of Education
Dr. Barry A. Kaufman, Dean
Programs in:
    curriculum and instruction • MS
    multiple subject credential • Certificate
    single subject credential • Certificate

School of Liberal and Professional Studies
Dr. LeAnn McGinley, Dean
Program in:
    strategic leadership • MBA

FRESNO PACIFIC UNIVERSITY
Fresno, CA 93702-4709

http://www.fresno.edu/grad/

Independent-religious coed comprehensive institution. *Enrollment:* 1,468 graduate, professional, and undergraduate students. Graduate faculty: *31 full-time, 73 part-time.* Computer facilities: *Campuswide network is available with full Internet access. Total number of PCs/ terminals supplied for student use: 70. Computer services are offered at no charge.* Library facilities: *Hiebert Library.* Graduate expenses: *$250 per unit.* General application contact: *Dr. John H. Yoder, Dean of the Graduate School, 209-453-2248.*

Graduate School
Dr. John H. Yoder, Dean
Programs in:
    administrative leadership • MA
    administrative services • MA Ed
    bilingual/cross-cultural education • MA Ed
    conflict management and peacemaking • MA
    curriculum and teaching • MA Ed
    individualized study • MA
    integrated mathematics/science education • MA Ed
    language development • MA Ed
    learning handicapped • MA Ed
    middle school mathematics • MA Ed
    physical and health impairments • MA Ed
    reading/English as a second language • MA Ed
    reading/language arts • MA Ed
    school counseling • MA Ed
    school library media • MA Ed
    school psychology • MA Ed
    science education • MA Ed
    secondary school mathematics • MA Ed
    severely handicapped • MA Ed
    teaching English to speakers of other languages • MA
    technology • MA Ed

GOLDEN GATE UNIVERSITY
San Francisco, CA 94105-2968

http://www.ggu.edu/

Independent coed university. *Enrollment:* 5,646 graduate, professional, and undergraduate students. Graduate faculty: *97 full-time, 398 part-time.* Computer facilities: *Campuswide network is available with full Internet access. Total number of PCs/terminals supplied for student use: 125. Computer service fees are included with tuition and fees.* Library facilities: *main library plus 1 additional on-campus library.* Graduate expenses: *$996 per course (minimum).* General application contact: *Enrollment Services, 415-442-7800.*

School of Business
Dr. Hamid Shomali, Dean
Programs in:
    accounting • M Ac, MBA
    business administration • DBA, EMBA
    economics • MS
    entrepreneurship • MBA
    finance • MBA, MS
    financial engineering • MS
    financial planning • Certificate
    human resource management • MBA, MS
    human resources management • Certificate
    information systems • MBA
    international business • MBA
    management • MBA
    manufacturing management • Certificate, MS
    marketing • MBA, MS
    operations management • MBA
    organizational behavior and development • MBA, MS
    procurement and logistics management • Certificate, MS
    professional export management • Certificate
    project and systems management • Certificate, MS
    public relations • Certificate, MS
    telecommunications • MBA

School of Law
Anthony J. Pagano, Dean
Programs in:
    environmental law • LL M
    international legal studies • LL M, SJD
    law • JD
    taxation • LL M
    U.S. legal studies • LL M

School of Liberal Studies and Public Affairs
Leonard Kooperman, Interim Dean
Programs in:
    applied psychology • Certificate
    arts administration • Certificate, MA
    counseling • MA
    health care management • Certificate, MHM
    industrial/organizational psychology • MA
    international relations • Certificate, MA
    liberal studies • MA
    liberal studies and public affairs • MBA
    marriage, family and child counseling • MA
    public administration • DPA, MPA

School of Taxation
Barbara Karlin, Dean
Program in:
    taxation • Certificate, MS

School of Technology and Industry
James Koerlin, Dean
Programs in:
    hospitality administration and tourism • MS
    information systems • Certificate, MS
    telecommunications management • Certificate, MS

HOLY NAMES COLLEGE
Oakland, CA 94619-1699

http://www.hnc.edu/

Independent-religious coed comprehensive institution. *Enrollment: 861 graduate, professional, and undergraduate students. Graduate faculty: 32 full-time, 33 part-time. Computer facilities: Campuswide network is available with full Internet access. Total number of PCs/terminals supplied for student use: 60. Computer service fees are included with tuition and fees. Library facilities: Paul J. Cushing Library. Graduate expenses: $7650 per year full-time, $425 per unit part-time. General application contact: Dr. David Fike, Vice President for Academic Affairs, 510-436-1040.*

Graduate Division
Dr. David Fike, Vice President for Academic Affairs
Programs in:
    community health nursing/case manager • MS
    education • M Ed
    English • MA
    family nurse practitioner • MS
    Kodály music education • Certificate
    management • MBA
    music education with a Kodály emphasis • MM
    performance • MM
    piano pedagogy • MM
    piano pedagogy with Suzuki emphasis • Certificate
    teaching English as a second language • Certificate

Institute in Pastoral Counseling
April Fernando, Program Co-Director
Programs in:
    counseling psychology with emphasis in pastoral
        counseling • MA
    pastoral counseling • Certificate, MA

Sophia Center: Spirituality for the New Millenium
James Conlon, Program Director
Programs in:
    creation spirituality • Certificate
    culture and creation spirituality • MA

HOPE INTERNATIONAL UNIVERSITY
Fullerton, CA 92831-3138

Independent-religious coed comprehensive institution. *Enrollment: 1,013 graduate, professional, and undergraduate students. Graduate faculty: 8 full-time, 57 part-time. Library facilities: Hurst Memorial Library. Graduate expenses: $341 per unit. General application contact: Connie Born, Director of Admissions, 800-762-1294 Ext. 626.*

Graduate Studies
Dr. Gene Sonnenberg, Dean
Programs in:
    church music • MA, MCM
    congregational leadership • MA
    education • ME
    family care and counseling • MA, MMFT
    field missions • MA
    intercultural studies • MA
    international development • MBA, MS
    management • MBA
    non-profit organizations management • MBA, MS

HUMBOLDT STATE UNIVERSITY
Arcata, CA 95521-8299

http://www.humboldt.edu/

Public coed comprehensive institution. *Enrollment: 7,492 graduate, professional, and undergraduate students. Graduate faculty: 319 full-time, 224 part-time. Computer facilities: Campuswide network is available with partial Internet access (e-mail only). Computer service fees are included with tuition and fees. Library facilities: main library. Graduate expenses: Tuition of $0 for state residents; $246 per unit for nonresidents. Fees of $1996 per year full-time, $1330 per year part-time. General application contact: Admissions and Records Office, 707-826-4402.*

Graduate Studies
Dr. Linda Parker, Interim Dean

College of Arts, Humanities, and Social Sciences
Dr. Karen Carlton, Dean
Programs in:
    art • MA
    English • MA
    social science • MA
    sociology • MA
    theatre arts • MA, MFA

College of Natural Resources and Sciences
Dr. James P. Smith Jr., Dean
Programs in:
    biological sciences • MA
    environmental systems • MS
    natural resources • MS
    psychology • MA

College of Professional Studies
Dr. Gail Fults, Dean
Programs in:
    business administration • MBA
    physical education • MA

 JOHN F. KENNEDY UNIVERSITY
Orinda, CA 94563-2689
http://www.jfku.edu/

Independent coed comprehensive institution. *Enrollment: 1,830 graduate, professional, and undergraduate students. Graduate faculty: 37 full-time, 701 part-time. Library facilities: Robert M. Fisher Library plus 4 additional on-campus libraries. Graduate expenses: Tuition of $316 per unit. Fees of $9 per quarter. General application contact: Ellena Bloedorn, Director of Admissions, 925-258-2213.*

Graduate School for Holistic Studies
K. Sue Duncan, Dean
Programs in:
    arts and consciousness • MA
    consciousness studies • MA
    holistic health education • MA
    studio arts • MFA
    transformative arts • MA
    transpersonal counseling psychology • MA

Graduate School of Professional Psychology
Dr. Ronald N. Levinson, Dean
Programs in:
    addiction studies • Certificate
    conflict resolution • Certificate
    counseling psychology • MA
    cross-cultural counseling • Certificate
    expressive arts • Certificate
    organizational psychology • Certificate, MA
    psychology • Psy D
    sport psychology • Certificate, MA

School of Law
Michael Guarino, Dean
Program in:
    law • JD

School of Liberal Arts
Jeremiah Hallisey, Dean
Programs in:
    administration • Certificate, MA
    collections management • Certificate, MA
    museum studies • Certificate, MA
    public programming • Certificate, MA
    teaching • MAT

School of Management
Craig Zachlod, Dean
Programs in:
    business administration • MBA
    career development • Certificate, MA
    executive management • Certificate
    management • MA
    organizational leadership • Certificate

LA SIERRA UNIVERSITY
Riverside, CA 92515-8247
http://www.lasierra.edu/

Independent-religious coed comprehensive institution. *Enrollment: 1,572 graduate, professional, and undergraduate students. Graduate faculty: 24 full-time, 22 part-time. Computer facilities: Campuswide network is available with full Internet access. Total number of PCs/terminals supplied for student use: 50. Computer services are offered at no charge. Library facilities: main library. General application contact: Myrna Costa-Casado, Director of Admissions, 909-785-2176.*

College of Arts and Sciences
Dr. Gary Bradley, Dean
Program in:
    English • MA

School of Business and Management
Dr. Henry E. Felder, Dean
Program in:
    business administration and management • MBA

School of Education
Dr. David S. Penner, Dean
Programs in:
    administration and leadership • Ed D, Ed S, MA
    counseling • MA
    curriculum and instruction • Ed D, Ed S, MA
    educational psychology • Ed S
    school psychology • Ed S
    special education • MA

School of Religion
Dr. John Jones, Dean
Programs in:
    religion • MA
    religious education • MA

LOMA LINDA UNIVERSITY
Loma Linda, CA 92350

Independent-religious coed university. *Enrollment: 3,492 graduate, professional, and undergraduate students. Graduate faculty: 972 full-time, 288 part-time. Computer facilities: Campuswide network is available with full Internet access. Total number of PCs/terminals supplied for student use: 100. Computer service fees are included with tuition and fees. Library facilities: Del Webb Library plus 2 additional on-campus libraries. Graduate expenses: $380 per unit. General application contact: Dr. W. Barton Rippon, Dean of the Graduate School, 909-824-4528.*

Graduate School
Dr. W. Barton Rippon, Dean
Programs in:
    adult and aging family nursing • MS
    anatomy • MS, PhD
    biochemistry • MS, PhD
    biology • MS, PhD
    biomedical and clinical ethics • MA
    clinical nutrition • MS
    clinical psychology • PhD, Psy D
    endodontics • Certificate, MS
    family studies • Certificate, MA
    geology • MS
    growing family nursing • MS
    implant dentistry • Certificate, MS
    marriage and family therapy • MS
    microbiology • MS, PhD
    nursing administration • MS
    nursing management • Certificate
    nutrition • MS
    nutritional science • MS
    nutrition care management • MS
    oral and maxillofacial surgery • Certificate, MS
    orthodontics • Certificate, MS
    periodontics • MS
    pharmacology • MS, PhD
    physiology • MS, PhD
    social work • MSW
    speech-language pathology and audiology • MS

School of Allied Health Professions
Dr. Joyce Hopp, Dean
Program in:
    allied health professions • DPT, MPT

School of Dentistry
Dr. Charles Goodacre, Dean
Program in:
    dentistry • DDS

School of Medicine
Dr. Brian Bull, Dean
Program in:
    medicine • MD

School of Public Health
Dr. Richard Hart, Dean
Programs in:
    biostatistics • MPH, MSPH
    environmental and occupational health • MPH, MSPH
    epidemiology • Dr PH, MPH
    health administration • MHA, MPH
    health promotion and education • Dr PH, MPH
    international health • MPH
    public health • MS
    public health nutrition • Dr PH, MPH

 # LOYOLA MARYMOUNT UNIVERSITY
Los Angeles, CA 90045-8350
http://www.lmu.edu/

Independent-religious coed comprehensive institution. *Enrollment:* 6,687 graduate, professional, and undergraduate students. Graduate faculty: *168 full-time, 237 part-time.* Computer facilities: *Campuswide network is available with full Internet access. Total number of PCs/terminals supplied for student use: 200. Computer service fees are included with tuition and fees.* Library facilities: *Charles Von der Ahe Library.* Graduate expenses: *Tuition of $500 per unit. Fees of $111 per year full-time, $28 per year part-time.* General application contact: *Chake Kouyoumjian, Director, Graduate Admissions Office, 310-338-2721.*

Graduate Division
Dr. Joseph G. Jabbra, Academic Vice President and Chair
Program in:
    marital and family therapy • MA

College of Business Administration
Dr. John T. Wholihan, Dean
Program in:
    business administration • MBA

College of Communication and Fine Arts
Thomas P. Kelly, Dean
Programs in:
    film production • MFA
    screenwriting • MFA
    TV production • MFA

College of Liberal Arts
Dr. Renee Harrangue, Acting Dean
Programs in:
    counseling psychology • MA
    creative writing • MA
    literature • MA
    pastoral studies • MA
    theology • MA

College of Science and Engineering
Dr. Gerald S. Jakubowski, Dean
Programs in:
    civil engineering • MSE
    computer science • MS
    electrical engineering • MSE
    engineering and production management • MS
    environmental engineering • MS
    environmental science • MS
    mechanical engineering • MSE

School of Education
Dr. Albert P. Koppes, Director
Programs in:
    administration • M Ed
    bilingual and bicultural education • MA
    biology education • MAT
    communications education • MAT
    counseling • MA

Loyola Marymount University (continued)
  elementary education • MA
  English education • MAT
  general education • M Ed
  history education • MAT
  Latin education • MAT
  literacy and language • M Ed
  mathematics education • MAT
  reading/language arts • M Ed
  school psychology • MA
  secondary education • MA
  social studies education • MAT
  special education • MA
  teaching English as a second language/multicultural
    education • MA

Loyola Law School

Gerald T. McLaughlin, Dean
Program in:
  law • JD

MOUNT ST. MARY'S COLLEGE

Los Angeles, CA 90049-1597

http://msmc.la.edu/

Independent-religious coed comprehensive institution. Library facilities: *Charles Willard Coe Memorial Library plus 1 additional on-campus library.* General application contact: *Dean of the Graduate Division, 213-477-2500.*

Graduate Division

Programs in:
  administrative studies • MS
  applied spiritual theology • MA
  counseling psychology • MS
  elementary education • MS
  physical therapy • MPT
  religious studies • MA
  secondary education • MS
  special education • MS

NATIONAL UNIVERSITY

La Jolla, CA 92037-1011

http://www.nu.edu/

Independent coed comprehensive institution. *Enrollment: 13,397 graduate, professional, and undergraduate students.* Computer facilities: *Campuswide network is available with full Internet access. Total number of PCs/terminals supplied for student use: 600. Computer services are offered at no charge.* Library facilities: *main library plus 1 additional on-campus library.* Graduate expenses: *$7830 per year full-time, $870 per course part-time.* General

application contact: *Nancy Rohland, Director of Enrollment Management, 619-563-7100.*

Graduate Studies

School of Education and Human Services

Dr. Ellen Curtis-Pierce, Dean
Programs in:
  bilingual crosscultural teaching • ME
  career development and community counseling •
    MCDCC
  counseling psychology • MA
  cross-cultural teaching • ME
  educational administration • MS
  educational counseling • MS
  educational technology • MS
  human behavior • MA
  human services • MHS
  instructional leadership • ME
  instructional leadership for adult learners • MS
  instructional leadership in curriculum and instruction •
    MS
  school psychology • MS
  special education • MS

School of Management and Technology

Dr. Azov Degan, Dean
Programs in:
  business administration • MBA
  criminal justice • MCJ
  environmental management • MEM
  forensic science • MFS
  global business administration • GMBA
  health care administration • MHCA
  human resource management • MA
  international business • MA
  management • MA
  public administration • MPA
  software engineering • MS
  technology management • MS
  telecommunication systems management • MS

PEPPERDINE UNIVERSITY

Culver City, CA 90230-7615

http://www.pepperdine.edu/

Independent-religious coed upper-level institution. *Enrollment: 7,802 graduate, professional, and undergraduate students.* Graduate faculty: *120 full-time, 139 part-time.* Computer facilities: *Campuswide network is available with full Internet access. Computer service fees are included with tuition and fees.* Library facilities: *Plaza Library plus 4 additional on-campus libraries.* Graduate expenses: *$540 per unit.* General application contact: *Director of Admissions for the appropriate school, 310-568-5600.*

Graduate School of Education and Psychology

Dr. Nancy Magnusson Fagan, Dean
Programs in:
    administration and educational technology • MS
    clinical psychology • MA, Psy D
    education • MA
    educational leadership, administration, and policy •
        Ed D
    educational technology • Ed D
    institutional management • Ed D
    organizational leadership • Ed D
    organization change • Ed D
    psychology • MA, Psy D
    school business administration • MS
    school management and administration • MS

School of Business and Management

Dr. Otis Baskin, Dean
Programs in:
    business • MBA, MIB
    business administration • MBA
    executive business administration • MBAA
    international business • MIB
    organizational development • MSOD
    technology management • MSTM

PEPPERDINE UNIVERSITY
Malibu, CA 90263-0001

http://www.pepperdine.edu/

Independent-religious coed university. *Enrollment: 7,802 graduate, professional, and undergraduate students. Graduate faculty: 76 full-time, 25 part-time. Computer facilities: Campuswide network is available with full Internet access. Computer service fees are included with tuition and fees. Library facilities: Payson Library plus 1 additional on-campus library. Graduate expenses: $22,050 per year (minimum) full-time, $690 per unit (minimum) part-time. General application contact: Paul Long, Dean of Enrollment Management, 310-456-4392.*

Malibu Graduate Business Programs

Dr. James A. Goodrich, Associate Dean
Programs in:
    business administration • MBA
    international business • MIB

School of Law

Dr. Richardson Lynn, Interim Dean
Programs in:
    dispute resolution • MDR
    law • JD

School of Public Policy

Dr. James Wilburn, Dean
Program in:
    public policy • MPP

Seaver College

Dr. David Baird, Dean
Programs in:
    American studies • MA
    communication • MA
    history • MA
    ministry • MS
    religion • M Div, MA

POINT LOMA NAZARENE UNIVERSITY
San Diego, CA 92106-2899

http://www.ptloma.edu/

Independent-religious coed comprehensive institution. *Enrollment: 2,534 graduate, professional, and undergraduate students. Graduate faculty: 6 full-time, 15 part-time. Computer facilities: Campuswide network is available with full Internet access. Total number of PCs/ terminals supplied for student use: 150. Computer service fees are included with tuition and fees. Library facilities: Ryan Library plus 1 additional on-campus library. Graduate expenses: Tuition of $450 per unit. Fees of $12.50 per unit. General application contact: Dr. Corlis McGee, Dean of Graduate Studies, 619-849-2284.*

Graduate Programs

Dr. Corlis McGee, Dean of Graduate Studies
Programs in:
    education • Ed D, Ed S, MA
    religion • M Min, MA

SAINT MARY'S COLLEGE OF CALIFORNIA
Moraga, CA 94575

http://www.stmarys-ca.edu/

Independent-religious coed comprehensive institution. *Enrollment: 4,238 graduate, professional, and undergraduate students. Graduate faculty: 136. Computer facilities: Campuswide network is available with full Internet access. Total number of PCs/terminals supplied for student use: 223. Computer service fees are included with tuition and fees. Library facilities: St. Albert Library. Graduate expenses: $1319 per course. General application contact: Michael Beseda, Assistant Vice President of Research, Planning, and Technology, 925-631-4060.*

School of Economics and Business Administration

Edwin M. Epstein, Dean
Programs in:
    business administration • MBA
    executive business administration • MBA
    international business • MBAIB

Saint Mary's College of California (continued)

School of Education
Dr. Fannie Preston, Dean
Programs in:
    administration and supervision • MA
    counseling leadership • MA
    early childhood education and Montessori teacher
        training • M Ed, MA
    reading leadership • MA
    special education • M Ed, MA

School of Extended Education
Dr. Penny Washbourn, Dean
Program in:
    health services administration • MS

School of Liberal Arts
Joseph Subbiondo, Dean
Programs in:
    creative writing • MFA
    health, physical education, and recreation • MA

School of Science
Dr. Keith Devlin, Dean
Programs in:
    general psychology • MA
    marriage, family and child counseling • MA
    organizational/personnel psychology • MS

SAN DIEGO STATE UNIVERSITY
San Diego, CA 92182
http://www.sdsu.edu/

Public coed university. *Enrollment:* 29,898 graduate, professional, and undergraduate students. Library facilities: *Malcolm A. Love Library plus 1 additional on-campus library. Graduate expenses: Tuition of $0 for state residents; $246 per unit for nonresidents. Fees of $1932 per year full-time, $1266 per year part-time.* General application contact: *Zac Hanscom III, Associate Dean, Graduate Division, 619-594-4162.*

Graduate Division and Research Affairs
James W. Cobble, Vice President for Research and Dean

College of Arts and Letters
Paul Strand, Dean
Programs in:
    anthropology • MA
    Asian studies • MA
    creative writing • MFA
    economics • MA
    English • MA
    French • MA
    geography • MA, PhD
    history • MA

    Latin American studies • MA
    liberal arts • MA
    linguistics and Oriental languages • CAL, MA
    philosophy • MA
    political science • MA
    sociology • MA
    Spanish • MA
    women's studies • MA

College of Education
Ann Morey, Dean
Programs in:
    counseling and school psychology • MS
    education • PhD
    educational administration and supervision • MA
    educational technology • MA
    elementary curriculum and instruction • MA
    policy studies in language and cross cultural education •
        MA
    reading education • MA
    rehabilitation counseling • MS
    secondary curriculum and instruction • MA
    special education • MA

College of Engineering
Pieter A. Frick, Dean
Programs in:
    aerospace engineering • MS
    civil engineering • MS
    electrical engineering • MS
    engineering mechanics • MS
    engineering sciences and applied mechanics • PhD
    flight dynamics • MS
    fluid dynamics • MS
    mechanical engineering • MS

College of Health and Human Services
Dolores A. Wozniak, Dean
Programs in:
    biostatistics • MPH
    communicative disorders • MA
    environmental health • MPH, MS
    epidemiology • MPH, PhD
    health promotion • MPH
    health services administration • MPH
    industrial hygiene • MS
    language and communicative disorders • PhD
    nursing • MS
    social work • MSW
    toxicology • MS

College of Professional Studies and Fine Arts
Joyce M. Gattas, Dean
Programs in:
    advertising and public relations • MA
    applied design • MA, MFA
    art history • MA
    city planning • MCP
    criminal justice administration • MPA
    critical-cultural studies • MA
    environmental design • MA, MFA
    exercise science • MA
    graphic design • MA, MFA
    interaction studies • MA

    intercultural and international studies • MA
    interior design • MA, MFA
    music and dance • MA, MM
    new media studies • MA
    news and information studies • MA
    nutritional science • MS
    painting and printmaking • MA, MFA
    public administration • MPA
    sculpture • MA, MFA
    studio arts • MA, MFA
    telecommunications and media management • MA
    television, film, and new media production • MA
    theater • MA, MFA

College of Sciences
Donald R. Short, Dean
Programs in:
    applied mathematics • MS
    astronomy • MS
    biology • MA, MS
    cell and molecular biology • PhD
    chemistry • MA, MS, PhD
    clinical psychology • MS, PhD
    computer science • MS
    ecology • MS, PhD
    geological sciences • MS
    industrial and organizational psychology • MS
    mathematics • MA
    mathematics and science education • PhD
    microbiology • MS
    molecular biology • MA, MS
    physics • MA, MS
    physiology • MS
    program evaluation • MS
    psychology • MA
    radiological health physics • MS
    statistics • MS
    systematics/evolution • MS

Graduate School of Business
Dr. Michael Hergert, Associate Dean, College of Business
    Administration
Programs in:
    accountancy • MBA, MS
    finance • MBA, MS
    information and decision systems • MBA, MS
    international business • MBA, MS
    management • MBA, MS
    marketing • MBA, MS

Interdisciplinary Studies
James W. Cobble, Vice President for Research and Dean,
    Graduate Division and Research Affairs
Program in:
    interdisciplinary studies • MA, MS

SAN FRANCISCO STATE UNIVERSITY
San Francisco, CA 94132-1722
http://www.sfsu.edu/

Public coed comprehensive institution. Computer facilities: *Campuswide network is available with full Internet access. Computer services are offered at no charge.* Library facilities: *J. Paul Leonard Library.* Graduate expenses: *Tuition of $0 for state residents; $246 per unit for nonresidents. Fees of $1982 per year full-time, $1316 per year part-time.* General application contact: *Director, Graduate Admissions and Evaluations, 415-338-2232.*

Graduate Division

College of Behavioral and Social Sciences
Programs in:
    anthropology • MA
    economics • MA
    environmental planning • MA
    geography • MA
    history • MA
    international relations • MA
    nonprofit administration • MPA
    policy analysis • MPA
    political science • MA
    psychology • MA, MS
    public management • MPA
    resource management • MA
    social science • MA
    urban administration • MPA

College of Business
Programs in:
    business administration • MBA
    taxation • MS

College of Creative Arts
Programs in:
    art • MA, MFA
    art history • MA
    broadcast and electronic communication arts • MA
    cinema • MFA
    cinema studies • MA
    industrial arts • MA
    music • MA, MM
    theatre arts • MA, MFA

College of Education
Programs in:
    adult education • AC, MA
    communicative disorders • MS
    early childhood education • MA
    educational administration • AC, MA
    educational technology • MA
    elementary education • MA
    mathematics education • MA
    secondary education • AC, MA
    special education • AC, Ed D, MA, PhD
    training systems development • AC

San Francisco State University (continued)

College of Ethnic Studies

Program in:
ethnic studies • MA

College of Health and Human Services

Programs in:
case management • MS
counseling • MS
ethnogerontology • MA
health science • MS
healthy aging • MA
home economics • MA
life-long learning • MA
long-term care • MS
long-term care administration • MA
marriage and family counseling • MS
nursing administration • MS
nursing education • MS
physical education • MA
physical therapy • MPT
primary care/family nurse practitioner • MS
recreation and leisure studies • MS
rehabilitation counseling • MS
social work education • MSW

College of Humanities

Programs in:
Chinese • MA
classics • MA
composition • Certificate, MA
creative writing • MA, MFA
English as a foreign/second language • MA
French • MA
German • MA
humanities • MA
Italian • MA
Japanese • MA
linguistics • MA
literature • MA
museum studies • MA
philosophy • MA
Russian • MA
Spanish • MA
speech and communication studies • MA
teaching composition • Certificate
teaching critical thinking • Certificate
teaching post-secondary reading • Certificate
women's studies • MA
world and comparative literature • MA

College of Science

Programs in:
biomedical laboratory science • MS
cell and molecular biology • MA
chemistry • MS
computer science • MS
conservation biology • MA
ecology and systematic biology • MA
engineering • MS
marine biology • MA
mathematics • MA
microbiology • MA
physics and astrophysics • MS
physiology and behavioral biology • MA

SAN JOSE STATE UNIVERSITY
San Jose, CA 95192-0001
http://www.sjsu.edu/

Public coed comprehensive institution. *Enrollment: 26,543 gradu-ate, professional, and undergraduate students. Graduate faculty: 933 full-time, 488 part-time. Computer facilities: Campuswide network is available with full Internet access. Computer services are offered at no charge.* Library facilities: *Clark Library plus 1 additional on-campus library.* Graduate expenses: *Tuition of $0 for state residents; $246 per unit for nonresidents. Fees of $2017 per year full-time, $1351 per year part-time.* General application contact: *Graduate Studies Office, 408-924-2480.*

Graduate Studies

Dr. Serena W. Stanford, Associate Vice President

College of Applied Arts and Sciences

Dr. Michael Ego, Dean
Programs in:
administration of justice • MS
community health nursing • MS
gerontology • MS
gerontology nurse practitioner • MS
health administration • Certificate
health science • MA
mass communication • MS
nursing administration • MS
nursing education • MS
nutritional science • MS
occupational therapy • MS
physical education • MA
public health • MPH
quality assurance • MS
recreation and leisure studies • MS

College of Business

Dr. Marshall Burak, Dean
Programs in:
accountancy • MS
business administration • MBA
taxation • MS
transportation management • MS

College of Education

Dr. Dolores Escobar, Dean
Programs in:
administration/higher education • Certificate, MA
audiology • MA
child development • MA
counseling • MA
education for the hearing impaired • MA
education for the severely handicapped • MA
elementary education • MA
instructional technology • Certificate, MA
learning handicapped • MA
secondary education • MA
special education • MA
speech pathology • MA

College of Engineering
Dr. Don Kirk, Dean
Programs in:
  aerospace engineering • MS
  chemical engineering • MS
  civil engineering and applied mechanics • MS
  computer engineering • MS
  computerized robots and computer applications • MS
  computer software • MS
  electrical engineering • MS
  general engineering • MS
  information and systems engineering • MS
  materials engineering • MS
  mechanical engineering • MS
  microprocessors and microcomputers • MS

College of Humanities and Arts
Dr. John Crane, Dean
Programs in:
  art education • MA
  art history • MA
  ceramics • MFA
  crafts • MFA
  drama • MA
  drawing • MFA
  environmental design • MA
  French • MA
  graphic arts • MA
  industrial design • MA
  interior design • MA
  linguistics • Certificate, MA
  literature • MA
  music • MA
  music performance • MA
  painting • MFA
  philosophy • Certificate, MA
  photography • MFA
  pictorial arts • MFA
  plastic arts • MFA
  printmaking • MFA
  sculpture • MFA
  Spanish • MA
  teaching English as a second language • MA
  technical writing • MA
  textiles • MA

College of Science
Dr. Gerald Selter, Dean
Programs in:
  analytical chemistry • MS
  biochemistry • MS
  biological sciences • MA, MS
  chemistry • MA
  computer science • MS
  geology • MS
  inorganic chemistry • MS
  marine science • MS
  mathematics • MA, MS
  meteorology • MS
  organic chemistry • MS
  physical chemistry • MS
  physics • MS
  polymer chemistry • MS
  radiochemistry • MS

College of Social Sciences
Dr. Lela Noble, Dean
Programs in:
  clinical psychology • MS
  counseling • MS
  criminology • MA
  economics • MA
  environmental studies • MS
  geography • MA
  history • MA
  industrial psychology • MS
  public administration • MPA
  research psychology • MA
  social sciences • MA
  speech communication • MA

College of Social Work
Dr. Sylvia Andrew, Dean
Programs in:
  Mexican-American studies • MA
  social work • MSW
  urban and regional planning • MUP

Graduate Studies Program
Dr. Serena W. Stanford, Associate Vice President, Graduate Studies
Programs in:
  human factors/ergonomics • MS
  interdisciplinary studies • MA, MS
  library and information science • MLIS

SANTA CLARA UNIVERSITY
Santa Clara, CA 95053-0001

http://www.scu.edu/

Independent-religious coed comprehensive institution. *Enrollment: 7,863 graduate, professional, and undergraduate students. Graduate faculty: 155 full-time, 93 part-time. Computer facilities: Campuswide network is available with full Internet access. Total number of PCs/terminals supplied for student use: 350. Computer service fees are included with tuition and fees. Library facilities: Orradre Library plus 1 additional on-campus library. Graduate expenses: $458 per unit. General application contact: Richard J. Toomey, Director, Enrollment Management, 408-554-4505.*

College of Arts and Sciences
Dr. Peter A. Facione, Dean
Programs in:
  catechetics • MA
  liturgical music • MA
  pastoral liturgy • MA
  spirituality • MA

Division of Counseling Psychology and Education
Dr. Peter A. Facione, Administrator
Programs in:
  counseling psychology • MA
  education • MA

Santa Clara University (continued)
educational administration • MA
health psychology • MA
marriage, family, and child counseling • MA
multiple subject teaching • Certificate
pastoral counseling • MA
single subject teaching • Certificate
special education • MA

Leavey School of Business and Administration

Dr. Barry Posner, Dean
Programs in:
agribusiness • MBA
business administration • MBA

School of Engineering

Dr. Terry E. Shoup, Dean
Programs in:
applied mathematics • MSAM
ASIC design and test • Certificate
civil engineering • MSCE
computer science and engineering • MSCSE, PhD
data storage technologies • Certificate
electrical engineering • Engineer, MSEE, PhD
engineering • MSE
engineering management • MSE Mgt
high performance computing • Certificate
mechanical engineering • Engineer, MSME, PhD
software engineering • Certificate

School of Law

Mack Player, Dean
Program in:
law • Certificate, JD, LL M

SONOMA STATE UNIVERSITY
Rohnert Park, CA 94928-3609

http://www.sonoma.edu/

Public coed comprehensive institution. *Enrollment: 7,050 graduate, professional, and undergraduate students. Graduate faculty: 240 full-time, 244 part-time. Computer facilities: Campuswide network is available with full Internet access. Total number of PCs/terminals supplied for student use: 300. Computer services are offered at no charge. Library facilities: Ruben Salazar Library. Graduate expenses: Tuition of $0 for state residents; $246 per unit for nonresidents. Fees of $2130 per year full-time, $1464 per year part-time. General application contact: Dr. Katharyn Crabbe, Dean of Academic Programs, 707-664-2831.*

Institute of Interdisciplinary Studies

Dr. Gardner Rust, Coordinator
Program in:
interdisciplinary studies • MA, MS

School of Arts and Humanities

Dr. William Babula, Dean
Programs in:
American literature • MA
creative writing • MA
English literature • MA
world literature • MA

School of Business and Economics

Lawrence Clark, Dean
Program in:
business administration • MBA

School of Education

Dr. Phyllis Fernlund, Dean
Programs in:
curriculum and instruction • MA
early childhood education • MA
educational administration • MA
reading • MA
special education • MA

School of Natural Sciences

Dr. Anne Swanson, Dean
Programs in:
environmental biology • MA
family nurse practitioner • MS
general biology • MA
kinesiology • MA

School of Social Sciences

Dr. Robert Karlsrud, Dean
Programs in:
counseling • MA
cultural resources management • MA
history • MA
marriage, family, and child counseling • MA
political science • MA
psychology • MA
public administration • MPA
pupil personnel services • MA

STANFORD UNIVERSITY
Stanford, CA 94305-9991

http://www.stanford.edu/

Independent coed university. *Enrollment: 14,084 graduate, professional, and undergraduate students. Graduate faculty: 1,535 full-time. Library facilities: Cecil H. Green Library plus 17 additional on-campus libraries. Graduate expenses: Tuition of $22,110 per year. Fees of $156 per year. General application contact: Mary Lue Eiche, Graduate Admissions Support Section, 650-723-4291.*

Graduate School of Business

A. Michael Spence, Dean
Program in:
business • MBA, PhD

Law School
Paul A. Brest, Dean
Program in:
  law • JD, JSD, JSM, MLS

School of Earth Sciences
Franklin M. Orr, Dean
Programs in:
  earth systems • MS
  geological and environmental sciences • Eng, MS, PhD
  geophysics • MS, PhD
  petroleum engineering • Eng, MS, PhD

School of Education
Richard Shavelson, Dean
Programs in:
  anthropology of education • PhD
  art • MAT
  art education • AM, PhD
  biology • MAT
  child and adolescent development • PhD
  counseling psychology • PhD
  curriculum studies and teacher education • AM, PhD
  dance education • AM
  economics of education • PhD
  educational psychology • PhD
  English • AM, PhD
  English education • AM
  French • MAT
  gender studies; interdisciplinary • AM
  German • MAT
  health psychology education • AM
  higher education administration • AM, Ed D, PhD
  history • MAT
  history of education • PhD
  international comparative education • AM, PhD
  international education administration and policy analysis • AM
  Italian • MAT
  Jewish education • PhD
  language, literacy, and culture • AM, PhD
  languages education • AM
  Latin American studies • MAT
  mathematics • MAT
  mathematics education • AM
  philosophy of education • PhD
  physics • MAT
  policy analysis • AM, Ed D, PhD
  prospective principal's program • AM
  science • AM, PhD
  science education • AM
  Slavic • MAT
  social science • AM, PhD
  social science in education • AM
  social sciences in education • PhD
  social studies education • AM
  sociology of education • PhD
  symbolic systems • PhD

School of Engineering
John L. Hennessy, Dean
Programs in:
  aeronautics and astronautics • Eng, MS, PhD
  biomechanical engineering • MS
  chemical engineering • Eng, MS, PhD
  civil and environmental engineering • Eng, MS, PhD
  computer science • MS, PhD
  electrical engineering • Eng, MS, PhD
  engineering-economic systems and operations research • Eng, MS, PhD
  engineering management • MS
  industrial engineering • Eng, MS, PhD
  manufacturing systems engineering • MS
  materials science and engineering • Eng, MS, PhD
  mechanical engineering • Eng, MS, PhD
  product design • MS
  scientific computing and computational mathematics • MS, PhD

School of Humanities and Sciences
John B. Shoven, Dean
Programs in:
  anthropology • AM, PhD
  applied physics • MS, PhD
  art • AM, MAT, MFA, PhD
  biological sciences • MAT, MS, PhD
  biophysics • PhD
  chemistry • PhD
  Chinese • AM, PhD
  classics • AM, PhD
  communication theory and research • PhD
  comparative literature • PhD
  computer-based music theory and acoustics • PhD
  drama • PhD
  economics • PhD
  film • AM
  French • AM, PhD
  French education • MAT
  German studies • AM, MAT, PhD
  history • AM, MAT, PhD
  humanities • AM
  international policy studies • AM
  Italian • AM, PhD
  Japanese • AM, PhD
  journalism • AM
  linguistics • AM, PhD
  mathematics • MAT, MS, PhD
  media studies • AM
  modern thought and literature • PhD
  musical acoustics, perception, and synthesis • AM
  music composition • AM, DMA
  musicology • AM, PhD
  performance practices • AM
  philosophy • AM, PhD
  physics • MAT, PhD
  political science • AM, PhD
  psychology • PhD
  religious studies • AM, PhD
  Russian • AM
  Slavic languages and literatures • MAT, PhD
  sociology • PhD

Stanford University (continued)
    Spanish • AM, PhD
    statistics • MS, PhD

Center for East Asian Studies
Harold Kahn, Director
Program in:
    East Asian studies • AM

Center for Latin American Studies
Jorge Ruffinelli-Altesor, Director
Program in:
    Latin American studies • AM, MAT

Center for Russian and East European Studies
Nancy Kollman, Director
Program in:
    Russian and East European studies • AM, MAT

Food Research Institute
Jeffrey C. Williams, Director
Program in:
    food research • AM, PhD

School of Medicine
Eugene Bauer, Dean
Programs in:
    biochemistry • PhD
    biology and biomedical sciences • PhD
    cancer biology • PhD
    developmental biology • PhD
    epidemiology • MS, PhD
    genetics • PhD
    health services research • MS
    immunology • PhD
    medical computer science • MS, PhD
    medical decision science • MS, PhD
    medicine • MD
    microbiology and immunology • PhD
    molecular and cellular physiology • PhD
    molecular pharmacology • PhD
    neurosciences • PhD
    structural biology • PhD

UNITED STATES INTERNATIONAL UNIVERSITY
San Diego, CA 92131-1799
http://www.usiu.edu/

Independent coed university. *Enrollment:* 1,331 graduate, professional, and undergraduate students. Graduate faculty: *58 full-time, 60 part-time.* Computer facilities: *Campuswide network is available with full Internet access. Total number of PCs/terminals supplied for student use: 69. Computer service fees are included with tuition and fees.* Library facilities: *Walter Library.* Graduate expenses: *Tuition of $255 per unit. Fees of $120 per year full-time, $33 per quarter part-time.* General application contact: *Susan Topham, Assistant Director of Admissions, 619-635-4885.*

College of Arts and Sciences
Programs in:
    clinical psychology • Psy D
    counseling psychology • MA
    developmental studies • MA
    educational administration • Ed D, MA
    industrial/organizational psychology • MA, Psy D
    international communication • MA
    international relations • MA
    leadership studies • MA
    marriage and family therapy • MA, Psy D
    peace and conflict studies • MA
    teaching • MA
    teaching English to speakers of other languages • Ed D, MA
    technology and learning • Ed D, MA

College of Business Administration
Dr. Mink H. Stavenga, Dean
Programs in:
    business administration • MBA
    finance • DBA
    international business • DBA, MIBA
    marketing • DBA
    strategic business • DBA

UNIVERSITY OF CALIFORNIA, BERKELEY
Berkeley, CA 94720-1500
http://www.berkeley.edu/

Public coed university. *Enrollment:* 30,372 graduate, professional, and undergraduate students. Graduate faculty: *1,654.* Computer facilities: *Campuswide network is available with full Internet access. Computer service fees are included with tuition and fees.* Library facilities: *Doe Library plus 55 additional on-campus libraries.* Graduate expenses: *Tuition of $0 for state residents; $9384 per year for nonresidents. Fees of $4409 per year.* General application contact: *Graduate Admissions Office, 510-642-7405.*

Graduate Division
Dr. Joseph Cerny, Vice Chancellor for Research and Dean
Programs in:
    ancient history and Mediterranean archaeology • MA, PhD
    applied science and technology • PhD
    Asian studies • PhD
    bioengineering • PhD
    biophysics • MA, PhD
    biostatistics • MA, PhD
    Buddhist studies • PhD
    comparative biochemistry • PhD
    demography • MA, PhD
    dramatic art • C Phil, PhD
    East Asian studies • MA
    endocrinology • MA, PhD
    energy and resources • MA, MS, PhD

epidemiology • MPH, MS, PhD
ethnic studies • PhD
folklore • MA
French • PhD
health services and policy analysis • PhD
Italian • PhD
Latin American studies • MA, PhD
logic and the methodology of science • PhD
microbiology • PhD
neurobiology • PhD
Northeast Asian studies • MA
nutrition • MS, PhD
ocean engineering • D Eng, M Eng, MS, PhD
range management • MS
Romance philology • PhD
South Asian studies • MA
Southeast Asian studies • MA
Spanish • PhD
vision science • MS, PhD
wood science and technology • MS, PhD

College of Chemistry
Dr. Alexis T. Bell, Dean
Programs in:
  chemical engineering • MS, PhD
  chemistry • PhD

College of Engineering
Dr. Paul R. Gray, Dean
Programs in:
  ceramic sciences and engineering • D Eng, M Eng, MS, PhD
  computer science • MS, PhD
  construction engineering and management • D Eng, M Eng, MS, PhD
  electrical engineering • D Eng, M Eng, MS, PhD
  engineering geoscience • D Eng, M Eng, MS, PhD
  environmental quality and environmental water resources engineering • D Eng, M Eng, MS, PhD
  geotechnical engineering • D Eng, M Eng, MS, PhD
  industrial engineering and operations research • D Eng, M Eng, MS, PhD
  materials engineering • D Eng, M Eng, MS, PhD
  mechanical engineering • D Eng, M Eng, MS, PhD
  mineral engineering • D Eng, M Eng, MS, PhD
  nuclear engineering • M Eng, MS, PhD
  petroleum engineering • D Eng, M Eng, MS, PhD
  physical metallurgy • D Eng, M Eng, MS, PhD
  structural engineering, mechanics and materials • D Eng, M Eng, MS, PhD
  transportation engineering • D Eng, M Eng, MS, PhD

College of Environmental Design
Harrison Fraker, Dean
Programs in:
  architecture • M Arch
  building science and urban design • MS, PhD
  city and regional planning • MCP, PhD
  design • MA
  design theories and methods • MS, PhD
  environmental design in developing countries • MS, PhD
  environmental planning • MLA, PhD
  history of architecture and urban design • MS, PhD
  landscape design and site planning • MLA
  social basis of architecture and urban design • MS, PhD
  structures and construction • MS, PhD
  the building process • MS, PhD
  urban and community design • MLA
  urban design • MUD

College of Letters and Science
Dr. Bonnie C. Wade, Chair of Deans
Programs in:
  African American studies • PhD
  anthropology • PhD
  applied mathematics • PhD
  art practice • MFA
  astrophysics • PhD
  biochemistry and molecular biology • PhD
  cell and developmental biology • PhD
  Chinese language • PhD
  classical archaeology • MA, PhD
  classics • MA, PhD
  comparative literature • MA, PhD
  Czech • MA, PhD
  Czech linguistics • MA, PhD
  Czech literature • MA, PhD
  economics • PhD
  endocrinology • PhD
  English • PhD
  French • MA, PhD
  genetics • PhD
  geography • PhD
  geology • MA, MS, PhD
  geophysics • MA, PhD
  German • MA, PhD
  Greek • MA
  Hindi-Urdu • MA, PhD
  Hispanic languages and literatures • MA, PhD
  history • C Phil, MA, PhD
  history of art • PhD
  immunology • PhD
  integrative biology • PhD
  Italian studies • MA, PhD
  Japanese language • PhD
  Latin • MA
  linguistics • MA, PhD
  Malay-Indonesian • MA, PhD
  mathematics • C Phil, MA, PhD
  medical anthropology • PhD
  music • MA, PhD
  Near Eastern religions • PhD
  Near Eastern studies • C Phil, MA, PhD
  neurobiology • PhD
  philosophy • PhD
  physics • PhD
  Polish • MA, PhD
  Polish linguistics • MA, PhD
  Polish literature • MA, PhD
  political science • PhD
  psychology • PhD
  rhetoric • PhD
  Russian • MA, PhD
  Russian linguistics • MA, PhD
  Russian literature • MA, PhD
  Sanskrit • MA, PhD

University of California, Berkeley (continued)
  Scandinavian languages and literatures • MA, PhD
  Serbo-Croatian • MA, PhD
  Serbo-Croatian linguistics • MA, PhD
  Serbo-Croatian literature • MA, PhD
  sociology • PhD
  South Asian civilization • MA
  statistics • MA, PhD
  Tamil • MA, PhD

College of Natural Resources
Dr. Gordon Rausser, Dean
Programs in:
  agricultural and environmental chemistry • MS, PhD
  agricultural and resource economics • PhD
  environmental science, policy, and management • MS, PhD
  forestry • MF
  natural resources • MA
  plant biology • PhD
  range management • MS

Graduate School of Journalism
Orville Schell, Dean
Program in:
  journalism • MJ

Graduate School of Public Policy
David Kirp, Acting Dean
Program in:
  public policy • MPP, PhD

Haas School of Business
William A. Hasler, Dean
Programs in:
  accounting • PhD
  business administration • MBA
  business and public policy • PhD
  finance • PhD
  marketing • PhD
  organizational behavior and industrial relations • PhD

School of Education
Dr. Eugene Garcia, Dean
Programs in:
  advanced reading and language leadership • MA
  athletes and academic achievement • MA
  educational leadership • Ed D
  education in mathematics, science, and technology • MA, PhD
  education/single subject teaching: mathematics • MA
  education/single subject teaching: science • MA
  education with a multiple subject credential • MA
  English • Certificate
  human development and education • MA, PhD
  language, literacy, and culture • Ed D, MA, PhD
  policy • MA
  policy research • PhD
  program evaluation and assessment • Ed D
  quantitative methods in education • PhD
  reading/reading and language arts • MA
  school psychology • PhD
  science and mathematics • PhD
  social and cultural analysis and social theory • MA, PhD
  special education • PhD

School of Information Management and Systems
Dr. Hal R. Varian, Dean
Program in:
  information management and systems • MIMS, PhD

School of Public Health
Dr. Edward E. Penhoet, Dean
Programs in:
  biostatistics • MA, PhD
  community health education • MPH
  environmental health sciences • MPH, MS, PhD
  epidemiology • MPH, MS, PhD
  epidemiology/biostatistics • MPH
  genetic counseling • MS
  health and medical sciences • MS
  health and social behavior • MPH
  health policy and administration • MPH
  infectious diseases • MA, MPH, PhD
  interdisciplinary • MPH
  maternal and child health • MPH
  public health • Dr PH
  public health nutrition • MPH

School of Social Welfare
Dr. James Midgley, Dean
Program in:
  social welfare • MSW, PhD

Boalt Hall School of Law
Herma Hill Kay, Dean
Programs in:
  jurisprudence and social policy • PhD
  law • JD, JSD, LL M

School of Optometry
Dr. Anthony J. Adams, Dean
Program in:
  optometry • OD

 # UNIVERSITY OF CALIFORNIA, DAVIS
Davis, CA 95616

http://www.ucdavis.edu/

Public coed university. *Enrollment: 24,299 graduate, professional, and undergraduate students. Graduate faculty: 1,371 full-time, 231 part-time. Computer facilities: Campuswide network is available with full Internet access. Total number of PCs/terminals supplied for student use: 300. Computer services are offered at no charge. Library facilities: Peter J. Shields Library plus 5 additional on-campus libraries. Graduate expenses: Tuition of $0 for state residents; $9384 per year for nonresidents. Fees of $4466 per year full-time, $2923 per year part-time. General application contact: Susan Chaffee, Publications Manager, 530-752-9300.*

Graduate Studies

Christina González, Dean
Programs in:
  acting • MFA
  agricultural and resource economics • MS, PhD
  agriculture and environmental chemistry • MS, PhD
  agronomy • MS
  animal behavior • PhD
  animal science • MAM, MS
  anthropology • MA, PhD
  applied linguistics • MA
  applied mathematics • MS, PhD
  art • MFA
  art history • MA
  atmospheric science • MS, PhD
  avian sciences • MS
  biochemistry and molecular biology • MS, PhD
  biophysics • MS, PhD
  cell and developmental biology • PhD
  chemistry • MS, PhD
  child development • MS
  community development • MS
  comparative literature • MA, PhD
  comparative pathology • MS, PhD
  composition • MA, PhD
  computer science • MS, PhD
  conducting • MA, PhD
  creative writing • MA
  dramatic art • PhD
  ecology • MS, PhD
  economics • MA, PhD
  education • Ed D
  endocrinology • MS, PhD
  English • MA, PhD
  entomology • MS, PhD
  epidemiology • MS, PhD
  exercise science • MS
  family and social organization • M Ed
  food science • MS, PhD
  French • MA, PhD
  genetics • MS, PhD
  geography • MA, PhD
  geology • MS, PhD
  German • MA, PhD
  history • MA, PhD
  horticulture • MS
  human development • PhD
  hydrologic sciences • MS, PhD
  immunology • MS, PhD
  instructional studies • PhD
  international agricultural development • MS
  linguistics • MA
  mathematics • MA, MAT, PhD
  microbiology • MS, PhD
  musicology • MA, PhD
  neuroscience • PhD
  nutrition • MS, PhD
  pharmacology/toxicology • MS, PhD
  philosophy • MA, PhD
  physics • MS, PhD
  physiology • MS, PhD
  plant biology • MS, PhD
  plant pathology • MS, PhD
  plant protection and pest management • MS
  plant sciences • MS
  political science • MA, PhD
  population biology • PhD
  psychological studies • PhD
  psychology • PhD
  sociocultural studies • PhD
  sociology • MA, PhD
  soil science • MS, PhD
  Spanish • MA, PhD
  statistics • MS, PhD
  textile arts and costume design • MFA
  textiles • MS
  transportation technology and policy • MS, PhD
  veterinary medicine • MPVM

College of Engineering

Dr. Alan Laub, Dean
Programs in:
  aeronautical engineering • Certificate, D Engr, M Engr, MS, PhD
  applied science • MS, PhD
  biological and agricultural engineering • D Engr, M Engr, MS, PhD
  biomedical engineering • MS, PhD
  chemical engineering • MS, PhD
  civil and environmental engineering • Certificate, D Engr, M Engr, MS, PhD
  electrical and computer engineering • MS, PhD
  materials science • Certificate, MS, PhD
  mechanical engineering • Certificate, D Engr, M Engr, MS, PhD

Graduate School of Management

Robert H. Smiley, Dean
Program in:
  management • MBA

School of Law

Bruce Wolk, Dean
Program in:
  law • JD, LL M

School of Medicine

Dr. Joseph Silva Jr., Dean
Program in:
  medicine • MD

School of Veterinary Medicine

Dr. Bennie I. Osburn, Dean
Program in:
  veterinary medicine • Certificate, DVM, MPVM

UNIVERSITY OF CALIFORNIA, IRVINE

Irvine, CA 92697

http://www.uci.edu/

Public coed university. *Enrollment: 17,153 graduate, professional, and undergraduate students. Graduate faculty: 1,438. Computer facilities: Campuswide network is available with full Internet access. Total number of PCs/terminals supplied for student use: 100. Computer service fees are included with tuition and fees. Library facilities: main library plus 2 additional on-campus libraries. Graduate expenses: Tuition of $0 for state residents; $9384 per year full-time, $1564 per quarter part-time for nonresidents. Fees of $4998 per year full-time, $1152 per quarter part-time. General application contact: Office of Research and Graduate Studies, 949-824-6761.*

Office of Research and Graduate Studies

Frederic Yui-Ming Wan, Vice Chancellor for Research and Dean of Graduate Studies
Programs in:
  comparative culture • MA, PhD
  educational administration • Ed D
  environmental toxicology • MS, PhD
  genetic counseling • MS
  information and computer science • MS, PhD
  pharmacology and toxicology • MS, PhD
  radiological sciences • MS, PhD

Graduate School of Management

David H. Blake, Dean
Program in:
  management • MBA, PhD

School of Biological Sciences

Dr. Susan Bryant, Interim Dean
Programs in:
  biological sciences • MS, PhD
  chemistry • PhD
  engineering • PhD

School of Engineering

Dr. John C. LaRue, Associate Dean
Programs in:
  chemical and biochemical engineering • MS, PhD
  electrical and computer engineering • MS, PhD
  engineering • MS, PhD
  mechanical and aerospace engineering • MS, PhD
  structures • MS, PhD
  transportation • MS, PhD
  water resources and environmental engineering • MS, PhD

School of Humanities

Karen Lawrence, Dean
Programs in:
  art history • PhD
  classics • MA, PhD
  comparative literature • MA, PhD
  East Asian languages and literatures • MA, PhD
  English • MA, PhD
  French • MA, PhD
  German • MA, PhD
  history • MA, PhD
  philosophy • MA, PhD
  Spanish • MA, MAT, PhD
  writing • MFA

School of Physical Sciences

Ralph J. Cicerone, Dean
Programs in:
  chemistry • MS, PhD
  earth system science • PhD
  mathematics • MS, PhD
  physics • MS, PhD

School of Social Ecology

Tom Crawford, Associate Dean
Programs in:
  criminology, law and society • PhD
  environmental analysis and design • PhD
  environmental health science and policy • MS, PhD
  health psychology • PhD
  human development • PhD
  social ecology • MA, PhD
  urban and regional planning • MURP, PhD

School of Social Sciences

William Schonfeld, Dean
Programs in:
  economics • MA, PhD
  political sciences • PhD
  psychology • PhD
  social networks • MA, PhD
  social relations • MA, PhD
  social science • MA, PhD

School of the Arts

Jill Beck, Dean
Programs in:
  dance • MFA
  drama • MFA
  music • MFA
  studio art • MFA

College of Medicine

Dr. Thomas Cesario, Dean
Programs in:
  biological sciences • MS, PhD
  environmental toxicology • MS, PhD
  genetic counseling • MS
  medicine • MD
  pharmacology and toxicology • MS, PhD
  radiological sciences • MS, PhD

UNIVERSITY OF CALIFORNIA, LOS ANGELES
Los Angeles, CA 90095

http://www.gdnet.ucla.edu/

Public coed university. *Enrollment: 32,625 graduate, professional, and undergraduate students. Graduate faculty: 1,906. Computer facilities: Campuswide network is available with full Internet access. Computer service fees are included with tuition and fees. Library facilities: University Research Library plus 13 additional on-campus libraries. Graduate expenses: Tuition of $0 for state residents; $9384 per year for nonresidents. Fees of $4551 per year. General application contact: Graduate Admissions, 310-825-1711.*

Graduate Division
Dr. Claudia Mitchell-Kernan, Dean
Programs in:
  anatomy and cell biology • PhD
  biological chemistry • MS, PhD
  biomathematics • MS, PhD
  biomedical physics • MS, PhD
  experimental pathology • MS, PhD
  human genetics • MS, PhD
  microbiology and immunology • PhD
  molecular and medical pharmacology • PhD
  molecular, cell and developmental biology • PhD
  neuroscience • PhD
  oral biology • MS, PhD
  physiology • MS, PhD

College of Letters and Science
Dr. Brian P. Copenhaver, Provost
Programs in:
  African area studies • MA
  Afro-American studies • MA
  American Indian studies • MA
  anthropology • MA, PhD
  applied linguistics • C Phil, PhD
  applied linguistics and teaching English as a second language • MA
  archaeology • C Phil, MA, PhD
  art history • MA, PhD
  Asian-American studies • MA
  astronomy • PhD
  atmospheric sciences • C Phil, MS, PhD
  biochemistry and molecular biology • C Phil, MS, PhD
  biology • C Phil, MA, PhD
  chemistry • C Phil, MS, PhD
  classics • C Phil, MA, PhD
  comparative literature • C Phil, MA, PhD
  East Asian languages and cultures • MA, PhD
  economics • PhD
  English • C Phil, PhD
  folklore and mythology • MA, PhD
  French • C Phil, MA, PhD
  geochemistry • C Phil, MS, PhD
  geography • C Phil, MA, PhD
  geology • C Phil, MS, PhD
  geophysics and space physics • MS, PhD
  German • MA
  Germanic languages • C Phil, PhD
  Greek • MA
  Hispanic languages and literature • PhD
  history • C Phil, MA, PhD
  Indo-European studies • C Phil, PhD
  Islamic studies • MA, PhD
  Italian • C Phil, MA, PhD
  Latin • MA
  Latin American studies • MA
  linguistics • C Phil, MA, PhD
  mathematics • C Phil, MA, MAT, PhD
  microbiology and molecular genetics • PhD
  molecular and cellular life sciences • PhD
  molecular biology • PhD
  musicology • MA, PhD
  Near Eastern languages and cultures • C Phil, MA, PhD
  philosophy • C Phil, PhD
  physics • PhD
  physics education • MAT
  physiological science • MS, PhD
  plant molecular biology • PhD
  political science • C Phil, MA, PhD
  Portuguese • MA
  psychology • C Phil, PhD
  Romance linguistics and literature • C Phil, MA, PhD
  Scandinavian • MA, PhD
  Slavic languages and literatures • C Phil, MA, PhD
  sociology • C Phil, MA, PhD
  Spanish • MA
  teaching English as a second language • Certificate

Graduate School of Education and Information Studies
Dr. Theodore R. Mitchell, Dean
Programs in:
  archive and preservation management • MLIS
  education • Ed D, M Ed, MA, PhD
  educational leadership • Ed D
  information access • MLIS
  information organization • MLIS
  information policy and management • MLIS
  information systems • MLIS
  library and information science • Certificate, PhD
  special education • PhD

John E. Anderson Graduate School of Management
Dr. John Mamer, Dean
Program in:
  management • MBA, MS, PhD

School of Engineering and Applied Science
Dr. Stephen E. Jacobsen, Associate Dean, Student Affairs
Programs in:
  aerospace engineering • MS, PhD
  biomedical engineering • MS, PhD
  ceramics engineering • MS, PhD
  chemical engineering • MS, PhD
  computer science • MS, PhD
  electrical engineering • MS, PhD
  environmental engineering • MS, PhD
  geotechnical engineering • MS, PhD
  integrated manufacturing engineering • M Engr
  manufacturing engineering • MS
  mechanical engineering • MS, PhD

University of California, Los Angeles (continued)
metallurgy • MS, PhD
operations research • MS, PhD
structural mechanics and earthquake engineering • MS, PhD
structures • MS, PhD
water resource systems engineering • MS, PhD

School of Nursing
Donna Vredevoe, Acting Dean
Program in:
nursing • MSN, PhD

School of Public Health
Dr. A. A. Afifi, Dean
Programs in:
biostatistics • MS, PhD
environmental health sciences • MS, PhD
environmental science and engineering • D Env
epidemiology • MS, PhD
health services • MS, PhD
public health • Dr PH, MPH, MS, PhD
public health for health and allied professionals • MPH

School of Public Policy and Social Research
Barbara Nelson, Dean
Programs in:
public policy • MPP
social welfare • MSW, PhD
urban planning • MA, PhD

School of the Arts and Architecture
Dr. Richard Weinstein, Dean
Programs in:
architecture • M Arch, MA, PhD
art • MA, MFA
composition • MA, PhD
dance • MA, MFA
dance/movement therapy • MA
design • MA, MFA
performance • DMA, MM

School of Theater, Film and Television
Robert Israel, Dean
Programs in:
film and television • MA, MFA, PhD
theater • MFA, PhD

School of Dentistry
Dr. Henry M. Cherrick, Dean
Programs in:
dentistry • Certificate, DDS
oral biology • MS, PhD

School of Law
Dr. Susan Westerberg-Prager, Dean
Program in:
law • JD, LL M

School of Medicine
Dr. Gerald S. Levey, Dean/Provost
Programs in:
anatomy and cell biology • PhD
biological chemistry • MS, PhD
biomathematics • MS, PhD
biomedical physics • MS, PhD
experimental pathology • MS, PhD
human genetics • MS, PhD
medicine • MD
microbiology and immunology • PhD
molecular and cellular life sciences • PhD
molecular and medical pharmacology • PhD
molecular, cell and developmental biology • PhD
neuroscience • PhD
physiology • MS, PhD

UNIVERSITY OF CALIFORNIA, RIVERSIDE
Riverside, CA 92521-0102
http://www.ucr.edu/

Public coed university. *Enrollment: 9,536 graduate, professional, and undergraduate students. Graduate faculty: 457 full-time. Computer facilities: Campuswide network is available with full Internet access. Computer services are offered at no charge. Library facilities: Tomas Rivera Library plus 4 additional on-campus libraries. Graduate expenses: Tuition of $0 for state residents; $9384 per year for nonresidents. Fees of $4861 per year. General application contact: Dr. Jean-Pierre Mileur, Dean of the Graduate Division, 909-787-3313.*

Graduate Division
Dr. Jean-Pierre Mileur, Dean

College of Engineering
Dr. Satish K. Tripathi, Dean
Programs in:
computer science • MS, PhD
electrical engineering • MS, PhD

College of Humanities, Arts and Social Sciences
Dr. Carlos Vélez-Ibáñez, Dean
Programs in:
anthropology • MA, MS, PhD
art history • MA
comparative literature • MA, PhD
dance history and theory • MA, PhD
economics • MA, PhD
English • MA, PhD
French • MA
history • MA, PhD
music • MA
philosophy • MA, PhD
political science • MA, PhD
psychology • MA, PhD
sociology • MA, PhD
Spanish • MA, PhD

College of Natural and Agricultural Sciences
Dr. Michael Clegg, Dean
Programs in:
    applied statistics • PhD
    biochemistry • MS, PhD
    biology • MS, PhD
    biomedical sciences • PhD
    botany • MS, PhD
    botany (plant genetics) • PhD
    chemistry • MS, PhD
    entomology • MS, PhD
    environmental toxicology • MS, PhD
    genetics • PhD
    geography • MS, PhD
    geological sciences • MS, PhD
    mathematics • MA, MS, PhD
    microbiology • MS, PhD
    pest management • MS
    physics • MA, MS, PhD
    plant pathology • MS, PhD
    plant science • MS
    population biology • PhD
    soil and environmental sciences • MS, PhD
    statistics • MS

Graduate School of Management
David Mayer, Interim Dean
Program in:
    management • MBA

School of Education
Dr. Robert Calfee, Dean
Program in:
    education • MA, PhD

UNIVERSITY OF CALIFORNIA, SAN DIEGO

La Jolla, CA 92093-5003

http://www.ucsd.edu/

Public coed university. *Enrollment:* 18,667 graduate, professional, and undergraduate students. *Graduate faculty:* 1,800. *Library facilities: Geisel Library plus 11 additional on-campus libraries.* *Graduate expenses: Tuition of $0 for state residents; $9384 per year full-time, $4692 per year part-time for nonresidents. Fees of $4887 per year full-time, $3344 per year part-time.* General application contact: *Graduate Admissions Office, 619-534-1193.*

Graduate Studies

Richard Attiyeh, Dean
Programs in:
    acting • MFA
    aerospace engineering • MS, PhD
    anthropology • PhD
    applied mathematics • MA
    applied mechanics • MS, PhD
    applied ocean science • MS, PhD

applied physics • MS, PhD
biochemistry • PhD
bioengineering • MS, PhD
biophysics • MS, PhD
cell and developmental biology • PhD
chemical engineering • MS, PhD
chemistry • PhD
clinical psychology • PhD
cognitive science • PhD
cognitive science/anthropology • PhD
cognitive science/communication • PhD
cognitive science/computer science and engineering • PhD
cognitive science/linguistics • PhD
cognitive science/neuroscience • PhD
cognitive science/philosophy • PhD
cognitive science/psychology • PhD
cognitive science/sociology • PhD
communication • MA, PhD
communication theory and systems • MS, PhD
comparative literature • MA, PhD
computational neurobiology • PhD
computer engineering • MS, PhD
computer science • MS, PhD
design • MFA
directing • MFA
ecology, behavior, and evolution • PhD
economics • PhD
electrical engineering • MS, PhD
electronic circuits and systems • MS, PhD
engineering physics • MS, PhD
ethnic studies • PhD
French literature • MA, PhD
genetics and molecular biology • PhD
German literature • MA, PhD
history • MA, PhD
immunology, virology, and cancer biology • PhD
intelligent systems, robotics and control • MS, PhD
language and communicative disorders • PhD
Latin American studies • MA
linguistics • PhD
literature • PhD
literatures and English • MA, PhD
materials science • MS, PhD
mathematics • MA, PhD
mechanical engineering • MS, PhD
molecular and cellular biology • PhD
molecular, cellular, and eukaryotic regulatory biology • PhD
molecular pathology • PhD
music • DMA, MA, PhD
neurobiology • PhD
neuroscience • PhD
pharmacology • PhD
philosophy • PhD
photonics • MS, PhD
physics • MS, PhD
physiology • PhD
plant molecular biology • PhD
playwriting • MFA
political science • PhD
psychology • PhD
public health and epidemiology • PhD

University of California, San Diego (continued)
regulatory biology • PhD
signal and image processing • MS, PhD
signal transduction • PhD
sociology • PhD
Spanish literature • MA, PhD
stage management • MFA
statistics • MS
structural engineering • MS, PhD
teacher education • MA
visual arts • MFA

Graduate School of International Relations and Pacific Studies
Dr. Miles Kahler, Interim Dean
Programs in:
international affairs • PhD
international technology management • MITM
Pacific international affairs • MPIA

Scripps Institution of Oceanography
W. Kendall Melville, Chair
Programs in:
biological oceanography • MS, PhD
geochemistry and marine chemistry • MS, PhD
marine biology • MS, PhD
physical oceanography and geological sciences • MS, PhD

School of Medicine
Programs in:
medicine • MD
molecular and cellular biology • PhD
molecular, cellular, and eukaryotic regulatory biology • PhD
molecular pathology • PhD
neuroscience • PhD
pharmacology • PhD
physiology • PhD
regulatory biology • PhD

UNIVERSITY OF CALIFORNIA, SAN FRANCISCO
San Francisco, CA 94143

http://www.ucsf.edu/

Public coed graduate-only institution. *Enrollment:* 2,394 matriculated graduate/professional students. Graduate faculty: 1,592. Library facilities: *main library.* Graduate expenses: *Tuition of $0 for state residents; $9384 per year for nonresidents. Fees of $4488 per year.* General application contact: *Dr. Clifford Attkisson, Dean of Graduate Studies, 415-476-2310.*

Graduate Division
Dr. Clifford Attkisson, Dean of Graduate Studies
Programs in:
anatomy • PhD
biochemistry and molecular biology • PhD
bioengineering • PhD
biophysics • PhD
cell biology • PhD
endocrinology • PhD
experimental pathology • PhD
genetics • PhD
history of health sciences • MA, PhD
medical anthropology • PhD
medical information science • MS, PhD
microbiology and immunology • PhD
neuroscience • PhD
oral biology • MS, PhD
pharmaceutical chemistry • PhD
physical therapy • MPT
physiology • PhD

School of Nursing
Jane S. Norbeck, Dean
Programs in:
nursing • MS, PhD
sociology • PhD

School of Dentistry
Program in:
dentistry • DDS

School of Medicine
Dr. Haile T. Debas, Dean
Programs in:
biochemistry and molecular biology • PhD
cell biology • PhD
genetics • PhD
medicine • MD

School of Pharmacy
George L. Kenyon, Dean
Programs in:
pharmaceutical chemistry • PhD
pharmacy • Pharm D

UNIVERSITY OF CALIFORNIA, SANTA BARBARA
Santa Barbara, CA 93106

http://www.ucsb.edu/

Public coed university. *Enrollment:* 18,531 graduate, professional, and undergraduate students. Graduate faculty: 684 full-time, 165 part-time. Computer facilities: *Campuswide network is available with full Internet access. Computer services are offered at no charge.* Library facilities: *Davidson Library.* Graduate expenses: *Tuition of $0 for state residents; $9384 per year for nonresidents. Fees of*

$4930 per year. General application contact: Mike Meraz, Director of Graduate Outreach Admissions and Retention, 805-893-3803.

Graduate Division
Charles Li, Dean

College of Engineering
Venkatesh Narayanamurti, Dean
Programs in:
   chemical engineering • MS, PhD
   computer science • MS, PhD
   electrical and computer engineering • MS, PhD
   materials • MS, PhD

College of Letters and Science
Gretchen Bataille, Provost
Programs in:
   anthropology • MA, PhD
   applied mathematics • MA
   art history • MA, PhD
   art studio • MFA
   biochemistry and molecular biology • PhD
   chemistry • MA, MS, PhD
   classics • MA, PhD
   communication • PhD
   comparative literature • MA, PhD
   dramatic art • MA, PhD
   East Asian languages and cultural studies • MA
   ecology, evolution, and marine biology • MA, PhD
   economics • MA, PhD
   English • MA, PhD
   French • MA, PhD
   geography • MA, PhD
   geological sciences • MA, PhD
   geophysics • MS
   Germanic languages and literature • MA, PhD
   Hispanic languages and literature • PhD
   history • MA, PhD
   history of science • PhD
   Latin American and Iberian studies • MA
   linguistics • MA, PhD
   marine science • MS, PhD
   mathematics • MA, PhD
   molecular, cellular, and developmental biology • MA, PhD
   music • MA, PhD
   performance • DMA, MM
   philosophy • PhD
   physics • PhD
   political science • MA, PhD
   Portuguese • MA
   psychology • MA, PhD
   religious studies • MA, PhD
   sociology • PhD
   Spanish • MA
   speech and hearing sciences • MA, PhD
   statistics and applied probability • MA, PhD

Graduate School of Education
Jules Zimmer, Dean
Programs in:
   clinical/school/counseling psychology • PhD
   education • M Ed, MA, PhD
   school psychology • M Ed

School of Environmental Science and Management
Jeff Dozier, Dean
Program in:
   environmental science and management • MESM

UNIVERSITY OF CALIFORNIA, SANTA CRUZ
Santa Cruz, CA 95064

http://www.ucsc.edu/

Public coed university. Enrollment: 10,117 graduate, professional, and undergraduate students. Graduate faculty: 499 full-time. Library facilities: McHenry Library plus 2 additional on-campus libraries. Graduate expenses: Tuition of $0 for state residents; $9384 per year for nonresidents. Fees of $5014 per year. General application contact: Graduate Admissions, 408-459-2301.

Graduate Division
Dr. Ron Henderson, Dean

Division of Arts
Dr. Ron Henderson, Dean, Graduate Division
Programs in:
   art • Certificate
   music • MA
   theatre arts • Certificate

Division of Humanities
Dr. Jorge Hankamer, Dean
Programs in:
   history • PhD
   history of consciousness • PhD
   linguistics • MA, PhD
   literature • MA, PhD

Division of Natural Sciences
Dr. David Kliger, Dean
Programs in:
   applied mathematics • MA, PhD
   astronomy and astrophysics • PhD
   biology • PhD
   chemistry • MS, PhD
   computer engineering • MS, PhD
   computer science • MS, PhD
   earth sciences • MS, PhD
   marine sciences • MS
   mathematics • MA, PhD
   molecular, cellular, and developmental biology • PhD
   physics • MS, PhD
   science communication • Certificate

Division of Social Sciences
Martin Chemers, Dean
Programs in:
   anthropology • MA, PhD
   applied economics • MS
   developmental psychology • PhD
   education • Certificate, MA

University of California, Santa Cruz (continued)
environmental studies • PhD
experimental psychology • PhD
international economics • PhD
social psychology • PhD
sociology • PhD

UNIVERSITY OF LA VERNE
La Verne, CA 91750-4443

http://www.ulaverne.edu/

Independent coed university. Library facilities: *Elvin and Betty Wilson Library plus 1 additional on-campus library. Graduate expenses: Tuition of $315 per unit (minimum). Fees of $60 per year. General application contact: Director, Graduate Student Services, 909-593-3511 Ext. 4244.*

College of Arts and Sciences
Programs in:
child development • MS
child development/child life • MS
counseling • MS
multiple subject/single subject teaching • Credential
reading • M Ed
school counseling • MS
special education • MS
special emphasis (classroom guidance) • M Ed

College of Law
Kenneth Held, Dean
Program in:
law • JD

School of Business and Economics
Programs in:
business administration • MBA
business organizational management • MS
operations management • MS

School of Continuing Education
Program in:
continuing education • M Ed, MBA, MS

School of Organizational Management
Programs in:
administrative services • Credential
educational management • Ed D, M Ed
health administration • MHA
leadership and management • MS
public administration • DPA, MPA

UNIVERSITY OF REDLANDS
Redlands, CA 92373-0999

http://www.redlands.edu/

Independent coed comprehensive institution. *Enrollment: 3,549 graduate, professional, and undergraduate students. Graduate faculty: 39 full-time, 313 part-time. Library facilities: Armacost Library plus 2 additional on-campus libraries. Graduate expenses: Tuition of $382 per unit. Fees of $158 per year. General application contact: Michael Kraft, Dean of Admissions, 909-793-2121 Ext. 4931.*

Graduate Studies
Dr. Philip Glotzbach, Vice President for Academic Affairs
Programs in:
communicative disorders • MS
music • MM

Alfred North Whitehead College for Lifelong Learning
Dr. Mary Boyce, Dean
Programs in:
administrative services • MA
adult education • MAHRM, MBA
curriculum leadership • MA
information systems • MBA
pupil personnel services • MA

 # UNIVERSITY OF SAN DIEGO
San Diego, CA 92110-2492

http://www.acusd.edu/

Independent-religious coed university. *Enrollment: 6,603 graduate, professional, and undergraduate students. Graduate faculty: 255. Library facilities: Copley Library plus 1 additional on-campus library. Graduate expenses: Tuition of $585 per unit (minimum). Fees of $50 per year full-time, $30 per year part-time. General application contact: Mary Jane Tiernan, Director of Graduate Admissions, 619-260-4524.*

College of Arts and Sciences
Dr. Patrick Drinan, Dean
Programs in:
dramatic arts • MFA
history • MA
international relations • MA
marine science • MS
pastoral care counseling • MA
pastoral ministry • MA
religious education • MA

Philip Y. Hahn School of Nursing
Dr. Janet Rodgers, Dean
Programs in:
    adult health nurse practitioner • MSN
    family health nurse practitioner • MSN
    nursing administration • MSN
    nursing science • DNS
    school health nurse practitioner • MSN

School of Business Administration
Dr. Curtis Cook, Dean
Program in:
    business administration • MBA, MIB

School of Education
Dr. Edward F. DeRoche, Dean
Programs in:
    counselor education • M Ed, MA
    curriculum and instruction • M Ed, MA, MAT
    educational leadership • Ed D, M Ed, MA
    marriage, family, and child counseling • MA
    special education • M Ed

School of Law
Kristine Strachan, Dean
Programs in:
    comparative law • MCL
    general studies • LL M
    international law • LL M
    law • JD
    taxation • Diploma, LL M

UNIVERSITY OF SAN FRANCISCO
San Francisco, CA 94117-1080

http://www.usfca.edu/

Independent-religious coed university. *Enrollment: 7,488 graduate, professional, and undergraduate students. Graduate faculty: 152 full-time, 248 part-time. Library facilities: Gleeson Library plus 2 additional on-campus libraries. Graduate expenses: $658 per unit (minimum). General application contact: Admissions Office, 415-422-6563.*

College of Arts and Sciences
Stanley Nel, Dean
Programs in:
    Asia Pacific studies • MA
    chemistry • MS
    computer science • MS
    environmental management • MS
    pastoral ministry • Certificate
    religious education • Certificate
    sports and fitness management • MA
    theology • MA
    writing • MA

College of Professional Studies
Betty Taylor, Dean
Programs in:
    health services administration • MPA
    human resources and organization development •
        MHROD
    nonprofit administration • MNA
    public administration • MPA

McLaren School of Business
Dr. Gary Williams, Dean
Programs in:
    executive business administration • EMBA
    finance and banking • MBA
    international business • MBA
    management • MBA
    marketing • MBA
    rehabilitation administration • EMRA
    telecommunications management and policy • MBA

School of Education
Dr. Paul Warren, Dean
Programs in:
    Catholic school teaching • MA
    counseling • MA
    counseling psychology • Psy D
    curriculum and instruction • Ed D, MA
    educational counseling • MA
    international and multicultural education • Ed D, MA
    life transitions counseling • MA
    marital and family therapy • MA
    private school administration • Ed D, MA
    teaching English as a second language • MA

School of Law
Jay Folberg, Dean
Program in:
    law • JD

School of Nursing
Dr. John Lantz, Interim Dean
Programs in:
    adult health nursing • MSN
    advanced practice nursing-nurse practitioner and clinical
        nurse specialist • MSN
    nursing administration • MSN

UNIVERSITY OF SOUTHERN CALIFORNIA
Los Angeles, CA 90089

http://www.usc.edu/

Independent coed university. *Enrollment: 28,342 graduate, professional, and undergraduate students. Graduate faculty: 2,398 full-time. Computer facilities: Campuswide network is available with full Internet access. Total number of PCs/terminals supplied for student use: 7,200. Computer services are offered at no charge. Library facilities: Dohenny Memorial Library plus 19 additional on-campus*

University of Southern California (continued)
libraries. Graduate expenses: *Tuition of $16,944 per year full-time, $706 per unit part-time. Fees of $414 per year full-time, $32 per year part-time. General application contact: Dr. Jonathan Kotler, Dean of Graduate Studies, 213-740-9033.*

Graduate School
Dr. Jonathan Kotler, Dean
Programs in:
    anatomy • PhD
    anatomy and cell biology • MS, PhD
    applied biometry/epidemiology • MS
    biochemistry and molecular biology • MS, PhD
    biometry • MS, PhD
    biometry/epidemiology • MPH
    cell biology • PhD
    craniofacial biology • MS, PhD
    epidemiology • PhD
    health behavior research • PhD
    health promotion • MPH
    molecular microbiology and immunology • MS, PhD
    molecular pharmacology and toxicology • MS, PhD
    pathobiology • MS, PhD
    pharmaceutical economics and policy • MS, PhD
    pharmaceutical sciences • MS, PhD
    pharmacology and nutrition • MS, PhD
    physiology and biophysics • MS, PhD
    preventive nutrition • MPH, MS

Annenberg School for Communication
Dr. Jonathan Kotler, Dean, Graduate School
Programs in:
    broadcast journalism • MA
    communication • MA, PhD
    communication management • MA
    international journalism • Certificate, MA
    interpersonal and social dynamics • PhD
    mass communication, technology, and public policy • PhD
    organizational communication • PhD
    print journalism • MA
    public relations • MA
    rhetorical and cultural studies • PhD

College of Letters, Arts and Sciences
Morton O. Schapiro, Dean
Programs in:
    applied demography • MS
    applied mathematics • MA, MS, PhD
    art history • Certificate, MA, PhD
    chemical physics • PhD
    chemistry • MA, MS, PhD
    classics • MA, PhD
    clinical psychology • PhD
    comparative literature • MA, PhD
    earth sciences • MS, PhD
    East Asian languages and cultures • MA, PhD
    East Asian studies • MA
    economic development programming • MA
    economics • MA, PhD
    English • MA, PhD
    exercise science • MA, MS, PhD
    film and literature • PhD

    French • MA, PhD
    geography • MA, MS, PhD
    German • MA, PhD
    history • MA, PhD
    international relations • MA, PhD
    linguistics • MA, PhD
    marine biology and biological oceanography • MS, PhD
    marriage and family therapy • PhD
    mathematics • MA, PhD
    molecular biology • MS, PhD
    neuroscience • PhD
    philosophy • MA, PhD
    physics • MA, MS, PhD
    political economy • MA
    political economy and public policy • PhD
    political science • MA, PhD
    professional writing • MPW
    psychology • PhD
    Slavic languages and literatures • MA, PhD
    social anthropology • PhD
    social ethics • MA, PhD
    sociology • MA, MS, PhD
    Spanish • MA, PhD
    statistics • MS
    visual anthropology • MA

Leonard Davis School of Gerontology
Dr. Edward Schneider, Dean
Program in:
    gerontology • Certificate, MS, PhD

Marshall School of Business
Dr. Randolph Westerfield, Dean
Programs in:
    accounting • M Acc
    business administration • MBA, MS, PhD
    business taxation • MBT
    finance and business economics • MBA
    information and operations management • MS
    international business • MBA

School of Architecture
Dr. Robert Timme, Dean
Programs in:
    architecture • M Arch
    building science • MBS
    landscape architecture • ML Arch

School of Cinema-Television
Dr. Elizabeth Daley, Dean
Programs in:
    critical studies • MA, PhD
    film and video production • MA, MFA
    film, video, and computer animation • MFA
    producing • MFA
    screen and television writing • MFA, PhD

School of Education
Dr. Guilbert Hentschke, Dean
Programs in:
    administration and policy • PhD
    college student personnel services • MS
    communication handicapped • MS
    counseling psychology • MS, PhD

curriculum and instruction • Ed D, PhD
curriculum and teaching • MS
educational leadership • MS
educational psychology • MS, PhD
instructional technology • MS
international and intercultural education • MS
language, literacy, and learning • PhD
learning handicapped • MS
marriage, family and child counseling • MFCC
pupil personnel services (K–12) • MS
teaching English as a second language • MS

School of Engineering
Dr. Leonard Silverman, Dean
Programs in:
    aerospace engineering • Engr, MS, PhD
    applied mechanics • MS
    biomedical engineering • MS, PhD
    biomedical imaging and telemedicine • MS
    chemical engineering • Engr, MS, PhD
    civil engineering • Engr, MS, PhD
    computer engineering • MS, PhD
    computer networks • MS
    computer science • MS, PhD
    construction engineering • MS
    construction management • MCM
    earthquake engineering • MS
    electrical engineering • Engr, MS, PhD
    engineering management • MS
    environmental engineering • MS, PhD
    industrial and systems engineering • Engr, MS, PhD
    manufacturing engineering • MS
    materials engineering • MS
    materials science • Engr, MS, PhD
    mechanical engineering • Engr, MS, PhD
    multimedia and creative technologies • MS
    ocean engineering • MS
    operations research • MS
    petroleum engineering • Engr, MS, PhD
    robotics and automation • MS
    software engineering • MS
    soil mechanics and foundations • MS
    structural engineering • MS
    structural mechanics • MS
    systems architecture and engineering • MS
    transportation engineering • MS
    VLSI design • MS
    water resources • MS

School of Fine Arts
Ruth Weisberg, Dean
Programs in:
    fine arts • MFA
    public art studies • MPAS

School of Health Affairs
Joseph P. Van Der Meulen, Vice President
Programs in:
    biokinesiology • MS, PhD
    nursing • Certificate, MS
    occupational science • PhD
    occupational therapy • MA
    physical therapy • DPT, MS

School of Music
Dr. Larry Livingston, Dean
Programs in:
    choral and church music • DMA, MM
    conducting • MM
    early music performance • MA
    historical musicology • PhD
    history and literature • MA
    jazz • MM
    music education • DMA, MM, MM Ed
    performance • DMA, MM
    theory and composition • DMA, MA, MM, PhD

School of Policy, Planning and Development
Dr. Edward Blakely, Dean
Programs in:
    planning • M Pl
    planning and development studies • DPDS, MPDS
    real estate development • MRED
    urban and regional planning • PhD

School of Public Administration
Dr. Jane Pisano, Dean
Programs in:
    health administration • MHA
    international public administration • MS
    public administration • Certificate, DPA, MPA, PhD
    public policy • MPP

School of Social Work
Dr. Marilyn L. Flynn, Dean
Program in:
    social work • MSW, PhD

School of Theatre
Dr. Robert Scales, Dean
Programs in:
    acting • MFA
    design • MFA
    directing • MFA
    playwriting • MFA

Law School
Scott H. Bice, Dean
Program in:
    law • JD

School of Dentistry
Dr. Howard Landesman, Dean
Programs in:
    craniofacial biology • MS, PhD
    dentistry • Certificate, DDS

School of Medicine
Dr. Stephen J. Ryan Jr., Dean
Programs in:
    anatomy • PhD
    anatomy and cell biology • MS, PhD
    applied biometry/epidemiology • MS
    biochemistry and molecular biology • MS, PhD
    biometry • MS, PhD
    biometry/epidemiology • MPH
    cell biology • PhD

University of Southern California (continued)
    epidemiology • PhD
    health behavior research • PhD
    health promotion • MPH
    medicine • MD
    molecular microbiology and immunology • MS, PhD
    pathobiology • MS, PhD
    pharmacology and nutrition • MS, PhD
    physiology and biophysics • MS, PhD
    preventive nutrition • MPH, MS

School of Pharmacy

Dr. Timothy M. Chan, Dean
Programs in:
    molecular pharmacology and toxicology • MS, PhD
    pharmaceutical economics and policy • MS, PhD
    pharmaceutical sciences • MS, PhD
    pharmacy • Pharm D

UNIVERSITY OF THE PACIFIC
Stockton, CA 95211-0197

http://www.uop.edu/graduate/

Independent coed university. *Enrollment: 5,850 graduate, professional, and undergraduate students. Graduate faculty: 378 full-time, 230 part-time. Computer facilities: Campuswide network is available with full Internet access. Computer services are offered at no charge. Library facilities: William Knox Holt Library plus 1 additional on-campus library.* Graduate expenses: *Tuition of $19,000 per year full-time, $594 per unit part-time. Fees of $30 per year (minimum).* General application contact: *Dr. Denis J. Meerdink, Interim Dean of the Graduate School, 209-946-2261.*

Graduate School

Dr. Denis J. Meerdink, Interim Dean
Programs in:
    biochemistry • MS, PhD
    biological sciences • MS
    biopharmaceutics/pharmacokinetics • MS, PhD
    chemistry • MS, PhD
    clinical pharmacy • MS, PhD
    communication • MA
    communicative disorders • MA
    English • MA
    history • MA
    industrial pharmacy • MS, PhD
    medicinal chemistry • MS, PhD
    nuclear pharmacy • MS, PhD
    pharmacology • MS, PhD
    physical therapy • MS
    physiology • MS, PhD
    psychology • MA
    sociology • MA
    sport sciences • MA

Conservatory of Music

Dr. Carl E. Nosse, Dean
Program in:
    music • MA, MAT, MM

Eberhardt School of Business

Mark Plovnick, Dean
Program in:
    business • MBA

School of Education

Dr. Fay B. Haisley, Dean
Programs in:
    counseling • MA
    counseling psychology • Ed D
    curriculum and instruction • Ed D, MA
    education • M Ed
    educational administration and foundations • Ed D, MA
    educational psychology • Ed D, MA
    educational research • MA
    school psychology • Ed D
    special education • Ed D, M Ed, MA

McGeorge School of Law

Gerald M. Caplan, Dean
Programs in:
    law • JD
    transnational business practice • LL M

School of Dentistry

Dr. Arthur A. Dugoni, Dean
Programs in:
    dentistry • DDS
    international dental studies • DDS
    orthodontics • MSD

School of Pharmacy

Dr. Philip Oppenheimer, Dean
Programs in:
    biopharmaceutics/pharmacokinetics • MS, PhD
    clinical pharmacy • MS, PhD
    industrial pharmacy • MS, PhD
    medicinal chemistry • MS, PhD
    nuclear pharmacy • MS, PhD
    pharmacology • MS, PhD
    pharmacy • Pharm D
    physiology • MS, PhD

WOODBURY UNIVERSITY
Burbank, CA 91510

http://www.woodburyu.edu/

Independent coed comprehensive institution. *Enrollment: 1,053 graduate, professional, and undergraduate students. Graduate faculty: 8 full-time, 9 part-time. Computer facilities: Campuswide network is available with full Internet access. Total number of PCs/terminals supplied for student use: 65. Computer service fees are included with tuition and fees. Library facilities: The Los Angeles Times Library.* Graduate expenses: *Tuition of $550 per unit. Fees of $360 per year.* General application contact: *Linda Parks, Graduate Admissions Assistant, 818-767-0888 Ext. 264.*

Business Administration Program
Richard King, Dean of Business and Management
Program in:
　business administration • MBA

COLORADO

ADAMS STATE COLLEGE
Alamosa, CO 81102

http://www.adams.edu/

Public coed comprehensive institution. *Enrollment: 2,350 graduate, professional, and undergraduate students. Graduate faculty: 42 full-time. Computer facilities: Campuswide network is available with full Internet access. Total number of PCs/terminals supplied for student use: 200. Computer service fees are applied as a separate charge. Library facilities: Nielson Library. Graduate expenses: $2164 per year full-time, $111 per credit part-time for state residents; $7284 per year full-time, $377 per credit part-time for nonresidents. General application contact: Dr. Scott Baldwin, Dean of Graduate Studies, 719-587-7936.*

Graduate Studies
Dr. Scott Baldwin, Dean

School of Arts and Letters
Dr. John D. Frazee, Dean
Program in:
　art • MA

School of Education and Graduate Studies
Dr. Scott Baldwin, Dean, Graduate Studies
Programs in:
　counseling • MA
　elementary education • MA
　health, physical education, and recreation • MA
　secondary education • MA
　special education • MA

COLORADO CHRISTIAN UNIVERSITY
Lakewood, CO 80226-7499

http://www.ccu.edu/

Independent-religious coed comprehensive institution. *Enrollment: 3,225 graduate, professional, and undergraduate students. Graduate faculty: 29. Library facilities: Clifton Fowler Library plus 1 additional on-campus library. General application contact: Thomas Yarney, Director of Graduate Studies, 303-697-8135.*

Graduate Division
Thomas Varney, Director of Graduate Studies
Programs in:
　biblical counseling • MA
　curriculum and instruction • MA
　management • MSM

 ## COLORADO SCHOOL OF MINES
Golden, CO 80401-1887

http://www.mines.edu/

Public coed university. *Enrollment: 3,283 graduate, professional, and undergraduate students. Graduate faculty: 97 full-time, 9 part-time. Computer facilities: Campuswide network is available with full Internet access. Total number of PCs/terminals supplied for student use: 350. Computer service fees are included with tuition and fees. Library facilities: Arthur Lakes Library. Graduate expenses: Tuition of $4508 per year full-time, $150 per semester hour part-time for state residents; $14,372 per year full-time, $479 per semester hour part-time for nonresidents. Fees of $573 per year. General application contact: Dr. Arthur J. Kidnay, Dean of Graduate Studies and Research, 303-273-3247.*

Graduate School
Dr. Arthur J. Kidnay, Dean of Graduate Studies and
　Research
Programs in:
　applied physics • PhD
　chemical engineering and petroleum refining • ME, MS,
　　PhD
　chemistry • MS, PhD
　engineering geology • Diploma
　engineering systems • ME, MS, PhD
　environmental science and engineering • MS, PhD
　exploration geosciences • Diploma
　geochemistry • MS, PhD
　geological engineering • Diploma, ME, MS, PhD
　geology • MS, PhD
　geophysical engineering • ME, MS, PhD
　geophysics • Diploma, MS, PhD
　hydrogeology • Diploma
　materials science • MS, PhD
　mathematical and computer sciences • MS, PhD
　metallurgical and materials engineering • ME, MS, PhD
　mineral economics • MS, PhD
　mining engineering • ME, MS, PhD
　petroleum economics and management • Diplôme
　　d'ingénieur, MS
　petroleum engineering • ME, MS, PhD
　physics • MS

COLORADO STATE UNIVERSITY
Fort Collins, CO 80523-0015

http://www.colostate.edu/

Public coed university. *Enrollment: 22,344 graduate, professional, and undergraduate students. Graduate faculty: 990 full-time. Computer facilities: Campuswide network is available with full Internet access. Total number of PCs/terminals supplied for student use: 8,000. Computer services are offered at no charge. Library facilities: Morgan Library. Graduate expenses: Tuition of $2632 per year full-time, $109 per credit hour part-time for state residents; $10,216 per year full-time, $425 per credit hour part-time for nonresidents. Fees of $708 per year full-time, $32 per semester (minimum) part-time. General application contact: Graduate School, 970-491-6817.*

Graduate School
Dean Jaros, Dean
Programs in:
anatomy and neurobiology • MS, PhD
cell and molecular biology • MS, PhD
cellular and molecular biology • MS, PhD
clinical sciences • MS, PhD
environmental health • MS, PhD
health physics • MS, PhD
immunology • MS, PhD
mammalian radiobiology • MS, PhD
microbiology • MS, PhD
nuclear-waste management • MS
pathology • MS, PhD
physiology • MS, PhD
radiobiology • MS
radioecology • MS, PhD
radiology • MS, PhD
veterinary radiology • MS

College of Agricultural Sciences
James C. Heird, Associate Dean
Programs in:
agricultural and resource economics • M Agr, MS, PhD
agricultural science • M Agr
animal breeding and genetics • MS, PhD
animal nutrition • MS, PhD
animal reproduction • MS, PhD
animal sciences • M Agr
crop science • MS, PhD
entomology • MS, PhD
floriculture • M Agr, MS, PhD
horticultural food crops • M Agr, MS, PhD
livestock handling • MS, PhD
meats • MS, PhD
nursery and landscape management • M Agr, MS, PhD
plant genetics • MS, PhD
plant pathology • MS, PhD
plant physiology • MS, PhD
production management • MS, PhD
soil science • MS, PhD
turf management • M Agr, MS, PhD
weed science • MS, PhD

College of Applied Human Sciences
Nancy Hartley, Dean
Programs in:
apparel and textiles individualized • MA, MS
automotive pollution control • MS
construction management • MS
design, merchandising, and consumer sciences • MA, MS
exercise science • MS
food science • MS, PhD
human development and family studies • MS
industrial sciences • MS
industrial sciences and technology education • MS
interior design • MS
manufacturing/industrial technology • MS
merchandising • MA, MS
nutrition • MS, PhD
occupational therapy • MS
social work • MSW
student affairs • MS
technology of industry • PhD
vocational education • M Ed, PhD
wellness management • MS

College of Business
Dr. Daniel Costello, Dean
Programs in:
accounting • MBA, MS
business administration • MBA
computer information systems • MBA, MS
finance and real estate • MBA
management • MBA, MS
marketing • MBA, MS
taxation • MBA, MS

College of Engineering
Johannes Gesler, Interim Dean
Programs in:
atmospheric science • MS, PhD
bioengineering • MS, PhD
bioresource and agricultural engineering • MS, PhD
chemical engineering • MS, PhD
electrical engineering • MS, PhD
energy and environmental engineering • MS, PhD
energy conversion • MS, PhD
engineering management • MS
environmental engineering • MS, PhD
heat and mass transfer • MS, PhD
hydraulics and wind engineering • MS, PhD
hydrology and water resources • MS, PhD
industrial and manufacturing systems engineering • MS, PhD
mechanical engineering • MS, PhD
mechanics and materials • MS, PhD
structural and geotechnical engineering • MS, PhD
water and infrastructure systems • MS, PhD

College of Liberal Arts
Robert Keller, Interim Dean
Programs in:
American history • MA
anthropology • MA
applied music • MM
archival science • MA

Asian history • MA
choral conducting • MM
communication development • MA
conducting • MM
creative writing • MFA
drawing • MFA
economics • MA, PhD
English as a second language • MA
European history • MA
fibers • MFA
French/TESL • MA
German/TESL • MA
graphic design • MFA
historic preservation • MA
Latin American history • MA
literature • MA
metalsmithing • MFA
music education • MM
music history and literature • MM
music theory • MM
music therapy • MM
orchestral conducting • MM
painting • MFA
performance • MM
philosophy • MA
political science • MA, PhD
printmaking • MFA
sculpture • MFA
sociology • MA, PhD
Spanish/TESL • MA
speech communication • MA
teaching • MA
technical communication • MS

College of Natural Resources
A. A. Dyer, Dean
Programs in:
commercial recreation and tourism • MS
earth resources • PhD
ecology • MS, PhD
fluvial geomorphology • MS
forestry • MF, MS, PhD
human dimensions in natural resources • PhD
hydrogeology • MS
petrology/geochemistry and economic geology • MS
rangeland ecosystem science • MS, PhD
recreation resource management • MS, PhD
resource interpretation • MS
stratigraphy/sedimentology • MS
structure/tectonics • MS
watershed science • MS

College of Natural Sciences
John C. Raich, Dean
Programs in:
biochemistry and molecular biology • MS, PhD
botany • MS, PhD
chemistry • MS, PhD
computer science • MS, PhD
counseling psychology • PhD
general/experimental psychology • PhD
industrial-organizational psychology • PhD
mathematics • MS, PhD

physics • MS, PhD
statistics • MS, PhD
zoology • MS, PhD

College of Veterinary Medicine and Biomedical Sciences
James L. Voss, Dean
Programs in:
anatomy and neurobiology • MS, PhD
cell and molecular biology • MS, PhD
cellular and molecular biology • MS, PhD
clinical sciences • MS, PhD
environmental health • MS, PhD
health physics • MS, PhD
immunology • MS, PhD
mammalian radiobiology • MS, PhD
microbiology • MS, PhD
nuclear-waste management • MS
pathology • MS, PhD
physiology • MS, PhD
radiobiology • MS
radioecology • MS, PhD
radiology • MS, PhD
veterinary medicine • DVM
veterinary radiology • MS

REGIS UNIVERSITY
Denver, CO 80221-1099

http://www.regis.edu/

Independent-religious coed comprehensive institution. *Enrollment: 7,837 graduate, professional, and undergraduate students. Graduate faculty: 27 full-time, 238 part-time. Computer facilities: Campuswide network is available with full Internet access. Total number of PCs/terminals supplied for student use: 221. Computer service fees are included with tuition and fees. Library facilities: Dayton Memorial Library plus 2 additional on-campus libraries. Graduate expenses: $322 per semester hour (minimum). General application contact: contact appropriate school.*

School for Professional Studies
Dr. Edward Cooper, Associate Academic Dean
Programs in:
business • MBA
community leadership • MACL
computer information systems • MSCIS
liberal studies • MLS
management • MSM

Regis College
Dr. Steve Doty, Dean
Program in:
whole learning education • MA

Regis University (continued)
School for Healthcare Professions
Dr. Patricia Ladewig, Academic Dean
Programs in:
    nursing • MSN
    physical therapy • MSPT

UNIVERSITY OF COLORADO AT BOULDER
Boulder, CO 80309
http://www.colorado.edu/

Public coed university. *Enrollment: 24,622 graduate, professional, and undergraduate students. Graduate faculty: 1,150 full-time. Computer facilities: Campuswide network is available with full Internet access. Computer service fees are included with tuition and fees. Library facilities: Norlin Library plus 6 additional on-campus libraries. Graduate expenses: Tuition of $3170 per year full-time, $531 per semester (minimum) part-time for state residents; $14,652 per year full-time, $2442 per semester (minimum) part-time for nonresidents. Fees of $667 per year full-time, $130 per semester (minimum) part-time. General application contact: Dean of the appropriate college.*

Graduate School
Carol Lynch, Dean
Program in:
    museum and field studies • MBS

College of Arts and Sciences
Peter D. Spear, Dean
Programs in:
    animal behavior • MA, PhD
    anthropology • MA, PhD
    applied mathematics • MS, PhD
    aquatic biology • MA, PhD
    art history • MA
    astrophysical and geophysical fluid dynamics • MS, PhD
    astrophysics • MS, PhD
    audiology • MA, PhD
    behavioral genetics • MA, PhD
    biochemistry • PhD
    cellular structure and function • MA, PhD
    chemical physics • PhD
    chemistry • MS, PhD
    classics • MA, PhD
    communication • MA, PhD
    comparative literature • MA, PhD
    creative writing • MA
    dance • MFA
    developmental biology • MA, PhD
    drawing • MFA
    East Asian languages and literature • MA
    ecology • MA, PhD
    economics • MA, PhD
    English literature • MA, PhD
    French • MA, PhD
    geography • MA, PhD
    geological sciences • MS, PhD
    geophysics • PhD
    German • MA
    history • MA, PhD
    international affairs • MA
    kinesiology • PhD
    linguistics • MA, PhD
    mathematical physics • PhD
    mathematics • MA, PhD
    medical physics • PhD
    microbiology • MA, PhD
    molecular biology • MA, PhD
    neurobiology • MA, PhD
    painting • MFA
    philosophy • MA, PhD
    photography • MFA
    physical education • MS
    physics • MS, PhD
    plant and animal physiology • MA, PhD
    plant and animal systematics • MA, PhD
    plasma physics • MS, PhD
    political science • MA, PhD
    population biology • MA, PhD
    population genetics • MA, PhD
    printmaking • MFA
    psychology • MA, PhD
    public policy analysis • MA
    religious studies • MA
    sculpture • MFA
    sociology • MA, PhD
    Spanish • MA, PhD
    speech-language pathology • MA, PhD
    theatre • MA, PhD

College of Engineering and Applied Science
Ross Corotis, Dean
Programs in:
    aerospace engineering sciences • ME, MS, PhD
    building systems • MS, PhD
    chemical engineering • ME, MS, PhD
    computer engineering • ME, MS, PhD
    computer science • ME, MS, PhD
    construction engineering and management • MS, PhD
    electrical engineering • ME, MS, PhD
    engineering management • ME
    environmental engineering • MS, PhD
    geoenvironmental engineering • MS, PhD
    geotechnical engineering • MS, PhD
    mechanical engineering • ME, MS, PhD
    structural engineering • MS, PhD
    telecommunications • ME, MS
    water resource engineering • MS, PhD

College of Music
Daniel P. Sher, Dean
Programs in:
    church music • M Mus
    composition • D Mus A, M Mus
    conducting • D Mus A, M Mus
    music education • M Mus Ed, PhD
    music literature • M Mus
    musicology • PhD

pedagogy • D Mus A, M Mus
performance • D Mus A, M Mus

School of Education
Lorrie Shepard, Interim Dean
Programs in:
educational and psychological studies • MA, PhD
instruction and curriculum • MA, PhD
research and evaluation methodologies • PhD
social multicultural and bilingual foundations • MA, PhD

School of Journalism and Mass Communication
Willard D. Rowland Jr., Dean
Programs in:
integrated marketing communications • MA
mass communication research • MA
media studies • PhD
newsgathering • MA

Graduate School of Business Administration
Larry Singell, Dean
Programs in:
accounting • MS
business administration • MBA, PhD
business self designed • MBA
finance • MBA, PhD
marketing • MBA, PhD
organization management • MBA, PhD
taxation • MS
technology and innovation management • MBA

School of Law
Harold H. Bruff, Dean
Program in:
law • JD

UNIVERSITY OF COLORADO AT COLORADO SPRINGS
Colorado Springs, CO 80933-7150

http://www.uccs.edu/

Public coed comprehensive institution. *Enrollment: 6,467 graduate, professional, and undergraduate students. Graduate faculty: 155 full-time, 14 part-time. Computer facilities: Campuswide network is available with full Internet access. Total number of PCs/terminals supplied for student use: 340. Computer service fees are included with tuition and fees. Library facilities: Kraemer Family Library. Graduate expenses: Tuition of $2760 per year full-time, $115 per credit hour part-time for state residents; $9960 per year full-time, $415 per credit hour part-time for nonresidents. Fees of $399 per year (minimum) full-time, $106 per year (minimum) part-time. General application contact: Admissions and Records Office, 719-262-3383.*

Department of Graduate Nursing
Barbara Joyce-Nagata, Chair
Programs in:
adult health nurse practitioner and clinical specialist • MSN
community clinical specialist • MSN
family practitioner • MSN
forensic clinical specialist • MSN
holistic clinical specialist • MSN
neonatal nurse practitioner and clinical specialist • MSN

Graduate School
Dr. Kenneth Rebman, Associate Vice Chancellor and Dean

College of Engineering and Applied Science
Dr. Ronald Sega, Dean
Programs in:
aerospace engineering • ME
applied mathematics • MS
computer science • MS
electrical and computer engineering • MS, PhD

College of Letters, Arts and Sciences
Dr. Elizabeth Grobsmith, Interim Dean
Programs in:
basic science • MBS
communications • MA
history • MA
physics • MBS, MS
psychology • MA
sociology • MA

School of Education
Dr. Greg R. Weisenstein, Dean
Programs in:
counseling and human services • MA
curriculum and instruction • MA
special education • MA

Graduate School of Business Administration
Dr. Richard Dicenza, Dean
Programs in:
accounting • MBA
finance • MBA
information systems • MBA
marketing • MBA
organizational management • MBA
production management • MBA

Graduate School of Public Affairs
Dr. Kathleen Beatty, Dean
Programs in:
criminal justice • MCJ
public administration • MPA

UNIVERSITY OF COLORADO AT DENVER
Denver, CO 80217-3364

http://www.cudenver.edu/

Public coed university. *Enrollment: 10,855 graduate, professional, and undergraduate students. Graduate faculty: 394. Computer facilities: Campuswide network is available with full Internet access. Total number of PCs/terminals supplied for student use: 480. Computer service fees are included with tuition and fees. Library facilities: Auraria Library. Graduate expenses: Tuition of $2996 per year full-time, $181 per semester hour part-time for state residents; $11,954 per year full-time, $717 per semester hour part-time for nonresidents. Fees of $252 per year. General application contact: Annette Beck, Program Specialist, 303-556-2663.*

Graduate School
Michael Murphy, Acting Vice Chancellor for Academic Affairs

College of Engineering and Applied Science
Peter Jenkins, Dean
Programs in:
civil engineering • MS, PhD
computer science • MS
electrical engineering • MS
engineering • ME
mechanical engineering • MS

College of Liberal Arts and Sciences
Marvin Loflin, Dean
Programs in:
anthropology • MA
applied mathematics • MS, PhD
basic science • MBS
biology • MA
chemistry • MS
communication and theatre • MA
economics • MA
environmental science • MS
health and behavioral science • PhD
history • MA
humanities • MH
literature • MA
political science • MA
psychology • MA
social sciences • MSS
sociology • MA
teaching English as a second language • MA
teaching of writing • MA
technical communication • MS

School of Education
G. Thomas Bellamy, Dean
Programs in:
administration, supervision, and curriculum development • MA
counseling psychology and counselor education • MA
curriculum and instruction • MA
early childhood education • MA
educational administration, curriculum and supervision • Ed S
educational leadership and innovation • PhD
educational psychology • MA
information and learning technologies • MA
special education • MA

College of Architecture and Planning
Patricia O'Leary, Dean
Programs in:
architecture • M Arch
design and planning • PhD
landscape architecture • MLA
urban and regional planning • MURP
urban design • M Arch UD

Graduate School of Business Administration
Yash P. Gupta, Dean
Programs in:
accounting • MS
business administration • Exec MBA, MBA
finance • MS
health administration • Exec MS, MS
information systems management • MS
international business • MS
management • MS
marketing • MS

Graduate School of Public Affairs
Kathleen Beatty, Dean
Programs in:
criminal justice • MCJ
public administration • Exec MPA, MPA, PhD

UNIVERSITY OF DENVER
Denver, CO 80208

http://www.du.edu/

Independent coed university. *Enrollment: 8,667 graduate, professional, and undergraduate students. Graduate faculty: 403 full-time, 20 part-time. Library facilities: Penrose Library plus 2 additional on-campus libraries. Graduate expenses: Tuition of $18,216 per year full-time, $506 per credit hour part-time. Fees of $159 per year. General application contact: contact individual schools, 303-871-2000.*

College of Education
Dr. Elinor Katz, Dean
Programs in:
child and family studies • MA, PhD
counseling psychology • MA, PhD
curriculum and instruction • MA, PhD
curriculum leadership • MA, PhD
educational psychology • Ed S, MA, PhD
higher education and adult studies • MA, PhD
quantitative research methods • MA, PhD
school administration • PhD
school psychology • Ed S, PhD

College of Law
Robert Yegge, Interim Dean
Programs in:
    American and comparative law • LL M
    law • JD
    legal administration • MSLA
    natural resources law • LL M, MRLS
    taxation • LL M, MT

Daniels College of Business
James R. Griesemer, Dean
Programs in:
    accountancy • M Acc
    accounting • MBA
    business administration • MBA
    education management • MSM
    finance • MBA, MS, MSF
    finance/real estate • MBA
    health care management • MSM
    information technology and electronic commerce •
        MBA, MIM
    management and communications • MSMC
    management and general engineering • MSMGEN
    management and telecommunications • MSMC
    marketing • MBA, MIM
    public health management • MSM
    real estate • MBA
    real estate and construction management • MRECM
    resort and tourism management • MS, MSRTM
    sports management • MSM

Graduate School of International Studies
Dr. Tom Farer, Dean
Program in:
    international studies • MA, MIM, PhD

Graduate School of Professional Psychology
Dr. Peter Buirski, Dean
Program in:
    clinical psychology • Psy D

Graduate School of Social Work
Dr. Catherine Alter, Dean
Program in:
    social work • MSW, PhD

Graduate Studies
Dr. Barry Hughes, Vice Provost
Programs in:
    advertising management • MS
    digital media studies • MA
    human communication studies • MA, PhD
    international and intercultural communication • MA
    mass communications • MA
    public relations • MS
    video production • MA

Faculty of Arts and Humanities/Social Sciences
Dr. Roscoe Hill, Dean
Programs in:
    anthropology • MA
    applied research and evaluation • MS
    art history • MA
    art history/museum studies • MA
    composition • MA
    conducting • MA
    economics • MA
    education • MA
    English • MA, PhD
    French • MA
    German • MA
    history • MA
    intern studies • MA
    Judaic studies • MA
    music education • MA
    music history and literature • MA
    Orff-Schulwerk • MA
    performance • MA
    philosophy • MA
    piano pedagogy • MA
    psychology • PhD
    religious studies • MA, PhD
    sociology • MA, PhD
    Spanish • MA
    studio art • MFA
    Suzuki pedagogy • MA
    theory • MA

Faculty of Natural Sciences, Mathematics and Engineering
Dr. Robert Coombe, Dean
Programs in:
    applied mathematics • MA, MS
    biological sciences • MS, PhD
    chemistry • MA, MS, PhD
    computer science • MS
    computer sicence and engineering • MS
    electrical engineering • MS
    geography • MA, PhD
    management and general engineering • MSMGEN
    materials science • PhD
    mathematics and computer science • PhD
    mechanical engineering • MS
    physics and astronomy • MS, PhD

University College
Peter Warren, Dean
Programs in:
    applied communication • MSS
    computer information systems • MCIS
    environmental policy and management • MEPM
    healthcare systems • MHS
    liberal studies • MLS
    library and information services • MLIS
    public health • MPH
    technology management • MoTM
    telecommunications • MTEL

UNIVERSITY OF NORTHERN COLORADO
Greeley, CO 80639

http://www.univnorthco.edu/

Public coed university. *Enrollment: 10,393 graduate, professional, and undergraduate students. Graduate faculty: 267 full-time, 19 part-time. Library facilities: Michener Library plus 2 additional on-campus libraries. Graduate expenses: Tuition of $2327 per year full-time, $129 per credit hour part-time for state residents; $9578 per year full-time, $532 per credit hour part-time for nonresidents. Fees of $752 per year full-time, $184 per semester (minimum) part-time. General application contact: Dr. Priscilla Kimboko, Associate Dean, 970-351-2831.*

Graduate School
Dr. Richard King, Interim Associate Vice President for Research and Dean
Programs in:
interdisciplinary education • MA
interdisciplinary studies • DA, Ed D, Ed S, MA, MS

College of Arts and Sciences
Dr. Sandra Flake, Dean
Programs in:
biological education • PhD
biological sciences • MA
chemical education • MA, PhD
chemical research • MA
communication • MA
earth sciences • MA
educational mathematics • MA, PhD
English • MA
history • MA
mathematics • MA, PhD
psychology • MA
social sciences • MA
Spanish • MA

College of Education
Dr. Allen Huang, Interim Dean
Programs in:
agency counseling • MA
applied statistics and research methods • MS, PhD
college student personnel administration • PhD
counseling psychology • Psy D
counselor education • Ed D
early childhood education • MA
educational leadership • Ed D, Ed S, MA
educational media • MA
educational psychology • MA, PhD
educational technology • MA, PhD
elementary education • Ed D, MA
elementary school counseling • MA
reading education • MA
school psychology • Ed S, PhD
secondary and postsecondary school counseling • MA
special education • Ed D, MA

College of Health and Human Sciences
Dr. Vincent Scalia, Dean
Programs in:
communication disorders • MA
community health • MPH
family nurse practitioner • MS
gerontology • MA
kinesiology and physical education • Ed D, MA
nursing education • MS
rehabilitation counseling • MA, PhD

College of Performing and Visual Arts
Dr. Shirley Howell, Interim Dean
Programs in:
music • DA, MM, MME
visual arts • MA

CONNECTICUT

CENTRAL CONNECTICUT STATE UNIVERSITY
New Britain, CT 06050-4010

http://www.ccsu.edu/

Public coed comprehensive institution. *Enrollment: 11,625 graduate, professional, and undergraduate students. Graduate faculty: 248 full-time, 306 part-time. Computer facilities: Campuswide network is available with full Internet access. Total number of PCs/terminals supplied for student use: 230. Computer service fees are applied as a separate charge. Library facilities: Elihu Burritt Library plus 1 additional on-campus library. Graduate expenses: Tuition of $4458 per year full-time, $175 per credit hour part-time for state residents; $9943 per year full-time, $175 per credit hour part-time for nonresidents. Fees of $45 per semester. General application contact: Drina M. Lynch, Assistant Dean, Graduate Studies, 860-832-2361.*

School of Graduate Studies
Dr. Elene Demos, Interim Dean
Programs in:
international studies • MS
social science • MS

School of Arts and Sciences
Dr. June Higgins, Interim Dean
Programs in:
art education • MS
biological sciences • MA, MS
chemistry • MS
communication • MS
criminal justice • MS
earth science • MS
English • MA, MS
French • MA
general science • MS
geography • MS

history • MA, MS
mathematics • MA, MS
music education • MS
physics • MS
psychology • MA
Spanish • MA, MS
teaching English to speakers of other languages • MS

School of Business
Dr. John Hampton, Dean
Programs in:
business education • MS
general business management • MS
international business administration • MBA

School of Education and Professional Studies
Dr. Richard Arends, Dean
Programs in:
administration, supervision and curriculum • MS
counseling • MS
early childhood education • MS
educational foundation and policy studies • MS
educational leadership • Sixth Year Certificate
educational technology and media • MS
elementary education • MS
physical education and health fitness • MS
reading • MS, Sixth Year Certificate
secondary education • MS
special education • MS

School of Technology
Dr. John R. Wright, Dean
Programs in:
industrial (technical) management • MS
technology education • MS

EASTERN CONNECTICUT STATE UNIVERSITY
Willimantic, CT 06226-2295

http://www.ecsu.ctstateu.edu/

Public coed comprehensive institution. *Enrollment: 4,632 graduate, professional, and undergraduate students. Graduate faculty: 17 full-time, 9 part-time. Computer facilities: Campuswide network is available with full Internet access. Total number of PCs/terminals supplied for student use: 290. Computer services are offered at no charge. Library facilities: J. Eugene Smith Library. Graduate expenses: Tuition of $2632 per year full-time, $175 per credit hour part-time for state residents; $7220 per year full-time, $175 per credit hour part-time for nonresidents. Fees of $1851 per year full-time, $20 per semester part-time for state residents; $2748 per year full-time, $20 per semester part-time for nonresidents. General application contact: Dr. David Stoloff, Interim Dean, 860-465-5293.*

School of Education and Professional Studies/ Graduate Division
Dr. David Stoloff, Interim Dean
Programs in:
early childhood education • MS
elementary education • MS
mathematics education • MS
organizational management • MS
reading and language arts • MS
science education • MS

FAIRFIELD UNIVERSITY
Fairfield, CT 06430-5195

http://www.fairfield.edu/

Independent-religious coed comprehensive institution. *Enrollment: 5,111 graduate, professional, and undergraduate students. Graduate faculty: 78 full-time, 45 part-time. Computer facilities: Campuswide network is available with full Internet access. Total number of PCs/terminals supplied for student use: 160. Computer service fees are included with tuition and fees. Library facilities: Nyselius Library. Graduate expenses: Tuition of $350 per credit hour (minimum). Fees of $20 per semester (minimum). General application contact: Dean of the appropriate school, 203-254-4000.*

College of Arts and Sciences
Dr. Orin Grossman, Dean
Program in:
American studies • MA

Graduate School of Education and Allied Professions
Dr. Margaret Deignan, Dean
Programs in:
applied psychology • MA
community counseling • MA
computers in education • CAS, MA
counselor education • CAS
early childhood education • CAS, MA
educational media • CAS, MA
elementary education • MA
marriage and family therapy • MA
school counseling • MA
school psychology • CAS, MA
special education • CAS, MA
student affairs • MA
teaching and foundation • CAS, MA
TESOL, foreign language and bilingual/multicultural education • CAS, MA

School of Business
Dr. Walter G. Ryba Jr., Acting Dean
Programs in:
accounting • CAS, MBA
finance • CAS, MBA
financial management • MSFM
human resource management • CAS, MBA

Fairfield University (continued)
  information technology • CAS, MBA
  international business • CAS, MBA
  marketing • CAS, MBA
  taxation • CAS, MBA

School of Nursing
Dr. Kathleen Wheeler, Director
Programs in:
  family nurse practitioner • CAS, MSN
  psychiatric nurse practitioner • MSN

QUINNIPIAC COLLEGE
Hamden, CT 06518-1904

http://www.quinnipiac.edu/

Independent coed comprehensive institution. *Enrollment: 5,571 graduate, professional, and undergraduate students. Graduate faculty: 121 full-time, 75 part-time. Computer facilities: Campuswide network is available with full Internet access. Total number of PCs/ terminals supplied for student use: 280. Computer services are offered at no charge. Library facilities: main library plus 1 additional on-campus library. Graduate expenses: Tuition of $395 per credit hour. Fees of $380 per year full-time. General application contact: Scott Farber, Director of Graduate Admissions, 203-287-5238.*

School of Business
Dr. Phillip Frese, Dean
Programs in:
  accounting • MBA
  computer information systems • MBA
  economics • MBA
  finance • MBA
  health administration • MHA
  health management • MBA
  international business • MBA
  long-term care administration • MHA
  management • MBA
  marketing • MBA

School of Health Sciences
Joseph Woods, Dean
Programs in:
  advanced clinical practice • MSPT
  biomedical sciences • MHS
  laboratory management • MHS
  microbiology • MHS
  molecular and cell biology • MS
  nurse practitioner • MSN
  orthopedic physical therapy • MSPT
  pathologists' assistant • MHS
  physician assistant • MHS

School of Law
Neil H. Cogan, Dean
Program in:
  law • JD

School of Liberal Arts
David Stineback, Dean
Programs in:
  biology • MAT
  chemistry • MAT
  English • MAT
  French • MAT
  history/social studies • MAT
  journalism • MS
  mathematics • MAT
  physics • MAT
  Spanish • MAT

SACRED HEART UNIVERSITY
Fairfield, CT 06432-1000

http://www.sacredheart.edu/

Independent-religious coed comprehensive institution. *Enrollment: 5,545 graduate, professional, and undergraduate students. Graduate faculty: 68 full-time, 128 part-time. Library facilities: Ryan-Matura Library plus 1 additional on-campus library. Graduate expenses: Tuition of $365 per credit. Fees of $78 per semester. General application contact: Linda B. Kirby, Dean of Graduate Admissions, 203-371-7880.*

Graduate Studies

College of Arts and Sciences
Programs in:
  chemistry • MS
  computer and information science • MS
  religious studies • MA

College of Business
Scott Colvin, Director
Programs in:
  business administration • MBA
  health care administration • MBA
  health systems management • MA

College of Education and Health Professions
Programs in:
  administration • CAS
  education • CAS
  elementary education • MAT
  nursing administration • MSN
  physical therapy • MSPT
  secondary education • MAT

SAINT JOSEPH COLLEGE
West Hartford, CT 06117-2700

http://www.sjc.edu/?homepage/

Independent-religious coed comprehensive institution. *Enrollment:* 1,938 graduate, professional, and undergraduate students. Graduate faculty: *40 full-time, 50 part-time.* Computer facilities: *Campuswide network is available with full Internet access. Total number of PCs/ terminals supplied for student use: 35. Computer service fees are included with tuition and fees.* Library facilities: *Pius XII Library.* Graduate expenses: *$395 per credit.* General application contact: *Dr. Mark Kosinski, Associate Dean, 860-232-4571 Ext. 261.*

Graduate Division
Dr. Mark Kosinski, Associate Dean

Division of Nursing
Dr. Virginia Knowlden, Director
Programs in:
    family health nursing • MS
    psychiatric/mental health nursing • MS

Field of Education and Counseling
Dr. Gerard Thibodeau, Co-Chair, Education Department
Programs in:
    counseling • Certificate, MA
    early childhood education/special education • MA
    elementary education • MA
    marriage and family therapy • MA
    secondary education • MA
    special education • MA
    special education/counseling • MA

Field of Natural Sciences
Dr. Billye Auclair, Chairman
Programs in:
    biology • Certificate, MS
    chemistry • Certificate
    chemistry and biological chemistry • MS
    general science • MS
    science education • MS

Field of Religious Studies
Dr. J. Milburn Thompson, Chairperson
Program in:
    religious studies • Certificate, MA

Field of Social Sciences
Dr. Mary Alice Wolf, Director
Programs in:
    human development/gerontology • MA
    nutrition • MS

SOUTHERN CONNECTICUT STATE UNIVERSITY
New Haven, CT 06515-1355

http://www.scsu.ctstateu.edu/

Public coed comprehensive institution. *Enrollment:* 11,412 graduate, professional, and undergraduate students. Graduate faculty: *374 full-time.* Computer facilities: *Campuswide network is available with full Internet access. Total number of PCs/terminals supplied for student use: 250. Computer service fees are included with tuition and fees.* Library facilities: *Hilton C. Buley Library.* Graduate expenses: *Tuition of $2632 per year full-time, $188 per credit part-time for state residents; $7200 per year full-time, $188 per credit part-time for nonresidents. Fees of $1806 per year full-time, $45 per semester part-time for state residents; $2703 per year full-time, $45 per semester part-time for nonresidents.* General application contact: *Roseann Diana, Associate Dean, 203-392-7000.*

Graduate Studies and Continuing Education
Dr. Sandra Holley, Dean

School of Arts and Sciences
Dr. Donna Jean Fredeen, Interim Dean
Programs in:
    art education • MS
    biology • MS, MS Ed
    chemistry • MS
    chemistry education • MS Ed
    English • MA, MS, MS Ed
    French • MA, MS Ed
    history • MA, MS Ed
    mathematics • MS Ed
    multicultural-bilingual education/teaching English to
      speakers of other languages • MS
    political science • MS
    psychology • MA
    Romance languages • MA, MS Ed
    sociology • MS
    Spanish • MA, MS Ed
    women's studies • MA

School of Business
Dr. James Finlay, Dean
Program in:
    business • MBA

School of Communication, Information and Library Science
Dr. Nancy Disbrow, Chairperson
Programs in:
    instructional technology • MS
    library/information studies • Diploma
    library science • MLS

School of Education
Dr. Rodney Lane, Dean
Programs in:
    classroom teacher specialist • Diploma
    counseling • Diploma, MS

Southern Connecticut State University (continued)
- counseling and school psychology • Diploma
- early childhood education • MS Ed
- educational leadership • Diploma
- elementary education • MS Ed
- environmental education • MS
- foundational studies • Diploma
- health science • MS Ed
- physical education • MS Ed
- physical education and recreation for the handicapped • MS Ed
- reading • Diploma, MS Ed
- research measurement and evaluation • MS
- school psychology • MS
- science education • Diploma, MS
- secondary education • MS Ed
- special education • Diploma, MS Ed

School of Professional Studies
Dr. Fay Miller, Dean
Programs in:
- marriage and family therapy • MFT
- nursing • MSN
- public health • MPH
- recreation and leisure studies • MS
- social work • MSW
- speech pathology and audiology • MS
- urban studies • MS

UNIVERSITY OF BRIDGEPORT
Bridgeport, CT 06601
http://www.bridgeport.edu/

Independent coed comprehensive institution. *Enrollment: 2,427 graduate, professional, and undergraduate students. Graduate faculty: 88 full-time, 219 part-time. Computer facilities: Campuswide network is available with full Internet access. Total number of PCs/ terminals supplied for student use: 300. Computer services are offered at no charge. Library facilities: Magnus Wahlstom Library plus 1 additional on-campus library. Graduate expenses: $340 per credit. General application contact: Suzanne D. Wilcox, Dean of Admissions and Financial Aid, 203-576-4552.*

College of Graduate and Undergraduate Studies
Anthony J. Guerra, Dean

Division of Allied Health Technology
Dr. Blonnie Y. Thompson, Director
Program in:
- human nutrition • MS

School of Business
Dr. Glenn A. Bassett, Director
Programs in:
- business • MS
- business administration • MBA

School of Education and Human Resources
Dr. James T. Ritchie, Director
Programs in:
- community agency counseling • MS
- computer specialist • Diploma, MS
- early childhood education • Diploma, MS
- education • MS
- educational management • Diploma, Ed D
- elementary education • Diploma, MS
- human resource development and counseling • MS
- international education • Diploma, MS
- reading specialist • Diploma, MS
- secondary education • Diploma, MS

School of Science, Engineering, and Technology
Dr. Steven F. Malary, Director
Programs in:
- computer engineering • MS
- computer science • MS
- electrical engineering • MS
- management engineering • MS
- mechanical engineering • MS

College of Chiropractic
Dr. Francis A. Zolli, Dean
Program in:
- chiropractic • DC

College of Naturopathic Medicine
Dr. Edward V. O'Connor, Dean
Program in:
- naturopathic medicine • ND

UNIVERSITY OF CONNECTICUT
Storrs, CT 06269
http://www.uconn.edu/

Public coed university. *Enrollment: 21,753 graduate, professional, and undergraduate students. Graduate faculty: 1,103. Computer facilities: Campuswide network is available with full Internet access. Total number of PCs/terminals supplied for student use: 10,004. Computer services are offered at no charge. Library facilities: Homer D. Babbidge Library plus 3 additional on-campus libraries. Graduate expenses: Tuition of $5272 per year full-time, $293 per credit part-time for state residents; $13,696 per year full-time, $761 per credit part-time for nonresidents. Fees of $948 per year full-time, $640 per year part-time. General application contact: Mary Lou Balinskas, Director of Graduate Admissions, 860-486-3617.*

Graduate School
Robert V. Smith, Dean
Programs in:
- biomedical science • PhD
- dental science • M Dent Sc
- public health • MPH

College of Agriculture and Natural Resources
Kirklyn M. Kerr, Dean
Programs in:
   agricultural and resource economics • MS, PhD
   animal science • MS, PhD
   natural resources: land, water, and air • MS
   nutritional sciences • MS, PhD
   pathobiology • MS, PhD
   plant and soil sciences • MS, PhD

College of Liberal Arts and Sciences
Ross D. MacKinnon, Dean
Programs in:
   African studies • MA
   anthropology • MA, PhD
   behavioral neuroscience • PhD
   biochemistry • MS, PhD
   biophysics • MS, PhD
   biopsychology • MA, PhD
   biotechnology • MS
   botany • MS, PhD
   cell and developmental biology • MS, PhD
   chemistry • MS, PhD
   child/developmental psychology • PhD
   clinical psychology • PhD
   cognition/instruction psychology • PhD
   communication processes and marketing
      communication • PhD
   comparative literature and cultural studies • MA, PhD
   developmental psychobiology • MS, PhD
   ecological psychology • PhD
   ecology • MS, PhD
   economics • MA, PhD
   English • MA, PhD
   entomology • MS, PhD
   French • MA, PhD
   general experimental psychology • PhD
   genetics • MS, PhD
   geography • MS, PhD
   geology • MS, PhD
   geophysics • MS, PhD
   history • MA, PhD
   industrial and organizational psychology • PhD
   international studies • MA
   interpersonal communication • MA
   Italian • MA, PhD
   language psychology • PhD
   Latin American studies • MA
   linguistics • MA, PhD
   mass communication • MA
   mathematics • MS, PhD
   medieval studies • MA, PhD
   microbiology • MS, PhD
   neurobiology • MS, PhD
   neuroscience • MA
   nonverbal communication • MA
   oceanography • MS, PhD
   organizational communication • MA
   philosophy • MA, PhD
   physics • MS, PhD
   physiology • MS, PhD
   plant molecular and cell biology • MS, PhD
   political science • MA, PhD

   public affairs • MPA
   Slavic and East European studies • MA
   social psychology • PhD
   sociology • MA, PhD
   Spanish • MA, PhD
   speech, language, and hearing • MA, PhD
   statistics • MS, PhD
   systematics • MS, PhD
   Western European studies • MA
   zoology • MS, PhD

School of Allied Health Professions
Joseph W. Smey, Dean
Program in:
   allied health professions • MS

School of Business Administration
Thomas G. Gutteridge, Dean
Programs in:
   accounting • MBA, PhD
   finance • PhD
   general business administration • MBA
   health care management • MBA
   human resources management • MBA
   management • MBA, PhD
   marketing • MBA, PhD

School of Education
Richard L. Schwab, Dean
Programs in:
   adult and vocational education • MA, PhD
   bilingual and bicultural education • MA, PhD
   cognition and instruction • PhD
   counseling psychology • MA, PhD
   curriculum and instruction • MA, PhD
   educational administration • MA, PhD
   educational psychology • MA, PhD
   educational studies • MA, PhD
   elementary education • MA, PhD
   English education • MA, PhD
   evaluation and measurement • MA, PhD
   foreign languages education • MA, PhD
   gifted and talented • MA, PhD
   history and social science education • MA, PhD
   instructional media and technology • MA, PhD
   leisure science • MA, PhD
   mathematics education • MA, PhD
   professional higher education administration • MA, PhD
   reading education • MA, PhD
   school psychology • MA, PhD
   science education • MA, PhD
   secondary education • MA, PhD
   special education • MA, PhD
   sport science • MA, PhD

School of Engineering
Harold Brody, Dean
Programs in:
   aerospace engineering • MS, PhD
   applied mechanics • PhD
   artificial intelligence • MS, PhD
   biological engineering • MS
   biomedical engineering • MS, PhD
   chemical engineering • MS, PhD

University of Connecticut (continued)

civil engineering • MS, PhD

computer architecture • MS, PhD

computer science • MS, PhD

control and communication systems • MS, PhD

electromagnetics and physical electronics • MS, PhD

environmental engineering • MS, PhD

fluid dynamics • PhD

material science • MS, PhD

mechanical engineering • MS, PhD

metallurgy • MS, PhD

ocean engineering • MS, PhD

operating systems • MS, PhD

polymer science • MS, PhD

robotics • MS, PhD

software engineering • MS, PhD

School of Family Studies

Charles M. Super, Dean

Programs in:

family studies • MS, PhD

human development and family relations • MA, PhD

School of Fine Arts

Robert H. Gray, Dean

Programs in:

art and art history • MFA

composition • M Mus

conducting • DMA, M Mus

dramatic arts • MA, MFA

historical musicology • MA

music education • M Mus, PhD

music theory and history • PhD

performance • DMA, M Mus

psychomusicology • PhD

theory • MA

School of Nursing

Barbara K. Redman, Dean

Programs in:

nurse education • MS

nursing • PhD

nursing management • MS

School of Pharmacy

Michael C. Gerald, Dean

Programs in:

medicinal chemistry • MS, PhD

natural products chemistry • MS, PhD

pharmaceutics • MS, PhD

pharmacology and toxicology • MS, PhD

School of Social Work

Mark Abrahamson, Dean

Program in:

social work • MSW

School of Law

Program in:

law • JD

UNIVERSITY OF HARTFORD
West Hartford, CT 06117-1599

http://www.hartford.edu/

Independent coed comprehensive institution. *Enrollment: 7,089 graduate, professional, and undergraduate students. Graduate faculty: 126 full-time, 88 part-time. Computer facilities: Campuswide network is available with full Internet access. Computer service fees are included with tuition and fees. Library facilities: W. H. Mortensen Library plus 3 additional on-campus libraries. Graduate expenses: Tuition of $260 per credit hour (minimum). Fees of $60 per year. General application contact: Nancy Clubb-Lazzerini, Coordinator of Graduate Applications, 860-768-4373.*

Barney School of Business and Public Administration

Corine T. Norgaard, Dean

Programs in:

accounting • MBA, MSPA

business administration • MBA

business and public administration • EMBA

finance • MBA

human resource management • MBA, MSOB

insurance • MBA

international business • MBA

life insurance • MSI

management information systems • MBA

marketing • MBA

operations management • MBA

organizational behavior • MBA

organizational development • MSOB

property and casualty insurance • MSI

quantitative decision making • MBA

strategy and policy • MBA

taxation • MST

College of Arts and Sciences

Dr. Edward Gray, Dean

Programs in:

biology • MS

biopsychology • MA

clinical practices • MA

clinical psychology • Psy D

communication • MA

health psychology • MA

industrial psychology • MA

school psychology • MS

College of Education, Nursing, and Health Professions

Dr. David A. Caruso, Dean

Programs in:

administration and supervision • CAGS, Certificate, M Ed

counseling • Certificate, M Ed, MS

early childhood education • M Ed

educational computing and technology • M Ed

educational leadership • Ed D

elementary education • M Ed

nursing • MSN
secondary education • M Ed
special education • M Ed

College of Engineering
Dr. Hemchandra M. Shertukde, Director of Graduate
Studies
Program in;
    engineering • M Eng

Hartford Art School
Stephen H. Keller, Assistant Dean
Program in:
    art • MFA

Hartt School of Music
Dr. Malcolm Morrison, Interim Dean
Programs in:
    accompanying • MM
    applied music • DMA, Diploma, MM
    choral • Diploma, MM
    composition • DMA, Diploma, MM
    conducting • Diploma, MM
    early childhood education • MM
    history • MM
    instrumental • Diploma, MM
    liturgical music • MM
    music education • DMA, MM
    opera • Diploma, MM
    pedagogy • MM
    performance • MM
    performance practice • MM
    research • MM
    scholarship and research • MM
    theory • MM

UNIVERSITY OF NEW HAVEN
West Haven, CT 06516-1916

http://www.newhaven.edu/

Independent coed university. *Enrollment: 4,753 graduate, professional, and undergraduate students. Graduate faculty: 150 full-time, 100 part-time. Library facilities: Marvin K. Peterson Library. Graduate expenses: Tuition of $1125 per course. Fees of $13 per trimester. General application contact: Joseph L. Spellman, Director of Admissions and Operations, 203-932-7133.*

Graduate School
Dr. Jerry L. Allen, Dean of Graduate Studies

College of Arts and Sciences
Dr. Nancy Carriuolo, Dean
Programs in:
    cellular and molecular biology • MS
    community psychology • Certificate, MA
    education • 6th Year Diploma, MS
    environmental sciences • MS

hospitality and tourism • MS
human nutrition • MS
industrial and organizational psychology • Certificate,
    MA

School of Business
Dr. Linda Martin, Dean
Programs in:
    accounting • MBA
    business administration • EMBA
    business policy and strategy • MBA
    computer and information science • MBA
    corporate taxation • MS
    finance • MBA
    finance and financial services • MS
    financial accounting • MS
    health care administration • MS
    health care management • MBA, MPA
    health care marketing • MBA
    hotel and restaurant management • MBA
    human resources management • MBA
    industrial relations • MS
    international business logistics • MBA
    management and organization • MBA
    management science • MBA
    management systems • Sc D
    managerial accounting • MS
    marketing • MBA
    operations research • MBA
    personnel and labor relations • MPA
    public relations • MBA
    public taxation • MS
    taxation • MS
    telecommunications • MBA
    travel and tourism administration • MBA

School of Engineering and Applied Science
Dr. M. Jerry Kenig, Dean
Programs in:
    applications software • MS
    civil engineering design • Certificate
    electrical engineering • MSEE
    environmental engineering • MS
    industrial engineering • MSIE
    logistics • Certificate
    management information systems • MS
    mechanical engineering • MSME
    operations research • MS
    systems software • MS

School of Public Safety and Professional Studies
Dr. Thomas Johnson, Dean
Programs in:
    advanced investigation • MS
    correctional counseling • MS
    criminalistics • MS
    criminal justice management • MS
    fire science • MS
    forensic science • MS
    industrial hygiene • MS
    occupational safety and health management • MS
    security management • MS

WESTERN CONNECTICUT STATE UNIVERSITY
Danbury, CT 06810-6885

http://www.wcsu.ctstate.edu/

Public coed comprehensive institution. *Enrollment: 5,421 graduate, professional, and undergraduate students. Graduate faculty: 41 full-time, 7 part-time. Computer facilities: Campuswide network is available with full Internet access. Computer service fees are applied as a separate charge. Library facilities: Ruth A. Haas Library plus 1 additional on-campus library. Graduate expenses: Tuition of $4127 per year (minimum) full-time, $178 per credit hour part-time for state residents; $9581 per year (minimum) full-time, $178 per credit hour part-time for nonresidents. Fees of $25 per year part-time. General application contact: William Hawkins, Acting Director of Graduate Studies, 203-837-8241.*

Division of Graduate Studies
William Hawkins, Acting Director of Graduate Studies

Ancell School of Business and Public Administration
Dr. Ronald Benson, Acting Dean
Program in:
   business and public administration • MBA, MHA, MSA

School of Arts and Sciences
Dr. Carol Hawkes, Dean
Programs in:
   biological and environmental sciences • MA
   English • MA
   history • MA
   mathematics and computer science • MA
   oceanography and limnology • MA
   theoretical mathematics • MA

School of Professional Studies
Walter Bernstein, Dean
Programs in:
   education • MS
   elementary education • MS
   music education • MS
   nursing • MSN
   reading • MS
   school counselor • MS
   secondary education • MS

YALE UNIVERSITY
New Haven, CT 06520

http://www.yale.edu/

Independent coed university. *Enrollment: 10,982 graduate, professional, and undergraduate students. Graduate faculty: 3,125. Computer facilities: Campuswide network is available with full Internet access. Total number of PCs/terminals supplied for student use: 350. Computer service fees are applied as a separate charge. Library facilities: Sterling Memorial Library plus 40 additional on-campus libraries. Graduate expenses: $22,760 per year. General application contact: Admissions Information, 203-432-2770.*

Divinity School
Dr. Richard J. Wood, Dean
Program in:
   theology • M Div, MAR, STM

Graduate School of Arts and Sciences
Dr. Susan Hockfield, Dean
Programs in:
   accounting • PhD
   African-American studies • MA, PhD
   African studies • MA
   American studies • MA, PhD
   anthropology • MA, PhD
   applied mathematics • M Phil, MS, PhD
   applied mechanics and mechanical engineering • M Phil, MS, PhD
   applied physics • MS, PhD
   archaeological studies • MA
   astronomy • MS, PhD
   biophysical chemistry • PhD
   cell biology • PhD
   cellular and molecular physiology • PhD
   chemical engineering • MS, PhD
   classics • PhD
   comparative literature • PhD
   computer science • PhD
   developmental biology • PhD
   East Asian languages and literatures • PhD
   East Asian studies • MA
   economics • PhD
   electrical engineering • MS, PhD
   English language and literature • MA, PhD
   environmental sciences • PhD
   experimental pathology • PhD
   financial economics • PhD
   forestry • PhD
   French • MA, PhD
   genetics • PhD
   genetics, development, and molecular biology • PhD
   geochemistry • PhD
   geophysics • PhD
   Germanic language and literature • MA, PhD
   history • MA, PhD
   history of art • PhD
   history of medicine and the life sciences • MS, PhD
   immunobiology • PhD
   immunology • PhD
   inorganic chemistry • PhD
   international and development economics • MA
   international relations • MA
   Italian language and literature • PhD
   linguistics • PhD
   marketing • PhD
   mathematics • MS, PhD
   medieval studies • MA, PhD
   meteorology • PhD
   microbiology • PhD
   mineralogy and crystallography • PhD
   molecular biology • PhD

molecular biophysics and biochemistry • MS, PhD
music • MA, PhD
Near Eastern languages and civilizations • MA, PhD
neurobiology • PhD
neuroscience • PhD
oceanography • PhD
operations research/management science • PhD
organic chemistry • PhD
paleoecology • PhD
paleontology and stratigraphy • PhD
petrology • PhD
pharmacological sciences and molecular medicine • PhD
pharmacology • PhD
philosophy • PhD
physical chemistry • PhD
physics • PhD
plant sciences • PhD
political science • PhD
psychology • MS, PhD
religious studies • PhD
Renaissance studies • PhD
Russian and East European studies • MA
Slavic languages and literatures • MA, PhD
sociology • PhD
Spanish and Portuguese • MA, PhD
statistics • MS, PhD
structural geology • PhD

Programs in Engineering and Applied Science
Dr. Susan Hockfield, Dean, Graduate School of Arts and
 Sciences
Programs in:
 applied mechanics and mechanical engineering •
  M Phil, MS, PhD
 applied physics • MS, PhD
 chemical engineering • MS, PhD
 electrical engineering • MS, PhD

Law School
Anthony T. Kronman, Dean
Program in:
 law • JD, JSD, LL M, MSL

School of Architecture
Fred Koetter, Dean
Program in:
 architecture • M Arch, M Env Des

School of Art
Richard Benson, Dean
Programs in:
 graphic design • MFA
 painting/printmaking • MFA
 photography • MFA
 sculpture • MFA

School of Drama
Dr. Stan Wojewodski Jr., Dean/Artistic Director
Program in:
 drama • Certificate, DFA, MFA

School of Forestry and Environmental Studies
Dr. John Gordon, Dean
Program in:
 forestry and environmental studies • DFES, MES, MF,
  MFS, PhD

School of Management
Jeffrey E. Garten, Dean
Programs in:
 accounting • PhD
 business administration • MBA
 financial economics • PhD
 marketing • PhD

School of Medicine
Dr. David A. Kessler, Dean
Programs in:
 biostatistics • Dr PH, MPH, PhD
 chronic disease epidemiology • Dr PH, MPH, PhD
 environmental health • Dr PH, MPH, PhD
 epidemiology of microbial diseases • Dr PH, MPH, PhD
 genetics, development, and molecular biology • PhD
 health policy and administration • Dr PH, MPH, PhD
 immunology • PhD
 international health • MPH
 medicine • MD
 microbiology • PhD
 molecular biophysics and biochemistry • PhD
 neuroscience • PhD
 parasitology • PhD
 pharmacological sciences and molecular medicine • PhD
 physician associate • Certificate

School of Music
Robert Blocker, Dean
Program in:
 music • AD, Certificate, DMA, MM, MMA

School of Nursing
Judith B. Krauss, Dean
Program in:
 nursing • DN Sc, MSN, Post Master's Certificate

DELAWARE

DELAWARE STATE UNIVERSITY
Dover, DE 19901-2277

http://www.dsc.edu/

Public coed comprehensive institution. Library facilities: *William C. Jason Library* plus 1 additional on-campus library. General application contact: *Dean of Graduate Studies and Research, 302-739-5143.*

Delaware State University (continued)
Graduate Programs
Programs in:
  applied chemistry • MS
  biology • MS
  biology education • MS
  business administration • MBA
  chemistry • MS
  curriculum and instruction • MA
  education • MA
  physics • MS
  physics teaching • MS
  science education • MA
  social work • MSW
  special education • MA

UNIVERSITY OF DELAWARE
Newark, DE 19716

http://www.udel.edu/

Public coed university. *Enrollment:* 21,722 graduate, professional, and undergraduate students. Graduate faculty: 964. Library facilities: *Hugh M. Morris Library plus 4 additional on-campus libraries.* Graduate expenses: *Tuition of $4250 per year full-time, $236 per credit hour part-time for state residents; $12,250 per year full-time, $681 per credit hour part-time for nonresidents. Fees of $466 per year full-time, $15 per semester (minimum) part-time. General application contact: Praria A. Stavis-Hicks, Associate Director for Graduate Admissions, 302-831-8486.*

College of Agriculture and Natural Resources
Dr. John C. Nye, Dean
Programs in:
  animal sciences • MS, PhD
  avian ecology • MS
  biology • PhD
  entomology • MS
  evolution and taxonomy • MS
  food and resource economics • MS
  food sciences • MS
  horticulture • MS
  insect biological control • MS
  insect ecology and behavior • MS
  insect genetics • MS
  operations research • MS, PhD
  pest management • MS
  plant and soil sciences • MS, PhD
  plant-insect interactions • MS
  plant science • PhD

College of Arts and Science
Margaret L. Andersen, Interim Dean
Programs in:
  acting • MFA
  American civilization • PhD
  applied mathematics • MA, MS, PhD
  art • MA, MFA

art conservation research • PhD
art history • MA, PhD
biochemistry • MA, MS, PhD
biopsychology • PhD
chemistry • MA, MS, PhD
climatology • PhD
clinical psychology • PhD
cognitive psychology • PhD
communication • MA
computer and information sciences • MS, PhD
criminology • MA, PhD
early American culture • MA
ecology • MS, PhD
English education • MA
English literature • MA
foreign language pedagogy • MA
French • MA
genetic and molecular biology • MS, PhD
geography • MA, MS
geology • MS, PhD
German • MA
history • MA, PhD
international relations • MA
liberal studies • MALS
linguistics • MA, PhD
literature • PhD
mathematics • MA, MS, PhD
microbiology • MS, PhD
museum studies • Certificate
neurobiology • MS, PhD
neuroscience and biology • PhD
neuroscience and psychology • PhD
physical therapy • MPT
physics and astronomy • MS, PhD
physiology/anatomy • MS, PhD
political science • MA, PhD
practicing art conservation • MS
social psychology • PhD
sociology • MA, PhD
Spanish • MA
stage management • MFA
technical production • MFA

College of Business and Economics
Dana J. Johnson, Dean
Programs in:
  accounting • MS
  business administration • MBA
  economics • MA, MS, PhD
  economics for educators • MA

College of Engineering
Stuart L. Cooper, Dean
Programs in:
  chemical engineering • M Ch E, PhD
  electrical engineering • MEE, PhD
  environmental engineering • MAS, MCE, PhD
  geotechnical engineering • MAS, MCE, PhD
  materials science and engineering • MMSE, PhD
  mechanical engineering • MME, PhD
  ocean engineering • MAS, MCE, PhD
  railroad engineering • MAS, MCE, PhD

structural engineering • MAS, MCE, PhD
transportation engineering • MAS, MCE, PhD
water resource engineering • MAS, MCE, PhD

College of Health and Nursing Sciences
Dr. Betty J. Paulanka, Dean
Programs in:
applied nutrition • MS
biomechanics • MS
biomechanics and movement science • MS, PhD
cardiac rehabilitation • MS
cardiopulmonary • Certificate, MSN
clinical nurse specialist • Certificate, MSN
clinical nurse specialist/nurse practitioner • Certificate
exercise physiology • MS
family nurse practitioner • Certificate, MSN
general human nutrition • MS
gerontology • Certificate, MSN
health promotion • MS
nursing • MSN
nursing administration • Certificate, MSN
nutrient metabolism and utilization • MS
oncology/immune deficiency • Certificate, MSN
pediatrics • Certificate, MSN
professional development • MA
women's health • Certificate, MSN

College of Human Resources, Education and Public Policy
Dr. Daniel Rich, Dean
Programs in:
college counseling • M Ed
family studies • PhD
individual and family studies • MS
student affairs practice in higher education • M Ed

Center for Energy and Environmental Policy
Dr. John Byrne, Director
Program in:
environmental and energy policy • MS, PhD

School of Education
Dr. Robert Hampel, Director
Programs in:
cognition and instruction • MA
cognition, development, and instruction • PhD
curriculum and instruction • M Ed, PhD
educational leadership • Ed D, M Ed
educational policy • MA, PhD
English as a second language/bilingualism • MA
exceptional children • M Ed
exceptionality • PhD
instruction • MI
measurements, statistics, and evaluation • MA, PhD
school counseling • M Ed
school psychology • MA
secondary education • M Ed

School of Urban Affairs and Public Policy
Dr. Jeffrey A. Raffel, Director
Programs in:
community development and nonprofit leadership • MA
energy and environmental policy • MA

governance, planning and management • PhD
historic preservation • MA
public administration • MPA
social and urban policy • PhD
technology, environment and society • PhD

College of Marine Studies
Dr. Carolyn A. Thoroughgood, Dean
Program in:
marine studies • MMP, MS, PhD

WILMINGTON COLLEGE
New Castle, DE 19720-6491

http://www.wilmcoll.edu/

Independent coed comprehensive institution. *Enrollment: 4,155 graduate, professional, and undergraduate students. Graduate faculty: 42 full-time, 146 part-time. Library facilities: main library. Graduate expenses: Tuition of $4410 per year full-time, $735 per course part-time. Fees of $50 per year. General application contact: Michael Lee, Director of Admissions and Financial Aid, 302-328-9401 Ext. 102.*

Division of Behavioral Science
Dr. Barbara Snyder, Chair
Programs in:
community counseling • MS
criminal justice studies • MS
rehabilitation counseling • MS

Division of Business
Dr. John Camp, Chair
Programs in:
business administration • MBA
human resource management • MS
management • MS
public administration • MS

Division of Education
Dr. Barbara Raetsch, Chair
Programs in:
elementary and secondary school counseling • M Ed
elementary special education • M Ed
elementary studies • M Ed
innovation and leadership • Ed D
school leadership • M Ed

Division of Nursing
Dr. Betty Caffo, Chair
Programs in:
family nurse practitioner • MSN
nursing • MSN

DISTRICT OF COLUMBIA

AMERICAN UNIVERSITY
Washington, DC 20016-8001
http://www.american.edu/

Independent-religious coed university. *Enrollment: 9,840 graduate, professional, and undergraduate students. Graduate faculty: 422 full-time, 215 part-time. Computer facilities: Campuswide network is available with full Internet access. Computer services are offered at no charge. Library facilities: University Library plus 1 additional on-campus library. Graduate expenses: Tuition of $687 per credit hour. Fees of $180 per year full-time, $110 per year part-time. General application contact: Office of Graduate Affairs and Admissions, 202-885-6000.*

College of Arts and Sciences
Dr. Howard M. Wachtel, Acting Dean
Programs in:
anthropology • MA, PhD
applied anthropology • MA
applied mathematics • MA
applied sociology • MA
applied statistics • Certificate
art history • MA
arts management • Certificate, MA
biology • MA, MS
chemistry • MS, PhD
clinical psychology • PhD
computer science • MS
creative writing • MFA
dance • MA
development banking • MA
economics • MA, PhD
environmental studies • MA, MS
experimental/biological psychology • MA
experimental psychology • PhD
financial economics for public policy • MA
French studies • MA
general psychology • MA
health fitness management • MS
history • MA, PhD
information systems • Certificate, MS
international training and education • MA
literature • MA
mathematics • MA
mathematics education • PhD
painting, sculpture and printmaking • MFA
personality/social psychology • MA
philosophy • MA
philosophy and social policy • MA
physics • MS, PhD
Russian studies • MA
sociology • MA, PhD
sociology/justice • PhD
Spanish: Latin American studies • MA
statistical computing • MS
statistics • MA, PhD
statistics for policy analysis • MS
teaching English to speakers of other languages • Certificate, MA
toxicology • Certificate, MS
translation • Certificate

School of Education
Dr. Charles Tesconi, Dean
Programs in:
education • PhD
educational leadership • MA
elementary education • MAT
English for speakers of other languages • MAT
learning disabilities • MA
mathematics education • PhD
secondary teaching • MAT
specialized studies • MA

Kogod College of Business Administration
Dr. Stevan R. Holmberg, Acting Dean
Programs in:
accounting • MBA, MS
entrepreneurship and management • MBA
finance • MBA, MS
human resource management • MBA
international business • MBA
management of global technology • MBA
marketing • MBA
real estate and urban development • MBA
taxation • MS

School of Communication
Sanford J. Ungar, Dean
Programs in:
broadcast journalism • MA
economic journalism • MA
film and electronic media • MFA
film and video production • MA
film criticism • MA
international journalism • MA
journalism and public affairs • MA
news media studies • MA
print journalism • MA
print journalism: radio and television • MA
producing for film and video • MA
public communication • MA
public policy journalism • MA
script writing • MA

School of International Service
Dr. Louis W. Goodman, Dean
Programs in:
comparative and regional studies • MA
development management • MS
environmental policy • MA
international communication • MA
international development • MA
international development management • Certificate
international economic policy • MA
international peace and conflict resolution • MA
international politics • MA
international relations • PhD
U.S. foreign policy • MA

School of Public Affairs
Dr. William Leo Grande, Acting Dean
Programs in:
    American politics • MA
    comparative politics • MA
    justice • MS
    organization development • MSOD
    personnel and human resource management • MS
    political science • MA, PhD
    public administration • MPA, PhD
    public policy • MPP
    sociology/justice • PhD

Washington College of Law
Claudio Grossman, Dean
Programs in:
    international legal studies • LL M
    law • JD
    law and government • LL M

THE CATHOLIC UNIVERSITY OF AMERICA
Washington, DC 20064
http://www.cua.edu/

Independent-religious coed university. *Enrollment: 5,616 graduate, professional, and undergraduate students. Graduate faculty: 360 full-time, 299 part-time. Computer facilities: Campuswide network is available with full Internet access. Total number of PCs/terminals supplied for student use: 400. Computer service fees are included with tuition and fees. Library facilities: Mullen Library plus 7 additional on-campus libraries. Graduate expenses: Tuition of $17,325 per year full-time, $668 per credit hour part-time. Fees of $680 per year full-time, $360 per year part-time. General application contact: Barbara J. Mullaney, Coordinator, Graduate Student Services, 202-319-5057.*

Columbus School of Law
Bernard Dobranski, Dean
Program in:
    law • JD

National Catholic School of Social Service
Dr. Ann Patrick Conrad, Dean
Program in:
    social service • MSW, PhD

School of Architecture and Planning
Gregory K. Hunt, Dean
Program in:
    architecture and planning • M Arch, M Arch Studies

School of Arts and Sciences
Dr. Antanas Suziedelis, Dean
Programs in:
    accounting • MA
    acting, directing, and playwriting • MFA
    administration, curriculum, and policy studies • MA
    American government • MA, PhD
    anthropology • MA, PhD
    applied experimental psychology • PhD
    Byzantine studies • Certificate, MA
    Catholic school leadership • MA
    cell biology • MS, PhD
    chemistry • MS, PhD
    classics • MA
    clinical laboratory science • MS, PhD
    clinical psychology • PhD
    comparative economic systems and planning • PhD
    comparative literature • MA, PhD
    congressional studies • MA
    counselor education • MA
    early Christian studies • Certificate, MA, PhD
    economic development • PhD
    economics • MA, PhD
    educational administration • PhD
    educational psychology • PhD
    English as a second language • MA
    English language and literature • MA, PhD
    financial management • MA
    French • MA, PhD
    general psychology • MA
    German • MA
    Greek and Latin • PhD
    history • MA, PhD
    human development • PhD
    human factors • MA
    human resource management • MA
    industrial organization • PhD
    international affairs • MA
    international economics • PhD
    international political economics • MA
    Irish studies • MA
    Italian • MA
    Latin • MA
    learning and instruction • MA
    medieval studies • Certificate, MA, PhD
    microbiology • MS, PhD
    physics • MS, PhD
    policy studies • PhD
    political theory • MA, PhD
    quantitative economics • PhD
    rhetoric • MA, PhD
    Romance languages and literatures • MA, PhD
    Semitic and Egyptian languages and literature • MA, PhD
    sociology • MA, PhD
    Spanish • MA, PhD
    teacher education • MA
    theatre history and criticism • MA
    world politics • MA, PhD

The Catholic University of America (continued)

School of Engineering

Dr. William E. Kelly, Dean
Programs in:
biomedical engineering • MBE, MS Engr, PhD
civil engineering • MCE
construction management • MCE, MS Engr
design • D Engr, PhD
design and robotics • D Engr, MME, PhD
electrical engineering and computer science • D Engr,
     MEE, MS Engr, PhD
engineering management • MS Engr
environmental engineering • MCE, MS Engr
fluid and solid mechanics • PhD
fluid mechanics and thermal science • D Engr, MME,
     PhD
geotechnical engineering • MCE
mechanical design • MME
ocean and structural acoustics • MME, MS Engr, PhD
structures and structural mechanics • MCE, PhD

School of Library and Information Science

Dr. Elizabeth Aversa, Dean
Program in:
library and information science • MSLS

School of Nursing

Sr. Mary Jean Flaherty, Dean
Programs in:
administration of nursing service • MSN
adult nurse practitioner • MSN
advanced practice nursing • MSN
clinical nursing • DN Sc
education • MSN
family nurse practitioner • MSN
geriatric nurse practitioner • MSN
pediatric nurse practitioner • MSN
psychiatric-mental health • MSN
school health nurse practitioner • MSN

School of Philosophy

Dr. Jude P. Dougherty, Dean
Program in:
philosophy • MA, Ph L, PhD

School of Religious Studies

Dr. Raymond F. Collins, Dean
Programs in:
biblical studies • MA, PhD
canon law • JCD, JCL
church history • MA, PhD
history of religion • MA
liturgical studies • MA, PhD, STD, STL
religion • MA, MRE, PhD
religious education • MA, MRE, PhD
theology • D Min, M Div, MA, PhD, STB, STD, STL

The Benjamin T. Rome School of Music

Dr. Elaine R. Walter, Dean
Programs in:
accompanying and chamber music • MM
chamber music • DMA
composition • DMA, MM
instrumental conducting • DMA, MM
liturgical music • DMA, M Lit M
music education • DMA, MM
musicology • MA, PhD
orchestral instruments • DMA, MM
organ • DMA, MM
performance • DMA, MM
piano pedagogy • DMA, MM
vocal accompanying • DMA
vocal pedagogy • MM
vocal performance • MM
voice pedagogy and performance • DMA

 # GALLAUDET UNIVERSITY
Washington, DC 20002-3625

http://www.gallaudet.edu/

Independent coed university. *Enrollment:* 2,145 graduate, professional, and undergraduate students. *Graduate faculty:* 55 full-time, 20 part-time. *Library facilities: Merrill Learning Center.* Graduate expenses: *Tuition of $7064 per year full-time, $392 per credit part-time. Fees of $50 (one-time charge).* General application contact: *Deborah DeStefano, Director of Admissions, 202-651-5253.*

The Graduate School

Dr. Robert E. Johnson, Director of Graduate Education

College of Arts and Sciences
Dr. Jane Dillehay, Dean
Programs in:
clinical psychology • PhD
developmental psychology • MA
school psychology • Psy S
social work • MSW

School of Communication
Dr. Patrick B. Cox, Dean
Programs in:
audiology • Au D, MS
interpretation • MA
linguistics • MA
speech and language pathology • MS

School of Education and Human Services
Dr. William P. McCrone, Dean
Programs in:
administration • MS
administration and supervision • Ed S, PhD
community counseling • MA
early childhood education • Ed S, MA

education of deaf and hard of hearing students and multihandicapped deaf and hard of hearing students • Ed S, MA
elementary education • Ed S, MA
individualized program of study • PhD
instructional supervision • Ed S
leadership training • MS
mental health counseling • MA
parent/infant specialty • Ed S, MA
research and evaluation • MA
school counseling • MA
secondary education • Ed S, MA
special education administration • PhD

GEORGETOWN UNIVERSITY
Washington, DC 20057
http://www.georgetown.edu/

Independent-religious coed university. Computer facilities: *Campuswide network is available with full Internet access. Total number of PCs/ terminals supplied for student use: 680. Computer service fees are included with tuition and fees.* Library facilities: *Lauinger Library plus 4 additional on-campus libraries.* Graduate expenses: *Tuition of $19,128 per year full-time, $797 per credit part-time. Fees of $99 (one-time charge).* General application contact: *Dean of the Graduate School, 202-687-5974.*

Graduate School
Programs in:
American government • MA, PhD
analytical chemistry • MS, PhD
Arabic language, literature, and linguistics • MS, PhD
Arab studies • Certificate, MA
bilingual education • Certificate
biochemistry • MS, PhD
biochemistry and molecular biology • PhD
biology • MS, PhD
biostatistics and epidemiology • MS
British and American literature • MA
business administration • MBA
cell biology • PhD
chemical physics • MS, PhD
communication, culture, and technology • MA
comparative government • PhD
demography • MA
economics • PhD
German • MS, PhD
health physics • MS
Hispanic literature • MS, PhD
history • MA, PhD
inorganic chemistry • MS, PhD
international relations • PhD
linguistics • MS, PhD
microbiology and immunology • PhD
national security studies • MA
neuroscience • PhD
organic chemistry • MS, PhD

pathology • MS, PhD
pharmacology • PhD
philosophy • MA, PhD
physical chemistry • MS, PhD
physiology and biophysics • MS, PhD
political theory • PhD
psychology • PhD
radiobiology • MS
Russian and East European studies • MA
Spanish • MS, PhD
Spanish linguistics • MS, PhD
Spanish literature • MS, PhD
teaching English as a second language • Certificate, MAT
theoretical chemistry • MS, PhD

Center for German and European Studies
Program in:
German and European studies • MA

Center for Latin American Studies
Program in:
Latin American studies • MA

Edmund A. Walsh School of Foreign Service
Program in:
foreign service • MS

School for Summer and Continuing Education
Program in:
summer and continuing education • MALS

School of Business
Program in:
business administration • MBA

School of Nursing
Program in:
nursing • MS

The Georgetown Public Policy Institute
Program in:
public policy • MPP

Law Center
Programs in:
advocacy • LL M
common law studies • LL M
general • LL M
international and comparative law • LL M
labor and employment law • LL M
law • JD, SJD
securities regulation • LL M
taxation • LL M

School of Medicine
Program in:
medicine • MD

THE GEORGE WASHINGTON UNIVERSITY
Washington, DC 20052
http://www.gwu.edu/

Independent coed university. *Enrollment: 19,356 graduate, professional, and undergraduate students. Graduate faculty: 1,373 full-time, 2,659 part-time. Computer facilities: Campuswide network is available with full Internet access. Total number of PCs/terminals supplied for student use: 550. Computer service fees are included with tuition and fees. Library facilities: Melvin Gelman Library plus 2 additional on-campus libraries. Graduate expenses: Tuition of $680 per semester hour. Fees of $35 per semester hour. General application contact: Kristin Williams, Director, Graduate Enrollment Support Services, 202-994-0467.*

Columbian School of Arts and Sciences
Dr. Lester Lefton, Dean
Programs in:
American • MA
American civilization • MA, PhD
American literature • MA, PhD
analytical chemistry • MS, PhD
anthropology • MA
applied mathematics • MA, MS
applied social psychology • MA, PhD
applied statistics • MS
art history • PhD
art history-museum training • MA
art therapy • MA
baroque • MA
biochemistry and molecular biology • MS, PhD
biology • MS, PhD
biostatistics • MS, PhD
botany • MS, PhD
ceramics • MFA
chemical toxicology • MS
classical • MA
clinical psychology • PhD, Psy D
cognitive neuropsychology • PhD
computational science • MA
crime and commerce • MA
criminal justice • MA
design • MFA
developmental psychology • MA, PhD
economics • MA, PhD
English literature • MA, PhD
environmental and resource policy • MA
environmental science • MS
epidemiology • MS, PhD
folklife • MA
forensic molecular biology • MFS
forensic sciences • MFS, MSFS
geobiology • MS, PhD
geochemistry • MS, PhD
geography and regional science • MA
geology • MS, PhD
historic preservation • MA
history • MA, PhD

history and public policy • MA
human resource management • MA
human sciences • PhD
industrial and engineering statistics • MS
industrial-organizational psychology • PhD
inorganic chemistry • MS, PhD
legislative affairs • MA
management information systems • MA
material culture • MA
materials science • MS, PhD
mathematical statistics • MS
mathematics • MA, PhD
medieval • MA
methods of policy analysis • MA
microbiology • MS, PhD
modern • MA
museum studies • Certificate, MA
organic chemistry • MS, PhD
organizational management • MA
painting • MFA
philosophy and social policy • MA
photography • MFA
physical chemistry • MS, PhD
physics • MA, PhD
political science • MA, PhD
printmaking • MFA
public policy • MA, PhD
public policy-women's studies • MA
radiological sciences • PhD
religion • MA
Renaissance • MA
sculpture • MFA
security management • MA
sociology • MA
speech pathology and audiology • MA
statistical computing • MS
statistics • PhD
telecommunication studies • MA
theatre • MFA
visual communication • MFA
women's studies • MA
zoology • MS, PhD

Graduate School of Political Management
Dr. Christopher Arterton, Dean
Program in:
political management • MA

Institute for Biomedical Sciences
Dr. Lester Lefton, Dean, Columbian School of Arts and Sciences
Programs in:
biochemistry • PhD
genetics • MS, PhD
molecular and cellular oncology • PhD
neuroscience • PhD
pharmacology • MS, PhD

Elliott School of International Affairs
Dr. Harry Harding, Dean
Programs in:
East Asian studies • MA
European studies • MA

international affairs • MA
international development studies • MA
Latin American studies • MA
Russian and East European studies • MA
science, technology, and public policy • MA, PhD
security policy studies • MA

Graduate School of Education and Human Development

Dr. Mary Futrell, Dean
Programs in:
counseling • Ed D, Ed S
counseling: school, community and rehabilitation • Ed D, MA Ed
curriculum and instruction • Ed D, Ed S, MA Ed
education administration and policy studies • Ed D
educational human development • MA Ed
educational technology leadership • MA Ed
education policy studies • MA Ed
elementary education • M Ed
elementary/secondary administration and supervision • MA Ed
executive leadership • Ed D
higher education • Ed D, Ed S
higher education administration • MA Ed
human development • Ed D, Ed S
human resource development • Ed S, MA Ed
infant special education • MA Ed
international education • MA Ed
museum education • MAT
secondary education • M Ed
special education • Ed D, Ed S
special education/early childhood • MA Ed
special education of seriously emotionally disturbed students • MA Ed
transitional special education • Certificate, MA Ed

Law School

Michael Young, Dean
Program in:
law • JD, LL M, SJD

School of Business and Public Management

Dr. Susan Philips, Dean
Programs in:
accountancy • M Accy, PhD
budget and public finance • MPA
business and public management • MA
business economics and public policy • MBA
destination management • MTA
event management • MTA
executive, legislative, and regulatory management • MPA
finance • MSF
finance and investments • MBA, PhD
human resources management • MBA
information systems • MSIS
information systems management • MBA
international business • MBA, PhD
logistics, operations, and materials management • MBA, MPA
management and organizations • PhD
management decision making • MBA, PhD

management of science, technology, and innovation • MBA
managing public organizations • MPA
managing state and local governments • MPA
marketing • MBA, PhD
organizational behavior and development • MBA
policy analysis and evaluation • MPA
project management • MS
public administration • MBA, MPA, PhD
real estate development • MBA
sport management • MTA
taxation • M Tax
tourism administration • MTA
tourism and hospitality management • MBA
travel marketing • MTA

School of Engineering and Applied Science

Dr. Thomas Mazzuchi, Interim Dean
Programs in:
civil engineering • App Sc, D Sc, Engr, MS
computer science • App Sc, D Sc, Engr, MS
electrical engineering • App Sc, D Sc, Engr, MS
engineering management • App Sc, D Sc, Engr, MEM, MS
environmental engineering • App Sc, D Sc, Engr, MS
mechanical engineering • App Sc, D Sc, Engr, MS
operations research • App Sc, D Sc, MS

School of Medicine and Health Sciences

Dr. Allan B. Weingold, Vice President for Academic Affairs
Program in:
medicine • MD

School of Public Health and Health Services

Dr. Richard Riegelman, Dean
Programs in:
community-oriented primary care • MPH
environmental-occupational health • MPH
exercise science • MS
health promotion • MPH
health promotion-disease prevention • MPH
health services management and policy • MHSA, Specialist
management • MPH
maternal and child health • MPH
policy • MPH
policy and programs • MPH
public health • Dr PH
public health and health services • MSHS

 # HOWARD UNIVERSITY
Washington, DC 20059-0002

http://www.howard.edu/

Independent coed university. *Enrollment:* 10,438 graduate, professional, and undergraduate students. Graduate faculty: *335.* Computer facilities: *Campuswide network is available with full Internet access. Computer services are offered at no charge.* Library facilities: *Founders Library plus 10 additional on-campus libraries.* Graduate

Howard University (continued)
expenses: *Tuition of $10,200 per year full-time, $567 per credit hour part-time. Fees of $405 per year. General application contact: Dr. Marlene McNeil, Associate Dean for Student Relations, 202-806-6800.*

College of Dentistry
Dr. Charles F. Sanders Jr., Dean
Program in:
  dentistry • Certificate, DDS

College of Engineering, Architecture, and Computer Sciences
Dr. James H. Johnson Jr., Dean

School of Architecture and Design
Victor Dzidzienyo, Associate Dean and Director
Program in:
  architecture • M Arch, MS Arch

School of Engineering and Computer Science
Dr. James H. Johnson Jr., Dean, College of Engineering, Architecture, and Computer Sciences
Programs in:
  aerospace engineering • M Eng, PhD
  applied mechanics • M Eng, PhD
  atmospheric sciences • MS, PhD
  CAD/CAM and robotics • M Eng, PhD
  chemical engineering • MS
  civil engineering • M Eng
  electrical engineering • M Eng, PhD
  fluid and thermal sciences • M Eng, PhD
  materials science and engineering • MS, PhD
  systems and computer science • MCS

College of Medicine
Dr. Floyd J. Malveaux, Interim Vice President for Health Affairs and Dean
Programs in:
  biochemistry and molecular biology • MS, PhD
  biotechnology • MS
  medicine • MD

College of Pharmacy, Nursing and Allied Health Sciences
Dr. Cecile H. Edwards, Interim Dean

Division of Nursing
Dr. Dorothy L. Powell, Associate Dean
Programs in:
  nurse practitioner • Certificate
  primary family health nursing • MSN

Division of Pharmacy
Dr. Vafant G. Telang, Associate Dean
Program in:
  pharmacy • Pharm D

Division of Fine Arts
Dr. Tritobia H. Benjamin, Interim Associate Dean
Programs in:
  applied music • MM
  art history • MA
  ceramics • MFA
  design • MFA
  experimental studio • MFA
  music • MM Ed
  music education • MM Ed
  painting • MFA
  photography • MFA
  printmaking • MFA
  sculpture • MFA

Graduate School of Arts and Sciences
Dr. Orlando L. Taylor, Dean
Programs in:
  African studies • MA, PhD
  analytical chemistry • MS, PhD
  anatomy • MS, PhD
  applied mathematics • MS, PhD
  arts and sciences • M Eng, MCS
  biochemistry • MS, PhD
  biology • MS, PhD
  biophysics • PhD
  clinical psychology • PhD
  developmental psychology • PhD
  economics • MA, PhD
  English • MA, PhD
  exercise physiology • MS
  experimental psychology • PhD
  French • MA
  genetics and human genetics • MS, PhD
  history • MA, PhD
  inorganic chemistry • MS, PhD
  mathematics • MS, PhD
  microbiology • PhD
  neuropsychology • PhD
  nutrition • MS, PhD
  organic chemistry • MS, PhD
  personality psychology • PhD
  pharmacology • MS, PhD
  philosophy • MA
  physical chemistry • MS, PhD
  physics • MS, PhD
  physiology • PhD
  political science • MA, PhD
  polymer chemistry • MS, PhD
  psychology • MS
  public administration • MAPA
  public affairs • MA
  recreation and leisure studies • MS
  school and community health education • MS
  social psychology • PhD
  sociology • MA, PhD
  Spanish • MA
  theoretical chemistry • MS, PhD

School of Business
Dr. Barron Harvey, Dean
Programs in:
    general management • MBA
    health services administration • MBA

School of Communications
Dr. Jannette L. Dates, Dean
Programs in:
    audiology • MS
    communication sciences and disorders • PhD
    film • MFA
    intercultural communication • MA, PhD
    mass communication • MA, PhD
    organizational communication • MA, PhD
    speech pathology • MS

School of Divinity
Dr. Clarence G. Newsome, Dean
Program in:
    theology • D Min, M Div, MARS

School of Education
Dr. Veronica G. Thomas, Interim Dean
Programs in:
    counseling psychology • CAGS, Ed D, M Ed, MA, PhD
    early childhood education • CAGS, M Ed, MA, MAT
    educational administration • CAGS, M Ed, MA
    educational psychology • CAGS, Ed D, M Ed, MA, PhD
    educational supervision • CAGS, M Ed, MA
    elementary education • M Ed
    guidance and counseling • CAGS, M Ed, MA
    human development • MS
    international development education • CAGS, M Ed, MA
    reading • CAGS, M Ed, MA, MAT
    school psychology • CAGS, Ed D, M Ed, MA, PhD
    secondary curriculum and instruction • CAGS, M Ed, MA, MAT
    special education • CAGS, M Ed, MA

School of Law
Alice Gresham Bullock, Dean
Program in:
    law • JD, LL M

School of Social Work
Dr. Fariyal Ross-Sheriff, Director, PhD Program
Program in:
    social work • DSW, MSW, PhD

⊚ TRINITY COLLEGE
Washington, DC 20017-1094
http://www.trinitydc.edu/

Independent-religious coed comprehensive institution. *Enrollment:* 1,440 graduate, professional, and undergraduate students. *Graduate faculty: 11 full-time, 28 part-time.* Computer facilities: *Campuswide network is available with full Internet access. Computer service fees*

are applied as a separate charge. Library facilities: *Sister Helen Sheehan Library.* Graduate expenses: *$460 per credit hour. General application contact: Karen Goodwin, Director of Graduate Admissions, 202-884-9400.*

School of Professional Studies
Dr. Mike Caruso, Acting Dean
Programs in:
    administration in non-profit management • MA
    community health promotion and education • MA
    curriculum and instruction • M Ed
    early childhood education • MAT
    educational administration • MSA
    elementary education • MAT
    entrepreneurial development • MSA
    guidance and counseling • MA
    human resource development • MSA
    human resource management • MSA
    human resources • MSA
    instructional leadership • MSA
    literacy • M Ed
    principalship • MSA
    secondary education • MAT
    special education • MAT
    student development in higher education • MA
    urban learner • M Ed

UNIVERSITY OF THE DISTRICT OF COLUMBIA
Washington, DC 20008-1175
http://www.udc.edu/

Public coed comprehensive institution. Library facilities: *main library plus 3 additional on-campus libraries.* Graduate expenses: *Tuition of $3564 per year full-time, $198 per credit part-time for district residents; $5922 per year full-time, $329 per credit part-time for nonresidents. Fees of $990 per year full-time, $55 per credit part-time. General application contact: Director of Graduate Admissions, 202-274-5011.*

Graduate Studies

College of Arts and Sciences
Programs in:
    counseling • MA
    early childhood education • MA
    English composition and rhetoric • MA
    mathematics • MST
    speech and language pathology • MS

College of Professional Studies
Programs in:
    business administration • MBA
    public administration • MPA

University of the District of Columbia (continued)
School of Law
William L. Robinson, Dean
Program in:
 law • JD

FLORIDA

 BARRY UNIVERSITY
Miami Shores, FL 33161-6695
http://www.barry.edu/

Independent-religious coed comprehensive institution. *Enrollment:* 6,899 graduate, professional, and undergraduate students. *Graduate faculty: 154 full-time, 128 part-time.* Library facilities: *Monsignor William A. Barry Memorial Library.* Graduate expenses: $450 per credit (minimum). General application contact: *Angela Scott, Enrollment Services, Assistant Dean, 305-899-3112.*

School of Adult and Continuing Education
Dr. Larry Bee, Academic Coordinator
Program in:
 information technology • MS

School of Arts and Sciences
Dr. Laura Armesto, Dean
Programs in:
 art therapy • MS
 art therapy/clinical psychology • MS
 business/communication • MS
 clinical psychology • MS
 communication • EMS
 corporate communication • MA
 media management • MA
 pastoral ministry for Hispanics • MA
 photography • MA, MFA, MS
 production and programming • MA
 public relations • MA
 school psychology • MS, SSP
 theology • D Min, MA

School of Business
Dr. Jack Scarborough, Dean
Programs in:
 business administration • MBA
 executive business administration • MBA

School of Education
Sr. Evelyn Piche, OP, Dean
Programs in:
 counseling • Ed S, MS, PhD
 educational computing and technology • Ed S, MS, PhD
 educational leadership • Ed S, MS
 elementary education • MS
 exceptional student education • Ed S, MS, PhD
 guidance and counseling • Ed S, MS
 higher education administration • MS, PhD
 human resource development • MS, PhD
 leadership • PhD
 marriage and family counseling • Ed S, MS
 mental health counseling • Ed S, MS
 Montessori education • Ed S, MS
 pre-kindergarten and primary education • MS
 reading • Ed S, MS
 rehabilitation counseling • Ed S, MS
 teaching • MAT

School of Graduate Medical Sciences
Dr. Chet Evans, Academic Dean
Programs in:
 physician assistant • MCMS
 podiatric medicine • DPM

School of Human Performance and Leisure Sciences
Dr. G. Jean Cerra, Dean, Associate Vice President for Academic Services
Programs in:
 athletic training • MS
 sport management • MS

School of Natural and Health Sciences
Sr. John Karen Frei, Dean
Programs in:
 anesthesiology • MS
 biology • MS
 biomedical sciences • MS
 health services administration • MS

School of Nursing
Dr. Judith Ann Balcerski, Dean
Programs in:
 advanced nursing completion • MSN
 nurse practitioner • MSN
 nursing • PhD
 nursing administration • MSN
 nursing education • MSN

School of Social Work
Dr. Stephen Holloway, Dean
Program in:
 social work • MSW, PhD

EMBRY–RIDDLE AERONAUTICAL UNIVERSITY
Daytona Beach, FL 32114-3900
http://www.db.erau.edu/

Independent coed comprehensive institution. *Enrollment: 4,586* graduate, professional, and undergraduate students. *Graduate faculty: 36 full-time, 3 part-time.* Computer facilities: *Campuswide network is available with full Internet access. Total number of PCs/*

terminals supplied for student use: 720. Computer services are offered at no charge. Library facilities: *Jack R. Hunt Memorial Library.* Graduate expenses: *Tuition of $425 per credit hour. Fees of $290 per year.* General application contact: *Ginny Tait, Graduate Admissions Specialist, 904-226-6115.*

Daytona Beach Campus Graduate Program
Dr. Andres G. Zellweger, Dean of Graduate Studies
Programs in:
   aeronautical science • MAS
   aerospace engineering • MSAE
   business administration in aviation • MBAA
   human factors engineering • MS
   industrial optimization • MSIO
   software engineering • MSE
   systems engineering • MS

EMBRY–RIDDLE AERONAUTICAL UNIVERSITY, EXTENDED CAMPUS
Daytona Beach, FL 32114-3900

http://ec.db.erau.edu/

Independent coed comprehensive institution. *Enrollment: 6,623 graduate, professional, and undergraduate students. Graduate faculty: 85 full-time, 2,158 part-time.* Computer facilities: *Campuswide network is available with full Internet access. Total number of PCs/terminals supplied for student use: 235. Computer services are offered at no charge.* Library facilities: *Jack R. Hunt Memorial Library.* Graduate expenses: *$220 per credit hour.* General application contact: *Pam Thomas, Director of Admissions and Records, 904-226-6910.*

Graduate Resident Centers
Dr. Leon E. Flancher, Associate Vice President and Chief Operating Officer
Programs in:
   aeronautical science • MAS
   aviation administration and management • MBAA
   technical management • MS

FLORIDA AGRICULTURAL AND MECHANICAL UNIVERSITY
Tallahassee, FL 32307-3200

http://www.famu.edu/

Public coed university. *Enrollment: 11,091 graduate, professional, and undergraduate students. Graduate faculty: 714 full-time, 111 part-time.* Computer facilities: *Campuswide network is available with full Internet access. Total number of PCs/terminals supplied for student use: 100. Computer services are offered at no charge.* Library facilities: *Coleman Library plus 8 additional on-campus libraries.* Graduate expenses: *Tuition of $140 per credit hour for*

state residents; *$484 per credit hour for nonresidents. Fees of $130 per year.* General application contact: *Dr. Theodore Hemmingway, Interim Dean of Graduate Studies, Research, and Continuing Education, 850-599-3315.*

Division of Graduate Studies, Research, and Continuing Education
Dr. Theodore Hemmingway, Interim Dean

College of Arts and Sciences
Dr. Aubrey M. Perry, Dean
Programs in:
   applied social science • MASS
   biology • MS
   chemistry • MS
   community psychology • MS
   physics • MS
   school psychology • MS

College of Education
Dr. Melvin Gadson, Dean
Programs in:
   administration and supervision • M Ed, MS Ed
   adult education • M Ed, MS Ed
   business education • MBE
   early childhood and elementary education • M Ed, MS Ed
   guidance and counseling • M Ed, MS Ed
   health, physical education, and recreation • M Ed, MS Ed
   industrial education • M Ed, MS Ed
   secondary education • M Ed, MS Ed

College of Engineering Science, Technology, and Agriculture
Dr. Robert Bradford, Dean
Program in:
   agricultural and extension education • M Ed, MS Ed

College of Pharmacy and Pharmaceutical Sciences
Dr. Henry Lewis, Dean
Programs in:
   environmental toxicology • PhD
   medicinal chemistry • MS, PhD
   pharmacology/toxicology • MS, PhD
   pharmacy and pharmaceutical sciences • Pharm D

FAMU-FSU College of Engineering
Dr. C. J. Chen, Dean
Programs in:
   chemical engineering • MS, PhD
   civil engineering • MS
   electrical engineering • MS, PhD
   industrial engineering • MS
   mechanical engineering • MS, PhD

School of Architecture
Rodner Wright, Dean
Program in:
   architecture • M Arch, MS Arch

Florida Agricultural and Mechanical University (continued)

School of Business and Industry
Dr. Sybil Mobley, Dean
Programs in:
    accounting • MBA
    finance • MBA
    management information systems • MBA
    marketing • MBA

School of Journalism Media and Graphic Arts
Robert Ruggles, Dean
Program in:
    journalism • MS

FLORIDA ATLANTIC UNIVERSITY
Boca Raton, FL 33431-0991

http://www.fau.edu/

Public coed university. *Enrollment: 19,669 graduate, professional, and undergraduate students. Graduate faculty: 680 full-time, 9 part-time. Computer facilities: Campuswide network is available with full Internet access. Total number of PCs/terminals supplied for student use: 180. Computer services are offered at no charge. Library facilities: S. E. Wimberly Library. Graduate expenses: Tuition of $2520 per year full-time, $140 per credit hour part-time for state residents; $8712 per year full-time, $484 per credit hour part-time for nonresidents. Fees of $5 per year (minimum). General application contact: Office of Admissions, 561-367-3040.*

Charles E. Schmidt College of Science
Dr. John Wiesenfeld, Dean
Programs in:
    biological sciences • MBS, MS, MST
    chemistry and biochemistry • MS, MST
    complex systems • PhD
    environmental sciences • MS
    geography • MA, MAT
    geology • MS
    mathematical science • MS, MST, PhD
    physics • MS, MST, PhD
    psychology • MA, MAT, PhD

College of Architecture, Urban and Public Affairs
Dr. Rosalyn Carter, Dean
Programs in:
    criminal justice • MJPM
    urban and regional planning • MURP

School of Public Administration
Dr. Charles W. Washington, Director
Program in:
    public administration • MPA, PhD

College of Arts and Letters
Dr. James Malek, Dean
Programs in:
    American literature • MA, MAT
    anthropology • MA, MAT
    art education • MAT
    ceramics • MFA
    communication • MA
    comparative literature • MA, MAT
    computer art • MFA
    English literature • MA, MAT
    French • MA
    German • MA
    graphics • MFA
    history • MA
    painting • MFA
    political science • MA, MAT
    sociology • MA, MAT
    Spanish • MA
    teaching French • MAT
    teaching German • MAT
    teaching Spanish • MAT
    theatre • MFA

College of Business
Dr. Bruce Mallen, Dean
Programs in:
    business administration • Exec MBA, MBA, PhD
    economics • MST

School of Accounting
Dr. Kenneth Wiant, Director
Program in:
    accounting • M Ac, M Tax

College of Education
Dr. Jerry Lafferty, Dean
Programs in:
    adult/community education • Ed D, Ed S, M Ed
    communication disorders • M Ed
    counselor education • Ed S, M Ed
    curriculum and instruction • Ed D, Ed S
    early childhood education • M Ed
    educational leadership • Ed D, Ed S, M Ed
    elementary education • Ed D, M Ed
    foundations-educational research • M Ed
    foundations-educational technology • M Ed
    foundations of education • M Ed
    learning disabilities, mental retardation, and emotional disturbance • M Ed
    physical therapy • MS
    reading education • M Ed
    special education • Ed D
    special education administration • Ed D

College of Engineering
Dr. John Jurewicz, Dean
Programs in:
    civil engineering • MS
    computer engineering • MS, PhD
    computer science • MS, PhD
    electrical engineering • MS, PhD

manufacturing systems engineering • MS
mechanical engineering • MS, PhD
ocean engineering • MS, PhD

College of Nursing
Dr. Anne Boykin, Dean
Programs in:
   adult health • MS
   adult practitioner • MS, Post Master's Certificate
   family health • MS
   family practitioner • MS, Post Master's Certificate
   nursing administration • MS

FLORIDA INSTITUTE OF TECHNOLOGY
Melbourne, FL 32901-6975

http://www.fit.edu/

Independent coed university. *Enrollment: 4,135 graduate, professional, and undergraduate students. Graduate faculty: 150 full-time, 152 part-time. Computer facilities: Campuswide network is available with full Internet access. Total number of PCs/terminals supplied for student use: 400. Computer services are offered at no charge. Library facilities: Evans Library. Graduate expenses: $550 per credit hour. General application contact: Carolyn P. Farrior, Associate Dean of Graduate Admissions, 407-674-7118.*

Graduate School
Dr. Norine E. Noonan, Dean and Vice President of Research

College of Engineering
Dr. Robert L. Sullivan, Dean
Programs in:
   aerospace engineering • MS, PhD
   biological oceanography • MS, PhD
   chemical engineering • MS, PhD
   chemical oceanography • MS, PhD
   civil engineering • PhD
   coastal zone management • MS
   computer engineering • MS, PhD
   computer information systems • MS
   computer science • MS, PhD
   construction engineering • MS
   electrical engineering • MS, PhD
   environmental engineering • MS
   environmental resource management • MS
   environmental science • MS, PhD
   geological oceanography • MS, PhD
   geotechnical engineering • MS
   mechanical engineering • MS, PhD
   ocean engineering • MS, PhD
   physical oceanography • MS, PhD
   structures engineering • MS
   water resources • MS

College of Science and Liberal Arts
Dr. Gordon L. Nelson, Dean
Programs in:
   biology education • Ed S, PhD
   biotechnology • MS
   cell and molecular biology • MS, PhD
   chemistry • MS, PhD
   chemistry education • Ed S, PhD
   computer science education • Ed S, MSE, PhD
   conservation biology • MS
   ecology • MS, PhD
   environmental education • MSE
   environmental science education • Ed S, PhD
   general science education • Ed S, MSE, PhD
   managerial communication • MS
   marine biology • MS, PhD
   mathematics education • Ed S, MSE, PhD
   physics • MS, PhD
   physics education • Ed S, MSE
   science education • Ed D, PhD
   space science • MS, PhD
   technical and professional communication • MS

School of Aeronautics
Dr. Nathaniel Villaire, Program Chairman of Graduate Studies
Programs in:
   aviation • MSA
   cognitive human factors • MS

School of Business
Dr. A. Thomas Hollingsworth, Dean
Program in:
   business • MBA, MHA, MS, MSM

School of Extended Graduate Studies
Dr. Ronald Marshall, Dean
Programs in:
   acquisition and contract management • MS, PMBA
   global management • PMBA
   health management • MS
   human resources management • MS, PMBA
   information systems • PMBA
   logistics management • MS
   management • MS
   materials acquisition management • MS
   operations research • MS
   public administration • MPA
   research • PMBA
   space systems • MS
   space systems management • MS

School of Psychology
Dr. Charles K. Prokop, Dean
Programs in:
   clinical psychology • Psy D
   industrial/organizational psychology • MS

FLORIDA INTERNATIONAL UNIVERSITY

Miami, FL 33199

http://www.fiu.edu/index2.html

Public coed university. *Enrollment:* 30,012 graduate, professional, and undergraduate students. *Graduate faculty:* 831 full-time, 27 part-time. *Computer facilities: Campuswide network is available with full Internet access. Total number of PCs/terminals supplied for student use: 1,500. Computer services are offered at no charge.* Library facilities: *University Park Campus Library.* Graduate expenses: *Tuition of $138 per credit hour for state residents; $482 per credit hour for nonresidents. Fees of $46 per semester. General application contact: Carmen Brown, Director of Admissions, 305-348-2363.*

College of Arts and Sciences

Arthur W. Herriot, Dean
Programs in:
biological management • MS
biological sciences • MS, PhD
chemistry • MS
comparative sociology • MA
creative writing • MFA
developmental psychology • PhD
economics • MA, PhD
energy • MS
English • MA
general psychology • MS
geology • MS, PhD
history • MA, PhD
international relations • PhD
international studies • MA
Latin American and Caribbean studies • MA
linguistics • MA
mathematical sciences • MS
physics • MS
political science • MS, PhD
pollution • MS
psychology • MS
religious studies • MA
sociology • PhD
Spanish • MA, PhD

School of Computer Science

Dr. Michael Evangelist, Director
Program in:
computer science • MS, PhD

School of Music

Fredrick Kaufman, Director
Programs in:
music • MM
music education • MS

College of Business Administration

Dr. Joyce Elam, Interim Dean
Programs in:
finance • MSF, PhD
international business • MIB, PhD
management • PhD
management information systems • MS
marketing and business environment • MBA, PhD

School of Accounting

Dr. James Scheiner, Director
Programs in:
accounting • M Acc, PhD
taxation • MST, PhD

College of Education

Dr. Ira Goldenberg, Dean
Programs in:
adult education • MS
art education • MS
community college teaching • Ed D
counselor education • MS
curriculum and instruction • Ed D, Ed S
early childhood education • MS
education • MA
educational administration and supervision • Ed D
educational leadership • Ed D, Ed S
elementary education • MS
emotional disturbances • MS
English education • MS
English for non-English speakers • MS
exceptional student education • Ed D
health education • MS
health occupations education • MS
human resource development • MS
international development education • MS
mathematics education • MS
modern language education • MS
non-school based home economics education • MS
parks and recreation administration • MS
physical education • MS
reading education • MS
school psychology • Ed S
science education • MS
social studies education • MS
specific learning disabilities • MS
technical education • MS
urban education • MS
vocational home economics education • MS
vocational industrial education • MS

College of Engineering

Dr. Gordon Hopkins, Dean
Programs in:
civil engineering • MS
computer engineering • MS
construction management • MS
electrical engineering • MS, PhD
environmental and urban systems • MS
environmental engineering • MS
industrial engineering • MS
mechanical engineering • MS, PhD

College of Health
Dr. Delois P. Weekes, Dean
Programs in:
    dietetics and nutrition • MS, PhD
    medical laboratory sciences • MS
    occupational therapy • MS
    physical therapy • MS
    public health • MPH

Department of Nursing
Dr. M. Velasco-Whetsell, Chair
Program in:
    nursing • MSN

College of Urban and Public Affairs
Dr. Ronald M. Berkman, Dean

School of Policy and Management
Dr. David Bergwall, Director
Programs in:
    criminal justice • MS
    health services administration • MHSA
    public administration • MPA, PhD

School of Social Work
Dr. Max Rothman, Acting Director
Program in:
    social work • MSW, PhD

School of Architecture
William McMinn, Dean
Programs in:
    architecture • MS
    landscape architecture • MS

School of Hospitality Management
Dr. Anthony G. Marshall, Dean
Program in:
    hotel and food service management • MS

School of Journalism and Mass Communication
Dr. J. Arthur Heise, Dean
Program in:
    mass communication • MS

 **FLORIDA STATE UNIVERSITY**
Tallahassee, FL 32306

http://www.fsu.edu/

Public coed university. *Enrollment:* 30,519 graduate, professional, and undergraduate students. Graduate faculty: *878 full-time, 137 part-time.* Library facilities: *Robert Manning Strozier Library plus 6 additional on-campus libraries.* Graduate expenses: *$139 per credit hour for state residents; $482 per credit hour for nonresidents.* General application contact: *Jessie Aloi, Director for Graduate and International Admissions, 850-644-3420.*

Graduate Studies
Dr. Alan R. Mabe, Dean

College of Arts and Sciences
Dr. Donald J. Foss, Dean
Programs in:
    American and Florida studies • MA
    analytical chemistry • MS, PhD
    anthropology • MA, MS
    applied mathematics • MA, MS, PhD
    applied statistics • MS
    archaeology • PhD
    biochemistry • MS, PhD
    cell biology • MS, PhD
    chemical physics • MS, PhD
    classical archaeology • MA
    classical civilization • MA, PhD
    classics • MA
    clinical psychology • PhD
    cognitive and behavioral science • PhD
    computer science • MA, MS, PhD
    developmental biology • MS, PhD
    ecology • MS, PhD
    English • MA, PhD
    evolutionary biology • MS, PhD
    French • MA, PhD
    genetics • MS, PhD
    geology • MS, PhD
    geophysical fluid dynamics • PhD
    German • MA
    Greek • MA
    Greek and Latin • MA
    historical administration • MA
    history • MA, PhD
    humanities • MA, PhD
    immunology • MS, PhD
    inorganic chemistry • MS, PhD
    Latin • MA
    literature and languages • PhD
    marine biology • MS, PhD
    mathematical sciences • MA, MS
    mathematical statistics • MS, PhD
    meteorology • MS, PhD
    microbiology • MS, PhD
    molecular biology • MS, PhD
    molecular biophysics • PhD
    neuroscience • PhD
    oceanography • MS, PhD
    organic chemistry • MS, PhD
    philosophy • MA, PhD
    physical chemistry • MS, PhD
    physics • MS, PhD
    physiology • MS, PhD
    plant sciences • MS, PhD
    pure mathematics • MA, MS, PhD
    radiation biology • MS, PhD
    religion • MA, PhD
    Slavic languages and literatures • MA
    Spanish • MA, PhD
    writing • MA, PhD
    zoology • MS, PhD

Florida State University (continued)

College of Business
Dr. Pamela L. Perrewé, Associate Dean for Graduate Studies
Programs in:
- accounting • M Acc
- business administration • MBA, PhD
- management • MS

College of Communication
Dr. John K. Mayo, Dean
Programs in:
- communication theory • MA, MS, PhD
- mass communication • MA, MS, PhD
- speech communication • MA, MS, PhD
- speech pathology • Adv M, MS, PhD

College of Education
Dr. John W. Miller, Dean
Programs in:
- adapted physical education • MS
- adult education • Ed D, Ed S, MS, PhD
- comprehensive vocational education • Ed S, PhD
- counseling and human systems • Ed S, MS
- counseling psychology • PhD
- early childhood education • Ed D, Ed S, MS, PhD
- educational administration/leadership • Ed D, Ed S, MS, PhD
- elementary education • Ed D, Ed S, MS, PhD
- emotional disturbance/learning disabilities • MS
- English education • Ed S, MS, PhD
- health education • MS
- higher education • Ed D, Ed S, MS, PhD
- history and philosophy of education • Ed S, MS, PhD
- institutional research • Ed D, Ed S, MS, PhD
- instructional systems • Ed S, MS, PhD
- international and intercultural education • Ed S, MS, PhD
- learning and cognition • Ed S, MS, PhD
- mathematics education • Ed S, MS, PhD
- measurement and statistics • Ed S, MS, PhD
- mental retardation • MS
- multilingual-multicultural education • Ed S, MS, PhD
- policy planning and analysis • Ed D, Ed S, MS, PhD
- program evaluation • Ed S, MS, PhD
- reading education/language arts • Ed D, Ed S, MS, PhD
- recreation and leisure services administration • MS
- rehabilitation services • Ed D, Ed S, MS, PhD
- school psychology • Ed S, MS
- science education • Ed S, MS, PhD
- social science and education • Ed S, PhD
- social science education • Ed D, Ed S, MS, PhD
- special education • Ed S, PhD
- sports administration • Ed D, Ed S, MS, PhD
- sports psychology • Ed S, MS, PhD
- teacher education • Ed D, Ed S, MS, PhD
- visual disabilities • MS

College of Human Sciences
Dr. Penny Ralston, Dean
Programs in:
- child development • MS, PhD
- clinical nutrition • MS
- exercise physiology • MS, PhD
- family and consumer sciences education • MS, PhD
- family relations • MS, PhD
- food science • MS
- human science • MS
- marriage and the family • PhD
- motor learning and control • MS, PhD
- movement science • MS, PhD
- nutrition and food science • PhD
- nutrition and sport • MS
- nutrition, education and health promotion • MS
- nutrition science • MS
- textiles and consumer sciences • MS, PhD

College of Social Sciences
Dr. Charles F. Cnudde, Dean
Programs in:
- Asian studies • MA
- demography • MS
- economics • MS, PhD
- geography • MA, MS, PhD
- international affairs • MA, MS
- political science • MA, MS, PhD
- public administration and policy • Certificate, MPA, PhD
- Russian and East European studies • MA
- social science • MA, MS
- sociology • MA, MS, PhD
- study of population • Certificate, MS
- urban and regional planning • MSP, PhD

FAMU/FSU College of Engineering
Dr. Sam Awoniyi, Assistant Dean
Programs in:
- chemical engineering • MS, PhD
- civil engineering • MS, PhD
- electrical engineering • MS, PhD
- industrial engineering • MS, PhD
- mechanical engineering • MS, PhD

School of Criminology and Criminal Justice
Daniel Maier-Katkin, Dean
Program in:
- criminology and criminal justice • MA, MSC, PhD

School of Information Studies
Dr. Jane B. Robbins, Dean
Programs in:
- information studies • Adv M, PhD
- library and information studies • MS, PhD

School of Motion Picture, Television, and Recording Arts
Dr. Raymond Fielding, Dean
Program in:
- motion picture, television, and record • MFA

School of Music
Jon R. Piersol, Dean
Programs in:
- accompanying • MM
- arts administration • MA
- choral conducting • MM
- composition • DM, MM
- ethnomusicology • MM, PhD
- historical musicology • MM, PhD
- instrumental accompanying • MM
- instrumental conducting • MM
- jazz studies • MM

music education • Ed D, MM Ed, PhD
musicology • MM, PhD
music theory • MM, PhD
music therapy • MM
opera • MM
performance • DM, MM
piano pedagogy • MM
vocal accompanying • MM

School of Nursing
Dr. Evelyn Singer, Dean
Programs in:
    adult nurse practitioner • MSN
    advanced registered nurse practitioner • MSN
    case manager • MSN
    family nurse practitioner • MSN
    family nursing • MSN
    nurse educator • MSN

School of Social Work
Dr. Dianne H. Montgomery, Dean
Programs in:
    administrative practice • MSW
    clinical social work • MSW
    marriage and the family • PhD
    social services practice • MSW
    social work • PhD

School of Theatre
Dr. Gil Lazier, Dean
Programs in:
    acting • MFA
    directing • MFA
    lighting, costume, and scenic design • MFA
    scenic technology • MFA
    theater management • MFA
    theatre • MA, MS, PhD

School of Visual Arts and Dance
Dr. Jerry Draper, Dean
Programs in:
    art education • Ed D, Ed S, MA, MS, PhD
    art history • MA, PhD
    dance • MFA
    fine arts • MFA
    interior design • MA, MFA, MS

College of Law
Paul A. Lebel, Dean
Program in:
    law • JD

JACKSONVILLE UNIVERSITY
Jacksonville, FL 32211-3394

http://www.ju.edu/

Independent coed comprehensive institution. *Computer facilities: Campuswide network is available with full Internet access. Total number of PCs/terminals supplied for student use: 167. Computer service fees are included with tuition and fees. Library facilities:* Carl S. Swisher Library. *General application contact: Director of Admission, 904-745-7000.*

College of Arts and Sciences

Division of Education
Programs in:
    art • MAT
    computer education • MAT
    early childhood education • Certificate
    educational leadership • MAT
    elementary education • MAT
    English • MAT
    exceptional child education • Certificate
    French • MAT
    gifted education • Certificate
    integrated learning with educational technology • MAT
    mathematics • MAT
    music • MAT
    reading • MAT
    secondary education • Certificate
    Spanish • MAT

College of Business
Program in:
    business administration • Exec MBA, MBA

NOVA SOUTHEASTERN UNIVERSITY
Fort Lauderdale, FL 33314-7721

http://www.nova.edu/

Independent coed university. *Enrollment: 15,782 graduate, professional, and undergraduate students. Graduate faculty: 435 full-time, 688 part-time. Computer facilities: Campuswide network is available with full Internet access. Total number of PCs/terminals supplied for student use: 450. Computer services are offered at no charge. Library facilities: Einstein Library plus 3 additional on-campus libraries. Graduate expenses: $245 per credit hour (minimum). General application contact: contact individual programs.*

Center for Psychological Studies
Dr. Ronald F. Levant, Interim Dean
Programs in:
    clinical psychology • PhD, Psy D
    mental health counseling • MS

Fischler Center for the Advancement of Education
Dr. H. Wells Singleton, Provost/Dean
Programs in:
    adult education • Ed D
    applied addictions studies • MS
    applied gerontology administration • MS
    audiology • Au D
    child and youth care administration • MS
    child and youth studies • Ed D

Nova Southeastern University (continued)
- computer education • Ed S, MS
- computer science education • Ed S, MS
- computing and information technology • Ed D
- early childhood education administration • MS
- educational leaders • Ed D
- educational leadership (administration K–12) • Ed S, MS
- educational media • Ed S, MS
- education technology • Ed S, MS
- elementary education • Ed S, MS
- emotionally handicapped • Ed S, MS
- English • Ed S, MS
- family support studies • MS
- health care education • Ed D
- higher education • Ed D
- instructional technology and distance education • Ed D, MS
- mathematics • Ed S, MS
- mentally handicapped • Ed S, MS
- pre-kindergarten/primary • Ed S, MS
- reading • Ed S, MS
- science • Ed S, MS
- social studies • Ed S, MS
- specific learning disabilities • Ed S, MS
- speech-language pathology • MS, SLPD
- teaching English to speakers of other languages • Ed S, MS
- varying exceptionalities • Ed S, MS
- vocational, occupational and technical education • Ed D

Health Professions Division
Dr. Morton Terry, Chancellor

College of Allied Health
Dr. Raul Cuadrado, Director
Programs in:
- occupational therapy • Dr OT, MOT
- physical therapy • MPT

College of Dental Medicine
Dr. Seymour Oliet, Dean
Program in:
- dental medicine • DMD

College of Medical Sciences
Dr. Harold E. Laubach, Dean
Program in:
- biomedical sciences • MBS

College of Optometry
Dr. David S. Loshin, Dean
Program in:
- optometry • OD

College of Osteopathic Medicine
Dr. Cyril Blavo, Interim Dean
Program in:
- osteopathic medicine • DO

College of Pharmacy
Dr. William Hardigan, Dean
Program in:
- pharmacy • Pharm D

Oceanographic Center
Dr. Julian P. McCreary, Dean
Programs in:
- coastal-zone management • MS
- marine biology • MS
- marine environmental science • MS
- oceanography • PhD

School of Business and Entrepreneurship
Dr. Randolph A. Pohlman, Dean
Programs in:
- accounting • M Acc
- business administration • MBA
- business and entrepreneurship • DBA
- health services administration • MS
- human resources management • MSHRM
- international business administration • DIBA, MIBA
- public administration • DPA, MPA

School of Computer and Information Sciences
Dr. Edward Lieblein, Dean
Programs in:
- computer information systems • MS, PhD
- computer science • MS, PhD
- computing technology in education • Ed D, MS, PhD
- information science • PhD
- information systems • PhD
- management information systems • MS

School of Social and Systemic Studies
Dr. Ronald Chenail, Dean
Program in:
- family therapy • Certificate, MS, PhD

Shepard Broad Law Center
Joseph D. Harbaugh, Dean
Program in:
- law • JD

ROLLINS COLLEGE
Winter Park, FL 32789-4499

http://www.rollins.edu/

Independent coed comprehensive institution. *Enrollment: 3,356 graduate, professional, and undergraduate students. Graduate faculty: 34 full-time, 23 part-time.* Computer facilities: *Campuswide network is available with full Internet access. Total number of PCs/ terminals supplied for student use: 150.* Computer service fees are included with tuition and fees. Library facilities: *Olin Library.* Graduate expenses: *$190 per hour.* General application contact: *contact individual programs.*

Crummer Graduate School of Business
Dr. Edward A. Moses, Dean
Program in:
- business • MBA

Hamilton Holt School
Dr. Robert D. Smither, Dean
Programs in:
    corporate communications and technology • MA
    elementary education • M Ed, MAT
    English • MAT
    human resources • MA
    liberal studies • MLS
    mathematics • MAT
    mental health counseling • MA
    music • MAT
    school counseling • MA
    secondary education • MAT

ST. THOMAS UNIVERSITY
Miami, FL 33054-6459

http://www.stu.edu/

Independent-religious coed comprehensive institution. Computer facilities: *Campuswide network is available with full Internet access. Total number of PCs/terminals supplied for student use: 44. Computer service fees are included with tuition and fees.* Library facilities: *main library.* Graduate expenses: *$410 per credit.* General application contact: *Associate Director of Graduate Admissions, 305-628-6614.*

School of Graduate Studies
Programs in:
    accounting • MBA
    elementary education • MS
    general management • Certificate, MSM
    guidance and counseling • Certificate, MS
    health management • Certificate, MBA, MSM
    human resource management • Certificate, MSM
    international business • Certificate, MBA, MSM
    justice administration • Certificate, MSM
    management • MBA
    marriage and family therapy • MS
    mental health counseling • MS
    pastoral ministries • Certificate, MA
    public management • Certificate, MSM
    sports administration • MBA

School of Law
Program in:
    law • JD

STETSON UNIVERSITY
DeLand, FL 32720-3781

http://www.stetson.edu/

Independent coed comprehensive institution. *Enrollment: 2,857 graduate, professional, and undergraduate students. Graduate faculty: 66 full-time, 55 part-time.* Computer facilities: *Campuswide network is available with full Internet access. Computer services are offered at no charge.* Library facilities: *DuPont Ball Library plus 2 additional on-campus libraries.* Graduate expenses: *$370 per credit hour.* General application contact: *Pat LeClaire, Office of Graduate Studies, 904-822-7075.*

College of Arts and Sciences
Dr. Gary Maris, Dean
Programs in:
    career teaching • Ed S
    education • MA
    educational leadership • Ed S, M Ed
    elementary education • M Ed
    English • MA, MAT
    exceptional student education • M Ed
    marriage and family therapy • MS
    mental health counseling • MS

College of Law
Lizabeth A. Moody, Dean
Program in:
    law • JD

School of Business Administration
Dr. Paul Dasher, Dean
Programs in:
    accounting • M Acc
    business administration • MBA

UNIVERSITY OF CENTRAL FLORIDA
Orlando, FL 32816

http://www.ucf.edu/

Public coed university. *Enrollment: 27,411 graduate, professional, and undergraduate students. Graduate faculty: 714.* Graduate expenses: *Tuition of $3288 per year full-time, $137 per credit hour part-time for state residents; $11,520 per year full-time, $480 per credit hour part-time for nonresidents. Fees of $105 per year.* General application contact: *Dr. Patricia Bishop, Director of Graduate Studies, 407-823-6432.*

College of Arts and Sciences
K. Seidel, Dean
Programs in:
    applied sociology • MA
    biological sciences • MS
    clinical psychology • MS, PhD
    communication • MA
    computer science • MS, PhD
    creative writing • MA
    history • MA
    human factors psychology • PhD
    industrial chemistry • MS
    industrial/organizational psychology • MS
    literature • MA

University of Central Florida (continued)
  mathematical science • MS
  mathematics • PhD
  physics • MS, PhD
  political science • MA
  Spanish • MA
  statistical computing • MS
  teaching English as a second language • MA
  technical writing • MA

College of Business Administration
Dr. Thomas Keon, Acting Dean
Programs in:
  accounting • MSA
  business administration • MBA
  economics • MAAE
  finance • PhD
  taxation • MST

College of Education
Dr. Sandra Robinson, Dean
Programs in:
  art education • M Ed, MA
  business education • M Ed, MA
  counselor education • M Ed, MA
  curriculum and instruction • Ed D, Ed S
  educational leadership • Ed D, Ed S, M Ed, MA
  educational media • M Ed
  educational technology • Ed D, MA
  elementary and secondary education • M Ed, MA
  elementary education • M Ed, MA
  English language education • M Ed, MA
  exceptional child education • M Ed
  foreign language education • M Ed, MA
  instructional systems • MA
  mathematics education • M Ed, MA
  music education • M Ed, MA
  physical education • M Ed, MA
  reading • M Ed
  school psychology • Ed S
  science education • M Ed, MA
  social science education • M Ed, MA
  teaching English as a second language • MA
  vocational education • M Ed, MA

College of Engineering
Dr. Martin Wanielista, Dean
Programs in:
  aerospace systems • MS, PhD
  civil engineering • MCE, MS, MSE, PhD
  computer engineering • MSE, PhD
  computer-integrated manufacturing • MS
  electrical engineering • MSE, PhD
  engineering management • MS
  environmental engineering • MS, MSE, PhD
  industrial engineering • MSIE
  industrial engineering and management systems • PhD
  manufacturing engineering • MS Mfg E
  materials science and engineering • MS, PhD
  mechanical systems • MS, PhD
  operations research • MS
  optical science and engineering • MS, PhD

  product assurance engineering • MS
  simulation systems • MS
  thermofluids • MS, PhD

College of Health and Public Affairs
Dr. B. R. McCarthy, Dean
Programs in:
  communicative disorders • MA
  criminal justice • MS
  health services administration • MS
  microbiology • MS
  molecular biology • MS
  nursing • MSN
  public administration • MPA
  public affairs • PhD
  social work • MSW

 # UNIVERSITY OF FLORIDA
Gainesville, FL 32611
http://www.ufl.edu/

Public coed university. *Enrollment:* 41,040 graduate, professional, and undergraduate students. Graduate faculty: 2,500. Library facilities: *University Library plus 8 additional on-campus libraries.* Graduate expenses: *$138 per credit hour for state residents; $481 per credit hour for nonresidents. General application contact: Julie W. F. Shih, Director of Graduate Program Research, 352-392-4646.*

Graduate School
Dr. Karen A. Holbrook, Vice President of Research and
  Dean of Graduate School
Programs in:
  biochemistry and molecular biology • PhD
  clinical chemistry • MS
  comparative law • LL M CL
  endodontics • MS
  genetics • PhD
  immunology and microbiology • PhD
  immunology and molecular pathology • PhD
  medicinal chemistry • PhD
  molecular cell biology • PhD
  neuroscience • MS, PhD
  oral biology • PhD
  orthodontics • MS
  periodontics • MS
  pharmaceutics • MSP, PhD
  pharmacodynamics • MSP, PhD
  pharmacology and therapeutics • PhD
  pharmacy • MSP, PhD
  pharmacy health care administration • MS, PhD
  physiology • PhD
  physiology and pharmacology • PhD
  prosthodontics • MS
  taxation • LL M T
  veterinary medical science • MS, PhD

Center for Nutritional Sciences
Dr. Douglas L. Archer, Director
Programs in:
  animal, dairy and poultry nutrition • MS, PhD
  human nutrition • MS, PhD
  nutritional biochemistry • MS, PhD
  nutritional sciences • MS, PhD

College of Agriculture
Dr. Joseph Joyce, Acting Vice President for Agriculture and
  Natural Resources
Programs in:
  agribusiness • MAB
  agricultural education and communication • M Ag, MS
  agricultural engineering • Engr, ME, MS, PhD
  agricultural operations management • MS, PhD
  agronomy • MS, PhD
  animal sciences • M Ag, MS, PhD
  botany • M Ag, MS, PhD
  botany education • MST
  cell biology • MS, PhD
  dairy and poultry science • M Ag, MS
  entomology and nematology • M Ag, MS, PhD
  environmental horticulture • MS, PhD
  fisheries and aquatic science • MFAS, MS, PhD
  food and resource economics • MS, PhD
  food science and human nutrition • M Ag, MS, PhD
  forest resources and conservation • MFRC, MS, PhD
  fruit crops • MS, PhD
  microbiology • MS, PhD
  plant molecular and cellular biology • MS, PhD
  plant pathology • M Ag, MS, PhD
  soil and water science • M Ag, MS, PhD
  vegetable crops and crop science • MS, PhD
  wildlife ecology • MS, PhD

College of Architecture
R. Wayne Drummond, Dean
Programs in:
  architecture • M Arch, MSAS, PhD
  building construction • MBC, MSBC, PhD
  landscape architecture • MLA
  urban and regional planning • MAURP, PhD

College of Business Administration
Dr. John Kraft, Dean
Programs in:
  accounting • M Acc, PhD
  business administration • MBA
  decision and information sciences • MA, PhD
  economics • MA, PhD
  finance • PhD
  health and hospital administration • MHA
  human resources management • PhD
  management • MA, PhD
  marketing • MA, PhD
  real estate and urban analysis • MA, PhD
  strategy • PhD

College of Education
Dr. Roderick McDavis, Dean
Programs in:
  bilingual education • Ed D, Ed S, M Ed, MAE, PhD
  comparative education • Ed D, Ed S, M Ed, MAE, PhD

computer education • Ed D, Ed S, M Ed, MAE, PhD
curriculum and instructional leadership • Ed D, Ed S,
  PhD
early childhood education • Ed D, Ed S, M Ed, MAE,
  PhD
economics education • Ed D, Ed S, M Ed, MAE, PhD
educational administration • Ed D, Ed S, M Ed, MAE,
  PhD
educational leadership • PhD
educational psychology • Ed D, Ed S, M Ed, MAE, PhD
elementary education • Ed D, Ed S, M Ed, MAE, PhD
English education • Ed D, Ed S, M Ed, MAE, PhD
foreign language education • Ed D, Ed S, M Ed, MAE,
  PhD
higher education • Ed D, Ed S, PhD
history, philosophy, and sociology of education • Ed D,
  Ed S, M Ed, MAE, PhD
marriage and family counseling • Ed D, Ed S, M Ed, PhD
mathematics education • Ed D, Ed S, M Ed, MAE, PhD
media and instructional design • Ed D, Ed S, M Ed,
  MAE, PhD
mental health counseling • Ed D, Ed S, M Ed, PhD
middle school education • Ed D, Ed S, M Ed, MAE, PhD
reading and language arts • Ed D, Ed S, M Ed, MAE,
  PhD
school counseling and guidance • Ed D, Ed S, M Ed
school psychology • Ed S, MAE, PhD
science education • Ed D, Ed S, M Ed, MAE, PhD
secondary education • Ed D, Ed S, M Ed, MAE, PhD
social studies education • Ed D, Ed S, M Ed, MAE, PhD
special education • Ed D, Ed S, M Ed, MAE, PhD
statistics, measurement, and evaluation methodology •
  Ed D, Ed S, M Ed, MAE, PhD
student counseling and guidance • PhD
student personnel services in higher education • Ed D,
  Ed S, M Ed, PhD

College of Engineering
Dr. Winifred M. Phillips, Dean
Programs in:
  aerospace engineering • Certificate, Engr, ME, MS, PhD
  agricultural engineering • Engr, ME, MS, PhD
  agricultural operations management • MS, PhD
  biomedical engineering • MS, PhD
  ceramic science and engineering • Engr, ME, MS, PhD
  chemical engineering • Engr, ME, MS, PhD
  civil engineering • Engr, MCE, ME, MS, PhD
  coastal and oceanographic engineering • Engr, ME, MS,
    PhD
  computer organization • Engr, MS, PhD
  electrical and computer engineering • Engr, ME, MS,
    PhD
  engineering management • ME, MS
  engineering mechanics • Engr, ME, MS, PhD
  engineering physics • Engr, ME, MS, PhD
  engineering science and engineering mechanics • Engr,
    ME, MS, PhD
  environmental engineering sciences • Engr, ME, MS,
    PhD
  facilities layout decision support systems energy • PhD
  health physics • MS, PhD
  health systems • ME, MS
  industrial and systems engineering • Engr, ME, MS, PhD

University of Florida (continued)

industrial engineering • Engr, PhD

information systems • Engr, MS, PhD

manufacturing systems engineering • Certificate, ME, MS, PhD

materials science and engineering • Certificate, Engr, ME, MS, PhD

mechanical engineering • Certificate, Engr, ME, MS, PhD

medical physics • MS, PhD

metallurgical and materials engineering • Engr, ME, MS, PhD

metallurgical engineering • Engr, ME, MS, PhD

nuclear power engineering • Engr, ME, MS, PhD

operations research • Engr, ME, MS, PhD

polymer science and engineering • Engr, ME, MS, PhD

production planning and control engineering management • PhD

quality and reliability assurance • ME, MS

software systems • Engr, MS, PhD

systems engineering • Engr, PhD

College of Fine Arts

Dr. Donald McGlothlin, Dean

Programs in:

art • MFA

art education • MA

art history • MA

music • MM, PhD

music education • MM, PhD

theatre • MFA, PhD

College of Health and Human Performance

Dr. Patrick J. Bird, Dean

Programs in:

exercise and sport science • MESS, MSESS, PhD

health and human performance • PhD

health science education • MHSE, MS, MSHSE, PhD

recreation • MSRS

recreation, parks and tourism • PhD

College of Health Professions

Dr. Robert Frank, Dean

Programs in:

audiology • Au D

clinical and health psychology • PhD

health and hospital administration • MHA

occupational therapy • MHS

physical therapy • MHS, MPT

rehabilitation counseling • MHS

rehabilitation sciences • PhD

College of Journalism and Communications

Dr. Terry Hynes, Dean

Programs in:

advertising • MAMC, PhD

journalism • MAMC, PhD

public relations • MAMC, PhD

telecommunication • MAMC, PhD

College of Liberal Arts and Sciences

Dr. Willard Harrison, Dean

Programs in:

African studies • Certificate

anthropology • MA, MAT, PhD

applied mathematics • MS, PhD

astronomy • MS, MST, PhD

audiology • Au D

botany • M Ag, MS, PhD

botany education • MST

chemistry • MS, MST, PhD

classics • MA, MAT

communication sciences and disorders • MA, PhD

creative writing • MFA

English • MA, PhD

French • MA, PhD

geography • MA, MAT, MS, MST, PhD

geology • MS, PhD

geology education • MST

German • MA, MAT, PhD

history • MA, PhD

international development policy • MA

international relations • MA, MAT, PhD

Latin American studies • Certificate, MA, MAT

linguistics • MA, PhD

mathematics • MA, MS, PhD

mathematics teaching • MAT, MST

philosophy • MA, MAT, PhD

physics • MS, PhD

physics education • MST

plant molecular and cellular biology • MS, PhD

political campaigning • Certificate, MA

political science • MA, MAT, PhD

psychology • MA, MAT, MS, MST, PhD

public affairs • Certificate, MA

religion • MA

sociology • MA, PhD

Spanish • MA, PhD

statistics • M Stat, MSTA, PhD

teaching English as a second language • Certificate

zoology • MS, MST, PhD

College of Nursing

Dr. Kathleen Long, Dean

Program in:

nursing • MS Nsg, PhD

College of Dentistry

Dr. Frank A. Catalanotto, Dean

Programs in:

dentistry • DMD

endodontics • MS

orthodontics • MS

periodontics • MS

prosthodontics • MS

College of Law

Richard A. Matasar, Dean

Programs in:

comparative law • LL M CL

law • JD

taxation • LL M T

College of Medicine
Dr. Kenneth I. Berns, Dean
Programs in:
    biochemistry and molecular biology • PhD
    clinical chemistry • MS
    genetics • PhD
    immunology and microbiology • PhD
    immunology and molecular pathology • PhD
    medicine • MD
    molecular cell biology • PhD
    neuroscience • MS, PhD
    oral biology • PhD
    pharmacology and therapeutics • PhD
    physician assistant studies • MPAS
    physiology • PhD
    physiology and pharmacology • PhD
    veterinary medical science • MS, PhD

College of Pharmacy
Dr. William H. Riffee, Dean
Programs in:
    medicinal chemistry • PhD
    pharmaceutics • MSP, PhD
    pharmacodynamics • MSP, PhD
    pharmacy • Pharm D
    pharmacy health care administration • MS, PhD

College of Veterinary Medicine
Dr. Joseph A. DiPietro, Dean
Programs in:
    veterinary medical science • MS, PhD
    veterinary medicine • DVM

UNIVERSITY OF MIAMI
Coral Gables, FL 33124

http://www.miami.edu/

Independent coed university. *Enrollment: 13,651 graduate, professional, and undergraduate students. Graduate faculty: 1,879 full-time, 700 part-time. Computer facilities: Campuswide network is available with full Internet access. Computer service fees are included with tuition and fees. Library facilities: Otto G. Richter Library plus 6 additional on-campus libraries. Graduate expenses: Tuition of $815 per credit hour. Fees of $174 per year. General application contact: Dean of the appropriate school.*

Graduate School
Dr. Steven G. Ullmann, Interim Dean
Programs in:
    biochemistry and molecular biology • PhD
    biomedical studies • PhD
    epidemiology • PhD
    microbiology and immunology • PhD
    molecular and cellular pharmacology • PhD
    molecular cell and developmental biology • PhD
    neuroscience • PhD
    physical therapy • MSPT, PhD

    physiology and biophysics • PhD
    public health • MPH
    radiology • MS

College of Arts and Sciences
Dr. Kumble R. Subbaswamy, Dean
Programs in:
    applied developmental psychology • PhD
    art history • MA
    behavioral neuroscience • PhD
    biology • MS, PhD
    ceramics • MFA
    chemistry • MS
    clinical psychology • PhD
    computer science • MA, MS
    English • MA, MFA, PhD
    French • MA, PhD
    genetics and evolution • MS, PhD
    graphic design/illustration • MFA
    health psychology • PhD
    history • MA, PhD
    inorganic chemistry • PhD
    liberal studies • MALS
    mathematics • DA, MA, MS, PhD
    organic chemistry • PhD
    painting • MFA
    philosophy • MA, MALS, PhD
    photography • MFA
    physical chemistry • PhD
    physics • DA, MS, PhD
    printmaking • MFA
    Romance languages • PhD
    sculpture • MFA
    sociology • MA, PhD
    Spanish • MA, PhD
    tropical biology, ecology, and behavior • MS, PhD

College of Engineering
Dr. M. Lewis Temares, Dean
Programs in:
    architectural engineering • MSAE
    biomedical engineering • MSBE, PhD
    civil engineering • DA, MSCE, PhD
    electrical and computer engineering • MSECE, PhD
    environmental health and safety • MSEH
    ergonomics • PhD
    industrial engineering • MSIE, PhD
    management of technology • MS
    mechanical engineering • DA, MS, MSME, PhD
    occupational ergonomics and safety • MS

Rosenstiel School of Marine and Atmospheric Science
Dr. Otis Brown, Dean
Programs in:
    applied marine physics • MS, PhD
    atmospheric science • MA, MS, PhD
    coastal ocean circulation dynamics • MS, PhD
    marine affairs • MA
    marine and atmospheric chemistry • MS, PhD
    marine biology and fisheries • MA, MS, PhD
    marine geology and geophysics • MA, MS, PhD
    ocean acoustics and geoacoustics • MS, PhD
    ocean engineering • MS
    physical oceanography • MA, MS, PhD

University of Miami (continued)
small-scale ocean surface dynamics and air-sea interaction physics • MS, PhD

School of Architecture
Denis Hecter, Director, Graduate Studies
Programs in:
architecture • M Arch
computing in design • M Arch
suburb and town design • M Arch

School of Business Administration
Dr. Harold W. Berkman, Vice Dean
Programs in:
accounting • MBA
business administration • Exec MBA
computer information systems • MS
economics • MA, PhD
health administration • Certificate
international business • MBA, MIBS
management science • Certificate, MS, PhD
political science • MPA
professional accounting • MP Acc
taxation • MS Tax
telecommunications management • Certificate

School of Communication
Edward J. Pfister, Dean
Programs in:
broadcast and print journalism • MA
communication studies • MA
film studies • MA
motion pictures • MFA
public relations • MA

School of Education
Dr. Samuel Yarger, Dean
Programs in:
counseling psychology • PhD
early childhood special education • Ed S, MS Ed
education • DA
educational leadership • Ed D, Ed S, MS Ed, PhD
educational research • PhD
educational research/exercise physiology • PhD
elementary education • Ed S, MS Ed
emotional handicaps/learning disabilities • MS Ed
exercise physiology • MS Ed
higher education • MS Ed
higher education/enrollment management • MS Ed
higher education/sports administration • Ed D, PhD
marriage and family therapy • MS Ed
mental health counseling • MS Ed
pre–K through primary education (age 3-grade 3) • MS Ed
research and evaluation • MS Ed
special education and reading • Ed S, MS Ed, PhD
sports administration • MS Ed
sports medicine • MS Ed, PhD
teaching English to speakers of other languages • Ed S, MS Ed

School of International Studies
Dr. Roger Kanet, Dean
Program in:
international studies • MA, PhD

School of Music
Dr. James William Hipp, Dean
Programs in:
accompanying and chamber music • DMA, MM
choral conducting • DMA, MM
composition • DMA, MM
electronic music • MM
instrumental conducting • DMA, MM
instrumental performance • ADP, DMA, MM
jazz pedagogy • MM
jazz performance • ADP, MM
keyboard performance and pedagogy • DMA, MM
media writing and production • MM
multiple woodwinds • DMA, MM
music business and entertaiment industries • MM
music education • Ed S, MM, PhD
music engineering • MS
musicology • MM
music theory • MM
music therapy • MM
piano/organ performance • ADP
piano performance • DMA, MM
studio jazz writing • MM
vocal performance • ADP, DMA, MM

School of Nursing
Dr. Diane Horner, Dean
Programs in:
adult nurse practitioner • MSN
family nurse practitioner • MSN
nurse midwifery • MSN
nursing • PhD
primary health care • MSN

School of Law
Michael Goodnight, Assistant Dean of Admissions
Programs in:
comparative law • LL M
estate planning • LL M
international law • LL M
law • JD
ocean and coastal law • LL M
real property and development • LL M

School of Medicine
Dr. John G. Clarkson, Vice President for Medical Affairs and Dean
Programs in:
biochemistry and molecular biology • PhD
biomedical studies • PhD
epidemiology • PhD
medicine • MD
microbiology and immunology • PhD
molecular and cellular pharmacology • PhD
molecular cell and developmental biology • PhD
neuroscience • PhD
physical therapy • MSPT, PhD
physiology and biophysics • PhD
public health • MPH
radiology • MS

UNIVERSITY OF NORTH FLORIDA
Jacksonville, FL 32224-2645

http://www.unf.edu/

Public coed comprehensive institution. *Enrollment: 11,389 graduate, professional, and undergraduate students. Graduate faculty: 210 full-time. Computer facilities: Campuswide network is available with full Internet access. Total number of PCs/terminals supplied for student use: 250. Computer service fees are included with tuition and fees. Library facilities: Thomas G. Carpenter Library. Graduate expenses: $3388 per year full-time, $141 per credit hour part-time for state residents; $11,634 per year full-time, $485 per credit hour part-time for nonresidents. General application contact: Deborah M. Kaye, Director of Enrollment Services and Admissions, 904-620-2624.*

College of Arts and Sciences
Dr. Lewis Radonovich, Dean
Programs in:
    computer science • MS
    counseling psychology • MAC
    criminal justice • MSCJ
    English • MA
    general psychology • MA
    history • MA
    mathematical sciences • MS
    public administration • MPA
    statistics • MS

College of Business Administration
Dr. Earle C. Traynham, Dean
Programs in:
    accounting • M Acct
    business administration • MBA
    human resource management • MHRM
    personnel management • MHRM

College of Computer Sciences and Engineering
Dr. Charles Winton, Interim Dean
Program in:
    computer and information sciences • MA

College of Education
Dr. Kathrine Kasten, Interim Dean
Programs in:
    administration • M Ed
    counselor education • M Ed
    educational leadership • Ed D
    elementary education • M Ed
    mathematics education • M Ed
    music education • M Ed
    science education • M Ed
    secondary education • M Ed
    special education • M Ed

College of Health
Dr. Joan Farrell, Dean
Programs in:
    addictions counseling • MS
    advanced practice nursing • MSN
    aging studies • Certificate
    employee health services • MS
    health administration • MHA
    health care administration • MS
    human ecology and nutrition • MS
    human performance • MS

UNIVERSITY OF SOUTH FLORIDA
Tampa, FL 33620-9951

http://www.usf.edu/

Public coed university. *Enrollment: 34,066 graduate, professional, and undergraduate students. Graduate faculty: 1,480 full-time, 603 part-time. Computer facilities: Campuswide network is available with full Internet access. Total number of PCs/terminals supplied for student use: 524. Computer services are offered at no charge. Library facilities: main library plus 5 additional on-campus libraries. Graduate expenses: $142 per credit hour for state residents; $486 per credit hour for nonresidents. General application contact: Dr. Dale E. Johnson, Dean, 813-974-2846.*

Graduate School
Dr. Dale E. Johnson, Dean
Programs in:
    anatomy • PhD
    biochemistry and molecular biology • PhD
    medical microbiology and immunology • PhD
    medical sciences • PhD
    pathology • PhD
    physiology and biophysics • PhD

College of Arts and Sciences
David Stamps, Dean
Programs in:
    aging studies • PhD
    American studies • MA
    analytical chemistry • MS, PhD
    applied anthropology • MA, PhD
    applied mathematics • PhD
    applied physics • MS
    audiology • MS
    aural rehabilitation • MS
    biochemistry • MS, PhD
    biology • MS, PhD
    botany • MS
    cellular and molecular biology • PhD
    clinical psychology • PhD
    communication • MA, PhD
    criminology • MA, PhD
    ecology • PhD
    engineering science/physics • PhD

University of South Florida (continued)
English • MA, PhD
experimental psychology • PhD
French • MA
geography • MA
geology • MS, PhD
gerontology • MA
history • MA
hydrogeology • Adv C, MS
industrial/organizational psychology • PhD
inorganic chemistry • MS, PhD
liberal arts • MLA
library and information sciences • MA
linguistics • MA
marine biology • MS, PhD
marine science • MS, PhD
mass communications • MA
mathematics • MA, PhD
microbiology • MS
oceanography • MS, PhD
organic chemistry • MS, PhD
philosophy • MA, PhD
physical chemistry • MS, PhD
physics • MA, MS
physiology • PhD
political science • MA
public administration • MPA
rehabilitation counseling • MA
religious studies • MA
school library media • MA
social work • MSW
sociology • MA
Spanish • MA
speech pathology • MS
teaching English as a second language • MA
women's studies • MA
zoology • MS

College of Business Administration
Robert L. Anderson, Dean
Programs in:
accounting • M Acc
business • PhD
business administration • Exec MBA, MBA
business administration for physicians • Exec MBA
economics • MA
management • MS
management information systems • MS

College of Education
Jane Applegate, Dean
Programs in:
adult education • Ed D, Ed S, MA, PhD
art education • MA
business and office education • MA
college student affairs • MA
counselor education • MA
distributive and marketing education • MA
early childhood education • M Ed, PhD
educational leadership • Ed D, Ed S, M Ed
educational measurement and research • Ed S, M Ed, PhD
education of the emotionally disturbed • MA

education of the mentally handicapped • MA
elementary education • Ed D, Ed S, MA, PhD
English education • Ed S, M Ed, MA, PhD
foreign language education • M Ed, MA
gifted education • MA
higher education • Ed S, PhD
industrial technical education • MA
instructional computing • M Ed, PhD
interdisciplinary education • Ed S, PhD
junior college teaching • MA
learning disabilities • MA
mathematics education • Ed S, M Ed, MA, PhD
middle school education • M Ed
music education • MA, PhD
physical education • MA
reading education • Ed S, MA, PhD
school psychology • Ed S, PhD
science education • Ed S, M Ed, MA, PhD
secondary education • PhD
social science education • M Ed, MA
special education • Ed D, Ed S, PhD
theater education • MA
varying exceptionalities • MA
vocational education • Ed D, Ed S, PhD

College of Engineering
Michael G. Kovac, Dean
Programs in:
chemical engineering • M Ch E, ME, MS Ch E, MSE, PhD
civil engineering • MCE, MSCE, PhD
computer engineering • M Cp E, MS Cp E
computer science • MCS, MSCS
computer science and engineering • PhD
electrical engineering • ME, MEE, MSE, MSEE, PhD
engineering • ME, MSE, MSES
engineering management • ME, MSE, MSEM, MSIE
engineering science • PhD
environmental engineering • MEVE, MSEV
industrial engineering • ME, MSE, MSEM, MSIE
mechanical engineering • MME, MSE, MSME, PhD

College of Fine Arts
John Smith, Dean
Programs in:
art • MFA
art history • MA
choral conducting • MM
composition • MM
instrumental conducting (wind instruments) • MM
jazz studies • MM
music education • MA, PhD
percussion • MM
performance • MM
piano • MM
string • MM
theory • MM
voice • MM
wind • MM

College of Nursing
Patricia A. Burns, Dean
Program in:
nursing • MS, PhD

College of Public Health

Dr. Charles Mahan, Dean
Programs in:
community and family health • MPH, MSPH, PhD
environmental and occupational health • MPH, MSPH, PhD
epidemiology and biostatistics • MPH, MSPH, PhD
health policy and management • MHA, MPH, MSPH, PhD

School of Architecture and Community Design

Alexander Ratensky, Dean
Program in:
architecture and community design • M Arch

College of Medicine

Dr. Martin Silbiger, Dean
Programs in:
anatomy • PhD
biochemistry and molecular biology • PhD
medical microbiology and immunology • PhD
medical sciences • PhD
medicine • MD
pathology • PhD
physiology and biophysics • PhD

THE UNIVERSITY OF TAMPA

Tampa, FL 33606-1490

http://www.utampa.edu/

Independent coed comprehensive institution. *Enrollment: 2,896 graduate, professional, and undergraduate students. Graduate faculty: 41 full-time, 8 part-time. Computer facilities: Campuswide network is available with full Internet access. Total number of PCs/ terminals supplied for student use: 160. Computer service fees are applied as a separate charge. Library facilities: Merl Kelce Library. General application contact: Barbara P. Strickler, Vice President for Enrollment, 800-733-4773.*

College of Business

Dr. Alfred N. Page, Dean and Co-Chief Academic Officer
Program in:
business administration • MBA

Nursing Program

Dr. Nancy Ross, Director
Programs in:
family nurse practitioner • MSN
nursing administration • MSN

UNIVERSITY OF WEST FLORIDA

Pensacola, FL 32514-5750

http://www.uwf.edu/

Public coed comprehensive institution. *Enrollment: 7,131 graduate, professional, and undergraduate students. Graduate faculty: 165 full-time, 47 part-time. Computer facilities: Campuswide network is available with full Internet access. Computer services are offered at no charge. Library facilities: Pace Library. Graduate expenses: $131 per credit hour (minimum) for state residents; $436 per credit hour (minimum) for nonresidents. General application contact: Susie Neeley, Director of Admissions, 850-474-2230.*

College of Arts and Social Sciences

Dr. Richard Doelker, Dean
Programs in:
applied politics • MA
communication arts • MA
English • MA
health • MS
health, leisure, and sports • MS
history • MA, MAT
humanities • MA
physical education • MS
political science • MA
psychology • MA
public administration • MPA

College of Business

Dr. William B. Carper, Dean
Programs in:
accounting • MA
business administration • MBA

College of Education

Dr. Wesley Little, Dean
Programs in:
clinical teaching • MA
curriculum and instruction • Ed D, Ed S
educational leadership • Ed S, M Ed
elementary education • M Ed
emotionally handicapped • MA
habilitative science • MA
learning disabled • MA
mentally handicapped • MA
middle level education • M Ed
primary education • M Ed
reading • M Ed
vocational education • M Ed

College of Science and Technology

K. Ranga Rao, Dean
Programs in:
biology • MS
biology education • MST
computer science • MS
mathematics • MA
mathematics education • MAT
statistics • MA
systems and control engineering • MS

GEORGIA

ALBANY STATE UNIVERSITY
Albany, GA 31705-2717

http://www.alsnet.peachnet.edu/

Public coed comprehensive institution. *Enrollment:* 3,226 graduate, professional, and undergraduate students. Graduate faculty: *75.* Library facilities: *Margaret Rood Hazard Library.* General application contact: *Diane P. Frink, Graduate Admissions Counselor, 912-430-5118.*

School of Arts and Sciences
Dr. James L. Hill, Dean
Programs in:
  criminal justice • MS
  fiscal management • MPA
  human resources management • MPA
  public policy • MPA

School of Business
Dr. Mollie Brown, Interim Dean
Program in:
  business • MBA

School of Education
Dr. Claude Perkins, Dean
Programs in:
  business education • M Ed
  early childhood education • M Ed
  educational administration and supervision • Certificate, M Ed
  English education • M Ed
  health and physical education • M Ed
  mathematics education • M Ed
  middle childhood education • M Ed
  music education • M Ed
  physical education • M Ed
  reading education • M Ed
  science education • M Ed
  secondary education • M Ed
  special education • M Ed

School of Nursing and Allied Health Sciences
Dr. Lucille B. Wilson, Dean
Program in:
  nursing • MS

ARMSTRONG ATLANTIC STATE UNIVERSITY
Savannah, GA 31419-1997

http://www.armstrong.edu/

Public coed comprehensive institution. *Enrollment:* 5,696 graduate, professional, and undergraduate students. Graduate faculty: *131.* Computer facilities: *Campuswide network is available with full Internet access. Total number of PCs/terminals supplied for student use: 126. Computer services are offered at no charge.* Library facilities: *Lane Library.* Graduate expenses: *Tuition of $83 per quarter hour for state residents; $250 per quarter hour for nonresidents. Fees of $145 per quarter hour for state residents; $228 per quarter hour for nonresidents.* General application contact: *Dr. Emma T. Simon, Dean of Graduate Studies, 912-927-5377.*

School of Graduate Studies
Dr. Emma T. Simon, Dean of Graduate Studies
Programs in:
  administration • MHS
  criminal justice • MS
  elementary education • M Ed
  history • MA
  middle grades education • M Ed
  nursing • MSN
  physical therapy • MSPT
  public health • MPH
  secondary education • M Ed
  special education • M Ed

AUGUSTA STATE UNIVERSITY
Augusta, GA 30904-2200

http://www.aug.edu/

Public coed comprehensive institution. *Enrollment:* 5,510 graduate, professional, and undergraduate students. Graduate faculty: *56 full-time, 1 part-time.* Computer facilities: *Campuswide network is available with full Internet access. Total number of PCs/terminals supplied for student use: 181. Computer services are offered at no charge.* Library facilities: *Reese Library.* Graduate expenses: *$2260 per year full-time, $83 per credit hour part-time for state residents; $8260 per year full-time, $333 per credit hour part-time for nonresidents.* General application contact: *Carol Giardina, Acting Director of Admissions, 706-737-1405.*

Graduate Studies
Dr. Bill E. Bompart, Vice President for Academic Affairs

College of Arts and Sciences
Dr. Elizabeth B. House, Dean
Programs in:
  psychology • MS
  public administration • MPA

College of Business Administration
Jackson K. Widener, Dean
Program in:
  business administration • MBA

College of Education
Dr. Robert Freeman, Dean
Programs in:
  counseling/guidance • Ed S, M Ed
  early childhood education • Ed S, M Ed
  middle grades education • Ed S, M Ed
  secondary education • Ed S, M Ed
  special education • Ed S, M Ed

BRENAU UNIVERSITY
Gainesville, GA 30501-3697

Independent primarily female comprehensive institution. *Enrollment:* 2,366 graduate, professional, and undergraduate students. *Graduate faculty: 26 full-time, 33 part-time. Computer facilities: Campuswide network is available with full Internet access. Total number of PCs/ terminals supplied for student use: 112. Computer service fees are included with tuition and fees. Library facilities: Brenau Trustee Library. Graduate expenses: $249 per semester hour. General application contact: Kathy Cobb, Director of Graduate Admissions, 770-534-6162.*

Graduate Programs
Dr. Helen Ray, Dean
Programs in:
  behavior disorders • M Ed
  business • MBA
  early childhood education • Ed S, M Ed
  family nurse practitioner • MSN
  learning disabilities • M Ed
  middle grades education • Ed S, M Ed
  special education interrelated • M Ed

CLARK ATLANTA UNIVERSITY
Atlanta, GA 30314
http://www.cau.edu/

Independent-religious coed university. *Enrollment:* 5,912 graduate, professional, and undergraduate students. Graduate faculty: 321 full-time. Library facilities: Robert W. Woodruff Library. Graduate expenses: *Tuition of $9672 per year full-time, $403 per credit hour part-time. Fees of $200 per year. General application contact: Michelle Clark-Davis, Graduate Program Assistant, 404-880-8709.*

School of Arts and Sciences
Dr. Larry Earvin, Dean
Programs in:
  African-American studies • MA
  Africana women's studies • DA, MA
  applied mathematics • MS
  biology • MS, PhD
  computer and information science • MS
  computer science • MS
  criminal justice • MA
  economics • MA
  English • MA
  history • MA
  humanities • DA
  inorganic chemistry • MS, PhD
  organic chemistry • MS, PhD
  physical chemistry • MS, PhD
  physics • MS
  political science • MA, PhD
  public administration • MPA
  Romance languages • MA
  science education • DA
  sociology • MA

School of Business Administration
Dr. Edward Davis, Acting Dean
Programs in:
  decision science • MBA
  finance • MBA
  marketing • MBA

School of Education
Dr. Trevor Turner, Dean
Programs in:
  counseling • MA, PhD
  curriculum • Ed S, MA
  educational leadership • Ed D, Ed S, MA
  education psychology • MA
  exceptional student education • Ed S, MA

School of International Affairs and Development
Dr. Herschelle Challenor, Dean
Programs in:
  international affairs and development • PhD
  international business and development • MA
  international development administration • MA
  international development education and planning • MA
  international relations • MA
  regional studies • MA

School of Library and Information Studies
Dr. Arthur C. Gunn, Acting Dean
Program in:
  library and information studies • MSLS, SLS

School of Social Work
Dr. Dorcas Bowles, Dean
Program in:
  social work • MSW, PhD

COLUMBUS STATE UNIVERSITY
Columbus, GA 31907-5645
http://www.colstate.edu/

Public coed comprehensive institution. *Enrollment: 5,405 graduate, professional, and undergraduate students. Graduate faculty: 110 full-time, 30 part-time. Computer facilities: Campuswide network is available with full Internet access. Total number of PCs/terminals supplied for student use: 430. Computer services are offered at no charge. Library facilities: Schwob Memorial Library. Graduate expenses: $1718 per year full-time, $151 per semester hour part-time for state residents; $6218 per year full-time, $401 per semester hour part-time for nonresidents. General application contact: Katie Thornton, Graduate Admissions, 706-568-2279.*

Graduate Studies
Dr. Thomas Z. Jones, Vice President for Academic Affairs

College of Arts and Letters
Paul J. Vander Gheynst, Dean
Programs in:
- art education • M Ed
- arts and letters • MPA
- music education • MM
- piano pedagogy • MM

College of Business
Dr. Robert S. Johnson, Dean
Program in:
- business • MBA

College of Education
Dr. Thomas E. Harrison, Dean
Programs in:
- behavioral disorders • M Ed
- biology • M Ed
- community counseling • MS
- early childhood education • Ed S, M Ed
- educational administration • Ed S, M Ed
- English • Ed S, M Ed
- general science • M Ed
- history • M Ed
- learning disabilities • M Ed
- mathematics • Ed S, M Ed
- mental retardation • M Ed
- middle grades education • Ed S, M Ed
- physical education • M Ed
- political science • M Ed
- reading • Ed S, M Ed
- school counseling • Ed S, M Ed
- science/biology • Ed S
- secondary education • Ed S, M Ed
- social science • Ed S, M Ed
- special education • Ed S, M Ed

College of Science
Dr. Arthur G. Cleveland, Dean
Programs in:
- applied computer science • MS
- environmental science • MS

 # EMORY UNIVERSITY
Atlanta, GA 30322-1100
http://www.emory.edu/

Independent-religious coed university. *Enrollment: 11,109 graduate, professional, and undergraduate students. Graduate faculty: 1,491 full-time, 192 part-time. Computer facilities: Campuswide network is available with full Internet access. Computer service fees are included with tuition and fees. Library facilities: Robert W. Woodruff Library plus 6 additional on-campus libraries. Graduate expenses: Tuition of $21,770 per year. Fees of $300 per year. General application contact: Admissions Office of the appropriate school, 404-727-6036.*

Graduate School of Arts and Sciences
Dr. Donald Stein, Dean
Programs in:
- anthropology • PhD
- art history • PhD
- biophysics • MA, MS, PhD
- biostatistics • MS, PhD
- chemistry • MS, PhD
- clinical psychology • PhD
- cognition and development • PhD
- comparative literature • Certificate, MA, PhD
- economics • MA, PhD
- English • MA, PhD
- film studies • MA
- French • MAT, PhD
- history • MA, PhD
- Jewish studies • MA
- mathematics • MA, MS, PhD
- mathematics/computer science • MS
- music • MM, MSM
- philosophy • MA, PhD
- physics • MA, MS, PhD
- political science • PhD
- psychobiology • PhD
- radiological physics • MA, MS, PhD
- sociology • MA, PhD
- solid-state physics • MA, MS, PhD
- Spanish • MA, MAT, PhD
- women's studies • Certificate, PhD

Division of Biological and Biomedical Sciences
Dr. Bryan D. Noe, Director
Programs in:
- biochemistry, cell and developmental biology • PhD
- genetics and molecular biology • PhD
- immunology and molecular pathogenesis • PhD
- microbiology and molecular genetics • PhD
- molecular therapeutics and toxicology • PhD
- neuroscience • PhD
- nutrition and health sciences • PhD
- physiological and pharmacological sciences • PhD
- population biology, ecology, and evolution • PhD

Division of Educational Studies
Dr. Robert Jensen, Acting Director
Programs in:
early childhood teaching • M Ed, MAT
educational studies • DAST, MA, PhD
middle grades teaching • M Ed, MAT
secondary teaching • M Ed, MAT

Division of Epidemiology
Dr. John Boring, Director
Program in:
quantitative epidemiology • PhD

Division of Religion
Dr. Jon P. Gunnemann, Director
Program in:
religion • PhD

Graduate Institute of Liberal Arts
Dr. Robert A. Paul, Chair
Program in:
liberal arts • PhD

Candler School of Theology
R. Kevin LaGree, Dean
Program in:
theology • M Div, MTS, Th D, Th M

Nell Hodgson Woodruff School of Nursing
Dr. Dyanne D. Affonso, Dean
Programs in:
adult health • MSN
adult medical/surgical/nurse practitioner • MSN
adult oncology/nurse practitioner • MSN
child health/pediatric nurse practitioner • MSN
critical care/nurse practitioner • MSN
family and adult nurse practitioner • MSN
gerontologic nurse practitioner • MSN
midwifery • MSN
nursing systems • MSN
occupational health nurse practitioner • MSN
pediatric oncology nurse practitioner • MSN
perinatal/neonatal nurse • MSN
psychosocial nurse practitioner • MSN
women and children • MSN

Roberto C. Goizueta Business School
Ronald E. Frank, Dean
Program in:
business • EMBA, MBA

School of Law
Howard O. Hunter, Dean
Program in:
law • JD, LL M

School of Medicine
Dr. Thomas J. Lawley, Dean
Programs in:
anesthesiology/patient monitoring systems • MM Sc
critical care medicine • MM Sc
general practice • Certificate

medicine • MD
ophthalmic technology • MM Sc
oral maxillofacial surgery • Certificate
oral pathology • Certificate
physical therapy • MM Sc, MPT
physician assistant • MM Sc
radiation oncology physics • MM Sc

The Rollins School of Public Health
Dr. James W. Curran, Dean
Programs in:
behavioral sciences and health education • MPH
biostatistics • MPH, MSPH
environmental/occupational health • MPH
epidemiology • MPH
health policy and management • MPH
international health • MPH
public health • MS, PhD

FORT VALLEY STATE UNIVERSITY
Fort Valley, GA 31030-3298

Public coed comprehensive institution. *Enrollment: 2,847 graduate, professional, and undergraduate students. Graduate faculty: 22. Library facilities: Hunt Memorial Library plus 1 additional on-campus library. Graduate expenses: $2486 per year full-time, $83 per semester hour part-time for state residents; $8486 per year full-time, $333 per semester hour part-time for nonresidents. General application contact: Harriet Steel, Acting Director of Admissions, 912-825-6307.*

Graduate Division
Dr. Curtis Martin, Dean
Programs in:
early childhood education • MS
guidance and counseling • Ed S, MS
mental health counseling • MS
middle grades education • MS
vocational rehabilitation counseling • MS

GEORGIA COLLEGE AND STATE UNIVERSITY
Milledgeville, GA 31061
http://www.gac.peachnet.edu/default.html

Public coed comprehensive institution. *Enrollment: 5,500 graduate, professional, and undergraduate students. Graduate faculty: 90 full-time. Computer facilities: Campuswide network is available with full Internet access. Computer services are offered at no charge. Library facilities: Ina Dillard Russell Library. General application contact: Dr. Ken Jones, Dean of the Graduate School, 912-471-2063.*

Georgia College and State University (continued)
Graduate School
Dr. Ken Jones, Dean

College of Arts and Sciences
Dr. Bernie L. Patterson, Dean
Programs in:
    biology • MS
    English, speech and journalism • MA
    history • MA
    logistics management • MSA
    logistics systems • MSLS
    psychology • MS
    public administration • MPA

School of Business
Dr. Melinda McCannon, Graduate Director
Program in:
    business • MBA, MIS

School of Education
Dr. W. Bee Crews, Graduate Coordinator
Programs in:
    administration and supervision • Ed S, M Ed
    behavior disorders • M Ed
    early childhood education • Ed S, M Ed
    foundations and secondary education • Ed S, M Ed,
       MAT
    instructional technology • M Ed
    middle grades education • Ed S, M Ed

School of Health Sciences
Dr. Pamela Levi, Dean
Programs in:
    health and physical education • Ed S, M Ed
    nursing • MSN

GEORGIA INSTITUTE OF TECHNOLOGY
Atlanta, GA 30332-0001
http://www.gatech.edu/

Public coed university. *Enrollment:* 13,086 graduate, professional, and undergraduate students. Graduate faculty: *672 full-time, 6 part-time.* Computer facilities: *Campuswide network is available with full Internet access. Computer service fees are included with tuition and fees.* Library facilities: *Price Gilbert Memorial Library.* Graduate expenses: *Tuition of $2670 per year full-time, $98 per credit hour part-time for state residents; $10,680 per year full-time, $298 per credit hour part-time for nonresidents. Fees of $681 per year full-time, $23 per credit hour (minimum) part-time.* General application contact: *Gail Potts, Manager, Graduate Academic and Enrollment Services, 404-894-4612.*

Graduate Studies and Research
Programs in:
    algorithms, combinatorics, and optimization • PhD
    statistics • MS Stat

College of Architecture
Thomas D. Galloway, Dean
Programs in:
    architecture • M Arch, MS, PhD
    city planning • MCP

College of Computing
Dr. Peter A. Freeman, Dean
Programs in:
    algorithms, combinatorics, and optimization • PhD
    computer science • MS, MSCS, PhD
    human computer interaction • MSHCI

College of Engineering
Dr. Jean-Lou Chameau, Dean
Programs in:
    aerospace engineering • MS, MSAE, PhD
    algorithms, combinatorics, and optimization • PhD
    biomedical engineering • Certificate, MS Bio E, PhD
    ceramic engineering • MSMSE, PhD
    chemical engineering • MS Ch E, PhD
    civil engineering • MS, MSCE, PhD
    construction management • MS, MSCE, PhD
    electrical and computer engineering • MS, MSEE, PhD
    engineering science and mechanics • MS, MSESM, PhD
    environmental engineering • MS, MS Env E, PhD
    health physics • MSHP
    health systems • MSHS
    industrial and systems engineering • PhD
    industrial engineering • MS, MSIE
    materials engineering • MS
    mechanical engineering • MS, MSME, PhD
    metallurgy • MSMSE, PhD
    nuclear engineering • MSNE, PhD
    operations research • MSOR
    polymers • MS Poly
    pulp and paper engineering • Certificate
    statistics • MS Stat
    textile chemistry • MS, MST Ch
    textile engineering • MS, MSTE, PhD
    textiles • MS, MS Text

College of Sciences
Dr. Gary B. Schuster, Dean
Programs in:
    algorithms, combinatorics, and optimization • PhD
    applied mathematics • MS
    applied physics • MSA Phy
    biology • MS, MS Biol, PhD
    chemistry and biochemistry • MS, MS Chem, PhD
    earth and atmospheric sciences • MS, MSEAS, PhD
    human computer interaction • MSHCI
    mathematics • MS Math, PhD
    physics • MS, MS Phys, PhD
    psychology • MS, MS Psy, PhD
    statistics • MS Stat

Dupree College of Management
Lloyd Byars, Acting Dean
Programs in:
    management • MS, MS Mgt, PhD
    management of technology • MSMOT

Ivan Allen College of Policy and International Affairs
Robert G. Hawkins, Dean
Programs in:
  economics • MS
  history of technology • MSHT, PhD
  human computer interaction • MSHCI
  information design and technology • MSIDT
  international affairs • MS Int A
  public policy • MS Pub P, PhD

GEORGIA SOUTHERN UNIVERSITY

Statesboro, GA 30460-8126

http://www.gasou.edu/

Public coed comprehensive institution. *Enrollment: 13,965 graduate, professional, and undergraduate students. Graduate faculty: 372 full-time, 26 part-time. Computer facilities: Campuswide network is available with full Internet access. Total number of PCs/terminals supplied for student use: 400. Computer service fees are applied as a separate charge. Library facilities: Henderson Library plus 1 additional on-campus library. Graduate expenses: $2619 per year full-time, $287 per semester (minimum) part-time for state residents; $8619 per year full-time, $1037 per semester (minimum) part-time for nonresidents. General application contact: Dr. John R. Diebolt, Associate Graduate Dean, 912-681-5384.*

College of Graduate Studies
Dr. G. Lane Van Tassell, Associate Vice President for
  Academic Affairs and Dean of Graduate Studies and
  Research

Allen E. Paulson College of Science and Technology
Dr. Jimmy Solomon, Dean
Programs in:
  biology • MS
  mathematics • MS
  technology • M Tech

College of Business
Dr. Michael McDonald, Director of Graduate Studies
Programs in:
  accounting • M Acc
  business administration • MBA

College of Education
Dr. Arnold Cooper, Dean
Programs in:
  adult and vocational education • M Ed
  art education • Ed S, M Ed
  business education • M Ed
  counselor education • Ed S, M Ed
  curriculum studies • Ed D
  early childhood education • Ed S, M Ed
  educational leadership • Ed D, Ed S, M Ed
  English • Ed S, M Ed
  French • M Ed
  German • M Ed

  health and physical education • Ed S, M Ed
  higher education and student services • M Ed
  instructional media • Ed S, M Ed
  mathematics • Ed S, M Ed
  middle grades education • Ed S, M Ed
  music • Ed S, M Ed
  reading specialist • Ed S, M Ed
  school psychology • Ed S, M Ed
  science • Ed S, M Ed
  social science • Ed S, M Ed
  Spanish • M Ed
  special education for exceptional children • Ed S, M Ed
  technology education • Ed S, M Ed

College of Health and Professional Studies
Dr. Frederick Whitt, Dean
Programs in:
  kinesiology • MS
  recreation administration • MS
  rural community health nurse specialist • MSN
  rural family nurse practitioner • Certificate, MSN
  sport management • MS

College of Liberal Arts and Social Sciences
Dr. Roosevelt Newson, Dean
Programs in:
  art • MFA
  English • MA
  history • MA
  music • MM
  political science • MA
  psychology • MS
  public administration • MPA
  sociology • MA

GEORGIA SOUTHWESTERN STATE UNIVERSITY

Americus, GA 31709-4693

http://gswrs6k1.gsw.peachnet.edu/

Public coed comprehensive institution. *Enrollment: 2,500 graduate, professional, and undergraduate students. Graduate faculty: 40 full-time, 3 part-time. Computer facilities: Campuswide network is available with full Internet access. Computer service fees are applied as a separate charge. Library facilities: James Earl Carter Library. General application contact: Dr. William L. Tietjen, Interim Vice President for Academic Affairs, 912-928-1361.*

Graduate Studies
Dr. William L. Tietjen, Interim Vice President for Academic
  Affairs
Programs in:
  business administration • MSA
  business education • M Ed
  computer and applied sciences • MS
  computer information systems • MSA
  early childhood education • Ed S, M Ed
  health and physical education • M Ed

Georgia Southwestern State University (continued)
- middle grades education • Ed S, M Ed
- psychology and sociology • MSA
- reading • M Ed
- secondary education • M Ed
- social administration • MSA

GEORGIA STATE UNIVERSITY
Atlanta, GA 30303-3083
http://www.gsu.edu/

Public coed university. *Enrollment:* 24,300 graduate, professional, and undergraduate students. Graduate faculty: *848 full-time, 57 part-time.* Computer facilities: *Campuswide network is available with full Internet access. Total number of PCs/terminals supplied for student use: 500. Computer services are offered at no charge.* Library facilities: *William R. Pullen Library plus 1 additional on-campus library.* Graduate expenses: *Tuition of $2673 per year full-time, $99 per semester hour part-time for state residents; $10,692 per year full-time, $396 per semester hour part-time for nonresidents. Fees of $228 per year.* General application contact: *Dr. Robert Sheinkopf, Director of Admissions, 404-651-2469.*

College of Arts and Sciences
Dr. Ahmed T. Abdelal, Dean
Programs in:
- analytical chemistry • PhD
- anthropology • MA
- applied linguistics/teaching English as a second language • MS
- astronomy • PhD
- biology • MS, PhD
- biophysical chemistry • PhD
- chemistry • MS
- community psychology • PhD
- creative writing • MA, MFA, PhD
- French • Certificate, MA
- geography • MA
- geology • MS
- German • Certificate, MA
- heritage preservation • MHP
- history • MA, PhD
- hydrogeology • Certificate
- journalism • MA
- literature • MA, PhD
- mathematics and computer science • MA, MAT, MS
- media studies • MA
- neuropsychology and behavioral neuroscience • PhD
- organic chemistry and biochemistry • PhD
- philosophy • MA
- physics • MS, PhD
- political science • MA, PhD
- psychological foundations • PhD
- sociology • MA, PhD
- Spanish • Certificate, MA
- speech • MA
- theatre • MA

School of Art and Design
John McWilliams, Director
Programs in:
- art and design • MFA
- art education • MA Ed
- art history • MA

School of Music
Dr. John Haberlen, Director
Programs in:
- choral conducting • M Mu
- composition • M Mu
- instrumental conducting • M Mu
- jazz studies • M Mu
- music education • M Mu
- music theory • M Mu
- performance • M Mu
- piano pedagogy • M Mu
- sacred music • M Mu

Women's Studies Institute
Dr. Diane L. Fowlkes, Director
Program in:
- women's studies • MA

College of Business Administration
Dr. Sidney E. Harris, Dean
Programs in:
- actuarial science • MAS
- computer information systems • MBA, MS, PhD
- decision sciences • MBA, MS, PhD
- economics • MBA
- finance • MBA, MS, PhD
- general business • MBA
- general business administration • MBA
- management • MBA, MS, PhD
- marketing • MBA, MS, PhD
- personal financial planning • MS
- real estate • MBA, MSRE, PhD
- risk management and insurance • MBA, MS, PhD

Institute of Health Administration
Dr. Everett A. Johnson, Director
Program in:
- health administration • MHA, MSHA

Institute of International Business
Kamal M. El-sheshai, Acting Director
Program in:
- international business • MBA, MIB

School of Accountancy
Dr. Fenwick Huss, Director
Programs in:
- accountancy • MBA, MPA, PhD
- taxation • MTX

W. T. Beebe Institute of Personnel and Employment Relations
Dr. Michael J. Jedel, Director
Program in:
- personnel and employment relations • MBA, MS, PhD

College of Education
Dr. Samuel M. Deitz, Dean
Programs in:
    art education • Ed S
    communication disorders • M Ed
    comprehensive business education • MBE
    counseling • PhD
    counseling psychology • PhD
    curriculum development and instruction processes •
       PhD
    educational psychology • MS, PhD
    educational research • MS
    education of behavior/learning disabled • M Ed
    education of the hearing impaired • M Ed
    English education • Ed S, M Ed
    exceptionalities • PhD
    exercise science • MS
    health and physical education • Ed S, M Ed
    higher education • PhD
    instructional technology • MS, PhD
    language and literacy education • PhD
    library media technology • Ed S, MLM, PhD
    mathematics education • Ed S, M Ed, PhD
    middle childhood education • Ed S, M Ed
    multiple/severe disabilities • M Ed
    music education • Ed S
    pastoral counseling • Ed S
    professional counseling • Ed S, MS
    reading instruction • Ed S, M Ed
    rehabilitation counseling • Ed S, MS
    research, measurements and statistics • PhD
    school counseling • Ed S, M Ed
    school psychology • Ed S, PhD
    school psychometry • M Ed
    science education • Ed S, M Ed, PhD
    social foundations of education • MS, PhD
    social science education • Ed S
    social studies education • M Ed, PhD
    special education • Ed S
    sports administration • MS
    sport science • PhD
    sports medicine • MS
    vocational education • Ed S, M Ed
    vocational leadership • PhD

College of Health and Human Sciences
Dr. Sherry K. Gaines, Dean
Programs in:
    criminal justice • MS
    immunohematology • MS
    laboratory management • MS
    orthopedics • MS
    respiratory care • MS

School of Nursing
Dr. Dee Baldwin, Director of Graduate Programs
Programs in:
    adult health • MS
    child and adolescent psychology • MS
    child health/pediatric nurse practitioner • MS
    community nursing • PhD
    family nurse practitioner • MS
    family nursing • PhD
    gerontology • MS
    health promotion, protection, and restoration • PhD
    perinatal women's health/practitioner • MS
    psychiatric/mental health nursing • MS

College of Law
Dr. Janice C. Griffith, Dean
Program in:
    law • JD

School of Policy Studies
Dr. Roy Bahl, Dean
Programs in:
    economics • MA, MS, PhD
    gerontology • MS
    human resource development • MS, PhD
    human resources • MS
    nonprofit administration • MS
    planning and economic development • MS
    public administration • MPA
    transportation • MS
    urban governance • MPA
    urban studies • MS

KENNESAW STATE UNIVERSITY
Kennesaw, GA 30144-5591

http://www.kennesaw.edu/

Public coed comprehensive institution. *Enrollment:* 13,094 graduate, professional, and undergraduate students. Graduate faculty: *121 full-time, 17 part-time.* Computer facilities: *Campuswide network is available with full Internet access. Total number of PCs/terminals supplied for student use: 950. Computer services are offered at no charge.* Library facilities: *Horace W. Sturgis Library.* Graduate expenses: *Tuition of $2398 per year full-time, $83 per credit hour part-time for state residents; $8398 per year full-time, $333 per credit hour part-time for nonresidents. Fees of $338 per year.* General application contact: *Dr. Susan N. Barrett, Administrative Specialist, Admissions, 770-423-6500.*

College of Arts, Humanities and Social Sciences
Dr. Donald W. Forrester, Interim Dean
Programs in:
    professional writing • MAPW
    public administration • MPA

Leland and Clarice C. Bagwell College of Education
Dr. Deborah Wallace, Dean
Programs in:
    early childhood • M Ed
    middle grades • M Ed
    special education • M Ed

Kennesaw State University (continued)
Michael J. Coles College of Business
Dr. Timothy Mescon, Dean
Programs in:
  accounting • M Acc, MBA
  business administration • MBA, MBA-EP, MBA-PE
  business information systems management • MBA
  entrepreneurship • MBA
  finance • MBA
  human resources management and development • MBA
  marketing • MBA

School of Nursing
Dr. Julia Perkins, Dean
Program in:
  primary care nurse practitioner • MSN

MERCER UNIVERSITY
Macon, GA 31207-0003

http://www.mercer.edu/

Independent-religious coed comprehensive institution. *Enrollment:* 2,605 graduate, professional, and undergraduate students. Library facilities: *main library plus 2 additional on-campus libraries.* Graduate expenses: *$180 per credit hour.* General application contact: *Director of Admissions, 912-752-2700.*

School of Education
Dr. Anne Hathaway, Dean
Programs in:
  early childhood education • Ed S, M Ed
  English education • M Ed
  mathematics education • M Ed
  middle grades education • Ed S, M Ed
  reading specialist • M Ed
  science education • M Ed
  social sciences education • M Ed

School of Engineering
Dr. Mogens Henriksen, Dean
Programs in:
  biomedical engineering • MSE
  electrical engineering • MSE
  engineering management • MSE
  mechanical engineering • MSE
  software engineering • MSE
  software systems • MS
  technical management • MS

School of Medicine
Program in:
  medicine • MD, MFS

Stetson School of Business and Economics
Dr. W. Carl Joiner, Dean
Program in:
  business and economics • MBA, MSM

Walter F. George School of Law
R. Lawrence Dessem, Dean
Program in:
  law • JD

MERCER UNIVERSITY, CECIL B. DAY CAMPUS
Atlanta, GA 30341-4155

http://www.mercer.edu/cbd/index.html

Independent-religious coed upper-level institution. *Enrollment:* 3,530 graduate, professional, and undergraduate students. Graduate faculty: *80 full-time, 57 part-time.* Computer facilities: *Campuswide network is available with full Internet access. Computer services are offered at no charge.* Library facilities: *Monroe F. Swilley Jr. Library.* Graduate expenses: *$220 per semester hour.* General application contact: *Director of Admissions, 770-986-3000.*

Graduate Education Programs
Dr. Anne Hathaway, Dean
Programs in:
  early childhood education • Ed S, M Ed
  middle grades education • Ed S, M Ed

Graduate Engineering Programs
Dr. Mogens Henriksen, Dean
Programs in:
  electrical engineering • MSE
  engineering management • MSE
  software engineering • MSE
  software systems • MS
  technical communication management • MS

James and Carolyn McAfee School of Theology
Dr. R. Alan Culpepper, Dean
Program in:
  theology • M Div

Southern School of Pharmacy
Dr. Hewitt W. Matthews, Dean
Programs in:
  pharmaceutical sciences • PhD
  pharmacy • Pharm D

Stetson School of Business and Economics
Dr. W. Carl Joiner, Dean
Programs in:
  business administration • MBA, XMBA
  health care policy and administration • MS
  technology management • MS

NORTH GEORGIA COLLEGE & STATE UNIVERSITY

Dahlonega, GA 30597-1001

http://www.ngc.peachnet.edu/

Public coed comprehensive institution. *Enrollment: 3,313 graduate, professional, and undergraduate students. Graduate faculty: 69 full-time, 14 part-time. Computer facilities: Campuswide network is available with full Internet access. Total number of PCs/terminals supplied for student use: 200. Computer service fees are included with tuition and fees. Library facilities: Stewart Library. General application contact: Mai-Lan Ledbetter, Coordinator of Graduate Admissions, 706-864-1543.*

Graduate School

Programs in:
- art education • M Ed
- behavior disorders • M Ed
- biology education • M Ed
- chemistry education • M Ed
- early childhood education • M Ed
- English education • M Ed
- family practitioner • MSN
- interrelated special education • M Ed
- learning disabilities • M Ed
- mathematics education • M Ed
- mental retardation • M Ed
- middle grades education • M Ed
- modern languages education • M Ed
- physical education • M Ed
- physical therapy • MS
- public administration • MPA
- science education • M Ed
- secondary education • M Ed
- social science education • M Ed
- special education • M Ed

STATE UNIVERSITY OF WEST GEORGIA

Carrollton, GA 30118

http://www.westga.edu/

Public coed comprehensive institution. *Enrollment: 8,422 graduate, professional, and undergraduate students. Graduate faculty: 219 full-time, 8 part-time. Computer facilities: Campuswide network is available with full Internet access. Total number of PCs/terminals supplied for student use: 1,500. Computer service fees are included with tuition and fees. Library facilities: Irvine Sullivan Ingram Library plus 1 additional on-campus library. Graduate expenses: Tuition of $2428 per year full-time, $83 per semester hour part-time for state residents; $8428 per year full-time, $250 per semester hour part-time for nonresidents. Fees of $428 per year. General application contact: Dr. Jack O. Jenkins, Dean of the Graduate School, 770-836-6419.*

Graduate School

Dr. Jack O. Jenkins, Dean

College of Arts and Sciences

Dr. Richard G. Miller, Dean
Programs in:
- art education • M Ed
- biology • MS
- English • MA
- gerontology • MA
- history • MA
- music education • MM
- music performance • MM
- psychology • MA
- public administration • MPA
- rural and small town planning • MS
- sociology • MA

College of Business

Dr. David H. Hovey, Dean
Programs in:
- accounting • MP Acc
- business administration • MBA
- business education • Ed S, M Ed

College of Education

Dr. Angela Lumpkin, Dean
Programs in:
- administration and supervision • Ed S, M Ed
- counseling and guidance • Ed S, M Ed
- early childhood education • Ed S, M Ed
- educational leadership • Ed D, Ed S
- library media • Ed S, M Ed
- middle grades education • Ed S, M Ed
- physical education • Ed S, M Ed
- reading • Ed S, M Ed
- school home services • Ed S, M Ed
- secondary education • Ed S, M Ed
- special education • Ed S, M Ed

 UNIVERSITY OF GEORGIA

Athens, GA 30602

http://www.uga.edu/

Public coed university. *Enrollment: 29,693 graduate, professional, and undergraduate students. Graduate faculty: 1,562. Library facilities: Ilah Dunlap Little Memorial Library. Graduate expenses: $3290 per year full-time, $643 per semester (minimum) part-time for state residents; $11,300 per year full-time, $1645 per semester (minimum) part-time for nonresidents. General application contact: Mary Ann Keller, Director of Graduate Admissions, 706-542-1739.*

Graduate School

Gordhan L. Patel, Dean
Programs in:
- avian medicine • MAM
- law • LL M
- medical microbiology • MS, PhD

University of Georgia (continued)
    parasitology • MS, PhD
    pathology • MS, PhD
    pharmacology • MS, PhD
    physiology • MS, PhD
    toxicology • MS, PhD
    veterinary anatomy • MS

College of Agricultural and Environmental Sciences
Dr. Gale A. Buchanan, Dean
Programs in:
    agricultural and applied economics • MAE, MS, PhD
    agricultural engineering • MS
    agricultural extension • MA Ext
    animal and dairy science • PhD
    animal nutrition • PhD
    animal science • MS
    biological and agricultural engineering • PhD
    biological engineering • MS
    crop and soil sciences • MPPPM, MS, PhD
    dairy science • MS
    entomology • MPPPM, MS, PhD
    environmental health science • MS
    food science • MS, PhD
    horticulture • MS, PhD
    plant pathology • MS, PhD
    plant protection and pest management • MPPPM
    poultry science • MS, PhD

College of Arts and Sciences
Wyatt W. Anderson, Dean
Programs in:
    analytical chemistry • MS, PhD
    anthropology • MA, PhD
    applied mathematical science • MAMS
    art • MFA, PhD
    art history • MA
    artificial intelligence • MS
    biochemistry and molecular biology • MS, PhD
    biological oceanography • MS, PhD
    botany • MS, PhD
    cellular biology • MS, PhD
    chemical oceanography • MS, PhD
    classics • MA
    clinical psychology • MS, PhD
    comparative literature • MA, PhD
    computer science • MS, PhD
    conservation ecology and sustainable development • MS
    drama • MFA, PhD
    ecology • MS, PhD
    English • MA, MAT, PhD
    French • MA, MAT
    genetics • MS, PhD
    geochemistry • MS, PhD
    geography • MA, PhD
    geophysics • MS, PhD
    German • MA
    Greek • MA
    history • MA, PhD
    inorganic chemistry • MS, PhD
    Latin • MA
    linguistics • MA, PhD
    mathematics • MA, PhD

    microbiology • MS, PhD
    music • DMA, MA, MM, PhD
    organic chemistry • MS, PhD
    philosophy • MA, PhD
    physical chemistry • MS, PhD
    physical oceanography • MS, PhD
    physics • MS, PhD
    political science • MA, PhD
    psychology • MS, PhD
    public administration • DPA, MPA
    religion • MA
    Romance languages • MA, MAT, PhD
    sociology • MA, PhD
    Spanish • MA, MAT
    speech communication • MA, PhD
    statistics • MS, PhD

College of Education
Dr. Russell H. Yeany, Dean
Programs in:
    adult education • Ed D, Ed S, M Ed, MA, PhD
    agricultural education • M Ed
    art education • Ed D, Ed S, MA Ed
    business education • M Ed
    communication sciences and disorders • Ed S, M Ed, MA, PhD
    computer-based education • M Ed
    counseling and student personnel services • PhD
    counseling psychology • PhD
    early childhood education • Ed D, Ed S, M Ed
    education • MA
    educational leadership • Ed D, Ed S, M Ed, MA
    educational psychology • M Ed, PhD
    education of the gifted • Ed D
    elementary and middle school education • Ed D, Ed S, M Ed
    English education • Ed S, M Ed
    exercise science • Ed D, M Ed, PhD
    guidance and counseling • M Ed
    health promotion and behavior • PhD
    health promotion and behavior and safety education • M Ed
    higher education • Ed D, PhD
    home economics education • M Ed
    human resource and organization development • M Ed
    instructional technology • Ed S, M Ed, PhD
    language education • Ed S, M Ed, PhD
    marketing education • M Ed
    mathematics education • Ed D, Ed S, M Ed, PhD
    middle school education • PhD
    music education • Ed D, Ed S, MM Ed
    occupational studies • Ed D, Ed S, M Ed
    physical education and sport studies • Ed D, Ed S, M Ed, MA, PhD
    reading education • Ed D, Ed S, M Ed, MA, PhD
    recreation and leisure studies • Ed D, M Ed, MA
    rehabilitation counseling • M Ed
    safety education • Ed S
    school psychology and school psychometry • Ed S, M Ed, MA
    science education • Ed D, Ed S, M Ed, PhD
    social science education • PhD
    social sciences education • Ed D, Ed S, M Ed

speech education • Ed S, M Ed
student personnel in higher education • M Ed
technological studies • M Ed

College of Family and Consumer Sciences
Sharon Y. Nickols, Dean
Programs in:
child and family development • MHE, MS, PhD
foods and nutrition • MHE, MS, PhD
housing and consumer economics • MS, PhD
textiles, merchandising, and interiors • MS, PhD

School of Environmental Design
John F. Crowley, Dean
Programs in:
historic preservation • MHP
landscape architecture • MLA

School of Forest Resources
Dr. Arnett C. Mace Jr., Dean
Program in:
forest resources • MFR, MS, PhD

School of Journalism and Mass Communication
J. Thomas Russell, Dean
Programs in:
journalism • MA
mass communication • MMC, PhD

School of Social Work
Dr. Bonnie L. Yegidis, Dean
Program in:
social work • MSW, PhD

Terry College of Business
Dr. P. George Benson, Dean
Programs in:
accounting • M Acc
applied mathematical science • MAMS
business administration • MA, MBA, PhD
economics • MA, PhD
marketing research • MMR

College of Pharmacy
Dr. Stuart Feldman, Dean
Programs in:
experimental therapeutics • MS, PhD
medicinal chemistry • MS, PhD
pharmaceutics • MS, PhD
pharmacology • MS, PhD
pharmacy • Pharm D
pharmacy care administration • MS, PhD
toxicology • MS, PhD

College of Veterinary Medicine
Dr. Keith W. Prasse, Dean
Programs in:
avian medicine • MAM
medical microbiology • MS, PhD
parasitology • MS, PhD
pathology • MS, PhD
pharmacology • MS, PhD
physiology • MS, PhD
toxicology • MS, PhD

veterinary anatomy • MS
veterinary medicine • DVM

School of Law
David E. Shipley, Dean
Program in:
law • JD, LL M

VALDOSTA STATE UNIVERSITY
Valdosta, GA 31698

http://www.valdosta.peachnet.edu/

Public coed university. *Enrollment: 9,807 graduate, professional, and undergraduate students. Graduate faculty: 171 full-time. Computer facilities: Campuswide network is available with full Internet access. Total number of PCs/terminals supplied for student use: 400. Computer service fees are included with tuition and fees. Library facilities: Odom Library plus 3 additional on-campus libraries. Graduate expenses: Tuition of $2472 per year full-time, $83 per semester hour part-time for state residents; $8472 per year full-time, $333 per semester hour part-time for nonresidents. Fees of $236 per year full-time. General application contact: Dr. Ernestine H. Clark, Dean of Graduate School, 912-333-5694.*

Graduate School
Dr. Ernestine H. Clark, Dean
Program in:
social work • MSW

College of Arts and Sciences
Dr. Thomas Dasher, Dean
Programs in:
anthropology • MS
criminal justice • MS
English • MA
history • MA
political science • MPA
social services • MS

College of Business Administration
Dr. Kenneth L. Stanley, Dean
Program in:
business administration • M Acc, MBA

College of Education
Dr. F. D. Toth, Dean
Programs in:
adult and vocational education • Ed D
art education • MAE
business education • Ed S, M Ed
curriculum and instruction • Ed D
early childhood education • Ed S, M Ed
educational leadership • Ed D, Ed S, M Ed
education of the multiply handicapped • Ed S, M Ed
guidance and counseling • Ed S, M Ed
health and physical education • M Ed
instructional technology • M Ed
middle grades education • Ed S, M Ed

Valdosta State University (continued)
music education • MME
psychology • MS
reading • Ed S, M Ed
school psychology • Ed S, M Ed
secondary education • Ed S, M Ed
special education • Ed S, M Ed
speech-language pathology • M Ed
vocational education • M Ed

College of Fine Arts
Dr. Lanny D. Milbrandt, Head
Programs in:
art education • MAE
music education • MME

College of Nursing
Dr. Maryann Reichenbach, Dean
Programs in:
administration • MSN
community health nursing • MSN

GUAM

UNIVERSITY OF GUAM
Mangilao, GU 96923

http://uog2.uog.edu/

Public coed comprehensive institution. Computer facilities: *Campuswide network is available with full Internet access. Computer service fees are included with tuition and fees.* Library facilities: *Robert F. Kennedy Memorial Library plus 1 additional on-campus library.* General application contact: *Dean, 671-735-2173.*

Graduate School

College of Agriculture and Life Sciences
Program in:
environmental science • MS

College of Arts and Sciences
Programs in:
ceramics • MA
graphics • MA
instructional leadership • MA
Micronesian studies • MA
painting • MA
tropical marine biology • MS

College of Business and Public Administration
Program in:
business and public administration • MBA, MPA

College of Education
Programs in:
administration and supervision • M Ed
counseling • MA
language and literacy • M Ed

secondary education • M Ed
special education • M Ed
teaching English to speakers of other languages • M Ed

HAWAII

CHAMINADE UNIVERSITY OF HONOLULU
Honolulu, HI 96816-1578

http://www.chaminade.edu/

Independent-religious coed comprehensive institution. *Enrollment: 2,225 graduate, professional, and undergraduate students. Graduate faculty: 19 full-time, 24 part-time. Library facilities: Sullivan Library.* General application contact: *Dr. Michael Fassiotto, Dean of Professional Studies and Lifelong Learning, 808-739-4674.*

Graduate Programs
Dr. Michael Fassiotto, Dean of Professional Studies and Lifelong Learning
Programs in:
business administration • MBA
counseling psychology • MSCP
criminal justice administration • MSCJA
Japanese business studies • MSJBS
public administration • MPA
social science via peace education • M Ed

 ## HAWAII PACIFIC UNIVERSITY
Honolulu, HI 96813-2785

http://www.hpu.edu/

Independent coed comprehensive institution. *Enrollment: 8,390 graduate, professional, and undergraduate students. Graduate faculty: 30 full-time, 12 part-time. Computer facilities: Campuswide network is available with full Internet access. Total number of PCs/terminals supplied for student use: 294. Computer service fees are applied as a separate charge. Library facilities: Meader Library plus 2 additional on-campus libraries. Graduate expenses: $7920 per year full-time, $330 per credit part-time.* General application contact: *Leina Danao, Admissions Coordinator, 808-544-1120.*

School of Business Administration
Dr. Richard Ward, Dean for Graduate Management Studies
Programs in:
accounting • MBA
finance • MBA
human resource management • MA, MBA
information systems management • MSIS
information systems technology • MSIS

international business • MBA
management • MA, MBA
marketing • MBA
organizational change • MA
quality management • MBA

School of Nursing
Dr. Carol Winters, Dean
Programs in:
community clinical nurse specialist • MSN
family nurse practitioner • MSN

UNIVERSITY OF HAWAII AT MANOA
Honolulu, HI 96822

http://www.hawaii.edu/

Public coed university. *Enrollment: 17,353 graduate, professional, and undergraduate students. Graduate faculty: 1,747. Computer facilities: Campuswide network is available with full Internet access. Total number of PCs/terminals supplied for student use: 500. Computer services are offered at no charge. Library facilities: Hamilton Library plus 1 additional on-campus library. Graduate expenses: $4029 per year full-time, $214 per credit hour part-time for state residents; $9957 per year full-time, $461 per credit hour part-time for nonresidents. General application contact: Raymond Jarman, Assistant Dean, 808-956-8950.*

Graduate Division
Dr. Alan H. Teramura, Senior Vice President for Research and Interim Dean
Programs in:
biochemistry • MS, PhD
biomedical sciences • PhD
biophysics • MS, PhD
biostatistics-epidemiology • PhD
cell, molecular, and neuro sciences • MS, PhD
ecology, evolution and conservation biology • MS, PhD
genetics and molecular biology • MS, PhD
marine biology • MS, PhD
pharmacology • MS, PhD
physiology • MS, PhD
reproductive biology • PhD
speech pathology and audiology • MS
tropical medicine • MS, PhD

College of Arts and Sciences
Dr. Alan H. Teramura, Senior Vice President for Research and Interim Dean, Graduate Division
Programs in:
American studies • MA, PhD
anthropology • MA, PhD
art • MA
art history • MA
Asian and Asian-Western theatre • PhD
botany • MS, PhD
chemistry • MS, PhD

classics • MA
clinical psychology • PhD
communication • MA
communication and information science • PhD
community planning and social policy • MURP
computer science • PhD
dance • MA, MFA
dance and theatre • PhD
East Asian languages and literature • MA, PhD
economics • MA, PhD
English • MA, PhD
English as a second language • MA
environmental planning and management • MURP
French • MA
geography • MA, PhD
German • MA
history • MA, PhD
land use and infrastructure planning • MURP
linguistics • MA, PhD
mathematics • MA, PhD
microbiology • MS, PhD
music • MA, MM, PhD
philosophy • MA, PhD
physics and astronomy • MS, PhD
political science • MA, PhD
psychology • MA, PhD
public administration • Certificate, MPA
religion • MA
second language acquisition • PhD
sociology • MA, PhD
Spanish • MA
speech • MA
theatre • MA, MFA
urban and regional planning in Asia and Pacific • MURP
visual arts • MFA
zoology • MS, PhD

College of Business Administration
H. David Bess, Dean
Programs in:
accountancy • M Acc
business administration • EMBA, MBA
China focused business administration • EMBA
international management • PhD
Japan focused business administration • EMBA

College of Education
Dr. Charles Araki, Interim Dean
Programs in:
counselor education • M Ed
curriculum and instruction • Ed D
educational administration • Ed D, M Ed
educational foundations • Ed D, M Ed
educational policy studies • Ed D
educational psychology • M Ed, PhD
educational technology • M Ed
education in teaching • M Ed T
elementary education • M Ed
exceptionalities • Ed D
secondary education • M Ed
special education • M Ed

University of Hawaii at Manoa (continued)

College of Engineering
Dr. Paul Yuen, Dean
Programs in:
civil engineering • MS, PhD
electrical engineering • MS, PhD
mechanical engineering • MS, PhD

College of Health Sciences and Social Welfare
Dr. Alan H. Teramura, Senior Vice President for Research
and Interim Dean, Graduate Division
Programs in:
adult health • MS
biostatistics • MPH, MS
biostatistics-epidemiology • PhD
chronic diseases • MPH, MS
clinical nurse specialist • MS
community health development and education • MPH,
MS
community mental health • MS
environmental health engineering • MPH, MS
environmental health management • MPH, MS
environmental/occupational health sciences • MPH, MS
epidemiology • MPH, MS
family nurse practitioner • MS
health services administration and planning • MPH, MS
health services development • Dr PH
infectious diseases • MPH, MS
international health • MPH, MS
maternal and child health • MPH, MS
nurse practitioner • MS
nursing • Certificate
nursing administration • MS
personal and community health maintenance and
promotion • Dr PH
social welfare • PhD
social work • MSW

College of Tropical Agriculture and Human Resources
Dr. Charles Laughlin, Dean
Programs in:
agricultural and resource economics • MS, PhD
agronomy and soil sciences • MS, PhD
animal sciences • MS
biosystems engineering • MS
botanical sciences • MS, PhD
entomology • MS, PhD
food science • MS
horticulture • MS, PhD
nutritional science • MS
plant pathology • MS, PhD
plant physiology • MS, PhD

School of Architecture
W. H. Raymond Yeh, Dean
Program in:
architecture • M Arch

School of Hawaiian, Asian and Pacific Studies
Willa Tanabe, Dean
Programs in:
Asian studies • MA
Pacific Island studies • MA

School of Library and Information Studies
Dr. Alan H. Teramura, Senior Vice President for Research
and Interim Dean, Graduate Division
Programs in:
advanced library and information studies • Certificate
communication and information science • PhD
library and information studies • MLIS

School of Ocean and Earth Science and Technology
C. Barry Raleigh, Dean
Programs in:
high-pressure geophysics and geochemistry • MS, PhD
hydrogeology and engineering geology • MS, PhD
marine geology and geophysics • MS, PhD
meteorology • MS, PhD
ocean engineering • MS, PhD
oceanography • MS, PhD
planetary geosciences and remote sensing • MS, PhD
seismology and solid-earth geophysics • MS, PhD
volcanology, petrology, and geochemistry • MS, PhD

School of Travel Industry Management
Dr. Alan H. Teramura, Senior Vice President for Research
and Interim Dean, Graduate Division
Program in:
travel industry management • MPS

John A. Burns School of Medicine
Dr. Sherrel L. Hammer, Interim Dean
Programs in:
biochemistry • MS, PhD
biomedical sciences • PhD
biophysics • MS, PhD
biostatistics-epidemiology • PhD
genetics and molecular biology • MS, PhD
medicine • MD
pharmacology • MS, PhD
physiology • MS, PhD
reproductive biology • PhD
speech pathology and audiology • MS
tropical medicine • MS, PhD

School of Law
Lawrence C. Foster, Dean
Program in:
law • JD

IDAHO

BOISE STATE UNIVERSITY
Boise, ID 83725-0399

http://www.idbsu.edu/

Public coed comprehensive institution. *Enrollment: 15,384 graduate, professional, and undergraduate students. Graduate faculty:
277 full-time, 115 part-time. Computer facilities: Campuswide
network is available with full Internet access. Total number of PCs/
terminals supplied for student use: 600. Computer services are*

offered at no charge. Library facilities: Albertsons Library. Graduate expenses: $3020 per year full-time, $135 per credit part-time for state residents; $8900 per year full-time, $135 per credit part-time for nonresidents. General application contact: Dr. Kenneth M. Hollenbaugh, Dean of the Graduate College, 208-385-3647.

Graduate College
Dr. Kenneth M. Hollenbaugh, Dean

College of Arts and Sciences
Dr. Phillip Eastman, Dean
Programs in:
    applied geophysics • MS
    biology • MA, MS
    computer science • MS
    English • MA
    geology • MS
    interdisciplinary studies • MA, MS
    music • MM
    music education • MM
    pedagogy • MM
    performance • MM
    raptor biology • MS
    technical communication • MA
    visual fine arts • MFA

College of Business and Economics
Dr. Harry White, Interim Dean
Programs in:
    accountancy • MS
    business administration • MBA
    management information systems • MS

College of Education
Dr. Glenn Potter, Interim Dean
Programs in:
    art education • MA
    athletic administration • MPE
    curriculum and instruction • Ed D, MA
    early childhood education • MA
    earth science education • MS
    educational technology • MS
    exercise and sport studies • MS
    mathematics education • MS
    reading • MA
    school counseling • MA
    special education • MA

College of Engineering
Dr. Lynn Russell, Dean
Program in:
    instructional and performance technology • MS

College of Health Science
Dr. James Taylor, Dean
Program in:
    health science • MHS

College of Social Science and Public Affairs
Dr. Jane C. Ollenburger, Dean
Programs in:
    communication • MA
    environmental and natural resources policy and administration • MPA

    general public administration • MPA
    history • MA
    social work • MSW
    state and local government policy and administration • MPA

IDAHO STATE UNIVERSITY
Pocatello, ID 83209

http://www.isu.edu/

Public coed university. Enrollment: 11,886 graduate, professional, and undergraduate students. Graduate faculty: 257 full-time, 55 part-time. Computer facilities: Campuswide network is available with full Internet access. Computer service fees are applied as a separate charge. Library facilities: Eli M. Oboler Library. Graduate expenses: $3130 per year full-time, $136 per credit hour part-time for state residents; $9370 per year full-time, $226 per credit hour part-time for nonresidents. General application contact: Dr. Paul Tate, Dean, 208-236-2150.

Graduate School
Dr. Paul Tate, Dean
Programs in:
    biology • MNS
    chemistry • MNS
    general interdisciplinary • M Ed, MA, MS
    geology • MNS
    hazardous waste management • MS
    mathematics • MNS
    physics • MNS

College of Arts and Sciences
Dr. Victor Hjelm, Dean
Programs in:
    anthropology • MA, MS
    art • MFA
    biology • DA, MS, PhD
    chemistry • MNS, MS
    clinical psychology • PhD
    English • DA, MA
    geology • MS
    geophysics/hydrology • MS
    mathematics • DA, MS
    microbiology • MS
    natural science • MNS
    physics • MS
    political science • DA, MA
    psychology • MS
    public administration • MPA
    sociology • MA
    speech communication • MA
    theatre • MA

College of Business
William Stratton, Dean
Program in:
    business • MBA

Idaho State University (continued)

College of Education
Dr. Larry Harris, Dean
Programs in:
   athletic administration • MPE
   curriculum and instruction • M Ed
   educational administration • Ed S, M Ed
   educational leadership • Ed D
   family and consumer sciences • M Ed
   human exceptionality–early childhood education • M Ed
   human exceptionality–school psychologial examiner •
      M Ed
   human exceptionality–special education • M Ed
   literacy • M Ed
   occupational training management • M Ed
   school psychology • Ed S
   special education • Ed S

College of Engineering
Dr. Jay Kunze, Dean
Programs in:
   engineering and applied science • PhD
   environmental engineering • MS
   hazardous waste management • MS
   measurement and control engineering • MS
   nuclear science and engineering • MS

College of Health Professions
Dr. Linda Hatzenbuehler, Dean
Programs in:
   audiology • MS
   counseling • Ed S
   counselor education and counseling • Ed D
   deaf education • MS
   family-centered practice • Certificate
   health education • MHE
   mental health counseling • M Coun
   nursing • Certificate, MS
   occupational therapy • MOT
   physical therapy • MPT
   public health • MPH
   school counseling • M Coun
   speech language pathology • MS
   student affairs and college counseling • M Coun

College of Pharmacy
Dr. Barbara Wells, Dean
Programs in:
   pharmaceutical chemistry • MS
   pharmaceutics • MS
   pharmaceutic science • PhD
   pharmacognosy • MS
   pharmacology • MS, PhD
   pharmacy • Pharm D
   pharmacy administration • MS, PhD

UNIVERSITY OF IDAHO
Moscow, ID 83844-4140
http://www.uidaho.edu/

Public coed university. *Enrollment: 11,027 graduate, professional, and undergraduate students. Graduate faculty: 495 full-time, 47 part-time. Computer facilities: Campuswide network is available with full Internet access. Total number of PCs/terminals supplied for student use: 800. Computer service fees are included with tuition and fees. Library facilities: main library plus 1 additional on-campus library. Graduate expenses: Tuition of $0 for state residents; $6000 per year full-time, $95 per credit part-time for nonresidents. Fees of $2676 per year full-time, $134 per credit part-time. General application contact: Dr. Roger P. Wallins, Associate Dean of the College of Graduate Studies, 208-885-6243.*

College of Graduate Studies
Dr. Jeanne M. Shreeve, Dean

College of Agriculture
Dr. David Lineback, Dean
Programs in:
   agricultural and extension education • MS
   agricultural economics • MS
   animal physiology • PhD
   biochemistry • MS, PhD
   biological and agricultural engineering • M Engr, MS,
      PhD
   entomology • MS, PhD
   food science • MS
   home economics • MS
   microbiology • MS, PhD
   microbiology, molecular biology and biochemistry • MS,
      PhD
   plant pathology • MS, PhD
   plant science • MS, PhD
   soil science • MS, PhD
   veterinary science • MS

College of Art and Architecture
Paul Windley, Dean
Programs in:
   architecture • M Arch, MA
   art • MFA
   art education • MAT

College of Business and Economics
Dr. Byron Dangerfield, Dean
Programs in:
   accounting • M Acct
   economics • MS

College of Education
Dr. Dale Gentry, Dean
Programs in:
   adult education • Ed D, M Ed, MS, PhD
   business education • M Ed
   counseling and human services • CHSS, Ed D, M Ed,
      MS, PhD
   education • Ed D, Ed S, MAT, PhD
   educational administration • EAS, Ed D, M Ed, MS, PhD

elementary education • M Ed
industrial technology education • Ed D, M Ed, MS, PhD
physical education • M Ed, MS, PhD
recreation • MS
school psychology • SPS
secondary education • M Ed, MS
special education • M Ed, MS, Sp Ed S
vocational education • Ed D, M Ed, MS, PhD, V Ed S

College of Engineering
Dr. Richard T. Jacobsen, Dean
Programs in:
  chemical engineering • M Engr, MS, PhD
  civil engineering • M Engr, MS, PhD
  computer engineering • M Engr, MS
  computer science • MS, PhD
  electrical engineering • M Engr, MS, PhD
  environmental science • MS
  mechanical engineering • M Engr, MS, PhD
  nuclear engineering • M Engr, MS, PhD
  waste management • MS

College of Forestry, Wildlife, and Range Sciences
Dr. Charles R. Hatch, Dean
Programs in:
  fishery management • MS
  fishery resources • PhD
  forest products • MS, PhD
  forest resources • MS, PhD
  forestry, wildlife, and range sciences • PhD
  range resources • MS, PhD
  resource recreation and tourism • MS, PhD
  wildlife resources • MS, PhD

College of Letters and Science
Dr. Kurt O. Olsson, Dean
Programs in:
  anthropology • MA
  biological sciences • M Nat Sci
  botany • MS, PhD
  chemistry • MS, PhD
  chemistry education • MAT
  creative writing • MFA
  English • MA
  English education • MAT
  French • MAT
  history • MA, PhD
  history education • MAT
  interdisciplinary studies • MA, MS
  mathematics • MS, PhD
  mathematics education • MAT
  music • M Mus, MA
  physics • MS, PhD
  physics education • MAT
  political science • MA, PhD
  psychology • MS
  public administration • MPA
  Spanish • MAT
  statistics • MS
  teaching English as a second language • MA
  theatre arts • MFA
  zoology • MS, PhD

College of Mines and Earth Resources
Dr. Earl H. Bennett, Dean
Programs in:
  geography • MS, PhD
  geography education • MAT
  geological engineering • MS
  geology • MS, PhD
  geophysics • MS
  hydrology • MS
  metallurgical engineering • MS, PhD
  metallurgy • MS
  metallurgy engineering • MS
  mining engineering • MS, PhD
  mining engineering: metallurgy • PhD

College of Law
Dr. John A. Miller, Dean
Program in:
  law • JD

ILLINOIS

AURORA UNIVERSITY
Aurora, IL 60506-4892

http://www.aurora.edu/

Independent coed comprehensive institution. *Enrollment: 2,122 graduate, professional, and undergraduate students. Graduate faculty: 70. Computer facilities: Campuswide network is available with full Internet access. Total number of PCs/terminals supplied for student use: 35. Computer service fees are included with tuition and fees.* Library facilities: *Charles B. Phillips Library.* Graduate expenses: *$408 per semester hour.* General application contact: *Office of Admissions, 630-844-5533.*

George Williams College
Programs in:
  administration of leisure services • MS
  education • MAT
  educational leadership • MEL
  outdoor pursuits recreation administration • MS
  outdoor therapeutic recreation administration • MS
  social work • MSW
  therapeutic recreation administration • MS

School of Business and Professional Studies
Dr. Forest Etheridge, Dean
Program in:
  business and professional studies • MBA

BENEDICTINE UNIVERSITY
Lisle, IL 60532-0900

http://www.ben.edu/

Independent-religious coed comprehensive institution. *Enrollment: 2,842 graduate, professional, and undergraduate students. Graduate faculty: 17 full-time, 107 part-time. Computer facilities: Campuswide network is available with full Internet access. Total number of PCs/terminals supplied for student use: 90. Computer service fees are applied as a separate charge. Library facilities: Lownik Library plus 1 additional on-campus library. General application contact: Dr. Ralph Meeker, Director of Graduate Admissions, 630-829-6200.*

Graduate Programs

Dr. John E. Eber, Dean
Programs in:
   business • MBA
   business administration • MBA
   counseling psychology • MS
   curriculum and instruction and collaborative teaching •
      M Ed
   elementary education • MA Ed
   exercise physiology • MS
   fitness management • MS
   management and organizational behavior • MS
   management information systems • MS
   organizational development • PhD
   public health • MPH
   special education • MA Ed

BRADLEY UNIVERSITY
Peoria, IL 61625-0002

http://www.bradley.edu/

Independent coed comprehensive institution. Library facilities: *Cullom-Davis Library. Graduate expenses: $13,240 per year full-time, $359 per semester hour (minimum) part-time. General application contact: Director of Graduate Admissions, 309-677-2371.*

Graduate School

College of Business Administration
Programs in:
   accounting • MS
   business administration • MBA

College of Communications and Fine Arts
Programs in:
   ceramics • MA, MFA
   painting • MA, MFA
   photography • MA, MFA
   printmaking • MA, MFA
   sculpture • MA, MFA

College of Education and Health Sciences
Programs in:
   community agency counseling • MA
   curriculum and instruction • MA
   education and learning disabilities • MA
   human development counseling • MA
   leadership in educational administration • MA
   leadership in human services administration • MA
   nursing • MSN
   school counseling • MA

College of Engineering and Technology
Programs in:
   civil engineering and construction • MSCE
   electrical engineering • MSEE
   industrial and manufacturing engineering and
      technology • MSIE, MSMFE
   mechanical engineering • MSME

College of Liberal Arts and Sciences
Programs in:
   biology • MS
   chemistry • MS
   computer information systems • MS
   computer science • MS
   English • MA
   liberal studies • MLS

CHICAGO STATE UNIVERSITY
Chicago, IL 60628

http://www.csu.edu/

Public coed comprehensive institution. Library facilities: *Paul and Emily Douglas Library. Graduate expenses: $2268 per year full-time, $95 per credit hour part-time for state residents; $6804 per year full-time, $284 per credit hour part-time for nonresidents. General application contact: Dean of Graduate Studies, 773-995-2404.*

Graduate Studies

College of Arts and Sciences
Programs in:
   biological sciences • MS
   criminal justice • MS
   English • MA
   geography • MA
   history • MA
   mathematics • MS
   school guidance and counseling • MA

College of Education
Programs in:
   bilingual/bicultural education • MS Ed
   curriculum and instruction • MS Ed
   early childhood education • MS Ed
   educational administration and supervision • MA
   elementary education • MS Ed
   library science and communications media • MS Ed

    occupational education • MS Ed
    physical education • MS Ed
    secondary education • MS Ed
    special education • MS Ed
    teaching in non-school settings • MS Ed
    teaching of reading • MS Ed

COLUMBIA COLLEGE
Chicago, IL 60605-1997

Independent coed comprehensive institution. Library facilities: *main library.* Graduate expenses: *Tuition of $392 per credit hour. Fees of $170 per year full-time, $150 per year part-time.* General application contact: *Associate Dean of the Graduate School, 312-663-1600 Ext. 5260.*

Graduate School
Programs in:
    architectural studies • MFA
    creative writing • MFA
    dance/movement therapy • MA
    elementary • MAT
    English • MAT
    film and video • MFA
    interdisciplinary arts • MA, MAT
    interdisciplinary book and paper arts • MFA
    interior design • MFA
    media management • MA
    multicultural education • MA
    music business • MA
    performing arts management • MA
    photography • MA, MFA
    public affairs journalism • MA
    teaching of writing • MA
    urban teaching • MA
    visual arts management • MA

CONCORDIA UNIVERSITY
River Forest, IL 60305-1499
http://www.curf.edu/

Independent-religious coed comprehensive institution. *Enrollment:* 1,806 graduate, professional, and undergraduate students. Graduate faculty: *97 full-time, 119 part-time.* Computer facilities: *Campuswide network is available with full Internet access. Total number of PCs/ terminals supplied for student use: 60. Computer services are offered at no charge.* Library facilities: *Klinck Memorial Library.* Graduate expenses: *$372 per semester hour.* General application contact: *Dr. Donald E. Gnewuch, Dean of Graduate Studies, 708-209-3454.*

Graduate Studies
Dr. Donald E. Gnewuch, Dean
Programs in:
    church music • CAS, MCM
    curriculum and instruction • CAS, MA
    early childhood education • CAS, MA
    gerontology • CAS, MA
    human services • CAS, MA
    mathematics/computer science education • CAS, MA
    professional counseling • CAS, MA
    psychology • CAS, MA
    reading instruction • CAS, MA
    religion • CAS, MA
    school administration • CAS, MA
    school guidance and counseling • CAS, MA
    supervision of instruction • CAS, MA
    urban teaching • MA

DEPAUL UNIVERSITY
Chicago, IL 60604-2287
http://www.depaul.edu/

Independent-religious coed university. *Enrollment: 17,804 graduate, professional, and undergraduate students. Graduate faculty: 441 full-time, 523 part-time.* Computer facilities: *Campuswide network is available with full Internet access. Total number of PCs/ terminals supplied for student use: 530. Computer services are offered at no charge.* Library facilities: *John T. Richardson Library plus 6 additional on-campus libraries.* Graduate expenses: *Tuition of $320 per credit hour. Fees of $30 per year.* General application contact: *Dean of the appropriate college, 312-362-8000.*

Charles H. Kellstadt Graduate School of Business
Dr. Ronald J. Patten, Dean
Programs in:
    business economics • MBA
    economics • MA
    entrepreneurship • MBA
    finance • MBA, MSF
    human resource management • MBA
    international business • MBA
    international marketing and finance • MBA
    leadership and change management • MBA
    management planning and strategy • MBA
    marketing • MBA
    operations management • MBA

School of Accountancy
Dr. Ray Whittington, Director
Programs in:
    accounting • M Acc, MBA, MSA, PMSA
    management information systems • MBA, MSMIS
    systems • MBA
    taxation • MST

College of Law
Teree E. Foster, Dean
Program in:
    law • JD, LL M

DePaul University (continued)
College of Liberal Arts and Sciences
Michael Mezey, Dean
Programs in:
    advanced practice nursing • MS
    applied mathematics • MS
    applied physics • MS
    biological sciences • MS
    business economics • MBA
    chemistry • MS
    clinical child psychology • MA, PhD
    clinical community psychology • MA, PhD
    communication • MA
    economics • MA
    English • MA
    experimental psychology • MA, PhD
    financial administration management • Certificate
    general psychology • MS
    health administration • Certificate
    health law and policy • MS
    history • MA
    industrial/organizational psychology • MA, PhD
    interdisciplinary studies • MA, MS
    international studies • MA
    liberal studies • MA
    mathematics education • MA
    metropolitan planning • Certificate
    nonprofit organization management • MS
    nurse anesthesia • MS
    philosophy • MA, PhD
    physics • MS
    public administration • MS
    public services • Certificate
    rehabilitation services • Certificate, MS
    sociology • MA
    teaching of physics • MS
    women's studies • Certificate
    writing • MA

School for New Learning
Dr. Suzanne Dumbleton, Dean
Program in:
    integrated professional studies • MA

School of Computer Science, Telecommunications, and Information Systems
Dr. Helmut Epp, Dean
Programs in:
    computer science • MS, PhD
    human-computer interaction • MS
    information systems • MS
    management information systems • MBA, MSMIS
    software engineering • MS
    telecommunications systems • MS

School of Education
Dr. Barbara Sizemore, Dean
Programs in:
    administration and supervision • M Ed, MA
    adolescent learning disabilities • M Ed, MA
    agencies, family concerns, and higher education • M Ed, MA

    bilingual multicultural learning disabilities • M Ed, MA
    Catholic school leadership • M Ed, MA
    curriculum development • M Ed, MA
    economic education • M Ed, MA
    elementary education • M Ed, MA
    elementary schools • M Ed, MA
    human development and learning • M Ed, MA
    human services management • M Ed, MA
    liberal studies • M Ed, MA
    physical education • M Ed, MA
    reading and learning disabilities • M Ed, MA
    secondary education • M Ed, MA
    secondary schools • M Ed, MA
    teaching and learning • M Ed, MA

School of Music
Dr. Donald E. Casey, Dean
Programs in:
    applied music (performance) • Certificate, MM
    composition • MM
    music composition • MM
    music education • MM
    performance • MM

Theatre School
Dr. John R. Watts, Dean
Programs in:
    acting • Certificate, MFA
    costume design • MFA
    directing • MFA
    lighting design • MFA
    scenic design • MFA

DOMINICAN UNIVERSITY
River Forest, IL 60305-1099
http://www.dom.edu/

Independent-religious coed comprehensive institution. *Enrollment:* 1,800 graduate, professional, and undergraduate students. *Graduate faculty: 33 full-time, 58 part-time.* Computer facilities: *Campuswide network is available with full Internet access. Total number of PCs/terminals supplied for student use: 120. Computer services are offered at no charge.* Library facilities: *Rebecca Crown Library.* Graduate expenses: *Tuition of $8280 per year full-time, $1380 per course part-time. Fees of $10 per course.* General application contact: *Marilyn Gerken Benakis, Registrar, 708-524-6803.*

Graduate School of Business
Dr. Molly Burke, Dean
Programs in:
    accounting • MSA
    business administration • MBA
    management information systems • MSMIS
    organization management • MSOM

Graduate School of Education

Sr. Colleen McNicholas, Dean
Programs in:
early childhood education • MS
education • MAT
educational administration • MA
special education • MS

Graduate School of Library and Information Science

Prudence Dalrymple, Dean
Programs in:
library and information science • CSS, MLIS
management information systems • MSMIS

EASTERN ILLINOIS UNIVERSITY
Charleston, IL 61920-3099

http://www.eiu.edu/

Public coed comprehensive institution. *Enrollment: 11,777 gradu-ate, professional, and undergraduate students. Graduate faculty: 362 full-time. Computer facilities: Campuswide network is available with full Internet access. Computer services are offered at no charge. Library facilities: Booth Library. Graduate expenses: Tuition of $3459 per year full-time, $96 per semester hour part-time for state residents; $10,377 per year full-time, $288 per semester hour part-time for nonresidents. Fees of $1566 per year full-time, $37 per semester hour part-time. General application contact: Dr. Robert M. Augustine, Acting Dean, Graduate School, 217-581-2220.*

Graduate School

Dr. Robert M. Augustine, Acting Dean

College of Arts and Humanities
James Johnson, Dean
Programs in:
art • MA
English • MA
historical administration • MA
history • MA
music • MA
speech-communication • MA

College of Education and Professional Studies
Dr. Elizabeth Hitch, Dean
Programs in:
business education • MS Ed
educational administration and supervision • Ed S, MS Ed
educational psychology and guidance • Ed S, MS Ed
elementary education • MS Ed
junior high education • MS Ed
physical education • MS
special education • MS Ed

College of Sciences
Dr. Lida Wall, Dean
Programs in:
biological sciences • MS
botany • MS
chemistry • MS
clinical psychology • MA
communication disorders and sciences • MS
economics • MA
environmental biology • MS
mathematics • MA
mathematics education • MA
political science • MA
school psychology • SSP
zoology • MS

Lumpkin College of Business and Applied Sciences
Dr. Theodore W. Ivarie, Dean
Programs in:
business administration • MBA
business education • MS Ed
dietetics • MS
gerontology • MA
home economics • MS
technology • MS

GOVERNORS STATE UNIVERSITY
University Park, IL 60466

http://www.govst.edu/

Public coed upper-level institution. *Enrollment: 6,180 graduate, professional, and undergraduate students. Graduate faculty: 150 full-time, 160 part-time. Computer facilities: Campuswide network is available with full Internet access. Total number of PCs/terminals supplied for student use: 162. Computer service fees are included with tuition and fees. Library facilities: University Library. Graduate expenses: Tuition of $1140 per trimester full-time, $95 per credit hour part-time for state residents; $3420 per trimester full-time, $285 per credit hour part-time for nonresidents. Fees of $95 per trimester. General application contact: William T. Craig, Admissions Officer, 708-534-4490.*

College of Arts and Sciences

Dr. Roger Oden, Dean
Programs in:
analytical chemistry • MS
art • MA
communication studies • MA
computer science • MS
English • MA
environmental biology • MS
instructional and training technology • MA
media communication • MA
political and justice studies • MA

Governors State University (continued)

College of Business and Public Administration
Dr. William Nowlin, Dean
Programs in:
    accounting • MS
    business administration • MBA
    public administration • MPA

College of Education
Dr. Larry Freeman, Acting Dean
Programs in:
    counseling • MA
    education • MA
    educational administration and supervision • MA
    multi-categorical special education • MA
    psychology • MA

College of Health Professions
Dr. Cecelia Rokusek, Dean
Programs in:
    addictions studies • MHS
    communication disorders • MHS
    health administration • MHA
    nursing • MSN
    occupational therapy • MOT
    physical therapy • MPT
    social work • MSW

ILLINOIS INSTITUTE OF TECHNOLOGY
Chicago, IL 60616-3793

http://www.iit.edu/

Independent coed university. *Enrollment: 6,100 graduate, professional, and undergraduate students. Graduate faculty: 271 full-time, 260 part-time. Computer facilities: Campuswide network is available with full Internet access. Total number of PCs/terminals supplied for student use: 250. Computer services are offered at no charge. Library facilities: Paul V. Galvin Library. Graduate expenses: Tuition of $17,250 per year full-time, $575 per credit hour part-time. Fees of $60 per year full-time, $1.50 per credit hour part-time. General application contact: Dr. S. M. Shahidehpour, Dean of Graduate College, 312-567-3024.*

Graduate College
Dr. S. M. Shahidehpour, Dean

Armour College of Engineering and Sciences
Dr. H. M. Nagib, Dean
Programs in:
    analytical chemistry • MS, PhD
    biochemistry • MS
    biology • PhD
    biotechnology • MS
    cell biology • MS
    chemical engineering • M Ch E, MS, PhD

    civil and architectural engineering • M Geoenv E, M Geotech E, M Struct E, M Trans E, MCE, MCM, MPW, MS
    computer science and applied mathematics • MS, PhD
    computer systems engineering • MS
    electrical and computer engineering • MECE
    electrical engineering • MS, PhD
    environmental engineering • M Env E, MS, PhD
    food safety and technology • MS
    health/medical physics • MS, PhD
    inorganic chemistry • MS, PhD
    manufacturing engineering • MME, MS
    mechanical and aerospace engineering • MMAE, MS, PhD
    metallurgical and materials engineering • MMME, MS, PhD
    microbiology • MS
    organic chemistry • MS, PhD
    physical chemistry • MS, PhD
    physics • MS, PhD
    polymer chemistry • MS, PhD
    social sciences • MPA, MPW
    technical communication and information design • MS
    theoretical chemistry • MS, PhD

College of Architecture
Donna Robertson, Dean
Program in:
    architecture • D Arch, M Arch

Institute of Design
Patrick Whitney, Director
Programs in:
    communication design • M Des, MS, PhD
    photography • M Des
    product design • M Des, MS, PhD

Institute of Psychology
Dr. M. Ellen Mitchell, Chairman
Programs in:
    clinical psychology • PhD
    industrial/organizational psychology • PhD
    personnel/human resource development • MS
    psychology • MS
    rehabilitation counseling • MS
    rehabilitation psychology • PhD

Stuart School of Business
Dr. M. Zia Hassan, Dean
Programs in:
    business administration • MBA
    environmental management • MS
    financial markets and trading • MS
    management science • PhD
    marketing communication • MS
    operations and technology management • MS

Chicago-Kent College of Law
Henry H. Perritt Jr., Dean
Program in:
    law • JD, LL M

ILLINOIS STATE UNIVERSITY
Normal, IL 61790-2200

http://www.ilstu.edu/

Public coed university. *Enrollment:* 20,331 graduate, professional, and undergraduate students. Graduate faculty: *516 full-time, 16 part-time.* Computer facilities: *Campuswide network is available with full Internet access. Computer service fees are included with tuition and fees.* Library facilities: *Milner Library.* Graduate expenses: *Tuition of $2454 per year full-time, $102 per hour part-time for state residents; $7362 per year full-time, $307 per hour part-time for nonresidents. Fees of $1048 per year full-time, $44 per hour part-time.* General application contact: *Dr. Sandra Little, Dean of the Graduate School, 309-438-2583.*

Graduate School
Dr. Sandra Little, Dean

College of Applied Science and Technology
Dr. J. Robert Rossman, Acting Dean
Programs in:
  agribusiness • MS
  applied computer science • MS
  criminal justice sciences • MA, MS
  family and consumer sciences • MA, MS
  health education • MA, MS
  industrial technology • MS
  physical education • MA, MS

College of Arts and Sciences
Dr. Paul Schollaert, Dean
Programs in:
  biological sciences • MS
  biology • PhD
  botany • PhD
  chemistry • MS
  clinical psychology • MA, MS
  communication • MA, MS
  counseling psychology • MA, MS
  developmental psychology • MA, MS
  ecology • PhD
  economics • MA, MS
  educational psychology • MA, MS
  English • MA, MS
  experimental psychology • MA, MS
  French • MA
  French and German • MA
  French and Spanish • MA
  genetics • PhD
  geohydrology • MS
  German • MA
  German and Spanish • MA
  history • MA, MS
  mathematics • MA, MS
  mathematics education • PhD
  measurement-evaluation • MA, MS
  microbiology • PhD
  organizational-industrial psychology • MA, MS
  physiology • PhD
  political science • MA, MS
  psychology • MA, MS
  school psychology • MA, MS, PhD, SSP
  sociology • MA, MS
  Spanish • MA
  speech pathology and audiology • MA, MS
  writing • MA, MS
  zoology • PhD

College of Business
Dr. Dixie Mills, Dean
Programs in:
  accounting • MS
  business • MA
  business administration • MBA

College of Education
Dr. Sally Pancrazio, Dean
Programs in:
  curriculum and instruction • Ed D, MA, MS, MS Ed
  educational administration • Ed D, MA, MS, MS Ed, PhD
  educational policies • Ed D
  guidance and counseling • MA, MS, MS Ed
  postsecondary education • Ed D
  reading education • MS Ed
  special education • Ed D, MA, MS, MS Ed
  supervision • Ed D

College of Fine Arts
Dr. Alvin Goldfarb, Dean
Programs in:
  aesthetics • Ed D
  art administration • Ed D
  art education research • Ed D
  art history • MA, MS
  arts for special needs • Ed D
  ceramics • MFA, MS
  drawing • MFA, MS
  fibers • MFA, MS
  glass • MFA, MS
  graphic design • MFA, MS
  instructional technology • Ed D
  metals • MFA, MS
  music • MM, MM Ed
  painting • MFA, MS
  photography • MFA, MS
  printmaking • MFA, MS
  sculpture • MFA, MS
  theater • MA, MFA, MS

LEWIS UNIVERSITY
Romeoville, IL 60446

http://www.lewisu.edu/

Independent-religious coed comprehensive institution. *Enrollment:* 4,293 graduate, professional, and undergraduate students. Graduate faculty: *107 full-time, 49 part-time.* Computer facilities: *Campuswide network is available with full Internet access. Computer services are offered at no charge.* Library facilities: *main library.* General applica-

Lewis University (continued)
tion contact: *Director of the appropriate department, 815-838-0500.*

College of Arts and Sciences
Programs in:
counseling psychology • MA
criminal/social justice • MS
education • M Ed, MAE
education administration • CAS
philosophy • MA

College of Business
Suzanne Benson, Executive Director of Graduate School of Management
Program in:
business • MBA

College of Nursing
Programs in:
community health • MSN
nursing administration • Certificate, MSN
nursing education • MSN

 LOYOLA UNIVERSITY CHICAGO
Chicago, IL 60611-2196
http://www.luc.edu/

Independent-religious coed university. *Enrollment: 13,759 graduate, professional, and undergraduate students. Graduate faculty: 1,382. Library facilities: Elizabeth M. Cudahy Memorial Library plus 4 additional on-campus libraries. Graduate expenses: $467 per semester hour. General application contact: Dr. James Brennan, Dean of the Graduate School, 773-508-3396.*

Graduate School
Dr. James Brennan, Dean
Programs in:
American politics and policy • MA, PhD
applied social psychology • MA, PhD
applied sociology • MA
biochemistry • MS, PhD
biology • MS
cell and molecular physiology • MS, PhD
cell biology, neurobiology and anatomy • MS, PhD
chemistry • MS, PhD
classical studies • PhD
clinical psychology • PhD
computer science • MS
criminal justice • MA
developmental psychology • PhD
English • MA, PhD
Greek • MA
history • MA, PhD
immunology • MS, PhD
international studies • MA, PhD
Latin • MA
mathematical science • MS
microbiology • MS, PhD
molecular biology • PhD
neurochemistry • PhD
neuroscience • MS, PhD
organizational development • MSOD
perception • PhD
pharmacology and experimental therapeutics • MS, PhD
philosophy • MA, PhD
political theory and philosophy • MA, PhD
sociology • MA, PhD
Spanish • MA
theology • MA, PhD
training and development • MSTD
virology • MS, PhD

Institute of Human Resources and Industrial Relations
Dr. Linda K. Stroh, Director
Program in:
human resources and industrial relatio • MSHR, MSIR

Institute of Pastoral Studies
Dr. Camilla Burns, Director
Programs in:
divinity • M Div
pastoral counseling • MA
pastoral studies • MPS
religious education • M Rel Ed

Marcella Niehoff School of Nursing
Dr. Shirley Dooling, Dean
Programs in:
adult nurse clinical nursing specialist • MSN
adult nurse practitioner • MSN
cardiac health/rehabilitation clinical nursing specialist • MSN
critical care/trauma clinical nursing specialist • MSN
critical care/trauma nurse practitioner • MSN
nursing • PhD
nursing service administration • MSN
oncology clinical nursing specialist • MSN
pediatric nurse practitioner • MSN
women's health nurse practitioner • MSN

Graduate School of Business
Paul Davidovitch, Director, MBA Program
Programs in:
accountancy • MS
business administration • MBA
information systems management • MS

School of Education
Dr. Margaret Fong, Dean
Programs in:
administration/supervision • Ed D, M Ed, MA, PhD
college student personnel • M Ed
community counseling • M Ed, MA
comparative-international education • Ed D, M Ed, MA, PhD
counseling psychology • PhD
curriculum and instruction • Ed D, M Ed, MA

early childhood development • Ed D
early childhood education • M Ed, PhD
educational psychology • M Ed, MA, PhD
family studies • M Ed
higher education • Ed D, PhD
history of education • Ed D, M Ed, MA, PhD
instructional leadership • M Ed
philosophy of education • Ed D, M Ed, MA, PhD
research methods/human development • M Ed, MA, PhD
school counseling • M Ed
school psychology • M Ed, PhD
sociology of education • Ed D, M Ed, MA, PhD
special education • M Ed

School of Law
Nina S. Appel, Dean
Programs in:
child law • LL M, MJ
corporate law • LL M, MJ
health law • D Law, LL M, MJ, SJD
law • JD

School of Social Work
Dr. Joseph A. Walsh, Dean
Program in:
social work • DSW, MSW

Stritch School of Medicine
Dr. Daniel H. Winship, Dean
Program in:
medicine • MD

NATIONAL–LOUIS UNIVERSITY
Evanston, IL 60201-1730

http://www.nl.edu/

Independent coed university. *Enrollment: 7,100 graduate, professional, and undergraduate students. Graduate faculty: 275 full-time, 1,595 part-time.* Computer facilities: *Campuswide network is available with full Internet access. Total number of PCs/terminals supplied for student use: 250. Computer services are offered at no charge.* Library facilities: *main library plus 4 additional on-campus libraries. Graduate expenses: $411 per semester hour.* General application contact: *Dr. David McCulloch, Vice President for University Services, 800-443-5522 Ext. 5127.*

College of Arts and Sciences
Dr. Edward Risinger, Dean
Programs in:
addictions counseling • Certificate, MS
addictions treatment • Certificate
adult education • Certificate, Ed D, M Ad Ed
adult education and developmental studies • Certificate
career counseling and development studies • Certificate
community wellness and prevention • Certificate, MS
counseling • Certificate, MS

developmental studies • M Ad Ed
eating disorders counseling • Certificate
employee assistance programs • Certificate, MS
gerontology administration • Certificate
gerontology counseling • Certificate, MS
human services administration • Certificate, MS
long-term care administration • Certificate
psychology • Certificate, MA
written communication • MS

College of Management and Business
Dr. Howard Zacks, Dean
Programs in:
business administration • MBA
human resource management and development • MS
managerial leadership • MS

National College of Education, McGaw Graduate School
Dr. Linda Tafel, Dean
Programs in:
administration and supervision • CAS, Ed S, M Ed
curriculum and instruction • CAS, M Ed, MS Ed
curriculum and social inquiry • Ed D
early childhood administration • CAS, M Ed
early childhood curriculum and instruction specialist • CAS, M Ed, MS Ed
early childhood education • CAS, MAT
early childhood leadership and advocacy • M Ed
educational leadership/superintendent endorsement • Ed D
educational psychology • CAS
educational psychology/human learning and development • Ed D, M Ed, MS Ed
educational psychology/school psychology • M Ed
elementary education • MAT
general special education • CAS, M Ed, MS Ed
language and literacy • CAS, M Ed, MS Ed
learning disabilities • CAS, M Ed, MS Ed
learning disabilities/behavior disorders • CAS, M Ed, MAT, MS Ed
mathematics education • CAS, M Ed, MS Ed
reading and language • Ed D
reading recovery • CAS
reading specialist • CAS, M Ed, MS Ed
school psychology • Ed D, Ed S
science education • CAS, M Ed, MS Ed
secondary education • MAT
superintendent endorsement • Ed S
technology in education • CAS, M Ed, MS Ed

NORTH CENTRAL COLLEGE
Naperville, IL 60566-7063

http://www.noctrl.edu/

Independent-religious coed comprehensive institution. *Enrollment: 2,716 graduate, professional, and undergraduate students. Graduate faculty: 40 full-time, 22 part-time.* Computer facilities: *Campuswide network is available with full Internet access. Total number of PCs/*

North Central College (continued)

terminals supplied for student use: 40. Computer service fees are included with tuition and fees. Library facilities: *Oesterle Library.* General application contact: *Dr. William Dunifan, Director of Graduate Programs, 630-637-5840.*

Graduate Programs

Dr. William Dunifon, Director
Programs in:
    business administration • MBA
    computer science • MS
    education • MA Ed
    leadership studies • MLD
    liberal studies • MALS
    management information systems • MS

NORTHEASTERN ILLINOIS UNIVERSITY
Chicago, IL 60625-4699

Public coed comprehensive institution. *Enrollment:* 10,306 graduate, professional, and undergraduate students. Graduate faculty: *240 full-time, 118 part-time.* Computer facilities: *Campuswide network is available with full Internet access. Total number of PCs/terminals supplied for student use: 280. Computer service fees are included with tuition and fees.* Library facilities: *Ronald Williams University Library plus 1 additional on-campus library.* Graduate expenses: *Tuition of $2226 per year full-time, $93 per credit hour part-time for state residents; $6678 per year full-time, $278 per credit hour part-time for nonresidents. Fees of $358 per year full-time, $14.90 per credit hour part-time.* General application contact: *Dr. Mohan K. Sood, Dean, 773-583-4050 Ext. 6143.*

Graduate College
Dr. Mohan K. Sood, Dean

College of Arts and Sciences
Dr. David Unumb, Acting Dean
Programs in:
    biology • MS
    chemistry • MS
    composition/writing • MA
    computer science • MS
    earth science • MS
    exercise science and cardiac rehabilitation • MS
    geography and environmental studies • MA
    gerontology • MA
    history • MA
    linguistics • MA
    literature • MA
    mathematics • MS
    mathematics for elementary school teachers • MA
    music • MA
    political science • MA
    speech • MA

College of Business and Management
Dr. Charles Falk, Dean
Programs in:
    accounting • MBA
    finance • MBA
    management • MBA
    marketing • MBA

College of Education
Dr. Michael Carl, Dean
Programs in:
    bilingual/bicultural • MAT, MSI
    career development • MA
    chief school business official • MA
    community and family counseling • MA
    community college administration • MA
    early childhood special education • MA
    educating children with behavior disorders • MA
    educating individuals with mental retardation • MA
    educational administration and supervision • MA
    elementary school counseling • MA
    gifted education • MA
    guidance and counseling • MA
    human resource development • MA
    inner city studies • MA
    language arts • MAT, MSI
    reading • MA
    secondary school counseling • MA
    teaching children with learning disabilities • MA
    teaching of language arts • M Ed

 # NORTHERN ILLINOIS UNIVERSITY
De Kalb, IL 60115-2854
http://www.niu.edu/

Public coed university. *Enrollment:* 22,082 graduate, professional, and undergraduate students. Graduate faculty: *757 full-time, 42 part-time.* Library facilities: *Founders Library plus 3 additional on-campus libraries.* Graduate expenses: *$3984 per year full-time, $154 per credit hour part-time for state residents; $8160 per year full-time, $328 per credit hour part-time for nonresidents.* General application contact: *Dr. Carla Montgomery, Associate Dean, 815-753-9402.*

Graduate School
Dr. Jerrold Zar, Dean and Associate Provost for Graduate Studies and Research

College of Business
David Graf, Dean
Programs in:
    accountancy • MAS, MST
    business administration • MBA
    finance • MS
    management information systems • MS

College of Education
Dr. Alfonzo Thurman, Dean
Programs in:
    adult continuing education • Ed D, MS Ed
    counseling • Ed D, MS Ed
    curriculum and instruction • Ed D, MS Ed
    early childhood education • MS Ed
    educational administration • Ed D, Ed S, MS Ed
    educational psychology • Ed D, MS Ed
    elementary education • MS Ed
    foundations of education • MS Ed
    instructional technology • Ed D, MS Ed
    physical education • MS Ed
    reading • Ed D, MS Ed
    school business management • MS Ed
    special education • Ed D, MS Ed

College of Engineering and Engineering Technology
Dr. Romualdas Kasuba, Dean
Programs in:
    electrical engineering • MS
    industrial engineering • MS
    industrial management • MS
    mechanical engineering • MS

College of Health and Human Sciences
Dr. James Lankford, Dean
Programs in:
    applied family and child studies • MS
    communicative disorders • MA
    home economics resources and services • MS
    nursing • MS
    nutrition and dietetics • MS
    public health • MPH

College of Liberal Arts and Sciences
Dr. Frederick Kitterle, Dean
Programs in:
    anthropology • MA
    applied probability and statistics • MS
    biological sciences • MS, PhD
    chemistry and biochemistry • MS, PhD
    communication studies • MA
    computer science • MS
    economics • MA, PhD
    English • MA, PhD
    French • MA
    geography • MS
    geology • MS, PhD
    history • MA, PhD
    mathematical sciences • PhD
    mathematics • MS
    philosophy • MA
    physics • MS
    political science • MA, PhD
    psychology • MA, PhD
    public administration • MPA
    sociology • MA
    Spanish • MA

College of Visual and Performing Arts
Dr. Harold Kafer, Dean
Programs in:
    art • MA, MFA, MS
    music • MM, Performer's Certificate
    theatre arts • MFA

College of Law
LeRoy Pernell, Dean
Program in:
    law • JD

NORTHWESTERN UNIVERSITY
Evanston, IL 60208

http://www.nwu.edu/

Independent coed university. *Enrollment: 17,478 graduate, professional, and undergraduate students. Graduate faculty: 1,990 full-time, 163 part-time. Computer facilities: Campuswide network is available with full Internet access. Total number of PCs/terminals supplied for student use: 605. Computer service fees are included with tuition and fees. Library facilities: University Library plus 6 additional on-campus libraries. Graduate expenses: $20,430 per year full-time, $2424 per course part-time. General application contact: Dorthea Reid, Coordinator of Graduate Admissions, 847-491-8532.*

The Graduate School
Carol Simpson Stern, Dean
Programs in:
    clinical health • PhD
    clinical neuropsychology • PhD
    clinical psychology • PhD
    general clinical • PhD
    genetic counseling • MS
    public health • MPH
    telecommunications science, management, and policy • Certificate, MA, MEM, MS

College of Arts and Sciences
Eric J. Sundquist, Dean
Programs in:
    anthropology • PhD
    applied mathematics • PhD
    art history • PhD
    astronomy • PhD
    astrophysics • PhD
    chemistry • PhD
    classics • MA, PhD
    clinical psychology • PhD
    cognitive psychology • PhD
    comparative literary studies • PhD
    drawing • MFA
    economics • MA, PhD
    English • MA, PhD
    French • PhD
    geological sciences • MS, PhD

Northwestern University (continued)
German literature and critical thought • PhD
Greek • MA
Hispanic studies • PhD
history • PhD
Italian • PhD
Latin • MA
linguistics • MA, PhD
mathematics • PhD
neurobiology and physiology • MS
painting • MFA
personality • PhD
philosophy • PhD
physics • PhD
political science • MA, PhD
printmaking • MFA
psychobiology • PhD
religion • MA, PhD
Slavic languages and literature • PhD
social psychology • PhD
sociology • PhD
statistics • MS, PhD

Division of Interdepartmental Programs
Carol Simpson Stern, Dean, The Graduate School
Programs in:
analytical methods • MS
biotechnology • MS, PhD
cell and molecular biology • PhD
environment and natural resources • MS
genetics and developmental biology • PhD
integrative biology • PhD
international issues • MS
liberal studies • MA
logistics and operations • MS
molecular biophysics • PhD
neuroscience • PhD
private sector management and decision making • MS
public transportation systems and analysis • MS
reproductive biology • PhD
sociology and organization behavior • PhD
structural biology • PhD

Integrated Graduate Programs in the Life Sciences
Dr. James M. Kramer, Director
Programs in:
cancer biology • PhD
cell biology • PhD
developmental biology • PhD
evolutionary biology • PhD
immunology and microbial pathogenesis • PhD
molecular biology and genetics • PhD
neurobiology • PhD
pharmacology and toxicology • PhD
structural biology and biochemistry • PhD

J. L. Kellogg Graduate School of Management
Dr. Donald P. Jacobs, Dean
Programs in:
accounting • PhD
business management • MM
finance • PhD
health services management • MM
manufacturing management • MMM

marketing • PhD
organization behavior • PhD
public and nonprofit management • MM
real estate management • MM
transportation management • MM

Robert R. McCormick School of Engineering and Applied Science
Jerome Cohen, Dean
Programs in:
biomedical engineering • MS, PhD
biosolid mechanics • MS, PhD
chemical engineering • MS, PhD
computer science • PhD
electrical and computer engineering • MS, PhD
engineering and applied science • MMM
engineering management • MEM
environmental health engineering • MS, PhD
fluid mechanics • MS, PhD
geotechnical engineering • MS, PhD
health physics/radiological health • MS, PhD
industrial engineering and management science • MS, PhD
information technology • MIT
manufacturing engineering • MME
materials science • PhD
materials science and engineering • MS
mechanical engineering • MS, PhD
project management • MPM
solid mechanics • MS, PhD
structural engineering • MS, PhD
structural mechanics • MS, PhD
transportation systems engineering • MS, PhD

School of Education and Social Policy
Jean Egmon, Assistant Dean
Programs in:
advanced teaching • MS
corporate training and development • MS
education and social policy • MS
education and social policy-counseling psychology • MA
education and social policy-learning sciences • MA, PhD
elementary teaching • MS
higher education administration • MS
human development and social policy • PhD
marital and family therapy • MS
school administration • MS
secondary teaching • MS

School of Speech
David Zarefsky, Dean
Programs in:
audiology and hearing sciences • MA, PhD
communication studies • MA, PhD
communication systems • MSC
directing • MFA
learning disabilities • MA, PhD
managerial communications • MSC
performance studies • MA, PhD
radio/television/film • MA, MFA, PhD
speech and language pathology • MA, PhD
speech and language pathology and learning disabilities • MA
stage design • MFA

theatre • MA

theatre and drama • PhD

Medical School

Programs in:

cancer biology • PhD

cell biology • PhD

clinical health • PhD

clinical neuropsychology • PhD

clinical psychology • PhD

developmental biology • PhD

evolutionary biology • PhD

general clinical • PhD

genetic counseling • MS

immunology and microbial pathogenesis • PhD

medicine • MD

molecular biology and genetics • PhD

neurobiology • PhD

pharmacology and toxicology • PhD

physical therapy • MPT

structural biology and biochemistry • PhD

Medill School of Journalism

Ken Bode, Dean

Programs in:

advertising/sales promotion • MSIMC

broadcast journalism • MSJ

direct marketing • MSIMC

general studies • MSIMC

magazine publishing • MSJ

new media • MSJ

newspaper management • MSJ

public relations • MSIMC

reporting and writing • MSJ

School of Law

David VanZandt, Dean

Program in:

law • JD, LL M, SJD

School of Music

Bernard J. Dobroski, Dean

Programs in:

chamber music and orchestral literature • MM

collaborative arts • DM

conducting • DM, MM

jazz pedagogy • MM

keyboard • CP, DM, MM

music composition • DM, MM

music education • MM, PhD

musicology • MM, PhD

music technology • MM, PhD

music theory • MM, PhD

performance • MM

piano performance and pedagogy • MM

string performance and pedagogy • MM

strings • DM, MM

strings, winds and percussion • CP

voice • CP, DM, MM

winds and percussion • DM, MM

OLIVET NAZARENE UNIVERSITY
Kankakee, IL 60901-0592

http://www.olivet.edu/

Independent-religious coed comprehensive institution. Library facilities: *Benner Library.* General application contact: *Dean of the Graduate School, 815-939-5291.*

Graduate School

Programs in:

business administration • MBA

practical ministries • MPM

Division of Education

Programs in:

curriculum and instruction • MAE

elementary education • MAT

secondary education • MAT

Division of Religion and Philosophy

Programs in:

biblical literature • MA

religion • MA

theology • MA

Institute for Church Management

Programs in:

church management • MCM

pastoral counseling • MPC

ROCKFORD COLLEGE
Rockford, IL 61108-2393

http://www.rockford.edu/

Independent coed comprehensive institution. *Enrollment: 1,299 graduate, professional, and undergraduate students. Graduate faculty: 33 full-time, 16 part-time. Library facilities: Howard Colman Library. Graduate expenses: $15,500 per year full-time, $400 per credit part-time. General application contact: Winston McKean, Dean, Continuing and Graduate Education, 815-226-4013.*

Graduate Studies

Winston McKean, Dean, Continuing and Graduate Education

Programs in:

art education • MAT

business administration • MBA

elementary education • MAT

English • MAT

history • MAT

learning disabilities • MAT

political science • MAT

remedial reading • MAT

secondary education • MAT

social sciences • MAT

ROOSEVELT UNIVERSITY
Chicago, IL 60605-1394

http://www.roosevelt.edu/

Independent coed comprehensive institution. *Enrollment: 6,587 graduate, professional, and undergraduate students. Graduate faculty: 168 full-time, 283 part-time. Library facilities: Murray-Green Library plus 1 additional on-campus library. Graduate expenses: Tuition of $445 per credit hour. Fees of $100 per year.* General application contact: *Joanne Canyon-Heller, Coordinator of Graduate Admissions, 312-341-3612.*

Graduate Division
Alice Zimring, Associate Dean

College of Arts and Sciences
Ronald Tallman, Dean
Programs in:
   actuarial science • MS
   applied economics • MA
   chemistry • MS
   clinical psychology • MA, Psy D
   computer science • MSC
   creative writing • MFA
   economics • MA
   English • MA
   general psychology • MA
   history • MA
   industrial/organizational psychology • MA
   integrated marketing communications • MSIMC
   journalism • MSJ
   mathematical sciences • MS
   political science • MA
   public administration • MPA
   sociology • MA
   sociology-gerontology • MA
   Spanish • MA
   telecommunications • MST
   women's studies • MA

College of Education
Dr. George Lowery, Dean
Programs in:
   early childhood education • MA
   educational administration and supervision • Ed D, MA
   elementary education • MA
   guidance and counseling • MA
   reading education • MA
   secondary education • MA

College of the Performing Arts
Donald Steven, Dean
Programs in:
   directing and dramaturgy • MFA
   music • MM
   musical theatre • MFA
   music education • MM Ed
   piano pedagogy • Diploma
   theatre • MA, MFA
   theatre-directing • MA
   theatre-performance • MFA

Evelyn T. Stone University College
Laura Evans, Dean
Programs in:
   general studies • MGS
   hospitality management • MS
   training and development • MA

Walter E. Heller College of Business Administration
Dr. James Cicarelli, Dean
Programs in:
   accounting • MSA
   business administration • MBA
   information systems • MSIS
   international business • MSIB

SAINT XAVIER UNIVERSITY
Chicago, IL 60655-3105

http://www.sxu.edu/

Independent-religious coed comprehensive institution. *Enrollment: 4,201 graduate, professional, and undergraduate students. Graduate faculty: 80. Library facilities: Byrne Memorial Library. Graduate expenses: Tuition of $450 per hour. Fees of $50 per year.* General application contact: *Sr. Evelyn McKenna, Vice President of Enrollment Services, 773-298-3050.*

Graduate Studies
Dr. George Matthews, Vice President of Academic Affairs
Programs in:
   adult counseling • Certificate
   adult health clinical nurse specialist • MS
   certified financial planner • Certificate, MBA
   child/adolescent counseling • Certificate
   core counseling • Certificate
   counseling psychology • MA
   curriculum and instruction • MA
   education • CAS
   educational administration • MA
   English • CAS
   family nurse practitioner • MS, PMC
   field-based education • MA
   finance • MBA
   financial trading and practice • Certificate, MBA
   general educational studies • MA
   generalist/administration • MBA
   healthcare management • Certificate, MBA
   leadership in community health nursing • MS
   learning disabilities • MA
   literary studies • MA
   management • MBA
   marketing • MBA
   psychiatric/mental health clinical nurse specialist • MS
   reading • MA
   speech-language pathology • MS
   taxation • Certificate, MBA
   teaching of writing • MA
   writing pedagogy • CAS

SOUTHERN ILLINOIS UNIVERSITY AT CARBONDALE

Carbondale, IL 62901-6806

http://www.siu.edu/cwis/

Public coed university. *Enrollment:* 21,908 graduate, professional, and undergraduate students. Graduate faculty: *1,074 full-time, 112 part-time. Computer facilities: Campuswide network is available with full Internet access. Computer services are offered at no charge.* Library facilities: *Morris Library.* Graduate expenses: *Tuition of $2964 per year full-time, $99 per semester hour part-time for state residents; $8892 per year full-time, $270 per semester hour part-time for nonresidents. Fees of $1034 per year full-time, $298 per semester (minimum) part-time.* General application contact: *Dr. Jack McKilli, Associate Dean of the Graduate School, 618-536-7791.*

Graduate School
Dr. Richard E. Falvo, Acting Dean
Programs in:
  molecular science • PhD
  pharmacology • MS, PhD
  physiology • MS, PhD

College of Agriculture
James McGuire, Dean
Programs in:
  agribusiness economics • MS
  animal science • MS
  food and nutrition • MS
  forestry • MS
  horticultural science • MS
  plant and soil science • MS

College of Business and Administration
Siva Balasubramanian, Acting Dean
Programs in:
  accountancy • DBA, M Acc
  business administration • DBA, MBA

College of Education
Nancy Quisenberry, Interim Dean
Programs in:
  behavioral analysis and therapy • MS
  communication disorders and sciences • MS
  counselor education • MS Ed, PhD
  curriculum and instruction • MS Ed, PhD
  educational administration • MS Ed, PhD
  educational psychology • PhD
  health education • MS Ed, PhD
  higher education • MS Ed
  human learning and development • MS Ed
  measurement and statistics • PhD
  physical education • MS Ed
  recreation • MS Ed
  rehabilitation • Rh D
  rehabilitation administration and services • MS
  rehabilitation counseling • MS
  social work • MSW
  special education • MS Ed
  workforce education and development • MS Ed, PhD

College of Engineering
Juh Wah Chen, Dean
Programs in:
  civil engineering and mechanics • MS
  electrical engineering • MS
  electrical systems • PhD
  fossil energy • PhD
  manufacturing systems • MS
  mechanical engineering and energy processes • MS
  mechanics • PhD
  mining engineering • MS

College of Liberal Arts
Dr. Robert Jensen, Acting Dean
Programs in:
  administration of justice • MA
  anthropology • MA, PhD
  applied linguistics • MA
  ceramics • MFA
  clinical psychology • MA, MS, PhD
  composition • MA, PhD
  composition and theory • MM
  counseling psychology • MA, MS, PhD
  creative writing • MFA
  drawing • MFA
  economics • MA, MS, PhD
  experimental psychology • MA, MS, PhD
  fiber/weaving • MFA
  foreign languages and literatures • MA
  geography • MS, PhD
  glass • MFA
  history • MA, PhD
  history and literature • MM
  jewelry • MFA
  literature • MA, PhD
  metals/blacksmithing • MFA
  music education • MM
  opera/music theater • MM
  painting • MFA
  performance • MM
  philosophy • MA, PhD
  piano pedagogy • MM
  political science • MA, PhD
  printmaking • MFA
  public administration • MPA
  rhetoric • MA, PhD
  sculpture • MFA
  sociology • MA, PhD
  speech communication • MA, MS, PhD
  speech/theater • PhD
  teaching English as a second language • MA
  theater • MFA

College of Mass Communication and Media Arts
Joe S. Foote, Dean
Programs in:
  cinema • MFA
  interactive multimedia • MA
  journalism • MA, PhD
  photography • MFA
  telecommunications • MA

Southern Illinois University at Carbondale (continued)

College of Science

Jack Parker, Dean

Programs in:

biological sciences • MS

chemistry and biochemistry • MS, PhD

computer science • MS

geology • MS, PhD

mathematics • MA, MS, PhD

molecular biology, microbiology, and biochemistry • MS, PhD

physics • MS

plant biology • MS, PhD

statistics • MS

zoology • MS, PhD

School of Law

Thomas F. Guernsey, Dean

Program in:

law • JD

School of Medicine

Dr. Carl J. Getto, Dean and Provost

Programs in:

medicine • MD

pharmacology • MS, PhD

physiology • MS, PhD

SOUTHERN ILLINOIS UNIVERSITY AT EDWARDSVILLE

Edwardsville, IL 62026-0001

http://www.siue.edu/

Public coed comprehensive institution. *Enrollment:* 11,207 graduate, professional, and undergraduate students. Graduate faculty: *458 full-time, 213 part-time.* Library facilities: *Lovejoy Library.* Graduate expenses: *Tuition of $1716 per year full-time, $95 per credit hour part-time for state residents; $5149 per year full-time, $286 per credit hour part-time for nonresidents. Fees of $463 per year full-time, $433 per year part-time.* General application contact: *Dr. Abdul M. Turay, Dean of the Graduate School, 618-692-3010.*

Graduate School

Dr. Abdul M. Turay, Dean

College of Arts and Sciences

Sharon Hahs, Dean

Programs in:

American and English literature • MA

art therapy • MA, MFA

biological sciences • MA, MS

ceramics • MFA

chemistry • MS

drawing • MFA

environmental studies • MS

fiber/fabrics • MFA

geography • MA, MS

history • MA

mass communication • MS

mathematics and statistics • MS

music • MM

painting • MFA

physics • MS

printmaking • MFA

public administration • MPA

sculpture • MFA

social work • MSW

sociology • MA

speech communication • MA

teaching English as a second language • MA

teaching of writing • MA

School of Business

Dr. M. Robert Carver, Dean

Programs in:

accountancy • MSA

business education • MS Ed

economics • MA, MS

management information systems • MBA

marketing research • MBA, MMR

School of Education

Dr. Gary Hull, Dean

Programs in:

business education • MS Ed

educational administration and supervision • Ed S, MS Ed

elementary education • MS Ed

health, recreation, and physical education • MS Ed

instructional process • Ed D

instructional technology • MS Ed

psychology • MA, MS

school psychology • Ed S

secondary education • MS Ed

special education • MS Ed

speech pathology • MS

School of Engineering

Dr. Harlan Bengtson, Dean

Programs in:

civil engineering • MS

computer information systems • MS

electrical engineering • MS

School of Nursing

Dr. Felissa Lashley, Dean

Programs in:

community health nursing • MS

medical-surgical nursing • MS

nurse anesthesia • MS

nurse practitioner nursing • MS

psychiatric nursing • MS

School of Dental Medicine

Dr. Patrick Ferrillo, Dean

Program in:

dental medicine • DMD

UNIVERSITY OF CHICAGO
Chicago, IL 60637-1513

http://www.uchicago.edu/

Independent coed university. *Enrollment:* 11,780 graduate, professional, and undergraduate students. *Graduate faculty:* 1,963 full-time, 338 part-time. *Computer facilities: Campuswide network is available with full Internet access. Computer services are offered at no charge. Library facilities: Joseph Regenstein Library plus 8 additional on-campus libraries. Graduate expenses: Tuition of $23,616 per year full-time, $3258 per course part-time. Fees of $378 per year. General application contact: Irene Staller, Manager, Office of Graduate Affairs, 773-702-7813.*

Divinity School
Dr. W. Clark Gilpin, Dean
Program in:
   theology • AM, AMRS, M Div, PhD

Division of Social Sciences
Dr. Richard Saller, Dean
Programs in:
   anthropology • PhD
   anthropology and linguistics • PhD
   economics • PhD
   education • AM, CAS, MAT
   history • PhD
   human development • PhD
   international relations • AM
   international relations with specialization • AM
   Latin American and Caribbean studies • AM
   Middle Eastern studies • AM
   political science • PhD
   psychology • PhD
   social sciences • AM
   social thought • PhD
   sociology • AM, PhD

Division of the Biological Sciences
Dr. Glenn D. Steele Jr., Dean
Programs in:
   biochemistry and molecular biology • PhD
   biopsychology • PhD
   cancer biology • PhD
   cell physiology • PhD
   cellular and molecular physiology • PhD
   cellular differentiation • PhD
   developmental endocrinology • PhD
   developmental genetics • PhD
   developmental neurobiology • PhD
   ecology and evolution • PhD
   functional and evolutionary biology • PhD
   gene expression • PhD
   genetics • PhD
   human nutrition and nutritional biology • PhD, SM
   immunology • PhD
   medical physics • PhD, SM
   neurobiology • PhD
   ophthalmology and visual science • PhD, SM
   organismal biology and anatomy • PhD
   pathology • PhD
   pharmacological and physiological sciences • PhD
   psychology • PhD
   virology • PhD

Division of the Humanities
Thomas B. Thuerer, Dean of Students
Programs in:
   ancient Mediterranean world • AM, PhD
   ancient philosophy • AM, PhD
   anthropology and linguistics • PhD
   art history • AM, PhD
   Bengali • PhD
   classical archaeology • AM, PhD
   classical languages and literatures • AM, PhD
   comparative literature • AM, PhD
   conceptual foundations of science • AM, PhD
   East Asian languages and civilizations • AM, PhD
   English language and literature • AM, PhD
   French • AM, PhD
   general studies in the humanities • AM
   Germanic languages and literatures • AM, PhD
   Hindi • PhD
   history of culture • AM, PhD
   humanities • AM
   Italian • AM, PhD
   Jewish history and culture • AM, PhD
   Jewish studies • AM
   Latin American and Caribbean studies • AM
   linguistics • AM, PhD
   Middle Eastern studies • AM
   music • AM, PhD
   Near Eastern languages and civilizations • AM, PhD
   New Testament and early Christian culture • AM, PhD
   philosophy • AM, PhD
   Sanskrit • PhD
   Slavic languages and literatures • AM, PhD
   South Asian languages and civilizations • AM, PhD
   Spanish • AM, PhD
   Tamil • PhD
   Urdu • PhD
   visual arts • MFA

Division of the Physical Sciences
David Oxtoby, Dean
Programs in:
   applied mathematics • PhD, SM
   astronomy and astrophysics • PhD, SM
   atmospheric sciences • PhD, SM
   chemistry • PhD, SM
   computer science • PhD, SM
   earth sciences • PhD, SM
   financial mathematics • MS
   mathematics • PhD, SM
   physical sciences • MS
   physics • PhD, SM
   planetary and space sciences • PhD, SM
   statistics • PhD, SM

University of Chicago (continued)

Graduate Program in Health Administration and Policy

Dr. Edward F. Lawlor, Director
Program in:
  health administration and policy • AM, Certificate, MBA

Graduate School of Business

Robert S. Hamada, Dean
Programs in:
  accounting • MBA
  business administration • EMBA, MBA, PhD
  international business administration • IEMBA, IMBA

Law School

Douglas Baird, Dean
Program in:
  law • JD, JSD, LL M, MCL

Pritzker School of Medicine

Dr. Glenn D. Steele Jr., Dean
Program in:
  medicine • MD

School of Social Service Administration

Dr. Jeanne C. Marsh, Dean
Programs in:
  social service administration • PhD
  social work • AM

The Irving B. Harris Graduate School of Public Policy Studies

Dr. Robert T. Michael, Dean
Program in:
  public policy studies • AM, MPP, PhD

UNIVERSITY OF ILLINOIS AT CHICAGO

Chicago, IL 60607-7128

http://www.uic.edu/

Public coed university. *Enrollment: 24,589 graduate, professional, and undergraduate students. Graduate faculty: 1,319 full-time, 94 part-time. Computer facilities: Campuswide network is available with full Internet access. Computer service fees are included with tuition and fees. Library facilities: University Library plus 4 additional on-campus libraries. Graduate expenses: $4616 per year full-time, $1014 per semester (minimum) part-time for state residents; $11,252 per year full-time, $2121 per semester (minimum) part-time for nonresidents. General application contact: Graduate College Receptionist, 312-413-2550.*

Graduate College

Dr. Mi Ja Kim, Dean
Programs in:
  anatomy and cell biology • MS, PhD
  biochemical mechanisms • PhD
  biochemistry and molecular biology • MS, PhD
  forensic science • MS
  medical education • MHPE
  medicinal chemistry • MS, PhD
  microbiology and immunology • PhD
  molecular biology and genetics • PhD
  neuroscience • PhD
  oral sciences • MS
  pathology • MS, PhD
  pharmaceutics • MS, PhD
  pharmacodynamics • MS, PhD
  pharmacognosy • MS, PhD
  pharmacokinetics • MS, PhD
  pharmacology • PhD
  pharmacy administration • MS, PhD
  physiology and biophysics • MS, PhD
  surgery • MS

College of Architecture and Art

Dr. Ellen Baird, Dean
Programs in:
  architecture • M Arch
  art history • MA
  art therapy • MA
  communications design • MFA
  computer graphics • MFA
  electronic visualization • MFA
  film animation • MFA
  graphic design • MFA
  industrial design • MFA
  painting • MFA
  printmaking • MFA
  sculpture • MFA
  theatre • MA

College of Associated Health Professions

Leopold Selker, Dean
Programs in:
  biomedical visualization • MAMS
  disability and human development • MS
  disability studies • PhD
  human nutrition and dietetics • MS, PhD
  medical laboratory sciences • MS
  occupational therapy • MS
  physical therapy • MS

College of Business Administration

Paul J. Uselding, Dean
Programs in:
  accounting • MS
  business administration • MBA
  business economics • PhD
  economics • MA
  finance • PhD
  human resources management • PhD
  management information systems • MS, PhD
  marketing • PhD
  public policy anaylsis • PhD

College of Education
Dr. Larry Braskamp, Dean
Programs in:
   curriculum and instruction • PhD
   educational policy and administration • PhD
   elementary education • M Ed
   instructional leadership • M Ed
   leadership and administration • M Ed
   reading • M Ed
   secondary education • M Ed
   special education • M Ed, PhD

College of Engineering
Lawrence A. Kennedy, Dean
Programs in:
   bioengineering • MS, PhD
   chemical engineering • MS, PhD
   computer science and engineering • MS, PhD
   electrical engineering • MS, PhD
   fluids engineering • MS, PhD
   industrial engineering • MS
   industrial engineering and operations research • PhD
   mechanical analysis and design • MS, PhD
   mechanical engineering • MS, PhD
   safety engineering • MS
   thermomechanical and power engineering • MS, PhD

College of Liberal Arts and Sciences
Sidney Simpson, Dean
Programs in:
   anthropology • MA, PhD
   applied linguistics (teaching English as a second
       language) • MA
   applied mathematics • DA, MS, PhD
   cell and developmental biology • PhD
   chemistry • MS, PhD
   communication • MA
   computer science • DA, MS, PhD
   creative writing • MA, PhD
   criminal justice • MA
   crystallography • MS, PhD
   ecology and evolution • DA, MS, PhD
   engineering • PhD
   English • MA, PhD
   environmental geology • MS, PhD
   environmental studies • MA
   French • MA
   genetics and development • PhD
   geochemistry • MS, PhD
   geology • MS, PhD
   geomorphology • MS, PhD
   geophysics • MS, PhD
   German • MA, PhD
   history • MA, MAT, PhD
   hydrogeology • MS, PhD
   language, literacy and rhetoric • PhD
   Latin American studies • MA, PhD
   liberal arts and sciences • MPA
   literature • MA, PhD
   low-temperature and organic geochemistry • MS, PhD
   mass communication • MA
   mineralogy • MS, PhD
   molecular biology • MS, PhD

neurobiology • MS, PhD
paleoclimatology • MS, PhD
paleontology • MS, PhD
petrology • MS, PhD
philosophy • MA, PhD
physics • MS, PhD
plant biology • DA, MS, PhD
political science • MA
probability and statistics • DA, MS, PhD
psychology • PhD
public policy analysis • PhD
pure mathematics • DA, MS, PhD
quaternary geology • MS, PhD
sedimentology • MS, PhD
Slavic languages and literatures • PhD
Slavic studies • MA
sociology • MA, PhD
teaching of English • MA
teaching of mathematics • MST
urban geography • MA
water resources • MS, PhD

College of Nursing
Dr. Kathleen Potempa, Dean
Programs in:
   administrative studies in nursing • MS
   maternity nursing/nurse midwifery • MS
   medical-surgical nursing • MS
   nursing sciences • PhD
   pediatric nursing • MS
   perinatal nursing • MS
   psychiatric nursing • MS
   public health nursing • MS

College of Urban Planning and Public Affairs
James Marek, Interim Dean
Programs in:
   public administration • MPA, PhD
   public policy analysis • PhD
   urban planning and policy • MUPP

Jane Addams College of Social Work
C. F. Hairston, Dean
Program in:
   social work • MSW, PhD

College of Dentistry
Allen Anderson, Dean
Programs in:
   dentistry • DDS
   oral sciences • MS

College of Medicine
Gerald S. Moss, Dean
Programs in:
   anatomy and cell biology • MS, PhD
   biochemical mechanisms • PhD
   biochemistry and molecular biology • MS, PhD
   medical education • MHPE
   medicine • MD
   microbiology and immunology • PhD
   molecular biology and genetics • PhD
   pathology • MS, PhD

University of Illinois at Chicago (continued)
  pharmacology • PhD
  physiology and biophysics • MS, PhD
  surgery • MS

College of Pharmacy
Rosalie Sagraves, Dean
Programs in:
  forensic science • MS
  medicinal chemistry • MS, PhD
  pharmaceutics • MS, PhD
  pharmacodynamics • MS, PhD
  pharmacognosy • MS, PhD
  pharmacokinetics • MS, PhD
  pharmacy • Pharm D
  pharmacy administration • MS, PhD

School of Public Health
Dr. Susan Scrimshaw, Dean
Programs in:
  biostatistics • MS, PhD
  community health sciences • Dr PH, MPH, MS, PhD
  environmental and occupational health sciences •
    Dr PH, MPH, MS, PhD
  epidemiology and biostatistics • Dr PH, MPH, MS, PhD
  health resources management • Dr PH, MPH, MS, PhD

UNIVERSITY OF ILLINOIS AT SPRINGFIELD
Springfield, IL 62794-9243

http://www.uis.edu/

Public coed upper-level institution. *Enrollment: 4,463 graduate, professional, and undergraduate students. Graduate faculty: 101 full-time, 57 part-time. Library facilities: Norris L. Brookens Library. Graduate expenses: Tuition of $99 per credit hour for state residents; $296 per credit hour for nonresidents. Fees of $242 per year full-time, $63 per semester (minimum) part-time. General application contact: Office of Admissions and Records, 217-786-6626.*

Graduate Programs
Dr. Wayne Penn, Provost/Vice Chancellor for Academic
  Affairs

School of Business and Management
Dr. John Munkirs, Dean
Programs in:
  accountancy • MA
  business administration • MBA
  economics • MA
  management information systems • MA

School of Health and Human Services
Dr. Steve Eggers, Dean
Programs in:
  child, family, and community services • MA
  educational administration • MA

  gerontology • MA
  human development counseling • MA
  public health • MPH

School of Liberal Arts and Sciences
William Bloemer, Dean
Programs in:
  biology • MA
  clinical psychology • MA
  communication • MA
  computer science • MA
  English • MA
  general psychology • MA
  individual option • MA
  mathematics • MA
  public affairs reporting • MA
  public history • MA
  statistics • MA

School of Public Affairs and Administration
Glen Cope, Dean
Programs in:
  community arts management • MA
  environmental studies • MA
  legal studies • MA
  political studies • MA
  public administration • MPA

UNIVERSITY OF ILLINOIS AT URBANA–CHAMPAIGN
Urbana, IL 61801

http://www.uiuc.edu/

Public coed university. *Enrollment: 36,019 graduate, professional, and undergraduate students. Graduate faculty: 1,991 full-time, 111 part-time. Computer facilities: Campuswide network is available with full Internet access. Computer service fees are included with tuition and fees. Library facilities: University Library plus 37 additional on-campus libraries. Graduate expenses: Tuition of $3884 per year full-time, $648 per semester (minimum) part-time for state residents; $10,760 per year full-time, $1784 per semester (minimum) part-time for nonresidents. Fees of $1053 per year full-time, $401 per semester (minimum) part-time. General application contact: Richard C. Alkire, Dean, Graduate College, 217-333-0035.*

Graduate College
Richard C. Alkire, Dean
Programs in:
  atmospheric science • MS, PhD
  biophysics and computational biology • PhD
  veterinary biosciences • MS, PhD
  veterinary pathobiology • MS, PhD

College of Agricultural, Consumer and Environmental Sciences
David L. Chicoine, Dean
Programs in:
- agricultural and consumer economics • MS, PhD
- animal sciences • MS, PhD
- crop sciences • MS, PhD
- extension education • MS
- food science and human nutrition • MS, PhD
- human and community development • AM, MS, PhD
- natural resources and environmental science • MS, PhD
- nutritional sciences • MS, PhD

College of Applied Life Studies
Michael J. Ellis, Dean
Programs in:
- community health • MSPH, PhD
- kinesiology • MS, MST, PhD
- leisure studies • MS, PhD
- rehabilitation • MS
- speech and hearing science • AM, MS, PhD

College of Commerce and Business Administration
Howard Thomas, Dean
Programs in:
- accountancy • MAS, MS, PhD
- business administration • MBA, MSBA, PhD
- economics • MS, PhD
- finance • MS, PhD

College of Communications
Kim B. Rotzoll, Dean
Programs in:
- advertising • MS
- communications • PhD
- journalism • MS

College of Education
Mildred Griggs, Dean
Programs in:
- curriculum and instruction • AC, AM, Ed D, Ed M, MS, PhD
- educational policy studies • AC, AM, Ed D, Ed M, MS, PhD
- educational psychology • AC, AM, Ed D, Ed M, MS, PhD
- education, organization and leadership • AC, AM, Ed D, Ed M, MS, PhD
- special education • AC, AM, Ed D, Ed M, MS, PhD
- vocational and technical education • AC, AM, Ed D, Ed M, MS, PhD

College of Engineering
Dr. William R. Schowalter, Dean
Programs in:
- aeronautical and astronautical engineering • MS, PhD
- agricultural engineering • MS, PhD
- civil engineering • MS, PhD
- computer engineering • MS, PhD
- computer science • MCS, MS, MST, PhD
- electrical engineering • MS, PhD
- environmental engineering • MS, PhD
- environmental science • MS, PhD
- general engineering • MS
- health physics • MS, PhD
- industrial engineering • MS, PhD
- materials science and engineering • MS, PhD
- mechanical engineering • MS, PhD
- nuclear engineering • MS, PhD
- physics • MS, PhD
- systems engineering and engineering design • MS
- theoretical and applied mechanics • MS, PhD

College of Fine and Applied Arts
Kathleen F. Conlin, Dean
Programs in:
- architecture • M Arch
- art education • AM, Ed D
- art history • AM, PhD
- dance • AM
- graphic design • MFA
- industrial design • MFA
- landscape architecture • MLA
- music • DMA, Ed D, M Mus, MS, PhD
- regional planning • PhD
- theatre • AM, MFA, PhD
- urban and regional planning • MUP

College of Liberal Arts and Sciences
Jesse Delia, Dean
Programs in:
- African studies • AM
- anthropology • AM, PhD
- applied mathematics • MS
- applied measurement • MS
- astronomy • MS, PhD
- biochemistry • MS, PhD
- biological psychology • AM, PhD
- cell and structural biology • PhD
- chemical engineering • MS, PhD
- chemistry • MS, PhD
- classics • AM, PhD
- clinical psychology • AM, PhD
- cognitive psychology • AM, PhD
- comparative literature • AM, MAT, PhD
- demography • AM, PhD
- developmental psychology • AM, PhD
- earth sciences • MS, PhD
- East Asian languages and cultures • AM, PhD
- ecology, ethology, and evolution • PhD
- engineering psychology • MS
- English • AM, PhD
- English as an international language • AM
- entomology • MS, PhD
- French • AM, MAT, PhD
- geochemistry • MS, PhD
- geography • AM, MS, PhD
- geology • MS, PhD
- geophysics • MS, PhD
- Germanic languages and literatures • AM, MAT, PhD
- history • AM, PhD
- insect pest management • MS
- Italian • AM, PhD
- Latin American and Caribbean studies • AM
- linguistics • AM, PhD
- mathematics • MS, PhD
- microbiology • MS, PhD
- molecular and integrative physiology • MS, PhD

University of Illinois at Urbana–Champaign (continued)

neuroscience • PhD

perception and performance psychology • AM, PhD

personality and social ecology psychology • AM, PhD

personnel psychology • MS

philosophy • AM, PhD

plant biology • MS, PhD

political science • AM, PhD

quantitative psychology • AM, PhD

Russian • AM, MAT, PhD

Russian and East European studies • AM

Slavic languages and literatures • AM, MAT, PhD

social/organizational, individual differences • AM, PhD

sociology • AM, PhD

Spanish • MAT

speech communication • AM, MAT, PhD

statistics • MS, PhD

teaching of mathematics • MS

Graduate School of Library and Information Science

Dr. Leigh S. Estabrook, Dean

Program in:

library and information science • CAS, MS, PhD

Institute of Labor and Industrial Relations

Peter Feuille, Director

Programs in:

human resources • AM, PhD

labor and industrial relations • AM, PhD

School of Social Work

Jill D. Kagle, Dean

Program in:

social work • MSW, PhD

College of Law

Thomas M. Mengler, Dean

Program in:

law • JD, JSD, LL M, MCL

College of Veterinary Medicine

Victor E. Valli, Dean

Programs in:

veterinary biosciences • MS, PhD

veterinary medicine • DVM

veterinary pathobiology • MS, PhD

UNIVERSITY OF ST. FRANCIS

Joliet, IL 60435-6188

http://www.stfrancis.edu/

Independent-religious coed comprehensive institution. *Enrollment:* 4,200 graduate, professional, and undergraduate students. *Graduate faculty:* 6 full-time, 62 part-time. *Computer facilities: Campuswide network is available with full Internet access. Computer services are offered at no charge. Library facilities: main library. Graduate expenses: $285 per credit hour. General application contact: Dr. F. William Kelley Jr., Dean of Graduate Studies, 800-735-4723.*

Graduate Studies

Dr. F. William Kelley Jr., Dean

Programs in:

business administration • MBA, MSM

continuing education training management • MS

curriculum in instruction in middle schools • MS

education • M Ed

health services administration • MS

long-term care administration • Certificate

 # WESTERN ILLINOIS UNIVERSITY

Macomb, IL 61455-1390

http://www.wiu.edu/

Public coed comprehensive institution. *Enrollment:* 12,200 graduate, professional, and undergraduate students. Graduate faculty: 438 full-time. *Computer facilities: Campuswide network is available with full Internet access. Total number of PCs/terminals supplied for student use: 800. Computer service fees are included with tuition and fees. Library facilities: University Library plus 3 additional on-campus libraries. Graduate expenses: Tuition of $2304 per year full-time, $96 per semester hour part-time for state residents; $6912 per year full-time, $288 per semester hour part-time for nonresidents. Fees of $944 per year full-time, $33 per semester hour part-time. General application contact: Barbara Baily, Director of Graduate Studies, 309-298-1806.*

School of Graduate Studies

Barbara Baily, Director of Graduate Studies

College of Arts and Sciences

Dr. Phyllis Rippey, Acting Dean

Programs in:

biological sciences • MS

chemistry • MS

clinical/community mental health • MS

general psychology • MS

geography • MA

gerontology • MA

history • MA

literature and language • MA

mathematics • MS

physics • MS

political science • MA

school psychology • MS, SSP

sociology • MA

writing • MA

College of Business and Technology

Dr. David Beveridge, Dean

Programs in:

accountancy • M Acct

business administration • MBA

computer science • MS

economics • MA

industrial technology • MS

College of Education and Human Services
Dr. David Taylor, Dean
Programs in:
  college student personnel • MS
  counseling • MS Ed
  education administration and supervision • Ed S, MS Ed
  elementary education • MS Ed
  health education and promotion • MS
  instructional technology and telecommunications • MS
  interdisciplinary studies • MS Ed
  law enforcement and justice administration • MA
  physical education • MS
  reading • MS Ed
  recreation, park, and tourism administration • MS
  special education • MS Ed
  sport management • MS

College of Fine Arts and Communication
Dr. James M. Butterworth, Dean
Programs in:
  communication sciences and disorders • MS
  music • MA
  public communication and broadcasting • MA
  theatre • MFA

INDIANA

BALL STATE UNIVERSITY
Muncie, IN 47306-1099

http://www.bsu.edu/

Public coed university. *Enrollment:* 19,500 graduate, professional, and undergraduate students. Graduate faculty: *670.* Library facilities: *Bracken Library plus 2 additional on-campus libraries.* Graduate expenses: *Tuition of $3454 per year full-time, $518 per semester (minimum) part-time for state residents; $9316 per year full-time, $1221 per semester (minimum) part-time for nonresidents. Fees of $242 per year full-time, $18 per semester (minimum) part-time.* General application contact: *Dr. Robert D. Habich, Acting Dean, 765-285-1300.*

Graduate School
Dr. Robert D. Habich, Acting Dean

College of Applied Science and Technology
Dr. Donald Smith, Dean
Programs in:
  applied gerontology • MA
  family and consumer sciences • MA, MAE, MS
  human bioenergetics • PhD
  industry and technology • MA, MAE
  nursing • MS
  physical education • MA, MAE, PhD
  wellness management • MS

College of Architecture and Planning
Dr. Eric Kelly, Dean
Programs in:
  architecture • M Arch
  historic preservation • M Arch, MS
  landscape architecture • MLA
  urban planning • MURP

College of Business
Dr. Neil A. Palomba, Dean
Programs in:
  accounting • MS
  business administration • MBA
  business education and office administration • MAE
  economics • MA
  management • MS

College of Communication, Information, and Media
Dr. Earl Conn, Dean
Programs in:
  information and communication sciences • MS
  journalism • MA
  public relations • MA
  speech, public address, forensics, and rhetoric • MA
  telecommunications • MA

College of Fine Arts
Dr. Margaret Merrion, Dean
Programs in:
  art • MA
  art education • MA, MAE
  music education • DA, MA, MM

College of Sciences and Humanities
Dr. Ronald L. Johnstone, Dean
Programs in:
  actuarial science • MA
  anthropology • MA
  applied linguistics • PhD
  biology • MA, MAE, MS
  biology education • Ed D
  chemistry • MA, MS
  clinical psychology • MA
  composition • MA, PhD
  computer science • MA, MS
  earth sciences • MA
  English • MA, PhD
  geology • MA, MS
  health education • MA, MAE
  history • MA
  linguistics • MA
  literature • PhD
  mathematical statistics • MA
  mathematics • MA, MS
  mathematics education • MAE
  natural resources • MA, MS
  physics • MA, MS
  physiology • MA, MS
  political science • MA
  psychological science • MA
  public administration • MPA
  social sciences • MA
  sociology • MA
  speech pathology and audiology • Au D, MA

Ball State University (continued)

Teachers College
Dr. Roy Weaver, Dean
Programs in:
    adult education • Ed D, MA
    counseling psychology • MA, PhD
    curriculum and instruction • Ed S, MAE
    early childhood education • Ed D, MAE
    educational administration • Ed D, MAE
    educational psychology • Ed S, MA, PhD
    elementary education • Ed D, MAE, PhD
    executive development • MA
    junior high/middle school education • MAE
    reading education • Ed D, MAE
    school psychology • Ed S, MA, PhD
    school superintendency • Ed S
    secondary education • MA
    social psychology • MA
    special education • Ed D, Ed S, MA, MAE
    student personnel administration in higher education •
      MA

BUTLER UNIVERSITY
Indianapolis, IN 46208-3485

http://www.butler.edu/

Independent coed comprehensive institution. *Enrollment:* 3,911 graduate, professional, and undergraduate students. Graduate faculty: *62 full-time, 37 part-time.* Computer facilities: *Campuswide network is available with full Internet access. Total number of PCs/ terminals supplied for student use: 230. Computer services are offered at no charge.* Library facilities: *Irwin Library plus 1 additional on-campus library.* Graduate expenses: *$220 per credit hour.* General application contact: *Carol Carmody, Director of Graduate Admissions, 317-940-8100.*

College of Business Administration
Dr. Lee Dahringer, Dean
Program in:
    business administration • MBA

College of Education
Dr. Saundra Tracy, Dean
Programs in:
    administration • Ed S, MS
    counseling psychology • Ed S
    elementary education • MS
    reading • MS
    school counseling • Ed S, MS
    school psychology • Ed S, MS
    secondary education • MS
    special education • MS

College of Liberal Arts and Sciences
Dr. Margriet Lacy, Dean
Programs in:
    chemistry • MS
    English • MA
    history • MA

College of Pharmacy
Dr. Robert A. Sandmann, Dean
Program in:
    pharmaceutical science • MS, Pharm D

Jordan College of Fine Arts
Dr. Michael B. Sells, Dean
Programs in:
    composition • MM
    conducting • MM
    music • MM
    music education • MM
    music history • MM
    organ • MM
    performance • MM

INDIANA STATE UNIVERSITY
Terre Haute, IN 47809-1401

http://www.isu.indstate.edu/

Public coed university. *Enrollment:* 10,784 graduate, professional, and undergraduate students. Graduate faculty: *455 full-time, 19 part-time.* Library facilities: *Cunningham Memorial Library plus 3 additional on-campus libraries.* Graduate expenses: *$143 per credit hour for state residents; $325 per credit hour for nonresidents.* General application contact: *Dr. Thomas E. Siefert, Associate Dean, School of Graduate Studies, 800-444-GRAD.*

School of Graduate Studies
Dr. Bernice Bass de Martinez, Dean

College of Arts and Sciences
Dr. Joseph Weixlmann, Dean
Programs in:
    applied linguistics • MA
    art history • MA
    ceramics • MA, MFA, MS
    chemistry • MS
    child and family relations • MS
    clinical laboratory sciences • MS
    clinical psychology • Psy D
    clothing and textiles • MS
    communication studies • MA, MS
    comparative and international administration • MPA
    composition • MA
    criminology • MA, MS
    dietetics • MS
    drawing • MA, MFA, MS
    earth sciences • MS
    ecology • MA, MS, PhD

economic geography • PhD
economics • MA, MS
English • MA, MS
French • MA
general psychology • MA, MS
geography • MA
geology • MA
graphic design • MA, MFA, MS
history • MA, MS
home management • MS
human resources and organizational development •
   MPA
interdisciplinary humanities • MA
language • CAS
Latin • MA
literature • CAS
mathematics • MA, MS
metalry • MA, MFA, MS
microbiology • MA, MS, PhD
music • MM
music education • MA, MME, MS
music history and literature • MA
music performance • MS
music theory • MA
national administration • MPA
nutrition and foods • MS
painting • MA, MFA, MS
photography • MA, MFA, MS
physical geography • PhD
physics • MA, MS
physiology • MA, MS, PhD
political science • MA, MS
printmaking • MA, MFA, MS
radio, television and film • MA, MS
religion • MA
rhetoric • CAS
science education • MA, MS
sculpture • MA, MFA, MS
sociology • MA, MS
Spanish • MA
state/local administration • MPA
theatre • MA, MS

School of Business
Dr. Donald Bates, Dean
Programs in:
   business • MBA
   business education • Ed S, MA, MS, PhD

School of Education
Dr. Richard Antonak, Dean
Programs in:
   agency counseling • MA, MS
   business education • Ed S, MA, MS, PhD
   college student personnel work • MA, MS
   counseling psychology • PhD
   counselor education • PhD
   curriculum and instruction • M Ed, PhD
   director of special education • M Ed
   early childhood education • Ed S, M Ed, PhD
   educational administration • Ed S, PhD
   educational media • Ed S, MA, MS
   educational psychology • MA, MS

elementary education • Ed S, M Ed, PhD
elementary school administration • M Ed
gifted/talented education • Ed S, MA, MS
guidance • Ed S, PhD
higher education • MA, MS
industrial arts education • PhD
marriage and family counseling • MA, MS
reading education • Ed S, M Ed, PhD
school counseling • M Ed
school psychology • Ed S, M Ed, PhD
secondary education • Ed S, M Ed, MS, PhD
secondary school administration • M Ed
special education • MA, MS, PhD
speech pathology and audiology • MA, MS
student personnel work in higher education • PhD

School of Health and Human Performance
Dr. Barbara Passmore, Dean
Programs in:
   athletic training • MA, MS
   health program and facility administration • MA, MS
   occupational safety management • MA, MS
   physical education • MA, MS
   school health and safety • MA, MS

School of Nursing
Dr. Judith Alexander, Acting Dean
Program in:
   nursing • MS

School of Technology
Clois Kicklighter, Dean
Programs in:
   curriculum and instruction • PhD
   electronics and computer technology • MA, MS
   human resource development • MS
   industrial technology • MA, MS
   technology education • MA, MS
   vocational technical education • MA, MS

INDIANA UNIVERSITY BLOOMINGTON
Bloomington, IN 47405

http://www.indiana.edu/iub/index.html

Public coed university. *Enrollment: 34,937 graduate, professional, and undergraduate students. Graduate faculty: 1,101 full-time, 5 part-time.* Computer facilities: *Campuswide network is available with full Internet access. Computer service fees are applied as a separate charge.* Library facilities: *main library plus 19 additional on-campus libraries.* Graduate expenses: *Tuition of $153 per credit hour for state residents; $446 per credit hour for nonresidents. Fees of $343 per year.* General application contact: *Dean of individual schools, 812-855-0211.*

Graduate School
George E. Walker, Vice President for Research and Dean
Program in:
   visual sciences and physiological optics • MS, PhD

Indiana University Bloomington (continued)
College of Arts and Sciences
Morton Lowengrub, Dean
Programs in:
   acting • MFA
   American studies • PhD
   anthropology • MA, PhD
   apparel studies • MS
   applied linguistics (teaching English as a second
      language) • Certificate, MA
   applied mathematics–numerical analysis • MA, PhD
   Arabic • MA, PhD
   arts administration • MA
   astronomy • MA, PhD
   astrophysics • PhD
   biochemistry and molecular biology • MS, PhD
   biology education • MAT
   chemistry • MAT, MS, PhD
   Chinese language and literature • MA, PhD
   classical archaeology • MA, PhD
   classical studies • MA, MAT, PhD
   clinical psychology • PhD
   comparative literature • MA, MAT, PhD
   computer science • MS, PhD
   costume design • MFA
   creative writing • MFA
   criticism • MA, PhD
   cross-cultural studies of crime and justice • MA, PhD
   directing • MFA
   East Asian studies • MA
   East European studies • Certificate
   economics • MA, MAT, PhD
   English • MA, PhD
   English education • MAT
   evolution, ecology, and organismal biology • MA, PhD
   French linguistics • MA, PhD
   French literature • MA, PhD
   genetics • PhD
   geochemistry • MS, PhD
   geography • MA, MAT, PhD
   geophysics • MS, PhD
   German and business studies • MA
   German literature and culture • MA
   German literature and linguistics • MA, PhD
   German studies • MA, PhD
   Hebrew • MA
   Hispanic linguistics • MA, PhD
   Hispanic literature • MA, PhD
   history • MA, MAT, PhD
   history and philosophy of science • MA, PhD
   Hungarian studies • Certificate
   interior design • MS
   Italian • MA, PhD
   Japanese language and literature • MA, PhD
   justice systems and processes • MA, PhD
   Latin American and Caribbean studies • MA
   law and society • MA, PhD
   lighting design • MFA
   linguistics • MA, PhD
   literature • MA, PhD
   Luso-Brazilian literature • MA, PhD
   mass communication • PhD
   mathematics education • MAT

   medieval German studies • PhD
   microbiology • MA, PhD
   molecular, cellular, and developmental biology • PhD
   nature of crime • MA, PhD
   neural sciences • PhD
   Persian • MA
   philosophy • MA, PhD
   physics • MAT, MS, PhD
   plant sciences • MA, PhD
   playwriting • MFA
   political science • MA, PhD
   probability-statistics • MA, PhD
   regional analysis and planning • PhD
   religious studies • MA, PhD
   Russian and East European studies • MA
   Russian area studies • Certificate
   scene design • MFA
   Slavic languages and literatures • MA, MAT, PhD
   social psychology • PhD
   sociology • MA, PhD
   speech and hearing sciences • MA, MAT, PhD
   speech communication • MA, MAT, PhD
   teaching French • MAT
   teaching German • MAT
   teaching Spanish • MAT
   technology • MFA
   telecommunications • MA, MS
   theater history • MA, PhD
   Uralic, Altaic, and Inner Asian studies • MA, PhD
   West European studies • Certificate, MA, PhD
   zoology • MA, PhD

School of Fine Arts
Jefferey Wolin, Director
Programs in:
   art education • MAT
   ceramics • MFA
   graphic design • MFA
   history of art • MA, PhD
   jewelry/metalsmithing • MFA
   painting • MFA
   photography • MFA
   printmaking • MFA
   sculpture • MFA
   textiles • MFA

School of Journalism
Trevor Brown, Dean
Programs in:
   journalism • MA
   mass communication • PhD

School of Business
Dr. Dan R. Dalton, Dean
Programs in:
   accounting • DBA, PhD
   business • EMBA
   business economics and public policy • DBA, PhD
   entrepreneurship • MBA
   finance • DBA, MBA, PhD
   human resources • MBA
   information and decision systems • DBA, PhD
   international business • MBA

management • DBA, MBA, PhD
management information systems • MBA
marketing • DBA, MBA, PhD
operations management • DBA, MBA, PhD
organizational behavior • DBA, PhD

School of Education

Donald Warren, Dean
Programs in:
art education • MS
college student personnel administration • MS
counseling/counselor education • Ed S, MS
counseling psychology • Ed D, PhD
curriculum and instruction • Ed D, PhD
early childhood education • Ed S, MS
educational leadership and policy • MS, PhD
educational psychology • Ed D, MS, PhD
elementary education • Ed S, MS
higher education • Ed D, PhD
history and philosophy of education • MS
history, philosophy, and policy studies in education • PhD
instructional systems technology • Ed D, Ed S, MS, PhD
international and comparative education • MS
language education • Ed D, Ed S, MS, PhD
school administration • Ed D, Ed S, MS
school psychology • Ed S
secondary education • Ed S, MS
social studies education • MS
special education • Ed D, Ed S, MS, PhD

School of Health, Physical Education and Recreation

Tony Mobley, Dean
Programs in:
adapted physical education • MS
administration • MS
applied sport science • MS
athletic administration/sport management • MS
athletic training • MS
biomechanics • MS
clinical exercise physiology • MS
exercise physiology • MS
health and safety studies • HS Dir, HSD
health behavior • PhD
health promotion • MS
human development/family studies • MS
human performance • PhD
leisure behavior • PhD
motor control • MS
motor development • MS
motor learning • MS
nutrition science • MS
outdoor recreation resources • MS
physical education • PE Dir, PED
public health • MPH
public health education • HS Dir
recreation • Re D, Re Dir
recreational sports administration • MS
safety management • MS
school and college health education • HS Dir
school health education • MS

social science of sport • MS
sport management • MS
therapeutic recreation • MS

School of Law

Alfred C. Aman Jr., Dean
Program in:
law • JD, LL M, MCL, SJD

School of Library and Information Science

Dr. Blaise Cronin, Dean
Program in:
library and information science • MIS, MLS, PhD, Spec

School of Music

David Woods, Dean
Programs in:
ballet • MS
music • AD, D Mus Ed, DM, MA, MM, MME, PD

School of Optometry

Jack W. Bennett, Dean
Programs in:
optometry • OD
visual sciences and physiological optics • MS, PhD

School of Public and Environmental Affairs

A. James Barnes, Dean
Programs in:
environmental science • MSES, PhD
public affairs • EMPA, MPA, PhD
public policy • PhD

INDIANA UNIVERSITY KOKOMO
Kokomo, IN 46904-9003

http://www.iuk.indiana.edu/

Public coed comprehensive institution. *Enrollment:* 2,927 graduate, professional, and undergraduate students. Graduate faculty: *17 full-time. Computer facilities: Campuswide network is available with full Internet access. Total number of PCs/terminals supplied for student use: 80. Computer service fees are applied as a separate charge. Library facilities: main library.* General application contact: *Admissions Office, 765-455-9357.*

Division of Business and Economics

Dr. Thomas Von der Embse, Dean
Program in:
business and economics • MBA

Division of Education

Dr. Steven Gilbert, Chair
Programs in:
education • MS
elementary education • MS

INDIANA UNIVERSITY NORTHWEST

Gary, IN 46408-1197

http://www.iun.indiana.edu/

Public coed comprehensive institution. *Enrollment: 6,000 graduate, professional, and undergraduate students. Graduate faculty: 43 full-time, 20 part-time. Computer facilities: Campuswide network is available with full Internet access. Total number of PCs/terminals supplied for student use: 200. Computer service fees are included with tuition and fees. General application contact: Marilyn Vasquez, Interim Vice Chancellor for Academic Affairs, 219-980-6967.*

Division of Business and Economics

Dr. Donald Coffin, Dean
Programs in:
    accountancy • M Acc
    accounting • Certificate
    business administration • MBA

Division of Education

Dr. William May, Interim Dean
Programs in:
    elementary education • MS Ed
    secondary education • MS Ed

Division of Public and Environmental Affairs

Joseph M. Pellicciotti, Director
Programs in:
    criminal justice • MPA
    health services administration • MPA
    human services administration • MPA
    management of public affairs • MPA
    non-profit management • NPMC
    public management • PMC

Program in Social Work

Dr. Grafton Hull Jr., Director
Program in:
    social work • MSW

INDIANA UNIVERSITY–PURDUE UNIVERSITY FORT WAYNE

Fort Wayne, IN 46805-1499

http://www.ipfw.edu/

Public coed comprehensive institution. *Enrollment: 10,749 graduate, professional, and undergraduate students. Graduate faculty: 127 full-time, 16 part-time. Computer facilities: Campuswide network is available with full Internet access. Total number of PCs/terminals supplied for student use: 300. Computer service fees are included with tuition and fees. Library facilities: Walter E. Helmke Library. Graduate expenses: Tuition of $2356 per year full-time, $131 per credit hour part-time for state residents; $5253 per year full-time,*

$292 per credit hour part-time for nonresidents. Fees of $183 per year full-time, $10.15 per credit hour part-time. General application contact: Karen Martin, Secretary for Graduate Studies, 219-481-6144.

Division of Public and Environmental Affairs

Dr. William Ludwin, Assistant Dean
Programs in:
    management of public affairs • MPA
    public management • Certificate

School of Arts and Sciences

Van Coufoudakis, Dean
Programs in:
    applied mathematics • MS
    biological sciences • MS
    chemistry • MS
    communication • MA, MS
    English • MA, MAT
    liberal studies • MLS
    mathematics • MS
    operations research • MS
    sociological practice • MA

School of Business and Management Sciences

Michael R. Lane, Dean
Program in:
    business • MBA

School of Education

Betty Steffy, Dean
Programs in:
    counselor education • MS Ed
    educational administration • MS Ed
    elementary education • MS Ed
    secondary education • MS Ed

School of Engineering, Technology, and Computer Science

G. Allen Pugh, Dean
Programs in:
    applied computer science • MS
    engineering • MS, MSE

School of Health Sciences

James E. Jones, Dean
Program in:
    nursing administration • MS

INDIANA UNIVERSITY–PURDUE UNIVERSITY INDIANAPOLIS

Indianapolis, IN 46202-2896

http://www.iupui.edu/

Public coed university. *Enrollment:* 27,036 *graduate, professional, and undergraduate students. Graduate faculty:* 491 *full-time, 1 part-time. Computer facilities: Campuswide network is available with full Internet access. Total number of PCs/terminals supplied for student use: 500. Computer service fees are included with tuition and fees. Library facilities: University Library plus 4 additional on-campus libraries. Graduate expenses: Tuition of $3602 per year full-time, $150 per credit hour part-time for state residents; $10,392 per year full-time, $433 per credit hour part-time for nonresidents. Fees of $100 per year (minimum) full-time, $40 per year (minimum) part-time. General application contact: Dr. Sheila Cooper, Director, Graduate Studies and Associate Dean, 317-274-4023.*

Center on Philanthropy
Dr. Eugene Tempel, Executive Director
Program in:
   philanthropic studies • MA

Herron School of Art
Robert Shay, Dean
Program in:
   art education • MAE

School of Business
Roger W. Schmenner, Associate Dean–Indianapolis
   Programs
Program in:
   business • MBA

School of Dentistry
Lawrence I. Goldblatt, Dean
Programs in:
   dental materials • MS, MSD
   dental sciences • PhD
   dentistry • DDS
   diagnostic sciences • MS, MSD
   oral biology • PhD
   orthodontics • MS, MSD
   pediatric dentistry • MSD
   periodontics • MSD
   preventive and community dentistry • PhD
   preventive dentistry • MS, MSD
   prosthodontics • MSD

School of Education
Barbara Wilcox, Executive Associate Dean
Programs in:
   counseling and counselor education • MS
   elementary education • MS
   language education • MS
   school administration • MS
   secondary education • MS
   special education • MS

School of Engineering and Technology
Dr. H. Oner Yurtseven, Dean
Programs in:
   biomedical engineering • MS Bm E, PhD
   electrical engineering • MSEE
   engineering • MS, MSE
   mechanical engineering • MSME

School of Law
Norman Lefstein, Dean
Program in:
   law • JD

School of Medicine
Dr. Robert W. Holden, Dean
Programs in:
   anatomy • MS, PhD
   biochemistry and molecular biology • MS, PhD
   medical and molecular genetics • MS, PhD
   medical biophysics • MS, PhD
   medical neurobiology • MS, PhD
   medicine • MD
   microbiology and immunology • MS, PhD
   nutrition and dietetics • MS
   pathology • MS, PhD
   pharmacology • MS, PhD
   physiology and biophysics • MS, PhD
   toxicology • MS, PhD

School of Nursing
Dr. Linda Finke, Associate Dean for Graduate Programs
Program in:
   nursing • MSN, PhD

School of Public and Environmental Affairs
Dr. Mark Rosentraub, Associate Dean
Programs in:
   environmental planning • M Pl
   health administration • MHA
   health planning • M Pl
   planning and public policy • M Pl
   public affairs • Certificate, MPA
   urban development planning • M Pl

School of Science
David L. Stocum, Dean
Programs in:
   applied mathematics • MS, PhD
   applied statistics • MS
   biology • MS, PhD
   chemistry • MS, PhD
   clinical rehabilitation psychology • MS, PhD
   computer science • MS
   geology • MS
   industrial/organizational psychology • MS
   mathematics • MS, PhD
   psychobiology of addictions • PhD

School of Social Work
Dr. Roberta Greene, Dean
Program in:
   social work • MSW, PhD

INDIANA UNIVERSITY SOUTH BEND

South Bend, IN 46634-7111

http://www.iusb.edu/

Public coed comprehensive institution. *Enrollment: 7,175 graduate, professional, and undergraduate students. Graduate faculty: 107 full-time, 50 part-time.* Computer facilities: *Campuswide network is available with full Internet access. Total number of PCs/terminals supplied for student use: 500. Computer service fees are included with tuition and fees.* Library facilities: *Schurz Library.* Graduate expenses: *Tuition of $3024 per year full-time, $126 per credit hour part-time for state residents; $7320 per year full-time, $305 per credit hour part-time for nonresidents. Fees of $222 per year full-time, $34 per semester (minimum) part-time.* General application contact: *Graduate Director, 219-237-4183.*

Division of Arts

Dr. Robert W. Demaree Jr., Dean
Programs in:
   music • MM
   music in secondary education • MS Ed

Division of Business and Economics

Dr. John R. Swanda Jr., Dean
Programs in:
   accounting • MS
   business administration • MBA

Division of Education

Dr. James Smith, Dean
Programs in:
   counseling and human services • MS Ed
   elementary education • MS Ed
   secondary education • MS Ed
   special education • MS Ed

Division of Liberal Arts and Sciences

Dr. Patrick J. Furlong, Director
Programs in:
   applied psychology • MA
   liberal studies • MLS

Program in Social Work

Program in:
   social work • MSW

School of Public and Environmental Affairs

Dr. William P. Hojnacki, Assistant Dean
Program in:
   public affairs • MPA

INDIANA UNIVERSITY SOUTHEAST

New Albany, IN 47150-6405

http://www.ius.indiana.edu/

Public coed comprehensive institution. *Enrollment: 5,520 graduate, professional, and undergraduate students. Graduate faculty: 18 full-time, 10 part-time.* Computer facilities: *Campuswide network is available with full Internet access. Total number of PCs/terminals supplied for student use: 175. Computer service fees are applied as a separate charge.* Library facilities: *main library.* Graduate expenses: *Tuition of $125 per credit hour (minimum) for state residents; $284 per credit hour (minimum) for nonresidents. Fees of $33 per year full-time, $2.75 per credit hour part-time.* General application contact: *Dr. Teesue H. Fields, Director of Graduate Studies, 812-941-2658.*

Division of Education

Dr. Carl DeGraaf, Dean
Programs in:
   counselor education • MS Ed
   elementary education • MS Ed
   secondary education • MS Ed

INDIANA WESLEYAN UNIVERSITY

Marion, IN 46953-4999

http://www.indwes.edu/

Independent-religious coed comprehensive institution. *Enrollment: 6,063 graduate, professional, and undergraduate students. Graduate faculty: 18 full-time, 125 part-time.* Library facilities: *Woodrow Goodman Library plus 1 additional on-campus library.* Graduate expenses: *$239 per hour.* General application contact: *Dr. Paul Collord, Vice President for Academic Affairs, 765-677-2104.*

Adult and Professional Studies Program

Dr. David Wright, Vice President
Programs in:
   business administration • MBA
   curriculum and instruction • M Ed
   management • MS

Graduate Programs

Dr. Paul Collord, Vice President for Academic Affairs
Programs in:
   counseling • MA
   ministry • MA

Division of Nursing Education

Dr. DeAnne Messias, Director of Graduate Nursing
Programs in:
   community health development • MS
   community health nursing • MS
   nursing education • MS
   primary care nursing • MS

PURDUE UNIVERSITY
West Lafayette, IN 47907

http://www.purdue.edu/

Public coed university. *Enrollment:* 34,591 graduate, professional, and undergraduate students. *Graduate faculty:* 1,739. *Computer facilities: Campuswide network is available with full Internet access. Computer services are offered at no charge. Library facilities:* main library plus 15 additional on-campus libraries. *Graduate expenses:* $3500 per year full-time, $126 per credit hour part-time for state residents; $11,720 per year full-time, $387 per credit hour part-time for nonresidents. *General application contact:* Graduate School Admissions, 765-494-2600.

Graduate School
Dr. Luis M. Proenza, Vice President for Research and Dean
Programs in:
   analytical medicinal chemistry • PhD
   anatomy • MS, PhD
   bacteriology • MS, PhD
   biochemistry and molecular biology • PhD
   biomedical engineering • MS Bm E, PhD
   clinical pharmacy • MS, PhD
   computational and biophysical medicinal chemistry • PhD
   epidemiology • MS, PhD
   immunology • MS, PhD
   industrial and physical pharmacy • PhD
   medicinal and bioorganic chemistry • PhD
   medicinal biochemistry and molecular biology • PhD
   molecular pharmacology and toxicology • PhD
   natural products and pharmacognosy • PhD
   neuroscience • PhD
   nuclear pharmacy • MS
   parasitology • MS, PhD
   pathology • MS, PhD
   pharmacology • MS, PhD
   pharmacy administration • MS, PhD
   physiology • MS, PhD
   plant biology • PhD
   radiopharmaceutical chemistry and nuclear pharmacy • PhD
   toxicology • MS, PhD
   veterinary clinical sciences • MS, PhD
   virology • MS, PhD

Krannert Graduate School of Management
Dr. Dennis J. Weidenaar, Dean
Programs in:
   accounting • MS, PhD
   applied optimization • PhD
   applied statistics • PhD
   economics • PhD
   finance • MSM, PhD
   general management • MSM
   human resource management • MS
   industrial administration • MSIA
   management information systems • MSM, PhD
   management science • MSM
   manufacturing management • MSM
   marketing • MSM, PhD
   operations management • MSM, PhD
   organizational behavior and human resource management • PhD
   quantitative methods • MSM, PhD
   strategic management • MSM, PhD

School of Agriculture
Dr. Victor L. Lechtenberg, Dean
Programs in:
   agricultural economics • MS, PhD
   agronomy • MS, PhD
   animal sciences • MS, PhD
   biochemistry • MS, PhD
   botany and plant pathology • MS, PhD
   entomology • MS, PhD
   food science • MS, PhD
   forestry and natural resources • MS, MSF, PhD
   horticulture • M Agr, MS, PhD

School of Consumer and Family Sciences
Dr. Dennis A. Savaiano, Dean
Programs in:
   consumer behavior • MS, PhD
   developmental studies • MS, PhD
   family and consumer economics • MS, PhD
   family studies • MS, PhD
   food sciences • MS, PhD
   marriage and family therapy • MS, PhD
   nutrition • MS, PhD
   restaurant, hotel, and institutional and tourism management • MS
   retail management • MS, PhD
   textile science • MS, PhD

School of Education
Dr. Marilyn J. Haring, Dean
Programs in:
   administration • Ed S, MS Ed, PhD
   agricultural and extension education • Ed S, PhD
   agriculture and extension education • MS Ed
   art education • PhD
   consumer and family sciences and extension education • Ed S, MS Ed, PhD
   counseling and development • Ed S, MS, MS Ed, PhD
   curriculum theory • Ed S, MS Ed, PhD
   educational psychology • MS, MS Ed, PhD
   educational technology • Ed S, MS Ed, PhD
   education of the gifted • MS Ed
   elementary education • MS Ed
   foreign language education • Ed S, MS Ed, PhD
   foundations of education • MS Ed
   instructional development • MS Ed
   language arts • Ed S, MS Ed, PhD
   literacy • Ed S, MS Ed, PhD
   mathematics/science education • MS Ed, PhD
   math/science education • Ed S
   social studies • MS Ed, PhD
   social studies education • Ed S
   special education • MS Ed
   vocational/industrial education • Ed S, MS Ed, PhD
   vocational/technical education • Ed S, MS Ed, PhD

Purdue University (continued)

School of Health Sciences
Dr. P. L. Ziemer, Head
Programs in:
  environmental health • MS, PhD
  health physics • MS, PhD
  industrial hygiene • MS, PhD
  medical physics • MS, PhD
  toxicology • MS, PhD

School of Liberal Arts
Dr. Margaret M. Rowe, Dean
Programs in:
  American studies • MA, PhD
  anthropology • MS, PhD
  art and design • MA
  audiology • MS, PhD
  communication • MA, MS, PhD
  comparative literature • MA, PhD
  creative writing • MFA
  exercise physiology • PhD
  French • MA, PhD
  French education • MAT
  German • MA, PhD
  German education • MAT
  health and fitness • MS
  health promotion • MS, PhD
  history • MA, PhD
  history/philosophy of sport • PhD
  linguistics • MA, MS, PhD
  literature • MA, PhD
  literature and philosophy • PhD
  motor control • PhD
  motor development • PhD
  movement and sport science • MS
  philosophy • MA, PhD
  political science • MA, PhD
  psychological sciences • PhD
  rhetoric and composition • MA, PhD
  sociology • MS, PhD
  Spanish • MA, PhD
  Spanish education • MAT
  speech and hearing science • MS, PhD
  speech-language pathology • MS, PhD
  sport biomechanics • PhD
  sport pedagogy • PhD
  sport psychology • PhD
  teaching and learning • MS
  theatre • MA, MFA

School of Science
Dr. Harry A. Morrison, Dean
Programs in:
  analytical chemistry • MS, PhD
  applied statistics • MS
  biochemistry • MS, PhD
  biophysics • PhD
  cell and developmental biology • PhD
  chemical education • MS, PhD
  computer sciences • MS, PhD
  earth and atmospheric sciences • MS, PhD
  ecology • MS, PhD
  evolutionary biology • MS, PhD

  genetics • MS, PhD
  inorganic chemistry • MS, PhD
  mathematics • MS, PhD
  microbiology • PhD
  molecular biology • PhD
  neurobiology • MS, PhD
  organic chemistry • MS, PhD
  physical chemistry • MS, PhD
  physics • MS, PhD
  plant physiology • PhD
  population biology • MS, PhD
  statistics • PhD
  statistics and computer science • MS
  theoretical statistics • MS

School of Technology
Dr. Don K. Gentry, Dean
Program in:
  industrial technology • MS

Schools of Engineering
Dr. Richard J. Schwartz, Dean
Programs in:
  aeronautics and astronautics • MS, MSAAE, MSE, PhD
  agricultural and biological engineering • MS, MSABE, MSE, PhD
  biomedical engineering • MS Bm E, PhD
  chemical engineering • MS Ch E, PhD
  civil engineering • MS, MSCE, MSE, PhD
  computer engineering • MS, MSE
  continuing engineering education • MS, MSE
  electrical engineering • MS, MSE, MSEE
  human factors in industrial engineering • MS, MSIE, PhD
  manufacturing engineering • MS, MSIE, PhD
  materials engineering • MS, MSE, PhD
  mechanical engineering • MS, MSE, MSME, PhD
  metallurgical engineering • MS Met E
  nuclear engineering • MS, MSNE, PhD
  operations research • MS, MSIE, PhD
  systems engineering • MS, MSIE, PhD

School of Pharmacy and Pharmacal Sciences
Dr. Charles O. Rutledge, Dean
Programs in:
  analytical medicinal chemistry • PhD
  clinical pharmacy • MS, PhD
  computational and biophysical medicinal chemistry • PhD
  environmental health • MS, PhD
  health physics • MS, PhD
  industrial and physical pharmacy • PhD
  industrial hygiene • MS, PhD
  medical physics • MS, PhD
  medicinal and bioorganic chemistry • PhD
  medicinal biochemistry and molecular biology • PhD
  molecular pharmacology and toxicology • PhD
  natural products and pharmacognosy • PhD
  nuclear pharmacy • MS
  pharmacy administration • MS, PhD
  pharmacy and pharmacal sciences • Pharm D
  radiopharmaceutical chemistry and nuclear pharmacy • PhD
  toxicology • MS, PhD

School of Veterinary Medicine

Dr. Alan H. Rebar, Dean
Programs in:
anatomy • MS, PhD
bacteriology • MS, PhD
epidemiology • MS, PhD
immunology • MS, PhD
parasitology • MS, PhD
pathology • MS, PhD
pharmacology • MS, PhD
physiology • MS, PhD
toxicology • MS, PhD
veterinary clinical sciences • MS, PhD
veterinary medicine • DVM
virology • MS, PhD

PURDUE UNIVERSITY CALUMET

Hammond, IN 46323-2094

http://www.calumet.purdue.edu/

Public coed comprehensive institution. General application contact: *Associate Vice Chancellor for Academic Affairs, 219-989-2257.*

Graduate School

School of Liberal Arts and Sciences

Programs in:
applied mathematics • MS
communication • MA
English • MA
general biology • MS
history and political science • MA
marriage and family therapy • MS

School of Professional Studies

Programs in:
counseling and personnel services • MS Ed
educational administration • MS Ed
elementary education • MS Ed
engineering • MSE
instructional development • MS Ed
management • MS
media sciences • MS Ed
nursing • MS
secondary education • MS Ed

UNIVERSITY OF EVANSVILLE

Evansville, IN 47722-0002

http://www.evansville.edu/

Independent-religious coed comprehensive institution. *Enrollment:* 3,264 graduate, professional, and undergraduate students. Graduate faculty: *3 full-time, 4 part-time.* Computer facilities: *Campuswide network is available with full Internet access. Total number of PCs/ terminals supplied for student use: 150. Computer services are*

offered at no charge. Library facilities: *Bower, Suhrheinrich, and Clifford Memorial Library.* Graduate expenses: *Tuition of $395 per credit hour. Fees of $30 per year.* General application contact: *Woody O'Cain, Associate Vice President for Admission and Financial Aid, 812-479-2683.*

Graduate Programs

Programs in:
counseling • MA, MS Coun
health services administration • MS
nursing • MS
special education • MA

UNIVERSITY OF INDIANAPOLIS

Indianapolis, IN 46227-3697

http://www.uindy.edu/

Independent-religious coed comprehensive institution. Library facilities: *Krannert Memorial Library.* General application contact: *Vice President and Provost, 317-788-3213.*

Graduate School

Programs in:
accounting • M Acc
business administration • MBA
occupational therapy • MS

College of Arts and Sciences

Programs in:
applied sociology • MA
art • MA
biology • MS
English language and literature • MA
history • MA

Krannert School of Physical Therapy

Program in:
physical therapy • MHS, MS

School of Education

Programs in:
art education • MA
education • MA
elementary education • MA
English education • MA
secondary education • MA
social studies education • MA

UNIVERSITY OF NOTRE DAME

Notre Dame, IN 46556

http://www.nd.edu/

Independent-religious coed university. Enrollment: 10,281 graduate, professional, and undergraduate students. Graduate faculty: 670. Computer facilities: Campuswide network is available with full Internet access. Total number of PCs/terminals supplied for student use: 600. Computer services are offered at no charge. Library facilities: Theodore M. Hesburgh Library plus 8 additional on-campus libraries. Graduate expenses: Tuition of $20,800 per year full-time, $1155 per credit hour part-time. Fees of $45 per year. General application contact: Dr. Terrence J. Akai, Director of Graduate Admissions, 219-631-7706.

Graduate School
Dr. James L. Merz, Vice President

College of Arts and Letters
Dr. Mark W. Roche, Dean
Programs in:
    art history • MA
    ceramics • MFA
    cognitive psychology • PhD
    counseling psychology • PhD
    creative writing • MFA
    developmental psychology • PhD
    economics • MA, PhD
    English • MA, PhD
    French • MA
    German • MA
    government and international studies • MA, PhD
    graphic design • MFA
    history • MA, PhD
    history and philosophy of science • MA, PhD
    industrial design • MFA
    international peace studies • MA
    Italian studies • MA
    medieval studies • MMS, PhD
    music • MA, MM
    painting • MFA
    philosophy • PhD
    photography • MFA
    printmaking • MFA
    quantitative psychology • PhD
    Romance literatures • MA
    sculpture • MFA
    social psychology • PhD
    sociology • MA, PhD
    Spanish • MA
    theology • M Div, MA, PhD

College of Engineering
Dr. Anthony N. Michel, Dean
Programs in:
    bioengineering • MS
    chemical engineering • MS, PhD
    civil engineering • MS, PhD
    computer science and engineering • MS, PhD
    electrical engineering • MS, PhD
    environmental engineering • MS
    geological sciences • MS, PhD
    mechanical engineering • MS, PhD

College of Science
Dr. Francis J. Castellino, Dean
Programs in:
    aquatic ecology, evolution and environmental biology • MS, PhD
    biochemistry • MS, PhD
    cellular and molecular biology • MS, PhD
    developmental biology • MS, PhD
    genetics • MS, PhD
    inorganic chemistry • MS, PhD
    mathematics • MS, PhD
    organic chemistry • MS, PhD
    physical chemistry • MS, PhD
    physics • MS, PhD
    physiology • MS, PhD
    vector biology and parasitology • MS, PhD

School of Architecture
Samir Younés, Director of Graduate Studies
Program in:
    architecture • M Arch

College of Business Administration
Dr. William Nichols, Associate Dean
Programs in:
    accountancy • MS
    business administration • MBA
    executive business administration • EMBA
    not-for-profit administration • MSA

Law School
Dr. David T. Link, Dean
Programs in:
    comparative law • LL M
    international law • JSD, LL M
    law • JD

UNIVERSITY OF SAINT FRANCIS

Fort Wayne, IN 46808-3994

http://www.sfc.edu/

Independent-religious coed comprehensive institution. Enrollment: 1,006 graduate, professional, and undergraduate students. Graduate faculty: 16 full-time, 13 part-time. Computer facilities: Campuswide network is available with full Internet access. Total number of PCs/terminals supplied for student use: 45. Computer service fees are applied as a separate charge. Library facilities: Bass Mansion. Graduate expenses: Tuition of $350 per semester hour. Fees of $390 per year full-time, $69 per semester (minimum) part-time. General application contact: Scott Flanagan, Director of Admissions, 219-434-3264.

Graduate School

Sr. M. Elaine Brothers, Vice President for Academic Affairs
Programs in:
  business administration • MBA, MSBA
  fine art • MA
  general psychology • MS
  mental health counseling • MS
  nursing • MSN
  reading • MS Ed
  school guidance and counseling • MS Ed
  special education • MS Ed

UNIVERSITY OF SOUTHERN INDIANA

Evansville, IN 47712-3590

http://www.usi.edu/

Public coed comprehensive institution. *Enrollment:* 8,300 graduate, professional, and undergraduate students. Graduate faculty: *72 full-time, 6 part-time.* Computer facilities: *Campuswide network is available with full Internet access. Total number of PCs/terminals supplied for student use: 450. Computer services are offered at no charge.* Library facilities: *David L. Rice Library.* Graduate expenses: *$129 per credit hour for state residents; $260 per credit hour for nonresidents.* General application contact: *Dr. Peggy F. Harrel, Director, Graduate Studies, 812-465-7015.*

Graduate Studies

Dr. Peggy F. Harrel, Director

School of Business

Dr. Philip C. Fisher, Dean
Programs in:
  accountancy • MSA
  business administration • MBA

School of Education and Human Services

Dr. Thomas Pickering, Dean
Programs in:
  elementary education • MS
  secondary education • MS
  social work • MSW

School of Liberal Arts

Dr. James R. Blevins, Dean
Program in:
  liberal studies • MA

School of Nursing and Health Professions

Dr. Nadine Coudret, Dean
Program in:
  nursing and health professions • MSN

School of Science and Engineering Technology

Dr. Jerome Cain, Dean
Program in:
  industrial management • MS

VALPARAISO UNIVERSITY

Valparaiso, IN 46383-6493

http://www.valpo.edu/

Independent-religious coed comprehensive institution. *Enrollment:* 3,603 graduate, professional, and undergraduate students. Graduate faculty: *82 full-time, 21 part-time.* Computer facilities: *Campuswide network is available with full Internet access. Total number of PCs/terminals supplied for student use: 417. Computer service fees are included with tuition and fees.* Library facilities: *Moellering Memorial Library plus 1 additional on-campus library.* Graduate expenses: *$3870 per year full-time, $215 per credit hour part-time.* General application contact: *Dr. James W. Albers, Dean, Graduate Studies and Continuing Education, 219-464-5313.*

Graduate Division

Dr. James W. Albers, Dean, Graduate Studies and
  Continuing Education
Programs in:
  clinical mental health counseling • MA
  counseling • MA
  emotionally handicapped • M Ed, MS Sp Ed
  English • MALS
  geography • MALS
  history • MALS
  human behavior and society • MALS
  learning disabilities • MS Sp Ed
  learning disability • M Ed
  mild disabilities • M Ed, MS Sp Ed
  mild mentally handicapped • M Ed, MS Sp Ed
  music • MALS, MM
  psychology • MALS
  school psychology • MA
  teaching and learning • M Ed

College of Nursing

Dr. Cynthia Russell, Acting Dean
Program in:
  nursing • MSN

School of Law

Ivan E. Bodensteiner, Dean
Program in:
  law • JD, LL M

IOWA

 # DRAKE UNIVERSITY

Des Moines, IA 50311-4516

http://www.drake.edu/admissions/grad/
grad_catalog.html

Independent coed university. *Enrollment:* 5,193 graduate, professional, and undergraduate students. Graduate faculty: *269 full-time.* Computer facilities: *Campuswide network is available with full*

Drake University (continued)

Internet access. Computer service fees are included with tuition and fees. Library facilities: *Cowles Library plus 1 additional on-campus library.* Graduate expenses: *$16,000 per year full-time, $260 per hour (minimum) part-time.* General application contact: *Thomas F. Willoughby, Director of Admissions, 515-271-3181.*

College of Arts and Sciences
Dr. Ron Troyer, Dean
Programs in:
    biology • MA
    psychology • MS

School of Fine Arts
Dr. Ron Troyer, Dean, College of Arts and Sciences
Programs in:
    conducting • MM
    instrumental • MM
    music • MME
    music education • MME
    painting • MFA
    printmaking • MFA
    voice • MM

College of Business and Public Administration
Antone F. Alber Jr., Dean
Program in:
    business and public administration • MBA, MPA

College of Pharmacy and Health Sciences
Stephen Hoag, Dean
Program in:
    pharmacy • Pharm D

Division of Nursing
Dr. Linda H. Brady, Chair
Program in:
    nursing • MSN

Law School
C. Peter Goplerud III, Dean
Program in:
    law • JD

School of Education
Dr. James P. Ferrare, Dean
Programs in:
    adult education • Ed D, Ed S, MSE
    adult education, training and development • MS
    counselor education • Ed D, MSE
    educational administration • Ed D, Ed S, MSE
    elementary education • MST
    higher education • Ed D, Ed S, MSE
    secondary education • MAT
    special education • MSE
    teacher education and curriculum studies • Ed D, Ed S, MSE
    vocational rehabilitation • MS

School of Journalism and Mass Communication
Janet Hill Keefer, Dean
Program in:
    mass communication • MA

IOWA STATE UNIVERSITY OF SCIENCE AND TECHNOLOGY
Ames, IA 50011
http://www.iastate.edu/

Public coed university. *Enrollment: 25,384 graduate, professional, and undergraduate students.* Graduate faculty: *1,410 full-time, 68 part-time.* Computer facilities: *Campuswide network is available with full Internet access. Total number of PCs/terminals supplied for student use: 2,300.* Computer service fees are included with tuition and fees. Library facilities: *University Library plus 5 additional on-campus libraries.* Graduate expenses: *Tuition of $3166 per year full-time, $176 per credit part-time for state residents; $9324 per year full-time, $518 per credit part-time for nonresidents. Fees of $200 per year.* General application contact: *Dr. Patricia B. Swan, Dean of the Graduate College, 515-294-6344.*

Graduate College
Dr. Patricia B. Swan, Dean
Programs in:
    biomedical engineering • MS, PhD
    microbiology, immunology, and preventive medicine • MS, PhD
    veterinary anatomy • MS, PhD
    veterinary clinical sciences • MS
    veterinary pathology • MS, PhD
    veterinary physiology • MS, PhD

College of Agriculture
Dr. David G. Topel, Dean
Programs in:
    agricultural economics • MS, PhD
    agricultural education and studies • MS, PhD
    agricultural meteorology • MS, PhD
    agriculture • M Ag
    agronomy • MS
    animal ecology • MS, PhD
    animal science • MS, PhD
    biochemistry • MS, PhD
    biophysics • MS, PhD
    crop production and physiology • MS, PhD
    entomology • MS, PhD
    fisheries and wildlife biology • MS, PhD
    food science • MS, PhD
    forestry • MS, PhD
    genetics • MS, PhD
    horticulture • MS, PhD
    microbiology, immunology, and preventive medicine • MS, PhD
    molecular, cellular, and developmental biology • MS, PhD
    nutrition • MS, PhD

plant breeding • MS, PhD
plant pathology • MS, PhD
rural sociology • MS, PhD
soil science • MS, PhD
toxicology • MS, PhD
zoology and genetics • MS, PhD

College of Business
Dr. Benjamin J. Allen, Dean
Program in:
business administration • MBA, MS

College of Design
Mark Engelbrecht, Dean
Programs in:
architectural studies • MSAS
architecture • M Arch
art and design • MA
community and regional planning • MCRP
graphic design • MFA
interior design • MFA
landscape architecture • MLA
transportation • MS

College of Education
Dr. Camilla P. Benbow, Interim Dean
Programs in:
adult and extension education • M Ed, MS, PhD
counselor education • MS
curriculum and instruction technology • M Ed, MS, PhD
educational administration • MS, PhD
elementary and secondary education • M Ed, MS
health and human performance • MS
higher education • MS, PhD
historical, philosophical and comparative studies in education • M Ed, MS
industrial education and technology • MS, PhD
research and evaluation • MS
special education • MS
vocational education • MS

College of Engineering
Dr. James L. Melsa, Dean
Programs in:
aerospace engineering • M Eng, MS, PhD
agricultural and biosystems engineering • M Eng, MS, PhD
chemical engineering • M Eng, MS, PhD
civil engineering • MS, PhD
civil engineering materials • MS, PhD
computer engineering • M Eng, MS, PhD
construction engineering and management • MS, PhD
electrical engineering • M Eng, MS, PhD
engineering mechanics • M Eng, MS, PhD
environmental engineering • MS, PhD
geometronics • MS, PhD
geotechnical engineering • MS, PhD
industrial and manufacturing systems engineering • M Eng
industrial engineering • MS, PhD
materials science and engineering • MS, PhD
operations research • MS
structural engineering • MS, PhD
transportation engineering • MS, PhD

College of Family and Consumer Sciences
Dr. Carol B. Meeks, Dean
Programs in:
family and consumer sciences education and studies • M Ed, MS, PhD
food science • MS, PhD
hotel, restaurant and institution management • MFCS, MS, PhD
human development and family studies • MS, PhD
marriage and family therapy • PhD
nutrition • MS, PhD
textiles and clothing • MFCS, MS, PhD

College of Liberal Arts and Sciences
Dr. Richard Hoffmann, Interim Dean
Programs in:
agricultural economics • MS, PhD
agricultural history and rural studies • PhD
anthropology • MA
applied mathematics • MS, PhD
biochemistry • MS, PhD
biophysics • MS, PhD
botany • MS, PhD
chemistry • MS, PhD
computer science • MS, PhD
earth science • MS, PhD
economics • MS, PhD
English • MA, PhD
genetics • MS, PhD
geology • MS, PhD
history • MA
history of technology and science • MA, PhD
journalism and mass communication • MS
materials science and engineering • MS, PhD
mathematics • MS, PhD
molecular, cellular, and developmental biology • MS, PhD
physics and astronomy • MS, PhD
political science • MA
psychology • MS, PhD
public administration • MPA
rural sociology • MS, PhD
school mathematics • MSM
school psychology • Spec
sociology • MS, PhD
statistics • MS, PhD
toxicology • MS, PhD
water resources • MS, PhD
zoology and genetics • MS, PhD

Interdisciplinary Programs
Patricia B. Swan, Dean of the Graduate College
Programs in:
agriculture • M Ag
biomedical engineering • MS, PhD
business administration • MBA, MS
ecology and evolutionary biology • MS, PhD
family and consumer sciences • MFCS
genetics • MS, PhD
immunobiology • MS, PhD
industrial relations • MS
interdisciplinary graduate studies • MA, MS

Iowa State University of Science and Technology (continued)
   molecular, cellular, and developmental biology • MS, PhD
   neuroscience • MS, PhD
   plant physiology • MS, PhD
   systems engineering • M Eng
   toxicology • MS, PhD
   transportation • MS
   water resources • MS, PhD

College of Veterinary Medicine
Dr. Richard F. Ross, Dean
Programs in:
   biomedical engineering • MS, PhD
   microbiology, immunology, and preventive medicine • MS, PhD
   veterinary anatomy • MS, PhD
   veterinary clinical sciences • MS
   veterinary medicine • DVM
   veterinary pathology • MS, PhD
   veterinary physiology • MS, PhD

MAHARISHI UNIVERSITY OF MANAGEMENT
Fairfield, IA 52557

http://miu.edu/

Independent coed university. *Enrollment: 796 graduate, professional, and undergraduate students. Graduate faculty: 39. Library facilities: main library plus 1 additional on-campus library.* General application contact: *Dr. John Fagan, Dean of Graduate Studies, 515-472-1111.*

Graduate Studies
Dr. John Fagan, Dean
Programs in:
   art • MA
   business administration • MBA, PhD
   ceramics/sculpture • MFA
   computer science • MS
   drawing/painting • MFA
   elementary education • MA
   English • MA
   foundations of education • MA
   mathematics • MS
   neuroscience of human consciousness • MS, PhD
   physics • MS, PhD
   physiology, molecular, and cell biology • MS, PhD
   professional writing • MA
   psychology • MS, PhD
   science of creative intelligence • MA, PhD
   secondary education • MA

MARYCREST INTERNATIONAL UNIVERSITY
Davenport, IA 52804-4096

Independent coed comprehensive institution. *Enrollment: 794 graduate, professional, and undergraduate students. Graduate faculty: 6 full-time, 3 part-time. Computer facilities: Campuswide network is available with full Internet access. Total number of PCs/terminals supplied for student use: 85. Computer service fees are included with tuition and fees. Library facilities: Cone Library.* Graduate expenses: *Tuition of $413 per credit hour. Fees of $5 per credit hour.* General application contact: *Dr. Laurence Conner, President, 319-326-9221.*

Graduate Studies
Dr. Marie Ven Horst, Interim Academic Dean
Programs in:
   computer science • MS
   early childhood education • MA, MS
   education • MA, MAT
   reading specialist • MA

ST. AMBROSE UNIVERSITY
Davenport, IA 52803-2898

http://www.sau.edu/sau.html

Independent-religious coed comprehensive institution. *Computer facilities: Campuswide network is available with full Internet access. Total number of PCs/terminals supplied for student use: 146. Computer service fees are included with tuition and fees. Library facilities: O'Keefe Library plus 1 additional on-campus library.* General application contact: *Vice President of Institutional Research, 319-333-6158.*

College of Business
Programs in:
   accounting • M Ac
   health care administration • MHCA
   management generalist • MBA
   technical management • MBA

College of Arts and Sciences
Programs in:
   pastoral studies • MPS
   social work • MSW

College of Human Services
Programs in:
   criminal justice • MCJ
   juvenile justice • M Ed
   physical therapy • MPT
   postsecondary disabilities services • M Ed
   special education • M Ed

UNIVERSITY OF DUBUQUE
Dubuque, IA 52001-5050

http://www.dbq.edu/

Independent-religious coed comprehensive institution. *Enrollment: 999 graduate, professional, and undergraduate students. Graduate faculty: 47. Computer facilities: Campuswide network is available with partial Internet access (e-mail only). Total number of PCs/terminals supplied for student use: 30. Computer service fees are included with tuition and fees. Library facilities: Ficke-Laird Library. General application contact: Clifford D. Bunting, Dean of Admissions and Records, 319-589-3270.*

Program in Business Administration
John Wiemers, Director
Programs in:
    aviation management • MBA
    business administration • MBA

Program in Communication
Dr. Mary Carol Harris, Chair
Program in:
    communication • MA

Program in Education
Dr. Sally Naylor, Director of Graduate Education
Programs in:
    multidisciplinary education • MA
    special education: multicategorical, elementary and
        secondary • MA

Theological Seminary
Dr. Jeffrey F. Bullock, Dean
Program in:
    theology • D Min, M Div, MAR

THE UNIVERSITY OF IOWA
Iowa City, IA 52242-1316

http://www.uiowa.edu/

Public coed university. *Enrollment: 27,871 graduate, professional, and undergraduate students. Graduate faculty: 1,645 full-time, 67 part-time. Computer facilities: Campuswide network is available with full Internet access. Total number of PCs/terminals supplied for student use: 932. Computer service fees are included with tuition and fees. Library facilities: main library plus 11 additional on-campus libraries. Graduate expenses: Tuition of $3166 per year full-time, $176 per semester hour part-time for state residents; $10,202 per year full-time, $176 per semester hour part-time for nonresidents. Fees of $202 per year full-time, $52 per year (minimum) part-time. General application contact: Betty Sawin, Assistant Director of Admissions, 319-335-1525.*

Graduate College
Leslie B. Sims, Dean
Programs in:
    anatomy and cell biology • PhD
    biochemistry • MS, PhD
    biostatistics • MS, PhD
    community health • MS
    dental public health • MS
    endodontics • Certificate, MS
    epidemiology • MS, PhD
    general microbiology and microbial physiology • MS,
        PhD
    genetics • PhD
    hospital and health administration • MA, PhD
    immunology • MS, PhD
    industrial hygiene • MS
    microbial genetics • MS, PhD
    molecular biology • PhD
    neuroscience • PhD
    occupational and environmental health • MS, PhD
    operative dentistry • Certificate, MS
    oral and maxillofacial surgery • MS
    oral science • MS, PhD
    orthodontics • Certificate, MS
    pathogenic bacteriology • MS, PhD
    pathology • MS
    pediatric dentistry • Certificate, MS
    periodontics • Certificate, MS
    pharmacology • PhD
    pharmacy • MS, PhD
    physical therapy • MA, MPT, PhD
    physician assistant • MPAS
    physiology and biophysics • PhD
    physiology and biophysiology • MS
    prosthodontics • Certificate, MS
    quality management and productivity • MS
    radiation biology • MS, PhD
    stomatology • Certificate, MS
    Third World development support • MA
    urban and regional planning • MA, MS
    virology • MS, PhD

College of Business Administration
Gary C. Fethke, Dean
Programs in:
    accountancy • M Ac
    business administration • PhD
    economics • PhD
    finance • PhD
    management • MBA
    management information systems • MA
    management sciences • PhD
    marketing • PhD

College of Education
Steven R. Yussen, Dean
Programs in:
    art education • MA, PhD
    college student development • Ed S
    counselor education • MA, PhD
    curriculum and instruction • Ed S
    curriculum and supervision • Ed S
    early childhood and elementary education • MA

The University of Iowa (continued)
    early childhood education • MA
    educational administration • Ed S, MA, PhD
    educational media • Ed S, MA, PhD
    elementary education • PhD
    higher education • Ed S, MA, PhD
    instructional design and technology • MA, PhD
    music education • MA, MAT, PhD
    psychological and quantitative foundations • Ed S, MA, PhD
    rehabilitation counseling • MA, PhD
    social foundations • MA, PhD
    special education • Ed S, MA, PhD

College of Engineering
Richard K. Miller, Dean
Programs in:
    biomedical engineering • MS, PhD
    chemical and biochemical engineering • MS, PhD
    civil and environmental engineering • MS, PhD
    electrical and computer engineering • MS, PhD
    engineering design and manufacturing • MS, PhD
    ergonomics • MS, PhD
    information and engineering management • MS, PhD
    mechanical engineering • MS, PhD
    operations research • MS, PhD
    quality engineering • MS, PhD

College of Liberal Arts
Linda Maxson, Dean
Programs in:
    African American world studies • MA
    American studies • MA, PhD
    anthropology • MA, PhD
    applied mathematical and computational sciences • PhD
    art • MA, MFA
    art history • MA, PhD
    Asian civilizations • MA
    astronomy • MS
    bibliography • PhD
    biological sciences • MS, PhD
    broadcasting and film • MA, PhD
    chemistry • MS, PhD
    classics • MA, PhD
    communication and mass communication • MA
    communication research • MA, PhD
    comparative literature • MA, PhD
    computer science • MS, PhD
    creative writing • MFA
    criminal justice and corrections • MA
    dance • MFA
    development support communication • MA
    English • MFA, PhD
    exercise science • MS, PhD
    expository writing • MA
    film and video production • MFA
    French • MA, PhD
    geography • MA, PhD
    geology • MS, PhD
    German • MA, PhD
    history • MA, PhD
    leisure studies • MA
    library and information science • MA

    linguistics • MA, PhD
    literary criticism • PhD
    literary history • PhD
    literary studies • MA
    mass communication • PhD
    mathematics • MS, PhD
    music • DMA, MA, MFA, PhD
    neural and behavioral sciences • PhD
    nonfiction writing • MFA
    pedagogy • PhD
    philosophy • MA, PhD
    physical education • PhD
    physical education and sports studies • MA, PhD
    physics • MS, PhD
    political science • MA, PhD
    professional journalism • MA
    psychology • MA, PhD
    religion • MA, PhD
    rhetorical studies • MA, PhD
    rhetorical theory and stylistics • PhD
    Russian • MA
    science education • MS, PhD
    social work • MSW, PhD
    sociology • MA, PhD
    Spanish • MA, PhD
    speech and hearing science • PhD
    speech pathology and audiology • MA
    statistics • MS, PhD
    theatre arts • MFA
    translation • MFA
    women's studies • PhD
    writer's workshop • MFA
    writing • PhD

College of Nursing
Melanie Dreher, Dean
Program in:
    nursing • MSN, PhD

College of Dentistry
Dr. David C. Johnsen, Dean
Programs in:
    dental public health • MS
    dentistry • DDS
    endodontics • Certificate, MS
    operative dentistry • Certificate, MS
    oral and maxillofacial surgery • MS
    oral science • MS, PhD
    orthodontics • Certificate, MS
    pediatric dentistry • Certificate, MS
    periodontics • Certificate, MS
    prosthodontics • Certificate, MS
    stomatology • Certificate, MS

College of Law
N. William Hines, Dean
Program in:
    law • JD, LL M

College of Medicine

Dr. Robert P. Kelch, Dean
Programs in:
- anatomy and cell biology • PhD
- biochemistry • MS, PhD
- biostatistics • MS, PhD
- community health • MS
- epidemiology • MS, PhD
- general microbiology and microbial physiology • MS, PhD
- genetics • PhD
- hospital and health administration • MA, PhD
- immunology • MS, PhD
- industrial hygiene • MS
- medicine • MD
- microbial genetics • MS, PhD
- molecular biology • PhD
- neuroscience • PhD
- occupational and environmental health • MS, PhD
- pathogenic bacteriology • MS, PhD
- pathology • MS
- pharmacology • PhD
- physical therapy • MA, MPT, PhD
- physician assistant • MPAS
- physiology and biophysics • PhD
- physiology and biophysiology • MS
- radiation biology • MS, PhD
- virology • MS, PhD

College of Pharmacy

Gilbert S. Banker, Dean
Program in:
- pharmacy • MS, PhD, Pharm D

UNIVERSITY OF NORTHERN IOWA
Cedar Falls, IA 50614

http://www.uni.edu/

Public coed comprehensive institution. *Enrollment:* 13,108 graduate, professional, and undergraduate students. Graduate faculty: *411 full-time. Computer facilities: Campuswide network is available with full Internet access. Computer service fees are included with tuition and fees. Library facilities: Rod Library. Graduate expenses: Tuition of $3166 per year full-time, $176 per hour part-time for state residents; $7805 per year full-time, $176 per hour part-time for nonresidents. Fees of $194 per year full-time, $12.50 per semester (minimum) part-time. General application contact: Dr. John W. Somervill, Graduate Dean, 319-273-2748.*

Graduate College

Dr. John W. Somervill, Dean
Programs in:
- public policy • MPP
- women's studies • MA

College of Education

Dr. Thomas J. Switzer, Dean
Programs in:
- college/university student services • MA Ed
- communication and training technology • MA Ed
- counseling • Ed D, MA
- curriculum and instruction • Ed D, MA Ed
- early childhood education • MA Ed
- educational administration • Ed D
- educational media • MA Ed
- educational psychology • MA Ed
- educational technology • MA
- education of the gifted • MA Ed
- elementary principal • MA Ed
- health education • MA
- middle school/junior high education • MA
- physical education • MA
- reading • MA Ed
- school counseling • MA Ed
- school library media studies • MA
- school psychology • Ed S
- secondary principal • MA Ed
- special education • MA Ed
- youth agency administration • MA

College of Humanities and Fine Arts

Dr. James F. Lubker, Dean
Programs in:
- art • MA
- art education • MA
- audiology • MA
- communication studies • MA
- composition • MM
- conducting • MM
- English • MA
- French • MA
- French/German • MA
- German • MA
- German/Spanish • MA
- jazz pedagogy • MM
- music • MA
- music education • MM
- music history • MM
- performance • MM
- Spanish • MA
- Spanish/French • MA
- speech pathology • MA
- teaching English to speakers of other languages • MA
- theatre • MA
- two languages • MA

College of Natural Sciences

Dr. Gerald W. Intemann, Dean
Programs in:
- biology • MA, MS
- chemistry • MA
- computer science • MS
- computer science education • MA
- environmental science/technology • MS
- industrial technology • DIT, MA
- mathematics • MA
- mathematics for elementary and middle school • MA
- physics education • MA
- science education • MA, SP

University of Northern Iowa (continued)

College of Social and Behavioral Sciences
Dr. Aaron M. Podelefsky, Dean
Programs in:
    geography • MA
    history • MA
    political science • MA
    psychology • MA
    sociology • MA

School of Business Administration
Dr. Willis Green, Dean
Program in:
    business administration • MBA

KANSAS

BAKER UNIVERSITY
Baldwin City, KS 66006-0065
http://www.bakeru.edu/

Independent-religious coed comprehensive institution. *Enrollment:* 2,012 graduate, professional, and undergraduate students. Graduate faculty: *34 full-time, 194 part-time.* Computer facilities: *Campuswide network is available with partial Internet access (e-mail only). Total number of PCs/terminals supplied for student use: 466. Computer service fees are included with tuition and fees.* Library facilities: *Collins Library.* Graduate expenses: *Tuition of $310 per credit hour (minimum). Fees of $40 per year.* General application contact: *Dr. Donald B. Clardy, Dean, School of Professional and Graduate Studies, 913-491-4432.*

School of Professional and Graduate Studies
Dr. Donald B. Clardy, Dean
Programs in:
    business • MBA, MSM
    education • MA Ed
    liberal arts • MLA

EMPORIA STATE UNIVERSITY
Emporia, KS 66801-5087
http://www.emporia.edu/

Public coed comprehensive institution. *Enrollment:* 5,320 graduate, professional, and undergraduate students. Graduate faculty: *172 full-time, 89 part-time.* Computer facilities: *Campuswide network is available with full Internet access. Total number of PCs/terminals supplied for student use: 156. Computer services are offered at no charge.* Library facilities: *William Allen White Library.* Graduate expenses: *$2300 per year full-time, $103 per credit hour part-time for state residents; $6012 per year full-time, $258 per credit hour*

part-time for nonresidents. General application contact: *Dr. John O. Schwenn, Dean, School of Graduate Studies, 316-341-5403.*

School of Graduate Studies
Dr. John O. Schwenn, Dean

College of Liberal Arts and Sciences
Dr. Lendley C. Black, Dean
Programs in:
    American history • MAT
    anthropology • MAT
    botany • MS
    chemistry • MS
    earth science • MS
    economics • MAT
    English • MA
    environmental biology • MS
    general biology • MS
    geography • MAT
    history • MA
    instrumental • MM
    mathematics • MS
    microbial and cellular biology • MS
    music education • MM
    performance theory • MM
    physics • MS
    political science • MAT
    social studies education • MAT
    sociology • MAT
    vocal • MM
    world history • MAT
    zoology • MS

School of Business
Dr. Sajjad Hashmi, Dean
Programs in:
    business education and general business • MS
    management, marketing, finance and economics • MBA

School of Library and Information Management
Dr. Faye N. Vowell, Dean
Program in:
    library and information management • MLS, PhD

The Teachers College
Dr. Teresa Mehring, Dean
Programs in:
    art therapy • MS
    behavior disorders • MS
    clinical psychology • MS
    early childhood education • MS
    elementary administration • MS
    elementary counseling • MS
    elementary education • MS
    general counseling • MS
    general psychology • MS
    industrial psychology • MS
    instructional design and technology • MS
    interrelated special education • MS
    learning disabilities • MS
    mental retardation • MS
    physical education • MS
    reading, elementary/secondary • MS

rehabilitation counseling • MS
school counseling • MS
school psychology • Ed S, MS
secondary administration • MS
secondary counseling • MS
secondary education • MS
student personnel • MS
supervision and curriculum • MS
teaching of the gifted, talented, and creative • MS

FORT HAYS STATE UNIVERSITY
Hays, KS 67601-4099

http://www.fhsu.edu/

Public coed comprehensive institution. *Enrollment: 5,627 graduate, professional, and undergraduate students. Graduate faculty: 112 full-time. Library facilities: Forsyth Library plus 1 additional on-campus library. Graduate expenses: $94 per credit hour for state residents; $249 per credit hour for nonresidents.* General application contact: *Dr. James L. Forsythe, Dean of the Graduate School, 785-628-4236.*

Graduate School
Dr. James L. Forsythe, Dean

College of Arts and Sciences
Dr. Larry Gould, Interim Dean
Programs in:
    communication • MS
    computer science • MAT
    English • MA
    geology • MS
    history • MA
    liberal studies • MS
    mathematics • MAT
    psychology • MS
    studio art • MFA

College of Business
Dr. Richard Peters, Acting Dean
Programs in:
    accounting • MBA
    computer information systems • MBA
    economics • MBA
    finance • MBA

College of Education
Dr. Charles Leftwich, Dean
Programs in:
    counseling • MS
    education administration • Ed S, MS
    elementary education • MS
    instructional technology • MS
    school psychology • Ed S
    secondary education • MS
    special education • MS

College of Health and Life Sciences
Dr. Tony Fernandez, Dean
Programs in:
    biology • MS
    health, physical education, and recreation • MS
    nursing • MSN
    speech-language pathology • MS

FRIENDS UNIVERSITY
Wichita, KS 67213

http://www.friends.edu/

Independent coed comprehensive institution. *Enrollment: 2,729 graduate, professional, and undergraduate students. Graduate faculty: 27. Library facilities: Edmund Stanley Library. Graduate expenses: Tuition of $326 per credit hour (minimum). Fees of $215 per year.* General application contact: *Director of Graduate Admissions, 800-794-6945 Ext. 5583.*

Graduate Programs
Dr. G. Robert Dove, Vice President of Academic Affairs

College of Arts and Sciences
Dr. G. Robert Dove, Vice President of Academic Affairs, Graduate Programs
Programs in:
    Christian ministries • MACM
    elementary education • MAT
    environmental studies • MS
    family development education • MS
    family therapy • MS
    school leadership • MSL
    secondary education • MAT

College of Business
Dr. Al Saber, Dean
Programs in:
    executive business administration • EMBA
    management • MS
    management information systems • MS

College of Continuing Education
Dr. G. Robert Dove, Vice President of Academic Affairs, Graduate Programs
Programs in:
    human resource development/occupational development • MHRDOD
    quality systems management • MSQSM

KANSAS STATE UNIVERSITY
Manhattan, KS 66506
http://www.ksu.edu/

Public coed university. *Enrollment:* 20,476 graduate, professional, and undergraduate students. *Graduate faculty:* 1,109. *Computer facilities:* Campuswide network is available with full Internet access. Total number of PCs/terminals supplied for student use: 500. Computer service fees are included with tuition and fees. *Library facilities:* Farrell Library plus 4 additional on-campus libraries. *Graduate expenses:* $2218 per year full-time, $401 per semester (minimum) part-time for state residents; $6336 per year full-time, $1087 per semester (minimum) part-time for nonresidents. *General application contact:* Paul D. Isaac, Associate Dean, 785-532-7927.

Graduate School
Timothy R. Donoghue, Dean
Programs in:
    anatomy • MS
    diagnostic medicine/pathobiology • MS, PhD
    food science • MS, PhD
    genetics • MS, PhD
    physiology • MS, PhD
    veterinary medicine and surgery • MS

College of Agriculture
Marc Johnson, Dean
Programs in:
    agricultural economics • MAB, MS, PhD
    animal nutrition • MS, PhD
    animal reproduction • MS, PhD
    animal sciences and industry • MS, PhD
    crop science • MS, PhD
    entomology • MS, PhD
    genetics • MS, PhD
    grain science and industry • MS, PhD
    horticulture • MS, PhD
    meat science • MS, PhD
    plant pathology • MS, PhD
    range management • MS, PhD
    soil science • MS, PhD
    weed science • MS, PhD

College of Architecture, Planning and Design
Lane Marshall, Dean
Programs in:
    architecture • M Arch
    landscape architecture • MLA
    regional and community planning • MRCP

College of Arts and Sciences
Peter Nicholls, Dean
Programs in:
    analytical chemistry • MS
    art • MFA
    biochemistry • MS, PhD
    cell biology • MS, PhD
    chemistry • PhD
    developmental biology and physiology • MS, PhD
    economics • MA, PhD
    English • MA

    French • MA
    geography • MA, MS, PhD
    geology • MS, PhD
    German • MA
    history • MA, PhD
    inorganic chemistry • MS
    kinesiology • MS
    mass communications • MS
    mathematics • MS, PhD
    microbiology and immunology • MS, PhD
    molecular biology and genetics • MS, PhD
    music • MM
    organic chemistry • MS
    physical chemistry • MS
    physics • MS, PhD
    political science • MA
    psychology • MS, PhD
    public administration • MPA
    sociology • MA, PhD
    Spanish • MA
    speech • MA
    statistics • MS, PhD
    systematics and ecology • MS, PhD
    virology and oncology • MS, PhD

College of Business Administration
Yar M. Ebadi, Interim Dean
Programs in:
    accounting • M Acc
    business administration • MBA

College of Education
Michael Holen, Dean
Programs in:
    counselor education • Ed D, PhD
    curriculum and instruction • Ed D, PhD
    educational administration and leadership • Ed D, MS
    educational psychology • Ed D
    elementary education • MS
    foundations and adult education • Ed D, MS, PhD
    school counseling • MS
    secondary education • MS
    special education • Ed D, MS
    student affairs in higher education • PhD
    student personnel services • MS

College of Engineering
Terry S. King, Dean
Programs in:
    architectural engineering • MS
    bioengineering • MS, PhD
    biological and agricultural engineering • MS, PhD
    chemical engineering • MS, PhD
    civil engineering • MS, PhD
    communications • MS, PhD
    computer engineering • MS, PhD
    computer science • MS, PhD
    control systems • MS, PhD
    electric energy systems • MS, PhD
    engineering • PhD
    industrial and manufacturing systems engineering •
      MEM, MS, PhD
    instrumentation • MS, PhD
    mechanical engineering • MS

nuclear engineering • MS
signal processing • MS, PhD
software engineering • MSE

College of Human Ecology

Barbara Stowe, Dean
Programs in:
clothing and textiles • MS
dietetics • MS
family studies and human services • MS
food science • MS, PhD
food service and hospitality management • MS, PhD
human ecology • PhD
nutrition • MS, PhD

College of Veterinary Medicine

Ronald J. Marler, Dean
Programs in:
anatomy • MS
diagnostic medicine/pathobiology • MS, PhD
physiology • MS, PhD
veterinary medicine • DVM
veterinary medicine and surgery • MS

MIDAMERICA NAZARENE UNIVERSITY

Olathe, KS 66062-1899

http://www.mnu.edu/

Independent-religious coed comprehensive institution. *Enrollment:* 1,400 graduate, professional, and undergraduate students. *Graduate faculty:* 17 full-time, 3 part-time. Computer facilities: *Campuswide network is available with full Internet access. Computer services are offered at no charge.* Library facilities: *Mabee Library.* Graduate expenses: *$7005 per year.* General application contact: *Delta Allen, Assistant Registrar, 913-782-3750.*

Graduate Studies in Education

Dr. Jim Burns, Director
Program in:
curriculum and instruction • M Ed

Graduate Studies in Management

Dr. Mark Stenger, Director
Program in:
management • MBA

PITTSBURG STATE UNIVERSITY

Pittsburg, KS 66762-5880

http://www.pittstate.edu/

Public coed comprehensive institution. *Enrollment:* 5,955 graduate, professional, and undergraduate students. *Graduate faculty:* 98 full-time, 41 part-time. Computer facilities: *Campuswide network is available with full Internet access. Total number of PCs/terminals supplied for student use: 64. Computer service fees are included with tuition and fees.* Library facilities: *Axe Library.* Graduate expenses: *$2418 per year full-time, $103 per credit hour part-time for state residents; $6130 per year full-time, $258 per credit hour part-time for nonresidents.* General application contact: *Dr. John McCrone, Dean of Graduate Studies and Research, 316-235-4221.*

Graduate School

Dr. John McCrone, Dean of Graduate Studies and Research

College of Arts and Sciences

Dr. Orville Brill, Dean
Programs in:
applied communication • MA
applied physics • MS
biology • MS
chemistry • MS
communication education • MA
English • MA
history • MA
instrumental music education • MM
mathematics • MS
music history/music literature • MM
nursing • MSN
orchestral performance • MM
organ • MM
performance • MM
physics • MS
piano • MM
professional physics • MS
social science • MS
studio art • MS
theatre • MA
theory and composition • MM
vocal music education • MM
voice • MM

Gladys A. Kelce School of Business and Economics

Dr. Terry Mendenhall, Dean
Programs in:
accounting • MBA
business and economics • MS
general administration • MBA

School of Education

Dr. Tom Bryant, Dean
Programs in:
behavioral disorders • MS
community college teaching • Ed S
counseling • MS
elementary education • MS
elementary reading • Ed S

Pittsburg State University (continued)
- elementary school administration • Ed S, MS
- elementary teaching • Ed S
- learning disabilities • MS
- mentally retarded • MS
- physical education • MS
- psychology • MS
- school psychology • Ed S
- secondary education • MS
- secondary reading • Ed S
- secondary school administration • Ed S, MS

School of Technology
Dr. Tom Baldwin, Dean
Programs in:
- graphics and imaging technologies • MS
- human resource development • MS
- industrial education • Ed S
- technical education • MS
- technical teacher education • MS
- technology • MS
- trade and technical education • Ed S

UNIVERSITY OF KANSAS
Lawrence, KS 66045

http://www.ukans.edu/

Public coed university. *Enrollment: 27,567 graduate, professional, and undergraduate students. Graduate faculty: 1,165 full-time, 96 part-time. Computer facilities: Campuswide network is available with full Internet access. Total number of PCs/terminals supplied for student use: 800. Computer service fees are applied as a separate charge. Library facilities: Watson Library plus 12 additional on-campus libraries. Graduate expenses: Tuition of $2400 per year full-time, $100 per credit hour part-time for state residents; $7890 per year full-time, $329 per credit hour part-time for nonresidents. Fees of $428 per year full-time, $31 per credit hour part-time. General application contact: Graduate Adviser in the appropriate department, 785-864-2700.*

Graduate School
Andrew Debicki, Dean

College of Liberal Arts and Sciences
Sally Frost-Mason, Dean
Programs in:
- American studies • MA, PhD
- anthropology • MA, PhD
- applied mathematics and statistics • MA, PhD
- biochemistry, cell, and molecular biology • MA, PhD
- botany • MA, PhD
- chemistry • MA, MS, PhD
- child language • MA, PhD
- classics • MA
- clinical child psychology • MA, PhD
- clinical psychology • PhD
- communication studies • MA, PhD
- computational physics and astronomy • MS
- developmental and child psychology • PhD
- early childhood education • MA, PhD
- East Asian languages and cultures • MA
- economics • MA, PhD
- English • MA, PhD
- entomology • MA, PhD
- experimental psychology • PhD
- French • MA, PhD
- genetics • MA, PhD
- geography • MA, PhD
- geology • MS, PhD
- German • MA, PhD
- historical administration and museum studies • MHAMS
- history • MA, PhD
- history of art • MA, PhD
- human development • MA, MHD
- Latin American area studies • MA
- linguistics • MA, PhD
- mathematics • MA, PhD
- microbiology • MA, PhD
- philosophy • MA, PhD
- physics • MS, PhD
- political science • MA, PhD
- psychology • MA, PhD
- public administration • MPA
- religious studies • MA
- Russian and East European studies • MA
- Slavic languages and literatures • MA, PhD
- social psychology • PhD
- sociology • MA, PhD
- Spanish • MA, PhD
- speech-language-hearing: sciences and disorders • MA, PhD
- systematics and ecology • MA, PhD
- theatre and film • MA, PhD

School of Architecture and Urban Design
John Gaunt, Dean
Programs in:
- architecture • M Arch
- urban planning • MUP

School of Business
Thomas W. Sarowski, Dean
Programs in:
- accounting • MAIS, PhD
- business administration and management • MBA
- finance • PhD
- marketing • PhD

School of Education
Karen Gallagher, Dean
Programs in:
- counseling psychology • MS Ed, PhD
- educational administration • Ed D, Ed S, MS Ed, PhD
- educational policy and leadership • Ed D, PhD
- education for the gifted, talented and creative • Ed D, Ed S, MS Ed, PhD
- foundations of education • Ed D, MS Ed, PhD
- health education • MS Ed
- higher education • Ed D, MS Ed, PhD
- physical education • Ed D, MS Ed, PhD
- reading • Ed D, Ed S, MS Ed, PhD
- school psychology • Ed S, PhD

special education • Ed D, Ed S, MS Ed, PhD
teaching English as a second language • Ed D, MA,
　MS Ed, PhD

School of Engineering
Carl E. Locke, Dean
Programs in:
　aerospace engineering • DE, ME, MS, PhD
　architectural engineering • MS
　chemical engineering • MS
　chemical/petroleum engineering • PhD
　civil engineering • DE, ME, MS, PhD
　computer science • MS, PhD
　electrical engineering • DE, MS, PhD
　engineering management • MS
　environmental engineering • MS, PhD
　environmental science • MS, PhD
　mechanical engineering • DE, ME, MS, PhD
　petroleum engineering • MS
　water resources engineering • MS
　water resources science • MS

School of Fine Arts
Peter Thompson, Dean
Programs in:
　art • MFA
　church music • DMA, MM
　composition • DMA, MM
　conducting • DMA, MM
　design • MFA
　music education • MME, PhD
　musicology • MM, PhD
　music theory • MM, PhD
　opera • MM
　performance • DMA, MM
　visual arts education • MA

School of Journalism and Mass Communications
James Gentry, Dean
Program in:
　journalism • MS

School of Pharmacy
Jack Fincham, Dean
Programs in:
　health services administration • MHSA
　medicinal chemistry • MS, PhD
　pharmaceutical chemistry • MS, PhD
　pharmacology • MS, PhD
　pharmacy practice • MS
　toxicology • MS, PhD

Graduate Studies Medical Center
Dr. A. L. Chapman, Vice Chancellor of Academic Affairs
　and Dean
Programs in:
　anatomy and cell biology • MA, PhD
　audiology • MA, PhD
　biochemistry and molecular biology • MS, PhD
　dietetics and nutrition • MS
　education of the deaf • MS
　microbiology, molecular genetics and immunology •
　　PhD
　molecular and integrative physiology • MS, PhD

nurse anesthesia • MS
occupational therapy • MS
pathology and laboratory medicine • MA, PhD
pharmacology • MS, PhD
physical therapy • MS
preventive medicine • MPH
speech and hearing science • PhD
speech language pathology • MA, PhD
toxicology • MS, PhD

School of Allied Health
Dr. Karen Miller, Dean
Programs in:
　audiology • MA, PhD
　dietetics and nutrition • MS
　education of the deaf • MS
　nurse anesthesia • MS
　occupational therapy • MS
　physical therapy • MS
　speech and hearing science • PhD
　speech-language pathology • MA, PhD

School of Nursing
Dr. Karen Miller, Dean
Program in:
　nursing • MS, PhD

School of Law
Michael H. Hoeflich, Dean
Program in:
　law • JD

School of Medicine
Dr. Deborah Powell, Executive Dean
Program in:
　medicine • MD

School of Social Welfare
Ann Weick, Dean
Program in:
　social work • MSW, PhD

WASHBURN UNIVERSITY OF TOPEKA
Topeka, KS 66621

http://www.wuacc.edu/

Public coed comprehensive institution. *Enrollment: 6,281 graduate, professional, and undergraduate students. Graduate faculty: 57 full-time, 54 part-time. Computer facilities: Campuswide network is available with full Internet access. Total number of PCs/terminals supplied for student use: 450. Computer services are offered at no charge. Library facilities: Mabee Library plus 1 additional on-campus library. General application contact: J. Karen Ray, Dean, College of Arts and Sciences, 785-231-1010 Ext. 1561.*

Washburn University of Topeka (continued)
College of Arts and Sciences
J. Karen Ray, Dean
Programs in:
    clinical psychology • MA
    curriculum and instruction • M Ed
    educational administration • M Ed
    reading • M Ed
    special education • M Ed

School of Business
Dr. Juliann Mazachek, Dean
Program in:
    business • MBA

School of Law
James M. Concannon, Dean
Program in:
    law • JD

WICHITA STATE UNIVERSITY
Wichita, KS 67260

http://www.twsu.edu/

Public coed university. *Enrollment:* 14,669 graduate, professional, and undergraduate students. Graduate faculty: *420 full-time, 340 part-time.* Computer facilities: *Campuswide network is available with full Internet access. Total number of PCs/terminals supplied for student use: 740. Computer service fees are included with tuition and fees.* Library facilities: *Ablah Library plus 2 additional on-campus libraries.* Graduate expenses: *Tuition of $2303 per year full-time, $96 per credit hour part-time for state residents; $7691 per year full-time, $321 per credit hour part-time for nonresidents. Fees of $490 per year full-time, $75 per semester (minimum) part-time.* General application contact: *Dr. Michael C. Vincent, Acting Dean of the Graduate School, 316-978-3095.*

Graduate School
Dr. Michael C. Vincent, Acting Dean

College of Education
Dr. Jon Engelhardt, Dean
Programs in:
    communications sciences • MA, PhD
    counseling • M Ed
    curriculum and instruction • M Ed
    education administration • Ed D, M Ed
    educational psychology • M Ed
    exercise science and wellness • M Ed
    physical education • M Ed
    school psychology • Ed S
    special education • M Ed
    sports administration • M Ed

College of Engineering
Dr. William J. Wilhelm, Dean
Programs in:
    aerospace engineering • MS, PhD
    electrical engineering • MS, PhD
    industrial and manufacturing engineering • MEM, MS, PhD
    mechanical engineering • MS, PhD

College of Fine Arts
Dr. Walter Myers, Dean
Programs in:
    art education • MA
    music • MM
    music education • MME
    studio arts • MFA

College of Health Professions
Dr. Michael C. Vincent, Acting Dean, Graduate School
Programs in:
    adult nursing • MSN
    clinical specialization • MSN
    maternal-child nursing • MSN
    nursing administration • MSN
    physical therapy • MPT
    psychiatric/mental health nursing • MSN
    public health • MPH
    teaching of nursing • MSN

Fairmount College of Liberal Arts and Sciences
Dr. David C. Glenn-Lewin, Dean
Programs in:
    anthropology • MA
    applied mathematics • PhD
    biological sciences • MS
    chemistry • MS, PhD
    communications • MA
    community/clinical psychology • PhD
    computer science • MS
    creative writing • MA, MFA
    criminal justice • MA
    English • MA, MFA
    environmental science • MS
    geology • MS
    gerontology • MA
    history • MA
    human factors • PhD
    liberal studies • MA
    mathematics • MS
    physics • MS
    political science • MA
    public administration • MPA
    sociology • MA
    Spanish • MA
    statistics • MS

W. Frank Barton School of Business
Dr. Gerald H. Graham, Dean
Programs in:
    business • EMBA, MBA, MS
    business economics • MA
    economic analysis • MA
    professional accountancy • MPA

KENTUCKY

BELLARMINE COLLEGE
Louisville, KY 40205-0671

http://www.bellarmine.edu/

Independent-religious coed comprehensive institution. *Enrollment:* 2,180 graduate, professional, and undergraduate students. Graduate faculty: *31.* Library facilities: *main library.* Graduate expenses: *$375 per credit hour.* General application contact: *Robert G. Pfaadt, Registrar, 502-452-8133.*

Allan and Donna Lansing School of Nursing
Dr. Susan Hockenberger, Dean
Programs in:
   advanced community health nursing • MSN
   nursing administration • MSN
   nursing education • MSN

College of Arts and Sciences
Dr. John Oppelt, Dean
Programs in:
   early elementary education • MA, MAT
   elementary education • MA
   learning and behavior disorders • MA
   liberal studies • MA
   middle school education • MA, MAT

W. Fielding Rubel School of Business
Laura Richardson, Director
Program in:
   business • EMBA, MBA

CUMBERLAND COLLEGE
Williamsburg, KY 40769-1372

http://cc.cumber.edu/

Independent-religious coed comprehensive institution. *Enrollment:* 1,614 graduate, professional, and undergraduate students. Graduate faculty: *4 full-time, 5 part-time.* Computer facilities: *Campuswide network is available with full Internet access. Total number of PCs/ terminals supplied for student use: 291. Computer services are offered at no charge.* Library facilities: *Hagan Memorial Library.* Graduate expenses: *$175 per credit.* General application contact: *Dr. Martha Johnson, Director, Graduate Programs in Education, 606-549-2200 Ext. 4432.*

Graduate Programs in Education
Dr. Martha Johnson, Director
Programs in:
   early childhood education • MA Ed
   early elementary K–4 • MA Ed
   elementary/secondary principalship • Certificate
   elementary/secondary teaching • Certificate
   middle school 5–8 • MA Ed
   middle school education • MA Ed
   reading specialist • MA Ed
   secondary general education • MA Ed
   special education • MA Ed

EASTERN KENTUCKY UNIVERSITY
Richmond, KY 40475-3101

http://www.eku.edu/

Public coed comprehensive institution. *Enrollment:* 16,866 graduate, professional, and undergraduate students. Graduate faculty: *416 full-time, 91 part-time.* Computer facilities: *Campuswide network is available with full Internet access. Total number of PCs/terminals supplied for student use: 1,000. Computer services are offered at no charge.* Library facilities: *John Grant Crabbe Library plus 2 additional on-campus libraries.* Graduate expenses: *$2390 per year full-time, $133 per credit hour part-time for state residents; $6630 per year full-time, $365 per credit hour part-time for nonresidents.* General application contact: *Dr. Virginia P. Falkenberg, Dean, The Graduate School, 606-622-1742.*

The Graduate School
Dr. Virginia P. Falkenberg, Dean

College of Allied Health and Nursing
Dr. David Gale, Dean
Programs in:
   occupational therapy • MS
   rural community health care • MSN
   rural health family nurse practitioner • MSN

College of Applied Arts and Technology
Glen Kleine, Dean
Programs in:
   community nutrition • MS
   industrial training • MS
   manufacturing technology • MS
   technology education • MS
   vocational administration • MS

College of Arts and Humanities
Danny Robinette, Dean
Programs in:
   choral conducting • MM
   English • MA
   performance • MM
   theory/composition • MM

College of Business
Dr. Jack Dyer, Coordinator
Program in:
   business • MBA

Eastern Kentucky University (continued)

College of Education
Dr. Kenneth Henson, Dean
Programs in:
administration and supervision • Ed S
agricultural education • MA Ed
allied health sciences education • MA Ed
art education • MA Ed
biological sciences education • MA Ed
business education • MA Ed
chemistry education • MA Ed
communication disorders • MA Ed
community counseling • MA
early elementary education • MA Ed
earth science education • MA Ed
elementary counseling • MA Ed
elementary education general • MA Ed
English education • MA Ed
general science education • MA Ed
geography education • MA Ed
history education • MA Ed
home economics education • MA Ed
industrial education • MA Ed
mathematical sciences education • MA Ed
music education • MA Ed
physical education • MA Ed
physics education • MA Ed
political science education • MA Ed
psychology education • MA Ed
reading • MA Ed
school health education • MA Ed
secondary counseling • MA Ed
sociology education • MA Ed
special education • Ed S, MA Ed
student personnel counseling • Ed S, MA

College of Health, Physical Education, Recreation and Athletics
Dr. Robert Baugh, Dean
Programs in:
physical education • MS
recreation and park administration • MS
sports administration • MS

College of Law Enforcement
Victor E. Kappeler, Director
Programs in:
corrections and juvenile services • MS
criminal justice • MS
criminal justice education • MS
loss prevention administration • MS
police studies • MS

College of Natural and Mathematical Sciences
Donald L. Batch, Dean
Programs in:
biological sciences • MS
chemistry • MS
ecology • MS
geology • MS, PhD
mathematical sciences • MS

College of Social and Behavioral Sciences
Dr. Vance Wisenbaker, Dean
Programs in:
clinical psychology • MS
community development • MPA
community health administration • MPA
general public administration • MPA
history • MA
political science • MA
school psychology • Psy S

KENTUCKY STATE UNIVERSITY
Frankfort, KY 40601

http://www.kysu.edu/

Public coed comprehensive institution. *Enrollment:* 2,288 graduate, professional, and undergraduate students. Graduate faculty: *6 full-time, 4 part-time.* Computer facilities: *Campuswide network is available with full Internet access. Total number of PCs/terminals supplied for student use: 170.* Computer service fees are included with tuition and fees. Library facilities: *Paul G. Blazer Library.* Graduate expenses: *Tuition of $2120 per year full-time, $125 per credit hour part-time for state residents; $6360 per year full-time, $360 per credit hour part-time for nonresidents. Fees of $250 per year full-time, $30 per year part-time.* General application contact: *Dr. Cassie Osborne, Dean, 502-227-6117.*

School of Public Affairs
Dr. Cassie Osborne, Dean
Program in:
public affairs • MPA

MOREHEAD STATE UNIVERSITY
Morehead, KY 40351

http://www.morehead-st.edu/

Public coed comprehensive institution. *Enrollment:* 8,208 graduate, professional, and undergraduate students. Graduate faculty: *131 full-time, 21 part-time.* Library facilities: *Camden-Carroll Library plus 1 additional on-campus library.* Graduate expenses: *$2470 per year full-time, $138 per semester hour part-time for state residents; $6710 per year full-time, $373 per semester hour part-time for nonresidents.* General application contact: *Dr. Marc Glasser, Dean of Graduate and Undergraduate Programs, 606-783-2039.*

Graduate Programs

Dr. Marc Glasser, Dean of Graduate and Undergraduate
Programs

Caudill College of Humanities
Dr. Lemuel Berry, Dean
Programs in:
  art education • MA
  communications • MA
  English • MA
  music education • MM
  music performance • MM
  studio art • MA

College of Business
Dr. Michael Carrell, Dean
Program in:
  business and management • MBA

College of Education and Behavioral Sciences
Dr. Harold Harty, Dean
Programs in:
  adult and higher education • Ed S, MA
  clinical psychology • MA
  counseling psychology • MA
  curriculum and instruction • Ed D, Ed S
  educational policy studies and evaluation • Ed D
  educational psychology and counseling • Ed D
  elementary teaching • MA Ed
  experimental/general psychology • MA
  guidance and counseling • Ed S, MA Ed
  health, physical education and recreation • Ed D, MA
  instructional leadership • Ed S
  instruction and administration • Ed D
  middle school education • MA Ed
  reading • MA Ed
  secondary teaching • MA Ed
  sociology • MA
  special education • Ed D, MA Ed
  sports administration • MS

College of Science and Technology
Dr. Gerald DeMoss, Dean
Programs in:
  biology • MS
  vocational education • Ed D, MS

MURRAY STATE UNIVERSITY
Murray, KY 42071-0009

http://www.murraystate.edu/

Public coed comprehensive institution. *Enrollment: 8,811 graduate, professional, and undergraduate students. Graduate faculty: 293 full-time. Library facilities: Waterfield Library plus 2 additional on-campus libraries. Graduate expenses: Tuition of $2500 per year full-time, $124 per hour part-time for state residents; $6740 per year full-time, $357 per hour part-time for nonresidents. Fees of $360 per year full-time, $180 per year part-time. General application contact: Dr. William F. Payne, Coordinator of Graduate Studies, 502-762-3744.*

College of Business and Public Affairs
Dr. Dannie Harrison, Dean
Programs in:
  business affairs • MBA
  economics • MS
  public affairs • MPA

College of Education
Dr. Bill Price, Interim Dean
Programs in:
  communication disorders • MS
  community and agency counseling • Ed S
  early childhood education • MS
  education • Ed D, PhD
  educational administration • Ed S
  elementary education • Ed S, MA Ed
  guidance and counseling • Ed S, MA Ed, MS
  human services • MS
  learning disabilities • MA Ed
  middle school education • Ed S, MA Ed
  physical education • MA
  reading education • MA Ed
  secondary education • Ed S, MA Ed

College of Fine Arts and Communications
Dr. Ted Wendt, Dean
Programs in:
  art • MA, MA Ed
  music • MME
  music education • MME
  speech • MA, MS

College of Humanistic Studies
Dr. Joseph H. Cartwright, Dean
Programs in:
  clinical psychology • MA, MS
  English • MA
  history • MA
  psychology • MA, MS
  teaching English to speakers of other languages • MA

College of Industry and Technology
Dr. Thomas B. Auer, Dean
Programs in:
  agriculture • MS
  environmental manufacturing • MS
  industrial and technical education • MA Ed, MS
  occupational safety and health • MS
  systems management technology • MS

College of Sciences
Dr. Marcia Hobbs, Interim Dean
Programs in:
  biological sciences • MAT, MS, PhD
  chemistry • MAT, MS
  geography • MA, MS
  mathematics • MA, MAT, MS
  nurse anesthesia • MSNA
  nursing • MSN
  physics • MAT, MS
  urban and regional planning • MS

NORTHERN KENTUCKY UNIVERSITY
Highland Heights, KY 41099

http://www.nku.edu/

Public coed comprehensive institution. *Enrollment:* 11,785 graduate, professional, and undergraduate students. Graduate faculty: *87 full-time.* Computer facilities: *Campuswide network is available with full Internet access. Computer services are offered at no charge.* Library facilities: *W. Frank Steely Library.* Graduate expenses: *$2420 per year full-time, $132 per semester hour part-time for state residents; $6660 per year full-time, $368 per semester hour part-time for nonresidents.* General application contact: *Peg Griffin, Coordinator, Graduate Program, 606-572-6364.*

School of Graduate Programs
Dr. Paul Reichardt, Associate Provost
Programs in:
> business administration • MBA
> elementary education • MA Ed
> nursing • MSN
> public administration • MPA
> secondary education • MA Ed
> technology • MST

Salmon P. Chase College of Law
Prof. David Short, Dean
Program in:
> law • JD

SPALDING UNIVERSITY
Louisville, KY 40203-2188

http://www.spalding.edu/

Independent-religious coed comprehensive institution. *Enrollment:* 1,574 graduate, professional, and undergraduate students. Graduate faculty: *35 full-time, 15 part-time.* Library facilities: *University Library.* Graduate expenses: *Tuition of $350 per credit hour (minimum). Fees of $48 per year full-time, $4 per credit hour part-time.* General application contact: *Jeanne Anderson, Assistant to the Provost and Director of Graduate Office, 502-585-7105.*

Graduate Studies
Dr. M. Janice Murphy, Provost and Dean

College of Arts and Sciences
Phyllis Passafiume, Dean
Programs in:
> ministry studies • MA
> religious studies • MA

School of Education
Dr. Mary Burns, Dean
Programs in:
> guidance • MA
> K–4 • MA, MAT
> leadership education • Ed D
> reading specialist • MA
> school media librarianship • MAML

School of Nursing and Health Sciences
Dr. Cynthia Crabtree, Dean
Programs in:
> administration • MSN
> family nurse practitioner • MSN

School of Professional Psychology and Social Work
Dr. M. Duncan Stanton, Dean
Programs in:
> psychology and social work • MA, Psy D
> social work • MSW

UNION COLLEGE
Barbourville, KY 40906-1499

http://www.unionky.edu/

Independent-religious coed comprehensive institution. *Enrollment:* 1,000 graduate, professional, and undergraduate students. Graduate faculty: *24 full-time, 5 part-time.* Library facilities: *Weeks-Townsend Memorial Library.* Graduate expenses: *$220 per hour.* General application contact: *Dr. William E. Bernhardt, Dean of Graduate Academic Affairs, 606-546-1210.*

Graduate Programs
Dr. William E. Bernhardt, Dean of Graduate Academic Affairs
Programs in:
> elementary education • MA Ed
> elementary principalship • Certificate
> health • MA Ed
> middle grades • MA Ed
> middle grades principalship • Certificate
> music education • MA Ed
> reading specialist • MA Ed
> secondary education • MA Ed
> secondary school principalship • Certificate
> special education • MA Ed
> supervisor of instruction • Certificate

UNIVERSITY OF KENTUCKY
Lexington, KY 40506-0032

http://www.uky.edu/

Public coed university. *Enrollment:* 23,540 graduate, professional, and undergraduate students. Graduate faculty: *1,373 full-time, 140 part-time.* Library facilities: *W. T. Young Library plus 14 additional*

on-campus libraries. Graduate expenses: $2976 per year full-time, $153 per credit hour part-time for state residents; $8256 per year full-time, $446 per credit hour part-time for nonresidents. General application contact: Dr. Constance L. Wood, Associate Dean, 606-257-4613.

Graduate School
Dr. Michael T. Nietzel, Dean
Programs in:
  anatomy and neurobiology • PhD
  biochemistry • PhD
  biomedical engineering • MSBE, PhD
  gerontology • PhD
  health administration • MHA
  microbiology and immunology • PhD
  molecular, cellular and integrative physiology • PhD
  nutritional sciences • PhD
  pharmaceutical sciences • MS, PhD
  pharmacology • MS, PhD
  public administration • MPA, PhD
  public health • MSPH
  toxicology • MS, PhD

College of Architecture
Dr. David Mohney, Dean
Program in:
  historic preservation • MHP

College of Communications and Information Studies
Dr. Douglas Boyd, Dean
Programs in:
  communication • MA, PhD
  library science • MA, MSLS

College of Human Environmental Sciences
Dr. Retia Scott Walker, Dean
Programs in:
  family studies • MSFAM
  human environment: interior design, merchandising, and textiles • MAIDM, MAIND, MATEX, MSIDM
  nutrition and food science • MS

College of Nursing
Dr. Carolyn Williams, Dean
Program in:
  nursing • MSN, PhD

College of Social Work
Dr. Edgar Sagan, Dean
Program in:
  social work • MSW, PhD

Graduate School Programs from the College of Agriculture
Dr. Oran Little, Dean
Programs in:
  agricultural economics • MS, PhD
  animal sciences • MS, PhD
  crop science • MS, MS Ag, PhD
  entomology • MS, PhD
  forestry • MSFOR
  plant and soil science • MS
  plant pathology • MS, PhD
  plant physiology • PhD
  soil science • PhD
  veterinary science • MS, PhD

Graduate School Programs from the College of Allied Health
Dr. Thomas Robinson, Dean
Programs in:
  clinical nutrition • MSCNU
  communication disorders • MSCD
  health physics • MSHP
  physical therapy • MSPT
  radiological medical physics • MSRMP

Graduate School Programs from the College of Arts and Sciences
Dr. Donald E. Sands, Acting Dean
Programs in:
  anthropology • MA, PhD
  biological sciences • MS, PhD
  chemistry • MS, PhD
  classical languages and literatures • MA
  English • MA, PhD
  French • MA
  geography • MA, PhD
  geology • MS, PhD
  German • MA
  history • MA, PhD
  mathematics • MA, MS, PhD
  philosophy • MA, PhD
  physics and astronomy • MS, PhD
  political science • MA, PhD
  psychology • MA, PhD
  sociology • MA, MS Ag, PhD
  Spanish • MA, PhD
  statistics • MS, PhD

Graduate School Programs from the College of Business and Economics
Dr. Richard Furst, Dean
Programs in:
  accounting • MSACC
  business administration • MBA, PhD
  economics • MS, PhD

Graduate School Programs from the College of Education
Dr. Shirley Raines, Dean
Programs in:
  administration and supervision • Ed D, Ed S
  clinical and college teaching • MS Ed
  curriculum and instruction • Ed D
  educational and counseling psychology • Ed D, Ed S, MA Ed, MS Ed, PhD
  educational policy studies and evaluation • Ed D, MS Ed, PhD
  instruction and administration • Ed D
  kinesiology and health promotion • Ed D, MS
  rehabilitation counseling • MRC
  special education • Ed D, Ed S, MA Ed, MS Ed
  vocational education • Ed D, Ed S, MA Ed, MS Ed, MSVE

Graduate School Programs from the College of Engineering
Dr. Thomas W. Lester, Dean
Programs in:
  agricultural engineering • MSAE, PhD
  chemical engineering • MS Ch E, PhD
  civil engineering • MCE, MSCE, PhD

University of Kentucky (continued)

    computer science • MS, PhD

    electrical engineering • MSEE, PhD

    engineering • M Eng

    engineering mechanics • MSEM, PhD

    manufacturing systems engineering • MSMSE

    materials science • MSMAE, PhD

    mechanical engineering • MSME, PhD

    mining engineering • MME, MS Min, PhD

Graduate School Programs from the College of Fine Arts

Dr. Rhoda-Gale Pollack, Dean

Programs in:

    art education • MA

    art history • MA

    art studio • MFA

    music • DMA, MA, MM, PhD

    theatre • MA

College of Dentistry

Leon A. Assael, Dean

Program in:

    dentistry • DMD, MS

College of Law

David E. Shipley, Dean

Program in:

    law • JD

College of Medicine

Dr. Carol Elam, Assistant Dean for Admissions

Programs in:

    anatomy and neurobiology • PhD

    biochemistry • PhD

    medicine • MD

    microbiology and immunology • PhD

    molecular, cellular and integrative physiology • PhD

    pharmacology • MS, PhD

    public health • MSPH

College of Pharmacy

Dr. Jordan Cohen, Dean

Programs in:

    pharmaceutical sciences • MS, PhD

    pharmacy • Pharm D

Patterson School of Diplomacy and International Commerce

Dr. John D. Stempel, Director of Graduate Studies

Program in:

    diplomacy and international commerce • MA

UNIVERSITY OF LOUISVILLE
Louisville, KY 40292-0001
http://www.louisville.edu/

Public coed university. *Enrollment: 21,020 graduate, professional, and undergraduate students. Graduate faculty: 1,233 full-time, 472 part-time. Computer facilities: Campuswide network is available with full Internet access. Total number of PCs/terminals supplied for student use: 1,000. Computer service fees are included with tuition and fees. Library facilities: Ekstrom Library plus 4 additional on-campus libraries. Graduate expenses: Tuition of $3180 per year full-time, $175 per credit hour part-time for state residents; $9060 per year full-time, $502 per credit hour part-time for nonresidents. Fees of $30 per year full-time, $7.50 per semester part-time. General application contact: Jenny Sawyer, Director of Admissions, 502-852-6531.*

Graduate School

Dr. Paul D. Jones, Acting Dean

Programs in:

    anatomy • MS, PhD

    biochemistry • MS, PhD

    communicative disorders • MS

    interdisciplinary studies • MA, MS

    microbiology and immunology • MS, PhD

    ophthalmology and visual sciences • PhD

    oral biology • MS

    pharmacology • MS, PhD

    physiology and biophysics • MS, PhD

College of Arts and Sciences

Randy Moore, Dean

Programs in:

    analytical chemistry • MS, PhD

    art history • MA, PhD

    biology • MS

    chemical physics • PhD

    clinical psychology • PhD

    English rhetoric and composition • PhD

    environmental biology • PhD

    experimental psychology • PhD

    fine arts • MA

    foreign language education • MA

    French • MA

    German • MA

    history • MA

    humanities • MA

    inorganic chemistry • MS, PhD

    justice administration • MS

    linguistics • MA

    mathematics • MA

    organic chemistry • MS, PhD

    philosophy • MA

    physical chemistry • MS, PhD

    physics • MS

    political science • MA

    psychology • MA

    sociology • MA

    Spanish • MA

    theatre arts • MA, MFA

College of Business and Public Administration
Dr. Robert L. Taylor, Dean
Programs in:
    business • MBA
    labor and public management • MPA
    public policy • MPA
    systems science • MA
    urban and public affairs • PhD
    urban and regional development • MPA

Raymond A. Kent School of Social Work
Dr. Terry Singer, Acting Dean
Program in:
    social work • MSSW, PhD

School of Allied Health Sciences
Alfred Thompson, Interim Dean
Program in:
    expressive therapies • MA

School of Education
Dr. Raphael O. Nystrand, Dean
Programs in:
    administration • Ed S
    art education • M Ed
    business education • MAT
    college student personnel services • M Ed
    community counseling • M Ed
    counseling and student personnel • Ed D
    early childhood education • M Ed
    early elementary education • MAT
    educational administration • Ed D
    educational supervision • Ed D, Ed S
    education policy studies and evaluation • Ed D
    elementary education • Ed S, M Ed, MA, MAT
    elementary school guidance • M Ed
    evaluation • Ed D
    exercise physiology • MS
    guidance and personnel • Ed S
    higher education • Ed S, MA
    middle school education • M Ed
    music education • MAT
    occupational and career education • M Ed
    physical education • M Ed, MAT
    reading education • M Ed
    secondary education • Ed S, M Ed, MA, MAT
    secondary school guidance • M Ed
    special education • Ed D, Ed S, M Ed

School of Music
Dr. Herbert L. Koerselman, Dean
Programs in:
    music composition • MM
    music education • MME
    music history • MA, MM, PhD
    music literature • PhD
    music performance • MM
    music theory • MM

School of Nursing
Dr. Mary H. Mundt, Dean
Program in:
    nursing • MSN

Speed Scientific School
Dr. Thomas R. Hanley, Dean
Programs in:
    chemical engineering • M Eng, MS, PhD
    civil engineering • M Eng, MS, PhD
    computer science and engineering • PhD
    electrical engineering • M Eng, MS
    engineering mathematics and computer science •
       M Eng, MS
    industrial engineering • M Eng, MS, PhD
    mechanical engineering • M Eng, MS

Louis D. Brandeis School of Law
Donald L. Burnett Jr., Dean
Program in:
    law • JD

School of Dentistry
Dr. Rowland A. Hutchinson Jr., Dean
Programs in:
    dentistry • DMD
    oral biology • MS

School of Medicine
Dr. Donald R. Kmetz, Dean
Programs in:
    anatomy • MS, PhD
    biochemistry • MS, PhD
    communicative disorders • MS
    medicine • MD
    microbiology and immunology • MS, PhD
    ophthalmology and visual sciences • PhD
    pharmacology • MS, PhD
    physiology and biophysics • MS, PhD

WESTERN KENTUCKY UNIVERSITY
Bowling Green, KY 42101-3576
http://www.wku.edu/

Public coed comprehensive institution. *Enrollment: 14,543 graduate, professional, and undergraduate students. Graduate faculty: 361 full-time, 9 part-time. Computer facilities: Campuswide network is available with full Internet access. Total number of PCs/terminals supplied for student use: 750. Computer service fees are included with tuition and fees. Library facilities: Helm-Cravens Library plus 3 additional on-campus libraries. Graduate expenses: $2460 per year full-time, $133 per credit hour part-time for state residents; $6700 per year full-time, $369 per credit hour part-time for nonresidents. General application contact: Dr. Elmer Gray, Dean, Graduate Studies, 502-745-2446.*

Graduate Studies
Dr. Elmer Gray, Dean
Program in:
    administration • MA

Western Kentucky University (continued)

College of Business Administration
Dr. Robert Jefferson, Dean
Programs in:
    accounting • MPA
    business administration • MA Ed, MBA
    economics and marketing • MA

College of Education
Dr. Carl Martray, Dean
Programs in:
    business education • MA Ed
    communication disorders • MS
    early childhood education • MA Ed
    education • Ed S, PhD
    elementary education • Ed S, MA Ed
    exceptional child education • MA Ed
    foods and nutrition • MS
    guidance and counseling • Ed S, MA Ed
    home economics education • MA Ed
    interior design and housing • MS
    library media education • MS
    middle grades education • MA Ed
    physical education • MA Ed, MS
    psychology • MA
    reading • MA Ed
    recreation • MS
    school administration • Ed D, Ed S
    school business administration • MA Ed
    school psychology • Ed S
    secondary education • Ed S, MA Ed
    textiles and clothing • MS

Ogden College of Science, Technology, and Health
Dr. Martin Houston, Dean
Programs in:
    agriculture • MA Ed, MS
    biology • MA Ed, MS
    chemistry • MA Ed, MS
    city and regional planning • MPA
    computer science • MS
    environmental health • MS
    fossil fuel chemistry • PhD
    geography • MA Ed, MS
    gerontology • MS
    health care administration • MS
    health education • MA Ed
    mathematics • MA Ed, MS
    mathematics and science • MA Ed
    nursing • MSN
    public health • MS
    public health education • MS
    science • MA Ed

Potter College of Arts and Humanities
Dr. David Lee, Dean
Programs in:
    American literature • MA
    art education • MA Ed
    British literature • MA
    communication • MA
    communication education • MA Ed
    communication theory and research • MA
    English • MA Ed

    folk studies • MA
    French • MA Ed
    German • MA Ed
    historic preservation • MA
    history • MA, MA Ed
    humanities • MA
    literary theory • MA
    literature • MA
    music • MA Ed
    organizational communication • MA
    public administration • MPA
    rhetoric and public address • MA
    sociology • MA, MA Ed
    Spanish • MA Ed
    teaching English as a second language • MA
    women writers • MA
    world literature • MA
    writing • MA

LOUISIANA

CENTENARY COLLEGE OF LOUISIANA
Shreveport, LA 71134-1188
http://www.centenary.edu/

Independent-religious coed comprehensive institution. *Enrollment: 1,014 graduate, professional, and undergraduate students. Graduate faculty: 11 full-time, 12 part-time. Computer facilities: Campuswide network is available with full Internet access. Total number of PCs/ terminals supplied for student use: 200. Computer service fees are included with tuition and fees. Library facilities: Magale Library plus 1 additional on-campus library. Graduate expenses: $600 per course. General application contact: Dr. Robert Bareikis, Provost and Dean, 318-869-5104.*

Graduate Programs
Dr. Robert Bareikis, Provost and Dean
Programs in:
    administration • M Ed
    business • MBA
    elementary education • M Ed
    supervision of instruction • M Ed

GRAMBLING STATE UNIVERSITY
Grambling, LA 71245

Public coed comprehensive institution. *Enrollment: 6,701 graduate, professional, and undergraduate students. Graduate faculty: 54 full-time, 21 part-time. Computer facilities: Campuswide network is available with full Internet access. Computer services are offered at no charge. Library facilities: A. C. Lewis Memorial Library. Gradu-*

ate expenses: *$1960 per year full-time, $297 per semester (minimum) part-time for state residents; $7110 per year full-time, $297 per semester (minimum) part-time for nonresidents.* General application contact: *Jacklen Greer, Administrative Assistant, Division of Graduate Studies, 318-274-2457.*

Division of Graduate Studies
Dr. Gerald L. Ellis, Dean

College of Business
Dr. Karim Dhanani, Dean
Program in:
  general administration • MBA

College of Education
Dr. Andolyn Harrison, Acting Dean
Programs in:
  curriculum and instruction • Ed D
  developmental education • Ed D, MS
  early childhood education • MS
  educational leadership • Ed D
  elementary education • MS
  sports administration • MS

College of Liberal Arts
Dr. Dardanella Ennis, Dean
Programs in:
  criminal justice • MS
  humanities • MA
  mass communication • MA
  public administration • MPA
  social sciences • MAT

College of Science and Technology
Dr. Emma Hill, Dean
Program in:
  natural sciences • MAT

School of Nursing
Dr. Betty E. Smith, Dean
Program in:
  nursing • MSN

School of Social Work
Dr. Birdex Copeland, Dean
Program in:
  social work • MSW

LOUISIANA STATE UNIVERSITY AND AGRICULTURAL AND MECHANICAL COLLEGE
Baton Rouge, LA 70803

http://www.lsu.edu/

Public coed university. *Enrollment:* 28,077 graduate, professional, and undergraduate students. *Graduate faculty: 1,118 full-time, 31 part-time. Computer facilities: Campuswide network is available with full Internet access. Computer services are offered at no charge. Library facilities: Troy H. Middleton Library plus 4 additional* on-campus libraries. Graduate expenses: *$2736 per year full-time, $285 per semester (minimum) part-time for state residents; $6636 per year full-time, $460 per semester (minimum) part-time for nonresidents.* General application contact: *Office of Graduate Admissions, 504-388-2311.*

Graduate School
John Larkin, Interim Dean
Programs in:
  liberal arts • MALA
  linguistics • MA, PhD

Center for Coastal, Energy and Environmental Resources
Dr. Russell L. Chapman, Interim Executive Director
Programs in:
  environmental planning and management • MS
  environmental toxicology • MS
  nuclear science and engineering • MS
  oceanography and coastal sciences • MS, PhD

College of Agriculture
Dr. Kenneth Koonce, Dean
Programs in:
  agricultural economics and agribusiness • MS, PhD
  agronomy • MS, PhD
  animal science • MS, PhD
  applied statistics • M App St
  biological and agricultural engineering • MSBAE
  comprehensive vocational education • MS, PhD
  dairy science • MS, PhD
  engineering science • MS, PhD
  entomology • MS, PhD
  extension and international education • MS, PhD
  fisheries • MS
  food science • MS, PhD
  forestry • MS, PhD
  horticulture • MS, PhD
  human ecology • MS, PhD
  industrial education • MS
  plant health • MS, PhD
  poultry science • MS
  vocational agriculture education • MS, PhD
  vocational business education • MS
  vocational home economics education • MS
  wildlife • MS
  wildlife and fisheries science • PhD

College of Arts and Sciences
Dr. Karl Roider, Dean
Programs in:
  anthropology • MA
  biological psychology • MA, PhD
  clinical psychology • MA, PhD
  cognitive psychology • MA, PhD
  communication sciences and disorders • MA, PhD
  comparative literature • MA, PhD
  creative writing • MFA
  developmental psychology • MA, PhD
  English • MA, PhD
  French literature and linguistics • MA, PhD
  geography • MA, MS, PhD
  history • MA, PhD
  industrial/organizational psychology • MA, PhD

Louisiana State University and Agricultural and Mechanical College (continued)

mathematics • MS, PhD
philosophy • MA
political science • MA, PhD
school psychology • MA, PhD
sociology • MA, PhD
Spanish • MA
speech communication • MA, PhD
theater • MFA, PhD

College of Basic Sciences
Dr. Peter Rabideau, Dean
Programs in:
astronomy • PhD
astrophysics • PhD
biochemistry • MS, PhD
chemistry • MS, PhD
computer science • MSSS, PhD
geology and geophysics • MS, PhD
microbiology • MS, PhD
natural sciences • MNS
physics • MS, PhD
plant biology • MS, PhD
systems science • MSSS
zoology • MS, PhD

College of Business Administration
Dr. Thomas D. Clark Jr., Dean
Programs in:
accounting • MS, PhD
business administration • MBA, PhD
economics • MS, PhD
finance • MS, PhD
information systems and decision sciences • MS, PhD
management • PhD
marketing • MS, PhD
public administration • MPA

College of Design
Christos Saccopoulas, Dean
Programs in:
architecture • MS
art history • MA
ceramics • MFA
landscape architecture • MLA
painting and drawing • MFA
photography • MFA
printmaking • MFA
sculpture • MFA

College of Education
Dr. F. Neil Matthews, Dean
Programs in:
counseling • Ed S, M Ed, MA
curriculum and instruction • Ed S, MA, PhD
educational administration • Ed S, M Ed, MA, PhD
elementary education • M Ed
kinesiology • MS, PhD
research methodology • PhD
secondary education • M Ed

College of Engineering
Dr. Adam Bourgoyne, Interim Dean
Programs in:
chemical engineering • MS Ch E, PhD
electrical and computer engineering • MSEE, PhD
engineering science • MSES, PhD
environmental engineering • MSCE, PhD
geotechnical engineering • MSCE, PhD
industrial engineering • MSIE
mechanical engineering • MSME, PhD
petroleum engineering • MS Pet E, PhD
structural engineering and mechanics • MSCE, PhD
transportation engineering • MSCE, PhD
water resources • MSCE, PhD

Manship School of Mass Communication
Dr. John Maxwell Hamilton, Dean
Program in:
mass communication • MMC

School of Library and Information Science
Dr. Bert R. Boyce, Dean
Program in:
library and information science • CLIS, MLIS

School of Music
Dr. Ronald Ross, Dean
Programs in:
music • DMA, MM, PhD
music education • PhD

Paul M. Hebert Law Center
Howard W. L'Enfant, Chancellor
Program in:
law • JD, LL M, MCL

School of Social Work
Dr. Kenneth A. Millar, Dean
Program in:
social work • MSW, PhD

School of Veterinary Medicine
Dr. David L. Huxsoll, Dean
Program in:
veterinary medicine • DVM, MS, PhD

LOUISIANA STATE UNIVERSITY IN SHREVEPORT
Shreveport, LA 71115-2399
http://www.lsus.edu/

Public coed comprehensive institution. *Enrollment: 4,259 graduate, professional, and undergraduate students. Graduate faculty: 90 full-time, 19 part-time. Computer facilities: Campuswide network is available with full Internet access. Total number of PCs/terminals supplied for student use: 225. Computer services are offered at no charge. Library facilities: Noel Library. General application contact:*

Kathleen G. Plante, Registrar and Director of Admissions, 318-797-5249.

College of Business Administration

Dr. Charlotte Jones, Interim Dean
Program in:
  business administration • MBA

College of Education

Dr. Gary S. Rush, Dean
Programs in:
  education • M Ed
  school psychology • SSP

College of Liberal Arts

Dr. Helen Clare Taylor, Director
Program in:
  liberal arts • MA

College of Sciences

Dr. Alfred McKinney, Dean
Programs in:
  biological sciences • MS
  environmental sciences • MS
  teaching • MST

LOUISIANA TECH UNIVERSITY

Ruston, LA 71272

http://www.latech.edu/

Public coed university. *Enrollment: 9,313 graduate, professional, and undergraduate students. Graduate faculty: 253 full-time.* Library facilities: *Prescott Memorial Library. Graduate expenses: $2382 per year full-time, $223 per quarter (minimum) part-time for state residents; $5307 per year full-time, $223 per quarter (minimum) part-time for nonresidents. General application contact: Dr. Stuart Deusch, Dean of the Graduate School, 318-257-2924.*

Graduate School

Dr. Stuart Deusch, Dean

College of Administration and Business

Dr. Anthony Inman, Interim Graduate Director
Programs in:
  business administration • MBA
  business economics • DBA, MBA
  finance • DBA, MBA
  management • DBA, MBA
  marketing • DBA, MBA
  professional accountancy • DBA, MBA, MPA
  quantitative analysis • DBA, MBA

College of Applied and Natural Sciences

Dr. Shirley Reagan, Dean
Programs in:
  biological sciences • MS
  dietetics • MS
  human ecology • MS

College of Education

Dr. Jerry W. Andrews, Dean
Programs in:
  business education • M Ed
  counseling • Ed S, MA
  counseling psychology • PhD
  curriculum and instruction • Ed D, MS
  educational leadership • Ed D
  English education • M Ed
  foreign language education • M Ed
  health and physical education • M Ed, MS
  industrial/organizational psychology • MA
  mathematics education • M Ed
  reading • Ed S
  science education • M Ed
  secondary education • M Ed
  social studies education • M Ed
  special education • MA
  speech education • M Ed

College of Engineering and Science

Dr. Barry A. Benedict, Dean
Programs in:
  applied computational analysis and modeling • PhD
  biomedical engineering • MS, PhD
  chemical engineering • D Eng, MS
  chemistry • MS
  civil engineering • D Eng, MS
  computer science • MS
  electrical engineering • D Eng, MS
  engineering • D Eng
  industrial engineering • D Eng, MS
  manufacturing systems engineering • MS
  mathematics and statistics • MS
  mechanical engineering • D Eng, MS
  operations research • MS
  physics • MS

College of Liberal Arts

Dr. Edward Jacobs, Director and Associate Dean
Programs in:
  art and graphic design • MFA
  English • MA
  history • MA
  interior design • MFA
  photography • MFA
  speech • MA
  speech pathology and audiology • MA
  studio art • MFA

LOYOLA UNIVERSITY NEW ORLEANS

New Orleans, LA 70118-6195

http://www.loyno.edu/

Independent-religious coed comprehensive institution. *Enrollment:* 5,161 graduate, professional, and undergraduate students. *Graduate faculty:* 273 full-time, 144 part-time. Computer facilities: *Campuswide network is available with full Internet access. Total number of PCs/terminals supplied for student use: 300. Computer service fees are included with tuition and fees.* Library facilities: *University Library plus 1 additional on-campus library.* Graduate expenses: *Tuition of $247 per credit hour. Fees of $556 per year full-time, $164 per year part-time.* General application contact: *Deborah C. Stiefel, Director of Admissions, 504-865-3240.*

College of Arts and Sciences

Dr. Robert J. Rowland Jr., Dean
Programs in:
    counseling • MS
    elementary education • MS
    mass communication • MA
    mathematics and computer science • MS
    reading education • MS
    religious studies • MA
    secondary education • MS

College of Music

Dr. Anthony Decuir, Interim Dean
Program in:
    music • MM, MME, MMT

Institute for Ministry

Barbara Fleischer, Director
Program in:
    ministry • MPS, MRE

Joseph A. Butt, S.J., College of Business Administration

Dr. J. Patrick O'Brien, Dean
Programs in:
    business administration • MBA
    quality management • MQM

Program in Nursing

Dr. Billie Ann Wilson, Director
Program in:
    family nurse practitioner • MSN

School of Law

John Makdisi Jr., Dean
Program in:
    law • JD

MCNEESE STATE UNIVERSITY

Lake Charles, LA 70609-2495

http://www.mcneese.edu/

Public coed comprehensive institution. *Enrollment:* 8,444 graduate, professional, and undergraduate students. *Graduate faculty:* 132 full-time. Library facilities: *Lether E. Frazar Memorial Library.* Graduate expenses: *$2118 per year full-time, $344 per semester (minimum) part-time for state residents; $7308 per year full-time, $344 per semester (minimum) part-time for nonresidents.* General application contact: *Kathy Bond, Admissions Counselor, 318-475-5147.*

Graduate School

Dr. Tom Wheeler, Dean for Graduate School and Research Services

College of Business

Dr. Elden Bailey, Dean
Program in:
    business administration • MBA

College of Education

Dr. Hugh Frugé, Dean
Programs in:
    administration and supervision • Ed S, M Ed
    biology education • M Ed
    business education • M Ed
    counseling and guidance • M Ed
    early childhood education • M Ed
    educational technology • M Ed
    elementary education • M Ed
    English education • M Ed
    health and physical education • M Ed
    mathematics education • M Ed
    psychology • MA
    reading education • M Ed
    social science education • M Ed
    special education • M Ed
    speech education • M Ed

College of Engineering and Technology

Dr. O. C. Karkalits, Dean
Programs in:
    chemical engineering • M Eng
    civil engineering • M Eng
    electrical engineering • M Eng
    mechanical engineering • M Eng

College of Liberal Arts

Dr. Millard T. Jones, Dean
Programs in:
    creative writing • MFA
    English • MA
    music education • MM Ed
    performance • MM

College of Nursing

Dr. Anita Fields, Dean
Program in:
    nursing • MSN

College of Science

Dr. George F. Mead Jr., Dean

Programs in:

    biology • MS

    chemistry • MS

    computer science • MS

    environmental sciences • MS

    mathematics • MS

    statistics • MS

NICHOLLS STATE UNIVERSITY

Thibodaux, LA 70310

http://www.nich.edu/

Public coed comprehensive institution. *Enrollment: 7,076 graduate, professional, and undergraduate students. Graduate faculty: 96 full-time. Computer facilities: Campuswide network is available with full Internet access. Computer service fees are included with tuition and fees. Library facilities: Allen Ellender Memorial Library plus 1 additional on-campus library. Graduate expenses: $2136 per year full-time, $283 per semester (minimum) part-time for state residents; $5376 per year full-time, $283 per semester (minimum) part-time for nonresidents. General application contact: Dr. J. B. Stroud, Director of Graduate Studies, 504-449-7014.*

Graduate Studies

Dr. J. B. Stroud, Director

College of Arts and Sciences

Dr. Donald M. Bardwell, Head

Programs in:

    applied mathematics • MS

    mathematics • MS

College of Business Administration

Dr. Ridley Gros, Dean

Program in:

    business administration • MBA

College of Education

Dr. Robert Clement, Dean

Programs in:

    administration and supervision • M Ed

    counselor education • M Ed

    curriculum and instruction • M Ed

    psychological counseling • MA

    school psychology • Ed S

NORTHEAST LOUISIANA UNIVERSITY

Monroe, LA 71209-0001

http://www.nlu.edu/

Public coed comprehensive institution. Library facilities: *Sandel Library. Graduate expenses: $2028 per year full-time, $240 per semester (minimum) part-time for state residents; $6852 per year full-time, $240 per semester (minimum) part-time for nonresidents. General application contact: Dean, Graduate Studies and Research, 318-342-1036.*

Graduate Studies and Research

College of Business Administration

Program in:

    business administration • MBA

College of Education

Programs in:

    administration and supervision • Ed S, M Ed

    counseling • Ed S, M Ed

    curriculum and instruction • Ed D

    educational leadership • Ed D

    elementary education • Ed S, M Ed

    English education • M Ed

    health and human performance • M Ed

    marriage and family therapy • MA, PhD

    psychology • MS

    psychology-applied psychometrics • MS

    psychology-applied school • MS

    psychology-general experimental • MS

    reading • M Ed

    school psychology • SSP

    secondary education • Ed S, M Ed

    special education • M Ed

    substance abuse counseling • MA

College of Liberal Arts

Programs in:

    communication • MA

    communicative disorders • MA

    criminal justice • MA

    gerontological studies • CGS

    gerontology • MA

    history • MA

    music • MM

College of Pharmacy and Health Sciences

Programs in:

    pharmaceutical sciences • MS

    pharmacy • PhD

College of Pure and Applied Sciences

Programs in:

    biology • MS

    chemistry • MS

    geosciences • MS

NORTHWESTERN STATE UNIVERSITY OF LOUISIANA
Natchitoches, LA 71497

http://www.nsula.edu/

Public coed comprehensive institution. *Enrollment:* 8,873 graduate, professional, and undergraduate students. Graduate faculty: *55 full-time, 12 part-time. Computer facilities: Campuswide network is available with full Internet access. Computer service fees are included with tuition and fees. Library facilities: Eugene P. Watson Memorial Library plus 2 additional on-campus libraries. Graduate expenses: $2147 per year full-time, $336 per semester (minimum) part-time for state residents; $6437 per year full-time, $336 per semester (minimum) part-time for nonresidents.* General application contact: *Dr. Tom Hanson, Dean, Graduate Studies and Research, 318-357-5851.*

Graduate Studies and Research
Dr. Tom Hanson, Dean
Programs in:
    art • MA
    business and distributive education • M Ed
    clinical psychology • MS
    community counseling psychology • MS
    counseling and guidance • Ed S, M Ed
    early childhood education • M Ed
    educational administration/supervision • Ed S, M Ed
    elementary teaching • Ed S, M Ed
    English • MA
    English education • MA
    health promotion • M Ed
    history • MA
    home economics education • M Ed
    mathematics education • M Ed
    music • MM
    nursing • MSN
    reading • Ed S, M Ed
    school psychology • Ed S
    science education • M Ed
    secondary teaching • Ed S, M Ed
    social sciences education • M Ed
    special education • Ed S, M Ed
    sport administration • M Ed
    student personnel services • MA

SOUTHEASTERN LOUISIANA UNIVERSITY
Hammond, LA 70402

http://www.selu.edu/

Public coed comprehensive institution. *Enrollment:* 15,330 graduate, professional, and undergraduate students. Graduate faculty: *219. Computer facilities: Campuswide network is available with full Internet access. Total number of PCs/terminals supplied for student use: 684. Computer service fees are included with tuition and fees.*

Library facilities: *Sims Memorial Library. Graduate expenses: Tuition of $2010 per year full-time, $287 per semester (minimum) part-time for state residents; $5232 per year full-time, $287 per semester (minimum) part-time for nonresidents. Fees of $5 per year.* General application contact: *Stephen C. Soutullo, Registrar and Director of Enrollment Services, 504-549-2066.*

College of Arts and Sciences
Dr. John S. Miller, Dean
Programs in:
    biological sciences • MS
    English • MA
    history • MA
    music theory • M Mus
    performance • M Mus
    psychology • MA

College of Business
Dr. Michael Budden, Dean
Program in:
    business • MBA

College of Education
Dr. Stephen Ragan, Dean
Programs in:
    counselor education • M Ed
    educational administration • Ed S
    elementary teaching • Ed S, M Ed
    health studies • MA
    kinesiology • MA
    reading • M Ed
    school administration and supervision • M Ed
    secondary teaching • M Ed
    special education • M Ed, MS

College of Nursing
Dr. S. Kay A. Thornhill, Director, Graduate Nursing
Program in:
    nursing • MSN

SOUTHERN UNIVERSITY AND AGRICULTURAL AND MECHANICAL COLLEGE
Baton Rouge, LA 70813

http://www.subr.edu/

Public coed comprehensive institution. *Enrollment:* 9,945 graduate, professional, and undergraduate students. Graduate faculty: *165 full-time. Library facilities: J. B. Cade Library. Graduate expenses: $2226 per year full-time, $267 per semester (minimum) part-time for state residents; $6262 per year full-time, $267 per semester (minimum) part-time for nonresidents.* General application contact: *Dr. Kweku K. Bentil, Associate Vice Chancellor for Academic Affairs and Dean of Graduate Studies, 504-771-5390.*

Graduate School
Dr. Kweku K. Bentil, Associate Vice Chancellor for Academic Affairs and Dean of Graduate Studies

College of Agricultural, Family and Consumer Sciences
Dr. Kirkland E. Mellad, Interim Dean
Program in:
    urban forestry • MS

College of Arts and Humanities
Dr. Richard Webb, Dean
Programs in:
    mass communications • MA
    social sciences • MA

College of Business
Dr. Brenda Birkett, Dean
Program in:
    professional accountancy • MPA

College of Education
Dr. Karen Webb, Dean
Programs in:
    administration and supervision • M Ed
    counselor education • MA
    elementary education • M Ed
    media • M Ed
    mental health counseling • MA
    secondary education • M Ed
    therapeutic recreation • MS

College of Sciences
Dr. Earl Doomes, Dean
Programs in:
    analytical chemistry • MS
    biochemistry • MS
    biology • MS
    environmental sciences • MS
    information systems • MS
    inorganic chemistry • MS
    mathematics • MS
    micro/minicomputer architecture • MS
    operating systems • MS
    organic chemistry • MS
    physical chemistry • MS
    physics • MS
    rehabilitation counseling • MS
    social sciences • MA

School of Public Policy and Urban Affairs
Dr. Damien Ejigiri, Dean
Programs in:
    public administration • MPA
    public policy • PhD
    social sciences • MA

Special Education Institute
Dr. Carolyn Person, Director
Program in:
    special education • M Ed, PhD

Law Center
Bhishma K. Agnihotri, Chancellor
Program in:
    law • JD

School of Nursing
Dr. Janet Rami, Dean
Program in:
    nursing • MSN

SOUTHERN UNIVERSITY AT NEW ORLEANS
New Orleans, LA 70126-1009

http://www.gnofn.org/~zaire/suno4.htm

Public coed comprehensive institution. *Enrollment: 4,700 graduate, professional, and undergraduate students. Graduate faculty: 21. Library facilities: main library. Graduate expenses: Tuition of $2448 per year full-time, $341 per semester (minimum) part-time for state residents; $4364 per year full-time, $494 per semester (minimum) part-time for nonresidents. Fees of $75 per year. General application contact: D. J. Smith, Director of Student Affairs, 504-286-5376.*

School of Social Work
Mille M. Charles, Dean
Program in:
    social work • MSW

TULANE UNIVERSITY
New Orleans, LA 70118-5669

http://www.tulane.edu/

Independent coed university. *Enrollment: 11,424 graduate, professional, and undergraduate students. Graduate faculty: 1,044 full-time, 351 part-time. Computer facilities: Campuswide network is available with full Internet access. Total number of PCs/terminals supplied for student use: 500. Computer services are offered at no charge. Library facilities: Howard Tilton Library plus 6 additional on-campus libraries. Graduate expenses: Tuition of $22,190 per year full-time, $1262 per hour part-time. Fees of $852 per year full-time. General application contact: Kay D. Orrill, Assistant Dean, Graduate School, 504-865-5100.*

Graduate School
Dr. Martha W. Gilliland, Dean
Programs in:
    anatomy • MS, PhD
    anthropology • MA, MS, PhD
    applied development • MA
    applied mathematics • MS
    art history • MA
    biochemistry • MS, PhD
    biology • MS, PhD
    chemistry • MS, PhD
    civic and cultural management • MA
    classical studies • MA

Tulane University (continued)
  economics • MA, PhD
  English • MA, PhD
  French and Italian • MA, PhD
  geology • MS, PhD
  German • MA, PhD
  history • MA, PhD
  human genetics • PhD
  Latin American studies • MA, PhD
  liberal arts • MLA
  mathematics • MS, PhD
  microbiology and immunology • MS, PhD
  molecular and cellular biology • PhD
  music • MA, MFA
  neuroscience • MS, PhD
  paleontology • PhD
  parasitology • MS, MSPH, PhD
  pharmacology • MS, PhD
  philosophy • MA, PhD
  physics • MS, PhD
  physiology • MS, PhD
  political science • MA, PhD
  psychology • MS, PhD
  sociology • MA, PhD
  Spanish and Portuguese • MA, PhD
  statistics • MS
  studio art • MFA
  theatre and dance • MFA

A. B. Freeman School of Business
James McFarland, Dean
Program in:
  business • EMBA, M Acct, MBA, PhD

School of Architecture
Don Gatzke, Dean
Program in:
  architecture • M Arch, MPS

School of Engineering
Dr. William C. Van Buskirk, Dean
Programs in:
  biomedical engineering • MS, MSE, PhD, Sc D
  chemical engineering • MS, MSE, PhD, Sc D
  civil and environmental engineering • MS, MSE, PhD,
    Sc D
  computer science • MS, MSCS, PhD, Sc D
  electrical engineering • MS, MSE, PhD, Sc D
  mechanical engineering • MS, MSE, PhD, Sc D

School of Law
Edward Sherman, Dean
Program in:
  law • JD, LL M, MCL, SJD

School of Medicine
Programs in:
  anatomy • MS, PhD
  biochemistry • MS, PhD
  human genetics • PhD
  medicine • MD

  microbiology and immunology • MS, PhD
  molecular and cellular biology • PhD
  neuroscience • MS, PhD
  parasitology • MS, MSPH, PhD
  pharmacology • MS, PhD
  physiology • MS, PhD

School of Public Health and Tropical Medicine
Dr. Paul K. Whelton, Dean
Programs in:
  biostatistics • MS, MSPH, PhD, Sc D
  environmental health sciences • MPH, MSPH, Sc D
  epidemiology • Dr PH, MPH, MS, PhD
  health communication/education • MPH
  health systems management • Dr PH, MHA, MMM, MPH
  international health and development • Dr PH, MADH,
    MPH
  maternal and child health • Dr PH, MPH
  nutrition • MPH
  parasitology • MS, MSPH, PhD
  population studies • MPH
  tropical medicine • Diploma, MPHTM, MSPH, Sc D

School of Social Work
Dr. Suzanne England, Dean
Program in:
  social work • Certificate, MSW, PhD

UNIVERSITY OF NEW ORLEANS
New Orleans, LA 70148

http://www.uno.edu/Welcome.shtml

Public coed university. *Enrollment:* 15,833 graduate, professional, and undergraduate students. Graduate faculty: 440. Library facilities: *Earl K. Long Library.* Graduate expenses: *Tuition of $2362 per year full-time, $373 per semester (minimum) part-time for state residents; $7888 per year full-time, $1423 per semester (minimum) part-time for nonresidents. Fees of $170 per year full-time, $25 per semester (minimum) part-time.* General application contact: *Dr. Robert Cashner, Dean, 504-286-6836.*

Graduate School
Dr. Robert Cashner, Dean

College of Business Administration
Dr. Tim Ryan, Dean
Programs in:
  accounting • MS
  business administration • MBA
  economics • MA
  financial economics • PhD
  taxation • MS

College of Education
Dr. Robert Wimpelberg, Dean
Programs in:
  adapted physical education • MA
  counselor education • Certificate, M Ed, PhD
  curriculum and instruction • Certificate, M Ed, PhD
  educational leadership and foundations • Certificate,
    M Ed, PhD
  exercise physiology • MA
  gerontology • Certificate
  health and physical education • Certificate
  physical education • M Ed
  science, pedagogy and coaching sport management •
    MA
  special education • Certificate, M Ed, PhD

College of Engineering
Dr. John N. Crisp, Dean
Programs in:
  civil engineering • MS
  electrical engineering • MS
  engineering and applied sciences • PhD
  engineering management • Certificate, MS
  mechanical engineering • MS
  naval architecture and marine engineering • MS

College of Liberal Arts
Philip B. Coulter, Dean
Programs in:
  applied sociology • MA
  archives and records administration • MA
  arts administration • MA
  communications • MA, MFA
  creative writing • MFA
  drama • MFA
  English • MA
  film • MA, MFA
  geography • MA
  graphic design • MFA
  graphics • MFA
  history • MA
  international relations • MA
  music • MM
  painting • MFA
  photography • MFA
  political science • MA, PhD
  Romance languages • MA
  sculpture • MFA
  sociology • MA
  television • MA, MFA

College of Sciences
Dr. Joe King, Dean
Programs in:
  applied biopsychology • PhD
  applied developmental psychology • PhD
  applied physics • MS
  applied psychology • PhD
  biological sciences • MS
  chemistry • MS, PhD
  computer science • MS
  geology • MS
  geophysics • MS
  mathematics • MS

  physics • MS
  psychology • MS
  science teaching • MA

College of Urban and Public Affairs
Dr. Fredrick Wagner, Dean
Programs in:
  public administration and policy • MPA
  urban and regional planning • MURP
  urban studies • MS, PhD

 **UNIVERSITY OF
SOUTHWESTERN LOUISIANA**
Lafayette, LA 70503

http://www.usl.edu/

Public coed university. *Enrollment: 17,020 graduate, professional,
and undergraduate students. Graduate faculty: 345 full-time.
Computer facilities: Campuswide network is available with full Internet
access. Computer service fees are included with tuition and fees.
Library facilities: Dupre Library. Graduate expenses: $2012 per
year full-time, $300 per semester (minimum) part-time for state
residents; $7244 per year full-time, $300 per semester (minimum)
part-time for nonresidents. General application contact: Dr. Lewis
Pyenson, Dean of the Graduate School, 318-482-6965.*

Graduate School
Dr. Lewis Pyenson, Dean

College of Applied Life Sciences
Dr. Lora Lana Goodeaux, Acting Dean
Program in:
  human resources • MS

College of Business Administration
Dr. C. William Roe, Graduate Coordinator
Programs in:
  business administration • MBA
  health care administration • MBA
  health care certification • MBA

College of Education
Dr. Mary Jane Ford, Acting Dean
Programs in:
  administration and supervision • M Ed
  curriculum and instruction • M Ed
  education of the gifted • M Ed
  guidance and counseling • M Ed

College of Engineering
Dr. Anthony B. Ponter, Dean
Programs in:
  chemical engineering • MSE
  civil engineering • MSE
  computer engineering • MS, PhD
  computer science • MS, PhD
  engineering management • MSET
  mechanical engineering • MSE
  petroleum engineering • MSE
  telecommunications • MSTC

University of Southwestern Louisiana (continued)

College of Liberal Arts
Dr. A. David Barry, Dean
Programs in:
British and American literature • MA
communicative disorders • MS
creative writing • MA, PhD
folklore • MA
francophone studies • PhD
French • MA
history • MA
literature • PhD
mass communications • MS
psychology • MS
rehabilitation counseling • MS
rhetoric • MA, PhD

College of Nursing
Dr. Gail Poirrier, Acting Dean
Program in:
nursing • MSN

College of Sciences
Dr. Duane D. Blumberg, Dean
Programs in:
applied physics • MS
biology • MS
computer science • MS
environmental and evolutionary biology • PhD
geology • MS
mathematics • MS, PhD
physics • MS
statistics • MS, PhD

College of the Arts
H. Gordon Brooks, Dean
Programs in:
conducting • MM
music • MM
pedagogy • MM
vocal and instrumental performance • MM

XAVIER UNIVERSITY OF LOUISIANA
New Orleans, LA 70125-1098

http://www.xavier.xula.edu/

Independent-religious coed comprehensive institution. *Enrollment:* 3,516 graduate, professional, and undergraduate students. *Graduate faculty: 29 full-time, 19 part-time.* Computer facilities: *Campuswide network is available with full Internet access. Total number of PCs/ terminals supplied for student use: 100. Computer service fees are included with tuition and fees.* Library facilities: *main library.* Graduate expenses: *$200 per semester hour.* General application contact: *Marlene Robinson, Director of Graduate Admissions, 504-483-7487.*

Graduate School
Dr. Alvin J. Richard, Dean
Programs in:
administration and supervision • MA
black Catholic studies • Th M
curriculum and instruction • MA
guidance and counseling • MA
nurse anesthesia • MS
teacher education • MAT

College of Pharmacy
Dr. Marcellus Grace, Dean
Program in:
pharmacy • Pharm D

MAINE

 # UNIVERSITY OF MAINE
Orono, ME 04469

http://www.ume.maine.edu/

Public coed university. *Enrollment:* 10,000 graduate, professional, and undergraduate students. *Graduate faculty: 600.* Computer facilities: *Campuswide network is available with full Internet access. Computer service fees are included with tuition and fees.* Library facilities: *Fogler Library plus 1 additional on-campus library.* Graduate expenses: *Tuition of $194 per credit hour for state residents; $548 per credit hour for nonresidents. Fees of $378 per year full-time, $33 per semester (minimum) part-time.* General application contact: *Scott Delcourt, Director of the Graduate School, 207-581-3218.*

Graduate School
Dr. Daniel J. Dwyer, Vice Provost for Research and Guaduate Studies
Program in:
liberal studies • MA

College of Business, Public Policy and Health
Dr. Virginia Gibson, Interim Dean
Programs in:
business • MBA
nursing • CAS, MS
public administration • MPA
social work • MSW

College of Education and Human Development
Dr. Robert A. Cobb, Dean
Programs in:
counselor education • CAS, M Ed, MAT, MS
educational leadership • CAS, Ed D, M Ed
elementary education • CAS, M Ed, MS
higher education • CAS, M Ed, MAT, MS
human development • MS
kinesiology and physical education • CAS, M Ed, MAT, MS

literacy education • CAS, Ed D, M Ed, MAT, MS
science education • CAS, M Ed, MS
secondary education • CAS, M Ed, MS
social studies education • CAS, M Ed, MAT, MS
special education • CAS, M Ed

College of Engineering
Dr. John Field, Interim Dean
Programs in:
chemical engineering • MS, PhD
civil engineering • MS, PhD
computer engineering • MS
electrical engineering • MS
engineering physics • M Eng
environmental engineering • MS, PhD
geotechnical engineering • MS, PhD
mechanical engineering • MS
spatial information science and engineering • MS, PhD
structural engineering • MS, PhD

College of Liberal Arts and Sciences
Dr. Rebecca Eilers, Dean
Programs in:
chemistry • MS, PhD
clinical psychology • PhD
communication • MA
communication disorders • MA
computer science • MS
developmental psychology • MA
economics • MA
engineering physics • M Eng
English • MA
experimental psychology • MA, PhD
French • MA, MAT
German • MAT
history • MA, PhD
mathematics • MA
music • MM
physics • MS, PhD
social psychology • MA
Spanish • MAT
theatre • MA

College of Natural Sciences, Forestry, and Agriculture
Dr. G. Bruce Wiersma, Dean
Programs in:
animal sciences • MPS, MS
biochemistry • MPS, MS
biochemistry and molecular biology • PhD
biological sciences • MS, PhD
bio-resource engineering • MS
ecology and environmental science • MS, PhD
ecology and environmental sciences • MS, PhD
entomology • MS
food and nutritional sciences • PhD
food science and human nutrition • MS
forest resources • PhD
forestry • MF, MS
geological sciences • MS, PhD
marine biology • MS, PhD
marine policy • MS
microbiology • MPS, MS, PhD
oceanography • MS, PhD
plant science • PhD

plant, soil, and environmental sciences • MS
resource economics and policy • MS
resource utilization • MS, PhD
wildlife conservation • MWC
wildlife ecology • MS, PhD
zoology • MS, PhD

Institute for Quaternary Studies
Dr. George Jacobson, Director
Program in:
quaternary studies • MS

UNIVERSITY OF NEW ENGLAND
Biddeford, ME 04005-9526
http://www.une.edu/

Independent coed comprehensive institution. *Enrollment: 2,296 graduate, professional, and undergraduate students. Graduate faculty: 34 full-time, 123 part-time. Computer facilities: Campuswide network is available with partial Internet access (e-mail only). Total number of PCs/terminals supplied for student use: 62. Computer services are offered at no charge. Library facilities: Jack S. Ketchum Library plus 1 additional on-campus library. Graduate expenses: Tuition of $335 per credit. Fees of $230 per year. General application contact: Patricia T. Cribby, Dean of Admissions and Enrollment Management, 207-283-0171 Ext. 2297.*

College of Health Professions
Dr. Vernon Moore, Acting Dean
Programs in:
education • MS Ed
nurse anesthesia • MS
physician assistant • MPA
social work • MSW

College of Osteopathic Medicine
Dr. Stephen Shannon, Dean
Program in:
osteopathic medicine • DO

UNIVERSITY OF SOUTHERN MAINE
Portland, ME 04104-9300
http://www.usm.maine.edu/

Public coed comprehensive institution. *Enrollment: 10,230 graduate, professional, and undergraduate students. Graduate faculty: 122. Computer facilities: Campuswide network is available with full Internet access. Computer service fees are included with tuition and fees. Library facilities: main library plus 2 additional on-campus libraries. Graduate expenses: Tuition of $178 per credit hour for state residents; $267 per credit hour (minimum) for nonresidents. Fees of $282 per year full-time, $83 per semester (minimum) part-*

University of Southern Maine (continued)
time. General application contact: *Mary Sloan, Assistant Director of Graduate Studies, 207-780-4386.*

College of Arts and Science
Dr. Steven Worchel, Dean
Program in:
American and New England studies • MA

College of Education and Human Development
Richard E. Barnes, Dean
Programs in:
adult education • CAS, MS
counselor education • CAS, MS
educational leadership • CAS, MS Ed
English as a second language • CAS, MS Ed
extended teacher education • Certificate, MS Ed
industrial/technology education • MS Ed
literacy education • CAS, MS Ed
school psychology • MS
special education • MS

College of Nursing
Dr. Marianne W. Rodgers, Interim Dean
Programs in:
adult health nursing • MS, PMC
family nursing • MS, PMC
management • MS
psychiatric-mental health nursing • MS, PMC

Edmund S. Muskie School of Public Service
Barton Wechsler, Dean
Programs in:
community planning and development • MCPD
health policy and management • MS
public policy and management • MA

School of Applied Science
Dr. Brian C. Hodgkin, Dean
Programs in:
applied immunology • MS
computer science • MS
manufacturing management • MS

School of Business
John M. Burt, Dean
Program in:
business • MBA

University of Maine School of Law
Donald Zillman, Dean
Program in:
law • JD

MARYLAND

BOWIE STATE UNIVERSITY
Bowie, MD 20715

http://www.bowiestate.edu/

Public coed comprehensive institution. Library facilities: *Thurgood Marshall Library.* Graduate expenses: *Tuition of $169 per credit hour for state residents; $304 per credit hour for nonresidents. Fees of $171 per year.* General application contact: *Graduate Dean, 301-464-6586.*

Graduate Programs
Programs in:
administration of nursing services • MS
business administration • M Adm Mgt
computer science • MS
counseling psychology • MA
elementary education • M Ed
family nurse practitioner • MS
guidance and counseling • M Ed
human resource development • MA
information systems analyst • Certificate
management information systems • MS
nursing education • MS
organizational communication • Certificate, MA
public administration • M Adm Mgt
reading education • M Ed
school administration and supervision • M Ed
secondary education • M Ed
special education • M Ed
teaching • MAT

COLLEGE OF NOTRE DAME OF MARYLAND
Baltimore, MD 21210-2476

http://www.ndm.edu/

Independent-religious primarily female comprehensive institution. *Enrollment: 3,300 graduate, professional, and undergraduate students. Graduate faculty: 62. Computer facilities: Campuswide network is available with partial Internet access (e-mail only). Total number of PCs/terminals supplied for student use: 24. Computer service fees are included with tuition and fees. Library facilities: Loyola/Notre Dame Library.* Graduate expenses: *$248 per credit.* General application contact: *Dr. Michael L. Storey, Interim Director of Graduate Studies, 410-532-5316.*

Graduate Studies
Dr. Michael L. Storey, Interim Director
Programs in:
adulthood and aging • MA
leadership in teaching • MA

liberal studies • MA
management • MA
teaching • MA

COPPIN STATE COLLEGE
Baltimore, MD 21216-3698

http://www.coppin.umd.edu/

Public coed comprehensive institution. *Enrollment:* 3,540 graduate, professional, and undergraduate students. Graduate faculty: *22 full-time, 23 part-time.* Library facilities: *Parlett L. Moore Library.* Graduate expenses: *Tuition of $140 per credit for state residents; $240 per credit for nonresidents. Fees of $504 per year.* General application contact: *Dr. Jerusa Wilson, Dean, Graduate Studies, 410-383-5535.*

Division of Graduate Studies
Dr. Jerusa Wilson, Dean

Division of Arts and Sciences
Dr. Thelma J. Bryan, Dean
Programs in:
    applied psychology and rehabilitation counseling • M Ed
    correctional education • M Ed
    criminal justice • MS

Division of Education
Dr. Julius Chapman, Chair
Programs in:
    adult and general education • M Ed, MS
    curriculum and instruction • M Ed
    special education • M Ed

FROSTBURG STATE UNIVERSITY
Frostburg, MD 21532-1099

Public coed comprehensive institution. Library facilities: *Lewis Ort Library.* General application contact: *Coordinator, Graduate Admissions, 301-689-7053.*

Graduate School

School of Arts and Humanities
Program in:
    modern humanities • MA

School of Business
Programs in:
    business • M Ed
    business administration • MBA

School of Education
Programs in:
    biology education • M Ed
    educational administration • M Ed
    elementary education • M Ed
    guidance and counseling • M Ed
    health and physical education • M Ed
    human performance • MS
    interdisciplinary education • M Ed
    parks and recreational management • MS
    reading • M Ed
    secondary education • M Ed

School of Natural and Social Sciences
Programs in:
    applied ecology and conservation biology • MS
    biology • MS
    counseling psychology • MS
    fisheries and wildlife management • MS

HOOD COLLEGE
Frederick, MD 21701-8575

http://www.hood.edu/

Independent-religious coed comprehensive institution. *Enrollment:* 1,856 graduate, professional, and undergraduate students. Graduate faculty: *26.* Computer facilities: *Campuswide network is available with full Internet access. Computer services are offered at no charge.* Library facilities: *Beneficial-Hodson Library.* Graduate expenses: *$285 per credit.* General application contact: *Dr. Ann Boyd, Dean of the Graduate School, 301-696-3600.*

Graduate School
Dr. Ann Boyd, Dean
Programs in:
    administration and management • MBA
    applied behavioral and social research • MA
    biomedical sciences • MS
    computer and information sciences • MS
    curriculum and instruction • MS
    early childhood education • MS
    educational leadership • MS
    elementary education • MS
    elementary school science and mathematics • MS
    environmental biology • MS
    psychology • MA
    reading • MS
    secondary education • MS
    special education • MS

JOHNS HOPKINS UNIVERSITY
Baltimore, MD 21218-2699
http://www.jhu.edu/

Independent coed university. *Enrollment: 15,677 graduate, professional, and undergraduate students. Graduate faculty: 2,262 full-time, 2,667 part-time. Computer facilities: Campuswide network is available with full Internet access. Total number of PCs/terminals supplied for student use: 300. Computer service fees are included with tuition and fees. Library facilities: Eisenhower Library plus 3 additional on-campus libraries. Graduate expenses: Tuition of $22,680 per year. Fees of $500 (one-time charge). General application contact: Nicole Kendzejewki, Graduate Admissions Coordinator, 410-516-8174.*

G. W. C. Whiting School of Engineering
Charles R. Westgate, Dean
Programs in:
- biomedical engineering • MSE, PhD
- chemical engineering • MS, MSE, PhD
- civil engineering • MSE, PhD
- computer science • MSE, PhD
- electrical and computer engineering • MSE, PhD
- geography and environmental engineering • MA, MS, MSE, PhD
- materials science and engineering • MMSE, MSE, PhD
- mathematical sciences • MA, MSE, PhD
- mechanical engineering • MS, MSE, PhD
- mechanics • MSE, PhD

Intercampus Program in Molecular Biophysics
Dr. George D. Rose, Director
Program in:
- molecular biophysics • PhD

Paul H. Nitze School of Advanced International Studies
Paul Wolfowitz, Dean
Programs in:
- African studies • MA, PhD
- American foreign policy • MA, PhD
- Asian studies • MA, PhD
- Canadian studies • MA, PhD
- European studies • MA, PhD
- interdisciplinary studies • MA, PhD
- international economics • MA
- international public policy • MIPP
- international relations • MA, PhD
- international studies • Certificate
- Latin American studies • MA, PhD
- Middle Eastern studies • MA, PhD
- Russian area and East European studies • MA, PhD
- social change and development • MA, PhD

Peabody Conservatory of Music
Dr. Robert Sirota, Director
Program in:
- music • AD, DMA, GPD, MM

School of Arts and Sciences
Dr. Richard McCarty, Acting Dean
Programs in:
- anthropology • MA, PhD
- astronomy • PhD
- biochemistry • PhD
- biophysics • MA, PhD
- cell biology • PhD
- chemistry • MA, PhD
- classics • MA, PhD
- cognitive science • MA, PhD
- comparative literature and intellectual history • PhD
- developmental biology • PhD
- economics • MA, PhD
- English and American literature • PhD
- experimental psychology • PhD
- French • PhD
- genetic biology • PhD
- geochemistry • MA, PhD
- geology • MA, PhD
- geophysics • MA, PhD
- German • MA, PhD
- groundwater • MA, PhD
- history • MA, PhD
- history of art • MA, PhD
- history of science • MA, PhD
- Italian • MA, PhD
- mathematics • MA, PhD
- molecular biology • PhD
- Near Eastern studies • MA, PhD
- oceanography • MA, PhD
- philosophy • MA, PhD
- physics • PhD
- planetary atmosphere • MA, PhD
- policy studies • MA
- political science • MA, PhD
- psychology • PhD
- sociology • PhD
- Spanish • MA, PhD
- writing • MA

School of Continuing Studies
Stanley C. Gabor, Dean

Division of Business and Management
Dr. Jon Heggan, Director
Programs in:
- business • MS
- change management • Certificate
- information and telecommunication systems for business • Certificate, MS
- investments • Certificate
- leadership development for minority managers • Certificate
- marketing • MS
- organizational development and human resources • MS
- real estate • MS
- skilled facilitator • Certificate
- the business of medicine • Certificate
- the business of nursing • Certificate
- women, leadership, and change • Certificate

Division of Education

Dr. Ralph Fessler, Director

Programs in:

    addictions counseling • Certificate

    administration and supervision • CAGS, MS

    assistive technology • Certificate

    autism • Certificate

    career counseling • Certificate

    computers for educators • CAGS

    counseling • CAGS, Ed D, MS

    counseling at-risk students • Certificate

    discipline and positive behavior management • Certificate

    early childhood education • MAT

    elementary education • MAT

    general education • CAGS, Ed D, MS

    gifted education • Certificate, MS

    inclusion • Certificate

    learning disabilities • CAGS

    organizations and counseling • Certificate

    reading • Certificate, MS

    school principalship • Certificate

    secondary education • MAT

    severely and profoundly handicapped • CAGS

    special education • Ed D, MS

    teacher leadership • MS

    technology for educators • MS

Program in Liberal Arts

Dr. Nancy Norris, Director

Program in:

    liberal arts • CAGS, MLA

School of Hygiene and Public Health

Dr. Alfred Sommer, Dean

Programs in:

    basic mechanisms of carcinogenesis • PhD

    biochemistry • PhD

    biophysics • PhD

    biostatistics • MHS, MPH, PhD, Sc M

    chronic disease epidemiology • Dr PH, MHS, PhD, Sc D, Sc M

    clinical epidemiology • Dr PH, MHS, PhD, Sc D, Sc M

    clinical investigation • PhD, Sc M

    disease control • Dr PH, MHS, PhD, Sc D

    environmental health engineering • Dr PH, MHS, PhD, Sc D, Sc M

    environmental health sciences • MPH

    epidemiology • Dr PH, MHS, MPH, PhD, Sc D, Sc M

    genetics • Dr PH, MHS, PhD, Sc D, Sc M

    health and public policy • Dr PH, MHS, PhD, Sc D

    health policy and management • MPH

    health services research • Dr PH, MHS, PhD, Sc D

    health systems • Dr PH, MHS, PhD, Sc D

    human nutrition • Dr PH, MHS, PhD, Sc D

    infectious disease • Dr PH, MHS, PhD, Sc D, Sc M

    interferon induction and herpes simplex viral transformation of mammalian cells • PhD

    international health • MPH

    international health policy, planning, and implementation • Dr PH, MHS, PhD, Sc D

    maternal and child health • MPH

    mental hygiene • Dr PH, MHS, MPH, Sc D, Sc M

    molecular microbiology and immunology • Dr PH, MHS, MPH, PhD, Sc D, Sc M

    nucleic acid structure, function, and interaction • PhD

    occupational and environmental health • Dr PH, PhD

    occupational/environmental epidemiology • Dr PH, MHS, PhD, Sc D, Sc M

    physiology • MHS, PhD, Sc M

    population dynamics • Dr PH, MHS, MPH, PhD, Sc D, Sc M

    public health/maternal and child health program planning, evaluation, and administration • Dr PH, MHS, PhD, Sc D

    radiation health sciences • Dr PH, MHS, PhD, Sc D, Sc M

    reproductive biology • MHS, PhD, Sc M

    research, administration, and teaching • PhD

    social and behavioral sciences • Dr PH, MHS, PhD, Sc D, Sc M

    social sciences and public health • Dr PH, MHS, Sc D

    structure and function of mammalian genetic apparatus • PhD

    structure and interaction of biopolymers and cells • PhD

    toxicological sciences • PhD

    vaccine sciences • Dr PH, PhD, Sc D

School of Medicine

Dr. Edward D. Miller, Dean of Medical Faculty and Chief Executive Officer

Programs in:

    art as applied to medicine • MA

    biochemistry, cellular and molecular biology • PhD

    biological chemistry • PhD

    biomedical engineering • MSE, PhD

    cell biology and anatomy • PhD

    cellular and molecular medicine • PhD

    cellular and molecular physiology • PhD

    human genetics • PhD

    immunology • PhD

    medicine • MD

    molecular biology and genetics • PhD

    neuroscience • PhD

    pharmacology and molecular sciences • PhD

    physiology • PhD

School of Nursing

Sue K. Donaldson, Dean

Programs in:

    adult acute/critical care • Certificate, MSN

    adult and pediatric primary care • MSN

    adult health • MSN

    adult or pediatric primary care • Certificate

    advanced practice nursing-nurse practitioner • MSN

    AIDS/HIV • MSN

    community health nursing • MSN

    family primary care • Certificate, MSN

    nurse practitioner • Certificate

    nursing • PhD

    nursing systems and management • MSN

    oncology nursing • MSN

LOYOLA COLLEGE
Baltimore, MD 21210-2699

http://www.loyola.edu/

Independent-religious coed comprehensive institution. *Enrollment: 6,241 graduate, professional, and undergraduate students. Graduate faculty: 79 full-time, 118 part-time. Computer facilities: Campuswide network is available with full Internet access. Total number of PCs/ terminals supplied for student use: 267. Computer service fees are included with tuition and fees. Library facilities: Loyola/Notre Dame Library. Graduate expenses: $222 per credit (minimum). General application contact: Emily Novak, Acting Director, Graduate Admissions, 410-617-2407.*

Graduate Programs
Rev. Harold Ridley, SJ, President

College of Arts and Sciences
Dr. John Hollwitz, Dean
Programs in:
    clinical psychology • CAS, MA, MS, Psy D
    counseling psychology • MA, MS
    curriculum and instruction • CAS, M Ed, MA
    educational management and supervision • CAS, M Ed, MA
    employee assistance and substance abuse • CAS
    engineering science • MES, MS
    foundations of education • CAS, M Ed, MA
    general psychology • CAS, MA
    guidance and counseling • CAS, M Ed, MA
    modern studies • MA
    pastoral counseling • CAS, MS, PhD
    reading • CAS, M Ed, MA
    special education • CAS, M Ed, MA
    speech pathology and audiology • CAS, MS
    spiritual and pastoral care • MA

Sellinger School of Business and Management
Dr. Peter Lorenzi, Dean
Programs in:
    decision sciences • MBA
    economics • MBA
    executive business administration • MBA, XMBA
    finance • MBA, MSF
    international business • MIB
    marketing/management • MBA

MORGAN STATE UNIVERSITY
Baltimore, MD 21251

http://www.morgan.edu/

Public coed university. *Enrollment: 5,909 graduate, professional, and undergraduate students. Graduate faculty: 70 full-time, 2 part-time. Computer facilities: Campuswide network is available with full Internet access. Total number of PCs/terminals supplied for student use: 100. Computer services are offered at no charge. Library facilities: Soper Library. Graduate expenses: Tuition of $160 per*

credit hour for state residents; $286 per credit hour for nonresidents. Fees of $326 per year. General application contact: James E. Waller, Admissions and Programs Officer, 410-319-3185.*

School of Graduate Studies
Dr. Richard F. Ochillo, Dean, Graduate Studies and
    Research

College of Arts and Sciences
Dr. Burney J. Hollis, Dean
Programs in:
    African-American studies • MA
    arts and sciences • PhD
    English • MA
    history • MA
    international studies • MA
    mathematics • MA
    music • MA
    sociology • MA, MS

Earl G. Graves School of Business and Management
Dr. Otis A. Thomas, Dean
Program in:
    business and management • MBA

Institute of Architecture and Planning
Melvin L. Mitchell Jr., Director
Programs in:
    architecture • M Arch, MS Arch
    city and regional planning • MCRP
    landscape architecture • MLA, MSLA

School of Education and Urban Studies
Dr. Patricia L. Morris, Dean
Programs in:
    educational administration and supervision • MS
    elementary and middle school education • MS
    teaching • MAT
    transportation • MS
    urban educational leadership • Ed D

School of Engineering
Dr. Eugene DeLoatch, Dean
Program in:
    engineering • D Eng, MS

MOUNT SAINT MARY'S COLLEGE AND SEMINARY
Emmitsburg, MD 21727-7799

http://www.msmary.edu/

Independent-religious coed comprehensive institution. *Enrollment: 1,798 graduate, professional, and undergraduate students. Graduate faculty: 12 full-time, 30 part-time. Computer facilities: Campuswide network is available with full Internet access. Total number of PCs/ terminals supplied for student use: 111. Computer service fees are included with tuition and fees. Library facilities: Phillips Library plus 1 additional on-campus library. Graduate expenses: Tuition of $250 per credit hour. Fees of $100 per year (minimum) full-time, $5 per*

credit hour part-time. General application contact: *Dr. Byron Stay, Associate Dean of the College, 301-447-5355.*

Graduate Program in Business
Dr. Raymond Speciale, Director
Program in:
    business • MBA

Graduate Program in Education
Dr. Marie Holahan, Director
Program in:
    education • M Ed

Graduate Seminary
Rev. Kevin Rhoades, Vice President/Rector
Program in:
    theology • M Div, MA

SALISBURY STATE UNIVERSITY
Salisbury, MD 21801-6837

http://www.ssu.edu/

Public coed comprehensive institution. *Enrollment: 6,022 graduate, professional, and undergraduate students. Graduate faculty: 62 full-time, 7 part-time.* Computer facilities: *Campuswide network is available with full Internet access. Total number of PCs/terminals supplied for student use: 202. Computer services are offered at no charge.* Library facilities: *Blackwell Library.* Graduate expenses: *Tuition of $158 per credit hour for state residents; $310 per credit hour for nonresidents. Fees of $4 per credit hour.* General application contact: *Jane H. Dané, Dean of Admissions, 410-543-6161.*

Graduate Division
Programs in:
    business administration • MBA
    composition • MA
    early childhood education • M Ed
    educational administration • M Ed
    elementary education • M Ed
    English • M Ed
    geography • M Ed
    history • M Ed
    literature • MA
    mathematics • M Ed
    media and technology • M Ed
    music • M Ed
    nursing • MS
    psychology • M Ed, MA
    reading education • M Ed
    science • M Ed
    secondary education • M Ed
    teaching English to speakers of other languages • MA

TOWSON UNIVERSITY
Towson, MD 21252-0001

http://www.towson.edu/

Public coed comprehensive institution. *Enrollment: 15,524 graduate, professional, and undergraduate students. Graduate faculty: 136 full-time, 19 part-time.* Computer facilities: *Campuswide network is available with full Internet access. Computer services are offered at no charge.* Library facilities: *Albert S. Cook Library.* Graduate expenses: *Tuition of $187 per credit hour for state residents; $364 per credit hour for nonresidents. Fees of $40 per credit hour.* General application contact: *Dr. Craig Weidemann, Dean of the Graduate School, 410-830-2078.*

Graduate School
Dr. Craig Weidemann, Dean
Programs in:
    accountancy • MS
    allied health professions • MS
    applied and industrial mathematics • MS
    art education • M Ed
    biology • MS
    clinical psychology • MA
    computer science • MS
    counseling psychology • MA
    Dalcroze • Certificate
    early childhood education • M Ed, Spec
    elementary education • M Ed, Spec
    experimental psychology • MA
    geography and environmental planning • MA
    human resource development • MS
    information systems project management • MS
    information technology • MS
    instructional technology • MS
    Kodály • Certificate
    liberal and professional studies • MA
    mass communication • MA
    music education • MS
    music performance • MM
    occupational therapy • MS
    operations management • MS
    Orff • Certificate
    professional writing • MS
    psychology • MA
    reading education • M Ed, Spec
    school psychology • CAS, MA
    secondary education • M Ed, Spec
    speech-language pathology and audiology • MS
    studio arts • MFA
    teaching • MAT
    theatre • MFA

UNIVERSITY OF BALTIMORE
Baltimore, MD 21201-5779

http://www.ubalt.edu/

Public coed upper-level institution. *Enrollment: 4,609 graduate, professional, and undergraduate students. Graduate faculty: 214 full-time, 161 part-time. Computer facilities: Campuswide network is available with full Internet access. Total number of PCs/terminals supplied for student use: 158. Computer services are offered at no charge. Library facilities: Langsdale Library plus 1 additional on-campus library. Graduate expenses: Tuition of $5592 per year full-time, $233 per credit part-time for state residents; $8544 per year full-time, $356 per credit part-time for nonresidents. Fees of $550 per year full-time, $208 per semester (minimum) part-time. General application contact: Tracey Jamison, Assistant Director of Admissions, 410-837-4809.*

Graduate School
Ronald Legon, Provost

College of Liberal Arts
Dr. Carl Stenberg, Dean
Programs in:
    applied psychology • MS
    counseling • MS
    criminal justice • MS
    government and public administration • MPA
    industrial and organizational psychology • MS
    legal and ethical studies • MA
    publications design • MA

School of Business
Dr. John Hatfield, Dean
Programs in:
    accounting • MS
    business administration • MBA
    business/management information systems • MS
    finance • MS
    taxation • MS

School of Law
John Sebert, Dean
Programs in:
    law • JD
    taxation • LL M

UNIVERSITY OF MARYLAND, BALTIMORE COUNTY
Baltimore, MD 21250-5398

http://www.umbc.edu/

Public coed university. *Computer facilities: Campuswide network is available with full Internet access. Total number of PCs/terminals supplied for student use: 400. Computer services are offered at no charge. Library facilities: Albin O. Kuhn Library. Graduate expenses: Tuition of $260 per credit hour for state residents; $468 per credit*

hour for nonresidents. Fees of $39 per credit hour. General application contact: Associate Dean, 410-455-3579.

Graduate School
Programs in:
    administration, planning, and policy • MS
    African-American studies • MA
    applied developmental psychology • PhD
    applied mathematics • MS, PhD
    applied molecular biology • MS
    applied physics • MS, PhD
    applied sociology • MA
    biochemistry • PhD
    biological sciences • MS, PhD
    chemical and biochemical engineering • MS, PhD
    chemistry • MS, PhD
    computer-integrated manufacturing and design • MS, PhD
    computer science • MS, PhD
    education • MA, MS
    electrical engineering • MS, PhD
    energy • MS, PhD
    engineering management • MS
    ethnomusicology • MA, PhD
    fluid mechanics • MS, PhD
    historical studies • MA
    imaging and digital arts • MFA
    instructional systems development • MA
    intercultural communications • MA
    marine-estuarine-environmental sciences • MS, PhD
    materials • MS, PhD
    medical sociology • MA
    molecular and cell biology • PhD
    neuroscience • MS, PhD
    operations analysis • MS, PhD
    optics • MS, PhD
    policy sciences • MPS, PhD
    preventive medicine and epidemiology • MS
    psychology • PhD
    solid mechanics • MS, PhD
    statistics • MS, PhD

UNIVERSITY OF MARYLAND, COLLEGE PARK
College Park, MD 20742-5045

http://www.umcp.umd.edu/

Public coed university. *Enrollment: 32,711 graduate, professional, and undergraduate students. Graduate faculty: 2,404 full-time, 665 part-time. Computer facilities: Campuswide network is available with full Internet access. Total number of PCs/terminals supplied for student use: 4,153. Computer services are offered at no charge. Library facilities: T. R. McKeldin Library plus 7 additional on-campus libraries. Graduate expenses: Tuition of $272 per credit hour for state residents; $400 per credit hour for nonresidents. Fees of $564 per year full-time, $342 per year part-time. General application*

contact: *John Mollish, Director, Graduate Admission and Records, 301-405-4198.*

Graduate School

Dr. Ilene Nagel, Associate Provost for Research and Dean of
the Graduate School
Program in:
textiles and consumer economics • MS, PhD

A. James Clark School of Engineering

Dr. William W. Destler Jr., Dean
Programs in:
aerospace engineering • M Eng, MS, PhD
chemical engineering • M Eng, MS, PhD
civil engineering • M Eng, MS, PhD
electrical engineering • M Eng, MS, PhD
electronic packaging and reliability • MS, PhD
fire protection engineering • M Eng, MS
manufacturing and design • MS, PhD
materials science and engineering • M Eng, MS, PhD
mechanical engineering • M Eng
mechanics and materials • MS, PhD
nuclear engineering • MS, PhD
reliability engineering • M Eng, MS, PhD
systems engineering • M Eng, MS
telecommunications • MS
thermal and fluid sciences • MS, PhD

College of Agriculture and Natural Resources

Dr. Thomas Fretz, Dean
Programs in:
agriculture economics • MS, PhD
agriculture education • AGSC, MS, PhD
agronomy • MS, PhD
animal sciences • MS, PhD
biological resources engineering • MS, PhD
environmental education • AGSC, MS, PhD
extension, adult, and continuing education • AGSC, MS,
PhD
food science • MS, PhD
horticulture • MS, PhD
human nutrition and food science • MS, PhD
nutrition • MS, PhD
poultry science • MS, PhD
resource economics • MS, PhD

College of Arts and Humanities

Dr. James Harris, Dean
Programs in:
American studies • MA, PhD
art • MFA
art history • MA, PhD
classics • MA
comparative literature • MA, PhD
creative writing • MFA
English • MA, PhD
French language and literature • MA, PhD
Germanic language and literature • MA, PhD
history • MA, PhD
linguistics • MA, PhD
music • DMA, Ed D, M Ed, M Mus, MM, PhD
philosophy • MA, PhD
public communication • PhD

Russian language and literature • MA
Spanish • MA, PhD
speech communication • MA, PhD
theatre • MA, MFA, PhD

College of Behavioral and Social Sciences

Dr. Irwin L. Goldstein, Dean
Programs in:
American politics • MA, PhD
applied anthropology • MAA
audiology • MA, PhD
behavioral and social sciences • MCP
clinical psychology • PhD
comparative politics • MA, PhD
criminal justice and criminology • MA, PhD
developmental psychology • PhD
economics • MA, PhD
experimental psychology • PhD
geography • MA, PhD
industrial psychology • MA, MS, PhD
international relations • MA, PhD
language pathology • MA, PhD
neurosciences and cognitive sciences • PhD
political economy • MA, PhD
political theory • MA, PhD
social psychology • PhD
sociology • MA, PhD
speech • MA, PhD
survey methodology • MS

College of Computer, Mathematical and Physical Sciences

Dr. Richard Herman, Dean
Programs in:
applied mathematics • MA, PhD
astronomy • MS, PhD
chemical physics • MS, PhD
computer science • MS, PhD
geology • MS, PhD
mathematical statistics • MA, PhD
mathematics • MA, PhD
meteorology • MS, PhD
physics • MS, PhD
software engineering • MSWE

College of Education

Dr. Willis Hawley, Dean
Programs in:
business education • CAGS, Ed D, M Ed, MA, PhD
college student personnel • M Ed, MA
college student personnel administration • PhD
community/career counseling • M Ed, MA
community counseling • CAGS
counseling and personnel services • M Ed, MA, PhD
counseling psychology • PhD
counselor education • PhD
curriculum and educational communications • Ed D,
M Ed, MA, PhD
early childhood/elementary education • CAGS, Ed D,
M Ed, MA, PhD
human development • CAGS, Ed D, M Ed, MA, PhD
industrial, technological, and occupational education •
CAGS, Ed D, M Ed, MA, PhD
measurement • MA, PhD
program evaluation • MA, PhD

University of Maryland, College Park (continued)
  reading • CAGS, M Ed, MA, PhD
  rehabilitation counseling • M Ed, MA
  school counseling • M Ed, MA
  school psychology • M Ed, MA, PhD
  secondary education • CAGS, Ed D, M Ed, MA, PhD
  social foundations of education • CAGS, Ed D, M Ed, MA, PhD
  special education • CAGS, Ed D, M Ed, MA, PhD
  statistics • MA, PhD
  teaching English to speakers of other languages • M Ed

College of Health and Human Performance
Dr. John Burt, Dean
Programs in:
  community development • MS
  consumer studies • MS
  family studies • MS
  health education • Ed D, MA, PhD
  kinesiology • MA, PhD
  recreation • Ed D, MA, PhD

College of Journalism
Dr. Reese Cleghorn, Dean
Programs in:
  advertising • MA, PhD
  broadcast journalism • MA, PhD
  international communication • MA, PhD
  journalism education • MA, PhD
  mass communication research • MA, PhD
  political communication • MA, PhD
  public affairs reporting • MA, PhD
  public communication • MA, PhD
  public relations • MA, PhD
  science communication • MA, PhD

College of Library and Information Services
Dr. Ann E. Prentice, Dean
Program in:
  library and information services • MA, MLS, MS, PhD

College of Life Sciences
Dr. Paul H. Mazzocchi, Dean
Programs in:
  analytical chemistry • MS, PhD
  biochemistry • MS, PhD
  entomology • MS, PhD
  inorganic chemistry • MS, PhD
  microbiology • MS, PhD
  molecular and cell biology • PhD
  organic chemistry • MS, PhD
  physical chemistry • MS, PhD
  plant biology • MS, PhD
  sustainable development and conservation biology • MS
  toxicology • MS, PhD
  zoology • MS, PhD

Robert H. Smith School of Business
Dr. Howard Frank, Dean
Program in:
  business • DBA, MBA, MS, PhD

School of Architecture
Steven Hurtt, Dean
Programs in:
  architecture • M Arch, MA
  community planning • MCP

School of Public Affairs
Dr. Susan C. Schwab, Dean
Programs in:
  policy studies • PhD
  public management • MPM
  public policy • MPP, PhD

 # UNIVERSITY OF MARYLAND EASTERN SHORE
Princess Anne, MD 21853-1299
http://www.umes.umd.edu/dept/acaddept.html

Public coed university. *Enrollment:* 3,209 graduate, professional, and undergraduate students. Graduate faculty: *59 full-time, 45 part-time.* Computer facilities: *Campuswide network is available with full Internet access. Total number of PCs/terminals supplied for student use: 60. Computer service fees are included with tuition and fees.* Library facilities: *Frederick Douglass Library.* Graduate expenses: *Tuition of $143 per credit hour for state residents; $253 per credit hour for nonresidents. Fees of $50 per year.* General application contact: *Dr. C. Dennis Ignasias, Dean of Graduate Studies, 410-651-6080.*

Graduate Programs
Dr. C. Dennis Ignasias, Dean of Graduate Studies
Programs in:
  agriculture education and extension • MS
  applied computer science • MS
  food and agricultural sciences • MS
  guidance and counseling • M Ed
  marine-estuarine-environmental sciences • MS, PhD
  physical therapy • MPT
  special education • M Ed
  teaching • MAT
  toxicology • MS, PhD

UNIVERSITY OF MARYLAND UNIVERSITY COLLEGE
College Park, MD 20742-1600
http://www.umuc.edu/

Public coed comprehensive institution. *Enrollment:* 13,786 graduate, professional, and undergraduate students. Graduate faculty: *0 full-time, 121 part-time.* Graduate expenses: *$277 per semester hour for state residents; $367 per semester hour for nonresidents.* General application contact: *Director of Graduate Admissions, 301-985-7155.*

Graduate School of Management and Technology

Nicholas H. Allen, Dean
Programs in:
    computer systems management • MS
    engineering management • MS
    environmental management • MS
    general administration • Exec MGA, MGA
    international management • Exec MIM, MIM
    management and technology • Senior Exec MGA
    software engineering • M Sw E
    technology management • Exec MS, MS
    telecommunications management • MS

MASSACHUSETTS

AMERICAN INTERNATIONAL COLLEGE

Springfield, MA 01109-3189

http://www.aic.edu/

Independent coed comprehensive institution. *Enrollment:* 1,825 graduate, professional, and undergraduate students. Graduate faculty: *18 full-time.* Library facilities: *James J. Shea Memorial Library.* Graduate expenses: *Tuition of $363 per credit hour. Fees of $25 per semester.* General application contact: *Dr. Elizabeth A. Ayres, Dean, 413-747-6525.*

School of Continuing Education and Graduate Studies

Dr. Elizabeth A. Ayres, Dean
Programs in:
    organization development • MSOD
    physical therapy • MPT
    public administration • MPA

School of Business Administration

Dr. Adam Zielinski, Dean
Program in:
    business administration • MBA

School of Psychology and Education

C. Gerald Weaver, Dean
Programs in:
    administration • CAGS, M Ed
    clinical psychology • MS
    criminal justice studies • MS
    educational psychology • Ed D, MA
    elementary education • CAGS, M Ed
    English • MAT
    history • MAT
    human resource development • CAGS, MA
    mathematics • MAT
    reading • CAGS, M Ed
    school psychology • CAGS, MA
    secondary education • CAGS, M Ed
    special education • CAGS, M Ed
    teaching • MA

ANNA MARIA COLLEGE

Paxton, MA 01612

Independent-religious coed comprehensive institution. *Enrollment:* 800 matriculated graduate/professional students. Graduate faculty: *96.* Library facilities: *Mondor-Eagen Library.* Graduate expenses: *$730 per course.* General application contact: *Dr. Cynthia Patterson, Dean, 508-849-3335.*

Graduate Division

Dr. Cynthia Patterson, Dean
Programs in:
    biological studies • MA
    business administration • MBA
    counseling psychology • CAGS, MA
    criminal justice • MA
    education • M Ed
    occupational and environmental health and safety • MS
    psychology • CAGS, MA

 # ASSUMPTION COLLEGE

Worcester, MA 01615-0005

http://www.assumption.edu/

Independent-religious coed comprehensive institution. Library facilities: *Emmanuel D'Alzon Library.* Graduate expenses: *Tuition of $297 per credit hour. Fees of $10 per semester.* General application contact: *Dean of Graduate Studies and Continuing Education, 508-767-7426.*

Graduate School

Programs in:
    business studies • CPS, MBA
    counseling psychology • CAGS, MA
    education • MA
    pastoral counseling • MA
    rehabilitation counseling • CAGS, MA
    religious education • MA
    special education • MA
    theology • CAGS, CAPS, MA
    theology/youth ministry • MA

 # BOSTON COLLEGE

Chestnut Hill, MA 02167-9991

http://infoeagle.bc.edu/

Independent-religious coed university. *Enrollment:* 14,830 graduate, professional, and undergraduate students. Graduate faculty: *591.* Library facilities: *O'Neill Library plus 5 additional on-campus libraries.* Graduate expenses: *Tuition of $626 per semester hour. Fees of $80 per year (minimum) full-time, $30 per semester part-*

Boston College (continued)
time. General application contact: *Emily Mills, Director of Graduate Admissions and Financial Aid, 617-552-3265.*

Graduate School of Arts and Sciences

Michael A. Smyer, Dean
Programs in:
  analytical chemistry • MS, PhD
  biochemistry • MS, PhD
  biology • MS, PhD
  chemistry • MS
  classics • MA
  economics • MA, PhD
  English • CAGS, MA, PhD
  European national studies • MA
  French • MA, PhD
  geology and geophysics • MS
  Greek • MA
  Hispanic ministry • MA
  history • MA, PhD
  inorganic chemistry • MS, PhD
  Italian • MA
  Latin • MA
  leadership/church management • MA
  linguistics • MA
  liturgy • MA
  mathematics • MA
  medieval language • PhD
  medieval studies • MA
  organic chemistry • MS, PhD
  pastoral counseling • MA
  pastoral ministry • MA
  philosophy • MA, PhD
  physical chemistry • MS, PhD
  physics • MS, PhD
  political science • MA, PhD
  psychology • PhD
  religious education • MA, PhD
  Russian and Slavic languages and literature • MA
  Slavic studies • MA
  social justice/social ministry • MA
  sociology • MA, PhD
  Spanish • MA, PhD
  spirituality • MA
  theology • MA, PhD

Graduate School of Education

Dr. Mary Brabeck, Dean
Programs in:
  biology • MST
  Catholic school leadership • CAES, M Ed
  chemistry • MST
  counseling psychology • MA, PhD
  curriculum and instruction • CAES, M Ed, PhD
  developmental and educational psychology • MA, PhD
  early childhood education/teacher option • M Ed
  early childhood/specialist option • MA
  educational administration • CAES, M Ed, PhD
  educational research, measurement, and evaluation •
    CAES, M Ed, PhD
  elementary teaching • M Ed
  English • MAT

  geology • MST
  higher education administration • MA, PhD
  history • MAT
  Latin and classics • MAT
  mathematics • MST
  moderate special needs • CAES, M Ed
  multihandicapped and deaf/blind • M Ed
  physics • MST
  professional school administrator • PhD
  reading specialist • CAES, M Ed
  religious education • M Ed
  Romance languages • MAT
  secondary teaching • M Ed
  severe special needs • M Ed
  special education and rehabilitation • PhD
  visually handicapped studies • M Ed

Graduate School of Social Work

Dr. June Gary Hopps, Dean
Program in:
  social work • MSW, PhD

Law School

Aviam Soifer, Dean
Program in:
  law • JD

School of Nursing

Dr. Barbara Munro, Dean
Programs in:
  adult health nursing • MS
  community health nursing • MS
  family health • MS
  gerontology • MS
  maternal/child health nursing • MS
  nursing • PhD
  pediatric and women's health • MS
  psychiatric-mental health nursing • MS

Wallace E. Carroll Graduate School of Management

Dr. Hassell McClellan, Associate Dean
Programs in:
  accounting • MBA
  business law • MBA
  computer science • MBA
  finance • MBA, MSF, PhD
  marketing • MBA
  operations and strategic management • MBA
  organization studies/human resources management •
    MBA, PhD

BOSTON UNIVERSITY
Boston, MA 02215

http://web.bu.edu/

Independent coed university. *Enrollment:* 29,857 graduate, professional, and undergraduate students. Library facilities: *Mugar Memorial Library plus 17 additional on-campus libraries.* Graduate expenses: *Tuition of $22,830 per year full-time, $713 per credit part-time. Fees of $218 per year full-time, $40 per semester part-time.* General application contact: *contact individual schools.*

College of Communication
Brent Baker, Dean
Programs in:
    broadcast journalism • MS
    business and economics reporting • MS
    film production • MS
    film studies • MS
    mass communication • MS
    print journalism • MS
    public relations • MS
    science journalism • MS
    screenwriting • MS
    television • MS
    television management • MS

College of Engineering
Dr. Charles DeLisi, Dean
Programs in:
    aerospace engineering • MS, PhD
    biomedical engineering • MS, PhD
    computer engineering • PhD
    computer systems engineering • MS
    electrical engineering • MS, PhD
    general engineering • MS
    manufacturing engineering • MS, PhD
    mechanical engineering • MS, PhD
    systems engineering • PhD

Graduate School of Arts and Sciences
J. Scott Whittaker, Associate Dean
Programs in:
    African American studies • MA
    African studies • Certificate
    American and New England studies • MA, PhD
    anthropology • MA, PhD
    applied linguistics • MA, PhD
    archaeology • MA, PhD
    art history • MA, PhD
    astronomy • MA, PhD
    biochemistry • MA, PhD
    biostatistics • MA, PhD
    botany • MA, PhD
    brain behavior and cognition • PhD
    cell and molecular biology • MA, PhD
    cell biology • MA, PhD
    cellular biophysics • PhD
    chemical physics • MA, PhD
    classical studies • MA, PhD

clinical psychology • PhD
cognitive and neural systems • MA, PhD
composition • MA
computer science • MA, PhD
creative writing • MA
earth sciences • MA, PhD
ecology • PhD
ecology, behavior, and evolution • MA, PhD
ecology/physiology, endocrinology and reproduction • MA
economics • MA, PhD
energy and environmental analysis • MA
English • MA, PhD
environmental remote sensing and geographic information systems • MA
French • MA, PhD
geography • MA, PhD
history • MA, PhD
human development • PhD
inorganic chemistry • MA, PhD
international relations • MA
international relations and communication • MA
international relations and resource and environmental management • MA
marine biology • MA, PhD
mathematics • MA, PhD
molecular biology, cell biology and biochemistry • MA, PhD
museum studies • Certificate
music • MA, PhD
music education • MA
music history theory • PhD
neurobiology, neuroendocrinology and reproduction • MA, PhD
organic chemistry • MA, PhD
philosophy • MA, PhD
photochemistry • MA, PhD
physical chemistry • MA, PhD
physics • MA, PhD
physiology, endocrinology, and neurobiology • MA, PhD
political science • MA, PhD
preservation studies • MA
psychology • MA
religious studies • MA, PhD
resource science • MA
social work and sociology • PhD
sociology • MA, PhD
Spanish • MA, PhD
statistics • MA, PhD
theoretical chemistry • MA, PhD
zoology • MA, PhD

Henry M. Goldman School of Dental Medicine
Dr. Spencer Frankl, Dean
Programs in:
    advanced general dentistry • CAGS
    dental public health • CAGS, D Sc D, MS, MSD
    dentistry • DMD
    endodontics • CAGS, D Sc D, MSD
    nutritional science • D Sc, D Sc D, MS
    operative dentistry • CAGS, D Sc D, MSD
    oral and maxillofacial surgery • CAGS, D Sc D, MSD

Boston University (continued)
    oral biology • D Sc, D Sc D, MSD
    orthodontics • CAGS, D Sc D, MSD
    pediatric dentistry • CAGS, D Sc D, MSD
    periodontology • CAGS, D Sc D, MSD
    prosthodontics • CAGS, D Sc D, MSD

Metropolitan College

Romualdas Skvarcius, Dean
Programs in:
    actuarial science • MS
    arts administration • MS
    city planning • MCP
    computer information systems • MS
    computer science • MS
    criminal justice • MCJ
    financial economics • MSAS
    innovation and technology • MSAS
    liberal arts • MLA
    multinational commerce • MSAS
    organizational policy • MSAS
    telecommunications • MS
    urban affairs • MUA

Sargent College of Health and Rehabilitation Sciences

Dr. Alan M. Jette, Dean
Programs in:
    applied anatomy and physiology • D Sc, MS
    applied kinesiology • D Sc
    audiology • D Sc
    nutrition • MS
    occupational therapy • CAGS, D Sc, MS, MSOT
    physical therapy • MS, MSPT
    rehabilitation counseling • CAGS, D Sc, MS
    speech-language pathology • CAGS, D Sc, MS

School for the Arts

Bruce MacCombie, Dean
Programs in:
    art education • MFA
    collaborative piano • Mus AD, Mus M
    composition • Mus AD, Mus M
    conducting • Diploma, Mus M
    costume design • MFA
    costume production • MFA
    directing • MFA
    graphic design • MFA
    historical performance • Diploma, Mus AD, Mus M
    lighting design • MFA
    music education • Mus AD, Mus M
    music history and literature • Mus M
    music theory • Mus M
    opera performance • Certificate
    painting • MFA
    performance • Diploma, Mus AD, Mus M
    scene design • MFA
    sculpture • MFA
    studio teaching • MFA
    technical production • Certificate, MFA
    theatre crafts • Certificate
    theatre education • MFA

School of Education

Dr. Edwin J. Delattre, Dean
Programs in:
    adult and continuing education • CAGS, Ed D, Ed M
    alternative community settings • CAGS, Ed D
    bilingual education • CAGS, Ed D, Ed M
    counseling • CAGS, Ed M
    counseling psychology • Ed D
    curriculum and teaching • Ed D
    early childhood education • CAGS, Ed D, Ed M
    educational media and technology • CAGS, Ed D, Ed M
    education of the deaf • CAGS, Ed M
    elementary education • Ed M
    English and language arts • CAGS, Ed D, Ed M
    English education • MAT
    health education • CAGS, Ed M
    higher education administration • Ed M
    human development and education • CAGS, Ed D, Ed M
    human movement • CAGS, Ed D, Ed M
    human resource education • CAGS, Ed D, Ed M
    international educational development • Ed M
    Latin and classical studies • MAT
    learning and behavioral disabilities • CAGS, Ed D
    leisure education • CAGS, Ed M
    literacy, language, and cultural studies • CAGS, Ed D, Ed M
    mathematics education • CAGS, Ed D, Ed M, MAT
    modern foreign language education • MAT
    policy, planning, and administration • CAGS, Ed D, Ed M
    reading • CAGS, Ed D, Ed M
    science education • CAGS, Ed D, Ed M, MAT
    severe disabilities • CAGS, Ed D
    social studies education • CAGS, Ed D, Ed M, MAT
    special education • CAGS, Ed D, Ed M
    teaching of English to speakers of other languages • CAGS, Ed M
    therapeutic recreation • CAGS, Ed D
    young children with special needs • CAGS, Ed D

School of Law

Ronald A. Cass, Dean
Programs in:
    American banking law • LL M
    international banking law • LL M
    law • JD
    taxation • LL M

School of Management

Therese M. Hofmann, Assistant Dean
Programs in:
    accounting • DBA
    business administration • Exec MBA
    finance • DBA
    general management • MBA
    health-care management • MBA
    management information systems • DBA, MSMIS
    management policy • DBA
    marketing • DBA
    nonprofit management • MBA
    operations management • DBA
    organizational behavior • DBA
    public management • MBA

School of Medicine
Dr. Aram V. Chobanian, Dean
Program in:
  medicine • MD

Division of Graduate Medical Sciences
Dr. Carl Franzblau, Chairman
Programs in:
  anatomy and neurobiology • MA, PhD
  behavioral neurosciences • PhD
  biochemistry • MA, PhD
  biophysics • MA, PhD
  cell and molecular biology • MA, PhD
  cellular, structural, and molecular biology • MA, PhD
  experimental pathology • PhD
  immunology • PhD
  medical sciences • MA
  microbiology • MA, PhD
  pharmacology and experimental therapeutics • MA, PhD
  physiology • MA, PhD

School of Public Health
Robert F. Meenan, Director
Programs in:
  biostatistics • MA, MPH, PhD
  environmental health • D Sc, MPH
  epidemiology • D Sc, M Sc, MPH
  health behavior, health promotion, and disease
    prevention • MPH
  health law • MPH
  health services • MPH
  international health • Certificate, MPH
  maternal and child health • MPH
  nurse midwifery education • Certificate

School of Social Work
Wilma Peebles-Wilkins, Dean
Programs in:
  clinical practice with groups • MSW
  clinical practice with individuals and families • MSW
  macro social work practice • MSW
  social work and sociology • PhD

School of Theology
Dr. Robert Neville, Dean
Program in:
  theology • D Min, M Div, MSM, MTS, STM, Th D

University Professors Program
Claudio Véliz, Director
Program in:
  self-designed • MA, PhD

 BRANDEIS UNIVERSITY
Waltham, MA 02454-2728

http://www.brandeis.edu/

Independent coed university. *Enrollment:* 4,008 graduate, professional, and undergraduate students. Graduate faculty: *360 full-time, 181 part-time.* Computer facilities: *Campuswide network is available with full Internet access. Total number of PCs/terminals* supplied for student use: 125. Computer services are offered at no charge. Library facilities: *Goldfarb/Farber Libraries plus 3 additional on-campus libraries.* Graduate expenses: *Tuition of $23,360 per year full-time, $2960 per course part-time. Fees of $45 per year.* General application contact: *Margaret Haley, Assistant Dean, Graduate Admissions, 781-736-3410.*

Graduate School of Arts and Sciences
Carolyn F. Locke, Associate Dean of Arts and Sciences for
  Graduate Education
Programs in:
  American history • MA, PhD
  anthropology • MA, PhD
  anthropology and women's studies • MA
  biochemistry • MS, PhD
  bioorganic chemistry • PhD
  biophysics • PhD
  cell biology • PhD
  comparative history • MA, PhD
  composition and theory • MA, MFA, PhD
  developmental biology • PhD
  English and American literature • MA, PhD
  English and women's studies • MA
  general psychology • MA
  genetic counseling • MS
  genetics • PhD
  inorganic chemistry • MS, PhD
  Jewish communal service • MA
  literary studies • MA, PhD
  mathematics • PhD
  microbiology • PhD
  molecular biology • PhD
  music and women's studies • MA, MFA
  musicology • MA, MFA, PhD
  Near Eastern and Judaic studies • MA, PhD
  Near Eastern and Judaic studies and women's studies •
    MA
  neurobiology • PhD
  neuroscience • MS, PhD
  organic chemistry • MS, PhD
  perception/cognition • PhD
  physical chemistry • MS, PhD
  physics • MS, PhD
  politics • MA, PhD
  postbaccalaureate premedical • Certificate
  social/developmental psychology • PhD
  sociology • MA, PhD
  sociology and women's studies • MA
  studio art • Certificate
  theater arts • MFA

Michtom School of Computer Science
Dr. James Pustejovsky, Director of Graduate Studies
Program in:
  computer science • MA, PhD

Graduate School of International Economics and Finance
Dr. Peter Petri, Dean
Programs in:
  finance • MSF
  international business • MBAi
  international economics and finance • MA, PhD

Brandeis University (continued)
The Heller Graduate School
Dr. Jack Shonkoff, Dean
Programs in:
    child, youth, and family services • MBA, MM
    health care administration • MBA, MM
    human services • MBA, MM
    social policy • PhD
    sustainable international development • MA

BRIDGEWATER STATE COLLEGE
Bridgewater, MA 02325-0001

http://www.bridgew.edu/

Public coed comprehensive institution. *Enrollment:* 8,926 graduate, professional, and undergraduate students. Graduate faculty: *140 full-time.* Library facilities: *Maxwell Library.* Graduate expenses: *Tuition of $1675 per year full-time, $70 per credit part-time for state residents; $6450 per year full-time, $269 per credit part-time for nonresidents. Fees of $1588 per year full-time, $66 per credit hour part-time for state residents; $1588 per year full-time, $66 per credit part-time for nonresidents. General application contact: Marilyn W. Barry, Dean, Graduate School, 508-697-1300.*

Graduate School
Marilyn W. Barry, Dean

School of Arts and Sciences
Dr. Howard London, Dean
Programs in:
    art • MAT
    biological sciences • MAT, MS
    chemical sciences • MAT, MS
    computer science • MS
    earth sciences • MAT
    English • MA, MAT
    geography • MAT
    history • MA, MAT
    mathematics • MAT
    physical sciences • MAT
    physics • MAT
    political science • MPA
    psychology • MA
    speech communication • MA, MAT

School of Education
Dr. Mary Lou Thornburg, Acting Dean
Programs in:
    counseling • M Ed
    early childhood education • M Ed
    elementary education • M Ed
    health promotion • M Ed
    library media • M Ed
    physical education • MS
    reading • M Ed
    school administration • CAGS, M Ed
    secondary education • MAT
    special education • M Ed

CLARK UNIVERSITY
Worcester, MA 01610-1477

http://www.clarku.edu/

Independent coed university. *Enrollment:* 3,083 graduate, professional, and undergraduate students. Graduate faculty: *161 full-time.* Computer facilities: *Campuswide network is available with full Internet access. Computer service fees are included with tuition and fees.* Library facilities: *Goddard Library.* Graduate expenses: *$21,300 per year full-time, $2663 per course part-time. General application contact: David P. Angel, Dean of Graduate Studies and Research, 508-793-7676.*

Graduate School
David P. Angel, Dean of Graduate Studies and Research
Programs in:
    biochemistry/molecular biology • MA, PhD
    biology • MA, PhD
    chemistry • MA, PhD
    clinical psychology • PhD
    cognition and experimental neuroscience • PhD
    developmental psychology • PhD
    economics • PhD
    education • MA Ed
    English • MA
    environmental science and policy • MA
    geography • PhD
    history • CAGS, MA, PhD
    holocaust history • PhD
    international development • MA
    physics • MA, PhD
    women's studies • PhD

College of Professional and Continuing Education
Dr. Thomas Massey, Director
Programs in:
    gerontology • CAGS, Certificate
    liberal studies • MALA
    professional communications • MSPC
    public administration • Certificate, MPA

Graduate School of Management
Dr. Maurry Tamarkin, Interim Dean
Programs in:
    business administration • MBA
    finance • MSF
    health administration • MHA

CURRY COLLEGE
Milton, MA 02186-9984

http://www.curry.edu:8080/

Independent coed comprehensive institution. *Enrollment:* 1,433 graduate, professional, and undergraduate students. Graduate faculty: *10.* Computer facilities: *Campuswide network is available with full Internet access. Computer service fees are included with tuition and fees.* Library facilities: *Louis R. Levin Memorial Library.*

Graduate expenses: *$325 per credit.* General application contact: *Dr. Jane Utley Adelizzi, Director, 617-333-2130.*

Graduate Program in Education

Dr. Jane Utley Adelizzi, Director
Programs in:
    adult education • Certificate, M Ed
    educational studies in and out of the classroom
        environment • M Ed
    learning disabilities across the lifespan • Certificate
    post-secondary learning disabilities • M Ed
    reading • Certificate, M Ed

EASTERN NAZARENE COLLEGE
Quincy, MA 02170-2999

http://www.enc.edu/

Independent-religious coed comprehensive institution. *Enrollment:* 1,508 graduate, professional, and undergraduate students. *Graduate faculty: 19 full-time, 15 part-time.* Computer facilities: *Campuswide network is available with full Internet access. Total number of PCs/ terminals supplied for student use: 70. Computer service fees are applied as a separate charge.* Library facilities: *Nease Library.* Graduate expenses: *Tuition of $350 per credit. Fees of $125 per semester full-time, $15 per semester part-time.* General application contact: *Cleo P. Cakridas, Graduate Enrollment Counselor, 617-745-3870.*

Graduate Studies

Patricia Shopland, Director of Graduate Studies
Programs in:
    bilingual education • Certificate, M Ed
    early childhood education • Certificate, M Ed
    elementary education • Certificate, M Ed
    English as a second language • Certificate, M Ed
    family counseling • MA
    instructional enrichment and development • Certificate,
        M Ed
    middle school education • Certificate, M Ed
    moderate special needs education • Certificate, M Ed
    music education • Certificate, M Ed
    physical education • Certificate, M Ed
    principal • Certificate
    program development and supervision • Certificate,
        M Ed
    secondary education • Certificate, M Ed
    special education administrator • Certificate
    supervisor • Certificate
    teacher of reading • Certificate, M Ed

 # EMERSON COLLEGE
Boston, MA 02116-1511

http://www.emerson.edu/

Independent coed comprehensive institution. *Enrollment: 3,885 graduate, professional, and undergraduate students.* Graduate faculty: *102 full-time, 41 part-time.* Computer facilities: *Campuswide network is available with full Internet access. Total number of PCs/ terminals supplied for student use: 160. Computer services are offered at no charge.* Library facilities: *main library.* Graduate expenses: *Tuition of $566 per credit. Fees of $30 per semester (minimum).* General application contact: *Lynn Terrell, Director of Graduate Admission, 617-824-8610.*

Graduate Studies

Dr. Marlene Fine, Dean

School of Communication, Management, and Public Policy
Dr. Stuart J. Sigman, Dean
Programs in:
    broadcast journalism • MA
    communications industries management • MA
    global marketing communication and advertising • MA
    health communication • MA
    management communication • MA
    political communication • MA
    print/multimedia journalism • MA
    speech communication studies • MA

School of Communication Sciences and Disorders
Dr. Dorothy Aram, Dean
Program in:
    speech-language pathology • MS, PhD

School of the Arts
Grafton J. Nunes, Dean
Programs in:
    creative writing • MFA
    new media production • MA
    radio/audio production • MA
    television/video production • MA
    theatre education • MA
    writing and publishing • MA

EMMANUEL COLLEGE
Boston, MA 02115

http://www.emmanuel.edu/

Independent-religious primarily female comprehensive institution. *Enrollment: 2,000 graduate, professional, and undergraduate students.* Graduate faculty: *11 full-time, 41 part-time.* Library facilities: *Cardinal Cushing Library.* General application contact: *Center for Adult Studies, 617-735-9918.*

Emmanuel College (continued)
Graduate Programs
Programs in:
    education • MAT
    education technology • M Ed
    human resource management • MA
    management • MSM
    ministry • Certificate

FITCHBURG STATE COLLEGE
Fitchburg, MA 01420-2697

http://www.fsc.edu/

Public coed comprehensive institution. *Enrollment: 3,644 graduate, professional, and undergraduate students. Graduate faculty: 0 full-time, 162 part-time. Computer facilities: Campuswide network is available with partial Internet access (e-mail only). Total number of PCs/terminals supplied for student use: 500. Computer service fees are included with tuition and fees. Library facilities: Hammond Library. Graduate expenses: Tuition of $147 per credit. Fees of $55 per semester. General application contact: Dr. Michele M. Zide, Associate Vice President, Academic Affairs and Dean of Graduate and Continuing Education, 978-665-3181.*

Division of Graduate and Continuing Education
Dr. Michele M. Zide, Associate Vice President, Academic
    Affairs and Dean
Programs in:
    adolescent and family therapy • Certificate
    arts in education • M Ed
    business administration • MBA
    child protective services • Certificate
    communications/media management • MS
    computer science • MS
    consultation and peer leadership • CAGS
    criminal justice • MS
    early childhood education • M Ed
    educational leadership and management • CAGS, M Ed
    elementary education • M Ed
    elementary school guidance counseling • MS
    forensic case work • Certificate
    forensic nursing • MS
    guided study • M Ed
    interdisciplinary studies • CAGS
    mental health counseling • MS
    middle school education • M Ed
    occupational education • M Ed
    professional staff development • CAGS
    school guidance counselor • Certificate
    science education • M Ed
    secondary education • M Ed
    secondary school guidance counseling • MS
    teaching biology • MA, MAT
    teaching earth science • MAT
    teaching English • MA, MAT
    teaching history • MA, MAT
    teaching mathematics • MAT
    teaching students with intensive special needs • M Ed
    teaching students with special needs • M Ed
    technology education • M Ed

FRAMINGHAM STATE COLLEGE
Framingham, MA 01701-9101

http://www.framingham.edu/

Public coed comprehensive institution. *Enrollment: 3,000 graduate, professional, and undergraduate students. Graduate faculty: 24 full-time, 32 part-time. Library facilities: Henry Whittemore Library. Graduate expenses: $4184 per year full-time, $523 per course part-time for state residents; $4848 per year full-time, $606 per course part-time for nonresidents. General application contact: Dr. Arnold Good, Associate Dean, 508-626-4562.*

Graduate Programs
Dr. Arnold Good, Associate Dean
Programs in:
    business administration • MA
    counseling • MA
    educational leadership • MA
    English • M Ed
    family and consumer sciences education • M Ed
    food science and nutrition science • MS
    health care administration • MA
    history • M Ed
    human resources administration • MA
    literacy and language • M Ed
    mathematics • M Ed
    museum administration • MA
    nutrition education • M Ed
    public administration • MA
    special education • M Ed

HARVARD UNIVERSITY
Cambridge, MA 02138

http://www.harvard.edu/

Independent coed university. *Enrollment: 18,597 graduate, professional, and undergraduate students. Graduate faculty: 2,170. Computer facilities: Campuswide network is available with full Internet access. Computer services are offered at no charge. Library facilities: Widener Library plus 90 additional on-campus libraries. Graduate expenses: Tuition of $21,342 per year. Fees of $686 per year. General application contact: Admissions Office of the appropriate school.*

Divinity School
Dr. Ronald Thiemann, Dean
Program in:
    theology • M Div, MTS, PhD, Th D, Th M

Extension School
Michael Shinagel, Dean
Programs in:
- applied sciences • CAS
- English for graduate and professional studies • DGP
- liberal arts • ALM
- museum studies • CMS
- premedical studies • Diploma
- publication and communication • CPC
- public health • CPH
- special studies in administration and management • CSS

Graduate School of Arts and Sciences
Dr. Christoph Wolff, Dean
Programs in:
- African history • PhD
- Akkadian and Sumerian • AM, PhD
- American history • PhD
- American politics • AM, PhD
- ancient art • PhD
- ancient, medieval, early modern, and modern Europe • PhD
- ancient Near Eastern art • PhD
- anthropology and Middle Eastern studies • PhD
- applied physics • PhD
- Arabic • AM, PhD
- archaeology • PhD
- architecture • PhD
- Armenian • AM, PhD
- astronomy • AM, PhD
- astrophysics • AM, PhD
- baroque art • PhD
- behavior and decision analysis • AM, PhD
- biblical history • AM, PhD
- biochemical chemistry • AM, PhD
- biological anthropology • PhD
- biological sciences in public health • PhD
- biology • PhD
- biophysics • PhD
- business economics • AM, PhD
- Byzantine art • PhD
- Byzantine Greek • PhD
- cell biology • PhD
- Celtic languages and literatures • AM, PhD
- Central Europe • PhD
- chemical physics • PhD
- chemistry • AM
- Chinese • AM, PhD
- Chinese studies • AM
- classical archaeology • AM, PhD
- classical art • PhD
- classical philology • AM, PhD
- classical philosophy • PhD
- cognition • AM, PhD
- comparative literature • PhD
- comparative politics • AM, PhD
- composition • AM, PhD
- critical theory • AM, PhD
- descriptive linguistics • AM, PhD
- developmental psychology • AM, PhD
- diplomatic history • PhD
- earth and planetary sciences • AM, PhD
- East Asian history • PhD
- economic and social history • PhD
- economics • AM, PhD
- economics and Middle Eastern studies • PhD
- eighteenth-century literature • AM, PhD
- engineering sciences • PhD
- experimental pathology • PhD
- experimental physics • AM, PhD
- experimental psychology • AM, PhD
- fine arts and Middle Eastern studies • PhD
- forest science • MFS
- French • AM, PhD
- genetics • PhD
- German • AM, PhD
- health policy • PhD
- Hebrew • AM, PhD
- historical linguistics • AM, PhD
- history and East Asian languages • PhD
- history and Middle Eastern studies • PhD
- history of American civilization • PhD
- history of science • AM, PhD
- immunology • PhD
- Indian art • PhD
- Indian philosophy • AM, PhD
- Indo-Muslim culture • AM, PhD
- Inner Asian and Altaic studies • PhD
- inorganic chemistry • AM, PhD
- intellectual history • PhD
- international relations • AM, PhD
- Iranian • AM, PhD
- Irish • AM, PhD
- Islamic art • PhD
- Italian • AM, PhD
- Japanese • AM, PhD
- Japanese and Chinese art • PhD
- Japanese studies • AM
- Jewish history and literature • AM, PhD
- Korean • AM, PhD
- Korean studies • AM
- landscape architecture • PhD
- Latin American history • PhD
- legal anthropology • AM
- literature: nineteenth-century to the present • AM, PhD
- mathematics • AM, PhD
- medical anthropology • AM
- medical engineering/medical physics • Sc D
- medical sciences • MD
- medieval art • PhD
- medieval Latin • PhD
- medieval literature and language • AM, PhD
- microbiology and molecular genetics • PhD
- modern art • PhD
- modern British and American literature • AM, PhD
- molecular and cellular biology • PhD
- Mongolian • AM, PhD
- Mongolian studies • AM
- musicology • AM
- musicology and ethnomusicology • PhD
- Near Eastern history • PhD
- neurobiology • PhD
- oceanic history • PhD
- oral literature • PhD
- organic chemistry • AM, PhD

Harvard University (continued)
organizational behavior • PhD
Pali • AM, PhD
Persian • AM, PhD
personality • AM, PhD
philosophy • PhD
physical chemistry • AM, PhD
physics • AM, PhD
Polish • AM, PhD
political economy and government • PhD
political science • AM, PhD
political thought • AM, PhD
Portuguese • AM, PhD
psychobiology • AM, PhD
psychology • AM, PhD
psychopathology • AM, PhD
public policy • PhD
quantitative methods • AM, PhD
regional studies–Middle East • AM
regional studies-Russia, Eastern Europe, and Central Asia • AM
Renaissance and modern architecture • PhD
Renaissance art • PhD
Renaissance literature • AM, PhD
Russia • PhD
Russian • AM, PhD
Sanskrit • AM, PhD
Scandinavian • AM, PhD
Semitic philology • AM, PhD
Serbo-Croatian • AM, PhD
Slavic philology • AM, PhD
social anthropology • AM, PhD
social change and development • AM
social psychology • AM, PhD
sociology • AM, PhD
Southeastern Europe • PhD
Spanish • AM, PhD
speech and hearing sciences • PhD, Sc D
statistics • AM, PhD
study of religion • AM, PhD
Syro-Palestinian archaeology • AM, PhD
theoretical linguistics • AM, PhD
theoretical physics • AM, PhD
theory • AM, PhD
Tibetan • AM, PhD
Turkish • AM, PhD
Ukrainian • AM, PhD
urban planning • PhD
Urdu • AM, PhD
Vietnamese • AM, PhD
Vietnamese studies • AM
virology • PhD
Welsh • AM, PhD
Western Europe • PhD

Division of Engineering and Applied Sciences
Dr. Paul C. Martin Jr., Dean
Programs in:
applied mathematics • ME, PhD, SM
applied physics • ME, PhD, SM
computer science • ME, PhD, SM
computing technology • PhD
engineering science • ME

engineering sciences • PhD, SM
medical engineering/medical physics • Sc D
physics • PhD

Graduate School of Business Administration
Kim B. Clark, Dean
Programs in:
business administration • DBA, MBA
business economics • PhD
organizational behavior • PhD

Graduate School of Design
Dr. Peter G. Rowe, Dean
Programs in:
architecture • M Arch
design • Dr DES, PhD
design studies • M Des S
landscape architecture • MLA
urban planning • MUP
urban planning and design • MAUD, MLAUD

Graduate School of Education
Jerome T. Murphy, Dean
Programs in:
acquisition of language and culture • Ed M
administration, planning and social policy • CAS, Ed M
arts in education • Ed M
children and adolescents at risk • Ed M
cognitive development • Ed M
community and lifelong learning • Ed D
curriculum development and evaluation • Ed D
education in the community • Ed D
elementary and secondary education • Ed D
experienced teachers program • CAS, Ed M
higher education • Ed D
human development and psychology • CAS, Ed D, Ed M
individualized program • Ed M
international education • Ed D, Ed M
language and literacy • CAS, Ed D, Ed M
learning and teaching • Ed D, Ed M
methodology in developmental research • Ed M
mid-career mathematics and science (teaching certification) • CAS, Ed M
philosophy of education and curriculum theory • Ed D
research • Ed D
risk and prevention • CAS
schools and schooling • Ed D
study of teaching • Ed D
teaching and curriculum (teaching certification) • Ed M
technology in education • Ed M
urban superintendency • Ed D

John F. Kennedy School of Government
Dr. Joseph Nye, Dean
Programs in:
political economy and government • PhD
public administration • MPA, Mid-Career MPA
public policy • MPP, PhD
public policy and urban planning • MPPUP

Law School

Robert Clark, Dean
Program in:
    law • JD, LL M, SJD

Medical School

Dr. Joseph Martin, Dean
Program in:
    medicine • MD

Division of Health Sciences and Technology

Dr. Joseph Bonventre, Director
Programs in:
    applied physics • PhD
    engineering sciences • PhD
    medical engineering/medical physics • Sc D
    medical sciences • MD
    physics • PhD
    speech and hearing sciences • PhD, Sc D

Division of Medical Sciences

Dr. Thomas Fox, Associate Dean for Graduate Education
Program in:
    medical sciences • PhD

School of Dental Medicine

Dr. R. Bruce Donoff, Dean
Programs in:
    advanced general dentistry • Certificate
    dental medicine • DMD
    general practice residency • Certificate
    oral biology • D Med Sc, M Med Sc
    oral surgery • Certificate
    pediatric dentistry • Certificate

School of Public Health

Dr. James Ware, Acting Dean
Programs in:
    biostatistics • DPH, SD, SM
    cancer biology • SD
    cancer cell biology • PhD
    carcinogenesis • SD
    environmental epidemiology • SD, SM
    environmental health • SM
    environmental health science • DPH
    environmental health sciences • SD, SM
    environmental science and risk management • SD, SM
    epidemiology • DPH, SD, SM
    epidemiology/international nutrition • DPH, SD
    health and social behavior • DPH, SD, SM
    health care and organizational management • MPH
    health policy and management • DPH, SD, SM
    immunology • SD
    immunology and infectious diseases • DPH, SD, SM
    industrial hygiene and occupational safety • SD, SM
    international health • MPH
    law and public health • MPH
    maternal and child health • DPH, SD, SM
    molecular genetics • SD
    occupational and environmental health • MPH
    occupational health • DPH, MOH, SD, SM
    population and international health • DPH, SD, SM
    public management and community health • MPH
    quantitative methods • MPH
    radiobiology • SD
    virology • SD

Division of Biological Sciences

Dr. Duann Wirth, Director
Program in:
    biological sciences • SD

 LESLEY COLLEGE
Cambridge, MA 02138-2790

http://www.lesley.edu/

Independent coed comprehensive institution. *Enrollment: 6,166 graduate, professional, and undergraduate students. Graduate faculty: 70 full-time, 888 part-time.* Computer facilities: *Campuswide network is available with full Internet access. Total number of PCs/terminals supplied for student use: 120. Computer services are offered at no charge.* Library facilities: *Eleanor DeWolfe Ludcke Library.* Graduate expenses: *$425 per credit.* General application contact: *Dean of Admissions and Enrollment Planning, 800-999-1959.*

Graduate School of Arts and Social Sciences

Dr. Martha B. McKenna, Dean
Programs in:
    art therapy • MA
    clinical mental health counseling • MA
    counseling psychology • CAGS, MA
    creative arts in learning • CAGS, M Ed
    dance therapy • MA
    development project administration • MA
    ecological literacy • MS
    environmental education • MS
    expressive therapies • CAGS, MA
    expressive therapies counseling • MA
    holistic counseling • MA
    independent studies • M Ed
    independent study • MA
    individually designed • M Ed, MA
    intercultural conflict resolution • MA
    intercultural health and human services • MA
    intercultural relations • CAGS, MA
    intercultural training and consulting • MA
    interdisciplinary studies • MA
    international education exchange • MA
    international student advising • MA
    managing culturally diverse human resources • MA
    mental health counseling • MA
    multicultural education • M Ed, MA
    music therapy • MA
    school and community counseling • MA
    school counseling • MA
    storytelling • M Ed
    theater studies • M Ed

Lesley College (continued)
School of Education
Dr. William L. Dandridge, Dean
Programs in:
computers in education • CAGS, M Ed
curriculum and instruction • CAGS, M Ed
early childhood education • M Ed
educational administration • CAGS, M Ed
educational studies • PhD
elementary education • M Ed
individually designed • M Ed
intensive special needs • M Ed
middle school education • M Ed
reading • CAGS, M Ed
special needs • CAGS, M Ed

School of Management
Dr. Earl Potter, Dean
Programs in:
fundraising management • MSM
health services management • MSM
human resources management • MSM
management • MSM
management of information technology • MSM
training and development • MS

MASSACHUSETTS INSTITUTE OF TECHNOLOGY
Cambridge, MA 02139-4307
http://web.mit.edu/

Independent coed university. *Enrollment: 9,690 graduate, professional, and undergraduate students. Graduate faculty: 900 full-time, 16 part-time. Computer facilities: Campuswide network is available with full Internet access. Total number of PCs/terminals supplied for student use: 900. Computer services are offered at no charge. Graduate expenses: $24,050 per year. General application contact: Marilee Jones, Dean of Admissions, 617-253-2917.*

Operations Research Center
Dr. Thomas L. Magnanti, Co-Director
Program in:
operations research • PhD, SM

Program in Oceanography/Applied Ocean Science and Engineering
Paola Rizzoli, Director
Programs in:
biological oceanography • PhD, Sc D
chemical oceanography • PhD, Sc D
marine geochemistry • PhD, Sc D
marine geology • PhD, Sc D
oceanographic engineering • Eng, MS, PhD, Sc D
physical oceanography • PhD, Sc D

School of Architecture and Planning
William Mitchell, Dean
Programs in:
architecture • M Arch, PhD, SM Arch S, SM Vis S, SMBT
city planning • MCP
media arts and sciences • MS, PhD
real estate • MSRED
urban studies and planning • MS, PhD

School of Engineering
Robert A. Brown, Dean
Programs in:
aeronautics and astronautics • EAA, M Eng, PhD, SM, Sc D
applied plasma physics • SM
ceramics • PhD, Sc D
chemical engineering • Chem E, PhD, SM, Sc D
civil and environmental engineering • CE, M Eng, MS Tr Pl, PhD, SM, Sc D
computer science • EE, M Eng, PhD, SM, Sc D
electrical engineering • EE
electrical engineering and computer science • M Eng, PhD, SM, Sc D
electronic materials • PhD, Sc D
engineering • SM
engineering and management • MSEM
fission reactor technology • SM
health physics • SM
logistics • MLOG
management • MBA, SM
materials engineering • Mat E, PhD, Sc D
materials science • PhD, Sc D
materials science and engineering • SM
mechanical engineering • Mech E, PhD, SM, Sc D
metallurgical engineering • Met E
metallurgy • PhD, Sc D
naval architecture and marine engineering • SM
naval engineering • Naval E
nuclear engineering • NE, PhD, SM, Sc D
nuclear materials engineering • SM
nuclear systems engineering • M Eng
ocean engineering • M Eng, Ocean E, PhD, SM, Sc D
ocean systems management • SM
polymers • PhD, Sc D
radiation science and technology • PhD, SM, Sc D
radiological health and industrial radiation engineering • M Eng
radiological sciences • PhD, Sc D
system design and management • Certificate
technology and policy • PhD, SM
transportation • MST, PhD

School of Humanities and Social Science
Philip S. Khoury, Dean
Programs in:
economics • PhD
history and social study of science and technology • PhD
linguistics • PhD
philosophy • PhD
political science • PhD, SM
technology and policy • PhD, SM

School of Science
Robert J. Birgeneau, Dean
Programs in:
   applied mathematics • PhD, Sc D
   atmospheres, oceans, and climate • PhD, SM, Sc D
   atmospheric chemistry • PhD, SM, Sc D
   biochemistry • PhD, SM
   biological chemistry • PhD, SM, Sc D
   biological oceanography • PhD, Sc D
   biophysical chemistry • PhD, SM
   biophysics • PhD
   cellular and developmental biology • PhD
   cellular/molecular neuroscience • PhD
   chemical physics • PhD, SM, Sc D
   cognitive neuroscience • PhD
   cognitive science • PhD
   computational neuroscience • PhD
   genetics • PhD
   geology and geochemistry • PhD, SM, Sc D
   geophysics • PhD, SM, Sc D
   immunology • PhD
   inorganic chemistry • PhD, SM, Sc D
   mathematics • PhD, Sc D
   microbiology • PhD
   neurobiology • PhD
   organic chemistry • PhD, SM, Sc D
   physical chemistry • PhD, SM, Sc D
   physics • PhD, SM, Sc D
   physiology • PhD
   planetary science • PhD, SM, Sc D
   systems neuroscience • PhD
   technology and policy • PhD, SM

Sloan School of Management
Dr. Glen L. Urban, Dean
Program in:
   management • MBA, PhD, SM

Whitaker College of Health Sciences and Technology
Dr. J. David Litster, Director
Programs in:
   medical engineering • PhD
   medical engineering and medical physics • Sc D
   medical informatics • SM
   medical physics • PhD
   medical sciences • MD
   radiological sciences • PhD, Sc D
   speech and hearing sciences • PhD, Sc D
   toxicology • PhD, SM, Sc D

NORTHEASTERN UNIVERSITY
Boston, MA 02115-5096

http://www.neu.edu/

Independent coed university. *Enrollment: 24,325 graduate, professional, and undergraduate students. Graduate faculty: 733 full-time.* Computer facilities: *Campuswide network is available with full Internet access. Computer services are offered at no charge.* Library

facilities: *Snell Library plus 5 additional on-campus libraries.* Graduate expenses: *Tuition of $440 per credit hour. Fees of $55 per quarter full-time, $13.25 per quarter part-time.* General application contact: *Dean of the appropriate school, 617-373-2000.*

Bouvé College of Pharmacy and Health Sciences Graduate School
Dr. Ena Vazquez-Nuttall, Director
Programs in:
   applied behavior analysis • MS
   audiology • MS
   biomedical sciences • MS
   cardiopulmonary science (perfusion technology) • MS
   clinical exercise physiology • MS
   college student development and counseling • MS
   counseling psychology • CAGS, MS, PhD
   general health professions • MHP
   health policy • MHP
   human resource counseling • MS
   medical laboratory science • MS, PhD
   medicinal chemistry • MS, PhD
   pharmaceutics • PhD
   pharmacology • MS, PhD
   pharmacy • Pharm D
   physician assistant • MHP
   regulatory toxicology • MHP
   rehabilitation counseling • MS
   school counseling • MS
   school psychology • CAGS, MS, PhD
   special needs and intensive special needs • MS Ed
   speech-language pathology • MS
   toxicology • MS, PhD

College of Computer Science
Dr. Larry A. Finkelstein, Dean
Program in:
   computer science • MS, PhD

Graduate School of Arts and Sciences
Dr. Kay D. Onan, Associate Dean and Director
Programs in:
   American government and politics • MA
   analytical chemistry • PhD
   biology • MS, PhD
   biology education • MAT
   chemistry • MAT, MS, PhD
   comparative government and politics • MA
   curriculum and instruction • M Ed
   development administration • MPA
   economic policy and planning • MS
   economics • MA, MAT, PhD
   educational research • M Ed
   English • MA, MAT, PhD
   health administration and policy • MPA
   historical agencies and administration • MA
   history • MA, MAT, PhD
   human development • M Ed
   inorganic chemistry • PhD
   international relations • MA
   law, policy, and society • MS, PhD
   linguistics • MA

Northeastern University (continued)
  literature • MA, PhD
  mathematics • MAT, MS, PhD
  operations managements • MS
  organic chemistry • PhD
  physical chemistry • PhD
  physics • MAT, MS, PhD
  political science • MAT
  political theory • MA
  psychology • MA, PhD
  public administration • MA
  public and international affairs • PhD
  public history • MA
  reading • M Ed
  sociology • MA, MAT, PhD
  technical and professional writing • MTPW
  technical writing • Certificate
  writing • MA, MAW, PhD

School of Journalism
Nicholas Daniloff, Director
Program in:
  journalism • MA

Graduate School of Business Administration
William I. Kelly, Interim Dean of Graduate Programs
Program in:
  finance • MSF

Graduate School of Professional Accounting
William I. Kelly, Interim Dean of Graduate Programs,
  Graduate School of Business Administration
Program in:
  taxation • CAS, MST

Graduate School of Criminal Justice
Dr. Robert D. Croatti, Director
Program in:
  criminal justice • MS

Graduate School of Engineering
Dr. Yaman Yener, Associate Dean for Research and
  Graduate Education
Programs in:
  chemical engineering • MS, PhD
  civil and environmental engineering • MS, PhD
  computer systems engineering • MS
  electrical and computer engineering • MS, PhD
  engineering management • MS
  industrial engineering • MS, PhD
  information systems • MS
  mechanical engineering • MS, PhD
  operations research • MS

Graduate School of Nursing
Carole A. Shea, Director and Associate Dean
Programs in:
  community health nursing • CAS, MS
  critical care-acute care nurse practitioner • CAS, MS
  critical care-neonatal nurse practitioner • CAS, MS
  nurse anesthesia • MS
  nursing administration • MS

  primary care nursing • CAS, MS
  psychiatric-mental health nursing • CAS, MS

School of Law
Daniel J. Givelber, Acting Dean
Program in:
  law • JD

SALEM STATE COLLEGE
Salem, MA 01970-5353

Public coed comprehensive institution. Library facilities: *main library.*
Graduate expenses: *Tuition of $140 per credit hour for state residents;
$230 per credit hour for nonresidents. Fees of $20 per credit hour.*
General application contact: *Dean of the Graduate School, 508-
741-6323.*

Division of Graduate and Continuing Education
Programs in:
  business administration • MBA
  chemistry • MAT
  counseling and psychological services • MS
  early childhood education • M Ed
  elementary education • M Ed
  English • MA, MAT
  English as a second language • MAT
  geography • MA, MAT
  geo-information science • MS
  guidance and counseling • M Ed
  history • MA, MAT
  library media studies • M Ed
  mathematics • MAT, MS
  nursing • MSN
  reading • M Ed
  school administration • M Ed
  social work • MSW
  special education • M Ed
  teaching English as a second language K–9 • M Ed

SIMMONS COLLEGE
Boston, MA 02115

http://www.simmons.edu/

Independent primarily female comprehensive institution. *Enrollment:*
3,494 graduate, professional, and undergraduate students. *Graduate faculty: 139 full-time, 195 part-time. Computer facilities:
Campuswide network is available with full Internet access. Total
number of PCs/terminals supplied for student use: 100. Computer
services are offered at no charge.* Library facilities: *Beatley Library
plus 5 additional on-campus libraries.* Graduate expenses: *Tuition
of $587 per credit hour. Fees of $20 per year.* General application
contact: *Director, Graduate Studies Admission, 617-521-2910.*

Graduate School
Chester D. Haskell, Dean
Programs in:
 children's literature • MA
 communications management • MS
 elementary school education • MAT
 English • M Phil, MA
 English as a second language • MAT
 French • MA
 gender/cultural studies • MA
 inclusion specialist • MS Ed
 intensive special needs • MS Ed
 middle school and high school teaching • MAT
 Spanish • MA
 special needs • MS Ed

Graduate School for Health Studies
Dr. Harriet G. Tolpin, Dean
Programs in:
 health care administration • CAGS, MS
 nutrition and health promotion • MS
 physical therapy • MS
 primary health care • CAGS, MS

Graduate School of Library and Information Science
Dr. James Matarazzo, Dean
Program in:
 library and information science • DA, MS

Graduate School of Management
Dr. Patricia O'Brien, Dean
Program in:
 management • MBA

School of Social Work
Dr. Joseph M. Regan, Dean
Program in:
 clinical social work • MSW, PhD

alcohol rehabilitation/substance abuse counseling • CAS, M Ed, MS
art therapy • CAS, M Ed, MS
athletic administration • CAS, M Ed, MPE, MS
athletic counseling • CAS, M Ed, MS
biomechanics • M Ed, MPE, MS
clinical exercise physiology • M Ed, MPE, MS
community physical education • CAS, M Ed, MPE, MS
counseling and secondary education • M Ed, MS
deaf counseling • CAS, M Ed, MS
developmental disabilities • CAS, M Ed, MS
education • M Ed, MS
exercise physiology • M Ed, MPE, MS
general counseling • CAS, M Ed, MS
general counseling and casework • CAS, M Ed, MS
general physical education • DPE
health care management • M Ed, MS
health fitness • M Ed, MPE, MS
health promotion/wellness management • CAS, M Ed, MS
human services • MS
industrial/organizational psychology • CAS, M Ed, MS
interdisciplinary studies • M Ed, MPE, MS
marriage and family therapy • CAS, M Ed, MS
mental health counseling • CAS, M Ed, MS
occupational therapy • CAS, M Ed, MS
outdoor recreational management • M Ed, MS
physical therapy • MS
psychiatric rehabilitation/mental health counseling • CAS, M Ed, MS
recreational management • M Ed, MS
school guidance and counseling • CAS, M Ed, MS
science and research • M Ed, MPE, MS
social work • MSW
special services • CAS, M Ed, MS
sport management • CAS, M Ed, MPE, MS
sport psychology • CAS, DPE, M Ed, MPE, MS
sports injury prevention and management • M Ed, MPE, MS
sport studies • CAS, M Ed, MPE, MS
student personnel in higher education • CAS, M Ed, MS
teaching and administration • CAS, M Ed, MPE, MS
therapeutic recreational management • M Ed, MS
vocational evaluation and work adjustment • CAS, M Ed, MS

SPRINGFIELD COLLEGE
Springfield, MA 01109-3797

http://www.spfldcol.edu/homepage.nsf

Independent coed comprehensive institution. *Enrollment: 3,826 graduate, professional, and undergraduate students. Graduate faculty: 103 full-time, 81 part-time. Library facilities: Babson Library. Graduate expenses: Tuition of $474 per credit. Fees of $25 per year. General application contact: Donald J. Shaw Jr., Director of Graduate Admissions, 413-748-3225.*

School of Graduate Studies
Dr. William J. Sullivan, Dean
Programs in:
 adapted physical education • CAS, M Ed, MPE, MS
 advanced level coaching • CAS, M Ed, MPE, MS

SUFFOLK UNIVERSITY
Boston, MA 02108-2770

http://www.suffolk.edu/

Independent coed comprehensive institution. *Enrollment: 6,209 graduate, professional, and undergraduate students. Graduate faculty: 67 full-time, 80 part-time. Computer facilities: Campuswide network is available with full Internet access. Total number of PCs/ terminals supplied for student use: 250. Computer service fees are included with tuition and fees. Library facilities: Sawyer Library plus 2 additional on-campus libraries. Graduate expenses: Tuition of $14,544 per year full-time, $1452 per course part-time. Fees of $20 per year full-time, $10 per year part-time. General application*

Suffolk University (continued)
contact: *Judy Reynolds, Acting Director of Graduate Admissions, 617-573-8302.*

College of Liberal Arts and Sciences
Michael Ronayne, Dean
Programs in:
adult and organizational learning • CAGS, MS
clinical-developmental psychology • PhD
communication • MA
computer science • MS
counseling and human relations • CAGS
criminal justice • MS
educational administration • M Ed
human resource development • CAGS, MS
international economics • MSIE
leadership • CAGS
mental health counseling • MS
political science • MS
professional teacher/trainer development • CAGS, M Ed
school counseling • M Ed
secondary school teaching • MS

Law School
Gail N. Ellis, Director of Admissions
Programs in:
civil litigation • JD
financial services • JD
health care/biotechnology law • JD
high technology/intellectual property law • JD
tax law • JD

Sawyer School of Management
John F. Brennan, Dean
Programs in:
accounting • GDPA, MSA
banking and financial services • MS
business administration • APC, EMBA, MBA
disability studies • MPA
entrepreneurial studies • MS
finance • MSF
health administration • MBAH, MHA, MPA
nonprofit management • MPA
public administration • CASPA
public finance and human resources • MPA
state and local government • MPA
taxation • MST

TUFTS UNIVERSITY
Medford, MA 02155

http://www.tufts.edu/

Independent coed university. *Enrollment:* 8,500 graduate, professional, and undergraduate students. *Graduate faculty:* 585 full-time, 416 part-time. *Library facilities:* Tisch Library plus 1 additional on-campus library. *Graduate expenses:* Tuition of $23,839 per

year. Fees of $1196 per year. General application contact: *Gretchen Inman, Administrative Director, 617-627-3395.*

Division of Graduate and Continuing Studies and Research
Robert M. Hollister, Dean

Graduate School of Arts and Sciences
Robert M. Hollister, Dean, Division of Graduate and Continuing Studies and Research
Programs in:
analytical chemistry • MS, PhD
applied developmental psychology • PhD
art history • MA
biology • MS, PhD
bioorganic chemistry • MS, PhD
chemical engineering • MS, PhD
child development • CAGS, MA
civil engineering • MS, PhD
classical archaeology • MA
classics • MA
community development • MA
computer science • MS, PhD
dance • MA, PhD
drama • MA
dramatic literature and criticism • PhD
early childhood education • MAT
economics • MA
electrical engineering • MS, PhD
elementary education • MAT
engineering management • MSEM
English • MA, PhD
environmental chemistry • MS, PhD
environmental engineering • MS, PhD
environmental engineering and environmental sciences • MS, PhD
environmental geotechnology • MS, PhD
environmental health • MS, PhD
environmental policy • MA
environmental science and management • MS, PhD
ethnomusicology • MA
French • MA
geotechnical engineering • MS, PhD
German • MA
hazardous materials management • MS, PhD
health and human welfare • MA
history • MA, PhD
housing policy • MA
human factors • MS
inorganic chemistry • MS, PhD
international environment/development policy • MA
mathematics • MA, MS, PhD
mechanical engineering • MS, PhD
middle and secondary education • MA, MAT
music history and literature • MA
music theory and composition • MA
occupational therapy • MA, MS
organic chemistry • MS, PhD
philosophy • MA
physical chemistry • MS, PhD
physics • MS, PhD
psychology • MS, PhD

public policy and citizen participation • MA
school psychology • CAGS, MA
secondary education • MA
structural engineering • MS, PhD
studio art • MFA
theater history • PhD
water resources engineering • MS, PhD

Professional and Continuing Studies

Robert M. Hollister, Dean, Division of Graduate and
   Continuing Studies and Research
Programs in:
   biotechnology • Certificate
   biotechnology engineering • Certificate
   community environmental studies • Certificate
   design for humans: assistive technology • Certificate
   design for humans: human-computer interaction •
      Certificate
   electro-optics technology • Certificate
   environmental management • Certificate
   management of community organizations • Certificate
   manufacturing engineering • Certificate
   microwave and wireless engineering • Certificate
   museum studies • Certificate
   occupational therapy • Certificate
   premedical studies • Certificate
   program evaluation • Certificate

Fletcher School of Law and Diplomacy

John R. Galvin, Dean
Program in:
   law and diplomacy • MA, MALD, PhD

Sackler School of Graduate Biomedical Sciences

Dr. Louis Lasagna, Dean
Programs in:
   biochemistry • PhD
   cell, molecular and developmental biology • PhD
   cellular and molecular physiology • PhD
   genetics • PhD
   immunology • PhD
   molecular biology • PhD
   molecular microbiology • PhD
   neuroscience • PhD
   pharmacology and experimental therapeutics • PhD

School of Dental Medicine

Dr. Lonnie H. Norris, Dean
Programs in:
   dental medicine • DMD, MS
   dentistry • Certificate

School of Medicine

Programs in:
   health communication • MS
   medicine • MD
   public health • MPH

School of Nutrition Science and Policy

Beatrice L. Rogers, Academic Affairs
Program in:
   nutrition science and policy • MS, PhD

School of Veterinary Medicine

Dr. Philip Kosch, Dean
Programs in:
   animals and public policy • MS
   veterinary medicine • DVM

UNIVERSITY OF MASSACHUSETTS AMHERST
Amherst, MA 01003-0001

http://www.umass.edu/gradschool/

Public coed university. *Enrollment: 23,932 graduate, professional, and undergraduate students. Graduate faculty: 1,151 full-time. Computer facilities: Campuswide network is available with full Internet access. Computer service fees are applied as a separate charge. Library facilities: University Library plus 4 additional on-campus libraries. Graduate expenses: Tuition of $2640 per year full-time, $110 per credit part-time for state residents; $3690 per year (minimum) full-time, $165 per credit (minimum) part-time for nonresidents. Fees of $2856 per year full-time, $422 per semester part-time for state residents; $3204 per year full-time, $480 per semester part-time for nonresidents. General application contact: Jean Ames, Supervisor of Admissions, 413-545-0721.*

Graduate School

Dr. Charlena M. Seymour, Dean
Programs in:
   communication disorders • MA, PhD
   exercise science • MS, PhD
   molecular and cellular biology • MS, PhD
   neuroscience and behavior • MS, PhD
   nutrition • MS, PhD
   organismic and evolutionary biology • MS, PhD
   public health • MPH, MS, PhD

College of Engineering

Dr. Joseph I. Goldstein, Dean
Programs in:
   chemical engineering • MS, PhD
   civil engineering • MS, PhD
   electrical and computer engineering • MS, PhD
   engineering management • MS
   environmental engineering • MS
   industrial engineering and operations research • MS,
      PhD
   manufacturing engineering • MS
   mechanical engineering • MS, PhD

College of Food and Natural Resources

Dr. Robert G. Helgeson, Dean
Programs in:
   consumer studies • MS
   entomology • MS, PhD
   food science • MS, PhD
   forestry and wood technology • MS, PhD
   hotel, restaurant, and travel administration • MS
   landscape architecture • MLA
   mammalian and avian biology • MS, PhD

University of Massachusetts Amherst (continued)
  microbiology • MS, PhD
  plant science • PhD
  regional planning • MRP, PhD
  resource economics • MS, PhD
  soil science • MS, PhD
  sport studies • MS, PhD
  wildlife and fisheries biology • MS, PhD

College of Humanities and Fine Arts
Dr. Lee Edwards, Dean
Programs in:
  Afro-American studies • MA, PhD
  ancient history • MA
  art history • MA
  British Empire history • MA
  Chinese • MA
  comparative literature • MA, PhD
  creative writing • MFA
  English and American literature • MA, PhD
  European (medieval and modern) history • MA, PhD
  French • PhD
  French and Francophone studies • MA, MAT
  Germanic languages and literatures • MA, PhD
  Hispanic literatures and linguistics • MA, PhD
  interior design • MS
  Islamic history • MA
  Italian studies • MAT
  Japanese • MA
  Latin American history • MA, PhD
  Latin and classical humanities • MAT
  linguistics • MA, PhD
  modern global history • MA
  music • MM, PhD
  philosophy • MA, PhD
  public history • MA
  science and technology history • MA
  studio art • MFA
  theater • MFA
  U.S. history • MA, PhD

College of Natural Sciences and Mathematics
Dr. Linda L. Slakey, Dean
Programs in:
  applied mathematics • MS
  astronomy • MS, PhD
  biochemistry • MS, PhD
  biology • MS, PhD
  chemistry • MS, PhD
  computer science • MS, PhD
  geography • MS
  geology • MS
  geosciences • PhD
  mathematics and statistics • MS, PhD
  physics • MS, PhD
  plant biology • MA, MS, PhD
  polymer science and engineering • MS, PhD

College of Social and Behavioral Sciences
Dr. Glen Gordon, Dean
Programs in:
  anthropology • MA, PhD
  clinical psychology • MS, PhD
  communication • MA, PhD

  economics • MA, PhD
  labor studies • MS
  political science • MA, PhD
  public administration • MPA
  sociology • MA, PhD

School of Education
Dr. Bailey Jackson, Dean
Programs in:
  cultural diversity and curriculum reform • CAGS, Ed D, M Ed
  early childhood education and development • CAGS, Ed D, M Ed
  educational administration • CAGS, Ed D, M Ed
  elementary teacher education • CAGS, Ed D, M Ed
  higher education • CAGS, Ed D, M Ed
  international education • CAGS, Ed D, M Ed
  mathematics, science, and instructional technology • CAGS, Ed D, M Ed
  physical education teacher education • CAGS, Ed D, M Ed
  reading and writing • CAGS, Ed D, M Ed
  research and evaluation methods • CAGS, Ed D, M Ed
  school psychology • PhD
  school psychology and school counseling • CAGS, Ed D, M Ed
  secondary teacher education • CAGS, Ed D, M Ed
  social justice education • CAGS, Ed D, M Ed
  special education • CAGS, Ed D, M Ed

School of Management
Dr. Thomas O'Brien, Dean
Programs in:
  business administration • PMBA
  management • MBA, MS, PhD

School of Nursing
Dr. Brenda Millette, Dean
Program in:
  nursing • MS, PhD

School of Public Health and Health Sciences
Dr. Stephen Gelhbach, Dean
Programs in:
  communication disorders • MA, PhD
  exercise science • MS, PhD
  nutrition • MS, PhD
  public health • MPH, MS, PhD

 UNIVERSITY OF MASSACHUSETTS BOSTON
Boston, MA 02125-3393

http://www.umb.edu/

Public coed university. *Enrollment: 10,342 graduate, professional, and undergraduate students. Graduate faculty: 452 full-time. Computer facilities: Campuswide network is available with full Internet access. Total number of PCs/terminals supplied for student use: 440. Computer service fees are included with tuition and fees. Library facilities: Joseph P. Healey Library. Graduate expenses:*

Tuition of $2640 per year full-time, $110 per credit part-time for state residents; $8930 per year full-time, $373 per credit part-time for nonresidents. Fees of $2650 per year full-time, $420 per semester (minimum) part-time for state residents; $2736 per year full-time, $420 per semester (minimum) part-time for nonresidents. General application contact: Lisa Lavely, Director of Graduate Admissions and Records, 617-287-6400.

Graduate Studies
Dr. Martin H. Quitt, Dean
Program in:
  public policy • PhD

College of Arts and Sciences
Dr. Martin H. Quitt, Dean, Graduate Studies
Programs in:
  American studies • MA
  applied physics • MS
  applied sociology • MA
  archival methods • MA
  bilingual education • MA
  biology • MS
  biotechnology and biomedical science • MS
  chemistry • MS
  clinical psychology • PhD
  computer science • MS, PhD
  English • MA
  English as a second language • MA
  environmental biology • PhD
  environmental, coastal and ocean sciences • PhD
  environmental sciences • MS
  historical archaeology • MA
  history • MA

College of Management
Dr. Philip Quaglieri, Dean
Program in:
  business administration • MBA

College of Nursing
Dr. Brenda Cherry, Dean
Program in:
  nursing • MS, PhD

College of Public and Community Service
Dr. Ismael Ramirez-Soto, Dean
Programs in:
  dispute resolution • Certificate, MA
  gerontology • PhD
  human services • MS

Division of Continuing Education
Dr. Theresa Mortimer, Associate Provost
Program in:
  women in politics and government • Certificate

Graduate College of Education
Dr. Richard Clark, Dean
Programs in:
  counseling • CAGS, M Ed
  critical and creative thinking • Certificate, MA
  educational administration • CAGS, M Ed
  elementary and secondary education • M Ed
  higher education administration • Ed D
  instructional design • M Ed
  school psychology • CAGS, M Ed
  special education • M Ed
  teacher certification • M Ed
  urban school leadership • Ed D

McCormack Institute for Public Affairs
Dr. Robert Woodbury, Director
Program in:
  public affairs • MS

UNIVERSITY OF MASSACHUSETTS DARTMOUTH
North Dartmouth, MA 02747-2300
http://www.umassd.edu/

Public coed comprehensive institution. Enrollment: 5,159 graduate, professional, and undergraduate students. Graduate faculty: 122. Computer facilities: Campuswide network is available with full Internet access. Computer services are offered at no charge. Library facilities: Library Communications Center. Graduate expenses: Tuition of $2950 per year full-time, $82 per credit part-time for state residents; $10,249 per year full-time, $285 per credit part-time for nonresidents. Fees of $5002 per year full-time, $143 per credit part-time for state residents; $6830 per year full-time, $194 per credit part-time for nonresidents. General application contact: Carol A. Novo, Graduate Admissions Office, 508-999-8604.

Graduate School
Dr. Richard J. Panofsky, Provost/Vice Chancellor for
  Academic Affairs

College of Arts and Sciences
Judy Schaaf, Dean
Programs in:
  biology • MS
  chemistry • MS
  clinical psychology • MA
  general psychology • MA
  marine biology • MS
  professional writing • MA
  teaching • MAT

College of Business and Industry
Dr. Ronald McNeil, Dean
Programs in:
  business administration • MBA
  textile science • MS
  textile technology • MS

College of Engineering
Dr. Thomas Curry, Dean
Programs in:
  computer science • MS
  electrical engineering • MS, PhD
  mechanical engineering • MS
  physics • MS, PhD

University of Massachusetts Dartmouth (continued)

College of Nursing

Dr. Elisabeth Pennington, Dean

Program in:
  nursing • MS

College of Visual and Performing Arts

Dr. Michael Taylor, Dean

Programs in:
  art education • MAE, MAT
  artisanry • MFA
  fine arts • MFA
  graphic design • MFA
  textile design • MFA

UNIVERSITY OF MASSACHUSETTS LOWELL

Lowell, MA 01854-2881

http://www.uml.edu/

Public coed university. *Enrollment:* 12,350 graduate, professional, and undergraduate students. Graduate faculty: *416 full-time, 115 part-time.* Computer facilities: *Campuswide network is available with full Internet access. Computer service fees are included with tuition and fees.* Library facilities: *Lydon Library plus 1 additional on-campus library.* Graduate expenses: *$4867 per year full-time, $618 per semester (minimum) part-time for state residents; $10,276 per year full-time, $1294 per semester (minimum) part-time for nonresidents.* General application contact: *Dr. Alan J. Lincoln, Assistant to the Dean, 978-934-2383.*

Graduate School

Dr. Jerome L. Hojnacki, Dean

College of Arts and Sciences

Dr. Nancy Kliniewski, Co-Dean

Programs in:
  applied mathematics • MS
  applied mechanics • PhD
  applied physics • MS, PhD
  biochemistry • PhD
  biological sciences • MS
  chemistry • MS, PhD
  community and social psychology • MA
  computer science • MS, PhD, Sc D
  criminal justice • MA
  energy engineering • PhD
  environmental studies • MS Eng, PhD
  mathematics • MS
  optical sciences • MS
  physics • MS, PhD
  polymer sciences • MS, PhD
  radiological sciences and protection • MS, PhD

College of Education

Dr. Donald Pierson, Dean

Programs in:
  curriculum and instruction • CAGS, Ed D, M Ed
  educational administration • CAGS, Ed D, M Ed
  language arts and literacy • Ed D
  leadership in schooling • Ed D
  math and science education • Ed D
  reading and language • CAGS, Ed D, M Ed

College of Health Professions

Dr. Janice Stecchi, Dean

Programs in:
  adult psychiatric nursing • MS
  clinical laboratory studies • MS
  family and community health nursing • MS
  gerontological nursing • MS
  health promotion • PhD
  health services administration • MS
  occupational health nursing • MS
  physical therapy • MS

College of Management

Dr. Kathryn Verreault, Dean

Programs in:
  business administration • MBA
  manufacturing management • MMS

College of Music

Gerald Lloyd, Dean

Programs in:
  music education • MM
  music theory • MM
  performance • MM
  sound recording technology • MMS

James B. Francis College of Engineering

Dr. Krishna Vedula, Dean

Programs in:
  chemical engineering • MS Eng
  chemistry • PhD
  civil engineering • MS Eng
  coatings and adhesives • MS Eng
  composites • MS Eng
  computer engineering • D Eng, MS Eng
  electrical engineering • D Eng, MS Eng
  energy engineering • MS Eng
  environmental studies • MS Eng
  mechanical engineering • D Eng, MS Eng
  plastics engineering • D Eng, MS Eng
  plastics processing • MS Eng
  polymer science/plastics engineering • PhD
  product design • MS Eng
  systems engineering • D Eng, MS Eng
  work environment • MS, Sc D

WESTERN NEW ENGLAND COLLEGE
Springfield, MA 01119-2654

http://www.wnec.edu/

Independent coed comprehensive institution. *Enrollment:* 4,583 graduate, professional, and undergraduate students. Graduate faculty: *64 full-time, 58 part-time.* Computer facilities: *Campuswide network is available with full Internet access. Total number of PCs/ terminals supplied for student use: 150. Computer services are offered at no charge.* Library facilities: *D'Amour Library plus 1 additional on-campus library.* Graduate expenses: *Tuition of $353 per credit hour. Fees of $44 per semester (minimum).* General application contact: *Rod Pease, Director of Student Administrative Services, 413-796-2080.*

School of Business
Dr. Stanley Kowalski Jr., Dean
Programs in:
    accounting • MBA, MSA
    business administration • MBA
    business administration (weekend) • MBA
    criminal justice administration • MSCJA
    finance • MBA
    health care management • MBA
    human resources • MBA
    information systems • MSIS
    international business • MBA
    management information systems • MBA
    marketing • MBA
    procurement and contracting • MBA

School of Engineering
Dr. Eric W. Haffner, Acting Dean
Programs in:
    electrical engineering • MSEE
    industrial and manufacturing engineering • MSEM
    mechanical engineering • MSME

School of Law
Donald J. Dunn, Interim Dean
Program in:
    law • JD

WESTFIELD STATE COLLEGE
Westfield, MA 01086

http://www.wsc.mass.edu/

Public coed comprehensive institution. *Enrollment:* 4,937 graduate, professional, and undergraduate students. Graduate faculty: *29 full-time, 39 part-time.* Computer facilities: *Campuswide network is available. Total number of PCs/terminals supplied for student use: 114. Computer services are offered at no charge.* Library facilities: *Joseph B. Ely Library.* Graduate expenses: *Tuition of $145 per credit for state residents; $155 per credit for nonresidents. Fees of*

$90 per semester. General application contact: *Marcia Davio, Graduate Records Clerk, 413-572-8024.*

Division of Graduate Studies and Continuing Education
Dr. Catherine Lilly, Dean
Programs in:
    counseling/clinical psychology • MA
    criminal justice • MS
    early childhood education • M Ed
    elementary education • M Ed
    English • MA
    history • M Ed
    intensive special needs education • M Ed
    middle school education • M Ed
    occupational education • M Ed
    reading • M Ed
    school administration • CAGS, M Ed
    secondary education • M Ed
    special education • M Ed
    special needs education • M Ed
    technology for educators • M Ed

WORCESTER POLYTECHNIC INSTITUTE
Worcester, MA 01609-2280

http://www.wpi.edu/

Independent coed university. *Enrollment:* 3,424 graduate, professional, and undergraduate students. Graduate faculty: *187 full-time, 54 part-time.* Computer facilities: *Campuswide network is available with full Internet access. Computer services are offered at no charge.* Library facilities: *Gordon Library.* Graduate expenses: *$636 per credit hour.* General application contact: *Donna Johnson, Graduate Admissions, 508-831-5248.*

Graduate Studies
Dianne E. Horgan, Director
Programs in:
    administration and management • MBA, MSM
    applied mathematics • MS
    applied statistics • MS
    biochemistry • MS, PhD
    biology • MS
    biomedical engineering • M Eng, MS, PhD
    biomedical sciences • PhD
    biotechnology • MS, PhD
    business administration • MBA
    chemical engineering • MS, PhD
    chemistry • MS, PhD
    civil and environmental engineering • M Eng, MS, PhD
    clinical engineering • MS
    computer science • MS, PhD
    electrical and computer engineering • MS, PhD
    engineering management • MBA, MSM
    fire protection engineering • MS, PhD

Worcester Polytechnic Institute (continued)
- manufacturing engineering • MS, PhD
- manufacturing management • MS
- marketing and technological innovation • MS
- materials science and engineering • MS, PhD
- mathematical science • PhD
- mathematics • MME
- mechanical engineering • M Eng, MS, PhD
- operations and information technology • MS
- physics • MS, PhD
- power systems engineering • MS, PhD

WORCESTER STATE COLLEGE
Worcester, MA 01602-2597

http://www.worc.mass.edu/

Public coed comprehensive institution. *Enrollment: 5,505 graduate, professional, and undergraduate students. Graduate faculty: 30 full-time, 11 part-time. Library facilities: Learning Resource Center. Graduate expenses: $127 per credit hour. General application contact: Andrea F. Wetmore, Graduate Admissions Counselor, 508-929-8120.*

Graduate Studies
Dr. Michael Massouh, Executive Director of Graduate Studies and Continuing Education
Programs in:
- biotechnology • MS
- early childhood education • M Ed
- elementary education • M Ed
- English • M Ed
- health education • M Ed
- history • M Ed
- leadership and administration • M Ed
- middle school education • Certificate, M Ed
- non-profit management • MS
- occupational therapy • MS
- physical therapy • MS
- reading • Certificate, M Ed
- secondary education • Certificate, M Ed
- speech-language pathology • MS

MICHIGAN

ANDREWS UNIVERSITY
Berrien Springs, MI 49104

http://www.cs.andrews.edu/

Independent-religious coed university. *Enrollment: 3,152 graduate, professional, and undergraduate students. Graduate faculty: 162 full-time, 20 part-time. Library facilities: James White Library plus 3 additional on-campus libraries. Graduate expenses: Tuition of $290 per quarter hour (minimum). Fees of $75 per quarter. General*

application contact: Dr. Dean W. Hunt, Vice President for Enrollment Services, 800-253-2874.

School of Graduate Studies
Dr. Lisa M. Beardsley, Dean
Program in:
- international development • MSA

College of Arts and Sciences
Dr. Patricia Mutch, Dean
Programs in:
- allied health • MSMT
- biology • MAT, MS
- communication • MA
- English • MA, MAT
- history • MA, MAT
- humanities • MA
- mathematics and physical science • MS
- modern languages • MAT
- music • M Mus, MA
- nursing • MS
- nutrition • MS
- physical therapy • MPT, MSPT
- physics • MS
- social work • MSW

School of Business
Dr. Ann Gibson, Dean
Programs in:
- information and computer science • MBA, MS
- management and marketing • MBA, MSA

School of Education
Dr. Karen R. Graham, Dean
Programs in:
- biology • MAT
- community counseling • MA
- counseling psychology • PhD
- curriculum and instruction • Ed D, Ed S, MA, PhD
- education • MAT
- educational administration and supervision • Ed D, Ed S, MA, PhD
- educational and developmental psychology • MA
- educational psychology • Ed D, PhD
- elementary education • MAT
- English • MAT
- English as a second language • MAT
- French • MAT
- history • MAT
- leadership • Ed D, PhD
- physics • MAT
- reading • MA
- religious education • Ed D, Ed S, MA, PhD
- school counseling • MA
- school psychology • Ed S
- secondary education • MAT

Seventh-day Adventist Theological Seminary
Werner K. Vyhmeister, Dean
Program in:
- theology • D Min, M Div, M Th, MA, PhD, Th D

AQUINAS COLLEGE
Grand Rapids, MI 49506-1799

http://www.aquinas.edu/

Independent-religious coed comprehensive institution. *Enrollment:* 2,458 graduate, professional, and undergraduate students. Graduate faculty: *28 full-time, 34 part-time.* Computer facilities: *Campuswide network is available with full Internet access. Total number of PCs/terminals supplied for student use: 130. Computer services are offered at no charge.* Library facilities: *Woodhouse Learning Resource Center.* Graduate expenses: *$310 per credit hour.* General application contact: *Dr. Joyce McNally, Dean of Graduate Studies, 616-459-8281 Ext. 5427.*

Graduate Education Program
Dr. Joyce McNally, Dean of Graduate Studies
Program in:
> education • MAT

Graduate Management Program
Dr. Joyce McNally, Dean of Graduate Studies
Program in:
> management • M Mgt

CALVIN COLLEGE
Grand Rapids, MI 49546-4388

http://www.calvin.edu/

Independent-religious coed comprehensive institution. *Enrollment:* 4,085 graduate, professional, and undergraduate students. Graduate faculty: *1 full-time, 15 part-time.* Computer facilities: *Campuswide network is available with full Internet access. Computer service fees are included with tuition and fees.* Library facilities: *Hekman Library.* Graduate expenses: *$250 per semester hour.* General application contact: *Dr. Robert S. Fortner, Director of Graduate Studies, 616-957-8533.*

Graduate Programs in Education
Dr. Robert S. Fortner, Director of Graduate Studies
Programs in:
> curriculum and instruction • M Ed
> learning disabilities • M Ed
> reading • M Ed
> school administration • M Ed

 # CENTRAL MICHIGAN UNIVERSITY
Mount Pleasant, MI 48859

http://www.cmich.edu/

Public coed university. *Enrollment:* 16,597 graduate, professional, and undergraduate students. Graduate faculty: *644 full-time, 1,399 part-time.* Computer facilities: *Campuswide network is available with full Internet access. Computer service fees are included with tuition and fees.* Library facilities: *Park Library.* Graduate expenses: *Tuition of $139 per credit hour (minimum) for state residents; $276 per credit hour (minimum) for nonresidents. Fees of $260 per year full-time, $150 per semester part-time.* General application contact: *Dr. Carole Beere, Dean, College of Graduate Studies, 517-774-6467.*

College of Graduate Studies
Dr. Carole Beere, Dean
Programs in:
> administration • MSA
> humanities • MA

College of Business Administration
Dr. Terry Arndt, Dean
Programs in:
> accounting • MBA
> business education • MBE
> economics • MA
> finance • MBA
> management and law • MBA
> marketing and hospitality services administration • MBA

College of Communication and Fine Arts
Sue Ann Martin, Dean
Programs in:
> art • MA, MFA
> broadcast and cinematic arts • MA
> interpersonal and public communications • MA, MSA
> music • MM
> music education and supervision • MM
> music performance • MM
> oral interpretation • MA
> theatre • MA

College of Education and Human Services
Dr. Kelvie Comer, Dean
Programs in:
> athletic administration • MA
> athletic coaching • Certificate
> coaching • MA
> counselor education • MA
> early childhood education • MA
> educational administration • Ed S, MA
> elementary education • MA
> exercise science • MA
> guidance and counselor education • Ed S
> human environmental studies • MA, MAV Ed
> library media • MA
> middle level education • MA

Central Michigan University (continued)
recreation, parks, and leisure studies administration •
MA, MS, MSA
secondary education • MA
special education • MA
sports administration • MSA
teaching • MA

College of Health Professions
Dr. Stephen Kopp, Dean
Programs in:
audiology • Au D
health promotion and program management • MA
health services administration • MSA
physical therapy • MS
physician assistant • MS
speech and language pathology • MA

College of Humanities and Social and Behavioral Sciences
Gary Shapiro, Dean
Programs in:
applied experimental psychology • PhD
clinical psychology • Psy D
comparative history • PhD
composition and communication • MA
English language and literature • MA
general/experimental psychology • MA
history • MA
industrial/organizational psychology • MA, PhD
political science • MA
public administration • MPA, MSA
school psychology • PhD, S Psy S
social and criminal justice • MA
social work administration • MSA
sociology • MA
teaching English to speakers of other languages • MA

College of Science and Technology
Dr. Robert E. Kohrman, Dean
Programs in:
biology • MS
chemistry • MS
computer science • MS
industrial education • MA
industrial education administration • MAV Ed
industrial management and technology • MA
mathematics • MA, MAT, PhD
physics • MS
teaching chemistry • MA

College of Extended Learning
Dr. Delbert Ringquist, Dean
Programs in:
education • MA
general administration • MSA
health services administration • Certificate, MSA
humanities • MA
human resources administration • Certificate, MSA
information resource management • Certificate, MSA
international administration • Certificate, MSA
public administration • Certificate, MSA
software engineering administration • Certificate, MSA
special education • MA

EASTERN MICHIGAN UNIVERSITY
Ypsilanti, MI 48197

http://www.emich.edu/

Public coed comprehensive institution. *Enrollment:* 23,400 graduate, professional, and undergraduate students. Graduate faculty: *680 full-time.* Library facilities: *University Library.* Graduate expenses: *Tuition of $2691 per year full-time, $150 per credit hour part-time for state residents; $6300 per year full-time, $350 per credit hour part-time for nonresidents. Fees of $368 per year full-time, $88 per semester (minimum) part-time.* General application contact: *Mary Ann Shichtman, Associate Director of Admissions, 734-487-3400.*

Graduate School
Dr. Robert Holkeboer, Interim Dean

College of Arts and Sciences
Dr. Barry Fish, Dean
Programs in:
applied economics • MA
art • MA
art education • MA
arts administration • MA
arts and sciences • SPA
biology • MS
chemistry • MS
children's literature • MA
clinical/behavioral services • MS
computer science • MS
criminology and criminal justice • MA
development, trade and planning • MA
drama/theatre for the young • MA, MFA
economics • MA
English linguistics • MA
fine arts • MFA
French • MA
general psychology • MS
general science • MS
geography • MA, MS
German • MA
historic preservation • MS
history • MA
interpretation/performance studies • MA
language and international trade • MA
literature • MA
mathematics • MA
music • MA
physics • MS
physics education • MS
public administration • MPA
social science • MA, MLS
social science and American culture • MLS
sociology • MA
Spanish • MA
Spanish (bilingual-bicultural education) • MA
studio art • MA
teaching English to speakers of other languages • MA
theatre arts • MA
women's studies • MLS
written communication • MA

College of Business
Dr. Stewart L. Tubbs, Dean
Programs in:
  accounting • MSA
  accounting and taxation • MBA
  accounting, financial, and operational control • MBA
  business administration • MBA
  computer-based information systems • MSIS
  computer information systems • MBA
  finance • MBA
  human resources management and organizational
    development • MSHROD
  international business • MBA
  management of human resources • MBA
  management organizational development • MBA
  marketing • MBA
  production and operations management • MBA
  strategic quality management • MBA

College of Education
Dr. Jerry Robbins, Dean
Programs in:
  advanced counseling • MA
  community counseling • MA
  curriculum and instruction • MA
  early childhood education • MA
  educational leadership • Ed D, MA, SPA
  educational psychology • MA
  elementary education • MA
  guidance and counseling • MA, SPA
  K–12 curriculum • MA
  middle school education • MA
  physical education • MS
  reading • MA
  secondary curriculum • MA
  secondary school teaching • MA
  social foundations of education • MA
  special education • MA, SPA
  speech and language pathology • MA

College of Health and Human Services
Dr. Elizabeth King, Dean
Programs in:
  human, environmental, and consumer resources • MS
  nursing education • MSN
  occupational therapy • MOT, MS
  social work • MSW

College of Technology
Dr. Thomas Harden, Dean
Programs in:
  business education • MBE
  industrial technology • MS
  liberal studies in technology • MLS
  polymer technology • MS
  technology education • MA

FERRIS STATE UNIVERSITY
Big Rapids, MI 49307-2742

http://www.ferris.edu/homepage.htm

Public coed comprehensive institution. *Enrollment: 9,468 graduate, professional, and undergraduate students. Graduate faculty: 49.* Computer facilities: *Campuswide network is available with full Internet access. Total number of PCs/terminals supplied for student use: 1,200. Computer services are offered at no charge.* Library facilities: *Timme Library plus 1 additional on-campus library.* Graduate expenses: *Tuition of $220 per credit hour for state residents; $450 per credit hour for nonresidents. Fees of $100 per year.* General application contact: *Don Mullens, Dean of Enrollment Services, 616-592-2100.*

College of Business
Joseph Rallo, Dean
Program in:
  information systems management • MS

College of Education
Dr. E. D. Cory, Acting Dean
Programs in:
  criminal justice • MS
  occupational education • MS

College of Optometry
Dr. Alan Lewis, Dean
Program in:
  optometry • OD

College of Pharmacy
Ian Mathison, Dean
Program in:
  pharmacy • Pharm D

GRAND RAPIDS BAPTIST SEMINARY
Grand Rapids, MI 49525-5897

Independent-religious coed graduate-only institution. *Enrollment: 216 matriculated graduate/professional students. Graduate faculty: 9 full-time, 6 part-time.* Library facilities: *Miller Library plus 1 additional on-campus library.* Graduate expenses: *Tuition of $245 per credit hour. Fees of $244 per year.* General application contact: *John F. VerBerkmoes, Director of Admissions, 616-222-1422 Ext. 1255.*

Graduate Programs
James M. Grier, Dean
Programs in:
  biblical counseling • MA
  Christian education • M Div, MA, MRE
  education/management • D Min

Grand Rapids Baptist Seminary (continued)
  intercultural studies • MA
  missions • M Div, MRE
  missions/cross-cultural • D Min
  New Testament • MA, MTS, Th M
  Old Testament • MA, MTS, Th M
  pastoral ministry • D Min
  pastoral studies • M Div, MRE
  religious education • MRE
  systematic theology • MA
  theology • MTS, Th M

GRAND VALLEY STATE UNIVERSITY
Allendale, MI 49401-9403

http://www.gvsu.edu/

Public coed comprehensive institution. *Enrollment: 15,676 graduate, professional, and undergraduate students. Graduate faculty: 108 full-time, 222 part-time. Computer facilities: Campuswide network is available with full Internet access. Total number of PCs/terminals supplied for student use: 791. Computer service fees are included with tuition and fees. Library facilities: Zumberge Library. General application contact: William Eilola, Director of Admissions, 616-895-2025.*

Division of Arts and Humanities
Dr. J. David McGee, Dean
Program in:
  communications • MS

Russell B. Kirkhof School of Nursing
Dr. Lorraine Rodrigues-Fisher, Dean
Program in:
  nursing • MSN

School of Education
Dr. Robert Hagerty, Dean
Programs in:
  biology • M Ed
  college student affairs leadership • M Ed
  early childhood education • M Ed
  educational leadership • M Ed
  educational technology • M Ed
  education of the gifted and talented • M Ed
  elementary education • M Ed
  English • M Ed
  history • M Ed
  learning disabilities • M Ed
  mathematics • M Ed
  physics • M Ed
  pre-primary impaired • M Ed
  reading/language arts • M Ed
  special education administration • M Ed

School of Social Work
Dr. Rodney Mulder, Dean
Program in:
  social work • MSW

Science and Mathematics Division
P. Douglas Kindschi, Dean
Programs in:
  health sciences • MHS
  information systems • MS
  occupational therapy • MS
  physical therapy • MS
  physician assistant studies • MS
  software engineering • MS

Seidman School of Business
Dr. Emery Turner, Dean
Programs in:
  business administration • MBA
  taxation • MST

Social Science Division
Dr. Nancy Harper, Dean
Program in:
  public and nonprofit administration • MPA

LAKE SUPERIOR STATE UNIVERSITY
Sault Sainte Marie, MI 49783-1629

http://www.lssu.edu/

Public coed comprehensive institution. *Enrollment: 3,392 graduate, professional, and undergraduate students. Graduate faculty: 35. Computer facilities: Campuswide network is available with full Internet access. Total number of PCs/terminals supplied for student use: 340. Computer services are offered at no charge. Library facilities: Kenneth Shouldice Library. Graduate expenses: $172 per credit hour. General application contact: Bruce Johnson, Director of Admissions, 906-635-2231.*

Program in Business Administration
Ray Adams, Dean of College of Engineering, Mathematics, and Business
Program in:
  business administration • MBA

Program in Public Administration
Richard Conboy, Director of Graduate and International Programs
Program in:
  public administration • MPA

MADONNA UNIVERSITY
Livonia, MI 48150-1173

http://www.munet.edu/

Independent-religious coed comprehensive institution. *Enrollment:* 4,400 graduate, professional, and undergraduate students. *Gradu ate faculty: 43 full-time, 28 part-time.* Computer facilities: *Campuswide network is available with full Internet access. Total number of PCs/ terminals supplied for student use: 78. Computer services are offered at no charge.* Library facilities: *main library.* Graduate expenses: *Tuition of $260 per credit hour (minimum). Fees of $50 per semester.* General application contact: *Dr. Edith Raleigh, Dean of Graduate Studies, 734-432-5457.*

Program in Business Administration
Dr. Stuart Arends, Dean of Business School
Programs in:
  international business • MSBA
  leadership studies • MSBA
  quality and operations management • MSBA

Program in Health Services
Ellen Oliver Smith, Dean
Program in:
  health services • MS

Program in Hospice
Sr. Cecilia Eagen, Coordinator
Program in:
  hospice • MSH

Program in Nursing
Dr. Mary Eddy, Coordinator of Graduate Nursing
Programs in:
  adult health: chronic health conditions • MSN
  nursing administration • MSN

Programs in Education
Dr. Robert Kimball, Chair, Education Department
Programs in:
  Catholic school leadership • MSA
  educational leadership • MSA
  learning disabilities • MAT
  literacy education • MAT

MARYGROVE COLLEGE
Detroit, MI 48221-2599

Independent-religious primarily female comprehensive institution. Library facilities: *main library.* General application contact: *Director of Graduate Studies, 313-864-8000 Ext. 445.*

Graduate Division
Programs in:
  educational administration • MA
  human resources management • MA
  pastoral ministry • MA

Division of Education
Programs in:
  art of teaching • MAT
  early childhood education • M Ed
  education of the emotionally impaired • M Ed
  modern language translation • M Ed
  reading education • M Ed

 # MICHIGAN STATE UNIVERSITY
East Lansing, MI 48824-1020

http://www.msu.edu/

Public coed university. *Enrollment: 42,603 graduate, professional, and undergraduate students. Graduate faculty: 1,982 full-time, 6 part-time.* Computer facilities: *Campuswide network is available with full Internet access. Computer service fees are included with tuition and fees.* Library facilities: *main library plus 15 additional on-campus libraries.* Graduate expenses: *Tuition of $4609 per year full-time, $223 per credit hour (minimum) part-time for state residents; $8704 per year full-time, $450 per credit hour (minimum) part-time for nonresidents. Fees of $576 per year full-time, $476 per year part-time.* General application contact: *Dr. Karen Klomparens, Acting Dean of the Graduate School, 517-355-0300.*

Graduate School
Dr. Karen Klomparens, Acting Dean
Programs in:
  administration and program evaluation-urban studies • MSW
  anatomy • MS, PhD
  audiology and speech sciences-urban studies • PhD
  biochemistry • MS, PhD
  civil engineering-urban studies • MS
  clinical social work-urban studies • MSW
  communication-urban studies • MA
  entomology-urban studies • MS, PhD
  environmental engineering-urban studies • MS
  environmental toxicology • PhD
  epidemiology • MS
  forestry-urban studies • MS, PhD
  geography-urban studies • MA
  history-urban studies • MA, PhD
  labor relations and human resources-urban studies • MLRHR
  large animal clinical sciences • MS, PhD
  microbiology • MS, PhD
  neuroscience • PhD
  neuroscience-anatomy • PhD
  neuroscience-audiology and speech • PhD
  neuroscience-biochemistry • PhD

Michigan State University (continued)

 neuroscience-chemistry • PhD
 neuroscience-electrical engineering • PhD
 neuroscience-pathology • PhD
 neuroscience-pharmacology • PhD
 neuroscience-physics • PhD
 neuroscience-physiology • PhD
 neuroscience-psychology • PhD
 neuroscience-systems science • PhD
 neuroscience-zoology • PhD
 park, recreation and tourism resources-urban studies •
   MS, PhD
 pathology • MS, PhD
 pharmacology • MS, PhD
 physical education and exercise science-urban studies •
   MS
 physiology • MS, PhD
 political science-urban studies • PhD
 psychology-urban studies • PhD
 public administration-urban studies • MPA
 resource development-urban studies • MS, PhD
 small animal clinical sciences • MS
 sociology-urban studies • PhD
 surgery • MS
 telecommunication-urban studies • MA

College of Agriculture and Natural Resources
Dr. Fred L. Poston, Dean
Programs in:
 agricultural economics • MS, PhD
 agricultural education • MS, PhD
 agricultural technology and systems management • MS,
   PhD
 animal science • MS, PhD
 biosystems engineering • MS, PhD
 building construction management • MS
 crop science • MS, PhD
 entomology • MS, PhD
 entomology-urban studies • MS, PhD
 extension education • MS, PhD
 fisheries and wildlife • MS, PhD
 food science • MS, PhD
 forestry • MS, PhD
 forestry-urban studies • MS, PhD
 horticulture • MS, PhD
 human nutrition • MS, PhD
 packaging • MS, PhD
 park, recreation and tourism resources • MS, PhD
 plant breeding and genetics-crop and soil sciences • MS,
   PhD
 plant breeding and genetics-forestry • MS, PhD
 plant breeding and genetics-horticulture • MS, PhD
 resource development • MS, PhD
 resource development-urban studies • MS, PhD
 soil science • MS, PhD

College of Arts and Letters
Wendy Wilkins, Dean
Programs in:
 acting • MFA
 American studies • MA, PhD
 applied music • M Mus
 ceramics • MFA

 comparative literature • MA
 conducting • M Mus
 creative writing • MA
 English • PhD
 English and American literature • MA
 French • MA
 French language and literature • PhD
 French secondary school teaching • MA
 German • MA, PhD
 graphic design • MFA
 health and humanities • MA
 history • MA, PhD
 history of art • MA
 history-secondary school teaching • MA
 history-urban studies • MA, PhD
 linguistics • MA, PhD
 music composition • DMA, M Mus
 music education • M Mus, PhD
 musicology • MA, PhD
 music, performance and conducting • DMA
 music theory • M Mus, PhD
 music therapy • M Mus
 painting • MFA
 philosophy • MA, PhD
 printmaking • MFA
 production design • MFA
 Russian • MA, PhD
 sculpture • MFA
 secondary school/community college teaching • MA
 Spanish • MA
 Spanish language and literature • PhD
 Spanish secondary school teaching • MA
 teaching of English to speakers of other languages • MA
 theatre • MA

College of Communication Arts and Sciences
Dr. James Spaniolo, Dean
Programs in:
 advertising • MA
 audiology and speech sciences • MA, PhD
 audiology and speech sciences-urban studies • PhD
 communication • MA, PhD
 communication-urban studies • MA
 journalism • MA
 mass media • PhD
 public relations • MA
 telecommunication • MA
 telecommunication-urban studies • MA

College of Education
Dr. Carole Ames, Dean
Programs in:
 adult and continuing education • MA
 counseling • MA
 counseling psychology • PhD
 curriculum and teaching • MA
 curriculum, teaching and education policy • Ed S, PhD
 educational psychology • MA, PhD
 higher, adult and lifelong education • PhD
 K–12 educational administration • Ed S, MA, PhD
 literacy instruction • MA
 measurement and quantitative methods • PhD

physical education and exercise science-urban studies • MS, PhD

rehabilitation counseling • MA

rehabilitation counseling and school counseling • PhD

school psychology • Ed S, PhD

special education • MA, PhD

student affairs administration • MA

College of Engineering

Dr. Theodore Bickart, Dean

Programs in:

agricultural technology and systems management • MS, PhD

biosystems engineering • MS, PhD

building construction management • MS

chemical engineering • MS, PhD

civil engineering • MS, PhD

civil engineering-urban studies • MS

computer science • MS, PhD

electrical engineering • MS, PhD

environmental engineering • MS, PhD

environmental engineering-urban studies • MS

materials science • MS, PhD

mechanical engineering • MS, PhD

mechanics • MS, PhD

College of Human Ecology

Dr. Julia R. Miller, Dean

Programs in:

apparel and textiles • MA

child development • MA

community services • MS

family and child ecology • PhD

family economics and management • MA

family studies • MA

food science • MS, PhD

home economics education • MA

human environment: design and management • PhD

human nutrition • MS, PhD

interior design and facilities management • MA

marriage and family therapy • MA

merchandising management • MS

College of Natural Science

Dr. George E. Leroi, Dean

Programs in:

analytical chemistry • MS, PhD

applied mathematics • MS, PhD

applied statistics • MS

astrophysics • PhD

biochemistry • MS, PhD

biological sciences • MS

botany and plant pathology • MS, PhD

cell and molecular biology • PhD

cellular and molecular biology • PhD

chemical physics • PhD

chemistry • MAT

clinical laboratory science • MS

computational statistics • MS

entomology • MS, PhD

entomology-urban studies • MS, PhD

environmental geosciences • MS, PhD

genetics • PhD

geological sciences • MA, MS, PhD

horticulture • PhD

inorganic chemistry • MS, PhD

mathematics • MAT, MS, PhD

mathematics education • PhD

microbiology • PhD

operations research-statistics • MS

organic chemistry • MS, PhD

physical chemistry • PhD

physical science • MS

physics • MAT, MS, PhD

physiology • MS, PhD

statistics • MA, MS, PhD

zoology • MS, PhD

College of Nursing

Dr. Marilyn Rothert, Dean

Program in:

nursing • MSN

College of Social Science

Kenneth E. Corey, Dean

Programs in:

administration and program evaluation • MSW

administration and program evaluation-urban studies • MSW

anthropology • MA, PhD

applied developmental science • MA, PhD

clinical social work • MSW

clinical social work-urban studies • MSW

criminal justice • MS, PhD

geography • MA, MS, PhD

geography-urban studies • MA

infant studies • MA, PhD

labor relations and human resources • MLRHR

labor relations and human resources-urban studies • MLRHR

neuroscience-psychology • MA, PhD

political science • MA, PhD

political science-urban studies • PhD

psychology • MA, PhD

psychology-urban studies • PhD

public administration • MPA

public administration-urban studies • MPA

social science • MA

social science-criminal justice • PhD

social science-labor relations and human resources • PhD

social science-social work • PhD

social science-urban and regional planning • PhD

sociology • MA, PhD

sociology-urban studies • PhD

urban and regional planning • MURP

Eli Broad Graduate School of Management

Dr. James Henry, Dean

Programs in:

accounting • PhD

business administration • MBA

economics • MA, PhD

finance • MBA, PhD

food service management • MS

general management • MBA

hospitality • MBA

human resources management • MBA

Michigan State University (continued)
  management policy and strategy • PhD
  marketing • MBA, PhD
  materials and logistics management-logistics • MBA
  materials and logistics management-operations
      management • MBA
  materials and logistics management-purchasing
      management • MBA
  organizational behavior-personnel • PhD
  production and operations management • PhD
  professional accounting • MBA
  transportation-distribution • PhD

Institute for Environmental Toxicology
Dr. Lawrence J. Fischer, Director
Program in:
  environmental toxicology • PhD

College of Human Medicine
Dr. William Abbett, Dean
Programs in:
  anatomy • MS, PhD
  biochemistry • MS, PhD
  epidemiology • MS
  human medicine • MD
  microbiology • MS, PhD
  pathology • MS, PhD
  pharmacology • MS, PhD
  physiology • MS, PhD
  surgery • MS

College of Osteopathic Medicine
Dr. Allen Jacobs, Acting Dean
Programs in:
  anatomy • MS, PhD
  biochemistry • MS, PhD
  environmental toxicology • PhD
  microbiology • PhD
  neuroscience • PhD
  neuroscience-anatomy • PhD
  neuroscience-audiology and speech • PhD
  neuroscience-biochemistry • PhD
  neuroscience-chemistry • PhD
  neuroscience-electrical engineering • PhD
  neuroscience-pathology • PhD
  neuroscience-pharmacology • PhD
  neuroscience-physics • PhD
  neuroscience-physiology • PhD
  neuroscience-psychology • PhD
  neuroscience-systems science • PhD
  neuroscience-zoology • PhD
  osteopathic medicine • DO
  pathology • MS, PhD
  pharmacology • MS, PhD
  physiology • MS, PhD

College of Veterinary Medicine
Dr. Lonnie J. King, Dean
Programs in:
  anatomy • MS, PhD
  large animal clinical sciences • MS, PhD
  microbiology • MS, PhD
  pathology • MS, PhD
  pharmacology • MS, PhD
  small animal clinical sciences • MS
  veterinary medicine • DVM

Urban Affairs Programs
Dozier W. Thornton, Acting Dean
Programs in:
  administration and program evaluation-urban studies •
      MSW
  audiology and speech sciences-urban studies • PhD
  civil engineering-urban studies • MS
  clinical social work-urban studies • MSW
  communication-urban studies • MA
  entomology-urban studies • MS, PhD
  environmental engineering-urban studies • MS
  forestry-urban studies • MS, PhD
  geography-urban studies • MA
  history-urban studies • MA, PhD
  labor relations and human resources-urban studies •
      MLRHR
  park, recreation and tourism resources-urban studies •
      MS, PhD
  physical education and exercise science-urban studies •
      MS
  political science-urban studies • PhD
  psychology-urban studies • PhD
  public administration-urban studies • MPA
  resource development-urban studies • MS, PhD
  sociology-urban studies • PhD
  telecommunication-urban studies • MA

MICHIGAN TECHNOLOGICAL UNIVERSITY
Houghton, MI 49931-1295

http://www.mtu.edu/

Public coed university. *Enrollment: 6,302 graduate, professional,
and undergraduate students. Graduate faculty: 319 full-time, 14
part-time. Computer facilities: Campuswide network is available
with full Internet access. Total number of PCs/terminals supplied for
student use: 1,241. Computer service fees are included with tuition
and fees. Library facilities: J. Robert Van Pelt Library. Graduate
expenses: Tuition of $3867 per year full-time, $216 per credit hour
part-time for state residents; $8307 per year full-time, $462 per
credit hour part-time for nonresidents. Fees of $360 per year
(minimum) full-time, $120 per quarter (minimum) part-time. General
application contact: Dr. Sung M. Lee, Vice Provost for Research and
Dean of the Graduate School, 906-487-2327.*

Graduate School
Dr. Sung M. Lee, Vice Provost for Research and Dean

College of Engineering
Dr. Robert Warrington, Dean
Programs in:
    chemical engineering • MS, PhD
    civil engineering • MS, PhD
    electrical engineering • MS, PhD
    engineering mechanics • MS
    environmental engineering • MS, PhD
    geological engineering • MS
    geology • MS, PhD
    geophysics • MS
    geotechnical engineering • PhD
    mechanical engineering • MS
    mechanical engineering-engineering mechanics • PhD
    metallurgical and materials engineering • MS, PhD
    mining engineering • MS, PhD
    sensing and signal processing • PhD

College of Sciences and Arts
Dr. Maximilian J. Seel, Dean
Programs in:
    applied physics • PhD
    biological sciences • MS, PhD
    chemistry • MS, PhD
    computer science • MS
    engineering-computational science • PhD
    environmental policy • MS
    industrial archaeology • MS
    mathematical sciences • MS, PhD
    physics • MS, PhD
    rhetoric and technical communication • MS, PhD

School of Business and Economics
Dr. R. Eugene Klippel, Dean
Programs in:
    mineral economics • MS
    operations management • MS

School of Forestry and Wood Products
Dr. Warren E. Frayer, Dean
Programs in:
    forestry • MS
    forest science • PhD

NORTHERN MICHIGAN UNIVERSITY
Marquette, MI 49855-5301

http://www.nmu.edu/

Public coed comprehensive institution. *Enrollment: 7,826 graduate, professional, and undergraduate students. Graduate faculty: 98 full-time, 7 part-time.* Computer facilities: *Campuswide network is available with full Internet access. Total number of PCs/terminals supplied for student use: 450. Computer services are offered at no charge.* Library facilities: *Lydia Olson Library.* Graduate expenses: *Tuition of $135 per credit hour for state residents; $215 per credit hour for nonresidents. Fees of $183 per year full-time, $94 per year*

(minimum) part-time. General application contact: *Dr. David J. Prior, Dean of Graduate Studies, 906-227-2300.*

College of Graduate Studies
Dr. David J. Prior, Dean

College of Arts and Sciences
Dr. Michael Marsden, Dean
Programs in:
    administrative services • MA
    biology • MS
    chemistry • MS
    English • MA
    public administration • MPA

College of Behavioral Sciences and Human Services
Dr. Stephen B. Christopher, Dean
Programs in:
    administration and supervision • MA Ed
    elementary education • MA Ed
    exercise science • MS
    secondary education • MA Ed
    special education • MA Ed

College of Nursing and Allied Health Science
Betty J. Hill, Dean
Programs in:
    communication disorders • MA
    nursing • MSN

 # OAKLAND UNIVERSITY
Rochester, MI 48309-4401

http://www.oakland.edu/

Public coed university. *Enrollment: 14,379 graduate, professional, and undergraduate students. Graduate faculty: 301 full-time, 93 part-time.* Library facilities: *Kresge Library plus 1 additional on-campus library.* Graduate expenses: *Tuition of $3852 per year full-time, $214 per credit hour part-time for state residents; $8532 per year full-time, $474 per credit hour part-time for nonresidents. Fees of $420 per year.* General application contact: *Dr. Brian Goslin, Acting Dean of Graduate Studies, 248-370-3168.*

Graduate Studies
Dr. Brian Goslin, Acting Dean

College of Arts and Sciences
Dr. David J. Downing, Dean
Programs in:
    applied statistics • MS
    biological sciences • MS
    cellular biology of aging • MS
    chemistry • MS, PhD
    English • MA
    health and environmental chemistry • PhD
    history • MA
    industrial applied mathematics • MS
    linguistics • MA

Oakland University (continued)
mathematics • MA
medical physics • PhD
music • MM
physics • MS
public administration • MPA
statistical methods • Certificate

School of Business Administration
Dr. John Gardner, Dean
Programs in:
accounting • M Acc
business administration • MBA

School of Education and Human Services
Dr. Mary L. Otto, Dean
Programs in:
counseling • Certificate, MA
early childhood education • Certificate, M Ed
educational specialist • Ed S
microcomputer applications in education • Certificate
reading • Certificate, MAT, PhD
special education • Certificate, M Ed
training and development • MTD

School of Engineering and Computer Science
Dr. Michael P. Polis, Dean
Programs in:
computer science • MS
electrical and computer engineering • MS
engineering management • MS
mechanical engineering • MS
software engineering • MS
systems engineering • MS, PhD

School of Health Sciences
Dr. Ronald E. Olson, Dean
Programs in:
exercise science • MS
physical therapy • MPT, MS

School of Nursing
Dr. Justine Speer, Dean
Programs in:
adult health • MSN
nurse anesthetist • MSN
nursing administration • MSN

SAGINAW VALLEY STATE UNIVERSITY
University Center, MI 48710

http://www.svsu.edu/

Public coed comprehensive institution. *Enrollment: 7,527 graduate, professional, and undergraduate students. Graduate faculty: 55 full-time.* Computer facilities: *Campuswide network is available with full Internet access. Total number of PCs/terminals supplied for student use: 300. Computer services are offered at no charge.* Library facilities: *Melvin J. Zahnow Library.* Graduate expenses: *Tuition of $159 per credit hour for state residents; $311 per credit*

hour for nonresidents. Fees of $8.70 per credit hour. General application contact: James P. Dwyer, Director of Admissions, 517-790-4200.

College of Arts and Behavioral Sciences
Dr. Donald Bachand, Dean
Programs in:
organizational leadership and administration • MA
political science/criminal justice • MA

College of Business and Management
Dr. Severin C. Carlson, Dean
Program in:
business and management • MBA

College of Education
Dr. Ken Wahl, Interim Dean
Programs in:
chief business officers • M Ed
early childhood education • MAT
educational administration and supervision • M Ed
education leadership • Ed S
elementary classroom teaching • MAT
learning and behavioral disorders • MAT
middle school classroom teaching • MAT
natural science teaching • MAT
principalship • M Ed
reading • MAT
secondary classroom teaching • MAT
superintendency • M Ed

College of Nursing
Dr. Cheryl Easley, Dean
Programs in:
client care management • MSN
clinical nurse specialist • MSN
nurse practitioner • MSN
nursing education • MSN

College of Science, Engineering, and Technology
Dr. Thomas Kullgren, Dean
Program in:
technological processes • MS

 # UNIVERSITY OF DETROIT MERCY
Detroit, MI 48219-0900

http://www.udmercy.edu/

Independent-religious coed university. Library facilities: *main library.* Graduate expenses: *Tuition of $490 per credit hour. Fees of $210 per year full-time, $75 per semester part-time.* General application contact: *Dean, Enrollment Management, 313-993-1245.*

College of Business Administration
Programs in:
　business administration • MBA
　computer information systems • MS

College of Education and Human Services
Programs in:
　addiction studies • Certificate
　counseling • MA
　criminal justice studies • MA, MS
　curriculum and instruction • MA
　early childhood education • MA
　educational administration • Ed S, MA
　emotionally impaired • MA
　learning disabilities • MA
　security administration • MS

College of Engineering and Science
Programs in:
　automotive engineering • DE
　biology • MS
　chemical engineering • DE, ME
　civil and environmental engineering • DE, ME
　computer science • MSCS
　economic aspects of chemistry • MSEC
　electrical engineering • DE, ME
　elementary mathematics education • MATM
　engineering management • M Eng Mgt
　junior high mathematics education • MATM
　macromolecular chemistry • MS, PhD
　manufacturing engineering • DE, ME
　mathematics • MA
　mechanical engineering • DE, M Eng Mgt, ME
　polymer engineering • ME
　secondary mathematics education • MATM

College of Health Professions
Programs in:
　health care education • MS
　health services administration • MS
　nurse anesthesiology • MS
　physician assistant • MS

College of Liberal Arts
Programs in:
　clinical psychology • MA, PhD
　economics • MA
　industrial/organizational psychology • MA
　international politics and economics • MA
　liberal studies • MA
　political science • MA
　public administration • MPA
　religious studies • MA
　school psychology • MA, Spec

School of Dentistry
Programs in:
　dentistry • DDS
　endodontics • Certificate, MS
　general practice residency • Certificate, MS
　orthodontics • Certificate, MS

School of Law
Program in:
　law • JD

UNIVERSITY OF MICHIGAN
Ann Arbor, MI 48109

http://www.umich.edu/

Public coed university. *Enrollment: 36,450 graduate, professional, and undergraduate students. Graduate faculty: 2,678. Library facilities: Hatcher Graduate Library plus 35 additional on-campus libraries. Graduate expenses: Tuition of $10,008 per year full-time, $1866 per semester (minimum) part-time for state residents; $20,300 per year full-time, $3580 per semester (minimum) part-time for nonresidents. Fees of $185 per year. General application contact: Admissions Office, 734-764-8129.*

College of Architecture and Urban Planning
Robert Beckley, Dean
Programs in:
　architecture • M Arch, M Sc, PhD
　gaming/simulation studies • Certificate
　urban planning • MUP
　urban, technological, and environmental planning •
　　PhD

College of Pharmacy
James W. Richards, Dean
Programs in:
　medicinal chemistry • MS, PhD
　pharmaceutical chemistry (computational) • MS, PhD
　pharmaceutics • MS, PhD
　pharmacy • Pharm D
　pharmacy administration • MS, PhD

Horace H. Rackham School of Graduate Studies
Earl Lewis, Dean of the Graduate School and Vice Provost
　for Academic Affairs-Graduate Studies
Programs in:
　American culture • AM, PhD
　biological chemistry • PhD
　biophysics • PhD
　cell, developmental and neural biology • PhD
　cellular and molecular biology • PhD
　education and psychology • PhD
　English and education • PhD
　human genetics • MS, PhD
　kinesiology • AM, Certificate, MS, PhD
　medical and biological illustration • MFA
　medicinal chemistry • MS, PhD
　microbiology • PhD
　microbiology and immunology • PhD
　modern Middle Eastern and North African studies • AM
　neuroscience • PhD
　pathology • PhD
　pharmaceutical chemistry (computational) • MS, PhD
　pharmaceutics • MS, PhD

University of Michigan (continued)
    pharmacology • PhD
    pharmacy administration • MS, PhD
    physiology • PhD

College of Engineering
Stephen W. Director, Dean
Programs in:
    aerospace engineering • Aerospace E, M Eng, MS, MSE, PhD
    applied mechanics • App ME, MSE, PhD
    applied physics • PhD
    atmospheric and space sciences • M Eng, MS, PhD
    atmospheric, oceanic and space sciences • MS, PhD
    automotive engineering • M Eng
    biomedical engineering and biomedical engineering research • MS, PhD
    chemical engineering • CE, MSE, PhD
    civil engineering • CE, MSE, PhD
    computer science and engineering • MS, MSE, PhD
    concurrent marine design • M Eng
    construction engineering and management • MSE
    electrical engineering • EE, MS, MSE, PhD
    electrical engineering: systems • MS, MSE, PhD
    environmental engineering • MSE, PhD
    financial engineering • MS
    industrial and operations engineering • IOE, MS, MSE, PhD
    macromolecular science and engineering • MS, PhD
    manufacturing • D Eng, M Eng
    materials science and engineering • MS, PhD
    mechanical engineering • ME, MSE, PhD
    naval architecture and marine engineering • MS, MSE, Mar Eng, Nav Arch, PhD
    nuclear engineering • MSE, Nuc E, PhD
    nuclear science • MS, PhD
    oceanography: physical • MS, PhD
    radiological health engineering • M Eng
    remote sensing and geoinformation • M Eng
    space systems • M Eng
    technical information design and management • MS
    transportation studies: intelligent transportation systems • Certificate

College of Literature, Science, and the Arts
Edie Goldenberg, Dean
Programs in:
    administration of archives • AM
    analytical chemistry • PhD
    ancient Israel/Hebrew Bible • AM, PhD
    anthropology • AM, PhD
    anthropology and history • PhD
    applied economics • AM
    applied physics • PhD
    applied social research • AM
    applied statistics • AM
    Arabic • AM, PhD
    astronomy • MS, PhD
    biology • MS, PhD
    biopsychology • PhD
    botany • PhD
    Buddhist studies • AM, PhD
    chemical biology • PhD

    Chinese literature • AM, PhD
    Chinese studies • AM
    classical art and archaeology • PhD
    classical studies • PhD
    clinical psychology • PhD
    cognition and perception • PhD
    comparative literature • PhD
    comparative studies in history • AM
    creative writing • MFA
    developmental psychology • PhD
    early Christian studies • AM, PhD
    economics • AM, PhD
    English and education • PhD
    English and women's studies • PhD
    English language and literature • PhD
    French • PhD
    geology • MS, PhD
    Germanic languages and literatures • AM, PhD
    Greek • AM
    Hebrew • AM, PhD
    history • AM, PhD
    history of art • PhD
    inorganic chemistry • PhD
    Islamic studies • AM, PhD
    Japanese literature • AM, PhD
    Japanese studies • AM
    Latin • AM
    linguistics • PhD
    mathematics • AM, MS, PhD
    Mesopotamian and ancient Near Eastern studies • AM, PhD
    mineralogy • MS, PhD
    museum practice • Certificate
    oceanography: marine geology and geochemistry • MS, PhD
    organic chemistry • PhD
    organizational psychology • PhD
    Persian • AM, PhD
    personality psychology • PhD
    philosophy • AM, PhD
    physical chemistry • PhD
    physics • MS, PhD
    plant biology • MS
    political science • AM, PhD
    psychology and women's studies • PhD
    Russian and East European studies • AM
    Slavic languages and literatures • PhD
    social psychology • PhD
    social work and economics • PhD
    social work and political science • PhD
    social work and sociology • PhD
    sociology • PhD
    South and Southeast Asian studies • AM
    Spanish • PhD
    statistics • AM, PhD
    teaching Latin • MAT
    teaching of Arabic as a foreign Language • AM
    Turkish • AM, PhD
    women's studies • Certificate

School of Art and Design
Allen J. Samuels, Dean
Programs in:
    art and design • AM, MFA
    medical and biological illustration • MFA

School of Education
Dr. Cecil Miskel, Dean
Programs in:
    academic affairs • Ed D, PhD
    community college administration • AM
    community college governance and leadership • Ed D
    curriculum development • AM
    early childhood education • AM, PhD
    educational administration and policy • AM, PhD
    educational foundations and policy • AM, PhD
    educational technology • AM, MS, PhD
    elementary education • MA-Certification
    English education • AM
    higher education administration • AM
    individually designed studies • Ed D, PhD
    learning disabilities and literacy • AM
    literacy education • AM, PhD
    mathematics education • AM, MS, PhD
    organizational behavior • Ed D, PhD
    public policy in postsecondary education • AM, Ed D, PhD
    research, evaluation, and assessment • PhD
    science education • AM, MS, PhD
    secondary education • MA-Certification
    social studies education • AM
    special education • PhD
    student development and academic support • AM
    teacher education • PhD

School of Information
Dr. Daniel E. Atkins III, Dean
Programs in:
    archives and records management • MS
    human-computer interaction • MS
    information • PhD
    information economics, management and policy • MS
    library and information services • MS

School of Nursing
Dr. Ada Sue Hinshaw, Dean
Programs in:
    acute care pediatric nurse practitioner • MS
    administration of nursing and patient care services • MS
    adult acute care nurse practitioner • MS
    adult primary care/adult nurse practitioner • MS
    community care/home care • MS
    family nurse practitioner • MS
    gerontology nursing • MS
    infant, child, adolescent health nurse practitioner • MS
    medical-surgical nursing • MS
    nurse midwifery • MS
    nursing • Certificate, PhD
    occupational health nursing • MS
    psychiatric mental health nurse practitioner • MS
    psychiatric mental health nursing • MS
    women's health/child-bearing families nurse practitioner • MS

School of Public Policy
Edward M. Gramlich, Dean
Program in:
    public policy • MPA, MPP, PhD

Law School
Jeffrey S. Lehman, Dean
Programs in:
    comparative law • MCL
    international economic law • LL M
    international law • LL M
    law • JD, LL M, SJD

Medical School
Dr. Giles G. Bole Jr., Dean
Programs in:
    biological chemistry • PhD
    cell, developmental and neural biology • PhD
    cellular and molecular biology • PhD
    human genetics • MS, PhD
    medicine • MD
    microbiology • PhD
    microbiology and immunology • PhD
    neuroscience • PhD
    pathology • PhD
    pharmacology • PhD
    physiology • PhD

School of Business Administration
Dr. B. Joseph White, Dean
Program in:
    business administration • MBA, PhD

School of Dentistry
William E. Kotowicz, Dean
Programs in:
    dentistry • Certificate, DDS, MS, PhD

School of Music
Paul C. Boylan, Dean
Programs in:
    composition • A Mus D, AM
    composition and theory • PhD
    conducting • A Mus D
    dance • MFA
    music • MM
    music education • PhD
    musicology • AM, PhD
    performance • A Mus D

School of Natural Resources and Environment
Dr. Paul Webb, Interim Dean
Programs in:
    forestry • MF
    landscape architecture • MLA, PhD
    natural resource economics • PhD
    natural resources and environment • MS, PhD
    resource ecology and management • MF, MS
    resource policy and behavior • MF, MS

University of Michigan (continued)
School of Public Health
Noreen M. Clark, Dean
Programs in:
  biostatistics • MPH, MS, PhD
  clinical research design and statistical analysis • MS
  dental public health • MPH
  environmental health • MPH, MS, PhD
  epidemiologic science • PhD
  epidemiology • Dr PH, MPH
  health behavior and health education • MPH, PhD
  health management and policy • MHSA, MPH
  health policy • Dr PH
  health services organization and policy • PhD
  hospital and molecular epidemiology • MPH
  human nutrition • MPH, MS
  industrial hygiene • MS, PhD
  international health • MPH
  occupational medicine • MPH
  toxicology • MPH, MS, PhD

School of Social Work
Paula Allen-Meares, Dean
Programs in:
  social work • MSW
  social work and social science • PhD

UNIVERSITY OF MICHIGAN–DEARBORN
Dearborn, MI 48128-1491

http://www.umd.umich.edu/univ/grad/

Public coed comprehensive institution. *Enrollment: 8,335 graduate, professional, and undergraduate students. Graduate faculty: 178. Computer facilities: Campuswide network is available with full Internet access. Total number of PCs/terminals supplied for student use: 1,100. Computer service fees are applied as a separate charge. Library facilities: Mardigian Library. Graduate expenses: Tuition of $4536 per year full-time, $252 per credit hour part-time for state residents; $13,086 per year full-time, $727 per credit hour part-time for nonresidents. Fees of $480 per year (minimum). General application contact: Vivian J. Ladd, Graduate Program Coordinator, 313-593-1494.*

College of Arts, Sciences, and Letters
John Presley, Dean
Program in:
  liberal studies • MA

School of Education
Dr. John Poster, Dean
Programs in:
  adult instruction and performance technology • MA
  education • MA
  public administration • MPA
  special education • M Ed

School of Engineering
Dr. S. Sengupta, Dean
Programs in:
  automotive systems engineering • MSE
  computer and information science • MS
  computer engineering • MSE
  electrical engineering • MSE
  engineering management • MS
  industrial and systems engineering • MSE
  manufacturing systems engineering • D Eng, MSE
  mechanical engineering • MSE

School of Management
Dr. Eric Brucker, Dean
Program in:
  management • MBA

UNIVERSITY OF MICHIGAN–FLINT
Flint, MI 48502-1950

http://www.flint.umich.edu/

Public coed comprehensive institution. *Computer facilities: Campuswide network is available with full Internet access. Computer service fees are applied as a separate charge. Library facilities: main library. General application contact: Dean of Graduate Programs and Research, 810-762-3171.*

Horace H. Rackham School of Graduate Studies
Programs in:
  liberal studies • MLS
  public administration • MPA

School of Health Professions and Studies
Dr. Suzanne M. Selig, Coordinator
Programs in:
  anesthesia • MSA
  health education • MS
  physical therapy • MPT

School of Management
Dr. Rod McGraw, Interim Dean
Program in:
  management • MBA

WAYNE STATE UNIVERSITY
Detroit, MI 48202

http://www.wayne.edu/

Public coed university. *Enrollment: 28,404 graduate, professional, and undergraduate students. Graduate faculty: 2,194. Computer facilities: Campuswide network is available with full Internet access. Computer services are offered at no charge. Library facilities: Purdy/Kresge Library plus 6 additional on-campus libraries. Graduate expenses: Tuition of $163 per credit hour for state residents; $355 per credit hour for nonresidents. Fees of $498 per year full-time,*

$114 per semester (minimum) part-time. General application contact: Michael Wood, Associate Director, 313-577-3596.

Graduate School

Daniel A. Walz, Dean

Programs in:

alcohol and drug abuse studies • Certificate
anatomy and cell biology • MS, PhD
archives administration • Certificate
basic medical science • MS
biochemistry • MS, PhD
cancer biology • PhD
cellular and clinical neurobiology • PhD
community health • MS
community health services • Certificate
developmental disabilities • Certificate
gerontology • Certificate
immunology and microbiology • MS, PhD
infant mental health • Certificate
interdisciplinary studies • PhD
library and information science • MLIS, Spec
medical physics • PhD
medical research • MS
molecular and cellular toxicology • MS, PhD
molecular biology and genetics • MS, PhD
pathology • PhD
pharmacology • MS, PhD
physiology • MS, PhD
radiological physics • MS

College of Education

Dr. Paula Wood, Dean

Programs in:

counseling • Ed D, Ed S, M Ed, MA, PhD
curriculum and instruction • Ed D, Ed S, PhD
educational evaluation and research • Ed D, M Ed, PhD
educational leadership • M Ed
educational psychology • Ed S, M Ed, PhD
elementary education • M Ed, MAT
general administration and supervision • Ed D, Ed S, PhD
health education • M Ed
higher education • Ed D, PhD
history, philosophy, and sociology of education • PhD
instructional technology • Ed D, Ed S, M Ed, PhD
marriage and family psychology • MA
physical education • M Ed
reading • Ed S
reading education • Ed D
recreation and park services • MA
school psychology • MA
science • Ed S
secondary education • M Ed, MAT
social studies • Ed S
special education • Ed D, Ed S, M Ed, PhD
sports administration • MA
vocational rehabilitation counseling • Ed S, MA

College of Engineering

Dr. Chin Kuo, Dean

Programs in:

biomedical engineering • MS, PhD
chemical engineering • MS, PhD
civil engineering • MS, PhD
computer engineering • MS, PhD
electrical engineering • MS, PhD
electronics and computer control systems • MS
engineering management • MS
engineering technology • MS
environmental auditing • Certificate
hazardous materials management on public lands • Certificate
hazardous waste control • Certificate
hazardous waste management • MS
industrial engineering • MS, PhD
manufacturing engineering • MS
materials science and engineering • MS, PhD
mechanical engineering • MS, PhD
operations research • MS
polymer engineering • Certificate

College of Fine, Performing and Communication Arts

Dr. Jack Kay, Interim Dean

Programs in:

art • MA, MFA
art history • MA
choral conducting • MM
communication studies • MA, PhD
composition • MM
design and merchandising • MA
fine, performing and communication art • MS
museology • PMC
music • MA
music education • MM
orchestral studies • Certificate
performance • MM
public relations and organizational communication • MA
radio-TV-film • MA, PhD
speech communication • MA, PhD
theatre • MA, MFA, PhD
theory • MM

College of Liberal Arts

Dr. Sondra O'Neale, Dean

Programs in:

anthropology • MA, PhD
archival administration • Certificate
classics • MA
comparative literature • MA
criminal justice • MPA, MS
economics • MA, PhD
English • MA, PhD
French • MA
German • MA
history • MA, PhD
interdisciplinary studies • PhD
Italian • MA
linguistics • MA
modern languages • PhD
Near Eastern studies • MA

Wayne State University (continued)
philosophy • MA, PhD
political science • MA, PhD
public administration • MPA
sociology • MA, PhD
Spanish • MA

College of Lifelong Learning
Dr. Robert Carter, Dean
Program in:
interdisciplinary studies • MIS

College of Nursing
Dr. Barbara Redman, Dean
Programs in:
adult primary care nursing • MSN
adult psychiatric-mental health nursing • MSN
advanced medical-surgical nursing • MSN
child/adolescent psychiatric nursing • MSN
community health nursing • MSN
neonatal nurse practitioner • Certificate
nursing • PhD
nursing care administration • MSN
nursing education • Certificate
nursing, parenting and families • MSN
transcultural nursing • MSN

College of Science
Dr. John D. Petersen, Dean
Programs in:
applied mathematics • MA, PhD
audiology and speech language pathology • MA, MS, PhD
biological sciences • MS, PhD
chemistry • MA, MS, PhD
clinical psychology • PhD
cognitive psychology • PhD
computer science • MA, MS, PhD
developmental psychology • PhD
electronics and computer control systems • MS
geology • MS
human development • MA
industrial/organizational psychology • PhD
mathematics • MA, PhD
molecular biotechnology • MS
nutrition and food science • MA, MS, PhD
physics • MA, MS, PhD
psychology • MA, PhD
social psychology • PhD
statistics • MA, PhD

College of Urban, Labor and Metropolitan Affairs
Dr. Sue Marx Smock, Dean
Programs in:
dispute resolution • Certificate, MADR
economic development • Certificate
geography • MA
industrial relations • MAIR
urban planning • MUP

Law School
James K. Robinson, Dean
Program in:
law • JD, LL M

School of Business Administration
Dr. Harvey Kahalos, Dean
Programs in:
business administration • MBA
taxation • MS

School of Social Work
Leon Chestang, Dean
Programs in:
social work • MSW
social work practice with families and couples • Certificate

College of Pharmacy and Allied Health Professions
Dr. George C. Fuller, Dean
Program in:
physician assistant • MS

Faculty of Allied Health Professions
Dr. George C. Fuller, Dean, College of Pharmacy and Allied Health Professions
Programs in:
anesthesia • MS
industrial hygiene • MS
industrial toxicology • MS
medical technology • MS
occupational health sciences • MS
occupational medicine • MS
occupational therapy • MS
physical therapy • MSPT

Faculty of Pharmacy
Dr. George C. Fuller, Dean, College of Pharmacy and Allied Health Professions
Programs in:
pharmaceutical sciences • MS, PhD
pharmacy practice • Pharm D

School of Medicine
Dr. Robert Sokol, Dean
Programs in:
anatomy and cell biology • MS, PhD
basic medical science • MS
biochemistry • MS, PhD
cancer biology • PhD
cellular and clinical neurobiology • PhD
community health • MS
community health services • Certificate
immunology and microbiology • MS, PhD
medical physics • PhD
medical research • MS
medicine • MD
molecular biology and genetics • MS, PhD
pathology • PhD
pharmacology • MS, PhD
physiology • MS, PhD
radiological physics • MS
rehabilitation sciences • MS

WESTERN MICHIGAN UNIVERSITY
Kalamazoo, MI 49008

http://www.wmich.edu/

Public coed university. *Enrollment: 26,132 graduate, professional, and undergraduate students. Graduate faculty: 817 full-time, 402 part-time. Computer facilities: Campuswide network is available with full Internet access. Total number of PCs/terminals supplied for student use: 2,000. Computer service fees are included with tuition and fees. Library facilities: Waldo Library plus 3 additional on-campus libraries. Graduate expenses: Tuition of $154 per credit hour for state residents; $372 per credit hour for nonresidents. Fees of $602 per year full-time, $132 per semester part-time. General application contact: Paula J. Boodt, Coordinator, Graduate Admissions and Recruitment, 616-387-2000.*

Graduate College
Dr. Shirley Clay Scott, Dean

College of Arts and Sciences
Dr. Elise B. Jorgens, Dean
Programs in:
    anthropology • MA
    applied behavior analysis • MA, PhD
    applied economics • PhD
    applied mathematics • MS
    biological sciences • MS, PhD
    biostatistics • MS
    chemistry • MA
    clinical psychology • MA, PhD
    comparative religion • MA, PhD
    computational mathematics • MS
    computer science • MS, PhD
    creative writing • MFA
    development administration • MDA
    earth science • MS
    economics • MA
    English • MA, PhD
    experimental analysis of behavior • PhD
    experimental psychology • MA
    geography • MA
    geology • MS, PhD
    graph theory and computer science • PhD
    history • MA, PhD
    industrial/organizational psychology • MA
    mathematics • MA
    mathematics education • MA, PhD
    medieval studies • MA
    organizational communication • MA
    philosophy • MA
    physics • MA, PhD
    political science • MA, PhD
    professional writing • MA
    public affairs and administration • DPA, MPA
    school psychology • Ed S, PhD
    science education • MA, PhD
    sociology • MA, PhD
    Spanish • MA
    statistics • MS, PhD

College of Education
Dr. Frank Rapley, Dean
Programs in:
    administration • MA
    athletic training • MA
    career and technical education • MA
    coaching and sports studies • MA
    counseling psychology • PhD
    counselor education • Ed D, MA, PhD
    counselor education and counseling psychology • MA, PhD
    counselor psychology • MA
    early childhood education • MA
    educational leadership • Ed D, Ed S, MA, PhD
    education and professional development • MA
    elementary education • MA
    exercise science • MA
    family and consumer sciences • MA
    middle school education • MA
    motor development • MA
    physical education • MA
    reading • MA
    special education • Ed D, MA
    special education for handicapped children • MA

College of Engineering and Applied Sciences
Dr. Leonard R. Lamberson, Dean
Programs in:
    computer engineering • MSE
    construction management • MS
    electrical engineering • MSE
    engineering management • MS
    industrial engineering • MSE
    manufacturing science • MS
    materials science and engineering • MS
    mechanical engineering • MSE, PhD
    operations research • MS
    paper, imaging and chemical engineering • MS

College of Fine Arts
Robert Luscombe, Dean
Programs in:
    graphic design • MFA
    music • MA, MM
    textile design • MA, MFA

College of Health and Human Services
Dr. Janet Pisaneschi, Dean
Programs in:
    audiology • MA
    blind rehabilitation • MA
    medicine • MS
    occupational therapy • MS
    social work • MSW
    speech pathology • MA

Haworth College of Business
Dr. James Schmotter, Dean
Programs in:
    accountancy • MSA
    business administration • MBA

MINNESOTA

BEMIDJI STATE UNIVERSITY
Bemidji, MN 56601-2699

http://bsuweb.bemidji.msus.edu/

Public coed comprehensive institution. *Enrollment: 4,587 graduate, professional, and undergraduate students. Graduate faculty: 0 full-time, 92 part-time. Computer facilities: Campuswide network is available with full Internet access. Total number of PCs/terminals supplied for student use: 250. Computer service fees are included with tuition and fees. Library facilities: A. C. Clark Library. Graduate expenses: Tuition of $128 per credit for state residents; $134 per credit (minimum) for nonresidents. Fees of $517 per year full-time, $35 per credit (minimum) part-time. General application contact: Dr. David Larkin, Dean of Graduate Studies, 218-755-3732.*

Graduate Studies
Dr. David Larkin, Dean

Division of Arts and Letters
Dr. Nancy Erickson, Dean
Program in:
English • MA, MS Ed

Division of Professional Studies
Dr. David Larkin, Dean, Graduate Studies
Programs in:
curriculum and instruction • MS Ed
industrial education • MS Ed
physical education • MS Ed
school administration • MS Ed
special education • MS Ed

Division of Social and Natural Sciences
Dr. Ken Lundberg, Dean
Programs in:
biology • MA
computer science • MS Ed
environmental studies • MA
mathematics • MS Ed
science • MS Ed

COLLEGE OF ST. CATHERINE
St. Paul, MN 55105-1789

http://www.stkate.edu/

Independent-religious primarily female comprehensive institution. *Enrollment: 2,803 graduate, professional, and undergraduate students. Graduate faculty: 95. Computer facilities: Campuswide network is available with full Internet access. Total number of PCs/terminals supplied for student use: 250. Computer service fees are included with tuition and fees. Library facilities: main library. Graduate expenses: Tuition of $460 per credit hour. Fees of $60 per year. General application contact: Office of Admission, 612-690-6505.*

Graduate Program
Dr. Jean Cameron, Acting Academic Dean
Programs in:
education • MA
library and information science • MA
nursing • MA
occupational therapy • MA
organizational leadership • MA
physical therapy • MPT
social work • MSW
theology • MA

COLLEGE OF ST. SCHOLASTICA
Duluth, MN 55811-4199

http://www.css.edu/

Independent-religious coed comprehensive institution. *Enrollment: 2,015 graduate, professional, and undergraduate students. Graduate faculty: 42 full-time, 22 part-time. Computer facilities: Campuswide network is available with full Internet access. Total number of PCs/terminals supplied for student use: 150. Computer service fees are included with tuition and fees. Graduate expenses: $7968 per year full-time, $332 per credit part-time. General application contact: Dr. Chandra M. N. Mehrotra, Dean of Graduate Studies, 218-723-6161.*

Graduate Studies
Dr. Chandra M. N. Mehrotra, Dean
Programs in:
education • M Ed
exercise physiology • MA
health information management • MA
management • MA
nursing • MA
occupational therapy • MA
physical therapy • MA

MANKATO STATE UNIVERSITY
Mankato, MN 56002-8400

http://www.mankato.msus.edu/

Public coed comprehensive institution. *Enrollment: 12,507 graduate, professional, and undergraduate students. Graduate faculty: 366 full-time, 80 part-time. Computer facilities: Campuswide network is available with full Internet access. Total number of PCs/terminals supplied for student use: 500. Computer service fees are included with tuition and fees. Library facilities: Memorial Library. Graduate expenses: $126 per credit (minimum) for state residents; $200 per credit for nonresidents. General application contact: Joni Roberts, Admissions Coordinator, 507-389-2321.*

College of Graduate Studies

Dr. Tony Filipovitch, Dean
Program in:
   multidisciplinary studies • MS

College of Allied Health and Nursing

Dr. Cheryl Samuels, Dean
Programs in:
   clinical nurse specialist • MSN
   communication disorders • MS
   community health • MS
   educator • MSN
   family consumer science and interior design • MS, MT
   family nurse practitioner • MSN
   family nursing • MSN
   health science • MS, MT
   human performance • MA, MS, MT, SP
   managed care • MSN
   manager • MSN
   rehabilitation counseling • MS

College of Arts and Humanities

Dr. Jane F. Earley, Dean
Programs in:
   art education • MS
   creative writing • MFA
   English • MA, MS
   French • MAT, MS
   German • MAT
   music • MM, MT
   Spanish • MAT, MS
   speech communication • MA, MS, MT
   studio art • MA
   teaching art • MAT, MT
   teaching English • MS, MT
   theatre arts • MA, MFA

College of Business

Dr. Gaber Abou El Enein, Dean
Programs in:
   business administration • MBA
   economics • MA

College of Education

M. Paula Stone, Interim Dean
Programs in:
   bilingual/bicultural education • MS
   business education • MS, MT
   computer services administration • MS
   counseling and student personnel • MS
   curriculum and instruction • MAT, MT
   early childhood education • MS
   early education for exceptional children • MS
   educational administration • Certificate
   educational leadership • MS
   education of the gifted and talented • MS
   education technology • MS
   elementary education • MS, SP
   elementary school administration • MS, SP
   emotional disturbance • MS
   experiential education • MS
   general educational administration • MS
   higher education administration • MS
   learning disabilities • MS

library media education • MS, SP
mental retardation • MS
reading consultant • MS
secondary administration • MS, SP
secondary teaching • MA, MS, SP
severely handicapped • MS
technology education • MS, MT
vocational-technical administration • MS

College of Science, Engineering and Technology

Dr. Gloria Dimoplon, Dean
Programs in:
   biology • MS
   chemistry • MA, MS
   computer science • MS
   ecology • MS
   economic and political systems • MS
   electrical engineering and electronic engineering technology • MSE
   human ecosystems • MS
   manufacturing • MS
   mathematics • MA, MS
   mathematics: computer science • MS
   physical science • MS
   physics and astronomy • MS, MT
   science • MS, MT
   statistics • MS
   teaching mathematics • MT
   technology • MS

College of Social and Behavioral Sciences

Dr. Susan Coultrap-McQuin, Acting Dean
Programs in:
   clinical psychology • MA
   geography • MA, MS, MT
   gerontology • MS
   history • MA, MS
   human services planning and administration • MA
   industrial psychology • MA
   political science • MA, MS, MT
   psychology • MT
   public administration • MAPA
   social studies • MS, MT
   sociology • MA, MT
   sociology: corrections • MS
   teaching history • MS, MT
   urban and regional studies • MA
   women's studies • MS

METROPOLITAN STATE UNIVERSITY
St. Paul, MN 55106-5000

Public coed comprehensive institution. *Enrollment: 9,000 graduate, professional, and undergraduate students. Graduate faculty: 23 full-time, 150 part-time. Computer facilities: Campuswide network is available with full Internet access. Total number of PCs/terminals supplied for student use: 80. Computer service fees are included with tuition and fees. Graduate expenses: $133 per credit for state*

Metropolitan State University (continued)
residents; $208 per credit for nonresidents. General application contact: *Gary Seiler, Graduate Coordinator, 612-373-2754.*

Management and Administration Program
Gary Seiler, Graduate Coordinator
Programs in:
    finance • MBA
    human resource management • MBA
    international business • MBA
    law enforcement • MMA
    management information systems • MBA
    manpower administration • MMA
    marketing • MBA
    organizational studies • MBA
    purchasing management • MBA

School of Nursing
Marilyn T. Molen, Dean
Program in:
    nursing • MSN

MOORHEAD STATE UNIVERSITY
Moorhead, MN 56563-0002

http://www.moorhead.msus.edu/

Public coed comprehensive institution. *Enrollment:* 5,717 graduate, professional, and undergraduate students. Graduate faculty: *148.* Computer facilities: *Campuswide network is available with full Internet access. Computer service fees are included with tuition and fees.* Library facilities: *Livingston Lord Library.* Graduate expenses: *$145 per credit hour for state residents; $220 per credit hour for nonresidents.* General application contact: *Graduate Admissions Office, 218-236-2164.*

Graduate Studies
Dr. Lawrence L. Reed, Dean of Academic Services
Programs in:
    art education • MS
    business administration • MBA
    counseling and student affairs • MS
    creative writing • MFA
    curriculum and instruction • MS
    educational administration • Ed S, MS
    elementary education • MS
    liberal studies • MLA
    music • MS
    music education • MS
    public and human services administration • MS
    reading • MS
    school psychology • MS, Spec
    special education • MS
    speech pathology and audiology • MS
    studio art • MA

ST. CLOUD STATE UNIVERSITY
St. Cloud, MN 56301-4498

http://www.stcloudstate.edu/

Public coed comprehensive institution. *Enrollment:* 13,994 graduate, professional, and undergraduate students. Graduate faculty: *341 full-time, 25 part-time.* Computer facilities: *Campuswide network is available with full Internet access. Computer service fees are included with tuition and fees.* Library facilities: *Centennial Hall Learning Resource Center.* Graduate expenses: *Tuition of $128 per credit for state residents; $203 per credit for nonresidents. Fees of $16.32 per credit.* General application contact: *Dr. Dennis Nunes, Dean of Graduate and Continuing Studies, 320-255-2113.*

School of Graduate and Continuing Studies
Dr. Dennis Nunes, Dean
Program in:
    special studies • MA, MS

College of Business
Dr. Wayne Wells, Coordinator of Graduate Programs
Programs in:
    accounting • MS
    finance • MBA
    marketing • MBA

College of Education
Dr. Joane McKay, Dean
Programs in:
    administration of special education • Spt
    behavior analysis • MS
    child and family studies • MS
    community counseling • MS
    educable mentally handicapped • MS
    educational administration and leadership • MS, Spt
    elementary education • MS
    emotionally disturbed • MS
    exercise science • MS
    gifted and talented • MS
    information media • MS
    junior high/middle school education • MS
    learning disabled • MS
    physical education • MS
    reading • MS
    rehabilitation counseling • MS
    secondary education • MS
    secondary school counseling • MS
    social responsibility • MS
    special education • MS
    sports management • MS
    trainable mentally retarded • MS

College of Fine Arts and Humanities
Dr. Roland Specht-Jarvis, Dean
Programs in:
    art • MA
    art education • MS
    communication disorders • MS
    communication management • MS

conducting and literature • MM
English • MA, MS
music education • MM
piano pedagogy • MM
teaching English as a second language • MA

College of Science and Engineering
Dr. A. I. Musah, Dean
Programs in:
    biological sciences • MA, MS
    computer science • MS
    environmental and technological studies • MS
    mathematics • MS

College of Social Sciences
Dr. Richard Lewis, Dean
Programs in:
    applied economics • MS
    criminal justice • MS
    geography • MS
    gerontology • MS
    history • MA, MS

SAINT MARY'S UNIVERSITY OF MINNESOTA
Winona, MN 55987-1399

http://www.smumn.edu/

Independent-religious coed comprehensive institution. Computer facilities: *Campuswide network is available with full Internet access. Total number of PCs/terminals supplied for student use: 24. Computer services are offered at no charge.* Library facilities: *Abbott-Northwestern Library.* General application contact: *Vice President, Graduate Programs, 612-874-9877.*

Graduate School
Programs in:
    arts administration • MA
    counseling and psychological services • MA
    developmental disabilities • MA
    education • MA
    educational administration • MA
    educational leadership • Ed D
    human and health services administration • MA
    human development • MA
    management • MA
    nurse anesthesia • MS
    pastoral ministries • Certificate, MA
    philanthropy and development • MA
    telecommunications • MS

UNIVERSITY OF MINNESOTA, DULUTH
Duluth, MN 55812-2496

http://www.d.umn.edu/

Public coed comprehensive institution. *Enrollment: 7,321 graduate, professional, and undergraduate students. Graduate faculty: 193 full-time, 61 part-time. Computer facilities: Campuswide network is available with full Internet access. Total number of PCs/terminals supplied for student use: 410. Computer service fees are included with tuition and fees. Library facilities: main library plus 3 additional on-campus libraries. Graduate expenses: Tuition of $5130 per year full-time, $299 per credit part-time for state residents; $10,074 per year full-time, $536 per credit part-time for nonresidents. Fees of $612 per year full-time, $76 per quarter part-time.* General application contact: *Dr. Stephen C. Hedman, Associate Graduate Dean, 218-726-7523.*

Graduate School
Dr. Stephen C. Hedman, Associate Graduate Dean
Program in:
    toxicology • MS, PhD

College of Education and Human Service Professions
Dr. Edmond Lundstrom, Acting Dean
Programs in:
    communication disorders • MA
    educational psychology • MA
    education and human service profession • M Ed
    social work • MSW

College of Liberal Arts
Dr. Harold Hellenbrand, Dean
Programs in:
    English • MA
    sociology/anthropology • MLS

College of Science and Engineering
Dr. Sabra Anderson, Dean
Programs in:
    applied and computational mathematics • MS
    archaeological studies • MA, MS, PhD
    biology • MS
    chemistry • MS
    computer science • MS
    geology • MS, PhD
    physics • MS

School of Business and Economics
Kjell Knudsen, Dean
Program in:
    business administration • MBA

School of Fine Arts
Dr. W. Robert Bucker, Dean
Programs in:
    art studies • MA
    graphic design • MFA
    music education • MM
    studio art • MA

University of Minnesota, Duluth (continued)
School of Medicine
Dr. Richard J. Ziegler, Interim Dean
Programs in:
anatomy and cell biology • MS, PhD
biochemistry and molecular biology • MS, PhD
medical microbiology and immunology • MS, PhD
medicine • MD
pharmacology • MS, PhD
physiology • MS, PhD

UNIVERSITY OF MINNESOTA, TWIN CITIES CAMPUS
Minneapolis, MN 55455-0213
http://www1.umn.edu/tc/

Public coed university. *Enrollment: 37,615 graduate, professional, and undergraduate students. Graduate faculty: 3,200. Library facilities: O. Meredith Wilson Library plus 16 additional on-campus libraries. Graduate expenses: Tuition of $5130 per year full-time, $773 per quarter (minimum) part-time for state residents; $10,074 per year full-time, $1484 per quarter (minimum) part-time for nonresidents. Fees of $677 per year full-time, $10.48 per quarter (minimum) part-time. General application contact: Dr. Christine Maziar, Vice President for Research and Dean, 612-625-3394.*

Graduate School
Dr. Christine Maziar, Vice President for Research and Dean
Programs in:
biochemistry, molecular biology and bi • PhD
biomedical engineering • MS, PhD
biophysical sciences and medical physics • MS, PhD
cellular and integrative physiology • MS, PhD
clinical laboratory sciences • MS
endodontics • MS
experimental and clinical pharmacology • MS, PhD
experimental surgery • MS
family practice and community health • MS
genetic counseling • MS
health informatics • MS, PhD
history of medicine • MA, PhD
hospital pharmacy • MS
medicinal chemistry • MS, PhD
microbial engineering • MS
microbiology • MS
microbiology, immunology, and molecular pathobiology • PhD
molecular, cellular and developmental biology and genetics • PhD
molecular veterinary biosciences • MS, PhD
neuroscience • PhD
oral biology • MS, PhD
oral health services for older adults • MS
orthodontics • MS
otolaryngology • MS, PhD
pediatric dentistry • MS
periodontology • MS

pharmaceutics • MS, PhD
pharmacology • MS, PhD
physical medicine and rehabilitation • MS, PhD
physical therapy • MS
prosthodontics • MS
scientific computation • MS, PhD
social and administrative pharmacy • MS, PhD
surgery • MS, PhD
temporal mandibular joint • MS
veterinary medicine • MS, PhD

College of Agricultural, Food, and Environmental Sciences
Dr. Michael V. Martin, Dean
Programs in:
agricultural and applied economics • MS, PhD
agricultural education • M Ed
agronomy • MS, PhD
animal science • MS, PhD
biosystems and agricultural engineering • MBAE, MSBAE, PhD
entomology • MS, PhD
food science • MS, PhD
horticultural science • MS, PhD
microbial ecology • MS, PhD
nutrition • MS, PhD
plant breeding • MS, PhD
plant pathology • MS, PhD
rhetoric and scientific and technical communication • MA, PhD
scientific and technical communication • MS
soil, water, and climate • MS, PhD

College of Architecture and Landscape Architecture
Thomas Fisher, Dean
Programs in:
architecture • M Arch
landscape architecture • MLA, MS

College of Biological Sciences
Dr. Robert Elde, Dean
Programs in:
biological sciences • MBS
ecology and animal behavior • MS, PhD
plant biology • MS, PhD
zoology • MS, PhD

College of Education and Human Development
Steve Yussen, Dean
Programs in:
adult education • M Ed
agricultural education • M Ed
art education • M Ed, MA, PhD
business and marketing education • M Ed
child development • PhD
communications • PhD
comparative and international development education • MA, PhD
curriculum studies • MA, PhD
early childhood education • M Ed, MA, PhD
educational administration • Ed D, Ed S
educational policy and administration • MA, PhD
educational psychology • Ed S, MA, PhD
elementary education • M Ed, MA, PhD
English education • M Ed, MA

evaluation studies • MA, PhD

higher education • MA, PhD

human resource development • M Ed

instructional systems • MA, PhD

kinesiology • M Ed, MA, PhD

literacy • MA

mathematics education • M Ed, MA, PhD

recreation, park, and leisure studies • M Ed, MA, PhD

remedial and reading supervisor endorsement • MA

science education • M Ed, MA, PhD

second languages and cultures • M Ed, MA, PhD

social studies education • M Ed, MA, PhD

special education • M Ed

teacher leadership • M Ed

vocational education • M Ed

work, community, and family education • Ed D, M Ed, MA, PhD

youth development leadership • M Ed

College of Human Ecology
Mary Heltsley, Dean

Programs in:

design, housing, and apparel • MA, MS, PhD

family social science • MA, PhD

food science • MS, PhD

nutrition • MS, PhD

social work • MSW, PhD

College of Liberal Arts
Steven J. Rosenstone, Dean

Programs in:

acting • MFA

American studies • MA, PhD

ancient and medieval art and archaeology • MA, PhD

anthropology • MA, PhD

art • MFA

art history • MA, PhD

biological psychopathology • PhD

Chinese • MA, PhD

classics • MA, PhD

clinical psychology • PhD

cognitive and biological psychology • PhD

communication disorders • MA, PhD

comparative literature • MA, PhD

comparative studies in discourse and society • MA, PhD

counseling psychology • PhD

design • MFA

differential psychology/behavior genetics • PhD

directing • MFA

East Asian studies • MA

economics • PhD

English • MA, MFA, PhD

French • MA, PhD

geographic information science • MGIS

geography • MA, PhD

German • MA, PhD

Germanic philology • MA, PhD

Greek • MA, PhD

Hispanic and Luso-Brazilian literatures and linguistics • PhD

Hispanic linguistics • MA

history • MA, PhD

industrial/organizational psychology • PhD

Italian • MA

Japanese • MA, PhD

Latin • MA, PhD

linguistics • MA, PhD

mass communication • MA, PhD

music • DMA, MA, MM, PhD

personality research • PhD

philosophy • MA, PhD

political science • MA, PhD

Portuguese • MA

psychometric methods • MA, PhD

Russian area studies • MA

Scandinavian studies • MA, PhD

school psychology • PhD

social psychology • PhD

sociology • MA, PhD

Spanish • MA

speech communication • MA, PhD

statistics • MS, PhD

theater arts and dance • PhD

theatre arts and dance • MA

College of Natural Resources
Dr. Alfred Sullivan, Dean

Programs in:

conservation biology • MS, PhD

fisheries • MS, PhD

forestry • MF, MS, PhD

wildlife conservation • MS, PhD

Hubert H. Humphrey Institute of Public Affairs
Dr. John Brandl, Interim Dean

Programs in:

public policy • MPP

science and technology policy • MS

urban and regional planning • MURP

Institute of Human Genetics
Anthony Faras, Director

Program in:

human genetics • MS, PhD

Institute of Technology
H. Ted Davis, Dean

Programs in:

aerospace engineering • M Aero E, MS, PhD

astrophysics • MS, PhD

biomedical engineering • MS, PhD

chemical engineering • M Ch E, MS Ch E, PhD

chemistry • MS, PhD

civil engineering • MCE, MSCE, PhD

computer and information sciences • MCIS, MS, PhD

computer engineering • M Comp E, MS

electrical and computer engineering • MEE, MSEE, PhD

geological engineering • M Geo E, MS Geo E, PhD

geology • MS, PhD

geophysics • MS, PhD

history of science and technology • MA, PhD

industrial engineering • MIE, MSIE, PhD

management of technology • MSMOT

manufacturing systems • MS

materials science and engineering • M Mat SE, MS Mat SE, PhD

mathematics • MS, PhD

University of Minnesota, Twin Cities Campus (continued)
mechanical engineering • MME, MSME, PhD
mechanics • MS, PhD
microbial engineering • MS
physics • MS, PhD
software engineering • MS

School of Nursing
Sandra Edwardson, Dean
Programs in:
adolescent nursing • MS
advanced clinical specialist in adult health nursing • MS
advanced clinical specialist in child and family nursing • MS
advanced clinical specialist in children with special health needs • MS
advanced clinical specialist in gerontology • MS
family nurse practitioner • MS
gerontology nurse practitioner • MS
midwifery • MS
nursing • PhD
nursing education • MS
nursing management • MS
oncology nursing • MS
pediatric nurse practitioner • MS
public health nursing • MS

Carlson School of Management
David Kidwell, Dean
Programs in:
accounting • MBA, PhD
business administration • MBA, PhD
business taxation • MBT
finance • MBA, PhD
healthcare management • MHA, PhD
human resources and industrial relations • MA, PhD
information and decision sciences • MBA, PhD
management • EMBA
management of technology • MSMOT
manufacturing systems • MS
marketing and logistics management • MBA, PhD
operations and management science • MBA, PhD
software engineering • MS
strategic management and organization • MBA, PhD

College of Pharmacy
Marilyn K. Speedie, Dean
Programs in:
experimental and clinical pharmacology • MS, PhD
hospital pharmacy • MS
medicinal chemistry • MS, PhD
pharmaceutics • MS, PhD
pharmacy • Pharm D
social and administrative pharmacy • MS, PhD

College of Veterinary Medicine
David Thawley, Dean
Programs in:
molecular veterinary biosciences • MS, PhD
veterinary medicine • DVM

Law School
E. Thomas Sullivan, Dean
Program in:
law • JD, LL M

Medical School
Programs in:
biochemistry, molecular biology and bi • PhD
biomedical engineering • MS, PhD
cellular and integrative physiology • MS, PhD
clinical laboratory sciences • MS
experimental surgery • MS
family practice and community health • MS
history of medicine • MA, PhD
medicine • MD
microbial engineering • MS
microbiology • MS
microbiology, immunology, and molecular pathobiology • PhD
otolaryngology • MS, PhD
pharmacology • MS, PhD
physical medicine and rehabilitation • MS, PhD
physical therapy • MS
surgery • MS, PhD

School of Dentistry
Dr. Michael J. Till, Dean
Programs in:
dentistry • DDS
endodontics • MS
oral biology • MS, PhD
oral health services for older adults • MS
orthodontics • MS
pediatric dentistry • MS
periodontology • MS
prosthodontics • MS
temporal mandibular joint • MS

School of Public Health
Dr. Edith Leyasmeyer, Dean
Programs in:
biostatistics • MPH, MS, PhD
community health education • MPH
environmental and occupational epidemiology • MPH, MS, PhD
environmental chemistry • MS, PhD
environmental health policy • MPH, MS, PhD
environmental microbiology • MPH, MS, PhD
environmental toxicology • MPH, MS, PhD
epidemiology • MPH, PhD
health services research and policy • MS
health services research, policy, and administration • PhD
industrial hygiene • MPH, MS, PhD
maternal and child health • MPH
occupational health nursing • MPH, MS, PhD
occupational medicine • MPH
public health administration • MPH
public health nutrition • MPH

UNIVERSITY OF ST. THOMAS
St. Paul, MN 55105-1096

http://www.stthomas.edu/

Independent-religious coed university. *Enrollment: 10,436 graduate, professional, and undergraduate students. Graduate faculty: 117 full-time, 300 part-time. Computer facilities: Campuswide network is available with full Internet access. Computer services are offered at no charge. Library facilities: O'Shaughnessy Frey Library plus 2 additional on-campus libraries. Graduate expenses: $410 per credit hour. General application contact: Dr. Miriam Q. Williams, Associate Vice President for Academic Affairs, 612-962-6032.*

Graduate Studies
Dr. Ralph Pearson, Vice President for Academic Affairs
Programs in:
    professional psychology • MA, Psy D
    social work • MSW

Graduate School of Applied Science and Engineering
Dr. Ralph Pearson, Vice President for Academic Affairs, Graduate Studies
Programs in:
    manufacturing systems engineering • Certificate, MMSE, MS
    software • Certificate, MS, MSDD, MSS

Graduate School of Arts and Sciences
Dr. Noreen Carrocci, Academic Dean
Programs in:
    art history • MA
    English • MA
    piano pedagogy and performance • MM

Graduate School of Business
Dr. Ted Fredrickson, Dean
Programs in:
    accounting • Certificate, MBA
    business administration • MBA
    business communication • MBC
    business writing • Certificate
    communication • Certificate
    environmental management • MBA
    finance • MBA
    financial services management • MBA
    franchise management • Certificate, MBA
    government contracts • Certificate, MBA
    health care management • Certificate, MBA
    human resource management • Certificate, MBA
    human resource management–compensation • Certificate
    human resource management–employee benefits • Certificate
    human resource management–generalist • Certificate
    human resource management–law • Certificate
    information management • MBA
    insurance and risk management • MBA
    internal communication • Certificate
    international finance • Certificate, MIM
    international human resource management • Certificate
    international human resources • Certificate, MIM
    international managerial communication • Certificate, MIM
    international marketing • Certificate, MIM
    management • MBA
    management communication • Certificate
    manufacturing systems • MBA
    marketing • Certificate, MBA
    medical group management • MBA
    nonprofit management • Certificate, MBA
    public relations • Certificate
    real estate appraisal • MS
    self-designed • MIM
    sports and entertainment management • MBA
    survey of professional communication • Certificate
    venture management • Certificate, MBA

School of Education
Dr. Richard Podemski, Dean
Programs in:
    curriculum and instruction • Ed S, MA
    educational leadership and administration • Certificate, Ed D, Ed S, MA
    gifted, creative and talented education • MA
    learning and human development technology • Certificate, MA
    special education • MA
    teaching • MA

St. Paul Seminary School of Divinity
Dr. Victor Klimoski, Dean
Programs in:
    divinity • M Div
    ministry • D Min
    pastoral studies • MA
    religious education • MA
    theology • MA

WINONA STATE UNIVERSITY
Winona, MN 55987-5838

http://www.winona.msus.edu/

Public coed comprehensive institution. *Enrollment: 7,013 graduate, professional, and undergraduate students. Graduate faculty: 76 full-time. Library facilities: Maxwell Library. General application contact: Dr. Pauline Christensen, Director of Graduate Studies, 507-457-5088.*

Graduate Studies
Dr. Pauline Christensen, Director

College of Business
Dr. Kenneth Gorman, Dean
Programs in:
    business administration • MBA
    business education • MS

Winona State University (continued)

College of Education
Dr. Carol Anderson, Dean
Programs in:
 counselor education • MS
 early childhood education • MS
 education • MS
 educational leadership • Ed S, MS
 elementary education • MS
 physical education • MS
 special education • MS

College of Liberal Arts
Dr. Peter Henderson, Dean
Program in:
 English • MA, MS

College of Nursing
Dr. Marjorie Smith, Graduate Director
Program in:
 nursing • MSN

MISSISSIPPI

ALCORN STATE UNIVERSITY
Lorman, MS 39096-9402

http://www.alcorn.edu/

Public coed comprehensive institution. Library facilities: *J. D. Boyd Library.* Graduate expenses: *$2470 per year full-time, $378 per semester (minimum) part-time for state residents; $5331 per year full-time, $855 per semester (minimum) part-time for nonresidents. General application contact: Dean, School of Graduate Studies, 601-877-6120.*

School of Graduate Studies
Programs in:
 administration and supervision • MS Ed
 agricultural economics • MS Ag
 agricultural education • MS Ed
 agronomy • MS Ag
 animal science • MS Ag
 computer and information sciences • MS
 elementary education • Ed S, MS Ed
 guidance and counseling • MS Ed
 health and physical education • MS Ed
 industrial education • MS Ed
 secondary education • MS Ed
 special education • MS Ed

School of Nursing
Program in:
 rural nursing • MSN

DELTA STATE UNIVERSITY
Cleveland, MS 38733-0001

http://www.deltast.edu/

Public coed comprehensive institution. *Enrollment: 4,085 graduate, professional, and undergraduate students. Graduate faculty: 129 full-time, 22 part-time. Computer facilities: Campuswide network is available with full Internet access. Total number of PCs/terminals supplied for student use: 280. Computer service fees are included with tuition and fees. Library facilities: W. B. Roberts Library.* Graduate expenses: *$2596 per year full-time, $121 per semester hour part-time for state residents; $5546 per year full-time, $285 per semester hour part-time for nonresidents. General application contact: Dr. John Thornell, Dean of Graduate Studies and Continuing Education, 601-846-4310.*

School of Graduate Studies
Dr. John Thornell, Dean of Graduate Studies and
 Continuing Education

School of Arts and Sciences
Dr. Richard S. Myers, Dean
Programs in:
 biological sciences • MSNS
 community development • MSCD
 criminal justice • MSCJ
 English education • M Ed
 history education • M Ed
 mathematics education • M Ed
 music education • MM Ed
 social science education • M Ed
 social work • MSW

School of Business
Dr. William Stewart, Dean
Programs in:
 accounting • MPA
 commercial aviation • MCA
 management and marketing • MBA

School of Education
Dr. Everett Caston, Dean
Programs in:
 administration • M Ed
 administration and supervision • Ed S
 elementary education • Ed S, M Ed
 elementary principalship • M Ed
 elementary supervision • M Ed
 guidance and counseling • M Ed
 physical education and recreation • M Ed
 professional studies • Ed D
 secondary principalship • M Ed
 secondary supervision • M Ed
 special education • M Ed

School of Nursing
Dr. Maureen Propst, Dean
Program in:
 nursing • MSN

JACKSON STATE UNIVERSITY
Jackson, MS 39217

http://www.jsums.edu/

Public coed university. *Enrollment: 6,333 graduate, professional, and undergraduate students. Graduate faculty: 213 full-time, 15 part-time. Computer facilities: Campuswide network is available with full Internet access. Total number of PCs/terminals supplied for student use: 900. Computer service fees are applied as a separate charge. Library facilities: H. T. Sampson Library plus 1 additional on-campus library. Graduate expenses: $2688 per year (minimum) full-time, $150 per semester hour part-time for state residents; $5546 per year (minimum) full-time, $309 per semester hour part-time for nonresidents. General application contact: Dr. Dorris R. Robinson-Gardner, Dean of the Graduate School, 601-968-2455.*

Graduate School
Dr. Doris Robinson-Gardner, Dean

School of Allied Health
Dr. Zenobia Bagli, Dean
Program in:
    communicative disorders • MS

School of Business
Dr. Glenda B. Glover, Dean
Programs in:
    accounting • MPA, PhD
    business administration • MBA, PhD
    business education • M Bus Ed
    systems management • MSSM

School of Education
Dr. Johnnie Mills-Jones, Dean
Programs in:
    community and agency counseling • MS
    early childhood education • Ed D, MS Ed
    education administration • Ed S
    educational administration • MS Ed, PhD
    educational technology • MS Ed
    elementary education • Ed S, MS Ed
    guidance and counseling • Ed S, MS, MS Ed
    health, physical education and recreation • MS Ed
    rehabilitation services • MS
    secondary education • Ed S, MS Ed
    special education and rehabilitative services • Ed S,
        MS Ed

School of Liberal Arts
Dr. Dollye M. E. Robinson, Dean
Programs in:
    clinical psychology • PhD
    criminology and justice service • MA
    English • MA
    history • MA
    mass communications • MS
    music education • MM Ed
    political science • MA
    public policy and administration • MPPA, PhD
    sociology • MA
    teaching English • MAT
    urban and regional planning • MS

School of Science and Technology
Dr. Abdul K. Mohamed, Dean
Programs in:
    biology education • MST
    chemistry • MS
    computer science • MS
    environmental science • MS, PhD
    hazardous materials management • MS
    industrial arts education • MS Ed
    mathematics • MS, MST
    science education • MST

School of Social Work
Dr. Gwendolyn S. Prater, Dean
Program in:
    social work • MSW, PhD

MISSISSIPPI COLLEGE
Clinton, MS 39058

http://www.mc.edu/

Independent-religious coed comprehensive institution. *Enrollment: 3,532 graduate, professional, and undergraduate students. Graduate faculty: 152 full-time, 95 part-time. Computer facilities: Campuswide network is available with full Internet access. Total number of PCs/terminals supplied for student use: 160. Computer services are offered at no charge. Library facilities: Leland Speed Library. Graduate expenses: Tuition of $6624 per year full-time, $276 per hour part-time. Fees of $230 per year full-time, $35 per semester (minimum) part-time. General application contact: Dr. Edward McMillan, Vice President and Graduate Dean, 601-925-3225.*

Graduate School
Dr. Edward McMillan, Vice President and Graduate Dean

College of Arts and Sciences
Dr. Richard G. Eaves, Dean
Programs in:
    applied music • MM
    art • MA
    combined sciences • MCS
    communication • MSC
    computer science • MS
    English • M Ed, MA
    general sociology • MS
    health care administration • MHS
    history • M Ed, MA, MSS
    marriage and family therapy • MS
    mathematics • MS
    music education • MM
    performance accompanying • MM
    social sciences • MSS
    sociology • MSS

School of Business Administration
Dr. Lloyd Roberts, Dean
Programs in:
    accounting • MBA
    business administration • MBA

Mississippi College (continued)

School of Education

Dr. Thomas Taylor, Dean
Programs in:
  art education • M Ed
  biology education • M Ed
  business education • M Ed
  computer science education • M Ed
  counseling psychology • MCP
  elementary education • M Ed
  guidance and counseling • Ed S, M Ed
  mathematics education • M Ed
  school administration • M Ed
  sciences education • M Ed
  secondary education • M Ed

School of Law

J. Richard Hurt, Dean
Program in:
  law • JD

MISSISSIPPI STATE UNIVERSITY
Mississippi State, MS 39762

http://www.msstate.edu/

Public coed university. *Enrollment:* 14,788 graduate, professional, and undergraduate students. *Graduate faculty:* 822. *Computer facilities: Campuswide network is available with full Internet access. Total number of PCs/terminals supplied for student use: 3,000. Computer services are offered at no charge. Library facilities: Mitchell Memorial Library plus 2 additional on-campus libraries. Graduate expenses: $3017 per year full-time, $168 per credit hour part-time for state residents; $6119 per year full-time, $340 per credit hour part-time for nonresidents. General application contact: Dr. Richard D. Koshel, Dean of Graduate School, 601-325-7400.*

Graduate School

Dr. Richard D. Koshel, Dean
Program in:
  veterinary medicine • MS, PhD

College of Agriculture and Life Sciences

Dr. Bill Fox, Dean
Programs in:
  agricultural economics • MABM, MS, PhD
  agricultural pest management • M Agr
  agriculture and extension education • ME Ed
  agriculture education and experimental statistics • Ed D, Ed S, MS, PhD
  animal physiology • MS, PhD
  biochemistry • MS
  entomology and plant pathology • MS, PhD
  food science and technology • MS, PhD
  genetics • MS
  molecular biology • PhD
  nutrition • MS, PhD
  plant and soil sciences • MS, PhD
  poultry science • MS

College of Arts and Sciences

Dr. Frank E. Saal, Dean
Programs in:
  analytical chemistry • MS, PhD
  biochemistry • PhD
  biological sciences • MS, PhD
  chemical physics • PhD
  electronic visualization • MFA
  engineering physics • PhD
  English • MA
  French • MA
  geosciences • MS
  history • MA, PhD
  inorganic chemistry • MS, PhD
  mathematical sciences • PhD
  mathematics • MS
  organic chemistry • MS, PhD
  physical chemistry • MS, PhD
  physics • MS
  political science • MA
  psychology • MS
  public policy and administration • MPPA, PhD
  rural administration • PhD
  sociology • MS, PhD
  Spanish • MA
  statistics • MS

College of Business and Industry

Dr. Garry O. Smith, Interim Dean
Programs in:
  accountancy • MPA, MTX
  business administration • DBA, MBA
  information systems • MSBA
  systems management • MSSM

College of Education

Dr. William H. Graves, Dean
Programs in:
  business education • MS
  church music education • MM Ed
  community counseling • MS
  counseling services • MS
  counselor education • MS, PhD
  education • M Ed
  elementary education • Ed D, Ed S, MS, PhD
  exercise science • MS
  general education psychology • MS, PhD
  health education/health promotion • MS
  industrial technology • MS
  instructional technology • MS, MSIT
  instrumental • MM Ed
  keyboard • MM Ed
  physical education • MS
  piano pedagogy • MM Ed
  rehabilitation • MS
  research and evaluation • MS
  school administration • Ed D, Ed S, MS, PhD
  school counseling • MS
  school psychology • PhD
  secondary education • Ed D, Ed S, MS, PhD
  special education • Ed S, MS, PhD
  sport administration • MS
  student development services • MS

teaching/coaching • MS
technology • MS
vocational education • MS
voice • MM Ed

College of Engineering
Dr. A. Wayne Bennett, Dean
Programs in:
    aerospace engineering • MS, PhD
    agricultural engineering • PhD
    biological engineering • MS, PhD
    chemical engineering • MS, PhD
    civil engineering • PhD
    computational engineering • MS, PhD
    computer engineering • MS, PhD
    computer science • MS, PhD
    electrical engineering • MS, PhD
    engineering • PhD
    engineering mechanics • MS
    engineering physics • PhD
    environmental engineering • MS
    industrial engineering • MS, PhD
    mechanical engineering • MS, PhD
    nuclear engineering • PhD
    petroleum engineering • PhD
    structural engineering • MS

College of Forest Resources
Dr. John E. Gunter, Dean
Programs in:
    forest products • MS, PhD
    forest resources • PhD
    forestry • MS, PhD
    genetics • MS
    wildlife ecology • MS

School of Architecture
Dr. John M. McRae, Dean
Program in:
    computer graphics/visualization • MS

College of Veterinary Medicine
Dr. H. Dwight Mercer, Dean
Program in:
    veterinary medicine • DVM, MS, PhD

UNIVERSITY OF MISSISSIPPI
University, MS 38677-9702

http://www.olemiss.edu/

Public coed university. *Enrollment:* 10,534 graduate, professional, and undergraduate students. Graduate faculty: *459 full-time.* Computer facilities: *Campuswide network is available with full Internet access. Total number of PCs/terminals supplied for student use: 200. Computer services are offered at no charge.* Library facilities: *John Davis Williams Library plus 4 additional on-campus libraries.* Graduate expenses: *$3053 per year full-time, $170 per hour part-time for state residents; $6155 per year full-time, $342 per hour*

part-time for nonresidents. General application contact: Dr. Donald R. Cole, Associate Dean of Graduate School, 601-232-7474.

Graduate School
Dr. Maurice Eftink, Acting Dean

College of Liberal Arts
Dr. H. Dale Abadie, Dean
Programs in:
    anthropology • MA
    art education • MA
    art history • MA
    biology • MS, PhD
    chemistry • DA, MS, PhD
    classics • MA
    clinical psychology • PhD
    communicative disorders • MS
    English • DA, MA, PhD
    experimental psychology • PhD
    fine arts • MFA
    French • MA
    German • MA
    history • MA, PhD
    journalism • MA
    mathematics • MA, MS, PhD
    music • DA, MM
    philosophy • MA
    physics • MA, MS, PhD
    political science • MA, PhD
    psychology • MA
    sociology • MA, MSS
    Southern studies • MA
    Spanish • MA
    theatre arts • MFA

School of Accountancy
Dr. James W. Davis, Dean
Programs in:
    accountancy • M Acc, PhD
    taxation accounting • M Tax

School of Business Administration
Dr. Randy Boxx, Dean
Programs in:
    business administration • MBA
    economics • MA, PhD
    systems management • MS

School of Education
Dr. James Chambless, Acting Dean
Programs in:
    curriculum and instruction • Ed D, Ed S, M Ed
    education • PhD
    educational leadership • PhD
    educational leadership and educational psychology •
       Ed D, Ed S, M Ed, MA
    educational psychology • PhD
    exercise science • MA, MS
    exercise science and leisure management • PhD
    higher education/student personnel • M Ed, MA
    leisure management • MA
    secondary education • MA
    wellness • MS

University of Mississippi (continued)

School of Engineering
Dr. Allie M. Smith, Dean
Programs in:
    computational engineering science • MS, PhD
    engineering science • MS, PhD

School of Pharmacy
Dr. Kenneth Roberts, Dean
Programs in:
    medicinal chemistry • MS, PhD
    pharmaceutics • MS, PhD
    pharmacognosy • MS, PhD
    pharmacology • MS, PhD
    pharmacy • Pharm D
    pharmacy administration • MS, PhD
    toxicology • PhD

School of Law
Dr. William Champion, Acting Dean
Program in:
    law • JD

UNIVERSITY OF SOUTHERN MISSISSIPPI
Hattiesburg, MS 39406-5167
http://www.usm.edu/

Public coed university. *Enrollment: 13,657 graduate, professional, and undergraduate students. Graduate faculty: 461 full-time, 59 part-time. Library facilities: Cook Memorial Library plus 2 additional on-campus libraries. Graduate expenses: $2870 per year full-time, $137 per credit hour part-time for state residents; $5972 per year full-time, $172 per credit hour part-time for nonresidents. General application contact: Dr. Margaret Carlin, Director of Graduate Admissions, 601-266-5137.*

Graduate School
Dr. Anselm C. Griffin III, Dean

College of Business Administration
Dr. Roderick Posey, Acting Dean
Programs in:
    business administration • MBA
    professional accountancy • MPA

College of Education and Psychology
Dr. Bruce Holliman, Acting Dean
Programs in:
    adult education • Ed D, Ed S, M Ed, PhD
    business technology education • MS
    early childhood education • Ed S, M Ed
    educational administration • Ed D, Ed S, M Ed, PhD
    education of the gifted • Ed D, Ed S, M Ed, PhD
    elementary education • Ed D, Ed S, M Ed, PhD
    psychology • Ed S, M Ed, MA, MS, PhD
    reading • Ed S, M Ed, MS
    secondary education • Ed D, Ed S, M Ed, MS, PhD
    special education • Ed D, Ed S, M Ed, PhD
    technical occupational education • MS

College of Health and Human Sciences
Dr. Jane Boudreaux, Interim Dean
Programs in:
    health education • MPH
    health policy/administration • MPH
    human nutrition • MS
    human performance • Ed D, PhD
    institution management • MS
    marriage and family therapy • MS
    occupational/environmental health • MPH
    physical education • MS
    public health nutrition • MPH
    recreation • MS
    social work • MSW

College of Liberal Arts
Dr. Glenn T. Harper, Dean
Programs in:
    anthropology • MA, MS
    communication • MA, MS, PhD
    corrections • MA, MS
    creative writing • MS
    economic development • MS
    English • MA, PhD
    foreign languages and literatures • MATL
    geography • MA, MS
    history • MA, MS, PhD
    juvenile justice • MA, MS
    law enforcement • MA, MS
    library science • MLS, SLS
    philosophy • MA
    political science • MA, MS
    public relations • MS
    speech and hearing sciences • MA, MS, PhD

College of Nursing
Dr. Gerry Cadenhead, Director
Programs in:
    community health nursing • MSN
    nursing service administration • MSN
    psychiatric nursing • MSN

College of Science and Technology
Dr. Steve Doblin, Dean
Programs in:
    analytical chemistry • MS, PhD
    biochemistry • MS, PhD
    engineering technology • MS
    environmental biology • MS, PhD
    geology • MS
    inorganic chemistry • MS, PhD
    marine biology • MS, PhD
    mathematics • MS
    medical technology • MS
    microbiology • MS, PhD
    molecular biology • MS, PhD
    organic chemistry • MS, PhD
    physical chemistry • MS, PhD
    physics and astronomy • MS
    polymer science • MS, PhD
    science education • Ed D, M Ed, MS, PhD
    scientific computing • PhD

College of the Arts
Dr. Peter Alexander, Dean
Programs in:
 art education • MAE
 church music • MM
 conducting • MM
 history and literature • MM
 music education • DME, MME, PhD
 performance • MM
 performance and pedagogy • DMA
 theatre and dance • MFA
 theory and composition • MM
 woodwind performance • MM

Institute of Marine Sciences
Dr. J. Grimes, Director
Program in:
 marine science • MS, PhD

WILLIAM CAREY COLLEGE
Hattiesburg, MS 39401-5499

http://www.wmcarey.edu/

Independent-religious coed comprehensive institution. *Enrollment:* 2,100 graduate, professional, and undergraduate students. Graduate faculty: *21 full-time, 11 part-time.* Library facilities: *Rouse Library.* Graduate expenses: *$130 per semester hour.* General application contact: *Dr. William Hetrick, Dean, College of Education and Psychology, 601-582-6217.*

Graduate Division
Dr. William Hetrick, Dean, College of Education and
 Psychology
Programs in:
 business • MBA
 educational leadership • M Ed
 elementary education • M Ed
 gifted education • M Ed
 secondary education • M Ed
 special education • M Ed
 teaching • MA Ed

MISSOURI

 AVILA COLLEGE
Kansas City, MO 64145-1698

http://www.avila.edu/

Independent-religious coed comprehensive institution. *Enrollment:* 1,305 graduate, professional, and undergraduate students. Graduate faculty: *12 full-time, 17 part-time.* Computer facilities: *Campuswide network is available with full Internet access. Total number of PCs/terminals supplied for student use: 71. Computer service fees are*

included with tuition and fees. Library facilities: *Hooley-Bundschu Library.* Graduate expenses: *Tuition of $295 per credit hour. Fees of $160 per year full-time, $6 per year part-time.* General application contact: *Sr. Marie Joan Harris, Vice President for Academic Affairs, 816-942-8400 Ext. 2358.*

Graduate Programs
Sr. Marie Joan Harris, Vice President for Academic Affairs
Programs in:
 business and economics • MBA
 education • MS
 psychology • MS

 # CENTRAL MISSOURI STATE UNIVERSITY
Warrensburg, MO 64093

http://www.cmsu.edu/

Public coed comprehensive institution. *Enrollment:* 10,320 graduate, professional, and undergraduate students. Graduate faculty: *432 full-time, 66 part-time.* Computer facilities: *Campuswide network is available with full Internet access. Total number of PCs/terminals supplied for student use: 1,441. Computer service fees are included with tuition and fees.* Library facilities: *Ward Edwards Library.* Graduate expenses: *$3288 per year full-time, $137 per credit hour part-time for state residents; $5928 per year full-time, $274 per credit hour part-time for nonresidents.* General application contact: *Dr. Novella Perrin, Dean, School of Graduate Studies, 660-543-4092.*

School of Graduate Studies
Dr. Novella Perrin, Dean
Programs in:
 human services/learning resources • Ed S
 library science and information services • MS

College of Applied Sciences and Technology
Dr. Art Rosser, Dean
Programs in:
 agricultural technology • MS
 aviation safety • MS
 human services/industrial arts and technology • Ed S
 human services/public services • Ed S
 industrial hygiene • MS
 industrial management • MS
 industrial safety management • MS
 industrial technology • MS
 industrial, vocational, and technical education • MS
 K–12 education/industrial arts and technology • MSE
 occupational safety management • MS
 public services administration • MS
 secondary education/safety education • MSE
 security • MS
 technology • PhD
 transportation safety • MS

Central Missouri State University (continued)

College of Arts and Sciences
Dr. Robert Schwartz, Dean
Programs in:
- art • MA
- art education • MSE
- biology • MS
- British and American literature • MA
- communication • MA
- English education • MSE
- history • MA
- mathematics • MS
- mathematics education • MSE
- music • MA
- social studies • MSE
- speech communication • MSE
- teaching English as a second language • MA
- theatre • MA

College of Education and Human Services
Dr. Jim Bowman, Dean
Programs in:
- administration • Ed S
- adult education • MSE
- communication disorders • MS
- criminal justice • MS
- curriculum and instruction • Ed S
- educational leadership • Ed D
- elementary • MSE
- elementary education • MSE
- human services • Ed S
- human services/guidance and counseling • Ed S
- human services-public services • Ed S
- K–12 education • MSE
- physical education • Ed S
- physical education/exercise and sports science • MS
- psychology • MS
- reading • MSE
- school administration • MSE
- school counseling • MS
- school principalship • Ed S
- secondary • MSE
- secondary education • MSE
- social gerontology • MS
- sociology • MA
- special education • MSE
- special education/human services • Ed S
- student personnel administration • MS
- superintendency • Ed S

Harmon College of Business Administration
Dr. Paul Shaffer, Dean
Programs in:
- accounting • MA
- economics • MA
- management • MBA

DRURY COLLEGE
Springfield, MO 65802-3791

http://www.drury.edu/

Independent coed comprehensive institution. *Enrollment: 3,843 graduate, professional, and undergraduate students. Graduate faculty: 38 full-time, 20 part-time. Computer facilities: Campuswide network is available with full Internet access. Total number of PCs/ terminals supplied for student use: 95. Computer services are offered at no charge. Library facilities: Olin Library plus 1 additional on-campus library. Graduate expenses: $170 per credit hour. General application contact: Dr. Daniel R. Beach, Director of Teacher Education, 417-873-7271.*

Breech School of Business Administration
Dr. Tom Zimmerer, Director
Program in:
- business and international management • MBA

Graduate Programs in Education
Dr. Daniel R. Beach, Director
Programs in:
- elementary education • M Ed
- gifted education • M Ed
- human services • M Ed
- middle school teaching • M Ed
- physical education • M Ed
- secondary education • M Ed

Program in Communication
Dr. Lynn Hinds, Chair
Program in:
- communication • MA

Program in Criminology/Criminal Justice
Dr. Victor Agruso, Chair, Behavioral Sciences
Programs in:
- criminal justice • MS
- criminology • MA

FONTBONNE COLLEGE
St. Louis, MO 63105-3098

http://www.fontbonne.edu/

Independent-religious coed comprehensive institution. *Enrollment: 2,054 graduate, professional, and undergraduate students. Graduate faculty: 15 full-time, 100 part-time. Computer facilities: Campuswide network is available with full Internet access. Total number of PCs/ terminals supplied for student use: 91. Computer service fees are included with tuition and fees. Library facilities: main library. Graduate expenses: Tuition of $10,650 per year full-time, $346 per credit hour part-time. Fees of $160 per year full-time, $7 per credit hour part-time. General application contact: Peggy Musen, Director of Admissions, 314-889-1400.*

Graduate Programs

Dr. Joan Lescinski, CSJ, Vice President and Dean for
　Academic Affairs
Programs in:
　　business administration • MBA
　　communication disorders • MS
　　computer education • MS
　　education • MA
　　fine arts • MA, MFA
　　management • MM
　　taxation • MST

LINCOLN UNIVERSITY
Jefferson City, MO 65102

http://www.lincolnu.edu/

Public coed comprehensive institution. *Enrollment:* 3,041 graduate, professional, and undergraduate students. Graduate faculty: *2 full-time, 27 part-time.* Computer facilities: *Campuswide network is available with full Internet access. Total number of PCs/terminals supplied for student use: 300. Computer services are offered at no charge.* Library facilities: *Page Library.* Graduate expenses: *Tuition of $117 per credit hour for state residents; $234 per credit hour for nonresidents. Fees of $552 per year (minimum) for state residents; $1104 per year (minimum) for nonresidents.* General application contact: *Rosemary Hearn, Vice President for Academic Affairs and Dean of Graduate Studies, 573-681-5074.*

Graduate School

Rosemary Hearn, Vice President for Academic Affairs and
　Dean of Graduate Studies

College of Arts and Sciences

Rosemary Hearn, Vice President for Academic Affairs and
　Dean of Graduate Studies, Graduate School
Programs in:
　　agency • M Ed
　　elementary • M Ed
　　elementary and secondary teaching • M Ed
　　guidance and counseling • M Ed
　　history • MA
　　school administration and supervision • M Ed
　　secondary • M Ed
　　sociology • MA

College of Business

Wayne Linhardt, Interim Dean, College of Business
Program in:
　　business • MBA

LINDENWOOD UNIVERSITY
St. Charles, MO 63301-1695

http://www.lindenwood.edu/

Independent-religious coed comprehensive institution. *Enrollment:* 4,293 graduate, professional, and undergraduate students. Graduate faculty: *42 full-time, 41 part-time.* Computer facilities: *Campuswide network is available with full Internet access. Total number of PCs/terminals supplied for student use: 70. Computer services are offered at no charge.* Library facilities: *Margaret Leggat Butler Memorial Library.* Graduate expenses: *$5880 per year full-time, $245 per credit hour part-time.* General application contact: *John Guffey, Director of Graduate Admissions, 314-949-4933.*

Graduate Programs

Dr. Larry Doyle, Vice President
Programs in:
　　administration • MSA
　　business administration • MBA, MS
　　corporate communication • MS
　　counseling psychology • MA
　　education • MA
　　gerontology • MA
　　health management • MS
　　human resource management • MS
　　human service agency management • MS
　　management • MSA
　　marketing • MSA
　　mass communication • MS
　　theatre arts • MA, MFA

MARYVILLE UNIVERSITY OF SAINT LOUIS
St. Louis, MO 63141-7299

http://www.maryvillestl.edu/

Independent coed comprehensive institution. *Enrollment:* 3,055 graduate, professional, and undergraduate students. Graduate faculty: *24 full-time, 20 part-time.* Computer facilities: *Campuswide network is available with full Internet access. Total number of PCs/terminals supplied for student use: 220. Computer service fees are included with tuition and fees.* Library facilities: *main library.* Graduate expenses: *Tuition of $11,480 per year full-time, $345 per credit hour part-time. Fees of $120 per year full-time, $60 per year part-time.* General application contact: *contact individual schools, 314-529-9300.*

School of Education

Dr. Kathe Rasch, Dean
Programs in:
　　art education • MA
　　early childhood education • MA
　　elementary education • MA
　　environmental education • MA

Maryville University of Saint Louis (continued)
    gifted education • MA
    middle grades education • MA
    multicultural education • MA
    secondary education • MA

The John E. Simon School of Business
Dr. Pamela Horwitz, Dean
Programs in:
    business administration and management • MBA
    management • MSM

NORTHWEST MISSOURI STATE UNIVERSITY
Maryville, MO 64468-6001

http://www.nwmissouri.edu/

Public coed comprehensive institution. *Enrollment:* 6,001 graduate, professional, and undergraduate students. Graduate faculty: *179 full-time.* Computer facilities: *Campuswide network is available with full Internet access. Total number of PCs/terminals supplied for student use: 3,000. Computer service fees are applied as a separate charge.* Library facilities: *B. D. Owens Library plus 1 additional on-campus library.* Graduate expenses: *Tuition of $113 per credit hour for state residents; $197 per credit hour for nonresidents. Fees of $3 per credit hour.* General application contact: *Dr. Frances Shipley, Dean of Graduate School, 816-562-1145.*

Graduate School
Dr. Frances Shipley, Dean

College of Arts and Sciences
Dr. C. Taylor Barnes, Dean
Programs in:
    agriculture • MS
    biology • MS
    English • MA
    history • MA
    mathematics education • MS Ed
    teaching art • MS Ed
    teaching English • MS Ed
    teaching history • MS Ed
    teaching music • MS Ed
    teaching secondary agriculture education • MS Ed

College of Education and Human Services
Dr. Max Ruhl, Dean
Programs in:
    counseling psychology • MS
    early childhood education • MS Ed
    educational administration and supervision • Ed S, MS Ed
    elementary education • MS Ed
    elementary education of the learning disabled • MS Ed
    elementary education of the mentally handicapped • MS Ed
    guidance and counseling • MS Ed
    health and physical education • MS Ed
    middle school education • MS Ed
    reading education • MS Ed
    science education • MS Ed
    secondary education • MS Ed
    secondary education of the learning disabled • MS Ed
    secondary education of the mentally handicapped • MS Ed

College of Professional and Applied Studies
Dr. Ron DeYoung, Dean
Programs in:
    accounting • MBA
    agricultural economics • MBA
    business administration • MBA
    educational uses of computer • MS Ed
    school computer studies • MS
    secondary business education • MS Ed
    teaching vocational business • MS Ed

PARK COLLEGE
Parkville, MO 64152-4358

Independent-religious coed comprehensive institution. *Enrollment:* 6,780 graduate, professional, and undergraduate students. Graduate faculty: *15.* Library facilities: *Carnegie Library.* Graduate expenses: *$210 per credit hour.* General application contact: *Erik Bergrud, Graduate Administrator, 816-421-1125.*

Graduate Program in Business Administration
Dr. J'Noel Ball, Director
Program in:
    business administration • MBA

Graduate Program in Education
Dr. Pat McClelland, Director
Program in:
    education • M Ed

Graduate School of Public Affairs
Dr. Jerzy Hauptmann, Dean
Program in:
    public affairs • MPA

Graduate School of Religion
Dr. John Noren, Director
Program in:
    religion • MAR

ROCKHURST COLLEGE
Kansas City, MO 64110-2561

http://www.rockhurst.edu/

Independent-religious coed comprehensive institution. *Enrollment: 2,792 graduate, professional, and undergraduate students. Graduate faculty: 32 full-time, 17 part-time. Computer facilities: Campuswide network is available with full Internet access. Total number of PCs/terminals supplied for student use: 300. Computer service fees are applied as a separate charge. Library facilities: Greenlease Library. Graduate expenses: Tuition of $335 per semester hour. Fees of $15 per year. General application contact: Director of Graduate Recruitment, 816-501-4100.*

College of Arts and Sciences
Corey Simmonds, Interim Dean
Programs in:
occupational therapy education • MOT
physical therapy • MPT

School of Management
Thomas L. Lyon, Interim Dean
Program in:
management • MBA

 # SAINT LOUIS UNIVERSITY
St. Louis, MO 63103-2097

http://www.slu.edu/

Independent-religious coed university. *Enrollment: 11,038 graduate, professional, and undergraduate students. Graduate faculty: 1,229 full-time, 1,826 part-time. Library facilities: Pius XII Memorial Library plus 5 additional on-campus libraries. Graduate expenses: $542 per credit hour. General application contact: Dr. Marcia Buresch, Assistant Dean of the Graduate School, 314-977-2240.*

Graduate School
Dr. Donald G. Brennan, Dean
Programs in:
aerospace engineering • MS, MS(R)
anatomy • MS(R), PhD
biochemistry and molecular biology • PhD
cell and molecular biology • PhD
dentistry • MS
molecular microbiology and immunology • PhD
neurobiology • PhD
pathology • MS(R), PhD
pharmacological and physiological science • MS(R), PhD

Center for Health Care Ethics
Dr. Gerard Magill, Department Chairman
Program in:
health care ethics • PhD

College of Arts and Sciences
Dr. Shirley Dowdy, Dean
Programs in:
American studies • MA, MA(R), PhD
applied experimental psychology • MS(R), PhD
arts and sciences • Ed D, Ed S
atmospheric science • M Pr Met, MS(R), PhD
biology • MS, MS(R), PhD
chemistry • MS, MS(R)
clinical psychology • MS(R), PhD
communication • MA, MA(R)
English • MA, MA(R), PhD
French • MA
geoscience • MS, MS(R), PhD
historical theology • MA, PhD
history • MA, MA(R), PhD
mathematics • MA, MA(R), PhD
philosophy • MA, MA(R), PhD
Spanish • MA
theology • MA

Institute for Leadership and Public Service
Dr. James Gilsinian, Director
Programs in:
communication disorders • MA
counseling and family therapy • PhD
curriculum and instruction • Ed D, MA, PhD
educational administration • Ed D, Ed S, MA, PhD
foundations • Ed D, MA, PhD
higher education • Ed D, Ed S, MA, PhD
human development counseling • MA
public administration • MAPA
public policy analysis • PhD
school counseling • MA
special education • MA
urban affairs • MAUA

School of Allied Health Professions
Dr. Frances Horvath, Dean
Programs in:
medical dietetics • MS
nutrition and physical performance • MS
physical therapy • MS(R)PT, MSPT

School of Nursing
Dr. Patsy Ruchala, Director
Programs in:
adult nurse practitioner • Certificate, MSN, MSN(R)
clinical health care specialist/case manager • Certificate, MSN, MSN(R)
clinical health specialist/case manager • Certificate, MSN, MSN(R)
family nurse practitioner • Certificate, MSN, MSN(R)
gerontological nurse practitioner • Certificate, MSN, MSN(R)
informatics nurse • Certificate, MSN, MSN(R)
nursing • PhD
pediatric nurse practitioner • Certificate, MSN, MSN(R)
public health nurse manager • Certificate, MSN, MSN(R)
public health nurse practice • Certificate, MSN, MSN(R)

Saint Louis University (continued)

School of Public Health
Dr. Richard S. Kurz, Dean
Programs in:
community health • MPH
health administration • MHA
health services research • PhD

School of Business and Administration
Dr. Neil E. Seitz, Dean
Programs in:
accounting • M Acct, MBA, PhD
business administration • MBA, PhD
decision sciences • M Dec S, MBA, PhD
economics • MBA, PhD
executive international business • EMIB
finance • M Fin, MBA, PhD
information systems management • MBA
international business • MBA, MIB, PhD
management • M Mgt, MBA, PhD
management information systems • MMIS
marketing • MBA, PhD

School of Law
John B. Attanasio, Dean
Program in:
law • JD, LL M

School of Medicine
Dr. Patricia Monteleone, Dean
Programs in:
anatomy • MS(R), PhD
biochemistry and molecular biology • PhD
cell and molecular biology • PhD
medicine • MD
molecular microbiology and immunology • PhD
neurobiology • PhD
pathology • MS(R), PhD
pharmacological and physiological science • MS(R), PhD

School of Social Services
Dr. Susan Tebb, Dean
Program in:
social services • MSW

SOUTHEAST MISSOURI STATE UNIVERSITY
Cape Girardeau, MO 63701-4799

http://www.semo.edu/

Public coed comprehensive institution. *Enrollment: 7,503 graduate, professional, and undergraduate students. Graduate faculty: 231 full-time. Computer facilities: Campuswide network is available with full Internet access. Total number of PCs/terminals supplied for student use: 200. Computer service fees are included with tuition and fees. Library facilities: Kent Library. Graduate expenses: $2034 per year full-time, $113 per credit hour part-time for state residents;*

$3672 per year full-time, $204 per credit hour part-time for nonresidents. General application contact: Dr. Sheila R. Caskey, Dean of the Graduate School, 573-651-2192.

Graduate School
Dr. Sheila R. Caskey, Dean
Programs in:
biology • MNS
business • MBA
business education • MA
chemistry • MNS
communication disorders • MA
criminal justice administration • MSA
educational administration • Ed D, Ed S, MA
elementary education • MA
English • MA
geosciences • MNS
guidance and counseling • MA
health care administration • MSA
history • MA
home economics • MA
human resources administration • MSA
mathematics • MNS
middle level education • MA
music education • MME
nursing • MSN
physical education • MA
psychological counseling • MA
public administration • MSA
science education • MNS
special education • MA
teaching English to speakers of other languages • MA

SOUTHWEST BAPTIST UNIVERSITY
Bolivar, MO 65613-2597

http://bearcat.sbuniv.edu/

Independent-religious coed comprehensive institution. *Enrollment: 3,986 graduate, professional, and undergraduate students. Graduate faculty: 11 full-time, 56 part-time. Computer facilities: Campuswide network is available with full Internet access. Total number of PCs/terminals supplied for student use: 122. Computer service fees are included with tuition and fees. Library facilities: Harriett K. Hutchens Library. Graduate expenses: $123 per credit hour. General application contact: Dr. M. Michael Awad, Provost, 417-326-1601.*

School of Graduate Studies
Dr. M. Michael Awad, Provost
Programs in:
accounting • MS
administration • MS
business administration • MS
education • MS
educational administration • MS
health services • MS
physical therapy • MSPT

SOUTHWEST MISSOURI STATE UNIVERSITY
Springfield, MO 65804-0094

http://www.smsu.edu/

Public coed comprehensive institution. *Enrollment: 15,343 graduate, professional, and undergraduate students. Graduate faculty: 385 full-time, 27 part-time. Computer facilities: Campuswide network is available with full Internet access. Computer services are offered at no charge. Library facilities: Meyer Library plus 2 additional on-campus libraries. Graduate expenses: Tuition of $1980 per year full-time, $110 per credit hour part-time for state residents; $3960 per year full-time, $220 per credit hour part-time for nonresidents. Fees of $274 per year full-time, $73 per semester part-time. General application contact: Frank A. Einhellig, Associate Vice President for Academic Affairs/Dean, 417-836-5335.*

Graduate College
Frank A. Einhellig, Associate Vice President for Academic Affairs/Dean

College of Arts and Letters
David Belcher, Dean
Programs in:
    communications • MA
    English • MA
    music • MM
    theatre • MA

College of Business Administration
Dr. Ronald Bottin, Dean
Programs in:
    accountancy • M Acc
    business administration • MBA
    computer information systems • MS

College of Education
Dr. Roger Bennett, Dean
Programs in:
    educational administration • Ed S, MS Ed
    elementary education • MS Ed
    guidance and counseling • MS
    reading and special education • MS Ed
    secondary education • MS Ed

College of Health and Human Services
Dr. Jeanne L. Thomas, Dean
Programs in:
    communication disorders • MS
    health promotion and wellness management • MS
    nurse anesthesia • MS
    nursing • MSN
    psychology • MS
    social work • MSW

College of Humanities and Public Affairs
Bernice S. Warren, Dean
Programs in:
    defense and strategic studies • MS
    history • MA
    public administration • MPA
    religious studies • MS

College of Natural and Applied Sciences
Dr. Lawrence E. Banks Jr., Dean
Programs in:
    biology • MS
    biology education • MS
    chemistry • MS
    materials science • MS
    mathematics • MA
    natural and applied sciences • MNAS
    resource planning • MS

TRUMAN STATE UNIVERSITY
Kirksville, MO 63501-4221

http://www.truman.edu/

Public coed comprehensive institution. *Computer facilities: Campuswide network is available with full Internet access. Computer services are offered at no charge. Library facilities: Pickler Library. Graduate expenses: $2718 per year full-time, $151 per credit part-time for state residents; $4824 per year full-time, $268 per credit part-time for nonresidents. General application contact: Graduate Office Secretary, 816-785-4109.*

Graduate School

Division of Business and Accountancy
Program in:
    accounting • M Ac

Division of Education
Program in:
    education • MAE

Division of Fine Arts
Program in:
    music • MA

Division of Human Potential and Performance
Program in:
    communication disorders • MA

Division of Language and Literature
Program in:
    English • MA

Division of Mathematics and Computer Science
Program in:
    mathematics • MA

Division of Science
Program in:
    biology • MS

Division of Social Science
Programs in:
    counseling • MA
    history • MA

UNIVERSITY OF MISSOURI–COLUMBIA
Columbia, MO 65211
http://www.missouri.edu/

Public coed university. *Enrollment: 22,483 graduate, professional, and undergraduate students. Graduate faculty: 1,644. Computer facilities: Campuswide network is available with full Internet access. Computer service fees are included with tuition and fees. Library facilities: Ellis Library plus 9 additional on-campus libraries. Graduate expenses: Tuition of $3240 per year full-time, $180 per credit hour part-time for state residents; $9108 per year full-time, $506 per credit hour part-time for nonresidents. Fees of $55 per year full-time. General application contact: contact individual programs, 573-882-2121.*

Graduate School
Dr. Charles Sampson, Interim Dean
Programs in:
  biochemistry • MS, PhD
  family and community medicine • MSPH
  health services management • MHA
  laboratory animal medicine • MS
  molecular microbiology and immunology • MS, PhD
  nutritional sciences • MS, PhD
  pathobiology • PhD
  pathology • MS
  pathology and anatomy • MA, PhD
  pharmacology • MS, PhD
  physiology • MS, PhD
  veterinary biomedical sciences • MS
  veterinary medicine and surgery • MS

College of Agriculture
Dr. Roger L. Mitchell, Dean
Programs in:
  agricultural economics • MS, PhD
  agricultural engineering • MS
  agronomy • MS, PhD
  animal sciences • MS, PhD
  biochemistry • MS, PhD
  biological engineering • MS, PhD
  entomology • MS, PhD
  foods and food systems management • MS
  food science • MS, PhD
  horticulture • MS, PhD
  human nutrition • MS
  plant pathology • MS, PhD
  rural sociology • MS, PhD

College of Arts and Sciences
Dr. Larry Clark, Dean
Programs in:
  analytical chemistry • MS, PhD
  anthropology • MA, PhD
  applied mathematics • MS
  art • MA, MFA
  art history and archaeology • MA, PhD
  biological sciences • MA, PhD
  classical studies • MA, PhD

communication • MA, PhD
economics • MA, PhD
English • MA, PhD
French • MA, PhD
genetics • MA, PhD
geography • MA
geological sciences • MS, PhD
German • MA
history • MA, PhD
inorganic chemistry • MS, PhD
literature • MA
mathematics • MA, MST, PhD
music • MA, MM
organic chemistry • MS, PhD
philosophy • MA, PhD
physical chemistry • MS, PhD
physics • MS, PhD
political science • MA, PhD
psychology • MA, MS, PhD
religious studies • MA
sociology • MA, PhD
Spanish • MA, PhD
statistics • MA, PhD
teaching • MA
theatre • MA, PhD

College of Business and Public Administration
Dr. Bruce Walker, Dean
Programs in:
  accountancy • M Acc, MA, MS, PhD
  business • MBA, PhD
  public administration • MPA

College of Education
Dr. Richard Andrews, Dean
Programs in:
  curriculum and instruction • Ed D, Ed S, M Ed, MA, PhD
  education administration • Ed D, Ed S, M Ed, MA, PhD
  educational and counseling psychology • Ed S, M Ed, MA, PhD
  higher and adult education • Ed D, Ed S, M Ed, MA, PhD
  library science • MA
  practical arts and vocational technical education • Ed D, Ed S, M Ed, MA, PhD
  special education • Ed D, Ed S, M Ed, MA, PhD

College of Engineering
Dr. James Thompson, Dean
Programs in:
  agricultural engineering • MS
  biological engineering • MS, PhD
  chemical engineering • MS, PhD
  civil engineering • MS, PhD
  computer engineering and computer science • MS
  electrical engineering • MS, PhD
  environmental engineering • MS, PhD
  geotechnical engineering • MS, PhD
  health physics • MS
  industrial engineering • MS, PhD
  mechanical and aerospace engineering • MS, PhD
  medical physics • MS
  nuclear engineering • MS, PhD

structural engineering • MS, PhD
transportation and highway engineering • MS
water resources • MS, PhD

College of Human Environmental Science
Dr. Bea Smith, Dean
Programs in:
consumer and family economics • MS
environmental design • MA, MS
exercise physiology • PhD
exercise science • MA
foods and food systems management • MS
food science • MS, PhD
human development and family studies • MA, MS
human environmental science • PhD
human nutrition • MS
social work • MSW
textiles and apparel management • MA, MS

School of Journalism
Dr. Esther Thorson, Director of Graduate Studies
Program in:
journalism • MA, PhD

School of Natural Resources
Dr. A. R. Vogt, Director
Programs in:
fisheries and wildlife • MS, PhD
forestry • MS, PhD
parks, recreation and tourism • MS
soil and atmospheric sciences • MS, PhD

School of Nursing
Dr. Rose Porter, Associate Dean
Program in:
nursing • MS, PhD

College of Veterinary Medicine
Dr. H. Richard Adams, Dean
Programs in:
laboratory animal medicine • MS
pathobiology • PhD
pathology • MS
physiology • PhD
veterinary biomedical sciences • MS
veterinary medicine • DVM
veterinary medicine and surgery • MS

School of Law
Timothy J. Heinsz, Dean
Program in:
law • JD

School of Medicine
Dr. Lester R. Bryant, Dean
Programs in:
biochemistry • MS, PhD
communication science and disorders • MHS
family and community medicine • MSPH
medicine • MD
molecular microbiology and immunology • MS, PhD
pathology and anatomy • MA, PhD
pharmacology • MS, PhD

physical therapy • MPT
physiology • MS, PhD

School of Health Related Professions
Dr. Gordon Brown, Director
Programs in:
communication science and disorders • MHS
physical therapy • MPT

UNIVERSITY OF MISSOURI–KANSAS CITY
Kansas City, MO 64110-2499
http://www.umkc.edu/

Public coed university. *Enrollment: 10,444 graduate, professional, and undergraduate students. Graduate faculty: 521 full-time, 240 part-time. Computer facilities: Campuswide network is available with full Internet access. Total number of PCs/terminals supplied for student use: 440. Computer service fees are included with tuition and fees. Library facilities: Miller Nichols Library plus 3 additional on-campus libraries. Graduate expenses: Tuition of $182 per credit hour for state residents; $508 per credit hour for nonresidents. Fees of $60 per year. General application contact: Mel Tyler, Director of Admissions, 816-235-1111.*

College of Arts and Sciences
Dr. James R. Durig, Dean
Programs in:
acting • MFA
administration of justice • MS
analytical chemistry • MS, PhD
art history • MA
communication studies • MA
community psychology • PhD
design technology • MFA
economics • MA, PhD
English • MA, PhD
geosciences • PhD
history • MA, PhD
inorganic chemistry • MS, PhD
mathematics and statistics • MA, MS, PhD
organic chemistry • MS, PhD
physical chemistry • MS, PhD
physics • MS, PhD
political science • MA, PhD
polymer chemistry • MS, PhD
psychology • MA, PhD
Romance languages and literatures • MA
sociology • MA, PhD
studio art • MA
theatre • MA
urban environmental geology • MS

University of Missouri–Kansas City (continued)

Conservatory of Music

Dr. Terry L. Applebaum, Dean
Programs in:
  choral music education • MME
  composition • DMA, MM
  conducting • DMA, MM
  elementary music education • MME
  instrumental music education • MME
  music • MA
  music education • PhD
  music history and literature • MM
  music theory • MM
  performance • DMA, MM

Program in Computer Science Telecommunications

Dr. Richard Hetherington, Director
Programs in:
  computer networking • MS, PhD
  software engineering • MS
  telecommunications networking • MS, PhD

School of Biological Sciences

Dr. Marino Martinez-Carrion, Dean
Programs in:
  biology • MA
  cell biology and biophysics • PhD
  cellular and molecular biology • MS, PhD
  molecular biology and biochemistry • PhD

School of Business and Public Administration

Dr. William B. Eddy, Dean
Programs in:
  accounting • MS
  business administration • MBA
  public affairs • MPA, PhD

School of Dentistry

Dr. Michael Reed, Dean
Programs in:
  advanced education in dentistry • Graduate Dental
    Certificate
  dental hygiene education • MS
  dentistry • DDS
  diagnostic sciences • Graduate Dental Certificate
  oral and maxillofacial surgery • Graduate Dental
    Certificate
  oral biology • MS, PhD
  orthodontics and dentofacial orthopedics • Graduate
    Dental Certificate
  pediatric dentistry • Graduate Dental Certificate
  periodontics • Graduate Dental Certificate
  prosthodontics • Graduate Dental Certificate

School of Education

Bernard Oliver, Dean
Programs in:
  counseling and guidance • Ed S, MA
  counseling psychology • PhD
  curriculum and instruction • Ed S
  education • PhD

  educational research and psychology • MA
  elementary education • MA
  language and literacy • Ed S, MA
  secondary education • MA
  special education • MA
  urban leadership and policy studies • Ed S, MA, PhD

School of Graduate Studies

Dr. Ronald MacQuarrie, Vice Provost/Dean
Programs in:
  cell biology and biophysics • PhD
  cellular and molecular biology • PhD
  chemistry • PhD
  computer science telecommunications • PhD
  curriculum and instruction • PhD
  economics • PhD
  engineering • PhD
  English • PhD
  geosciences • PhD
  history • PhD
  interdisciplinary studies • PhD
  mathematics and statistics • PhD
  molecular biology and biochemistry • PhD
  music education • PhD
  oral biology • PhD
  pharmaceutical sciences • PhD
  pharmacology • PhD
  philosophy • PhD
  physics • PhD
  political science • PhD
  public affairs • PhD
  sociology • PhD
  urban leadership and policy • PhD

School of Law

Dr. Burnele Powell, Dean
Programs in:
  general • LL M
  law • JD
  taxation • LL M

School of Medicine

Dr. Marjorie Sirridge, Interim Dean
Program in:
  medicine • MD

School of Nursing

Dr. Nancy Mills, Dean
Programs in:
  health care for adults • MSN
  health care for children • MSN
  health care for women • MSN
  nurse practitioner • MSN
  nursing • PhD

School of Pharmacy

Dr. Robert W. Piepho, Dean
Programs in:
  pharmaceutical sciences • MS
  pharmacy • Pharm D

UNIVERSITY OF MISSOURI–ROLLA
Rolla, MO 65409-0910

http://www.umr.edu/

Public coed university. *Enrollment: 4,976 graduate, professional, and undergraduate students. Graduate faculty: 231 full-time, 2 part time. Computer facilities: Campuswide network is available with full Internet access. Total number of PCs/terminals supplied for student use: 812. Computer service fees are included with tuition and fees. Library facilities: Curtis Laws Wilson Library. Graduate expenses: Tuition of $3902 per year full-time, $163 per credit hour part-time for state residents; $11,738 per year full-time, $489 per credit hour part-time for nonresidents. Fees of $610 per year (minimum) full-time, $146 per year (minimum) part-time. General application contact: Julie Sibley, Admissions Adviser, 573-341-4315.*

Graduate School
Dr. W. J. Gajda Jr., Vice Chancellor of Academic Affairs

College of Arts and Sciences
Dr. Russell Buhite, Dean
Programs in:
    applied mathematics • MS
    chemistry • MS, PhD
    chemistry education • MST
    computer science • MS, PhD
    mathematics • PhD
    mathematics education • MST
    physics • MS, PhD

School of Engineering
Dr. O. Robert Mitchell, Dean
Programs in:
    aerospace engineering • MS, PhD
    chemical engineering • MS, PhD
    civil engineering • MS, PhD
    construction engineering • DE, MS, PhD
    electrical engineering • DE, MS, PhD
    engineering management • MS, PhD
    engineering mechanics • MS, PhD
    environmental engineering • MS
    fluid mechanics • DE, MS, PhD
    geotechnical engineering • DE, MS, PhD
    hydrology and hydraulic engineering • DE, MS, PhD
    mechanical engineering • DE, MS, PhD
    sanitary engineering and environmental health • DE, MS, PhD
    structural analysis and design • DE, MS, PhD
    structural materials • MS
    structural methods • DE, PhD

School of Mines and Metallurgy
Dr. Lee W. Saperstein, Dean
Programs in:
    ceramic engineering • MS, PhD
    geochemistry • MS, PhD
    geological engineering • DE, MS, PhD
    geology • MS, PhD
    geophysics • MS, PhD
    groundwater and environmental geology • MS, PhD
    metallurgical engineering • MS, PhD
    mining engineering • DE, MS, PhD
    nuclear engineering • DE, MS, PhD
    petroleum engineering • DE, MS, PhD

 # UNIVERSITY OF MISSOURI–ST. LOUIS
St. Louis, MO 63121-4499

http://www.umsl.edu/

Public coed university. *Enrollment: 11,858 graduate, professional, and undergraduate students. Graduate faculty: 404. Computer facilities: Campuswide network is available with full Internet access. Total number of PCs/terminals supplied for student use: 1,000. Computer services are offered at no charge. Library facilities: Thomas Jefferson Library plus 3 additional on-campus libraries. Graduate expenses: Tuition of $3903 per year full-time, $167 per credit hour part-time for state residents; $11,745 per year full-time, $489 per credit hour part-time for nonresidents. Fees of $816 per year full-time, $34 per credit hour part-time. General application contact: Graduate Admissions, 314-516-5458.*

Graduate School
Dr. Douglas Wartzok, Associate Vice Chancellor for Research and Dean
Programs in:
    gerontological social work • Certificate
    gerontology • Certificate, MS
    physiological optics • MS, PhD
    public policy administration • MPPA

College of Arts and Sciences
Dr. Martin Sage, Interim Dean
Programs in:
    applied psychology • PhD
    biology • MS, PhD
    biotechnology • Certificate
    chemistry • MS, PhD
    clinical psychology • Certificate, PhD
    criminology and criminal justice • MA, PhD
    economics • MA
    English • MA, MFA
    experimental psychology • PhD
    general psychology • MA
    history • MA
    international studies • Certificate
    managerial economics • Certificate
    mathematical sciences • MA, PhD
    music education • MME
    physics • MS, PhD
    political science • MA, PhD
    sociology • MA
    tropical biology and conservation • Certificate
    women's and gender studies • Certificate

University of Missouri–St. Louis (continued)

School of Business Administration
Dr. Donald Kummer, Director of Graduate Studies
Programs in:
    accounting • M Acc, MBA
    finance • MBA
    human resource management • Certificate
    management information science • MBA
    management information systems • MSMIS
    marketing • Certificate, MBA
    organizational behavior • MBA
    quantitative management science • MBA
    taxation • Certificate

School of Education
Dr. Kathleen Haywood, Director of Graduate Studies
Programs in:
    counseling • M Ed
    education • Ed D
    educational administration • M Ed
    elementary education • M Ed
    secondary education • M Ed
    special education • M Ed

School of Nursing
Dr. Jean Bachman, Associate Dean
Program in:
    nursing • MSN, ND, PhD

School of Optometry
Dr. Ralph P. Garzia, Interim Dean
Programs in:
    optometry • OD
    physiological optics • MS, PhD

WASHINGTON UNIVERSITY IN ST. LOUIS
St. Louis, MO 63130-4899
http://www.wustl.edu/

Independent coed university. *Enrollment:* 11,636 graduate, professional, and undergraduate students. Graduate faculty: 2,248. Library facilities: *John M. Olin Library plus 13 additional on-campus libraries.* Graduate expenses: *$22,200 per year full-time, $925 per credit hour part-time. General application contact: Graduate School of Arts and Sciences, 314-935-6880.*

Graduate School of Arts and Sciences
Robert E. Thach, Dean
Programs in:
    American history • MA, PhD
    anthropology • MA, PhD
    art history • MA, PhD
    Asian history • MA, PhD
    Asian language • MA
    Asian studies • MA
    audiology • MS
    British history • MA, PhD
    chemistry • MA, PhD
    Chinese • MA, PhD
    Chinese and comparative literature • PhD
    classical archaeology • MA, PhD
    classics • MA, MAT
    clinical psychology • PhD
    communication sciences • MA, PhD
    comparative literature • MA, PhD
    drama • MA
    early childhood education • AGC, MA Ed
    earth and planetary sciences • MA
    East Asian studies • MA
    economics • MA, PhD
    educational research • PhD
    elementary education • AGC, MA Ed
    English and American literature • MA, PhD
    environmental science • MA
    European history • MA, PhD
    European studies • MA
    French • MA, PhD
    general experimental psychology • MA, PhD
    geochemistry • PhD
    geology • MA, PhD
    geophysics • PhD
    Germanic languages and literature • MA, PhD
    history • PhD
    Islamic and Near Eastern studies • MA
    Japanese • MA, PhD
    Japanese and comparative literature • PhD
    Jewish studies • MA
    Latin American history • MA, PhD
    mathematics • MA, PhD
    mathematics education • MAT
    Middle Eastern history • MA, PhD
    movement science • PhD
    music • MA, MM, PhD
    philosophy • MA, PhD
    philosophy/neuroscience/psychology • PhD
    physics • MA, PhD
    planetary sciences • PhD
    political economy and public policy • MA
    political science • MA, PhD
    Romance languages • MA, PhD
    secondary education • MA Ed, MAT
    social psychology • MA, PhD
    Spanish • MA, PhD
    speech and hearing • MS
    statistics • MA, PhD
    writing • MFAW

Division of Biology and Biomedical Sciences
Robert E. Thach, Dean, Graduate School of Arts and Sciences
Programs in:
    biochemistry • PhD
    bioorganic chemistry • PhD
    developmental biology • PhD
    ecology • PhD
    environmental biology • PhD
    evolutionary biology • PhD
    genetics • PhD
    immunology • PhD

molecular biophysics • PhD
molecular cell biology • PhD
molecular genetics • PhD
molecular microbiology and microbial pathogenesis •
PhD
neurosciences • PhD
plant biology • PhD

George Warren Brown School of Social Work
Dr. Shanti K. Khinduka, Dean
Program in:
social work • MSW, PhD

John M. Olin School of Business
Stuart I. Greenbaum, Dean
Program in:
business • EMBA, MBA, PhD

School of Architecture
Cynthia Weese, Dean
Programs in:
architecture • M Arch
urban design • MAUD

School of Art
Joe Deal, Dean
Programs in:
ceramics • MFA
painting • MFA
photography • MFA
printmaking/drawing • MFA
sculpture • MFA

School of Engineering and Applied Science
Program in:
biomedical engineering • D Sc, MS

Sever Institute of Technology
Programs in:
chemical engineering • D Sc
chemical enginering • MS
civil engineering • MSCE
computer science • D Sc, MS
construction engineering • MCE
construction management • MCM
control engineering • MCE
electrical engineering • D Sc, MSEE
engineering and policy • D Sc, MA, MS
environmental engineering • D Sc, MS, MSEE
materials science and engineering • D Sc, MS
materials science engineering • D Sc
mechanical engineering • D Sc, MS
structural engineering • D Sc, MSE
systems science and mathematics • D Sc, MS
systems science, mathematics, and economics • D Sc
transportation and urban systems engineering • D Sc

School of Law
Dorsey D. Ellis Jr., Dean
Program in:
law • JD, JSD, LL M, MJS

School of Medicine
Dr. William A. Peck, Dean
Programs in:
health administration • MHA
medicine • MD
occupational therapy • MA, MSOT
physical therapy • MHS, MSPT, PhD

WEBSTER UNIVERSITY
St. Louis, MO 63119-3194
http://www.websteruniv.edu/

Independent coed comprehensive institution. *Enrollment: 11,756 graduate, professional, and undergraduate students. Graduate faculty: 61 full-time, 299 part-time. Computer facilities: Campuswide network is available with full Internet access. Total number of PCs/ terminals supplied for student use: 175. Computer service fees are included with tuition and fees. Library facilities: Eden-Webster Library. Graduate expenses: $350 per credit hour. General application contact: Beth Russell, Director of Graduate Admissions, 314-968-7089.*

College of Arts and Sciences
William Eidson, Dean
Programs in:
counseling • MA
environmental management • MS
family systems nursing • MSN
gerontology • MA
international relations • MA
legal studies • MA
nurse anesthesia • MS
paralegal studies • Certificate

College of Fine Arts
Peter Sargent, Dean
Programs in:
art • MA, MFA
arts management and leadership • MFA
church music • MM
composition • MM
conducting • MM
jazz studies • MM
music education • MM
performance • MM
piano • MM

School of Business and Technology
Dr. Wilford G. Miles Jr., Dean
Programs in:
business • MA, MBA
computer distributed systems • Certificate
computer resources and information management • MA, MBA
computer science • MS
computer science/distributed systems • MS
finance • MA, MBA

Webster University (continued)
   health care management • MA
   health services management • MA, MBA
   human resources development • MA, MBA
   human resources management • MA
   international business • MA, MBA
   management • DM, MA, MBA
   marketing • MA, MBA
   procurement and acquisitions management • MA, MBA
   public administration • MA
   real estate management • MA, MBA
   security management • MA, MBA
   space systems management • MA, MBA, MS
   telecommunications management • MA, MBA

School of Communications
Debra Carpenter, Dean
Programs in:
   interactive media • MA
   media communication • MA

School of Education
Judith Walker DeFelix, Dean
Programs in:
   communication education • MAT
   communications • MAT
   computer studies • MAT
   early childhood education • MAT
   mathematics education • MAT
   multidisciplinary studies • MAT
   science education • MAT
   social science education • MAT
   special education • MAT

MONTANA

MONTANA STATE UNIVERSITY–BILLINGS
Billings, MT 59101-9984

http://www.msubillings.edu/

Public coed comprehensive institution. Library facilities: *main library.* Graduate expenses: *Tuition of $2253 per year full-time, $397 per semester (minimum) part-time for state residents; $5313 per year full-time, $907 per semester (minimum) part-time for nonresidents. Fees of $378 per year full-time, $105 per semester (minimum) part-time.* General application contact: *Director of Graduate Studies and Research, 406-657-2238.*

College of Education and Human Services
Programs in:
   community counseling • MS Sp Ed
   early childhood education • M Ed
   educational technology • M Ed
   emotionally disturbed • MS Sp Ed

   general curriculum • M Ed
   health care administration • MS
   K–12 education • M Ed
   learning disabilities • MS Sp Ed
   mental retardation • MS Sp Ed
   multi-disciplinary studies • M Ed
   multiply handicapped • MS Sp Ed
   personal guidance service • MSRC
   reading • M Ed
   rehabilitation counseling • MSRC
   school counseling • M Ed
   secondary education • M Ed
   special education generalist • MS Sp Ed
   teaching as a second career • M Ed

College of Business
Program in:
   information processing and communications • MSIPC

MONTANA STATE UNIVERSITY–BOZEMAN
Bozeman, MT 59717

http://www.montana.edu/

Public coed university. *Enrollment:* 11,662 graduate, professional, and undergraduate students. Graduate faculty: *422 full-time, 18 part-time.* Computer facilities: *Campuswide network is available with full Internet access. Total number of PCs/terminals supplied for student use: 850. Computer service fees are applied as a separate charge.* Library facilities: *Renne Library plus 1 additional on-campus library.* Graduate expenses: *$3994 per year full-time, $367 per semester (minimum) part-time for state residents; $9507 per year full-time, $957 per semester (minimum) part-time for nonresidents.* General application contact: *Dr. Joseph Fedock, Interim Dean, 406-994-4145.*

College of Graduate Studies
Dr. Joseph Fedock, Interim Dean

College of Agriculture
Dr. Thomas J. McCoy, Dean
Programs in:
   agronomy • MS
   animal science • MS
   applied economics • MS
   crop and soil science • PhD
   entomology • MS
   land rehabilitation • MS
   plant pathology • MS, PhD
   range science • MS
   soils • MS
   veterinary molecular biology • MS, PhD

College of Arts and Architecture
Dr. Jerry Bancroft, Dean
Programs in:
   architecture • M Arc
   art • MFA

College of Business
Michael Owen, Dean
Programs in:
  business education • MS
  professional accountancy • MPA

College of Education, Health, and Human Development
Dr. Larry Baker, Interim Dean
Programs in:
  education • Ed D, Ed S, M Ed
  health and human development • M Ed, MS

College of Engineering
Dr. David F. Gibson, Dean
Programs in:
  chemical engineering • MS
  civil engineering • MS
  computer science • MS
  construction engineering management • MCEM
  electrical and computer engineering • PhD
  electrical engineering • MS
  engineering • PhD
  environmental engineering • MS, PhD
  industrial and management engineering • MS
  mechanical engineering • MS
  project engineering and management • MPEM

College of Letters and Science
Dr. James McMillan, Interim Dean
Programs in:
  applied psychology • MS
  biochemistry • MS, PhD
  biological sciences • MS, PhD
  chemistry • MS, PhD
  earth sciences • MS
  fish and wildlife management • MS
  history • MA
  mathematics • MS, PhD
  microbiology • MS, PhD
  physics • MS, PhD
  public administration • MPA
  statistics • MS, PhD
  wildlife biology • PhD

College of Nursing
Dr. Lea Acord, Dean
Programs in:
  health administration • MHA
  nursing • MN

MONTANA STATE UNIVERSITY–NORTHERN
Havre, MT 59501-7751

http://www.nmclites.edu/

Public coed comprehensive institution. *Enrollment:* 1,742 graduate, professional, and undergraduate students. *Graduate faculty: 26 full-time. Library facilities: Vande Bogart Library. Graduate expenses: $3090 per year full-time, $696 per semester (minimum) part-time for state residents; $8044 per year full-time, $1758 per semester*

(minimum) part-time for nonresidents. General application contact: Dr. Ben Johnson, Director of Education and Graduate Programs, 406-265-3738.

Department of Education
Dr. Ben Johnson, Director of Education and Graduate Programs
Programs in:
  counseling and development • M Ed
  elementary education • M Ed
  general science • M Ed
  learning development • M Ed
  vocational education • M Ed

MONTANA TECH OF THE UNIVERSITY OF MONTANA
Butte, MT 59701-8997

http://www.mtech.edu/

Public coed comprehensive institution. *Enrollment:* 1,823 graduate, professional, and undergraduate students. *Graduate faculty: 61 full-time. Computer facilities: Campuswide network is available with full Internet access. Total number of PCs/terminals supplied for student use: 800. Computer service fees are applied as a separate charge. Library facilities: main library plus 1 additional on-campus library. Graduate expenses: $2976 per year full-time, $373 per semester (minimum) part-time for state residents; $8857 per year full-time, $1118 per semester (minimum) part-time for nonresidents. General application contact: Cindy Dunstan, Administrative Assistant, 406-496-4128.*

Graduate School
John Brower, Director
Programs in:
  engineering science • MS
  environmental engineering • MS
  geochemistry • MS
  geological engineering • MS
  geology • MS
  geophysical engineering • MS
  hydrogeological engineering • MS
  hydrogeology • MS
  industrial hygiene • MS
  metallurgical/mineral processing engineering • MS
  mineral economics • MS
  mining engineering • MS
  petroleum engineering • MS
  project engineering and management • MPEM
  technical communications • MTC

THE UNIVERSITY OF MONTANA–MISSOULA
Missoula, MT 59812-0002

http://www.umt.edu/

Public coed university. *Enrollment: 11,935 graduate, professional, and undergraduate students. Graduate faculty: 450 full-time, 31 part-time. Computer facilities: Campuswide network is available with full Internet access. Computer service fees are included with tuition and fees. Library facilities: Maureen and Mike Mansfield Library plus 2 additional on-campus libraries. Graduate expenses: $2499 per year (minimum) full-time, $376 per semester (minimum) part-time for state residents; $6528 per year (minimum) full-time, $1048 per semester (minimum) part-time for nonresidents. General application contact: Dr. David A. Strobel, Associate Graduate Dean, 406-243-2572.*

Graduate School
Robert Kindrick, Dean
Program in:
 interdisciplinary studies • MIS

College of Arts and Sciences
Dr. James Flightner, Dean
Programs in:
 algebra • MA, PhD
 analysis • MA, PhD
 anthropology • MA
 applied mathematics • MA, PhD
 chemistry • MS, PhD
 chemistry teaching • MST
 clinical psychology • PhD
 communication studies • MA
 computer science • MS
 creative writing • MFA
 economics • MA
 English education • MA
 English literature • MA
 environmental chemistry • PhD
 environmental studies • MS
 experimental psychology • PhD
 French • MA
 geography • MA
 geology • MS, PhD
 German • MA
 history • MA
 inorganic chemistry • PhD
 linguistics • MA
 mathematics • MAT
 mathematics education • PhD
 operations research • MA, PhD
 organic chemistry • PhD
 philosophy • MA
 physical chemistry • PhD
 political science • MA
 public administration • MPA
 rural, town and regional planning • MA
 school psychology • Ed S, MA
 sociology • MA
 Spanish • MA
 statistics • MA, PhD

Division of Biological Sciences
Dr. Don Christian, Associate Dean
Programs in:
 biochemistry and microbiology • MS, PhD
 organismal biology and ecology • MS, PhD
 teaching biological sciences • MST

School of Business Administration
Dr. Larry Gianchetta, Dean
Programs in:
 accounting and finance • M Acct
 business administration • MBA

School of Education
Dr. Don Robson, Dean
Programs in:
 curriculum and instruction • Ed S, M Ed, MA
 education • Ed D
 guidance and counseling • Ed D, Ed S, M Ed, MA
 health and human performance • MS
 school administration and supervision • Ed S, M Ed, MA

School of Fine Arts
Dr. James Kriley, Dean
Programs in:
 art • MA, MFA
 composition • MM
 drama • MA, MFA
 music and literature • MA
 music education • MME
 performance • MM

School of Forestry
Dr. Perry Brown, Dean
Programs in:
 ecosystem management • MEM
 forestry • PhD
 recreation management • MS
 resource conservation • MS
 wildlife biology • MS

School of Journalism
Clemens P. Work, Director of Graduate Studies
Program in:
 journalism • MA

School of Pharmacy and Allied Health Sciences
Dr. David Forbes, Dean
Programs in:
 pharmaceutical sciences • MS
 pharmacology • PhD
 physical therapy • MS

School of Law
E. Edwin Eck, Dean
Program in:
 law • JD

NEBRASKA

BELLEVUE UNIVERSITY
Bellevue, NE 68005-3098

http://bruins.bellevue.edu/

Independent coed comprehensive institution. *Enrollment:* 2,928 graduate, professional, and undergraduate students. Graduate faculty: 22 full-time, 13 part-time. Computer facilities: *Campuswide network is available with full Internet access. Computer service fees are included with tuition and fees.* Library facilities: *Freeman/Lozier Library.* General application contact: *Elizabeth Wall, Director of Marketing and Enrollment, 402-293-3702.*

Graduate School
Dr. Douglas Frost, Dean
Programs in:
    business • MBA
    computer information systems • MS
    health care administration • MS
    human services • MS
    leadership • MA
    management • MA

CHADRON STATE COLLEGE
Chadron, NE 69337

http://www.csc.edu/

Public coed comprehensive institution. *Enrollment:* 3,003 graduate, professional, and undergraduate students. Graduate faculty: 23. Computer facilities: *Campuswide network is available with full Internet access. Total number of PCs/terminals supplied for student use: 120. Computer service fees are applied as a separate charge.* Library facilities: *Reta King Library.* Graduate expenses: *Tuition of $1788 per year full-time, $75 per credit hour part-time for state residents; $3588 per year full-time, $149 per credit hour part-time for nonresidents. Fees of $388 per year full-time, $1232 per year part-time.* General application contact: *Dr. Pat Colgate, Dean of Graduate Studies, 308-432-6330.*

School of Graduate Studies
Dr. Pat Colgate, Dean
Programs in:
    business • MA Ed
    business and economics • MBA
    counseling • MA Ed, Sp Ed
    educational administration • MS Ed, Sp Ed
    elementary education • MS Ed
    history • MA Ed
    language and literature • MA Ed
    secondary administration • MS Ed
    secondary education • MS Ed

CREIGHTON UNIVERSITY
Omaha, NE 68178-0001

http://www.creighton.edu/

Independent-religious coed university. *Enrollment:* 6,292 graduate, professional, and undergraduate students. Graduate faculty: 251. Computer facilities: *Campuswide network is available with full Internet access. Computer service fees are included with tuition and fees.* Library facilities: *Alumni Memorial Library.* Graduate expenses: *Tuition of $402 per credit hour. Fees of $536 per year full-time, $28 per semester part-time.* General application contact: *Dr. Barbara J. Braden, Dean, Graduate School, 402-280-2870.*

Graduate School
Dr. Barbara J. Braden, Dean
Programs in:
    biomedical sciences • MS, PhD
    medical microbiology and immunology • MS, PhD
    pharmaceutical sciences • MS
    pharmacology • PhD

College of Arts and Sciences
Rev. Michael Proterra, Dean
Programs in:
    atmospheric sciences • MS
    Christian spirituality • MA
    computer sciences • MCS
    educational administration • MS
    guidance and counseling • MS
    international relations • MA
    liberal studies • MLS
    mathematics and statistics • MS
    medical microbiology and immunology • MS, PhD
    ministry • MA
    pharmaceutical sciences • MS
    pharmacology • PhD
    physics • MS
    theology • MA

Eugene C. Eppley College of Business Administration
Dr. Robert Pitts, Dean
Program in:
    business administration • MBA, MSITM

School of Dentistry
Dr. Wayne W. Barkmeier, Dean
Program in:
    dentistry • DDS

School of Law
Lawrence Raful, Dean
Program in:
    law • JD

School of Medicine
Dr. Roderick Nairn, Dean
Programs in:
    biomedical sciences • MS, PhD
    medical microbiology and immunology • MS, PhD

Creighton University (continued)
    medicine • MD
    pharmaceutical sciences • MS
    pharmacology • PhD

School of Nursing
Dr. Edeth K. Kitchens, Dean
Program in:
    nursing • MS

School of Pharmacy and Allied Health Professions
Dr. Sidney J. Stohs, Dean
Programs in:
    occupational therapy • OTD
    pharmacy • Pharm D
    physical therapy • DPT

UNIVERSITY OF NEBRASKA AT KEARNEY
Kearney, NE 68849-0001

http://www.unk.edu/

Public coed comprehensive institution. *Enrollment: 7,133 graduate, professional, and undergraduate students. Graduate faculty: 110 full-time. Computer facilities: Campuswide network is available with full Internet access. Computer service fees are included with tuition and fees. Library facilities: Calvin T. Ryan Library. Graduate expenses: Tuition of $1494 per year full-time, $83 per credit hour part-time for state residents; $2826 per year full-time, $157 per credit hour part-time for nonresidents. Fees of $229 per year full-time, $11.25 per semester (minimum) part-time. General application contact: Dr. Kenneth Nikels, Graduate Dean, 308-865-8500.*

College of Graduate Study
Dr. Kenneth Nikels, Dean

College of Business and Technology
Dr. Galen Hadley, Dean
Programs in:
    business administration • MBA
    business administration/education • MS Ed

College of Education
Dr. Jean Ramage, Dean
Programs in:
    adapted physical education • MA Ed
    counseling • Ed S, MS Ed
    curriculum and instruction • MS Ed
    early childhood education • MA Ed
    early childhood special education • MA Ed
    educational administration • Ed S, MA Ed
    education of behaviorally disordered • MA Ed
    education of the gifted and talented • MA Ed
    elementary education • MA Ed
    exercise science • MA Ed
    instructional technology • MS Ed
    master teacher • MA Ed
    middle school education • MA Ed
    mild/moderate handicapped • MA Ed
    reading education • MA Ed
    school psychology • Ed S
    special education • MA Ed
    specific learning disabilities • MA Ed
    speech pathology • MS Ed
    supervisor of educational media • MA Ed

College of Fine Arts and Humanities
Dr. Harold Nichols, Dean
Programs in:
    art education • MA Ed
    English • MA
    English education • MA Ed
    French • MA Ed
    German • MA Ed
    music education • MA Ed
    Spanish • MA Ed
    speech • MA Ed

College of Natural and Social Sciences
Dr. Michael Schuyler, Dean
Programs in:
    biology education • MS Ed
    general biology • MS
    history • MA
    history education • MA Ed
    mathematics education • MS Ed
    science/mathematics teaching • MS Ed

UNIVERSITY OF NEBRASKA AT OMAHA
Omaha, NE 68182

http://www.unomaha.edu/

Public coed university. *Enrollment: 15,000 graduate, professional, and undergraduate students. Graduate faculty: 308 full-time, 9 part-time. Computer facilities: Campuswide network is available with partial Internet access (e-mail only). Total number of PCs/terminals supplied for student use: 450. Computer service fees are included with tuition and fees. Library facilities: University Library. Graduate expenses: Tuition of $1670 per year full-time, $94 per credit hour part-time for state residents; $4082 per year full-time, $227 per credit hour part-time for nonresidents. Fees of $302 per year full-time, $108 per semester (minimum) part-time. General application contact: John Flemming, Director of Admissions, 402-554-2709.*

Graduate Studies and Research
Dr. Ernest Peck, Dean

College of Arts and Sciences
Dr. John Flocken, Dean
Programs in:
    biology • MA, MS
    communication • MA
    computer science • MA, MS

developmental psychobiology • PhD
educational psychology • MS
English • MA
experimental child psychology • PhD
geography • MA
history • MA
industrial/organizational psychology • MS, PhD
mathematics • MA, MAT, MS
political science • MA, MS
psychology • MA
school psychology • Ed S
sociology • MA

College of Business Administration
Dr. Stan Hille, Dean
Programs in:
accounting • MPA
business administration • MBA
economics • MA, MS

College of Education
Dr. Richard B. Flynn, Dean
Programs in:
behavioral disorders • MS
community counseling • MA, MS
counseling gerontology • MA, MS
educational administration and supervision • Ed D, Ed S, MS
elementary education • MA, MS
health, physical education and recreation • MA, MS
mental retardation • MA
reading education • MA, MS
resource teaching and learning disabilities • MS
school counseling-elementary • MA, MS
school counseling-secondary • MA, MS
secondary education • MA, MS
speech-language pathology • MA, MS
student affairs practice in higher education • MA, MS
teaching the hearing impaired • MS
teaching the mentally retarded • MS
urban education • MS

College of Fine Arts
Dr. Karen White, Dean
Programs in:
dramatic arts • MA
music • MM

College of Public Affairs and Community Service
Dr. David Hinton, Dean
Programs in:
criminal justice • MA, MS, PhD
gerontology • Certificate, MA
public administration • MPA, PhD
social work • MSW

UNIVERSITY OF NEBRASKA–LINCOLN
Lincoln, NE 68588
http://www.unl.edu/

Public coed university. Enrollment: 22,827 graduate, professional, and undergraduate students. Graduate faculty: *902 full-time, 38 part-time.* Computer facilities: *Campuswide network is available with full Internet access. Computer service fees are included with tuition and fees.* Library facilities: *Love Memorial Library plus 11 additional on-campus libraries.* Graduate expenses: *Tuition of $110 per credit hour for state residents; $270 per credit hour for nonresidents. Fees of $480 per year full-time, $110 per semester part-time.* General application contact: *Dr. Merlin P. Lawson, Dean of Graduate Studies, 402-472-2875.*

Graduate College
Dr. Merlin P. Lawson, Dean of Graduate Studies
Programs in:
legal studies • MLS
museum studies • MA, MS

Center for Biological Chemistry
Dr. Robert Klucas, Head
Program in:
biochemistry • MS, PhD

College of Agricultural Sciences and Natural Resources
Dr. Donald M. Edwards, Dean
Programs in:
agricultural economics • MS, PhD
agricultural leadership, education and communication • MS
agronomy • MS, PhD
animal science • MS, PhD
biometry • MS
entomology • MS, PhD
food science and technology • MS, PhD
forestry, fisheries, and wildlife • MS
horticulture • MS
horticulture and forestry • PhD
mechanized systems management • MS
nutrition • MS, PhD
veterinary and biomedical sciences • MS, PhD

College of Architecture
W. Cecil Steward, Dean
Programs in:
architecture • M Arch
community and regional planning • MCRP

College of Arts and Sciences
Dr. Brian Foster, Dean
Programs in:
analytical chemistry • PhD
anthropology • MA
astronomy • MS, PhD
chemistry • MS
classics • MA
communications studies • MA
communication studies and theatre arts • PhD

University of Nebraska–Lincoln (continued)
  computer science and engineering • MS, PhD
  English • MA, PhD
  French • MA, PhD
  geography • MA, PhD
  geosciences • MS, PhD
  German • MA, PhD
  history • MA, PhD
  inorganic chemistry • PhD
  mathematics and statistics • M Sc T, MA, MAT, MS, PhD
  organic chemistry • PhD
  philosophy • MA, PhD
  physical chemistry • PhD
  physics • MS, PhD
  political science • MA, PhD
  psychology • MA, PhD
  sociology • MA, PhD
  Spanish • MA, PhD
  survey research and methodology • MS

College of Business Administration
Dr. John Goebel, Dean
Programs in:
  accountancy • MPA, PhD
  actuarial science • MS
  business • MA, MBA, PhD
  economics • MA, PhD

College of Engineering and Technology
Dr. James L. Hendrix, Dean
Programs in:
  agricultural and biological systems engineering • MS
  chemical engineering • MS
  civil engineering • MS
  electrical engineering • MS
  engineering • PhD
  engineering mechanics • MS
  environmental engineering • MS
  industrial and management systems engineering • MS
  manufacturing systems engineering • MS
  materials science engineering • MS
  mechanical engineering • MS

College of Fine and Performing Arts
Dr. Richard Durst, Dean
Programs in:
  art and art history • MFA
  music • DMA, MM
  theatre arts and dance • MFA

College of Human Resources and Family Sciences
Dr. Karen E. Craig, Dean
Programs in:
  family and consumer sciences • MS
  human resources and family sciences • MS, PhD
  nutritional science and dietetics • MS
  textiles, clothing, and design • MA, MS

College of Journalism and Mass Communications
Dr. Will Norton Jr., Dean
Program in:
  journalism and mass communications • MA

School of Biological Sciences
Dr. T. Jack Morris, Director
Program in:
  biological sciences • MA, MS, PhD

Teachers College
Dr. James P. O'Hanlon, Dean
Programs in:
  administration, curriculum and instruction • Ed D, PhD
  community and human resources • Ed D, PhD
  curriculum and instruction • Ed S, M Ed, MA, MST
  educational administration • Certificate, Ed D, M Ed, MA
  educational psychology • Ed S, MA
  health, physical education, and recreation • M Ed, MPE
  psychological and cultural studies • Ed D, PhD
  special education • M Ed, MA
  special education and communication disorders • Ed S
  speech-language pathology and audiology • MS
  vocational and adult education • M Ed, MA

College of Law
Harvey S. Perlman, Dean
Program in:
  law • JD

WAYNE STATE COLLEGE
Wayne, NE 68787

http://www.wsc.edu/

Public coed comprehensive institution. *Enrollment:* 3,838 graduate, professional, and undergraduate students. Graduate faculty: *0 full-time, 85 part-time.* Computer facilities: *Campuswide network is available with full Internet access. Total number of PCs/terminals supplied for student use: 200. Computer services are offered at no charge.* Library facilities: *U. S. Conn Library plus 1 additional on-campus library.* Graduate expenses: *Tuition of $1788 per year full-time, $75 per credit hour part-time for state residents; $3576 per year full-time, $149 per credit hour part-time for nonresidents. Fees of $360 per year full-time, $15 per credit hour part-time.* General application contact: *Dr. Robert McCue, Dean of Graduate Studies, 402-375-7232.*

Graduate School
Dr. Robert McCue, Dean of Graduate Studies

Division of Business
Dr. Vaughn Benson, Head
Program in:
  business • MBA

Division of Education
Dr. Diane Alexander, Head
Programs in:
  art education • MSE
  business education • MSE
  communication arts education • MSE
  counselor education • MSE

curriculum and instruction • MSE
educational administration • Ed S
elementary administration • MSE
elementary education • MSE
English as a second language • MSE
health and physical education/health • MSE
health and physical education/pedagogy • MSE
industrial technology education • MSE
mathematics education • MSE
music education • MSE
science education • MSE
secondary administration • MSE
special education • MSE

Division of Fine Arts
Dr. James O'Leary, Head
Program in:
    art education • MSE

Division of Humanities
Dr. Ed Battistella, Head
Programs in:
    communication arts • MSE
    English education • MSE

Division of Math and Science
Dr. J. S. Johar, Head
Program in:
    math and science • MSE

Division of Physical Education
Dr. Ralph Barclay, Head
Program in:
    physical education • MSE

Division of Social Sciences
Dr. Jean Karlen, Head
Programs in:
    history • MSE
    social science • MSE

NEVADA

UNIVERSITY OF NEVADA, LAS VEGAS
Las Vegas, NV 89154-9900
http://www.unlv.edu/

Public coed university. *Enrollment: 20,232 graduate, professional, and undergraduate students. Graduate faculty: 542 full-time, 25 part-time. Computer facilities: Campuswide network is available with full Internet access. Computer services are offered at no charge. Library facilities: James R. Dickinson Library. Graduate expenses: Tuition of $93 per credit for state residents; $93 per credit full-time, $190 per credit part-time for nonresidents. Fees of $5570 per year full-time for nonresidents. General application contact: Dr. Penny Amy, Interim Dean, Graduate College, 702-895-4391.*

Graduate College
Dr. Penny Amy, Interim Dean

College of Business
Elvin C. Lashbrooke, Dean
Programs in:
    accounting • MS
    business administration • MBA
    economics • MA
    public administration • MPA

College of Education
Dr. John Readence, Dean
Programs in:
    assessment and evaluation techniques for the
        exceptional • Ed D
    educational administration • Ed D, Ed S, M Ed
    educational computing and technology • M Ed, MS
    educational psychology • M Ed, MS
    emotional disturbance • Ed D
    English/language arts • M Ed, MS
    general elementary curriculum • M Ed, MS
    general secondary education • M Ed, MS
    general special education • Ed D
    instructional and curricular studies • Ed D, Ed S, PhD
    language and literacy education • M Ed, MS
    learning disabilities • Ed D
    library science and audiovisual education • M Ed, MS
    mathematics education • M Ed, MS
    mental retardation • Ed D
    middle school education • M Ed, MS
    postsecondary education • M Ed, MS
    school psychology • Ed S
    special education • Ed S, M Ed, MA, MS
    teaching English as a second language • M Ed, MS
    vocational education • M Ed, MS

College of Fine Arts
Dr. Jeffrey Koep, Dean
Programs in:
    acting • MA
    architecture • M Arch
    art • MFA
    composition/theory • MM
    dance • MM
    design and technical • MA
    directing • MA
    music education • MM
    performance • MM
    playwriting • MA
    theatre arts • MFA

College of Health Sciences
Dr. Carolyn Sabo, Dean
Programs in:
    acute and chronic health problems • MS
    exercise physiology • MS
    family nurse practitioner • MS
    health physics • MS
    kinesiology • MS
    terminal illness • MS

University of Nevada, Las Vegas (continued)

College of Liberal Arts
Dr. James Frey, Interim Dean
Programs in:
    amelioration and social policy • MA
    anthropology • MA
    counseling • MA
    English • PhD
    English and American literature • MA
    ethics and policy studies • MA
    French • MA
    general psychology • MA
    history • MA, PhD
    language studies • MA
    political science • MA
    preclinical • MA
    sociology • PhD
    Spanish • MA
    theoretical • MA
    writing • MA

College of Science
Dr. Raymond Alden, Dean
Programs in:
    applied mathematics • MS
    biological sciences • MS
    environmental analytical chemistry • MS
    environmental biology • PhD
    general chemistry • MS
    geoscience • MS
    mathematics • MS
    physics • MS, PhD
    pure mathematics • MS
    science • MA
    statistics • MS
    water resources management • MS

Greenspun College of Urban Affairs
Dr. Martha Watson, Dean
Programs in:
    community agency counseling • MS
    criminal justice • MS
    environmental sciences • MS
    marriage and family counseling • MS
    mass communications • MA
    rehabilitation couseling • MS
    social work • MSW

Howard R. Hughes College of Engineering
Dr. William Wells, Dean
Programs in:
    civil and environmental engineering • MSE, PhD
    computer science • MS, PhD
    electrical and computer engineering • MSE, PhD
    mechanical engineering • MSE, PhD

William F. Harrah College of Hotel Administration
Dr. David Christianson, Dean
Programs in:
    hospitality administration • PhD
    hotel administration • MS
    leisure studies • MS

UNIVERSITY OF NEVADA, RENO
Reno, NV 89557

http://www.unr.edu/grad/

Public coed university. *Enrollment:* 12,000 graduate, professional, and undergraduate students. Graduate faculty: *556.* Computer facilities: *Campuswide network is available with full Internet access. Computer services are offered at no charge.* Library facilities: *Getchell Library plus 7 additional on-campus libraries.* Graduate expenses: *Tuition of $0 for state residents; $5770 per year full-time, $200 per credit part-time for nonresidents. Fees of $93 per credit.* General application contact: *Dr. Kenneth W. Hunter, Vice President of Research and Dean of Graduate School, 702-784-6869.*

Graduate School
Dr. Kenneth Hunter, Vice President of Research and Dean
Programs in:
    biochemistry • MS, PhD
    biomedical engineering • MS, PhD
    cell and molecular biology • MS, PhD
    cellular and molecular pharmacology and physiology • MS, PhD
    ecology, evolution, and conservation biology • PhD
    hydrogeology • MS, PhD
    hydrology • MS, PhD
    land use planning • MS
    social psychology • PhD
    speech pathology • PhD
    speech pathology and audiology • MS

Center for Environmental Sciences and Engineering
Dr. James N. Seiber, Director
Programs in:
    atmospheric sciences • MS, PhD
    ecology, evolution and conservation biology • PhD
    environmental sciences and health • MS, PhD

College of Arts and Science
Dr. Robert W. Mead, Dean
Programs in:
    anthropology • MA, PhD
    Basque studies • PhD
    chemistry • MS, PhD
    English • MA, MATE, PhD
    French • MA
    geography • MS
    German • MA
    history • MA, PhD
    mathematics • MS
    music • MA, MM
    philosophy • MA
    physics • MS, PhD
    political science • MA, PhD
    public administration • MPA
    sociology • MA
    Spanish • MA
    speech communication • MA
    teaching English as a second language • MA
    teaching mathematics • MATM

College of Business Administration
Dr. H. Michael Reed, Dean
Programs in:
　accountancy • M Acc
　business administration • MBA
　economics • MA, MS

College of Education
Dr. Stephen Rock, Acting Dean
Programs in:
　counseling and educational psychology • Ed D, Ed S,
　　M Ed, MA, MS, PhD
　curriculum and instruction • Ed D, Ed S, PhD
　educational leadership • Ed D, Ed S, M Ed, MA, MS,
　　PhD
　elementary education • M Ed, MA, MS
　secondary education • M Ed, MA, MS
　special education • M Ed, MA, MS

College of Engineering
Dr. Theodore Batchman, Dean
Programs in:
　chemical engineering • MS, PhD
　civil engineering • MS, PhD
　computer science • MS
　electrical engineering • MS, PhD
　mechanical engineering • MS, PhD

College of Human and Community Sciences
Dr. Jean L. Perry, Dean
Programs in:
　human development and family studies • MS
　nursing • MS
　nutrition • MS
　physical education • MS
　social work • MSW

Donald W. Reynolds School of Journalism
Dr. Travis Linn, Acting Dean
Program in:
　journalism • MA

Mackay School of Mines
Dr. Jane Long, Dean
Programs in:
　geochemistry • MS, PhD
　geological engineering • Geol E, MS
　geology • MS, PhD
　geophysics • MS, PhD
　metallurgical engineering • MS, Met E, PhD
　mining engineering • EM, MS

M. C. Fleischmann College of Agriculture
Dr. Bernard M. Jones, Dean
Programs in:
　agriculture • PhD
　animal science • MS
　environmental and natural resource science • MS
　resource and applied economics • MS

School of Medicine
Dr. Robert Daugherty Jr., Dean
Programs in:
　biomedical engineering • MS, PhD

cellular and molecular pharmacology and physiology •
　MS, PhD
medicine • MD
speech pathology • PhD
speech pathology and audiology • MS

NEW HAMPSHIRE

 DARTMOUTH COLLEGE
Hanover, NH 03755
http://www.dartmouth.edu/

Independent coed university. Enrollment: 5,249 graduate, professional, and undergraduate students. Graduate faculty: 336 full-time, 716 part-time. Computer facilities: Campuswide network is available with full Internet access. Computer service fees are included with tuition and fees. Library facilities: Baker Library plus 8 additional on-campus libraries. Graduate expenses: $31,719 per year. General application contact: Dorothea French, Assistant Dean of Graduate Studies, 603-646-2107.

School of Arts and Sciences
Roger D. Sloboda, Dean
Programs in:
　biochemistry • PhD
　biological sciences • MS, PhD
　chemistry • PhD
　cognitive neuroscience • PhD
　comparative literature • AM
　computer science • MS, PhD
　earth sciences • MS, PhD
　electro-acoustic music • AM
　evaluative clinical science • MS, PhD
　liberal studies • MALS
　mathematics • PhD
　pharmacology and toxicology • PhD
　physics and astronomy • PhD
　physiology • PhD
　psychology • PhD

Amos Tuck School of Business Administration
Paul Danos, Dean
Program in:
　business administration • MBA

Dartmouth Medical School
Dr. John C. Baldwin, Dean
Program in:
　medicine • MD

Thayer School of Engineering
Dr. Charles E. Hutchinson, Dean
Programs in:
　biomedical engineering • MS, PhD
　biotechnology and biochemical engineering • MS, PhD

Dartmouth College (continued)
    computer engineering • MS, PhD
    electrical engineering • MS, PhD
    engineering management • MEM
    environmental engineering • MS, PhD
    materials sciences and engineering • MS, PhD
    mechanical engineering • MS, PhD

KEENE STATE COLLEGE
Keene, NH 03435

http://www.keene.edu/

Public coed comprehensive institution. *Enrollment:* 3,876 graduate, professional, and undergraduate students. Graduate faculty: *184 full-time, 169 part-time.* Computer facilities: *Campuswide network is available with full Internet access. Total number of PCs/terminals supplied for student use: 285. Computer service fees are included with tuition and fees.* Library facilities: *Mason Library.* General application contact: *Peter Tandy, Academic Counselor, 603-358-2332.*

Division of Graduate and Professional Studies
Dr. Ann Britt Waling, Dean
Programs in:
    counseling and consultation • M Ed
    curriculum and instruction • M Ed
    educational administration • M Ed

 # NOTRE DAME COLLEGE
Manchester, NH 03104-2299

http://www.notredame.edu

Independent-religious coed comprehensive institution. *Enrollment:* 1,316 graduate, professional, and undergraduate students. Graduate faculty: *10 full-time, 52 part-time.* Library facilities: *Paul Harvey Library.* Graduate expenses: *$299 per credit.* General application contact: *Graduate Admissions Office, 603-669-4298 Ext. 194.*

Division of Sciences
Dr. Jane Walter, Dean
Program in:
    counseling psychology • MA

Education Division
Sandra S. Metes, Dean
Programs in:
    advanced reading • M Ed
    curriculum and instruction • M Ed
    elementary teaching • M Ed
    emotional and behavioral disorders • M Ed
    interdisciplinary studies • M Ed
    learning and language disabilities • M Ed

    school administration and supervision • M Ed
    school counseling • M Ed
    secondary teaching • M Ed
    teaching English as a second language • M Ed

Humanities Division
Dr. Barbara Radtke, Dean
Program in:
    theology • MA

PLYMOUTH STATE COLLEGE OF THE UNIVERSITY SYSTEM OF NEW HAMPSHIRE
Plymouth, NH 03264-1595

http://www.plymouth.edu/

Public coed comprehensive institution. *Enrollment:* 3,779 graduate, professional, and undergraduate students. Graduate faculty: *47 full-time, 28 part-time.* Computer facilities: *Campuswide network is available with full Internet access. Computer service fees are included with tuition and fees.* Library facilities: *Lamson Library.* Graduate expenses: *$232 per credit for state residents; $254 per credit for nonresidents.* General application contact: *Maryann Szabadics, Administrative Secretary, 603-535-2636.*

Graduate Studies
Programs in:
    business studies • MBA
    educational administration • M Ed
    educational computing • M Ed
    elementary education • M Ed
    environmental science education • M Ed
    guidance and counseling • M Ed
    health education • M Ed
    heritage studies • M Ed
    integrated arts • M Ed
    mathematics education • M Ed
    reading specialist • M Ed
    secondary education • M Ed

RIVIER COLLEGE
Nashua, NH 03060-5086

Independent-religious coed comprehensive institution. Library facilities: *Regina Library.* General application contact: *Dean of the Graduate School, 603-888-1311 Ext. 8234.*

School of Graduate Studies
Programs in:
    business administration • MBA
    computer science • MS

computers in education • MA
counseling and psychotherapy • MA
counselor education • M Ed
early childhood education • M Ed
educational administration • M Ed
elementary education • M Ed
employee relations • MBA
English • MA, MAT
general education • M Ed
human resources management • MBA, MS
information science • MS
learning disabilities • M Ed
mathematics • MS
modern languages • MAT
nursing • MS
professional development • MS
reading • M Ed
secondary education • M Ed
writing and literature • MA

UNIVERSITY OF NEW HAMPSHIRE
Durham, NH 03824

http://www.unh.edu/

Public coed university. *Enrollment:* 12,701 graduate, professional, and undergraduate students. Graduate faculty: *577 full-time.* Computer facilities: *Campuswide network is available with full Internet access. Computer services are offered at no charge.* Library facilities: *Dimond Library plus 4 additional on-campus libraries.* Graduate expenses: *Tuition of $5440 per year full-time, $302 per credit hour part-time for state residents; $8160 per year (minimum) full-time, $453 per credit hour (minimum) part-time for nonresidents. Fees of $868 per year full-time, $15 per year part-time.* General application contact: *Dr. Harry J. Richards, Associate Dean, Graduate School, 603-862-3000.*

Graduate School
Dr. Harry J. Richards, Associate Dean

College of Engineering and Physical Sciences
Dr. Roy B. Torbert, Dean
Programs in:
applied mathematics • MS
chemical engineering • MS, PhD
chemistry • MS, MST, PhD
civil engineering • MS, PhD
computer science • MS, PhD
earth sciences • MS, PhD
electrical engineering • MS, PhD
geochemical • MS
geology • MS, PhD
hydrology • MS, PhD
mathematics • MS, MST, PhD
mathematics education • PhD
mechanical engineering • MS, PhD
ocean engineering • MS

oceanography • MS, PhD
physics • MS, PhD
systems design engineering • PhD

College of Liberal Arts
Dr. Paul T. Brockelman, Graduate Coordinator
Programs in:
counseling • M Ed, MA
early childhood education • M Ed
education • PhD
educational administration • CAGS, M Ed
elementary education • M Ed, MAT
English • MA, PhD
English education • MST
history • MA, PhD
liberal studies • MALS
music • MA
music education • MS
political science • MA
psychology • PhD
public administration • MPA
reading • M Ed
reading and writing instruction • PhD
secondary education • M Ed, MAT
sociology • MA, PhD
Spanish • MA
special education • M Ed

College of Life Sciences and Agriculture
Dr. William Mautz, Interim Dean
Programs in:
adult and occupational education • MAOE
animal and nutritional sciences • MS, PhD
biochemistry and molecular biology • MS, PhD
biology • MS
environmental conservation • MS
forestry • MS
genetics • MS, PhD
microbiology • MS, PhD
natural resources • PhD
plant biology • MS, PhD
resource administration and management • MS
resource economics • MS
soil science • MS
water resources management • MS
wildlife • MS
zoology • MS, PhD

School of Health and Human Services
Roger A. Ritvo, Dean
Programs in:
communication disorders • MS, MST
family studies • MS
health management and policy • MHA
kinesiology • MS
marriage and family therapy • MS
nursing • MS
occupational therapy • MS
social work • MSW

Whittemore School of Business and Economics
Dr. Lyndon Goodridge, Dean
Programs in:
business administration • MBA
economics • MA, PhD

NEW JERSEY

THE COLLEGE OF NEW JERSEY
Ewing, NJ 08628

http://www.tcnj.edu/

Public coed comprehensive institution. *Enrollment: 6,780 graduate, professional, and undergraduate students. Graduate faculty: 41 full-time, 12 part-time. Computer facilities: Campuswide network is available with full Internet access. Total number of PCs/terminals supplied for student use: 800. Computer service fees are included with tuition and fees. Library facilities: Roscoe L. West Library. Graduate expenses: Tuition of $6892 per year full-time, $287 per credit hour part-time for state residents; $9602 per year full-time, $402 per credit hour part-time for nonresidents. Fees of $799 per year full-time, $33 per credit hour part-time. General application contact: Office of Graduate Studies, 609-771-2300.*

Graduate Division
Dr. Suzanne Pasch, Dean

School of Arts and Sciences
Dr. Richard Kamber, Dean
Programs in:
English • MA
music • M Ed, MA, MAT

School of Education
Dr. Suzanne Pasch, Dean, Graduate Division
Programs in:
alcohol and chemical dependency counseling • Certificate
audiology • MA
community counseling • MA
developmental reading • M Ed
educational leadership • M Ed
elementary education • M Ed, MAT
English as a second language • M Ed
health • MAT
health and physical education • M Ed
instructional computing coordinator • Certificate
physical education • M Ed
school counseling • MA
secondary education • MAT
special education • M Ed, MAT
special education with learning disabilities • M Ed
speech pathology • MA
teaching English as a second language • Certificate

School of Nursing
Dr. Laurie N. Sherwen, Dean
Program in:
nursing • MSN

FAIRLEIGH DICKINSON UNIVERSITY, FLORHAM–MADISON CAMPUS
Madison, NJ 07940-1099

http://www.fdu.edu/

Independent coed comprehensive institution. *Enrollment: 3,307 graduate, professional, and undergraduate students. Graduate faculty: 62 full-time, 84 part-time. Library facilities: Friendship Library. Graduate expenses: Tuition of $522 per credit. Fees of $302 per year full-time, $138 per year part-time. General application contact: Michael Hendricks, Director of Admissions, 973-443-8905.*

Maxwell Becton College of Arts and Sciences
Dr. Martin Green, Dean
Programs in:
addictions counseling • MA
applied social and community psychology • MA
biology • MS
chemistry • MS
clinical psychology • MA
computer science • MS
corporate and organizational communication • MA
general experimental psychology • MA
industrial psychology • MA
mathematics • MS
organizational behavior • MA
psychology personnel • MA
teaching • MAT

Samuel J. Silberman College of Business Administration
Dr. Paul Lerman, Dean
Programs in:
accounting • MBA
economics • MA, MBA
finance • MBA
human resource management • MBA
industrial management • MBA
international business • MBA
management • MBA
marketing • MBA
pharmaceutical-chemical studies • MBA
quantitative analysis • MBA
taxation • MS

FAIRLEIGH DICKINSON UNIVERSITY, TEANECK–HACKENSACK CAMPUS
Teaneck, NJ 07666-1914

http://www.fdu.edu/

Independent coed comprehensive institution. *Enrollment: 5,330 graduate, professional, and undergraduate students. Graduate faculty: 148 full-time, 185 part-time. Computer facilities: Campuswide network is available with full Internet access. Total number of PCs/terminals supplied for student use: 210. Computer service fees are included with tuition and fees. Library facilities: Weiner Library plus 1 additional on-campus library. Graduate expenses: Tuition of $522 per credit. Fees of $302 per year full-time, $138 per year part-time. General application contact: Dale Herold, Vice President for Enrollment Management, 800-338-8803.*

Samuel J. Silberman College of Business Administration
Dr. Paul Lerman, Dean
Programs in:
  accounting • MBA, MS
  administrative science • MAS
  economics • MBA
  finance • MBA
  human resource administration • MBA
  industrial management • MBA
  international business • MBA
  management • MBA
  marketing • MBA
  pharmaceutical-chemical studies • MBA
  public administration • MPA
  quantitative analysis • MBA
  taxation • MS

University College: Arts, Sciences, and Professional Studies
Dr. Dario A. Cortes, Dean
Programs in:
  computer engineering • MS
  environmental studies • MS

Peter Sammartino School of Education
Dr. Eloise Forster, Interim Director
Programs in:
  bilingual/bicultural education • MAT
  biological science education • MAT
  elementary education • MAT
  English education • MAT
  learning disabilities • MA
  mathematics education • MAT
  multilingual education • MA
  physical education • MAT
  science education • MAT
  social studies education • MAT
  teaching • MAT
  teaching English as a second language • MAT

School of Communication Arts
Dr. Duane Edwards, Director
Programs in:
  corporate and organizational communication • MA
  English and literature • MA

School of Computer Science and Information Systems
Dr. Gilbert Steiner, Director
Programs in:
  computer science • MS
  management information systems • MS
  mathematics • MS

School of Engineering and Engineering Technology
Dr. Alfredo Tan, Director
Program in:
  electrical engineering • MSEE

School of Natural Sciences
Dr. Irwin R. Isquith, Director
Programs in:
  biology • MS
  chemistry • MS
  physics • MS
  science • MA

School of Nursing and Allied Health
Dr. Caroline Jordet, Director
Program in:
  nursing • MS

School of Political and International Studies
Dr. Faramarz Fatemi, Director
Programs in:
  history • MA
  international studies • MA
  political science • MA

School of Psychology
Dr. Christopher Capuano, Director
Programs in:
  clinical psychology • PhD
  psychology • MA
  school psychology • MA, Psy D

GEORGIAN COURT COLLEGE
Lakewood, NJ 08701-2697

http://www.georgian.edu/

Independent-religious primarily female comprehensive institution. *Enrollment: 2,422 graduate, professional, and undergraduate students. Graduate faculty: 8 full-time, 47 part-time. Library facilities: main library. Graduate expenses: $350 per credit. General application contact: Sr. Mary Arthur Beal, Dean of the Graduate School, 732-367-1717.*

Georgian Court College (continued)
Graduate School
Sr. Mary Arthur Beal, Dean
Programs in:
  administration, supervision, and curriculum planning •
    MA
  administration, supervision and curriculum planning
    (management specialization) • MA
  biology • MS
  business administration • MBA
  counseling psychology • MA
  mathematics • MA
  reading specialization • MA
  special education • MA
  teaching certificate • MA
  theology • MA

KEAN UNIVERSITY
Union, NJ 07083

http://www.kean.edu/

Public coed comprehensive institution. *Enrollment:* 11,537 graduate, professional, and undergraduate students. Graduate faculty: *351 full-time, 532 part-time.* Library facilities: *Nancy Thompson Library plus 1 additional on-campus library.* Graduate expenses: *$5926 per year full-time, $248 per credit part-time for state residents; $7312 per year full-time, $304 per credit part-time for nonresidents.* General application contact: *Joanne Morris, Director of Graduate Admissions, 908-527-2665.*

School of Business, Government, and Technology
Dr. Charles Anderson, Dean
Programs in:
  health services administration • MPA
  management systems analysis • MSMSA
  public administration • MPA

School of Education
Dr. Ana Maria Schuhmann, Dean
Programs in:
  administration in early childhood and family studies •
    MA
  advanced curriculum and teaching • MA
  alcohol and drug abuse counseling • MA
  bilingual/bicultural education • MA
  bilingual education • Certificate
  business and industry counseling • MA, PMC
  classroom instruction • MA
  community/agency counseling • MA
  developmental disabilities • MA
  earth science • MA
  educational administration • Certificate, MA
  education for family living • MA
  emotionally disturbed and socially maladjusted • MA
  English as a second language • Certificate
  learning disabilities • MA
  mathematics/science/computer education • MA

pre-school handicapped • MA
reading specialization • MA
school counseling • MA
speech pathology • MA
teaching • MA
teaching English as a second language • MA
teaching of reading • Certificate

School of Liberal Arts
Edward B. Weil, Dean
Programs in:
  behavioral sciences • MA
  business and industry counseling • MA, PMC
  educational psychology • MA
  fine arts education • MA
  human behavior and organizational psychology • MA
  liberal studies • MA
  psychological services • MA
  school psychology • Diploma
  social work • MSW

School of Natural Sciences, Mathematics, and Nursing
Dr. Betty Barber, Dean
Programs in:
  mathematics education • MA
  nursing • MS

MONMOUTH UNIVERSITY
West Long Branch, NJ 07764-1898

http://www.monmouth.edu/

Independent coed comprehensive institution. *Enrollment:* 5,177 graduate, professional, and undergraduate students. Graduate faculty: *67 full-time, 27 part-time.* Computer facilities: *Campuswide network is available with full Internet access. Total number of PCs/ terminals supplied for student use: 375. Computer service fees are included with tuition and fees.* Library facilities: *Guggenheim Memorial Library.* Graduate expenses: *Tuition of $459 per credit. Fees of $274 per semester full-time, $137 per semester part-time.* General application contact: *Office of Graduate Admissions, 732-571-3452.*

Graduate School
Dr. Datta V. Naik, Dean, Graduate School
Programs in:
  computer science • MS
  corporate and public communication • MA
  criminal justice • MA
  electronic engineering • MS
  history • MA
  human resources communication • Certificate
  liberal studies • MALS
  media studies • Certificate
  nursing • MSN
  professional counseling • PMC
  psychological counseling • MA

public relations • Certificate
software engineering • MS

School of Business Administration
Dr. William Dempsey, Dean
Program in:
business administration • MBA

School of Education
Dr. Bernice Willis, Dean
Programs in:
certified teachers • MAT
elementary education • MAT
learning disabilities-teacher consultant • Certificate
non-certified teachers • MAT
principalship • MS Ed
reading specialist • Certificate, MS Ed
special education • Certificate, MS Ed
student personnel services • MS Ed
supervision • Certificate

MONTCLAIR STATE UNIVERSITY
Upper Montclair, NJ 07043-1624
http://www.montclair.edu/

Public coed comprehensive institution. *Enrollment:* 12,851 graduate, professional, and undergraduate students. Graduate faculty: 444 full-time. Computer facilities: *Campuswide network is available with full Internet access. Total number of PCs/terminals supplied for student use:* 450. Computer service fees are included with tuition and fees. Library facilities: *Sprague Library.* Graduate expenses: Tuition of $201 per credit for state residents; $257 per credit for nonresidents. Fees of $22.05 per credit. General application contact: *Dr. Carla Narrett, Dean of Graduate Studies, 973-655-5147.*

Office of Graduate Studies
Dr. Carla Narrett, Dean

College of Education and Human Services
Dr. Nicholas M. Michelli, Dean
Programs in:
administration and supervision • MA
coaching and sports administration • MA
counseling and guidance • MA
critical thinking • M Ed
exercise science • MA
family life education • MA
family relations/child development • MA
health education • MA
home economics education • MA
home management/consumer economics • MA
industrial technology and education • MA
reading • MA
teaching and administration of physical education • MA
teaching middle school philosophy • MAT

College of Humanities and Social Sciences
Dr. Rachel Fordyce, Dean
Programs in:
anthropology • MA
applied linguistics • MA
applied sociology • MA
clinical psychology • MA
dispute resolution • MA
early childhood special education • MA
economics • MA
educational psychology • MA
English and comparative literature • MA
French • MA
geography • MA
history • MA
industrial and organizational psychology • MA
law office management and technology • MA
learning disabilities • MA
political science • MA
practical anthropology • MA
sociology • MA
Spanish • MA
speech/language pathology • MA
urban studies • MA

College of Science and Mathematics
Dr. Vaughn Vandegrift, Dean
Programs in:
applied mathematics • MS
applied statistics • MS
biology • MS
chemistry • MS
computer science • MS
environmental education • MS
environmental health • MS
environmental management • MS
environmental science • MS
environmental studies • MS
geoscience • MS
mathematics education • MS
pure and applied mathematics • MS
statistics • MS

School of Business
Dr. Alan Oppenheim, Acting Dean
Programs in:
accounting • MBA, MS
business economics • MBA
distributive education • MA
economics and finance • MA
finance • MBA
international business • MBA
management • MBA
marketing • MBA
quantitative analysis • MBA

School of the Arts
Dr. Geoffrey Newman, Dean
Programs in:
art history • MA
communication arts • MA
music education • MA
performance • MA
studio art • MA

Montclair State University (continued)
theatre • MA
theory/composition • MA

NEW JERSEY CITY UNIVERSITY
Jersey City, NJ 07305-1957
http://www.jcstate.edu/

Public coed comprehensive institution. Computer facilities: *Campuswide network is available with full Internet access. Total number of PCs/ terminals supplied for student use: 495.* Computer service fees are included with tuition and fees. Library facilities: *Forrest A. Irwin Library.* General application contact: *Director of Graduate Studies, 201-200-3409.*

Graduate Studies

School of Arts and Sciences
Programs in:
art • MA
art education • MA
counseling • MA
educational psychology • MA, PD
mathematics education • MA
music education • MA
school psychology • PD

School of Professional Studies and Education
Programs in:
administration and supervision • MA
basics and urban studies • MA
bilingual/bicultural education and English as a second
language • MA
community health education • MS
criminal justice • MS
early childhood education • MA
health administration • MS
literary education • MA
professional studies and education • Certificate
special education • MA
urban education • MA

NEW JERSEY INSTITUTE OF TECHNOLOGY
Newark, NJ 07102-1982
http://www.njit.edu/

Public coed university. *Enrollment: 6,752 graduate, professional, and undergraduate students. Graduate faculty: 358 full-time, 216 part-time.* Computer facilities: *Campuswide network is available with full Internet access.* Computer service fees are included with tuition and fees. Library facilities: *Van Houten Library plus 1 additional on-campus library.* Graduate expenses: *Tuition of $6952 per year full-time, $1104 per semester (minimum) part-time for*

state residents; $9770 per year full-time, $1527 per semester (minimum) part-time for nonresidents. Fees of $938 per year full-time, $196 per semester (minimum) part-time. General application contact: *Kathy Kelly, Director of Admissions, 973-596-3300.*

Office of Graduate Studies
Dr. Ron Kane, Dean of Graduate Studies
Programs in:
applied chemistry • MS
applied mathematics • MS
applied physics • MS, PhD
applied science • MS
bioinformatics • MS, PhD
biomedical engineering • MS
biomedical systems • MS, PhD
chemical engineering • Engineer, MS, PhD
chemistry • PhD
civil engineering • Engineer, MS, PhD
communication and signal processing • MS, PhD
computer and information science • PhD
computer engineering • MS
computer science • MS
computer systems • MS, PhD
control systems • MS, PhD
electrical engineering • Engineer, MS, PhD
engineering management • MS
engineering science • MS
environmental engineering • MS, PhD
environmental policy studies • MS
environmental science • MS, PhD
history • MA, MAT
history of technology, environment and medicine • MA
industrial engineering • MS, PhD
information systems • MS
manufacturing systems engineering • MS
materials science and engineering • MS, PhD
mathematical science • PhD
mechanical engineering • Engineer, MS, PhD
microwave and lightwave engineering • MS, PhD
occupational safety and health engineering • MS
power engineering • MS
professional and technical communication • MS
solid-state materials and devices • MS, PhD
telecommunications • MS
transportation • MS, PhD

School of Architecture
Urs Gauchat, Dean
Programs in:
architectural studies • MS
architecture • M Arch
infrastructure planning • MIP

School of Management
Dr. Alok Chakrabarti, Dean
Program in:
management • MS, PhD

PRINCETON UNIVERSITY
Princeton, NJ 08544-1019

http://www.princeton.edu/

Independent coed university. *Enrollment: 6,400 graduate, professional, and undergraduate students. Graduate faculty: 709 full-time. Computer facilities: Campuswide network is available with full Internet access. Computer services are offered at no charge. Library facilities: Firestone Library plus 18 additional on-campus libraries. Graduate expenses: $24,330 per year. General application contact: Director of Graduate Admission, 609-258-3034.*

Graduate School
John F. Wilson, Dean
Programs in:
 African-American studies • PhD
 ancient history • PhD
 ancient Near Eastern studies • PhD
 anthropology • PhD
 applied and computational mathematics • PhD
 archaeology • PhD
 astrophysical sciences • PhD
 atmospheric and oceanic sciences • PhD
 biology • PhD
 cell biology • PhD
 chemistry • PhD
 Chinese and Japanese art and archaeology • PhD
 classical archaeology • PhD
 classical philosophy • PhD
 community college history teaching • PhD
 comparative literature • PhD
 composition • PhD
 demography • Certificate, PhD
 demography and public affairs • PhD
 developmental biology • PhD
 East Asian civilizations • PhD
 East Asian studies • PhD
 economics • PhD
 economics and demography • PhD
 English • PhD
 environmental engineering and water resources • PhD
 French • PhD
 geological and geophysical sciences • PhD
 Germanic languages and literatures • PhD
 history • PhD
 history, archaeology and religions of the ancient world • PhD
 history of science • PhD
 industrial chemistry • MS
 Islamic studies • PhD
 Latin American studies • PhD
 mathematical physics • PhD
 mathematics • PhD
 modern Near Eastern studies • MA
 molecular biology • PhD
 molecular biophysics • PhD
 musicology • PhD
 neuroscience • PhD
 philosophy • PhD
 physics • PhD
 physics and chemical physics • PhD
 plasma physics • PhD
 political philosophy • PhD
 politics • PhD
 polymer sciences and materials • MSE, PhD
 psychology • PhD
 religion • PhD
 Slavic languages and literatures • PhD
 sociology • PhD
 sociology and demography • PhD
 Spanish • PhD

School of Architecture
John F. Wilson, Dean, Graduate School
Program in:
 architecture • M Arch, PhD

School of Engineering and Applied Science
James Wei, Dean
Programs in:
 applied and computational mathematics • PhD
 applied physics • M Eng, MSE, PhD
 chemical engineering • M Eng, MSE, PhD
 computational methods • M Eng, MSE
 computer engineering • MSE, PhD
 computer science • M Eng, MSE, PhD
 dynamics and control systems • M Eng, MSE, PhD
 electrical engineering • M Eng
 electronic materials and devices • MSE, PhD
 energy and environmental policy • M Eng, MSE, PhD
 energy conversion, propulsion, and combustion • M Eng, MSE, PhD
 environmental engineering and water resources • PhD
 financial engineering • M Eng
 flight science and technology • M Eng, MSE, PhD
 fluid mechanics • M Eng, MSE, PhD
 information sciences and systems • MSE, PhD
 optoelectronics • MSE, PhD
 plasma science and technology • MSE, PhD
 polymer sciences and materials • MSE, PhD
 statistics and operations research • MSE, PhD
 structural engineering • M Eng
 structures and mechanics • MSE, PhD
 transportation systems • MSE, PhD

Woodrow Wilson School of Public and International Affairs
Dr. Michael Rothschild, Dean
Programs in:
 public affairs • MPA, MPA-URP, PhD
 public affairs and urban and regional planning • MPA-URP, PhD
 public and international affairs • MPP

RIDER UNIVERSITY
Lawrenceville, NJ 08648-3001

http://www.rider.edu/

Independent coed comprehensive institution. *Enrollment:* 5,128 graduate, professional, and undergraduate students. *Graduate faculty:* 109 full-time, 32 part-time. Library facilities: *Franklin Moore Library.* Graduate expenses: *$329 per credit hour. General application contact: Dr. John Carpenter, Dean, College of Continuing Studies, 609-896-5036.*

College of Business Administration
Tom Kelly, Associate Dean
Program in:
  business administration • M Acc, MBA

School of Graduate Education and Human Services
Dr. Jesse DeEsch, Assistant Dean
Programs in:
  business education • MA
  counseling services • Ed S, MA
  curriculum, instruction and supervision • MA
  educational administration • MA
  human services administration • MA
  reading/language arts • MA

Westminster Choir College of Rider University
Dr. James Goldsworthy, Associate Dean
Program in:
  music • MM

ROWAN UNIVERSITY
Glassboro, NJ 08028-1701

http://www.rowan.edu/

Public coed comprehensive institution. *Enrollment:* 8,038 graduate, professional, and undergraduate students. *Graduate faculty:* 76 full-time. Computer facilities: *Campuswide network is available with full Internet access. Total number of PCs/terminals supplied for student use: 400. Computer service fees are included with tuition and fees.* Library facilities: *main library plus 1 additional on-campus library.* Graduate expenses: *$5728 per year full-time, $258 per credit hour part-time for state residents; $8968 per year full-time, $393 per credit hour part-time for nonresidents. General application contact: Marion Rilling, Dean, Graduate Studies, 609-256-4050.*

Graduate Studies
Marion Rilling, Dean

College of Business Administration
Dr. Steven McNeil, Dean
Program in:
  business administration • MBA

College of Communication
Dr. Antoinette Libro, Dean
Program in:
  public relations • MA

College of Education
Dr. David Kapel, Dean
Programs in:
  administration and supervision in health and physical education or athletics • MA
  art education • MA
  biological science education • MA
  computers in education • Certificate
  educational leadership • Ed D
  education media specialist • Certificate
  elementary education • MA, MST
  elementary mathematics achievement • Certificate
  English as a second language/bilingual • Certificate
  health and exercise science • Certificate
  higher education administration • MA
  learning disabilities • Certificate, MA
  mathematics education • MA
  music education • MA
  physical science education • MA
  reading education • MA
  school administration • MA
  school administration-business administration • MA
  school and public librarianship • MA
  school business administration • Certificate
  school psychology • Certificate, MA
  special education • MA, MST
  student personnel services • Certificate, MA
  supervision and curriculum development • Certificate, MA
  teaching-secondary • MST

School of Engineering
Dr. James Tracey, Dean
Program in:
  engineering • MS

School of Liberal Arts and Sciences
Dr. Pearl Bartelt, Dean
Programs in:
  applied psychology • MA
  environmental education • MA
  mathematics • MA

RUTGERS, THE STATE UNIVERSITY OF NEW JERSEY, CAMDEN
Camden, NJ 08102-1401

http://camden-www.rutgers.edu/

Public coed university. *Enrollment:* 4,833 graduate, professional, and undergraduate students. Library facilities: *Paul Robeson Library.* Graduate expenses: *Tuition of $6492 per year full-time, $268 per credit part-time for state residents; $9520 per year full-time, $395 per credit part-time for nonresidents. Fees of $891 per year full-*

time, $160 per semester (minimum) part-time. General application contact: Dr. Deborah B. Bowles, Director of Admissions, 609-225-6056.

Graduate School
Dr. Margaret Marsh, Dean
Programs in:
    American and public history • MA
    biology • MS, MST
    English • MA
    health care management and policy • MPA
    international development policy and administration •
      MPA
    liberal studies • MA
    mathematics • MS
    physical therapy • MPT
    public management • MPA

School of Business
Milton Leontiades, Dean
Program in:
    business • MBA

School of Law
Jay Feinman, Acting Dean
Program in:
    law • JD

RUTGERS, THE STATE UNIVERSITY OF NEW JERSEY, NEWARK
Newark, NJ 07102-3192

http://info.rutgers.edu/newark/rutgers-newark.html

Public coed university. *Enrollment:* 9,326 graduate, professional, and undergraduate students. *Library facilities: John Cotton Dana Library.* Graduate expenses: *Tuition of $6248 per year full-time, $257 per credit part-time for state residents; $9160 per year full-time, $380 per credit part-time for nonresidents. Fees of $738 per year full-time, $107 per semester (minimum) part-time.* General application contact: *Bruce C. Neimeyer, Director of Admissions, 973-353-5205.*

Graduate School
Dr. Norman Samuels, Dean
Programs in:
    accounting • PhD
    accounting information systems • PhD
    American political system • MA
    analytical chemistry • MS, PhD
    applied economics • MA
    behavioral and neural sciences • PhD
    biochemistry • MS, PhD
    biology • MS, PhD
    cognitive science • PhD
    computer information systems • PhD
    environmental geology • MS
    finance • PhD
    health care administration • MPA
    history • MA, MAT
    human resources administration • MPA
    information technology • PhD
    inorganic chemistry • MS, PhD
    international business • PhD
    international relations • MA
    jazz history and research • MA
    liberal studies • MALS
    management science • PhD
    marketing • PhD
    mathematical sciences • PhD
    organic chemistry • MS, PhD
    organization management • PhD
    perception • PhD
    physical chemistry • MS, PhD
    psychobiology • PhD
    public administration • PhD
    public management • MPA
    public policy analysis • MPA
    social cognition • PhD
    urban systems and issues • MPA

Center for Global Change and Governance
Prof. Richard Langhorne, Director
Programs in:
    global studies • MA
    international studies • MS

College of Nursing
Dr. Hurdis Griffith, Dean/Director
Programs in:
    acute care of adults and aged • MS
    advanced practice in pediatric nursing • MS
    community health nursing • MS
    family nurse practitioner • MS
    nursing research • PhD
    primary care of adults and aged • MS
    psychiatric/mental health nursing • MS

School of Criminal Justice
Dr. Ronald Clarke, Director
Program in:
    criminal justice • MA, PhD

Graduate School of Management
Dr. P. George Benson, Dean, Faculty of Management
Programs in:
    finance and economics • MBA
    international business • MBA
    management • MA, PhD
    management science/computer information systems •
      MBA
    marketing • MBA
    organization management • MBA
    professional accounting • MBA

School of Law
Eric Neisser, Acting Dean
Program in:
    law • JD

RUTGERS, THE STATE UNIVERSITY OF NEW JERSEY, NEW BRUNSWICK

New Brunswick, NJ 08903

http://www.rutgers.edu/

Public coed university. *Enrollment: 34,420 graduate, professional, and undergraduate students. Computer facilities: Campuswide network is available with full Internet access. Computer service fees are included with tuition and fees. Library facilities: Alexander Library plus 18 additional on-campus libraries. Graduate expenses: Tuition of $6492 per year full-time, $268 per credit part-time for state residents; $9520 per year full-time, $395 per credit part-time for nonresidents. Fees of $208 per year (minimum). General applica- tion contact: Dr. Donald J. Taylor, Director of Graduate Admissions, 732-932-7711.*

College of Pharmacy
Dr. Joseph Barone, Director
Program in:
   pharmacy • Pharm D

Edward J. Bloustein School of Planning and Public Policy
James W. Hughes, Dean
Programs in:
   public health • Dr PH, MPH, PhD
   public policy • MS
   urban planning and policy development • MCRP, MS, PhD

Graduate School
Programs in:
   agricultural economics • MS
   air resources • MS, PhD
   American political institutions • PhD
   analytical chemistry • MS, PhD
   anthropology • MA, PhD
   applied mathematics • MS, PhD
   applied microbiology • MS, PhD
   aquatic biology • MS, PhD
   aquatic chemistry • MS, PhD
   art history • MA, PhD
   astrophysics • MS, PhD
   biochemistry • MS, PhD
   biological chemistry • PhD
   biomedical engineering • MS, PhD
   biopsychology and behavioral neuroscience • PhD
   bioresource engineering • MS
   cell biology • MS, PhD
   cellular and molecular pharmacology • PhD
   ceramic science and engineering • MS, PhD
   chemical and biochemical engineering • MS, PhD
   chemistry and physics of aerosol and hydrosol systems • MS, PhD
   chemistry education • MST
   civil and environmental engineering • MS, PhD
   classics • MA, MAT, PhD

clinical microbiology • MS, PhD
clinical psychology • PhD
cognitive psychology • PhD
communication, information and library studies • PhD
communications and solid-state electronics • MS, PhD
comparative literature • PhD
comparative politics • PhD
composition • MA, PhD
computational fluid dynamics • MS, PhD
computational molecular biology • PhD
computer engineering • MS, PhD
computer science • MS, PhD
condensed matter physics • MS, PhD
control systems • MS, PhD
design and dynamics • MS, PhD
developmental biology • MS, PhD
digital signal processing • MS, PhD
diplomatic history • PhD
direct intervention in interpersonal situations • PhD
early American history • PhD
early modern European history • PhD
ecology and evolution • MS, PhD
economics • MA, PhD
elementary particle physics • MS, PhD
endocrine control of growth and metabolism • MS, PhD
English • PhD
entomology • MS, PhD
environmental chemistry • MS, PhD
environmental microbiology • MS, PhD
environmental toxicology • MS, PhD
exposure assessment • PhD
fluid mechanics • MS, PhD
food science • M Phil, MS, PhD
French • MA, PhD
French studies • MAT
geological sciences • MS, PhD
German • PhD
global/comparative history • PhD
heat transfer • MS, PhD
history • PhD
history of technology, medicine, and science • PhD
horticulture • MS, PhD
immunology • MS, PhD
industrial and systems engineering • MS, PhD
industrial-occupational toxicology • MS, PhD
industrial pharmacy • MS, PhD
inorganic chemistry • MS, PhD
interdisciplinary developmental psychology • PhD
interdisciplinary health psychology • PhD
intermediate energy nuclear physics • MS, PhD
international relations • PhD
Italian • MA
Italian history • PhD
Italian literature and literary criticism • MA, PhD
language, literature and civilization • MAT
Latin American history • PhD
linguistics • PhD
literature • MA, PhD
mathematics • MS, PhD
mechanics • MS, PhD
medicinal chemistry • MS, PhD
medieval history • PhD
microbial biochemistry • MS, PhD

modern American history • PhD
modern British history • PhD
modern European history • PhD
molecular and cell biology • PhD
molecular biology • MS, PhD
molecular biology and biochemistry • MS, PhD
molecular genetics • MS, PhD
museum studies • MA
music history • MA, PhD
nuclear physics • MS, PhD
nutritional sciences • MS, PhD
nutritional toxicology • MS, PhD
nutrition of ruminant and nonruminant animals • MS, PhD
oceanography • MS, PhD
operations research • PhD
organic chemistry • MS, PhD
pathology • MS, PhD
pharmaceutical chemistry • MS, PhD
pharmaceutical toxicology • MS, PhD
pharmaceutics • MS, PhD
philosophy • PhD
physical chemistry • MS, PhD
physical metallurgy • MS, PhD
physics • MST
physiology and neurobiology • PhD
plant ecology • MS, PhD
plant genetics • PhD
plant physiology • MS, PhD
political and cultural history • PhD
political economy • PhD
political theory • PhD
politics • MS
polymer science • MS, PhD
production and management • MS
public law • PhD
quality and productivity management • MS
reproductive endocrinology and neuroendocrinology • MS, PhD
social policy analysis and administration • PhD
social psychology • PhD
social work • PhD
sociology • MA, PhD
solid mechanics • MS, PhD
Spanish • MA, MAT, PhD
Spanish-American literature • MA, PhD
statistics • MS, PhD
structure and plant groups • MS, PhD
theoretical physics • MS, PhD
translation • MA
virology • MS, PhD
water and wastewater treatment • MS, PhD
water resources • MS, PhD
women and politics • PhD
women's history • PhD
women's studies • MA

Graduate School of Applied and Professional Psychology

Sandra L. Harris, Dean
Programs in:
    clinical psychology • Psy D, Psy M
    organizational psychology • Psy D, Psy M
    school psychology • Psy D, Psy M

Graduate School of Education

Dr. Louise Cherry Wilkinson, Dean
Programs in:
    adult and continuing education • Ed D, Ed M
    counseling psychology • Ed D, Ed M
    early childhood/elementary education • Ed D, Ed M, Ed S
    education administration • Ed M
    educational administration and supervision • Ed D, Ed S
    educational statistics and measurement • Ed D, Ed M
    English as a second language education • Ed D, Ed M
    English education • Ed M
    language education • Ed D, Ed M, Ed S
    learning cognition and development • Ed D, Ed M
    literacy education • Ed D, Ed M, Ed S
    mathematics education • Ed D, Ed M, Ed S
    school business administration • Ed M
    science education • Ed D, Ed M, Ed S
    social and philosophical foundations of education • Ed D, Ed M, Ed S
    social studies education • Ed D, Ed M, Ed S
    special education • Ed D, Ed M
    vocational-technical education • Ed D, Ed M, Ed S

Mason Gross School of the Arts

Marilyn Feller Somville, Dean
Programs in:
    arts • MTA
    music • AD, DMA, MM
    theater arts • MFA
    visual arts • MFA

Programs in Engineering

Program in:
    engineering • MS, PhD

School of Communication, Information and Library Studies

Todd Hunt, Dean
Programs in:
    communication and information studies • MCIS
    library and information studies • MLS

School of Management and Labor Relations

Dr. John F. Burton Jr., Dean
Programs in:
    human resource management • MHRM
    industrial relations and human resources • PhD
    labor and industrial relations • MLIR

School of Social Work

Mary E. Davidson, Dean
Program in:
    social work • MSW, PhD

SAINT PETER'S COLLEGE
Jersey City, NJ 07306-5997

http://www.spc.edu/

Independent-religious coed comprehensive institution. *Enrollment:* 3,698 graduate, professional, and undergraduate students. *Graduate faculty:* 24 full-time, 36 part-time. *Computer facilities: Campuswide network is available with full Internet access. Total number of PCs/ terminals supplied for student use: 150. Computer services are offered at no charge. Library facilities: O'Toole Library plus 1 additional on-campus library. Graduate expenses: $516 per credit. General application contact: Nancy P. Campbell, Associate Vice President for Enrollment, 201-915-9213.*

Graduate Programs in Education
Dr. Joseph McLaughlin, Director
Programs in:
  administration and supervision • MA
  elementary teacher • Certificate
  reading specialist • MA
  supervisor of instruction • Certificate
  teaching • MA
  urban education • MA

MBA Programs
Sr. Jeanne Gilligan, Associate Vice President for Academic Affairs
Programs in:
  international business • MBA
  management • MBA
  management information systems • MBA

Program in Accountancy
Sr. Jeanne Gilligan, Associate Vice President for Academic Affairs
Program in:
  accountancy • Certificate, MS

Program in Nursing
Dr. Marylou Yam, Director
Program in:
  nursing • MSN

SETON HALL UNIVERSITY
South Orange, NJ 07079-2697

http://www.shu.edu/

Independent-religious coed university. *Computer facilities: Campuswide network is available with full Internet access. Total number of PCs/ terminals supplied for student use: 300. Computer services are offered at no charge. Library facilities: Walsh Library plus 2 additional on-campus libraries. Graduate expenses: Tuition of $500 per credit. Fees of $610 per year full-time, $185 per semester part-time. General application contact: Director, Graduate Services, 201-761-2036.*

College of Arts and Sciences
Dr. James Van Oosting, Dean
Programs in:
  American, European, and Third World history • MA
  American studies • MA
  analytical chemistry • MS, PhD
  Asian studies • MA
  biochemistry • MS, PhD
  biology • MS
  chemistry • MS
  corporate and public communication • MA
  criminal justice/judicial administration • MPA
  English • MA
  French • MA
  healthcare administration • MHA
  health policy and management • MPA
  inorganic chemistry • MS, PhD
  Jewish-Christian studies • MA
  management of nonprofit organizations • MPA
  microbiology • MS
  museum professions • MA
  operations research • MA, MS
  organic chemistry • MS, PhD
  physical chemistry • MS, PhD
  public service administration and policy • MPA
  religious organization management • MPA
  Spanish • MA

College of Education and Human Services
Dr. Sylvester Kohut Jr., Dean
Programs in:
  bilingual education • Ed S, MA
  Catholic school leadership • MA
  clinical psychology • Psy D
  counseling psychology • PhD
  counselor preparation • MA
  educational administration and supervision • Ed D, Exec Ed D, PhD
  elementary and secondary educational administration • Ed D, Ed S, MA
  elementary education • MA
  English as a second language • Ed S, MA
  higher education administration • Ed D, Ed S, Exec Ed D, PhD
  human resource training and development • MA
  instructional design • Ed S, MA
  marriage and family counseling • Ed S, MS, PhD
  professional development • Ed S, MA
  psychological studies • MA
  school psychology • Ed S
  secondary education • Ed S, MA
  student personnel services (K-12) • MA

College of Nursing
Dr. Barbara Beeker, Dean
Programs in:
  acute care nurse practitioner • MSN
  adult nurse practitioner • MSN
  gerontological nurse practitioner • MSN
  nursing administration • MSN
  nursing case management • MSN
  nursing education • MA

pediatric nurse practitioner • MSN
school nurse practitioner • MSN
women's health nurse practitioner • MSN

Immaculate Conception Seminary School of Theology
Programs in:
pastoral ministry • M Div, MA
theology • Certificate, MA

School of Diplomacy and International Relations
Terence L. Blackburn, Acting Dean
Program in:
diplomacy • MA

School of Graduate Medical Education
Dr. John A. Paterson, Dean
Programs in:
health sciences • MS, PhD
occupational therapy • MS
physician assistant • MS
speech-language pathology • MS

School of Law
Ronald J. Riccio, Dean
Program in:
law • JD, LL M, MSJ

W. Paul Stillman School of Business
Sheldon Epstein, Dean
Programs in:
accounting • MBA, MS
economics • MBA
finance • MBA
human resource management • MBA, MS
information systems • MBA, MS
international business • Certificate, MS
management • MBA
marketing • MBA
professional accounting • MS
quantitative analysis • MBA
sports management • MBA
taxation • Certificate, MS

 STEVENS INSTITUTE OF TECHNOLOGY
Hoboken, NJ 07030

http://www.stevens-tech.edu/

Independent coed university. *Enrollment: 3,248 graduate, professional, and undergraduate students. Graduate faculty: 104 full-time, 80 part-time. Computer facilities: Campuswide network is available with full Internet access. Total number of PCs/terminals supplied for student use: 200. Computer services are offered at no charge. Library facilities: Samuel C. Williams Library. Graduate expenses: Tuition of $13,500 per year full-time, $675 per credit*

part-time. Fees of $160 per year. General application contact: Dr. Charles L. Suffel, Dean of the Graduate School, 201-216-5234.

Graduate School
Dr. Charles L. Suffel, Dean
Program in:
interdisciplinary sciences and engineering • M Eng, MS, PhD

Charles V. Schaefer Jr. School of Engineering
Dr. Bernard Gallois, Dean
Programs in:
advanced manufacturing • Certificate
air pollution technology • Certificate
analysis of polymer processing methods • Certificate
biochemical engineering • Engr, M Eng, PhD
building energy systems • Certificate
coastal and ocean engineering • Engr, M Eng, PhD
computational methods in fluid mechanics and heat transfer • Certificate
computer and communications security • Certificate
computer and information engineering • Engr, M Eng, PhD
computer architecture and digital system design • Engr, M Eng, PhD
concurrent design management • M Eng
concurrent engineering • Certificate, PhD
construction accounting/estimating • Certificate
construction engineering • Certificate, Engr, M Eng, PhD
construction law/disputes • Certificate
construction management • MS
construction/quality management • Certificate
controls in aerospace and robotics • Certificate
design and production management • Certificate, MS
digital systems and VLSI design • Certificate
environmental compatibility in engineering • Certificate
environmental process • Certificate, M Eng, PhD
finite-element analysis • Certificate
fundamentals of modern chemical engineering • Certificate
geotechnical engineering • Certificate
geotechnical/geoenvironmental engineering • Engr, M Eng, PhD
groundwater and soil pollution control • Certificate, M Eng, PhD
image and signal processing • Engr, M Eng, PhD
information networks • Certificate
inland and coastal environmental hydrodynamics • Certificate, M Eng, PhD
integrated production design • Certificate
materials engineering • M Eng, PhD
materials science • MS, PhD
mechanical engineering • Engr, M Eng, PhD
mechanism design • Certificate
ocean engineering • M Eng, PhD
polymer engineering • Engr, M Eng, PhD
polymer processing • Certificate
power generation • Certificate
process control • Engr, M Eng, PhD
process engineering • Certificate, Engr, M Eng, PhD
robotics and automation • Engr, M Eng, PhD

Stevens Institute of Technology (continued)
  robotics and control • Certificate
  robotics/control/instrumentation • Engr, M Eng, PhD
  signal and image processing • Engr, M Eng, PhD
  software engineering • Engr, M Eng, PhD
  stress analysis and design • Certificate
  structural analysis of materials • Certificate
  structures • Engr, M Eng, PhD
  surface modification of materials • Certificate
  telecommunications engineering • Engr, M Eng, PhD
  telecommunications management • Certificate, MS, PhD
  vibration and noise control • Certificate
  water quality • Certificate

School of Applied Sciences and Liberal Arts
Dr. Patrick W. Flanagan, Dean
Programs in:
  advanced programming: theory, design and verification • Certificate
  algebra • PhD
  analysis • PhD
  analytical chemistry • Certificate, MS, PhD
  applied mathematics • MS, PhD
  applied optics • Certificate
  applied statistics • Certificate, MS
  artificial intelligence and robotics • MS, PhD
  chemical biology • Certificate, MS, PhD
  chemical physiology • Certificate
  chemistry • Certificate, MS, PhD
  computer and information systems • MS, PhD
  computer architecture and digital system design • MS, PhD
  database systems • Certificate
  elements of computer science • Certificate
  engineering optics • M Eng
  engineering physics • M Eng
  information systems • Certificate, MS
  instrumental analysis • Certificate
  mathematics • MS
  network and graph theory • Certificate
  organic chemistry • MS, PhD
  physical chemistry • MS, PhD
  physics • MS, PhD
  polymer chemistry • Certificate, MS, PhD
  software design • MS, PhD
  software engineering • Certificate
  surface physics • Certificate
  theoretical computer science • Certificate, MS, PhD
  wireless communications • Certificate

Wesley J. Howe School of Technology Management
Dr. James Teitjen, Head
Programs in:
  concurrent design management • M Eng
  construction management • MS
  design and production management • Certificate, MS
  general management • MS
  information management • Certificate, MIM, MS, PhD
  information systems • Certificate, MS
  management planning • MS
  network planning and evaluation • MS, PhD
  project management • Certificate, MS, PhD
  technology management • Certificate, MS, MTM, PhD

  technology management marketing • MS, PhD
  telecommunications management • Certificate

WILLIAM PATERSON UNIVERSITY OF NEW JERSEY
Wayne, NJ 07470-8420
http://www.wilpaterson.edu/

Public coed comprehensive institution. *Enrollment: 9,207 graduate, professional, and undergraduate students. Graduate faculty: 87 full-time, 54 part-time. Computer facilities: Campuswide network is available with full Internet access. Total number of PCs/terminals supplied for student use: 500. Computer service fees are included with tuition and fees. Library facilities: Sarah Byrd Askew Library. Graduate expenses: Tuition of $230 per credit for state residents; $327 per credit for nonresidents. Fees of $3.25 per credit. General application contact: Ann Marie Duffy, Director of Graduate Services, 973-720-2698.*

College of Business
Frank Grippo, Dean
Program in:
  business • MBA

College of Education
Susan Kuveke, Interim Dean
Programs in:
  counseling • M Ed
  elementary education • M Ed, MAT
  reading • M Ed
  special education • M Ed

College of Science and Health
Dr. Eswar Phadia, Dean
Programs in:
  biotechnology • MS
  general biology • MA
  limnology and terrestrial ecology • MA
  molecular biology • MA
  nursing • MSN
  physiology • MA
  speech pathology • MS

College of the Arts and Communication
Ofelia Garcia, Dean
Programs in:
  communication arts • MA
  visual arts • MA

College of the Humanities and Social Sciences
Leslie Agard-Jones, Interim Dean
Programs in:
  English • MA
  history • MA
  sociology • MA

NEW MEXICO

EASTERN NEW MEXICO UNIVERSITY
Portales, NM 88130

http://www.enmu.edu/

Public coed comprehensive institution. *Enrollment:* 3,221 graduate, professional, and undergraduate students. Graduate faculty: *67 full-time, 32 part-time.* Computer facilities: *Campuswide network is available with full Internet access. Total number of PCs/terminals supplied for student use: 325. Computer services are offered at no charge.* Library facilities: *Golden Library.* Graduate expenses: *$1956 per year full-time, $82 per credit hour part-time for state residents; $6702 per year full-time, $280 per credit hour part-time for nonresidents.* General application contact: *Dr. Renee Neely, Dean, 505-562-2147.*

Graduate School
Dr. Renee Neely, Dean

College of Business
Dr. Dolores Martin, Dean
Program in:
    business • MBA

College of Education and Technology
Dr. Lawrence Byrnes, Dean
Programs in:
    counseling and guidance • M Ed
    education • M Ed
    physical education • MS
    psychology • M Ed, MA
    special education • M Sp Ed

College of Fine Arts
Dr. Patrick Rucker, Acting Dean
Program in:
    performance and pedagogy • MM

College of Liberal Arts and Sciences
Dr. Thurman Elder, Acting Dean
Programs in:
    anthropology • MA
    biology • MS
    chemistry • MS
    English • MA
    mass communication • MA
    mathematical sciences • MA
    speech communication • MA
    speech pathology and audiology • MS

NEW MEXICO HIGHLANDS UNIVERSITY
Las Vegas, NM 87701

http://www.nmhu.edu/

Public coed comprehensive institution. *Enrollment:* 2,839 graduate, professional, and undergraduate students. Graduate faculty: *114 full-time, 1 part-time.* Library facilities: *Donnelly Library.* Graduate expenses: *Tuition of $1816 per year full-time, $227 per hour part-time for state residents; $7468 per year full-time, $227 per hour part-time for nonresidents. Fees of $10 per year.* General application contact: *Dr. Glen W. Davidson, Academic Vice President, 505-454-3311.*

Graduate Division
Dr. Glen W. Davidson, Academic Vice President

College of Arts and Sciences
Dr. Tomas Salazar, Dean
Programs in:
    anthropology • MA
    applied chemistry • MS
    computer graphics • MS
    creative writing • MA
    design studies • MA
    digital audio and video production • MA
    English • MA
    Hispanic language and literature • MA
    historical and cross cultural perspective • MA
    history and political science • MA
    language, rhetoric and composition • MA
    life sciences • MS
    literature • MA
    media arts and computer science • MA, MS
    networking technologies • MS
    political and governmental processes • MA
    psychology • MS
    social and organizational processes • MA

School of Business
Dr. Ronald Maestas, Dean
Program in:
    business • MBA

School of Education
Dr. James Abreu, Dean
Programs in:
    curriculum and instruction • MA
    education administration • MA
    guidance and counseling • MA
    human performance and sport • MA
    special education • MA

School of Social Work
Dr. Alfredo Garcia, Dean
Program in:
    social work • MSW

NEW MEXICO STATE UNIVERSITY
Las Cruces, NM 88003-8001

http://www.nmsu.edu/

Public coed university. *Enrollment: 15,067 graduate, professional, and undergraduate students. Graduate faculty: 521 full-time, 13 part-time. Computer facilities: Campuswide network is available with full Internet access. Computer service fees are included with tuition and fees. Library facilities: New Library. Graduate expenses: $2514 per year full-time, $105 per credit hour part-time for state residents; $7848 per year full-time, $327 per credit hour part-time for nonresidents. General application contact: Dr. Timothy J. Pettibone, Dean of the Graduate School, 505-646-2834.*

Graduate School
Dr. Timothy J. Pettibone, Dean
Programs in:
  interdisciplinary studies • MA, MS, PhD
  molecular biology • MS, PhD

College of Agriculture and Home Economics
Dr. Jerry Schickedanz, Interim Dean
Programs in:
  agricultural business • MS
  agricultural economics • MS
  agriculture and extension education • MA
  animal science • M Ag, MS, PhD
  economics • MA
  entomology, plant pathology and weed science • MS
  family and consumer sciences • MS
  fishery science • MS
  general agronomy • MS, PhD
  horticulture • MS
  range science • M Ag, MS, PhD
  wildlife science • MS

College of Arts and Sciences
Dr. E. Rene Casillas, Dean
Programs in:
  anthropology • MA
  art • MA, MFA
  astronomy • MS, PhD
  biology • MS, PhD
  chemistry and biochemistry • MS, PhD
  communication studies • MA
  computer science • MS, PhD
  criminal justice • MCJ
  English • MA, PhD
  geography • MAG
  geological sciences • MS
  government • MA, MPA
  history • MA
  mathematical sciences • MS, PhD
  music • MM
  physics • MS, PhD
  psychology • MA, PhD
  sociology • MA
  Spanish • MA

College of Business Administration and Economics
Dr. Danny Arnold, Dean
Programs in:
  accounting and business computer systems • M Acct
  business administration • MBA, PhD
  economics • MA, MBA, MS
  experimental statistics • MS

College of Education
Dr. H. Prentice Baptiste, Dean
Programs in:
  counseling and guidance • Ed S, MA
  counseling psychology • PhD
  curriculum and instruction • Ed D, Ed S, MAT, PhD
  educational administration • Ed S, MA, PhD
  educational management and development • Ed D
  general education • MA
  reading • Ed S
  special education/communication disorders • MA

College of Engineering
Dr. J. Derald Morgan, Dean
Programs in:
  chemical engineering • MS Ch E, PhD
  civil engineering • MSCE, PhD
  electrical and computer engineering • MSEE, PhD
  environmental engineering • MS Env E
  industrial engineering • MSIE, PhD
  mechanical engineering • MSME, PhD

College of Health and Social Services
Dr. Virginia Higbie, Dean
Programs in:
  health science • MPH
  nursing • MSN
  social work • MSW

 # UNIVERSITY OF NEW MEXICO
Albuquerque, NM 87131-2039

http://www.unm.edu/

Public coed university. *Enrollment: 23,770 graduate, professional, and undergraduate students. Graduate faculty: 862 full-time, 1,170 part-time. Computer facilities: Campuswide network is available with full Internet access. Computer service fees are included with tuition and fees. Library facilities: Zimmerman Library plus 9 additional on-campus libraries. Graduate expenses: Tuition of $2442 per year full-time, $103 per credit hour part-time for state residents; $8691 per year full-time, $103 per credit hour (minimum) part-time for nonresidents. Fees of $32 per year. General application contact: Nasir Ahmed, Interim Dean, 505-277-2711.*

Graduate School
Nasir Ahmed, Interim Dean
Programs in:
  biochemistry and molecular biology • MS, PhD
  cell biology and physiology • MS, PhD
  molecular genetics and microbiology • MS, PhD
  neuroscience • MS, PhD

pathology • MS, PhD

public health • MPH

College of Arts and Sciences

Michael Fischer, Dean

Programs in:

air land ecology • MS, PhD

American studies • MA, PhD

behavioral ecology • MS, PhD

biology • MS, PhD

botany • MS, PhD

cellular and molecular biology • MS, PhD

chemistry • MS, PhD

clinical psychology • MS, PhD

communication • MA, PhD

communicative disorders • MS

community ecology • MS, PhD

comparative immunology • MS, PhD

comparative literature • MA

comparative physiology • MS, PhD

conservation biology • MS, PhD

earth and planetary sciences • MS, PhD

ecology • MS, PhD

ecosystem ecology • MS, PhD

educational linguistics • PhD

English • MA, PhD

evolutionary biology • MS, PhD

evolutionary genetics • MS, PhD

experimental psychology • MS, PhD

French • MA, PhD

geography • MA

German • MA

Hispanic linguistics • PhD

Hispanic literature • PhD

history • MA, PhD

Latin American studies • MALAS, PhD

linguistics • MA, PhD

mathematics • MA, PhD

microbiology • MS, PhD

molecular genetics • MS, PhD

optical sciences • PhD

parasitology • MS, PhD

philosophy • MA, PhD

physics • MS, PhD

physiological ecology • MS, PhD

physiology • MS, PhD

political science • MA, PhD

population biology • MS, PhD

Portuguese • MA, PhD

Romance languages • PhD

sociology • MA, PhD

Southwest Hispanic studies • PhD

Spanish • MA

vertebrate and invertebrate zoology • MS, PhD

College of Education

Dr. Viola E. Florez Tighe, Dean

Programs in:

administration and supervision • Ed D, PhD

curriculum and instruction • Ed S

educational administration • Ed S, MA

educational foundations • MA

educational linguistics • PhD

educational thought and sociocultural studies • Ed D, PhD

elementary education • MA

family studies • MA, PhD

health education • MS

multicultural teacher and childhood education • Ed S, PhD

nutrition/dietetics • MS

parks and recreation • MA

physical education • Certificate, Ed S, MS

recreation • Ed S

secondary education • MA

special education • Ed D, Ed S, MA, PhD

College of Fine Arts

Thomas A. Dodson, Dean

Programs in:

art of the Americas • MA, PhD

art of the Modern Age • MA, PhD

music • MM

painting/drawing • MFA

photography • MFA

printmaking • MFA

sculpture and ceramics • MFA

theatre and dance • MA

College of Nursing

Dr. Sandra Ferketich, Dean

Programs in:

administration of nursing • Certificate, MSN

adult health nursing • MSN

advanced nurse practice • Certificate

advanced nursing practice • MSN

community health nursing • MSN

family nurse practitioner • MSN

gerontological nursing • MSN

nurse midwifery • MSN

parent-child nursing • MSN

primary care nursing • MSN

psychiatric-mental health nursing • MSN

College of Pharmacy

Dr. William Hadley, Dean

Programs in:

hospital pharmacy • MS

pharmaceutical sciences • MS, PhD

pharmacy • Pharm D

pharmacy administration • MS, PhD

radiopharmacy • MS

toxicology • MS, PhD

Robert O. Anderson Graduate School of Management

Howard L. Smith, Dean

Programs in:

accounting • M Acc, MBA

business administration • EMBA

financial management • MBA

general management • MBA

human resources management • MBA

international management • MBA

international management in Latin America • MBA

management information systems • MBA

management of technology • EMBA, MBA

marketing management • MBA

University of New Mexico (continued)
  operations and management science • MBA
  policy and planning • MBA
  tax accounting • MBA

School of Architecture and Planning
James Richardson, Dean
Programs in:
  architecture • M Arch
  community and regional planning • MCRP

School of Engineering
Paul Fleury, Dean
Programs in:
  chemical engineering • MS
  civil engineering • MS
  computer engineering • MS, PhD
  computer science • MS, PhD
  engineering • PhD
  hazardous waste engineering • ME
  manufacturing engineering • ME, MS
  mechanical engineering • MS
  microelectronics • MS, PhD
  network and control systems • MS, PhD
  nuclear engineering • MS
  optoelectronics • MS, PhD
  pulsed power and plasma science • MS, PhD
  signal processing and communications • MS, PhD

School of Public Administration
T. Zane Reeves, Director
Programs in:
  public administration • MPA
  water resources administration • MWRA

School of Law
Robert J. Desiderio, Dean
Program in:
  law • JD

School of Medicine
Program in:
  medicine • MD

WESTERN NEW MEXICO UNIVERSITY
Silver City, NM 88062-0680
http://www.wnmu.edu/

Public coed comprehensive institution. *Enrollment: 2,580 graduate, professional, and undergraduate students. Graduate faculty: 38 full-time, 2 part-time. Computer facilities: Campuswide network is available with full Internet access. Total number of PCs/terminals supplied for student use: 85. Computer services are offered at no charge. Library facilities: J. Cloyd Miller Library plus 1 additional on-campus library. Graduate expenses: $1516 per year full-time, $55 per credit part-time for state residents; $5604 per year full-time, $55 per credit part-time for nonresidents. General application*

contact: *Dr. Kathie S. Gilbert, Vice President for Academic Affairs, 505-538-6317.*

Graduate Division
Dr. Kathie S. Gilbert, Vice President for Academic Affairs
Programs in:
  business • MBA
  counselor education • MA
  elementary education • MAT
  reading • MAT
  school administration • MA
  secondary education • MAT
  special education • MAT

NEW YORK

 # ADELPHI UNIVERSITY
Garden City, NY 11530
http://www.adelphi.edu/

Independent coed university. *Enrollment: 5,594 graduate, professional, and undergraduate students. Graduate faculty: 203 full-time, 307 part-time. Library facilities: Swirbul Library plus 1 additional on-campus library. Graduate expenses: Tuition of $16,000 per year full-time, $485 per credit part-time. Fees of $500 per year full-time, $150 per semester part-time. General application contact: Jennifer Spiegel, Associate Director of Graduate Admissions, 516-877-3055.*

Derner Institute of Advanced Psychological Studies
Dr. Robert Mendelsohn, Dean
Programs in:
  clinical psychology • Diploma, PhD
  experimental psychology • PhD
  general psychology • MA
  psychotherapy and psychoanalysis • Diploma

Graduate School of Arts and Sciences
Gail Insler, Dean
Programs in:
  biochemistry • MS
  biology • MS
  chemistry • MS
  earth sciences • MS
  English • MA
  environmental management • Certificate
  mathematics • DA, MS
  physics • MS
  studio art • MA

School of Education
Dr. Elaine Sands, Interim Dean
Programs in:
  art • MA
  biology • MA

chemistry • MA

coaching (advanced) • Certificate

communicative disorders • DA, MS

community health education • Certificate, MA

early childhood/elementary education • MA

early childhood/elementary education-special education • MS

early childhood special education • MS

educational assessment • Certificate

education of the speech and hearing handicapped • MS

elementary education • MA

English • MA

exercise physiology • Certificate

mathematics • MA

music • MA

physical education • MA

physics • MA

reading • MS, PD

school health education • MA

secondary education • MA

social studies • MA

Spanish • MA

special education • MS

special physical education • Certificate

sports management • Certificate

teaching English to speakers of other languages • Certificate, MA

School of Management and Business

Rakesh Gupta, Dean

Programs in:

accounting and law • MS Acct

administrative sciences • MBA

banking • Certificate

finance and banking • MS

human resource management • Certificate

management for non-business majors • Certificate

management for women • Certificate

School of Nursing

Dr. Caryle G. Wolahan, Director

Programs in:

adult health nursing • MS, PMC

nursing • PhD

nursing service administration • MS, PMC

parent-child nursing • MS, PMC

psychiatric nursing • MS, PMC

teaching • MS, PMC

School of Social Work

Dr. Roger Levin, Associate Dean

Programs in:

clinical practice • Certificate

social welfare • DSW

social work • MSW

ALFRED UNIVERSITY
Alfred, NY 14802-1205

http://www.alfred.edu/

Independent coed university. *Enrollment: 2,397 graduate, profes sional, and undergraduate students. Graduate faculty: 103. Computer facilities: Campuswide network is available with full Internet access. Computer services are offered at no charge. Library facilities: Herrick Library plus 1 additional on-campus library. Graduate expenses: Tuition of $20,376 per year full-time, $390 per credit hour (minimum) part-time. Fees of $546 per year. General application contact: Cathleen R. Johnson, Assistant Director of Admissions, 607-871-2141.*

Graduate School and New York State College of Ceramics

Dr. W. Richard Ott, Provost and Director of Graduate Studies

Graduate School

Dr. W. Richard Ott, Provost and Director of Graduate Studies, Graduate School and New York State College of Ceramics ,

Programs in:

biology education • MS Ed

business • MBA

business education • MS Ed

chemistry education • MS Ed

college student development • MS Ed

community services administration • MPS

counseling • MS Ed

earth science education • MS Ed

electrical engineering • MS

elementary education • MS Ed

English education • MS Ed

industrial engineering • MS

mathematics education • MS Ed

mechanical engineering • MS

physics education • MS Ed

reading • MS Ed

school psychology • CAS, MA, Psy D

secondary education • MS Ed

social studies education • MS Ed

New York State College of Ceramics

Dr. L. David Pye, Dean

Programs in:

ceramic engineering • MS

ceramics • MFA, PhD

ceramic science • MS

glass • MFA

glass science • MS, PhD

sculpture • MFA

BARUCH COLLEGE OF THE CITY UNIVERSITY OF NEW YORK
New York, NY 10010-5585

http://www.baruch.cuny.edu/

Public coed comprehensive institution. *Enrollment:* 15,091 graduate, professional, and undergraduate students. Graduate faculty: *285.* Computer facilities: *Campuswide network is available. Total number of PCs/terminals supplied for student use: 650. Computer services are offered at no charge.* Library facilities: *William and Anita Newman Library.* Graduate expenses: *Tuition of $4350 per year full-time, $185 per credit part-time for state residents; $7600 per year full-time, $320 per credit part-time for nonresidents. Fees of $53 per year.* General application contact: *Lois Cronholm, Provost, 212-802-2820.*

Department of Education
Dr. Jeffrey H. Golland, Chairperson
Programs in:
early childhood education • MS Ed
elementary education • MS Ed

School of Business
Sidney I. Lirtzman, Dean
Programs in:
accounting • MBA, MS, PhD
business administration • EMBA
computer information systems • MBA, MS
economics • MBA
finance • EMSF, MBA, MS, PhD
general business • MBA
general management and policy • MBA
health care administration • MBA
human resources management • MBA
industrial and organizational psychology • Certificate, MBA, MS, PhD
industrial and service management • MBA
international business • MBA
management planning systems • PhD
management science • MBA
marketing • MBA, MS, PhD
operations research • MBA, MS
organizational behavior • MBA
organization and policy studies • PhD
statistics • MBA, MS
taxation • MBA, MS

School of Public Affairs
Carroll Seron, Acting Dean
Programs in:
collective bargaining, labor law and labor history • EMSILR
educational administration and supervision • MS Ed
higher education administration • MS Ed
personnel and human resources management • EMSILR
public administration • MPA

 # BROOKLYN COLLEGE OF THE CITY UNIVERSITY OF NEW YORK
Brooklyn, NY 11210-2889

http://www.brooklyn.cuny.edu/

Public coed comprehensive institution. *Enrollment:* 13,236 graduate, professional, and undergraduate students. Graduate faculty: *432 full-time, 284 part-time.* Computer facilities: *Campuswide network is available with full Internet access. Computer service fees are included with tuition and fees.* Library facilities: *Harry D. Gideonse Library.* Graduate expenses: *Tuition of $4350 per year full-time, $185 per credit part-time for state residents; $7600 per year full-time, $320 per credit part-time for nonresidents. Fees of $500 per year for state residents; $806 per year for nonresidents.* General application contact: *Pasquale Leonardo, Director of Admissions, 718-951-5914.*

Division of Graduate Studies
Dr. Louise Hainline, Acting Dean
Programs in:
accounting • MA
acting • MFA
applied biology • MA
applied chemistry • MA
applied geology • MA
applied physics • MA
art history • MA
audiology • MS
biology • MA, PhD
chemistry • MA, PhD
community health • MA, MPH
computer and information science • MA, PhD
computer science and health science • MS
criticism • MA
design and technical production • MFA
directing • MFA
dramaturgy • MFA
drawing and painting • MFA
economics • MA
economics and computer and information science • MPS
English • MA
exercise science and rehabilitation • MS
experimental psychology • MA
fiction • MFA
geology • MA
health and nutrition sciences • MS Ed
health care management • MA, MPH
health care policy and administration • MA, MPH
history • MA
human relations psychology • MA
industrial and organizational psychology • MA
industrial and organizational psychology-human relations • MA
information systems • MS
Judaic studies • MA
liberal studies • MA
management and programming • MS

mathematics • MA
nutrition • MS
pathology • MS
performing arts management • MFA
photography • MFA
physical education • MS, MS Ed
physics • MA, PhD
playwriting • MFA
poetry • MFA
political science • MA
printmaking • MFA
psychology • PhD
psychology-organizational psychology and behavior • MA
psychosocial aspects of physical activity • MS
sculpture • MFA
secondary mathematics education • MA
sociology • MA
Spanish • MA
speech • MA
speech and hearing science • MS
sports management • MS
television and radio • MS
television production • MFA
thanatology • MA
theater history • MA
urban policy and administration • MA

Conservatory of Music
Dr. Nancy Hager, Chairperson
Programs in:
    composition • MM
    music education • MA
    musicology • MA
    performance • MM
    performance practice • MA

School of Education
Dr. Rosamond Welchman, Acting Dean
Programs in:
    art education • MA, MS Ed
    bilingual education • MS Ed
    bilingual special education • MS Ed
    biology education • MA
    chemistry education • MA
    children with emotional handicaps • MS Ed
    children with neuropsychological learning disabilities • MS Ed
    children with retarded mental development • MS Ed
    early childhood education • MS Ed
    elementary mathematics education • MS Ed
    English education • MA
    French • MA
    general science education • MA
    guidance and counseling • CAS, MS Ed
    health and nutrition sciences • MS Ed
    home economics education • MS Ed
    humanities education • MS Ed
    mathematics education • MA
    music • MS Ed
    music education • MS Ed
    physics education • MA
    reading and language arts • MS Ed
    school administration and supervision • CAS

school psychology • CAS, MS Ed
science and environmental education • MS Ed
social science • MS Ed
social studies education • MA
Spanish education • MA
speech • MA
speech and hearing handicapped education • MS Ed

CANISIUS COLLEGE
Buffalo, NY 14208-1098

http://gort.canisius.edu/

Independent-religious coed comprehensive institution. *Enrollment: 4,598 graduate, professional, and undergraduate students. Graduate faculty: 49 full-time, 96 part-time. Computer facilities: Campuswide network is available with full Internet access. Computer service fees are included with tuition and fees. Library facilities: Bouwhuis Library. Graduate expenses: Tuition of $415 per credit hour. Fees of $15 per credit hour. General application contact: Dr. Herbert Nelson, Vice President, Graduate Division, 716-888-2120 Ext. 109.*

Graduate Division
Dr. Herbert Nelson, Vice President

College of Arts and Sciences
Dr. Ellen O. Conley, Dean
Program in:
    organizational communication and development • MS

School of Education and Human Services
Dr. James M. McDonnell, Acting Dean
Programs in:
    counselor education • CAS, MS
    educational administration and supervision • MS, SAS
    physical education • MS
    reading • MS Ed
    secondary education • MS
    special education—preparation of teachers of the deaf • MS
    sport administration • MS
    teacher education • MS Ed

Wehle School of Business
Dr. Richard Shick, Dean
Programs in:
    business administration • MBA, MBAPA
    professional accounting • MBA

CITY COLLEGE OF THE CITY UNIVERSITY OF NEW YORK
New York, NY 10031-6977

http://www.ccny.cuny.edu/

Public coed university. Enrollment: 12,093 graduate, professional, and undergraduate students. Graduate faculty: 497 full-time, 484 part-time. Computer facilities: Campuswide network is available with full Internet access. Total number of PCs/terminals supplied for student use: 3,000. Computer services are offered at no charge. Library facilities: Cohen Library plus 3 additional on-campus libraries. Graduate expenses: Tuition of $4350 per year full-time, $185 per credit part-time for state residents; $7600 per year full-time, $320 per credit part-time for nonresidents. Fees of $41 per year. General application contact: Graduate Admissions Office, 212-650-6977.

Graduate School
Ellen Smiley, Assistant Provost for Graduate Studies and
 Research

College of Liberal Arts and Science
Ellen Smiley, Assistant Provost for Graduate Studies and
 Research, Graduate School
Programs in:
 advertising design • MFA
 applied urban anthropology • MA
 art history • MA
 biochemistry • MA, PhD
 biology • MA, PhD
 ceramic design • MFA
 chemistry • MA, PhD
 clinical psychology • PhD
 creative writing • MA
 earth and environmental science • PhD
 earth systems science • MA
 economics • MA
 English and American literature • MA
 experimental cognition • PhD
 general psychology • MA
 history • MA
 international relations • MA
 language and literacy • MA
 liberal arts and science • MS
 mathematics • MA
 museum studies • MA
 music • MA
 new forms/intermedia • MFA
 painting • MFA
 physics • MA, PhD
 printmaking • MFA
 sculpture • MFA
 sociology • MA
 Spanish • MA
 wood and metal design • MFA

School of Architecture and Environmental Studies
Ellen Smiley, Assistant Provost for Graduate Studies and
 Research, Graduate School
Programs in:
 architecture • PD
 urban design • MUP

School of Education
Oliver Patterson, Acting Dean
Programs in:
 art education • MA
 bilingual education • MS
 early childhood education • MS
 educational administration • AC, MS
 elementary education • MS
 English education • MA
 environmental education • MA
 guidance and counseling • MS
 mathematics education • MA
 reading • AC, MS
 school psychology • AC, MS
 secondary science education • MA
 social studies education • MA
 special education • MS
 technology education • MA, MS Ed

School of Engineering
Dr. Gerard G. Lowen, Associate Dean for Graduate Studies
Programs in:
 chemical engineering • ME, MS, PhD
 civil engineering • ME, MS, PhD
 computer sciences • MS, PhD
 electrical engineering • ME, MS, PhD
 mechanical engineering • ME, MS, PhD

CLARKSON UNIVERSITY
Potsdam, NY 13699

http://www.clarkson.edu/

Independent coed university. Enrollment: 2,745 graduate, professional, and undergraduate students. Graduate faculty: 153 full-time, 20 part-time. Computer facilities: Campuswide network is available with full Internet access. Total number of PCs/terminals supplied for student use: 110. Computer services are offered at no charge. Library facilities: Andrew S. Schuler Educational Resources Center. Graduate expenses: Tuition of $19,075 per year full-time, $635 per credit hour part-time. Fees of $178 per year. General application contact: Dr. Philip K. Hopke, Dean of the Graduate School, 315-268-6447.

Graduate School
Dr. Philip K. Hopke, Dean
Program in:
 engineering and manufacturing management • MS

School of Business
Dr. Victor P. Pease, Dean
Programs in:
 business administration • MBA
 human resource management • MS
 management information systems • MS
 manufacturing management • MS

School of Engineering
Dr. Anthony Collins, Dean
Programs in:
- chemical engineering • ME, MS, PhD
- civil and environmental engineering • PhD
- civil engineering • ME, MS
- computer engineering • ME, MS
- electrical and computer engineering • PhD
- electrical engineering • ME, MS
- engineering science • MS, PhD
- mechanical engineering • ME, MS, PhD

School of Science
Dr. Jim H. Thorp III, Dean
Programs in:
- analytical chemistry • MS, PhD
- computer science • MS
- inorganic chemistry • MS, PhD
- mathematics • MS, PhD
- organic chemistry • MS, PhD
- physical chemistry • MS, PhD
- physics • MS, PhD

COLLEGE OF NEW ROCHELLE
New Rochelle, NY 10805-2308

http://cnr.edu/

Independent coed comprehensive institution. *Enrollment: 7,061 graduate, professional, and undergraduate students. Graduate faculty: 22 full-time, 90 part-time. Library facilities: Gill Library. Graduate expenses: $329 per credit. General application contact: Ann Fitzpatrick, Associate Dean of the Graduate School, 914-654-5389.*

Graduate School
Dr. Laura S. Ellis, Dean
Programs in:
- art education • MA
- art museum education • Certificate
- art therapy • MS
- career development • Certificate, MS
- communication arts • Certificate, MS
- community-school psychology • MS
- elementary education/early childhood education • MS Ed
- fine art • MS
- gerontology • Certificate, MS
- gifted education • Certificate, MS Ed
- graphic art • MS
- guidance and counseling • MS
- nursing • Certificate, MS
- reading/adult communication skills • MS Ed
- reading/special education • MS Ed
- school administration and supervision • Certificate, MS Ed, PD
- special education • MS Ed
- teaching English as a second language • MS Ed
- therapeutic education • MS Ed

THE COLLEGE OF SAINT ROSE
Albany, NY 12203-1419

http://www.strose.edu/

Independent coed comprehensive institution. *Enrollment: 3,973 graduate, professional, and undergraduate students. Graduate faculty: 96 full-time, 28 part-time. Computer facilities: Campuswide network is available with full Internet access. Total number of PCs/terminals supplied for student use: 202. Computer services are offered at no charge. Library facilities: Neil Hellman Library. Graduate expenses: Tuition of $338 per credit. Fees of $60 per year. General application contact: Anne Tully, Dean of Graduate and Adult and Continuing Education Admissions, 518-454-5136.*

Graduate Studies
Dr. Margaret Kirwin, Dean of Studies

School of Arts and Humanities
Dr. Margaret Kirwin, Dean of Studies, Graduate Studies
Programs in:
- art education • MS Ed
- English • MA
- history/political science • MA
- music • MA
- music education • MS Ed
- public communications • MA

School of Business
Dr. Michael Hurley, Associate Dean
Programs in:
- accounting • MS
- business administration • MBA

School of Education
Dr. Penny Axelrod, Associate Dean
Programs in:
- college student personnel • MS Ed
- communication disorders • MS Ed
- community counseling • MS Ed
- early childhood education • MS Ed
- educational administration and supervision • Certificate, MS Ed
- educational psychology • MS Ed
- elementary education • MS Ed
- reading • MS Ed
- school counseling • MS Ed
- school psychology • Certificate, MS Ed
- secondary education • MS Ed
- special education • MS Ed

COLLEGE OF STATEN ISLAND OF THE CITY UNIVERSITY OF NEW YORK
Staten Island, NY 10314-6600
http://www.csi.cuny.edu/

Public coed comprehensive institution. *Enrollment:* 12,023 graduate, professional, and undergraduate students. *Graduate faculty:* 55 full-time, 51 part-time. *Computer facilities: Campuswide network is available with full Internet access. Total number of PCs/terminals supplied for student use: 1,200. Computer services are offered at no charge.* Library facilities: *main library. Graduate expenses: Tuition of $4350 per year full-time, $185 per credit part-time for state residents; $7600 per year full-time, $320 per credit part-time for nonresidents. Fees of $106 per year full-time, $54 per year part-time. General application contact: Earl Teasley, Director of Admissions, 718-982-2010.*

Graduate Programs
Dr. Mirella Affron, Vice President for Academic Affairs/
    Provost
Programs in:
    biology • PhD
    cinema studies • MA
    computer science • MS, PhD
    educational supervision and administration • 6th Year
        Certificate
    elementary education • MS Ed
    English • MA
    environmental science • MA
    liberal studies • MA
    polymer chemistry • PhD
    psychology • PhD
    secondary education • MS Ed
    special education • MS Ed

COLUMBIA UNIVERSITY
New York, NY 10027
http://www.columbia.edu/

Independent coed university. *Enrollment:* 21,102 graduate, professional, and undergraduate students. *Graduate faculty:* 2,639 full-time, 727 part-time. *Computer facilities: Campuswide network is available with full Internet access. Computer service fees are included with tuition and fees.* Library facilities: *Butler Library plus 23 additional on-campus libraries. Graduate expenses: $22,700 per year full-time, $12,844 per year part-time. General application contact: Admissions Office of the appropriate school.*

College of Physicians and Surgeons
Dr. Herbert Pardes, Dean, Faculty of Medicine
Programs in:
    medicine • MD
    occupational therapy administration or education
        (post-professional) • MS

    occupational therapy (professional) • MS
    physical therapy • MS

Graduate School of Arts and Sciences at the College of Physicians and Surgeons
Dr. David Figurski, Associate Dean of Graduate Students
Programs in:
    anatomy • M Phil, MA, PhD
    anatomy and cell biology • PhD
    biochemistry and molecular biophysics • M Phil, PhD
    biomedical sciences • M Phil, MA, PhD
    biophysics • PhD
    cellular, molecular and biophysical studies • M Phil, MA,
        PhD
    genetics • M Phil, MA, PhD
    medical informatics • M Phil, MA, PhD
    neurobiology and behavior • M Phil, PhD
    nutrition • M Phil, MA, PhD
    pathobiology • M Phil, MA, PhD
    pharmacology • M Phil, MA, PhD
    pharmacology-toxicology • M Phil, MA, PhD

Institute of Human Nutrition
Dr. Richard Deckelbaum, Director
Program in:
    nutrition • M Phil, MA, MS, PhD

Fu Foundation School of Engineering and Applied Science
C. J. Colombo, Dean
Programs in:
    applied physics • Eng Sc D, MS, PhD
    biomedical engineering • Eng Sc D, MS
    chemical engineering • Eng Sc D, Engr, MS, PhD
    civil engineering • Eng Sc D, Engr, MS, PhD
    computer science • CSE, MS, PhD
    earth resources engineering • MS
    electrical engineering • EE, Eng Sc D, MS, PhD
    engineering and applied science • Minl E
    industrial engineering • Eng Sc D, Engr, MS, PhD
    materials engineering • Eng Sc D, MS
    materials science • EM, Eng Sc D, PhD
    materials science and engineering • MS
    mechanical engineering • Eng Sc D, ME, MS, PhD
    mechanics • Eng Sc D, Engr, MS, PhD
    metallurgical engineering • Engr
    metallurgy • Met E
    mineral engineering • Engr
    minerals engineering and materials science • Eng Sc D,
        PhD
    mines • Engr
    operations research • Eng Sc D, MS, PhD
    solid state science and engineering • Eng Sc D, MS, PhD
    telecommunications • MS

Graduate School of Architecture, Planning, and Preservation
Bernard Tschumi, Dean
Programs in:
    advanced architectural design • MS
    architecture • M Arch
    architecture and urban design • MS
    historic preservation • MS

real estate development • MS
urban planning • MS, PhD

Graduate School of Arts and Sciences

Dr. Eduardo R. Macagno, Dean and Associate Vice President
Programs in:
American studies • MA
anatomy • M Phil, MA, PhD
anatomy and cell biology • PhD
ancient studies • MA
biochemistry and molecular biophysics • M Phil, PhD
biomedical sciences • M Phil, MA, PhD
biophysics • PhD
cellular, molecular and biophysical studies • M Phil, MA, PhD
clinical specialty • MA
conservation biology • Certificate
East Asian studies • MA
ecology and evolutionary biology • PhD
environmental policy • Certificate
French cultural studies • MA
genetics • M Phil, MA, PhD
Islamic culture studies • MA
Jewish studies • MA
medical informatics • M Phil, MA, PhD
medieval studies • MA
modern European studies • MA
neurobiology and behavior • M Phil, PhD
nutrition • M Phil, MA, PhD
pathobiology • M Phil, MA, PhD
pharmacology • M Phil, MA, PhD
pharmacology-toxicology • M Phil, MA, PhD
South Asian studies • MA
theatre • M Phil, MA, PhD

Division of Humanities

Dr. Eduardo R. Macagno, Dean and Associate Vice President, Graduate School of Arts and Sciences
Programs in:
archaeology • M Phil, MA, PhD
art history and archaeology • M Phil, MA, PhD
classics • M Phil, MA, PhD
comparative literature • M Phil, MA, PhD
East Asian languages and cultures • M Phil, MA, PhD
English literature • M Phil, MA, PhD
French and Romance philology • M Phil, MA, PhD
Germanic languages • M Phil, MA, PhD
Hebrew language and literature • M Phil, MA, PhD
Italian • M Phil, MA, PhD
Jewish studies • M Phil, MA, PhD
literature-writing • M Phil, MA, PhD
Middle Eastern languages and cultures • M Phil, MA, PhD
music • DMA, M Phil, MA, PhD
Oriental studies • M Phil, MA, PhD
philosophy • M Phil, MA, PhD
religion • M Phil, MA, PhD
Russian literature • M Phil, MA, PhD
Slavic languages • M Phil, MA, PhD
Spanish and Portuguese • M Phil, MA, PhD

Division of Natural Sciences

Dr. Eduardo R. Macagno, Dean and Associate Vice President, Graduate School of Arts and Sciences
Programs in:
astronomy • M Phil, MA, PhD
atmospheric and planetary science • M Phil, PhD
biological sciences • M Phil, MA, PhD
chemical physics • M Phil, PhD
epidemiology • M Phil, MA, PhD
experimental psychology • M Phil, MA, PhD
geochemistry • M Phil, MA, PhD
geodetic sciences • M Phil, MA, PhD
geophysics • M Phil, MA, PhD
inorganic chemistry • M Phil, MS, PhD
mathematics • M Phil, MA, PhD
oceanography • M Phil, MA, PhD
organic chemistry • M Phil, MS, PhD
physics • M Phil, MA, PhD
psychobiology • M Phil, MA, PhD
social psychology • M Phil, MA, PhD
statistics • M Phil, MA, PhD

Division of Social Sciences

Dr. Eduardo R. Macagno, Dean and Associate Vice President, Graduate School of Arts and Sciences
Programs in:
American history • M Phil, MA, PhD
anthropology • M Phil, MA, PhD
economics • M Phil, MA, PhD
history • M Phil, MA, PhD
political science • M Phil, MA, PhD
sociology • M Phil, MA, PhD

Graduate School of Business

Prof. Meyer Feldberg, Dean
Programs in:
accounting • MBA, PhD
business • PhD
business administration • MBA
construction management • MBA
entrepreneurship • MBA
finance and economics • MBA, PhD
human resource management • MBA
international business • MBA
management of organizations • MBA, PhD
management science • MBA
management science/operations research • PhD
marketing • MBA, PhD
media, entertainment and communications • MBA
production and operations management • MBA
public and nonprofit management • MBA
real estate • MBA

Graduate School of Journalism

Program in:
journalism • MS

School of Dental and Oral Surgery

Dr. Allan J. Formicola, Dean
Programs in:
clinical specialty • MA
dental and oral surgery • DDS

Columbia University (continued)

School of International and Public Affairs
Dr. Lisa Anderson, Dean
Programs in:
    international affairs • MIA
    public policy and administration • MPA

East Asian Institute
Dr. Madeleine Zelin, Director
Program in:
    Asian studies • Certificate

Institute of African Studies
Dr. George Bond, Director
Program in:
    African studies • Certificate

Institute of Latin American and Iberian Studies
Dr. Consuelo Cruz, Director
Program in:
    Latin American and Iberian studies • Certificate

Institute on East Central Europe
Dr. John Micgiel, Director
Program in:
    East Central Europe • Certificate

Middle East Institute
Dr. Richard Bulliet, Director
Program in:
    Middle East studies • Certificate

Southern Asian Institute
Dr. Philip Oldenburg, Director
Program in:
    Southern Asian studies • Certificate

W. Averell Harriman Institute for Advanced Study of the Soviet Union
Dr. Mark von Hagen, Director
Program in:
    Soviet studies • Certificate

Western Europe Institute
Dr. Glenda Rosenthal, Director
Program in:
    Western Europe studies • Certificate

School of Law
David W. Leebron, Dean of Faculty of Law
Program in:
    law • JD, JSD, LL M

School of Nursing
Dr. Mary O. Mundinger, Dean
Programs in:
    adult nurse practitioner • Adv C, MS
    critical care nurse practitioner • MS
    emergency nurse practitioner • Adv C, MS
    family nurse practitioner • Adv C, MS
    geriatric nurse practitioner • Adv C, MS
    HIV nursing • Adv C, MS
    neonatal nurse practitioner • Adv C, MS
    nurse anesthesia • MS
    nurse midwifery • MS

    nursing science • DN Sc
    oncology nursing • Adv C, MS
    pediatric nurse practitioner • Adv C, MS
    psychiatric-community mental health nursing • Adv C, MS
    women's health nurse practitioner • Adv C, MS

School of Public Health
Dr. Allan Rosenfield, Dean
Programs in:
    biostatistics • Dr PH, MPH, MS, PhD
    epidemiology • Dr PH, MPH, MS, PhD
    health • Dr PH, MPH
    health policy and management • Dr PH, Exec MPH, MPH
    medical physics • Dr PH, MPH
    population and family health • MPH
    public health • Dr PH, MPH
    sociomedical sciences • Dr PH, MPH, PhD

School of Social Work
Dr. Ronald A. Feldman, Dean
Program in:
    social work • MSSW, PhD

School of the Arts
Robert Fitzpatrick, Dean
Programs in:
    digital media • MFA
    directing • MFA
    drawing • MFA
    fiction • MFA
    history/theory • MFA
    installation • MFA
    mixed media • MFA
    nonfiction • MFA
    painting • MFA
    photography • MFA
    poetry • MFA
    printmaking • MFA
    producing • MFA
    screen writing • MFA
    sculpture • MFA

Oscar Hammerstein Center for Theatre Studies
Dr. Arnold Aronson, Chairman
Programs in:
    acting • MFA
    directing • MFA
    drama and theater arts • PhD
    dramaturgy • MFA
    playwriting • MFA
    theater management • MFA

CORNELL UNIVERSITY
Ithaca, NY 14853-0001

http://www.gradschool.cornell.edu/

Independent coed university. *Enrollment: 18,428 graduate, professional, and undergraduate students. Graduate faculty: 1,463 full-time, 69 part-time. Computer facilities: Campuswide network is available with full Internet access. Total number of PCs/terminals supplied for student use: 700. Computer services are offered at no charge. Library facilities: Olin Library plus 17 additional on-campus libraries. Graduate expenses: Tuition of $22,780 per year. Fees of $48 per year. General application contact: Graduate School Application Requests, Caldwell Hall, 607-255-4884.*

Graduate School
Dr. Walter Cohen, Dean
Programs in:
    biophysics • PhD
    hotel administration • MMH, MS, PhD

Graduate Field in the Law School
Dr. Walter Cohen, Dean, Graduate School
Program in:
    law • JSD

Graduate Field of Management
Dr. Walter Cohen, Dean, Graduate School
Programs in:
    accounting • PhD
    behavioral decision theory • PhD
    finance • PhD
    management information systems • PhD
    managerial economics • PhD
    marketing • PhD
    organizational behavior • PhD
    production and operations management • PhD
    quantitative analysis • PhD

Graduate Fields of Agriculture and Life Sciences
Dr. Daryl B. Lund, Dean
Programs in:
    acarology • MS, PhD
    agricultural economics • MPS, MS, PhD
    agricultural education • MAT
    agricultural, extension, and adult education • MPS, MS, PhD
    agricultural finance • MPS, MS, PhD
    agronomy • MPS, MS, PhD
    animal breeding • MS, PhD
    animal cytology • PhD
    animal ecology • PhD
    animal genetics • MS, PhD
    animal nutrition • MPS, MS, PhD
    animal science • MPS, MS, PhD
    apiculture • MS, PhD
    applied ecology • PhD
    applied econometrics and quantitative analysis • MPS, MS, PhD
    applied entomology • MS, PhD
    aquatic entomology • MS, PhD
    aquatic science • MPS, MS, PhD

atmospheric sciences • MPS, MS, PhD
behavioral biology • PhD
behavioral ecology • PhD
biochemistry • PhD
biogeochemistry • PhD
biological control • MS, PhD
biological engineering • M Eng, MPS, MS, PhD
biology • MAT
biometry • MS, PhD
biophysics • PhD
cell biology • PhD
cellular and biochemical toxicology • MS, PhD
cellular and molecular neurobiology • PhD
chemical ecology • PhD
chemistry • MAT
clinical nutrition • MPS, MS, PhD
communication • MPS, MS, PhD
communication research methods • MS, PhD
community and ecosystem ecology • PhD
community and regional sociology • MPS, PhD
community development process • MPS
community nutrition • MPS, MS, PhD
comparative and functional anatomy • PhD
controlled environmental horticulture • MPS, MS, PhD
curriculum and instruction • MPS, MS, PhD
cytology • PhD
dairy science • MPS, MS, PhD
decision theory • MS, PhD
developmental biology • PhD
earth science • MAT
ecological and environmental plant pathology • MPS, MS, PhD
ecological genetics • PhD
ecology • PhD
economic and social statistics • MS, PhD
economic development • MPS
economics of development • MPS, MS, PhD
ecotoxicology and environmental chemistry • MS, PhD
educational psychology and measurement • MPS, MS, PhD
educational research methodology • MPS, MS, PhD
energy • M Eng, MPS, MS, PhD
engineering statistics • MS, PhD
environmental economics • PhD
environmental engineering • M Eng, MPS, MS, PhD
environmental management • M Eng, MPS, MS, PhD
epidemiological plant pathology • MPS, MS, PhD
ethology • PhD
evolutionary biology • PhD
experimental design • MS, PhD
farm management and production economics • MPS, MS
field crop science • MPS, MS, PhD
fishery science • MPS, MS, PhD
floriculture crop production • MPS, MS, PhD
food and nutritional toxicology • MS, PhD
food chemistry • MPS, MS, PhD
food engineering • MPS, MS, PhD
food management and production economics • PhD
food microbiology • MPS, MS, PhD
food processing engineering • M Eng, MPS, MS, PhD
food processing waste technology • MPS, MS, PhD
foods • MPS, MS, PhD

Cornell University (continued)

food science • MFS, MPS, MS, PhD
forest science • MPS, MS, PhD
genetics • PhD
horticultural physiology • MS, PhD
horticulture physiology • MPS
human nutrition • MPS, MS, PhD
insect behavior • MS, PhD
insect biochemistry • MS, PhD
insect ecology • MS, PhD
insect genetics • MS, PhD
insect morphology • MS, PhD
insect pathology • MS, PhD
insect physiology • MS, PhD
insect systematics • MS, PhD
insect toxicology and insecticide chemistry • MS, PhD
integrated pest management • MS, PhD
international agriculture • M Eng, MPS, MS, PhD
international agriculture and rural development • MPS
international and intercultural communication • MS, PhD
international food science • MPS, MS, PhD
international nutrition • MPS, MS, PhD
landscape architecture • MLA
landscape horticulture • MPS, MS, PhD
limnology • PhD
local government organizations and operation • MPS
local roads • M Eng, MPS, MS, PhD
machine systems • M Eng, MPS, MS, PhD
marketing and food distribution • MPS, MS, PhD
mathematical statistics • MS, PhD
mathematics • MAT, MS
medical and veterinary entomology • MS, PhD
microbiology • PhD
molecular biology • PhD
molecular plant pathology • MPS, MS, PhD
mycology • MPS, MS, PhD
neuroanatomy • PhD
neurobiology • PhD
neurochemistry • PhD
neuroethology • PhD
neuropharmacology • PhD
neurophysiology • PhD
nursery crop production • MPS, MS, PhD
nutritional biochemistry • MPS, MS, PhD
nutrition of horticultural crops • MPS, MS, PhD
oceanography • PhD
paleobiology • PhD
paleobotany • PhD
philosophical and social foundations: educational administration • MPS, MS, PhD
physics • MAT
physiological ecology • PhD
physiology of reproduction • MPS, MS, PhD
plant breeding • MPS, MS, PhD
plant cell biology • PhD
plant disease epidemiology • MPS, MS, PhD
plant ecology • PhD
plant genetics • MPS, MS, PhD
plant materials and horticultural taxonomy • MPS, MS, PhD
plant molecular biology • PhD
plant morphology, anatomy and biomechanics • PhD

plant pathology • MPS, MS, PhD
plant physiology • PhD
plant propagation • MPS, MS, PhD
plant protection • MPS
pomology • MPS, MS, PhD
population and development • MPS, PhD
population biology • PhD
population ecology • PhD
probability • MS, PhD
program development and planning • MPS
public policy analysis • MPS, MS, PhD
resource economics • MPS, MS, PhD
resource policy and management • MPS, MS, PhD
rural and environmental sociology • MPS, PhD
sampling • MS, PhD
science and environmental communication • MS, PhD
sensory evaluation • MPS, MS, PhD
sensory physiology • PhD
social psychology of communication • MS, PhD
sociobiology • PhD
soil and water engineering • M Eng, MPS, MS, PhD
soil science • MPS, MS, PhD
state, economy, and society • MPS, PhD
statistical computing • MS, PhD
stochastic processes • MS, PhD
structures and environment • M Eng, MPS, MS, PhD
systematic botany • PhD
systematics • PhD
theoretical ecology • PhD
turfgrass science • MPS, MS, PhD
urban horticulture • MPS, MS, PhD
uses and effects of communication media • MS, PhD
vegetable crops • MPS, MS, PhD
vertebrate zoology • PhD
weed science • MPS, MS, PhD
wildlife science • MPS, MS, PhD

Graduate Fields of Architecture, Art and Planning
Dr. Anthony Vidler, Acting Dean
Programs in:
architectural science • MS
city and regional planning • MRP, PhD
creative visual arts • MFA
design • M Arch
environmental studies • MA, MS, PhD
historic preservation planning • MA
history of architecture and urban development • MA, PhD
international spatial problems • MA, MS, PhD
landscape architecture • MLA
location theory • MA, MS, PhD
multiregional economic analysis • MA, MS, PhD
painting • MFA
peace science • MA, MS, PhD
photography • MFA
planning methods • MA, MS, PhD
planning theory and systems analysis • MRP, PhD
printmaking • MFA
real estate • MPSRE
regional science • MRP, PhD
sculpture • MFA
urban and regional economics • MA, MS, PhD
urban and regional theory • MRP, PhD
urban planning history • MRP, PhD

Graduate Fields of Arts and Sciences
Dr. Philip E. Lewis, Dean
Programs in:

African-American studies • MPS
African history • MA, PhD
African studies • MPS
Afro-American literature • PhD
American art • PhD
American history • MA, PhD
American literature after 1865 • PhD
American literature to 1865 • PhD
American politics • PhD
American studies • MA, PhD
analytical chemistry • PhD
ancient art and archaeology • PhD
ancient history • MA, PhD
ancient Near Eastern studies • MA, PhD
ancient philosophy • PhD
animal cytology • PhD
animal ecology • PhD
applied anthropology • MA, PhD
applied ecology • PhD
applied economics • PhD
applied mathematics • PhD
Arabic and Islamic studies • MA, PhD
archaeology • MA, PhD
Asian religions • MA, PhD
astronomy • PhD
astrophysics • PhD
baroque art • PhD
behavioral biology • PhD
behavioral ecology • PhD
biblical studies • MA, PhD
biochemistry • PhD
biogeochemistry • PhD
bio-organic chemistry • PhD
biophysical chemistry • PhD
biophysics • PhD
biopsychology • PhD
cell biology • PhD
cellular and molecular neurobiology • PhD
chemical ecology • PhD
chemical physics • PhD
Chinese philology • MA, PhD
classical archaeology • PhD
classical Chinese literature • MA, PhD
classical Japanese literature • MA, PhD
colonial and postcolonial literature • PhD
community and ecosystem ecology • PhD
comparative and functional anatomy • PhD
comparative literature • PhD
comparative politics • PhD
composition • DMA, MFA
creative writing • MFA
cultural studies • PhD
culture and meaning • MA, PhD
cytology • PhD
developmental biology • PhD
development policy • MPS
drama and the theater • PhD
dramatic literature • PhD
early modern European history • MA, PhD
East Asian art • PhD

East Asian studies • MA
ecological genetics • PhD
ecology • PhD
econometrics and economic statistics • PhD
economic development and planning • PhD
economic history • PhD
economics of participation and labor-managed systems • PhD
economic systems • PhD
economic theory • PhD
economy and society • MA, PhD
eighteenth-century performance practice • DMA, MFA
English history • MA, PhD
English poetry • PhD
English Renaissance to 1660 • PhD
environmental archaeology • MA
ethology • PhD
evolutionary biology • PhD
experimental physics • MS, PhD
French history • MA, PhD
French linguistics • PhD
French literature • PhD
gender and life course • MA, PhD
general linguistics • MA, PhD
general psychology • PhD
general space sciences • PhD
genetics • PhD
German area studies • MA, PhD
German history • MA, PhD
Germanic linguistics • MA, PhD
Germanic literature • MA, PhD
German intellectual history • MA, PhD
Greek and Latin language and linguistics • PhD
Greek language and literature • PhD
Hebrew and Judaic studies • MA, PhD
Hispanic literature • PhD
historical anthropology • MA, PhD
historical archaeology • MA
history and philosophy of science and technology • MA, PhD
history of science • MA, PhD
human experimental psychology • PhD
industrial organization and control • PhD
infrared astronomy • PhD
inorganic chemistry • PhD
international economics • PhD
international nutrition • MPS
international planning • MPS
international population • MPS
international relations • PhD
Italian linguistics • PhD
Italian literature • PhD
Korean literature • MA, PhD
labor economics • PhD
Latin American archaeology • MA
Latin American history • MA, PhD
Latin language and literature • PhD
lesbian, bisexual, and gay literature studies • PhD
limnology • PhD
literary criticism and theory • PhD
material chemistry • PhD
mathematics • PhD
medieval and Renaissance Latin literature • PhD

Cornell University (continued)
medieval archaeology • MA, PhD
medieval art • PhD
medieval Chinese history • MA, PhD
medieval history • MA, PhD
medieval literature • PhD
medieval music • PhD
medieval philology and linguistics • PhD
medieval philosophy • PhD
Mediterranean and Near Eastern archaeology • MA
microbiology • PhD
modern art • PhD
modern Chinese history • MA, PhD
modern Chinese literature • MA, PhD
modern European history • MA, PhD
modern Japanese history • MA, PhD
modern Japanese literature • MA, PhD
molecular biology • PhD
monetary and macroeconomics • PhD
musicology • MA, PhD
neuroanatomy • PhD
neurobiology • PhD
neurochemistry • PhD
neuroethology • PhD
neuropharmacology • PhD
neurophysiology • PhD
nineteenth century • PhD
oceanography • PhD
Old and Middle English • PhD
organic chemistry • PhD
organizations • MA, PhD
organometallic chemistry • PhD
paleobiology • PhD
paleobotany • PhD
peace science • PhD
philosophy • PhD
physical anthropology • MA, PhD
physical chemistry • PhD
physics • MS, PhD
physiological ecology • PhD
planetary studies • PhD
plant cell biology • PhD
plant ecology • PhD
plant molecular biology • PhD
plant morphology, anatomy and biomechanics • PhD
plant physiology • PhD
political sociology/social movements • MA, PhD
political thought • PhD
polymer chemistry • PhD
population biology • PhD
population ecology • PhD
premodern Islamic history • MA, PhD
premodern Japanese history • MA, PhD
prose fiction • PhD
psychological anthropology • MA, PhD
public affairs • MPA
public finance • PhD
public policy • MPA
racial and ethnic relations • MA, PhD
radio astronomy • PhD
radiophysics • PhD
Renaissance art • PhD
Renaissance history • MA, PhD

Restoration and eighteenth century • PhD
Romance linguistics • PhD
Russian history • MA, PhD
Russian literature • MA, PhD
science and technology policy • MPS
sensory physiology • PhD
Slavic linguistics • MA, PhD
social and personality psychology • PhD
social anthropology • MA, PhD
social networks • MA, PhD
social psychology • MA, PhD
social stratification • MA, PhD
social studies of science and technology • MA, PhD
sociobiology • PhD
South Asian studies • MA
Southeast Asian art • PhD
Southeast Asian history • MA, PhD
Southeast Asian studies • MA
Spanish linguistics • PhD
Stone Age archaeology • MA
systematic botany • PhD
systematics • PhD
theater history • PhD
theater theory and aesthetics • PhD
theoretical astrophysics • PhD
theoretical chemistry • PhD
theoretical ecology • PhD
theoretical physics • MS, PhD
theory and criticism • PhD
twentieth century • PhD
vertebrate zoology • PhD
women's literature • PhD

Graduate Fields of Engineering
Dr. John Hopcroft, Dean
Programs in:
advanced materials processing • M Eng, MS, PhD
aerospace engineering • M Eng, MS, PhD
algorithms • M Eng, PhD
applied logic and automated reasoning • M Eng, PhD
applied mathematics and computational methods • M Eng, MS, PhD
applied physics • PhD
applied probability and statistics • PhD
artificial intelligence • M Eng, PhD
biochemical engineering • M Eng, MS, PhD
biological engineering • M Eng, MPS, MS, PhD
biomechanical engineering • M Eng, MS, PhD
biomedical engineering • PhD
chemical reaction engineering • M Eng, MS, PhD
classical and statistical thermodynamics • M Eng, MS, PhD
combustion • M Eng, MS, PhD
computer engineering • M Eng, PhD
computer graphics • M Eng, PhD
computer science • M Eng, PhD
computer vision • M Eng, PhD
concurrency and distributed computing • M Eng, PhD
economic geology • MS, PhD
electrical engineering • M Eng, PhD
electrical systems • M Eng, PhD
electrophysics • M Eng, PhD
energy • M Eng, MPS, MS, PhD

energy and power systems • M Eng, MS, PhD
engineering geology • MS, PhD
engineering physics • M Eng, PhD
environmental engineering • M Eng, MPS, MS, PhD
environmental geophysics • M Eng
environmental management • M Eng, MPS, MS, PhD
environmental systems engineering • M Eng, MS, PhD
fluid dynamics, rheology and biorheology • M Eng, MS, PhD
fluid mechanics • M Eng, MS, PhD
food processing engineering • M Eng, MPS, MS, PhD
general geology • MS, PhD
geobiology • MS, PhD
geochemistry and isotope geology • MS, PhD
geohydrology • M Eng, MS, PhD
geomorphology • MS, PhD
geophysics • MS, PhD
geotechnical engineering • M Eng, MS, PhD
geotectonics • MS, PhD
heat and mass transfer • M Eng, MS, PhD
heat transfer • M Eng, MS, PhD
hydraulics and hydrology • M Eng, MS, PhD
information organization and retrieval • M Eng, PhD
international agriculture • M Eng, MPS, MS, PhD
kinetics and catalysis • M Eng, MS, PhD
local roads • M Eng, MPS, MS, PhD
machine systems • M Eng, MPS, MS, PhD
manufacturing systems engineering • PhD
materials and manufacturing engineering • M Eng, MS, PhD
materials engineering • M Eng, PhD
materials science • M Eng, PhD
mathematical programming • PhD
mechanical systems and design • M Eng, MS, PhD
mineralogy • MS, PhD
multiphase flows • M Eng, MS, PhD
nuclear engineering • M Eng
nuclear science and engineering • MS, PhD
operating systems • M Eng, PhD
operations research and industrial engineering • M Eng
paleontology • MS, PhD
parallel computing • M Eng, PhD
petroleum geology • MS, PhD
petrology • MS, PhD
planetary geology • MS, PhD
polymers • M Eng, MS, PhD
Precambrian geology • MS, PhD
programming environments • M Eng, PhD
programming languages and methodology • M Eng, PhD
Quaternary geology • MS, PhD
remote sensing • M Eng, MS, PhD
robotics • M Eng, PhD
rock mechanics • MS, PhD
scientific computing • M Eng, PhD
sedimentology • MS, PhD
seismology • MS, PhD
soil and water engineering • M Eng, MPS, MS, PhD
stratigraphy • MS, PhD
structural engineering • M Eng, MS, PhD
structural geology • MS, PhD
structures and environment • M Eng, MPS, MS, PhD
surface science • M Eng, MS, PhD
theoretical and applied mechanics • M Eng, MS, PhD

theory of computation • M Eng, PhD
transportation engineering • M Eng, MS, PhD
water resource systems • M Eng, MS, PhD

Graduate Fields of Human Ecology
Dr. Francille Firebaugh, Dean
Programs in:
animal nutrition • MPS, MS, PhD
apparel design • MA, MPS
applied research in human-environment relations • MS
clinical nutrition • MPS, MS, PhD
community nutrition • MPS, MS, PhD
consumer economics • MS, PhD
developmental psychology • PhD
facilities planning and management • MS
family economics • MS, PhD
fiber science • MS, PhD
foods • MPS, MS, PhD
health services administration • MHA
housing • MS, PhD
housing and design • MS
human development and family studies • PhD
human factors and ergonomics • MS
human nutrition • MPS, MS, PhD
human service administration • MPS, MS, PhD
interior design • MA
international nutrition • MPS, MS, PhD
nutritional biochemistry • MPS, MS, PhD
polymer science • MS, PhD
program evaluation and planning • MPS, MS, PhD
textile science • MS, PhD

Graduate Fields of Industrial and Labor Relations
Dr. Walter Cohen, Dean, Graduate School
Programs in:
collective bargaining, labor law and labor history • MILR, MPS, MS, PhD
economic and social statistics • MILR, MPS, MS, PhD
human resource studies • MILR, MPS, MS, PhD
international and comparative labor • MILR, MPS, MS, PhD
labor economics • MILR, MPS, MS, PhD
organizational behavior • MILR, MPS, MS, PhD

Graduate Fields of Veterinary Medicine
Dr. Donald F. Smith, Dean
Programs in:
anatomy • MS, PhD
behavioral physiology • MS, PhD
cancer biology • MS, PhD
cardiovascular and respiratory physiology • MS, PhD
cellular immunology • MS, PhD
clinical sciences • MS, PhD
endocrinology • MS, PhD
environmental and comparative physiology • MS, PhD
gastrointestinal and metabolic physiology • MS, PhD
immunochemistry • MS, PhD
immunogenetics • MS, PhD
immunopathology • MS, PhD
infection and immunity • MS, PhD
infectious diseases • MS, PhD
membrane and epithelial physiology • MS, PhD
molecular and cellular physiology • MS, PhD
neural and sensory physiology • MS, PhD

Cornell University (continued)
  pathology • MS, PhD
  pharmacology • MS, PhD
  reproductive physiology • MS, PhD
  veterinary physiology • MS, PhD
  virology • MS, PhD

Graduate School of Medical Sciences

Dr. David P. Hajjar, Dean
Programs in:
  biochemistry and structural biology • PhD
  cell biology and genetics • PhD
  clinical epidemiology and health services research • MS
  immunology • MS, PhD
  microbiology • MS, PhD
  molecular biology • MS, PhD
  molecular medicine • PhD
  neuroscience • PhD
  pathology • MS, PhD
  pharmacology • PhD
  physiology and biophysics • PhD

Professional Field of the Johnson Graduate School of Management

Alan G. Merten, Dean
Program in:
  management • MBA

Professional Field of the Law School

Russell K. Osgood, Dean
Program in:
  law • JD, LL M

Professional School of Veterinary Medicine

Donald F. Smith, Dean
Program in:
  veterinary medicine • DVM

DOWLING COLLEGE
Oakdale, NY 11769-1999

http://www.dowling.edu/

Independent coed comprehensive institution. *Enrollment:* 5,998 graduate, professional, and undergraduate students. Graduate faculty: *177.* General application contact: *Kate Rowe, Director of Admissions, 516-244-3030.*

Graduate Programs in Education

Dr. Kathryn Padovano, Dean
Programs in:
  computers in education • PD
  elementary education • MS Ed
  reading • MS Ed
  reading/special education • MS Ed
  school administration and supervision • PD
  school district administration • PD

  secondary education • MS Ed
  special education • MS Ed

School of Business

Dr. Anthony F. Libertella, Interim Dean
Programs in:
  aviation management • Certificate, MBA
  banking and finance • Certificate, MBA
  general management • MBA
  public management • Certificate, MBA
  total quality management • Certificate, MBA

 # D'YOUVILLE COLLEGE
Buffalo, NY 14201-1084

http://www.dyc.edu/

Independent coed comprehensive institution. *Enrollment:* 1,870 graduate, professional, and undergraduate students. Graduate faculty: *88 full-time, 73 part-time.* Computer facilities: *Campuswide network is available with full Internet access. Total number of PCs/terminals supplied for student use: 100. Computer service fees are applied as a separate charge.* Library facilities: *Library Resources Center.* Graduate expenses: *Tuition of $357 per credit hour. Fees of $350 per year.* General application contact: *Joseph Syracuse, Graduate Admissions Director, 716-881-7676.*

Division of Business

Dr. Jayanti Sen, Interim Director
Programs in:
  health services administration • MS
  international business • MS

Division of Education

Dr. Robert DiSibio, Graduate Director
Programs in:
  elementary education • MS Ed
  secondary education • MS Ed
  special education • MS Ed

Division of Nursing

Dr. Carol Gutt, Chairperson
Programs in:
  nurse practitioner • MS
  nursing • MSN

Division of Physical Therapy

Dr. Penelope Klein, Chair
Program in:
  physical therapy • MS

ELMIRA COLLEGE
Elmira, NY 14901

http://www.elmira.edu/

Independent coed comprehensive institution. *Enrollment: 2,141 graduate, professional, and undergraduate students. Graduate faculty: 20 full-time, 31 part-time. Library facilities: Gannett-Tripp Library. Graduate expenses: $344 per credit hour. General application contact: Judith B. Clack, Associate Dean for Graduate Studies, 607-735-1825.*

Graduate Programs in Education
Dr. Ronald Sundberg, Dean of Continuing Education
Programs in:
  adult education • MS Ed
  elementary education • MS Ed
  general education • MS Ed
  reading • MS Ed
  secondary education • MS Ed

FORDHAM UNIVERSITY
New York, NY 10458

http://www.fordham.edu/

Independent-religious coed university. *Enrollment: 13,668 graduate, professional, and undergraduate students. Graduate faculty: 370 full-time, 470 part-time. Computer facilities: Campuswide network is available with full Internet access. Total number of PCs/ terminals supplied for student use: 400. Computer services are offered at no charge. Library facilities: The William D. Walsh Family Library plus 4 additional on-campus libraries. Graduate expenses: Tuition of $560 per credit. Fees of $200 per year. General application contact: Dr. Craig W. Pilant, Assistant Dean, 718-817-4420.*

Graduate School of Arts and Sciences
Dr. Robert F. Himmelberg, Dean
Programs in:
  American • MA
  American politics • MA, PhD
  biblical studies • MA, PhD
  biological sciences • MS, PhD
  cell and molecular biology • MS, PhD
  classical Greek and Latin literature • MA
  classical Greek literature • MA
  classical Latin literature • MA
  classical philology • PhD
  clinical psychology • PhD
  comparative politics • MA
  computer science • MS
  demography • MA, PhD
  developmental psychology • PhD
  early modern Europe • PhD
  ecology • MS, PhD
  economic development • MA, PhD
  economics • MA, PhD
  economics of public policy • MA, PhD
  ethnic minorities • MA, PhD
  financial economics • MA, PhD
  historical theology • MA, PhD
  history • MA, PhD
  industrial organization • MA, PhD
  international economics • MA, PhD
  international political economy and development • CIF, MA
  international politics • MA
  liberal studies • MA
  medieval Europe • MA, PhD
  medieval Latin • PhD
  medieval studies • MA
  modern Europe • MA
  monetary economics • MA, PhD
  philosophical resources • MA
  philosophy • MA, PhD
  political philosophy • MA, PhD
  political science • MA, PhD
  psychometrics • PhD
  public communications • MA
  sociology • MA, PhD
  sociology of religions • MA, PhD
  systematics • MA, PhD

Graduate School of Business Administration
Dr. Ernest J. Scalberg, Dean
Programs in:
  accounting • GPMBA, MBA
  business administration • TMBA
  communications and media management • GPMBA, MBA
  finance • GPMBA, MBA
  information and communication systems • GPMBA, MBA
  management • MBA
  management systems • GPMBA
  marketing • GPMBA, MBA
  taxation • MS
  total quality management • Certificate

Graduate School of Education
Dr. Regis Bernhardt, Dean
Programs in:
  administration and supervision • Adv C, MSE
  administration and supervision for church leaders • PhD
  adult education • MS, MSE
  bilingual teacher education • MSE
  counseling and personnel services • Adv C, MSE
  counseling psychology • PhD
  curriculum and teaching • MSE
  early childhood education • MSE
  educational administration and supervision • Ed D, PhD
  educational psychology • MSE, PhD
  elementary education • MST
  human resource program administration • MS
  language, literacy, and learning • PhD
  reading education • Adv C, MSE
  school psychology • PhD
  secondary education • MAT, MSE
  special education • Adv C, MSE

Fordham University (continued)
teaching English as a second language • MSE
urban and urban bilingual school psychology • Adv C

Graduate School of Religion and Religious Education
Rev. Vincent M. Novak, SJ, Dean
Program in:
religion and religious education • MA, MS, PD

Graduate School of Social Service
Dr. Mary Ann Quaranta, Dean
Program in:
social service • MSW, PhD

School of Law
John Feerick, Dean
Programs in:
banking, corporate and finance law • LL M
international business and trade law • LL M
law • JD

GRADUATE SCHOOL AND UNIVERSITY CENTER OF THE CITY UNIVERSITY OF NEW YORK
New York, NY 10036-8099

http://www.gc.cuny.edu/

Public coed graduate-only institution. *Enrollment: 3,541 matriculated graduate/professional students.* Graduate faculty: *1,471 full-time.* Library facilities: *Mina Rees Library.* Graduate expenses: *Tuition of $4350 per year full-time, $185 per credit (minimum) part-time for state residents; $7600 per year full-time, $320 per credit (minimum) part-time for nonresidents. Fees of $69 per year.* General application contact: *Les Gribben, Director of Admissions, 212-642-2812.*

Graduate Studies
Dr. Geoffrey Marshall, Provost and Senior Vice President for Academic Affairs
Programs in:
accounting • PhD
anthropological linguistics • PhD
archaeology • PhD
architecture • PhD
basic applied neurocognition • PhD
behavioral science • PhD
biochemistry • PhD
biology • PhD
biomedical science • PhD
biopsychology • PhD
chemical engineering • PhD
chemistry • PhD
civil engineering • PhD
classical studies • MA, PhD

classics • PhD
clinical psychology • PhD
comparative literature • MA, PhD
computer science • PhD
criminal justice • PhD
cultural anthropology • PhD
developmental psychology • PhD
earth and environmental sciences • PhD
economics • PhD
educational psychology • PhD
electrical engineering • PhD
English • PhD
environmental psychology • PhD
experimental psychology • PhD
finance • PhD
French • PhD
German • PhD
Germanic languages and literatures • MA, PhD
graphic arts • PhD
history • PhD
industrial psychology • PhD
Italian • PhD
language in social context • PhD
learning processes • PhD
liberal studies • MA
linguistics • MA, PhD
management planning systems • PhD
mathematics • PhD
mechanical engineering • PhD
medieval studies • PhD
music • DMA, PhD
neuropsychology • PhD
painting • PhD
philosophy • MA, PhD
photography • PhD
physical anthropology • PhD
physics • PhD
political science • MA, PhD
psychology • PhD
public policy • MA, PhD
sculpture • PhD
social personality • PhD
social welfare • DSW
sociology • PhD
Spanish • PhD
speech and hearing sciences • PhD
theatre • PhD
urban studies • MA, PhD
women's studies • MA, PhD

HOFSTRA UNIVERSITY
Hempstead, NY 11549

http://www.hofstra.edu/

Independent coed university. *Enrollment: 12,591 graduate, professional, and undergraduate students.* Graduate faculty: *187 full-time, 135 part-time.* Computer facilities: *Campuswide network is available with full Internet access. Total number of PCs/terminals supplied for student use: 350. Computer services are offered at no charge.* Library facilities: *Axinn Library plus 1 additional on-campus*

library. Graduate expenses: Tuition of $10,968 per year full-time, $457 per credit hour part-time. Fees of $670 per year full-time, $112 per semester (minimum) part-time. General application contact: Mary Beth Carey, Dean of Admissions, 516-463-6700.

College of Liberal Arts and Sciences
Dr. Bernard J. Firestone, Interim Dean

Division of Humanities
Dr. Bernard J. Firestone, Interim Dean, College of Liberal Arts and Sciences
Programs in:
    applied linguistics • MA
    audiology • MA
    bilingualism • MA
    comparative literature and languages • MA
    English • MA
    humanities • MA
    speech-language pathology • MA

Division of Natural Sciences, Mathematics, Engineering, and Computer Science
Dr. Bernard J. Firestone, Interim Dean, College of Liberal Arts and Sciences
Programs in:
    applied mathematics • MA, MS
    biology • MA
    computer science • MA, MS
    human cytogenetics • MS

Division of Social Sciences
Dr. Bernard J. Firestone, Interim Dean, College of Liberal Arts and Sciences
Programs in:
    clinical and school psychology • MA, PhD
    industrial/organizational psychology • MA
    school-community psychology • MA, MS, Psy D

Frank G. Zarb School of Business
Dr. Ralph Polimeni, Dean of Academics
Programs in:
    accounting • MBA
    business • Exec MBA
    business computer information systems/quantitative methods • MBA
    finance and banking • MBA
    international business • MBA
    management • MBA
    marketing • MBA
    taxation • MBA

New College
David C. Christman, Dean
Program in:
    interdisciplinary studies • MA

School of Education and Allied Human Services
James Johnson, Dean
Programs in:
    art education • MA, MS Ed
    art therapy • MA
    art therapy and special education • MA

    bilingual education • MS Ed
    consultation in special education • CAS
    counseling • CAS, MS Ed, PD
    early childhood education • MA
    early childhood special education • CAS, MS Ed
    educational administration • CAS, Ed D, MS Ed, PD
    elementary education • MA, MS Ed
    emotional disturbance • MS Ed
    foundations of education • CAS, MS Ed
    gerontology • MS
    health administration • MA
    health education • MS Ed
    learning disability • MS Ed
    marriage and family therapy • CAS, MA, PD
    mathematics, science, and technology in elementary education • MA
    mental retardation • MS Ed
    music education • MA, MS Ed
    physical disability • MS Ed
    physical education • MS
    program evaluation • MS Ed
    reading • CAS, Ed D, MA, MS Ed, PD, PhD
    rehabilitation counseling • MS Ed
    secondary education • MA, MS Ed
    special education • MA, MPS, PD
    special education and reading • PD
    special education assessment and diagnosis • CAS
    teaching English as a second language • MS Ed
    teaching of writing • CAS, MA

School of Law
Dr. Stuart Rabinowitz, Dean
Program in:
    law • JD

HUNTER COLLEGE OF THE CITY UNIVERSITY OF NEW YORK
New York, NY 10021-5085

http://www.hunter.cuny.edu/

Public coed comprehensive institution. Enrollment: 19,689 graduate, professional, and undergraduate students. Graduate faculty: 644 full-time, 679 part-time. Library facilities: Jacqueline Grennan Wexler Library plus 2 additional on-campus libraries. Graduate expenses: Tuition of $4350 per year full-time, $185 per credit part-time for state residents; $7600 per year full-time, $320 per credit part-time for nonresidents. Fees of $26 per year. General application contact: William Slata, Director of Admissions, 212-772-4490.

Hunter College of the City University of New York (continued)

Graduate School
William Zlata, Director of Admissions

Division of Education
William Zlata, Director of Admissions, Graduate School
Programs in:
   bilingual education • MS
   biology and general science education • MA
   corrective reading (K–12) • MS Ed
   early childhood education • MS Ed
   educational supervision and administration • AC
   elementary education • MS
   English education • MA
   French education • MA
   guidance and counseling • MS Ed
   Italian education • MA
   mathematics education • MA
   music education • MA
   rehabilitation counseling • MS Ed
   social studies education • MA
   Spanish education • MA
   special education • MS Ed
   teaching English as a second language • MA

Division of Humanities and the Arts
William Zlata, Director of Admissions, Graduate School
Programs in:
   art history • MA
   communications and mass culture • MA
   composition • MA
   English and American literature • MA
   English education • MA
   ethnomusicology • MA
   fine arts • MFA
   French • MA
   French education • MA
   Italian • MA
   Italian education • MA
   music education • MA
   music history • MA
   music performance • MA
   Spanish • MA
   Spanish education • MA
   teaching Latin • MA
   theater • MA

Division of Sciences and Mathematics
William Zlata, Director of Admissions, Graduate School
Programs in:
   analytical geography • MA
   applied mathematics • MA
   biochemistry • MA
   biological sciences • MA, PhD
   computer science • MA, PhD
   physics • MA, PhD
   pure mathematics • MA

Division of Social Sciences
William Zlata, Director of Admissions, Graduate School
Programs in:
   anthropology • MA
   applied social-organizational psychology • MA
   biopsychology and comparative psychology • MA

   developmental psychology • MA
   economics • MA
   experimental and physiological psychology • MA
   history • MA
   personality and clinical psychology • MA
   Russian area studies • MA
   social research • MS
   urban affairs • MS
   urban planning • MUP

Hunter-Bellevue School of Nursing
Dr. Evelynn Gioiella, Dean
Programs in:
   adult nurse practitioner • MS
   community health nursing • MS
   gerontological nurse practitioner • MS
   maternal child-health nursing • MS
   medical/surgical nursing • MS
   nursing administration • MS
   pediatric nurse practitioner • AC, MS
   psychiatric nursing • MS

School of Health Sciences
Dr. Lynne W. Clark, Director
Programs in:
   audiology • MS
   community health education • MPH
   environmental and occupational health sciences • MS
   nutrition • MS
   speech language pathology • MS
   teacher of speech and hearing handicapped • MS

School of Social Work
Bogart R. Leashore, Dean
Program in:
   social work • DSW, MSW

IONA COLLEGE
New Rochelle, NY 10801-1890
http://www.iona.edu/

Independent coed comprehensive institution. *Enrollment: 4,897 graduate, professional, and undergraduate students. Graduate faculty: 66 full-time, 44 part-time. Computer facilities: Campuswide network is available with full Internet access. Computer service fees are included with tuition and fees. Library facilities: Ryan Library. Graduate expenses: Tuition of $455 per credit hour. Fees of $25 per semester. General application contact: John Braunstein, Vice Provost, 914-633-2461.*

School of Arts and Science
Brian Fernandes, Assistant Dean for Graduate Programs
Programs in:
   biology education • MS Ed, MST
   business education • MST
   communication arts • CAS
   computer science • MS
   criminal justice • MS
   educational computing • Certificate, MS

elementary education • MST
elementary school science • MS Ed
English • MA
English education • MS Ed, MST
family counseling • Certificate, MS
health service administration • Certificate, MS
history • MA
journalism • MS
mathematics education • MS Ed, MST
multicultural education • MS Ed
organizational communication • MS
pastoral counseling • MS
psychology • MA
public relations • MS
school administration and supervision • MS Ed
school district administration • Diploma
social studies education • MS Ed, MST
Spanish • MA
Spanish education • MS Ed, MST
telecommunications • Certificate, MS

Hagan Graduate School of Business

Dr. Nicholas J. Beutell, Dean
Programs in:
  accounting • MBA
  financial management • MBA, PMC
  human resource management • MBA, PMC
  international business • MBA, PMC
  management • MBA, PMC
  management information systems • MBA, PMC
  management science • MBA, PMC
  marketing • MBA, PMC
  production and operations management • MBA, PMC

ITHACA COLLEGE
Ithaca, NY 14850-7020

http://www.ithaca.edu/

Independent coed comprehensive institution. *Enrollment: 5,897 graduate, professional, and undergraduate students. Graduate faculty: 81 full-time, 5 part-time. Computer facilities: Campuswide network is available with full Internet access. Total number of PCs/ terminals supplied for student use: 400. Computer service fees are included with tuition and fees. Library facilities: main library. Graduate expenses: $552 per credit hour. General application contact: Dr. Garry Brodhead, Assistant Provost and Dean of Graduate Studies, 607-274-3527.*

Graduate Studies

Dr. Garry Brodhead, Assistant Provost and Dean

Roy H. Park School of Communications

Dr. Thomas W. Bohn, Dean
Program in:
  communications • MS

School of Health Sciences and Human Performance

Dr. Richard Miller, Dean
Programs in:
  audiology • MS
  exercise and sport sciences • MS
  occupational therapy • MS
  physical therapy • MS
  speech pathology • MS
  teacher of the speech and hearing handicapped • MS

School of Music

Dr. Arthur Ostrander, Dean
Programs in:
  composition • MM
  conducting • MM
  music education • MM, MS
  music theory • MM
  performance • MM
  strings, woodwinds, or brasses • MM
  Suzuki pedagogy • MM

LEHMAN COLLEGE OF THE CITY UNIVERSITY OF NEW YORK
Bronx, NY 10468-1589

http://www.lehman.cuny.edu/

Public coed comprehensive institution. *Enrollment: 10,352 graduate, professional, and undergraduate students. Graduate faculty: 110 full-time, 36 part-time. Computer facilities: Campuswide network is available. Total number of PCs/terminals supplied for student use: 400. Computer service fees are included with tuition and fees. Library facilities: main library. Graduate expenses: Tuition of $4350 per year full-time, $185 per credit part-time for state residents; $7600 per year full-time, $320 per credit part-time for nonresidents. Fees of $120 per year full-time, $80 per year part-time. General application contact: Clarence Wilkes, Director of Admissions, 718-960-8706.*

Division of Arts and Humanities

Marlene Gottlieb, Acting Dean
Programs in:
  art • MA, MFA
  English • MA
  history • MA
  music • MAT
  Spanish • MA
  speech-language pathology and audiology • MA

Division of Education

James V. Bruni, Dean
Programs in:
  bilingual special education • MS Ed
  business education • MS Ed
  early childhood education • MS Ed
  early special education • MS Ed
  elementary education • MS Ed
  emotional handicaps • MS Ed

Lehman College of the City University of New York (continued)
  English education • MS Ed
  guidance and counseling • MS Ed
  learning disabilities • MS Ed
  mathematics 7–12 • MS Ed
  mental retardation • MS Ed
  reading teacher • MS Ed
  science education • MS Ed
  social studies 7–12 • MA
  teaching English to speakers of other languages • MS Ed

Division of Natural and Social Sciences
Joseph Rachlin, Dean
Programs in:
  accounting • MS
  adult health nursing • MS
  approved preprofessional practice • MS
  biology • MA
  clinical nutrition • MS
  community nutrition • MS
  computer science • MS
  health education and promotion • MA
  health N–12 teacher • MS Ed
  mathematics • MA
  nursing of old adults • MS
  parent-child nursing • MS
  pediatric nurse practitioner • MS
  plant sciences • PhD
  recreation education • MA, MS Ed

LONG ISLAND UNIVERSITY, BROOKLYN CAMPUS
Brooklyn, NY 11201-8423
http://www.brooklyn.liunet.edu/cwis/bklyn/bklyn.html

Independent coed comprehensive institution. *Enrollment:* 8,044 graduate, professional, and undergraduate students. Computer facilities: *Campuswide network is available with full Internet access. Total number of PCs/terminals supplied for student use: 400. Computer service fees are included with tuition and fees.* Library facilities: *Salena Library Learning Center.* Graduate expenses: *Tuition of $480 per credit. Fees of $415 per year full-time, $73 per semester (minimum) part-time.* General application contact: *Bernard W. Sullivan, Associate Director of Admissions, 718-488-1011.*

Arnold and Marie Schwartz College of Pharmacy and Health Sciences
Dr. Stephen M. Gross, Dean
Programs in:
  cosmetic science • MS
  drug information and communication • MS
  drug regulatory affairs • MS
  hospital pharmacy administration • MS
  industrial pharmacy • MS
  pharmaceutical and health care marketing administration • MS
  pharmaceutics • PhD
  pharmacology/toxicology • MS
  pharmacotherapeutics • MS
  pharmacy • Pharm D

Richard L. Conolly College of Liberal Arts and Sciences
Dr. David Cohen, Dean
Programs in:
  biology • MS
  chemistry • MS
  clinical psychology • PhD
  economics • MA
  English literature • MA
  history • MS
  political science • MA
  professional and creative writing • MA
  psychology • MA
  sociology • MA
  speech-language pathology • MA
  teaching of writing • MA
  United Nations studies • Certificate
  urban studies • MA

School of Business and Public Administration
Harry Stucke, Acting Dean
Programs in:
  accounting • MS
  business administration • MBA
  computer science • MS
  public administration • MPA
  taxation • MS

School of Education
Dr. Ofelia Garcia, Dean
Programs in:
  alcoholism counseling • Certificate
  bilingual education • MS Ed
  computers in education • MS
  counseling and development • MS Ed
  educational leadership • PD
  elementary education • MS Ed
  family counseling • MS
  gerontological counseling • Certificate
  mathematics education • MS Ed
  reading • MS Ed
  school psychology • MS Ed
  special education • MS Ed
  teaching English to speakers of other languages • MS Ed

School of Health Professions
Dr. Stephen M. Gross, Dean
Programs in:
  adapted physical education • MS
  athletic training and sports sciences • MS
  community mental health • MS
  exercise physiology • MS
  family health • MS
  health management • MS
  health sciences • MS
  physical therapy • MS

School of Nursing
Dr. Esther Siegel, Dean
Program in:
 adult nurse practitioner • MS

LONG ISLAND UNIVERSITY, C.W. POST CAMPUS
Brookville, NY 11548-1300

http://www.liu.edu/

Independent coed comprehensive institution. *Enrollment:* 8,171 graduate, professional, and undergraduate students. *Graduate faculty:* 215 full-time, 170 part-time. *Computer facilities: Campuswide network is available with full Internet access. Total number of PCs/ terminals supplied for student use: 400. Computer services are offered at no charge. Library facilities: B. Davis Schwartz Memorial Library. Graduate expenses: Tuition of $480 per credit. Fees of $316 per year full-time, $71 per semester (minimum) part-time. General application contact: Sally Luzader, Associate Director of Graduate Admissions, 516-299-2417.*

College of Liberal Arts and Sciences
Dr. Paul Sherwin, Dean
Programs in:
 applied mathematics • MS
 biology • MS
 classical mathematics • MS
 clinical psychology • Psy D
 computer mathematics • MS
 computer science education • MS
 English and American literature • MA
 environmental management • MS
 environmental science • MS
 general experimental psychology • MA
 history • MA
 information systems • MS
 interdisciplinary studies • MA, MS
 management engineering • MS
 mathematics for secondary school teachers • MS
 political science/international studies • MA
 Spanish • MA

College of Management
Dr. Robert J. Sanator, Dean

School of Business
Mary K. Dillon, Coordinator
Programs in:
 business administration • MBA
 finance • CAS, MBA
 human resource management • MBA
 international business • MBA
 management information systems • MBA
 marketing • MBA

School of Professional Accountancy
Dr. Philip H. Siegel, Director
Programs in:
 accounting • MS
 accounting/taxation • CAS
 strategic management accounting • MS
 taxation • MS

School of Public Service
Dr. Carl Figliola, Chair
Programs in:
 criminal justice • MS
 gerontology • CG
 health administration • MPA
 health administration/gerontology • MPA
 health systems finance • Certificate, MPA
 public administration • MPA

Palmer School of Library and Information Science
Anne Woodsworth, Dean
Programs in:
 archives • Certificate
 information studies • PhD
 library and information science • MS
 records management • Certificate

School of Education
Dr. Jeffrey Kane, Dean
Programs in:
 art education • MS
 bilingual education • MS
 biology education • MS
 college student development counseling • MS
 computers in education • CAS, MS
 earth science • MS
 educational administration • PD
 elementary education • MS Ed
 English education • MS
 history education • MS
 mathematics education • MS
 mental health counseling • MS
 middle school education • MS
 music education • MS
 reading • MS
 school administration and supervision • MS
 school business administration • PD
 school counseling • MS
 secondary education • MS
 Spanish education • MS
 special education • MS
 speech-language pathology • MA
 teaching English as a second language • MS

School of Health Professions
Stephen Gross, Dean
Programs in:
 advanced practical nursing • MS
 clinical laboratory management • MS
 dietetic internship • Certificate
 family nurse practitioner • Certificate, MS
 hematology • MS
 immunology • MS

Long Island University, C.W. Post Campus (continued)
    medical chemistry • MS
    microbiology • MS
    nutrition • MS

School of Visual and Performing Arts
Lynn Croton, Dean
Programs in:
    art • MA
    art education • MS
    clinical art therapy • MA
    fine arts • MFA
    music • MA
    music education • MS
    theatre • MA

LONG ISLAND UNIVERSITY, SOUTHAMPTON COLLEGE
Southampton, NY 11968-9822

http://www.southampton.liunet.edu/sc_framo.htm

Independent coed comprehensive institution. *Enrollment:* 1,288 graduate, professional, and undergraduate students. Graduate faculty: *14 full-time, 19 part-time.* Computer facilities: *Campuswide network is available with full Internet access. Computer service fees are included with tuition and fees.* General application contact: *Dr. R. Lawrence McCann, Director, Education Division, 516-287-8211 Ext. 211.*

Education Division
Dr. R. Lawrence McCann, Director
Programs in:
    elementary education • MS Ed
    reading • MS Ed

Humanities Division
Dr. Robert Pattison, Director
Program in:
    English and writing • MFA

MANHATTAN COLLEGE
Riverdale, NY 10471

http://www.manhattan.edu/

Independent-religious coed comprehensive institution. *Enrollment:* 3,038 graduate, professional, and undergraduate students. Graduate faculty: *62 full-time, 29 part-time.* Library facilities: *Cardinal Hayes Library plus 1 additional on-campus library.* Graduate expenses: *Tuition of $385 per credit. Fees of $100 per year.* General application contact: *Dr. Weldon Jackson, Provost, 718-862-7303.*

Graduate Division
Dr. Weldon Jackson, Provost
Programs in:
    accounting • MBA
    finance • MBA
    international business • MBA
    management • MBA
    management information systems • MBA
    marketing • MBA

Leo School of Engineering
Dr. John D. Patterson, Dean
Programs in:
    biotechnology • MS
    chemical engineering • MS
    civil engineering • MS
    computer engineering • MS
    electrical engineering • MS
    environmental engineering • ME, MS
    mechanical engineering • MS

School of Education
Dr. Elizabeth Kosky, Director, Graduate Education Programs
Programs in:
    administration and supervision • Diploma, MS Ed
    counseling • Diploma, MA
    special education • Diploma, MS Ed

MANNES COLLEGE OF MUSIC, NEW SCHOOL UNIVERSITY
New York, NY 10024-4402

http://www.newschool.edu/academic/mannes.htm

Independent coed comprehensive institution. *Enrollment:* 281 graduate, professional, and undergraduate students. Graduate faculty: *15 full-time, 145 part-time.* Library facilities: *Harry Scherman Library.* Graduate expenses: *Tuition of $16,600 per year. Fees of $200 per year (minimum).* General application contact: *Lisa Crissman Wright, Director of Admissions, 212-580-0210.*

Graduate Program
Joel Lester, Dean
Program in:
    music • Certificate, MM

MARIST COLLEGE
Poughkeepsie, NY 12601-1387

http://www.marist.edu/

Independent coed comprehensive institution. *Enrollment:* 4,618 graduate, professional, and undergraduate students. Graduate faculty: *32 full-time, 23 part-time.* Computer facilities: *Campuswide network is available with full Internet access. Total number of PCs/terminals supplied for student use: 258. Computer services are*

offered at no charge. Library facilities: *main library.* Graduate expenses: *Tuition of $419 per credit hour. Fees of $50 per year (minimum).* General application contact: *Dr. H. Griffin Walling, Dean of Graduate and Continuing Education, 914-575-3530.*

Graduate Programs

Dr. Artin Arslanian, Academic Vice President
Programs in:
  business administration • MBA, PGC
  computer science • MS
  counseling/community psychology • MA
  education psychology • MA
  information systems • MS
  public administration • Certificate, MPA
  school psychology • Adv C, MA
  software development • MS

MOUNT SAINT MARY COLLEGE
Newburgh, NY 12550-3494

http://www.msmc.edu/

Independent coed comprehensive institution. *Enrollment: 1,975* graduate, professional, and undergraduate students. Graduate faculty: *19 full-time, 21 part-time.* Library facilities: *Curtin Memorial Library.* Graduate expenses: *Tuition of $367 per credit. Fees of $30 per year.* General application contact: *Graduate Coordinator, 914-561-0800.*

Division of Business

Dr. Mattson Atsunyo, Coordinator
Program in:
  business • MBA

Division of Education

Dr. Lucy DiPaola, Chairperson
Programs in:
  elementary education • MS Ed
  elementary/special education • MS Ed
  secondary education • MS Ed
  special education • MS Ed

Division of Nursing

Sr. Leona DeBoer, Coordinator
Programs in:
  adult nurse practitioner • MS
  clinical nurse specialist-adult health • MS
  nursing education • MS
  nursing management • MS

NAZARETH COLLEGE OF ROCHESTER
Rochester, NY 14618-3790

http://www.naz.edu/

Independent coed comprehensive institution. *Enrollment: 2,760* graduate, professional, and undergraduate students. Graduate faculty: *40 full-time, 77 part-time.* Computer facilities: *Campuswide network is available with full Internet access. Total number of PCs/ terminals supplied for student use: 50. Computer service fees are included with tuition and fees.* Library facilities: *Lorette Wilmont Library plus 1 additional on-campus library.* Graduate expenses: *Tuition of $436 per credit hour. Fees of $20 per semester.* General application contact: *Dr. Kay F. Marshman, Dean of Graduate Studies, 716-389-2815.*

Graduate Studies

Dr. Kay F. Marshman, Dean
Programs in:
  art education • MS Ed
  art therapy • MS
  business education • MS Ed
  computer education • MS Ed
  early childhood education • MS Ed
  elementary education • MS Ed
  general secondary education • MS Ed
  gerontological nurse practitioner • MS
  management • MS
  music education • MS Ed
  reading • MS Ed
  special education • MS Ed
  speech pathology • MS
  teaching English to speakers of other languages • MS Ed

NEW SCHOOL UNIVERSITY
New York, NY 10011-8603

http://www.newschool.edu/

Independent coed university. *Enrollment: 6,528* graduate, professional, and undergraduate students. Graduate faculty: *104 full-time, 390 part-time.* Computer facilities: *Campuswide network is available with full Internet access. Total number of PCs/terminals supplied for student use: 400. Computer service fees are included with tuition and fees.* Library facilities: *Raymond Fogelman Library plus 5 additional on-campus libraries.* Graduate expenses: *$920 per credit.* General application contact: *Dean of the appropriate school, 212-229-5600.*

Adult Division

Dr. Elizabeth Dickey, Dean
Programs in:
  communication theory • MA
  creative writing • MFA
  media studies • MA
  teacher education • MST

New School University (continued)

Graduate Faculty of Political and Social Science
Dr. Judith Friedlander, Dean
Programs in:
    anthropology • DS Sc, MA, PhD
    clinical psychology • PhD
    gender studies • MA
    general psychology • MA, PhD
    historical studies • MA, PhD
    liberal studies • MA
    philosophy • DS Sc, MA, PhD
    political science • DS Sc, MA, PhD
    psychoanalytic studies • MS Sc
    sociology • DS Sc, MA, PhD

Parsons School of Design
H. Randolph Swearer, Dean
Programs in:
    architecture • M Arch
    design • MS Ed
    design and technology • MFA
    history of decorative arts • MA
    lighting design • MFA
    painting • MFA
    sculpture • MFA

Robert J. Milano Graduate School of Management and Urban Policy
James A. Krauskopf, Dean
Programs in:
    health services management and policy • MS
    human resources management • MS
    labor relations • Adv C
    management of medical services • Adv C
    materials management • Adv C
    mental health administration • Adv C
    nonprofit management • MS
    organization development • Adv C
    public and urban policy • PhD
    training • Adv C
    urban policy analysis and management • MS

School of Dramatic Arts/Actors Studio
James Lipton, Dean
Programs in:
    acting • MFA
    directing • MFA
    playwriting • MFA

NEW YORK INSTITUTE OF TECHNOLOGY
Old Westbury, NY 11568-8000

http://www.nyit.edu/

Independent coed comprehensive institution. *Enrollment:* 8,982 graduate, professional, and undergraduate students. Graduate faculty: *116 full-time, 493 part-time.* Computer facilities: *Campuswide network is available with full Internet access. Total number of PCs/*

terminals supplied for student use: 550. Computer services are offered at no charge. Library facilities: *Wisser Library plus 2 additional on-campus libraries.* Graduate expenses: *$413 per credit.* General application contact: *Glenn Berman, Executive Director of Admissions, 516-686-7519.*

Graduate Division
Dr. Edward Guiliano, Vice President for Academic Affairs

School of Allied Health and Life Sciences
Stanley Schiowitz, Dean
Programs in:
    clinical nutrition • MS
    human relations • MPS

School of Architecture
Jonathon Friedman, Dean
Program in:
    urban and regional design • M Arch

School of Arts, Sciences, and Communication
Dr. Robert Vogt, Dean
Program in:
    communication arts • MA

School of Education
Dr. Helen Greene, Dean
Programs in:
    elementary education • MS
    instructional technology • Certificate, MS

School of Engineering and Technology
Dr. Heskia Heskiaoff, Dean
Programs in:
    computer science • MS
    electrical engineering • MS
    energy management • MS
    environmental technology • Certificate, MS
    mechanical engineering • MS

School of Management
Dr. J. C. Spender, Dean
Programs in:
    business administration • MBA
    human resources management and labor relations • Certificate, MS

New York College of Osteopathic Medicine
Dr. Stanley Schiowitz, Dean
Program in:
    osteopathic medicine • DO

NEW YORK UNIVERSITY
New York, NY 10012-1019

http://www.nyu.edu/

Independent coed university. *Enrollment:* 36,606 graduate, professional, and undergraduate students. Graduate faculty: *2,381 full-time, 3,128 part-time.* Computer facilities: *Campuswide network is available with full Internet access. Computer service fees are included*

with tuition and fees. Library facilities: Elmer H. Bobst Library plus 6 additional on-campus libraries. Graduate expenses: Tuition of $715 per credit. Fees of $1048 per year full-time, $229 per semester (minimum) part-time. General application contact: New York University Information Center, 212-998-1212.

College of Dentistry
Dr. Edward G. Kaufman, Dean
Programs in:
  dental materials science • MS
  dentistry • DDS
  endodontics • Certificate
  implantology • Certificate
  oral and maxillofacial surgery • Certificate
  orthodontics • Certificate
  pediatric dentistry • Certificate
  periodontics • Certificate
  prosthodontics • Certificate

Gallatin School of Individualized Study
Dr. E. Frances White, Dean
Program in:
  individualized study • MA

Graduate School of Arts and Science
Catharine R. Stimpson, Dean
Programs in:
  Africana studies • MA
  American studies • MA, PhD
  anatomy • MS, PhD
  anthropology • M Phil
  anthropology and French studies • PhD
  applied economic analysis • Adv C
  applied recombinant DNA technology • MS
  archaeological anthropology • MA, PhD
  archival management and historical editing • Certificate
  biochemistry • MS, PhD
  biomedical journalism • MA
  biophysics • PhD
  cell and developmental biology • PhD
  cell biology • PhD
  chemistry • MS, PhD
  cinema studies • MA, PhD
  classics • MA, PhD
  clinical psychology • PhD
  cognition and perception • PhD
  community psychology • PhD
  comparative literature • MA, PhD
  computers in biological research • MS
  creative writing • MFA
  cultural anthropology • MA, PhD
  cultural reporting and criticism • MA
  dental materials science • MS
  early music performance • Certificate
  economics • MA, PhD
  English and American literature • MA, PhD
  environmental biology • PhD
  environmental carcinogenesis • PhD
  ethnomusicology • MA, PhD
  European history • PhD
  French studies and politics • PhD
  French studies and sociology • PhD
  French studies/history • PhD
  French studies/journalism • MA
  general biology • MS
  general psychology • MA
  Germanic languages and literatures • MA, PhD
  Hebrew and Judaic studies • MA, PhD
  Hebrew and Judaic studies/history • PhD
  Hebrew and Judaic studies/museum studies • MA
  histology and cell biology • MS, PhD
  history • MA, PhD
  humanities and social thought • MA
  immunology • PhD
  industrial/organizational psychology • PhD
  international politics and international business • MA
  Italian literature • MA, PhD
  Italian studies • MA
  journalism • MA
  Latin American and Caribbean history • PhD
  Latin American and Carribean studies/journalism • MA
  linguistic anthropology • MA, PhD
  linguistics • MA, PhD
  medical and molecular parasitology • PhD
  microbiology • MS, PhD
  Middle Eastern studies/history • PhD
  molecular biology and biochemistry • PhD
  molecular oncology • PhD
  museum studies • Certificate
  museum studies and Africana studies • MA
  museum studies and Hebrew and Judaic studies • MA
  museum studies and Latin American and Caribbean studies • MA
  museum studies and Middle Eastern studies • MA
  musicology • MA, PhD
  music theory and composition • MA, PhD
  Near Eastern studies/journalism • MA
  Near Eastern studies/politics • PhD
  neural sciences and physiology • PhD
  neuroscience • PhD
  oral biology • MS
  parasitology • PhD
  pathology • PhD
  performance studies • MA, PhD
  personnel psychology • MA
  pharmacology • PhD
  philosophy • MA, PhD
  physical anthropology • MA, PhD
  physics • MS, PhD
  physiology • MS, PhD
  politics • MA, PhD
  population and evolutionary biology • PhD
  Portuguese • PhD
  Portuguese literature • MA
  psychoanalysis • Certificate
  public history • Certificate, MA
  religion • Certificate
  religious studies • MA
  Romance languages and literatures • MA
  Russian literature • MA
  science and environmental reporting • CAS, MA
  Slavic literature • MA
  social/personality psychology • PhD
  social theory • Certificate

New York University (continued)
> sociology • MA, PhD
> Spanish • PhD
> Spanish Peninsular literature • MA
> United States history • PhD
> urban anthropology • MA, PhD
> women's history • MA

Alexander S. Onassis Center for Hellenic Studies
Speros Vryonis Jr., Director
Program in:
> Hellenic studies • MA, PhD

Center for European Studies
Martin Schain, Director
Program in:
> European studies • MA

Center for French Civilization and Culture
Thomas Bishop, Director
Programs in:
> French language and civilization • MA
> French literature • MA, PhD
> French studies • Adv C, MA, PhD
> French studies and anthropology • PhD
> French studies and French • PhD
> French studies and history • PhD
> French studies and journalism • MA
> French studies and politics • PhD
> French studies and sociology • PhD
> French studies/French literature • PhD
> Romance languages and literatures • MA, PhD

Center for Latin American and Caribbean Studies
Christopher Mitchell, Director
Programs in:
> Latin American and Caribbean studies • MA
> Latin American and Caribbean studies/journalism • MA
> Latin American and Caribbean studies/museum studies
>   • MA

Center for Neural Science
Anthony Movshon, Chairman
Program in:
> neural science • PhD

Courant Institute of Mathematical Sciences
Catharine R. Stimpson, Dean, Graduate School of Arts and
>   Science
Programs in:
> applied science • MS, PhD
> computer science • MS, PhD
> information systems • MS
> mathematics • MS, PhD
> mathematics and statistics/operations research • MS
> mathematics in finance • MS
> scientific computing • MS

Hagop Kevorkian Center for Near Eastern Studies
Timothy Mitchell, Director
Programs in:
> Middle Eastern studies • MA, PhD
> Middle Eastern studies/history • PhD
> Near Eastern studies • MA
> Near Eastern studies/journalism • MA
> Near Eastern studies/museum studies • MA

Institute for Law and Society
Paul Chevigny, Director
Program in:
> law and society • PhD

Institute of Fine Arts
James McCredie, Chair
Programs in:
> classical art and archaeology • PhD
> conservation • Diploma
> curatorial studies • PhD
> history of art • PhD
> history of art and archaeology • MA
> Near Eastern art and archaeology • PhD

Nelson Institute of Environmental Medicine
Dr. Max Costa, Director
Programs in:
> aquatic toxicology • PhD
> environmental biology • PhD
> environmental carcinogenesis • PhD
> environmental epidemiology and biostatistics • PhD
> environmental-occupational hygiene • MS
> environmental radiation • PhD
> ergonomics and biomechanics • PhD
> molecular toxicology • PhD
> occupational-environmental hygiene • PhD
> systemic toxicology • PhD
> toxicology • MS

Leonard N. Stern School of Business
George G. Daly, Dean
Programs in:
> accounting • APC, MBA, PhD
> economics • APC, MBA, PhD
> finance • APC, MBA, PhD
> information systems • APC, MBA, MS, PhD
> international business • APC, MBA, PhD
> management • APC, MBA, PhD
> marketing • APC, MBA, PhD
> operations management • MBA
> statistics and operations research • APC, MBA, MS, PhD
> taxation • APC, MBA, PhD

Robert F. Wagner Graduate School of Public Service
Dr. Jo Ivey Boufford, Dean
Programs in:
> developmental administration • APC, MPA
> financial management • APC, MPA
> financial management and public finance • APC, MPA
> health policy analysis • APC, MPA
> health policy and management • AMPC, MS, PhD
> health services management • APC, MPA
> housing • APC
> human resources management • APC, MPA
> international administration • APC, MPA
> management for public and nonprofit organizations •
>   APC, MPA
> public administration • MS, PhD
> public economics • APC
> public policy analysis • APC, MPA
> quantitative analysis and computer applications • APC

urban planning • MUP
urban policy analysis • MPA
urban public policy • APC

School of Continuing Education

Gerald A. Heeger, Dean
Program in:
information systems auditing • APC

Center for Direct Marketing

Pierre Passavant, Director
Program in:
direct marketing communications • MS

Center for Hospitality, Tourism and Travel Administration

Dr. Lalia Rich, Associate Dean
Programs in:
hospitality industries studies • MS
tourism and travel management • MS

Center for Publishing

Robert Baensch, Director
Program in:
publishing • MS

Real Estate Institute

Dr. Arthur Margon, Director
Program in:
real estate • MS

The Virtual College

Richard Vigilante, Senior Director, Information
Technologies Institute
Programs in:
information technology • APC
management control and systems • MS

School of Education

Dr. Ann Marcus, Dean
Programs in:
administrators and supervisors of health education •
CAS
alcohol studies • MPH
art education • Ed D, MA, PhD
arts and humanities education • MA, PhD
art therapy • MA
Asian studies • MA
bilingual education • CAS, MA, PhD
bilingual school counseling • MA
bilingual special education • MA
community health education • Ed D, MPH, PhD
costume studies • MA
counseling and guidance • CAS, MA, PhD
counseling psychology • PhD
dance education • Ed D, MA, PhD
deafness rehabilitation • MA
drama therapy • MA
early childhood and elementary education • CAS, Ed D,
MA, PhD
early childhood special education • MA
educational administration and supervision • CAS, Ed D,
MA, PhD
educational communication and technology • CAS,
Ed D, MA, PhD

educational sociology • MA, PhD
educational theatre • CAS, Ed D, MA, PhD
English education • CAS, MA, PhD
environmental art • MA
environmental conservation education • MA
folk art studies • MA
food and food management • PhD
food management • MA
food, nutrition, and dietetics • MS, PhD
food studies • MA
foreign language education • CAS, MA
for-profit sector • MA
general applied psychology • MA
graphic communications management and technology •
Ed D, MA, PhD
higher education • Ed D, PhD
history of education • MA, PhD
human sexuality education • CAS, Ed D, MA, PhD
international community health education • Ed D, MPH,
PhD
international education • MA, PhD
learning disabilities and reading • MA
mathematics education • MA, PhD
measurement and evaluation • MA
media ecology • MA, PhD
music education • CAS, Ed D, MA, PhD
music entertainment professions • MA
music performance and composition • MA, PhD
music technology • MM
music therapy • DA, MA
occupational therapy • MA, PhD
pathokinesiology • MA
pediatrics • MA
performing arts administration • MA
philosophy of education • MA, PhD
physical therapy • DPS, PhD
professional child/school psychology • Psy D
psychological development • PhD
psychological foundations of reading • MA, PhD
psychology of parenthood • MA
public health nutrition • MPH
recreation and leisure studies • CAS, MA, PhD
rehabilitation counseling • MA, PhD
school and college health education • CAS, Ed D, MA,
PhD
school business administration • CAS
school psychologist • CAS
school psychology • PhD
science education • MA
social studies • MA
special education • MA
special education learning consultant • CAS
speech communication • CAS, MA
speech-language pathology and audiology • MA, PhD
student personnel administration in higher education •
MA
studio art • MA, MFA
supervisors of reading • MA
teachers of business subjects in higher education • CAS,
Ed D, MA, PhD
teachers of reading • MA
teaching English to speakers of other languages • CAS,
MA, PhD

New York University (continued)
Division of Nursing
Diane McGivern, Chairperson
Programs in:
    adult nurse practitioner acute care • MA
    adult nurse practitioner primary care • MA
    advanced practice nursing: adult • AC
    advanced practice nursing: elderly • AC, MA
    advanced practice nursing: infants, children, and
        adolescents • AC, MA
    advanced practice nursing: mental health • AC, MA
    delivery of nursing services • MA
    nurse midwifery • AC, MA
    nursing • PhD
    teaching of nursing • MA

School of Law
John Sexton, Dean
Programs in:
    law • JD, JSD, LL M, MCJ, PhD

School of Medicine
Dr. David D. Scotch, Associate Dean
Program in:
    medicine • MD

Sackler Institute of Graduate Biomedical Sciences
Dr. Joel D. Oppenheim, Associate Dean for Graduate
    Studies
Programs in:
    biochemistry • PhD
    biophysics • PhD
    cell biology • PhD
    immunology • PhD
    medical and molecular parasitology • PhD
    microbiology • PhD
    molecular oncology • PhD
    neuroscience • PhD
    pathology • PhD
    pharmacology • PhD
    physiology • PhD

Shirley M. Ehrenkranz School of Social Work
Thomas Meenaghan, Dean
Program in:
    social work • MSW, PhD

Tisch School of the Arts
Mary Schmidt Campbell, Dean
Programs in:
    acting • MFA
    cinema studies • MA, PhD
    dance • MFA
    design • MFA
    dramatic writing • MFA
    film • MFA
    musical theatre writing • MFA
    performance studies • MA, PhD
    telecommunications • MPS

NIAGARA UNIVERSITY
Niagara University, NY 14109

http://www.niagara.edu/

Independent coed comprehensive institution. *Enrollment: 3,079
graduate, professional, and undergraduate students. Graduate
faculty: 27 full-time, 24 part-time. Computer facilities: Campuswide
network is available with full Internet access. Total number of PCs/
terminals supplied for student use: 150. Computer service fees are
included with tuition and fees. Library facilities: main library. Graduate expenses: Tuition of $4950 per year full-time, $275 per credit
hour part-time. Fees of $25 per semester. General application contact:
George Pachter, Dean of Admissions, 716-286-8721.*

Graduate Division of Arts and Sciences
Dr. Edward W. Sieh, Director
Program in:
    criminal justice administration • MS

Graduate Division of Business Administration
Dr. Charles G. Smith, Director
Programs in:
    business • MBA
    commerce • MBA

Graduate Division of Education
Rev. Daniel F. O'Leary, OMI, Dean
Programs in:
    administration and supervision • MS Ed, PD
    biology • MAT
    elementary education • MS Ed
    foundations and teaching • MA, MS Ed
    mental health counseling • MS Ed
    school counseling • MS Ed, PD
    secondary education • MS Ed

Graduate Division of Nursing
Nancy Shaffer, Acting Dean
Program in:
    family nurse practitioner • MS

PACE UNIVERSITY
New York, NY 10038

http://www.pace.edu/newhome.html

Independent coed university. *Computer facilities: Campuswide
network is available with full Internet access. Computer services are
offered at no charge. Library facilities: main library plus 3 additional
on-campus libraries. Graduate expenses: Tuition of $520 per credit.
Fees of $360 per year full-time, $53 per semester (minimum) part-
time. General application contact: University Director of Graduate
Admission, 212-346-1531.*

Dyson College of Arts and Sciences
Programs in:
    counseling-substance abuse • MS
    environmental science • MS
    government management • MPA
    health care administration • MPA
    nonprofit management • MPA
    psychology • MA
    publishing • MS
    school-clinical child psychology • Psy D
    school-community psychology • MS Ed, Psy D

Lienhard School of Nursing
Program in:
    nursing • Advanced Certificate, MS

Lubin School of Business
Programs in:
    banking and finance • MBA
    business • APC
    corporate economic planning • MBA
    corporate financial management • MBA
    economics • MS
    financial economics • MBA
    financial management • MBA
    health systems management • MBA
    information systems • MBA
    international business • MBA
    international economics • MBA
    investment management • MBA, MS
    management • MBA
    management science • MBA
    managerial accounting • MBA
    marketing management • MBA
    marketing research • MBA
    operations management • MBA
    professional studies • DPS
    public accounting • MBA, MS
    taxation • MBA, MS

School of Computer Science and Information Systems
Programs in:
    computer communications and networks • Certificate
    computer science • MS
    information systems • MS
    object-oriented programming • Certificate
    telecommunications • Certificate, MS

School of Education
Programs in:
    administration and supervision • MS Ed
    curriculum and instruction • MS
    education • MST
    school business management • Certificate

School of Law
Program in:
    law • JD, LL M, SJD

PLATTSBURGH STATE UNIVERSITY OF NEW YORK
Plattsburgh, NY 12901-2681

http://www.plattsburgh.edu/

Public coed comprehensive institution. *Enrollment: 5,920 graduate, professional, and undergraduate students. Computer facilities: Campuswide network is available with full Internet access. Total number of PCs/terminals supplied for student use: 278. Computer service fees are included with tuition and fees. Library facilities: B. F. Feinberg Library. Graduate expenses: Tuition of $5100 per year full-time, $213 per credit hour part-time for state residents; $8416 per year full-time, $351 per credit hour part-time for nonresidents. Fees of $395 per year full-time, $15.10 per credit hour part-time. General application contact: Richard Higgins, Director of Admissions, 518-564-2040.*

Center for Lifelong Learning
Dr. Janet Worthington, Director
Programs in:
    administration and leadership • MA
    educational studies • MA
    English language and literature • MA
    historical studies • MA
    liberal studies • MA
    natural sciences • MA

Faculty of Arts and Science
Dr. Kathleen Lavoie, Dean
Programs in:
    psychology • MA
    school psychology • CAS

Faculty of Professional Studies
Dr. Virginia Barker, Dean
Programs in:
    college/agency counseling • MS
    community counseling • MS
    school counseling • CAS
    speech-language pathology • MA
    student affairs practice • MS

Center for Educational Studies and Services
Dr. Raymond Domenico, Director and Associate Dean
Programs in:
    biology • MST
    earth sciences • MST
    educational administration • CAS, MS
    elementary education • MS, MST
    English • MS Ed, MST
    French • MST
    mathematics • MST
    physics • MST
    reading • MS
    social studies • MS Ed, MST
    Spanish • MST
    special education • MS

POLYTECHNIC UNIVERSITY, BROOKLYN CAMPUS
Brooklyn, NY 11201-2990

http://www.poly.edu/brooklyn.html

Independent coed university. *Enrollment:* 3,354 graduate, professional, and undergraduate students. Graduate faculty: *178 full-time, 122 part-time.* Computer facilities: *Campuswide network is available with full Internet access. Total number of PCs/terminals supplied for student use: 110. Computer services are offered at no charge. Library facilities: Bern Dibner Library of Science and Technology.* Graduate expenses: *Tuition of $19,530 per year full-time, $675 per credit part-time. Fees of $600 per year full-time, $135 per semester part-time.* General application contact: *John S. Kerge, Dean of Admissions, 718-260-3200.*

Department of Applied Mathematics and Physics
Dr. Eric Grinberg, Head
Programs in:
  mathematics • MS, PhD
  physics • MS, PhD

Department of Chemical Engineering, Chemistry and Materials Science
Dr. Kalle Levon, Head
Programs in:
  chemical engineering • MS, PhD
  chemical physics • PhD
  materials chemistry • PhD
  polymer science and engineering • MS, PhD

Department of Civil and Environmental Engineering
Dr. Ilan Juran, Head
Programs in:
  civil engineering • MS, PhD
  environmental engineering • MS
  environmental health science • MS
  transportation management • MS
  transportation planning and engineering • MS

Department of Computer and Information Science
Dr. Stuart Steele, Head
Programs in:
  computer science • MS, PhD
  information systems engineering • MS

Department of Electrical Engineering
Dr. Zivan Zabar, Head
Programs in:
  electrical engineering • MS, PhD
  electrophysics • MS
  systems engineering • MS
  telecommunication networks • MS

Department of Humanities and Social Sciences
Dr. Richard Wener, Head
Programs in:
  environment behavior studies • MS
  history of science • MS
  specialized journalism • MS

Department of Management
Mel Horwitch, Head
Programs in:
  financial engineering • MS
  management • MS
  management of technology • MS
  operations management • MS
  organizational behavior • MS
  telecommunications and computing management • MS

Department of Mechanical, Aerospace and Manufacturing Engineering
Dr. Sunil Kumar, Head
Programs in:
  aeronautics and astronautics • MS
  industrial engineering • MS
  manufacturing engineering • MS
  mechanical engineering • MS, PhD

POLYTECHNIC UNIVERSITY, FARMINGDALE CAMPUS
Farmingdale, NY 11735-3995

http://rama.poly.edu/

Independent coed university. *Enrollment:* 257 graduate, professional, and undergraduate students. Graduate faculty: *178 full-time, 122 part-time.* Computer facilities: *Campuswide network is available with full Internet access. Total number of PCs/terminals supplied for student use: 40. Computer services are offered at no charge. Library facilities: Long Island Center Library.* Graduate expenses: *Tuition of $19,530 per year full-time, $675 per credit part-time. Fees of $600 per year full-time, $135 per semester part-time.* General application contact: *John S. Kerge, Dean of Admissions, 718-260-3200.*

Graduate Programs
David Doucette, Associate Dean for Long Island Campus
Programs in:
  aeronautics and astronautics • MS
  chemistry • MS, PhD
  civil engineering • MS, PhD
  computer science • MS, PhD
  distributed informations systems engineering • MS
  electrical engineering • MS, PhD
  electrophysics • MS
  environmental engineering • MS
  information systems engineering • MS
  mathematics • MS, PhD
  mechanical engineering • MS, PhD

physics • MS, PhD
telecommunication networks • MS
transportation planning and engineering • MS

Department of Management
Dr. Mel Horwitch, Head
Programs in:
financial engineering • MS
management • MS
operations management • MS

POLYTECHNIC UNIVERSITY, WESTCHESTER GRADUATE CENTER
Hawthorne, NY 10532-1507

http://west.poly.edu/~www/

Independent coed graduate-only institution. *Enrollment:* 367 graduate, professional, and undergraduate students. Graduate faculty: *178 full-time, 122 part-time.* Library facilities: *Richard Laster Library.* Graduate expenses: *Tuition of $19,530 per year full-time, $675 per credit part-time. Fees of $600 per year full-time, $135 per semester part-time.* General application contact: *John S. Kerge, Dean of Admissions, 718-260-3200.*

Graduate Programs
Ifay Chang, Dean
Programs in:
chemistry • MS
civil engineering • MS, PhD
computer science • MS, PhD
electrical engineering • MS, PhD
electrophysics • MS
environmental engineering • MS
information systems engineering • MS
manufacturing engineering • MS
systems engineering • MS
telecommunication networks • MS
transportation management • MS

Division of Management
Mel Horwitch, Dean
Programs in:
financial engineering • MS
management • MS
management of technology • MS
operations management • MS
organizational behavior • MS
telecommunication and computing management • MS

QUEENS COLLEGE OF THE CITY UNIVERSITY OF NEW YORK
Flushing, NY 11367-1597

http://www.qc.edu/

Public coed comprehensive institution. *Enrollment:* 16,807 graduate, professional, and undergraduate students. Graduate faculty: *504 full-time, 489 part-time.* Computer facilities: *Campuswide network is available with full Internet access. Total number of PCs/ terminals supplied for student use: 345. Computer services are offered at no charge.* Library facilities: *Benjamin Rosenthal Library plus 1 additional on-campus library.* Graduate expenses: *Tuition of $4350 per year full-time, $185 per credit part-time for state residents; $7600 per year full-time, $320 per credit part-time for nonresidents. Fees of $104 per year.* General application contact: *Mario Caruso, Director of Graduate Admissions, 718-997-5200.*

Division of Graduate Studies
Dr. Hamid Shirvani, Vice President for Graduate Studies and Research

Arts Division
Dr. Raymond Erickson, Dean
Programs in:
applied linguistics • MA
art history • MA
creative writing • MA
English language and literature • MA
fine arts • MFA
French • MA
Italian • MA
media studies • MA
music • MA
Spanish • MA
speech pathology • MA
teaching English to speakers of other languages • MS Ed

Mathematics and Natural Sciences Division
Dr. Norman Goldman, Dean
Programs in:
biochemistry • MA
biology • MA
chemistry • MA
clinical behavioral applications in mental health settings • MA
computer science • MA
geology • MA
home economics • MS Ed
mathematics • MA
physical education and exercise sciences • MS Ed
physics • MA
psychology • MA

Social Science Division
Dr. Donald Scott, Dean
Programs in:
administration and supervision • AC
art • MS Ed
bilingual education • MS Ed

Queens College of the City University of New York (continued)

biology • AC, MS Ed
chemistry • AC, MS Ed
counselor education • MS Ed
earth sciences • AC, MS Ed
economics • MA
elementary education • AC, MS Ed
English • AC, MS Ed
French • AC, MS Ed
history • MA
Italian • AC, MS Ed
liberal studies • MALS
library and information studies • AC, MLS
mathematics • AC, MS Ed
music • AC, MS Ed
physics • AC, MS Ed
political science • MA
reading • MS Ed
school psychology • AC, MS Ed
social sciences • MASS
social studies • AC, MS Ed
sociology • MA
Spanish • AC, MS Ed
special education • MS Ed
urban studies • MA

RENSSELAER POLYTECHNIC INSTITUTE

Troy, NY 12180-3590

http://www.rpi.edu/

Independent coed university. *Enrollment: 6,356 graduate, professional, and undergraduate students. Graduate faculty: 345 full-time, 135 part-time. Computer facilities: Campuswide network is available with full Internet access. Total number of PCs/terminals supplied for student use: 600. Computer service fees are included with tuition and fees. Library facilities: Richard G. Folsom Library plus 1 additional on-campus library. Graduate expenses: Tuition of $630 per credit hour. Fees of $1000 per year. General application contact: Gail Gere, Director, Graduate Academic and Enrollment Services, 518-276-6789.*

Graduate School
Dr. Jack Wilson, Acting Dean

Lally School of Management and Technology
Dr. Joseph G. Ecker, Dean
Programs in:
accounting/finance • PhD
applied economics • PhD
business administration • MBA, PhD
business policy and strategy • PhD
environmental management and policy • MS, PhD
finance and accounting • MBA
human resource • PhD
information systems management • MBA
management • PhD

management information systems • PhD
management of technology and entrepreneurships • MBA
managerial economics • PhD
manufacturing • PhD
manufacturing management • MBA
marketing management • MBA
operations research • MBA
organizational behavior and human resource management • MBA
statistical methods for management • MBA

School of Architecture
Dr. Alan Balfour, Dean
Programs in:
architecture • M Arch
building sciences • MS
informatics • M Arch
lighting • MS

School of Engineering
Dr. James M. Tien Jr., Acting Dean
Programs in:
aeronautical engineering • D Eng, M Eng, MS, PhD
biomedical engineering • D Eng, M Eng, MS, PhD
ceramics and glass science • D Eng, M Eng, MS, PhD
chemical engineering • D Eng, M Eng, MS, PhD
composites • D Eng, M Eng, MS, PhD
computer and systems engineering • D Eng, M Eng, MS, PhD
electrical engineering • D Eng, M Eng, MS, PhD
electric power engineering • D Eng, M Eng, MS, PhD
electronic materials • D Eng, M Eng, MS, PhD
engineering physics • M Eng, MS, PhD
environmental engineering • M Eng, MS, PhD
geotechnical engineering • D Eng, M Eng, MS, PhD
industrial and management engineering • M Eng, MS, PhD
manufacturing systems engineering • M Eng, MS, PhD
mechanical engineering • D Eng, M Eng, MS, PhD
mechanics • MS, PhD
mechanics of composite materials and structures • D Eng, M Eng, MS, PhD
metallurgy • D Eng, M Eng, MS, PhD
nuclear engineering • D Eng, M Eng, MS
nuclear engineering and science • PhD
operations research and statistics • M Eng, MS, PhD
plasma physics • D Eng, M Eng, MS, PhD
polymers • D Eng, M Eng, MS, PhD
structural engineering • D Eng, M Eng, MS, PhD
transportation engineering • D Eng, M Eng, MS, PhD

School of Humanities and Social Sciences
Dr. Faye Duchin, Dean
Programs in:
communication and rhetoric • MS, PhD
ecological economics • PhD
ecological economics, values, and policy • MS
economics • MS
electronic arts • MFA
human factors • MS
industrial-organizational psychology • MS
philosophy • MS
psychopharmacology • MS

science and technology studies • MS, PhD
technical communication • MS

School of Science
Dr. G. Doyle Daves Jr., Dean
Programs in:
applied mathematics • MS
biochemistry • MS, PhD
biophysics • MS, PhD
cell biology • MS, PhD
computer science • MS, PhD
developmental biology • MS, PhD
environmental chemistry • MS, PhD
geochemistry • MS, PhD
geophysics • MS, PhD
hydrogeology • MS
inorganic chemistry • MS, PhD
mathematics • MS, PhD
microbiology • MS, PhD
molecular biology • MS, PhD
organic chemistry • MS, PhD
petrology • MS, PhD
physical chemistry • MS, PhD
physics • MS, PhD
planetary geology • MS, PhD
plant science • MS, PhD
tectonics • MS, PhD

ROCHESTER INSTITUTE OF TECHNOLOGY
Rochester, NY 14623-5604

http://www.rit.edu/

Independent coed comprehensive institution. Enrollment: 13,230 graduate, professional, and undergraduate students. Computer facilities: Campuswide network is available with full Internet access. Total number of PCs/terminals supplied for student use: 2,000. Computer service fees are included with tuition and fees. Library facilities: Wallace Memorial Library. Graduate expenses: Tuition of $18,765 per year full-time, $527 per credit hour part-time. Fees of $126 per year full-time. General application contact: Daniel Shelley, Director of Admissions, 716-475-6631.

Part-time and Graduate Admissions
Joseph Nairn, Director

College of Applied Science and Technology
Dr. Wiley McKinzie, Dean
Programs in:
applied computer studies • AC
career and human resource development • MS
computer integrated manufacturing • MS
computer science • MS
cross-disciplinary professional studies • MS
health systems administration • MS
health systems-finance • AC
hospitality-tourism management • MS
information technology • MS

instructional technology • MS
interactive media design • AC
packaging science • MS
service management • MS
software development and management • MS
telecommunications software technology • MS

College of Business
Dr. Lyn D. Pankoff, Dean
Programs in:
accounting • MBA, MS
business administration • MBA
executive business administration • Exec MBA
finance • MS
international business • MS
manufacturing management and leadership • MS

College of Engineering
Dr. Paul Petersen, Dean
Programs in:
applied statistics • MS
computer engineering • ME
electrical engineering • MSEE
engineering management • ME
industrial engineering • ME
manufacturing engineering • ME
mechanical engineering • MSME
microelectronic engineering • ME
statistical quality • AC
systems engineering • ME

College of Imaging Arts and Sciences
Dr. Joan Stone, Interim Dean
Programs in:
art education • MST
ceramics and ceramic sculpture • MFA, MST
computer graphics design • MFA
glass • MFA, MST
graphic arts publishing • MS
graphic arts systems • MS
graphic design • MFA, MST
imaging arts • MFA
industrial design • MFA, MST
interior design • MFA, MST
medical illustration • MFA
metal crafts and jewelry • MFA, MST
painting • MFA, MST
printing technology • MS
printmaking • MFA, MST
weaving and textile design • MFA, MST
woodworking and furniture design • MFA, MST

College of Liberal Arts
Dr. William J. Daniels, Dean
Programs in:
school psychology • MS
school psychology and deafness • AC

College of Science
Dr. Robert Clark, Dean
Programs in:
chemistry • MS
clinical chemistry • MS
color science • MS

Rochester Institute of Technology (continued)
    imaging science • MS, PhD
    industrial and applied mathematics • MS
    materials science and engineering • MS

National Technical Institute for the Deaf
Dr. James DeCaro, Dean
Program in:
    secondary education • MS

ROCKEFELLER UNIVERSITY
New York, NY 10021-6399

http://www.rockefeller.edu/

Independent coed graduate-only institution. *Enrollment:* 137 matriculated graduate/professional students. Graduate faculty: *216 full-time, 170 part-time.* Computer facilities: *Campuswide network is available with full Internet access. Total number of PCs/terminals supplied for student use: 13. Computer services are offered at no charge.* Library facilities: *main library.* Graduate expenses: *$0.* General application contact: *Dr. George Cross, Dean of Graduate Studies, 212-327-8086.*

Program in Biomedical Sciences
Dr. George Cross, Dean of Graduate Studies
Program in:
    biomedical sciences • PhD

SAGE GRADUATE SCHOOL
Troy, NY 12180-4115

http://www.sage.edu/

Independent coed graduate-only institution. *Enrollment:* 1,123 matriculated graduate/professional students. Graduate faculty: *25 full-time, 42 part-time.* Computer facilities: *Campuswide network is available with full Internet access. Total number of PCs/terminals supplied for student use: 194. Computer services are offered at no charge.* Library facilities: *James Wheelock Clark Library.* Graduate expenses: *Tuition of $360 per credit hour. Fees of $50 per semester.* General application contact: *Melissa Robertson, Associate Director of Admissions, 518-244-6878.*

Graduate School
Barbara R. Grumet, Dean
Programs in:
    chemical dependency • MA
    child care and children's services • MA
    community counseling • MA
    community health • MS
    community health educator • MA
    community health nursing • MS
    community psychology • MA
    elementary education • MS Ed

family nurse practitioner • MS
finance • MBA
general psychology • MA
gerontology • MS
guidance and counseling • MS Ed, PMC
health education • MS
human resources management • MBA
human services administration • MS
management • MBA, MS
marketing • MBA
medical-surgical nursing • MS
nursing • MS, PMC
nutrition and dietetics • MS
psychiatric–mental health nurse practitioner • MS
psychology • MA
public management • MS
reading • MS Ed
reading/special education • MS Ed
school health • MS
secondary education • MS Ed, PMC
special education • MS Ed
visual art therapy • MA

ST. BONAVENTURE UNIVERSITY
St. Bonaventure, NY 14778-2284

http://www.sbu.edu/

Independent-religious coed comprehensive institution. *Enrollment:* 2,723 graduate, professional, and undergraduate students. Graduate faculty: *65 full-time, 28 part-time.* Computer facilities: *Campuswide network is available with full Internet access. Total number of PCs/terminals supplied for student use: 60. Computer services are offered at no charge.* Library facilities: *Friedsam Memorial Library.* Graduate expenses: *$8100 per year full-time, $450 per credit hour part-time.* General application contact: *Dean of Graduate Studies, 716-375-2200.*

Graduate School

School of Arts and Sciences
Dr. James White, Dean
Programs in:
    English • MA
    history • MA
    psychology • MA
    theology • Adv C, MA

School of Business Administration
Dr. Michael Fischer, Dean
Programs in:
    accounting and finance • MBA
    business administration • Adv C
    management and marketing • MBA

School of Education
Dr. Carol Anne Pierson, Dean
Programs in:
    advanced instructional processes • MS Ed
    counseling education • Adv C
    counseling education-agency • MS, MS Ed
    counseling education-school • MS, MS Ed
    educational administration, supervision, and curriculum
        • Adv C, MS Ed
    reading • MS Ed
    secondary education • MS Ed
    special education • MS Ed

School of Franciscan Studies
Fr. Michael Blastic, OFM, Dean
Program in:
    Franciscan studies • Adv C, MA

ST. JOHN FISHER COLLEGE
Rochester, NY 14618-3597

http://www.sjfc.edu/

Independent-religious coed comprehensive institution. *Enrollment:* 2,286 graduate, professional, and undergraduate students. Graduate faculty: *20 full-time, 4 part-time.* Computer facilities: *Campuswide network is available with full Internet access. Total number of PCs/ terminals supplied for student use: 150. Computer services are offered at no charge.* Library facilities: *Charles J. Lavery Library.* Graduate expenses: *$13,500 per year full-time, $375 per credit hour part-time.* General application contact: *Dr. Kathleen A. Powers, Associate Vice President, School of Adult and Graduate Education, 716-385-8161.*

School of Adult and Graduate Education
Dr. Kathleen A. Powers, Associate Vice President
Programs in:
    family nurse practitioner • Certificate
    human resources development • MS
    international studies • MS
    management • MBA
    mathematics/science/technology education • MS
    nursing • MS

 # ST. JOHN'S UNIVERSITY
Jamaica, NY 11439

http://www.stjohns.edu/

Independent-religious coed university. *Enrollment:* 18,523 graduate, professional, and undergraduate students. Graduate faculty: *589 full-time, 499 part-time.* Computer facilities: *Campuswide network is available with full Internet access. Total number of PCs/ terminals supplied for student use: 817. Computer service fees are included with tuition and fees.* Library facilities: *St. Augustine Hall plus 2 additional on-campus libraries.* Graduate expenses: *Tuition of $525 per credit. Fees of $150 per year.* General application

contact: *Shamus McGrenra, TOR, Associate Director, Graduate Admissions, 718-990-6107.*

Graduate School of Arts and Sciences
Dr. Willard Gingerich, Dean
Programs in:
    algebra • MA
    analysis • MA
    applied mathematics • MA
    Asian studies • MA
    biological sciences • MS, PhD
    chemistry • MS
    clinical child psychology • PhD
    clinical psychology • PhD
    computer science • MA
    divinity • M Div
    English • DA, MA
    general experimental psychology • MA
    geometry-topology • MA
    government and politics • MA
    history • MA
    library and information science • Adv C, MLS
    logic and foundations • MA
    modern world history • DA
    pastoral ministry • Adv C
    probability and statistics • MA
    public administration • MA
    school psychology • MS
    sociology • MA
    Spanish • MA
    speech pathology and audiology • MA
    theology • MA

College of Business Administration
Peter J. Tobin, Dean
Programs in:
    accounting • Adv C, MBA
    computer information systems and decision sciences •
        Adv C, MBA
    economics • Adv C, MBA
    finance • Adv C, MBA
    management • Adv C, MBA
    marketing • Adv C, MBA
    taxation • Adv C, MBA

College of Pharmacy and Allied Health Professions
Dr. Thomas H. Wiser, Dean
Programs in:
    clinical pharmacy • MS
    cosmetic sciences • MS
    industrial pharmacy • MS, PhD
    medical chemistry • MS, PhD
    medical technology • MS
    pharmaceutical • MS
    pharmacology • MS
    pharmacology/toxicology • PhD
    pharmacotherapeutics • MS
    pharmacy • Pharm D
    pharmacy administration • MS
    toxicology • MS, PhD

St. John's University (continued)
Metropolitan College
Dr. George Ansalone, Associate Vice President and
Executive Dean
Program in:
liberal studies • MS

School of Education and Human Services
Dr. Jerrold Ross, Dean
Programs in:
administration and supervision • Ed D, MS Ed, PD
bilingual/multicultural education/teaching English to
speakers of other languages • MS Ed
elementary education • MS Ed
instructional leadership • Ed D, PD
reading specialist • MS Ed, PD
rehabilitation counseling • MS Ed
school counseling/bilingual school counseling • MS Ed
secondary education • MS Ed
special education/bilingual special education • MS Ed,
PD
student development practice in higher education •
MS Ed

School of Law
Prof. Brian Tamanaha, Acting Dean
Program in:
law • JD

STATE UNIVERSITY OF NEW YORK AT ALBANY
Albany, NY 12222-0001

http://www.albany.edu/

Public coed university. *Enrollment: 16,051 graduate, professional, and undergraduate students. Graduate faculty: 618 full-time, 277 part-time. Computer facilities: Campuswide network is available with full Internet access. Total number of PCs/terminals supplied for student use: 500. Computer service fees are included with tuition and fees. Library facilities: University Library plus 1 additional on-campus library. Graduate expenses: Tuition of $5100 per year full-time, $213 per credit hour part-time for state residents; $8416 per year full-time, $351 per credit hour part-time for nonresidents. Fees of $705 per year full-time, $26.85 per credit hour part-time. General application contact: Jon Bartow, Director, Graduate Admissions, 518-442-3980.*

College of Arts and Sciences
Cyril Knoblauch, Interim Dean
Programs in:
African studies • MA
Afro-American studies • MA
anthropology • MA, PhD
art • MA, MFA
atmospheric science • MS, PhD
biodiversity, conservation, and policy • MS

biopsychology • PhD
chemistry • MS, PhD
classics • MA
clinical psychology • PhD
communication • MA
computer science • MS, PhD
demography • Certificate
ecology, evolution, and behavior • MS, PhD
economics • Certificate, MA, PhD
English • MA, PhD
French • MA, PhD
general/experimental psychology • PhD
geographic information systems and spatial analysis •
Certificate
geography • MA
geology • MS, PhD
history • MA, PhD
humanistic studies • DA
industrial/organizational psychology • PhD
Italian • MA
Latin American and Caribbean studies • Certificate, MA
liberal studies • MA
mathematics • PhD
molecular, cellular, developmental, and neural biology •
MS, PhD
philosophy • MA, PhD
physics • MS, PhD
psychology • MA
public history • Certificate
regional planning • MRP
Russian • MA
Russian translation • Certificate
secondary teaching • MA
social/personality psychology • PhD
sociology • MA, PhD
sociology and communication • PhD
Spanish • MA, PhD
statistics • MA
theatre • MA
urban policy • Certificate

Nelson A. Rockefeller College of Public Affairs and Policy
Dr. Frank Thompson, Interim Provost
Program in:
information science • MS, PhD

Graduate School of Public Affairs
Frank J. Thompson, Dean
Programs in:
administrative behavior • PhD
comparative and development administration • MPA,
PhD
human resources • MPA
legislative administration • MPA
planning and policy analysis • CAS
policy analysis • MPA
political science • MA, PhD
program analysis and evaluation • PhD
public affairs and policy • MA
public finance • MPA, PhD
public management • MPA, PhD

School of Criminal Justice
David Bayley, Dean
Program in:
  criminal justice • MA, PhD

School of Information Science and Policy
Philip Eppard, Interim Dean
Program in:
  information science and policy • CAS, MLS

School of Social Welfare
Lynn Videka-Sherman, Dean
Program in:
  social welfare • MSW, PhD

School of Business
Donald Bourque, Interim Dean
Programs in:
  accounting • MS
  finance • MBA
  human resource systems • MBA
  management science and information systems • MBA
  marketing • MBA
  organizational studies • PhD
  taxation • MS

School of Education
James Fleming, Interim Dean
Programs in:
  counseling psychology • CAS, MS, PhD
  curriculum and instruction • CAS, Ed D, MS
  curriculum planning and development • MA
  educational administration • CAS, Ed D, MS
  educational communications • CAS, MS
  educational psychology • Ed D
  educational psychology and statistics • MS
  measurements and evaluation • Ed D
  reading • CAS, Ed D, MS
  rehabilitation counseling • MS
  school counselor • CAS
  school psychology • CAS, Psy D
  special education • MS
  statistics and research design • Ed D

School of Public Health
Dr. John Conway, Interim Dean
Programs in:
  biochemistry, molecular biology, and genetics • MS, PhD
  biometry and statistics • MS, PhD
  cell and molecular structure • MS, PhD
  environmental and occupational health • MS, PhD
  environmental chemistry • MS, PhD
  epidemiology • MS, PhD
  health policy and management • MS
  immunobiology and immunochemistry • MS, PhD
  molecular pathogenesis • MS, PhD
  neuroscience • MS, PhD
  public health • Dr PH, MPH
  toxicology • MS, PhD

 # STATE UNIVERSITY OF NEW YORK AT BINGHAMTON
Binghamton, NY 13902-6000

http://www.binghamton.edu/

Public coed university. Enrollment: 12,138 graduate, professional, and undergraduate students. Graduate faculty: 466 full-time, 234 part-time. Computer facilities: Campuswide network is available with full Internet access. Total number of PCs/terminals supplied for student use: 500. Computer service fees are included with tuition and fees. Library facilities: Glenn G. Bartle Library plus 5 additional on-campus libraries. Graduate expenses: Tuition of $5100 per year full-time, $213 per credit hour part-time for state residents; $8416 per year full-time, $351 per credit hour part-time for nonresidents. Fees of $654 per year full-time, $75 per semester (minimum) part-time. General application contact: Dr. Susan Strehle, Vice Provost for Graduate Studies and Research, 607-777-2239.

Graduate School
Dr. Susan Strehle, Vice Provost for Graduate Studies and Research

School of Arts and Sciences
Dr. Solomon Polachek, Dean
Programs in:
  analytical chemistry • PhD
  anthropology • MA, PhD
  applied physics • MS
  art history • MA, PhD
  behavioral neuroscience • MA, PhD
  biological sciences • MA, PhD
  chemistry • MA, MS
  clinical psychology • MA, PhD
  cognitive and behavioral science • MA, PhD
  comparative literature • MA, PhD
  computer science • MA, PhD
  economics • MA, PhD
  economics and finance • MA, PhD
  English • MA, PhD
  French • MA
  geography • MA
  geological sciences • MA, PhD
  history • MA, PhD
  inorganic chemistry • PhD
  Italian • MA
  music • MA, MM
  organic chemistry • PhD
  philosophy • MA, PhD
  physical chemistry • PhD
  physics • MA, MS
  political science • MA, PhD
  probability and statistics • MA, PhD
  public administration • MPA
  public policy • MA, PhD
  sociology • MA, PhD
  Spanish • MA
  theater • MA
  translation • Certificate
  translation research and instruction • Certificate

State University of New York at Binghamton (continued)

School of Education and Human Development

Dr. Linda B. Biemer, Dean
Programs in:
- biology education • MAT, MS Ed, MST
- early childhood and elementary education • MS Ed
- earth science education • MAT, MS Ed, MST
- educational theory and practice • Ed D
- English education • MAT, MS Ed, MST
- French education • MAT, MST
- mathematical sciences education • MAT, MS Ed, MST
- physics • MAT, MS Ed, MST
- reading education • MS Ed
- social science • MASS
- social studies • MAT, MS Ed, MST
- Spanish education • MAT, MST
- special education • MS Ed

School of Management

Dr. Glenn Pittman, Dean
Programs in:
- accounting • MS, PhD
- arts administration • MBA Arts
- business administration • MBA, PhD
- health care professional executive • MBA

School of Nursing

Dr. Mary Collins, Dean
Program in:
- nursing • Certificate, MS, PhD

Thomas J. Watson School of Engineering and Applied Science

Dr. Lyle D. Feisel, Dean
Programs in:
- applied science • PhD
- computer science • MS, PhD
- electrical engineering • M Eng, MS, PhD
- mechanical engineering • M Eng, MS, PhD
- systems science and industrial engineering • M Eng, MS, MSAT, PhD

STATE UNIVERSITY OF NEW YORK AT BUFFALO

Buffalo, NY 14260

http://www.buffalo.edu/

Public coed university. *Enrollment:* 23,429 graduate, professional, and undergraduate students. *Graduate faculty:* 1,298 full-time, 735 part-time. *Computer facilities: Campuswide network is available with full Internet access. Total number of PCs/terminals supplied for student use: 1,800. Computer service fees are included with tuition and fees. Library facilities: Lockwood Library plus 8 additional on-campus libraries. Graduate expenses: $5970 per year full-time, $288 per credit hour part-time for state residents; $9286 per year full-time, $426 per credit hour part-time for nonresidents. General application contact: Dr. Myron Thompson, Associate Provost and Executive Director, 716-645-6227.*

Graduate School

Dr. Myron Thompson, Associate Provost and Executive Director

Faculty of Arts and Letters

Dr. Kerry Grant, Dean
Programs in:
- American studies • MA, PhD
- art history • MA
- classics • MA, PhD
- communication design • MFA
- comparative literature • MA, PhD
- English • MA, PhD
- French • MA, PhD
- German • MA, PhD
- humanities • MA
- illustration • MFA
- music composition • MA, PhD
- music education • CAS, MA, MM
- music history • MA, PhD
- music performance • MM
- music theory • MA, PhD
- painting • MFA
- photography • MFA
- printmaking • MFA
- sculpture • MFA
- Spanish • MA, PhD
- women's studies • MA

Faculty of Natural Sciences and Mathematics

Dr. Joseph J. Tufariello, Dean
Programs in:
- cell and developmental biology • MA, PhD
- cellular, comparative, and endocrine physiology • MA, PhD
- chemistry • MA, PhD
- computer science • MS, PhD
- ecology • MA, PhD
- geology • MA, PhD
- mathematics • MA, PhD
- molecular biology, genetics, and biological chemistry • MA, PhD
- natural science • MS
- physics • MA, PhD
- plant science • MA, PhD

Faculty of Social Sciences

Dr. Mark B. Kristal, Dean
Programs in:
- anthropology • MA, PhD
- behavioral neuroscience • PhD
- clinical psychology • PhD
- cognitive psychology • PhD
- communication theory • MA, PhD
- communicative disorders and sciences • PhD
- economics • MA, PhD
- general psychology • MA
- geography • MA, PhD
- history • MA, PhD
- linguistics • MA, PhD
- philosophy • MA, PhD
- political science • MA, PhD
- social psychology • PhD
- social sciences • MS

sociology • MA, PhD
speech-language pathology and audiology • MA

Graduate Programs in Biomedical Sciences at Roswell Park
Dr. Arthur M. Michalek, Dean
Programs in:
　biochemistry • MA, MS, PhD
　biometry • MS
　biophysics • MS, PhD
　cellular and molecular biology • MA, PhD
　cellular molecular biology • MS
　chemistry • MA, MS, PhD
　clinical chemistry • PhD
　experimental pathology • MA, PhD
　immunology • MS
　microbiology/immunology • MA, PhD
　molecular pharmacology and cancer therapeutics • PhD
　pathology • MS
　pharmacology • MS
　physiology • MA, MS, PhD

Graduate School of Education
Dr. Jacquelyn Mitchell, Dean
Programs in:
　bilingual education/teaching English to speakers of
　　other languages • Ed M
　counseling psychology • PhD
　counselor education • PhD
　early childhood education • Ed D, Ed M
　educational administration • Certificate, Ed D, Ed M,
　　PhD
　educational psychology • MA, PhD
　elementary education • Ed D, Ed M, PhD
　English education • Ed D, PhD
　foreign language education • Ed D, PhD
　mathematics education • Ed D, PhD
　reading education • Ed D, Ed M, PhD
　rehabilitation counseling • MS
　school administrator and supervisor • Certificate
　school counseling • Certificate, Ed M
　school psychology • MA
　science education • PhD
　secondary education • Ed D, Ed M, PhD
　social, philosophical, and historical foundations • Ed D,
　　PhD
　teaching English as a second language • Ed D, PhD

School of Architecture and Planning
Bruno Freschi, Dean
Programs in:
　architecture • M Arch
　planning • MUP
　urban studies • MS

School of Dental Medicine
Dr. Louis J. Goldberg, Dean
Programs in:
　advanced education in general dentistry • Certificate
　biomaterials • MS
　dental medicine • DDS
　endodontics • Certificate
　general practice residency • Certificate
　oral and maxillofacial surgery • Certificate
　oral biology • PhD

oral sciences • MS
orthodontics • Certificate, MS
pediatric dentistry • Certificate
periodontology • Certificate
prosthodontics • Certificate

School of Engineering and Applied Sciences
Dr. Mark Karwan, Dean
Programs in:
　aerospace engineering • M Eng, MS, PhD
　applied physics • MS, PhD
　chemical engineering • M Eng, MS, PhD
　computational engineering and mechanics • MS, PhD
　construction • M Eng, MS, PhD
　electrical and computer engineering • M Eng, MS, PhD
　geoenvironmental and geotechnical engineering •
　　M Eng, MS, PhD
　industrial engineering • M Eng, MS, PhD
　mechanical engineering • M Eng, MS, PhD
　structural and earthquake engineering • M Eng, MS,
　　PhD
　water resources and environmental engineering •
　　M Eng, MS, PhD

School of Health Related Professions
Dr. Barry S. Eckert, Dean
Programs in:
　clinical laboratory science • MS
　clinical nutrition • MS
　exercise science • MS, PhD
　nutrition science • MS
　occupational therapy • MS, PhD
　rehabilitation science • PhD

School of Information and Library Studies
Dr. George S. Bobinski, Dean
Program in:
　information and library studies • Certificate, MLS

School of Law
Barry B. Boyer, Dean
Program in:
　law • JD

School of Management
John M. Thomas, Interim Dean
Program in:
　management • MBA, PhD

School of Medicine
Dr. John R. Wright, Interim Dean
Programs in:
　anatomy and cell biology • MA, PhD
　biochemistry • MA, PhD
　biomedical sciences • PhD
　biophysical sciences • MS, PhD
　epidemiology • MS
　epidemiology and community health • PhD
　medicine • MD
　microbiology • MA, PhD
　molecular cell biology • PhD
　pathology • MA, PhD
　pharmacology and toxicology • MA, PhD
　physiology • MA, PhD
　statistics • MA, PhD

State University of New York at Buffalo (continued)

School of Nursing
Dr. Mecca S. Cranley, Dean
Programs in:
　　adult health nursing • MS
　　child health nursing • MS
　　clinical nurse specialist • MS
　　clinical specialist • MS
　　nurse anesthesia • MS
　　nurse practitioner • MS
　　nursing • DNS
　　pediatric nurse practitioner • MS

School of Pharmacy
Dr. Wayne K. Anderson, Dean
Programs in:
　　biochemical pharmacology • MS, PhD
　　medicinal chemistry • MS, PhD
　　pharmaceutics • MS, PhD
　　pharmacy • Pharm D

School of Social Work
Dr. Lawrence Shulman, Dean
Program in:
　　social work • MSW, PhD

STATE UNIVERSITY OF NEW YORK AT NEW PALTZ
New Paltz, NY 12561-2499

http://www.newpaltz.edu/

Public coed comprehensive institution. *Enrollment: 7,641 graduate, professional, and undergraduate students. Graduate faculty: 270 full-time, 264 part-time. Computer facilities: Campuswide network is available with full Internet access. Total number of PCs/terminals supplied for student use: 400. Computer services are offered at no charge. Library facilities: Sojourner Truth Library. Graduate expenses: Tuition of $5100 per year full-time, $213 per credit hour part-time for state residents; $8416 per year full-time, $351 per credit hour part-time for nonresidents. Fees of $493 per year full-time, $48 per semester (minimum) part-time. General application contact: Dr. Robert Mumper, Dean of the Graduate School, 914-257-3287.*

Graduate School
Dr. Robert Mumper, Dean

Faculty of Education
Dr. Robert Michael, Interim Dean
Programs in:
　　early childhood education • MS Ed
　　educational administration • CAS, MS Ed
　　elementary education • MST
　　English as a second language • MS Ed
　　environmental education • MS Ed
　　general education • MS Ed
　　humanistic education • MPS
　　reading • MS Ed
　　secondary education • MAT, MS Ed
　　special education • MS Ed

Faculty of Engineering and Business
Dr. Owen Hill, Dean
Programs in:
　　business administration • MS
　　engineering • MS

Faculty of Fine and Performing Arts
Dr. Patricia Phillips, Dean
Programs in:
　　art education • MS
　　ceramics • MA, MFA
　　metal • MA, MFA
　　painting • MA, MFA
　　photography • MA, MFA
　　piano pedagogy • MA, MFA
　　printmaking • MA, MFA
　　sculpture • MA, MFA

Faculty of Liberal Arts and Sciences
Dr. Gerald Benjamin, Interim Dean
Programs in:
　　biology • MA, MAT, MS Ed
　　chemistry • MA, MAT, MS Ed
　　communication disorders • MS Ed
　　computer science • MS
　　English • MA, MAT, MS Ed
　　geological sciences • MA, MAT, MS Ed
　　gerontological nursing • MS
　　mathematics • MA, MAT, MS Ed
　　physics • MA, MAT, MS Ed
　　psychology • MA
　　sociology • MA

 # STATE UNIVERSITY OF NEW YORK AT OSWEGO
Oswego, NY 13126

http://www.oswego.edu/

Public coed comprehensive institution. *Enrollment: 7,802 graduate, professional, and undergraduate students. Graduate faculty: 85 full-time, 29 part-time. Computer facilities: Campuswide network is available with full Internet access. Total number of PCs/terminals supplied for student use: 160. Computer services are offered at no charge. Library facilities: Penfield Library. Graduate expenses: Tuition of $5100 per year full-time, $213 per credit hour part-time for state residents; $8416 per year full-time, $351 per credit hour part-time for nonresidents. Fees of $135 per year (minimum). General application contact: Dr. Jack Y. Narayan, Interim Dean of Graduate Studies, 315-341-3152.*

Graduate Studies
Dr. Jack Y. Narayan, Interim Dean

Division of Arts and Sciences
Dr. Sara Varhus, Interim Dean
Programs in:
　　art • MA
　　chemistry • MS

English • MA
history • MA

School of Business
Dr. Lanny A. Karns, Dean
Programs in:
    business administration • MBA
    management • MS

School of Education
Dr. Linda Markert, Interim Dean
Programs in:
    art education • MAT
    counseling services • CAS, MS
    educational administration • PhD
    elementary education • MS Ed
    human services/counseling • MS
    instructional administration • CAS, MS Ed
    reading education • MS Ed
    school psychology • CAS, MS
    secondary education • MS Ed
    special education • MS Ed
    vocational-technical education • MS Ed

STATE UNIVERSITY OF NEW YORK AT STONY BROOK
Stony Brook, NY 11794

http://www.sunysb.edu/

Public coed university. Enrollment: 17,831 graduate, professional, and undergraduate students. Graduate faculty: 1,226 full-time, 456 part-time. Computer facilities: Campuswide network is available with full Internet access. Total number of PCs/terminals supplied for student use: 1,550. Computer service fees are included with tuition and fees. Library facilities: F. Melville Memorial Library plus 7 additional on-campus libraries. Graduate expenses: Tuition of $5100 per year full-time, $213 per credit hour part-time for state residents; $8416 per year full-time, $351 per credit hour part-time for nonresidents. Fees of $529 per year full-time, $77 per semester (minimum) part-time. General application contact: Ann Carvalho, Assistant Vice Provost, 516-632-7040.

Graduate School
Dr. Lawrence B. Martin, Dean
Programs in:
    anatomical sciences • PhD
    immunology and pathology • PhD
    molecular and cellular pharmacology • PhD
    molecular microbiology • PhD
    oral biology and pathology • PhD
    physiology and biophysics • PhD

College of Arts and Sciences
Dr. Paul Armstrong, Dean
Programs in:
    anthropology • MA, PhD
    art history and criticism • MA, PhD
    biological sciences • MA

biopsychology • PhD
cellular and developmental biology • PhD
chemistry • MAT, MS, PhD
clinical psychology • PhD
dramaturgy • MFA
earth and space science • MS, PhD
earth and space sciences • MS, PhD
earth science • MAT
ecology and evolution • PhD
economics • MA, PhD
English • MA, MAT, PhD
experimental psychology • PhD
foreign languages • DA
French • DA, MAT
genetics • PhD
German • DA, MAT
Germanic languages and literatures • MA
history • MA, MAT, PhD
Italian • DA, MAT
linguistics • MA, PhD
mathematics • MA, PhD
molecular and cellular biology • PhD
molecular biology and biochemistry • PhD
music • MA, PhD
music performance • DMA, MM
neurobiology and behavior • PhD
philosophy • MA, PhD
physics • MA, MAT, MS, PhD
political science • MA, PhD
psychology • MA
romance languages and literature • MA
Russian • DA
Slavic languages and literature • MA
social/health psychology • PhD
sociology • MA, PhD
studio art • MFA
teaching English to speakers of other languages • DA, MA
theatre • MA

College of Engineering and Applied Sciences
Dr. Yacov Shamash, Dean
Programs in:
    biomedical engineering • Certificate
    computer science • MS, PhD
    electrical engineering • MS, PhD
    information systems management • Certificate
    materials science and engineering • MS, PhD
    mechanical engineering • MS, PhD
    technological systems management • MS

Institute for Terrestrial and Planetary Atmospheres
Marvin A. Geller, Director
Program in:
    terrestrial and planetary atmospheres • PhD

Marine Sciences Research Center
Dr. Marvin A. Geller, Dean
Programs in:
    coastal oceanography • PhD
    marine environmental sciences • MS

State University of New York at Stony Brook (continued)

Health Sciences Center

Dr. Norman H. Edelman, Dean of the School of Medicine

School of Dental Medicine

Dr. B. R. Pollack, Dean

Programs in:
    dental medicine • DDS
    oral biology and pathology • PhD
    orthodontics • Certificate
    periodontics • Certificate

School of Health Technology and Management

Dr. Lorna McBarnette, Dean

Programs in:
    health care management • Advanced Certificate
    health care policy and management • MS

School of Medicine

Dr. Norman H. Edelman, Dean of the School of Medicine, Health Sciences Center

Programs in:
    anatomical sciences • PhD
    immunology and pathology • PhD
    medicine • MD
    molecular and cellular pharmacology • PhD
    molecular microbiology • PhD
    physiology and biophysics • PhD

School of Nursing

Dr. Lenora J. McClean, Dean

Programs in:
    adult health nurse practitioner • Certificate
    adult health/primary care nursing • MS
    child health nurse practitioner • Certificate
    child health nursing • MS
    gerontological nursing • MS
    mental health nurse practitioner • Certificate
    mental health/psychiatric nursing • MS
    neonatal nurse practitioner • Certificate
    neonatal nursing • MS
    nurse-midwifery • Certificate, MS
    perinatal/women's health nurse practitioner • Certificate
    perinatal/women's health nursing • MS

School of Social Welfare

Dr. Frances L. Brisbane, Dean

Programs in:
    social welfare • PhD
    social work • MSW

School of Professional Development and Continuing Studies

Dr. Paul J. Edelson, Dean

Programs in:
    chemistry-grade 7-12 • MAT
    coaching • Certificate
    earth science-grade 7-12 • MAT
    educational computing • Certificate
    English-grade 7-12 • MAT
    environmental/occupational health and safety • Certificate
    French-grade 7-12 • MAT

German-grade 7-12 • MAT
Italian-grade 7-12 • MAT
labor management • MPS
labor management studies • Certificate
liberal studies • MA
physics-grade 7-12 • MAT
public affairs • MPS
Russian-grade 7-12 • MAT
school administration and supervision • Certificate
school district administration • Certificate
social science and the professions • MPS
social studies • MAT
software engineering • Certificate
waste management • Certificate, MPS

STATE UNIVERSITY OF NEW YORK COLLEGE AT BROCKPORT

Brockport, NY 14420-2997

http://www.brockport.edu/

Public coed comprehensive institution. Enrollment: 7,519 graduate, professional, and undergraduate students. Graduate faculty: 112 full-time, 62 part-time. Computer facilities: Campuswide network is available with full Internet access. Total number of PCs/terminals supplied for student use: 660. Computer service fees are included with tuition and fees. Library facilities: Drake Library. Graduate expenses: Tuition of $5100 per year full-time, $213 per credit hour part-time for state residents; $8416 per year full-time, $351 per credit hour part-time for nonresidents. Fees of $440 per year full-time, $22.60 per credit hour part-time. General application contact: Scott Atkinson, Interim Director of Admissions, 716-395-2751.

School of Arts and Performance

Ginny L. Studer, Dean

Programs in:
    communication • MA
    dance • MA
    physical education • MS Ed
    visual studies • MFA

School of Letters and Sciences

Dr. Robert McLean, Dean

Programs in:
    biological sciences • MS
    English • MA
    history • MA
    liberal studies • MA
    mathematics • MA
    psychology • MA

School of Professions

Dr. Diane Elliott, Interim Dean

Programs in:
    bilingual education • MS Ed
    biology education • MS Ed
    chemistry education • MS Ed

counselor education • CAS, MS Ed
earth science education • MS Ed
elementary education • MS Ed
English education • MS Ed
health science • MS Ed
mathematics education • MS Ed
physics education • MS Ed
professional studies • MSW
public administration • MPA
reading • MS Ed
recreation and leisure studies • MS
school administration and supervision • CAS, MS Ed
school business administration • CAS
school district administration • CAS
social studies education • MS Ed

STATE UNIVERSITY OF NEW YORK COLLEGE AT BUFFALO
Buffalo, NY 14222-1095

http://www.snybuf.edu/

Public coed comprehensive institution. *Enrollment:* 10,843 graduate, professional, and undergraduate students. Graduate faculty: *231 full-time, 13 part-time.* Computer facilities: *Campuswide network is available with full Internet access. Total number of PCs/terminals supplied for student use: 200. Computer service fees are included with tuition and fees.* Library facilities: *Butler Library.* Graduate expenses: *Tuition of $5100 per year full-time, $213 per credit hour part-time for state residents; $8416 per year full-time, $351 per credit hour part-time for nonresidents. Fees of $195 per year full-time, $8.60 per credit hour part-time.* General application contact: *Mary Lou Hartnett, Graduate Admissions Counselor, 716-878-5601.*

Graduate Studies and Research
Dr. Thomas G. Kinsey, Interim Dean
Program in:
    multidisciplinary studies • MA, MS

Faculty of Applied Science and Education
Dr. Daniel King, Dean
Programs in:
    business and distributive education • MS Ed
    business education • MS Ed
    creative studies • MS
    criminal justice • MS
    educational computing • MS Ed
    elementary education • MS Ed
    English education • MS Ed
    general science education • MS Ed
    industrial technology • MS
    mathematics education • MS Ed
    reading • MPS, MS Ed
    school administration and supervision • CAS
    social studies education • MS Ed
    special education • MS Ed
    student personnel administration • MS

teaching bilingual exceptional individuals • MS Ed
technology education • MS Ed
vocational technical education • MS Ed

Faculty of Arts and Humanities
Dr. Dennis McCarty, Interim Dean
Programs in:
    art conservation • CAS
    art education • MS Ed
    conservation of historic works and art works • MA
    English • MA, MS Ed
    secondary education • MS Ed

Faculty of Natural and Social Sciences
Dr. Gail Dinter-Gottlieb, Interim Dean
Programs in:
    biology • MA, MS Ed
    chemistry • MA
    geoscience • MS Ed
    history • MA
    mathematics education • MS Ed
    science • MS Ed
    secondary education • MS Ed
    social studies • MS Ed

STATE UNIVERSITY OF NEW YORK COLLEGE AT CORTLAND
Cortland, NY 13045

http://www.cortland.edu/

Public coed comprehensive institution. *Enrollment: 6,306 graduate, professional, and undergraduate students.* Computer facilities: *Campuswide network is available with full Internet access. Total number of PCs/terminals supplied for student use: 832. Computer service fees are included with tuition and fees.* Library facilities: *Memorial Library.* Graduate expenses: *Tuition of $5100 per year full-time, $213 per credit hour part-time for state residents; $8416 per year full-time, $351 per credit hour part-time for nonresidents. Fees of $644 per year full-time, $79 per semester (minimum) part-time.* General application contact: *Jeanne M. Bechtel, Associate Director of Admissions, 607-753-4711.*

Graduate Studies
Programs in:
    American civilization and culture • CAS
    biology • MAT, MS Ed
    chemistry • MAT, MS Ed
    earth science • MAT, MS Ed
    English • MA, MAT, MS Ed
    English education • MS Ed
    French • MS Ed
    general science education • MS Ed
    health education • MS Ed
    history • MA
    mathematics • MAT, MS Ed
    mathematics education • MS Ed
    physical education • MS Ed
    physics • MAT, MS Ed

State University of New York College at Cortland (continued)

  reading • MS Ed

  recreation education • MS, MS Ed

  school administration and supervision • CAS

  school business administrator • CAS

  secondary education • MS Ed

  social studies • MS Ed

  social studies education • MS Ed

STATE UNIVERSITY OF NEW YORK COLLEGE AT FREDONIA
Fredonia, NY 14063

http://www.fredonia.edu/

Public coed comprehensive institution. *Enrollment: 4,465 graduate, professional, and undergraduate students. Graduate faculty: 34 full-time, 9 part-time. Computer facilities: Campuswide network is available with full Internet access. Total number of PCs/terminals supplied for student use: 300. Computer service fees are included with tuition and fees. Library facilities: Reed Library. Graduate expenses: Tuition of $5100 per year full-time, $213 per credit hour part-time for state residents; $8416 per year full-time, $351 per credit hour part-time for nonresidents. Fees of $725 per year full-time, $30 per credit hour part-time. General application contact: J. Denis Bolton, Director of Graduate Admissions, 716-673-3251.*

Graduate Studies
Dr. Thomas Rywick, Interim Dean, Natural and Social Sciences and Professional Studies
Programs in:
  biology • MS, MS Ed
  business administration • MBA
  chemistry • MS, MS Ed
  educational administration • CAS
  elementary education • MS Ed
  English • MA, MS Ed
  mathematics • MS Ed
  reading • MS Ed
  secondary education • MS Ed
  social sciences • MA, MS
  speech pathology and audiology • MS

School of Music
Dr. Peter Schoenbach, Director
Programs in:
  music • MM
  music education • MM

STATE UNIVERSITY OF NEW YORK COLLEGE AT GENESEO
Geneseo, NY 14454-1401

http://www.geneseo.edu

Public coed comprehensive institution. *Enrollment: 5,560 graduate, professional, and undergraduate students. Graduate faculty: 38 full-time, 20 part-time. Computer facilities: Campuswide network is available with full Internet access. Total number of PCs/terminals supplied for student use: 650. Computer service fees are applied as a separate charge. Library facilities: Milne Library plus 1 additional on-campus library. Graduate expenses: Tuition of $5100 per year full-time, $213 per credit hour part-time for state residents; $8416 per year full-time, $351 per credit hour part-time for nonresidents. Fees of $375 per year full-time, $15.35 per credit hour part-time. General application contact: Dr. Kathleen Broikou, Director of Graduate Studies, 716-245-5546.*

Graduate Studies
Dr. Kathleen Broikou, Director of Graduate Studies
Program in:
  communicative disorders and sciences • MA

School of Education
Dr. Gary DeBolt, Head
Programs in:
  elementary education • MS Ed
  reading • MPS, MS Ed
  secondary education • MS Ed

STATE UNIVERSITY OF NEW YORK COLLEGE AT ONEONTA
Oneonta, NY 13820-4015

http://www.oneonta.edu/

Public coed comprehensive institution. *Enrollment: 5,406 graduate, professional, and undergraduate students. Computer facilities: Campuswide network is available with full Internet access. Total number of PCs/terminals supplied for student use: 200. Computer services are offered at no charge. Library facilities: James M. Milne Library plus 1 additional on-campus library. Graduate expenses: Tuition of $5100 per year full-time, $213 per credit hour part-time for state residents; $8416 per year full-time, $351 per credit hour part-time for nonresidents. Fees of $482 per year full-time, $6.85 per credit hour part-time. General application contact: Dr. Carolyn Haessig, Coordinator of Graduate Programs, 607-436-2523.*

Graduate Studies
Dr. Carolyn Haessig, Coordinator of Graduate Programs
Programs in:
  biology • MA
  biology education • MS Ed
  business • MS
  chemistry education • MS Ed

counseling • CAS, MS, MS Ed
early secondary English (N–9) • MS Ed
early secondary math (N–9) • MS Ed
early secondary social science (N–9) • MS Ed
earth science • MA
earth science education • MS Ed
English • MA
English education • MS Ed
general science (N–9) • MS Ed
history • MA
history museum studies • MA
home economics education • MS Ed
mathematics education • MS Ed
physics education • MS Ed
reading • MS Ed
school nurse teacher • MS Ed
social science education • MS Ed

STATE UNIVERSITY OF NEW YORK COLLEGE AT POTSDAM

Potsdam, NY 13676

http://www.potsdam.edu/

Public coed comprehensive institution. *Enrollment:* 4,038 graduate, professional, and undergraduate students. Graduate faculty: *48 full-time, 19 part-time.* Computer facilities: *Campuswide network is available with full Internet access. Total number of PCs/terminals supplied for student use: 375. Computer service fees are included with tuition and fees.* Library facilities: *F. W. Crumb Memorial Library plus 1 additional on-campus library.* Graduate expenses: *Tuition of $5100 per year full-time, $213 per credit hour part-time for state residents; $8416 per year full-time, $351 per credit hour part-time for nonresidents. Fees of $315 per year full-time, $12.50 per credit hour part-time.* General application contact: *Dr. William Amoriell, Dean of Education and Graduate Studies, 315-267-2515.*

Crane School of Music

Dr. James Stoltie, Dean
Programs in:
   composition • MM
   history and literature • MM
   music education • MM
   music theory • MM
   performance • MM

School of Arts and Sciences

Dr. Galen K. Pletcher, Dean
Programs in:
   English • MA
   mathematics • MA

School of Education

Dr. William Amoriell, Dean of Education and Graduate Studies
Programs in:
   educational technology • MS Ed
   elementary education • MS Ed, MST
   reading education • MS Ed
   secondary education • MS Ed, MST
   special education • MS Ed

STATE UNIVERSITY OF NEW YORK COLLEGE OF ENVIRONMENTAL SCIENCE AND FORESTRY

Syracuse, NY 13210-2779

http://www.esf.edu/

Public coed university. *Enrollment:* 1,694 graduate, professional, and undergraduate students. Graduate faculty: *124 full-time, 9 part-time.* Computer facilities: *Campuswide network is available with full Internet access. Computer services are offered at no charge.* Library facilities: *F. Franklin Moon Library.* Graduate expenses: *Tuition of $5100 per year full-time, $213 per credit hour part-time for state residents; $8416 per year full-time, $351 per credit hour part-time for nonresidents. Fees of $308 per year full-time, $48 per semester (minimum) part-time.* General application contact: *Dr. Robert H. Frey, Dean, Instruction and Graduate Studies, 315-470-6599.*

Faculty of Chemistry

Dr. John P. Hassett, Chairperson
Program in:
   chemistry • MS, PhD

Faculty of Environmental and Forest Biology

Dr. Neil H. Ringler, Chairperson
Program in:
   environmental and forest biology • MPS, MS, PhD

Faculty of Environmental and Resource Engineering

Dr. Robert Brock, Chairperson
Program in:
   environmental and resource engineering • MPS, MS, PhD

Faculty of Environmental Science

Dr. Richard Smardon, Chairperson
Program in:
   environmental science • MPS, MS, PhD

Faculty of Forestry

Dr. William Bentley, Chair
Programs in:
   agronomy and soil sciences management • MPS, MS, PhD

State University of New York College of Environmental Science and Forestry (continued)

    forest resources management • MPS, MS, PhD

    forestry • MPS, MS, PhD

    natural resources management • MPS, MS, PhD

Faculty of Landscape Architecture

Richard Hawks, Chairperson

Program in:

    landscape architecture • MLA, MS

STATE UNIVERSITY OF NEW YORK INSTITUTE OF TECHNOLOGY AT UTICA/ROME

Utica, NY 13504-3050

http://www.sunyit.edu/

Public coed upper-level institution. *Enrollment: 1,877 graduate, professional, and undergraduate students. Graduate faculty: 42 full-time, 10 part-time. Computer facilities: Campuswide network is available with full Internet access. Total number of PCs/terminals supplied for student use: 275. Computer service fees are included with tuition and fees. Library facilities: main library. Graduate expenses: Tuition of $5100 per year full-time, $213 per credit hour part-time for state residents; $8416 per year full-time, $351 per credit hour part-time for nonresidents. Fees of $570 per year full-time, $17.60 per credit hour part-time. General application contact: Marybeth Lyons, Director of Admissions, 315-792-7500.*

School of Business

Dr. Richard Havranek, Dean

Programs in:

    accountancy • MS

    business management • MS

School of Information Systems and Engineering Technology

Dr. Rosemary Mullick, Acting Dean

Programs in:

    advanced technology • MS

    computer and information science • MS

    telecommunications • MS

School of Nursing

Dr. Elizabeth Kellogg Walker, Dean

Programs in:

    adult nurse practitioner • Certificate, MS

    nursing administration • MS

SYRACUSE UNIVERSITY

Syracuse, NY 13244-0003

http://www.syr.edu/

Independent coed university. *Enrollment: 18,387 graduate, professional, and undergraduate students. Graduate faculty: 807 full-time, 570 part-time. Computer facilities: Campuswide network is available with full Internet access. Total number of PCs/terminals supplied for student use: 700. Computer service fees are included with tuition and fees. Library facilities: Ernest Stevenson Bird Library plus 6 additional on-campus libraries. Graduate expenses: $13,320 per year full-time, $555 per credit hour part-time. General application contact: Dr. Howard Johnson, Dean of the Graduate School, 315-443-5012.*

Graduate School

Dr. Howard Johnson, Dean

College for Human Development

Susan Crockett, Dean

Programs in:

    child and family studies • MA, MS, PhD

    consumer studies • MA, MS

    environmental arts • MA, MS

    marriage and family therapy • MA, PhD

    nutrition science and food management • MA, MS, PhD

College of Arts and Sciences

Robert Jensen, Dean

Programs in:

    anthropology • MA, PhD

    applied statistics • MS

    art history • MA

    biology • MS, PhD

    biophysics • PhD

    chemistry • MS, PhD

    classics • MA

    clinical psychology • MA, MS, PhD

    composition/rhetoric • PhD

    creative writing • MFA

    English • PhD

    experimental psychology • MA, MS, PhD

    foreign languages • DA

    French language, literature and culture • MA

    geology • MA, MS, PhD

    German language, literature and culture • MA

    Greek literature • MA

    humanities • MA, PhD

    hydrogeology • MS

    linguistic studies • MA

    literature and critical theory • MA

    mathematics • MS, PhD

    mathematics education • MS, PhD

    music history • MA

    philosophy • MA, PhD

    physics • MS, PhD

    psychology • MA, MS, PhD

    religion • MA, PhD

    Romance language • DA, MA

    Romance languages • MA

Russian language, literature and culture • MA
school psychology • PhD
Slavic language and literature • MA
social psychology • PhD
Spanish language, literature and culture • MA, PhD

College of Nursing
Grace Chickadonz, Dean
Program in:
nursing • MS

College of Visual and Performing Arts
Donald Lantzy, Dean
Programs in:
advertising design • MFA
art photography process • MFA
ceramics • MFA
cinema/drama • MFA
computer graphics • MFA
design • MFA
directing/acting • MFA
drama • MA, MFA
experimental studios • MFA
fiber structure interlocking • MFA
film-art/drama • MFA
illustration • MFA
industrial design • MID
interior design • MFA
metalsmithing • MFA
museum studies • MA
music composition • M Mus
organ • M Mus
painting • MFA
percussion • M Mus
piano • M Mus
printmaking • MFA
sculpture • MFA
speech communication • MA, MS
strings • M Mus
surface pattern design • MFA
technical theater • MFA
theory • M Mus
video research • MFA
voice • M Mus
wind instruments • M Mus

L. C. Smith College of Engineering and Computer Science
Dr. Edward Bogucz, Dean
Programs in:
aerospace engineering • MS, PhD
bioengineering • MS
chemical engineering • MS, PhD
civil engineering • MS, PhD
computer and information science • PhD
computer engineering • CE, MS, PhD
computer science • MS
electrical engineering • EE, MS, PhD
engineering management • MS
environmental engineering • MS
hydrogeology • MS
manufacturing engineering • MS
mechanical engineering • MS, PhD
neuroscience • MS, PhD
solid-state science and technology • MS, PhD
systems and information science • MS, PhD

Maxwell School of Citizenship and Public Affairs
John Palmer, Dean
Programs in:
anthropology • MA, PhD
economics • MA, PhD
geography • MA, PhD
history • MA, PhD
international relations • MA, PhD
political science • MA, PhD
public administration • MA, MPA, PhD
social sciences • MS Sc, PhD
sociology • MA, PhD

School of Architecture
Bruce Abbey, Dean
Program in:
architecture • M Arch

School of Education
Dr. Steven T. Bossert, Dean
Programs in:
art education • CAS, MS
audiology and speech pathology • MS, PhD
counselor education • CAS, Ed D, MS, PhD
cultural foundations of education and curriculum • CAS, MS, PhD
educating infants and young children with special needs • MS
educational administration • CAS, Ed D, MS, PhD
educational leadership • CAS, Ed D, MS
elementary education • CAS, MS
English education • CAS, Ed D, MS, PhD
exercise science • CAS, MS
health and physical education • CAS, MS
higher education • CAS, Ed D, MS, PhD
instructional design, development, and evaluation • CAS, Ed D, MS, PhD
learning disabilities • MS
mathematics education • CAS, Ed D, MS, PhD
music education • M Mu, MS
reading and language arts • CAS, Ed D, MS, PhD
rehabilitation counseling • Ed D, MS, PhD
science education • CAS, Ed D, MS, PhD
social studies education • CAS, MS
special education (emotional disorders and severe disabilities) • Ed D, MS, PhD
teaching and curriculum • CAS, Ed D, MS, PhD

School of Information Studies
Dr. Raymond F. von Dram, Dean
Programs in:
information and library science • CAS, MLS
information resources management • MS
information transfer • PhD
telecommunications and network management • MS

School of Management
George Burman, Dean
Programs in:
accounting • MBA, MS Acct, PhD
business administration • MBA
finance • MBA, PhD
human resource management • MBA
innovation management • PhD

Syracuse University (continued)
  international business • MBA
  management • MPS
  management information systems • MBA, PhD
  managerial statistics • MBA
  marketing • MBA, PhD
  operations management • MBA, PhD
  organizational behavior • PhD
  organization and management • MBA
  strategy • PhD
  transportation and distribution management • MBA

School of Social Work
William Pollard, Dean
Programs in:
  family mental health • MSW
  gerontology • MSW
  health care • MSW
  occupational social work • MSW

S. I. Newhouse School of Public Communications
David Rubin, Dean
Programs in:
  advertising • MA, MS
  broadcast journalism • MA, MS
  communications management • MS
  magazine journalism • MA, MS
  mass communications • PhD
  media administration • MPS
  newspaper journalism • MA, MS
  photography • MA, MS
  television-radio • MA, MS

College of Law
Daan Braveman, Dean
Program in:
  law • JD

TEACHERS COLLEGE, COLUMBIA UNIVERSITY
New York, NY 10027-6696

http://www.tc.columbia.edu/

Independent coed graduate-only institution. *Enrollment: 5,045 matriculated graduate/professional students. Graduate faculty: 128 full-time, 218 part-time. Computer facilities: Campuswide network is available with full Internet access. Computer service fees are included with tuition and fees. Library facilities: Milbank Memorial Library. Graduate expenses: Tuition of $640 per credit. Fees of $120 per semester. General application contact: John Fisher, Executive Director of Admissions and Financial Aid, 212-678-3710.*

Graduate Faculty of Education
Arthur Levine, President
Programs in:
  adult education • Ed D, MA
  anthropology • Ed D, Ed M, MA, PhD

applied educational psychology—school psychology • Ed D, Ed M, MA, PhD
applied linguistics • Ed D, Ed M, MA
applied physiology • Ed D, Ed M, MA, MS
art and art education • Ed D, Ed DCT, Ed M, MA
arts administration • MA
audiology • Ed D, Ed M, MS, PhD
behavioral disorders • Ed D, MA, PhD
bilingual and bicultural education • MA
blind and visual impairment • Ed D, MA
clinical psychology • PhD
college teaching and academic leadership • Ed D
communications • Ed D, Ed M, MA
community nutrition education • Ed M
comparative and international education • Ed D, Ed M, MA, PhD
computing in education • MA
counseling psychology • Ed D, Ed M, PhD
cross categorical studies in special education • Ed D, Ed M, MA, PhD
curriculum and teaching • Ed D, Ed M, MA
curriculum and teaching in physical education • Ed D, Ed M, MA
dance and dance education • MA
developmental psychology • Ed D, MA, PhD
early childhood education • Ed D, Ed M, MA
early childhood special education • Ed M, MA
economics and education • Ed D, Ed M, MA, PhD
educational administration • Ed D, Ed M, MA, PhD
educational media/instructional technology • Ed D, Ed M, MA
educational psychology-human cognition and learning • Ed D, Ed M, MA, PhD
elementary/childhood education, preservice • MA
giftedness • Ed D, MA
health education • Ed D, MA, MS
hearing impairment • Ed D, MA
higher education • Ed D, Ed M, MA, PhD
history and education • Ed D, Ed M, MA, PhD
inquiry in educational administration • Ed D
interdisciplinary studies • Ed D, Ed M, MA
international educational development • Ed D, Ed M, MA, PhD
learning disabilities • Ed D, Ed M, MA
mathematics education • Ed D, Ed DCT, Ed M, MA, MS, PhD
measurement, evaluation, and statistics • Ed D, MA, MS, PhD
mental retardation • Ed D, MA, PhD
motor learning • Ed D, Ed M, MA
music and music education • Ed D, Ed DCT, Ed M, MA
neuroscience and education • Ed M
nurse executive • Ed D, Ed M, MA
nursing, professional role • Ed D, Ed M, MA
nutrition and public health • Ed D, MS
nutrition education • Ed D, Ed M, MS
nutrition education and public health nutrition • Ed D, Ed M, MS
organizational psychology • Ed D, MA, PhD
philosophy and education • Ed D, Ed M, MA, PhD
physical disabilities • Ed D, MA, PhD
politics and education • Ed D, Ed M, MA, PhD
reading/learning disability • Ed M

reading specialist • MA

religion and education • Ed D, Ed M, MA

research in special education • Ed D

science education • Ed D, Ed DCT, Ed M, MA, MS, PhD

social psychology • Ed D, PhD

social studies education • Ed D, Ed M, MA, PhD

sociology and education • Ed D, Ed M, MA, PhD

special education administration and supervision, instructional practice • Ed D, Ed M, MA

speech-language pathology • Ed D, Ed M, MS, PhD

student personnel administration • Ed D, Ed M, MA

teaching English to speakers of other languages • Ed D, Ed M, MA

teaching of English and English education • Ed D, Ed M, MA, PhD

teaching of Spanish • Ed D, Ed DCT, Ed M, MA, PhD

UNIVERSITY OF ROCHESTER
Rochester, NY 14627-0001

http://www.rochester.edu/

Independent coed university. Enrollment: 8,451 graduate, professional, and undergraduate students. Graduate faculty: 1,263. Computer facilities: Campuswide network is available with full Internet access. Total number of PCs/terminals supplied for student use: 300. Computer service fees are included with tuition and fees. Library facilities: University Library plus 7 additional on-campus libraries. Graduate expenses: Tuition of $21,485 per year full-time, $672 per credit hour part-time. Fees of $336 per year. General application contact: Dean of the appropriate school, 716-275-2121.

Eastman School of Music
James Undercofler, Director
Programs in:
composition • DMA, MA, MM, PhD
conducting • DMA, MM
education • MA, PhD
jazz studies/contemporary media • MM
music education • DMA, MM
musicology • MA, PhD
opera • MM
performance and literature • DMA, MM
piano accompanying and chamber music • DMA, MM
theory • MA, PhD
woodwinds • MM

Margaret Warner Graduate School of Education and Human Development
Philip Wexler, Dean
Program in:
education and human development • Ed D, MAT, MS, PhD

School of Medicine and Dentistry
Dr. Lowell Goldsmith, Dean
Programs in:
anatomy • MS, PhD
biochemistry • MS, PhD
biomedical engineering • MS, PhD
biophysics • MS, PhD
environmental studies and industrial hygiene • MS
health services research • PhD
marriage and family therapy • MS
medical statistics • MS
medicine • MD
medicine and dentistry • Certificate
microbiology • MS, PhD
neuroscience • MS, PhD
oral biology • MS
pathology • MS, PhD
pharmacology • MS, PhD
physiology • MS, PhD
public health • MPH
statistics • MA, PhD
toxicology • MS, PhD

School of Nursing
Sheila A. Ryan, Dean
Program in:
nursing • MS, PhD

The College, Arts and Sciences
Thomas LeBlanc, Vice Provost and Dean
Programs in:
anthropology • MA, PhD
brain and cognitive sciences • MS, PhD
cellular and molecular biology • MS, PhD
chemistry • MS, PhD
clinical psychology • PhD
comparative literature • MA, PhD
computer science • MS, PhD
developmental psychology • PhD
ecology and evolutionary biology • MS, PhD
economics • MA, PhD
English literature • MA, PhD
French • MA
genetics and developmental biology • MS, PhD
geology • MS, PhD
German • MA
history • MA, PhD
linguistics • MA, PhD
mathematics • MA, MS, PhD
philosophy • MA, PhD
physics • MA, MS, PhD
physics and astronomy • PhD
political science • MA, PhD
psychology • MA
public policy analysis • MS
social psychology • PhD
Spanish • MA
visual and cultural studies • MA, PhD

University of Rochester (continued)
The College, School of Engineering and Applied Sciences
Kevin Parker, Dean
Programs in:
    biomedical engineering • MS, PhD
    chemical engineering • MS, PhD
    electrical engineering • MS, PhD
    materials science • MS, PhD
    mechanical engineering • MS, PhD
    optics • MS, PhD

William E. Simon Graduate School of Business Administration
Charles Plosser, Dean
Program in:
    business administration • MBA, MS, PhD

WAGNER COLLEGE
Staten Island, NY 10301
http://www.wagner.edu/

Independent coed comprehensive institution. *Enrollment: 2,002 graduate, professional, and undergraduate students. Graduate faculty: 32 full-time, 25 part-time. Computer facilities: Campuswide network is available with full Internet access. Computer services are offered at no charge. Library facilities: Hormann Library plus 2 additional on-campus libraries. Graduate expenses: $580 per credit. General application contact: Dr. Constance B. Schuyler, Associate Provost and Dean of Graduate Studies, 718-390-3104.*

Division of Graduate Studies
Dr. Constance B. Schuyler, Associate Provost and Dean
Programs in:
    bacteriology • MS
    elementary education • MS Ed
    family nurse practitioner • Certificate
    finance and banking • MBA
    international business • MBA
    management • Exec MBA, MBA
    marketing • MBA
    nursing • MS
    secondary education • MS Ed
    special education • MS Ed

YESHIVA UNIVERSITY
New York, NY 10033-3201
http://www.yu.edu/

Independent coed university. *Computer facilities: Campuswide network is available with full Internet access. Total number of PCs/ terminals supplied for student use: 300. Computer services are offered at no charge. Library facilities: Mendel Gottesman Library of Hebraica-Judaica plus 5 additional on-campus libraries. Gradu-*

ate expenses: Tuition of $815 per credit (minimum). Fees of $150 per year. General application contact: Associate Director of Admissions, 212-960-5277.

Albert Einstein College of Medicine
Program in:
    medicine • MD

Sue Golding Graduate Division of Medical Sciences
Programs in:
    anatomy • PhD
    biochemistry • PhD
    cell and developmental biology • PhD
    cell biology • PhD
    developmental and molecular biology • PhD
    microbiology and immunology • PhD
    molecular genetics • PhD
    molecular pharmacology • PhD
    neuroscience • PhD
    pathology • PhD
    physiology and biophysics • PhD

Azrieli Graduate School of Jewish Education and Administration
Dr. Yitzchak Handel, Director
Program in:
    Jewish education and administration • Ed D, MS, Specialist

Benjamin N. Cardozo School of Law
Paul Verkuil, Dean
Program in:
    law • JD

Bernard Revel Graduate School
Dr. Arthur Hyman, Dean
Program in:
    Jewish studies • MA, PhD

Ferkauf Graduate School of Psychology
Dr. Lawrence J. Siegel, Dean
Programs in:
    clinical psychology • Psy D
    developmental psychology • PhD
    general psychology • MA
    health psychology • PhD
    school psychology • Psy D

Wurzweiler School of Social Work
Dr. Sheldon R. Gelman, Dean
Program in:
    social work • DSW, MSW

NORTH CAROLINA

APPALACHIAN STATE UNIVERSITY
Boone, NC 28608

http://www.appstate.edu/

Public coed comprehensive institution. *Enrollment:* 11,641 graduate, professional, and undergraduate students. Graduate faculty: *433 full-time, 33 part-time.* Computer facilities: *Campuswide network is available with full Internet access. Total number of PCs/terminals supplied for student use: 600. Computer service fees are included with tuition and fees.* Library facilities: *Carol Grotnes Belk Library plus 2 additional on-campus libraries.* Graduate expenses: *$1811 per year full-time, $354 per semester (minimum) part-time for state residents; $9081 per year full-time, $2171 per semester (minimum) part-time for nonresidents.* General application contact: *Dr. E. D. Huntley, Associate Dean for Graduate Studies, 704-262-2130.*

Cratis D. Williams Graduate School
Dr. Judith E. Domer, Dean of Graduate Studies and
　Research

College of Arts and Sciences
Dr. Don Sink, Dean
Programs in:
　Appalachian studies • MA
　applied physics • MS
　biology • MA, MS
　clinical psychology • MA
　computer science • MS
　English • MA
　general theoretical psychology • MA
　geography • MA
　gerontology • MA
　history • MA
　industrial and organizational psychology • MA
　mathematics • MA
　political science • MA
　public administration • MPA
　rehabilitation training • MA
　romance languages • MA
　school psychology • CAS, MA
　social sciences • MA

College of Education
Dr. Charles Duke, Dean
Programs in:
　adult education • Ed S, MA
　community counseling • MA
　early childhood education • MA
　educational leadership • Ed D
　educational media • MA
　elementary education • MA
　higher education • Ed S, MA
　library science • Ed S, MA, MLS
　marriage and family therapy • MA
　reading education • Ed S, MA
　school administration • MSA

　school counseling • Ed S, MA
　secondary education • MA
　special education • MA
　speech pathology and audiology • MA
　student development • Ed S, MA

College of Fine and Applied Arts
Dr. Ming Land, Dean
Programs in:
　exercise science • MS
　family and consumer sciences • MA
　industrial education • MA
　industrial technology • MA
　master teacher • MA
　sports management • MA

John A. Walker College of Business
Dr. Ken Peacock, Dean
Programs in:
　accounting • MS
　business administration • MBA
　industrial organization/human resource management •
　　MA

School of Music
Dr. Arthur Unsworth, Dean
Program in:
　music education • MM

CAMPBELL UNIVERSITY
Buies Creek, NC 27506

http://www.campbell.edu/

Independent-religious coed university. *Enrollment:* 5,976 graduate, professional, and undergraduate students. Graduate faculty: *72 full-time, 48 part-time.* Computer facilities: *Campuswide network is available with full Internet access. Total number of PCs/terminals supplied for student use: 65. Computer services are offered at no charge.* Library facilities: *Carrie Rich Library plus 2 additional on-campus libraries.* Graduate expenses: *$168 per credit hour (minimum).* General application contact: *James S. Farthing, Director of Graduate Admissions, 910-893-1200 Ext. 1318.*

Graduate and Professional Programs
Dr. Jerry M. Wallace, Vice President for Academic Affairs
　and Provost

Divinity School
Dr. Michael Cogdill, Dean
Programs in:
　Christian education • MA
　divinity • M Div

Lundy-Fetterman School of Business
Thomas H. Folwell Jr., Dean
Program in:
　business • MBA

Campbell University (continued)

School of Education
Dr. Margaret Giesbrecht, Dean
Programs in:
administration • MSA
community counseling • MA
elementary education • M Ed
English education • M Ed
mathematics education • M Ed
middle grades education • M Ed
physical education • M Ed
school counseling • M Ed
secondary education • M Ed
social science education • M Ed

School of Law
Patrick K. Hetrick, Dean
Program in:
law • JD

School of Pharmacy
Dr. Ronald Maddox, Dean
Program in:
pharmacy • Pharm D

DUKE UNIVERSITY
Durham, NC 27708-0586

http://www.duke.edu/

Independent-religious coed university. *Enrollment: 12,346 graduate, professional, and undergraduate students. Graduate faculty: 3,466. Computer facilities: Campuswide network is available with full Internet access. Total number of PCs/terminals supplied for student use: 225. Computer service fees are included with tuition and fees. Library facilities: William R. Perkins Library plus 12 additional on-campus libraries. Graduate expenses: Tuition of $16,632 per year full-time, $693 per unit part-time. Fees of $2884 per year. General application contact: Donna Lee Giles, Assistant Dean for Admissions, 919-684-3913.*

Graduate School
Lewis M. Siegel, Dean
Programs in:
art and art history • PhD
biological chemistry • Certificate
biological psychology • PhD
botany • PhD
business administration • PhD
cell biology • PhD
cellular and molecular biology • Certificate, PhD
chemistry • PhD
classical studies • PhD
clinical psychology • PhD
cognitive psychology • PhD
comparative morphology of human and non-human primates • PhD
computer science • MS, PhD
crystallography of macromolecules • PhD

developmental psychology • PhD
East Asian studies • AM, Certificate
economics • AM, PhD
English • PhD
enzyme mechanisms • PhD
experimental psychology • PhD
French • PhD
genetics • PhD
geology • MS, PhD
German studies • PhD
gross anatomy and physical anthropology • PhD
health psychology • PhD
history • PhD
humanities • AM
human social development • PhD
immunology • PhD
international development policy • AM
Latin American studies • Certificate, PhD
liberal studies • AM
lipid biochemistry • PhD
literature • PhD
mathematics • PhD
medieval and Renaissance studies • Certificate
membrane structure and function • PhD
microbiology • PhD
molecular biophysics • Certificate
molecular cancer biology • PhD
molecular genetics • PhD
music composition • AM, PhD
musicology • AM, PhD
natural resource economics/policy • AM, PhD
natural resource science/ecology • AM, PhD
natural resource systems science • AM, PhD
neuroanatomy • PhD
neurobiology • PhD
neurochemistry • PhD
nucleic acid structure and function • PhD
pathology • PhD
performance practice • AM, PhD
pharmacology • PhD
philosophy • PhD
physical anthropology • PhD
physical therapy • MS
physics • PhD
physiology and cellular biophysics • PhD
political science • AM, PhD
primate social behavior • PhD
protein structure and function • PhD
religion • PhD
Slavic languages and literatures • AM, PhD
social/cultural anthropology • PhD
sociology • AM, PhD
Spanish • PhD
teaching • MAT
toxicology • Certificate
vertebrate paleontology • PhD
women's studies • Certificate
zoology • PhD

Center for Demographic Studies
Dr. George C. Myers, Director
Program in:
demographic studies • PhD

Institute of Statistics and Decision Sciences
Dr. Michael Lavine, Director of Graduate Studies
Program in:
  statistics and decision sciences • PhD

School of Engineering
Dr. Earl H. Dowell, Dean
Programs in:
  biomedical engineering • MS, PhD
  civil and environmental engineering • MS, PhD
  electrical and computer engineering • MS, PhD
  engineering management • MEM
  environmental engineering • MS, PhD
  materials science • MS, PhD
  mechanical engineering • MS, PhD

Terry Sanford Institute of Public Policy
Dr. Francis Lethem, Director of Graduate Studies
Program in:
  public policy • MPP

Divinity School
Dr. L. Gregory Jones, Dean
Program in:
  theology • M Div, MCM, MTS, Th M

Fuqua School of Business
Blair H. Sheppard, Senior Associate Dean for Academic
  Programs
Programs in:
  business • PhD, WEMBA
  health services management • MBA

Nicholas School of the Environment
Dr. Norman L. Christensen Jr., Dean
Programs in:
  coastal environmental management • MEM
  environmental science and policy • PhD
  environmental toxicology, chemistry, and risk assessment
    • MEM
  forest resource management • MF
  resource ecology • MEM
  resource economics and policy • MEM
  water and air resources • MEM

School of Law
Pamela B. Gann, Dean
Program in:
  law • JD, LL M, MLS, SJD

School of Medicine
Dr. Dan G. Blazer, Dean for Medical Education
Programs in:
  clinical research • MHS
  medicine • MD
  pathologists' assistant • MHS
  physician assistant • MHS

School of Nursing
Dr. Mary T. Champagne, Dean
Programs in:
  acute care adult • Certificate, MSN
  acute care pediatric • Certificate, MSN
  adult cardiovascular • Certificate, MSN
  adult oncological/HIV • Certificate, MSN
  clinical nurse specialist • MSN
  family • Certificate, MSN
  gerontological • Certificate, MSN
  health systems leadership and outcomes • Certificate,
    MSN
  neonatal • Certificate, MSN
  nurse practitioner • MSN
  nursing informatics • Certificate
  pediatric • Certificate, MSN

 # EAST CAROLINA UNIVERSITY
Greenville, NC 27858-4353

http://www.ecu.edu/

Public coed university. *Enrollment:* 17,022 graduate, professional, and undergraduate students. Graduate faculty: *526 full-time, 4 part-time.* Computer facilities: *Campuswide network is available with full Internet access. Total number of PCs/terminals supplied for student use: 4,100. Computer service fees are included with tuition and fees.* Library facilities: *Joyner Library plus 1 additional on-campus library.* Graduate expenses: *$1886 per year full-time, $472 per semester (minimum) part-time for state residents; $9156 per year full-time, $2289 per semester (minimum) part-time for nonresidents.* General application contact: *Dr. Paul D. Tschetter, Associate Dean of the Graduate School, 252-328-6012.*

Graduate School
Dr. Thomas L. Feldbush, Vice Chancellor for Research and
  Graduate Studies
Programs in:
  anatomy and cell biology • PhD
  biochemistry • PhD
  microbiology and immunology • PhD
  pathology and laboratory medicine • PhD
  pharmacology • PhD
  physiology • PhD

College of Arts and Sciences
Dr. Keats Sparrow, Dean
Programs in:
  American history • MA, MA Ed
  anthropology • MA
  applied and biomedical physics • MS
  applied mathematics • MA
  applied resource economics • MS
  biology • MS
  chemistry • MS
  clinical psychology • MA
  computer science • MS
  English • MA, MA Ed
  European history • MA, MA Ed

East Carolina University (continued)
  general psychology • MA
  geography • MA
  geology • MS
  international studies • MA
  maritime history • MA
  mathematics • MA, MA Ed
  medical physics • MS
  molecular biology/biotechnology • MS
  public administration • MPA
  school psychology • CAS
  social studies • MA Ed
  sociology • MA

School of Allied Health Sciences
Dr. Harold Jones, Dean
Programs in:
  communication sciences and disorders • MSSL, PhD
  environmental health • MSEH
  occupational therapy • MS
  physical therapy • MPT
  rehabilitation studies • MS

School of Art
Jackie Leebrick, Director of Graduate Studies
Program in:
  art • MA, MA Ed, MFA

School of Business
Donald B. Boldt, Director of Graduate Studies
Programs in:
  accounting • MSA
  decision sciences • MBA
  finance • MBA
  management • MBA
  marketing • MBA

School of Education
Dr. Marilyn Sheerer, Dean
Programs in:
  adult education • MA Ed
  counselor education • CAS, MA Ed
  educational administration • Ed S
  educational leadership • Ed D
  elementary education • MA Ed
  instruction technology specialist • MA Ed
  learning disabilities • MA Ed
  library science • CAS, MLS
  mental retardation • MA Ed
  middle grade education • MA Ed
  reading education • MA Ed
  school administration • MSA
  science education • MA, MA Ed
  supervision • Ed S, MA Ed
  vocational education • MS

School of Health and Human Performance
Dr. Christian Zauner, Dean
Programs in:
  exercise and sports science • MA, MA Ed
  health education • MA, MA Ed

School of Human Environmental Sciences
Dr. Helen Grove, Dean
Programs in:
  child development and family relations • MS
  marriage and family therapy • MS
  nutrition • MS

School of Industry and Technology
Dr. Elmer Poe, Director of Graduate Studies
Program in:
  industry and technology • MS

School of Music
Dr. Rodney Schmidt, Director of Graduate Studies
Programs in:
  accompanying • MM
  church music • MM
  composition/theory • MM
  music education • MM
  music therapy • MM
  performance • MM
  piano pedagogy • MM
  string pedagogy • MM

School of Nursing
Dr. Lou Everett, Director of Graduate Studies
Program in:
  nursing • MSN

School of Social Work
Dr. Linner Griffin, Director of Graduate Studies
Program in:
  social work • MSW

School of Medicine
Dr. James A. Hallock, Dean
Programs in:
  anatomy and cell biology • PhD
  biochemistry • PhD
  medicine • MD
  microbiology and immunology • PhD
  pathology and laboratory medicine • PhD
  pharmacology • PhD
  physiology • PhD

ELON COLLEGE
Elon College, NC 27244
http://www.elon.edu/

Independent-religious coed comprehensive institution. *Enrollment:* 3,685 graduate, professional, and undergraduate students. Graduate faculty: 40. Computer facilities: *Campuswide network is available with full Internet access. Total number of PCs/terminals supplied for student use: 225. Computer services are offered at no charge.* Library facilities: *McEwen Library.* Graduate expenses: *$210 per credit hour.* General application contact: *Alice N. Essen, Director of Graduate Admissions, 800-334-8448.*

Program in Business Administration
Dr. Kevin J. O'Mara, Chair
Program in:
> business administration • MBA

Program in Education
Dr. Glenda W. Beamon, Director
Programs in:
> elementary education • M Ed
> special education • M Ed

Program in Physical Therapy
Dr. Elizabeth A. Rogers, Director
Program in:
> physical therapy • MPT

FAYETTEVILLE STATE UNIVERSITY
Fayetteville, NC 28301-4298

Public coed comprehensive institution. Library facilities: *Charles Waddell Chesnutt Library.* Graduate expenses: *$1498 per year full-time, $327 per semester (minimum) part-time for state residents; $8768 per year full-time, $2144 per semester (minimum) part-time for nonresidents. General application contact: Director of the Graduate Center, 910-486-1498.*

Graduate School
Programs in:
> biology • MAT, MS
> business administration • MBA
> education • Ed D
> educational leadership and secondary education • MA Ed
> elementary education • MA Ed
> English • MA
> history • MA, MAT
> mathematics • MAT, MS
> middle grades education • MA Ed
> political science • MA, MAT
> psychology • MA
> sociology • MA, MAT
> special education • MA Ed

GARDNER–WEBB UNIVERSITY
Boiling Springs, NC 28017

Independent-religious coed comprehensive institution. *Enrollment: 2,755 graduate, professional, and undergraduate students. Graduate faculty: 39 full-time, 13 part-time. Computer facilities: Campuswide network is available with full Internet access. Total number of PCs/ terminals supplied for student use: 115. Computer service fees are included with tuition and fees. Library facilities: John R. Dover Memorial Library.* Graduate expenses: *$178 per semester hour*

full-time, *$220 per semester hour part-time. General application contact: Dr. Darlene J. Gravett, Dean, Graduate School, 704-434-4723.*

Graduate Studies
Dr. Darlene J. Gravett, Dean
Programs in:
> agency counseling • MA
> elementary education • MA
> English education • MA
> middle grades education • MA
> physical education • MA
> school administration • MA
> school counseling • MA

Broyhill School of Management
Dr. Anthony Negbenebor, Director
Program in:
> management • MBA

School of Divinity
Dr. R. Wayne Stacy, Dean
Program in:
> theology • M Div

LENOIR–RHYNE COLLEGE
Hickory, NC 28601

http://www.lrc.edu/

Independent-religious coed comprehensive institution. *Enrollment: 1,617 graduate, professional, and undergraduate students. Graduate faculty: 16. Computer facilities: Campuswide network is available with full Internet access. Total number of PCs/terminals supplied for student use: 60. Computer service fees are included with tuition and fees. Library facilities: Carl Augustus Rudisill Library.* Graduate expenses: *$190 per credit hour. General application contact: Dr. Thomas W. Fauquet, Dean of Graduate Studies, 828-328-7275.*

Division of Graduate Programs
Dr. Thomas W. Fauquet, Dean
Programs in:
> academically gifted • MA
> business • MBA
> counselor education • Ed S, MA
> early childhood education • MA
> elementary education • MA
> middle school education • MA
> reading • MA

MEREDITH COLLEGE
Raleigh, NC 27607-5298

http://www.meredith.edu/

Independent-religious female only comprehensive institution. *Enrollment: 2,552 graduate, professional, and undergraduate students. Graduate faculty: 15 full-time, 8 part-time. Computer facilities: Campuswide network is available with full Internet access. Total number of PCs/terminals supplied for student use: 120. Computer service fees are included with tuition and fees. Library facilities: Carlyle Campbell Library plus 2 additional on-campus libraries. Graduate expenses: $4680 per year full-time, $260 per credit hour part-time. General application contact: Dr. Mary Johnson, Dean of Graduate School, 919-829-8423.*

John E. Weems Graduate School
Dr. Mary Johnson, Dean
Programs in:
  business administration • MBA
  education • M Ed
  music • MM

NORTH CAROLINA AGRICULTURAL AND TECHNICAL STATE UNIVERSITY
Greensboro, NC 27411

http://www.ncat.edu/

Public coed university. *Enrollment: 7,468 graduate, professional, and undergraduate students. Graduate faculty: 442 full-time, 91 part-time. Computer facilities: Campuswide network is available with full Internet access. Computer services are offered at no charge. Library facilities: F. D. Bluford Library. Graduate expenses: $1662 per year full-time, $272 per semester (minimum) part-time for state residents; $8790 per year full-time, $2054 per semester (minimum) part-time for nonresidents. General application contact: Dr. Thoyd Melton, Dean of the Graduate School and Associate Vice Chancellor for Academic Affairs, 336-334-7920.*

Graduate School
Dr. Thoyd Melton, Dean and Associate Vice Chancellor for Academic affairs

College of Arts and Sciences
Dr. Ethel F. Taylor, Interim Dean
Programs in:
  applied mathematics • MS
  art education • MS
  biology • MS
  chemistry • MS
  English • MA
  English and Afro-American literature • MA
  history education • MS
  mathematics education • MS
  mathematics, secondary education • MS
  social science education • MS
  sociology and social work • MSW

College of Engineering
Dr. Lonnie Sharpe, Dean
Programs in:
  architectural engineering • MSAE
  chemical engineering • MSE
  civil engineering • MSE
  computer science • MSCS
  electrical engineering • MSEE, PhD
  industrial engineering • MSIE, PhD
  mechanical engineering • MSME, PhD

School of Agriculture
Dr. Daniel Godfrey, Dean
Programs in:
  agricultural economics • MS
  agricultural education • MS
  food and nutrition • MS
  plant science • MS

School of Education
Dr. David Boger, Dean
Programs in:
  adult education • MS
  biology education • MS
  chemistry education • MS
  early childhood education • MS
  educational administration • MS
  educational media • MS
  educational supervision • MS
  elementary education • MS
  English education • MS
  guidance and counseling • MS
  health and physical education • MS
  history education • MS
  human resources • MS
  reading • MS
  social science education • MS

School of Technology
Dr. Earl Yarborough, Dean
Programs in:
  industrial arts education • MS
  industrial technology • MS, MSIT
  safety and driver education • MS
  technology education • MS
  vocational-industrial education • MS

NORTH CAROLINA CENTRAL UNIVERSITY
Durham, NC 27707-3129

http://www.nccu.edu/

Public coed comprehensive institution. *Enrollment: 5,664 graduate, professional, and undergraduate students. Graduate faculty: 243 full-time, 78 part-time. Library facilities: James E. Shepard Memorial Library plus 3 additional on-campus libraries. Graduate*

expenses: *$2027 per year full-time, $508 per semester (minimum) part-time for state residents; $9155 per year full-time, $2290 per semester (minimum) part-time for nonresidents. General application contact: Dr. Patsy B. Perry, Interim Vice Chancellor for Academic Affairs and Provost, 919-560-6230.*

Division of Academic Affairs
Dr. Patsy B. Perry, Interim Vice Chancellor for Academic
　　Affairs and Provost

College of Arts and Sciences
Dr. Bernice D. Johnson, Interim Dean
Programs in:
　　biology • MS
　　chemistry • MS
　　criminal justice • MS
　　earth sciences • MS
　　English • MA
　　French • MA
　　general physical education • MS
　　history • MA
　　human sciences • MS
　　mathematics • MS
　　music • MA
　　psychology • MA
　　public administration • MPA
　　recreation administration • MS
　　sociology • MA
　　special physical education • MS
　　therapeutic recreation • MS

School of Business
Dr. Sundar Flemming, Dean
Program in:
　　business • MBA

School of Education
Dr. Sammie C. Parrish, Dean
Programs in:
　　agency counseling • MA
　　career counseling • MA
　　educational leadership • MA
　　education of the emotionally handicapped • M Ed
　　education of the mentally handicapped • M Ed
　　elementary education • M Ed, MA
　　instructional media • MA
　　school counseling • MA
　　speech pathology and audiology • M Ed

School of Law
Percy Luney, Dean
Program in:
　　law • JD

School of Library and Information Sciences
Dr. Benjamin F. Speller Jr., Dean
Program in:
　　library and information sciences • MIS, MLS

NORTH CAROLINA STATE UNIVERSITY
Raleigh, NC 27695
http://www.ncsu.edu/

Public coed university. *Enrollment: 27,529 graduate, professional, and undergraduate students. Graduate faculty: 1,480 full-time, 782 part-time. Computer facilities: Campuswide network is available. Total number of PCs/terminals supplied for student use: 2,500. Computer service fees are included with tuition and fees. Library facilities: D. H. Hill Library plus 5 additional on-campus libraries. Graduate expenses: $2370 per year full-time, $517 per semester (minimum) part-time for state residents; $11,536 per year full-time, $2809 per semester (minimum) part-time for nonresidents. General application contact: Graduate Admissions, 919-515-2871.*

Graduate School
Dr. Debra W. Stewart, Dean
Programs in:
　　cell biology and morphology • MS, PhD
　　epidemiology and population medicine • MS, PhD
　　immunology • MS, PhD
　　microbiology and immunology • MS, PhD
　　pathology • MS, PhD
　　pharmacology • MS, PhD
　　specialized veterinary medicine • MS

College of Agriculture and Life Sciences
Dr. James L. Oblinger, Interim Dean
Programs in:
　　adult and community college education • Ed D, M Ed,
　　　MS
　　agricultural and extension education • MS
　　agricultural economics • M Econ, MS, PhD
　　agriculture and life sciences • MA
　　animal science • M Ag, MS, PhD
　　biochemistry • MS, PhD
　　biological and agricultural engineering • MBAE, MS,
　　　PhD
　　botany • MLS, MS, PhD
　　crop science • M Ag, MS, PhD
　　ecology • MS
　　entomology • M Ag, MS, PhD
　　food science • M Ag, MS, PhD
　　genetics • MS, PhD
　　horticultural science • M Ag, MS, PhD
　　microbiology • MLS, MS, PhD
　　nutrition • MS, PhD
　　physiology • MLS, MS, PhD
　　plant pathology • M Ag, MLS, MS, PhD
　　poultry science • MS
　　rural sociology • MS
　　sociology • M Soc, PhD
　　soil science • M Ag, MS, PhD
　　toxicology • M Tox, MS, PhD
　　zoology • MAWB, MLS, MS, PhD

North Carolina State University (continued)

College of Education and Psychology

Dr. Joan J. Michael, Dean

Programs in:

  adult and community college education • Ed D, M Ed, MS

  agricultural education • CAGS, M Ed, MS

  counselor education • CAGS, Ed D, M Ed, MS, PhD

  curriculum and instruction • Ed D, M Ed, MS

  education and psychology • Certificate

  health occupations education • M Ed, MS

  mathematics education • M Ed, MS, PhD

  middle years education • M Ed, MS

  occupational education • CAGS, Ed D, M Ed, MS

  psychology • MS, PhD

  science education • M Ed, MS, PhD

  special education • M Ed, MS

  technology education • M Ed, MS

  training and development • MS

College of Engineering

Dr. Nino A. Masnari III, Dean

Programs in:

  aerospace engineering • MS, PhD

  biological and agricultural engineering • MBAE, MS, PhD

  chemical engineering • M Ch E, MS, PhD

  civil engineering • MCE, MS, PhD

  computer science • MC Sc, MS, PhD

  electrical and computer engineering • MS, PhD

  engineering • M Eng, PD

  industrial engineering • MIE, MSIE, PhD

  integrated manufacturing systems engineering • MIMS

  materials science and engineering • MMSE, MS, PhD

  mechanical engineering • MME, MS, PhD

  nuclear engineering • MNE, MS, PhD

  operations research • MOR, MS, PhD

College of Forest Resources

Dr. Larry W. Tombaugh, Dean

Programs in:

  fisheries and wildlife management • MS

  forestry • MF, MS, PhD

  geographic information systems • MS

  maintenance management • MRRA, MS

  recreation/park management • MRRA, MS

  recreation planning • MRRA, MS

  recreation resources administration/public administration • MRRA

  sports management • MRRA, MS

  travel and tourism management • MS

  wood and paper science • MS, MWPS, PhD

College of Humanities and Social Sciences

Dr. Margaret A. Zahn, Dean

Programs in:

  English • MA

  history • MA

  international studies • MAIS

  liberal studies • MA

  political science • MA

  public administration • MPA, PhD

  public history • MA

  rural sociology • MS

  sociology • M Soc, PhD

  technical communication • MS

College of Management

Dr. Richard J. Lewis, Dean

Programs in:

  accounting • MAC

  biotechnology • MS

  computer science • MS

  economics • M Econ, MA, PhD

  engineering • MS

  forest resources management • MS

  general business • MS

  management information systems • MS

  operations research • MS

  statistics • MS

  telecommunications systems engineering • MS

  textile management • MS

  total quality management • MS

College of Physical and Mathematical Sciences

Dr. Jerry L. Whitten, Dean

Programs in:

  applied mathematics • MS, PhD

  biomathematics • M Biomath, MS, PhD

  chemistry • MCH, MS, PhD

  ecology • PhD

  geology • MS, PhD

  geophysics • MS, PhD

  marine, earth, and atmospheric sciences • MS, PhD

  mathematics • MS, PhD

  meteorology • MS, PhD

  oceanography • MS, PhD

  physical and mathematical sciences • MA

  physics • MS, PhD

  statistics • M Stat, MS, PhD

College of Textiles

Dr. Robert A. Barnhardt, Dean

Programs in:

  fiber and polymer science • PhD

  textile chemistry • MS, MT

  textile engineering • MS

  textiles • MS, MT, MTE

  textile technology management • PhD

School of Design

Dr. Marvin Malecha, Dean

Programs in:

  architecture • M Arch

  graphic design • MGD

  industrial design • MID

  landscape architecture • MLA

College of Veterinary Medicine

Dr. Oscar J. Fletcher, Dean

Programs in:

  cell biology and morphology • MS, PhD

  epidemiology and population medicine • MS, PhD

  immunology • MS, PhD

  microbiology and immunology • MS, PhD

  pathology • MS, PhD

  pharmacology • MS, PhD

  physiology • MLS, MS, PhD

specialized veterinary medicine • MS
veterinary medicine • DVM

PFEIFFER UNIVERSITY
Misenheimer, NC 28109-0960

http://www.pfeifferuniv.edu/

Independent-religious coed comprehensive institution. *Enrollment:* 1,214 graduate, professional, and undergraduate students. Graduate faculty: *11 full-time, 8 part-time.* Computer facilities: *Campuswide network is available. Total number of PCs/terminals supplied for student use: 35. Computer service fees are included with tuition and fees.* Library facilities: *G. A. Pfeiffer Library.* Graduate expenses: *$245 per hour (minimum).* General application contact: *Dan Owens, Director of Graduate Admissions, 704-521-9116.*

Program in Business Administration
Dr. Muhammed Abdullah, Director
Programs in:
business administration • MBA
organizational management • MS

Program in Religion, Philosophy, and Christian Education
Kay Kilbourne, Coordinator
Program in:
religion, philosophy, and Christian ed • MACE

QUEENS COLLEGE
Charlotte, NC 28274-0002

Independent-religious coed comprehensive institution. *Enrollment:* 1,652 graduate, professional, and undergraduate students. Graduate faculty: *11 full-time, 6 part-time.* Computer facilities: *Campuswide network is available with partial Internet access (e-mail only). Computer service fees are included with tuition and fees.* Library facilities: *Everett Library.* Graduate expenses: *Tuition of $260 per credit hour. Fees of $40 per year.* General application contact: *Katie M. Wireman, Director of Adult Admissions, 704-337-2242.*

Hayworth College
Dr. Darrel Miller, Dean
Program in:
elementary education • MAT

Division of Nursing
Dr. Joan McGill, Chair
Program in:
nursing management • MSN

McColl School of Business
Dr. Sid Adkins, Dean
Program in:
business • MBA

 # THE UNIVERSITY OF NORTH CAROLINA AT CHAPEL HILL
Chapel Hill, NC 27599

http://www.unc.edu/

Public coed university. *Enrollment:* 24,189 graduate, professional, and undergraduate students. Graduate faculty: *2,371.* Computer facilities: *Campuswide network is available with full Internet access. Computer service fees are included with tuition and fees.* Library facilities: *Davis Library plus 21 additional on-campus libraries.* Graduate expenses: *Tuition of $1428 per year full-time, $357 per semester (minimum) part-time for state residents; $10,414 per year full-time, $2604 per semester (minimum) part-time for nonresidents. Fees of $782 per year full-time, $332 per semester (minimum) part-time.* General application contact: *Peggy O. Berryhill, Director for Admissions and Student Records, 919-962-6312.*

Graduate School
Dr. Linda Dykstra, Dean
Programs in:
applied and materials science • MS, PhD
biochemistry and biophysics • MS, PhD
biomedical engineering • MS, PhD
cell biology and anatomy • PhD
dental hygiene education • MS
dentistry • MS
experimental pathology • MS, PhD
genetics and molecular biology • MS, PhD
human movement science • MS
immunology • MS, PhD
microbiology • MS, PhD
neurobiology • PhD
occupational science • MS
oral biology • MS, PhD
oral epidemiology • PhD
pharmacology • PhD
pharmacy • MS, PhD
physical therapy • MPT
physiology • PhD
public policy analysis • PhD
rehabilitation psychology and counseling • MS
speech and hearing sciences • MS
toxicology • MS, PhD

College of Arts and Sciences
Dr. Linda Dykstra, Dean, Graduate School
Programs in:
acting • MFA
anthropology • MA, PhD
art history • MA, PhD
astronomy and astrophysics • MS, PhD
athletic training • MA

The University of North Carolina at Chapel Hill (continued)

botany • MA, MS, PhD

cell biology, development, and physiology • MA, MS, PhD

chemistry • MA, MS, PhD

city and regional planning • MRP

classical archaeology • MA, PhD

classics • MA, PhD

clinical psychology • MA, PhD

communication studies • MA

comparative literature • MA, PhD

computer science • MS, PhD

costume technology • MFA

developmental psychology • PhD

development psychology • MA

ecology • MA, MS, PhD

ecology and behavior • MA, MS, PhD

economics • MS, PhD

English • MA, PhD

exercise physiology • MA

experimental psychology • MA, PhD

folklore • MA

French • MA, PhD

genetics and molecular biology • MA, MS, PhD

geography • MA, PhD

geology • MS, PhD

Germanic languages • MA, PhD

history • MA, PhD

Italian • MA, PhD

Latin American studies • Certificate

leisure studies and recreation administration • MSRA

linguistics • MA, PhD

marine sciences • MS, PhD

mathematics • MA, MS, PhD

morphology, systematics, and evolution • MA, MS, PhD

music • MA, PhD

operations research • MS, PhD

philosophy • MA, PhD

planning • PhD

political science • MA, PhD

Portuguese • MA, PhD

public administration • MPA

public policy analysis • PhD

quantitative psychology • MA, PhD

religious studies • MA, PhD

Romance languages • MA, PhD

Romance philology • MA, PhD

Russian literature • MA, PhD

Slavic languages • MA, PhD

social psychology • MA, PhD

sociology • MA, PhD

Spanish • MA, PhD

sports administration • MA

sports psychology • MA

statistics • MS, PhD

studio art • MFA

technical production • MFA

School of Education
Dr. Madeline R. Grumet, Dean

Programs in:

culture, curriculum and change • PhD

curriculum and instruction • Ed D, MA

early childhood, family, and literacy studies • PhD

early intervention and family support • M Ed

educational leadership • Ed D

educational psychology • M Ed, MA

elementary education • M Ed

English • MAT

French • MAT

German • MAT

Japanese • MAT

Latin • MAT

learning disabilities • M Ed

mathematics • MAT

music • MAT

psychological studies in education • PhD

school administration • MSA

school counseling • M Ed, MA

school psychology • M Ed, MA, PhD

science • MAT

social studies/social science • MAT

Spanish • MAT

special education • M Ed, MA

School of Information and Library Science
Dr. Barbara B. Moran, Dean

Program in:

information and library science • CAS, MSIS, MSLS, PhD

School of Journalism and Mass Communication
Dr. Richard R. Cole, Dean

Program in:

mass communication • MA, PhD

School of Nursing
Dr. Cynthia M. Freund, Dean

Program in:

nursing • MSN, PhD

School of Public Health
Dr. William L. Roper, Dean

Programs in:

biostatistics • Dr PH, MPH, MS, PhD

environmental engineering • MSEE

environmental sciences and engineering • MS, PhD

epidemiology • Dr PH, MPH, MSPH, PhD

health behavior and health education • Dr PH, MPH, PhD

health policy and administration • Dr PH, MHA, MPH, MSPH, PhD

maternal and child health • Dr PH, MPH, MSPH

nutrition • Dr PH, MPH, PhD

professional practice program • MPH

public health • MPH, MSPH

public health leadership • Dr PH, MPH, MS

public health nursing • MPH, MS

School of Social Work
Dr. Richard Edwards, Dean

Program in:

social work • Certificate, MSW

Kenan-Flagler Business School
Robert S. Sullivan, Dean
Programs in:
  accounting • MAC, PhD
  business • MBA
  business administration • MBA
  business policy/strategy • PhD
  finance • PhD
  marketing • PhD
  operations management/quantitative methods • PhD
  organizational behavior • PhD

School of Dentistry
Dr. John Stamm, Dean
Programs in:
  dental hygiene education • MS
  dentistry • DDS
  oral biology • MS, PhD
  oral epidemiology • PhD

School of Law
Judith W. Wegner, Dean
Program in:
  law • JD

School of Medicine
Dr. Jeffrey Houpt, Dean
Programs in:
  biochemistry and biophysics • MS, PhD
  biomedical engineering • MS, PhD
  cell biology and anatomy • PhD
  experimental pathology • MS, PhD
  genetics and molecular biology • MS, PhD
  human movement science • MS
  immunology • MS, PhD
  medicine • MD
  microbiology • MS, PhD
  neurobiology • PhD
  occupational science • MS
  pharmacology • PhD
  physical therapy • MPT
  physiology • PhD
  rehabilitation psychology and counseling • MS
  speech and hearing sciences • MS

School of Pharmacy
Dr. William H. Campbell, Dean
Program in:
  pharmacy • MS, PhD

UNIVERSITY OF NORTH CAROLINA AT CHARLOTTE
Charlotte, NC 28223-0001
http://www.uncc.edu/

Public coed university. *Enrollment:* 16,370 graduate, professional, and undergraduate students. Graduate faculty: *482 full-time, 27 part-time.* Computer facilities: *Campuswide network is available*

with full Internet access. Total number of PCs/terminals supplied for student use: 750. Computer service fees are included with tuition and fees. Library facilities: *J. Murrey Atkins Library.* Graduate expenses: *$1786 per year full-time, $339 per semester (minimum) part-time for state residents; $8914 per year full-time, $2121 per semester (minimum) part-time for nonresidents.* General application contact: *Dr. Robert J. Mundt, Interim Dean, 704-547-3372.*

Graduate School
Dr. Robert J. Mundt, Interim Dean
Program in:
  health administration • MHA

College of Architecture
Charles Hight, Dean
Program in:
  architecture • M Arch

College of Arts and Sciences
Dr. Schley R. Lyons, Dean
Programs in:
  applied mathematics • MS, PhD
  applied physics • MS
  applied statistics • MS
  biology • MA, MS
  chemistry • MS
  community/clinical psychology • MA
  criminal justice • MS
  English • MA
  geography and earth sciences • MA
  gerontology • MA
  history • MA
  industrial/organizational psychology • MA
  liberal studies • MA
  mathematics • MA
  mathematics education • MA
  political science • MPA
  psychology • MA
  sociology • MA

College of Business Administration
Dr. Edward M. Mazze, Dean
Programs in:
  accounting • M Acc
  business administration • MBA
  economics • MS

College of Education
Dr. John M. Nagle, Dean
Programs in:
  counseling and guidance • MA
  educational administration • CAS
  educational leadership • Ed D
  elementary education • M Ed
  instructional systems technology • M Ed
  middle school education • M Ed
  reading education • M Ed
  school administration • MSA
  secondary education • M Ed
  special education • M Ed
  teaching English as a second language • M Ed

University of North Carolina at Charlotte (continued)
College of Nursing and Health Professions
Dr. Sue M. Bishop, Dean
Programs in:
    health education • M Ed
    nursing • MSN

School of Information Technology
Dr. Robert J. Mundt, Interim Dean, Graduate School
Program in:
    information technology • PhD

The William States Lee College of Engineering
Dr. Robert D. Snyder, Dean
Programs in:
    civil engineering • MSCE
    computer science • MS
    electrical engineering • MSEE, PhD
    engineering • ME, MSE
    mechanical engineering and engineering science •
        MSME, PhD

UNIVERSITY OF NORTH CAROLINA AT GREENSBORO
Greensboro, NC 27412-0001

http://www.uncg.edu/

Public coed university. *Enrollment:* 12,500 graduate, professional, and undergraduate students. *Graduate faculty:* 559 full-time, 146 part-time. *Computer facilities: Campuswide network is available with full Internet access. Computer service fees are included with tuition and fees. Library facilities: Walter Clinton Jackson Library plus 1 additional on-campus library. Graduate expenses: Tuition of $1842 per year full-time, $370 per semester (minimum) part-time for state residents; $10,296 per year full-time, $2484 per semester (minimum) part-time for nonresidents. Fees of $806 per year full-time, $111 per semester (minimum) part-time. General application contact: Dr. Anne P. Saab, Associate Dean, 336-334-5596.*

Graduate School
Dr. Brad Bartel, Dean
Programs in:
    gerontology • Certificate
    interdisciplinary studies • MALS

College of Arts and Sciences
Walter Beale, Dean
Programs in:
    applied communication • MA
    art • M Ed
    biology • M Ed, MS
    chemistry • M Ed, MS
    clinical psychology • MA, PhD
    creative writing • MFA
    drama • M Ed, MFA
    English • M Ed, MA, PhD
    film and video • MFA
    French • M Ed, MA

    geography • MA
    history • M Ed, MA
    Latin • M Ed
    mathematics • M Ed, MA
    political science • MA
    psychology • MA, PhD
    public affairs • MPA
    sociology • MA
    Spanish • M Ed, MA
    speech communication • M Ed, MA
    studio arts • MFA

Joseph M. Bryan School of Business and Economics
James K. Weeks, Dean
Programs in:
    accounting • MS
    applied economics • MA
    business administration • Certificate, MBA
    business marketing education • MSBE
    economics • MA
    information systems and operations management • MS
    international business administration • Certificate

School of Education
Dr. David Armstrong, Dean
Programs in:
    curriculum and teaching • PhD
    deaf education • M Ed, MA
    educational leadership • Ed D, Ed S, PhD
    educational research, measurement and evaluation •
        M Ed, PhD
    education and welfare of exceptional individuals • M Ed
    elementary curriculum and teaching • M Ed
    gerontological counseling • PMC
    guidance and counseling • Ed D, MS, PhD
    higher education • M Ed
    library and information studies • MLIS
    marriage and family counseling • PMC
    middle grades education • M Ed
    school administration • MSA
    school counseling • PMC
    secondary curriculum and teaching • M Ed
    supervision • M Ed

School of Health and Human Performance
Robert Christina, Dean
Programs in:
    dance • MA, MFA
    exercise and sports science • M Ed, MS, PhD
    parks and recreation management • MS
    public health education • MPH

School of Human Environmental Sciences
Dr. Helen A. Shaw, Dean
Programs in:
    food service management • M Ed, MS
    home economics education • M Ed, MS, PhD
    housing and interior design • MS
    human development and family studies • M Ed, MS,
        PhD
    human nutrition • M Ed, MS, PhD
    social work • MSW
    textile products design and marketing • M Ed, MS, PhD

School of Music
Arthur Tollefson, Dean
Programs in:
    composition • MM
    education • MM
    music education • PhD
    performance • DMA, MM

School of Nursing
Dr. Lynne Pearcey, Dean
Programs in:
    administration of nursing in health agencies • MSN
    gerontological nurse practitioner • PMC
    nurse anesthesia • MSN, PMC

UNIVERSITY OF NORTH CAROLINA AT PEMBROKE
Pembroke, NC 28372-1510

http://www.uncp.edu/

Public coed comprehensive institution. *Enrollment:* 3,034 graduate, professional, and undergraduate students. Graduate faculty: *51 full-time, 6 part-time.* Computer facilities: *Campuswide network is available with full Internet access. Total number of PCs/terminals supplied for student use: 400. Computer service fees are included with tuition and fees.* Library facilities: *Sampson-Livermore Library. Graduate expenses: $1554 per year full-time, $610 per semester (minimum) part-time for state residents; $8824 per year full-time, $2122 per semester (minimum) part-time for nonresidents.* General application contact: *Dean of Graduate Studies, 910-521-6271.*

Graduate Studies
Programs in:
    business administration • MBA
    educational administration and supervision • MA Ed
    elementary education • MA Ed
    English education • MA
    mathematics education • MA Ed
    middle grades education • MA Ed
    organizational leadership and management • MS
    reading education • MA Ed
    school administration • MSA
    school counseling • MA
    service agency counseling • MA

UNIVERSITY OF NORTH CAROLINA AT WILMINGTON
Wilmington, NC 28403-3201

http://www.uncwil.edu/

Public coed comprehensive institution. *Enrollment:* 9,176 graduate, professional, and undergraduate students. Graduate faculty: *109 full-time, 12 part-time.* Library facilities: *Randall Library.* Graduate

expenses: *$1748 per year full-time, $270 per semester (minimum) part-time for state residents; $8882 per year full-time, $2058 per semester (minimum) part-time for nonresidents.* General application contact: *Neil F. Hadley, Dean, Graduate School, 910-962-4117.*

College of Arts and Sciences
Dr. JoAnn Seiple, Dean
Programs in:
    biology • MS
    chemistry • MS
    creative writing • MFA
    English • MA
    geology • MS
    history • MA
    marine biology • MS
    mathematical sciences • MA, MS
    psychology • MA

School of Business
Dr. Howard Rockness, Dean
Programs in:
    accountancy • MS
    business administration • MBA

School of Education
Dr. Robert Tyndall, Dean
Programs in:
    educational administration and supervision • M Ed
    elementary education • M Ed
    reading education • M Ed
    special education • M Ed
    teaching • MAT

WAKE FOREST UNIVERSITY
Winston-Salem, NC 27109

http://www.wfu.edu/

Independent coed university. *Enrollment:* 5,748 graduate, professional, and undergraduate students. Graduate faculty: *1,448.* Library facilities: *Z. Smith Reynolds Library plus 3 additional on-campus libraries. Graduate expenses: $17,150 per year full-time, $550 per hour part-time.* General application contact: *Dr. Gordon A. Melson, Dean of the Graduate School, 336-758-5301.*

Graduate School
Dr. Gordon A. Melson, Dean
Programs in:
    accountancy • MSA
    analytical chemistry • MS, PhD
    anthropology • MA
    biochemistry • PhD
    biology • MS, PhD
    bioorganic and macromolecular structure • PhD
    cancer biology • PhD
    comparative medicine • MS
    computer science • MS

Wake Forest University (continued)

English • MA
epidemiology • MS
guidance and counseling • MA Ed
health and exercise science • MS
health services research • MS
history • MA
inorganic chemistry • MS, PhD
liberal studies • MALS
mathematics • MA
medical engineering • PhD
medical genetics • MS
microbiology and immunology • PhD
molecular and cellular pathobiology • MS, PhD
molecular genetics • PhD
neurobiology and anatomy • PhD
neuroscience • PhD
organic chemistry • MS, PhD
pastoral counseling • MA
pharmacology • PhD
physical chemistry • MS, PhD
physics • MS, PhD
physiology • PhD
psychology • MA
religion • MA
secondary education • MA Ed
speech communication • MA

Babcock Graduate School of Management

R. Charles Moyer, Dean
Program in:
business administration • MBA

School of Law

Robert K. Walsh, Dean
Program in:
law • JD, LL M

School of Medicine

Dr. James N. Thompson, Dean
Programs in:
biochemistry • PhD
bioorganic and macromolecular structure • PhD
cancer biology • PhD
comparative medicine • MS
epidemiology • MS
health services research • MS
medical engineering • PhD
medical genetics • MS
medicine • MD
microbiology and immunology • PhD
molecular and cellular pathobiology • MS, PhD
molecular genetics • PhD
neurobiology and anatomy • PhD
neuroscience • PhD
pharmacology • PhD
physiology • PhD

WESTERN CAROLINA UNIVERSITY

Cullowhee, NC 28723

http://www.wcu.edu/

Public coed comprehensive institution. *Enrollment: 6,511 graduate, professional, and undergraduate students. Graduate faculty: 275. Computer facilities: Campuswide network is available with full Internet access. Total number of PCs/terminals supplied for student use: 400. Computer service fees are included with tuition and fees. Library facilities: Hunter Library. Graduate expenses: $1799 per year full-time, $144 per credit hour (minimum) part-time for state residents; $9069 per year full-time, $1053 per credit hour (minimum) part-time for nonresidents. General application contact: Kathleen Owen, Assistant to the Dean, 828-227-7398.*

Graduate School

College of Applied Science

Dale Pounds, Dean
Programs in:
family and consumer sciences • MAT, MS
health sciences • MHS
industrial and engineering technology • MS
physical therapy • MPT

College of Arts and Sciences

J. C. Alexander, Dean
Programs in:
American history • MA
art education • MAT
biology • MA Ed, MAT, MS
chemistry and physics • MAT, MS
English • MA, MA Ed, MAT
mathematics and computer science • MA Ed, MAT, MS
music • MA
public affairs • MPA
social sciences • MAT
studio art • MA

College of Business

Dr. Ronald E. Shiffler, Dean
Programs in:
accountancy • M Ac
business administration • MBA
project management • MPM

College of Education and Allied Professions

Gurney Chambers, Dean
Programs in:
art education • MAT
behavioral disorders • MA Ed
biology • MAT
chemistry • MAT
clinical psychology • MA
communication disorders • MS
community college education • MA Ed
community counseling • MS
counseling • MA Ed
educational administration • MA Ed
educational leadership • Ed D, Ed S

educational supervision • MA Ed
elementary education • MA Ed
English • MAT
family and consumer sciences • MAT
human resource development • MS
learning disabilities • MA Ed
mathematics • MAT
mental retardation • MA Ed
middle grades education • MA Ed
physical education • MA Ed, MAT
reading • MAT
reading education • MAT
school administration • MSA
school counseling • MA Ed
school psychology • MA
social sciences • MAT

NORTH DAKOTA

MINOT STATE UNIVERSITY
Minot, ND 58707-0002

http://warp6.cs.misu.nodak.edu/

Public coed comprehensive institution. *Enrollment:* 3,294 graduate, professional, and undergraduate students. *Graduate faculty:* 80 full-time, 14 part-time. *Computer facilities: Campuswide network is available with full Internet access. Computer service fees are included with tuition and fees. Library facilities: Gordon B. Olson Library. Graduate expenses: $2714 per year for state residents; $3235 per year (minimum) for nonresidents. General application contact: Dr. Jack L. Rasmussen, Dean of Graduate School, 800-777-0750 Ext. 3150.*

Graduate School
Dr. Jack L. Rasmussen, Dean
Programs in:
　　audiology • MS
　　criminal justice • MS
　　education of the deaf • MS
　　elementary education • MS
　　English • MAT
　　infant/toddler • MS
　　learning disabilities • MS
　　management • MS
　　mathematics • MAT
　　music education • MME
　　science • MAT
　　severely multihandicapped • MS
　　special education • MS
　　speech-language pathology • MS

 # NORTH DAKOTA STATE UNIVERSITY
Fargo, ND 58105

http://www.ndsu.nodak.edu/index.nojs.shtml

Public coed university. *Enrollment.* 9,502 graduate, professional, and undergraduate students. *Graduate faculty: 425 full-time, 15 part-time. Computer facilities: Campuswide network is available with full Internet access. Total number of PCs/terminals supplied for student use: 350. Computer services are offered at no charge. Library facilities: main library plus 3 additional on-campus libraries. Graduate expenses: $2572 per year full-time, $107 per credit part-time for state residents; $6868 per year full-time, $286 per credit part-time for nonresidents. General application contact: Dr. William D. Slanger, Interim Dean, 701-231-7033.*

Graduate Studies and Research
Dr. William D. Slanger, Interim Dean
Program in:
　　natural resource management • MS

College of Agriculture
Dr. Glen Statler, Interim Associate Dean and Director of Academic Programs
Programs in:
　　agricultural economics • MS
　　animal science • MS, PhD
　　cellular and molecular biology • PhD
　　cereal science • MS, PhD
　　crop and weed sciences • MS
　　entomology • MS, PhD
　　horticulture • MS
　　microbiology • MS
　　natural resource management • MS
　　plant pathology • MS, PhD
　　plant sciences • PhD
　　range science • MS, PhD
　　soil sciences • MS, PhD
　　veterinary sciences • MS

College of Arts, Humanities and Social Sciences
Dr. Thomas J. Riley, Dean
Programs in:
　　acting • MA
　　directing • MA
　　dramatic theory • MA
　　English • MA, MS
　　history • MA, MS
　　mass communication • MA, MS
　　political science • MA, MS
　　sociology • MA, MS
　　speech communication • MA, MS
　　technical direction and stage design • MA

College of Business Administration
Dr. Jay Leitch, Dean
Program in:
　　business administration • MBA

North Dakota State University (continued)

College of Engineering and Architecture

Dr. Otto J. Helweg, Dean

Programs in:

agricultural and biosystems engineering • MS

civil engineering • MS

electrical engineering • MS

engineering • PhD

environmental engineering • MS

industrial engineering and management • MS

mechanical engineering and applied mechanics • MS

natural resource management • MS

College of Human Development and Education

Dr. Virginia L. Clark, Dean

Programs in:

agricultural education • M Ed, MS

agricultural extension education • MS

apparel/textiles • MS

cellular and molecular biology • PhD

child development and family science • MS

counselor education • M Ed, MA, MS

educational administration • Ed S, MS

family and consumer sciences education • M Ed, MS

food and nutrition • MS

pedagogy • M Ed, MS

physical education and athletic administration • M Ed, MS

College of Pharmacy

Dr. Charles Peterson, Dean

Programs in:

pharmaceutical sciences • PhD

pharmacology/toxicology • MS

College of Science and Mathematics

Dr. Allan Fischer, Dean

Programs in:

applied mathematics • MS, PhD

biochemistry • MS, PhD

botany • MS, PhD

cellular and molecular biology • PhD

chemistry • MS, PhD

clinical psychology • MS

computer science • MS, PhD

general psychology • MS

general science • MS

mathematics • MS, PhD

natural resource management • MS

operations research • MS

physics • MS, PhD

polymers and coatings • MS, PhD

psychology • MS

statistics • MS, PhD

zoology • MS, PhD

UNIVERSITY OF MARY
Bismarck, ND 58504-9652

Independent-religious coed comprehensive institution. *Enrollment:* 1,847 graduate, professional, and undergraduate students. *Graduate faculty: 27 full-time, 122 part-time.* Computer facilities: *Campuswide network is available with full Internet access. Total number of PCs/ terminals supplied for student use: 30. Computer service fees are applied as a separate charge.* Library facilities: *main library plus 1 additional on-campus library.* Graduate expenses: *$265 per credit.* General application contact: *Dr. Diane Fladeland, Director, Graduate Programs, 701-255-7500.*

Division of Nursing

Dr. Betty Rembur, Chair

Programs in:

family nurse practitioner • MSN

nursing administration • MSN

nursing education • MSN

Program in Education

Ramona Klein, Director

Programs in:

elementary education • MS

elementary education administration • MS Ed

higher education • MS Ed

secondary education administration • MS Ed

secondary teaching • MS Ed

special education • MS

Program in Management

Lawrence P. Brown, Director

Program in:

management • M Mgmt

Program in Physical Therapy

Michael Parker, Chairperson

Program in:

physical therapy • MPT

UNIVERSITY OF NORTH DAKOTA
Grand Forks, ND 58202

http://www.und.edu/

Public coed university. *Enrollment:* 11,512 graduate, professional, and undergraduate students. *Graduate faculty: 416 full-time.* Computer facilities: *Campuswide network is available with full Internet access. Computer services are offered at no charge.* Library facilities: *Chester Fritz Library plus 5 additional on-campus libraries.* Graduate expenses: *$3040 per year full-time, $153 per credit hour part-time for state residents; $7336 per year full-time, $332 per credit hour part-time for nonresidents.* General application contact: *Dr. Harvey Knull, Dean of the Graduate School, 701-777-2786.*

Graduate School
Dr. Harvey Knull, Dean
Programs in:
   anatomy • MS, PhD
   biochemistry • MS, PhD
   microbiology and immunology • MS, PhD
   pharmacology and toxicology • MS, PhD
   physical therapy • MPT
   physiology • MS, PhD

Center for Aerospace Studies
John Odegard, Dean
Programs in:
   atmospheric sciences • MS
   computer science • MS
   space studies • MS

College of Arts and Sciences
Dr. John Ettling, Dean
Programs in:
   botany • DA, MS, PhD
   chemistry • MS, PhD
   clinical psychology • PhD
   ecology • DA, MS, PhD
   English • MA, PhD
   entomology • DA, MS, PhD
   environmental biology • DA, MS, PhD
   fisheries/wildlife • DA, MS, PhD
   genetics • DA, MS, PhD
   geography • M Ed, MA, MS
   history • DA, MA
   linguistics • MA
   mathematics • M Ed, MS
   physics • MS, PhD
   psychology • MA, PhD
   sociology • MA
   speech-language pathology • MS
   zoology • DA, MS, PhD

College of Business and Public Administration
Dr. Dennis Elbert, Dean
Programs in:
   business administration • MBA
   business education • MS
   industrial technology • MS
   political science • MA
   public administration • MPA
   vocational education • MS

College of Education and Human Development
Dr. Mary Harris, Dean
Programs in:
   counseling • MA
   counseling psychology • PhD
   early childhood education • MS
   educational leadership • Ed D, Ed S, M Ed, MS, PhD
   education/general studies • MS
   elementary education • Ed D, M Ed, MS, PhD
   kinesiology • MS
   measurement and statistics • Ed D, PhD
   reading education • M Ed, MS
   secondary education • Ed D, PhD
   social work • MSW
   special education • Ed D, M Ed, MS, PhD

College of Fine Arts
Dr. Bruce Jacobsen, Dean
Programs in:
   communication • MA
   music • M Mus
   music education • M Mus
   theatre arts • MA
   visual arts • MFA

School of Engineering and Mines
Dr. Don Richard, Dean
Programs in:
   chemical engineering • M Engr, MS
   civil engineering • M Engr
   electrical engineering • M Engr, MS
   energy engineering • PhD
   geology • MA, MS, PhD
   mechanical engineering • M Engr, MS
   sanitary engineering • M Engr
   soils and structures engineering • M Engr
   surface mining engineering • M Engr

School of Nursing
Dr. Regina Monnig, Director
Program in:
   nursing • MS

School of Law
W. Jeremy Davis, Dean
Program in:
   law • JD

School of Medicine
Dr. H. David Wilson, Dean
Programs in:
   anatomy • MS, PhD
   biochemistry • MS, PhD
   medicine • MD
   microbiology and immunology • MS, PhD
   pharmacology and toxicology • MS, PhD
   physical therapy • MPT
   physiology • MS, PhD

OHIO

ASHLAND UNIVERSITY
Ashland, OH 44805-3702

http://www.ashland.edu/

Independent-religious coed comprehensive institution. *Enrollment:* 5,737 graduate, professional, and undergraduate students. Graduate faculty: 86 full-time, 74 part-time. Computer facilities: *Campuswide network is available with full Internet access. Total number of PCs/terminals supplied for student use: 400. Computer service fees are applied as a separate charge.* Library facilities: *main library plus 1 additional on-campus library.* Graduate expenses: *$275 per credit*

Ashland University (continued)
hour. General application contact: *Dr. Mary Ellen Drushal, Provost, 419-289-5099.*

College of Business Administration and Economics
Dr. Paul A. Sears, Dean
Program in:
    executive management • MBA

College of Education
Dr. Gene A. Telego, Associate Provost and Dean
Programs in:
    administration • M Ed
    business manager • M Ed
    classroom instruction • M Ed
    computer education • M Ed
    developmentally handicapped education • M Ed
    early childhood education • M Ed
    early education of the handicapped child • M Ed
    economics education • M Ed
    gifted education • M Ed
    multihandicapped education • M Ed
    reading • M Ed
    school treasurer • M Ed
    special education • M Ed
    specific learning disabled education • M Ed
    sports science • M Ed
    supervision • M Ed

Theological Seminary
Dr. Frederick J. Finks, President
Programs in:
    biblical studies • MA, MABS
    black church studies • MA
    Christian education • MACE
    church history • MA
    church music • MA
    ministry • D Min
    ministry management • MAMM
    missions • MA
    New Testament • MA
    Old Testament • MA
    pastoral counseling • MAPC
    philosophical studies • MA
    spiritual formation • MA
    theological studies • MA
    theology • M Div

BALDWIN-WALLACE COLLEGE
Berea, OH 44017-2088

http://www.bw.edu/

Independent-religious coed comprehensive institution. *Enrollment: 4,539 graduate, professional, and undergraduate students. Graduate faculty: 31 full-time, 32 part-time. Computer facilities: Campuswide network is available with full Internet access. Total number of PCs/terminals supplied for student use: 350. Computer services are offered at no charge. Library facilities: Ritter Library plus 1 additional*

on-campus library. Graduate expenses: $355 per credit hour (minimum). General application contact: *Dr. Jane F. Cavanaugh, Director of Continuing Education, 440-826-2222.*

Graduate Programs
Dr. Mark Collier, Academic Dean

Division of Business Administration
Dr. Thomas A. Riemenschneider, Director
Programs in:
    business management • MBA
    executive health care management • MBA
    executive management • MBA
    international management • MBA

Division of Education
Dr. Patrick F. Cosiano, Chairman
Programs in:
    reading • MA Ed
    specific learning disabilities • MA Ed
    supervision or administration • MA Ed

 # BOWLING GREEN STATE UNIVERSITY
Bowling Green, OH 43403

http://www.bgsu.edu/

Public coed university. *Enrollment: 17,328 graduate, professional, and undergraduate students. Graduate faculty: 531 full-time, 111 part-time. Computer facilities: Campuswide network is available with full Internet access. Total number of PCs/terminals supplied for student use: 700. Computer service fees are included with tuition and fees. Library facilities: William T. Jerome Library plus 6 additional on-campus libraries. Graduate expenses: $6070 per year full-time, $284 per credit hour part-time for state residents; $11,358 per year full-time, $536 per credit hour part-time for nonresidents. General application contact: Terry L. Lawrence, Director of Graduate Admissions, 419-372-7713.*

Graduate College
Dr. Steven Ballard, Associate Vice President for Research and Dean
Program in:
    interdisciplinary studies • MA, MS, PhD

College of Arts and Sciences
Dr. C. J. Cranny, Dean
Programs in:
    American culture studies • MA, MAT, PhD
    applied biology • Specialist
    applied philosophy • PhD
    applied statistics • MS
    art • MA
    art history • MA
    astrophysics • MS
    biological sciences • MAT, MS, PhD
    chemistry • MAT, MS

clinical psychology • MA, PhD
computer science • MS
creative writing • MFA
developmental psychology • MA, PhD
English • MA, PhD
experimental psychology • MA, PhD
French • MA
French education • MAT
geology • MAT, MS
German • MA, MAT
history • MA, MAT, PhD
industrial/organizational psychology • MA, PhD
interpersonal communication • MA, PhD
mass communication • MA, MAT, PhD
mathematics • MA, MAT, PhD
mathematics supervision • Ed S
philosophy • MA
photochemical sciences • PhD
physics • MAT, MS
physics and astronomy • MAT
popular culture • MA
public administration • MPA
quantitative psychology • MA, PhD
rhetoric composition • PhD
scientific and technical communication • MA
sociology • MA, PhD
Spanish • MA
Spanish education • MAT
statistics • MA, MAT, PhD
studio art • MA, MFA
teaching English as a second language • MA
theatre • MA, PhD

College of Business Administration
Dr. James Sullivan, Dean
Programs in:
    accountancy • M Acc
    applied statistics • MS
    business • MBA
    economics • MA
    organization development • MOD

College of Education and Allied Professions
Dr. Les Sternberg, Dean
Programs in:
    business education • M Ed
    classroom technology • M Ed
    college student personnel • MA
    development kinesiology • M Ed
    educational administration and supervision • Ed S, M Ed
    elementary education • M Ed
    food and nutrition • MFCS
    guidance and counseling • M Ed, MA
    higher education administration • PhD
    human development and family studies • MFCS
    leadership studies • Ed D
    math supervision • Ed S
    reading • Ed S, M Ed
    recreation and leisure • M Ed
    rehabilitation counseling • MRC
    school psychology • M Ed
    secondary education • M Ed
    special education • M Ed
    sport administration • M Ed

College of Health and Human Services
Dr. Clyde Willis, Dean
Programs in:
    communication disorders • MS, PhD
    public health • MPH

College of Musical Arts
Dr. H. Lee Riggins, Dean
Programs in:
    composition • MM
    music education • MM
    music history • MM
    music theory • MM
    performance • MM

College of Technology
Dr. Thomas Erekson, Dean
Programs in:
    career and technology education • M Ed
    manufacturing technology • MIT

CAPITAL UNIVERSITY
Columbus, OH 43209-2394

http://www.capital.edu/

Independent-religious coed comprehensive institution. *Enrollment: 3,988 graduate, professional, and undergraduate students. Graduate faculty: 55 full-time, 63 part-time. Library facilities: main library plus 1 additional on-campus library. Graduate expenses: $260 per credit hour. General application contact: Dr. John Wellington, Dean, Graduate School of Administration, 614-236-6679.*

Graduate School of Administration
Dr. John Wellington, Dean
Program in:
    administration • MBA

Law School
Steven C. Bahls, Dean
Programs in:
    law • JD
    taxation • LL M, MT

School of Nursing
Dr. Doris Edwards, Dean
Programs in:
    administration • MSN
    family and community • MSN
    legal studies • MSN
    theological studies • MSN

CASE WESTERN RESERVE UNIVERSITY
Cleveland, OH 44106
http://www.cwru.edu/

Independent coed university. *Enrollment: 9,344 graduate, professional, and undergraduate students. Graduate faculty: 1,949 full-time. Computer facilities: Campuswide network is available with full Internet access. Total number of PCs/terminals supplied for student use: 200. Computer services are offered at no charge. Library facilities: Kelvin Smith Library plus 5 additional on-campus libraries. Graduate expenses: $18,400 per year full-time, $767 per credit hour part-time. General application contact: Joy Eisen, Assistant Dean of Graduate Studies, 216-368-4390.*

Frances Payne Bolton School of Nursing
Dr. Dorothy Brooten, Dean
Programs in:
    acute care adult nurse practitioner • MSN
    acute care pediatric nurse practitioner • MSN
    adult practitioner • MSN
    community health nursing • MSN
    critical care nursing • MSN
    family nurse practitioner • MSN
    gerontological nurse practitioner • MSN
    medical-surgical nursing • MSN
    neonatal practitioner • MSN
    nurse anesthesia • MSN
    nurse midwifery • MSN
    nursing • ND, PhD
    oncology nursing • MSN
    pediatric nurse practitioner • MSN
    psychiatric-mental health nurse practitioner • MSN
    women's health nurse practitioner • MSN

Mandel School of Applied Social Sciences
Dr. Darlyne Bailey, Dean
Programs in:
    nonprofit organizations • CNM, MNO
    social administration • MSSA
    social welfare • PhD

School of Dentistry
Dr. Jerold Goldberg, Dean
Programs in:
    advanced general dentistry • Certificate
    dentistry • DDS
    endodontics • MSD
    oral surgery • Certificate
    orthodontics • MSD
    pedodontics • Certificate
    periodontics • MSD

School of Graduate Studies
Dr. Joyce E. Jentoft, Dean
Programs in:
    acting • MFA
    advanced general dentistry • Certificate

American studies • MA, PhD
analytical chemistry • MS, PhD
anesthesiology • MS
anthropology • MA, PhD
applied anatomy • MS
applied mathematics • MS, PhD
art education • MA
art history • MA, PhD
art history and museum studies • MA, PhD
astronomy • MS, PhD
biochemical research • MS
biochemistry • MS, PhD
bioethics • MA
biological anthropology • MS, PhD
biology • MS, PhD
biomedical sciences • PhD
biophysics and bioengineering • PhD
biostatistics • MS, PhD
cell biology • MS, PhD
cell physiology • PhD
cellular biology • MS, PhD
clinical psychology • PhD
comparative literature • MA
contemporary dance • MFA
developmental biology • PhD
dietetics • MS
early music • D Mus A
endodontics • MSD
English and American literature • MA, PhD
environmental toxicology • MS, PhD
experimental psychology • PhD
French • MA, PhD
genetic counseling • MS
geological sciences • MS, PhD
gerontology • Certificate
health services research • MS, PhD
history • MA, PhD
human, molecular, and developmental genetics • PhD
immunology • MS, PhD
inorganic chemistry • MS, PhD
mathematics • MS, PhD
mental retardation • PhD
microbiology • PhD
molecular biology • PhD
molecular toxicology • MS, PhD
museum studies • MA
music • MA, PhD
music education • MA, PhD
neurobiology • PhD
neuroscience • PhD
nutrition • MS, PhD
nutrition and biochemistry • PhD
oral surgery • Certificate
organic chemistry • MS, PhD
orthodontics • MSD
pathology • MS, PhD
pedodontics • Certificate
periodontics • MSD
pharmacology • PhD
physical chemistry • MS, PhD
physics • MS, PhD
physiology and biophysics • PhD
political science • MA, PhD

public health nutrition • MS
sociology • PhD
speech-language pathology • MA, PhD
statistics • MS, PhD
systems physiology • PhD
theater • MFA

The Case School of Engineering
James W. Wagner, Dean
Programs in:
applied physics • MS, PhD
biomedical engineering • MS, PhD
chemical engineering • ME, MS, PhD
clinical engineering • MS
computer engineering • MS, PhD
computing and information science • MS, PhD
electrical engineering • MS, PhD
engineering • ME
engineering mechanics • MS, PhD
environmental engineering • MS, PhD
fluid and thermal sciences • MS, PhD
geotechnical engineering • MS, PhD
macromolecular science • MS, PhD
materials science and engineering • MS, PhD
mechanical engineering • MS, PhD
structural engineering • MS, PhD
systems and control engineering • MS, PhD

School of Law
Gerald Korngold, Dean
Programs in:
law • JD
taxation • LL M
U.S. legal studies • LL M

School of Medicine
Dr. Nathan A. Berger, Dean
Programs in:
anesthesiology • MS
applied anatomy • MS
biochemical research • MS
biochemistry • MS, PhD
bioethics • MA
biological anthropology • MS, PhD
biomedical sciences • PhD
biophysics and bioengineering • PhD
biostatistics • MS, PhD
cell biology • MS, PhD
cell physiology • PhD
cellular biology • MS, PhD
developmental biology • PhD
dietetics • MS
environmental toxicology • MS, PhD
genetic counseling • MS
health services research • MS, PhD
human, molecular, and developmental genetics • PhD
immunology • MS, PhD
medicine • MD
microbiology • PhD
molecular biology • PhD
molecular toxicology • MS, PhD
neurobiology • PhD

neuroscience • PhD
nutrition • MS, PhD
nutrition and biochemistry • PhD
pathology • MS, PhD
pharmacology • PhD
physiology and biophysics • PhD
public health nutrition • MS
systems physiology • PhD

Weatherhead School of Management
Kim S. Cameron, Dean
Programs in:
accountancy • M Acc, PhD
banking and finance • MBA, PhD
economics • MBA
finance • MS
information systems • MS
labor and human resource policy • MBA, PhD
management • EDM
management information and decision systems • MBA, MSM, PhD
management policy • MBA, PhD
management science • MS
marketing • MBA, MS, PhD
operations management • MBA, MS
operations research • MS, PhD
organizational behavior and analysis • MBA, MS, PhD
quality management • MS

Mandel Center for Nonprofit Organizations
John Palmer Smith, Director
Program in:
nonprofit organizations • CNM, MNO

 CLEVELAND STATE UNIVERSITY
Cleveland, OH 44115-2440

http://www.csuohio.edu/

Public coed university. *Enrollment:* 13,817 graduate, professional, and undergraduate students. Graduate faculty: *440 full-time.* Computer facilities: *Campuswide network is available with full Internet access. Computer service fees are included with tuition and fees.* Library facilities: *main library plus 1 additional on-campus library.* Graduate expenses: *Tuition of $5252 per year full-time, $202 per credit hour part-time for state residents; $10,504 per year full-time, $404 per credit hour part-time for nonresidents. Fees of $2.25 per credit hour (minimum).* General application contact: *Gail H. Banes, Manager of Graduate Admissions, 216-687-3594.*

Cleveland State University (continued)
College of Graduate Studies
Dr. A. Harry Andrist, Dean

College of Arts and Sciences
Dr. Karen Steckol, Dean
Programs in:
  analytical chemistry • MS, PhD
  applied mathematics • MS
  applied optics • MS
  art history • MA
  biological, geological and environmental sciences • MS, PhD
  clinical and counseling psychology • MA
  clinical chemistry • MS, PhD
  communication • MACTM
  composition • MM
  condensed matter physics • MS
  consumer/industrial research • MA
  economics • MA
  education and performance • MM
  English • MA
  history • MA
  inorganic chemistry • MS
  mathematics • MA, MS
  music history • MM
  organic chemistry • MS
  philosophy • MA
  physical chemistry • MS
  research psychology • MA
  social work • MSW
  sociology • MA
  Spanish • MA
  speech and hearing • MA
  structural analysis • MS, PhD

College of Education
Dr. James McLoughlin, Dean
Programs in:
  adult learning and development • M Ed
  bilingual education • M Ed
  community health • M Ed
  computer uses in education • M Ed
  curriculum and instruction • M Ed
  early childhood education • M Ed
  early childhood/special education • M Ed
  educational administration and supervision • Ed S, M Ed
  educational research • M Ed
  education of emerging adolescents • M Ed
  elementary education • M Ed
  English as a second language • M Ed
  exercise science • M Ed
  gifted education • M Ed
  health education • M Ed
  human performance • M Ed
  learning disabilities • M Ed
  Montessori education • M Ed
  multihandicapped • M Ed
  pedagogy • M Ed
  reading • M Ed
  recreation • M Ed
  school and professional counseling • Ed S, M Ed
  secondary education • M Ed

  sport education • M Ed
  sport management • M Ed
  sport management/exercise science • M Ed
  urban education • PhD

Fenn College of Engineering
Dr. Kenneth Lloyd Keys, Dean
Programs in:
  chemical engineering • D Eng, MS
  civil engineering • D Eng, MS
  electrical and computer engineering • D Eng, MS
  industrial engineering • D Eng, MS
  mechanical engineering • D Eng, MS

James J. Nance College of Business Administration
Dr. Robert L. Minter, Dean
Programs in:
  accounting and financial information systems • MAFIS
  business administration • DBA, MBA
  health care administration • MBA
  information systems • DBA
  labor relations and human resources • MLRHR
  management and organization analysis • MCIS
  systems programming • MCIS

Maxine Goodman Levin College of Urban Affairs
Dr. David C. Sweet, Dean
Programs in:
  public administration • MPA
  urban planning, design, and development • MUPDD
  urban studies • MS, PhD

Cleveland-Marshall College of Law
Steven S. Steinglass, Dean
Program in:
  law • JD, LL M

COLLEGE OF MOUNT ST. JOSEPH
Cincinnati, OH 45233-1670
http://www.msj.edu/index.html

Independent-religious coed comprehensive institution. *Enrollment:* 2,470 graduate, professional, and undergraduate students. *Graduate faculty:* 20. Computer facilities: *Campuswide network is available with partial Internet access (e-mail only). Computer services are offered at no charge.* Library facilities: *Archbishop Alter Library.* Graduate expenses: *$320 per credit hour.* General application contact: *Dr. Barbara J. Reid, Chairperson, Education Department, 513-244-4812.*

Education Department
Dr. Barbara Reid, Chairperson
Programs in:
  art • MA Ed
  educational foundations • MA Ed
  elementary education • MA Ed
  inclusive early childhood education • MA Ed
  professional effectiveness • MA Ed

reading • MA Ed
special education • MA Ed

Program in Pastoral Studies

Dr. John Trokan, Chair
Program in:
   religious studies • MA

FRANCISCAN UNIVERSITY OF STEUBENVILLE
Steubenville, OH 43952-6701

http://www.franuniv.edu/

Independent-religious coed comprehensive institution. *Enrollment:* 1,997 graduate, professional, and undergraduate students. *Graduate faculty: 5 full-time, 6 part-time. Computer facilities: Campuswide network is available with full Internet access. Total number of PCs/ terminals supplied for student use: 83. Computer services are offered at no charge.* Library facilities: *John Paul II Library.* Graduate expenses: *Tuition of $410 per credit hour. Fees of $280 per year.* General application contact: *Mark McGuire, Associate Director of Graduate Admissions, 800-783-6220.*

Graduate Programs

Virginia Zoric, Assistant Dean of Faculty
Programs in:
   administration • MS Ed
   business • MBA
   counseling • MA
   philosophy • MA
   theology and Christian ministry • MA

JOHN CARROLL UNIVERSITY
University Heights, OH 44118-4581

http://www.jcu.edu/

Independent-religious coed comprehensive institution. *Enrollment:* 4,080 graduate, professional, and undergraduate students. *Graduate faculty: 133 full-time, 61 part-time. Computer facilities: Campuswide network is available with full Internet access. Total number of PCs/ terminals supplied for student use: 304. Computer service fees are included with tuition and fees.* Library facilities: *Grasselli Library.* Graduate expenses: *$450 per credit.* General application contact: *Dr. Sally H. Wertheim, Dean, Graduate School, 216-397-4284.*

Graduate School

Dr. Sally H. Wertheim, Dean
Programs in:
   administration supervision • M Ed, MA
   biology • MA, MS
   chemistry • MS

clinical counseling • Certificate
communication management • MA
counseling • MA
educational psychology • M Ed, MA
English • MA
guidance and counseling • M Ed, MA
history • MA
humanities • MA
mathematics • MA, MS
physics • MS
professional teacher education • M Ed, MA
religious studies • MA
school based elementary education • M Ed
school based secondary education • M Ed

School of Business

Dr. James M. Daley, Associate Dean
Program in:
   business • MBA

KENT STATE UNIVERSITY
Kent, OH 44242-0001

http://www.kent.edu/

Public coed university. *Enrollment:* 20,743 graduate, professional, and undergraduate students. *Graduate faculty: 765.* Library facilities: *main library plus 4 additional on-campus libraries.* Graduate expenses: *$4752 per year full-time, $216 per credit hour part-time for state residents; $9213 per year full-time, $419 per credit hour part-time for nonresidents.* General application contact: *Division of Research and Graduate Studies, 330-672-2661.*

College of Arts and Sciences

Dr. John W. Watson, Associate Dean
Programs in:
   American politics • MA, PhD
   analytical chemistry • MS, PhD
   anthropology • MA
   applied mathematics • MA, MS, PhD
   biochemistry • PhD
   botany • MA, MS, PhD
   chemical physics • MS, PhD
   chemistry • MA, MS, PhD
   clinical psychology • MA, PhD
   comparative politics • MA
   computer science • MA, MS, PhD
   criminal justice studies • MA
   ecology • MS, PhD
   English • MA, PhD
   experimental psychology • MA, PhD
   French • MA
   geography • MA, PhD
   geology • MS, PhD
   German • MA
   history • MA, PhD
   inorganic chemistry • MS, PhD
   international politics • PhD
   international relations • MA

Kent State University (continued)
Latin • MA
liberal studies • MLS
organic chemistry • MS, PhD
philosophy • MA
physical chemistry • MS, PhD
physics • MA, MS, PhD
physiology • MS, PhD
political theory • MA, PhD
public administration • MPA
pure mathematics • MA, MS, PhD
sociology • MA, PhD
Spanish • MA
zoology • MA, PhD

College of Fine and Professional Arts
Dr. Gary S. Nieman, Associate Dean

Hugh A. Glauser School of Music
Dr. John M. Lee, Director
Programs in:
composition • MA
conducting • MM
ethnomusicology • MA, PhD
music education • MM, PhD
musicology • MA, PhD
performance • MM
piano pedagogy • MM
theory • MA
theory and composition • PhD

School of Architecture and Environmental Design
James Dalton, Director
Program in:
architecture • M Arch

School of Art
William Quinn, Director
Programs in:
art education • MA
fiber arts • MA, MFA
graphic design/illustration • MA, MFA

School of Communication Studies
Dr. Keith L. Ewing, Interim Director
Program in:
communication studies • MA, PhD

School of Exercise, Leisure and Sport
Dr. Gary S. Nieman, Associate Dean, College of Fine and
Professional Arts
Programs in:
exercise physiology • PhD
physical education • MA

School of Family and Consumer Studies
Dr. Jeannie D. Sneed, Director
Programs in:
child and family relations • MA
nutrition • MS

School of Journalism and Mass Communication
Pamela J. Creedon, Director
Program in:
journalism and mass communication • MA

School of Library and Information Science
Dr. Danny P. Wallace, Director
Program in:
library and information science • MLS

School of Speech Pathology and Audiology
Dr. Peter B. Mueller, Director
Program in:
speech pathology and audiology • MA, PhD

School of Theatre and Dance
Dr. John R. Crawford, Director
Program in:
theatre • MA, MFA

Graduate School of Education
Dr. Joanne R. Whitmore, Dean
Programs in:
community counseling • M Ed, MA
counseling • Ed S
counseling and human development services • PhD
cultural foundations • M Ed, MA, PhD
curriculum and instruction • Ed S, M Ed, MA, PhD
developmentally handicapped education • M Ed, MA
early childhood education • M Ed, MA
educational psychology • M Ed, MA
elementary education • M Ed, MA, MAT
evaluation and measurement • M Ed, MA, PhD
gifted education • M Ed, MA
health education • M Ed, MA
hearing impaired education • M Ed, MA
higher education administration and student personnel
    • Ed S, M Ed, MA, PhD
instructional technology • M Ed, MA, PhD
K–12 leadership • Ed S, M Ed, MA, PhD
learning and development • M Ed, MA
multiply handicapped/orthopedically handicapped
    education • M Ed, MA
organization development • Ed S, M Ed, MA, PhD
reading • M Ed, MA
rehabilitation counseling • Ed S, M Ed, MA
school counseling • M Ed, MA
school psychology • Ed S, M Ed, PhD
secondary education • M Ed, MA, MAT
severe behavior disordered education • M Ed, MA
special education • Ed S, PhD
specific learning disabled education • M Ed, MA
vocational education • M Ed, MA

Graduate School of Management
Frederick W. Schroath, Associate Dean
Programs in:
accounting • MS, PhD
business administration • MBA
economics • MA, PhD
finance • PhD
management systems • PhD
marketing • PhD

School of Biomedical Sciences

Dr. James L. Blank, Director
Programs in:
biological anthropology • PhD
cellular and molecular biology • MS, PhD
neuroscience • MS, PhD
pharmacology • MS, PhD
physiology • MS, PhD

School of Nursing

Dr. Davina Gosnell, Dean
Programs in:
clinical nursing • MSN
nursing administration • MSN
nursing education • MSN
nursing of the adult (medical/surgical nursing) • MSN
parent-child nursing • MSN
psychiatric mental health nursing • MSN

School of Technology

Dr. A. Raj Chowdhury, Dean
Program in:
technology • MA

LAKE ERIE COLLEGE
Painesville, OH 44077-3389

http://www.lakeerie.edu/

Independent coed comprehensive institution. *Enrollment:* 708 graduate, professional, and undergraduate students. Graduate faculty: *11 full-time, 2 part-time.* Computer facilities: *Campuswide network is available with full Internet access. Total number of PCs/terminals supplied for student use: 45. Computer service fees are included with tuition and fees.* Library facilities: *Lincoln Learning Resource Center.* Graduate expenses: *Tuition of $391 per credit hour. Fees of $20 per credit hour.* General application contact: *Admissions Office, 440-639-7879.*

Division of Education

Dr. Carol Ramsay, Associate Dean of Teacher Education and Certification
Programs in:
education • MS Ed
effective teaching • MS Ed
reading • MS Ed

Division of Management Studies

Dr. William Blanchard, Associate Dean
Program in:
management studies • MBA

MIAMI UNIVERSITY
Oxford, OH 45056

http://www.muohio.edu/

Public coed university. *Enrollment:* 19,743 graduate, professional, and undergraduate students. Graduate faculty: *798.* Computer facilities: *Campuswide network is available with full Internet access. Computer service fees are included with tuition and fees.* Library facilities: *King Library plus 4 additional on-campus libraries.* Graduate expenses: *$5932 per year full-time, $255 per credit hour part-time for state residents; $12,392 per year full-time, $524 per credit hour part-time for nonresidents.* General application contact: *Dr. Robert C. Johnson, Associate Provost and Dean of the Graduate School, 513-529-4125.*

Graduate School

Dr. Robert C. Johnson, Associate Provost and Dean

College of Arts and Sciences
Karl Mattox, Dean
Programs in:
arts and sciences • M En S
biochemistry • MS, PhD
botany • MA, MAT, MS, PhD
chemistry • MS, PhD
clinical psychology • PhD
composition and rhetoric • PhD
creative writing • MA
criticism • PhD
English and American literature and language • PhD
English education • MAT
experimental psychology • PhD
French • MA, MAT
geography • MA, MAT
geology • MA, MS, PhD
gerontology • MGS
history • MA, MAT
language and linguistics • MA
mass communication • MA, MS
mathematics • MA, MAT, MS
mathematics/operations research • MS
microbiology • MS, PhD
philosophy • MA
physics • MA, MAT, MS
political science • MA, MAT, PhD
religion • MA, MAT
social psychology • PhD
Spanish • MA
speech communication • MA
speech pathology and audiology • MA, MS
statistics • MS
technical and scientific communication • MTSC
zoology • MA, MS, PhD

Institute of Environmental Sciences
Dr. Gene Willeke, Director
Program in:
environmental sciences • M En S

Miami University (continued)

Richard T. Farmer School of Business Administration
Judy Barille, Director of Graduate Programs
Programs in:
accountancy • M Acct
decision sciences • MBA
economics • MA
finance • MBA
general management • MBA
management information systems • MBA
marketing • MBA

School of Applied Science
David C. Haddad, Dean
Programs in:
paper science and engineering • MS
systems analysis • MS

School of Education and Allied Professions
Dr. Curtis Ellison, Acting Dean
Programs in:
child and family studies • MS
college student personnel services • MS
curriculum • Ed D, PhD
curriculum and teacher leadership • M Ed
educational administration • Ed D, M Ed, PhD
educational psychology • M Ed
elementary education • M Ed, MAT
exercise science • MS
reading education • M Ed, MS
school psychology • Ed S, MS
secondary education • M Ed, MAT
special education • M Ed
sports studies • MS

School of Fine Arts
Pamela Fox, Dean
Programs in:
architecture • M Arch
art education • M Ed, MA
composition • MM
fibers • MA, MFA
music • MM
music education • MM
performance • MM
studio art • MA, MFA
theatre • MA

THE OHIO STATE UNIVERSITY
Columbus, OH 43210
http://www.ohio-state.edu/

Public coed university. *Enrollment:* 54,818 graduate, professional, and undergraduate students. *Graduate faculty:* 2,985. *Computer facilities: Campuswide network is available with full Internet access. Total number of PCs/terminals supplied for student use:* 3,000. *Computer services are offered at no charge. Library facilities: William Oxley Thompson Library plus 12 additional on-campus libraries. Graduate expenses:* $5472 per year full-time, $554 per quarter (minimum) part-time for state residents; $14,172 per year full-time,

$1424 per quarter (minimum) part-time for nonresidents. General application contact: *Marie Taris, Associate Director, Graduate Admissions, 614-292-5995.*

Graduate School
Susan L. Huntington, Vice Provost for Graduate Studies and Dean
Programs in:
allied medicine • MS
anatomy and cellular biology • MS, PhD
cell biology, neurobiology, and anatomy • MS, PhD
dentistry • MS
experimental pathobiology • MS, PhD
health administration • MHA, PhD
hospital pharmacy • MS
medical microbiology and immunology • MS, PhD
neuroscience • PhD
nutrition • PhD
oral biology • PhD
pathobiology • MS, PhD
pharmaceutical administration • MS, PhD
pharmacology • MS, PhD
pharmacy • MS, PhD
physiological optics • MS, PhD
physiology • PhD
public health • MPH, MS, PhD
Slavic and East European studies • MA
toxicology • MS, PhD
veterinary clinical sciences • MS, PhD
veterinary physiology • MS, PhD
veterinary preventive medicine • MS, PhD

College of Biological Sciences
Alan G. Goodridge, Dean
Programs in:
biochemistry • MS, PhD
biophysics • MS, PhD
cell and developmental biology • MS, PhD
entomology • MS, PhD
environmental science • MS, PhD
genetics • MS, PhD
microbiology • MS, PhD
molecular biology • MS, PhD
molecular, cellular and developmental biology • MS, PhD
plant biology • MS, PhD
zoology • MS, PhD

College of Education
Dr. Nancy Zimpher, Dean
Programs in:
educational administration • Certificate
educational policy and leadership • M Ed, MA, PhD
educational services and research • M Ed, MA, PhD
educational studies: humanities, science, technological and vocational • M Ed, MA, PhD
educational theory and practice • M Ed, MA, PhD
health, physical education, and recreation • M Ed, MA, PhD

College of Engineering
David B. Ashley Jr., Dean
Programs in:
  aeronautical and astronautical engineering • MS, PhD
  architecture • M Arch
  biomedical engineering • MS, PhD
  ceramic engineering • MS, PhD
  chemical engineering • MS, PhD
  city and regional planning • MCRP, PhD
  civil engineering • MS, PhD
  computer and information science • MS, PhD
  electrical engineering • MS, PhD
  engineering mechanics • MS, PhD
  geodetic science and surveying • MS, PhD
  industrial and systems engineering • MS, PhD
  landscape architecture • M Land Arch
  mechanical engineering • MS, PhD
  metallurgical engineering • MS, PhD
  nuclear engineering • MS, PhD
  welding engineering • MS, PhD

College of Food, Agricultural, and Environmental Sciences
Bobby Moser, Dean
Programs in:
  agricultural economics and rural sociology • MS, PhD
  agricultural education • MS, PhD
  animal science • MS, PhD
  dairy science • MS, PhD
  food, agricultural, and biological engineering • MS, PhD
  food science and nutrition • MS, PhD
  horticulture and crop science • MS, PhD
  natural resources • MS
  plant pathology • MS, PhD
  poultry science • MS, PhD
  soil science • MS, PhD
  vocational education • PhD

College of Human Ecology
Denis Medeiros, Interim Dean
Programs in:
  family and consumer sciences education • MS, PhD
  family relations and human development • MS, PhD
  family resource management • MS, PhD
  foods • MS, PhD
  food service management • MS, PhD
  nutrition • MS, PhD
  textiles and clothing • MS, PhD

College of Humanities
Kermit L. Hall, Dean
Programs in:
  African-American and African studies • MA
  comparative studies • MA
  East Asian languages and literatures • MA, PhD
  English • MA, PhD
  French and Italian • MA, PhD
  Germanic languages and literatures • MA, PhD
  Greek and Latin • MA, PhD
  history • MA, PhD
  Latin American studies • Certificate
  linguistics • MA, PhD
  Near Eastern languages and cultures • MA
  philosophy • MA, PhD
  Russian area studies • Certificate

  Slavic and East European languages and literatures •
    MA, PhD
  Spanish and Portuguese • MA, PhD
  women's studies • MA

College of Mathematical and Physical Sciences
Robert Gold, Acting Dean
Programs in:
  astronomy • MS, PhD
  biostatistics • PhD
  chemical physics • MS, PhD
  chemistry • MS, PhD
  geological sciences • MS, PhD
  mathematics • MS, PhD
  physics • MS, PhD
  statistics • M Appl Stat, MS, PhD

College of Nursing
Dr. Carole A. Anderson, Dean
Program in:
  nursing • MS, PhD

College of Social and Behavioral Sciences
Randall Ripley, Dean
Programs in:
  anthropology • MA, PhD
  atmospheric sciences • MS, PhD
  clinical psychology • PhD
  cognitive/experimental psychology • PhD
  communication • MA, PhD
  counseling psychology • PhD
  developmental psychology • PhD
  economics • MA, PhD
  geography • MA, PhD
  industrial/organizational psychology • PhD
  journalism • MA
  Latin American studies • Certificate
  mental retardation and developmental disabilities • PhD
  political science • MA, PhD
  psychobiology • PhD
  psychology • MA
  public policy and management • MA, MPA, PhD
  quantitative psychology • PhD
  Russian area studies • Certificate
  social psychology • PhD
  sociology • MA, PhD
  speech and hearing science • MA, PhD

College of Social Work
Tony Tripodi, Dean
Program in:
  social work • MSW, PhD

College of the Arts
Judith S. Koroscik, Dean
Programs in:
  art • MA, MFA
  art education • MA, PhD
  arts policy and administration • MA
  dance • MA, MFA
  history of art • MA, PhD
  industrial design • MA
  music • DMA, M Mus, MA, PhD
  theatre • MA, MFA, PhD

The Ohio State University (continued)

Max M. Fisher College of Business
Joseph A. Alutto, Dean
Programs in:
  accounting and management information systems • MA, PhD
  business administration • MA, MBA, PhD
  labor and human resources • MLHR, PhD

College of Dentistry
Henry W. Fields, Dean
Programs in:
  dentistry • DDS, MS
  oral biology • PhD

College of Law
Gregory H. Williams, Dean
Program in:
  law • JD

College of Medicine and Public Health
Dr. Bernadine Healy, Dean
Programs in:
  allied medicine • MS
  cell biology, neurobiology, and anatomy • MS, PhD
  experimental pathobiology • MS, PhD
  health administration • MHA, PhD
  medical microbiology and immunology • MS, PhD
  medicine • MD
  pharmacology • MS, PhD
  physiology • PhD
  public health • MPH, MS, PhD
  toxicology • MS, PhD

College of Optometry
Dr. John Schoessler, Dean
Programs in:
  optometry • OD
  physiological optics • MS, PhD

College of Pharmacy
Dr. John M. Cassady, Dean
Programs in:
  hospital pharmacy • MS
  pharmaceutical administration • MS, PhD
  pharmacology • MS, PhD
  pharmacy • Pharm D

College of Veterinary Medicine
Programs in:
  anatomy and cellular biology • MS, PhD
  pathobiology • MS, PhD
  pharmacology • MS, PhD
  toxicology • MS, PhD
  veterinary clinical sciences • MS, PhD
  veterinary medicine • DVM
  veterinary physiology • MS, PhD
  veterinary preventive medicine • MS, PhD

OHIO UNIVERSITY
Athens, OH 45701-2979
http://www.ohiou.edu/

Public coed university. *Enrollment: 27,605 graduate, professional, and undergraduate students. Graduate faculty: 949 full-time, 656 part-time. Library facilities: Alden Library plus 1 additional on-campus library. Graduate expenses: $5430 per year full-time, $216 per quarter hour part-time for state residents; $10,431 per year full-time, $423 per quarter hour part-time for nonresidents. General application contact: Dr. Gordon Schanzenbach, Assistant Vice President for Graduate Studies, 740-593-2800.*

Graduate Studies
Dr. Carol J. Blum, Interim Vice President for Research and Graduate Studies

Center for International Studies
Dr. Joseph Rota, Director
Programs in:
  African studies • MA
  communications and development studies • MA
  development studies • MA
  Latin American studies • MA
  Southeast Asian studies • MA

College of Arts and Sciences
Dr. Leslie Flemming, Dean
Programs in:
  chemistry • MS, PhD
  clinical psychology • PhD
  economics • MA
  English language and literature • MA, PhD
  environmental and plant biology • MS, PhD
  environmental science • MS
  experimental psychology • PhD
  French • MA
  geography • MA
  geological sciences • MS
  history • MA, PhD
  industrial and organizational psychology • PhD
  linguistics • MA
  mathematics • MS, PhD
  microbiology • MS, PhD
  molecular and cellular biology • MS, PhD
  philosophy • MA
  physics • MS, PhD
  political science • MA
  public administration • MPA
  social sciences • MSS
  sociology • MA
  Spanish • MA
  zoology • MS, PhD

College of Business
Dr. Glenn Corlett, Dean
Programs in:
  accounting • MS
  business administration • EMBA, MBA

College of Communication
Dr. Kathy Krendl, Dean
Programs in:
  interpersonal communication • MA, PhD
  journalism • MS, PhD
  telecommunications • MA, PhD
  visual communication • MA

College of Education
Dr. Karen Viechnicki, Interim Dean
Programs in:
  computers in education • M Ed
  economic education • MA, PhD
  educational administration • Ed S, M Ed, PhD
  educational media • M Ed
  education of the gifted • M Ed
  elementary education • M Ed
  guidance and counseling • M Ed, PhD
  higher education • M Ed, PhD
  instructional technology • PhD
  mathematics education • M Ed, PhD
  middle school education • M Ed
  reading • M Ed, PhD
  rehabilitation counseling • M Ed
  research and evaluation • M Ed, PhD
  secondary education • M Ed
  social sciences • PhD
  special education • M Ed
  student personnel • M Ed, PhD
  supervision • PhD

College of Engineering and Technology
Dr. Warren K. Wray, Dean
Programs in:
  CAD/CAM • MS
  chemical engineering • MS, PhD
  electrical engineering • MS, PhD
  geotechnical and environmental engineering • MS, PhD
  industrial and manufacturing systems engineering • MS
  intelligent systems • PhD
  manufacturing • MS
  manufacturing engineering • MS
  materials processing • PhD
  mechanical engineering • MS, PhD
  mechanical systems • MS
  technology management • MS
  thermal systems • MS
  water resources and structures • MS

College of Fine Arts
Dr. James Stewart, Interim Dean
Programs in:
  art education • MA
  art history • MFA
  art history/studio • MFA
  ceramics • MFA
  comparative arts • PhD
  film • MA, MFA
  music • MM
  painting • MFA
  photography • MFA
  printmaking • MFA
  sculpture • MFA
  theater • MA, MFA

College of Health and Human Services
Dr. Barbara Chapman, Dean
Programs in:
  child and family studies • MSHCS
  early childhood education • MSHCS
  exercise physiology • MSP Ex
  family studies • MSHCS
  health and human services • MS
  health sciences • MHA
  international and community nutrition • MSHCS
  nutrition science • MSHCS
  physical education • MSPE
  physical therapy • MPT
  speech pathology and audiology • MA, PhD
  sports administration • MSA

College of Osteopathic Medicine
Dr. Barbara Ross-Lee, Dean
Program in:
  osteopathic medicine • DO

THE UNION INSTITUTE
Cincinnati, OH 45206-1925

http://www.tui.edu/

Independent coed university. *Enrollment: 2,036 graduate, professional, and undergraduate students. Graduate faculty: 56 full-time, 28 part-time. Computer facilities: Campuswide network is available with full Internet access. Total number of PCs/terminals supplied for student use: 16. Computer services are offered at no charge. Library facilities: main library. General application contact: Michael J. Z. Robertson, Associate Registrar, 800-486-3116.*

Graduate School
Dr. Gail Brophy, Dean
Programs in:
  clinical psychology • PhD
  interdisciplinary studies • PhD

THE UNIVERSITY OF AKRON
Akron, OH 44325-0001

http://www.uakron.edu/

Public coed university. *Enrollment: 23,538 graduate, professional, and undergraduate students. Graduate faculty: 521 full-time, 337 part-time. Computer facilities: Campuswide network is available with full Internet access. Computer services are offered at no charge. Library facilities: Bierce Library plus 2 additional on-campus libraries. Graduate expenses: Tuition of $178 per credit hour for state residents; $333 per credit hour for nonresidents. Fees of $145 per year full-time, $32 per semester (minimum) part-time. General application contact: Charles M. Dye, Dean, 330-972-7664.*

The University of Akron (continued)
Graduate School
Charles M. Dye, Dean

Buchtel College of Arts and Sciences
Dr. Roger Creel, Dean
Programs in:
analytical chemistry • MS, PhD
applied cognitive aging • MA, PhD
applied mathematics • MS
applied politics • MAP
biochemistry • MS, PhD
biology • MS
cartography/geography • MS
chemistry • MS, PhD
computer science • MS
counseling psychology • MA, PhD
earth science • MS
economics • MA
engineering geology • MS
English composition • MA
environmental geology • MS
geography • MA
geography/urban planning • MA
geophysics • MS
history • MA, PhD
industrial and gerontological psychology • MA, PhD
industrial/organizational psychology • PhD
inorganic chemistry • MS, PhD
labor and industrial relations • MA
literature • MA
organic chemistry • MS, PhD
personnel psychology • MA
physical chemistry • MS, PhD
physics • MS
policy analysis • PhD
political science • MA
psychology • MA, PhD
public administration • MPA
social research methodology • MA
sociology • MA, PhD
Spanish • MA
statistics • MS
urban planning • PhD
urban studies • MA

College of Business Administration
Stephen F. Hallam, Dean
Programs in:
accountancy • MS
accounting • MBA
finance • MBA
international business • MBA
management • MBA
management-human resources • MSM
management-information systems • MSM
marketing • MBA
taxation • MT

College of Education
Dr. Rita Saslaw, Dean
Programs in:
adapted physical education • MA, MS
administrative specialist • MA, MS

athletic training/sports medicine • MA, MS
classroom guidance for teachers • MA, MS
community counseling • MA, MS
counseling psychology • PhD
educational administration • Ed D, MA, MS
elementary education • MA, PhD
elementary education with certification • MS
elementary school administration • MA, MS
elementary school counseling • MA, MS
exercise physiology/adult fitness • MA, MS
guidance and counseling • PhD
higher education administration • MA, MS
marriage and family therapy • MA, MS
outdoor education • MA, MS
school superintendent • MA, MS
secondary education • MA, PhD
secondary education with certification • MS
secondary school administration • MA, MS
secondary school counseling • MA, MS
special education • MA Ed, MS Ed
supervisor • MA, MS
technical education administration • MSTE
technical education guidance • MSTE
technical education instructional technology • MSTE
technical education supervision • MSTE
technical education teaching • MSTE
technical education training • MSTE

College of Engineering
Dr. Max S. Willis Jr., Interim Dean
Programs in:
biomedical engineering • MS, MSE, PhD
chemical engineering • MS Ch E, PhD
civil engineering • MSCE, PhD
electrical engineering • MSEE, PhD
engineering-applied mathematics • PhD
engineering (management specialization) • MSE
mechanical engineering • MS, PhD

College of Fine and Applied Arts
Dr. Linda Moore, Dean
Programs in:
accompanying • MM
arts administration • MA
audiology • MA
child development • MA
child life • MA
clothing, textiles and interiors • MA
communication • MA
composition • MM
family development • MA
food science • MA
music education • MM
music history and literature • MM
music technology • MM
nutrition and dietetics • MS
performance • MM
social work • MSW
speech-language pathology • MA
theatre arts • MA
theory • MM

College of Nursing
Cynthia Capers, Dean
Programs in:
nursing administration • MSN
nursing clinical specialist • MSN
nursing education • MSN

College of Polymer Science and Polymer Engineering
Frank Kelley, Dean
Programs in:
polymer engineering • MS, MSE, PhD
polymer science • MS, PhD

School of Law
Richard L. Aynes Jr., Dean
Program in:
law • JD

 # UNIVERSITY OF CINCINNATI
Cincinnati, OH 45221

http://www.uc.edu/

Public coed university. *Enrollment: 36,184 graduate, professional, and undergraduate students. Graduate faculty: 774. Library facilities: Walter C. Langsam Library plus 16 additional on-campus libraries. Graduate expenses: $7228 per year full-time, $185 per credit hour part-time for state residents; $13,812 per year full-time, $352 per credit hour part-time for nonresidents. General application contact: Dr. Robert C. Gesteland, Vice President and University Dean, 513-556-4336.*

Division of Research and Advanced Studies
Dr. Robert C. Gesteland, Vice President and University Dean
Program in:
interdisciplinary studies • PhD

Center for Health Related Programs
Dr. Andrea Lindell, Dean
Programs in:
communication sciences and disorders • MA, PhD
nutrition sciences • M Ed

College-Conservatory of Music
Robert J. Werner, Dean
Programs in:
arts administration • MA
choral conducting • DMA, MM
composition • DMA, MM
directing • MFA
music education • DME, MM
music history • MM
musicology • PhD
music theory • MM, PhD
orchestral conducting • DMA, MM
performance • AD, DMA, MM
theater design and production • MFA
theater performance • MFA
wind conducting • DMA, MM

College of Business Administration
Dr. Frederick Russ, Dean
Programs in:
accounting • MBA, PhD
finance • MBA, PhD
information systems • MBA, PhD
international business • MBA
management • MBA, PhD
marketing • MBA, PhD
operations management • MBA, PhD
quantitative analysis • MBA, MS, PhD
real estate • MBA

College of Design, Architecture, Art and Planning
Jayanta Chatterjee, Dean
Programs in:
architecture • MS Arch
art education • MA
art history • MA
community planning • MCP
fashion design • M Des
fine arts • MFA
graphic design • M Des
health planning/administration • MS
industrial design • M Des
interior design • M Des

College of Education
Dr. Louis Castenell Jr., Dean
Programs in:
community health • M Ed
counselor education • CAGS, Ed D, M Ed
criminal justice • MS, PhD
curriculum and instruction • Ed D, M Ed
early childhood education • M Ed
education administration • Ed D, Ed S, M Ed
educational foundations • Ed D, M Ed
elementary education • Ed D, M Ed
health promotion and education • M Ed
reading/literacy • Ed D, M Ed
rehabilitation counseling • CAGS, MA
school psychology • M Ed, PhD
secondary education • M Ed
special education • Ed D, M Ed

College of Engineering
Robert Jenkins, Dean
Programs in:
aerospace engineering • MS, PhD
ceramic science and engineering • MS, PhD
chemical engineering • MS, PhD
civil engineering • MS, PhD
computer engineering • MS, PhD
computer science • MS
computing sciences • MS, PhD
electrical engineering • MS, PhD
engineering mechanics • MS, PhD
environmental engineering • MS, PhD
environmental sciences • MS, PhD
health physics • MS, PhD
industrial engineering • MS, PhD
materials science and engineering • MS, PhD
mechanical engineering • MS, PhD
metallurgical engineering • MS, PhD

University of Cincinnati (continued)
    nuclear engineering • MS, PhD
    polymer science and engineering • MS, PhD
    solid state electronics • MS, PhD

College of Medicine
Dr. John Hutton, Dean
Programs in:
    anatomic pathology • PhD
    anatomy • PhD
    biophysics • MS, PhD
    blood transfusion medicine • MS
    cell and molecular biology • PhD
    cell biology • PhD
    cell biophysics • PhD
    environmental and industrial hygiene • MS
    environmental and occupational medicine • MS
    environmental health • PhD
    environmental hygiene science and engineering • MS,
        PhD
    epidemiology and biostatistics • MS
    genetic counseling • MS
    laboratory medicine • PhD
    medicine • MD
    molecular and cellular pathophysiology • D Sc
    molecular and developmental biology • MS, PhD
    molecular genetics, biochemistry and microbiology •
        PhD
    neurobiology • PhD
    neuroscience • PhD
    occupational safety • MS
    pathobiology and molecular medicine • PhD
    pathology • PhD
    pharmacology • PhD
    physiology • MS, PhD
    radiological sciences • MS
    teratology • MS, PhD
    toxicology • MS, PhD

College of Nursing and Health
Dr. Andrea Lindell, Dean
Programs in:
    adult health nursing • MSN
    community health nursing • MSN
    nurse anesthesia • MSN
    nurse midwifery • MSN
    nurse practitioner studies • MSN
    nursing • PhD
    nursing administration • MSN
    parent/child nursing • MSN
    psychiatric nursing • MSN

College of Pharmacy
Dr. Daniel Acosta Jr., Dean
Programs in:
    pharmaceutical sciences • MS, PhD
    pharmacy practice • Pharm D

McMicken College of Arts and Sciences
Dr. Joseph Caruso, Dean
Programs in:
    analytical chemistry • MS, PhD
    anthropology • MA
    applied mathematics • MS, PhD

    biochemistry • MS, PhD
    biological sciences • MS, PhD
    classics • MA, PhD
    clinical psychology • PhD
    communication • MA
    economics • MA, PhD
    English • MA, PhD
    experimental psychology • MA, PhD
    French • MA, PhD
    geography • MA, PhD
    geology • MS, PhD
    Germanic languages and literature • MA, MAT, PhD
    history • MA, MAT, PhD
    inorganic chemistry • MS, PhD
    labor and employment relations • MALER
    mathematics education • MAT
    organic chemistry • MS, PhD
    philosophy • MA, PhD
    physical chemistry • MS, PhD
    physics • MS, PhD
    political science • MA, PhD
    polymer chemistry • MS, PhD
    public affairs • MPA
    pure mathematics • MS, PhD
    social psychology • PhD
    sociology • MA, PhD
    Spanish • MA, PhD
    statistics • MS, PhD
    women's studies • Certificate, MA

School of Social Work
Dr. Philip Jackson, Director
Program in:
    social work • MSW

College of Law
Dr. Joseph Tomain, Dean
Program in:
    law • JD

 UNIVERSITY OF DAYTON
Dayton, OH 45469-1611

http://www.udayton.edu/

Independent-religious coed university. *Enrollment:* 10,198 graduate, professional, and undergraduate students. Graduate faculty: 341. Computer facilities: *Campuswide network is available with full Internet access. Total number of PCs/terminals supplied for student use: 480. Computer service fees are included with tuition and fees.* Library facilities: *Roesch Library plus 1 additional on-campus library.* Graduate expenses: *Tuition of $4896 per year full-time, $408 per semester hour part-time. Fees of $50 per year.* General application contact: *Nancy A. Wilson, Office for Graduate Studies and Research, 937-229-2390.*

Graduate School

Dr. Gordon A. Sargent, Vice President for Graduate Studies and Research and Dean of the Graduate School

College of Arts and Sciences
Dr. Paul J. Morman, Dean
Programs in:
- applied mathematics • MS
- biology • MS, PhD
- clinical psychology • MA
- communication • MA
- computer science • MCS
- general psychology • MA
- human factors and research • MA
- pastoral ministries • MA
- public administration • MPA
- theological studies • MA

School of Business Administration
Dr. Sam Gould, Dean
Program in:
- business administration • MBA

School of Education
Dr. Thomas J. Lasley, Dean
Programs in:
- college student personnel services • MS Ed
- educational leadership • Ed S, PhD
- physical education • MS Ed
- school administration • MS Ed
- school counseling • MS Ed
- school psychology • MS Ed
- school social worker • MS Ed
- social agency counseling • MS Ed
- teacher education • MS Ed, MST

School of Engineering
Dr. Blake Cherrington, Dean
Programs in:
- aerospace engineering • DE, MSAE, PhD
- chemical engineering • MS Ch E
- electrical engineering • DE, MSEE, PhD
- electro-optics • MSEO, PhD
- engineering • MSE
- engineering management • MSEM
- engineering mechanics • MSCE
- environmental engineering • MSCE
- management science • MSMS
- materials engineering • DE, MS Mat E, PhD
- mechanical engineering • DE, MSME, PhD
- soil mechanics • MSCE
- structural engineering • MSCE
- transport engineering • MSCE

School of Law
Francis J. Conte, Dean
Program in:
- law • JD

UNIVERSITY OF TOLEDO
Toledo, OH 43606-3398

http://www.utoledo.edu/

Public coed university. *Enrollment: 20,307 graduate, professional, and undergraduate students. Graduate faculty: 501 full-time, 47 part-time. Computer facilities: Campuswide network is available with full Internet access. Total number of PCs/terminals supplied for student use: 300. Computer services are offered at no charge. Library facilities: William S. Carlson Library. Graduate expenses: $5907 per year full-time, $246 per hour part-time for state residents; $11,835 per year full-time, $493 per hour part-time for nonresidents. General application contact: Dr. Heinz Bulmahn, Associate Vice President and Dean of the Graduate School, 419-530-4723.*

Graduate School
Dr. Heinz Bulmahn, Associate Vice President and Dean

College of Arts and Sciences
Dr. Patricia Cummins, Dean
Programs in:
- analytical chemistry • MS, MS Ed, PhD
- anthropology • MA Ed
- applied mathematics • MS
- biological chemistry • MS, MS Ed, PhD
- biology • MS, MS Ed, PhD
- clinical psychology • PhD
- economics • MA, MA Ed
- English as a second language • MA Ed
- English language and literature • MA, MA Ed, PhD
- experimental psychology • MA, PhD
- French • MA, MA Ed
- geography • MA
- geology • MS
- German • MA, MA Ed
- history • MA, MA Ed, PhD
- inorganic chemistry • MS, MS Ed, PhD
- liberal studies • MLS
- mathematics • MA, MS Ed, PhD
- music education • MM
- organic chemistry • MS, MS Ed, PhD
- performance • MM
- philosophy • MA
- physical chemistry • MS, MS Ed, PhD
- physics • MS, MS Ed, PhD
- planning • MA
- political science • MA
- public administration • MPA
- sociology • MA, MA Ed
- Spanish • MA, MA Ed
- statistics • MS

College of Education and Allied Professions
Dr. Philip J. Rusche, Dean
Programs in:
- art education • M Ed
- business education • M Ed
- counselor education • Ed D, M Ed, PhD
- curriculum and instruction • Ed D, Ed S, M Ed, MA Ed, MS Ed, PhD

University of Toledo (continued)

early childhood education • M Ed
educational administration and supervision • Ed D, Ed S, M Ed
educational psychology • M Ed
educational technology • M Ed
educational theory and social foundations • M Ed
elementary education • M Ed
exercise science • MS
foundations of education • Ed D, PhD
guidance and counseling • Ed D, Ed S, PhD
health education • Ed D, M Ed, PhD
higher education • M Ed, PhD
physical education • Ed D, M Ed, PhD
public health • M Ed, MPH
recreation and leisure education • M Ed
research • M Ed
school psychology • Ed D, Ed S, M Ed, PhD
secondary education • M Ed
special education services • M Ed
speech-language pathology • M Ed
vocational education • M Ed

College of Engineering
Dr. Vik J. Kapoor, Dean
Programs in:
bioengineering • MS, PhD
chemical engineering • MS Ch E
civil engineering • MSCE
computer science • MSES
electrical engineering • MSEE
engineering sciences • PhD
industrial engineering • MSIE
mechanical engineering • MSME

College of Pharmacy
Dr. Norman F. Billups, Dean
Programs in:
administrative pharmacy • MSPS
industrial pharmacy • MSPS
medicinal and biological chemistry • MS, PhD
pharmacology • MSPS
pharmacy • Pharm D

Graduate School of Business
Dr. Robert Deans, Dean
Programs in:
accounting • MBA, MS Acct
business • EMBA
decision sciences • MBA
finance • MBA
information systems • MBA
international business • MBA
management • MBA
manufacturing management • MS, PhD
marketing • MBA
operations management • MBA

College of Law
Albert T. Quick, Dean
Program in:
law • JD

WALSH UNIVERSITY
North Canton, OH 44720-3396

http://www.walsh.edu/

Independent-religious coed comprehensive institution. *Enrollment:* 1,376 graduate, professional, and undergraduate students. Gradu-ate faculty: *12 full-time, 10 part-time.* Computer facilities: *Campuswide network is available with full Internet access. Total number of PCs/terminals supplied for student use: 100. Computer services are offered at no charge.* Library facilities: *main library.* Graduate expenses: *Tuition of $363 per credit hour. Fees of $10 per credit hour.* General application contact: *Dr. James C. Foster, Vice President of Academic Affairs, 330-490-7122.*

Graduate Studies
Dr. James C. Foster, Vice President of Academic Affairs
Programs in:
counseling and human development • MA
management • MA
physical therapy • M Sc
teacher education • MA

 # WRIGHT STATE UNIVERSITY
Dayton, OH 45435

http://www.wright.edu/

Public coed university. *Enrollment:* 16,033 graduate, professional, and undergraduate students. Graduate faculty: *718 full-time, 339 part-time.* Computer facilities: *Campuswide network is available with full Internet access. Total number of PCs/terminals supplied for student use: 500. Computer service fees are included with tuition and fees.* Library facilities: *Paul Laurence Dunbar Library plus 2 additional on-campus libraries.* Graduate expenses: *$5109 per year full-time, $161 per credit hour part-time for state residents; $9039 per year full-time, $282 per credit hour part-time for nonresidents.* General application contact: *Gerald C. Malicki, Assistant Dean and Director of Graduate Admissions and Records, 937-775-2976.*

School of Graduate Studies
Dr. Joseph F. Thomas Jr., Dean and Associate Provost
Program in:
aerospace medicine • MS

College of Business and Administration
Dr. Rishi Kumar, Dean
Programs in:
accountancy • M Acc
finance and financial administration • MBA
health care management • MBA
international business • MBA
logistics management • MBA, MS
management • MBA
management information systems • MBA
marketing • MBA

operations management • MBA
project management • MBA
social and applied economics • MS

College of Education and Human Services
Dr. Gregory Bernhardt, Dean
Programs in:
advanced educational leadership • Ed S
business and industrial • MA, MS
business education • M Ed, MA
chemical dependency • MRC
classroom teacher education • M Ed, MA
community counseling • MA, MS
counseling • MA, MS
developmentally handicapped • M Ed, MA
early childhood education • M Ed, MA
educational leadership • M Ed, MA
education and human services • PhD
exceptional children • MA, MS
gerontology • MA, MS
gifted • M Ed, MA
health, physical education, and recreation • M Ed, MA
marriage and family • MA, MS
mental health • MA, MS
multiple handicapped • M Ed, MA
orthopedically handicapped • M Ed, MA
school counseling • M Ed, MA
severe behavior handicapped • M Ed, MA
severe disabilities • MRC
specific learning disabilities • M Ed, MA
student affairs in higher education counseling • MA, MS
student personnel services • M Ed, MA
vocational education • M Ed, MA

College of Engineering and Computer Science
Dr. James E. Brandeberry, Dean
Programs in:
biomedical engineering • MSE
computer engineering • MSCE
computer science • MSCS
computer science and engineering • PhD
electrical engineering • MSE
engineering • PhD
human factors engineering • MSE
materials science and engineering • MSE
mechanical engineering • MSE

College of Liberal Arts
Dr. Perry D. Moore, Dean
Programs in:
applied behavioral science • MA
English • MA
history • MA
humanities • M Hum
music education • M Mus
teaching students of other languages • MA
urban affairs and geography • MUA

College of Nursing and Health
Dr. Jane Swart, Dean
Programs in:
adult health and illness • MS
child and adolescent health • MS
community health • MS

family nurse practitioner • MS
nursing administration • MS
nursing education • MS

College of Science and Mathematics
Dr. Roger K. Gilpin, Dean
Programs in:
anatomy • MS
applied mathematics • MS
applied statistics • MS
biochemistry and molecular biology • MS
biological sciences • MS
biomedical sciences • PhD
chemistry • MS
earth science education • MST
environmental geology • MS
environmental sciences • MS
geological sciences • MS
geophysics • MS
human factors psychology • MS, PhD
hydrogeology • MS
industrial/organizational psychology • MS, PhD
mathematics • MS
medical physics • MS
microbiology and immunology • MS
petroleum geology • MS
physics • MS
physics education • MST
physiology and biophysics • MS

Interdisciplinary Programs
Dr. Joseph F. Thomas Jr., Dean and Associate Provost, School of Graduate Studies
Program in:
interdisciplinary studies • MA, MS

School of Medicine
Dr. Howard Part, Interim Dean
Programs in:
aerospace medicine • MS
biomedical sciences • PhD
medicine • MD

School of Professional Psychology
Dr. Leon VandeCreek, Dean
Program in:
professional psychology • Psy D

XAVIER UNIVERSITY
Cincinnati, OH 45207-2111
http://www.xu.edu/

Independent-religious coed comprehensive institution. *Enrollment:* 6,504 graduate, professional, and undergraduate students. Graduate faculty: *154 full-time, 95 part-time.* Computer facilities: *Campuswide network is available with full Internet access. Total number of PCs/ terminals supplied for student use: 180. Computer service fees are included with tuition and fees.* Library facilities: *McDonald Library plus 1 additional on-campus library.* Graduate expenses: *$400 per*

Xavier University (continued)

credit hour. General application contact: *David M. Sauter, Registrar, 513-745-2966.*

College of Arts and Sciences

Dr. Max Keck, Dean
Programs in:
English • MA
history • MA
humanities • MA
theology • MA

College of Business Administration

Dr. Michael Webb, Dean
Program in:
business administration • Exec MBA, MBA

College of Social Sciences

Dr. Neil Heighberger, Dean
Programs in:
agency and community counseling • M Ed
art • M Ed
classics • M Ed
clinical psychology • Psy D
counseling • M Ed
criminal justice • MS
developmentally handicapped • M Ed
early childhood education of handicapped • M Ed
educational administration • M Ed
elementary education • M Ed
English • M Ed
experimental psychology • MA
gifted • M Ed
health services administration • MHSA
human resource development • M Ed
industrial/organizational psychology • MA
mathematics • M Ed
Montessori • M Ed
multicultural literature for children • M Ed
multiple handicapped • M Ed
music • M Ed
nursing administration • MSN
occupational therapy • Certificate
reading specialist • M Ed
school counseling • M Ed
secondary education • M Ed
severe behavior handicapped • M Ed
specific learning disabilities • M Ed
sport administration • M Ed
theology • M Ed

YOUNGSTOWN STATE UNIVERSITY

Youngstown, OH 44555-0002
http://www.ysu.edu/

Public coed comprehensive institution. *Enrollment:* 12,324 graduate, professional, and undergraduate students. *Graduate faculty:* 273 full-time, 91 part-time. *Library facilities: Maag Library* plus 1 additional on-campus library. *Graduate expenses: Tuition* of $90 per credit hour for state residents; $144 per credit hour (minimum) for nonresidents. *Fees* of $528 per year full-time, $244 per year (minimum) part-time. General application contact: *Dr. Peter J. Kasvinsky, Dean of Graduate Studies, 330-742-3091.*

Graduate School

Dr. Peter J. Kasvinsky, Dean of Graduate Studies

College of Arts and Sciences

Dr. Barbara Brothers, Dean
Programs in:
biological sciences • MS
chemistry • MS
economics • MA
English • MA
history • MA
mathematics • MS

College of Education

Dr. Clara M. Jennings, Dean
Programs in:
counseling • MS Ed
educational administration • MS Ed
educational leadership • Ed D
gifted and talented education • MS Ed
secondary education • MS Ed
special education • MS Ed
teaching—elementary education • MS Ed
teaching—secondary reading • MS Ed

College of Fine and Performing Arts

Dr. George McCloud, Dean
Programs in:
music education • MM
music history and literature • MM
music theory and composition • MM
performance • MM

College of Health and Human Services

Dr. John J. Yemma, Dean
Programs in:
criminal justice • MS
health and human services • MHHS
nursing • MSN

Warren P. Williamson Jr. College of Business Administration

Dr. Betty Jo Licata, Dean
Programs in:
accounting • MBA
executive business administration • EMBA
finance • MBA
management • MBA
marketing • MBA

William Rayen College of Engineering
Dr. Charles A. Stevens, Dean
Programs in:
chemical engineering • MSE
civil and environmental engineering • MSE
electrical engineering • MSE
industrial and manufacturing systems engineering • MSE
materials science • MSE
mechanical engineering • MSE

OKLAHOMA

EAST CENTRAL UNIVERSITY
Ada, OK 74820-6899

http://www.ecok.edu/

Public coed comprehensive institution. *Enrollment:* 4,387 graduate, professional, and undergraduate students. Computer facilities: *Campuswide network is available with full Internet access. Total number of PCs/terminals supplied for student use: 170. Computer services are offered at no charge.* Library facilities: *Linscheid Library.* Graduate expenses: *Tuition of $75 per semester hour for state residents; $177 per semester hour for nonresidents. Fees of $39 per year full-time, $31 per year part-time.* General application contact: *Dr. Jack W. Paschall, Dean of the Graduate School, 405-332-8000 Ext. 709.*

Graduate School
Dr. Jack W. Paschall, Dean
Programs in:
administration • MSHR
counseling • MSHR
criminal justice • MSHR
education • M Ed
psychology • MSPS
rehabilitation counseling • MSHR

NORTHEASTERN STATE UNIVERSITY
Tahlequah, OK 74464-2399

http://www.nsuok.edu/

Public coed comprehensive institution. *Enrollment:* 8,660 graduate, professional, and undergraduate students. Graduate faculty: *32 full-time, 130 part-time.* Library facilities: *John Vaughn Library/ Learning Resources Center plus 1 additional on-campus library.* Graduate expenses: *Tuition of $74 per credit hour for state residents; $176 per credit hour for nonresidents. Fees of $30 per year.* General application contact: *Dr. J. Ross Underwood, Dean of the Graduate College, 918-456-5511 Ext. 3690.*

Graduate College
Dr. J. Ross Underwood, Dean

College of Arts and Letters
Dr. Greg Combs, Dean
Program in:
communication • MA

College of Behavioral and Social Sciences
Dr. Lyle Haskins, Dean
Programs in:
American studies • MA
counseling psychology • MS
criminal justice • MS
school counseling • M Ed

College of Business and Industry
Dr. Earl Williams, Dean
Programs in:
business administration • MBA
industrial management • MS

College of Education
Dr. Mark Clark, Dean
Programs in:
college teaching • MS
curriculum and instruction • M Ed
early childhood education • M Ed
elementary education • M Ed
reading • M Ed
school administration • M Ed
secondary education • M Ed
special education • M Ed
teaching • M Ed

College of Optometry
Dr. Bill Monaco, Dean
Program in:
optometry • OD

NORTHWESTERN OKLAHOMA STATE UNIVERSITY
Alva, OK 73717

http://www.nwalva.edu/

Public coed comprehensive institution. *Enrollment:* 1,787 graduate, professional, and undergraduate students. Graduate faculty: *51 full-time, 1 part-time.* Library facilities: *J. W. Martin Library.* Graduate expenses: *$73 per semester hour for state residents; $175 per semester hour for nonresidents.* General application contact: *Dr. Ed Huckeby, Dean of Graduate School, 405-327-8410.*

School of Education, Psychology, and Health and Physical Education
Dr. James Bowen, Dean
Programs in:
behavioral sciences • MBS
education: non-certificate option • M Ed

Northwestern Oklahoma State University (continued)
- elementary education • M Ed
- guidance and counseling K–12 • M Ed
- library media specialist • M Ed
- psychometry • M Ed
- reading specialist • M Ed
- secondary education • M Ed

OKLAHOMA CITY UNIVERSITY
Oklahoma City, OK 73106-1402

http://www.okcu.edu/

Independent-religious coed comprehensive institution. *Enrollment:* 4,323 graduate, professional, and undergraduate students. Graduate faculty: *155 full-time, 83 part-time.* Computer facilities: *Campuswide network is available with full Internet access. Total number of PCs/ terminals supplied for student use: 130. Computer service fees are applied as a separate charge.* Library facilities: *Dulaney-Browne Library plus 1 additional on-campus library.* Graduate expenses: *Tuition of $318 per hour. Fees of $124 per year.* General application contact: *Laura L. Rahhal, Director of Graduate Admissions, 800-633-7242 Ext. 2.*

Petree College of Arts and Sciences
Dr. Leo Werneke, Dean
Programs in:
- computer science • MS
- costume design • MPA
- counseling • MACP
- criminal justice administration • MCJA
- drama • MPA
- early childhood education • M Ed
- elementary education • M Ed
- gifted and talented education • M Ed
- liberal arts • MLA
- performing arts • MPA
- secondary education • M Ed
- social sciences • MCJA
- teaching English as a second language • M Ed
- technical theater • MPA

School of Law
Jay Conison, Interim Dean
Program in:
- law • JD

School of Management and Business Sciences
Dr. David Carmichael, Dean
Programs in:
- accounting • MSA
- arts and public service/management • MBA
- finance • MBA
- health administration • MBA
- information systems management • MBA
- international business • MBA
- management • MBA
- marketing and advertising • MBA

School of Music
Mark Parker, Dean
Programs in:
- musical theatre • MM
- music composition • MM
- opera performance • MM
- performance • MM

School of Religion and Church Vocations
Dr. Donald Emler, Dean
Programs in:
- church business management • MAR
- religious education • M Rel
- religious studies • MAR

OKLAHOMA STATE UNIVERSITY
Stillwater, OK 74078

http://www.okway.okstate.edu

Public coed university. *Enrollment:* 19,350 graduate, professional, and undergraduate students. Graduate faculty: *1,138 full-time, 113 part-time.* Computer facilities: *Campuswide network is available with full Internet access. Computer service fees are included with tuition and fees.* Library facilities: *Edmond Low Library.* Graduate expenses: *Tuition of $80 per credit hour for state residents; $255 per credit hour for nonresidents. Fees of $392 per year (minimum) full-time, $101 per semester (minimum) part-time.* General application contact: *Dr. Wayne Powell, Dean, 405-744-6368.*

Graduate College
Dr. Wayne Powell, Dean
Programs in:
- biophotonics • MS
- chemistry • MS
- electrical engineering • MS
- environmental sciences • MS, PhD
- natural and applied science • MS
- physics • MS
- veterinary biomedical sciences • MS, PhD

College of Agricultural Sciences and Natural Resources
Dr. Samuel S. Curl, Dean
Programs in:
- agricultural economics • M Ag, MS, PhD
- agricultural education, communication and 4H • Ed D, M Ag, MS, PhD
- agronomy • M Ag, MS, PhD
- animal breeding • PhD
- animal nutrition • PhD
- animal sciences • M Ag, MS
- biochemistry and molecular biology • MS, PhD
- biosystems and agricultural engineering • M Bio E, MS, PhD
- crop science • PhD
- entomology • MS, PhD
- food science • MS, PhD

forestry • M Ag, MS
horticulture and landscape architecture • M Ag, MS
plant pathology • M Ag, MS, PhD
soil science • PhD

College of Arts and Sciences
Dr. Smith L. Holt, Dean
Programs in:
applied mathematics • MS
botany • MS, PhD
chemistry • MS, PhD
clinical psychology • PhD
communications sciences and disorders • MA
computer education • Ed D
computer science • MS, PhD
corrections • MS
English • MA, PhD
experimental psychology • PhD
fire and emergency management • MS
general psychology • MS
geography • MS
geology • MS
history • MA, PhD
mass communication • Ed D, MS
mathematics • Ed D, MS, PhD
microbiology and molecular genetics • MS, PhD
music pedagogy • MM
philosophy • MA
physics • MS, PhD
political science • MA
sociology • MS, PhD
speech communication • MA
statistics • MS, PhD
theatre • MA
wildlife and fisheries ecology • MS, PhD
zoology • MS, PhD

College of Business Administration
Dr. Gary L. Trannepohl, Dean
Programs in:
accounting • MS, PhD
economics and legal studies in business • MS, PhD
finance • MBA, PhD
management • MBA, PhD
marketing • MBA, PhD
telecommunications management • MS

College of Education
Dr. Ann C. Candler-Lotven, Dean
Programs in:
applied behavioral studies • Ed D, MS, PhD
applied educational studies • Ed D
counseling and student personnel • MS
curriculum and instruction • Ed D, Ed S, MS
educational administration • Ed S, MS
educational psychology • PhD
health • Ed D, MS
higher education • Ed D, MS
leisure sciences • Ed D, MS
physical education • Ed D, MS
physical education and leisure sciences • Ed D
technical education • Ed D, Ed S, MS
trade and industrial education • Ed D, Ed S, MS

College of Engineering, Architecture and Technology
Dr. Karl N. Reid, Dean
Programs in:
architectural engineering • M Arch E
biosystems and agricultural engineering • M Bio E, MS, PhD
chemical engineering • M Chem E, MS, PhD
civil engineering • M Civil E, MS, PhD
electrical and computer engineering • M Elec E, MS, PhD
engineering, architecture and technolo • M Arch, MIE Mgmt
environmental engineering • M Envir E, MS, PhD
general engineering • M Gen E, MS, PhD
manufacturing systems engineering • MMSE
mechanical engineering • M Mech E, MS, PhD

College of Human Environmental Sciences
Dr. Patricia Knaub, Dean
Programs in:
design, housing and merchandising • MS, PhD
family relations and child development • MS, PhD
hotel and restaurant administration • MS, PhD
nutritional sciences • MS, PhD

College of Veterinary Medicine
Dr. Joseph W. Alexander, Dean
Programs in:
veterinary biomedical sciences • MS, PhD
veterinary medicine • DVM

ORAL ROBERTS UNIVERSITY
Tulsa, OK 74171-0001

http://www.oru.edu/

Independent-religious coed university. *Enrollment: 4,714 graduate, professional, and undergraduate students. Graduate faculty: 43 full-time, 21 part-time. Library facilities: John D. Messick Learning Resource Center. General application contact: Dr. Ralph Fagin, Vice President for Academic Affairs, 918-495-6529.*

School of Business
Programs in:
accounting • MBA
business administration • MBA
finance • MBA
international business • MBA
management • MBA
marketing • MBA

School of Education
Dr. David Hand, Dean
Programs in:
Christian school administration • MA Ed
Christian school teaching • MA Ed
curriculum and instruction • MA Ed
early childhood education • MA Ed

Oral Roberts University (continued)
> public school administration • MA Ed
> public school teaching • MA Ed
> teaching English as a second language • MA Ed

School of Theology
Dr. Jerry W. Horner, Dean
Programs in:
> biblical literature • MA
> Christian counseling • MA
> Christian education • MA
> divinity • M Div
> missions • MA
> practical theology • MA
> theological/historical studies • MA
> theology • D Min

PHILLIPS UNIVERSITY
Enid, OK 73701-6439

http://www.phillips.edu/

Independent-religious coed comprehensive institution. *Enrollment:* 621 graduate, professional, and undergraduate students. Graduate faculty: *10 full-time, 6 part-time.* Library facilities: *Zollars Memorial Library plus 1 additional on-campus library.* Graduate expenses: *Tuition of $97 per credit hour. Fees of $10 per credit hour.* General application contact: *Dr. Donna Payne, Vice President for Academic Affairs, 405-237-4433 Ext. 207.*

School of Business
Program in:
> business • MBA

School of Education
Dr. Donna Payne, Dean
Programs in:
> elementary education • M Ed
> secondary education • M Ed

SOUTHEASTERN OKLAHOMA STATE UNIVERSITY
Durant, OK 74701-0609

Public coed comprehensive institution. *Enrollment:* 3,946 graduate, professional, and undergraduate students. Graduate faculty: *94 full-time, 3 part-time.* Library facilities: *Henry G. Bennett Library.* Graduate expenses: *$76 per credit hour for state residents; $178 per credit hour for nonresidents.* General application contact: *Dr. Jack Robinson, Assistant Vice President, Academic Affairs, 580-924-0121 Ext. 2428.*

Graduate School
Dr. Jack Robinson, Assistant Vice President, Academic Affairs
Programs in:
> business • MBA
> educational administration • M Ed
> elementary education • M Ed
> guidance and counseling • MBS
> school counseling • M Ed
> secondary education • M Ed
> technology • MT

SOUTHERN NAZARENE UNIVERSITY
Bethany, OK 73008-2694

http://www.snu.edu/

Independent-religious coed comprehensive institution. *Enrollment:* 1,799 graduate, professional, and undergraduate students. Graduate faculty: *33 full-time, 15 part-time.* Library facilities: *R. T. Williams Learning Resources Center.* General application contact: *Dr. Wayne L. Murrow, Dean of Graduate College, 405-491-6316.*

Graduate College
Dr. Wayne L. Murrow, Dean
Programs in:
> practical theology • M Min
> religion • MA

School of Business
Dr. Scott Morris, Chair
Program in:
> business • MBA, MS Mgt

School of Education
Dr. Rex Tullis, Director
Program in:
> education • MA

School of Psychology
Dr. Phil Budd, Chair
Program in:
> counseling psychology • MSCP

SOUTHWESTERN OKLAHOMA STATE UNIVERSITY
Weatherford, OK 73096-3098

http://www.swosu.edu/

Public coed comprehensive institution. *Enrollment:* 4,945 graduate, professional, and undergraduate students. Graduate faculty: *206 full-time.* Computer facilities: *Campuswide network is available with full Internet access. Total number of PCs/terminals supplied for student use: 550. Computer service fees are included with tuition*

and fees. Library facilities: *Al Harris Library.* Graduate expenses: *Tuition of $60 per credit hour (minimum) for state residents; $147 per credit hour (minimum) for nonresidents. Fees of $109 per year full-time, $24 per semester (minimum) part-time. General application contact: Dr. Dan Dill, Associate Vice President for Academic Affairs and Dean of Graduate School, 580-774-3769.*

Graduate School

Dr. Dan Dill, Associate Vice President for Academic Affairs and Dean

School of Arts and Sciences

Dr. Dan Dill, Associate Vice President for Academic Affairs and Dean, Graduate School
Programs in:
    music • MM
    psychology • MSAP

School of Business

Dr. Ralph May, Director
Program in:
    business • MBA

School of Education

Dr. Greg Moss, Dean
Programs in:
    agency counseling • M Ed
    early childhood education • M Ed
    educational administration • M Ed
    elementary education • M Ed
    health, physical education and recreation • M Ed
    library media • M Ed
    psychometry • M Ed
    school counseling • M Ed
    secondary education • M Ed
    special education • M Ed
    teaching • M Ed

UNIVERSITY OF CENTRAL OKLAHOMA
Edmond, OK 73034-5209

http://www.ucok.edu/

Public coed comprehensive institution. Library facilities: *Max Chambers Library.* Graduate expenses: *$76 per credit hour for state residents; $178 per credit hour for nonresidents. General application contact: Interim Dean, Graduate College, 405-341-2980 Ext. 3341.*

Graduate College

College of Business Administration

Program in:
    business administration • MBA

College of Education

Programs in:
    community counseling • M Ed
    community services • M Ed
    early childhood education • M Ed
    elementary education • M Ed
    family and child studies • MS
    family and consumer science education • MS
    fashion marketing • MS
    general education • M Ed
    gerontology • M Ed
    guidance and counseling • M Ed
    instructional media • M Ed
    interior design • MS
    nutrition-food management • MS
    professional health occupations • M Ed
    professional services—home economics • MS
    psychology • MA
    reading • M Ed
    school administration • M Ed
    secondary education • M Ed
    special education • M Ed
    speech-language pathology • M Ed

College of Liberal Arts

Programs in:
    creative studies • MA
    criminal justice management and administration • MA
    English • MA
    history • MA
    international affairs • MA
    museum studies • MA
    music education • MM
    performance • MM
    political science • MA
    Southwestern studies • MA
    urban affairs • MA

College of Mathematics and Science

Programs in:
    applied mathematical sciences • MS
    biology • MS
    computer science • MS
    industrial and applied physics • MS
    mathematics • MS
    mathematics/computer science teaching • MS
    statistics • MS

 # UNIVERSITY OF OKLAHOMA
Norman, OK 73019-0390

http://www.ou.edu/

Public coed university. *Enrollment: 20,509 graduate, professional, and undergraduate students. Graduate faculty: 848 full-time, 193 part-time. Library facilities: Bizzell Memorial Library plus 8 additional on-campus libraries. Graduate expenses: Tuition of $1920 per year full-time, $80 per credit hour part-time for state residents; $6108 per year full-time, $255 per credit hour part-time for nonresidents. Fees of $468 per year full-time, $12 per semester (minimum) part-*

University of Oklahoma (continued)
time. General application contact: Marc Borish, Director of Admissions, 405-325-2251.

Graduate College
Dr. Eddie C. Smith, Dean

College of Architecture
Eleanor F. Weinel, Interim Dean
Programs in:
   architecture • M Arch
   construction science • MS
   landscape architecture • MLA
   regional and city planning • MRCP

College of Arts and Sciences
Dr. Paul B. Bell Jr., Dean
Programs in:
   advertising • MA
   anthropology • MA, PhD
   astrophysics • M Nat Sci, MS, PhD
   botany • M Nat Sci, MS, PhD
   broadcasting and electronic media • MA
   chemistry and biochemistry • MS, PhD
   communication • MA, PhD
   economics • MA, PhD
   engineering physics • M Nat Sci, MS, PhD
   English • MA, PhD
   French • MA, PhD
   German • MA
   health and exercise science • MS
   history • MA, PhD
   history of science • MA, PhD
   human relations • MHR
   library and information studies • Certificate, MALIS, MLIS
   mathematics • MA, MS, PhD
   microbiology • M Nat Sci, MS, PhD
   newspaper • MA
   philosophy • MA, PhD
   physics • M Nat Sci, MS, PhD
   political science • MA, PhD
   professional writing • MA
   psychology • MS, PhD
   public administration • MPA
   public relations • MA
   social work • MSW
   sociology • MA, PhD
   Spanish • MA, PhD
   sport management and behavior • MS
   women's studies • MA
   zoology • M Nat Sci, MS, PhD

College of Business Administration
Dr. Richard Cosier, Dean
Programs in:
   accounting • M Acc
   business administration • MBA, PhD

College of Education
Dr. Joan Karen Smith, Dean
Programs in:
   adult and higher education • Ed D, M Ed, PhD
   community counseling • M Ed
   counseling psychology • PhD
   early childhood education • M Ed, PhD
   educational psychology • M Ed, PhD
   elementary education • M Ed, PhD
   elementary school administration • Ed D, M Ed, PhD
   English education • M Ed, PhD
   foundations of education • Ed D, M Ed, PhD
   general school administration • Ed D, M Ed, PhD
   instructional psychology • Ed D, M Ed, PhD
   math education • M Ed, PhD
   reading education • M Ed, PhD
   science education • M Ed, PhD
   secondary education • M Ed, PhD
   secondary school administration • Ed D, M Ed, PhD
   social studies education • M Ed, PhD
   special education • Ed D, M Ed, PhD

College of Engineering
Dr. William Crynes, Dean
Programs in:
   aerospace engineering • MS, PhD
   air • M Env Sc
   chemical engineering • MS, PhD
   civil engineering • PhD
   computer science • MS, PhD
   electrical engineering • MS, PhD
   engineering • D Engr, MS, PhD
   environmental engineering • MS
   environmental science • PhD
   geotechnical engineering • MS
   groundwater management • M Env Sc
   hazardous solid waste • M Env Sc
   industrial engineering • MS, PhD
   mechanical engineering • MS, PhD
   occupational safety and health • M Env Sc
   petroleum and geological engineering • MS, PhD
   process design • M Env Sc
   structures • MS
   transportation • MS
   water quality resources • M Env Sc

College of Fine Arts
Mary Margaret Holt, Interim Dean
Programs in:
   art history • MA
   ceramics • MFA
   choreography • MFA
   drama • MA, MFA
   film and video • MFA
   music • M Mus
   music education • M Mus Ed, PhD
   painting and drawing • MFA
   performance and composition • DMA
   photography • MFA
   printmaking • MFA
   sculpture • MFA
   visual communications • MFA

College of Geosciences
Dr. John T. Snow, Dean
Programs in:
geography • MA, PhD
geology • MS, PhD
geophysics • MS
meteorology • MS Metr, PhD

College of Liberal Studies
Dr. George Henderson, Dean
Program in:
liberal studies • MLS

College of Law
Dr. Andrew M. Coats, Dean
Program in:
law • JD

UNIVERSITY OF TULSA
Tulsa, OK 74104-3189

http://www.utulsa.edu/

Independent-religious coed university. Enrollment: 4,150 graduate, professional, and undergraduate students. Graduate faculty: 230 full-time, 26 part-time. Computer facilities: Campuswide network is available with full Internet access. Computer services are offered at no charge. Library facilities: McFarlin Library plus 1 additional on-campus library. Graduate expenses: Tuition of $480 per credit hour. Fees of $2 per credit hour. General application contact: Dr. Janet A. Haggerty, Dean of Research and Graduate Studies, 918-631-2336.

Graduate School
Dr. Janet A. Haggerty, Dean of Research and Graduate Studies

College of Arts and Sciences
Dr. Thomas A. Horne, Dean
Programs in:
anthropology • MA
art • MA, MFA
biological sciences • MS, PhD
clinical psychology • MA, PhD
education • MA
English language and literature • MA, PhD
history • MA
industrial/organizational psychology • MA, PhD
math/science education • MSMSE
music • MM
music education • MME
speech-language pathology • MA
teaching arts • MTA

College of Business Administration
Dr. Rodney H. Mabry, Dean
Programs in:
accounting • M Acct
accounting and information systems • MAIS

business administration • MBA
chemical engineering • METM
computer science • METM
electrical engineering • METM
geological science • METM
mathematics • METM
mechanical engineering • METM
nursing administration • MNA
petroleum engineering • METM
taxation • M Tax

College of Engineering and Applied Sciences
Dr. Steve J. Bellovich, Dean
Programs in:
chemical engineering • ME, METM, MSE, PhD
computer science • METM, MS, PhD
electrical engineering • ME, METM, MSE
geological science • METM
geosciences • MS, PhD
mathematical sciences • MS
mathematics • METM
mechanical engineering • ME, METM, MSE, PhD
petroleum engineering • ME, METM, MSE, PhD

College of Law
Martin H. Belsky, Dean
Program in:
law • JD

OREGON

MARYLHURST UNIVERSITY
Marylhurst, OR 97036-0261

Independent-religious coed comprehensive institution. Enrollment: 1,157 graduate, professional, and undergraduate students. Graduate faculty: 3 full-time, 66 part-time. Computer facilities: Campuswide network is available with full Internet access. Total number of PCs/terminals supplied for student use: 25. Computer service fees are included with tuition and fees. Library facilities: Shoen Library. Graduate expenses: Tuition of $265 per credit hour. Fees of $195 per year full-time, $29 per quarter (minimum) part-time. General application contact: John Rolston, Registrar, 503-699-6246 Ext. 3316.

Graduate Program in Management
Program in:
management • MBA, MS

Graduate Program in Art Therapy
Christine Turner, Director
Program in:
art therapy • MA

Marylhurst University (continued)
Program in Interdisciplinary Studies
Dr. Mary E. Olszewski, Chair
Program in:
   interdisciplinary studies • MA

OREGON STATE UNIVERSITY
Corvallis, OR 97331

http://osu.orst.edu/

Public coed university. *Enrollment:* 14,127 graduate, professional, and undergraduate students. Graduate faculty: *1,330 full-time, 527 part-time.* Library facilities: *The Valley Library.* Graduate expenses: *$6207 per year full-time, $810 per quarter (minimum) part-time for state residents; $10,551 per year full-time, $1293 per quarter (minimum) part-time for nonresidents. General application contact: Dr. Thomas J. Maresh, Dean of the Graduate School, 541-737-4881.*

Graduate School
Dr. Thomas J. Maresh, Dean
Programs in:
   interdisciplinary studies • MAIS
   plant physiology • MS, PhD

College of Agricultural Sciences
Dr. Thayne R. Dutson, Dean
Programs in:
   agricultural and resource economics • M Agr, MAIS, MS, PhD
   agricultural education • M Agr, MAIS, MAT, MS
   agriculture • M Agr
   animal science • M Agr, MAIS, MS, PhD
   crop science • M Agr, MAIS, MS, PhD
   economics • MS, PhD
   fisheries science • M Agr, MAIS, MS, PhD
   food science and technology • M Agr, MAIS, MS, PhD
   genetics • MA, MAIS, MS, PhD
   horticulture • M Ag, MAIS, MS, PhD
   poultry science • M Agr, MAIS, MS, PhD
   rangeland resources • M Agr, MAIS, MS, PhD
   soil science • M Agr, MAIS, MS, PhD
   toxicology • MS, PhD
   wildlife science • MAIS, MS, PhD

College of Business
Dr. Donald F. Parker, Dean
Program in:
   business • Certificate, MAIS, MBA

College of Engineering
Thomas M. West, Dean
Programs in:
   bioresource engineering • M Agr, MAIS, MS, PhD
   chemical engineering • MAIS, MS, PhD
   civil engineering • MAIS, MS, PhD
   computer science • MA, MAIS, MS, PhD
   industrial engineering • MAIS, MS, PhD
   manufacturing engineering • M Eng
   materials science • MAIS, MS
   mechanical engineering • MS, PhD
   nuclear engineering • MAIS, MS, PhD
   ocean engineering • M Oc E
   radiation health physics • MS

College of Forestry
Dr. George W. Brown, Dean
Programs in:
   agricultural and resource economics • M Agr, MAIS, MS, PhD
   economics • MS, PhD
   forest engineering • MAIS, MF, MS, PhD
   forest products • MAIS, MF, MS, PhD
   forest resources • MAIS, MF, MS, PhD
   forest science • MAIS, MF, MS, PhD
   wood science and technology • MF, MS, PhD

College of Health and Human Performance
Dr. Timothy P. White, Dean
Programs in:
   environmental health management • MAIS, MS
   health • MS, PhD
   health and safety administration • MAIS, MS
   health education • MAIS, MAT, MS
   human performance • MAIS, MS, PhD
   movement studies for the disabled • MAIS, MS
   physical education • MAT
   public health • MPH

College of Home Economics and Education
Dr. Kinsey B. Green, Dean
Programs in:
   adult education • Ed M, MAIS
   college student service administration • Ed M, MS
   counseling • MS, PhD
   elementary education • MAT
   family resource management • MAIS, MS, PhD
   general education • Ed D, Ed M, MAIS, MS, PhD
   gerontology • MAIS
   home economics • MAIS, MS
   home economics and education • MA
   home economics education • MAT, MS
   human development and family studies • MS, PhD
   nutrition and food management • MAIS, MS, PhD
   professional technical education • MAT
   teaching • MAT

College of Liberal Arts
Dr. Kay F. Schaffer, Dean
Programs in:
   anthropology • MAIS
   applied anthropology • MA
   economics • MA, MS, PhD
   English • MA, MAIS
   language arts education • MAT
   music education • MAT
   scientific and technical communication • MA, MAIS, MS

College of Oceanic and Atmospheric Sciences
Dr. G. Brent Dalrymple, Dean
Programs in:
  atmospheric sciences • MA, MS, PhD
  geophysics • MA, MS, PhD
  marine resource management • MA, MS
  oceanography • MA, MS, PhD

College of Pharmacy
Dr. Richard A. Ohvall, Dean
Program in:
  pharmacy • MAIS, MS, PhD, Pharm D

College of Science
Dr. Frederick H. Horne, Dean
Programs in:
  advanced mathematics education • MAT
  analytical chemistry • MS, PhD
  biochemistry and biophysics • MA, MAIS, MS, PhD
  biology education • MAT
  biometry • MA, MS, PhD
  botany and plant pathology • M Agr, MAIS
  chemistry • MA, MAIS
  chemistry education • MAT
  entomology • M Agr, MA, MAIS, MS, PhD
  environmental statistics • MA, MS, PhD
  general science • MA, MS, PhD
  geography • MA, MAIS, MS, PhD
  geology • MA, MAIS, MS, PhD
  inorganic chemistry • MS, PhD
  integrated science education • MAT
  mathematics • MA, MAIS, MS, PhD
  mathematics education • MA, MAT, MS, PhD
  microbiology • M Agr, MA, MAIS, MS, PhD
  molecular and cellular biology • PhD
  nuclear and radiation chemistry • MS, PhD
  operations research • MA, MAIS, MS
  organic chemistry • MS, PhD
  pathology • MA, MS, PhD
  physical chemistry • MS, PhD
  physics • MA, MS, PhD
  physics education • MAT
  science education • MA, MAT, MS, PhD
  statistics • MA, MS, PhD
  structural botany • MA, MS, PhD
  systematics and ecology • MA, MS, PhD
  zoology • MA, MAIS, MS, PhD

College of Veterinary Medicine
Dr. Robert C. Wilson, Dean
Programs in:
  comparative veterinary medicine • PhD
  microbiology • MS
  pathology • MS
  toxicology • MS
  veterinary medicine • DVM

PACIFIC UNIVERSITY
Forest Grove, OR 97116-1797

http://www.pacificu.edu/

Independent coed comprehensive institution. *Enrollment: 1,854 graduate, professional, and undergraduate students. Graduate faculty: 52 full-time, 57 part-time. Library facilities: Harvey W. Scott Memorial Library. Graduate expenses: Tuition of $9704 per year full-time, $350 per credit hour part-time. Fees of $345 per year. General application contact: Lisa Lutero, Director of Admissions, 503-359-2900.*

College of Optometry
Programs in:
  clinical optometry • MS
  optometry • OD
  visual function in learning • M Ed

School of Education
Dr. Willard Kniep, Program Director
Programs in:
  early childhood education/elementary education • MAT
  education • MAE
  elementary/middle school education • MAT
  secondary education • MAT

School of Occupational Therapy
Molly McEwen, Director
Program in:
  occupational therapy • MOT

School of Physical Therapy
Dr. Daiva Banaitis, Director
Program in:
  physical therapy • MSHS, MSPT

School of Physician Assistant Studies
Christine Legler, Director
Program in:
  physician assistant studies • MS

School of Professional Psychology
Dr. James Lane, Program Director
Program in:
  professional psychology • MS, Psy D

PORTLAND STATE UNIVERSITY
Portland, OR 97207-0751

http://www.pdx.edu/

Public coed university. *Enrollment: 12,746 graduate, professional, and undergraduate students. Graduate faculty: 577 full-time, 225 part-time. Computer facilities: Campuswide network is available with full Internet access. Total number of PCs/terminals supplied for student use: 420. Computer service fees are included with tuition*

Portland State University (continued)
and fees. Library facilities: *Branford Millar Library.* Graduate expenses: *$6101 per year full-time, $689 per semester (minimum) part-time for state residents; $10,445 per year full-time, $689 per semester (minimum) part-time for nonresidents.* General application contact: *Agnes A. Hoffman, Interim Director of Admissions and Records, 503-725-3511.*

Graduate Studies
William Feyerherm, Vice Provost for Research and Dean
Programs in:
- systems science/anthropology • PhD
- systems science/business administration • PhD
- systems science/civil engineering • PhD
- systems science/economics • PhD
- systems science/engineering management • PhD
- systems science/general • PhD
- systems science/mathematical sciences • PhD
- systems science/mechanical engineering • PhD
- systems science/psychology • PhD
- systems science/sociology • PhD

College of Liberal Arts and Sciences
Dr. Marvin Kaiser, Dean
Programs in:
- anthropology • MA, PhD
- applied economics • MA, MS
- biology • MA, MS, PhD
- chemistry • MA, MS, PhD
- economics • PhD
- English • MA, MAT
- environmental management • MEM
- environmental sciences/biology • PhD
- environmental sciences/chemistry • PhD
- environmental sciences/civil engineering • PhD
- environmental sciences/economics • PhD
- environmental sciences/geography • PhD
- environmental sciences/geology • PhD
- environmental sciences/physics • PhD
- environmental studies • MS
- foreign literature and language • MA
- French • MA
- general arts and letters education • MAT, MST
- general economics • MA, MS
- general science education • MAT, MST
- general social science education • MAT, MST
- general speech communication • MA, MS
- geography • MA, MS, PhD
- geology • MA, MS, PhD
- German • MA
- history • MA
- mathematical sciences • MA, MAT, MS, MST, PhD
- mathematics education • PhD
- physics • MA, MS, PhD
- psychology • MA, MS, PhD
- science/geology • MAT, MST
- sociology • MA, MS, PhD
- Spanish • MA
- speech and hearing sciences • MA, MS
- teaching English to speakers of other languages • MA

College of Urban and Public Affairs
Dr. Nohad A. Toulan, Dean
Programs in:
- administration of justice • MS, PhD
- gerontology • Certificate
- health administration • MPA
- health administration and policy • MPH
- health education • MA, MS
- health education and health promotion • MPH
- political science • MA, MAT, MS, MST, PhD
- public administration • MPA
- public administration and policy • PhD
- urban and regional planning • MURP
- urban studies • MUS, PhD

Graduate School of Social Work
Dr. James Ward, Dean
Programs in:
- social work • MSW
- social work and social research • PhD

School of Business Administration
Dr. Roger Ahlbrandt, Dean
Programs in:
- business administration • PhD
- international business • MBA
- international management • MIM
- taxation • M Tax

School of Education
Dr. Robert Everhart, Dean
Programs in:
- counselor education • MA, MS
- early childhood education • MA, MS
- education • M Ed, MA, MS
- educational administration • MA, MS
- educational leadership: curriculum and instruction • Ed D
- educational leadership/educational administration • Ed D
- educational leadership/postsecondary adult and continuing education • Ed D
- educational media/school librarianship • MA, MS
- elementary education • M Ed, MAT, MST
- reading • MA, MS
- secondary education • M Ed, MAT, MST
- special education • MA, MS

School of Engineering and Applied Science
Dr. Robert D. Dryden, Dean
Programs in:
- civil engineering • MS, PhD
- computer science • MS
- electrical and computer engineering • MS, PhD
- engineering management • MS, PhD
- manufacturing engineering • ME
- mechanical engineering • MS, PhD

School of Fine and Performing Arts
Dr. Barbara Sestak, Interim Dean
Programs in:
- ceramics • MFA
- conducting • MM
- music education • MAT, MST

painting • MFA
performance • MM
sculpture • MFA
theater arts • MA

SOUTHERN OREGON UNIVERSITY
Ashland, OR 97520

http://www.sou.edu/

Public coed comprehensive institution. *Enrollment: 4,726 graduate, professional, and undergraduate students. Graduate faculty: 119 full-time. Computer facilities: Campuswide network is available. Total number of PCs/terminals supplied for student use: 300. Computer service fees are included with tuition and fees. Library facilities: main library. Graduate expenses: $5187 per year full-time, $586 per quarter (minimum) part-time for state residents; $9228 per year full-time, $586 per quarter (minimum) part-time for nonresidents. General application contact: Allen H. Blaszak, Director of Admissions, 541-552-6411.*

Graduate Office
Sara Hopkins-Powell, Associate Provost

School of Arts and Letters
Dr. Kathryn Robinson, Dean
Program in:
arts and letters • MA, MS

School of Business
Dr. John Laughlin, Director
Program in:
business • MA Ed, MBA, MS Ed

School of Sciences
Dr. Joseph Graf, Dean
Programs in:
environmental education • MA, MS
mathematics/computer science • MA, MS
science • MA, MS

School of Social Science, Health and Physical Education
Neil Kunze, Dean
Programs in:
classroom teacher • MA Ed, MS Ed
early childhood • MA Ed, MS Ed
elementary education • MA Ed, MS Ed
handicapped learner • MA Ed, MS Ed
professional counseling • MA, MS
psychology • MA, MS
reading • MA Ed, MS Ed
secondary education • MA Ed, MS Ed
social science • MA, MS
supervision • MA Ed, MS Ed
teaching • MAT

UNIVERSITY OF OREGON
Eugene, OR 97403

http://www.uoregon.edu/

Public coed university. *Enrollment: 17,207 graduate, professional, and undergraduate students. Graduate faculty: 777 full time, 391 part-time. Computer facilities: Campuswide network is available with full Internet access. Total number of PCs/terminals supplied for student use: 1,000. Computer service fees are included with tuition and fees. Library facilities: Knight Library plus 5 additional on-campus libraries. Graduate expenses: $6429 per year full-time, $873 per quarter (minimum) part-time for state residents; $10,857 per year full-time, $1360 per quarter (minimum) part-time for nonresidents. General application contact: Graduate School, 541-346-5129.*

Graduate School
Steadman Upham, Vice Provost for Research and Graduate
Education/Dean

Charles H. Lundquist College of Business
Dale Morse, Dean
Programs in:
accounting • PhD
decision sciences • MA, MS, PhD
finance • MA, MS, PhD
human resources and industrial relations • MHRIR
information management • MS
management • MA, MS, PhD
management: general business • MBA
marketing • MA, MS, PhD

College of Arts and Sciences
Joe Stone, Dean
Programs in:
anthropology • MA, MS, PhD
Asian studies • MA
biochemistry • MA, MS, PhD
chemistry • MA, MS, PhD
Chinese • MA, PhD
classical civilization • MA
classics • MA
clinical psychology • PhD
cognitive psychology • MA, MS, PhD
comparative literature • MA, PhD
computer and information science • MA, MS, PhD
creative writing • MFA
developmental psychology • MA, MS, PhD
ecology and evolution • MA, MS, PhD
economics • MA, MS, PhD
English • MA, PhD
environmental studies • MA, MS
exercise and movement science • MS, PhD
French • MA
geography • MA, MS, PhD
geological sciences • MA, MS, PhD
Germanic languages and literatures • MA, PhD
Greek • MA
history • MA, PhD
independent study: folklore • MA, MS
international studies • MA

University of Oregon (continued)
Italian • MA
Japanese • MA, PhD
Latin • MA
linguistics • MA, PhD
marine biology • MA, MS, PhD
mathematics • MA, MS, PhD
molecular, cellular and genetic biology • PhD
neuroscience and development • PhD
philosophy • MA, PhD
physics • MA, MS, PhD
physiological psychology • MA, MS, PhD
political science • MA, MS, PhD
psychology • MA, MS, PhD
Romance languages • MA, PhD
Russian • MA
social/personality psychology • MA, MS, PhD
sociology • MA, MS, PhD
Spanish • MA
theater arts • MA, MFA, MS, PhD

College of Education
Martin J. Kaufman, Dean
Programs in:
communication disorders and sciences • D Ed, M Ed, MA, MS, PhD
computer and education • PhD
counseling psychology • D Ed, M Ed, MA, MS, PhD
developmental disabilities • MA, MS, PhD
early intervention • D Ed, M Ed, MA, MS, PhD
educational administration • D Ed, MS
educational policy and foundations • MS
exceptional learner • D Ed, M Ed, MA, MS, PhD
foundations and research • PhD
higher education • MS
management and leadership • PhD
organization and governance • PhD
school psychology • M Ed, MA, MS, PhD
special education • D Ed, M Ed, MA, MS, PhD

School of Architecture and Allied Arts
Robert Melnick, Dean
Programs in:
architecture • M Arch
art history • MA, PhD
arts management • MA, MS
community and regional planning • MCRP
fine and applied arts • MFA
historic preservation • MS
interior architecture • MI Arch
landscape architecture • MLA
public affairs • MA, MS

School of Journalism and Communication
Tim Gleason, Acting Dean
Program in:
journalism • MA, MS, PhD

School of Music
Anne Dhu McLucas, Dean
Programs in:
choral conducting • M Mus
composition • DMA, M Mus
dance • MA, MS

music • MA
music education • DMA, M Mus, PhD
music history • DMA, MA, PhD
music theory • DMA, MA, PhD
performance • DMA
performance and music literature • M Mus
performance in woodwind or brass instruments • M Mus
piano pedagogy • M Mus
wind ensemble conducting • M Mus

School of Law
Rennard Strickland, Dean
Program in:
law • JD

UNIVERSITY OF PORTLAND
Portland, OR 97203-5798

http://www.up.edu/

Independent-religious coed comprehensive institution. *Enrollment: 2,659 graduate, professional, and undergraduate students. Graduate faculty: 84 full-time, 11 part-time. Computer facilities: Campuswide network is available with full Internet access. Total number of PCs/ terminals supplied for student use: 419. Computer service fees are included with tuition and fees. Library facilities: Wilson W. Clark Library. Graduate expenses: $515 per semester hour. General application contact: Dr. Patricia L. Chadwick, Assistant Academic Vice President, 503-283-7107.*

Graduate School
Dr. Patricia L. Chadwick, Assistant Academic Vice President

College of Arts and Sciences
Dr. Marlene Moore, Dean
Programs in:
communication studies • MA
drama • MFA
management communication • MS
music • MA
music education • MM Ed

Multnomah School of Engineering
Dr. Zia Yamayee, Dean
Programs in:
civil engineering • MSCE
electrical engineering • MSEE
mechanical engineering • MSME

School of Business Administration
Dr. Ronald P. Hill, Dean
Program in:
business administration • MBA

School of Education
Dr. Maria Ciriello, OP, Dean
Programs in:
early childhood education • M Ed, MA, MAT
religious education • M Ed, MA

secondary education • M Ed, MA, MAT

special education • M Ed, MA

School of Nursing

Dr. Terry Misener, Dean

Programs in:

family nurse practitioner • Post Master's Certificate

leadership in health care systems • Post Master's Certificate

nursing • MS

WESTERN OREGON UNIVERSITY
Monmouth, OR 97361

http://www.wou.edu/

Public coed comprehensive institution. *Enrollment: 4,088 graduate, professional, and undergraduate students. Graduate faculty: 102 full-time, 84 part-time. Computer facilities: Campuswide network is available with full Internet access. Total number of PCs/terminals supplied for student use: 177. Computer service fees are included with tuition and fees. Library facilities: main library. Graduate expenses: $3198 per year full-time, $272 per semester (minimum) part-time for state residents; $9738 per year full-time, $272 per semester (minimum) part-time for nonresidents.* General application contact: *Alison Marshall, Director of Admissions, 503-838-8211.*

Graduate Programs

Dr. Linda Stonecipher, Director

School of Education

Dr. Meredith Brodsky, Dean

Programs in:

early childhood education • MS Ed

early intervention/special education • MS Ed

English for speakers of other languages • MS Ed

humanities • MAT, MS Ed

information technology • MS Ed

learning disabilities • MS Ed

mathematics • MAT, MS Ed

middle school education • MS Ed

multihandicapped education • MS Ed

reading education • MS Ed

rehabilitation counseling • MS Ed

science • MAT, MS Ed

socially and educationally different • MS Ed

social science • MAT, MS Ed

teacher preparation: deafness • MS Ed

School of Liberal Arts and Sciences

Dr. John Minahan, Dean, Interim Provost

Program in:

correctional administration • MA, MS

PENNSYLVANIA

ALLEGHENY UNIVERSITY OF THE HEALTH SCIENCES
Philadelphia, PA 19102-1192

http://www.auhs.edu/homepage.html

Independent coed university. *Enrollment: 3,295 graduate, professional, and undergraduate students. Graduate faculty: 1,593 full-time, 274 part-time. Computer facilities: Campuswide network is available with full Internet access. Total number of PCs/terminals supplied for student use: 130. Computer services are offered at no charge. Library facilities: main library plus 3 additional on-campus libraries. Graduate expenses: Tuition of $11,500 per year full-time, $640 per credit part-time. Fees of $125 per year.* General application contact: *Paula Greenberg, Director of Admissions and Recruitment, 215-762-8288.*

School of Health Professions

Dr. Will Green, Dean

Programs in:

art therapy • MA

clinical psychology • MA, MS, PhD

couples and family therapy • PhD

emergency medical service • MEMS

family therapy • MFT

group counseling and organizational dynamics • MGCOD, MGPGP, MS

health care education technology • MS

movement science in physical therapy • MS, PhD

movement therapy • MA

music therapy • MA

orthopedic physical therapy • MS, PhD

pediatric physical therapy • MS, PhD

physical therapy • MPT

School of Medicine

Dr. Barbara Atkinson, Dean

Programs in:

anatomy and neurobiology • MS, PhD

biochemistry • MS, PhD

bioengineering • PhD

biomedical nutrition • PhD

cardiovascular biology • MS, PhD

clinical microbiology • MS

laboratory animal science • MLAS

medical physics • MS, PhD

medical science • MBS, MMS

medicine • MD

microbiology and immunology • MS, PhD

molecular and cell biology • MS, PhD

molecular and human genetics • MS, PhD

molecular pathobiology • PhD

neuroscience • PhD

pharmacology • MS, PhD

physiology • PhD

radiation science • MS, PhD

Allegheny University of the Health Sciences (continued)

School of Nursing
Dr. Gloria Donnelly, Dean
Program in:
  nursing • Certificate, MSN

School of Public Health
William E. Welton, Acting Dean
Program in:
  public health • MPH

BEAVER COLLEGE
Glenside, PA 19038-3295

http://www.beaver.edu/

Independent-religious coed comprehensive institution. Library facilities: *Eugenia Fuller Atwood Library.* Graduate expenses: *Tuition of $6570 per year full-time, $365 per credit part-time. Fees of $35 per year.* General application contact: *Dean of Graduate Studies, 215-572-2925.*

Graduate Studies
Programs in:
  allied health • MA Ed, MHA, MSH Ed
  art education • M Ed, MA Ed
  biology education • MA Ed
  chemistry education • MA Ed
  child development • CAS
  community counseling • MAC
  computer education • CAS, M Ed, MA Ed
  counseling • MAC
  curriculum • CAS
  early childhood education • CAS, M Ed
  educational leadership • CAS, M Ed
  educational psychology • CAS
  elementary education • CAS, M Ed
  English • MAE
  English education • MA Ed
  environmental education • CAS, MA Ed
  fine arts, theater, and music • MAH
  genetic counseling • MSGC
  history education • MA Ed
  history, philosophy, and religion • MAH
  individualized • M Ed
  international peace and conflice management • MA
  language arts • CAS, M Ed
  literature and language • MAH
  master teacher • M Ed
  mathematics education • CAS, M Ed, MA Ed
  music education • MA Ed
  physical therapy • DPT, MSPT
  physician assistant studies • MSPAS
  reading • CAS, M Ed
  research in child development • M Ed
  school counseling • MAC
  school library science • M Ed
  science education • CAS, M Ed

secondary education • CAS, M Ed
special education • CAS, M Ed
written communication • MA Ed

BLOOMSBURG UNIVERSITY OF PENNSYLVANIA
Bloomsburg, PA 17815-1905

http://www.bloomu.edu/

Public coed comprehensive institution. *Enrollment: 7,499 graduate, professional, and undergraduate students. Graduate faculty: 207 full-time. Computer facilities: Campuswide network is available with full Internet access. Total number of PCs/terminals supplied for student use: 510. Computer service fees are included with tuition and fees. Library facilities: Harvey A. Andruss Library.* Graduate expenses: *Tuition of $3468 per year full-time, $193 per credit part-time for state residents; $6236 per year full-time, $346 per credit part-time for nonresidents. Fees of $748 per year full-time, $166 per semester (minimum) part-time.* General application contact: *Patrick J. Schloss, Assistant Vice President and Dean for Graduate Studies and Research, 217-389-4015.*

School of Graduate Studies
Patrick J. Schloss, Assistant Vice President and Dean for Graduate Studies and Research

College of Arts and Sciences
Dr. Hsien-Tung Liu, Dean
Programs in:
  art history • MA
  biology • MS
  biology education • M Ed
  communication • MA
  exercise science and adult fitness • MS
  instructional technology • MS
  studio art • MA

College of Business
David Long, Dean
Programs in:
  accounting • MS
  business administration • MBA
  business education • M Ed

College of Professional Studies
Dr. Ann L. Lee, Dean
Programs in:
  communication disorders/audiology • MS
  communication disorders/education of deaf/hard of
    hearing • MS
  communication disorders/speech pathology • MS
  curriculum and instruction • M Ed
  early childhood education • MS
  elementary education • M Ed
  nursing • MSN
  reading • M Ed
  special education • MS

CABRINI COLLEGE
Radnor, PA 19087-3698

http://www.cabrini.edu/

Independent-religious coed comprehensive institution. *Enrollment: 2,054 graduate, professional, and undergraduate students. Graduate faculty: 9 full-time, 16 part-time. Computer facilities: Campuswide network is available with full Internet access. Total number of PCs/ terminals supplied for student use: 92. Computer service fees are included with tuition and fees. Library facilities: Holy Spirit Library. General application contact: William Firman, Associate Director of Admissions, 610-902-8552.*

Graduate Education Programs
Dr. Dawn Middleton, Chairperson
Program in:
   education • M Ed

CALIFORNIA UNIVERSITY OF PENNSYLVANIA
California, PA 15419-1394

http://www.cup.edu/

Public coed comprehensive institution. *Enrollment: 5,300 graduate, professional, and undergraduate students. Graduate faculty: 10 full-time, 93 part-time. Computer facilities: Campuswide network is available with full Internet access. Total number of PCs/terminals supplied for student use: 300. Computer services are offered at no charge. Library facilities: Louis L. Manderino Library. Graduate expenses: Tuition of $3468 per year full-time, $193 per credit part-time for state residents; $6236 per year full-time, $346 per credit part-time for nonresidents. Fees of $886 per year full-time, $153 per semester (minimum) part-time. General application contact: Dr. George W. Crane, Dean of Graduate Studies, 724-938-4187.*

School of Graduate Studies
Dr. George W. Crane, Dean

School of Education
Dr. Stephen A. Pavlak, Dean
Programs in:
   athletic training • MS
   communication disorders • MS
   early childhood education • M Ed
   educational administration • M Ed
   elementary education • M Ed
   guidance and counseling • M Ed, MS
   mentally and/or physically handicapped education •
      M Ed
   reading specialist • M Ed
   school psychology • MS
   social work • MSW
   technology education • M Ed

School of Liberal Arts
Dr. Jess Cignetti, Dean
Programs in:
   communication • MA
   earth science • MS
   English • M Ed, MA
   geography • M Ed, MA
   social science • MA

School of Science and Technology
Richard B. Hart, Dean
Programs in:
   biology • M Ed, MS
   business administration • MS
   computer science • M Ed
   mathematics • M Ed

CARNEGIE MELLON UNIVERSITY
Pittsburgh, PA 15213-3891

http://www.cmu.edu/

Independent coed university. *Enrollment: 7,912 graduate, professional, and undergraduate students. Graduate faculty: 920 full-time, 108 part-time. Computer facilities: Campuswide network is available with full Internet access. Computer service fees are included with tuition and fees. Library facilities: Hunt Library plus 2 additional on-campus libraries. Graduate expenses: Tuition of $21,275 per year full-time, $295 per unit part-time. Fees of $130 per year. General application contact: Mike Steidel, Admissions Office, 412-268-2000.*

Carnegie Institute of Technology
John Anderson, Dean
Programs in:
   biomedical engineering • MS, PhD
   chemical engineering • MS, PhD
   civil engineering • MS, PhD
   civil engineering and industrial management • MS
   civil engineering and robotics • PhD
   civil engineering/bioengineering • PhD
   civil engineering/engineering and public policy • MS,
      PhD
   colloids, polymers and surfaces • MS
   electrical and computer engineering • MS, PhD
   engineering and public policy • MS, PhD
   materials science and engineering • ME, MS, PhD
   mechanical engineering • ME, MS, PhD
   robotics • PhD
   technology • MOM

Center for Innovation in Learning
Dr. John R. Hayes, Director
Program in:
   instructional science • PhD

Carnegie Mellon University (continued)

College of Fine Arts
Dr. Martin Prekop, Dean
Programs in:
architecture • MSA
art • MFA
arts management • MAM
building performance and diagnostics • M Sc, PhD
communication planning and design • M Des
composition • MM
computational design • M Sc, PhD
conducting • MM
design • MFA
directing • MFA
dramatic writing • MFA
interaction design • M Des
performance • MM
performance technology and management • MFA

College of Humanities and Social Sciences
Dr. Peter Stearns, Dean
Programs in:
applied statistics • PhD
behavioral decision theory • MS, PhD
business • MAPW
cognitive neuropsychology • PhD
cognitive psychology • PhD
computational statistics • PhD
developmental psychology • PhD
English • MA
history • MA
history and policy • MS, PhD
literary and cultural theory • MA, PhD
logic and computation • MS
mathematical finance • PhD
organization science • MS, PhD
philosophy • MA, MS
pure and applied logic • PhD
research • MAPW
rhetoric • MA, PhD
rhetorical theory • MAPW
second language acquisition • PhD
social and cultural history • MA, PhD
social and decision science • MS, PhD
social/personality psychology • PhD
statistics • MS, PhD
technical • MAPW
theoretical statistics • PhD

Graduate School of Industrial Administration
Douglas Dunn, Dean
Programs in:
accounting • PhD
administration and public management • MSIA
algorithms, combinatorics, and optimization • PhD
business management and software engineering • MBMSE
civil engineering and industrial management • MS
computational finance • MSCF
economics • PhD
environmental engineering and management • MEEM
finance • PhD

financial economics • PhD
industrial administration • MSIA, PhD
information science • PhD
manufacturing • MOM
marketing • PhD
mathematical finance • PhD
operations research • PhD
organizational behavior and theory • PhD
political economy • PhD
public policy and management • MIS, MS
robotics • PhD

H. John Heinz III School of Public Policy and Management
Mark Kamlet, Dean
Programs in:
arts management • MAM
health care policy and management • MSHCPM
public management • MPM
public policy analysis • PhD
public policy and management • MIS, MS
sustainable economic development • MSED

Information Networking Institute
Bernard Bennington, Director
Program in:
information networking • MS

Mellon College of Science
Dr. Susan A. Henry, Dean
Programs in:
algorithms, combinatorics, and optimization • PhD
applied physics • PhD
biochemistry • PhD
biophysics • PhD
cell biology • PhD
chemical instrumentation • MS
chemistry • MS, PhD
colloids, polymers and surfaces • MS
developmental biology • PhD
genetics • PhD
mathematical finance • PhD
mathematical sciences • DA, MS, PhD
molecular biology • PhD
physics • MS, PhD
polymer science • MS
pure and applied logic • PhD

School of Computer Science
Raj Reddy, Dean
Programs in:
algorithms, combinatorics, and optimization • PhD
computer science • PhD
human-computer interaction • MHCI
language technologies • MS, PhD
pure and applied logic • PhD
robotics • PhD
software engineering • MSE

CHESTNUT HILL COLLEGE
Philadelphia, PA 19118-2693

Independent-religious coed comprehensive institution. *Enrollment:* 1,340 graduate, professional, and undergraduate students. Graduate faculty: *17 full-time, 37 part-time.* Library facilities: *Logue Library.* Graduate expenses: *Tuition of $365 per credit. Fees of $25 per semester.* General application contact: *Sr. Mary Anne Celenza, OFM, Dean, 215-248-7161.*

Graduate Division
Sr. Mary Anne Celenza, OFM, Dean
Programs in:
    applied technology • MS
    early childhood education • M Ed
    elementary education • M Ed
    holistic spirituality • MA
    holistic spirituality and spiritual direction • MA
    professional psychology • MA, MS, Psy D

CHEYNEY UNIVERSITY OF PENNSYLVANIA
Cheyney, PA 19319
http://www.cheyney.edu/

Public coed comprehensive institution. *Enrollment:* 1,430 graduate, professional, and undergraduate students. Graduate faculty: *5 full-time, 7 part-time.* Library facilities: *L. P. Hill Library.* Graduate expenses: *$3848 per year full-time, $193 per credit hour part-time for state residents; $6616 per year full-time, $346 per credit hour part-time for nonresidents.* General application contact: *Dean of Graduate Studies, 610-399-2400.*

School of Education
Programs in:
    adult and continuing education • MS
    educational administration and supervision • M Ed
    elementary education • M Ed
    special education • M Ed, MS

 # CLARION UNIVERSITY OF PENNSYLVANIA
Clarion, PA 16214
http://www.clarion.edu/

Public coed comprehensive institution. *Enrollment:* 5,948 graduate, professional, and undergraduate students. Graduate faculty: *134 full-time.* Computer facilities: *Campuswide network is available with full Internet access. Total number of PCs/terminals supplied for student use: 350. Computer services are offered at no charge.* Library facilities: *Carlson Library.* Graduate expenses: *Tuition of*

$3468 per year full-time, $193 per credit hour part-time for state residents; $6236 per year full-time, $346 per credit hour part-time for nonresidents. Fees of $921 per year full-time, $90 per credit hour part-time for state residents; $921 per year full-time, $89 per credit hour part-time for nonresidents. General application contact: *Dr. Brenda Dédé, Coordinator of Graduate Studies, 814-226-2337.*

College of Graduate Studies
Dr. Brenda Dédé, Coordinator

College of Arts and Sciences
Dr. Stan Green, Dean
Programs in:
    biology • MS
    communication • MS
    English • MA
    mathematics • M Ed
    science education • M Ed

College of Business Administration
Dr. Robert Balough, Coordinator
Program in:
    business administration • MBA

College of Education and Human Services
Dr. Gail Grejda, Interim Dean
Programs in:
    communication sciences and disorders • MS
    elementary education • M Ed
    library science • MSLS
    reading • M Ed
    special education • MS

School of Nursing
Dr. Audean Duespohl, Dean
Program in:
    nursing • MSN

COLLEGE MISERICORDIA
Dallas, PA 18612-1098
http://miseri.edu/

Independent-religious coed comprehensive institution. *Enrollment:* 1,697 graduate, professional, and undergraduate students. Graduate faculty: *48.* Library facilities: *Sister Francesca McLaughlin Memorial Library.* Graduate expenses: *Tuition of $13,780 per year full-time, $345 per credit part-time. Fees of $740 per year.* General application contact: *Barbara Leggat, Continuing Education Specialist, 800-852-7675.*

Division of Health Sciences
Dr. Catherine Perry Wilkinson, Chair
Programs in:
    nursing • MSN
    occupational therapy • MSOT
    physical therapy • MSPT

College Misericordia (continued)
Division of Professional Studies
Dr. Linda Trompeter, Director of Graduate Programs
Programs in:
- education/curriculum • MS
- organizational management • MS

DREXEL UNIVERSITY
Philadelphia, PA 19104-2875

http://www.drexel.edu/

Independent coed university. *Enrollment: 9,590 graduate, professional, and undergraduate students. Graduate faculty: 400 full-time, 442 part-time. Computer facilities: Campuswide network is available with full Internet access. Computer services are offered at no charge. Library facilities: W. W. Hagerty Library. Graduate expenses: Tuition of $565 per credit hour. Fees of $121 per quarter full-time, $65 per quarter part-time. General application contact: Director of Graduate Admissions, 215-895-6700.*

Graduate School
Dr. Richard Haracz, Associate Provost for Research and Graduate Studies

College of Arts and Sciences
Dr. Cecilie Goodrich, Dean
Programs in:
- biological science • MS, PhD
- chemistry • MS, PhD
- clinical neuropsychology • MS, PhD
- computer science • MS
- food science • MS
- mathematics • MS, PhD
- nutrition science • MS, PhD
- physics and atmospheric science • MS, PhD
- science of instruction • MS
- software engineering • MS
- technical and science communication • MS

College of Business and Administration
Dr. Pamela Lewis, Dean
Programs in:
- accounting • MBA, MS, PhD
- business administration • APC, MBA, PhD
- decision sciences • MS, PhD
- economics • MBA, PhD
- finance • MBA, MS, PhD
- legal studies • MBA
- management • MBA
- marketing • MBA, MS, PhD
- organizational sciences • PhD
- quantitative methods • MBA, MS
- strategic management • PhD
- taxation • MS

College of Engineering
Dr. Y. T. Shah, Dean
Programs in:
- biochemical engineering • MS
- chemical engineering • MS, PhD
- civil engineering • MS, PhD
- electrical and computer engineering • PhD
- electrical engineering • MSEE
- engineering geology • MS
- engineering management • MS, PhD
- manufacturing engineering • MS, PhD
- materials engineering • MS, PhD
- mechanical engineering and mechanics • MS, PhD
- telecommunications engineering • MSEE

College of Information Science and Technology
Dr. Richard Lytle, Dean
Programs in:
- information studies • CAS, PhD
- information systems • MSIS
- library and information science • MS

Nesbitt College of Design Arts
Dr. J. Michael Adams, Dean
Programs in:
- arts administration • MS
- fashion design • MS
- interior design • MS
- publication management • MS

School of Biomedical Engineering, Science and Health Systems
Dr. Banu Onaral, Director
Programs in:
- biomedical engineering • MS, PhD
- biomedical science • MS, PhD
- biostatistics • MS
- clinical/rehabilitation engineering • MS

School of Environmental Science, Engineering and Policy
Dr. Michael Gealt, Director
Programs in:
- environmental engineering • MS, PhD
- environmental science • MS, PhD

DUQUESNE UNIVERSITY
Pittsburgh, PA 15282-0001

http://www.duq.edu/

Independent-religious coed university. *Enrollment: 9,500 graduate, professional, and undergraduate students. Graduate faculty: 255 full-time, 90 part-time. Computer facilities: Campuswide network is available with full Internet access. Total number of PCs/terminals supplied for student use: 525. Computer service fees are included with tuition and fees. Library facilities: Gumberg Library plus 1 additional on-campus library. Graduate expenses: Tuition of $481 per credit. Fees of $39 per credit. General application contact: Dr. Michael P. Weber, Provost and Academic Vice President, 412-396-6054.*

Graduate School of Liberal Arts

Dr. Constance Ramirez, Dean
Programs in:
    archival, museum, and editing studies • MA
    clinical psychology • PhD
    communication • MA
    English • MA, PhD
    general phenomenological psychology • MA
    health care ethics • DHCE, MA, PhD
    history • MA
    liberal studies • M Phil, MALS
    multimedia technology • MS
    philosophy • MA, PhD
    philosophy for theological studies • MA
    theology • MA, PhD

Graduate Center for Social and Public Policy

Dr. Evan Stoddard, Director
Programs in:
    conflict resolution and peace studies • Certificate
    social and public policy • MA

Bayer School of Natural and Environmental Sciences

Dr. Heinz Machatzke, Dean
Programs in:
    biochemistry • MS, PhD
    biological sciences • MS
    chemistry • MS, PhD
    environmental science and management • Certificate, MS

Graduate School of Business Administration

Thomas J. Murrin, Dean
Programs in:
    business administration • MBA
    information systems management • MS
    taxation • MS

John G. Rangos, Sr. School of Health Sciences

Dr. Jerome L. Martin, Dean
Programs in:
    health management systems • MHMS
    occupational therapy • MOT
    physical therapy • MPT
    physician assistant • MPA
    speech-language pathology • MSLP

School of Education

Dr. James Henderson, Dean
Programs in:
    counselor education • MS Ed
    educational leaders • Ed D
    educational studies • MS Ed
    elementary administration • MS Ed
    elementary education • MS Ed
    instructional leadership excellence • Ed D
    reading and language arts • MS Ed
    school administration • MS Ed
    school psychology • CAGS, MS Ed
    school supervision • MS Ed
    secondary administration • MS Ed
    secondary education • MS Ed
    special education • MS Ed

School of Law

Nicholas P. Cafardi, Dean
Program in:
    law • JD

School of Music

Dr. Robert Shankovich, Graduate Chair
Programs in:
    applied music • MM
    composition • MM
    music • AD
    music education • MM
    music theory • MM
    sacred music • MM

School of Nursing

Dr. Jeri A. Milstead, Chair
Programs in:
    family nurse practitioner • MSN
    nursing • PhD
    nursing administration • MSN
    nursing education • MSN

School of Pharmacy

Dr. P. Randall L. Vanderveen, Dean
Programs in:
    medicinal chemistry • MS, PhD
    pharmaceutical administration • MS
    pharmaceutical chemistry • MS, PhD
    pharmaceutics • MS, PhD
    pharmacology/toxicology • MS, PhD
    pharmacy • Pharm D

EASTERN COLLEGE
St. Davids, PA 19087-3696

http://www.eastern.edu/

Independent-religious coed comprehensive institution. *Enrollment:* 2,496 graduate, professional, and undergraduate students. *Graduate faculty: 30 full-time, 60 part-time. Computer facilities: Campuswide network is available with full Internet access. Total number of PCs/ terminals supplied for student use: 100. Computer services are offered at no charge. Library facilities: Warner Memorial Library plus 1 additional on-campus library.* General application contact: *Leonard N. Jamison, Director of Graduate Admissions, 610-341-5972.*

Graduate Business Programs

Dr. John Stapleford, Chair
Programs in:
    accounting • MBA
    business administration • MBA
    economic development • MBA, MS

Eastern College (continued)
    economics • MBA
    finance • MBA
    management • MBA
    marketing • MBA
    nonprofit management • MBA, MS

Graduate Education Programs
Dr. Helen Loeb, Director
Programs in:
    English as a second or foreign language • Certificate
    multicultural education • M Ed
    school health services • M Ed

Programs in Counseling
Dr. Michele Nouomi, Head
Programs in:
    community/clinical counseling • MA
    school counseling • MA
    school psychology • MS
    spiritual formation • MA
    student development • MA

EAST STROUDSBURG UNIVERSITY OF PENNSYLVANIA
East Stroudsburg, PA 18301-2999

http://www.esu.edu/

Public coed comprehensive institution. Computer facilities: *Campuswide network is available with full Internet access. Total number of PCs/terminals supplied for student use: 250. Computer service fees are included with tuition and fees.* Library facilities: *Kemp Library.* Graduate expenses: *Tuition of $3468 per year full-time, $193 per credit part-time for state residents; $6236 per year full-time, $346 per credit part-time for nonresidents. Fees of $700 per year full-time, $39 per credit part-time.* General application contact: *Dean of Graduate Studies and Continuing Education, 717-422-3536.*

Graduate School

School of Arts and Sciences
Programs in:
    biology • M Ed, MS
    computer science • MS
    general science • M Ed, MS
    history • M Ed, MA
    political science • M Ed, MA

School of Health Sciences and Human Performance
Programs in:
    cardiac rehabilitation and exercise science • MS
    community health education • MPH
    health and physical education • M Ed
    health education • MS
    physical education • MS
    speech pathology and audiology • MS
    sports management • M Ed

School of Professional Studies
Programs in:
    elementary education • M Ed
    professional and secondary education • M Ed
    reading • M Ed
    special education • M Ed

EDINBORO UNIVERSITY OF PENNSYLVANIA
Edinboro, PA 16444

http://www.edinboro.edu/

Public coed comprehensive institution. *Enrollment: 7,083 graduate, professional, and undergraduate students. Graduate faculty: 93 full-time. Computer facilities: Campuswide network is available with full Internet access. Total number of PCs/terminals supplied for student use: 300. Computer services are offered at no charge. Library facilities: Baron-Forness Library plus 1 additional on-campus library. Graduate expenses: Tuition of $3468 per year full-time, $193 per credit part-time for state residents; $6236 per year full-time, $346 per credit part-time for nonresidents. Fees of $898 per year full-time, $50 per semester (minimum) part-time. General application contact: Dr. Philip Kerstetter, Dean of Graduate Studies, 814-732-2856.*

Graduate Studies
Dr. Philip Kerstetter, Dean

School of Education
Dr. Philip Kerstetter, Dean, Graduate Studies
Programs in:
    counseling-elementary guidance • MA
    counseling-rehabilitation • MA
    counseling-secondary guidance • MA
    counseling-student personnel services • MA
    early childhood • M Ed
    educational psychology • M Ed
    elementary education • M Ed
    elementary education clinical • M Ed
    elementary school administration • Certificate, M Ed
    health and physical education • Certificate
    language arts • M Ed
    mathematics • M Ed
    middle and secondary instruction • M Ed
    reading • Certificate, M Ed
    school psychology • Certificate
    science • M Ed
    secondary school administration • Certificate, M Ed
    social studies • M Ed
    special education • M Ed

School of Liberal Arts
Dr. Terry Smith, Dean
Programs in:
    art • MA
    ceramics • MFA
    clinical psychology • MA
    communication studies • MA

jewelry • MFA
painting • MFA
printmaking • MFA
sculpture • MFA
social sciences • MA
speech-language pathology • MA

School of Science, Management and Technology
Dr. Eric Randall, Dean
Programs in:
   biology • MS
   family nurse practitioner • MSN

GANNON UNIVERSITY
Erie, PA 16541
http://www.gannon.edu/

Independent-religious coed comprehensive institution. *Enrollment:* *3,227 graduate, professional, and undergraduate students. Graduate faculty: 45 full-time, 17 part-time. Computer facilities: Campuswide network is available with full Internet access. Total number of PCs/ terminals supplied for student use: 380. Computer service fees are included with tuition and fees. Library facilities: Nash Library. Graduate expenses: Tuition of $405 per credit. Fees of $200 per year full-time, $8 per credit part-time. General application contact: Beth Nemenz, Director of Admissions, 814-871-7240.*

School of Graduate Studies
Rev. Paul DeSante, Dean

College of Humanities, Business, and Education
Dr. Gregor Reinhard, Dean
Programs in:
   accounting • Certificate
   business administration • Certificate, MBA
   counseling psychology • MS
   curriculum and instruction • M Ed
   early intervention • Certificate, MS
   educational computing technology • M Ed
   English • M Ed, MA
   finance • Certificate
   gerontology • Certificate
   human resources management • Certificate
   pastoral studies • Certificate, MA
   public administration • Certificate, MPA
   reading • Certificate, M Ed
   secondary education • M Ed
   social sciences • M Ed, MA

College of Sciences, Engineering, and Health Sciences
Dr. Loretta Seigley, Dean
Programs in:
   administration • MSN
   anesthesia • MSN
   electrical engineering • MS
   embedded software engineering • MS
   family nurse practitioner • Certificate, MSN
   gerontology • MSN

health services administration • Certificate, MS
mechanical engineering • MS
medical-surgical nursing • MSN
natural sciences/environmental education • Certificate,
   M Ed
physical therapy • MPT

GWYNEDD–MERCY COLLEGE
Gwynedd Valley, PA 19437-0901
http://www.gmc.edu/

Independent-religious coed comprehensive institution. *Enrollment:* *1,722 graduate, professional, and undergraduate students. Graduate faculty: 13 full-time, 19 part-time. Computer facilities: Campuswide network is available with full Internet access. Total number of PCs/ terminals supplied for student use: 43. Computer services are offered at no charge. Library facilities: Lourdes Library. Graduate expenses: Tuition of $299 per credit. Fees of $50 per year. General application contact: Dr. Ralph Hoffmann, Associate Vice President for Academic Affairs, 215-646-7300.*

Graduate Education Programs
Dr. Lorraine Cavaliere, Dean
Programs in:
   educational administration • MS
   mental health counseling • MS
   reading • MS
   school counseling • MS
   teaching • MS

Graduate Program in Nursing
Dr. Mary Dressler, Dean
Programs in:
   adult • MSN
   gerontology • MSN
   nurse practitioner • MSN
   oncology • MSN
   pediatric • MSN
   pediatrics • MSN

 # IMMACULATA COLLEGE
Immaculata, PA 19345-0500
http://www.immaculata.edu/

Independent-religious coed comprehensive institution. *Enrollment:* *2,400 graduate, professional, and undergraduate students. Graduate faculty: 67 full-time, 116 part-time. Computer facilities: Campuswide network is available with full Internet access. Computer services are offered at no charge. Library facilities: Gabriele Library. Graduate expenses: Tuition of $345 per credit (minimum). Fees of $60 per year. General application contact: Dr. Ann M. Heath, Dean, 610- 647-4400 Ext. 3211.*

Immaculata College (continued)

Graduate Division

Dr. Ann M. Heath, Dean
Programs in:
- clinical psychology • Psy D
- counseling psychology • Certificate, MA
- cultural and linguistic diversity • MA
- educational leadership and administration • Ed D, MA
- elementary education • Certificate
- intermediate unit director • Certificate
- music therapy • MA
- nutrition education • MA
- nutrition education/approved pre-professional practice program • MA
- school guidance counselor • Certificate
- school principal • Certificate
- school psychologist • Certificate
- school superintendent • Certificate

 INDIANA UNIVERSITY OF PENNSYLVANIA

Indiana, PA 15705-1087

http://www.iup.edu/

Public coed university. *Enrollment: 13,680 graduate, professional, and undergraduate students. Graduate faculty: 322 full-time. Computer facilities: Campuswide network is available with full Internet access. Total number of PCs/terminals supplied for student use: 350. Computer service fees are included with tuition and fees. Library facilities: Stapleton Library. Graduate expenses: Tuition of $3468 per year full-time, $193 per credit part-time for state residents; $6236 per year full-time, $346 per credit part-time for nonresidents. Fees of $313 per year (minimum) full-time, $84 per year part-time. General application contact: Cheryl Vaneman, Acting Assistant Dean, 724-357-2222.*

Graduate School

Dr. David M. Lynch, Dean

College of Business

Dr. Robert Camp, Dean
Programs in:
- business administration • MBA
- business education • M Ed

College of Education

Dr. John Butzow, Dean
Programs in:
- administration and leadership studies • Certificate, D Ed
- administration and supervision • D Ed
- adult and community education • MA
- community counseling • MA
- counseling services • MA
- counselor education • M Ed
- early childhood education • M Ed
- education • M Ed
- educational psychology • Certificate, M Ed
- education of exceptional persons • M Ed
- elementary education • D Ed
- elementary science • M Ed
- literacy • Certificate, M Ed
- school psychology • D Ed
- speech-language pathology • MS
- student affairs in higher education • MA
- student personnel services • MA

College of Fine Arts

Dr. Charles Cullum, Acting Dean
Programs in:
- art • MA, MFA
- music education • MA
- music history and literature • MA
- music theory and composition • MA
- performance • MA

College of Health and Human Services

Dr. Harold Wingard, Dean
Programs in:
- aquatics administration and facilities management • MS
- food and nutrition • MS
- industrial and labor relations • MA
- nursing • MS
- safety sciences • MS
- sport broadcast journalism • MS
- sport management • MS
- sports studies • MS

College of Humanities and Social Sciences

Dr. Brenda Carter, Dean
Programs in:
- administration and leadership studies • PhD
- criminology • MA, PhD
- generalist • MA
- geography • MA, MS
- history • MA
- international studies • MA
- literature • MA
- literature and criticism • PhD
- public affairs • MA
- rhetoric and linguistics • PhD
- sociology • MA
- teaching English • MAT
- teaching English to speakers of other languages • MA

College of Natural Sciences and Mathematics

Dr. John S. Eck, Dean
Programs in:
- applied mathematics • MS
- biology • MS
- chemistry • MA, MS
- elementary and middle school mathematics education • M Ed
- mathematics education • M Ed
- physics • MA, MS
- psychology • MA, Psy D

KUTZTOWN UNIVERSITY OF PENNSYLVANIA
Kutztown, PA 19530
http://www.kutztown.edu/

Public coed comprehensive institution. *Enrollment: 7,920 graduate, professional, and undergraduate students. Graduate faculty: 54 full-time. Computer facilities: Campuswide network is available with full Internet access. Computer services are offered at no charge. Library facilities: Rohrbach Library. Graduate expenses: $4111 per year full-time, $225 per credit hour part-time for state residents; $6879 per year full-time, $393 per credit hour part-time for nonresidents. General application contact: Dr. William Bruce Ezell Jr., Dean, 610-683-4200.*

Graduate School
Dr. William Bruce Ezell Jr., Dean

College of Business
Theodore Hartz, Dean
Program in:
   business administration • MBA

College of Education
Dr. U. Mae Reck, Dean
Programs in:
   agency counseling • MA
   art education • M Ed
   biology • M Ed
   counselor education • M Ed
   curriculum and instruction • M Ed
   elementary counseling • M Ed
   elementary education • M Ed
   English • M Ed
   library science • MLS
   marital and family therapy • MA
   mathematics • M Ed
   reading • M Ed
   secondary counseling • M Ed
   social studies • M Ed
   student affairs in higher education • M Ed

College of Liberal Arts and Sciences
Dr. Carl Brunner, Acting Dean
Programs in:
   computer and information science • MS
   English • MA
   mathematics • MA
   public administration • MPA
   telecommunications • MS

LA ROCHE COLLEGE
Pittsburgh, PA 15237-5898
http://www.laroche.edu/

Independent-religious coed comprehensive institution. *Enrollment: 1,560 graduate, professional, and undergraduate students. Graduate faculty: 13 full-time, 23 part-time. Computer facilities: Campuswide network is available with full Internet access. Total number of PCs/terminals supplied for student use: 32. Computer service fees are applied as a separate charge. Library facilities: John Wright Library. Graduate expenses: $385 per credit. General application contact: Roland Gagne, Director of Graduate Studies, 412-536-1260.*

Graduate Studies
Roland Gagne, Director
Programs in:
   community health nursing • MSN
   critical care nursing • MSN
   family nurse practitioner • MSN
   gerontological nursing • MSN
   human resources management • MS
   nurse anesthesia • MS
   nursing management • MSN
   science education • MS

LA SALLE UNIVERSITY
Philadelphia, PA 19141-1199
http://www.lasalle.edu/

Independent-religious coed comprehensive institution. *Enrollment: 5,408 graduate, professional, and undergraduate students. Graduate faculty: 76 full-time, 38 part-time. Computer facilities: Campuswide network is available with full Internet access. Total number of PCs/terminals supplied for student use: 200. Computer service fees are included with tuition and fees. Library facilities: Connelly Library. General application contact: Brian W. Niles, Director of Marketing/Graduate Enrollment, 215-951-1057.*

School of Arts and Sciences
Dr. Barbara C. Millard, Dean
Programs in:
   bilingual/bicultural studies (Spanish) • MA
   Central and Eastern European studies • MA
   clinical-counseling psychology • MA
   clinical geropsychology • Psy D
   clinical psychology • Psy D
   computer information science • MA
   education • MA
   family psychology • Psy D
   pastoral studies • MA
   professional communication • MA
   rehabilitation psychology • Psy D
   religion • MA
   theological studies • MA

La Salle University (continued)

Business Administration Program
Joseph Y. Ugras, Associate Dean
Program in:
    business administration • Certificate, MBA

Program in Nursing
Dr. Zane R. Wolf, Dean
Programs in:
    clinical nurse specialist, adult health and illness • MSN
    nurse practitioner/primary care of adults • MSN
    nursing administration • MSN
    nursing education • MSN
    nursing informatics • MSN
    public health nursing • MSN
    wound, ostomy, and continence nursing • MSN

LEHIGH UNIVERSITY
Bethlehem, PA 18015-3094

http://www.lehigh.edu/

Independent coed university. *Enrollment: 6,316 graduate, professional, and undergraduate students. Graduate faculty: 397 full-time, 86 part-time. Computer facilities: Campuswide network is available with full Internet access. Total number of PCs/terminals supplied for student use: 400. Computer services are offered at no charge. Library facilities: Fairchild-Martindale Library and Computing Center plus 2 additional on-campus libraries. Graduate expenses: Tuition of $830 per credit. Fees of $12 per semester full-time, $6 per semester part-time. General application contact: contact individual colleges, 610-758-3000.*

College of Arts and Sciences
Dr. Bobb Carson, Dean
Programs in:
    applied mathematics • MS, PhD
    behavioral and evolutionary bioscience • MS, PhD
    behavioral neuroscience • MS, PhD
    biochemistry • MS, PhD
    biochemistry and analytical chemistry • MS, PhD
    biology • MS, PhD
    chemistry • DA
    clinical chemistry • MS
    English • MA, PhD
    environmental science • MS, PhD
    experimental psychology • MS, PhD
    geological sciences • MS, PhD
    history • MA, PhD
    inorganic chemistry • MS, PhD
    mathematics • MS, PhD
    molecular biology • MS, PhD
    organic chemistry • MS, PhD
    physical chemistry • MS, PhD
    physics • MS, PhD
    physiological chemistry • PhD
    political science • MA
    polymer science and engineering • MS, PhD

    sociology and anthropology • MA
    statistics • MS

College of Business and Economics
Patti Ota, Dean
Programs in:
    business administration • MBA
    business and economics • PhD
    economics • MS, PhD
    management of technology • MS

College of Education
Roland K. Yoshida, Dean
Programs in:
    bilingual/bicultural education • M Ed
    counseling and human services • M Ed
    counseling psychology • PhD
    curriculum and instruction • Ed D
    educational leadership • Certificate, Ed D, M Ed
    educational technology • Ed D, MS
    elementary education • Certificate, Ed D, M Ed
    school counseling • Certificate, M Ed
    school psychology • Certificate, Ed S, PhD
    secondary education • Certificate, M Ed, MA
    special education • Certificate, M Ed, PhD

College of Engineering and Applied Science
Dr. Harvey Stenger, Dean
Programs in:
    applied mathematics • MS, PhD
    chemical engineering • M Eng, MS, PhD
    civil and environmental engineering • M Eng, MS, PhD
    computer engineering • MS
    computer science • MS, PhD
    electrical engineering • M Eng, MS, PhD
    industrial engineering • M Eng, MS, PhD
    manufacturing systems engineering • MS
    materials science and engineering • M Eng, MS, PhD
    mechanical engineering • M Eng, MS, PhD
    mechanics • M Eng, MS, PhD
    polymer science and engineering • MS, PhD

LINCOLN UNIVERSITY
Lincoln University, PA 19352

http://www.lincoln.edu/

Public coed comprehensive institution. *Enrollment: 2,065 graduate, professional, and undergraduate students. Graduate faculty: 6 full-time, 15 part-time. Library facilities: Langston Hughes Memorial Library. Graduate expenses: $5175 per year for state residents; $7790 per year for nonresidents. General application contact: Dr. Szabi Ishtai-Zee, Acting Director, Graduate Program in Human Services, 610-932-8300 Ext. 3360.*

Graduate Program in Human Services
Dr. Szabi Ishtai-Zee, Acting Director
Program in:
    human services • M Hum Svcs

MANSFIELD UNIVERSITY OF PENNSYLVANIA
Mansfield, PA 16933

http://www.mnsfld.edu/

Public coed comprehensive institution. *Enrollment: 2,907 graduate, professional, and undergraduate students. Graduate faculty: 1 full-time, 58 part-time. Computer facilities: Campuswide network is available with full Internet access. Computer service fees are included with tuition and fees. Library facilities: main library plus 2 additional on-campus libraries. Graduate expenses: Tuition of $3468 per year full-time, $193 per credit part-time for state residents; $6236 per year full-time, $346 per credit part-time for nonresidents. Fees of $236 per year full-time, $18.25 per semester (minimum) part-time for state residents; $266 per year full-time, $18.25 per semester (minimum) part-time for nonresidents. General application contact: Dr. Sandra Linck, Associate Provost, 717-662-4807.*

Graduate Studies
Dr. Sandra Linck, Associate Provost
Programs in:
    art education • M Ed
    community-clinical psychology • MA
    elementary education • M Ed
    mentally/physically handicapped • M Ed
    music education • MM
    secondary education • MS
    special education • M Ed, MS

MARYWOOD UNIVERSITY
Scranton, PA 18509-1598

http://www.marywood.edu/

Independent-religious coed comprehensive institution. *Enrollment: 2,523 graduate, professional, and undergraduate students. Graduate faculty: 96 full-time, 92 part-time. Computer facilities: Campuswide network is available with full Internet access. Total number of PCs/terminals supplied for student use: 210. Computer services are offered at no charge. Library facilities: Learning Resources Center. Graduate expenses: Tuition of $449 per credit hour. Fees of $530 per year full-time, $180 per year part-time. General application contact: Deborah M. Flynn, Coordinator of Admissions, 717-340-6002.*

Graduate School of Arts and Sciences
Dr. James L. Gearity, Dean
Programs in:
    art education • MA
    art therapy • MA
    church music • MA
    communication arts • MA
    counseling • MA
    counselor education-elementary • MS
    counselor education-secondary • MS

    early childhood education • MS
    elementary education • MAT, MS
    finance and investments • MBA
    general management • MBA
    health services administration • MHSA
    human development • PhD
    instructional technology • MS
    management information systems • MBA, MS
    music education • MA
    musicology • MA
    nutrition and dietetics • MS
    public administration • MPA
    reading education • MS
    school leadership • MS
    special education • MS
    special education administration and supervision • MS
    speech language pathology • MS
    studio art • MA
    theological studies • MA
    visual arts • MFA

Graduate School of Social Work
Dr. William Whitaker, Dean
Program in:
    social work • MSW

MILLERSVILLE UNIVERSITY OF PENNSYLVANIA
Millersville, PA 17551-0302

http://www.millersv.edu/

Public coed comprehensive institution. *Enrollment: 7,564 graduate, professional, and undergraduate students. Graduate faculty: 191 full-time, 77 part-time. Computer facilities: Campuswide network is available with full Internet access. Total number of PCs/terminals supplied for student use: 350. Computer services are offered at no charge. Library facilities: Helen Ganser Library. Graduate expenses: $3468 per year full-time, $234 per credit part-time for state residents; $6236 per year full-time, $387 per credit part-time for nonresidents. General application contact: Dr. Robert J. Labriola, Dean of Graduate Studies, 717-872-3030.*

Graduate School
Dr. Robert J. Labriola, Dean

School of Education
Dr. Bennett Berhow, Dean
Programs in:
    clinical psychology • MS
    counselor education • M Ed
    elementary education • M Ed
    gifted education • M Ed
    industrial arts/technology education • M Ed
    psychological services • MS
    reading/language arts education • M Ed
    school psychology • Certificate
    special education • M Ed

Millersville University of Pennsylvania (continued)

School of Humanities and Social Sciences
Dr. Linda Clark-Neuman, Acting Dean
Programs in:
art • M Ed
English • MA
English education • M Ed
French • M Ed, MA
German • M Ed, MA
history • MA
Spanish • M Ed, MA

School of Science and Mathematics
Dr. Albert Hoffman, Dean
Programs in:
biology • MS
mathematics • M Ed
nursing • MSN
science and mathematics • Certificate

PENNSYLVANIA STATE UNIVERSITY AT ERIE, THE BEHREND COLLEGE
Erie, PA 16563

http://www.pserie.psu.edu/

Public coed comprehensive institution. *Enrollment: 3,327 graduate, professional, and undergraduate students. Graduate expenses: Tuition of $7632 per year full-time, $318 per credit hour part-time for state residents; $14,664 per year full-time, $611 per credit hour part-time for nonresidents. Fees of $252 per year full-time, $43 per semester (minimum) part-time. General application contact: John M. Lilley, Dean and Provost, 814-898-6319.*

Graduate Center
John M. Lilley, Dean and Provost
Programs in:
business administration • MBA
engineering and engineering technology • M Eng

PENNSYLVANIA STATE UNIVERSITY HARRISBURG CAMPUS OF THE CAPITAL COLLEGE
Middletown, PA 17057-4898

http://www.hbg.psu.edu/

Public coed comprehensive institution. *Enrollment: 3,466 graduate, professional, and undergraduate students. Library facilities: Richard H. Heindel Library. Graduate expenses: Tuition of $6534 per year full-time, $276 per credit part-time for state residents; $12,516 per year full-time, $523 per credit part-time for nonresidents. Fees of*

$232 per year (minimum) full-time, $40 per semester (minimum) part-time. General application contact: John Bruhn, Provost and Dean, 717-948-6100.

Graduate Center
John Bruhn, Provost and Dean

Division of Behavioral Sciences and Education
Dr. William A. Henk, Head
Programs in:
adult education • D Ed
applied psychology • MA
community psychology • MCP
health education • M Ed
teaching and curriculum • M Ed
training and development • M Ed

Division of Humanities
Dr. William J. Mahar, Coordinator
Programs in:
American studies • MA
humanities • MA

School of Business Administration
Dr. Mukund Kulkarni, Acting Director
Programs in:
business administration • MBA
information systems • MS

School of Public Affairs
Dr. Steven A. Peterson, Director
Programs in:
health administration • MHA
public administration • MPA, PhD

School of Science, Engineering and Technology
Dr. William Welsh, Director
Programs in:
computer science • MS
electrical engineering • M Eng
engineering science • M Eng
environmental pollution control • M Eng, MEPC, MS

PENNSYLVANIA STATE UNIVERSITY UNIVERSITY PARK CAMPUS
University Park, PA 16802-1503

http://www.psu.edu/UniversityPark/UniversityPark.html

Public coed university. *Enrollment: 40,471 graduate, professional, and undergraduate students. Library facilities: Pattee Library plus 7 additional on-campus libraries. Graduate expenses: Tuition of $6534 per year full-time, $276 per credit part-time for state residents; $13,460 per year full-time, $561 per credit part-time for nonresidents. Fees of $252 per year (minimum) full-time, $43 per semester (minimum) part-time. General application contact: Dr. Graham Spanier, President, 814-865-1795.*

Graduate School
Dr. Rodney A. Erickson, Vice President, Research and Dean

College of Agricultural Sciences
Dr. Robert D. Steele, Dean
Programs in:
  agricultural economics • M Agr
  agricultural economics and demography • MS, PhD
  agricultural education • D Ed, M Ed, MS, PhD
  agronomy • M Agr, MS, PhD
  animal science • M Agr, MS, PhD
  entomology • M Agr, MS, PhD
  extension education • M Agr, M Ed
  food science • MS, PhD
  forest resources • M Agr, MFR, MS, PhD
  horticulture • M Agr, MS, PhD
  pathobiology • MS, PhD
  plant pathology • M Agr, MS, PhD
  rural sociology • M Agr, MS, PhD
  soil science • M Agr, MS, PhD
  wildlife and fisheries sciences • M Agr, MFR, MS, PhD

College of Arts and Architecture
Dr. Neil Porterfield, Dean
Programs in:
  architecture • MS
  art • MA
  art education • D Ed, M Ed, MS, PhD
  art history • MA, PhD
  composition/theory • M Mus
  conducting • M Mus
  graphic design • MFA
  landscape architecture • MLA
  music • M Mus
  music education • M Ed, PhD
  musicology • MA
  music theory and history • MA
  performance • M Mus
  piano pedagogy and performance • M Mus
  theatre arts • MFA
  voice performance and pedagogy • M Mus

College of Communications
Dr. Terri Brooks, Dean
Programs in:
  communications • PhD
  media studies • MA
  telecommunications studies • MA

College of Earth and Mineral Sciences
Dr. John A. Dutton, Dean
Programs in:
  ceramic science • MS, PhD
  fuel science • MS, PhD
  geochemistry • MS, PhD
  geography • MS, PhD
  geology • MS, PhD
  geophysics • MS, PhD
  metals science and engineering • MS, PhD
  meteorology • MS, PhD
  mineral economics • MS, PhD
  mineral engineering management • M Eng
  mineral processing • MS, PhD
  mining engineering • M Eng, MS, PhD

  petroleum and natural gas engineering • MS, PhD
  polymer science • MS, PhD

College of Education
Dr. Rodney J. Reed, Dean
Programs in:
  adult education • D Ed, M Ed
  bilingual education • D Ed, M Ed, MS, PhD
  counseling psychology • PhD
  counselor education • D Ed
  early childhood education • D Ed, M Ed, MS, PhD
  educational administration • D Ed, M Ed, MS, PhD
  educational psychology • MS, PhD
  educational theory and policy • MA, PhD
  elementary counseling • M Ed, MS
  elementary education • D Ed, M Ed, MS, PhD
  higher education • D Ed, M Ed, PhD
  instructional systems • D Ed, M Ed, MS, PhD
  language arts and reading • D Ed, M Ed, MS, PhD
  school psychology • M Ed, MS, PhD
  science education • D Ed, M Ed, MS, PhD
  social studies education • D Ed, MS, PhD
  special education • M Ed, MS, PhD
  supervisor and curriculum development • D Ed, M Ed, MS, PhD
  workforce education and development • D Ed, M Ed, MS, PhD

College of Engineering
Dr. David Wormley, Dean
Programs in:
  acoustics • M Eng, MS, PhD
  aerospace engineering • M Eng, MS, PhD
  agricultural engineering • MS, PhD
  architectural engineering • M Eng, MS, PhD
  chemical engineering • MS, PhD
  civil engineering • M Eng, MS, PhD
  computer science and engineering • M Eng, MS, PhD
  engineering mechanics • M Eng, MS
  engineering science • MS
  engineering science and mechanics • PhD
  environmental engineering • M Eng, MS, PhD
  industrial engineering • MS, PhD
  mechanical engineering • M Eng, MS, PhD
  nuclear engineering • M Eng, MS, PhD
  structural engineering • M Eng, MS, PhD
  transportation and highway engineering • M Eng, MS, PhD
  water resources engineering • M Eng, MS, PhD

College of Health and Human Development
Dr. Barbara Shannon, Dean
Programs in:
  biobehavioral health • MS, PhD
  communication disorders • M Ed, MS, PhD
  health policy and administration • MHA, MS, PhD
  hotel, restaurant, and institutional management • MHRIM
  human development and family studies • MS, PhD
  kinesiology • D Ed, M Ed, MS, PhD
  leisure studies • M Ed, MS, PhD
  man-environment relations • D Ed, M Ed, MS, PhD
  nursing • MS

Pennsylvania State University University Park Campus (continued)

College of Liberal Arts
Dr. Susan Welch, Dean
Programs in:
  anthropology • MA, PhD
  classical American philosophy • MA, PhD
  clinical psychology • MS, PhD
  comparative literature • MA, PhD
  contemporary European philosophy • MA, PhD
  crime, law, and justice • MA, PhD
  developmental psychology • MS, PhD
  economics • MA, PhD
  English • M Ed, MA, MFA, PhD
  experimental psychology • MS, PhD
  German • M Ed, MA, PhD
  history • D Ed, M Ed, MA, PhD
  history of philosophy • MA, PhD
  industrial/organizational psychology • MS, PhD
  industrial relations and human resources • MS
  liberal arts • MPA
  political science • MA, PhD
  Russian and comparative literature • MA
  social psychology • MS, PhD
  sociology • MA, PhD
  Spanish • M Ed, MA, PhD
  speech communication • MA, PhD
  teaching English as a second language • MA

Eberly College of Science
Dr. Howard Grotch, Interim Dean
Programs in:
  applied mathematics • MA, PhD
  astronomy and astrophysics • MS, PhD
  biochemistry, microbiology, and molecular biology • MS, PhD
  biology • MS, PhD
  chemistry • MS, PhD
  mathematics • D Ed, M Ed, MA, PhD
  molecular evolutionary biology • MS, PhD
  physics • D Ed, M Ed, MS, PhD
  statistics • MA, MS, PhD

Intercollege Graduate Programs
Dr. Rodney Erickson, Dean of the Graduate School
Programs in:
  acoustics • M Eng, MS, PhD
  applied human nutrition • MS
  bioengineering • MS, PhD
  biomolecular transport dynamics • MS, PhD
  cell and developmental biology • MS, PhD
  cellular and molecular mechanisms of toxicity • MS, PhD
  chemical biology • MS, PhD
  ecological and molecular plant physiology • MS, PhD
  ecology • MS, PhD
  environmental pollution control • M Eng, MEPC, MS
  genetics • MS, PhD
  human nutrition • M Ed
  immunobiology • MS, PhD
  integrative biosciences • MS, PhD
  mass communications • PhD
  materials • MS, PhD
  molecular medicine • MS, PhD

  neuroscience • MS, PhD
  nutrition • MS, PhD
  nutrition and public health • M Ed, MS
  nutrition education • M Ed, MS
  nutrition science • MS, PhD
  physiology • MS, PhD
  plant physiology • MS, PhD
  quality and manufacturing management • MMM

The Mary Jean and Frank P. Smeal College of Business Administration
Dr. J. D. Hammond, Dean
Programs in:
  accounting • MS
  business administration • MBA
  business logistics • MS
  finance • MS
  finance/insurance and real estate • PhD
  insurance • MS
  management and organization • PhD
  management science and information systems • MS
  management science/operations/logistics • PhD
  marketing • MS
  marketing and distribution • PhD
  real estate • MS

PHILADELPHIA COLLEGE OF TEXTILES AND SCIENCE
Philadelphia, PA 19144-5497

http://www.philacol.edu/

Independent coed comprehensive institution. *Enrollment: 3,423 graduate, professional, and undergraduate students. Graduate faculty: 59 full-time, 60 part-time.* Computer facilities: *Campuswide network is available with full Internet access. Computer services are offered at no charge.* Library facilities: *Paul Gutman Library plus 1 additional on-campus library.* Graduate expenses: *$448 per credit hour.* General application contact: *Robert J. Reed, Director of Graduate Admissions, 215-951-2943.*

School of Business
Dr. Raymond Poteau, Dean
Programs in:
  accounting • MBA
  business administration • MBA
  finance • MBA
  health care management • MBA
  international business • MBA
  marketing • MBA
  taxation • MBA, MS

School of Science and Health
Dr. Paul Berberian, Dean
Programs in:
  instructional technology • MS
  midwifery • MS
  occupational therapy • MS

School of Textiles and Materials Science

Dr. David Brookstein, Dean of School of Textiles and
    Materials Technology
Programs in:
    fashion-apparel studies • MS
    fibrous materials science • MS
    global textile marketing • MS
    textile design • MS
    textile engineering • MS
    textile marketing • MS

SAINT FRANCIS COLLEGE

Loretto, PA 15940-0600

http://www.sfcpa.edu/

Independent-religious coed comprehensive institution. *Enrollment:*
1,891 graduate, professional, and undergraduate students. Graduate faculty: *15 full-time, 71 part-time.* Computer facilities: *Campuswide*
network is available with full Internet access. Total number of PCs/
terminals supplied for student use: 70. Computer service fees are
included with tuition and fees. Library facilities: *Pasquerilla Library.*
General application contact: *Dr. Peter Skoner, Assistant Vice President*
for Academic Affairs, 814-472-3085.

Business Administration Program

Randy L. Frye, Director
Program in:
    business administration • MBA

Graduate School of Human Resource Management and Industrial Relations

Dr. Philip Benham, Director
Program in:
    human resource management and industri • MA

Medical Science Program

Dr. William Duryea, Director
Program in:
    medical science • MMS

Occupational Therapy Program

Donald Walkovich, Chair
Program in:
    occupational therapy • MOT

Pastoral Ministry Program

Dr. Michael McKale, Chairperson
Program in:
    pastoral ministry • MAPM

Physical Therapy Program

Dr. Edward Pisarski, Chair
Program in:
    physical therapy • MPT

Physician Assistant Program

Albert Simon, Chair
Program in:
    physician assistant • MPAS

Program in Education

Dr. Elizabeth Gensante, Department Chair
Program in:
    leadership • M Ed

 # SAINT JOSEPH'S UNIVERSITY

Philadelphia, PA 19131-1395

http://www.sju.edu/

Independent-religious coed comprehensive institution. *Enrollment:*
7,027 graduate, professional, and undergraduate students. Graduate faculty: *88 full-time, 83 part-time.* Computer facilities: *Campuswide*
network is available with full Internet access. Total number of PCs/
terminals supplied for student use: 143. Computer services are
offered at no charge. Library facilities: *Francis A. Drexel Library*
plus 1 additional on-campus library. Graduate expenses: *$470 per*
credit hour. General application contact: *Dr. Robert H. Palestini,*
Dean of Graduate and Continuing Studies, 610-660-1289.

College of Arts and Sciences

Dr. Robert H. Palestini, Dean of Graduate and Continuing
    Studies
Programs in:
    biology • MS
    chemistry • MS
    chemistry education • MS
    computer science • MS
    criminal justice • MS
    education • Certificate, MS
    gerontological services • MS
    health administration • MS
    health education • MS
    mathematics education • MS
    nurse anesthesia • MS
    professional education • MS
    psychology • MS
    reading • MS
    secondary education • MS
    special education • MS
    training and development • MS

Erivan K. Haub School of Business

Dr. Gregory G. Dell'Omo, Dean
Programs in:
    accounting • MBA
    business • MBA
    environmental protection and safety management • MS
    finance • MBA
    food marketing • MS
    general business • MBA
    health and medical services administration • MBA
    information systems • MBA

Saint Joseph's University (continued)
    international business • MBA
    international marketing • MBA, MS
    management • MBA
    marketing • MBA
    pharmaceutical marketing • MBA
    public safety • MS

SHIPPENSBURG UNIVERSITY OF PENNSYLVANIA
Shippensburg, PA 17257-2299

http://www.ship.edu/

Public coed comprehensive institution. *Enrollment: 6,683 graduate, professional, and undergraduate students. Graduate faculty: 115 full-time, 16 part-time. Computer facilities: Campuswide network is available. Total number of PCs/terminals supplied for student use: 300. Computer services are offered at no charge. Library facilities: Ezra Lehman Memorial Library plus 1 additional on-campus library. Graduate expenses: Tuition of $3468 per year full-time, $193 per credit hour part-time for state residents; $6236 per year full-time, $346 per credit hour part-time for nonresidents. Fees of $678 per year full-time, $108 per semester (minimum) part-time. General application contact: A. Renee Mims, Assistant Dean of Graduate Studies and Research, 717-532-1213.*

School of Graduate Studies and Research
Dr. Robert B. Bartos, Dean

College of Arts and Sciences
Dr. Janet Gross, Dean
Programs in:
    biology • M Ed, MS
    communication studies • MS
    computer education • M Ed
    computer science • MS
    English • M Ed, MA
    geoenvironmental studies • MS
    history/philosophy • MA
    information systems • MS
    mathematics • M Ed, MS
    political science • MPA
    psychology • MS

College of Business
Dr. James A. Pope III, Dean
Program in:
    business education • M Ed

College of Education and Human Services
Dr. Robert B. Bartos, Dean, School of Graduate Studies and Research
Programs in:
    administration of justice • MS
    computer education • M Ed
    counseling • MS
    elementary education • M Ed
    elementary school administration • M Ed

    guidance and counseling • M Ed
    reading • M Ed
    secondary school administration • M Ed
    special education • M Ed

SLIPPERY ROCK UNIVERSITY OF PENNSYLVANIA
Slippery Rock, PA 16057

http://www.sru.edu/depts/graduate/

Public coed comprehensive institution. *Library facilities: Matilda Bailey Library. Graduate expenses: $4484 per year full-time, $247 per credit part-time for state residents; $7667 per year full-time, $423 per credit part-time for nonresidents. General application contact: Dean, Graduate Studies and Research, 724-738-2051.*

Graduate School
Program in:
    public administration • MPA

College of Arts and Sciences
Programs in:
    English • MA
    history • MA

College of Education
Programs in:
    child and youth counseling • MA
    counseling psychology • MA
    early childhood education • M Ed
    elementary education • M Ed
    elementary guidance • M Ed
    gerontological counseling • MA
    reading • M Ed
    secondary education in math/science • M Ed
    secondary guidance • M Ed
    special education • M Ed
    student personnel • MA
    substance abuse counseling • MA

College of Human Service Professions
Programs in:
    allied health • MS
    environmental education • M Ed
    nursing • MSN
    physical education • M Ed, MS
    physical therapy • DPT
    recreation programming • MS
    resource management • MS
    sustainable systems • MS
    therapeutic recreation • MS

College of Information Science and Business Administration
Program in:
    accounting • MS

TEMPLE UNIVERSITY
Philadelphia, PA 19122-6096
http://www.temple.edu/

Public coed university. *Enrollment: 28,369 graduate, professional, and undergraduate students. Graduate faculty: 1,851. Computer facilities: Campuswide network is available with full Internet access. Computer service fees are applied as a separate charge. Library facilities: Paley Library plus 12 additional on-campus libraries. Graduate expenses: Tuition of $323 per semester hour for state residents; $444 per semester hour for nonresidents. Fees of $170 per year full-time, $28 per semester (minimum) part-time. General application contact: Dr. Pete Goodwin, Acting Dean of the Graduate School, 215-204-1380.*

Graduate School
Dr. Pete Goodwin, Acting Dean
Programs in:
    advanced education in general dentistry • Certificate
    anatomy and cell biology • PhD
    applied communication • MA
    biochemistry • MS, PhD
    communication sciences • PhD
    endodontology • Certificate
    linguistics • MA
    microbiology and immunology • MS, PhD
    molecular biology and genetics • PhD
    nursing • MSN
    occupational therapy • MS
    oral and maxillofacial surgery • Certificate
    oral biology • MS
    orthodontics • Certificate
    pathology and laboratory medicine • PhD
    periodontology • Certificate
    pharmacology • MS, PhD
    physical therapy • MPT, MS, PhD
    physiology • MS, PhD
    prosthodontics • Certificate
    speech-language-hearing • MA

College of Education
Dr. Trevor Sewell, Dean
Programs in:
    adult and organizational development • Ed M
    behavioral science • Ed M, PhD
    counseling psychology • PhD
    counselor education • Ed M
    early childhood education • Certificate
    early childhood education and elementary education •
        Ed M, MS
    educational administration • Ed D, Ed M
    educational psychology • Ed M, PhD
    elementary education • Certificate
    kinesiology • PhD
    mathematics/science education • Ed M
    math/science education • Ed D
    physical education • Ed M
    reading and language education • Ed D, Ed M, MS
    school psychology • Ed M, PhD
    secondary education • Certificate, Ed M, MS

    somatic science • Ed M, PhD
    special education • Ed M, MS
    urban education • Ed D, Ed M
    vocational education • Ed M, MS

College of Liberal Arts
Dr. Carolyn T. Adams, Dean
Programs in:
    African-American studies • MA, PhD
    anthropology • MA, PhD
    art history • MA, PhD
    clinical psychology • PhD
    cognitive psychology • PhD
    creative writing • MA
    criminal justice • MA, PhD
    developmental psychology • PhD
    English • MA, PhD
    experimental psychology • PhD
    geography • MA
    history • MA, PhD
    liberal arts • MLA
    philosophy • MA, PhD
    political science • MA, PhD
    religion • MA, PhD
    social and organizational psychology • PhD
    sociology • MA, PhD
    Spanish • MA, PhD
    urban studies • MA

College of Science and Technology
Dr. Chris Platsoucas, Acting Dean
Programs in:
    applied and computational mathematics • MA, PhD
    biology • MA, PhD
    chemistry • MA, PhD
    civil and environmental engineering • MSE
    computer and information sciences • MS, PhD
    electrical and computer engineering • MSE
    engineering • PhD
    environmental health • MS
    geology • MA
    mechanical engineering • MSE
    physics • MA, PhD
    pure mathematics • MA, PhD

Esther Boyer College of Music
Dr. Jeffrey Cornelius, Dean
Programs in:
    composition • DMA, MM
    dance • M Ed, MFA, PhD
    music education • MM, PhD
    music history • MM
    music performance • DMA, MM
    music theory • MM
    music therapy • MMT

School of Business and Management
Dr. M. Moshe Porat, Dean
Programs in:
    accounting • MBA, MS, PhD
    actuarial science • MBA, MS
    chemistry • MBA
    computer and information sciences • MBA, MS
    economics • MA, MBA, MS, PhD

Temple University (continued)

finance • MBA, MS, PhD
general and strategic management • MBA, PhD
healthcare financial management • MS
healthcare management • MBA
human resource administration • MBA, MS, PhD
international business • MS
international business administration • MBA
legal studies • MBA
management science/operations management • MBA, MS
marketing • MBA, MS, PhD
physical distribution • MBA
real estate and urban land studies • MBA, MS
risk management insurance • MBA, MS
statistics • MBA, MS, PhD

School of Communications and Theater
Dr. Joseph Folger, Assistant Dean
Programs in:
acting • MFA
broadcasting, telecommunications and mass media • MA
design • MFA
film and media arts • MFA
journalism • MJ
mass media and communication • PhD

School of Social Administration
Dr. Phillip Jaslow, Associate Dean
Programs in:
community health education • MPH
health studies • PhD
school health education • Ed M
social work • MSW
therapeutic recreation • Ed M

School of Tourism and Hospitality
Dr. M. Moshe Porat, Interim Head
Programs in:
sport and recreation administration • Ed M
tourism and hospitality management • MTHM

Tyler School of Art
Rochelle Toner, Dean
Programs in:
art education • M Ed
ceramics • MFA
fibers • MFA
glass • MFA
metalworking • MFA
painting/drawing • MFA
photography • MFA
printmaking • MFA
sculpture • MFA
visual design • MFA

Health Sciences Center

College of Allied Health Professions
Amy Hecht, Dean
Programs in:
applied communication • MA
communication sciences • PhD
linguistics • MA

nursing • MSN
occupational therapy • MS
physical therapy • MPT, MS, PhD
speech-language-hearing • MA

School of Dentistry
Dr. Martin F. Tansy, Dean
Programs in:
advanced education in general dentistry • Certificate
dentistry • DMD
endodontology • Certificate
oral and maxillofacial surgery • Certificate
oral biology • MS
orthodontics • Certificate
periodontology • Certificate
prosthodontics • Certificate

School of Medicine
Dr. Leon Malmud, Dean
Programs in:
anatomy and cell biology • PhD
biochemistry • MS, PhD
medicine • MD
microbiology and immunology • MS, PhD
molecular biology and genetics • PhD
pathology and laboratory medicine • PhD
pharmacology • MS, PhD
physiology • MS, PhD

School of Pharmacy
Dr. Peter Doukas, Dean
Programs in:
medicinal and pharmaceutical chemistry • MS, PhD
pharmaceutics • MS, PhD
pharmacy • Pharm D
quality assurance/regulatory affairs • MS

School of Podiatric Medicine
Dr. Richard M. Englert, Acting Chief Administrative Officer
Program in:
podiatric medicine • DPM

School of Law
Robert J. Reinstein, Dean
Programs in:
law • JD
taxation • LL M
transnational law • LL M
trial advocacy • LL M

UNIVERSITY OF PENNSYLVANIA
Philadelphia, PA 19104
http://www.upenn.edu/

Independent coed university. *Enrollment:* 21,642 graduate, professional, and undergraduate students. *Graduate faculty:* 2,140 full-time. *Computer facilities:* Campuswide network is available with full Internet access. Computer services are offered at no charge. *Library facilities:* Van Pelt Library plus 14 additional on-campus libraries.

Graduate expenses: *Tuition of $22,716 per year full-time, $2876 per course part-time. Fees of $1484 per year full-time, $181 per course part-time. General application contact: Patricia Rea, Admissions Assistant, 215-898-5720.*

Annenberg School for Communication
Dr. Kathleen Hall Jamieson, Dean
Program in:
    communication • MAC, PhD

Fels Center of Government
Dr. John J. Mulhern, Administrator
Program in:
    government • MGA

Graduate School of Education
Dr. Susan Fuhrman, Dean
Programs in:
    clinical child psychology • PhD
    community psychology • PhD
    counseling psychology • MS Ed
    early childhood education • MS Ed
    educational linguistics • PhD
    educational policy and leadership • Ed D, MS Ed, PhD
    education, culture, and society • Ed D, MS Ed, PhD
    elementary education • MS Ed
    higher education • Ed D, MS Ed, PhD
    human development • MS Ed, PhD
    human sexuality education • Ed D, MS Ed, PhD
    intercultural communication • MS Ed
    policy research, evaluation, and measurement • MS Ed, PhD
    reading, writing, and literacy • Ed D, MS Ed, PhD
    school psychology • PhD
    secondary education • MS Ed
    teaching English to speakers of other languages • MS Ed

Graduate School of Fine Arts
Gary Hack, Dean
Programs in:
    architecture • M Arch, MS, PhD
    city and regional planning • Certificate, MCP, PhD
    conservation and heritage management • Certificate
    fine arts • MFA
    historic conservation • Certificate
    historic preservation • Certificate, MS
    landscape architecture and regional planning • MLA
    landscape studies • Certificate
    real estate design and development • Certificate
    urban design • Certificate

Law School
Colin S. Diver, Dean
Program in:
    law • JD, LL M, SJD

School of Arts and Sciences
Walter Licht, Associate Dean for Graduate Studies
Programs in:
    American civilization • AM, PhD
    ancient history • AM, PhD
    anthropology • AM, MS, PhD
    art and archaeology of the Mediterranean world • AM, PhD
    Asian and Middle Eastern studies • AM, PhD
    biblical studies • AM, PhD
    cell, molecular, and developmental biology • PhD
    chemistry • MS, PhD
    classical studies • AM, PhD
    comparative literature • AM, PhD
    conflict analysis and peace science • AM, PhD
    demography • AM, PhD
    ecology and population biology • PhD
    economics • PhD
    English • AM, PhD
    folklore and folklife • AM, PhD
    French • AM, PhD
    geology • MS, PhD
    Germanic languages • AM, PhD
    Hellenistic Judaism • AM, PhD
    history • AM, PhD
    history and sociology of science • AM, PhD
    history of art • AM, PhD
    Italian • AM, PhD
    linguistics • AM, PhD
    literary theory • AM, PhD
    mathematics • AM, PhD
    medieval Hebrew literature • AM, PhD
    modern Hebrew literature • AM
    modern Judaism • AM, PhD
    music • AM, PhD
    neurobiology/physiology and behavior • PhD
    organizational dynamics • MS
    philosophy • AM, PhD
    physics • PhD
    plant science • PhD
    political science • AM, PhD
    psychology • PhD
    rabbinic literature • AM, PhD
    regional science • AM, PhD
    religious studies • PhD
    sociology • AM, PhD
    South Asian regional studies • AM, PhD
    Spanish • AM, PhD

Joseph H. Lauder Institute of Management and International Studies
Dr. Stephen Kobrin, Director
Programs in:
    international studies • MA
    management and international studies • MBA

School of Dental Medicine
Dr. Raymond Fonseca, Dean
Program in:
    dental medicine • DMD

University of Pennsylvania (continued)

School of Engineering and Applied Science

Eduardo D. Glandt, Interim Dean
Programs in:
applied mechanics • MSE, PhD
bioengineering • MSE, PhD
biotechnology • MS
chemical engineering • MSE, PhD
computer and information science • MSE, PhD
electrical engineering • MSE, PhD
management of technology • MSE
materials science and engineering • MSE, PhD
mechanical engineering • MSE, PhD
systems engineering • MSE, PhD
telecommunications and networking • MSE

School of Medicine

Dr. William N. Kelley, Dean
Programs in:
biochemistry and molecular biophysics • PhD
cell growth and cancer • PhD
cell structure and function • PhD
clinical epidemiology • MSCE
comparative medical sciences • MS, PhD
developmental biology • PhD
epidemiology • PhD
gene therapy • PhD
genetics and gene regulation • PhD
immunology • PhD
medicine • MD
microbiology and virology • PhD
neuroscience • PhD
parasitology • PhD
pathology • PhD
pharmacology • PhD
physiology • PhD

School of Nursing

Dr. Marla Salmon, Associate Dean and Director of Graduate
    Studies
Programs in:
administration/consulting • MSN
adult and special populations • MSN
adult critical care nurse practitioner • MSN
cardiopulmonary • MSN
child and family • MSN
gerontological nurse practitioner • MSN
geropsychiatrics • MSN
health care of women nurse practitioner • MSN
neonatal nurse practitioner • MSN
neuroscience • MSN
nurse midwifery • MSN
nursing • Certificate, PhD
nursing administration • MSN, PhD
occupational health administration/consultation • MSN
oncology advanced practice nurse • MSN
pediatric critical care nurse practitioner • MSN
pediatric oncology nurse practitioner • MSN
perinatal advanced practice nurse specialist • MSN
perinatal nurse practitioner • MSN
primary care • MSN
primary care nurse practitioner: adult • MSN
primary care nurse practitioner: pediatrics • MSN
renal metabolic • MSN
surgical • MSN
tertiary nurse practitioner • MSN

School of Social Work

Ira M. Schwartz, Dean
Programs in:
social welfare • PhD
social work • MSW

School of Veterinary Medicine

Dr. Alan M. Kelly, Dean
Program in:
veterinary medicine • VMD

Wharton School

Dr. Thomas P. Gerrity, Dean
Programs in:
accounting • MBA, PhD
business administration • MBA
executive business administration • Exec MBA
finance • PhD
health care systems • MBA, PhD
insurance and risk management • MBA, PhD
international studies • MA
legal studies • MBA
management • MBA, PhD
marketing • PhD
operations and information management • MBA, PhD
public policy and management • PhD
real estate • MBA
risk and insurance • PhD
statistics • AM, MBA, PhD

UNIVERSITY OF PITTSBURGH
Pittsburgh, PA 15260

http://www.pitt.edu/

Public coed university. *Enrollment:* 25,461 graduate, professional,
and undergraduate students. *Graduate faculty:* 2,848 full-time, 546
part-time. *Computer facilities:* Campuswide network is available
with full Internet access. Total number of PCs/terminals supplied for
student use: 620. Computer service fees are included with tuition
and fees. *Library facilities:* Hillman Library plus 26 additional
on-campus libraries. *Graduate expenses:* Tuition of $8018 per year
full-time, $329 per credit part-time for state residents; $16,508 per
year full-time, $680 per credit part-time for nonresidents. Fees of
$480 per year full-time, $180 per year part-time. *General application contact:* Dean of the appropriate school, 412-624-4141.

Center for Neuroscience

Program in:
neuroscience • PhD

Faculty of Arts and Sciences
Mary Louise Soffa, Dean, Graduate Studies
Programs in:
anthropology • MA, PhD
applied mathematics • MA, MS
applied statistics • MA, MS
astronomy • MS, PhD
chemistry • MS, PhD
classics • MA, PhD
clinical psychology • PhD
cognitive psychology • PhD
computer science • MS, PhD
developmental psychology • PhD
East Asian studies • MA
ecology and evolution • MS, PhD
economics • MA, PhD
English • MA, MFA, PhD
French • MA, PhD
geology and planetary science • MS, PhD
Germanic languages and literatures • MA, PhD
health psychology • PhD
Hispanic languages and literatures • MA, PhD
history • MA, PhD
history and philosophy of science • MA, PhD
history of art and architecture • MA, PhD
intelligent systems • MS, PhD
Italian • MA
Latin American studies • Certificate
linguistics • MA, PhD
mathematics • MA, MS, PhD
medical ethics • MA
molecular, cellular, and developmental biology • PhD
music • MA, PhD
neuroscience • MS, PhD
philosophy • MA, PhD
physics • MS, PhD
political science • MA, PhD
psychology • MS
religion • PhD
religious studies • MA
rhetoric and communication • MA, PhD
Slavic languages and literatures • MA, PhD
social psychology • PhD
sociology • MA, PhD
statistics • MA, MS, PhD
theatre arts • MA, MFA, PhD
women's studies • Certificate

Graduate School of Public and International Affairs
Dr. Carolyn Ban, Dean
Programs in:
applied policy analysis • Certificate
city management • Certificate
community information management • Certificate
diplomacy and international administration • Certificate
economic and social development • MPIA
financial management • Certificate
information services management • Certificate
international affairs • MPIA
international political economy • Certificate
international security studies • Certificate
management science • Certificate
personnel and labor relations • Certificate
public and international affairs • MPIA, PhD
public management and policy • MPA
public policy and management • MPPM
urban and regional development • Certificate
urban and regional planning • MURP

Graduate School of Public Health
Dr. Donald R. Mattison, Dean
Programs in:
biostatistics • Dr PH, MPH, MS, PhD
community health services • MPH
environmental and occupational health • MPH, MS, PhD
epidemiology • Dr PH, MPH, MS, PhD
genetic counseling • MS
health administration • MHA
health services administration • Dr PH
human genetics • MS, PhD
infectious diseases and microbiology • Dr PH, MPH, MS, PhD
occupational medicine • MPH
public health • MHPE, MPH
radiation health • Certificate

Joseph M. Katz Graduate School of Business
Dr. Frederick W. Winter, Dean
Programs in:
business • EMBA, MHA
business administration • MBA, PhD
management of information systems • MS

School of Dental Medicine
Dr. Jon B. Suzuki, Dean
Programs in:
anesthesiology • Certificate
dental medicine • DMD
endodontics • Certificate, MDS
maxillofacial prosthodontics • Certificate
orthodontics • Certificate
pediatric dentistry • Certificate, MDS
periodontics • Certificate, MDS
prosthodontics • Certificate, MDS

School of Education
Dr. Kenneth F. Metz, Dean
Programs in:
cognitive studies • PhD
deaf and hard of hearing • M Ed
developmental/educational psychology • PhD
developmental movement • MS, PhD
early childhood education • M Ed
early education of disabled students • M Ed
educational leadership • Ed D, M Ed, MA
education of students with mental and physical disabilities • M Ed
education of the visually impaired • M Ed
elementary education • M Ed, MAT
English/communications education • Ed D, M Ed, MAT, PhD

University of Pittsburgh (continued)
    exercise physiology • MS, PhD
    foreign languages education • Ed D, M Ed, MA, MAT, PhD
    general special education • M Ed
    health promotion and education • MHPE
    international developmental education • M Ed
    international development education • MA, PhD
    mathematics education • Ed D, M Ed, MAT
    movement science • MHPE, MS, PhD
    reading education • Ed D, M Ed, PhD
    research methodology • M Ed, MA, PhD
    school counseling • M Ed, MA
    science education • Ed D, M Ed, MAT, MS, PhD
    social, philosophical, and historical foundations of education • M Ed, MA, PhD
    social studies education • Ed D, M Ed, MAT, PhD
    special education • Ed D, PhD
    sports medicine • MS, PhD

School of Engineering
Dr. Gerald D. Holder, Dean
Programs in:
    bioengineering • MSBENG, PhD
    chemical engineering • MS Ch E, PhD
    civil and environmental engineering • MSCEE, PhD
    electrical engineering • MSEE, PhD
    energy resources • MER, MSER
    engineering • Certificate
    industrial engineering • MSIE, PhD
    manufacturing systems engineering • MSMfSE
    materials science and engineering • MSMSE, PhD
    mechanical engineering • MSME, PhD
    metallurgical engineering • MS Met E, PhD
    petroleum engineering • MSPE

School of Health and Rehabilitation Sciences
Dr. Clifford Brubaker, Dean
Programs in:
    clinical laboratory sciences • MS
    communication science and disorders • MA, MS, PhD
    health and rehabilitation sciences • MS
    health care supervision and management • MS
    health information systems • MS
    occupational therapy • MS
    physical therapy • MPT, MS
    rehabilitation engineering • Certificate
    rehabilitation science • PhD
    rehabilitation science and technology • MS
    rehabilitation sciences • PhD
    rehabilitation technology • Certificate
    rehabilitation technology service delivery • Certificate

School of Information Sciences
Dr. Toni Carbo, Dean
Programs in:
    information science • Certificate, MSIS, PhD
    library and information science • Certificate, MLIS, PhD
    telecommunications • Certificate, MST

School of Law
Dr. David Herring, Interim Dean
Programs in:
    health law • Certificate
    international and comparative law • LL M
    law • JD

School of Medicine
Dr. George K. Michalopoulos, Interim Dean
Programs in:
    biochemistry and molecular genetics • MS, PhD
    immunology • MS, PhD
    medicine • MD
    molecular virology and microbiology • MS, PhD
    neurobiology • MS, PhD
    pathology • MS, PhD
    pathology/neuroscience • PhD
    pharmacology • MS, PhD
    physiology • MS, PhD
    physiology/neuroscience • PhD

School of Nursing
Dr. Ellen B. Rudy, Dean
Programs in:
    acute and tertiary care • MSN
    acute care nurse practitioner • MSN
    administration • MSN
    anesthesia nursing • MSN
    family nurse practitioner • MSN
    health and community systems • MSN
    health promotion and development • MSN
    individualized options • MSN
    informatics • MSN
    nursing • PhD
    nursing education • MSN
    pediatric nurse practitioner • MSN
    psychiatric primary care nurse practitioner • MSN
    research • MSN
    women's health nurse practitioner • MSN

School of Pharmacy
Dr. Randy P. Juhl, Dean
Programs in:
    pharmaceutical sciences • MS, PhD
    pharmacy • Pharm D

School of Social Work
Dr. David E. Epperson, Dean
Programs in:
    child development and child care • MS
    family and marital therapy • Certificate
    gerontology • Certificate
    social work • MSW, PhD

UNIVERSITY OF SCRANTON
Scranton, PA 18510-4622

http://www.uofs.edu/

Independent-religious coed comprehensive institution. *Enrollment:* 4,816 *graduate, professional, and undergraduate students. Graduate faculty:* 139 *full-time,* 34 *part-time. Computer facilities: Campuswide network is available with full Internet access. Total number of PCs/ terminals supplied for student use:* 300. *Computer service fees are included with tuition and fees. Library facilities: Harry and Jeanette Weinberg Memorial Library. Graduate expenses: Tuition of* $465 *per credit. Fees of* $25 *per semester. General application contact: James L. Goonan, Director of Admissions, 717-941-6304.*

Graduate School
Dr. Robert E. Powell, Dean
Programs in:
- accounting • MBA
- biochemistry • MA, MS
- chemistry • MA, MS
- clinical chemistry • MA, MS
- community counseling • MS
- elementary education • MS
- elementary school administration • MS
- English • MA
- family nurse practitioner • MS
- finance • MBA
- general business administration • MBA
- health administration • MHA
- history • MA
- human resources • MS
- human resources development • MS
- international business • MBA
- marketing • MBA
- organizational leadership • MS
- personnel/labor • MBA
- reading • MS
- rehabilitation counseling • MS
- school counseling • MS
- secondary education • MS
- secondary school administration • MS
- software engineering • MS
- theology • MA

 # VILLANOVA UNIVERSITY
Villanova, PA 19085-1699

http://www.vill.edu/

Independent-religious coed comprehensive institution. *Enrollment:* 10,061 *graduate, professional, and undergraduate students. Graduate faculty:* 172 *full-time,* 126 *part-time. Library facilities: Falvey Memorial Library plus 2 additional on-campus libraries. Graduate expenses: Tuition of* $400 *per credit. Fees of* $60 *per year. General application contact: Dr. Gerald Long, Dean, Graduate School of Liberal Arts and Sciences, 610-519-7090.*

Graduate School of Liberal Arts and Sciences
Dr. Gerald Long, Dean
Programs in:
- applied statistics • MS
- biology • MA, MS
- chemistry • MA, MS, PhD
- classical languages • MA
- computing sciences • MS
- counseling and human relations • MS
- criminal justice administration • MS
- elementary education • MA
- English • MA
- health care administration • MS
- history • MA
- human resource development • MS
- human services administration • MS
- liberal studies • MA
- mathematical sciences • MA, MS
- philosophy • MA, PhD
- political science • MA
- psychology • MS
- public administration • MS
- school administration • MA
- secondary education • MA
- Spanish • MA
- supervisory certification • MA
- teaching of mathematics • MATM
- theatre • Certificate, MA
- theology and religious studies • MA

College of Commerce and Finance
Dr. Thomas F. Monahan, Dean
Programs in:
- business administration • MBA
- taxation • LL M in Tax, MT

College of Engineering
Robert D. Lynch, Dean
Programs in:
- chemical engineering • M Ch E
- civil engineering • MCE
- computer engineering • MSCE
- electrical engineering • MSEE
- manufacturing • Certificate
- mechanical engineering • MME
- transportation engineering • MSTE
- virtual manufacturing • Certificate
- water resources and environmental engineering • MSWREE

College of Nursing
Dr. Claire Manfredi, Graduate Director
Programs in:
- adult nurse practitioner • MSN
- clinical case management • MSN, Post Master's Certificate
- health care administration • MSN
- nurse anesthetist • MSN, Post Master's Certificate
- nurse practitioner • Post Master's Certificate
- nursing education • MSN
- pediatric nurse practitioner • MSN

Villanova University (continued)
School of Law
Mark A. Sargent, Dean
Program in:
law • JD, LL M in Tax

WEST CHESTER UNIVERSITY OF PENNSYLVANIA
West Chester, PA 19383

http://www.wcupa.edu/

Public coed comprehensive institution. *Enrollment:* 10,607 graduate, professional, and undergraduate students. Computer facilities: *Campuswide network is available with full Internet access. Computer service fees are included with tuition and fees.* Library facilities: *Francis Harvey Green Library plus 1 additional on-campus library.* Graduate expenses: *Tuition of $3468 per year full-time, $193 per credit part-time for state residents; $6236 per year full-time, $346 per credit part-time for nonresidents. Fees of $660 per year full-time, $38 per credit part-time.* General application contact: *Office of Graduate Studies, 610-436-2943.*

Graduate Studies
Dr. Gary Knock, Dean

College of Arts and Sciences
Dr. David H. Buchanan, Dean
Programs in:
biology • MA
chemistry • MS
clinical chemistry • MS
communication studies • MA
computer science • MS
English • M Ed, MA
French • M Ed, MA
German • M Ed
history • M Ed, MA
Latin • M Ed
mathematics • M Ed, MA
philosophy • MA
physical science • MA
psychology • MA
Spanish • M Ed, MA
teaching English as a second language • MA

School of Business and Public Affairs
Dr. Christopher Fiorentino, Dean
Programs in:
criminal justice • MS
economics/finance • MBA
executive business administration • MBA
general business • MBA
geography • MA
health services • MSA
human research management • MSA
leadership for women • MSA
longterm care • MSA
management • MBA

public administration • MSA
social work • MSW
sport and athletic administration • MSA
training and development • MSA
urban and regional planning • MSA

School of Education
Dr. Tony Johnson, Dean
Programs in:
educational research • MS
elementary education • M Ed
instructional media • M Ed, MS
reading • M Ed
school counseling • M Ed, MS
secondary education • M Ed
special education • M Ed

School of Health Sciences
Dr. Donald E. Barr, Dean
Programs in:
coaching • Certificate
communicative disorders • MA
community health nursing • MSN
driver education • Certificate
exercise and sport physiology • MS
general exercise science • MS
health • M Ed, MS
nursing • MS
physical education • MS
safety • Certificate
sport and athletic administration • MSA

School of Music
Dr. Timothy Blair, Dean
Programs in:
accompanying • MM
composition • MM
music education • MM
music history • MA
music theory • MM
performance • MM
piano pedagogy • MM

WIDENER UNIVERSITY
Chester, PA 19013-5792

http://www.widener.edu/widener.html

Independent coed comprehensive institution. *Enrollment:* 8,517 graduate, professional, and undergraduate students. Graduate faculty: *242 full-time, 226 part-time.* Library facilities: *Wolfgram Library plus 1 additional on-campus library.* Graduate expenses: *$455 per credit.* General application contact: *Dr. Stephen C. Wilhite, Assistant Provost for Graduate Studies, 610-499-4351.*

College of Arts and Sciences
Dr. Kenneth Skinner, Dean
Programs in:
criminal justice • MA
liberal studies • MA
public administration • MPA

School of Business Administration

Lisa Bussom Jr., Director, Graduate Programs in Business
Programs in:
  accounting • MS
  business administration • MBA
  health and medical services administration • MBA, MHA
  human resource management • MS
  taxation • MS

School of Engineering

Dr. David H. T. Chen, Assistant Dean for Graduate
  Programs and Research
Programs in:
  chemical engineering • ME
  civil engineering • ME
  computer, software, and telecommunication engineering
    • ME
  electrical engineering • ME
  engineering management • ME
  mechanical engineering • ME

School of Human Service Professions

Dr. Stephen C. Wilhite, Dean
Programs in:
  clinical psychology • Psy D
  education • Ed D, M Ed
  physical therapy education • MS
  social work education • MSW

School of Nursing

Dr. Mary B. Walker, Assistant Dean for Graduate Studies
Program in:
  nursing • DN Sc, MSN, PMC

Widener University School of Law

Dr. Arthur Frakt, Dean
Program in:
  law • JD, LL M

WILKES UNIVERSITY
Wilkes-Barre, PA 18766-0002

http://www.wilkes.edu/

Independent coed comprehensive institution. *Enrollment:* 2,824 graduate, professional, and undergraduate students. Graduate faculty: *59 full-time, 17 part-time.* Computer facilities: *Campuswide network is available with full Internet access. Computer service fees are included with tuition and fees.* Library facilities: *E. S. Farley Library plus 1 additional on-campus library.* Graduate expenses: *Tuition of $12,552 per year full-time, $523 per credit hour part-time. Fees of $240 per year full-time, $10 per credit hour part-time.* General application contact: *Dr. Jack Meyers, Associate Dean of Academic Affairs and Graduate Studies, 717-408-4857.*

Graduate Studies

Dr. Jack Meyers, Associate Dean of Academic Affairs and
  Graduate Studies
Programs in:
  accounting • MBA
  biology • MS Ed
  chemistry • MS Ed
  educational computing • MS Ed
  educational development and strategies • MS Ed
  educational leadership • MS Ed
  elementary education • MS Ed
  English • MS Ed
  finance • MBA
  health administration • MHA
  health care • MBA
  history • MS Ed
  human resource management • MBA
  international business • MBA
  management • MBA
  management information systems • MBA
  marketing • MBA
  mathematics • MS, MS Ed
  nursing • MSN
  physics • MS, MS Ed
  secondary education • MS Ed

School of Pharmacy

Dr. Bernard Graham, Dean
Program in:
  pharmacy • Pharm D

School of Science and Engineering

Dr. Umid Nejib, Dean
Program in:
  electrical engineering • MSEE

PUERTO RICO

INTER AMERICAN UNIVERSITY OF PUERTO RICO, METROPOLITAN CAMPUS
San Juan, PR 00919-1293

http://coqui.metro.inter.edu/

Independent coed comprehensive institution. *Enrollment:* 12,156 graduate, professional, and undergraduate students. Graduate faculty: *57 full-time, 79 part-time.* Computer facilities: *Campuswide network is available with full Internet access. Total number of PCs/ terminals supplied for student use: 400. Computer services are offered at no charge.* Library facilities: *main library.* Graduate expenses: *Tuition of $3272 per year full-time, $1740 per year part-time. Fees of $328 per year full-time, $176 per year part-time.* General application contact: *Dr. Carmen T. Muñiz, Coordinator of Graduate Programs, 787-250-1912.*

Inter American University of Puerto Rico, Metropolitan Campus (continued)

Graduate Programs

Dr. Carmen T. Muñiz, Coordinator

Division of Behavioral Science and Allied Professions

Dr. Miguel Poupart, Dean
Programs in:
    criminal justice • MA
    psychology • MA
    social work • MA

Division of Economics and Business Administration

Dr. Angel Ruiz, Dean
Programs in:
    accounting • MBA
    business education • MA
    finance • MBA
    human resources • MBA
    industrial management • MBA
    labor relations • MA
    marketing • MBA

Division of Education

Dr. Amalia Charneco, Director
Programs in:
    administration and supervision • MA
    education • Ed D
    elementary education • MA
    guidance and counseling • MA
    health and physical education • MA
    higher education • MA Ed
    occupational education • MA
    special education • MA Ed
    teaching of science • MA Ed
    vocational evaluation • MA

Division of Humanities

Dr. Dalia Rodriguez, Dean
Programs in:
    Spanish • MA
    teaching English as a second language • MA

Division of Science and Technology

Dr. Lillian Gayá-González, Dean
Programs in:
    educational computing • MA
    medical technology • MS

School of Law

Carlos E. Ramos-González, Dean
Program in:
    law • JD

School of Optometry

Dr. Hector Santiago, Dean
Program in:
    optometry • OD

INTER AMERICAN UNIVERSITY OF PUERTO RICO, SAN GERMÁN CAMPUS
San Germán, PR 00683-5008

http://www.sg.inter.edu/

Independent coed comprehensive institution. *Enrollment:* 6,022 graduate, professional, and undergraduate students. Graduate faculty: *32 full-time, 45 part-time.* Computer facilities: *Campuswide network is available with full Internet access. Total number of PCs/ terminals supplied for student use: 265. Computer service fees are included with tuition and fees.* Library facilities: *Juan Cancio Ortiz Library.* Graduate expenses: *Tuition of $150 per credit. Fees of $177 per semester.* General application contact: *Mildred Camacho, Admissions Director, 787-892-3090.*

Graduate Programs

Dr. Waldemar Velez, Acting Director of Graduate Studies
    Center
Programs in:
    accounting • MBA
    administration of higher education institutions • MA
    business education • MA
    curriculum and instruction • MA Ed
    educational administration • MA Ed
    environmental sciences • MS
    finance • MBA
    guidance and counseling • MA Ed
    human resources • MBA
    industrial relations • MBA
    library science • MA
    marketing • MBA
    medical technology • Certificate
    physical education and scientific analysis of human body
        movement • MA Ed
    psychology • MA, MS
    science education • MA
    special education • MS Ed
    teaching English as a second language • MA

PONTIFICAL CATHOLIC UNIVERSITY OF PUERTO RICO
Ponce, PR 00731-6382

http://www.pucpr.edu/

Independent-religious coed comprehensive institution. *Enrollment:* 10,819 graduate, professional, and undergraduate students. Graduate faculty: *47 full-time, 41 part-time.* Computer facilities: *Campuswide network is available with full Internet access. Total number of PCs/ terminals supplied for student use: 29. Computer service fees are included with tuition and fees.* Library facilities: *Encarnación Valdés Library plus 1 additional on-campus library.* Graduate expenses: *Tuition of $3360 per year. Fees of $550 per year.* General applica-

tion contact: *Manuel Luciano, Director of Admissions, 787-841-2000 Ext. 426.*

College of Arts and Humanities
Jose J. Baez, Chairperson
Programs in:
criminology • MA
divinity • MA
history • MA
public administration • MA
social work • MSW
theology • MA

College of Business Administration
Dr. Kenya Carrasquillo, Chairperson
Program in:
business administration • MBA

College of Education
Dr. Gilbert Toro, Chairperson
Program in:
education • M Ed, MA Ed, MRE

College of Sciences
Julio Rivera, Dean
Programs in:
chemistry • MS
clinical psychology • MS
industrial psychology • MS
medical-surgical nursing • MS
mental health and psychiatric nursing • MS

School of Law
Charles Cuprill, Dean
Program in:
law • JD, LL M

UNIVERSIDAD DEL TURABO
Gurabo, PR 00778-3030

Independent coed comprehensive institution. Library facilities: *Recursos De Aprendizaje.* General application contact: *Admissions Officer, 787-746-3009.*

Graduate Programs
Programs in:
accounting • MBA
bilingual education • MA
criminal justice studies • MPA
education administration and supervision • MA
environmental studies • MES
human resources • MBA
human services administration • MPA
logistics and materials management • MBA
management • MBA
marketing • MBA

school libraries administration • MA
special education • MA
teaching English as a second language • MA

UNIVERSIDAD METROPOLITANA
Río Piedras, PR 00928-1150

http://umet_mie.suagm.edu/

Independent coed comprehensive institution. *Enrollment: 4,864 graduate, professional, and undergraduate students. Graduate faculty: 2 full-time, 30 part-time. Computer facilities: Campuswide network is available with full Internet access. Total number of PCs/terminals supplied for student use: 300. Computer service fees are applied as a separate charge.* Library facilities: *main library.* General application contact: *Dr. Pedro Rivera Villegas, Assistant Vice Chancellor, Evaluation and Development, 787-766-1717 Ext. 6440.*

Graduate Programs in Education
Dr. Ana Delgado, Dean
Programs in:
administration of pre-school • MA
environmental education • MA
teaching • MA

School of Business Administration
Pedro Hernández, Dean
Programs in:
accounting • MBA
management • MBA
marketing • MBA

School of Environmental Affairs
Dr. Carlos Padin, Head
Program in:
environmental management • MS

UNIVERSITY OF PUERTO RICO, MAYAGÜEZ CAMPUS
Mayagüez, PR 00681-5000

http://www_rum.upr.clu.edu/

Public coed university. *Enrollment: 12,771 graduate, professional, and undergraduate students. Graduate faculty: 416 full-time, 3 part-time. Computer facilities: Campuswide network is available with full Internet access. Total number of PCs/terminals supplied for student use: 1,000. Computer services are offered at no charge.* Library facilities: *main library plus 1 additional on-campus library. Graduate expenses: Tuition of $75 per credit for commonwealth residents; $75 per credit (minimum) for nonresidents. Fees of $35 per semester (minimum).* General application contact: *Dr. Zulma Toro Ramos, Director of Graduate Studies, 787-265-3809.*

University of Puerto Rico, Mayagüez Campus (continued)
Graduate Studies
Dr. Zulma Toro Ramos, Director

College of Agricultural Sciences
Dr. Alejandro Ayala, Dean
Programs in:
- agricultural economics • MS
- agricultural education • MS
- agricultural extension • MS
- animal industry • MS
- crop protection • MS
- crops • MS
- food technology • MS
- horticulture • MS
- soils • MS

College of Arts and Sciences
Dr. Ismael Scott, Dean
Programs in:
- applied mathematics • MS
- biological oceanography • MMS, PhD
- biology • MS
- chemical oceanography • MMS, PhD
- chemistry • MS
- computational sciences • MS
- English • MA
- geological oceanography • MMS, PhD
- geology • MS
- Hispanic studies • MA
- physical oceanography • MMS, PhD
- physics • MS
- pure mathematics • MS
- statistics • MS

College of Business Administration
Prof. Jaime Pabón, Dean
Program in:
- business administration • MBA

College of Engineering
Dr. Jack Allison, Dean
Programs in:
- chemical engineering • M Ch E, MS
- civil engineering • MCE, MS, PhD
- computer engineering • M Co E, MS
- electrical engineering • MEE, MS
- industrial engineering • MMSE
- mechanical engineering • MME, MS

UNIVERSITY OF PUERTO RICO, RÍO PIEDRAS
San Juan, PR 00931

Public coed university. Library facilities: *Jose M. Lazaro Library plus 19 additional on-campus libraries.* General application contact: *Dean of the appropriate school.*

College of Education
Programs in:
- biology education • M Ed
- chemistry education • M Ed
- child education • M Ed
- curriculum and teaching • Ed D
- educational research and evaluation • M Ed
- elementary education • M Ed
- English education • M Ed
- guidance and counseling • Ed D, M Ed
- history education • M Ed
- home economics • M Ed
- mathematics education • M Ed
- physics education • M Ed
- school administration • Ed D, M Ed
- secondary education • M Ed
- Spanish education • M Ed
- special education • M Ed
- teaching English as a second language • M Ed

College of Humanities
Programs in:
- comparative literature • MA
- English • MA
- Hispanic studies • MA, PhD
- history • MA, PhD
- interpretation • Certificate
- linguistics • MA
- philosophy • MA
- specialization in translation • Certificate
- translation • MA

College of Social Sciences
Programs in:
- economics • MA
- psychology • MA, PhD
- public administration • MPA
- rehabilitation counseling • MRC
- social work • MSW
- sociology • MA

Faculty of Natural Sciences
Programs in:
- applied physics • MS
- biology • MS, PhD
- chemical physics • PhD
- chemistry • MS, PhD
- mathematics • MA
- physics • MS

Graduate School of Business Administration
Program in:
- business administration • MBA

Graduate School of Librarianship
Program in:
- librarianship • M Bibl

Graduate School of Planning
Program in:
- planning • MP

School of Architecture
Program in:
   architecture • M Arch

School of Law
Program in:
   law • JD

School of Public Communication
Program in:
   public communication • MA

UNIVERSITY OF THE SACRED HEART
San Juan, PR 00914-0383

Independent-religious coed comprehensive institution. *Enrollment:* 4,943 graduate, professional, and undergraduate students. Graduate faculty: *17 full-time, 18 part-time.* Computer facilities: *Campuswide network is available with full Internet access. Total number of PCs/ terminals supplied for student use: 300. Computer service fees are applied as a separate charge.* Library facilities: *Madre María Teresa Guevara Library.* Graduate expenses: *Tuition of $150 per credit. Fees of $240 per credit.* General application contact: *Dr. Blanca Villamil, Acting Director, 787-727-5500.*

Graduate Programs
Dr. Cesar A. Rey, Dean, Academic and Student Affairs
Programs in:
   human resource management • MBA
   instruction systems and education technology • M Ed
   management information systems • MBA
   marketing • MBA
   medical technology • Certificate
   natural science • Certificate
   public relations • MA
   taxation • MBA

RHODE ISLAND

BROWN UNIVERSITY
Providence, RI 02912

http://www.brown.edu/

Independent coed university. *Enrollment: 7,372 graduate, professional, and undergraduate students.* Library facilities: *John D. Rockefeller Library plus 4 additional on-campus libraries.* Graduate expenses: *Tuition of $23,616 per year. Fees of $436 per year.* General application contact: *Admission Office, 401-863-2600.*

Graduate School
Peder J. Estrup, Dean
Programs in:
   American civilization • AM, PhD
   anthropology • AM, PhD
   art history • AM, PhD
   biochemistry • PhD
   chemistry • PhD, Sc M
   classics • AM, PhD
   cognitive science • PhD, Sc M
   comparative literature • AM, PhD
   comparative study of development • AM
   computer science • PhD, Sc M
   economics • AM, PhD
   Egyptology • AM, PhD
   elementary education K–6 • MAT
   English literature and language • AM, PhD
   French studies • AM, PhD
   geological sciences • MA, PhD, Sc M
   German • AM, PhD
   Hispanic studies • AM, PhD
   history • AM, PhD
   history of mathematics • AM, PhD
   Italian studies • AM, PhD
   Judaic studies • AM, PhD
   linguistics • AM, PhD
   mathematics • AM, PhD, Sc M
   music • AM, PhD
   philosophy • AM, PhD
   physics • PhD, Sc M
   political science • AM, PhD
   population studies • PhD
   psychology • AM, PhD, Sc M
   religious studies • AM, PhD
   Russian • AM, PhD
   secondary biology • MAT
   secondary English • MAT
   secondary social studies • MAT
   Slavic languages • AM, PhD
   sociology • AM, PhD
   theatre arts • AM
   writing • MFA

Center for Environmental Studies
Harold Ward, Director
Program in:
   environmental studies • AM

Center for Old World Archaeology and Art
R. Ross Holloway, Director
Program in:
   old world archaeology and art • AM, PhD

Center for Portuguese and Brazilian Studies
Onesimo Almeida, Chair
Programs in:
   Brazilian studies • AM
   Luso-Brazilian studies • PhD
   Portuguese studies and bilingual education • AM

Division of Applied Mathematics
David Gottlieb, Chair
Program in:
   applied mathematics • PhD, Sc M

Brown University (continued)

Division of Biology and Medicine
Dr. Donald Marsh, Dean
Programs in:
  artificial organs/biomaterials/cellular technology • MA, PhD, Sc M
  biochemistry • M Med Sc, PhD, Sc M
  biology • MA, PhD, Sc M
  biomedical engineering • Sc M
  cancer biology • PhD
  cell biology • M Med Sc, PhD, Sc M
  developmental biology • M Med Sc, PhD, Sc M
  ecology and evolutionary biology • PhD, Sc M
  epidemiology and gerontology • PhD, Sc M
  health services research • MS, PhD
  immunology • M Med Sc, PhD, Sc M
  immunology and infection • PhD
  medical science • M Med Sc, PhD
  molecular microbiology • M Med Sc, PhD, Sc M
  molecular pharmacology and physiology • MA, PhD, Sc M
  neuroscience • PhD, Sc M
  pathobiology • Sc M
  toxicology and environmental pathology • PhD

Division of Engineering
Dr. Harvey F. Silverman, Chairman
Programs in:
  aerospace engineering • PhD, Sc M
  biomedical engineering • Sc M
  electrical sciences • PhD, Sc M
  fluid mechanics, thermodynamics, and chemical processes • PhD, Sc M
  materials science • PhD, Sc M
  mechanics of solids and structures • PhD, Sc M

Program in Medicine
Donald Marsh, Dean
Program in:
  medicine • MD

PROVIDENCE COLLEGE
Providence, RI 02918

Independent-religious coed comprehensive institution. *Enrollment:* 4,575 graduate, professional, and undergraduate students. Graduate faculty: *47 full-time, 42 part-time.* Computer facilities: *Campuswide network is available with full Internet access. Total number of PCs/ terminals supplied for student use: 200. Computer services are offered at no charge.* Library facilities: *Phillips Memorial Library.* Graduate expenses: *$621 per course.* General application contact: *Dr. Thomas F. Flaherty, Dean, 401-865-2247.*

Graduate School
Dr. Thomas F. Flaherty, Dean
Programs in:
  biblical studies • MA
  business administration • MBA

elementary administration • M Ed
guidance and counseling • M Ed
history • MA, PhD
mathematics • MAT
pastoral ministry • MA
religious education • MA
religious studies • MA
secondary administration • M Ed
special education • M Ed

 # RHODE ISLAND COLLEGE
Providence, RI 02908-1924

http://www.ric.edu/

Public coed comprehensive institution. *Enrollment: 6,976 graduate, professional, and undergraduate students. Graduate faculty: 222 full-time, 62 part-time.* Computer facilities: *Campuswide network is available with full Internet access. Total number of PCs/terminals supplied for student use: 250. Computer service fees are included with tuition and fees.* Library facilities: *James P. Adams Library plus 1 additional on-campus library.* Graduate expenses: *$4064 per year full-time, $214 per credit part-time for state residents; $7658 per year full-time, $376 per credit part-time for nonresidents.* General application contact: *Dr. James D. Turley, Dean of Graduate Studies, 401-456-8700.*

School of Graduate Studies
Dr. James D. Turley, Dean

Center for Management and Technology
Dr. Nazanin Sahba, Director
Program in:
  industrial technology • MS

Faculty of Arts and Sciences
Dr. Richard R. Weiner, Dean
Programs in:
  art education • MAT
  art studio • MA
  biology • MA, MAT
  English • MA, MAT
  French • MA, MAT
  general science • MAT
  history • MA, MAT
  mathematics • CAGS, MA, MAT
  music • MM
  music education • MAT
  physical science • MAT
  psychology • MA
  Spanish • MAT

School of Education and Human Development
Dr. David Nelson, Dean
Programs in:
  agency counseling • MA
  bilingual/bicultural education • M Ed
  counselor education • CAGS, M Ed
  curriculum • CAGS
  early childhood education • M Ed

education • PhD
educational administration • CAGS, M Ed
educational psychology • MA
education and human development • MS
elementary education • M Ed, MAT
English as a second language • M Ed
health education • M Ed
reading education • CAGS, M Ed
school psychology • CAGS
secondary education • M Ed
special education • CAGS, M Ed
teaching of the handicapped • CAGS, M Ed
technology education • M Ed

School of Social Work
Dr. George Metrey, Dean
Program in:
social work • MSW

SALVE REGINA UNIVERSITY
Newport, RI 02840-4192

http://www.salve.edu/

Independent-religious coed comprehensive institution. *Enrollment:* 2,108 graduate, professional, and undergraduate students. Graduate faculty: *11 full-time, 36 part-time.* Computer facilities: *Campuswide network is available with full Internet access. Total number of PCs/terminals supplied for student use: 163. Computer service fees are included with tuition and fees.* Library facilities: *McKillop Library.* Graduate expenses: *Tuition of $275 per credit hour. Fees of $70 per year.* General application contact: *Laura E. McPhie, Dean of Enrollment Services, 401-847-6650 Ext. 2908.*

Graduate School
Dr. Judith M. Mills, Vice President of Academic Affairs
Programs in:
accounting • MS
administration of justice • MS
biomedical technology/management • MS
business administration • MBA
education • M Ed
health services administration • MS
holistic counseling • CAGS, MA
humanities • CAGS, MA, PhD
human resources management • MA, MS
information systems science • MS
international relations • MA

UNIVERSITY OF RHODE ISLAND
Kingston, RI 02881

http://www.uri.edu/

Public coed university. Library facilities: *main library plus 2 additional on-campus libraries.* Graduate expenses: *Tuition of $3446 per year full-time, $191 per credit part-time for state residents; $9850 per year full-time, $547 per credit part-time for nonresidents. Fees of $1276 per year full-time, $135 per semester (minimum) part-time.* General application contact: *Associate Dean of the Graduate School, 401-874-2262.*

Graduate School

College of Arts and Sciences
Programs in:
American government • MA
American politics • MA
biochemistry • MS, PhD
biodegradation • MS
botany • MS, PhD
cellular development • MS
chemistry • MS, PhD
clinical psychology • PhD
comparative government • MA
computer science and statistics • MS, PhD
economics • MA
electron microscopy and ultrastructure • MS
English • MA, PhD
experimental psychology • PhD
French • MA
genetics and molecular biology • MS
geology • MS
history • MA
immunology • MS
international development studies • Certificate
international relations • MA
marine affairs • MA, MMA
marine and freshwater ecosystems • MS
mathematics • MS, PhD
microbial pathogenesis • MS
microbial physiology • MS
microbiology • MS, PhD
music • MM
philosophy • MA
physics • MS, PhD
political science • MA
protozoology • MS
public policy • MA
public policy and administration • MPA
school psychology • MS, PhD
Spanish • MA
virology • MS
water-pollution microbiology • MS
zoology • MS, PhD

College of Business Administration
Programs in:
accounting • MS
applied mathematics • PhD
finance • MBA
international business • MBA
international sports management • MBA
management • MBA
management information systems • MBA
management science • MBA
manufacturing • MBA
marketing • MBA

University of Rhode Island (continued)

College of Continuing Education
Programs in:
 clinical laboratory sciences • MS
 continuing education • Exec MBA

College of Engineering
Programs in:
 chemical engineering • MS, PhD
 design/systems • MS, PhD
 electrical and computer engineering • MS, PhD
 environmental engineering • MS, PhD
 fluid mechanics • MS, PhD
 geotechnical engineering • MS, PhD
 industrial engineering • MS
 manufacturing engineering • MS
 ocean engineering • MS, PhD
 solid mechanics • MS, PhD
 structural engineering • MS, PhD
 thermal sciences • MS, PhD
 transportation engineering • MS, PhD

College of Human Science and Services
Programs in:
 adult education • MA
 communicative disorders • MA, MS
 elementary education • MA
 guidance and counseling • MS
 health • MS
 home economics education • MS
 marriage and family therapy • MS
 physical education • MS
 physical therapy • MS
 reading • MA
 recreation • MS
 secondary education • MA
 textiles, fashion merchandising and design • MS

College of Nursing
Programs in:
 nursing • PhD
 nursing service administration • MS
 teaching of nursing • MS

College of Pharmacy
Programs in:
 medicinal chemistry • MS, PhD
 pharmaceutics • MS, PhD
 pharmacognosy • MS, PhD
 pharmacology and toxicology • MS, PhD
 pharmacy • Pharm D
 pharmacy administration • MS

College of Resource Development
Programs in:
 animal science • MS
 community planning and area development • MCP
 entomology • MS, PhD
 food and nutrition science • MS, PhD
 food science and technology, nutrition and dietetics • MS, PhD
 plant pathology • MS, PhD
 resource economics and marine resources • MS, PhD

Graduate Library School
Program in:
 library science • MLIS

Graduate School of Oceanography
Program in:
 oceanography • MS, PhD

Labor Research Center
Program in:
 labor and industrial relations • MS

SOUTH CAROLINA

CHARLESTON SOUTHERN UNIVERSITY
Charleston, SC 29423-8087

http://www.csuniv.edu/

Independent-religious coed comprehensive institution. *Enrollment:* 2,481 graduate, professional, and undergraduate students. *Graduate faculty: 26. Computer facilities: Campuswide network is available with full Internet access. Total number of PCs/terminals supplied for student use: 150. Computer service fees are included with tuition and fees. Library facilities: L. Mendel Rivers Library. Graduate expenses: $9821 per year full-time, $173 per hour (minimum) part-time. General application contact: Debbie Williamson, Office of Admissions, 803-863-7050.*

Program in Business
Dr. Al Parish, MBA Director
Programs in:
 accounting • MBA
 finance • MBA
 health care administration • MBA
 marketing • MBA
 organizational development • MBA

Programs in Education
Dr. Martha Watson, Director of Graduate Programs
Programs in:
 administration and supervision • M Ed
 elementary • M Ed
 elementary education • M Ed
 English • MAT
 science • MAT
 secondary • M Ed
 secondary education • M Ed
 social studies • MAT

THE CITADEL, THE MILITARY COLLEGE OF SOUTH CAROLINA

Charleston, SC 29409

http://www.citadel.edu/

Public coed comprehensive institution. *Enrollment: 2,592 graduate, professional, and undergraduate students. Graduate faculty: 49 full-time, 20 part-time. Library facilities: Daniel Memorial Library plus 1 additional on-campus library. Graduate expenses: Tuition of $130 per credit hour for state residents; $260 per credit hour for nonresidents. Fees of $30 per semester. General application contact: Dr. David H. Reilly, Dean of Graduate Studies, 803-953-7118.*

Graduate Studies

Dr. David H. Reilly, Dean
Programs in:
　biology education • MAE
　business administration • MBA
　curriculum and instruction • M Ed
　educational administration • Ed S, M Ed
　English • MA
　guidance and counseling • M Ed
　health and physical education • M Ed
　history • MA
　mathematics education • MAE
　psychology • Ed S, M Ed
　reading • M Ed
　school psychology • Ed S
　secondary education • MAT
　social studies education • MAE
　special education • M Ed

CLEMSON UNIVERSITY

Clemson, SC 29634

http://www.clemson.edu/

Public coed university. *Enrollment: 16,396 graduate, professional, and undergraduate students. Graduate faculty: 825 full-time, 77 part-time. Computer facilities: Campuswide network is available with full Internet access. Total number of PCs/terminals supplied for student use: 1,700. Computer service fees are included with tuition and fees. Library facilities: Robert Muldrow Cooper Library plus 4 additional on-campus libraries. Graduate expenses: Tuition of $3154 per year full-time, $130 per credit hour part-time for state residents; $6452 per year full-time, $264 per credit hour part-time for nonresidents. Fees of $190 per year. General application contact: Dr. Mark A. McKnew, Assistant Dean of the Graduate School, 864-656-3196.*

Graduate School

Dr. Debra Jackson, Acting Dean

College of Agriculture, Forestry and Life Sciences
Dr. William Wehrenberg, Dean
Programs in:
　agricultural and applied economics • MS
　agricultural economics • M Ag
　agricultural education • M Ag Ed
　agricultural engineering • M Engr, MS, PhD
　agricultural mechanization and business • M Ag
　agronomy • MS, PhD
　animal and food industries • MS
　animal industries • M Ag
　animal physiology • MS, PhD
　applied economics • PhD
　aquaculture, fisheries and wildlife • MS
　biochemistry • MS, PhD
　botany • MS
　entomology • MS, PhD
　environmental toxicology • MS, PhD
　food technology • PhD
　forest resources • MFR, MS, PhD
　genetics • MS, PhD
　horticulture • MS
　microbiology • MS, PhD
　nutrition • MS, PhD
　plant health • M Ag
　plant pathology • MS, PhD
　plant physiology • PhD
　soils and land use • MS
　zoology • MS, PhD

College of Architecture, Arts, and Humanities
Dr. James F. Barker, Dean
Programs in:
　architecture • M Arch, MS
　construction science and management • MCSM
　English • MA
　environmental planning • MCRP
　history • MA
　land development planning • MCRP
　professional communication • MA
　visual arts • MA

College of Business and Public Affairs
Dr. Jerry Trapnell, Dean
Programs in:
　accountancy and legal studies • MP Acc
　applied economics • PhD
　applied psychology • MS
　applied sociology • MS
　business administration • MBA
　economics • MA
　industrial management • MS, PhD
　industrial/organizational psychology • PhD
　management science • PhD
　public administration • MPA

College of Engineering and Science
Dr. Thomas M. Keinath, Dean
Programs in:
　applied and pure mathematics • MS, PhD
　astronomy and astrophysics • MS, PhD

Clemson University (continued)
  atmospheric physics • MS, PhD
  bioengineering • MS, PhD
  biophysics • MS, PhD
  ceramic engineering • M Engr, MS, PhD
  chemical engineering • M Engr, MS, PhD
  chemistry • MS, PhD
  civil engineering • M Engr, MS, PhD
  computational mathematics • MS, PhD
  computer engineering • MS, PhD
  computer science • MS, PhD
  electrical engineering • M Engr, MS, PhD
  engineering mechanics • MS, PhD
  environmental systems engineering • M Engr, MS, PhD
  environmental toxicology • MS, PhD
  hydrogeology • MS
  industrial engineering • MS, PhD
  management science • PhD
  materials science and engineering • MS, PhD
  mechanical engineering • M Engr, MS, PhD
  operations research • MS, PhD
  physics • MS, PhD
  statistics • MS, PhD
  textile and polymer science • PhD
  textile chemistry • MS
  textile science • MS

College of Health, Education, and Human Development
Dr. Harold E. Cheatham, Dean
Programs in:
  administration and supervision • Ed S, M Ed
  counseling and guidance services • M Ed
  curriculum and instruction • PhD
  educational leadership • PhD
  elementary education • M Ed
  English • M Ed
  foundations and special education • M Ed
  history and government • M Ed
  human resource development • MHRD
  industrial education • M In Ed
  mathematics • M Ed
  natural sciences • M Ed
  nursing • MS
  parks, recreation, and tourism management • MPRTM, MS, PhD
  public health • MHA
  reading • M Ed
  vocational/technical education • Ed D

CONVERSE COLLEGE
Spartanburg, SC 29302-0006

http://www.converse.edu/

Independent coed comprehensive institution. *Enrollment: 1,496 graduate, professional, and undergraduate students. Graduate faculty: 72 full-time, 11 part-time. Library facilities: Mickel Library. Graduate expenses: $185 per credit. General application contact: Dr. Martha T. Lovett, Dean of Graduate Education and Special Programs, 864-596-9082.*

Department of Education
Dr. Martha T. Lovett, Dean of Graduate Education and Special Programs
Programs in:
  educational administration • Ed S
  educational curriculum and instruction • Ed S
  elementary education • M Ed
  gifted education • M Ed
  marriage and family therapy • Ed S
  secondary education • M Ed
  special education • M Ed

School of Music
Dr. Jack Bowman, Dean
Programs in:
  composition • MM
  instrumental performance • MM
  music education • MM
  music history • MM
  music theory • MM
  piano pedagogy • MM
  vocal performance • MM

FRANCIS MARION UNIVERSITY
Florence, SC 29501-0547

http://www.fmarion.edu/

Public coed comprehensive institution. *Enrollment: 4,103 graduate, professional, and undergraduate students. Graduate faculty: 106 full-time, 1 part-time. Computer facilities: Campuswide network is available with full Internet access. Computer service fees are applied as a separate charge. Library facilities: James A. Rogers Library. General application contact: Provost Office, 803-661-1281.*

Graduate Programs
Programs in:
  applied clinical psychology • MS
  applied community psychology • MS
  business • MBA
  early childhood education • M Ed
  elementary education • M Ed
  learning disabilities • M Ed, MAT
  remediation education • M Ed
  school psychology • MS
  secondary education • M Ed
  substance abuse counseling • MS

LANDER UNIVERSITY
Greenwood, SC 29649-2099

http://www.lander.edu/

Public coed comprehensive institution. *Enrollment: 2,731 graduate, professional, and undergraduate students. Graduate faculty: 9 full-time. Library facilities: Larry A. Jackson Library. Graduate expenses:*

$3700 per year full-time, $148 per semester hour part-time for state residents; $6326 per year full-time, $253 per semester hour part-time for nonresidents. General application contact: *Dr. Phil Bennett, Dean, School of Education, 864-388-8225.*

School of Education
Dr. Phil Bennett, Dean
Programs in:
    art • MAT
    elementary education • M Ed
    English • MAT
    science • MAT

SOUTH CAROLINA STATE UNIVERSITY
Orangeburg, SC 29117-0001

http://www.scsu.edu/

Public coed comprehensive institution. *Enrollment: 4,980 graduate, professional, and undergraduate students. Graduate faculty: 80. Computer facilities: Campuswide network is available with full Internet access. Total number of PCs/terminals supplied for student use: 125. Computer service fees are included with tuition and fees. Library facilities: Miller F. Whittaker Library. Graduate expenses: $2974 per year full-time, $165 per credit hour part-time. General application contact: Dr. Howard Hill, Dean of the School of Graduate Studies, 803-536-7064.*

School of Graduate Studies
Dr. Howard Hill, Dean

School of Applied Professional Sciences
Dr. Leola Adams, Dean
Programs in:
    individual and family development • MS
    nutritional sciences • MS
    rehabilitation counseling • MA
    speech/language pathology • MA

School of Business
Dr. Lucy J. Rueben, Dean
Program in:
    agribusiness • MS

School of Education
Dr. Casimir Kawalski, Dean
Programs in:
    biology education • M Ed
    business education • M Ed
    counselor education • M Ed
    early childhood and special education • M Ed
    early childhood education • MAT
    educational administration • Ed D, Ed S
    elementary counselor education • M Ed
    elementary education • M Ed, MAT
    emotionally handicapped • M Ed
    engineering • MAT

    English education • M Ed
    general science • MAT
    home economics education • M Ed
    industrial education • M Ed
    learning disabilities • M Ed
    mathematics • MAT
    mathematics education • M Ed
    mentally handicapped • M Ed
    science education • M Ed
    secondary counselor education • M Ed
    secondary education • M Ed
    social studies education • M Ed
    special education • M Ed
    speech pathology • MAT

UNIVERSITY OF SOUTH CAROLINA
Columbia, SC 29208

http://www.sc.edu

Public coed university. *Enrollment: 25,447 graduate, professional, and undergraduate students. Graduate faculty: 1,125 full-time, 324 part-time. Computer facilities: Campuswide network is available with full Internet access. Total number of PCs/terminals supplied for student use: 2,500. Computer service fees are included with tuition and fees. Library facilities: Thomas Cooper Library plus 6 additional on-campus libraries. Graduate expenses: Tuition of $3894 per year full-time, $193 per credit hour part-time for state residents; $8114 per year full-time, $404 per credit hour part-time for nonresidents. Fees of $125 per year full-time, $37 per semester (minimum) part-time. General application contact: Dr. Marcia G. Welsh, Dean of the Graduate School, 803-777-4811.*

Graduate School
Dr. Marcia G. Welsh, Dean
Programs in:
    anatomy • PhD
    experimental pathology • PhD
    genetic counseling • MS
    gerontology • Certificate
    microbiology and immunology • PhD
    nurse anesthesia • MBS
    pharmaceutical sciences • MS, PhD
    pharmacology • PhD
    physiology • PhD
    rehabilitation counseling • MRC

College of Applied Professions Sciences
Dr. John Duffy, Interim Dean
Program in:
    hotel, restaurant and tourism administration • MHRTA

College of Business Administration
Dr. David L. Shrock, Dean
Programs in:
    business administration • IMBA, M Acc, MBA, MS, PhD
    economics • MA, PhD
    human resources • MHR

University of South Carolina (continued)
   international business • MIBS
   taxation • M Tax

College of Criminal Justice
Cole Blease Graham, Dean
Program in:
   criminal justice • MCJ

College of Education
Dr. Frederic Melway, Interim Dean
Programs in:
   community and occupational education • M Ed, MA
   counseling education • Ed S, PhD
   curriculum and instruction • Ed D
   early childhood education • M Ed, MA, MAT, PhD
   educational administration • Ed S, M Ed, MA, PhD
   elementary education • M Ed, MA, MAT, PhD
   elementary school counseling • M Ed, MA
   foundations in education • PhD
   health education administration • Ed D
   higher education leadership • Certificate
   instructional technology • M Ed
   physical education • IMA, MAT, MS, PhD
   reading education • M Ed, MA, PhD
   secondary education • Ed D, IMA, M Ed, MA, MAT, MT
   secondary school counseling • M Ed, MA
   special education • MAT, PhD
   student and personnel services in higher education •
      M Ed, MA
   teaching • Ed S

College of Engineering
Dr. Craig A. Rogers, Dean
Programs in:
   chemical engineering • ME, MS, PhD
   civil and environmental engineering • ME, MS, PhD
   computer engineering • ME, MS, PhD
   electrical engineering • ME, MS, PhD
   mechanical engineering • ME, MS, PhD

College of Journalism
Judy VanSlyke Turk, Dean
Program in:
   journalism • MA, MMC, PhD

College of Liberal Arts
Dr. Gordon Smith, Interim Dean
Programs in:
   anthropology • MA
   art education • IMA, MA, MAT
   art history • MA
   art studio • MA
   clinical/community psychology • PhD
   comparative literature • MA, PhD
   creative writing • MFA
   English • MA, PhD
   English education • MAT
   experimental psychology • MA, PhD
   French • IMA, MA, MAT
   French education • IMA, MAT
   geography • MA, MS, PhD
   geography education • IMA, MAT
   German • MA

   German education • IMA, MAT
   historic preservation • MA
   history • MA, PhD
   history education • IMA, MAT
   international studies • MA, PhD
   linguistics • MA, PhD
   media arts • MMA
   museum management • Certificate
   philosophy • MA, PhD
   political science • MA, PhD
   public administration • MPA
   religious studies • MA
   school psychology • PhD
   sociology • MA, PhD
   Spanish • IMA, MA, MAT
   studio art • MFA
   teaching English as a foreign language • Certificate
   theater • IMA, MA, MAT, MFA
   women's studies • Certificate

College of Library and Information Science
Dr. Fred W. Roper, Dean
Program in:
   library and information science • Certificate, MLIS,
      Specialist

College of Nursing
Dr. Mary Ann Parsons, Dean
Programs in:
   advanced practice nursing • Certificate
   clinical nursing • MSN
   community mental health and psychiatric health nursing
      • MSN
   health nursing • MSN
   nursing administration • Certificate, MSN
   nursing science • PhD

College of Science and Mathematics
Dr. Gary Crawley, Dean
Programs in:
   biology • MS, PhD
   biology education • IMA, MAT
   chemistry and biochemistry • IMA, MAT, MS, PhD
   computer science • MS, PhD
   ecology/organismic biology • MS, PhD
   geological sciences • IMA, MAT, MS, PhD
   marine science • MS, PhD
   mathematics • MA, MS, PhD
   mathematics education • M Math, MAT
   molecular/cellular/developmental biology • MS, PhD
   physics and astronomy • IMA, MAT, MS, PhD
   statistics • MIS, MS, PhD

College of Social Work
Dr. Frank B. Raymond III, Dean
Program in:
   social work • MSW, PhD

School of Music
Dr. Manuel Alvarez, Dean
Programs in:
   composition • DMA, MM
   conducting • DMA, MM
   jazz studies • MM

music education • MM Ed, PhD
music history • MM
music performance • Certificate
music theory • MM
opera theater • MM
performance • DMA, MM
piano pedagogy • DMA, MM

School of Public Health
Dr. Harris Pastides, Dean
Programs in:
    alcohol and drug studies • Certificate
    biostatistics • Dr PH, MPH, MSPH, PhD
    environmental quality • MPH, MSPH, PhD
    epidemiology • Dr PH, MPH, MSPH, PhD
    exercise science • DPT, MS, PhD
    general public health • MPH
    hazardous materials management • MPH, MSPH, PhD
    health administration • Dr PH, MHA, MPH, PhD
    health education administration • Ed D
    health promotion and education • Dr PH, MAT, MPH,
        MS, MSPH, PhD
    industrial hygiene • MPH, MSPH, PhD
    school health education • Certificate
    speech language pathology and audiology • MCD, MSP,
        PhD

School of the Environment
Dr. Bruce C. Coull, Dean
Program in:
    earth and environmental resources management •
        MEERM

College of Pharmacy
Dr. Farid Sadik, Dean
Programs in:
    pharmaceutical sciences • MS, PhD
    pharmacy • Pharm D

Law School
John Montgomery, Dean
Program in:
    law • JD

School of Medicine
Dr. Larry R. Faulkner, Dean
Programs in:
    anatomy • PhD
    experimental pathology • PhD
    genetic counseling • MS
    medicine • MD
    microbiology and immunology • PhD
    nurse anesthesia • MBS
    pharmacology • PhD
    physiology • PhD
    rehabilitation counseling • MRC

WINTHROP UNIVERSITY
Rock Hill, SC 29733

http://www.winthrop.edu/

Public coed comprehensive institution. *Enrollment: 5,574 graduate, professional, and undergraduate students. Graduate faculty: 14/ full-time. Computer facilities: Campuswide network is available with full Internet access. Total number of PCs/terminals supplied for student use: 236. Computer service fees are included with tuition and fees. Library facilities: Ida Jane Dacus Library. Graduate expenses: $3928 per year full-time, $164 per credit hour part-time for state residents; $7060 per year full-time, $294 per credit hour part-time for nonresidents. General application contact: Sharon Johnson, Director of Graduate Studies, 803-323-2204.*

College of Arts and Sciences
Dr. Betsy Brown, Dean
Programs in:
    biology • MS
    English • MA
    history • MA
    human nutrition • MS
    liberal arts • MLA
    mathematics • M Math
    psychology • MS, SSP
    Spanish • MA

College of Education
Dr. Thomas Powell, Dean
Programs in:
    agency counseling • M Ed
    business education • MAT, MS
    curriculum development • Ed S
    educational administration • Ed S, M Ed
    educational media • M Ed
    elementary education • Ed S, M Ed
    family and consumer sciences • MS
    physical education • MS
    reading education • M Ed
    school counseling • M Ed
    secondary education • Ed S, M Ed, MAT
    special education • Ed S, M Ed

School of Business Administration
Dr. Roger Weikle, Dean
Program in:
    business administration • MBA

School of Visual and Performing Arts
Dr. David Franklin, Dean
Programs in:
    art • MFA
    art education • MA
    music education • MME
    performance • MM

SOUTH DAKOTA

NORTHERN STATE UNIVERSITY
Aberdeen, SD 57401-7198

http://www.northern.edu/

Public coed comprehensive institution. *Enrollment: 2,464 graduate, professional, and undergraduate students. Graduate faculty: 98 full-time. Computer facilities: Campuswide network is available with full Internet access. Total number of PCs/terminals supplied for student use: 397. Computer service fees are included with tuition and fees. Library facilities: Williams Library and Learning Resources Center. Graduate expenses: Tuition of $1999 per year full-time, $83 per credit hour part-time for state residents; $6034 per year full-time, $251 per credit hour part-time for nonresidents. Fees of $954 per year full-time, $40 per credit hour part-time. General application contact: Dr. Sharon Tebben, Director of Graduate Studies, 605-626-2558.*

Division of Graduate Studies in Education

Dr. Sharon Tebben, Director of Graduate Studies
Programs in:
elementary classroom teaching • MS Ed
elementary school administration • MS Ed
guidance and counseling • MS Ed
health, physical education, and coaching • MS Ed
language and literacy • MS Ed
secondary classroom teaching • MS Ed
secondary school administration • MS Ed
special education • MS Ed

SOUTH DAKOTA STATE UNIVERSITY
Brookings, SD 57007

http://www.sdstate.edu/

Public coed university. *Enrollment: 8,162 graduate, professional, and undergraduate students. Graduate faculty: 285 full-time. Computer facilities: Campuswide network is available with full Internet access. Total number of PCs/terminals supplied for student use: 300. Computer service fees are included with tuition and fees. Library facilities: Briggs Library. Graduate expenses: Tuition of $82 per credit hour for state residents; $242 per credit hour for nonresidents. Fees of $37 per credit hour. General application contact: David Hilderbrand, Dean of the Graduate School, 605-688-4181.*

Graduate School
David Hilderbrand, Acting Dean

College of Agriculture and Biological Sciences
Dr. Fred Cholick, Dean
Programs in:
agronomy • MS, PhD
analytical chemistry • MS, PhD
animal science • MS, PhD
biochemistry • MS, PhD
biological sciences • PhD
biology • MS
chemistry • MS, PhD
dairy science • MS, PhD
economics • MS
entomology • MS
inorganic chemistry • MS, PhD
microbiology • MS
organic chemistry • MS, PhD
physical chemistry • MS, PhD
plant pathology • MS
rural sociology • MS, PhD
wildlife and fisheries sciences • MS

College of Arts and Science
Dr. Herbert Cheever, Dean
Programs in:
analytical chemistry • MS, PhD
biochemistry • MS, PhD
chemistry • MS, PhD
communication studies and theatre • MS
English • MA
geography • MS
health, physical education and recreation • MS
inorganic chemistry • MS, PhD
journalism • MS
organic chemistry • MS, PhD
physical chemistry • MS, PhD

College of Education and Counseling
Dr. Dee Hopkins, Dean
Programs in:
counseling and human resource development • MS
curriculum and instruction • M Ed
educational administration • M Ed

College of Engineering
Dr. Duane Sander, Dean
Programs in:
agricultural engineering • MS, PhD
atmospheric, environmental, and water resources • PhD
civil engineering • MS
computer science • MS
electrical engineering • MS
engineering • MS
environmental engineering • MS
industrial management • MS
mathematics • MS
mechanical engineering • MS
physics • MS

College of Family and Consumer Sciences
Dr. Laurie Stenberg Nichols, Dean
Program in:
family and consumer sciences • MS

College of Nursing

Dr. Roberta Olson, Dean
Program in:
nursing • MS

College of Pharmacy

Dr. Danny Lattin, Dean
Programs in:
pharmaceutical sciences • MS
pharmacy • Pharm D

UNIVERSITY OF SOUTH DAKOTA
Vermillion, SD 57069-2390

http://www.usd.edu/

Public coed university. *Enrollment: 7,750 graduate, professional, and undergraduate students. Graduate faculty: 369 full-time, 309 part-time. Library facilities: I. D. Weeks Library plus 2 additional on-campus libraries. Graduate expenses: Tuition of $1530 per year full-time, $85 per credit hour part-time for state residents; $4518 per year full-time, $251 per credit hour part-time for nonresidents. Fees of $792 per year full-time, $44 per credit hour part-time. General application contact: Shirley Andersen, Administrative Assistant, 605-677-6498.*

Graduate School

Dr. Charles N. Kaufman, Dean
Programs in:
administrative studies • MS
anatomy • MA, PhD
biochemistry and molecular biology • MA, PhD
interdisciplinary studies • MA
microbiology • MA, PhD
occupational therapy • MS
pharmacology • MA, PhD
physical therapy • MS
physiology • MA, PhD

College of Arts and Sciences

Dr. John Carlson, Dean
Programs in:
audiology • MA
biology • MA, MNS, PhD
chemistry • MA, MNS
clinical psychology • MA, PhD
computer science • MA
English • MA, PhD
history • MA
mathematics • MA, MNS
political science • MA
psychology • MA, PhD
public administration • MPA
social behavior • MA
speech communication • MA
speech-language pathology • MA

College of Fine Arts

John A. Day, Dean
Programs in:
art • MFA
mass communications • MA
music • MM
theatre • MA, MFA

School of Business

Dr. Jerry Johnson, Dean
Programs in:
accounting • MP Acc
business administration • MBA

School of Education

Dr. Larry Bright, Dean
Programs in:
counseling and psychology in education • Ed D, Ed S, MA
curriculum and instruction • Ed D, Ed S
educational administration • Ed D, Ed S, MA
elementary education • MA
health, physical education and recreation • MA
secondary education • MA
special education • MA

School of Law

Barry R. Vickrey, Dean
Program in:
law • JD

School of Medicine

Dr. Robert Talley, Vice President, Health Affairs/Dean
Programs in:
anatomy • MA, PhD
biochemistry and molecular biology • MA, PhD
medicine • MD
microbiology • MA, PhD
occupational therapy • MS
pharmacology • MA, PhD
physical therapy • MS
physiology • MA, PhD

TENNESSEE

AUSTIN PEAY STATE UNIVERSITY
Clarksville, TN 37044-0001

http://www.apsu.edu/

Public coed comprehensive institution. *Enrollment: 7,803 graduate, professional, and undergraduate students. Graduate faculty: 71 full-time, 18 part-time. Computer facilities: Campuswide network is available with full Internet access. Total number of PCs/terminals supplied for student use: 395. Computer service fees are included with tuition and fees. Library facilities: Felix Woodward Library. Graduate expenses: Tuition of $2438 per year full-time, $123 per semester hour part-time for state residents; $7034 per year full-time, $324 per semester hour part-time for nonresidents. Fees of*

Austin Peay State University (continued)
$484 per year (minimum) full-time, $154 per semester (minimum) part-time. General application contact: Gaines Hunt, Assistant Vice President for Academic Affairs, 931-648-7414.

Graduate School
Gaines Hunt, Assistant Vice President for Academic Affairs
Program in:
  health and human performance • MA Ed, MS

College of Arts and Sciences
Richard Hogan, Dean
Programs in:
  biology • MS
  clinical psychology • MA
  communication arts • MA
  corporate communication • MA
  English • MA, MA Ed
  guidance and counseling • MS
  journalism • MA
  music • M Mu
  music education • M Mu
  psychological science • MA
  public relations • MA
  radio, television • MA
  school psychology • MA
  speech • MA
  theatre • MA

College of Education
Sutton Flynt, Dean
Programs in:
  administration and supervision • Ed S, MA Ed
  counseling and guidance • Ed S
  curriculum and instruction • MA Ed
  elementary education • Ed S, MA Ed
  reading • MA Ed
  school psychology • Ed S
  secondary education • Ed S
  special education • MA

BELMONT UNIVERSITY
Nashville, TN 37212-3757

http://www.belmont.edu/

Independent-religious coed comprehensive institution. *Enrollment: 2,986 graduate, professional, and undergraduate students. Graduate faculty: 43 full-time, 27 part-time. Computer facilities: Campuswide network is available with full Internet access. Total number of PCs/ terminals supplied for student use: 200. Computer services are offered at no charge. Library facilities: Lila D. Bunch Library. Graduate expenses: $560 per credit hour. General application contact: Dean of the appropriate school, 615-385-6785.*

Graduate Program in Nursing
Dr. Debra Wollaber, Acting Dean
Program in:
  nursing • MSN

Graduate Studies in Education
Dr. Norma Stevens, Associate Dean
Programs in:
  childcare administration • M Ed
  elementary education • M Ed
  English • M Ed
  music education • MME

Jack C. Massey Graduate School of Business
Dr. James Clapper, Dean
Program in:
  business • M Acc, MBA

Program in Occupational Therapy
Dr. Scott D. McPhee, Chair
Program in:
  occupational therapy • MS

Program in Physical Therapy
Dr. David G. Greathouse, Chair
Program in:
  physical therapy • MPT

CHRISTIAN BROTHERS UNIVERSITY
Memphis, TN 38104-5581

http://www.cbu.edu/

Independent-religious coed comprehensive institution. *Enrollment: 1,869 graduate, professional, and undergraduate students. Graduate faculty: 16 full-time, 11 part-time. Computer facilities: Campuswide network is available with full Internet access. Total number of PCs/ terminals supplied for student use: 150. Computer services are offered at no charge. Library facilities: Plough Library. Graduate expenses: Tuition of $325 per hour. Fees of $30 per semester. General application contact: Michael T. Smith, Director, MBA Program, 901-321-3317.*

Graduate Programs
Programs in:
  business administration • MBA
  engineering • MEM
  liberal arts • M Ed
  telecommunications and information systems
    management • MS

EAST TENNESSEE STATE UNIVERSITY
Johnson City, TN 37614-0734

http://www.etsu-tn.edu/

Public coed university. *Enrollment:* 10,823 graduate, professional, and undergraduate students. *Graduate faculty:* 290 full-time, 50 part-time. *Library facilities: Sherrod Library* plus 2 additional on-campus libraries. *Graduate expenses:* $2944 per year full-time, $158 per credit hour part-time for state residents; $7770 per year full-time, $369 per credit hour part-time for nonresidents. *General application contact: Dr. Peggy Cantrell, Interim Dean, 423-439-6146.*

School of Graduate Studies
Dr. Peggy Cantrell, Interim Dean
Programs in:
  anatomy and cell biology • MS, PhD
  biochemistry and molecular biology • MS, PhD
  biological sciences • MS
  chemistry • MS
  microbiology • MS, PhD
  pharmacology • MS, PhD
  physiology • MS, PhD

College of Applied Science and Technology
Dr. James Hales, Dean
Programs in:
  clinical nutrition • MS
  computer science • MS
  geography • MA
  information sciences • MS
  technology • MS

College of Arts and Sciences
Dr. Don Johnson, Interim Dean
Programs in:
  art and design • MA, MFA
  biological sciences • MS
  chemistry • MS
  clinical psychology • MA
  criminal justice and criminology • MA
  English • MA
  general psychology • MA
  history • MA
  mathematics • MS
  music • M Mu Ed
  psychology • MA
  sociology • MA

College of Business
Dr. Allan D. Spritzer, Dean
Programs in:
  accountancy • M Acc
  business administration • MBA
  public management • MCM, MPM

College of Education
Dr. Martha Collins, Dean
Programs in:
  counseling • M Ed, MA
  early childhood learning and development • M Ed, MA
  educational leadership • Ed D, Ed S, M Ed
  elementary education • M Ed, MAT
  media services • M Ed
  physical education • M Ed, MA
  reading • M Ed, MA
  secondary education • M Ed, MAT
  special education • M Ed, MA
  story arts • M Ed, MA
  supervision of instruction • M Ed

College of Nursing
Dr. Joellen Edwards, Dean
Programs in:
  advanced nursing practice • Post Master's Certificate
  nursing • MSN

College of Public and Allied Health
Dr. Wilsie Bishop, Dean
Programs in:
  communicative disorders • MS
  environmental health • MSEH
  microbiology • MS
  public health • MPH

James H. Quillen College of Medicine
Dr. Joellen Edwards, Interim Vice President for Health Affairs
Programs in:
  anatomy and cell biology • MS, PhD
  biochemistry and molecular biology • MS, PhD
  biological sciences • MS
  chemistry • MS
  medicine • MD
  microbiology • MS, PhD
  pharmacology • MS, PhD
  physiology • MS, PhD

LINCOLN MEMORIAL UNIVERSITY
Harrogate, TN 37752-1901

http://www.lmu.edu/

Independent coed comprehensive institution. *Enrollment:* 1,811 graduate, professional, and undergraduate students. *Graduate faculty:* 10 full-time, 12 part-time. *Library facilities: Bert Vincent Memorial Library. Graduate expenses: Tuition of $7800 per year full-time, $210 per semester hour part-time. Fees of $300 per year full-time, $100 per year part-time. General application contact: Barbara McCune, Senior Assistant, Graduate Office, 423-869-6374.*

Program in Business Administration
Chet Brisley, Dean
Program in:
  business administration • MBA

Lincoln Memorial University (continued)
Program in Education
Dr. Fred Bedelle, Dean, School of Graduate Studies
Program in:
  education • Ed S, M Ed

MIDDLE TENNESSEE STATE UNIVERSITY
Murfreesboro, TN 37132

http://www.mtsu.edu/

Public coed university. *Enrollment: 18,366 graduate, professional, and undergraduate students. Graduate faculty: 389 full-time, 22 part-time. Computer facilities: Campuswide network is available with full Internet access. Total number of PCs/terminals supplied for student use: 3,000. Computer service fees are included with tuition and fees. Library facilities: Todd Library. Graduate expenses: Tuition of $2560 per year full-time, $129 per semester hour part-time for state residents; $7386 per year full-time, $340 per semester hour part-time for nonresidents. Fees of $486 per year full-time, $17 per semester (minimum) part-time. General application contact: Dr. Donald L. Curry, Dean of the College of Graduate Studies, 615-898-2840.*

College of Graduate Studies
Dr. Donald L. Curry, Dean

College of Basic and Applied Sciences
Dr. Earl E. Keese, Dean
Programs in:
  aerospace education • M Ed
  airport/airline management • MS
  asset management • MS
  biology • MS, MST
  chemistry • DA, MS
  computer science • MS
  engineering technology and industrial studies • MS, MVTE
  mathematics • MS
  mathematics education • MST
  natural science • MS

College of Business
Dr. Rick Elam, Dean
Programs in:
  accounting • MS
  business administration • MBA
  business education • MBE
  computer information systems • MS
  economics • DA, MA
  finance • MBA
  industrial relations • MA
  information systems • MS

College of Education
Dr. Robert Eaker, Dean
Programs in:
  administration and supervision • Ed S, M Ed
  business education • MBE
  child development and family studies • MS
  criminal justice administration • MCJ
  curriculum specialist • Ed S, M Ed
  early childhood education • M Ed
  elementary education • Ed S, M Ed
  health, physical education, recreation and safety • DA, MS
  industrial/organizational psychology • MA
  middle school education • M Ed
  nutrition and food science • MS
  psychology • MA
  reading • M Ed
  school counseling • Ed S, M Ed
  school psychology • Ed S
  secondary education • Ed S, M Ed
  special education • M Ed

College of Liberal Arts
Dr. John McDaniel, Dean
Programs in:
  English • DA, MA
  foreign languages and literatures • MAT
  historic preservation • DA
  history • DA, MA
  music • MA
  sociology • MA

College of Mass Communications
Dr. Deryl Leaming, Dean
Program in:
  mass communications • MS

TENNESSEE STATE UNIVERSITY
Nashville, TN 37209-1561

http://www.tnstate.edu/

Public coed comprehensive institution. *Enrollment: 8,625 graduate, professional, and undergraduate students. Graduate faculty: 208 full-time, 35 part-time. Computer facilities: Campuswide network is available with full Internet access. Computer service fees are included with tuition and fees. Library facilities: Brown-Daniel Library. Graduate expenses: $2962 per year full-time, $182 per credit hour part-time for state residents; $7788 per year full-time, $393 per credit hour part-time for nonresidents. General application contact: Dr. Clinton M. Lipsey, Dean of the Graduate School, 615-963-5901.*

Graduate School
Dr. Clinton M. Lipsey, Dean

College of Arts and Sciences
Dr. Bobby L. Lovett, Dean
Programs in:
   biology • MS, PhD
   chemistry • MS
   criminal justice • MCJ
   English • MA
   mathematics • MS
   music education • MS

College of Business
Dr. Tilden J. Curry, Dean
Program in:
   business • MBA

College of Education
Dr. Franklin Jones, Dean
Programs in:
   adult education • M Ed
   counseling • MS
   counseling and guidance • MS
   counseling psychology • PhD
   curriculum and instruction • M Ed
   curriculum planning • Ed D
   educational administration • Ed D, M Ed, MA Ed
   educational technology • M Ed
   elementary education • Ed D, M Ed, MA Ed
   elementary school counseling • MS
   health, physical education and recreation • MA Ed
   organizational counseling • MS
   psychology • MS, PhD
   reading • M Ed
   school psychology • MS, PhD
   secondary education • Ed D, MA Ed
   secondary instruction • M Ed
   secondary school counseling • MS
   special education • Ed D, M Ed, MA Ed

College of Engineering and Technology
Dr. Decatur B. Rogers, Dean
Program in:
   engineering and technology • ME

Institute of Government
Dr. A. Robert Thoeny, Director
Program in:
   public administration • MPA, PhD

School of Agriculture and Family Services
Dr. Troy Wakefield, Dean
Program in:
   agriculture and family services • MS

School of Allied Health Professions
Dr. Andrew Bond, Dean
Program in:
   allied health professions • M Ed

School of Nursing
Dr. Marion Anema, Dean
Program in:
   nursing • MS

TENNESSEE TECHNOLOGICAL UNIVERSITY
Cookeville, TN 38505

http://www.tntech.edu/

Public coed university. *Enrollment:* 8,163 graduate, professional, and undergraduate students. *Graduate faculty:* 341 full-time. *Library facilities: University Library. Graduate expenses: $2960 per year full-time, $147 per semester hour part-time for state residents; $7786 per year full-time, $358 per semester hour part-time for nonresidents. General application contact: Dr. Rebecca F. Quattlebaum, Dean of the Graduate School, 931-372-3233.*

Graduate School
Dr. Rebecca F. Quattlebaum, Dean

College of Arts and Sciences
Dr. Jack Armistead III, Dean
Programs in:
   chemistry • MS
   English • MA
   environmental biology • MS
   environmental sciences • PhD
   fish, game, and wildlife management • MS
   mathematics • MS

College of Business Administration
Dr. Virginia Moore, Director
Program in:
   business administration • MBA

College of Education
Dr. Karen I. Adams, Dean
Programs in:
   curriculum • Ed S, MA
   early childhood education • Ed S, MA
   educational psychology • Ed S, MA
   educational psychology and student personnel • Ed S, MA
   elementary education • Ed S, MA
   health and physical education • MA
   instructional leadership • Ed S, MA
   reading • Ed S, MA
   secondary education • Ed S, MA
   special education • Ed S, MA

College of Engineering
Dr. Charles Hickman, Interim Dean
Programs in:
   chemical engineering • MS, PhD
   civil engineering • MS, PhD
   electrical engineering • MS, PhD
   engineering • PhD
   industrial engineering • MS, PhD
   mechanical engineering • MS, PhD

TREVECCA NAZARENE UNIVERSITY
Nashville, TN 37210-2834

http://www.trevecca.edu/

Independent-religious coed comprehensive institution. *Enrollment: 1,457 graduate, professional, and undergraduate students.* Graduate faculty: *8 full-time, 18 part-time.* Computer facilities: *Campuswide network is available with full Internet access. Total number of PCs/terminals supplied for student use: 150. Computer service fees are included with tuition and fees.* Library facilities: *Mackey Library.* Graduate expenses: *Tuition of $230 per hour. Fees of $60 per year.* General application contact: *Dr. Stephen Pusey, Vice President of Academic Affairs, 615-248-1258.*

Graduate Division
Dr. Stephen Pusey, Vice President of Academic Affairs
Program in:
   organizational management • MA

Division of Education
Dr. Melvin Welch, Dean of Education
Programs in:
   educational leadership • M Ed
   elementary education • M Ed
   instructional effectiveness • M Ed

Division of Natural and Applied Sciences
Dr. Mike Movedock, Dean
Program in:
   physician assistant • MS

Division of Religious Studies
Dr. Tim Green, Dean
Program in:
   religion • MA

Division of Social and Behavioral Sciences
Dr. Randy Carden, Dean
Programs in:
   counseling • MA
   counseling psychology • MA
   marriage and family therapy • MMFT

TUSCULUM COLLEGE
Greeneville, TN 37743-9997

http://www.tusculum.edu/

Independent-religious coed comprehensive institution. *Enrollment: 1,516 graduate, professional, and undergraduate students.* Graduate faculty: *19 full-time, 33 part-time.* Computer facilities: *Campuswide network is available with full Internet access. Total number of PCs/terminals supplied for student use: 34. Computer service fees are included with tuition and fees.* Library facilities: *Albert Columbus Tate Library plus 1 additional on-campus library.* Graduate expenses:

$190 per credit hour (minimum). General application contact: *Dr. Suzanne T. Hine, Dean, 423-693-1177.*

Graduate School
Dr. Suzanne T. Hine, Vice President for Graduate and
   Professional Studies
Programs in:
   adult education • MA Ed
   K–12 • MA Ed
   organizational management • MAOM

THE UNIVERSITY OF MEMPHIS
Memphis, TN 38152

http://www.memphis.edu/

Public coed university. *Enrollment: 19,851 graduate, professional, and undergraduate students.* Computer facilities: *Campuswide network is available with full Internet access. Total number of PCs/terminals supplied for student use: 319. Computer service fees are included with tuition and fees.* Library facilities: *Ned R. McWherter Library plus 5 additional on-campus libraries.* Graduate expenses: *$2862 per year full-time, $166 per credit hour part-time for state residents; $6696 per year full-time, $379 per credit hour part-time for nonresidents.* General application contact: *Dianne Horgan, Associate Dean of Graduate School, 901-678-2531.*

Graduate School
Dr. Linda L. Brinkley, Dean

College of Arts and Sciences
Dr. Ralph J. Faudree, Dean
Programs in:
   anthropology • MA
   applied mathematics • MS
   applied statistics • PhD
   biology • MS, PhD
   botany • MS, PhD
   chemistry • MS, PhD
   city and regional planning • MCRP
   clinical psychology • PhD
   computer science • PhD
   computer sciences • MS
   creative writing • MFA
   criminology and criminal justice • MA
   English • MA
   experimental psychology • PhD
   French • MA
   geography • MA, MS
   geology • MS
   geophysics • MS, PhD
   health administration • MHA
   health services administration • MPA
   history • MA, PhD
   human resources administration • MPA
   invertebrate zoology • MS, PhD
   mathematics • PhD

non-profit administration • MPA
philosophy • MA, PhD
physics • MS
political science • MA
psychology • MS
public administration • MPA
school psychology • MA, PhD
sociology • MA
Spanish • MA
statistics • MS, PhD
urban management and planning • MPA
vertebrate zoology • MS, PhD

College of Communication and Fine Arts
Dr. Richard R. Ranta, Dean
Programs in:
applied music • M Mu
ceramics • MFA
communication • MA
communication arts • PhD
composition • DMA
Egyptian art and archaeology • MA
film and video production • MA
general art history • MA
general journalism • MA
graphic design • MFA
interior design • MFA
journalism administration • MA
music education • DMA, M Mu
music history • M Mu
musicology • PhD
music theory • M Mu
Orff-Schulwerk • M Mu
painting • MFA
performance • DMA
piano pedagogy • M Mu
printmaking/photography • MFA
sacred music • DMA, M Mu
sculpture • MFA
Suzuki pedagogy-piano • M Mu
theatre • MFA

College of Education
Dr. Nathan L. Essex, Dean
Programs in:
adult education • Ed D
clinical nutrition • MS
community agency counseling • MS
community education • Ed D
consumer science and education • MS
counseling and personnel services • Ed D, MS
counseling psychology • PhD
early childhood education • Ed D, MAT, MS
education • Ed S
educational leadership • Ed D
educational psychology • Ed D, MS
educational psychology and research • Ed D, MS, PhD
educational research • Ed D, MS
elementary education • MAT
exercise and sport science • MS
health promotion • MS
higher education • Ed D
instruction and curriculum • Ed D, MS

instruction design and technology • Ed D, MS
leadership • MS
policy studies • Ed D
reading • Ed D, MS
rehabilitation counseling • MS
school administration and supervision • MS
school counseling • MS
secondary education • MAT
special education • Ed D, MAT, MS
sport and leisure commerce • MS
student personnel services • MS

Division of Audiology and Speech Pathology
Dr. Maurice Mendel, Dean
Program in:
audiology and speech pathology • MA, PhD

Fogelman College of Business and Economics
Dr. Donna Randall, Dean
Programs in:
accounting • MBA, MS, PhD
accounting systems • MS
economics • MA, MBA, PhD
executive business administration • MBA
finance • PhD
finance, insurance, and real estate • MBA, MS
international business administration • MBA
management • MBA, MS, PhD
management information systems • MBA, MS
management information systems and decision sciences • PhD
management science • MBA
marketing • MBA, MS, PhD
real estate development • MS
taxation • MS

Herff College of Engineering
Dr. Richard C. Warder Jr., Dean
Programs in:
architectural engineering • MS
automatic control systems • MS
biomedical engineering • MS, PhD
biomedical systems • MS
civil engineering • PhD
communications and propagation systems • MS
design and mechanical engineering • MS
electrical engineering • PhD
electronics • MS
energy systems • MS
engineering computer systems • MS
environmental engineering • MS
foundation engineering • MS
industrial and systems engineering • MS
manufacturing engineering • MS
mechanical engineering • PhD
mechanical systems • MS
power systems • MS
structural engineering • MS
transportation engineering • MS
water resources engineering • MS

The University of Memphis (continued)
Cecil C. Humphreys School of Law
Donald J. Polden, Dean
Program in:
   law • JD

UNIVERSITY OF TENNESSEE AT CHATTANOOGA
Chattanooga, TN 37403-2598

http://www.utc.edu/

Public coed comprehensive institution. *Enrollment: 8,528 graduate, professional, and undergraduate students. Graduate faculty: 101 full-time, 21 part-time. Library facilities: T. Carter and Margaret Rawlings Lupton Library. Graduate expenses: $2864 per year full-time, $160 per credit hour part-time for state residents; $6806 per year full-time, $379 per credit hour part-time for nonresidents. General application contact: Dr. Deborah Arfken, Assistant Provost for Graduate Studies, 423-755-4667.*

Graduate Division
Dr. Deborah Arfken, Assistant Provost for Graduate Studies

College of Arts and Sciences
Dr. Timothy Summerlin, Dean
Programs in:
   English • MA
   environmental sciences • MS
   industrial/organizational psychology • MS
   music • MM
   public administration • MPA
   research psychology • MS
   school psychology • MS

School of Business Administration
Dr. Linda Fletcher, Dean
Programs in:
   accountancy • M Acc
   business administration • MBA
   economics • MBA
   finance • MBA
   marketing • MBA
   operations/production • MBA
   organizational management • MBA

School of Education
Dr. Mary Tanner, Dean
Programs in:
   athletic training • MS
   curriculum and instruction • M Ed
   early childhood education • M Ed
   elementary administration • M Ed
   guidance and counseling • M Ed
   reading • M Ed
   secondary administration • M Ed
   secondary education • M Ed
   special education • M Ed

School of Engineering
Dr. Greg Sedrick, Acting Dean
Programs in:
   computer science • MS
   engineering • MS
   engineering management • MS

School of Human Services
Dr. Galan Janeksela, Dean
Programs in:
   administration • MSN
   adult health • MSN
   criminal justice • MSCJ
   education • MSN
   family nurse practitioner • MSN
   nurse anesthesia • MSN
   physical therapy • MSPT

THE UNIVERSITY OF TENNESSEE AT MARTIN
Martin, TN 38238-1000

http://www.utm.edu/

Public coed comprehensive institution. *Enrollment: 6,012 graduate, professional, and undergraduate students. Graduate faculty: 128 full-time, 11 part-time. Computer facilities: Campuswide network is available with full Internet access. Total number of PCs/terminals supplied for student use: 400. Computer service fees are included with tuition and fees. Library facilities: Paul Meek Library. Graduate expenses: $2962 per year full-time, $165 per semester hour part-time for state residents; $7788 per year full-time, $434 per semester hour part-time for nonresidents. General application contact: Dr. K. Paul Jones, Associate Vice Chancellor and Dean, 901-587-7012.*

Graduate Studies
Dr. K. Paul Jones, Associate Vice Chancellor and Dean

School of Agriculture and Human Environment
Dr. James Byford, Dean
Programs in:
   child development and family relations • MSHES
   food science and nutrition • MSHES

School of Business Administration
Dr. Gary Young, Dean
Programs in:
   accounting • M Ac
   business administration • MBA

School of Education
Dr. Linda Murphy, Dean
Programs in:
   counseling • MS Ed
   teaching • MS Ed

UNIVERSITY OF TENNESSEE, KNOXVILLE
Knoxville, TN 37996

http://www.utk.edu/

Public coed university. Enrollment: 25,410 graduate, professional, and undergraduate students. Graduate faculty: 1,254 full-time, 205 part-time. Computer facilities: Campuswide network is available with full Internet access. Computer service fees are applied as a separate charge. Library facilities: John C. Hodges Library plus 4 additional on-campus libraries. Graduate expenses: $3354 per year full-time, $181 per semester hour part-time for state residents; $8410 per year full-time, $462 per semester hour part-time for nonresidents. General application contact: Diana Lopez, Director of Graduate Admissions, 423-947-3251.

Graduate School
Dr. C. W. Minkel, Dean

College of Agricultural Sciences and Natural Resources
Dr. John Riley, Dean
Programs in:
  agribusiness • MS
  agricultural economics • MS, PhD
  agricultural education • MS
  agricultural extension education • MS
  animal anatomy • PhD
  biosystems engineering • MS, PhD
  biosystems engineering technology • MS
  breeding • MS, PhD
  crop physiology and ecology • MS, PhD
  entomology • MS
  floricultural science and technology • MS
  food chemistry • PhD
  food microbiology • PhD
  food processing • PhD
  food science and technology • MS, PhD
  forestry • MS
  management • MS, PhD
  nursery science and technology • MS
  nutrition • MS, PhD
  physiology • MS, PhD
  plant breeding and genetics • MS, PhD
  plant pathology • MS
  rural sociology • MS
  sensory evaluation of foods • PhD
  soil science • MS, PhD
  turfgrass science and technology • MS
  wildlife and fisheries science • MS

College of Architecture and Planning
Marleen Davis, Dean
Programs in:
  architecture • M Arch
  environmental planning • MSP
  land-use planning • MSP
  real estate development planning • MSP
  transportation planning • MSP

College of Arts and Sciences
Dr. Lorayne Lester, Dean
Programs in:
  accompanying • MM
  acting • MFA
  American history • PhD
  analytical chemistry • MS, PhD
  applied linguistics • PhD
  applied mathematics • MS
  archaeology • MA, PhD
  audiology • MA, PhD
  behavior • MS, PhD
  biochemistry and cellular and molecular biology • MS, PhD
  biological anthropology • MA, PhD
  biotechnology • MS
  botany • MS, PhD
  ceramics • MFA
  chemical physics • PhD
  choral conducting • MM
  clinical psychology • PhD
  composition • MM
  computer science • MS, PhD
  costume design • MFA
  criminology • MA, PhD
  cultural anthropology • MA, PhD
  drawing • MFA
  ecology • MS, PhD
  energy, environment, and resources policy • MA, PhD
  English • MA, PhD
  environmental chemistry • MS, PhD
  European history • PhD
  evolutionary biology • MS, PhD
  experimental psychology • MA, PhD
  French • MA, PhD
  geography • MS, PhD
  geology • MS, PhD
  German • MA, PhD
  graphic design • MFA
  hearing science • PhD
  history • MA
  inorganic chemistry • MS, PhD
  instrumental conducting • MM
  inter-area • MFA
  Italian • PhD
  jazz • MM
  lighting design • MFA
  mathematical ecology • PhD
  mathematics • M Math, MS, PhD
  media arts • MFA
  medical ethics • MA, PhD
  microbiology • MS, PhD
  music education • MM
  musicology • MM
  organic chemistry • MS, PhD
  painting • MFA
  performance • MM
  philosophy • MA, PhD
  physical chemistry • MS, PhD
  physics • MS, PhD
  piano pedagogy and literature • MM
  plant physiology and genetics • MS, PhD
  political economy • MA, PhD

University of Tennessee, Knoxville (continued)
　　political science • MA, PhD
　　polymer chemistry • MS, PhD
　　Portuguese • PhD
　　printmaking • MFA
　　psychology • MA
　　public administration • MPA
　　religious studies • MA
　　Russian • PhD
　　sacred music • MM
　　scene design • MFA
　　sculpture • MFA
　　Spanish • MA, PhD
　　speech and language pathology • PhD
　　speech and language science • PhD
　　speech pathology • MA
　　string pedagogy • MM
　　theatre technology • MFA
　　theoretical chemistry • PhD
　　theory • MM
　　watercolor • MFA
　　zooarchaeology • MA, PhD

College of Business Administration
Warren Neel, Dean
Programs in:
　　accounting • M Acc, PhD
　　business administration • Exec MBA, PMBA
　　economics • MA, MBA, PhD
　　entrepreneurship/new venture analysis • MBA
　　environmental management • MBA
　　finance • MBA, PhD
　　financial auditing • M Acc
　　forest industries management • MBA
　　global business • MBA
　　industrial/organizational psychology • MS, PhD
　　industrial statistics • MS
　　logistics and transportation • MBA, PhD
　　management • MBA, PhD
　　manufacturing management • MBA
　　marketing • MBA, PhD
　　statistics • MBA, MS, PhD
　　systems • M Acc
　　taxation • M Acc

College of Communications
Dr. Dwight Teeter, Dean
Programs in:
　　advertising • MS, PhD
　　broadcasting • MS, PhD
　　communications • MS, PhD
　　information sciences • PhD
　　journalism • MS, PhD
　　public relations • MS, PhD
　　speech communication • PhD

College of Education
Dr. Glennon Rowell, Dean
Programs in:
　　adult education • Ed D, MS, PhD
　　art education • MS
　　college student personnel • MS
　　community counseling • MS
　　counseling psychology • PhD

　　cultural studies in education • MS, PhD
　　curriculum • Ed D, Ed S, MS
　　early childhood education • PhD
　　early childhood special education • MS
　　educational administration and supervision/higher education • Ed D, Ed S, MS, PhD
　　educational psychology • PhD
　　educational psychology: collaborative learning • Ed D
　　educational research • Ed D
　　education of deaf and hard of hearing • MS
　　elementary education • Ed D, Ed S, MS, PhD
　　English education • Ed D, Ed S, MS
　　English, foreign language and ESL education • PhD
　　exercise science • MS, PhD
　　foreign language/ESL education • Ed D, Ed S, MS
　　higher education • Ed D
　　individual and collaborative learning • MS
　　instructional media and technology • Ed D, Ed S, MS
　　instructional technology/curriculum • PhD
　　leadership for teaching and learning • Ed D
　　literacy studies • PhD
　　mathematics education • Ed D, Ed S, MS
　　math science and social studies education • PhD
　　modified and comprehensive special education • MS
　　reading education • Ed D, Ed S, MS
　　rehabilitation and special education • PhD
　　rehabilitation counseling • MS
　　research/assessment/evaluation • PhD
　　school counseling • Ed S, MS
　　school psychology • Ed S, PhD
　　science education • Ed D, Ed S, MS
　　social foundations • MS
　　social sciences education • Ed D, Ed S, MS
　　sport management • MS
　　teaching and learning • Ed S

College of Engineering
Dr. Jerry Stoneking, Dean
Programs in:
　　aerospace engineering • MS, PhD
　　biomedical engineering • MS, PhD
　　chemical engineering • MS, PhD
　　civil engineering • MS, PhD
　　composite materials • MS, PhD
　　computational mechanics • MS, PhD
　　engineering management • MS
　　engineering science • MS, PhD
　　environmental engineering • MS
　　fluid mechanics • MS, PhD
　　industrial engineering • MS, PhD
　　manufacturing systems • MS
　　mechanical engineering • MS, PhD
　　metallurgical engineering • MS, PhD
　　nuclear engineering • MS, PhD
　　optical engineering • MS, PhD
　　polymer engineering • MS, PhD
　　radiological engineering • MS
　　solid mechanics • MS, PhD
　　traditional industrial engineering • MS

College of Human Ecology

Dr. Jacky DeJonge, Dean
Programs in:
child development • MS, PhD
community health • PhD
community health education • MPH
family studies • MS, PhD
gerontology • MPH
health education • Ed D
health planning/administration • MPH
health promotion and health education • MS
hospitality management • MS
human ecology • Ed S, MS
human resource development • PhD
interior design • MS
nutrition • MS
nutrition science • MS, PhD
public health nutrition • MS
recreation administration • MS
retail and consumer sciences • MS
retailing and consumer sciences • PhD
safety education and service • MS
textile science • MS, PhD
therapeutic recreation • MS
tourism • MS
training and development • MS

College of Nursing

Dr. Joan L. Creasia, Dean
Program in:
nursing • MSN, PhD

College of Social Work

Dr. Karen Sowers-Hoag, Dean
Programs in:
clinical social work practice • MSSW
management and community practice • MSSW
social work • PhD

College of Veterinary Medicine

Dr. G. M. H. Shires, Dean
Program in:
veterinary medicine • DVM

School of Biomedical Sciences

Dr. Raymond Popp, Director
Program in:
biomedical sciences • MS, PhD

School of Information Sciences

Dr. C. W. Minkel, Acting Head
Program in:
information sciences • MS

College of Law

Karen R. Britton, Director of Admissions and Career
Services
Program in:
law • JD

VANDERBILT UNIVERSITY
Nashville, TN 37240-1001

http://www.vanderbilt.edu/

Independent coed university. *Enrollment:* 10,253 graduate, professional, and undergraduate students. *Graduate faculty:* 1,930 full-time, 1,274 part-time. Computer facilities: *Campuswide network is available with full Internet access. Total number of PCs/terminals supplied for student use: 400. Computer services are offered at no charge.* Library facilities: *Central Library plus 8 additional on-campus libraries.* Graduate expenses: *Tuition of $16,452 per year full-time, $914 per semester hour part-time. Fees of $236 per year.* General application contact: *Peter W. Reed, Associate Dean, Graduate Studies and Research, 615-322-3943.*

Divinity School

Dr. Joseph C. Hough Jr., Dean
Program in:
theology • M Div, MTS

Graduate School

Russell G. Hamilton, Dean for Graduate Studies and
Research
Programs in:
anthropology • MA, PhD
astronomy • MS
biochemistry • MS, PhD
biology • MAT, MS, PhD
biomedical engineering • MS, PhD
biomedical sciences • PhD
cell biology • MS, PhD
cellular and molecular pathology • PhD
chemistry • MA, MAT, MS, PhD
classical studies • MA, MAT, PhD
comparative literature • MA, PhD
economics • MA, MAT, PhD
educational leadership • MS, PhD
English • MA, MAT, PhD
finance • PhD
fine arts • MA, MAT
French • MA, MAT, PhD
geology • MS
German • MA, MAT, PhD
hearing and speech sciences • MS, PhD
history • MA, MAT, PhD
Latin American studies • MA
liberal arts and science • MLAS
marketing • PhD
mathematics • MA, MAT, MS, PhD
microbiology and immunology • MS, PhD
molecular biology • MS, PhD
molecular physiology and biophysics • PhD
neuroscience • PhD
nursing science • PhD
operations management • PhD
organizational studies • PhD
pharmacology • PhD
philosophy • MA, PhD
physics • MA, MAT, MS, PhD

Vanderbilt University (continued)

> policy development and program evaluation • MS, PhD
> political science • MA, MAT, PhD
> Portuguese • MA
> psychology • MA, PhD
> psychology and human development • MS, PhD
> religion • MA, PhD
> sociology • MA, PhD
> Spanish • MA, MAT, PhD
> Spanish and Portuguese • PhD
> special education • MS, PhD
> teaching and learning • MS, PhD

Owen Graduate School of Management

Martin S. Geisel, Dean
Programs in:
> business administration • MBA
> executive business administration • MBA
> finance • PhD
> international executive business administration • MBA
> marketing • PhD
> operations management • PhD
> organizational studies • PhD

Peabody College

Dr. James W. Pellegrino, Dean
Programs in:
> curriculum and instruction • M Ed
> early childhood education • Ed D, M Ed
> elementary education • Ed D, M Ed
> English education • Ed D, M Ed
> general administrative leadership • Ed D, Ed S, M Ed
> health promotion education • M Ed
> higher education • Ed D, Ed S, M Ed
> human development counseling • M Ed
> human resource development • Ed D, M Ed
> mathematics education • Ed D, M Ed
> policy development and program evaluation • MPP
> psychology and human development • MS, PhD
> reading education • Ed D, M Ed
> school administration • Ed D, Ed S, M Ed
> science education • Ed D, M Ed
> secondary education • M Ed
> social studies education • Ed D, M Ed
> special education • Ed D, Ed S, M Ed, MS, PhD

School of Engineering

Kenneth F. Galloway, Dean
Programs in:
> biomedical engineering • MS, PhD
> chemical engineering • M Eng, MS, PhD
> civil engineering • M Eng, MS, PhD
> computer science • M Eng, MS, PhD
> electrical engineering • M Eng, MS, PhD
> environmental engineering • M Eng, MS, PhD
> management of technology • M Eng, MS, PhD
> materials science and engineering • MS, PhD
> mechanical engineering • M Eng, MS, PhD

School of Law

Kent D. Syverud, Dean
Program in:
> law • JD

School of Medicine

Dr. John E. Chapman, Dean
Programs in:
> medicine • MD
> public health • MPH

School of Nursing

Dr. Colleen Conway-Welch, Dean
Programs in:
> adult acute care nurse practitioner • MSN
> family nurse practitioner • MSN
> gerontology nurse practitioner • MSN
> health systems management • MSN
> neonatal critical care practitioner • MSN
> neonatal nurse practitioner • MSN
> nurse midwifery • MSN
> nursing science • PhD
> occupational health/adult health nurse practitioner • MSN
> pediatric nurse practitioner • MSN
> psychiatric-mental health nurse practitioner • MSN
> women's health nurse practitioner • MSN

TEXAS

ABILENE CHRISTIAN UNIVERSITY
Abilene, TX 79699-9100

http://www.acu.edu/

Independent-religious coed comprehensive institution. *Enrollment:* 4,542 graduate, professional, and undergraduate students. Graduate faculty: *1 full-time, 157 part-time.* Computer facilities: *Campuswide network is available with full Internet access. Total number of PCs/terminals supplied for student use: 500. Computer service fees are included with tuition and fees.* Library facilities: *Margaret and Herman Brown Library.* Graduate expenses: *Tuition of $308 per credit hour. Fees of $430 per year full-time, $85 per semester (minimum) part-time.* General application contact: *Danelle Brand, Assistant Dean of the Graduate School, 915-674-2355.*

Graduate School

Dr. Carley Dodd, Dean
Program in:
> organizational and human resource development • MS

College of Arts and Sciences

Dr. Coleen Durrington, Dean
Programs in:
> American religious history • MA
> associate school psychology • MS

clinical counseling • MS
counseling psychology • MS
educational diagnosis • M Ed
elementary teaching • M Ed
family studies • MS
general psychology • MS
gerontology • MS
guidance services • M Ed
history • MA
human communication • MA
journalism and mass communication • MA
liberal arts • MLA
literature • MA
reading specialist • M Ed
religious communication • MS
school administration • M Ed
school supervision • M Ed
secondary teaching • M Ed
social services administration • MS
writing • MA

College of Biblical and Family Studies
Dr. Jack Reese, Dean
Programs in:
biblical and related studies • MA, MS
Christian education • MS
Christian ministry • MS
Christian youth and family ministry • MS
church history • MA
divinity • M Div
doctrinal studies • MA
history of Christian thought • MA
marriage and family therapy • MMFT
ministry • D Min
missions • M Miss, MA, MS
New Testament • MA
New Testament Greek • MA
Old Testament • MA
theology • MA

College of Business Administration
Dr. Monty Lynn, Graduate Adviser
Programs in:
accountancy • M Acc
business administration • MBA

School of Nursing
Dr. Corinne Bonnett, Dean
Program in:
nursing • MS, MSN

AMBER UNIVERSITY
Garland, TX 75041-5595

http://www.amberu.edu/

Independent-religious coed upper-level institution. *Enrollment: 1,500 graduate, professional, and undergraduate students. Graduate faculty: 16 full-time, 45 part-time. Library facilities: main library. Graduate expenses: Tuition of $150 per semester hour. Fees of $25*

per year. General application contact: Dr. Algia Allen, Academic Dean, 972-279-6511 Ext. 135.

Graduate School
Dr. Algia Allen, Academic Dean
Programs in:
counseling • MA
general business • MBA
human relations and business • MA, MS
management • MBA
professional development • MA

 # ANGELO STATE UNIVERSITY
San Angelo, TX 76909

http://www.angelo.edu/

Public coed comprehensive institution. *Enrollment: 6,234 graduate, professional, and undergraduate students. Graduate faculty: 112 full-time, 8 part-time. Computer facilities: Campuswide network is available with full Internet access. Total number of PCs/terminals supplied for student use: 305. Computer service fees are included with tuition and fees. Library facilities: Porter Henderson Library. Graduate expenses: Tuition of $1022 per year full-time, $36 per semester hour part-time for state residents; $7382 per year full-time, $246 per semester hour part-time for nonresidents. Fees of $1140 per year full-time, $165 per semester (minimum) part-time. General application contact: Jackie Droll, Secretary, Office of the Graduate Dean, 915-942-2169.*

Graduate School
Dr. Carol B. Diminnie, Graduate Dean
Program in:
interdisciplinary studies • MA, MS

College of Liberal and Fine Arts
Dr. E. James Holland, Dean
Programs in:
art and music • MME
English • MA
history • MA
international studies • MA
public administration • MPA

College of Professional Studies
Dr. Robert K. Hegglund, Dean
Programs in:
accounting • MBA
computer science • MBA
curriculum and instruction • MA
educational diagnostics • M Ed
guidance and counseling • M Ed
management • MBA
reading specialist • M Ed
school administration • M Ed
supervision • M Ed

Angelo State University (continued)
College of Sciences
Dr. David Loyd, Dean
Programs in:
    animal science • MS
    biology • MS
    kinesiology • MS
    mathematics • MS
    nursing • MSN
    physical education • MAT
    psychology • MS

BAYLOR UNIVERSITY
Waco, TX 76798

http://www.baylor.edu/

Independent-religious coed university. *Enrollment: 12,472 gradu-ate, professional, and undergraduate students. Graduate faculty: 350. Computer facilities: Campuswide network is available with full Internet access. Total number of PCs/terminals supplied for student use: 800. Computer service fees are included with tuition and fees. Library facilities: Moody Memorial Library plus 5 additional on-campus libraries. Graduate expenses: Tuition of $7392 per year full-time, $308 per semester hour part-time. Fees of $1024 per year. General application contact: Dr. Darden Powers, Interim Dean of the Graduate School, 254-710-3588.*

Graduate School
Dr. Darden Powers, Interim Dean
Programs in:
    American studies • MA
    Christian theology • MCT
    environmental economics • MS

Academy of Health Sciences
Col. T. R. Byrne, Dean
Programs in:
    health care administration • MHA
    physical therapy • MPT

College of Arts and Sciences
Dr. Wallace Daniel Jr., Dean
Programs in:
    anthropology • MA, MAA
    applied sociology • PhD
    biology • MA, MS, PhD
    chemistry • MS, PhD
    clinical gerontology • MCG
    clinical psychology • MSCP, Psy D
    communication sciences and disorders • MA, MSCSD
    communication studies • MA
    directing • MFA
    earth science • MA
    economics • MA
    English • MA, PhD
    environmental biology • MS
    environmental studies • MES, MS
    geology • MS, PhD

gerontology • MSG
history • MA
international economics • MA, MIE, MS
international journalism • MIJ
international relations • MA
journalism • MA
limnology • MSL
mathematics • MA, MS
museum studies • MA
neuroscience • MA, PhD
philosophy • MA
physics • MA, MS, PhD
political science • MA
public policy and administration • MPPA
religion • MA, PhD
social work • MA
Spanish • MA
theater arts • MA

Hankamer School of Business
Dr. Donald F. Cunningham, Associate Dean for Graduate Programs
Programs in:
    accounting • M Acc, MT
    business administration • MBA
    economics • MS Eco
    information systems • MSIS
    information systems management • MBA
    international management • MIM

Institute for Graduate Statistics
Dr. Roger E. Kirk, Director
Program in:
    statistics • MA, PhD

Institute of Biomedical Studies
Dr. Darden Powers, Director
Program in:
    biomedical studies • MS, PhD

J. M. Dawson Institute of Church-State Studies
Dr. Derek H. Davis, Chairman
Program in:
    church-state studies • MA, PhD

School of Education
Dr. Fred Curtis, Director of Graduate Studies
Programs in:
    curriculum and instruction • Ed D, Ed S, MA, MS Ed
    educational administration • Ed D, Ed S, MA, MS Ed
    educational psychology • Ed S, MA, MS Ed, PhD
    health, human performance and recreation • MS Ed

School of Engineering and Computer Science
Dr. Greg Speegle, Director of Graduate Studies
Program in:
    computer science • MS

School of Music
Dr. Harry Elzinga, Director of Graduate Studies
Programs in:
    choral conducting • MM
    church music • MM
    composition • MM
    music education • MM

music history and literature • MM
music theory • MM
performance • MM
piano accompanying • MM
piano pedagogy and performance • MM
string pedagogy and performance • MM

School of Nursing
Dr. Phyllis S. Karns, Dean
Programs in:
family nurse practitioner • MSN
patient care management • MSN

George W. Truett Seminary
Dr. Bradley Creed, Dean
Program in:
theology • M Div

School of Law
Dr. Bradley J. B. Toben, Dean
Program in:
law • JD

DALLAS BAPTIST UNIVERSITY
Dallas, TX 75211-9299

http://www.dbu.edu/

Independent-religious coed comprehensive institution. *Enrollment:* 3,493 graduate, professional, and undergraduate students. *Graduate faculty: 40 full-time, 40 part-time.* Library facilities: *Vance Memorial Library.* Graduate expenses: *$285 per hour.* General application contact: *Travis Bundrick, Director of Graduate Programs, 214-333-5243.*

College of Business
Dr. Larry W. Rottmeyer, Dean
Programs in:
accounting • MBA
business administration • MBA
conflict resolution management • MA
finance • MBA
general management • MA
human resource management • MA
international business • MBA
management • MBA
management information systems • MBA
marketing • MBA

College of Humanities and Social Sciences
Dr. Michael E. Williams, Dean
Programs in:
counseling • MA
liberal arts • MLA

Dorothy M. Bush College of Education
Dr. Mike Rosato, Dean
Programs in:
early childhood education • M Ed
educational organization and administration • M Ed
elementary reading education • M Ed
general elementary education • M Ed
higher education • M Ed
reading specialist • M Ed
school counseling • M Ed

HARDIN–SIMMONS UNIVERSITY
Abilene, TX 79698-0001

http://www.hsutx.edu/

Independent-religious coed comprehensive institution. *Enrollment:* 2,312 graduate, professional, and undergraduate students. Graduate faculty: *67 full-time, 14 part-time.* Library facilities: *Richardson Library plus 1 additional on-campus library.* Graduate expenses: *Tuition of $280 per semester hour. Fees of $630 per year full-time.* General application contact: *Dr. J. Paul Sorrels, Dean of Graduate Studies, 915-670-1298.*

Graduate School
Dr. J. Paul Sorrels, Dean
Programs in:
English • MA
environmental management • MS
family ministry • MA
family psychology • MA
history • MA
physical therapy • MPT

Irvin School of Education
Dr. Peter Gilman, Dean
Programs in:
counseling and human development • M Ed
gifted education • M Ed
psychology • M Ed
reading • M Ed
reading specialist • M Ed
secondary physical education • M Ed
Spanish • M Ed
speech • M Ed
sports and recreation management • M Ed

Logsdon School of Theology
Dr. H. K. Neely, Dean
Programs in:
family ministry • MA
religion • MA
theology • M Div

School of Business and Finance
Dr. Lynn Gillette, Dean
Program in:
business and finance • MBA

Hardin–Simmons University (continued)

School of Music
Dr. Loyd Hawthorne, Dean
Programs in:
   applied literature • MM
   music education • MM
   theory-composition • MM

School of Nursing
Dr. Corine Bonnet, Dean
Program in:
   nursing • MSN

HOUSTON BAPTIST UNIVERSITY
Houston, TX 77074-3298

Independent-religious coed comprehensive institution. *Enrollment:* 2,109 graduate, professional, and undergraduate students. Graduate faculty: *48 full-time, 63 part-time.* Computer facilities: *Campuswide network is available with full Internet access. Total number of PCs/terminals supplied for student use: 120. Computer service fees are included with tuition and fees.* Library facilities: *Moody Library.* Graduate expenses: *Tuition of $300 per semester hour. Fees of $235 per quarter.* General application contact: *Ida Thompson, Acting Director of Graduate Admissions, 281-649-3302.*

Center for Health Studies
Dr. Betty Souther, Director
Programs in:
   congregational care nurse • MSN
   family nurse practitioner • MSN
   family nurse practitioner-congregational nurse • MSN
   health administration • MS

College of Arts and Humanities
Dr. Harold Raley, Dean
Programs in:
   liberal arts • MLA
   theological studies • MA

College of Business and Economics
Dr. R. Bruce Garrison, Dean
Programs in:
   accounting • MBA
   business administration • EMBA
   finance • MBA
   human resources management • MSHRM
   management, computing and systems • MSMCS
   marketing • MBA

College of Education and Behavioral Sciences
Dr. Bill Borgers, Dean
Programs in:
   bilingual education • M Ed
   counselor education • M Ed
   education • M Ed
   educational administration • M Ed
   educational diagnostician • M Ed
   elementary education • M Ed
   generic special education • M Ed
   psychology • MAP
   reading education • M Ed
   secondary education • M Ed

LAMAR UNIVERSITY
Beaumont, TX 77710

http://www.lamar.edu/

Public coed university. *Enrollment:* 8,143 graduate, professional, and undergraduate students. Graduate faculty: *148 full-time, 19 part-time.* Computer facilities: *Campuswide network is available with full Internet access. Total number of PCs/terminals supplied for student use: 751. Computer service fees are included with tuition and fees.* Library facilities: *Mary and John Gray Library.* Graduate expenses: *Tuition of $1296 per year full-time, $360 per year part-time for state residents; $6432 per year full-time, $1608 per year part-time for nonresidents. Fees of $238 per year full-time, $103 per year part-time.* General application contact: *Alicia Satre, Graduate Admissions Coordinator, 409-880-8350.*

College of Graduate Studies
Dr. Robert D. Moulton, Associate Vice President for Research and Dean

College of Arts and Sciences
Dr. Miriam J. Shillingsburg, Dean
Programs in:
   biology • MS
   chemistry • MS
   English and foreign languages • MA
   government • MPA
   history • MA
   psychology • MS
   public administration • MPA

College of Business
Dr. Robert A. Swerdlow, Associate Dean
Program in:
   business • MBA

College of Education and Human Development
Dr. LeBland McAdams, Dean
Programs in:
   administration • M Ed
   counseling and development • M Ed
   elementary education • Certificate, M Ed
   family and consumer sciences • MS
   health, kinesiology, and dance • MS
   secondary education • Certificate, M Ed
   special education • Certificate, M Ed
   supervision • M Ed

College of Engineering
Dr. Fred M. Young, Dean
Programs in:
chemical engineering • DE, ME, MES
civil engineering • DE, ME, MES
computer science • MS
electrical engineering • DE, ME, MES
engineering management • MEM
environmental engineering • MS
environmental studies • MS
industrial engineering • DE, ME, MES
mathematics • MS
mechanical engineering • DE, ME, MES

College of Fine Arts and Communication
Dr. James Simmons, Dean
Programs in:
art history • MA
deaf education • Ed D, MS
music education • MM Ed
music performance • MM
photography • MA
speech language pathology and audiology • MS
studio art • MA
theatre • MS
visual design • MA

MIDWESTERN STATE UNIVERSITY
Wichita Falls, TX 76308-2096

http://www.mwsu.edu/

Public coed comprehensive institution. *Enrollment: 5,770 graduate, professional, and undergraduate students. Graduate faculty: 75 full-time, 1 part-time. Computer facilities: Campuswide network is available with full Internet access. Total number of PCs/terminals supplied for student use: 250. Computer service fees are included with tuition and fees. Library facilities: Moffett Library. Graduate expenses: Tuition of $44 per hour for state residents; $259 per hour for nonresidents. Fees of $90 per year (minimum) full-time, $9 per semester (minimum) part-time. General application contact: Darla Inglish, Assistant Registrar, 940-397-4321.*

Graduate Studies
Dr. Jesse W. Rogers, Vice President for Academic Affairs

Division of Business Administration
Dr. Yoshi Fukasawa, Director
Program in:
business administration • MBA

Division of Education
Dr. Emerson Capps, Director
Programs in:
educational administration • M Ed
elementary education • M Ed
general counseling • MA
human resource development • MA
physical education • MSK
reading education • M Ed
school counseling • M Ed
secondary education • M Ed
special education • M Ed
teaching • M Ed

Division of Health Sciences
Dr. Susan Sportsman, Director
Programs in:
family nurse practitioner • MSN
nurse educator • MSN
radiologic administration • MS
radiologic education • MS

Division of Humanities
Dr. Michael L. Collins, Director
Programs in:
English • MA
history • MA

Division of Mathematical Sciences
Dr. William E. Hinds, Director
Program in:
computer science • MS

Division of Political Science and Public Administration
Dr. Michael Preda, Director
Programs in:
political science • MA
political science and public administration • MA

Division of Sciences
Dr. Norman V. Horner, Director
Program in:
biology • MS

Division of Social and Behavioral Sciences
Dr. Robert E. Clark, Director
Program in:
psychology • MA

OUR LADY OF THE LAKE UNIVERSITY OF SAN ANTONIO
San Antonio, TX 78207-4689

http://www.ollusa.edu/

Independent-religious coed comprehensive institution. *Enrollment: 3,668 graduate, professional, and undergraduate students. Graduate faculty: 121 full-time, 115 part-time. Computer facilities: Campuswide network is available with full Internet access. Total number of PCs/terminals supplied for student use: 150. Computer service fees are included with tuition and fees. Library facilities: St. Florence Library plus 3 additional on-campus libraries. Graduate expenses: Tuition of $371 per credit hour. Fees of $57 per semester full-time, $32 per semester part-time. General application contact: Debbie Hamilton, Director of Admissions, 210-434-6711 Ext. 314.*

Our Lady of the Lake University of San Antonio (continued)
College of Arts and Sciences
Sr. Isabel Ball, Dean
Programs in:
   English communication arts • MA
   language and literature • MA

School of Business and Public Administration
Dr. W. Earl Walker, Dean
Programs in:
   finance • MBA
   general • MBA
   health care management • MBA
   international business • MBA
   management • MBA

School of Education and Clinical Studies
Dr. Jacquelyn Alexander, Dean
Programs in:
   administration/supervision • M Ed
   communication and learning disorders • MA
   counseling psychology • MS, Psy D
   curriculum and instruction • M Ed
   human sciences • MA
   learning resources • M Ed
   psychology • MS, Psy D
   school counseling • MS
   school supervision • M Ed
   sociology • MA
   special education • MA

Worden School of Social Service
Dr. Santos Hernandez, Dean
Program in:
   social service • MSW

PRAIRIE VIEW A&M UNIVERSITY
Prairie View, TX 77446-0188

http://www.pvamu.edu/

Public coed comprehensive institution. *Enrollment: 6,004 graduate, professional, and undergraduate students. Graduate faculty: 107 full-time.* Computer facilities: *Campuswide network is available with full Internet access. Total number of PCs/terminals supplied for student use: 504. Computer service fees are included with tuition and fees.* Library facilities: *John B. Coleman Library plus 1 additional on-campus library.* Graduate expenses: *$2202 per year full-time, $336 per semester (minimum) part-time for state residents; $6000 per year full-time, $963 per semester (minimum) part-time for nonresidents.* General application contact: *Dr. Willie F. Trotty, Dean, Graduate School and Research, 409-857-2315.*

Graduate School
Dr. Willie F. Trotty, Dean, Graduate School and Research

College of Agriculture and Human Sciences
Dr. Elizabeth Noel, Dean
Programs in:
   agricultural economics • MS
   agriculture • MS
   human sciences • MS
   sociology • MA

College of Arts and Sciences
Edward Martin, Dean
Programs in:
   applied music • MA
   biology • MS
   chemistry • MS
   English • MA
   mathematics • MS
   social and political science • MA

College of Business
Dr. David Kruegel, Interim Dean
Program in:
   general business administration • MBA

College of Education
Dr. M. Paul Mehta, Dean
Programs in:
   counseling • MA, MS Ed
   curriculum and instruction • M Ed, MS Ed
   health education • MA Ed, MS Ed
   media technology • M Ed, MS Ed
   physical education • MA Ed, MS Ed
   school administration • M Ed, MS Ed
   school supervision • M Ed, MS Ed
   special education • M Ed, MS Ed

College of Engineering and Architecture
Dr. Milton R. Bryant, Interim Dean
Program in:
   engineering and architecture • MS Engr

RICE UNIVERSITY
Houston, TX 77005

http://www.ruf.rice.edu/~graduate/

Independent coed university. Library facilities: *Fondren Library plus 5 additional on-campus libraries.* Graduate expenses: *Tuition of $15,300 per year full-time, $850 per credit hour part-time. Fees of $238 per year.*

Graduate Programs

George R. Brown School of Engineering
Programs in:
   bioengineering • MS, PhD
   chemical engineering • M Ch E, MS, PhD
   circuits, controls, and communication systems • MS, PhD

civil engineering • MCE, MS, PhD
computational and applied mathematics • MA, MAM Sc, PhD
computer science • MCS, MS, PhD
computer science and engineering • MS, PhD
electrical engineering • MEE
environmental engineering • MEE, MES, MS, PhD
environmental science • MEE, MES, MS, PhD
lasers, microwaves, and solid-state electronics • MS, PhD
materials science • MME, MMS, MS, PhD
mechanical engineering • MEE, MMS, MS, PhD
statistics • M Stat, MA, PhD
structural engineering • MCE, MS, PhD

Jesse H. Jones Graduate School of Management
Dr. Gilbert R. Whitaker Jr., Dean
Program in:
business administration • MBA

School of Architecture
Programs in:
architecture • D Arch, M Arch
urban design • M Arch UD

School of Humanities
Programs in:
art history • MA
education • MAT
English • MA, PhD
French studies • MA, PhD
German and Slavic studies • MA, PhD
Hispanic and classical studies • MA
history • MA, PhD
linguistics • MA, PhD
philosophy • MA, PhD
religious studies • MA, PhD

School of Social Sciences
Programs in:
anthropology • MA, PhD
economics • MA, PhD
industrial-organizational/social psychology • MA, PhD
political science • MA, PhD
psychology • MA, PhD

Shepherd School of Music
Programs in:
composition • DMA, MM
conducting • MM
history • MM
performance • DMA, MM
theory • MM

Wiess School of Natural Sciences
Programs in:
applied physics • MS, PhD
biochemistry and cell biology • MA, PhD
chemistry • MA, PhD
ecology and evolutionary biology • MA, PhD
geology and geophysics • MA, PhD
mathematics • MA, PhD
physics • MA, PhD
space physics and astronomy • MS, PhD

ST. EDWARD'S UNIVERSITY
Austin, TX 78704-6489

http://www.stedwards.edu/

Independent-religious coed comprehensive institution. *Enrollment: 3,101 graduate, professional, and undergraduate students. Graduate faculty: 20 full-time, 24 part-time. Computer facilities: Campuswide network is available with full Internet access. Total number of PCs/terminals supplied for student use: 275. Computer services are offered at no charge. Library facilities: Scarborough-Phillips Library. General application contact: Tom Evans, Director of Graduate Admissions, 512-448-8600.*

School of Business Administration
Dr. David Kendall, Dean
Programs in:
accounting • Certificate
business administration • MBA

School of Education
Dr. J. Frank Smith, Dean
Program in:
human services • MA

ST. MARY'S UNIVERSITY OF SAN ANTONIO
San Antonio, TX 78228-8507

http://www.stmarytx.edu/

Independent-religious coed comprehensive institution. *Computer facilities: Campuswide network is available with full Internet access. Total number of PCs/terminals supplied for student use: 125. Computer service fees are included with tuition and fees. Library facilities: main library plus 1 additional on-campus library. Graduate expenses: Tuition of $383 per credit hour (minimum). Fees of $217 per year full-time, $58 per semester part-time. General application contact: Dean of the Graduate School, 210-436-3101.*

Graduate School
Programs in:
Catholic school leadership • MA
clinical psychology • MA, MS
computer information systems • MS
correctional administration • MJA
counseling • PhD, Sp C
economics • MA
educational leadership • MA
electrical/computer engineering • MS
electrical engineering • MS
engineering administration • MS
engineering computer application • MS
history • MA
industrial engineering • MS
industrial psychology • MA, MS

St. Mary's University of San Antonio (continued)
  international relations • MA
  marriage and family relations • Certificate
  marriage and family therapy • MA
  mental health • MA
  mental health and substance abuse counseling •
    Certificate
  operations research • MS
  pastoral administration • MA
  police administration • MJA
  political science • MA
  public administration • MPA
  reading • MA
  speech communication • MA
  substance abuse • MA
  systems administration • MS
  theology • MA

School of Business Administration
Program in:
  business administration • MBA

School of Law
Program in:
  law • JD

SAM HOUSTON STATE UNIVERSITY
Huntsville, TX 77341

http://www.shsu.edu/

Public coed comprehensive institution. *Enrollment:* 12,709 graduate, professional, and undergraduate students. Computer facilities:
*Campuswide network is available with full Internet access. Computer
service fees are included with tuition and fees.* Library facilities:
Newton Gresham Library. Graduate expenses: *$1810 per year
full-time, $297 per semester (minimum) part-time for state residents;
$6922 per year full-time, $924 per semester (minimum) part-time
for nonresidents.* General application contact: *Dr. Christopher
Baldwin, Dean, College of Arts and Sciences, 409-294-1401.*

College of Arts and Sciences
Dr. Christopher Baldwin, Dean
Programs in:
  applied music and literature • MM
  art education • M Ed
  biological sciences • M Ed, MA, MS
  ceramics • MA, MFA
  chemistry • M Ed, MS
  computing science • M Ed, MS
  conducting • MM
  dance • MFA
  drawing • MA, MFA
  English • M Ed, MA
  history • MA
  jewelry • MA
  Kodály pedagogy • MM

  mathematics • M Ed, MA, MS
  music education • M Ed
  musicology • MM
  painting • MA, MFA
  physics • MS
  political science • MA
  printmaking • MA, MFA
  sculpture • MA, MFA
  sociology • MA
  theory and composition • MM

College of Business Administration
Dr. R. Dean Lewis, Dean
Program in:
  business administration • MBA

College of Criminal Justice
Dr. Timothy J. Flanagan, Dean and Director
Program in:
  criminal justice • MA, MS, PhD

College of Education and Applied Science
Dr. Kenneth Craycraft, Dean
Programs in:
  agricultural business • MS
  agricultural education • M Ed
  agricultural mechanization • MS
  agriculture • MS
  bilingual education and English as a second language •
    Certificate
  clinical psychology • MA
  counseling • M Ed, MA
  curriculum and instruction • Ed D
  early childhood education • M Ed
  educational administration • M Ed
  elementary education • Certificate, M Ed
  general psychology • MA
  health education • MA
  home economics • MA
  industrial education • M Ed, MA
  industrial technology • MA
  kinesiology • M Ed, MA
  library science • MLS
  reading • M Ed
  school psychology • MA
  secondary education • Certificate, M Ed, MA
  special education • M Ed
  supervision • M Ed
  vocational education • M Ed, MS

 # SOUTHERN METHODIST UNIVERSITY
Dallas, TX 75275

http://www.smu.edu/

Independent-religious coed university. *Enrollment:* 9,708 graduate,
professional, and undergraduate students. Graduate faculty: *432
full-time, 222 part-time.* Computer facilities: *Campuswide network*

is available with full Internet access. Total number of PCs/terminals supplied for student use: 409. Computer services are offered at no charge. Library facilities: *Central University Library plus 9 additional on-campus libraries.* Graduate expenses: *Tuition of $11,754 per year full-time, $653 per credit part-time. Fees of $1512 per year full-time, $84 per credit part-time.* General application contact: *Dr. Narayan U. Bhat, Dean of Research and Graduate Studies, 214-768-3268.*

Dedman College

Dr. Jasper Neel, Dean
Programs in:
    anthropology • MA, PhD
    applied economics • MA
    applied mathematics • MS
    archaeology • MA, PhD
    biological sciences • MA, MS, PhD
    chemistry • MS
    clinical and counseling psychology • MA, MS
    economics • MA, PhD
    English • MA
    exploration geophysics • MS
    geological sciences • MS, PhD
    geology • MS, PhD
    geophysics • MS, PhD
    history • MA
    Latin American studies • MA
    liberal arts • MBE, MLA
    mathematical sciences • PhD
    mathematics • MA
    medical anthropology • MA, PhD
    medieval studies • MA
    physics • MS, PhD
    psychology • MA, PhD
    religious studies • MA, PhD
    statistical science • MS, PhD

Edwin L. Cox School of Business

Dr. Albert Neimi Jr., Dean
Program in:
    business • Exec MBA, MBA

Meadows School of the Arts

Carole Brandt, Dean
Programs in:
    acting • MFA
    art history • MA
    ceramics • MFA
    dance • MFA
    design • MFA
    directing • MFA
    drawing • MFA
    music • MM, MMT, MSM
    painting • MFA
    photography • MFA
    printmaking • MFA
    sculpture • MFA
    studio art • MFA
    TV/radio • MA, MFA

Perkins School of Theology

Dr. Robin Lovin Jr., Dean
Program in:
    theology • D Min, M Div, MRE, MSM, MTS

School of Engineering and Applied Science

Dr. Andre G. Vacroux, Dean
Programs in:
    applied science • MS, PhD
    computer engineering • MS Cp E, PhD
    computer science • MS, PhD
    electrical engineering • MS, MSEE, PhD
    engineering management • DE, MSEM
    hazardous and waste materials management • MS
    manufacturing systems management • MS
    material science and engineering • MS
    mechanical engineering • MSME, PhD
    operations research • MS, PhD
    software engineering • MS
    systems engineering • MS

School of Law

Dr. Harvey Wingo, Interim Dean
Programs in:
    comparative and international law • LL M
    law • JD, LL M, SJD
    taxation • LL M

 SOUTHWEST TEXAS STATE UNIVERSITY
San Marcos, TX 78666

http://www.swt.edu/

Public coed comprehensive institution. *Enrollment: 20,652 graduate, professional, and undergraduate students. Graduate faculty: 287 full-time, 30 part-time.* Computer facilities: *Campuswide network is available with full Internet access. Total number of PCs/terminals supplied for student use: 600.* Computer service fees are included with tuition and fees. Library facilities: *Alkek Library.* Graduate expenses: *Tuition of $648 per year full-time, $120 per semester (minimum) part-time for state residents; $4500 per year full-time, $750 per semester (minimum) part-time for nonresidents. Fees of $1264 per year full-time, $314 per semester (minimum) part-time.* General application contact: *Dr. J. Michael Willoughby, Dean of the Graduate School, 512-245-2581.*

Graduate School

Dr. J. Michael Willoughby, Dean
Program in:
    interdisciplinary studies • MAIS, MSIS

School of Applied Arts and Technology

Dr. G. Eugene Martin, Dean
Programs in:
    agriculture education • M Ed
    criminal justice • MSCJ
    industrial technology • MST

Southwest Texas State University (continued)

School of Business
Dr. Paul R. Gowens, Dean
Programs in:
   accounting • M Acy
   business administration • MBA

School of Education
Dr. John Beck, Dean
Programs in:
   counseling and guidance • M Ed
   developmental education • MA
   educational administration • M Ed, MA
   elementary education • M Ed, MA
   health and physical education • MA
   health education • M Ed
   management of vocational/technical education • M Ed
   physical education • M Ed
   professional counseling • MA
   reading education • M Ed
   school psychology • MA
   secondary education • M Ed, MA
   special education • M Ed

School of Fine Arts and Communication
Dr. T. Richard Cheatham, Dean
Programs in:
   mass communication • MA
   music education • MM
   music performance • MM
   speech communication • MA
   theatre arts • MA

School of Health Professions
Dr. Rumaldo Z. Juarez, Dean
Programs in:
   allied health research • MSHP
   communication disorders • MA, MSCDIS
   health care administration • MSHP
   healthcare human resources • MSHP
   physical therapy • MSPT
   social work • MSW

School of Liberal Arts
Dr. G. Jack Gravitt, Dean
Programs in:
   applied geography • MAG
   cartography/geographic information systems • MAG
   creative writing • MFA
   English • MA
   environmental geography • PhD
   geography education • PhD
   history • M Ed, MA
   land/area studies • MAG
   political science • MA
   political science education • M Ed
   public administration • MPA
   resource and environmental studies • MAG
   sociology • MA
   Spanish • MA
   Spanish education • MAT

School of Science
Dr. Stanley C. Israel, Dean
Programs in:
   aquatic biology • MS
   biology • M Ed, MA, MS
   chemistry • M Ed, MA, MS
   computer science • MA, MS
   mathematics • M Ed, MA, MS
   physics • MA, MS

STEPHEN F. AUSTIN STATE UNIVERSITY
Nacogdoches, TX 75962
http://www.sfasu.edu/

Public coed comprehensive institution. *Enrollment:* 11,890 graduate, professional, and undergraduate students. Graduate faculty: *214 full-time, 75 part-time.* Computer facilities: *Campuswide network is available with full Internet access. Computer service fees are included with tuition and fees.* Library facilities: *Ralph W. Steen Library.* Graduate expenses: *$1465 per year full-time, $263 per semester (minimum) part-time for state residents; $5299 per year full-time, $890 per semester (minimum) part-time for nonresidents.* General application contact: *Dr. David Jeffrey, Associate Vice President for Graduate Studies and Research, 409-468-2807.*

Graduate School
Dr. David Jeffrey, Associate Vice President for Graduate Studies and Research

College of Applied Arts and Science
Dr. James O. Standley, Dean
Programs in:
   communication • MA
   interdisciplinary studies • MIS
   mass communication • MA
   social work • MSW

College of Business
Dr. Marlin C. Young, Dean
Programs in:
   business • MBA
   computer science • MS
   management and marketing • MBA
   professional accountancy • MPA

College of Education
Dr. Thomas Franks, Dean
Programs in:
   agriculture • MS
   counseling • MA
   early childhood education • M Ed
   educational leadership • Ed D
   elementary education • M Ed
   health education • M Ed
   human sciences • MS
   physical education • M Ed
   school psychology • MA

secondary education • M Ed
special education • M Ed
speech pathology • MS

College of Fine Arts
Dr. Ron Jones, Dean
Programs in:
art • MA
design • MFA
drawing • MFA
music • MA, MM
painting • MFA
sculpture • MFA
theatre • MA

College of Forestry
Dr. Scott Beasley, Dean
Program in:
forestry • DF, MF, MSF

College of Liberal Arts
Dr. James Speer, Dean
Programs in:
English • MA
history • MA
psychology • MA

College of Sciences and Mathematics
Dr. Thomas Atchison, Dean
Programs in:
biology • MS
biotechnology • MS
chemistry • MS
environmental science • MS
geology • MS, MSNS
mathematics • MS
mathematics education • MS
physics • MS
statistics • MS

SUL ROSS STATE UNIVERSITY
Alpine, TX 79832

http://www.sulross.edu/

Public coed comprehensive institution. *Enrollment:* 3,296 graduate, professional, and undergraduate students. Graduate faculty: *71 full-time, 14 part-time.* Library facilities: *Bryan Wildenthal Memorial Library.* Graduate expenses: *Tuition of $864 per year full-time, $120 per semester (minimum) part-time for state residents; $5976 per year full-time, $747 per semester (minimum) part-time for nonresidents. Fees of $754 per year full-time, $105 per semester (minimum) part-time.* General application contact: *Robert Cullins, Dean of Admissions and Records, 915-837-8050.*

Division of Range Animal Science
Dr. Robert Kinucan, Director
Programs in:
animal science • M Ag, MS
range and wildlife management • M Ag, MS

Rio Grande College of Sul Ross State University
Dr. Frank Abbott, Dean
Programs in:
bilingual education • M Ed
business administration • MBA
counseling • M Ed
educational diagnostics • M Ed
elementary education • M Ed
general education • M Ed
reading • M Ed
school administration • M Ed
secondary education • M Ed
teacher education • M Ed

School of Arts and Sciences
Dr. Bruce Glasrud, Dean
Programs in:
art education • M Ed
art history • M Ed
biology • MS
ceramics • M Ed
design • M Ed
drawing • M Ed
English • MA
geology and chemistry • MS
history • MA
jewelry • M Ed
painting • M Ed
political science • MA
printmaking • M Ed
psychology • MA
public administration • MA
sculpture • M Ed
studio art • M Ed
weaving • M Ed

School of Professional Studies
Dr. Chet Sample, Dean
Programs in:
bilingual education • M Ed
counseling • M Ed
criminal justice • MS
educational diagnostics • M Ed
elementary education • M Ed
industrial arts • M Ed
international trade • MBA
management • MBA
physical education • M Ed
reading specialist • M Ed
school administration • M Ed
secondary education • M Ed
supervision • M Ed

TARLETON STATE UNIVERSITY
Stephenville, TX 76402

http://www.tarleton.edu/

Public coed comprehensive institution. *Enrollment: 6,034 graduate, professional, and undergraduate students. Graduate faculty: 104 full-time. Computer facilities: Campuswide network is available with full Internet access. Computer service fees are included with tuition and fees. Library facilities: Dick Smith Library. Graduate expenses: Tuition of $46 per hour for state residents; $249 per hour for nonresidents. Fees of $49 per hour. General application contact: Dr. Ronald D. Bradberry, Dean, 254-968-9104.*

College of Graduate Studies
Dr. Ronald D. Bradberry, Dean

College of Agriculture
Jesse L. Tackett, Dean
Program in:
    agriculture • MS, MST

College of Arts and Sciences
Lamar Johanson, Dean
Programs in:
    arts and sciences • MAT, MST
    biological sciences • MS
    English and languages • MA
    environmental science • MS
    history • MA
    mathematics • MA
    political science • MA

College of Business Administration
Dan Collins, Dean
Program in:
    business administration • MBA

College of Education
Dr. Joe Gillespie, Dean
Programs in:
    educational administration • Certificate, M Ed
    elementary education • Certificate, M Ed
    guidance and counseling • M Ed
    health and physical education • Certificate, M Ed
    reading • Certificate
    secondary education • Certificate, M Ed
    special education • Certificate

TEXAS A&M INTERNATIONAL UNIVERSITY
Laredo, TX 78041-1900

http://www.tamu.edu/

Public coed comprehensive institution. *Library facilities: Yeary Library. General application contact: Director of Admissions and Advancement, 210-326-2200.*

Division of Graduate Studies

Division of Arts and Humanities
Programs in:
    criminal justice • MAIS, MSCJ
    English • MA, MAIS
    history • MA, MAIS
    mathematics • MAIS
    political science • MAIS
    psychology • MA, MAIS
    sociology • MA, MAIS
    Spanish • MAIS

Division of Business Administration
Programs in:
    business administration • MBA
    information systems • MSIS
    international banking • MBA
    international logistics • MSIL
    international trade • MBA
    professional accountancy • MP Acc

Division of Teacher Education and Psychology
Programs in:
    administration • MS Ed
    bilingual education • MS Ed
    business education • MS Ed
    early childhood education • MS Ed
    education • MS Ed
    elementary education • MS Ed
    gifted and talented • MS Ed
    guidance and counseling • MS Ed
    reading • MS Ed
    secondary education • MS Ed
    supervision • MS Ed

TEXAS A&M UNIVERSITY
College Station, TX 77843

http://www.tamu.edu/researchandgradstudies/

Public coed university. *Enrollment: 41,790 graduate, professional, and undergraduate students. Graduate faculty: 2,054 full-time, 482 part-time. Computer facilities: Campuswide network is available with full Internet access. Total number of PCs/terminals supplied for student use: 1,200. Computer service fees are included with tuition and fees. Library facilities: Sterling C. Evans Library plus 4 additional on-campus libraries. Graduate expenses: Tuition of $2160 per year full-time, $228 per semester (minimum) part-time for state residents; $8550 per year full-time, $855 per semester (minimum) part-time for nonresidents. Fees of $1821 per year full-time, $293 per semester (minimum) part-time. General application contact: Annette M. Hardin, Assistant Director, 888-826-8647.*

Office of Graduate Studies
Dan H. Robertson, Director
Programs in:
    anatomy • MS, PhD
    epidemiology • MS

genetics • MS, PhD
human anatomy and medical neurobiology • PhD
immunology • PhD
medical biochemistry and genetics • PhD
medical pharmacology and toxicology • PhD
medical physiology • PhD
microbiology • PhD
molecular biology • PhD
molecular pathology • PhD
neuroscience • PhD
pathology • MS, PhD
physiology • MS, PhD
veterinary large animal medicine and surgery • MS
veterinary microbiology • MS, PhD
veterinary public health • MS
veterinary small animal medicine and surgery • MS
virology • PhD

College of Agriculture and Life Sciences
Edward A. Hiler, Dean
Programs in:
agricultural chemistry • M Agr
agricultural economics • M Agr, MS, PhD
agricultural education • Ed D, M Ed, MS, PhD
agricultural engineering • M Agr, M Eng, MS, PhD
agronomy • M Agr, MS, PhD
animal breeding • MS, PhD
animal science • M Agr, MS, PhD
biochemistry • MS, PhD
biophysics • MS
dairy science • M Agr, MS
entomology • M Agr, MS, PhD
food science and technology • M Agr, MS, PhD
forest science • MS, PhD
genetics • MS, PhD
horticulture • PhD
horticulture and floriculture • M Agr, MS
natural resources development • M Agr
nutrition • MS, PhD
physiology of reproduction • MS, PhD
plant breeding • MS, PhD
plant pathology • MS, PhD
plant physiology and plant biotechnology • MS, PhD
plant protection • M Agr
poultry science • M Agr, MS, PhD
range science • M Agr, MS, PhD
recreation and resources development • M Agr, MS, PhD
soil science • MS, PhD
wildlife and fisheries sciences • M Agr, MS, PhD

College of Architecture
Ward Wells Jr., Interim Dean
Programs in:
architectural design • M Arch
architectural history and preservation • M Arch
architecture • MS, PhD
construction management • MS
health facilities planning and design • M Arch
interior architecture • M Arch
land development • MS
landscape architecture • MLA
management in architecture • M Arch
urban and regional science • PhD

urban planning • MUP
visualization sciences • MS

College of Education
Jane Conerly, Dean
Programs in:
adult education • Ed D, M Ed, MS, PhD
bilingual education • M Ed, MS, PhD
counseling psychology • PhD
curriculum development • Ed D, M Ed, MS, PhD
educational administration • Ed D, M Ed, MS, PhD
educational human resource development • Ed D, M Ed, MS, PhD
educational psychology • MS
educational technology • M Ed
gifted and talented education • M Ed, MS
health education • M Ed, MS, PhD
human learning and development • PhD
industrial education • Ed D, M Ed, MS, PhD
kinesiology • MS, PhD
math/science • Ed D, M Ed, MS, PhD
physical education • Ed D, M Ed
reading • Ed D, M Ed, MS, PhD
research, measurement, and statistics • M Ed, MS, PhD
school psychology • PhD
social foundation • Ed D, M Ed, MS, PhD
special education • M Ed, PhD
vocational education • Ed D, PhD
vocational education/school counseling • M Ed

College of Engineering
C. Roland Haden, Dean
Programs in:
aerospace engineering • M Eng, MS, PhD
agricultural engineering • M Agr, M Eng, MS, PhD
bioengineering • D Eng, M Eng, MS, PhD
chemical engineering • M Eng, MS, PhD
computer engineering • MS, PhD
computer science • MCS, MS, PhD
construction engineering and project management • D Eng, M Eng, MS, PhD
electrical engineering • M Eng, MS, PhD
engineering mechanics • M Eng, MS, PhD
environmental engineering • D Eng, M Eng, MS, PhD
geotechnical engineering • D Eng, M Eng, MS, PhD
health physics • MS
hydraulic engineering • M Eng, MS, PhD
hydrology • M Eng, MS, PhD
industrial engineering • D Eng, M Eng, MS, PhD
industrial hygiene • MS
materials engineering • D Eng, M Eng, MS, PhD
mechanical engineering • D Eng, M Eng, MS, PhD
nuclear engineering • M Eng, MS, PhD
ocean engineering • D Eng, M Eng, MS, PhD
petroleum engineering • D Eng, M Eng, MS, PhD
public works engineering and management • M Eng, MS, PhD
safety engineering • MS
structural engineering and structural mechanics • D Eng, M Eng, MS, PhD
transportation engineering • D Eng, M Eng, MS, PhD
water resources engineering • D Eng, M Eng, MS, PhD

Texas A&M University (continued)

College of Geosciences
David Prior, Dean
Programs in:
geography • MS, PhD
geology and geophysics • MS, PhD
meteorology • MS, PhD
oceanography • MS, PhD

College of Liberal Arts
Woodrow Jones Jr., Dean
Programs in:
anthropology • MA, PhD
clinical psychology • MS, PhD
economics • MS, PhD
English • MA, PhD
general psychology • MS, PhD
government and public service • MPSA
history • MA, PhD
industrial/organizational psychology • MS, PhD
philosophy • MA
political science • MA, PhD
sociology • MS, PhD
Spanish • MA
speech communication • MA

College of Science
Richard E. Ewing, Dean
Programs in:
biology • MS, PhD
botany • MS, PhD
chemistry • MS, PhD
mathematics • MS, PhD
microbiology • MS, PhD
molecular and cell biology • PhD
physics • MS, PhD
statistics • MS, PhD
zoology • MS, PhD

Intercollegiate Faculty in Nutrition
David N. McMurray, Chair
Program in:
nutrition • MS, PhD

Intercollegiate Faculty in Toxicology
Kenneth S. Ramos, Chair
Program in:
toxicology • MS, PhD

Lowry Mays Graduate School of Business
Dr. A. Benton Cocanougher, Dean
Programs in:
accounting • MS, PhD
business administration • MBA
finance • MS, PhD
management • MS, PhD
management information systems • MS, PhD
marketing • MS, PhD

College of Medicine
Dr. Elvin Smith, Interim Dean
Programs in:
human anatomy and medical neurobiology • PhD
immunology • PhD

medical biochemistry and genetics • PhD
medical pharmacology and toxicology • PhD
medical physiology • PhD
medicine • MD
microbiology • PhD
molecular biology • PhD
molecular pathology • PhD
neuroscience • PhD
virology • PhD

College of Veterinary Medicine
Dr. John A. Shadduck, Dean
Programs in:
anatomy • MS, PhD
epidemiology • MS
genetics • MS, PhD
pathology • MS, PhD
physiology • MS, PhD
toxicology • MS, PhD
veterinary large animal medicine and surgery • MS
veterinary medicine • DVM
veterinary microbiology • MS, PhD
veterinary public health • MS
veterinary small animal medicine and surgery • MS

TEXAS A&M UNIVERSITY–COMMERCE
Commerce, TX 75429-3011

http://www.tamu-commerce.edu/

Public coed university. *Enrollment: 7,457 graduate, professional, and undergraduate students. Graduate faculty: 166 full-time, 36 part-time. Computer facilities: Campuswide network is available with full Internet access. Total number of PCs/terminals supplied for student use: 500. Computer service fees are included with tuition and fees. Library facilities: James G. Gee Library. Graduate expenses: $2382 per year full-time, $343 per semester (minimum) part-time for state residents; $7518 per year full-time, $343 per semester (minimum) part-time for nonresidents. General application contact: Pam Hammonds, Graduate Admissions Adviser, 903-886-5167.*

Graduate School
Dr. R. N. Singh, Interim Dean

College of Arts and Sciences
Dr. Stephen Razniak, Dean
Programs in:
agricultural education • M Ed, MS
agricultural sciences • M Ed, MS
art • MA, MFA, MS
biological and earth sciences • M Ed, MS
chemistry • M Ed, MS
college teaching of English • Ed D
computer science • MS
English • M Ed, MA, MS
French • MA
history • MA, MS

journalism • MA, MS
mathematics • MA, MS
music • MS
music composition • MM
music education • MM, MS
music performance • MM
music theory • MM
physics • M Ed, MS
social sciences • M Ed, MS
sociology • MA, MS
Spanish • MA
speech communications • MA, MS
theatre • MA, MS

College of Business and Technology
Dr. Lee Schmidt, Dean
Programs in:
business administration • MBA
economics • MA, MS
industry and technology • MS

College of Education
Dr. Donald Coker, Dean
Programs in:
administration • MS
counseling • Ed D, M Ed, MS
early childhood education • M Ed, MA, MS
educational administration • Ed D, M Ed, MS
educational computing • M Ed, MA, MS
educational psychology • PhD
elementary education • M Ed, MS
health and physical education • M Ed, MS
higher education • MS
learning technology and information systems • M Ed, MA, MS
library and information science • M Ed, MA, MS
media and technology • M Ed, MA, MS
psychology • MA, MS
reading • M Ed, MA, MS
secondary education • M Ed, MA, MS
special education • M Ed, MA, MS
supervision of curriculum and instruction: elementary education • Ed D, PhD
teaching • MS
training and development • MS
vocational/technical education • M Ed, MA, MS

semester (minimum) part-time for state residents; *$4482 per year full-time, $747 per semester (minimum) part-time for nonresidents. Fees of $1010 per year full-time, $205 per semester part-time. General application contact: Mary Margaret Dechant, Director of Admissions, 512-994-2624.*

Graduate Programs
Dr. Sandra Harper, Provost

College of Arts and Humanities
Dr. Paul Hain, Dean
Programs in:
English • MA
interdisciplinary studies • MA
psychology • MA
public administration • MPA

College of Business Administration
Dr. Moustafa H. Abdelsamad, Dean
Programs in:
accounting • M Acc
management • MBA

College of Education
Dr. Robert Cox, Dean
Programs in:
curriculum and instruction • MS
educational administration • MS
educational leadership • Ed D
elementary education • MS
guidance and counseling • MS
occupational education • MS
secondary education • MS
special education • MS

College of Science and Technology
Dr. Diana Marinez, Dean
Programs in:
biology • MS
computer science • MS
environmental sciences • MS
mariculture • MS
mathematics • MS
nursing administration • MSN

TEXAS A&M UNIVERSITY–CORPUS CHRISTI
Corpus Christi, TX 78412-5503

http://www.tamucc.edu/

Public coed comprehensive institution. *Enrollment: 6,025 graduate, professional, and undergraduate students. Graduate faculty: 206 full-time, 199 part-time. Computer facilities: Campuswide network is available with full Internet access. Total number of PCs/terminals supplied for student use: 500. Computer service fees are applied as a separate charge. Library facilities: Mary and Jeff Bell Library. Graduate expenses: Tuition of $648 per year full-time, $120 per*

TEXAS A&M UNIVERSITY– KINGSVILLE
Kingsville, TX 78363

http://www.tamuk.edu/

Public coed university. *Enrollment: 6,050 graduate, professional, and undergraduate students. Graduate faculty: 157. Computer facilities: Campuswide network is available with full Internet access. Total number of PCs/terminals supplied for student use: 350. Computer service fees are included with tuition and fees. Library facilities: James C. Jernigan Library. Graduate expenses: $1822 per year full-time, $281 per semester (minimum) part-time for state residents; $6934 per year full-time, $908 per semester (minimum)*

Texas A&M University–Kingsville (continued)
part-time for nonresidents. General application contact: Dr. Alberto
M. Olivares, Dean, College of Graduate Studies, 512-593-2808.

College of Graduate Studies
Dr. Alberto M. Olivares, Dean

College of Agriculture and Home Economics
Dr. Charles DeYoung, Dean
Programs in:
  agribusiness • MS
  agricultural education • MS
  animal sciences • MS
  human sciences • MS
  plant and soil sciences • MS
  range and wildlife management • MS
  wildlife science • PhD

College of Arts and Sciences
Dr. Mary Mattingly, Dean
Programs in:
  applied geology • MS
  art • MA, MS
  biology • MS
  chemistry • MS
  communication sciences and disorders • MS
  English • MA, MS
  gerontology • MS
  history and political science • MA, MS
  mathematics • MS
  music education • MM
  psychology • MA, MS
  sociology • MA, MS
  Spanish • MA

College of Business Administration
Dr. Darvin Hoffman, Graduate Coordinator
Program in:
  business administration • MBA, MS

College of Education
Dr. Francisco Hidalgo, Dean
Programs in:
  adult education • M Ed
  bilingual education • Ed D, MA, MS
  early childhood education • M Ed
  elementary education • MA, MS
  English as a second language • M Ed
  guidance and counseling • MA, MS
  health and kinesiology • MA, MS
  higher education administration • PhD
  reading • MS
  school administration • Ed D, MA, MS
  secondary education • MA, MS
  special education • M Ed
  supervision • MA, MS

College of Engineering
Dr. Phil V. Compton, Dean
Programs in:
  chemical engineering • ME, MS
  civil engineering • ME, MS
  computer science • MS
  electrical engineering • ME, MS
  environmental engineering • ME, MS
  industrial engineering • ME, MS
  mechanical engineering • ME, MS
  natural gas engineering • ME, MS

TEXAS A&M UNIVERSITY–TEXARKANA
Texarkana, TX 75505-5518

http://www.tamut.edu/

Public coed upper-level institution. *Enrollment: 1,045 graduate,
professional, and undergraduate students. Graduate faculty: 19
full-time, 5 part-time. Computer facilities: Campuswide network is
available with full Internet access. Total number of PCs/terminals
supplied for student use: 104. Computer service fees are included
with tuition and fees. Library facilities: John F. Moss Library. Graduate expenses: $2136 per year for state residents; $7248 per year
for nonresidents. General application contact: Pat Black, Registrar,
903-223-3068.*

Graduate School
Dr. John Anderson, Vice President for Academic Affairs
Programs in:
  behavioral sciences and business administration • MBA, MS
  counseling psychology • MS
  elementary education • M Ed, MA, MS
  interdisciplinary studies • MA, MS
  secondary education • M Ed, MA, MS
  special education • M Ed, MA, MS

TEXAS CHRISTIAN UNIVERSITY
Fort Worth, TX 76129-0002

http://www.tcu.edu/

Independent-religious coed university. *Enrollment: 7,273 graduate,
professional, and undergraduate students. Graduate faculty: 209
full-time. Computer facilities: Campuswide network is available with
full Internet access. Total number of PCs/terminals supplied for
student use: 1,452. Computer services are offered at no charge.
Library facilities: Mary Couts Burnett Library. Graduate expenses:
Tuition of $10,350 per year full-time, $345 per credit hour part-
time. Fees of $1240 per year full-time, $50 per credit hour part-
time. General application contact: Dean of the appropriate school,
817-257-7000.*

Add Ran College of Arts and Sciences
Dr. Michael McCracken, Dean
Programs in:
  biology • MA, MS
  chemistry • MA, MS, PhD

economics • MA
English • MA, PhD
environmental sciences • MS
geology • MS
history • MA, PhD
mathematics • MS
physics • MA, MS, PhD
psychology • MA, MS, PhD
software engineering • MSE

Brite Divinity School
Dr. Leo G. Perdue, Dean
Program in:
theology • CTS, D Min, M Div, MTS

College of Fine Arts and Communication
Dr. Robert P. Garwell, Dean
Programs in:
art • MFA
ballet and modern dance • MFA
media studies • MS
music • M Mus
music education • MM Ed
speech communication • MS
speech-language pathology • MS

Graduate Studies and Research
Program in:
liberal arts • MLA

M. J. Neeley School of Business
Dr. Rob Rhodes, Director, MBA Academic Programs
Programs in:
accounting • M Ac
business administration • MBA

School of Education
Dr. Douglas J. Simpson, Dean
Programs in:
administration education • M Ed
educational research and collaboration • M Ed
elementary education • M Ed
general education • M Ed
kinesiology and physical education • MS
secondary education • M Ed
special education • M Ed

TEXAS SOUTHERN UNIVERSITY
Houston, TX 77004-4584

http://www.tsu.edu/

Public coed university. *Enrollment:* 7,593 graduate, professional, and undergraduate students. Library facilities: *Robert J. Terry Library plus 2 additional on-campus libraries.* Graduate expenses: *Tuition of $2067 per year (minimum) full-time, $453 per semester (minimum) part-time for state residents; $5469 per year (minimum) full-time,* $1020 per semester (minimum) part-time for nonresidents. Fees of $100 per year (minimum). General application contact: *Dr. Joseph Jones, Dean of the Graduate School, 713-313-7232.*

Graduate School
Dr. Joseph Jones, Dean

College of Arts and Sciences
Dr. John Sapp, Acting Dean
Programs in:
biology • MS
chemistry • MS
child development • MS
city planning • MCP
English • MA, MS
foods and nutrition • MS
history • MA
home economics education • MA, MS
journalism • MA
mathematics • MA, MS
music • MA
public administration • MPA
sociology • MA
speech communications • MA
telecommunications • MA

College of Education
William Nealy, Acting Dean
Programs in:
bilingual education • M Ed
counseling and guidance • MA
counseling, guidance, and psychology • Ed D, M Ed, MA
curriculum, instruction, and urban education • Ed D
early childhood education • M Ed
educational administration • Ed D, M Ed
elementary education • M Ed
health education • MS
higher education administration • Ed D
physical education • MS
reading education • M Ed
secondary education • M Ed
special education • M Ed

School of Business
Dr. Priscilla Slade, Dean
Programs in:
business administration • MBA
business education • M Ed

School of Technology
Dr. Josua Hill, Dean
Programs in:
constructional technology • M Ed
educational technology • M Ed
transportation • MS

College of Pharmacy and Health Sciences
Dr. Pedro Lecca, Acting Dean
Program in:
pharmacy and health sciences • Pharm D

Texas Southern University (continued)
Thurgood Marshall School of Law
L. Darnell Weeden, Acting Dean
Program in:
  law • JD

 TEXAS TECH UNIVERSITY
Lubbock, TX 79409

http://www.ttu.edu/

Public coed university. *Enrollment: 25,022 graduate, professional, and undergraduate students. Graduate faculty: 724 full-time, 27 part-time. Computer facilities: Campuswide network is available with full Internet access. Total number of PCs/terminals supplied for student use: 1,460. Computer services are offered at no charge. Library facilities: main library plus 4 additional on-campus libraries. Graduate expenses: Tuition of $864 per year full-time, $120 per semester (minimum) part-time for state residents; $5976 per year full-time, $747 per semester (minimum) part-time for nonresidents. Fees of $1961 per year full-time, $257 per semester (minimum) part-time. General application contact: Troy Johnson, Graduate Admissions Director, 806-742-2787.*

Graduate School
Dr. David J. Schmidly, Dean
Program in:
  museum science • MA

College of Agricultural Sciences and Natural Resources
Dr. John R. Abernathy, Dean
Programs in:
  agricultural and applied economics • M Agr, MS, PhD
  agricultural education • M Agr, MS
  agronomy • PhD
  animal breeding • MS
  animal nutrition • MS
  animal science • MS, PhD
  animal science and food technology • M Agr
  crop science • MS
  entomology • MS
  fishery science • MS, PhD
  food technology • MS
  horticulture • MS
  landscape architecture • MLA
  meat science • MS
  plant and soil science • M Agr
  range science • MS, PhD
  soil science • MS
  wildlife science • MS, PhD

College of Architecture
Dr. James E. White, Dean
Programs in:
  architecture • M Arch
  community planning and design • PhD
  environmental/natural resource planning and
    management • PhD
  historic preservation • PhD
  public policy administration • PhD

College of Arts and Sciences
Dr. Jane Winer, Dean
Programs in:
  anthropology • MA
  applied physics • MS, PhD
  art • MFA
  art education • MAE
  atmospheric sciences • MS, PhD
  biology • MS, PhD
  chemistry • MS, PhD
  classical humanities • MA
  communication studies • MA
  economics • MA, PhD
  English • MA, PhD
  fine arts • PhD
  fine arts management • MA, PhD
  geoscience • MS, PhD
  German • MA
  history • MA, PhD
  interdisciplinary studies • MA, MS, PhD
  mass communications • MA
  mathematics • MA, MS, PhD
  microbiology • MS
  music education • MME
  music history and literature • MM
  music performance • MM
  music theory • MM
  philosophy • MA
  physical education • MS
  physics • MS, PhD
  political science • MA, PhD
  psychology • MA, PhD
  public administration • MPA
  Romance languages • MA
  sociology • MA
  Spanish • MA, PhD
  sports health • MS
  statistics • MS
  technical communication • MA
  technical communication and rhetoric • PhD
  theatre arts • MA, MFA
  zoology • MS, PhD

College of Business Administration
Dr. Roy D. Howell, Interim Dean
Programs in:
  accounting • PhD
  business administration • MBA
  business statistics • MSBA, PhD
  controllership • MSA
  finance • MSBA, PhD
  health organization management • Certificate, MBA
  health organization management/controllership • MSA
  management • MSBA, PhD
  management information systems • MSBA, PhD
  marketing • MSBA, PhD
  operations management • PhD
  professional accounting • MSA
  taxation • MSA

College of Education

Dr. Elaine Jarchow, Dean

Programs in:

    art education • Certificate

    bilingual education • Ed D, M Ed

    counselor education • Certificate, Ed D, M Ed

    curriculum and instruction • Ed D, M Ed

    early childhood education • Certificate, M Ed

    educational leadership • Ed D, M Ed

    educational psychology • Ed D, M Ed

    education diagnostician • Certificate

    elementary education • Certificate, Ed D, M Ed

    higher education • Ed D, M Ed

    instructional technology • Ed D, M Ed

    music education • Certificate

    physical education • Certificate

    principal • Certificate

    reading education • Ed D, M Ed

    reading specialist • Certificate

    secondary education • Certificate, Ed D, M Ed

    special education • Ed D, M Ed

    special education counselor • Certificate

    special education supervisor • Certificate

    superintendent • Certificate

    supervision • M Ed

    supervisor • Certificate

College of Engineering

Dr. Jorge I. Auñon, Dean

Programs in:

    chemical engineering • MS Ch E, PhD

    civil engineering • MSCE, PhD

    computer science • MS, PhD

    electrical engineering • MSEE, PhD

    engineering • M Engr

    environmental engineering • MENVEGR

    environmental technology and management • MSETM

    industrial engineering • MSIE, PhD

    mechanical engineering • MSME, PhD

    petroleum engineering • MS Pet E

College of Human Sciences

Dr. Elizabeth Haley, Dean

Programs in:

    clothing, textiles and merchandising • MS, PhD

    environmental design • MS

    environmental design and consumer economics • PhD

    family and consumer sciences education • MS, PhD

    family financial planning • MS

    food and nutrition • MS, PhD

    human development and family studies • MS, PhD

    marriage and family therapy • PhD

    restaurant, hotel, and institutional management • MS

School of Law

W. Frank Newton, Dean

Program in:

    law • JD

TEXAS WESLEYAN UNIVERSITY
Fort Worth, TX 76105-1536

http://www.txwesleyan.edu/

Independent-religious coed comprehensive institution. *Enrollment: 3,136 graduate, professional, and undergraduate students. Graduate faculty: 30 full-time, 53 part-time. Computer facilities: Campuswide network is available. Computer services are offered at no charge. Library facilities: James and Eunice West Library plus 1 additional on-campus library. Graduate expenses: Tuition of $275 per hour. Fees of $200 per semester. General application contact: Joyce Breeden, Dean of Admissions, 817-531-4458.*

Graduate Programs

Dr. Thomas Armstrong, Provost

Programs in:

    business administration • MBA

    education • MA Ed, MAT, MS Ed

    nurse anesthesia • MHS

Law School

Frank Walwer, Dean

Program in:

    law • JD

 # TEXAS WOMAN'S UNIVERSITY
Denton, TX 76204

http://www.twu.edu/

Public primarily female university. *Enrollment: 9,378 graduate, professional, and undergraduate students. Computer facilities: Campuswide network is available with full Internet access. Total number of PCs/terminals supplied for student use: 332. Computer service fees are included with tuition and fees. Library facilities: Mary Evelyn Blagg Huey Library plus 1 additional on-campus library. Graduate expenses: $1973 per year (minimum) full-time, $415 per semester (minimum) part-time for state residents; $5807 per year (minimum) full-time, $1029 per semester (minimum) part-time for nonresidents. General application contact: Dr. Leslie M. Thompson, Dean for Graduate Studies and Research, 940-898-3400.*

Graduate School

Dr. Leslie M. Thompson, Dean for Graduate Studies and Research

College of Arts and Sciences

Dr. Susan Buckley, Dean

Programs in:

    acting • MA

    advertising design • MA

    applied music • MA

    art • MA

    art education • MA

    art history • MA

    bacteriology • MS

Texas Woman's University (continued)

biology • MS
biology teaching • MS
business administration • MBA
ceramics • MA, MFA
chemistry • MS
counseling psychology • MA, PhD
dance • MA, MFA, PhD
directing • MA
English • MA
English and rhetoric • PhD
fashion and textiles • PhD
fashion design • MA
fashion merchandising • MS, PhD
fibers • MA
fibers and handmade paper • MFA
general psychology • MA
government • MA
history • MA
jewelry/metal smithing • MA
mathematics • MA, MS
molecular biology • PhD
music education • MA
music pedagogy • MA
music therapy • MA
neuroscience • PhD
painting • MA, MFA
photography • MA
photography and typographic bookmaking • MFA
school psychology • MA, PhD
sculpture • MA, MFA
sociology • MA, PhD
technical theater • MA
textiles and apparel • MS
zoology • MS

College of Education and Human Ecology
Dr. Michael Wiebe, Dean
Programs in:
administration and supervision • M Ed, MA
child development • MS, PhD
counseling and development • M Ed, MS
early childhood education • Ed D, M Ed, MA, MS
family studies • MS, PhD
family therapy • MS, PhD
general elementary education • M Ed, MA
reading • Ed D, M Ed, MA, MS, PhD
special education • M Ed, MA, PhD
vocational-technical education • Ed D, M Ed, MA, MS, PhD

College of Health Sciences
Dr. Jean Pyfer, Interim Dean
Programs in:
adapted physical education • MS, PhD
administration • MS, PhD
biomechanics • MS, PhD
education of the hearing impaired • MS
exercise and sports nutrition • MS, PhD
exercise physiology • MS, PhD
food science • MS
health care administration • MS
health education • Ed D, PhD

health studies • MS
institutional administration • MS
motor behavior • MS, PhD
nutrition • MS, PhD
nutrition/dietetic internship • MS
pedagogy • MS, PhD
speech-language pathology • MS

College of Nursing
Dr. Carolyn S. Gunning, Dean
Programs in:
adult health nurse • MS
adult health nurse practitioner • MS
community health nursing • MS
family nurse practitioner • MS
nursing • PhD
pediatric nurse practitioner • MS
pediatric nursing • MS
psychiatric-mental health nursing • MS
women's health nurse • PhD
women's health nurse practitioner • PhD

School of Library and Information Studies
Dr. Keith Swigger, Dean
Program in:
library and information studies • MA, MLS, PhD

School of Occupational Therapy
Dr. Janette Schkade, Dean
Program in:
occupational therapy • MA, MOT, PhD

School of Physical Therapy
Dr. Carolyn Rozier, Dean
Program in:
physical therapy • MS, PhD

TRINITY UNIVERSITY
San Antonio, TX 78212-7200
http://www.trinity.edu/

Independent-religious coed comprehensive institution. *Enrollment:* 2,560 graduate, professional, and undergraduate students. *Graduate faculty: 23 full-time, 18 part-time.* Computer facilities: *Campuswide network is available with full Internet access. Total number of PCs/ terminals supplied for student use: 100. Computer service fees are included with tuition and fees.* Library facilities: *Elizabeth Huth Coates Library.* Graduate expenses: *Tuition of $14,580 per year full-time, $608 per hour part-time. Fees of $18 per year full-time, $6 per hour part-time.* General application contact: *Dr. Mary E. Stefl, Dean, 210-736-7521.*

Division of Behavioral and Administrative Studies
Dr. Mary E. Stefl, Dean
Programs in:
accounting • MS
educational administration • M Ed
health care administration • MS
school psychology • MA

teacher education • MAT

urban administration • MS

UNIVERSITY OF CENTRAL TEXAS
Killeen, TX 76540-1416

http://www.vvm.com/uct/

Independent coed upper-level institution. *Enrollment:* 1,113 graduate, professional, and undergraduate students. Graduate faculty: *19 full-time, 6 part-time.* Computer facilities: *Total number of PCs/ terminals supplied for student use: 35. Computer service fees are applied as a separate charge.* Library facilities: *Ovetta Culp Hobby Library.* Graduate expenses: *$150 per hour.* General application contact: *Julie Reynolds, Dean of University Student Services, 254- 526-8262 Ext. 258.*

Graduate Programs
Dr. Roger Alford, Dean of Faculty
Programs in:
    business administration • MBA
    criminal justice administration • MCJ
    general studies • MS
    management science • MS
    public administration • MS

UNIVERSITY OF HOUSTON
Houston, TX 77204-2163

http://www.uh.edu/

Public coed university. *Enrollment:* 31,602 graduate, professional, and undergraduate students. Graduate faculty: *762 full-time, 285 part-time.* Computer facilities: *Campuswide network is available with full Internet access. Total number of PCs/terminals supplied for student use: 850. Computer service fees are included with tuition and fees.* Library facilities: *M. D. Anderson Library plus 5 additional on-campus libraries.* Graduate expenses: *Tuition of $1152 per year full-time, $120 per semester (minimum) part-time for state residents; $4482 per year full-time, $747 per semester (minimum) part-time for nonresidents. Fees of $977 per year full-time, $119 per semester (minimum) part-time.* General application contact: *Susan Zwieg, Director of Student Outreach Services, 713-743-1010.*

College of Architecture
Bruce Webb, Dean
Program in:
    architecture • M Arch

College of Business Administration
Dr. Sara M. Freedman, Dean
Programs in:
    accountancy • MS Accy
    accounting • MBA, PhD
    business administration • MBA, MS Admin, PhD
    finance • MBA, PhD
    international business • MBA
    management • MBA, PhD
    management information systems • MBA, PhD
    marketing and entrepreneurship • MBA, PhD
    operations management • MBA, PhD
    statistics and operations research • MBA, PhD
    taxation • MBA

College of Education
Allen R. Warner, Dean
Programs in:
    allied health • Ed D, M Ed
    art education • M Ed
    bilingual education • M Ed
    counseling psychology • M Ed, PhD
    curriculum and instruction • Ed D
    early childhood education • M Ed
    educational administration • Ed D, M Ed
    educational psychology • M Ed
    educational psychology and individual differences • PhD
    education of the gifted • M Ed
    elementary education • M Ed
    exercise science • MS
    health education • M Ed
    higher education • M Ed
    historical, social, and cultural foundations of education • Ed D, M Ed
    mathematics education • M Ed
    physical education • Ed D, M Ed
    reading and language arts education • M Ed
    science education • M Ed
    secondary education • M Ed
    second language education • M Ed
    social studies education • M Ed
    special education • Ed D, M Ed
    teaching • M Ed

College of Humanities, Fine Arts and Communication
Dr. Lois Zamora, Dean
Programs in:
    applied English linguistics • MA
    English and American literature • MA, PhD
    French • MA
    graphic communications • MFA
    history • MA, PhD
    interior design • MFA
    literature and creative writing • MA, MFA, PhD
    painting • MFA
    philosophy • MA
    photography • MFA
    printmaking • MFA
    public history • MA
    sculpture • MFA
    Spanish • MA, PhD

University of Houston (continued)

Moores School of Music
David Tomatz, Director
Programs in:
    accompanying • MM
    applied music • MM
    composition • DMA, MM
    conducting • DMA
    music education • DMA, MM
    music literature • MM
    music performance and pedagogy • MM
    music theory • MM
    performance • DMA

School of Communication
Robert Musburger, Director
Programs in:
    audiology • MA
    communication sciences research • MA
    mass communication studies • MA
    medical speech pathology • MA
    public relations studies • MA
    speech communication • MA

School of Theatre
Sidney Berger, Director
Program in:
    theatre • MA, MFA

College of Law
Stephen Zamora, Dean
Program in:
    law • JD, LL M

College of Natural Sciences and Mathematics
Dr. John L. Bear, Dean
Programs in:
    applied mathematics • MS
    biochemistry • MS, PhD
    biology • MS, PhD
    chemistry • MS, PhD
    computer science • MS, PhD
    geology • MS, PhD
    geophysics • MS, PhD
    mathematics • MS, PhD
    physics • MS, PhD

College of Optometry
Jerald Strickland, Dean
Programs in:
    optometry • OD
    physiological optics/vision science • MS Phys Op, PhD

College of Pharmacy
Dr. M. F. Lokhandwala, Dean
Programs in:
    hospital pharmacy • MSPHR
    medical chemistry and pharmacology • MS
    pharmaceutics • MS, PhD
    pharmacology • MS, PhD
    pharmacy • Pharm D
    pharmacy administration • MSPHR

College of Social Sciences
Dr. Richard M. Rozelle, Dean
Programs in:
    anthropology • MA
    clinical neuropsychology • PhD
    clinical psychology • PhD
    developmental psychology • PhD
    economics • MA, PhD
    general psychology • PhD
    industrial/organizational psychology • PhD
    political science • MA, PhD
    public administration • MA
    social psychology • PhD
    sociology • MA

College of Technology
Bernard McIntyre, Dean
Programs in:
    construction management • MT
    manufacturing systems • MT
    microcomputer systems • MT
    occupational technology • MSOT

Conrad N. Hilton College of Hotel and Restaurant Management
Alan T. Stutts, Dean
Program in:
    hotel and restaurant management • MHM

Cullen College of Engineering
Dr. John Wolfe, Dean
Programs in:
    aerospace engineering • MSAER, PhD
    biomedical engineering • MS
    chemical engineering • M Ch E, MS Ch E, PhD
    civil and environmental engineering • MCE, MS Env E, MSCE, PhD
    computer and systems engineering • MSCSE, PhD
    electrical and computer engineering • MEE, MSEE, PhD
    environmental engineering • MS, PhD
    industrial engineering • MIE, MSIE, PhD
    materials engineering • MS Mat, PhD
    mechanical engineering • MME, MSME, PhD
    petroleum engineering • MSPE

Graduate School of Social Work
Dr. Karen A. Holmes, Dean
Program in:
    social work • MSW, PhD

 UNIVERSITY OF HOUSTON–CLEAR LAKE
Houston, TX 77058-1098
http://www.cl.uh.edu/

Public coed upper-level institution. *Enrollment: 6,947 graduate, professional, and undergraduate students. Graduate faculty: 78. Library facilities: Neumann Library. Graduate expenses: $207 per*

credit hour for state residents; $336 per credit hour for nonresidents. General application contact: Darella L. Banks, Executive Director of Enrollment Services, 281-283-2517.

School of Business and Public Administration
Programs in:
    accounting • MS
    administration of health services • MS
    business administration • MBA
    environmental management • MS
    finance • MS
    healthcare administration • MHA
    human resource management • MA
    public management • MA

School of Education
Dr. Dennis Spuck, Dean
Programs in:
    counseling • MS
    curriculum and instruction • MS
    early childhood education • MS
    educational management • MS
    instructional technology • MS
    learning resources • MS
    multicultural education • MS
    reading • MS
    secondary education • MA

School of Human Sciences and Humanities
Dr. Shirley Paolini, Dean
Programs in:
    behavioral sciences • MA
    behavioral sciences-general • MA
    behavioral sciences-psychology • MA
    behavioral sciences-sociology • MA
    clinical psychology • MA
    cross-cultural studies • MA
    family therapy • MA
    fitness and human performance • MA
    history • MA
    humanities • MA
    literature • MA
    school psychology • MA
    studies of the future • MS

School of Natural and Applied Sciences
Dr. Charles McKay, Dean
Programs in:
    biological sciences • MS
    chemistry • MS
    computer engineering • MS
    computer information systems • MA
    computer science • MS
    environmental science • MS
    mathematical sciences • MS
    physical science • MS
    software engineering • MS
    statistics • MS

UNIVERSITY OF HOUSTON–VICTORIA
Victoria, TX 77901-4450

Public coed upper-level institution. *Enrollment: 1,491 graduate, professional, and undergraduate students. Graduate faculty: 40 full-time. Computer facilities: Campuswide network is available with full Internet access. Total number of PCs/terminals supplied for student use: 100. Computer service fees are included with tuition and fees. Library facilities: Victoria College Library. Graduate expenses: Tuition of $1026 per year full-time, $57 per semester hour part-time for state residents; $4464 per year full-time, $248 per semester hour part-time for nonresidents. Fees of $540 per year full-time, $30 per semester hour part-time. General application contact: Carol Alxander, Enrollment Management, 512-788-6222.*

College of Arts and Sciences
Dr. Horace Fairlamb, Chair
Programs in:
    interdisciplinary studies • MAIS
    psychology • MA

Division of Business Administration
Charles Bullock, Chair
Program in:
    business administration • MBA

Division of Education
Dr. Cheryl Hines, Chair
Program in:
    education • M Ed

UNIVERSITY OF MARY HARDIN–BAYLOR
Belton, TX 76513

http://www.umhb.edu/

Independent-religious coed comprehensive institution. *Enrollment: 2,313 graduate, professional, and undergraduate students. Graduate faculty: 21 full-time, 12 part-time. Library facilities: Townsend Library. Graduate expenses: Tuition of $270 per semester hour. Fees of $15 per semester hour. General application contact: Dr. Kenneth Johnson, Vice President for Administration and Academic Affairs, 254-939-4505.*

Graduate Program in Health Services Management
Dr. Michael P. West, Chair
Program in:
    health services management • MHSM

University of Mary Hardin–Baylor (continued)

School of Business

Dr. Lee E. Baldwin, Dean
Program in:
 business • MBA

School of Education

Dr. Clarence E. Ham, Dean
Programs in:
 educational administration • M Ed
 educational psychology • M Ed
 general studies • M Ed
 reading education • M Ed

School of Sciences and Humanities

Dr. Darrell G. Watson, Dean
Programs in:
 counseling • MA
 psychology • MA

 # UNIVERSITY OF NORTH TEXAS

Denton, TX 76203-6737

http://www.unt.edu/

Public coed university. *Enrollment: 25,013 graduate, professional, and undergraduate students. Graduate faculty: 671 full-time, 104 part-time. Computer facilities: Campuswide network is available with full Internet access. Computer service fees are applied as a separate charge. Library facilities: A. M. Willis Library plus 5 additional on-campus libraries. Graduate expenses: $2063 per year full-time, $815 per year part-time for state residents; $5897 per year full-time, $2100 per year part-time for nonresidents. General application contact: Dr. C. Neal Tate, Dean of the Graduate School, 940-565-2383.*

Robert B. Toulouse School of Graduate Studies

Dr. C. Neal Tate, Dean
Programs in:
 information science • PhD
 interdisciplinary studies • MA, MS

College of Arts and Sciences

Dr. William Kamman, Interim Dean
Programs in:
 biochemistry • MS, PhD
 biology • MA, MS, PhD
 chemistry • MS, PhD
 clinical psychology • PhD
 communication studies • MA, MS
 computer sciences • MA, MS, PhD
 counseling psychology • MA, MS, PhD
 drama • MA, MS
 economic research • MS
 economics • MA
 engineering technology • MS
 English • MA, PhD

 environmental science • MS, PhD
 experimental psychology • MA, MS, PhD
 French • MA
 health psychology and behavioral medicine • PhD
 history • MA, MS, PhD
 industrial psychology • MA, MS
 journalism • MA, MJ
 labor and industrial relations • MS
 materials science • MS, PhD
 mathematics • MA, MS, PhD
 molecular biology • MA, MS, PhD
 physics • MA, MS, PhD
 political science • MA, MS, PhD
 psychology • MA, MS, PhD
 radio/television/film • MA, MS
 school psychology • MA, MS, PhD
 Spanish • MA
 speech-language pathology/audiology • MA, MS

College of Business Administration

Dr. Henry Hays, Dean
Programs in:
 accounting • MS, PhD
 administrative management • MBA
 banking • MBA, PhD
 finance • MBA, PhD
 information systems • MBA, PhD
 insurance • MBA
 management • MBA
 management science • MBA, PhD
 marketing • MBA, PhD
 organization theory and policy • PhD
 personnel and industrial relations • MBA, PhD
 production/operations management • MBA, PhD
 real estate • MBA

College of Education

Dr. Jean Keller, Dean
Programs in:
 applied technology and training development • Ed D,
  M Ed, MS, PhD
 community health • MS
 computer education and cognitive systems • MS
 counseling and student services • M Ed, MS, PhD
 counselor education • MS
 curriculum and instruction • Ed D, PhD
 development and family studies • MS
 early childhood education • M Ed, MS, PhD
 educational administration • Ed D, M Ed, PhD
 educational research • PhD
 elementary education • M Ed, MS
 elementary school supervision • M Ed
 higher education • Ed D, PhD
 kinesiology • MS
 reading • Ed D, M Ed, MS, PhD
 recreation and leisure studies • Certificate, MS
 school health • MS
 secondary education • M Ed, MS
 secondary school supervision • M Ed
 special education • M Ed, MS, PhD
 special subject supervision • M Ed
 vocational counselor • Certificate

College of Music

Dr. David L. Shrader, Dean
Programs in:
  composition • DMA, MM, PhD
  conducting • DMA, MM
  jazz studies • MM
  music • MA
  music education • MM, MME, PhD
  musicology • MM, PhD
  music theory • MM, PhD
  performance • DMA, MM

School of Community Service

Dr. David W. Hartman, Interim Dean
Programs in:
  administration of aging organizations • MA, MS
  administration of retirement facilities • MA, MS
  aging • Certificate, MA, MS
  applied economics • MS
  behavior analysis • MS
  public administration • MPA
  rehabilitation counseling • MS
  rehabilitation studies • MS
  sociology • MA, MS, PhD
  vocational evaluation • MS
  work adjustment services • MS

School of Library and Information Sciences

Dr. Philip M. Turner, Dean
Programs in:
  information science • MS, PhD
  library science • MS

School of Merchandising and Hospitality Management

Dr. Suzanne V. LaBrecque, Dean
Programs in:
  hotel/restaurant management • MS
  merchandising and fabric analytics • MS

School of Visual Arts

Dr. D. Jack Davis, Dean
Programs in:
  art • PhD
  art education • MA, MFA, PhD
  art history • MA, MFA
  ceramics • MFA
  communication design • MFA
  fashion design • MFA
  fibers • MFA
  interior design • MFA
  metalsmithing and jewelry • MFA
  painting and drawing • MFA
  photography • MFA
  printmaking • MFA
  sculpture • MFA

UNIVERSITY OF ST. THOMAS
Houston, TX 77006-4696

http://www.stthom.edu/

Independent-religious coed comprehensive institution. *Enrollment:* 2,506 graduate, professional, and undergraduate students. Graduate faculty: *98 full-time, 97 part-time.* Computer facilities: *Campuswide network is available with full Internet access. Total number of PCs/terminals supplied for student use: 186. Computer services are offered at no charge.* Library facilities: *Doherty Library plus 2 additional on-campus libraries.* Graduate expenses: *Tuition of $410 per credit hour. Fees of $33 per year full-time, $22.50 per year part-time.* General application contact: *Elsie P. Biron, Director of Admissions, 713-525-3505.*

Cameron School of Business

Dr. Yhi-Min Ho, Dean
Program in:
  business • MBA, MIB, MSA

Center for Thomistic Studies

Rev. John Gallagher, CSB, Director
Program in:
  philosophy • MA, PhD

Program in Liberal Arts

Dr. Janice Gordon-Kelter, Director
Program in:
  liberal arts • MLA

School of Education

Dr. Anna Dewald, Dean
Program in:
  education • M Ed

School of Theology

Rev. Louis T. Brusatti, CM, Dean
Program in:
  theology • Diploma, M Div, MAPS

THE UNIVERSITY OF TEXAS AT ARLINGTON
Arlington, TX 76019-0407

http://www.uta.edu/

Public coed university. *Enrollment:* 19,286 graduate, professional, and undergraduate students. Graduate faculty: *437 full-time, 43 part-time.* Computer facilities: *Campuswide network is available with full Internet access. Total number of PCs/terminals supplied for student use: 600. Computer service fees are included with tuition and fees.* Library facilities: *Central Library plus 2 additional on-campus libraries.* Graduate expenses: *$3206 per year full-time, $468 per semester (minimum) part-time for state residents; $8612 per year full-time, $1137 per semester (minimum) part-time for*

The University of Texas at Arlington (continued)
nonresidents. General application contact: *Dr. Dale Anderson, Vice Provost for Research and Graduate Studies, 817-272-2681.*

Graduate School
Dr. Dale Anderson, Vice Provost for Research and Graduate Studies
Programs in:
  environmental science and engineering • MS
  interdisciplinary studies • MA, MS

Center for Professional Teacher Education
Dr. Jeanne Gerlach, Director
Program in:
  teacher education • MET

College of Business Administration
Dr. Dan Worrell, Interim Dean
Programs in:
  accounting • MBA, MPA, MS
  business administration • PhD
  economics • MA
  finance • MBA
  information systems • MBA, MS, PhD
  management • MBA
  management sciences • MBA
  marketing • MBA
  marketing research • MS
  personnel and human resources management • MS
  real estate • MBA, MS
  taxation • MS

College of Engineering
Dr. J. Ronald Bailey, Dean
Programs in:
  aerospace engineering • M Engr, MS, PhD
  biomedical engineering • MS, PhD
  civil and environmental engineering • M Engr, MS, PhD
  computer science and engineering • M Engr, M Sw En, MCS, MS, PhD
  electrical engineering • M Engr, MS, PhD
  engineering mechanics • MS
  industrial engineering • M Engr, MS, PhD
  materials science and engineering • MS, PhD
  mechanical engineering • M Engr, MS, PhD

College of Liberal Arts
Dr. Ben Agger, Dean
Programs in:
  anthropology • MA
  criminal justice • MA
  English • MA
  French • MA
  German • MA
  history • MA
  humanities • MA, MAT, PhD
  linguistics • MA
  literature • PhD
  political science • MA
  rhetoric • PhD
  sociology • MA
  Spanish • MA

College of Science
Dr. Verne Cox, Interim Dean
Programs in:
  applied chemistry • PhD
  biology • MS, PhD
  chemistry • MS, PhD
  geology • MS
  mathematical sciences • PhD
  mathematics • MS
  physics • MS, PhD
  psychology • MS, PhD
  radiological physics • MS

School of Architecture
Edward Baum, Dean
Programs in:
  architecture • M Arch
  landscape architecture • MLA

School of Nursing
Dr. Elizabeth C. Poster, Dean
Programs in:
  administration/supervision of nursing • MSN
  teaching of nursing • MSN

School of Social Work
Dr. Santos Hernandez, Dean
Program in:
  social work • MSSW, PhD

School of Urban and Public Affairs
Dr. Richard L. Cole, Dean
Programs in:
  city and regional planning • MCRP
  public administration • MPA
  public and urban administration • PhD
  urban and regional affairs • MA

THE UNIVERSITY OF TEXAS AT AUSTIN
Austin, TX 78712

http://www.utexas.edu/

Public coed university. *Enrollment:* 48,008 graduate, professional, and undergraduate students. Graduate faculty: *1,774.* Computer facilities: *Campuswide network is available. Computer service fees are included with tuition and fees.* Library facilities: *Perry-Castaneda Library plus 18 additional on-campus libraries.* Graduate expenses: *Tuition of $2592 per year full-time, $324 per semester (minimum) part-time for state residents; $7704 per year full-time, $963 per semester (minimum) part-time for nonresidents. Fees of $778 per year full-time, $161 per semester (minimum) part-time.* General application contact: *Dr. William Paver, Director, Graduate and International Admissions Center, 512-475-7390.*

Graduate School
Dr. Teresa A. Sullivan, Vice President and Dean
Programs in:
  computational and applied mathematics • MA, PhD
  neuroscience • MA, PhD
  post-Soviet and East European studies • MA
  science and technology commercialization • MS
  writing • MFA

College of Business Administration
Robert G. May, Dean
Programs in:
  accounting • MPA, PhD
  business • MBA
  finance • PhD
  management • PhD
  management sciences and information systems • PhD
  marketing administration • PhD

College of Communication
Dr. Ellen Wartella, Dean
Programs in:
  advertising • MA, PhD
  communication sciences and disorders • MA, PhD
  communication studies • MA, PhD
  film/video production • MFA
  journalism • MA, PhD
  radio-television-film • MA, PhD

College of Education
Dr. Manuel J. Justiz, Dean
Programs in:
  educational administration • Ed D, M Ed, PhD
  educational psychology • M Ed, MA, PhD
  foreign language education • MA, PhD
  health education • Ed D, M Ed, MA, PhD
  kinesiology • Ed D, M Ed, MA, PhD
  mathematics education • M Ed, MA, PhD
  science education • M Ed, MA, PhD
  special education • Ed D, M Ed, MA, PhD

College of Engineering
Dr. Ben G. Streetman, Dean
Programs in:
  aerospace engineering • MSE, PhD
  architectural engineering • MSE
  biomedical engineering • MSE, PhD
  chemical engineering • MSE, PhD
  civil engineering • MSE, PhD
  electrical and computer engineering • MSE, PhD
  engineering mechanics • MSE, PhD
  environmental and water resources engineering • MSE
  manufacturing systems engineering • MSE
  materials science and engineering • MSE, PhD
  mechanical engineering • MSE, PhD
  operations research and industrial engineering • MSE, PhD
  petroleum and geosystems engineering • MSE, PhD

College of Fine Arts
David L. Deming, Interim Dean
Programs in:
  art education • MA
  art history • MA, PhD
  music • DMA, M Music, PhD
  studio art • MFA
  theatre • MA, MFA, PhD

College of Liberal Arts
Dr. Sheldon Ekland-Olson, Dean
Programs in:
  American civilization • MA, PhD
  Arabic studies • MA, PhD
  archaeology • MA, PhD
  Asian cultures and languages • MA, PhD
  Asian studies • MA
  classics • MA, PhD
  comparative literature • MA, PhD
  economics • MA, MS Econ, PhD
  English • MA, PhD
  folklore • MA, PhD
  French • MA, PhD
  geography • MA, PhD
  Germanic languages • MA, PhD
  government • MA, PhD
  Hebrew studies • MA, PhD
  history • MA, PhD
  Latin American studies • MA, PhD
  linguistic anthropology • MA, PhD
  linguistics • MA, PhD
  Middle Eastern studies • MA
  Persian studies • MA, PhD
  philosophy • MA, PhD
  physical anthropology • MA, PhD
  Portuguese • MA, PhD
  psychology • PhD
  Slavic languages • MA, PhD
  social anthropology • MA, PhD
  sociology • MA, PhD
  Spanish • MA, PhD

College of Natural Sciences
Mary Ann Rankin, Dean
Programs in:
  analytical chemistry • MA, PhD
  astronomy • MA, PhD
  biochemistry • MA, PhD
  biological sciences • MA, PhD
  botany • MA, PhD
  child development and family relations • MA, PhD
  computer sciences • MA, MSCS, PhD
  geological sciences • MA, MS, PhD
  inorganic chemistry • MA, PhD
  marine science • MA, PhD
  mathematics • MA, PhD
  microbiology • MA, PhD
  molecular biology • MA, PhD
  nutrition • MA
  nutritional sciences • PhD
  organic chemistry • MA, PhD
  physical chemistry • MA, PhD
  physics • MA, MS, PhD
  statistics • MS Stat
  zoology • MA, PhD

Graduate School of Library and Information Science
Glynn Harmon, Interim Dean
Program in:
  library and information science • MLIS, PhD

The University of Texas at Austin (continued)

Lyndon B. Johnson School of Public Affairs
Dr. Edwin Dorn, Dean
Programs in:
 public affairs • MP Aff
 public policy • PhD

School of Architecture
Lawrence Speck, Dean
Programs in:
 architecture • M Arch, MS Arch St
 community and regional planning • MSCRP, PhD

School of Nursing
Dr. Dolores Sands, Dean
Program in:
 nursing • MSN, PhD

School of Social Work
Dr. Barbara White, Dean
Program in:
 social work • MSSW, PhD

College of Pharmacy
Programs in:
 pharmacy • MS Phr, PhD, Pharm D

School of Law
M. Michael Sharlot, Dean
Program in:
 law • JD, LL M

THE UNIVERSITY OF TEXAS AT BROWNSVILLE
Brownsville, TX 78520-4991

http://www.utb.edu/

Public coed upper-level institution. *Enrollment: 2,473 graduate, professional, and undergraduate students. Graduate faculty: 71 full-time, 2 part-time. Computer facilities: Campuswide network is available with full Internet access. Total number of PCs/terminals supplied for student use: 748. Computer service fees are included with tuition and fees. Library facilities: Arnulfo L. Oliveira Library. Graduate expenses: Tuition of $648 per year full-time, $120 per semester hour part-time for state residents; $4698 per year full-time, $783 per semester hour part-time for nonresidents. Fees of $593 per year full-time, $109 per year part-time. General application contact: Dr. Mimosa Stephenson, Interim Dean, Graduate Studies, 956-544-8812.*

Graduate Studies
Dr. Mimosa Stephenson, Interim Dean

College of Liberal Arts
Dr. Anthony N. Zavaleta, Dean
Programs in:
 behavioral sciences • MAIS
 English • MA

 interdisciplinary studies • MAIS
 social sciences • MAIS
 Spanish • MA

College of Science, Mathematics and Technology
Dr. José G. Martin, Dean
Program in:
 biological sciences • MSIS

School of Business
Dr. Betsy V. Boze, Dean
Program in:
 business • MBA

School of Education
Dr. Sylvia C. Peña, Dean
Programs in:
 counseling and guidance • M Ed
 curriculum and instruction • M Ed
 early childhood education • M Ed
 education • Ed D
 educational administration • M Ed
 educational technology • M Ed
 elementary education • M Ed
 English as a second language • M Ed
 reading • M Ed
 special education • M Ed
 supervision • M Ed

THE UNIVERSITY OF TEXAS AT DALLAS
Richardson, TX 75083-0688

http://www.utdallas.edu/

Public coed university. *Enrollment: 9,327 graduate, professional, and undergraduate students. Graduate faculty: 288 full-time, 138 part-time. Computer facilities: Campuswide network is available with full Internet access. Total number of PCs/terminals supplied for student use: 380. Computer service fees are applied as a separate charge. Library facilities: Eugene McDermott Library. Graduate expenses: $3489 per year full-time, $536 per semester (minimum) part-time for state residents; $8600 per year full-time, $1175 per semester (minimum) part-time for nonresidents. General application contact: Jean Stuart, Director of Admissions and Records, 972-883-2346.*

Erik Jonsson School of Engineering and Computer Science
Dr. William P. Osborne, Dean
Programs in:
 computer science • MS, PhD
 electrical engineering • MSEE, PhD
 microelectronics • MSEE
 telecommunications • MSEE

School of Arts and Humanities
Dr. Dennis M. Kratz, Dean
Programs in:
  aesthetic studies • MA, MAT, PhD
  history of ideas • MA, MAT, PhD
  humanities • MA, MAT, PhD
  studies in literature • MA, MAT, PhD

School of General Studies
Dr. George Fair, Dean
Program in:
  interdisciplinary studies • MA

School of Human Development
Dr. Bert Moore, Dean
Programs in:
  applied cognition and neuroscience • MS
  communications disorders • MS
  human development and communication sciences • PhD
  human development and early childhood disorders • MS

School of Management
Dr. Hasan Pirkul, Dean
Programs in:
  business administration • MBA
  international management studies • MA, PhD
  management • MBA
  management and administrative sciences • MS
  management and administrative services • MS
  management science • PhD

School of Natural Sciences and Mathematics
Dr. Richard Caldwell, Dean
Programs in:
  applied mathematics • MS, PhD
  applied statistics • MS, PhD
  biology • MS, PhD
  biotechnology • MS, PhD
  chemistry • MS
  environmental applications of geochemistry and
    geophysics • MS, PhD
  geochemistry-petrology-mineral resources • MS, PhD
  geophysics-sedimentology • MS, PhD
  hydrogeology • MS, PhD
  industrial chemistry • D Chem
  mathematics • MAT
  mathematics education • MAT
  molecular and cell biology • MS, PhD
  physics • MS, PhD
  pure mathematics • MS
  science education • MAT
  sedimentology • MS, PhD
  stratigraphy-micropaleontology • MS, PhD
  structural geology • MS, PhD
  tectonics • MS, PhD
  theoretical statistics • MS, PhD

School of Social Sciences
Dr. Rita Mae Kelly, Dean
Programs in:
  political economy • PhD
  public affairs • MPA

THE UNIVERSITY OF TEXAS AT EL PASO
El Paso, TX 79968-0001

http://www.utep.edu/

Public coed university. *Computer facilities:* Campuswide network is available with full Internet access. Computer service fees are included with tuition and fees. *Library facilities:* main library. Graduate expenses: *$1559 per year full-time, $230 per credit hour part-time for state residents; $5393 per year full-time, $405 per credit hour part-time for nonresidents.* General application contact: *Director, Graduate Student Services, 915-747-5491.*

Graduate School
Programs in:
  environmental science and engineering • PhD
  materials science and engineering • PhD

College of Business Administration
Programs in:
  accounting • MACY
  business administration • MBA, MS

College of Education
Programs in:
  education • MA
  educational leadership and foundations • Ed D
  educational psychology and special services • M Ed

College of Engineering
Programs in:
  civil engineering • MS
  computer engineering • MS, PhD
  computer science • MS
  electrical engineering • MS, PhD
  engineering • MEENE, MSENE
  industrial engineering • MS
  manufacturing engineering • MS
  mechanical engineering • MS
  metallurgical engineering • MS

College of Liberal Arts
Programs in:
  art • MA
  border history • MA
  clinical psychology • MA
  communication • MA
  creative writing in English • MFA
  creative writing in Spanish • MFA
  English and American literature • MA
  experimental psychology • MA
  history • MA
  liberal arts • MAIS
  linguistics • MA
  music education • MM
  music performance • MM
  political science • MA, MPA
  psychology • PhD
  sociology • MA
  Spanish • MA
  theatre arts • MA

The University of Texas at El Paso (continued)

College of Nursing and Health Science
Programs in:
adult health • MSN
community health • MSN
community health/family nurse practitioner • MSN
health sciences • MS
kinesiology and sports studies • MS
nurse midwifery • MSN
nursing administration • MSN
nursing and health science • MPH
parent-child nursing • MSN
psychiatric/mental health nursing • MSN
speech language pathology • MS
womens health care/nurse practitioner • MSN

College of Science
Programs in:
biological sciences • MS
chemistry • MS
geological sciences • MS, PhD
geophysics • MS
interdisciplinary studies • MSIS
mathematical sciences • MAT, MS
physics • MS
statistics • MS

THE UNIVERSITY OF TEXAS AT SAN ANTONIO
San Antonio, TX 78249-0617

http://www.utsa.edu/

Public coed comprehensive institution. *Enrollment: 17,497 graduate, professional, and undergraduate students. Graduate faculty: 387 full-time, 480 part-time. Computer facilities: Campuswide network is available with full Internet access. Total number of PCs/terminals supplied for student use: 800. Computer service fees are included with tuition and fees. Library facilities: John Peace Library plus 1 additional on-campus library. Graduate expenses: Tuition of $2476 per year full-time, $309 per semester (minimum) part-time for state residents; $7584 per year full-time, $948 per semester (minimum) part-time for nonresidents. Fees of $361 per year full-time, $133 per semester (minimum) part-time. General application contact: Dr. John H. Brown, Director of Admissions and Registrar, 210-458-4530.*

College of Business
James F. Gaertner, Dean
Programs in:
accounting • MP Acct
business administration • MBA
management of technology • MSMOT
taxation • MT

College of Fine Arts and Humanities
Dr. Alan Craven, Dean
Programs in:
architecture and interior design • M Arch
art • MFA
art history • MA
English • MA
music • MM
Spanish • MA

College of Sciences and Engineering
Dr. Rey Elizondo, Dean
Programs in:
biology • MS
biotechnology • MS
chemistry • MS
civil engineering • MS
computer science • MS, PhD
electrical engineering • MS
environmental sciences • MS
geology • MS
mathematics • MS
mathematics education • MS
mechanical engineering • MS
neurobiology • PhD
statistics • MS

College of Social and Behavioral Sciences
Dr. Dwight Henderson, Dean
Programs in:
anthropology • MA
bicultural-bilingual studies • MA
bicultural studies • MA
education • MA
history • MA
political science • MA
psychology • MS
public administration • MPA
sociology • MS
teaching English as a second language • MA

THE UNIVERSITY OF TEXAS AT TYLER
Tyler, TX 75799-0001

http://www.uttyl.edu/

Public coed upper-level institution. *Enrollment: 3,390 graduate, professional, and undergraduate students. Graduate faculty: 115 full-time, 33 part-time. Library facilities: Robert R. Muntz Library. Graduate expenses: $2144 per year full-time, $337 per semester (minimum) part-time for state residents; $7256 per year full-time, $964 per semester (minimum) part-time for nonresidents. General application contact: Martha D. Wheat, Director of Admissions and Student Records, 903-566-7201.*

Graduate Studies

Dr. Don Killebrew, Graduate Coordinator

School of Business Administration

Dr. Jim Tarter, Dean
Programs in:
   business administration • MBA
   health care • MBA

School of Education and Psychology

Dr. J. Milford Clark, Dean
Programs in:
   allied health/interdisciplinary studies • MS
   biology • Certificate, M Ed
   clinical exercise physiology • MS
   early childhood education • M Ed, MA
   educational administration • Certificate, M Ed
   English • Certificate, M Ed
   health and kinesiology • M Ed
   history • Certificate, M Ed
   interdisciplinary studies • MS
   kinesiology • MS
   kinesiology/interdisciplinary studies • MS
   mathematics • Certificate, M Ed
   psychology • Certificate, MA, MS
   reading • Certificate, M Ed, MA
   secondary teaching • MAT
   special education • Certificate, M Ed, MA
   technology • MS

School of Engineering

Dr. Leonard Hale, Dean
Program in:
   engineering • M Engr

School of Liberal Arts

Dr. Vincent Falzone, Interim Dean
Programs in:
   history • Certificate, MA, MAT
   interdisciplinary studies • MA, MS
   political science • MA
   public administration • MPA

School of Nursing

Dr. Linda Klotz, Dean
Program in:
   nursing • MSN

School of Sciences and Mathematics

Dr. L. Lynn Sherrod, Dean
Programs in:
   biology • MS
   computer science • MS
   interdisciplinary studies • MA, MS
   mathematics • MS

THE UNIVERSITY OF TEXAS OF THE PERMIAN BASIN
Odessa, TX 79762-0001

http://www.utpb.edu/

Public coed comprehensive institution. Computer facilities: *Campuswide network is available with full Internet access. Total number of PCs/ terminals supplied for student use: 75. Computer service fees are included with tuition and fees.* Library facilities: *J. Conrad Dunagan Library plus 1 additional on-campus library.* Graduate expenses: *Tuition of $1314 per year full-time, $73 per hour part-time for state residents; $4896 per year full-time, $272 per hour part-time for nonresidents. Fees of $383 per year full-time, $111 per semester (minimum) part-time.* General application contact: *Director of Graduate Studies, 915-552-2530.*

Graduate School

College of Arts and Sciences

Programs in:
   applied behavioral analysis • MA
   biology • MS
   clinical psychology • MA
   criminal justice administration • MS
   English • MA
   geology • MS
   history • MA
   physical education • MA

School of Business

Programs in:
   accountancy • MPA
   management • MBA

School of Education

Programs in:
   counseling • MA
   early childhood education • MA
   educational administration • MA
   elementary education • MA
   reading • MA
   secondary education • MA
   special education • MA
   supervision • MA

 # THE UNIVERSITY OF TEXAS– PAN AMERICAN
Edinburg, TX 78539-2999

http://www.panam.edu/

Public coed comprehensive institution. *Enrollment: 12,501 graduate, professional, and undergraduate students. Graduate faculty: 88 full-time, 3 part-time.* Library facilities: *main library.* Graduate expenses: *$2156 per year full-time, $283 per semester (minimum) part-time for state residents; $6788 per year full-time, $862 per semester (minimum) part-time for nonresidents.* General application

The University of Texas–Pan American (continued)
contact: *David Zuniga, Director of Admissions and Records, 956-381-2206.*

College of Business Administration
Program in:
   business administration • MBA, PhD

College of Education
Programs in:
   administration • M Ed
   counseling and guidance • M Ed
   early childhood education • M Ed
   education • Ed D
   educational diagnostics • M Ed
   elementary bilingual education • M Ed
   elementary education • M Ed
   gifted and talented education • M Ed
   kinesiology • M Ed
   reading • M Ed
   school psychology • MA
   secondary education • M Ed
   special education • M Ed
   supervision • M Ed

College of Health and Human Services
Dr. Helen M. Castillo, Dean
Programs in:
   communication disorders • MA
   nursing • MSN
   social work • MSSW

College of Liberal and Performing Arts
Programs in:
   English • MA, MAIS
   English as a second language • MA
   history • MA, MAIS
   Spanish • MA
   speech communication • MA
   theatre • MA

College of Science and Engineering
Programs in:
   biology • MS
   computer science • MS
   mathematics • MS, MSIS

College of Social and Behavioral Sciences
Dr. James W. Lamare, Dean
Programs in:
   clinical psychology • MA
   criminal justice • MS
   experimental psychology • MA
   psychology • MA
   public administration • MPA
   sociology • MS

Program in Interdisciplinary Studies
Program in:
   interdisciplinary studies • MAIS, MSIS

UNIVERSITY OF THE INCARNATE WORD
San Antonio, TX 78209-6397

http://www.uiw.edu/

Independent-religious coed comprehensive institution. *Enrollment:* 3,312 graduate, professional, and undergraduate students. Graduate faculty: *42 full-time, 11 part-time.* Computer facilities: *Campuswide network is available with full Internet access. Total number of PCs/terminals supplied for student use: 200. Computer services are offered at no charge.* Library facilities: *J. E. and L. E. Mabee Library.* Graduate expenses: *Tuition of $350 per semester hour. Fees of $180 per year full-time, $111 per semester (minimum) part-time.* General application contact: *Andrea Cyterski, Director of Admissions, 210-829-6005.*

School of Graduate Studies
Dr. D. Reginald Traylor, Dean
Program in:
   multidisciplinary studies • MA

College of Arts and Sciences
Gilberto M. Hinojosa, Dean
Programs in:
   biology • MA, MS
   communication arts • MA
   English • MA
   mathematics • MAMT, MS
   nutrition • MS
   religious studies • MA

College of Professional Studies
Dr. Bill Platzer, Dean
Programs in:
   adult education • M Ed, MA
   business administration • MBA
   deaf education • M Ed
   early childhood education • M Ed, MA
   educational diagnostics • M Ed, MA
   elementary education • M Ed, MA
   general management • MAA
   international administration • MAA
   nursing • MSN
   organization development • MAA
   physical education • M Ed, MA
   reading • M Ed, MA
   reading specialist • M Ed, MA
   secondary teaching • M Ed, MA
   social gerontology • MA
   special education • M Ed, MA
   sports management • MAA

WEST TEXAS A&M UNIVERSITY
Canyon, TX 79016-0001

http://www.wtamu.edu/

Public coed comprehensive institution. *Enrollment: 6,189 graduate, professional, and undergraduate students. Graduate faculty: 115 full-time, 74 part-time. Computer facilities: Campuswide network is available with full Internet access. Total number of PCs/terminals supplied for student use: 350. Computer service fees are included with tuition and fees. Library facilities: Cornette Library plus 1 additional on-campus library. Graduate expenses: Tuition of $46 per semester hour for state residents; $259 per semester hour for nonresidents. Fees of $156 per semester (minimum). General applica-tion contact: Dr. Vaughn Nelson, Dean of the Graduate School, 806-651-2730.*

College of Agriculture, Nursing, and Natural Sciences
Dr. James Clark, Dean
Programs in:
agricultural business and economics • MS
agriculture • MS
animal science • MS
biology • MS
chemistry • MS
engineering technology • MS
environmental science • MS
mathematics • MS
nursing • MSN
plant science • MS

College of Education and Social Sciences
Dr. Ted Guffy, Dean
Programs in:
administration • M Ed
counseling education • M Ed
curriculum and instruction • M Ed, MA
educational diagnostician • M Ed
educational technology • M Ed
elementary education • M Ed, MA
history • MA
political science • MA
professional counseling • M Ed
psychology • MA
reading • M Ed
secondary education • M Ed, MA
sports and exercise science • MS

College of Fine Arts and Humanities
Dr. Sue Park, Dean
Programs in:
art • MA
communication • MA
English • MA
music • MA
performance • MM
studio art • MFA

Program in Interdisciplinary Studies
Dr. Vaughn Nelson, Dean of the Graduate School
Program in:
interdisciplinary studies • MA, MS

T. Boone Pickens College of Business
Dr. Jerry Miller, Dean
Programs in:
accounting • MP Acc
business administration • MBA
finance and economics • MS

UTAH

BRIGHAM YOUNG UNIVERSITY
Provo, UT 84602-1001

http://www.byu.edu/

Independent-religious coed university. *Enrollment: 31,249 gradu-ate, professional, and undergraduate students. Graduate faculty: 1,176. Computer facilities: Campuswide network is available with full Internet access. Total number of PCs/terminals supplied for student use: 1,800. Computer service fees are applied as a separate charge. Library facilities: Harold B. Lee Library plus 2 additional on-campus libraries. Graduate expenses: $3200 per year full-time, $178 per credit hour part-time for state residents; $4800 per year full-time, $266 per credit hour part-time for nonresidents. General application contact: Adviser, 801-378-4541.*

Graduate School
Addie Fuhriman, Dean

College of Biological and Agricultural Sciences
Addie Fuhriman, Dean, Graduate School
Programs in:
agronomy • MS
animal science • MS
biological science education • MS
botany • MS, PhD
food science • MS
horticulture • MS
microbiology • MS, PhD
molecular biology • MS, PhD
nutrition • MS
range science • MS
wildlife and range resources • MS, PhD
zoology • MS, PhD

College of Engineering and Technology
Dr. Douglas M. Chabries, Dean
Programs in:
chemical engineering • MS
civil engineering • MS
electrical engineering • MS
engineering • PhD
engineering management • MEM

Brigham Young University (continued)
    engineering technology • MS
    manufacturing engineering • MS
    mechanical engineering • MS, PhD
    technology education and construction management •
        MS

College of Family, Home, and Social Sciences
Dr. Clayne L. Pope, Dean
Programs in:
    American studies • MA
    anthropology • MA
    Asian studies • MA
    clinical psychology • PhD
    family sciences and human development • MS, PhD
    family studies • PhD
    general psychology • MS
    geography • MS
    history • MA, PhD
    international development • MA
    international relations • MA
    marriage and family therapy • MS, PhD
    Near Eastern ancient studies • MA
    psychology • PhD
    social work • MSW

College of Fine Arts and Communications
Dr. Bruce L. Christensen, Dean
Programs in:
    art education • MA
    art history • MA
    ceramics • MFA
    communications • MA
    composition • MM
    conducting • MM
    music education • MA, MM
    musicology • MA, PhD
    painting-drawing • MFA
    performance • MM
    printmaking-drawing • MFA
    sculpture • MFA
    theatre and film • MA, PhD
    theatre design and technology • MFA

College of Humanities
Dr. Van C. Gessel, Dean
Programs in:
    American studies • MA
    Arabic • MA
    Asian studies • MA
    Chinese • MA
    comparative literature • MA
    English • MA
    Finnish • MA
    French • MA
    French studies • MA
    general linguistics • MA
    German • MA
    German literature • MA
    humanities • MA
    international development • MA
    international relations • MA
    Japanese • MA
    Korean • MA

    Near Eastern ancient studies • MA
    Portuguese • MA
    Portuguese linguistics • MA
    Portuguese literature • MA
    Russian • MA
    Scandinavian • MA
    Spanish linguistics • MA
    Spanish literature • MA
    Spanish teaching • MA
    teaching English as a second language • Certificate, MA

College of Nursing
Dr. Sandra Rogers, Dean
Program in:
    nursing • MS

College of Physical and Mathematical Sciences
Bill R. Hays, Dean
Programs in:
    analytical chemistry • MS, PhD
    applied statistics • MS
    biochemistry • MS, PhD
    computer science • MS, PhD
    inorganic chemistry • MS, PhD
    organic chemistry • MS, PhD
    physical and mathematical sciences • MA
    physical chemistry • MS, PhD
    physics • MS, PhD
    physics and astronomy • PhD

College of Physical Education
Dr. Robert K. Conlee, Dean
Programs in:
    athletic training • MS
    corrective physical education • PhD
    curriculum and instruction • PhD
    dance • MA
    exercise physiology • M Ed, MS
    exercise science/wellness • PhD
    health promotion • M Ed, MS
    health sciences • MS
    physical education • M Ed, MS
    recreation management and youth leadership • MS

David O. McKay School of Education
Dr. Robert S. Patterson, Dean
Programs in:
    audiology • MS
    counseling and school psychology • MS
    counseling psychology • PhD
    educational leadership and foundations • Ed D, M Ed,
        PhD
    instructional psychology and technology • MS, PhD
    reading • Ed D
    special education • MS
    speech-language pathology • MS
    teaching and learning • M Ed, MA
    teaching English to speakers of other languages •
        Certificate

J. Reuben Clark Law School
Dr. H. Reese Hansen, Dean
Program in:
    law • JD, LL M

Marriott School of Management
Dr. K. Fred Skousen, Dean
Programs in:
    accountancy and information systems • M Acc, MISM
    business administration • MBA
    executive business administration • MBA
    organizational behavior • MOB
    public management • MPA

SOUTHERN UTAH UNIVERSITY
Cedar City, UT 84720-2498

http://www.suu.edu/

Public coed comprehensive institution. *Enrollment: 6,007 graduate, professional, and undergraduate students. Graduate faculty: 25 full-time, 3 part-time. Computer facilities: Campuswide network is available with full Internet access. Total number of PCs/terminals supplied for student use: 1,000. Computer service fees are included with tuition and fees. Library facilities: main library. Graduate expenses: Tuition of $1581 per year full-time, $59 per credit hour part-time for state residents; $5985 per year full-time, $204 per credit hour part-time for nonresidents. Fees of $414 per year full-time, $20 per semester (minimum) part-time. General application contact: Dr. Terry D. Alger, Provost, 435-586-7704.*

School of Business
Carl Templin, Dean
Program in:
    business • M Acc

School of Education
Dr. Paul Wilford, Director
Programs in:
    elementary education • M Ed
    secondary education • M Ed

UNIVERSITY OF UTAH
Salt Lake City, UT 84112-1107

http://www.utah.edu/

Public coed university. *Enrollment: 26,193 graduate, professional, and undergraduate students. Graduate faculty: 1,456 full-time. Computer facilities: Campuswide network is available with full Internet access. Total number of PCs/terminals supplied for student use: 1,000. Computer service fees are included with tuition and fees. Library facilities: Marriott Library plus 2 additional on-campus libraries. Graduate expenses: $2045 per year full-time, $562 per semester (minimum) part-time for state residents; $6129 per year full-time, $1607 per semester (minimum) part-time for nonresidents. General application contact: Dr. Ann W. Hart, Dean of the Graduate School, 801-581-7642.*

Graduate School
Dr. Ann W. Hart, Dean
Programs in:
    biochemistry • MS, PhD
    biological chemistry • PhD
    biostatistics • M Stat
    medical informatics • MS, PhD
    medical laboratory science • MS
    medicinal chemistry • MS, PhD
    microbiology and immunology • PhD
    molecular biology • PhD
    molecular evolutionary biology • PhD
    neurobiology and anatomy • MS, PhD
    neuroscience • PhD
    oncological sciences • MS, PhD
    pathology • PhD
    pharmaceutics and pharmaceutical chemistry • MS, PhD
    pharmacology and toxicology • MS, PhD
    pharmacy practice • MS
    physiology • PhD
    public health • MPH, MSPH
    statistics • M Stat

College of Engineering
David Pershing, Dean
Programs in:
    applied mechanics • MS
    bioengineering • ME, MS, PhD
    chemical engineering • M Phil, ME, MS, PhD
    civil engineering • ME, MS, PhD
    computer science • M Phil, ME, MS, PhD
    electrical engineering • EE, M Phil, ME, MS, PhD
    engineering administration • MEA
    fuels engineering • ME, MS, PhD
    materials science and engineering • ME, MS, PhD
    mechanical engineering • M Phil, ME, MS, PhD
    nuclear engineering • ME, MS, PhD

College of Fine Arts
Phyllis Haskell, Dean
Programs in:
    art education • MA
    art history • MA
    ballet • MA, MFA
    ceramics • MFA
    drawing • MFA
    film • MFA
    graphic design • MFA
    illustration • MFA
    metal sculpture • MFA
    modern dance • MA, MFA
    music • M Mus, MA, PhD
    painting • MFA
    photography • MFA
    printmaking • MFA
    sculpture • MFA
    theatre • MFA, PhD

College of Health
John Dunn, Dean
Programs in:
    audiology • MA, MS
    exercise and sport science • Ed D, M Phil, MS, PhD
    foods and nutrition • MS

University of Utah (continued)
    health promotion and education • Ed D, M Phil, MS, PhD
    physical therapy • MPT
    recreation and leisure • Ed D, M Phil, MS, PhD
    speech-language pathology • MA, MS
    speech-language pathology and audiology • M Phil, PhD

College of Humanities
Patricia L. Hanna, Dean
Programs in:
    communication • M Phil, MA, MS, PhD
    comparative literature • MA, PhD
    creative writing • MFA
    English • MA, PhD
    French • MA, MAT, PhD
    German • MA, MAT, PhD
    history • MA, MS, PhD
    language pedagogy • MAT
    linguistics • MA
    Middle East studies • MA, PhD
    philosophy • MA, MS, PhD
    Spanish • MA, MAT, PhD

College of Mines and Earth Sciences
Francis Brown, Dean
Programs in:
    geological engineering • ME, MS, PhD
    geology • MS, PhD
    geophysics • MS, PhD
    metallurgy and metallurgical engineering • ME, MS, PhD
    meteorology • MS, PhD
    mining engineering • ME, MS, PhD

College of Nursing
Linda K. Amos, Dean
Programs in:
    gerontology • Certificate, MS
    nursing • MS, PhD

College of Science
Peter Stang, Dean
Programs in:
    biological chemistry • PhD
    biology • M Phil
    cell biology • PhD
    chemical physics • PhD
    chemistry • M Phil, MA, MS, PhD
    ecology and evolutionary biology • MS, PhD
    genetics • MS, PhD
    mathematics • M Phil, M Stat, MA, MS, PhD
    molecular biology • PhD
    molecular evolutionary biology • PhD
    physics • M Phil, MA, MS, PhD
    science • MS
    science teacher education • MS

College of Social and Behavioral Science
Donna M. Gelfand, Dean
Programs in:
    anthropology • MA, MS, PhD
    economics • M Phil, M Stat, MA, MS, PhD
    family and consumer studies • MS

    geography • MA, MS, PhD
    political science • MA, MS, PhD
    psychology • M Stat, MA, MS, PhD
    public administration • Certificate, MPA
    sociology • MA, MS, PhD

Graduate School of Architecture
William C. Miller, Dean
Program in:
    architecture • M Arch, MS

Graduate School of Business
John Seybolt, Dean
Programs in:
    accounting • M Pr A, MBA, PhD
    business • M Stat
    business administration • MBA, PhD
    finance • MBA, MS, PhD
    human resources management • MHRM
    management • MBA, PhD
    marketing • MBA, PhD

Graduate School of Education
Colleen S. Kennedy, Dean
Programs in:
    cultural foundations • M Ed, PhD
    educational administration • Ed D, M Ed, PhD
    educational psychology • M Ed, M Stat, MA, MS, PhD
    educational studies • M Ed, MA, MS, PhD
    elementary and secondary education • M Ed
    special education • M Ed, MS, PhD

Graduate School of Social Work
Kay L. Dea, Dean
Program in:
    social work • MSW, PhD

College of Law
Lee E. Teitelbaum, Dean
Program in:
    law • JD, LL M

College of Pharmacy
Programs in:
    medicinal chemistry • MS, PhD
    pharmaceutics and pharmaceutical chemistry • MS, PhD
    pharmacology and toxicology • MS, PhD
    pharmacy • Pharm D
    pharmacy practice • MS

School of Medicine
Dr. John M. Matsen, Senior Vice President for Health Sciences and Dean
Programs in:
    biochemistry • MS, PhD
    biological chemistry • PhD
    biostatistics • M Stat
    medical informatics • MS, PhD
    medical laboratory science • MS
    medicine • MD
    microbiology and immunology • PhD
    molecular biology • PhD
    molecular evolutionary biology • PhD

neurobiology and anatomy • MS, PhD
neuroscience • PhD
oncological sciences • MS, PhD
pathology • PhD
physiology • PhD
public health • MPH, MSPH

UTAH STATE UNIVERSITY
Logan, UT 84322

http://www.usu.edu/

Public coed university. Enrollment: 21,234 graduate, professional, and undergraduate students. Computer facilities: Campuswide network is available with full Internet access. Total number of PCs/terminals supplied for student use: 800. Computer service fees are included with tuition and fees. Library facilities: Merrill Library and Learning Resource Center plus 5 additional on-campus libraries. Graduate expenses: Tuition of $1448 per year full-time, $624 per year part-time for state residents; $5082 per year full-time, $2192 per year part-time for nonresidents. Fees of $421 per year full-time, $165 per year part-time. General application contact: Diana Thimmes, Admissions Officer, School of Graduate Studies, 435-797-1190.

School of Graduate Studies
James P. Shaver, Dean

College of Agriculture
Dr. Rodney Brown, Dean
Programs in:
  agricultural economics • MA, MS
  agricultural extension education • MS
  agricultural mechanization • MS
  agricultural systems technology • MA, MS
  animal science • MA, MS, PhD
  biometeorology • MA, MS, PhD
  bioveterinary science • MA, MS
  community economic development • MCED
  dairy science • MA, MS
  economics • MA, MS, MSS, PhD
  farm systems research • MS
  international agricultural extension • MS
  molecular biology • MS, PhD
  nutrition and food sciences • MA, MS, PhD
  physical ecology • MS, PhD
  plant ecology • MS, PhD
  plant science • MA, MS, PhD
  secondary and postsecondary agricultural education •
    MS
  soil science • MA, MS, PhD
  toxicology • MS, PhD

College of Business
Dr. David B. Stephens, Dean
Programs in:
  accountancy • M Acc
  agricultural economics • MA, MS
  business administration • MBA

business education • MS
business information systems • Ed D, MS, PhD
community economic development • MCED
economics • MA, MS, MSS, PhD
human resource management • MSS
marketing education • MS
training and development • MS

College of Education
Ron Thorkildsen, Interim Dean
Programs in:
  business information systems and education • Ed D, PhD
  communicative disorders • M Ed, MA, MS
  curriculum and instruction • Ed D, PhD
  educational audiology • Ed S
  elementary education • M Ed, MA, MS
  health education • MS
  instructional technology • Ed S, M Ed, MS, PhD
  physical education • M Ed, MS
  psychology • MA, MS, PhD
  research and evaluation • Ed D, PhD
  secondary education • M Ed, MA, MS
  special education • Ed D, M Ed, MS, PhD

College of Engineering
A. Bruce Bishop, Dean
Programs in:
  aerospace engineering • MS, PhD
  biological and agricultural engineering • MS, PhD
  civil and environmental engineering • CE, ME, MS, PhD
  electrical engineering • EE, ME, MES, MS, PhD
  industrial technology • MS
  irrigation engineering • MS, PhD
  mechanical engineering • ME, MS, PhD

College of Family Life
Bonita W. Wyse, Dean
Programs in:
  family life • PhD
  human environments • MS
  molecular biology • MS, PhD
  nutrition and food sciences • MA, MS, PhD

College of Humanities, Arts and Social Sciences
Ann Leffler, Interim Dean
Programs in:
  advanced technical practice • MFA
  communication • MA, MS
  designing • MFA
  directing • MFA
  English • MA, MS
  folklore • MA, MS
  history • MA, MS, MSS
  landscape architecture • MLA, MS
  literary studies • MS
  literature • MA, MS
  political economy • MA, MS
  sociology • MA, MS, MSS, PhD
  studio art • MA, MFA
  technical writing • MS
  theatre arts • MA
  theory of writing • MS
  town and regional planning • MS

Utah State University (continued)

College of Natural Resources
Dr. John Kadlec, Acting Dean
Programs in:
 aquatic ecology • MS, PhD
 fisheries and wildlife • MNR, MS, PhD
 fisheries and wildlife ecology • MS, PhD
 forest ecology • MS, PhD
 forest management • MF
 forest resources • MNR
 forestry • MS, PhD
 forest soils • PhD
 geography • MA, MS
 geography and earth resources • MNR
 range ecology • MS, PhD
 rangeland resources • MNR
 range science • MS, PhD
 recreation resources management • MS, PhD
 science program • MS, PhD

College of Science
James MacMahon, Dean
Programs in:
 applied statistics • MS
 biochemistry • MS, PhD
 bio-ecology • MS, PhD
 biology • MS, PhD
 chemistry • MS, PhD
 computer science • MS
 geology • MS
 geology-ecology • MS
 hydrogeology • MS
 mathematical sciences • PhD
 mathematics • M Math, MS
 molecular biology • MS, PhD
 physics • MS, PhD

WEBER STATE UNIVERSITY
Ogden, UT 84408-1001

http://www.weber.edu/

Public coed comprehensive institution. *Enrollment: 14,613 graduate, professional, and undergraduate students. Graduate faculty: 39 full-time, 8 part-time. Computer facilities: Campuswide network is available with full Internet access. Total number of PCs/terminals supplied for student use: 563. Computer service fees are included with tuition and fees. Library facilities: Stewart Library plus 1 additional on-campus library. Graduate expenses: Tuition of $1490 per year full-time, $290 per semester (minimum) part-time for state residents; $5214 per year full-time, $1016 per semester (minimum) part-time for nonresidents. Fees of $402 per year full-time, $83 per semester (minimum) part-time. General application contact: Christopher C. Rivera, Director of Admissions, 801-626-6046.*

College of Business and Economics
Dr. Michael Vaughan, Dean
Program in:
 accountancy • MP Acc

College of Education
Dr. David M. Greene, Dean
Program in:
 curriculum and instruction • M Ed

WESTMINSTER COLLEGE OF SALT LAKE CITY
Salt Lake City, UT 84105-3697

http://www.wcslc.edu/

Independent coed comprehensive institution. *Enrollment: 2,140 graduate, professional, and undergraduate students. Graduate faculty: 29 full-time, 13 part-time. Computer facilities: Campuswide network is available with full Internet access. Total number of PCs/terminals supplied for student use: 175. Computer service fees are included with tuition and fees. Library facilities: Ginger Gore Giovale Library. Graduate expenses: Tuition of $448 per credit hour. Fees of $200 per year full-time, $65 per semester (minimum) part-time. General application contact: Philip J. Alletto, Vice President for Student Development and Enrollment Management, 801-488-4200.*

School of Arts and Sciences
Dr. Ray Ownbey, Dean
Program in:
 professional communication • MPC

School of Education
Dr. Janice R. Fauske, Dean
Program in:
 education • M Ed

St. Mark's-Westminster School of Nursing and Health Sciences
Dr. A. Gretchen McNeely, Dean
Program in:
 nursing • MSN

The Bill and Vieve Gore School of Business
Dr. James Seidelman, Dean
Program in:
 business administration • MBA

VERMONT

CASTLETON STATE COLLEGE
Castleton, VT 05735

http://www.csc.vsc.edu/

Public coed comprehensive institution. *Enrollment: 1,800 graduate, professional, and undergraduate students. Graduate faculty: 10 full-time, 9 part-time. Library facilities: Calvin Coolidge Library.*

Graduate expenses: *Tuition of $3924 per year full-time, $164 per credit part-time for state residents; $9192 per year full-time, $383 per credit part-time for nonresidents. Fees of $902 per year full-time, $26 per credit part-time. General application contact: Mary Frucelli, Graduate Assistant, 802-468-1441.*

Division of Graduate Studies
Dr. John E. Larkin Jr., Director of Graduate Studies
Programs in:
    curriculum and instruction • MA Ed
    educational leadership • CAGS, MA Ed
    forensic psychology • MA
    language arts and reading • CAGS, MA Ed
    special education • MA Ed

GODDARD COLLEGE
Plainfield, VT 05667

http://www.goddard.edu/

Independent coed comprehensive institution. *Enrollment: 534 graduate, professional, and undergraduate students. Graduate faculty: 8 full-time, 46 part-time. Computer facilities: Campuswide network is available with full Internet access. Total number of PCs/terminals supplied for student use: 20. Computer services are offered at no charge. Library facilities: Eliot Pratt Library. General application contact: Ellen Codling, Admissions Office, 802-454-8311.*

Graduate Programs
Dr. Terry Keeney, Dean
Programs in:
    education and teaching • MA
    individually designed liberal arts • MA
    interdisciplinary arts • MFA
    psychology and counseling • MA
    social ecology • MA
    writing • MFA

JOHNSON STATE COLLEGE
Johnson, VT 05656-9405

Public coed comprehensive institution. *Enrollment: 1,622 graduate, professional, and undergraduate students. Graduate faculty: 15 full-time, 6 part-time. Computer facilities: Campuswide network is available with full Internet access. Total number of PCs/terminals supplied for student use: 100. Computer service fees are included with tuition and fees. Library facilities: John Dewey Library. Graduate expenses: Tuition of $164 per credit for state residents; $383 per credit for nonresidents. Fees of $15.90 per credit. General application contact: Catherine H. Higley, Administrative Assistant, 802-635-2356 Ext. 1244.*

Graduate Program in Education
Programs in:
    counseling • MA
    curriculum and instruction • MA Ed
    early childhood education • MA Ed
    education of the gifted • MA Ed
    public school principal • MA Ed
    reading education • MA Ed
    school business management • MA Ed
    special education • MA Ed

Program in Fine Arts
Programs in:
    drawing • MFA
    painting • MFA
    sculpture • MFA

NORWICH UNIVERSITY
Northfield, VT 05663

http://www.norwich.edu/

Independent coed comprehensive institution. *Enrollment: 2,200 graduate, professional, and undergraduate students. Graduate faculty: 39 full-time, 270 part-time. Computer facilities: Campuswide network is available with full Internet access. Computer service fees are included with tuition and fees. Library facilities: Chaplin Memorial Library. Graduate expenses: $4485 per semester. General application contact: Susan Bradt, Associate Director of Admissions, 800-336-6794.*

Vermont College
Dr. Jackson Kytle, Dean
Programs in:
    art therapy • MA
    visual art • MFA
    writing • MFA
    writing for children • MFA

Military Graduate Program
Dr. Fariborz L. Mokhtari, Director
Program in:
    diplomacy and military science • MA

SAINT MICHAEL'S COLLEGE
Colchester, VT 05439

http://www.smcvt.edu/

Independent-religious coed comprehensive institution. *Enrollment: 2,683 graduate, professional, and undergraduate students. Graduate faculty: 24 full-time, 137 part-time. Library facilities: Durick Library. General application contact: Dr. Susan Kuntz, Dean of The Prevel School, 802-654-2223.*

Saint Michael's College (continued)
The Prevel School
Dr. Susan Kuntz, Dean
Programs in:
>   administration • CAGS, M Ed
>   administration and management • CAMS, MSA
>   clinical psychology • MA
>   curriculum and instruction • CAGS, M Ed
>   integrating the arts into education • M Ed
>   reading • M Ed
>   self designed • M Ed
>   special education • CAGS, M Ed
>   teaching English as a second language • MATESL
>   technology • M Ed
>   theology • CAS, Certificate, MA

UNIVERSITY OF VERMONT
Burlington, VT 05405-0160

http://www.uvm.edu/indexbasic.html

Public coed university. *Enrollment: 9,341 graduate, professional, and undergraduate students. Graduate faculty: 702 full-time, 604 part-time. Library facilities: Bailey-Howe Library plus 2 additional on-campus libraries. Graduate expenses: Tuition of $302 per credit for state residents; $755 per credit for nonresidents. Fees of $434 per year full-time, $46 per semester (minimum) part-time. General application contact: Ralph M. Swenson, Director of Admissions and Administration, 802-656-3160.*

Graduate College
Dr. Andrew Bodman, Dean
Programs in:
>   anatomy and neurobiology • PhD
>   biochemistry • MS, PhD
>   cell and molecular biology • MS, PhD
>   microbiology and molecular genetics • MS, PhD
>   molecular physiology and biophysics • MS, PhD
>   pathology • MS
>   pharmacology • MS, PhD

College of Agriculture and Life Sciences
Dr. Donald McLean, Dean
Programs in:
>   agricultural biochemistry • MS, PhD
>   animal sciences • MS, PhD
>   biology • MST
>   botany • MAT, MS, PhD
>   community development and applied economics • M Ext Ed, MS
>   field naturalist • MS
>   nutritional sciences • MS
>   occupational and practical arts • MAT
>   plant and soil science • MS, PhD

College of Arts and Sciences
Dr. H. Ball, Dean
Programs in:
>   biology • MS, PhD
>   biology education • MAT, MST
>   chemistry • MS, MST, PhD
>   chemistry education • MAT
>   clinical psychology • PhD
>   communication sciences • MS
>   engineering physics • MS
>   English • MA
>   English education • MAT
>   French • MA
>   French education • MAT
>   geography • MA, MAT
>   geology • MS
>   geology education • MAT, MST
>   German • MA
>   German education • MAT
>   Greek • MA
>   Greek and Latin • MAT
>   historic preservation • MS
>   history • MA
>   history education • MAT
>   Latin • MA
>   physical sciences • MST
>   physics • MAT, MS
>   political science • MA
>   psychology • PhD
>   public administration • MPA

College of Education and Social Services
Dr. Jill Tarule, Dean
Programs in:
>   counseling • MS
>   curriculum and instruction • M Ed
>   educational leadership • M Ed
>   educational leadership and policy studies • Ed D
>   educational studies • M Ed
>   higher education and student affairs administration • M Ed
>   interdisciplinary studies • M Ed
>   reading and language arts • M Ed
>   social work • MSW
>   special education • M Ed

College of Engineering and Mathematics
Dr. R. Foote, Acting Dean
Programs in:
>   biomedical engineering • MS
>   biostatistics • MS
>   civil engineering • MS, PhD
>   computer science • MS
>   electrical engineering • MS, PhD
>   materials science • MS, PhD
>   mathematics • MS, PhD
>   mathematics education • MAT, MST
>   mechanical engineering • MS, PhD
>   statistics • MS

School of Allied Health Sciences
Dr. L. McCrorey, Dean
Programs in:
>   biomedical technologies • MS
>   physical therapy • MS

School of Business Administration
Dr. Larry E. Shirland, Dean
Program in:
business administration • MBA

School of Natural Resources
Dr. Larry Forcier, Dean
Programs in:
forestry • MS
natural resources planning • MS, PhD
water resources • MS
wildlife and fisheries biology • MS

School of Nursing
M. McGrath, Interim Dean
Program in:
nursing • MS

College of Medicine
Dr. John W. Frymoyer, Interim Dean
Programs in:
anatomy and neurobiology • PhD
biochemistry • MS, PhD
medicine • MD
microbiology and molecular genetics • MS, PhD
molecular physiology and biophysics • MS, PhD
pathology • MS
pharmacology • MS, PhD

VIRGIN ISLANDS

UNIVERSITY OF THE VIRGIN ISLANDS
Charlotte Amalie, St. Thomas, VI 00802-9990
http://www.uvi.edu/

Public coed comprehensive institution. *Enrollment:* 2,610 graduate, professional, and undergraduate students. Graduate faculty: *19 full-time, 14 part-time.* Computer facilities: *Campuswide network is available with full Internet access. Total number of PCs/terminals supplied for student use: 100. Computer service fees are included with tuition and fees.* Library facilities: *Ralph Paiewonsky Library plus 1 additional on-campus library.* Graduate expenses: *$205 per credit for territory residents; $410 per credit for nonresidents.* General application contact: *Judith Edwin, Director of Enrollment Management, 340-693-1151.*

Graduate Programs
Dr. Denis Paul, Vice President, Academic Affairs
Programs in:
business administration • MBA
education • MAE
public administration • MPA

VIRGINIA

AVERETT COLLEGE
Danville, VA 24541-3692
http://www.averett.edu/

Independent-religious coed comprehensive institution. *Enrollment:* 2,369 graduate, professional, and undergraduate students. Graduate faculty: *20 full-time, 82 part-time.* Library facilities: *Mary B. Blount Library.* Graduate expenses: *$225 per credit hour.* General application contact: *Dr. Elizabeth Compton, Academic Vice President, 804-791-5630.*

Division of Education
Dr. Elizabeth Compton, Academic Vice President
Programs in:
curriculum and instruction • M Ed
reading • M Ed
teaching • MAT

Program in Business Administration
Dr. Brian Satterlee, Dean of Adult Education
Program in:
business administration • MBA

 ## COLLEGE OF WILLIAM AND MARY
Williamsburg, VA 23187-8795
http://www.wm.edu/

Public coed university. *Enrollment: 7,572 graduate, professional, and undergraduate students.* Graduate faculty: *578 full-time, 139 part-time.* Computer facilities: *Campuswide network is available with full Internet access. Total number of PCs/terminals supplied for student use: 300. Computer services are offered at no charge.* Library facilities: *Swem Library plus 8 additional on-campus libraries.* Graduate expenses: *$5262 per year full-time, $165 per semester hour part-time for state residents; $16,138 per year full-time, $500 per semester hour part-time for nonresidents.* General application contact: *Office of Graduate Studies, 757-221-2467.*

Faculty of Arts and Sciences
Franz Gross, Dean of Research and Graduate Studies
Programs in:
American studies • MA, PhD
anthropology • MA
applied science • MA, MS, PhD
biology • MA
chemistry • MA, MS
clinical psychology • Psy D
computational operations research • MS
computational science • PhD
computer science • MS, PhD

College of William and Mary (continued)
English • MA
general experimental psychology • MA
history • MA, PhD
physics • MA, MS, PhD
public policy • MPP

Marshall-Wythe School of Law
Paul Marcus, Acting Dean
Program in:
law • JD, LL M

School of Business
Dr. Lawrence Pulley, Interim Dean
Program in:
business • MBA

School of Education
Dr. Virginia McLaughlin, Dean
Programs in:
counseling • Ed D, M Ed, PhD
gifted education • MA Ed
school psychology • Ed D, M Ed, PhD
special education • MA Ed

School of Marine Science/Virginia Institute of Marine Science
Dr. L. Donelson Wright, Dean and Director
Program in:
marine science • MS, PhD

 GEORGE MASON UNIVERSITY
Fairfax, VA 22030-4444

http://www.gmu.edu/

Public coed university. *Enrollment: 23,826 graduate, professional, and undergraduate students. Graduate faculty: 795 full-time, 525 part-time. Library facilities: Fenwick Library plus 1 additional on-campus library. Graduate expenses: $4344 per year full-time, $181 per credit hour part-time for state residents; $12,504 per year full-time, $521 per credit hour part-time for nonresidents. General application contact: Graduate School Admissions Office, 703-993-2402.*

College of Arts and Sciences
Danielle Struppa, Interim Dean
Programs in:
applied and engineering physics • MS
bioinformatics • MS
chemistry • MS
clinical psychology • PhD
creative writing • MFA
cultural studies • PhD
developmental psychology • PhD
ecology, systematics and evolution • MS
economics • MA, PhD

English • MA
environmental science and public policy • MS, PhD
experimental neuropsychology • MA
foreign languages • MA
geography and cartographic sciences • MS
history • MA
human factors engineering psychology • MA, PhD
industrial/organizational psychology • MA, PhD
interpretive biology • MS
life-span development psychology • MA
linguistics • MA
mathematics • MS
molecular, microbial, and cellular biology • MS
music • MA
music education • MA
organismal biology • MS
public administration • DPA, MPA
school psychology • MA
social and organizational learning • MA
sociology • MA
telecommunications • MA

College of Nursing and Health Science
Dr. Rita M. Carty, Dean
Programs in:
advanced clinical nursing • MSN
nurse practitioner • MSN
nursing • MSN, PhD
nursing administration • MSN

Graduate School of Education
Gary Galluzzo, Dean
Programs in:
bilingual/multicultural/English as a second language education • M Ed
community college education • DA Ed
counseling and development • M Ed
early childhood education • M Ed
education • PhD
education leadership • M Ed
exercise science and health • MS
instructional technology • M Ed
middle education • M Ed
reading • M Ed
secondary education • M Ed
special education • M Ed

Institute for Computational Sciences and Informatics
Dr. W. Murray Black, Director
Program in:
computational sciences and informatics • PhD

Institute for Conflict Analysis and Resolution
Dr. Kevin P. Clements, Director
Program in:
conflict analysis and resolution • MS, PhD

Institute of Public Policy
Dr. Kingsley Haynes, Director
Programs in:
public policy • MA, PhD

Institute of the Arts

Sarah Lawless, Director
Programs in:
   dance • MFA
   visual information technologies • MA, MFA

Interdisciplinary Studies Program

Catherine A. McCormick, Coordinator
Programs in:
   archaeology • MAIS
   gerontology • MAIS
   interdisciplinary studies • MAIS
   liberal studies • MALS
   regional economic development and technology • MAIS
   video-based production • MAIS

School of Information Technology and Engineering

Lloyd Griffiths, Dean
Programs in:
   computer science • MS
   electrical engineering • MS
   information systems • MS
   information technology • PhD
   operations research and management science • MS
   software systems engineering • MS
   statistical science • MS
   systems engineering • MS

School of Law

Dr. Mark F. Grady, Dean
Program in:
   law • JD

School of Management

Jack High, Dean
Programs in:
   accounting • MS
   business administration • EMBA, MBA
   taxation • MS

HAMPTON UNIVERSITY
Hampton, VA 23668

http://www.hamptonu.edu/

Independent coed comprehensive institution. *Enrollment: 5,705 graduate, professional, and undergraduate students. Graduate faculty: 90 full-time, 11 part-time. Library facilities: William R. and Norma B. Harvey Library plus 4 additional on-campus libraries. Graduate expenses: Tuition of $9038 per year full-time, $220 per credit part-time. Fees of $70 per year. General application contact: Dr. Calvin Lowe, Vice President for Research and Dean of Graduate College, 757-727-5310.*

Graduate College

Dr. Calvin Lowe, Vice President for Research and Dean
Programs in:
   applied mathematics • MS
   biological sciences • MA, MS
   business • MBA
   chemistry • MS
   college student development • MA
   communicative sciences and disorders • MA
   community agency counseling • MA
   computer science • MS
   elementary education • MA
   museum studies • MA
   nursing • MS
   physics • MS, PhD
   special education • MA
   teaching • MT

JAMES MADISON UNIVERSITY
Harrisonburg, VA 22807

http://www.jmu.edu/

Public coed comprehensive institution. *Enrollment: 13,714 graduate, professional, and undergraduate students. Graduate faculty: 141 full-time, 29 part-time. Computer facilities: Campuswide network is available with full Internet access. Total number of PCs/terminals supplied for student use: 500. Computer services are offered at no charge. Library facilities: Carrier Library plus 1 additional on-campus library. Graduate expenses: $134 per credit hour for state residents; $404 per credit hour for nonresidents. General application contact: Dr. Dorothy Boyd-Rush, Dean of the Graduate School, 540-568-6131.*

Graduate School

Dr. Dorothy Boyd-Rush, Dean

College of Arts and Letters

Dr. Richard F. Whitman, Dean
Programs in:
   art education • MA
   art history • MA
   ceramics • MFA
   conducting • MM
   drawing/painting • MFA
   English • MA
   history • MA
   metal/jewelry • MFA
   music education • MM
   performance • MM
   photography • MFA
   printmaking • MFA
   public administration • MPA
   sculpture • MFA
   studio art • MA
   technical and scientific communication • MA, MS
   theory-composition • MM
   weaving/fibers • MFA

James Madison University (continued)

College of Business
Dr. Robert D. Reid, Dean
Programs in:
    accounting • MS
    business administration • MBA

College of Education and Psychology
Dr. A. Jerry Benson, Dean
Programs in:
    counseling psychology • Ed S, M Ed
    early childhood education • M Ed
    education • M Ed, MAT
    educational leadership • M Ed
    general psychology • MA, Psy D
    kinesiology • MS
    library science and educational media • M Ed
    middle school education • M Ed
    reading education • M Ed
    school psychology • Ed S, MA
    secondary education • M Ed
    special education • M Ed
    vocational education • MS Ed

College of Integrated Science and Technology
Dr. Jackson E. Ramsey, Dean
Programs in:
    computer science • MS
    health sciences • MS, MS Ed
    hearing disorders • M Ed
    speech pathology • MS

College of Science and Mathematics
Dr. Norman E. Garrison, Dean
Program in:
    biology • MS

 LIBERTY UNIVERSITY
Lynchburg, VA 24502

http://www.liberty.edu/

Independent-religious coed comprehensive institution. *Enrollment:* 6,646 graduate, professional, and undergraduate students. Graduate faculty: *14 full-time, 12 part-time.* Computer facilities: *Campuswide network is available with full Internet access. Total number of PCs/ terminals supplied for student use: 200. Computer services are offered at no charge.* Graduate expenses: *$280 per credit hour.* General application contact: *Bill Wegert, Coordinator of Graduate Admissions, 804-582-2175.*

Liberty Baptist Theological Seminary
Dr. Danny Lovett, Dean
Program in:
    theology • D Min, M Div, MAR, MRE, Th M

School of Arts and Science
Dr. R. Terry Spohn, Dean
Program in:
    counseling • MA

School of Education
Dr. Pauline Donaldson, Dean
Programs in:
    educational administration • M Ed
    elementary education • M Ed
    reading • M Ed
    secondary education • M Ed

School of Religion
Dr. Elmer Towns, Dean
Program in:
    religious studies • MA

LONGWOOD COLLEGE
Farmville, VA 23909-1800

http://www.lwc.edu/

Public coed comprehensive institution. *Enrollment:* 3,300 graduate, professional, and undergraduate students. Graduate faculty: *0 full-time, 69 part-time.* Computer facilities: *Campuswide network is available with full Internet access. Total number of PCs/terminals supplied for student use: 110. Computer services are offered at no charge.* Library facilities: *main library.* Graduate expenses: *Tuition of $3048 per year full-time, $127 per credit hour part-time for state residents; $8160 per year full-time, $340 per credit hour part-time for nonresidents. Fees of $920 per year full-time, $31 per credit hour part-time.* General application contact: *Norman J. Bregman, Director of Graduate Studies, 804-395-2707.*

Graduate Programs
Norman J. Bregman, Director
Programs in:
    administration/supervision • MS
    community and college counseling • MS
    criminal justice • MS
    curriculum and instruction specialist-elementary • MS
    English • MA, MS
    guidance and counseling • MS
    library science media specialist • MS
    mild disabilities • MS
    modern language • MS
    natural sciences • MS
    physical education • MS
    reading specialist • MS
    speech and drama • MS

LYNCHBURG COLLEGE
Lynchburg, VA 24501-3199

http://www.lynchburg.edu/

Independent-religious coed comprehensive institution. Library facilities: *Knight-Capron Library.* General application contact: *Academic Dean, 804-522-8232.*

Graduate Studies

School of Business
Programs in:
 administration • M Ad
 business • MBA
 industrial management • M Ad
 personnel management • M Ad

School of Education and Human Development
Programs in:
 adapted physical education • M Ed
 agency counseling • M Ed
 curriculum and instruction • M Ed
 curriculum and instruction: early childhood education • M Ed
 curriculum and instruction: middle education • M Ed
 early childhood special education • M Ed
 English education • M Ed
 mental retardation • M Ed
 middle school education • M Ed
 physical education • M Ed
 reading • M Ed
 school administration • M Ed
 school counseling • M Ed
 secondary education • M Ed
 severely/profoundly handicapped education • M Ed
 supervision • M Ed
 teaching children with learning disabilities • M Ed
 teaching the emotionally disturbed • M Ed

MARYMOUNT UNIVERSITY
Arlington, VA 22207-4299
http://www.marymount.edu/

Independent-religious coed comprehensive institution. *Enrollment: 3,695 graduate, professional, and undergraduate students. Graduate faculty: 61 full-time, 62 part-time. Computer facilities: Campuswide network is available with full Internet access. Total number of PCs/ terminals supplied for student use: 550. Computer service fees are applied as a separate charge. Library facilities: Reinsch Library plus 1 additional on-campus library. Graduate expenses: Tuition of $465 per credit hour. Fees of $120 per year full-time, $5 per credit hour part-time. General application contact: Chris E. Domes, Dean of Admissions, 703-284-1500.*

School of Arts and Sciences
Dr. Rosemary Hubbard, Dean
Programs in:
 computer science • MS
 humanities • MA
 interior design • MA

School of Business Administration
Dr. Robert Sigethy, Dean
Programs in:
 business administration • MBA
 health care management • MS

human performance systems • MA
 human resources management • MA
 information management • MS
 legal administration • MA
 organizational leadership and innovation • MS
 organization development • MA

School of Education and Human Services
Dr. Wayne Lesko, Dean
Programs in:
 counseling psychology • MA
 elementary education • M Ed
 English as a second language • M Ed
 learning disabilities • M Ed
 school counseling • MA
 secondary education • M Ed

School of Health Professions
Dr. Catherine Connelly, Dean
Programs in:
 critical care nursing • MSN
 health promotion management • MS
 nursing administration • MSN
 nursing education • MSN
 physical therapy • MS
 primary care family practitioner • MSN

MARY WASHINGTON COLLEGE
Fredericksburg, VA 22401-5358
http://www.mwc.edu/

Public coed comprehensive institution. *Enrollment: 3,840 graduate, professional, and undergraduate students. Graduate faculty: 36 full-time, 2 part-time. Computer facilities: Campuswide network is available with full Internet access. Computer service fees are applied as a separate charge. Library facilities: Simpson Library. Graduate expenses: $147 per credit hour for state residents; $338 per credit hour for nonresidents. General application contact: Dr. Roy Weinstock, Vice President of Planning, Assessment, and Institutional Research, 540-654-1048.*

Center for Graduate and Continuing Education
Meta R. Braymer, Dean
Program in:
 liberal studies • MALS

NORFOLK STATE UNIVERSITY
Norfolk, VA 23504-3907
http://www.nsu.edu/

Public coed comprehensive institution. *Enrollment: 7,659 graduate, professional, and undergraduate students. Graduate faculty: 67 full-time, 42 part-time. Library facilities: Lyman Beecher Brooks Library. Graduate expenses: $3718 per year full-time, $198 per*

Norfolk State University (continued)
credit hour part-time for state residents; $7668 per year full-time, $404 per credit hour part-time for nonresidents. General application contact: *Dr. Ann McKinney-Morris, Dean, School of Graduate Studies, 757-683-8015.*

School of Graduate Studies
Dr. Ann W. McKinney-Morris, Dean

School of Arts and Letters
Dr. Thelma Thompson, Dean
Programs in:
    broadcasting • MA
    communication • MA
    interpersonal communication • MA
    journalism • MA
    music • MM
    music education • MM
    performance • MM
    theory and composition • MM
    visual studies • MA, MFA

School of Education
Dr. Denise Littleton, Acting Dean
Programs in:
    early childhood education • MAT
    education of the gifted • MA
    orthopedic education and education of the multiply
      handicapped and health impaired • MA
    pre-elementary education • MA
    principal preparation • MA
    secondary education • MAT
    urban education/administration • MA

School of Health Related Professions and Natural Sciences
Dr. Clarence D. Coleman, Dean
Program in:
    materials science • MS

School of Social Sciences
Dr. Elsie Barnes, Dean
Programs in:
    applied sociology • MS
    community/clinical psychology • MA
    psychology • Psy D
    urban affairs • MA

School of Social Work
Dr. Moses Newsome, Dean
Program in:
    social work • DSW, MSW

OLD DOMINION UNIVERSITY
Norfolk, VA 23529
http://www.odu.edu/

Public coed university. *Enrollment: 18,557 graduate, professional, and undergraduate students. Graduate faculty: 372 full-time, 138 part-time. Computer facilities: Campuswide network is available with full Internet access. Total number of PCs/terminals supplied for student use: 400. Computer services are offered at no charge. Library facilities: University Library. Graduate expenses: Tuition of $180 per credit hour for state residents; $477 per credit hour for nonresidents. Fees of $140 per year full-time, $32 per semester part-time.* General application contact: *Michael T. O'Connor, Director of Admissions, 757-683-3637.*

College of Arts and Letters
Dr. Karen Gould, Dean
Programs in:
    applied linguistics • MA
    applied sociology • MA
    creative writing • MFA
    English • MA
    history • MA
    humanities • MA
    international studies • MA, PhD
    visual studies • MFA

College of Business and Public Administration
Dr. J. Taylor Sims, Dean
Programs in:
    accounting • MS
    business administration • MBA, PhD
    economics • MA
    policy analysis/program evaluation • MUS
    public administration • MPA
    public planning analysis • MUS
    taxation • MTX
    urban administration • MUS
    urban services/urban management • PhD

College of Engineering and Technology
Dr. William Swart, Dean
Programs in:
    aerospace engineering • ME, MS, PhD
    civil and environmental engineering • ME, MS, PhD
    design manufacturing • ME
    electrical and computer engineering • ME, MS, PhD
    engineering management • MEM, MS, PhD
    engineering mechanics • ME, MS, PhD
    mechanical engineering • ME, MS, PhD
    operations research/systems analysis • ME

College of Health Sciences
Dr. Lindsay L. Rettie, Dean
Programs in:
    community health professions • MS
    dental hygiene • MS
    long-term care administration • Certificate
    medical laboratory sciences and environmental health •
      MS
    nursing • Certificate, MSN
    physical therapy • MS
    professional preparation • MS
    public health • MPH
    urban services/urban health services • PhD

College of Sciences

Dr. Terry L. Hickey, Dean
Programs in:
analytical chemistry • MS
applied mathematics • MS, PhD
biochemistry • MS
biology • MS
biomedical sciences • PhD
clinical chemistry • MS
clinical psychology • Psy D
computer science • MS, PhD
ecological sciences • PhD
environmental chemistry • MS
general psychology • MS
geological sciences • MS
industrial/organizational psychology • PhD
oceanography • MS, PhD
organic chemistry • MS
physical chemistry • MS
physics • MS, PhD
statistics • MS, PhD

Darden College of Education

Dr. Donna Evans, Dean
Programs in:
administration • MS Ed
athletic training • MS Ed
business and distributive education • MS Ed
community agency counseling • MS
counseling • CAS
curriculum and instruction • MS Ed
early childhood education • MS Ed
educational administration • CAS, MS
educational media • MS Ed
elementary education • MS Ed
exercise science and wellness • MS Ed
industrial education • MS Ed
instructional technology • MS Ed
physical education • MS Ed
reading • MS
recreation administration • MS Ed
school counseling • MS
special education • MS Ed
speech pathology and audiology • MS Ed
sports management • MS Ed
student development counseling in higher education •
MS
urban services/urban education • PhD

RADFORD UNIVERSITY
Radford, VA 24142

http://www.runet.edu/

Public coed comprehensive institution. *Enrollment:* 8,534 graduate, professional, and undergraduate students. *Graduate faculty:* 252 full-time, 13 part-time. Computer facilities: *Campuswide network is available with full Internet access. Total number of PCs/terminals supplied for student use: 1,700. Computer service fees are included with tuition and fees. Library facilities: McConnell Library. Graduate*

expenses: *Tuition of $2302 per year full-time, $147 per credit hour part-time for state residents; $5672 per year full-time, $287 per credit hour part-time for nonresidents. Fees of $1222 per year full-time. General application contact: Dr. Wilbur W. Stanton, Dean of the Graduate College, 540-831-5431.*

Graduate College

Dr. Wilbur W. Stanton, Dean

College of Arts and Sciences

Dr. Ivan B. Liss, Dean
Programs in:
clinical psychology • MA
computational science • MS
corporate and professional communication • MS
counseling psychology • MA
criminal justice • MA, MS
engineering geosciences • MS
English • MA, MS
general psychology • MA, MS
industrial-organizational psychology • MA
school psychology • Ed S

College of Business and Economics

Dr. Bruce K. Blaylock, Dean
Programs in:
business administration • MBA
international economics • MS

College of Education and Human Development

Dr. Robert C. Small Jr., Dean
Programs in:
counselor education • MS
curriculum and instruction • MS
educational leadership • MS
educational media • MS
education and human development • MSW
education of the emotionally disturbed • MS
learning disabilities • MS
mentally retarded • MS
physical education • MS
reading • MS

College of Nursing and Health Services

Dr. Stephen L. Heater, Dean
Programs in:
communication science and disorders • MA, MS
leisure services • MS
nursing • MS
social work • MSW

College of Visual and Performing Arts

Dr. Joseph P. Scartelli, Dean
Programs in:
art • MFA
art education • MS
music • MA
music education • MS

SHENANDOAH UNIVERSITY
Winchester, VA 22601-5195

http://www.su.edu/

Independent-religious coed comprehensive institution. *Enrollment: 1,927 graduate, professional, and undergraduate students. Graduate faculty: 81 full-time, 31 part-time. Computer facilities: Campuswide network is available with full Internet access. Total number of PCs/ terminals supplied for student use: 150. Computer services are offered at no charge. Library facilities: Alson H. Smith Jr. Library. Graduate expenses: $470 per credit. General application contact: Michael Carpenter, Director of Admissions, 540-665-4581.*

Byrd School of Business
Dr. Daniel A. Pavsek, Dean
Program in:
  business • MBA

Department of Occupational Therapy
Dr. Gretchen Stone, Chair
Program in:
  occupational therapy • MS

Department of Physical Therapy
Dr. Camilla Wilson, Chair
Program in:
  physical therapy • MPT

Division of Nursing
Dr. Martha Erbach, Interim Chair
Program in:
  nursing • MSN

School of Arts and Sciences
Dr. Catherine Tisinger, Dean
Programs in:
  computer education • MSC
  education • MSE

School of Pharmacy
Dr. Alan McKay, Dean
Program in:
  pharmacy • Pharm D

Shenandoah Conservatory
Dr. Charlotte A. Collins, Dean
Programs in:
  arts management • MS
  church music • MM
  composition • MM
  conducting • MM
  dance accompanying • MM
  dance choreography and performance • MFA
  music education • DMA, MME
  performance • MM
  piano accompanying • MM

UNIVERSITY OF RICHMOND
University of Richmond, VA 23173

http://www.urich.edu/

Independent coed comprehensive institution. *Enrollment: 4,366 graduate, professional, and undergraduate students. Graduate faculty: 228 full-time, 38 part-time. Computer facilities: Campuswide network is available with full Internet access. Computer services are offered at no charge. Library facilities: Boatwright Memorial Library plus 3 additional on-campus libraries. Graduate expenses: $18,695 per year full-time, $320 per credit hour part-time. General application contact: Dr. Barbara J. Griffin, Director of the Graduate School, 804-289-8417.*

Graduate School
Dr. Barbara J. Griffin, Director
Programs in:
  biology • MS
  early childhood education • M Ed
  elementary education • MT
  English • MA
  history • MA
  learning disabilities • M Ed
  learning disabled • MT
  liberal arts • MLA
  political science • MA
  psychology • MA
  reading specialization • M Ed
  secondary education • M Ed, MT

T. C. Williams School of Law
John R. Pagan, Dean
Program in:
  law • JD

The E. Claiborne Robins School of Business
Dr. J. Randolph New, Dean
Program in:
  business administration • MBA

UNIVERSITY OF VIRGINIA
Charlottesville, VA 22903

http://www.virginia.edu/

Public coed university. *Enrollment: 17,941 graduate, professional, and undergraduate students. Graduate faculty: 1,818 full-time, 174 part-time. Computer facilities: Campuswide network is available with full Internet access. Total number of PCs/terminals supplied for student use: 1,859. Computer service fees are included with tuition and fees. Library facilities: Alderman Library plus 12 additional on-campus libraries. Graduate expenses: $4870 per year full-time, $941 per semester (minimum) part-time for state residents; $15,818 per year full-time, $2745 per semester (minimum) part-time for nonresidents. General application contact: Dean of the appropriate school, 804-924-0311.*

Colgate Darden Graduate School of Business Administration

Edward A. Snyder Jr., Dean
Program in:
 business administration • DBA, MBA, PhD

Curry School of Education

David W. Breneman, Dean
Programs in:
 administration and supervision • Ed D, Ed S, M Ed
 clinical psychology • PhD
 communication disorders • M Ed
 counselor education • Ed D, Ed S, M Ed
 curriculum and instruction • Ed D, Ed S, M Ed
 education • MT, PhD
 educational policy studies • Ed D, M Ed
 educational psychology • Ed D, Ed S, M Ed
 health and physical education • Ed D, M Ed
 higher education • Ed D, Ed S
 special education • Ed D, Ed S, M Ed

Graduate School of Arts and Sciences

Stephen E. Schnatterly, Vice Provost for Graduate Studies
Programs in:
 anthropology • MA, PhD
 art history • MA, PhD
 Asian and Middle Eastern languages and cultures • MA
 astronomy • MA, PhD
 biochemistry • PhD
 biological and physical sciences • MS
 biology • MA, MS, PhD
 biology education • MAT
 biophysics • PhD
 cell biology • PhD
 cell biology/anatomy • PhD
 chemistry • MA, MS, PhD
 chemistry education • MAT
 classical art and archaeology • MA, PhD
 classics • MA, MAT, PhD
 clinical ethics • MA
 clinical investigation • MS
 clinical psychology • PhD
 creative writing • MFA
 drama • MFA
 economics • MA, PhD
 English • MA, MAT, PhD
 environmental sciences • MA, MS, PhD
 epidemiology • MS
 foreign affairs • MA, PhD
 French • MA, MAT, PhD
 Germanic languages and literatures • MA, MAT, PhD
 government • MA, MAT, PhD
 health care informatics • MS
 health care resource management • MS
 health services research and outcomes evaluation • MS
 history • MA, MAT, PhD
 Italian • MA
 linguistics • MA
 mathematics • MA, MS, PhD
 microbiology • MS, PhD
 molecular genetics • PhD
 molecular physiology and biological physics • PhD
 music • MA, MAT
 neuroscience • PhD
 pharmacology • PhD
 philosophy • MA, PhD
 physics • MA, MAT, MS, PhD
 physiology • PhD
 psychology • MA, PhD
 religious studies • MA, PhD
 Slavic languages and literatures • MA, PhD
 sociology • MA, PhD
 Spanish • MA, PhD
 statistics • MS, PhD
 surgery • MS
 teaching Spanish • MAT

McIntire School of Commerce

Robert S. Kemp, Director of Graduate Studies
Programs in:
 accounting • MS
 management information systems • MS

School of Architecture

William McDonough, Dean
Programs in:
 architectural history • M Arch H, PhD
 architecture • M Arch
 landscape architecture • M Land Arch
 urban and environmental planning • MP

School of Engineering and Applied Science

Richard W. Miksad Jr., Dean
Programs in:
 applied mechanics • MAM, MS
 biomedical engineering • ME, MS, PhD
 chemical engineering • ME, MS, PhD
 computer science • MCS, MS, PhD
 electrical engineering • ME, MS, PhD
 engineering and applied science • M Ap Ma
 engineering physics • MEP, MS, PhD
 environmental engineering • ME, MS, PhD
 materials science • MMSE, MS, PhD
 mechanical and aerospace engineering • ME, MS, PhD
 nuclear engineering • ME, MS, PhD
 structural engineering • ME, MS, PhD
 systems engineering • ME, MS, PhD
 transportation engineering and management • ME, MS, PhD
 water resources • ME, MS, PhD

School of Law

Robert E. Scott, Dean
Program in:
 law • JD, LL M, SJD

School of Medicine

Robert M. Carey, Dean
Program in:
 medicine • MD

University of Virginia (continued)
School of Nursing
B. Jeanette Lancaster, Dean
Program in:
   nursing • MSN, PhD

VIRGINIA COMMONWEALTH UNIVERSITY
Richmond, VA 23284-9005
http://www.vcu.edu/

Public coed university. *Enrollment: 21,349 graduate, professional, and undergraduate students. Graduate faculty: 817. Computer facilities: Campuswide network is available with full Internet access. Computer services are offered at no charge. Library facilities: Cabell/ Tompkins-McCaw Libraries. Graduate expenses: $4960 per year full-time, $257 per credit part-time for state residents; $12,652 per year full-time, $684 per credit part-time for nonresidents. General application contact: Dr. Sherry T. Sandkam, Associate Dean, 804-828-6916.*

School of Graduate Studies
Dr. Jack L. Haar, Dean

Center for Environmental Studies
Greg Garman, Director
Programs in:
   environmental communication • MIS
   environmental health • MIS
   environmental planning • MIS
   environmental sciences • MIS

Center for Public Policy
Dr. Robert D. Holsworth, Director
Program in:
   public policy and administration • PhD

College of Humanities and Sciences
Dr. Stephen D. Gottfredson, Dean
Programs in:
   account management • MS
   applied mathematics • MS
   applied physics • MS
   applied social research • CASR
   art direction • MS
   biology • MS
   chemistry • MS, PhD
   clinical psychology • PhD
   computer science • MS
   copywriting • MS
   counseling psychology • PhD
   creative writing • MFA
   criminal justice • CCJA, MS
   forensic science • MS
   general psychology • PhD
   history • MA
   human resources management • MPA
   literature • MA
   mass communications • MS
   mathematics • MS
   operations research • MS
   physics • MS
   planning information • CPI
   policy analysis • MPA
   public finance • MPA
   public management • CPM
   public personnel • MPA
   sociology • MS
   statistics • Certificate, MS
   urban planning • MURP
   urban revitalization • CURP
   writing and rhetoric • MA

Program in Interdisciplinary Studies
Dr. Sherry T. Sandkam, Director
Program in:
   interdisciplinary studies • MIS

School of Allied Health Professions
Dr. Cecil B. Drain, Interim Dean
Programs in:
   advanced physical therapy • MS
   aging studies • CAS
   alcohol and drug education/rehabilitation • CPC, MS
   anatomy and physical therapy • PhD
   clinical laboratory sciences • MS
   entry-level physical therapy • MS
   executive health administration • MSHA
   gerontology • MS
   health administration • MHA
   health services organization and research • PhD
   nurse anesthesia • MSNA
   occupational therapy • MS, MSOT
   physiology and physical therapy • PhD
   rehabilitation and counseling • MS

School of Business
Dr. Howard P. Tuckman, Dean
Programs in:
   accounting/taxation • PhD
   business administration • MBA, PhD
   decision sciences • MS, PhD
   economics • MA, MS, PhD
   finance • MS, PhD
   human resources management and industrial relations • MS
   information systems • Certificate, MS, PhD
   international business • PhD
   marketing and business law • MS, PhD
   real estate and urban land development • Certificate, MS
   risk management and insurance • MS
   taxation • M Tax

School of Education
Dr. John S. Oehler, Dean
Programs in:
   administration and supervision • M Ed
   adult education and human resource development • M Ed
   counselor education • M Ed
   curriculum and instruction • M Ed

early education • MT
emotionally disturbed • M Ed, MT
learning disabilities • M Ed
mathematics education • M Ed
mentally retarded • M Ed, MT
middle education • MT
physical education • MS
preschool handicapped • M Ed
reading • M Ed
recreation, parks and tourism • MS
secondary education • Certificate, MT
severely/profoundly handicapped • M Ed
urban services • PhD

School of Engineering
Dr. Henry A. McGee Jr., Dean
Program in:
biomedical engineering • MS, PhD

School of Medicine Graduate Programs
Dr. Hermes A. Kontos, Dean
Programs in:
anatomy • CBHS, MS
anatomy and physical therapy • PhD
biochemistry and molecular biophysics • CBHS, MS, PhD
biostatistics • MS, PhD
genetic counseling • MS
human genetics • CBHS, PhD
microbiology and immunology • CBHS, MS, PhD
neuroscience • MS
pathology • MS, PhD
pharmacology and toxicology • CBHS, MS, PhD
physiology • CBHS, MS, PhD
preventive medicine • MPH

School of Nursing
Dr. Nancy F. Langston, Dean
Programs in:
adult health nursing • MS
biology of health and illness • PhD
child health nursing • MS
clinical nurse manager • MS
family health nursing • MS
human health and illness • PhD
nurse executive • MS
nurse practitioner • Certificate
nursing administration • MS
nursing systems • PhD
psychiatric-mental health nursing • MS
women's health nursing • MS

School of Pharmacy Graduate Programs
Dr. Victor A. Yanchick, Dean
Program in:
pharmacy and pharmaceutics • MS, PhD

School of Social Work
Dr. Frank R. Baskind, Dean
Program in:
social work • MSW, PhD

School of the Arts
Dr. Richard Toscan, Dean
Programs in:
acting • MFA
art education • MAE
art history • MA, PhD
composition • MM
conducting • MM
costume design • MFA
crafts • MFA
directing • MFA
education • MFA, MM
interior environments • MFA
painting and printmaking • MFA
performance • MM
photography/film • MFA
scene design/technical theater • MFA
sculpture • MFA
visual communications • MFA

Medical College of Virginia-Professional Programs

Dr. John E. Jones, Vice President for Health Sciences

School of Dentistry
Dr. Lindsay M. Hunt, Dean
Program in:
dentistry • DDS

School of Medicine
Dr. Hermes A. Kontos, Dean
Programs in:
anatomy • CBHS, MS
anatomy and physical therapy • PhD
biochemistry and molecular biophysics • CBHS, MS, PhD
biostatistics • MS, PhD
genetic counseling • MS
human genetics • CBHS, PhD
medicine • MD
microbiology and immunology • CBHS, MS, PhD
neuroscience • MS
pathology • MS, PhD
pharmacology and toxicology • CBHS, MS, PhD
physiology • CBHS, MS, PhD
preventive medicine • MPH

School of Pharmacy
Dr. Victor A. Yanchick, Dean
Programs in:
pharmacy • Pharm D
pharmacy and pharmaceutics • MS, PhD

VIRGINIA POLYTECHNIC INSTITUTE AND STATE UNIVERSITY
Blacksburg, VA 24061
http://milieu.grads.vt.edu/rgs.html

Public coed university. *Enrollment:* 27,235 graduate, professional, and undergraduate students. Library facilities: *Carol M. Newman Library plus 3 additional on-campus libraries.* Graduate expenses: *$4927 per year full-time, $792 per semester (minimum) part-time for state residents; $7537 per year full-time, $1227 per semester (minimum) part-time for nonresidents.* General application contact: *Graduate School Receptionist, 877-453-1405.*

Graduate School
Dr. John L. Eaton, Associate Provost
Program in:
    veterinary medical sciences • MS, PhD

College of Agriculture and Life Sciences
Dr. L. A. Swiger, Dean
Programs in:
    agricultural and applied economics • MS, PhD
    animal science • MS, PhD
    behavior • MS, PhD
    biochemistry • MS, PhD
    cell and molecular biology • PhD
    crop and soil environmental sciences • MS, PhD
    dairy science • MS, PhD
    entomology • MS, PhD
    food science and technology • MS, PhD
    genetics • MS, PhD
    horticulture • MS, PhD
    management • MS, PhD
    nutrition • MS, PhD
    physiology • MS, PhD
    plant pathology • MS, PhD
    plant physiology • MS, PhD
    poultry science • MS, PhD

College of Architecture and Urban Studies
Dr. Paul L. Knox, Dean
Programs in:
    architecture • M Arch, MS
    environmental design and planning • PhD
    landscape architecture • MLA
    public administration and policy • CAGS, MPA, PhD
    urban affairs • MUA
    urban and regional planning • MURPL

College of Arts and Sciences
Dr. Robert C. Bates, Dean
Programs in:
    applied behavioral science • MS
    applied experimental psychology • PhD
    applied mathematics • MS, PhD
    botany • MS, PhD
    chemistry • MS, PhD
    clinical psychology • PhD
    computer science • MS, PhD

    developmental psychology • MS, PhD
    ecology • MS, PhD
    economics • MA, PhD
    English • MA
    environmental psychology • MS
    genetics • PhD
    geography • MS
    geological sciences • MS, PhD
    geophysics • MS, PhD
    history • MA
    human performance • MS
    industrial/organizational psychology • MS, PhD
    information systems • MIS
    mathematical physics • MS, PhD
    microbiology • MS, PhD
    philosophy • MA
    physics • MS, PhD
    political science • MA
    psychology • PhD
    pure mathematics • MS, PhD
    school psychology • PhD
    science and technology studies • MS, PhD
    sociology • MS, PhD
    statistics • MS, PhD
    theatre arts • MFA
    zoology • MS, PhD

College of Engineering
Dr. F. William Stephenson, Dean
Programs in:
    aerospace engineering • M Eng, MS, PhD
    biological systems engineering • M Eng, MS, PhD
    chemical engineering • MS, PhD
    civil engineering • M Eng, MS, PhD
    electrical and computer engineering • MS, PhD
    engineering administration • MEA
    engineering mechanics • M Eng, MS, PhD
    environmental engineering • MS
    environmental sciences and engineering • MS, PhD
    industrial engineering • M Eng, MS, PhD
    materials engineering science • PhD
    materials science and engineering • M Eng, MS
    mechanical engineering • M Eng, MS, PhD
    mining and minerals engineering • M Eng, MS, PhD
    ocean engineering • MS
    operations research • M Eng, MS, PhD
    systems engineering • M Eng, MS

College of Forestry and Wildlife Resources
Gregory N. Brown, Dean
Programs in:
    aquaculture • MS, PhD
    conservation biology • MS, PhD
    fisheries science • MS, PhD
    forest biology • MF, MS, PhD
    forest biometry • MF, MS, PhD
    forest management/economics • MF, MS, PhD
    forest products marketing • MF, MS, PhD
    industrial forestry operations • MF, MS, PhD
    outdoor recreation • MF, MS, PhD
    wildlife science • MS, PhD
    wood science and engineering • MF, MS, PhD

College of Human Resources and Education

Dr. J. M. Johnson, Dean

Programs in:

administration and supervision of special education • CAGS, Ed D, PhD

adult and continuing education • CAGS, Ed D, MA Ed, MS Ed, PhD

adult development and aging • MS, PhD

adult learning and human resource development • MS, PhD

apparel product design and analysis • MS, PhD

child development • MS, PhD

clinical exercise physiology • MS, PhD

community and international nutrition • MS, PhD

consumer studies • MS, PhD

curriculum and instruction • CAGS, Ed D, MA Ed, PhD

educational administration • CAGS, Ed D, MA Ed, PhD

educational research and evaluation • PhD

family studies • MS, PhD

foods • MS, PhD

health and physical education • MS Ed

hospitality and tourism management • MS, PhD

household equipment • MS, PhD

housing • MS, PhD

interior design • MS, PhD

management/family economics • MS, PhD

management, marketing, and economic analysis of textiles and apparel • MS, PhD

marriage and family therapy • MS, PhD

muscle physiology and biochemistry • MS, PhD

nutrition • MS, PhD

nutrition in sports and chronic disease • MS, PhD

student personnel services • CAGS, Ed D, MA Ed, PhD

vocational-technical education • CAGS, Ed D, MS Ed, PhD

Pamplin College of Business

Dr. Richard E. Sorensen, Dean

Programs in:

accounting • M Acct, PhD

business administration • MBA

business administration/finance • PhD

business administration/management • PhD

business administration/management science • PhD

business administration/marketing • PhD

Virginia-Maryland Regional College of Veterinary Medicine

Dr. Peter Eyre, Dean

Programs in:

veterinary medical sciences • MS, PhD

veterinary medicine • DVM

VIRGINIA STATE UNIVERSITY
Petersburg, VA 23806-2096

http://www.vsu.edu/

Public coed comprehensive institution. Enrollment: 4,220 graduate, professional, and undergraduate students. Graduate faculty: 48 full-time, 5 part-time. Computer facilities: Campuswide network is available with full Internet access. Total number of PCs/terminals supplied for student use: 20. Computer services are offered at no charge. Library facilities: Johnston Memorial Library. Graduate expenses: $3739 per year full-time, $133 per credit hour part-time for state residents; $9056 per year full-time, $364 per credit hour part-time for nonresidents. General application contact: Dr. Wayne F. Virag, Dean, Graduate Studies and Continuing Education, 804-524-5985.

School of Graduate Studies and Continuing Education

Dr. Wayne F. Virag, Dean

Program in:

interdisciplinary studies • MIS

School of Agriculture, Science and Technology

Dr. Lorenza W. Lyons, Dean

Programs in:

biology • MS

mathematics • MS

mathematics education • M Ed

physics • MS

psychology • MS

vocational technical education • CAGS, M Ed, MS

School of Business

Dr. Sadie Gregory, Dean

Program in:

economics and finance • MA

School of Liberal Arts and Education

Dr. Samuel Creighton, Dean

Programs in:

educational administration and supervision • M Ed, MS

educational media • M Ed, MS

elementary education • M Ed, MS

English • MA

guidance • M Ed, MS

history • MA

special education • M Ed, MS

WASHINGTON

CENTRAL WASHINGTON UNIVERSITY
Ellensburg, WA 98926
http://www.cwu.edu/

Public coed comprehensive institution. *Enrollment:* 8,569 graduate, professional, and undergraduate students. Graduate faculty: *269 full-time.* Library facilities: *main library.* Graduate expenses: *Tuition of $4200 per year full-time, $140 per credit hour part-time for state residents; $12,780 per year full-time, $426 per credit hour part-time for nonresidents. Fees of $240 per year.* General application contact: *Dr. Duncan M. Perry, Dean of Graduate Studies and Research, 509-963-3103.*

Graduate Studies and Research
Dr. Duncan M. Perry, Dean
Program in:
    individual studies • M Ed, MA, MS

College of Arts and Humanities
Dr. Liahna Babener, Dean
Programs in:
    art • MA, MFA
    English • MA
    English language learning • MA
    history • MA
    music • MM
    teaching English as a foreign language • MA
    teaching English as a second language • MA
    theatre production • MA

College of Education and Professional Studies
Dr. Lin Douglas, Dean
Programs in:
    apparel design • MS
    business and distributive education • M Ed
    curriculum and instruction • M Ed
    educational administration • M Ed
    elementary education • M Ed
    family and consumer sciences education • MS
    family studies • MS
    health, physical education and recreation • MS
    nutrition • MS
    reading education • M Ed
    special education • M Ed

College of the Sciences
Dr. Anne Denman, Dean
Programs in:
    biology • MS
    chemistry • MS
    counseling psychology • MS
    experimental psychology • MS
    geology • MS
    guidance and counseling • M Ed
    mathematics • MAT, MS
    organizational development • MS
    resource management • MS
    school psychology • M Ed

CITY UNIVERSITY
Bellevue, WA 98004-6442
http://www.cityu.edu/

Independent coed comprehensive institution. *Enrollment:* 13,172 graduate, professional, and undergraduate students. Graduate faculty: *41 full-time, 1,079 part-time.* Computer facilities: *Campuswide network is available with full Internet access. Total number of PCs/terminals supplied for student use: 100. Computer services are offered at no charge.* Library facilities: *main library.* Graduate expenses: *$280 per credit hour.* General application contact: *Nabil El-Khatib, Vice President, Admissions, 800-426-5596.*

Graduate Division
Dr. Steven Stargardter, Acting Vice President of Academic Affairs

School of Business and Management Professions
Dr. Roman Borboa, Dean
Programs in:
    computer systems • MS
    financial management • Certificate, MBA
    general business administration • MBA
    general public administration • MPA
    information systems • Certificate, MBA
    management • Certificate, MA
    managerial leadership • Certificate, MBA
    marketing • Certificate, MBA
    project management • Certificate, MS
    public administration • Certificate

School of Education
Roxanne Kelly, Dean
Programs in:
    curriculum and instruction • M Ed
    education technology • M Ed
    ESL counseling • Certificate
    ESL instructional methods • M Ed
    guidance and counseling • M Ed
    school administration • M Ed
    school principal • Certificate
    special education • M Ed
    teaching • MIT

School of Human Services and Applied Behavioral Sciences
Dr. Roman Borboa, Dean
Programs in:
    human behavior • MA
    management and leadership • XMA
    marriage and family counseling • MA
    marriage, family, child counseling • MA
    mental health counseling • MA
    organizational and human systems design • XMA
    vocational rehabilitation counseling • Certificate, MA

EASTERN WASHINGTON UNIVERSITY
Cheney, WA 99004-2431

http://www.ewu.edu/

Public coed comprehensive institution. *Enrollment: 7,537 graduate, professional, and undergraduate students. Graduate faculty: 288. Computer facilities: Campuswide network is available with full Internet access. Computer service fees are applied as a separate charge. Library facilities: John F. Kennedy Library plus 3 additional on-campus libraries. Graduate expenses: $4200 per year full-time, $140 per credit part-time for state residents; $12,780 per year full-time, $415 per credit part-time for nonresidents. General application contact: Dr. Larry Briggs, Director, Graduate Office, 509-359-6297.*

Graduate School

Dr. Ronald Dalla, Dean
Program in:
    interdisciplinary studies • MA, MS

College of Business Administration

Dr. John Schleede, Dean
Programs in:
    business administration • MBA
    business education • M Ed
    public administration • MPA
    urban and regional planning • MURP
    vocational administration • M Ed

College of Education and Human Development

Dr. Phyllis Edmundson, Dean
Programs in:
    administration—school principal • M Ed
    adult education • M Ed
    college instruction • MA, MS
    college instruction in physical education • MS
    counseling psychology • MS
    curriculum and instruction • M Ed
    developing psychology • MS
    early childhood education • M Ed
    elementary teaching • M Ed
    foundations of education • M Ed
    instructional communications: community services •
        M Ed
    literacy specialist • M Ed
    physical education • MS
    school counseling • MS
    school library media administration • M Ed
    school psychology • MS
    science education • M Ed
    social science education • M Ed
    special education • M Ed
    supervising (clinic) teaching • M Ed

College of Letters and Social Sciences

Dr. Edmund Yarwood, Dean
Programs in:
    college instruction • MA
    communications • MS

composition • MA
creative writing • MFA
English • MA
French education • M Ed
history • MA
instrumental/vocal performance • MA
music education • MA
music history and literature • MA
psychology • MS
school psychology • MS
social work and human services • MSW

College of Science, Mathematics and Technology

Dr. Ray Soltero, Dean
Programs in:
    biology • MS
    communication disorders • MS
    computer science • M Ed, MS
    geology • MS
    mathematics • M Ed, MS
    medical technology • MS
    physical therapy • MPT
    technology • M Ed

Intercollegiate Center for Nursing Education

Dr. Dorothy Detlor, Dean
Program in:
    nursing education • MN

GONZAGA UNIVERSITY
Spokane, WA 99258-0001

http://www.gonzaga.edu/

Independent-religious coed comprehensive institution. *Enrollment: 4,613 graduate, professional, and undergraduate students. Graduate faculty: 154 full-time, 45 part-time. Computer facilities: Campuswide network is available with full Internet access. Computer service fees are applied as a separate charge. Library facilities: Foley Center plus 2 additional on-campus libraries. Graduate expenses: $7380 per year (minimum) full-time, $410 per credit (minimum) part-time. General application contact: Dr. Leonard Doohan, Dean of the Graduate School, 509-328-4220 Ext. 3546.*

Graduate School

Dr. Leonard Doohan, Dean

College of Arts and Sciences

Michael McFarland, SJ, Dean
Programs in:
    art • MAT
    English • MA, MAT
    history • MAT
    mathematics and computer science • MAT
    pastoral ministry • MA
    philosophy • MA
    religious studies • M Div, MA
    spirituality • MA

Gonzaga University (continued)

School of Business Administration
Dr. Clarence H. Barnes, Dean
Programs in:
    accounting • M Acc
    business administration • MBA

School of Education
Dr. Corrine McGuigan, Dean
Programs in:
    administration and curriculum • MAA
    anesthesiology education • M Anesth Ed
    computer education • MACE
    counseling psychology • MAP
    educational leadership • PhD
    initial teaching • MIT
    special education • MES
    sports and athletic administration • MASPAA
    teaching • MTA

School of Engineering
Dr. William Ilgen, Dean
Program in:
    electrical engineering • MSEE

School of Professional Studies
Dr. Richard Wolfe, Dean
Programs in:
    nursing • MSN
    organizational leadership • MOL

School of Law
John E. Clute, Dean
Program in:
    law • JD

HERITAGE COLLEGE
Toppenish, WA 98948-9599

http://www.heritage.edu/

Independent coed comprehensive institution. *Enrollment:* 1,152 graduate, professional, and undergraduate students. Graduate faculty: *9 full-time, 21 part-time.* Library facilities: *main library.* Graduate expenses: *$270 per credit.* General application contact: *Dean, Education Division, 509-865-2244 Ext. 1306.*

Graduate Program in Education
Programs in:
    bilingual education/ESL • M Ed
    community and human resource development • M Ed
    counseling • M Ed
    early childhood education • M Ed
    educational administration • M Ed
    special education • M Ed

PACIFIC LUTHERAN UNIVERSITY
Tacoma, WA 98447

http://www.plu.edu/

Independent-religious coed comprehensive institution. *Enrollment:* 3,555 graduate, professional, and undergraduate students. Graduate faculty: *37 full-time, 8 part-time.* Computer facilities: *Campuswide network is available with full Internet access. Total number of PCs/terminals supplied for student use: 180.* Computer services are offered at no charge. Library facilities: *Robert Mortvedt Library.* Graduate expenses: *$490 per semester hour.* General application contact: *Marjo Burdick, Office of Admissions, 253-535-7151.*

Division of Graduate Studies
Dr. Paul Menzel, Provost and Dean

Division of Social Sciences
Dr. Earl Smith, Dean
Program in:
    marriage and family therapy • MA

School of Business Administration and Management
Dr. Joseph McCann, Dean
Programs in:
    business administration • MBA
    technology and innovation management • MBA

School of Education
Dr. John L. Brickell, Acting Dean
Programs in:
    classroom language and literacy focus • MA
    early childhood • MA
    education administration • MA
    elementary education • MA
    kindergarten through twelfth grade • MA
    language and literacy • MA
    school library media • MA
    secondary education • MA
    teaching • MA

School of Nursing
Dr. Terry Miller, Dean
Programs in:
    client systems management • MSN
    family nurse practitioner • MSN
    gerontology • MSN
    health care systems management • MSN
    women's health care • MSN

SAINT MARTIN'S COLLEGE
Lacey, WA 98503-7500

http://www.stmartin.edu/

Independent-religious coed comprehensive institution. *Enrollment:* 1,568 graduate, professional, and undergraduate students. Graduate faculty: *20 full-time, 12 part-time.* Computer facilities: *Campuswide*

network is available with full Internet access. Total number of PCs/ terminals supplied for student use: 35. Computer services are offered at no charge. Graduate expenses: $450 per credit. General application contact: Administrative Assistant of the appropriate department, 360-491-4700.

Graduate Programs

Dr. Lillian V. Cady, Vice President, Academic Affairs
Programs in:
    business administration • MBA
    computers in education • M Ed
    counseling and community psychology • MAC
    counseling and guidance • M Ed
    economics and business administration • MBA
    engineering management • M Eng Mgt
    family nurse practitioner • MSN
    instruction • M Ed
    leadership in health policy • MSN
    reading • M Ed
    special education • M Ed
    teaching • MIT

SEATTLE PACIFIC UNIVERSITY
Seattle, WA 98119-1997

http://www.spu.edu/

Independent-religious coed comprehensive institution. Enrollment: 3,293 graduate, professional, and undergraduate students. Graduate faculty: 51 full-time, 54 part-time. Computer facilities: Campuswide network is available with full Internet access. Computer service fees are included with tuition and fees. Library facilities: main library. Graduate expenses: $268 per credit. General application contact: Admissions Office of the appropriate program, 206-281-2000.

Graduate Studies

Dr. Bruce G. Murphy, Provost

College of Arts and Sciences
Dr. Martin L. Abbott, Dean
Programs in:
    arts and sciences • MS
    clinical family psychology • Psy D
    teaching English as a second language • MA

School of Business and Economics
Gary Karns, Associate Dean
Programs in:
    business and economics • MBA
    information systems management • MS

School of Education
Dr. Ginger MacDonald, Director of Graduate Studies
Programs in:
    education • Ed D
    educational leadership • M Ed
    reading/language arts education • M Ed
    school counseling • M Ed
    secondary teaching • MAT

School of Health Sciences
Dr. Annalee Oakes, Dean
Program in:
    leadership in advanced nursing practice • MSN

SEATTLE UNIVERSITY
Seattle, WA 98122

http://www.seattleu.edu/Home.html

Independent-religious coed comprehensive institution. Enrollment: 5,739 graduate, professional, and undergraduate students. Graduate faculty: 162 full-time. Computer facilities: Campuswide network is available with full Internet access. Computer services are offered at no charge. Library facilities: A. A. Lemieux Library plus 1 additional on-campus library. Graduate expenses: Tuition of $339 per credit hour (minimum). Fees of $70 per year. General application contact: Michael McKeon, Dean of Admissions, 206-296-5900.

Albers School of Business and Economics

Dr. Fred DeKay, Acting Dean
Programs in:
    applied economics • Certificate, MAE
    business administration • Certificate, MBA
    finance • Certificate, MSF
    international business • Certificate, MIB

College of Arts and Sciences

Dr. Stephen Rowan, Dean
Program in:
    existential and phenomenological therapeutic
        psychology • MA Psych

Institute of Public Service
Dr. John Collins, Director
Programs in:
    not-for-profit leadership • MNPL
    public administration • MPA

School of Education

Dr. Sue Schmitt, Dean
Programs in:
    adult education and training • M Ed, MA
    counseling • MA
    curriculum and instruction • M Ed, MA
    educational administration • Ed S, M Ed, MA
    educational diagnostics/school psychology • Ed S
    educational leadership • Ed D
    student development administration • M Ed, MA
    teacher education • MIT
    teaching English to speakers of other languages • M Ed,
        MA

School of Law

James E. Bond, Dean
Program in:
    law • JD

Seattle University (continued)

School of Nursing
Dr. Constance Nakao, Director
Program in:
   nursing • Certificate, MSN

School of Science and Engineering
Dr. George Simmons, Dean
Program in:
   software engineering • MSE

School of Theology and Ministry
Dr. Loretta Jancoski, Dean
Programs in:
   divinity • M Div
   pastoral studies • MAPS
   transforming spirituality • MATS

UNIVERSITY OF WASHINGTON
Seattle, WA 98195

http://www.washington.edu/

Public coed university. *Enrollment: 37,362 graduate, professional, and undergraduate students. Graduate faculty: 4,526. Computer facilities: Campuswide network is available with full Internet access. Total number of PCs/terminals supplied for student use: 3,000. Computer service fees are included with tuition and fees. Library facilities: Suzzallo Library plus 18 additional on-campus libraries. Graduate expenses: $5433 per year full-time, $775 per quarter (minimum) part-time for state residents; $13,479 per year full-time, $1925 per quarter (minimum) part-time for nonresidents. General application contact: Dean/Chair of the academic unit, 206-543-2100.*

Graduate School
Marsha L. Landolt, Dean and Vice Provost
Programs in:
   biochemistry • PhD
   bioengineering • MS, MSE, PhD
   biological structure • PhD
   dentistry • MS, MSD, PhD
   immunology • PhD
   laboratory medicine • MS
   medical/health care ethics • MA
   medicinal chemistry • PhD
   microbiology • PhD
   molecular and cellular biology • PhD
   molecular basis of disease • PhD
   molecular biotechnology • PhD
   museology • MA
   Near and Middle Eastern studies • PhD
   neurobiology and behavior • PhD
   occupational therapy • MS
   pathology • MS
   pharmaceutics • MS, PhD
   pharmacology • MS, PhD
   physical therapy • MPT, MS
   physiology and biophysics • PhD
   plant molecular integration and function • PhD
   preservation planning and design • Certificate
   quantitative ecology and resource management • MS, PhD
   rehabilitation medicine • MS
   urban design • Certificate

College of Architecture and Urban Planning
Marsha L. Landolt, Dean and Vice Provost, Graduate School
Programs in:
   architecture and urban planning • M Arch
   construction management • MS
   historic preservation • Certificate
   landscape architecture • MLA
   urban design • Certificate
   urban design and planning • PhD
   urban planning • MUP

College of Arts and Sciences
John B. Simpson, Dean
Programs in:
   acting • MFA
   anthropology • MA, PhD
   applied mathematics • MS, PhD
   art history • MA, PhD
   arts and sciences • DMA, MM
   astronomy • MS, PhD
   atmospheric sciences • MS, PhD
   botany • MS, PhD
   Central Asian studies • MAIS
   chemistry • MS, PhD
   China studies • MAIS
   Chinese language and literature • MA, PhD
   classics • MA, PhD
   classics and philosophy • PhD
   communications • MA, MC, PhD
   communication theory • PhD
   comparative literature • MA, PhD
   comparative religion • MAIS
   costume design • MFA
   dance • MFA
   directing • MFA
   East European studies • MAIS
   economics • MA, PhD
   English • MA, MAT, MFA, PhD
   English as a second language • MAT
   French literature • MA, PhD
   genetics • PhD
   geography • MA, PhD
   geological sciences • MS, PhD
   geophysics • MS, PhD
   Germanics • MA, PhD
   history • MA, PhD
   international studies • MAIS
   Italian literature • MA
   Japanese language and literature • MA, PhD
   Japan studies • MAIS
   Korean language and literature • MA, PhD
   Korea studies • MAIS
   lighting design • MFA
   linguistics • MA, PhD

mathematics • MA, MS, PhD

medical ethics • PhD

Middle Eastern studies • MAIS

music education • MA, PhD

Near Eastern languages and civilization • MA

philosophy • MA, PhD

physics • MS, PhD

political science • MA, PhD

psychology • PhD

Romance languages and literature • PhD

Romance linguistics • MA, PhD

Russian literature • MA, PhD

Russian studies • MAIS

Scandinavian languages and literatures • MA, PhD

scene design • MFA

Slavic linguistics • MA, PhD

sociology • MA, PhD

South Asian language and literature • MA, PhD

South Asian studies • MAIS

Spanish literature • MA, PhD

speech and hearing sciences • MS, PhD

speech communication • MA, PhD

statistics • MS, PhD

theory and criticism • PhD

zoology • PhD

College of Education
Dr. Allen Glenn, Dean
Programs in:
    curriculum and instruction • Ed D, M Ed, PhD
    educational leadership and policy studies • Ed D, M Ed, PhD
    human development and cognition • M Ed, PhD
    measurement and research • M Ed, PhD
    school counseling • M Ed, PhD
    school psychology • M Ed, PhD
    special education • Ed D, M Ed, PhD

College of Engineering
Dr. Denice D. Denton, Dean
Programs in:
    aeronautics and astronautics • MSAA, PhD
    bioengineering • MS, MSE, PhD
    ceramic engineering • MS, MSE
    chemical engineering • MS Ch E, PhD
    computer science • MS, PhD
    electrical engineering • MSEE, PhD
    engineering • M Eng, MAE
    environmental engineering • MS, MSCE, MSE, PhD
    hydraulic engineering • MSCE, MSE, PhD
    materials science • MSE
    materials science and engineering • MS, PhD
    mechanical engineering • MSE, MSME, PhD
    metallurgical engineering • MS, MSE
    structural and geotechnical engineering and mechanics • MS, MSCE, MSE, PhD
    technical communication • MS
    transportation and construction engineering • MS, MSCE, MSE, PhD

College of Forest Resources
Dr. David B. Thorud, Dean
Programs in:
    forest economics • MS, PhD
    forest ecosystem analysis • MS, PhD
    forest engineering/forest hydrology • MS, PhD
    forest products marketing • MS, PhD
    forest soils • MS, PhD
    pulp and paper science • MS, PhD
    quantitative resource management • MS, PhD
    silviculture • MFR
    silviculture and forest protection • MS, PhD
    social sciences • MS, PhD
    urban horticulture • MFR, MS, PhD
    wildlife science • MS, PhD

College of Ocean and Fishery Sciences
Arthur R. M. Nowell, Dean
Programs in:
    biological oceanography • MS, PhD
    chemical oceanography • MS, PhD
    fisheries • MS, PhD
    marine affairs • MMA
    marine geology and geophysics • MS, PhD
    physical oceanography • MS, PhD

Graduate School of Library and Information Science
Betty G. Bengtson, Acting Director
Program in:
    library and information science • MLIS

Graduate School of Public Affairs
Dr. Marc M. Lindenberg, Dean
Program in:
    public affairs • MPA

School of Business Administration
William Bradford, Dean
Program in:
    business administration • MBA, MP Acc, PhD

School of Nursing
Marsha L. Landolt, Dean and Vice Provost, Graduate School
Program in:
    nursing • MN, MS, PhD

School of Public Health and Community Medicine
Gilbert S. Omenn, Dean
Programs in:
    biostatistics • MS, PhD
    epidemiology • MPH, MS, PhD
    health services administration and planning • MHA
    industrial hygiene • PhD
    industrial hygiene and safety • MS
    nutritional sciences • MPH, MS, PhD
    occupational medicine • MPH
    pathobiology • MS, PhD
    preventive medicine • MPH
    technology • MS
    toxicology • MS, PhD

School of Social Work
Nancy R. Hooyman, Dean
Program in:
    social work • MSW, PhD

University of Washington (continued)

School of Dentistry

Dr. Paul B. Robertson, Dean
Program in:
  dentistry • DDS, MS, MSD, PhD

School of Law

Roland L. Hjorth, Dean
Programs in:
  Asian law • LL M, PhD
  international environmental law • LL M
  law • JD
  law and marine affairs • LL M
  law of sustainable international development • LL M
  taxation • LL M

School of Medicine

Dr. Paul G. Ramsey, Acting Vice President for Medical
  Affairs and Acting Dean
Programs in:
  biochemistry • PhD
  bioengineering • MS, MSE, PhD
  biological structure • PhD
  immunology • PhD
  laboratory medicine • MS
  medical/health care ethics • MA
  medicine • MD
  microbiology • PhD
  molecular and cellular biology • PhD
  molecular basis of disease • PhD
  molecular biotechnology • PhD
  neurobiology and behavior • PhD
  occupational therapy • MS
  pathology • MS
  pharmacology • MS, PhD
  physical therapy • MPT, MS
  physiology and biophysics • PhD
  plant molecular integration and function • PhD
  rehabilitation medicine • MS

School of Pharmacy

Dr. Sid Nelson, Dean
Programs in:
  medicinal chemistry • PhD
  pharmaceutics • MS, PhD
  pharmacy • Pharm D

WALLA WALLA COLLEGE
College Place, WA 99324-1198

http://www.wwc.edu/

Independent-religious coed comprehensive institution. *Enrollment:* 1,653 graduate, professional, and undergraduate students. *Graduate faculty:* 28 full-time, 16 part-time. *Computer facilities: Campuswide network is available with full Internet access. Computer service fees are included with tuition and fees. Library facilities: Peterson Memorial Library plus 1 additional on-campus library.* Graduate expenses:

$346 per quarter hour. General application contact: *Dr. Joe Galusha, Dean of Graduate Studies, 509-527-2421.*

Graduate School

Dr. Joe Galusha, Dean
Programs in:
  biological science • MS
  counseling psychology • MA
  curriculum and instruction • M Ed, MA
  educational leadership • M Ed, MA
  literacy instruction • M Ed, MA
  school counseling • M Ed, MA
  sociology and social work • MSW
  special education • M Ed, MA
  students at risk • M Ed, MA

WASHINGTON STATE UNIVERSITY
Pullman, WA 99164-1610

http://www.wsu.edu:8080/~gradsch/

Public coed university. *Enrollment:* 17,500 graduate, professional, and undergraduate students. *Graduate faculty: 721 full-time, 49 part-time. Computer facilities: Campuswide network is available with full Internet access. Computer service fees are applied as a separate charge. Library facilities: Holland Library plus 5 additional on-campus libraries.* Graduate expenses: $5334 per year full-time, $267 per credit hour part-time for state residents; $13,380 per year full-time, $677 per credit hour part-time for nonresidents. General application contact: *Dr. Steven R. Burkett, Assistant Dean of the Graduate School, 509-335-6424.*

Graduate School

Dr. Karen De Pauw, Interim Dean
Programs in:
  neuroscience • MS, PhD
  veterinary clinical sciences • MS, PhD
  veterinary microbiology and pathology • MS, PhD
  veterinary science • MS, PhD

College of Agriculture and Home Economics

Dr. James Zuiches, Dean
Programs in:
  agribusiness • MA
  agricultural economics • MA, PhD
  animal sciences • MS, PhD
  apparel design • MA
  apparel, merchandising and textiles • MA
  crop sciences • MS, PhD
  entomology • MS, PhD
  food science • MS, PhD
  genetics and cell biology • MS, PhD
  horticulture • MS, PhD
  human development • MA
  human nutrition • MS
  interior design • MA, MS
  natural resources sciences • MS, PhD
  nutrition • PhD

plant pathology • MS, PhD
plant physiology • MS, PhD
soil sciences • MS, PhD

College of Business and Economics
Dr. Gale Sullenberger, Dean
Programs in:
accounting and business law • M Acc
business administration • MBA, PhD
economics • MA, PhD

College of Education
Dr. Walter Gmelch, Interim Dean
Programs in:
counseling psychology • MA, PhD
curriculum development • Ed D, PhD
educational leadership • Ed D, M Ed, MA, PhD
educational psychology • Ed D, M Ed, MA, MAT, MIT, PhD
elementary education • Ed D, M Ed, MA, MAT, MIT, PhD
kinesiology • M Ed, MS
recreation and leisure studies • M Ed, MS
secondary education • Ed D, M Ed, MA, MAT, MIT, PhD

College of Engineering and Architecture
Dr. Robert Altenkirch, Dean
Programs in:
architecture • MS
chemical engineering • MS, PhD
civil engineering • MS, PhD
computer science • MS, PhD
electrical engineering • MS, PhD
environmental engineering • MS
materials science • PhD
materials science and engineering • MS
mechanical engineering • MS, PhD

College of Liberal Arts
Dr. Gail Chermack, Interim Dean
Programs in:
American studies • MA, PhD
anthropology • MA, PhD
clinical psychology • PhD
communications • MA
composition • MA
criminal justice • MA
English • MA, PhD
fine arts • MFA
history • MA, PhD
music • MA
political science • MA, PhD
psychology • MS, PhD
public affairs • MPA
sociology • MA, PhD
Spanish • MA
speech and hearing sciences • MA
teaching of English • MA
theater arts and drama • MA, MAT

College of Pharmacy
Dr. Dennis Clifton, Interim Dean
Programs in:
pharmaceutical science • Pharm D
pharmacology and toxicology • MS, PhD

College of Sciences
Dr. Leon Radziemski, Dean
Programs in:
analytical chemistry • MS, PhD
biochemistry and biophysics • MS, PhD
biology • MS
botany • MS, PhD
chemical physics • PhD
environmental science • MS, PhD
genetics and cell biology • MS, PhD
geology • MS, PhD
inorganic chemistry • MS, PhD
material science • MS, PhD
microbiology • MS, PhD
nuclear chemistry • MS, PhD
organic chemistry • MS, PhD
physical chemistry • MS, PhD
physics • MS, PhD
pure and applied mathematics • DA, MS, PhD
regional planning • MRP
zoology • MS, PhD
zoophysiology • PhD

School of Nursing
Dr. Dorothy Detlor, Dean
Program in:
nursing • M Nurs

College of Veterinary Medicine
Terry F. McElwain, Interim Dean
Programs in:
neuroscience • MS, PhD
veterinary clinical sciences • MS, PhD
veterinary medicine • DVM
veterinary microbiology and pathology • MS, PhD
veterinary science • MS, PhD

WESTERN WASHINGTON UNIVERSITY
Bellingham, WA 98225-5996

http://www.wwu.edu/

Public coed comprehensive institution. *Enrollment: 10,708 graduate, professional, and undergraduate students. Graduate faculty:
303. Computer facilities: Campuswide network is available with full
Internet access. Total number of PCs/terminals supplied for student
use: 1,000. Computer service fees are included with tuition and
fees. Library facilities: Mabel Zoe Wilson Library plus 1 additional
on-campus library. Graduate expenses: Tuition of $4200 per year
full-time, $140 per credit part-time for state residents; $12,780 per
year full-time, $426 per credit part-time for nonresidents. Fees of
$249 per year full-time, $83 per quarter part-time. General applica-*
tion contact: *Graduate Office, 360-650-3170.*

Western Washington University (continued)
Graduate School
Dr. Moheb Ghali, Dean

College of Arts and Sciences
Dr. Peter J. Elich, Dean
Programs in:
- anthropology • MA
- biology • MS
- chemistry • MS
- computer science • MS
- English • MA
- geology • MS
- history • MA
- mathematics • MS
- mental health counseling • MS
- physical education • M Ed
- political science • MA
- psychology • MS
- school counseling • M Ed
- science education • M Ed
- sociology • MA
- speech pathology and audiology • MA

College of Business and Economics
Dr. Dennis R. Murphy, Dean
Program in:
- business and economics • MBA

College of Fine and Performing Arts
Dr. Bertil H. van Boer, Dean
Programs in:
- art education • M Ed
- music • M Mus
- theatre • MA

Huxley College of Environmental Studies
Dr. Brad Smith, Dean
Programs in:
- behavioral toxicology • MS
- environmental science • MS
- geography • MS

Woodring College of Education
Dr. Larry Marrs, Dean
Programs in:
- adult education administration • M Ed
- elementary and secondary educational administration • M Ed
- elementary education • M Ed
- instructional technology • M Ed
- reading • M Ed
- secondary education • M Ed
- special education • M Ed
- student personnel administration • M Ed

WHITWORTH COLLEGE
Spokane, WA 99251-0001
http://www.whitworth.edu/

Independent-religious coed comprehensive institution. *Enrollment: 2,043 graduate, professional, and undergraduate students. Graduate faculty: 15 full-time, 60 part-time. Computer facilities: Campuswide network is available with full Internet access. Total number of PCs/terminals supplied for student use: 90. Computer service fees are included with tuition and fees. Library facilities: Harriet Cheney Cowles Memorial Library plus 3 additional on-campus libraries.* Graduate expenses: $230 per semester hour. General application contact: *Fred Pfursich, Office of Admissions, 509-777-1000 Ext. 3212.*

School of Education
Programs in:
- education administration • M Ed
- English as a second language • MAT
- gifted and talented • MAT
- physical education and sport administration • MA
- reading • MAT
- school counselors • M Ed
- social agency/church setting • M Ed
- special education • MAT
- teaching • MIT

Department of International Management
Dr. Dan Sanford, Director
Program in:
- international management • MIM

WEST VIRGINIA

MARSHALL UNIVERSITY
Huntington, WV 25755-2020
http://www.marshall.edu/

Public coed comprehensive institution. *Enrollment: 15,280 graduate, professional, and undergraduate students. Graduate faculty: 331 full-time, 78 part-time. Computer facilities: Campuswide network is available with full Internet access. Total number of PCs/terminals supplied for student use: 741. Computer service fees are included with tuition and fees. Library facilities: James E. Morrow Library plus 1 additional on-campus library.* Graduate expenses: $2364 per year full-time, $132 per hour part-time for state residents; $6894 per year full-time, $383 per hour part-time for nonresidents. General application contact: *Dr. James Harless, Director of Admissions, 304-696-3160.*

Graduate College

Dr. Leonard J. Deutsch, Dean
Programs in:
    biomedical sciences • MS, PhD
    forensic science • MS

College of Business

Dr. Calvin Kent, Dean
Program in:
    business • MBA

College of Education

Dr. Larry Froelich, Dean
Programs in:
    adult and technical education • MS
    athletic training • MS
    counseling • MA
    early childhood education • MA
    education • MAT
    educational administration • Ed D, Ed S, MA
    educational supervision • MA
    elementary education • MA
    exercise science • MS
    family and consumer sciences • MA
    health and physical education • MS
    library science education • MA
    reading education • MA
    safety • MS
    secondary education • MA
    social studies • MA
    special education • MA

College of Fine Arts

Dr. Donald Van Horn, Dean
Programs in:
    art • MA
    music • MA

College of Liberal Arts

Dr. Joan Mead, Dean
Programs in:
    clinical psychology • MA
    communication disorders • MA
    communication studies • MA
    criminal justice • MS
    English • MA
    general psychology • MA
    geography • MA, MS
    history • MA
    journalism • MAJ
    political science • MA
    sociology • MA

College of Science

Dr. Thomas Storch, Dean
Programs in:
    biological science • MA, MS
    chemistry • MS
    mathematics • MA, MS
    physical science • MS

Graduate School of Education and Professional Studies

Dr. James Ranson, Dean
Programs in:
    counseling • Ed S, MA
    elementary education • MA
    humanities • MA
    leadership studies • Ed S, MA
    psychology • Ed S, MA
    reading education • Ed S, MA
    secondary education • MA
    special education • MA

Graduate School of Engineering and Information Technology

Dr. William E. Crockett, Dean
Programs in:
    chemical engineering • MSE
    control systems engineering • MSE
    engineering management • MSE
    environmental engineering • MSE
    environmental science • MS
    information systems • MS
    technology management • MS

Graduate School of Management

Dr. Kurt Olmosk, Associate Dean
Programs in:
    business administration • MBA
    employee relations • MSM
    health care administration • MSM
    industrial relations • MSIR
    public administration • MSM

School of Nursing

Dr. Lynne Welch, Dean
Program in:
    nursing • MSN

School of Medicine

Dr. Charles H. McKown Jr., Dean and Vice President
Programs in:
    biomedical sciences • MS, PhD
    forensic science • MS
    medicine • MD

UNIVERSITY OF CHARLESTON
Charleston, WV 25304-1099

http://www.uchaswv.edu/

Independent coed comprehensive institution. *Enrollment:* 1,450 graduate, professional, and undergraduate students. Graduate faculty: *8 full-time, 9 part-time. Computer facilities: Campuswide network is available with full Internet access. Total number of PCs/ terminals supplied for student use: 90. Computer service fees are included with tuition and fees. Library facilities: A. S. Thomas Memorial Library. Graduate expenses: $365 per credit hour.* General application contact: *Lynn Jackson, Director of Admissions, 304-357-4750.*

University of Charleston (continued)
Jones-Benedum Division of Business
Dennis McMillen, Chair of MBA Program
Programs in:
    business administration • MBA
    human resource management • MHRM

WEST VIRGINIA UNIVERSITY
Morgantown, WV 26506
http://www.wvu.edu/

Public coed university. *Enrollment: 22,238 graduate, professional, and undergraduate students. Graduate faculty: 1,313 full-time, 262 part-time. Computer facilities: Campuswide network is available with full Internet access. Total number of PCs/terminals supplied for student use: 1,500. Computer services are offered at no charge. Library facilities: Charles C. Wise Jr. Library plus 9 additional on-campus libraries. Graduate expenses: $2820 per year full-time, $149 per credit hour part-time for state residents; $8104 per year full-time, $443 per credit hour part-time for nonresidents. General application contact: Evie G. Brantmayer, Interim Director of Records, 800-344-WVU1.*

College of Agriculture, Forestry and Consumer Sciences
Dr. Rosemary R. Haggett, Dean
Programs in:
    agricultural and environmental education • MS
    agricultural and resource economics • MS
    agricultural sciences • PhD
    agriculture • M Agr
    animal and veterinary sciences • MS
    family and consumer sciences • MS
    forest resource science • PhD
    forestry • MSF
    natural resource economics • PhD
    recreation and parks management • MS
    wildlife and fisheries resources • MS

College of Business and Economics
Dr. Sydney Stern, Dean
Programs in:
    business administration • MBA
    economics • MA, PhD
    industrial relations • MS
    professional accountancy • MPA

College of Creative Arts
Dr. Philip Faini, Dean
Programs in:
    art • MA
    art education • MA
    art history • MA
    fine arts • MFA
    music • DMA, MM, PhD
    visual art • MFA

College of Engineering and Mineral Resources
Dr. Allen Cogley, Dean
Programs in:
    aerospace engineering • MSAE
    chemical engineering • MS Ch E
    civil engineering • MSCE, MSE
    computer science • MS, PhD
    electrical engineering • MSEE
    engineering • MSE, PhD
    engineering of mines • MSEM
    industrial engineering • MSIE
    mechanical engineering • MSME
    mineral engineering • PhD
    occupational hygiene and occupational safety • MS
    petroleum and natural gas engineering • MSPNGE
    safety and environmental management • MS
    software engineering • MS

College of Human Resources and Education
Dr. William L. Deaton, Dean
Programs in:
    counseling psychology • PhD
    curriculum and instruction • Ed D
    education • Ed D
    educational leadership studies • MA
    educational psychology • Ed D, MA
    elementary education • MA
    reading • MA
    rehabilitation counseling • MS
    secondary education • MA
    special education • MA
    speech pathology and audiology • MS
    technology education • Ed D, MA

College of Law
John W. Fisher II, Interim Dean
Program in:
    law • JD

Eberly College of Arts and Sciences
Dr. M. Duane Nellis, Dean
Programs in:
    animal behavior • MS
    biology • MS
    cellular and molecular biology • MS, PhD
    chemistry • MS, PhD
    communication studies • MA
    comparative literature • MA
    English • MA, PhD
    environmental ecology • MS
    environmental plant biology • PhD
    French • MA
    geography • MA, PhD
    geology • MS, PhD
    German • MA
    history • MA, PhD
    linguisitics • MA
    mathematics • MS, PhD
    physics • MS, PhD
    plant ecology • MS, PhD
    plant systematics • MS
    political science • MA, PhD

population genetics • MS
psychology • MA, PhD
public administration • MPA
sociology and anthropology • MA
Spanish • MA
statistics • MS
teaching English to speakers of other languages • MA

Interdisciplinary Programs

Programs in:
genetics and developmental biology • MS, PhD
liberal studies • MALS
reproductive physiology • MS, PhD

Perley Isaac Reed School of Journalism

Dr. William T. Slater, Dean
Program in:
journalism • MSJ

School of Dentistry

Dr. Robert Moore, Dean
Programs in:
dental hygiene • MS
dental specialities • MS
dentistry • DDS

School of Medicine

Dr. Robert M. D'Alessandri, Dean
Programs in:
anatomy • MS, PhD
biochemistry • MS, PhD
community health promotion • MS
exercise physiology • MS
medical technology • MS
medicine • MD
microbiology and immunology • MS, PhD
occupational therapy • MOT
pharmacology and toxicology • MS, PhD
physical therapy • MPT
physiology • MS, PhD
public health • MPH

School of Nursing

Dr. E. Jane Martin, Dean
Programs in:
nurse practitioner • Certificate
nursing • MSN

School of Pharmacy

Dr. George R. Spratto, Dean
Programs in:
pharmaceutical sciences • MS, PhD
pharmacy • Pharm D

School of Physical Education

Dr. Lynn Housner, Assistant Dean
Program in:
physical education • Ed D, MS

School of Social Work

Dr. Karen V. Harper, Dean
Program in:
social work • MSW

WEST VIRGINIA WESLEYAN COLLEGE
Buckhannon, WV 26201

http://www.wvwc.edu/

Independent-religious coed comprehensive institution. *Enrollment:* 1,600 graduate, professional, and undergraduate students. Graduate faculty: *4 full-time, 5 part-time.* Computer facilities: *Campuswide network is available with full Internet access. Total number of PCs/ terminals supplied for student use: 200. Computer services are offered at no charge. Library facilities: A. M. Pfeiffer Library plus 1 additional on-campus library.* General application contact: *David W. McCauley, Director, MBA Program, 304-473-8MBA.*

Faculty of Business

David W. McCauley, Director, MBA Program
Program in:
business • MBA

WHEELING JESUIT UNIVERSITY
Wheeling, WV 26003-6295

http://www.wju.edu/

Independent-religious coed comprehensive institution. *Enrollment:* 1,556 graduate, professional, and undergraduate students. Graduate faculty: *17 full-time, 11 part-time.* Computer facilities: *Campuswide network is available with full Internet access. Total number of PCs/ terminals supplied for student use: 45. Computer service fees are included with tuition and fees. Library facilities: Bishop Hodges Library plus 2 additional on-campus libraries. Graduate expenses: $360 per credit hour.* General application contact: *Carol Carroll, Graduate Secretary, 304-243-2344.*

Department of Mathematics

Programs in:
mathematics education • MS
science education • MS

Department of Nursing

Dr. Judith A. Lemire, Coordinator
Program in:
nursing • MSN

Department of Physical Therapy

Mary Jo Wisniewski, Director
Program in:
physical therapy • MSPT

Wheeling Jesuit University (continued)
Department of Theology and Religious Studies
Dr. David Hammond, Director
Program in:
  applied theology • MA

Graduate Business Program
Dr. Edward W. Younkins, Director
Programs in:
  accounting • MS
  business administration • MBA

WISCONSIN

CARDINAL STRITCH UNIVERSITY
Milwaukee, WI 53217-3985
http://www.stritch.edu/

Independent-religious coed comprehensive institution. *Enrollment:* 5,316 *graduate, professional, and undergraduate students. Graduate faculty:* 65 *full-time,* 493 *part-time. Library facilities: main library plus 1 additional on-campus library. Graduate expenses: Tuition of* $338 *per credit. Fees of* $25 *per semester. General application contact: Amy Knox, Graduate Admissions Officer, 414-410-4042.*

College of Arts and Sciences
Dr. Dickson Smith, Associate Dean
Programs in:
  adult and family ministry • ME
  computer science education • MS
  educational computing • M Ed
  professional development • ME
  religious studies • MA
  special needs ministry • ME
  youth ministry • ME

College of Business and Management
Dr. Arthur Wasserman, Associate Dean
Programs in:
  business administration • MBA
  health services administration • MS
  international business • MBA
  management • MS

College of Education
Dr. Tia Bojar, Associate Dean
Programs in:
  administration • MS
  Catholic urban educator • ME
  education • M Ed
  educational leadership • MS
  English as a second language • ME
  leadership • Ed D
  professional development • ME
  special education • MA

  staff development • MS
  teaching • ME

CARTHAGE COLLEGE
Kenosha, WI 53140-1994
http://www.carthage.edu/

Independent-religious coed comprehensive institution. *Enrollment:* 2,250 *graduate, professional, and undergraduate students. Graduate faculty:* 6 *full-time,* 13 *part-time. Computer facilities: Campuswide network is available with full Internet access. Total number of PCs/ terminals supplied for student use:* 45. *Computer service fees are included with tuition and fees. Library facilities: John M. Ruthrauff Library. Graduate expenses:* $230 *per credit hour. General application contact: Dr. Judith B. Schaumberg, Director of Graduate Programs, 414-551-5876.*

Division of Teacher Education
Dr. Judith B. Schaumberg, Director of Graduate Programs
Programs in:
  classroom guidance and counseling • M Ed
  creative arts • M Ed
  gifted and talented children • M Ed
  language arts • M Ed
  modern language • M Ed
  natural sciences • M Ed
  reading • Certificate, M Ed
  social sciences • M Ed

EDGEWOOD COLLEGE
Madison, WI 53711-1998
http://www.edgewood.edu/

Independent-religious coed comprehensive institution. *Enrollment:* 1,842 *graduate, professional, and undergraduate students. Graduate faculty:* 19 *full-time,* 17 *part-time. Computer facilities: Campuswide network is available with partial Internet access (e-mail only). Total number of PCs/terminals supplied for student use:* 20. *Computer service fees are included with tuition and fees. Library facilities: Oscar Rennebohm Library. Graduate expenses:* $330 *per credit. General application contact: Dr. Raymond Schultz, Associate Dean of Graduate Programs, 608-257-4861 Ext. 2377.*

Program in Business
Dr. Gary Schroeder, Chair
Program in:
  business • MBA

Program in Education
Dr. Joseph Schmiedicke, Chair
Programs in:
  director of instruction • Certificate

director of special education and pupil services •
  Certificate
education • MA Ed
educational administration • MA
emotional disturbances • Certificate, MA
learning disabilities • Certificate, MA
learning disabilities and emotional disturbances •
  Certificate, MA
school business administration • Certificate
school principalship K-12 • Certificate

Program in Marriage and Family Therapy
Dr. Peter Fabian, Director
Program in:
  marriage and family therapy • MS

Program in Nursing
Dr. Virginia Wirtz, Chair
Program in:
  nursing • MNA

Program in Religious Studies
Dr. John Leonard, OP, Chairperson
Program in:
  religious studies • MA

MARIAN COLLEGE OF FOND DU LAC
Fond du Lac, WI 54935-4699

Independent-religious coed comprehensive institution. *Enrollment:* 2,263 graduate, professional, and undergraduate students. Graduate faculty: *9 full-time, 37 part-time.* Library facilities: *Cardinal Meyer Library.* Graduate expenses: *$220 per credit hour.* General application contact: *Dr. Nancy C. Riley, Chair, Educational Studies, 920-923-8143.*

Business Division
Richard M. Dienesch, Assistant Dean of Evening/Weekend
  Programs
Program in:
  organizational leadership and quality • MS

Education Division
Dr. Nancy C. Riley, Chair, Educational Studies
Programs in:
  educational leadership • MA
  teacher development • MA

 # MARQUETTE UNIVERSITY
Milwaukee, WI 53201-1881
http://www.mu.edu/

Independent-religious coed university. *Enrollment:* 10,527 graduate, professional, and undergraduate students. Graduate faculty: *519 full-time, 290 part-time.* Computer facilities: *Campuswide network is available with full Internet access. Computer service fees are included with tuition and fees.* Library facilities: *Memorial Library plus 2 additional on-campus libraries.* Graduate expenses: *$490 per credit.* General application contact: *Graduate School Staff, 414-288-7137.*

Graduate School
Rev. Thaddeus J. Burch, SJ, Dean
Programs in:
  advanced education in general dentistry • MS
  dental biomaterials • MS
  endodontics • MS
  interdisciplinary studies • PhD
  orthodontics • MS
  physical therapy • MPT
  physician assistant studies • MS
  prosthodontics • MS

College of Arts and Sciences
Dr. Thomas Hachey, Dean
Programs in:
  algebra • PhD
  American literature • PhD
  American politics • MA
  analytical chemistry • MS, PhD
  ancient philosophy • MA, PhD
  bioanalytical chemistry • MS, PhD
  bio-mathematical modeling • PhD
  biophysical chemistry • MS, PhD
  British and American literature • MA
  British empiricism and analytic philosophy • MA, PhD
  British literature • PhD
  cell biology • MS, PhD
  Christian philosophy • MA, PhD
  clinical psychology • MS
  comparative politics • MA
  developmental biology • MS, PhD
  early modern European philosophy • MA, PhD
  ecology • MS, PhD
  endocrinology • MS, PhD
  ethics • MA, PhD
  European history • MA, PhD
  genetics • MS, PhD
  German philosophy • MA, PhD
  historical theology • MA, PhD
  inorganic chemistry • MS, PhD
  international affairs • MA
  international political economy • MA
  international politics • MA
  mathematics • MS
  mathematics education • MS
  medieval history • MA
  medieval philosophy • MA, PhD

Marquette University (continued)
   microbiology • MS, PhD
   molecular biology • MS, PhD
   muscle and exercise physiology • MS, PhD
   neurobiology • MS, PhD
   organic chemistry • MS, PhD
   phenomenology and existentialism • MA, PhD
   philosophy of religion • MA, PhD
   physical chemistry • MS, PhD
   political philosophy • MA
   political science • MA
   psychology • PhD
   religious studies • PhD
   Renaissance and Reformation • MA
   reproductive physiology • MS, PhD
   scriptural theology • MA, PhD
   Spanish • MA, MAT
   statistics • MS
   systematic theology • MA, PhD
   theology • MA
   theology and society • PhD
   United States • MA, PhD

College of Business Administration
Dr. Lewis Mandell, Dean
Programs in:
   business administration • MBA
   business economics • MSAE
   financial economics • MSAE
   human resources • MSHR
   international economics • MSAE
   public policy economics • MSAE

College of Communication
Dr. William R. Elliot, Dean
Programs in:
   advertising • MA
   broadcasting and electronic communication • MA
   interpersonal communication • MA
   journalism • MA
   mass communication • MA
   mass communications • MA
   organizational communication • MA
   public relations • MA
   religious communications • MA
   speech education • MA
   speech-language pathology • MS
   theatre arts • MA

College of Engineering
Dr. Robert L. Reid, Dean
Programs in:
   bioinstrumentation/computers • MS, PhD
   biomechanics/biomaterials • MS, PhD
   construction and public works management • MS, PhD
   electrical and computer engineering • MS, PhD
   engineering management • MS
   environmental/water resources engineering • MS, PhD
   manufacturing systems engineering • MS, PhD
   materials science and engineering • MS, PhD
   mechanical engineering • MS, PhD
   structural/geotechnical engineering • MS, PhD
   systems physiology • MS, PhD
   transportation planning and engineering • MS, PhD

College of Nursing
Dr. Madeline Wake, Dean
Programs in:
   adult • MSN
   adult nurse practitioner • Certificate
   advanced practice nursing • MSN
   children • MSN
   gerontological nurse practitioner • Certificate
   neonatal nurse practitioner • Certificate, MSN
   nurse-midwifery • Certificate, MSN
   older adult • MSN
   pediatric nurse practitioner • Certificate

School of Education
Dr. Mary P. Hoy, Dean
Program in:
   education • Ed D, M Ed, MA, PhD, Spec

Law School
Howard B. Eisenberg, Dean
Program in:
   law • JD

School of Dentistry
Dr. William L. Lobb, Dean
Programs in:
   advanced education in general dentistry • MS
   dental biomaterials • MS
   dentistry • DDS
   endodontics • MS
   orthodontics • MS
   prosthodontics • MS

UNIVERSITY OF WISCONSIN–EAU CLAIRE

Eau Claire, WI 54702-4004

http://www.uwec.edu/

Public coed comprehensive institution. *Enrollment:* 10,484 graduate, professional, and undergraduate students. Graduate faculty: *391 full-time.* Library facilities: *William D. McIntyre Library.* Graduate expenses: *$3651 per year full-time, $611 per semester (minimum) part-time for state residents; $11,295 per year full-time, $1886 per semester (minimum) part-time for nonresidents.* General application contact: *Roger Groenewold, Director of Admissions, 715-836-5415.*

College of Arts and Sciences
Carl Haywood, Dean
Programs in:
   biology • MS
   English • MA
   history • MA
   psychology • MSE
   school psychology • MSE

College of Business

V. Thomas Dock, Dean
Program in:
 business administration • MBA

College of Professional Studies

Ronald N. Satz, Dean

School of Education

Stephen Kurth, Associate Dean
Programs in:
 biology • MAT, MST
 education and professional development • MEPD
 elementary education • MST
 English • MAT, MST
 history • MAT, MST
 mathematics • MAT, MST
 reading • MST
 special education • MSE

School of Human Sciences and Services

Carol Klun, Associate Dean
Programs in:
 communicative disorders • MS
 environmental and public health • MS

School of Nursing

Dr. Marjorie Bottoms, Associate Dean
Program in:
 nursing • MSN

UNIVERSITY OF WISCONSIN– GREEN BAY

Green Bay, WI 54311-7001

http://www.uwgb.edu/

Public coed comprehensive institution. *Enrollment: 5,159 graduate, professional, and undergraduate students. Graduate faculty: 22 full-time, 10 part-time. Computer facilities: Campuswide network is available with full Internet access. Total number of PCs/terminals supplied for student use: 250. Computer services are offered at no charge. Library facilities: Cofrin Library plus 1 additional on-campus library. Graduate expenses: $3774 per year full-time, $183 per credit part-time for state residents; $11,418 per year full-time, $425 per credit part-time for nonresidents. General application contact: Ronald D. Stieglitz, Associate Dean of Graduate Studies, 920-465-2123.*

Graduate Studies

Ronald D. Stieglitz, Associate Dean
Programs in:
 administrative science • MS
 applied leadership in teaching and learning • MS Ed
 environmental science and policy • MS

 # UNIVERSITY OF WISCONSIN– LA CROSSE

La Crosse, WI 54601-3742

http://www.uwlax.edu/

Public coed comprehensive institution. *Enrollment: 9,088 graduate, professional, and undergraduate students. Graduate faculty: 214 full-time, 16 part-time. Computer facilities: Campuswide network is available with full Internet access. Total number of PCs/terminals supplied for student use: 350. Computer service fees are included with tuition and fees. Library facilities: Murphy Library plus 3 additional on-campus libraries. Graduate expenses: $3737 per year full-time, $208 per credit part-time for state residents; $11,921 per year full-time, $633 per credit part-time for nonresidents. General application contact: Admissions Office, 608-785-8939.*

Graduate Studies

Dr. Garth Tymeson, Director of University Graduate Studies
Program in:
 social work • MSW

College of Business Administration

Rex Fuller, Dean
Program in:
 business administration • MBA

College of Health, Physical Education and Recreation

Douglas Hastad, Interim Dean
Programs in:
 adult fitness/cardiac rehabilitation • MS
 community health • MS
 community health education • MPH
 general pedagogy • MS
 general sports administration • MS
 human performance • MS
 recreation • MS
 recreation administration • MS
 school health • MS
 special adaptive physical education • MS
 therapeutic recreation • MS

College of Liberal Studies

Dr. John Magerus, Interim Dean
Program in:
 school psychology • CAGS, MS Ed

College of Science and Allied Health

Dr. C. Richard Kistner, Interim Dean
Programs in:
 biology • MS
 clinical microbiology • MS
 nurse anesthetist • MS
 physical therapy • MSPT

School of Education

Dr. Paul Theobald, Associate Dean
Programs in:
 college student development and administration • MS Ed
 elementary education • MEPD
 grades 1 through 6 • MEPD

University of Wisconsin–La Crosse (continued)
  K–12 • MEPD
  professional development • MEPD
  reading • MS Ed
  secondary education • MEPD
  special education • MS Ed

UNIVERSITY OF WISCONSIN–MADISON

Madison, WI 53706-1380

http://www.wisc.edu/

Public coed university. *Enrollment: 40,196 graduate, professional, and undergraduate students. Graduate faculty: 1,883 full-time, 276 part-time. Computer facilities: Campuswide network is available with full Internet access. Total number of PCs/terminals supplied for student use: 1,100. Computer services are offered at no charge. Library facilities: Memorial Library plus 44 additional on-campus libraries. Graduate expenses: $4928 per year full-time, $926 per semester (minimum) part-time for state residents; $15,190 per year full-time, $2849 per semester (minimum) part-time for nonresidents. General application contact: Graduate Admissions, 608-262-2433.*

Graduate School

Virginia Hinshaw, Dean
Programs in:
  administrative medicine • MS, PhD
  analytical clinical chemistry • MS
  biomolecular chemistry • MS, PhD
  biophysics • PhD
  cancer biology • MS, PhD
  cellular and molecular biology • PhD
  clinical microbiology and immunology • MS
  continuing education in pharmacy • PhD
  developmental biology • PhD
  endocrinology-reproductive physiology • MS, PhD
  epidemiology • MS, PhD
  genetics • PhD
  health physics • MS
  health services research • MS, PhD
  history of pharmacy • PhD
  hospital pharmacy • MS
  legal institutions • MLI
  medical genetics • MS
  medical physics • MS, PhD
  microbiology • PhD
  molecular and cellular pharmacology • PhD
  neurophysiology • PhD
  neuroscience • PhD
  oncology • PhD
  pathology • PhD
  pharmaceutical biochemistry • PhD
  pharmaceutical chemistry • PhD
  pharmaceutics • PhD
  pharmacology-pharmacy • PhD
  pharmacy administration • PhD
  physiology • PhD
  social and administrative sciences in pharmacy • PhD

College of Agricultural and Life Sciences

Elton D. Aberle, Dean
Programs in:
  agricultural and applied economics • MA, MS, PhD
  agricultural and life sciences • MBA
  agricultural journalism • MS
  agronomy • MS, PhD
  anatomy • MS, PhD
  animal sciences • MS, PhD
  bacteriology • MS, PhD
  biochemistry • MS, PhD
  biological systems engineering • MS, PhD
  biometry • MS
  cellular and molecular biology • MS, PhD
  continuing and vocational education • MS, PhD
  dairy science • MS, PhD
  development • PhD
  entomology • MS, PhD
  environmental toxicology • MS, PhD
  family and consumer journalism • MS
  food science • MS, PhD
  forest ecology and management • MS, PhD
  genetics • PhD
  horticulture • MS, PhD
  landscape architecture • MA, MS
  mass communication • PhD
  medical genetics • MS
  molecular and environmental toxicology • MS, PhD
  neurosciences • MS, PhD
  nutritional sciences • MS, PhD
  pharmacology • MS, PhD
  physiology • MS, PhD
  plant breeding and plant genetics • MS, PhD
  plant pathology • MS, PhD
  recreation resources management • MS
  rural sociology • MS
  soil science • MS, PhD
  wildlife ecology • MS, PhD

College of Engineering

John G. Bollinger, Dean
Programs in:
  chemical engineering • MS, PhD
  civil and environmental engineering • MS, PhD
  electrical engineering • MS, PhD
  engineering • PDD
  engineering mechanics • MS, PhD
  geological engineering • MS, PhD
  industrial engineering • MS, PhD
  manufacturing systems engineering • MS
  materials science • MS, PhD
  mechanical engineering • MS, PhD
  metallurgical engineering • MS, PhD
  nuclear engineering and engineering physics • MS, PhD
  oceanography and limnology • MS, PhD
  professional practice • ME
  technical Japanese • ME
  water chemistry • MS, PhD

College of Letters and Science
Phillip R. Certain, Dean
Programs in:
African languages and literature • MA, PhD
Afro-American studies • MA
anthropology • MA, MS, PhD
applied English linguistics • MA
art history • MA, PhD
astronomy • PhD
atmospheric and oceanic sciences • MS, PhD
biological psychology • PhD
botany • MS, PhD
Buddhist studies • PhD
cartography and geographic information systems • MS
chemistry • MS, PhD
Chinese • MA, PhD
choral • DMA, MM
classics • MA, PhD
clinical psychology • PhD
cognitive and perceptual sciences • PhD
communication arts • MA, PhD
communicative disorders • MS, PhD
comparative literature • MA, PhD
composition • DMA, MM
composition studies • PhD
computer sciences • MS, PhD
curriculum and instruction • PhD
developmental psychology • PhD
development policy and public administration • MA
economics • PhD
English language and linguistics • PhD
ethnomusicology • MM, PhD
family and consumer journalism • PhD
French • MA, PhD
geographic information systems • Certificate
geography • MS, PhD
geology • MS, PhD
geophysics • MS, PhD
German • MA, PhD
Greek • MA
Hebrew and Semitic studies • MA, PhD
history • MA, PhD
history of science • MA, PhD
industrial relations • MA, MS, PhD
instrumental • DMA, MM
Italian • MA, PhD
Japanese • MA, PhD
journalism and mass communication • MA
Latin • MA
Latin American and Iberian studies • MA
library and information studies • Certificate, MA, PhD
linguistics • MA, PhD
literature • MA, PhD
mass communication • PhD
mathematics • MA, PhD
music education • MM
musicology • MA, MM, PhD
performance • DMA, MM
philosophy • MA, PhD
physics • MA, MS, PhD
political science • MA, PhD
Portuguese • MA, PhD
public affairs and administration • MA

public affairs and policy analysis • MA
rural sociology • MS
Scandinavian studies • MA, PhD
Slavic languages and literature • MA, PhD
social and personality psychology • PhD
social welfare • PhD
social work • MSSW
sociology • MS, PhD
South Asian language and literature • PhD
South Asian studies • MA
Southeast Asian studies • MA
Spanish • MA, PhD
statistics • MS, PhD
theatre and drama • MA, MFA, PhD
theory • MA, MM, PhD
urban and regional planning • MS, PhD
zoology • MA, MS, PhD

Institute for Environmental Studies
Thomas M. Yuill, Director
Programs in:
conservation biology and sustainable development • MS
environmental monitoring • MS, PhD
land resources • MS, PhD
water resources management • MS

School of Business
Virginia Hinshaw, Dean, Graduate School
Programs in:
accounting • M Acc, MBA, MS, PhD
actuarial science • MS, PhD
agribusiness • MBA
arts administration • MA
business • PhD
distribution management • MBA, MS
diversified business • MBA
finance, investment, and banking • MBA, MS, PhD
information systems analysis and design • MBA, MS, PhD
international business • MBA, MS
management and human resources • MBA, MS
manufacturing and technology management • MS
marketing • MBA
marketing research • MS
operations and information management • MBA, MS, PhD
real estate and urban land economics • MBA, MS, PhD
real estate appraisal and investment analysis • MS
risk management and insurance • MBA, MS, PhD

School of Education
Virginia Hinshaw, Dean, Graduate School
Programs in:
art • MA, MFA
art education • MA
chemistry education • MS
commercial arts education • MA
continuing and vocational education • MS, PhD
counseling • MS
counseling psychology • PhD
curriculum and instruction • MS, PhD
educational administration • MS, PhD
educational policy studies • MA, PhD
educational psychology • MS, PhD

University of Wisconsin–Madison (continued)
education and mathematics • MA
English education • MA
French education • MA
geography education • MS
German education • MA
kinesiology • MS, PhD
Latin education • MA
music education • MS
physics education • MS
rehabilitation psychology • MA, MS, PhD
science education • MS
Spanish education • MA
special education • MA, MS, PhD
therapeutic science • MS

School of Human Ecology
Virginia Hinshaw, Dean, Graduate School
Programs in:
child and family studies • MS, PhD
consumer science • MS
continuing and vocational education • MS, PhD
family and consumer journalism • MS, PhD
interior environments • MS
textiles and clothing • MS
textiles and design • PhD

Law School
Kenneth B. Davis Jr., Dean
Programs in:
law • JD, LL M, SJD
legal institutions • MLI

Medical School
Dr. Phillip M. Farrell, Dean
Programs in:
administrative medicine • MS, PhD
biomolecular chemistry • MS, PhD
cancer biology • MS, PhD
clinical microbiology and immunology • MS
epidemiology • MS, PhD
genetics • PhD
health physics • MS
health services research • MS, PhD
medical genetics • MS
medical physics • MS, PhD
medicine • MD
microbiology • PhD
molecular and cellular pharmacology • PhD
neurophysiology • PhD
neuroscience • PhD
oncology • PhD
pathology • PhD
physiology • PhD

School of Nursing
Dr. Vivian M. Littlefield, Dean
Program in:
nursing • MS, PhD

School of Pharmacy
Programs in:
continuing education in pharmacy • PhD
history of pharmacy • PhD
hospital pharmacy • MS
pharmaceutical biochemistry • PhD
pharmaceutical chemistry • PhD
pharmaceutics • PhD
pharmacology-pharmacy • PhD
pharmacy • Pharm D
pharmacy administration • PhD
social and administrative sciences in pharmacy • PhD

School of Veterinary Medicine
Dr. Daryl Buss, Dean
Program in:
veterinary medicine • DVM, MS, PhD

 # UNIVERSITY OF WISCONSIN–MILWAUKEE
Milwaukee, WI 53201-0413

http://www.uwm.edu/

Public coed university. *Enrollment: 21,877 graduate, professional, and undergraduate students. Graduate faculty: 773 full-time. Computer facilities: Campuswide network is available with full Internet access. Total number of PCs/terminals supplied for student use: 320. Computer services are offered at no charge. Library facilities: Golda Meir Library. Graduate expenses: $4996 per year full-time, $1030 per semester (minimum) part-time for state residents; $15,216 per year full-time, $2947 per semester (minimum) part-time for nonresidents. General application contact: Wendy Fall, Director of Student Services, 414-229-4133.*

Graduate School
Wiliam R. Rayburn, Dean of the Graduate School and Associate Provost for Research

College of Engineering and Applied Science
Dr. Chan Shih-Hung, Interim Dean
Programs in:
computer science • MS, PhD
engineering • MS, PhD

College of Letters and Sciences
Marshall Goodman, Dean
Programs in:
anthropology • MS, PhD
art history • MA
art museum studies • Certificate
biological sciences • MS, PhD
chemistry • MS, PhD
classics and Hebrew studies • MAFLL
clinical psychology • MS, PhD
communication • MA
comparative literature • MAFLL
economics • MA, PhD

English and comparative literature • MA, PhD
French and Italian • MAFLL
geography • MA, MS, PhD
geological sciences • MS, PhD
German • MAFLL
history • MA
industrial and labor relations • MHRLR, MILR
mass communication • MA
mathematics • MS, PhD
philosophy • MA
physics • MS, PhD
political science • MA, PhD
psychology • MS, PhD
public administration • MPA
Slavic studies • MAFLL
sociology • MA
Spanish • MAFLL
urban studies • MS, PhD

School of Allied Health Professions
Fred Pairent, Dean
Programs in:
    clinical laboratory science • MS
    communication sciences and disorders • MS
    human kinetics • MS
    occupational therapy • MS

School of Architecture and Urban Planning
Robert Greenstreet, Dean
Programs in:
    architecture • M Arch, PhD
    urban planning • MUP

School of Business Administration
Charles Kroncke, Dean
Program in:
    business administration • MBA, MS, PhD

School of Education
William Harvey, Dean
Programs in:
    administrative leadership and supervision in education •
      MS
    cultural foundations of education • MS
    curriculum planning and instruction improvement • MS
    early childhood education • MS
    educational psychology • MS
    educational rehabilitation counseling • MS
    elementary education • MS
    exceptional education • MS
    junior high/middle school education • MS
    reading education • MS
    secondary education • MS
    teaching in an urban setting • MS
    urban education • PhD

School of Fine Arts
Catherine Davy, Dean
Programs in:
    art • MA, MFA
    art education • MA, MFA, MS
    dance • MFA
    film • MFA
    music • MM
    theatre • MFA

School of Library and Information Science
Dr. Mohammed Aman, Dean
Program in:
    library and information science • CAS, MLIS

School of Multidisciplinary Studies
Wiliam R. Rayburn, Dean of the Graduate School and
    Associate Provost for Research, Graduate School
Program in:
    multidisciplinary studies • PhD

School of Nursing
Sharon Hoffman, Dean
Program in:
    nursing • MS, PhD

School of Social Welfare
James A. Blackburn, Dean
Programs in:
    criminal justice • MS
    social work • MSW

UNIVERSITY OF WISCONSIN–OSHKOSH
Oshkosh, WI 54901-8602

http://www.uwosh.edu/

Public coed comprehensive institution. *Enrollment:* 9,601 graduate, professional, and undergraduate students. Graduate faculty: *148 full-time, 38 part-time.* Computer facilities: *Campuswide network is available with full Internet access. Total number of PCs/terminals supplied for student use: 375. Computer service fees are included with tuition and fees.* Library facilities: *Polk Library.* Graduate expenses: *$3638 per year full-time, $609 per semester (minimum) part-time for state residents; $11,282 per year full-time, $1884 per semester (minimum) part-time for nonresidents.* General application contact: *Gregory B. Wypiszynski, Coordinator of Graduate Studies, 920-424-1223.*

Graduate School
Dr. Patricia J. Koll, Assistant Vice Chancellor

College of Business Administration
Dr. E. Alan Hartman, Dean
Program in:
    business administration • MBA

College of Education and Human Services
Dr. Donald W. Mocker, Dean
Programs in:
    counseling • MSE
    curriculum and instruction • MSE
    early childhood: exceptional education needs • MSE
    educational leadership • MS
    emotionally disturbed • MSE
    learning disabilities • MSE
    mental retardation • MSE
    reading education • MSE
    special education • MSE

University of Wisconsin–Oshkosh (continued)

College of Letters and Science

Dr. Michael Zimmerman, Dean

Programs in:

audiology • MS

biology • MS

botany • MS

experimental psychology • MS

health care • MPA

industrial/organizational psychology • MS

instrumentation • MS

mathematics education • MS

microbiology • MS

physics • MS

physics education • MS

public administration • MPA

speech and hearing science • MS

speech pathology • MS

zoology • MS

College of Nursing

Dr. Merritt Knox, Dean

Programs in:

family nurse practitioner • MSN

primary health care • MSN

UNIVERSITY OF WISCONSIN– PARKSIDE

Kenosha, WI 53141-2000

http://www.uwp.edu/

Public coed comprehensive institution. *Enrollment: 4,696 graduate, professional, and undergraduate students. Graduate faculty: 28 full-time. Computer facilities: Campuswide network is available with full Internet access. Computer services are offered at no charge. Library facilities: main library. Graduate expenses: $3698 per year full-time, $1242 per semester part-time for state residents; $11,342 per year full-time, $3792 per semester part-time for nonresidents. General application contact: Dr. Donald Creff, Dean, College of Arts and Sciences, 414-595-2140.*

College of Arts and Sciences

Dr. Donald Creff, Dean

Program in:

applied molecular biology • MAMB

School of Business and Technology

Dr. Richard Stolz, Dean

Program in:

business and technology • MBA

UNIVERSITY OF WISCONSIN– PLATTEVILLE

Platteville, WI 53818-3099

http://www.uwplatt.edu/

Public coed comprehensive institution. *Enrollment: 5,022 graduate, professional, and undergraduate students. Graduate faculty: 4 full-time, 133 part-time. Library facilities: Karrmann Library. General application contact: Laurie Schuler, Admissions and Enrollment Management, 608-342-1125.*

School of Graduate Studies

Judy Paul, Interim Dean

College of Business, Industry, Life Science, and Agriculture

Dr. Jerry Strohm, Interim Dean

Programs in:

agricultural industries • MS

industrial technology management • MS

College of Liberal Arts and Education

Dr. Charlotte Stokes, Dean

Programs in:

adult education • MSE

counselor education • MSE

elementary education • MSE

middle school education • MSE

secondary education • MSE

vocational and technical education • MSE

UNIVERSITY OF WISCONSIN– RIVER FALLS

River Falls, WI 54022-5001

http://www.uwrf.edu/

Public coed comprehensive institution. *Enrollment: 5,441 graduate, professional, and undergraduate students. Graduate faculty: 234 full-time, 5 part-time. Computer facilities: Campuswide network is available with full Internet access. Total number of PCs/terminals supplied for student use: 90. Computer service fees are included with tuition and fees. Library facilities: Chalmer Davee Library. General application contact: Graduate Admissions, 715-425-3843.*

School of Graduate and Professional Studies

Kathleen Daly, Dean

College of Agriculture, Food, and Environmental Sciences

Gary E. Rohde, Dean

Program in:

agricultural education • MS

College of Arts and Science
Neal Prochnow, Dean
Programs in:
    language, literature, and communication education •
      MSE
    mathematics education • MSE
    science education • MSE
    social science education • MSE

College of Education and Graduate Studies
Kathleen Daly, Dean, School of Graduate and Professional
    Studies
Programs in:
    communicative disorders • MS
    counseling • MSE
    elementary education • MSE
    reading • MSE
    school psychology • MSE

UNIVERSITY OF WISCONSIN–STEVENS POINT
Stevens Point, WI 54481-3897

http://www.uwsp.edu/

Public coed comprehensive institution. *Enrollment: 8,362 graduate, professional, and undergraduate students. Graduate faculty: 298 full-time, 28 part-time. Computer facilities: Campuswide network is available with full Internet access. Total number of PCs/terminals supplied for student use: 405. Computer services are offered at no charge. Library facilities: University Library. Graduate expenses: $3702 per year full-time, $664 per semester (minimum) part-time for state residents; $11,346 per year full-time, $1938 per semester (minimum) part-time for nonresidents. General application contact: David Eckholm, Director of Admissions, 715-346-2441.*

College of Fine Arts and Communication
Gerard McKenna, Dean
Programs in:
    interpersonal communication • MA
    mass communication • MA
    music • MM Ed
    organizational communication • MA
    public relations • MA

College of Letters and Science
Justus Paul, Dean
Programs in:
    business and economics • MBA
    English • MST
    history • MST

College of Natural Resources
Dr. Richard Wilke, Associate Dean
Program in:
    natural resources • MS

College of Professional Studies
Joan North, Dean
Programs in:
    communicative disorders • MS
    educational administration • MSE
    education—general/reading • MSE
    elementary education • MSE
    guidance and counseling • MSE
    human and community resources • MS
    nutritional sciences • MS

UNIVERSITY OF WISCONSIN–STOUT
Menomonie, WI 54751

http://www.uwstout.edu/

Public coed comprehensive institution. *Enrollment: 7,412 graduate, professional, and undergraduate students. Graduate faculty: 212 full-time. Computer facilities: Campuswide network is available with full Internet access. Total number of PCs/terminals supplied for student use: 470. Computer service fees are included with tuition and fees. Library facilities: Library Learning Center. Graduate expenses: $3284 per year full-time, $183 per credit hour part-time for state residents; $7644 per year full-time, $425 per credit hour part-time for nonresidents. General application contact: Myrna McRoberts, Graduate Student Evaluator, 715-232-1322.*

Graduate Studies
Robert A. Sedlak, Associate Vice Chancellor

College of Human Development
Dr. Edwin Biggerstaff, Dean
Programs in:
    applied psychology • MS
    education • MS
    food science and nutrition • MS
    guidance and counseling • Ed S, MS
    home economics • MS
    hospitality and tourism • MS
    marriage and family therapy • MS
    school psychology • MS Ed
    vocational rehabilitation • MS

College of Technology, Engineering, and Management
Dr. Bruce Siebold, Dean
Programs in:
    industrial and vocational education • Ed S
    industrial/technology education • MS
    management technology • MS
    media technology • MS
    risk control • MS
    training and development • MS
    vocational education • MS

UNIVERSITY OF WISCONSIN–SUPERIOR
Superior, WI 54880-2873

http://www.uwsuper.edu/

Public coed comprehensive institution. *Enrollment: 2,329 graduate, professional, and undergraduate students. Graduate faculty: 87 full-time, 28 part-time. Computer facilities: Campuswide network is available with full Internet access. Total number of PCs/terminals supplied for student use: 100. Computer service fees are included with tuition and fees. Library facilities: Jim Dan Hill Library. Graduate expenses: $3628 per year full-time, $222 per credit hour part-time for state residents; $11,272 per year full-time, $647 per credit hour part-time for nonresidents. General application contact: Nancy M. Minahan, Director of Graduate Studies, 715-394-8296.*

Graduate Division
Dr. Diane J. Garsombke, Interim Dean of Faculties
Programs in:
art education • MA
art history • MA
art therapy • MA
counselor education • MSE
educational administration • Ed S, MSE
emotionally disturbed learners • MSE
instruction • MSE
learning disabilities • MSE
mass communication • MA
school psychology • MSE
speech communication • MA
studio arts • MA
teaching reading • MSE
theater • MA

UNIVERSITY OF WISCONSIN–WHITEWATER
Whitewater, WI 53190-1790

http://www.uww.edu/

Public coed comprehensive institution. Computer facilities: *Campuswide network is available with full Internet access. Total number of PCs/terminals supplied for student use: 2,000. Computer service fees are included with tuition and fees. Library facilities: Andersen Library. General application contact: Dean of Graduate Studies, 414-472-5200.*

School of Graduate Studies

College of Arts and Communications
Programs in:
communicative disorders • MS
corporate/public communication • MS
mass communication • MS
music • MME

College of Business and Economics
Programs in:
accounting • MPA
business administration • MBA
business and economics • MS
school business management • MS Ed

College of Education
Programs in:
counselor education • MS
curriculum and instruction • MS
education • MAT
professional development • MEPD
reading • MS Ed
safety • MS
special education • MS Ed

College of Letters and Sciences
Programs in:
letters and sciences • MS
professional development • MEPD
school psychology • MS Ed

VITERBO COLLEGE
La Crosse, WI 54601-4797

http://www.viterbo.edu/

Independent-religious coed comprehensive institution. *Enrollment: 1,640 graduate, professional, and undergraduate students. Graduate faculty: 1 full-time, 120 part-time. Library facilities: Wehr Library plus 5 additional on-campus libraries. General application contact: John R. Schroeder, Director of Graduate Studies, 608-796-3090.*

Graduate Program in Education
John R. Schroeder, Director of Graduate Studies
Program in:
education • MA

Graduate Program in Nursing
Bonnie Nesbitt, Director
Program in:
nursing • MSN

WYOMING

 # UNIVERSITY OF WYOMING
Laramie, WY 82071

http://www.uwyo.edu/

Public coed university. *Enrollment: 11,251 graduate, professional, and undergraduate students. Graduate faculty: 649. Computer facilities: Campuswide network is available with full Internet access. Total number of PCs/terminals supplied for student use: 372.*

Computer service fees are included with tuition and fees. Library facilities: *Coe Library plus 5 additional on-campus libraries. Graduate expenses: Tuition of $2430 per year full-time, $135 per credit hour part-time for state residents; $7518 per year full-time, $418 per credit hour part-time for nonresidents. Fees of $386 per year full-time, $9.25 per credit hour part-time. General application contact: Dr. Donald S. Warder, Dean of the Graduate School, 307-766-2287.*

Graduate School
Dr. Donald S. Warder, Dean

College of Agriculture
Steven Horn, Dean
Programs in:
- agricultural economics • MS
- agronomy • MS, PhD
- animal sciences • MS, PhD
- entomology • MS, PhD
- family and consumer economics • MS
- food science and human nutrition • MS
- molecular biology • MS, PhD
- pathobiology • MS
- plant pathology • MS
- rangeland ecology and watershed management • MS, PhD
- reproductive biology • MS, PhD

College of Arts and Sciences
Oliver Walter, Dean
Programs in:
- American studies • MA
- anthropology • MA
- art • MA, MAT, MFA
- botany • MS, PhD
- botany/water resources • MS
- chemistry • MS, MST, PhD
- communication • MA
- community and regional planning and natural resources • MP
- computer science • MS, PhD
- English • MA
- French • MA
- geography • MA, MP, MST
- geography/water resources • MA
- geology and geophysics • MS, PhD
- geology/water resources • MS
- geophysics • MS, PhD
- German • MA
- history • MA, MAT
- history and literature • MA
- international studies • MA
- mathematics • MA, MAT, MS, MST, PhD
- mathematics-computer science • PhD

- music education • MA
- natural science • MS, MST
- performance • MM
- philosophy • MA
- physics and astronomy • MS, MST, PhD
- political science • MA
- psychology • MA, MS, PhD
- public administration • MPA
- recreation and park administration • MS
- sociology • MA
- Spanish • MA
- statistics • MS, PhD
- theory and composition • MA
- zoology and physiology • MS, PhD

College of Business
Dr. Bruce Forster, Dean
Programs in:
- business administration • MBA
- economics • MS, PhD
- finance • MS

College of Education
Dr. Charles Ksir, Dean
Programs in:
- leadership and human development • Ed D, Ed S, MA, MS, PhD
- lifelong learning and instruction • Ed D, Ed S, MA, MS, PhD

College of Engineering
Dr. Kynric Pell, Dean
Programs in:
- atmospheric science • MS, PhD
- chemical engineering • MS, PhD
- civil engineering • MS, PhD
- electrical engineering • MS, PhD
- environmental engineering • MS
- mechanical engineering • MS, PhD
- petroleum engineering • MS, PhD

College of Health Sciences
Dr. Martha S. Williams, Dean
Programs in:
- audiology • MS
- nursing • MS
- physical and health education • MS
- social work • MSW
- speech-language pathology • MS

College of Law
John M. Burman, Dean
Program in:
- law • JD

Appendix

ALABAMA

BIRMINGHAM–SOUTHERN COLLEGE
Birmingham, AL 35254
http://www.bsc.edu/
General application contact: Eleanor F. Terry, Director of Graduate Studies, 205-226-4840.

FAULKNER UNIVERSITY
Montgomery, AL 36109-3398
http://www.faulkner.edu/
General application contact: Paul M. Smith, Director, 334-260-6210.

SOUTHERN CHRISTIAN UNIVERSITY
Montgomery, AL 36124-0240
http://www.southernchristian.edu/
General application contact: Mac Adkins, Director of Admissions, 800-351-4040.

UNITED STATES SPORTS ACADEMY
Daphne, AL 36526-7055
http://www.sport.ussa.edu/
General application contact: Assistant Dean of Student Services, 334-626-3303.

ARIZONA

ARIZONA SCHOOL OF PROFESSIONAL PSYCHOLOGY
Phoenix, AZ 85021
http://www.aspp.edu/loc_ariz.html
General application contact: Dr. Michael Horowitz, Dean, 602-216-2600.

ARIZONA STATE UNIVERSITY EAST
Mesa, AZ 85206-0903
http://www.east.asu.edu/
General application contact: C. Vinette Cowart, Director of Academic Services, 602-727-1028.

FRANK LLOYD WRIGHT SCHOOL OF ARCHITECTURE
Scottsdale, AZ 85261-4430
General application contact: Pamela S. Stefansson, Director of Admissions, 602-860-2700.

GRAND CANYON UNIVERSITY
Phoenix, AZ 85017-3030
General application contact: contact individual colleges, 602-249-3300.

INTERNATIONAL BAPTIST COLLEGE
Tempe, AZ 85282
General application contact: Dr. Stan Bushey, Registrar, 602-838-7070.

PRESCOTT COLLEGE
Prescott, AZ 86301-2990
General application contact: Joan Clingan, Graduate Director, 520-776-5130.

SOUTHWEST COLLEGE OF NATUROPATHIC MEDICINE AND HEALTH SCIENCES
Tempe, AZ 85282
http://www.scnm.edu/
General application contact: Melissa Frownfelter, Assistant Dean of Students, 602-858-9100.

THUNDERBIRD, THE AMERICAN GRADUATE SCHOOL OF INTERNATIONAL MANAGEMENT
Glendale, AZ 85306-3236
http://www.t-bird.edu/
General application contact: Judy Johnson, Director of Admissions, 602-978-7100.

UNIVERSITY OF PHOENIX
Phoenix, AZ 85072-2069
General application contact: Campus Information Center, 602-966-9577.

WESTERN INTERNATIONAL UNIVERSITY
Phoenix, AZ 85021-2718
General application contact: Enrollment Department, 602-943-2311.

ARKANSAS

JOHN BROWN UNIVERSITY
Siloam Springs, AR 72761-2121
General application contact: Gil Pineira, Graduate Admissions Counselor, 501-524-7169.

UNIVERSITY OF ARKANSAS AT MONTICELLO
Monticello, AR 71656
http://cotton.uamont.edu/
General application contact: Jo Beth Johnson, Office of
Admission Records, 870-460-1034.

UNIVERSITY OF ARKANSAS AT PINE BLUFF
Pine Bluff, AR 71601-2799
General application contact: Dr. Calvin Johnson, Dean of
the School of Education, 870-543-8256.

**UNIVERSITY OF ARKANSAS FOR MEDICAL
SCIENCES**
Little Rock, AR 72205-7199
General application contact: Paul Carter, Assistant to the
Vice Chancellor for Academic Affairs, 501-686-5454.

CALIFORNIA

ACADEMY OF ART COLLEGE
San Francisco, CA 94105-3410
http://www.academyart.edu/
General application contact: Jim Short, Graduate
Admissions Manager, 415-274-2285.

**ACADEMY OF CHINESE CULTURE AND HEALTH
SCIENCES**
Oakland, CA 94612
http://www.acchs.edu/
General application contact: Wei Tsuei, President/Founder,
510-763-7787.

AMERICAN BAPTIST SEMINARY OF THE WEST
Berkeley, CA 94704-3029
http://www.gtu.edu/Schools/absw.html
General application contact: Joanne Pike, Registrar,
510-841-1905 Ext. 14.

**AMERICAN COLLEGE OF TRADITIONAL
CHINESE MEDICINE**
San Francisco, CA 94107
General application contact: Lori Long, Admissions Officer,
415-282-7600 Ext. 14.

AMERICAN CONSERVATORY THEATER
San Francisco, CA 94108-5800
General application contact: Jack F. Sharrar, Registrar and
Director of MFA Program, 415-439-2350.

**AMERICAN FILM INSTITUTE CENTER FOR
ADVANCED FILM AND TELEVISION STUDIES**
Los Angeles, CA 90027-1657
http://www.afionline.org/
General application contact: Admissions Coordinator,
213-856-7628.

AMERICAN INTERCONTINENTAL UNIVERSITY
Los Angeles, CA 90024-5603
General application contact: Allan Gueco, Director of
Admissions, 800-333-2652.

**AMERICAN SCHOOL OF PROFESSIONAL
PSYCHOLOGY, ROSEBRIDGE CAMPUS**
Corte Madera, CA 94925

**ANTIOCH SOUTHERN CALIFORNIA/LOS
ANGELES**
Marina del Rey, CA 90292-7090
http://www.antiochla.edu/
General application contact: MeHee Hyun, Director of
Admissions, 310-578-1090.

**ANTIOCH SOUTHERN CALIFORNIA/SANTA
BARBARA**
Santa Barbara, CA 93101-1580
General application contact: Carol Flores, Admissions
Officer, 805-962-8179.

ARMSTRONG UNIVERSITY
Oakland, CA 94612
http://www.armstrong-u.edu/
General application contact: Judy Battle, Director of
Admissions, 510-835-7900.

ART CENTER COLLEGE OF DESIGN
Pasadena, CA 91103-1999
http://www.artcenter.edu/main/mm.html
General application contact: Dr. Richard Hertz, Chair of
Graduate Studies, 818-396-2335.

**BETHANY COLLEGE OF THE ASSEMBLIES OF
GOD**
Scotts Valley, CA 95066-2820
General application contact: Faith Alpher, Admissions
Coordinator for Teacher Education, 408-438-3800 Ext.
1503.

BROOKS INSTITUTE OF PHOTOGRAPHY
Santa Barbara, CA 93108-2399
General application contact: Inge B. Kautzmann, Director
of Admissions, 805-966-3888 Ext. 217.

CALIFORNIA BAPTIST COLLEGE
Riverside, CA 92504-3206
http://www.calbaptist.edu/
General application contact: Gail Ronveaux, Director of
Graduate Services, 909-343-4249.

CALIFORNIA COLLEGE FOR HEALTH SCIENCES
National City, CA 91950-6605
http://www.cchs.edu/
General application contact: Lisa J. Davis, Dean of Student
Affairs, 800-221-7374.

CALIFORNIA COLLEGE OF ARTS AND CRAFTS
San Francisco, CA 94107

General application contact: Sheri McKenzie, Director, Enrollment Services, 415-703-9535.

CALIFORNIA COLLEGE OF PODIATRIC MEDICINE
San Francisco, CA 94115

General application contact: Frank L. Jimenez, Director of Admissions, 800-334-2276.

CALIFORNIA INSTITUTE OF INTEGRAL STUDIES
San Francisco, CA 94109

http://www.ciis.edu/

General application contact: Dr. Cathy Coleman, Director of Admissions, 415-674-5500 Ext. 215.

CALIFORNIA INSTITUTE OF THE ARTS
Valencia, CA 91355-2340

http://www.calarts.edu/

General application contact: Kenneth Young, Director of Admissions, 805-253-7863.

CALIFORNIA SCHOOL OF PROFESSIONAL PSYCHOLOGY
Alameda, CA 94501-1148

http://www.cspp.edu/

General application contact: Patricia J. Mullen, Vice President, Marketing and Enrollment, 800-457-1273.

CALIFORNIA SCHOOL OF PROFESSIONAL PSYCHOLOGY–FRESNO
Fresno, CA 93727

http://www.cspp.edu/

General application contact: Patricia J. Mullen, Vice President, Marketing and Enrollment, 800-457-1273.

CALIFORNIA SCHOOL OF PROFESSIONAL PSYCHOLOGY–LOS ANGELES
Alhambra, CA 91803-1360

http://www.cspp.edu/

General application contact: Patricia J. Mullen, Vice President, Marketing and Enrollment, 800-457-1273.

CALIFORNIA SCHOOL OF PROFESSIONAL PSYCHOLOGY–SAN DIEGO
San Diego, CA 92121-3725

http://www.cspp.edu/

General application contact: Patricia J. Mullen, Vice President, Marketing and Enrollment, 800-457-1273.

CALIFORNIA WESTERN SCHOOL OF LAW
San Diego, CA 92101-3046

http://www.cwsl.edu/

General application contact: Nancy C. Ramsayer, Assistant Dean for Admissions, 619-525-1401.

CHARLES R. DREW UNIVERSITY OF MEDICINE AND SCIENCE
Los Angeles, CA 90059

General application contact: American Medical College Admission Service, 202-828-0635.

CHURCH DIVINITY SCHOOL OF THE PACIFIC
Berkeley, CA 94709-1217

General application contact: Margo Webster, Registrar and Director of Admissions, 510-204-0715.

CLAREMONT SCHOOL OF THEOLOGY
Claremont, CA 91711-3199

General application contact: Mark Hobbs, Director of Admissions, 800-626-7821.

CLEVELAND CHIROPRACTIC COLLEGE OF LOS ANGELES
Los Angeles, CA 90004-2196

General application contact: Paul Forgetta, Director of Admissions, 800-466-CCLA.

COLEMAN COLLEGE
La Mesa, CA 91942-1532

General application contact: William Fall, Registrar, 619-465-3990.

CONCORDIA UNIVERSITY
Irvine, CA 92612-3299

http://www.cui.edu/

General application contact: Dr. Thomas Doyle, Dean of the School of Graduate Studies, 949-854-8002.

DOMINICAN SCHOOL OF PHILOSOPHY AND THEOLOGY
Berkeley, CA 94709-1295

General application contact: Dr. Eugene Ludwig, Academic Dean, 510-883-2084.

DONGGUK–ROYAL UNIVERSITY
Los Angeles, CA 90017

General application contact: Xianze Zhao, Dean of Admission, 213-482-6646.

EMPEROR'S COLLEGE OF TRADITIONAL ORIENTAL MEDICINE
Santa Monica, CA 90403

General application contact: Catherine Allen, Director of Development, 310-453-8300.

FIELDING INSTITUTE
Santa Barbara, CA 93105-3538

General application contact: Sylvia Williams, Director, Enrollment Management Services Center, 805-687-1099 Ext. 4006.

FIVE BRANCHES INSTITUTE: COLLEGE OF TRADITIONAL CHINESE MEDICINE
Santa Cruz, CA 95062
http://www.fivebranches.com/
General application contact: Meredith Bigley, Admissions Director, 408-476-9424.

FRANCISCAN SCHOOL OF THEOLOGY
Berkeley, CA 94709-1294
General application contact: Dale Gilson, SFO, Coordinator of Student Services, 510-848-5232.

FULLER THEOLOGICAL SEMINARY
Pasadena, CA 91182
http://www.fuller.edu/
General application contact: Office of Admission, 800-238-5537.

GOLDEN GATE BAPTIST THEOLOGICAL SEMINARY
Mill Valley, CA 94941-3197
http://www.ggbts.edu/
General application contact: Director of Admissions, 415-380-1600.

GRADUATE THEOLOGICAL UNION
Berkeley, CA 94709-1212
http://www.gtu.edu/
General application contact: A. K. Anderson, Director of Admissions, 800-826-4488.

HARVEY MUDD COLLEGE
Claremont, CA 91711-5994
http://www.hmc.edu/
General application contact: J. R. Phillips, Chairman, Program in Engineering, 909-621-8019.

HEBREW UNION COLLEGE–JEWISH INSTITUTE OF RELIGION
Los Angeles, CA 90007-3796
General application contact: Rabbi Sheldon Marder, Associate Dean, 213-749-3424.

HUMPHREYS COLLEGE
Stockton, CA 95207-3896
General application contact: Lance Hall, Law Registrar, 209-478-0800.

HURON INTERNATIONAL UNIVERSITY
San Diego, CA 92108-3801
General application contact: Susan Edyburne, Admissions Coordinator, 619-298-9040.

ICR GRADUATE SCHOOL
Santee, CA 92071
http://www.icr.org/
General application contact: Dr. Jack Kriege, Registrar, 619-448-0900.

INSTITUTE OF TRANSPERSONAL PSYCHOLOGY
Palo Alto, CA 94303
http://www.itp.edu/
General application contact: Brian Lieske, Registrar, 650-493-4430 Ext. 14.

INTERNATIONAL SCHOOL OF THEOLOGY
San Bernardino, CA 92414-0001
http://www.leaderu.com/isot/
General application contact: Randy Harrell, Director of Admissions, 909-886-7876 Ext. 138.

JESUIT SCHOOL OF THEOLOGY AT BERKELEY
Berkeley, CA 94709-1193
General application contact: Alice Ducey, Director of Admissions, 510-841-8804.

KYUNG SAN UNIVERSITY USA
Garden Grove, CA 92644
General application contact: E. S. Lee, Acting Registrar, 714-636-0337.

LIFE CHIROPRACTIC COLLEGE WEST
San Lorenzo, CA 94580-1315
http://www.lifewest.edu/
General application contact: Jeffrey D. Cook, Director of Admissions, 800-788-4476.

LINCOLN UNIVERSITY
San Francisco, CA 94118-4498
http://www.lincolnuca.edu/
General application contact: Dr. Pete Bogue, Director of Admissions/Registrar, 415-221-1212.

LOS ANGELES COLLEGE OF CHIROPRACTIC
Whittier, CA 90604-4051
General application contact: Dr. Charlene Frontiera, Director of Admissions, 562-947-8755 Ext. 321.

THE MASTER'S COLLEGE AND SEMINARY
Santa Clarita, CA 91321-1200
http://www.mastersem.edu/
General application contact: Jim George, Director of Admissions and Placement, 805-909-5710.

MEIJI COLLEGE OF ORIENTAL MEDICINE
San Francisco, CA 94115
General application contact: Teresa Voelker, Admissions Officer, 415-771-1019.

MENNONITE BRETHREN BIBLICAL SEMINARY
Fresno, CA 93727-5097
General application contact: Janet Enns, Director of Admissions, 209-452-1710.

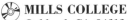 **MILLS COLLEGE**
Oakland, CA 94613-1000
http://www.mills.edu/
General application contact: La Vonna S. Brown, Coordinator of Graduate Studies, 510-430-3309.

MONTEREY INSTITUTE OF INTERNATIONAL STUDIES
Monterey, CA 93940-2691

http://www.miis.edu/

General application contact: Admissions Office, 408-647-4123.

NAVAL POSTGRADUATE SCHOOL
Monterey, CA 93943

http://www.nps.navy.mil/

General application contact: Theodore H. Calhoon, Director of Admissions, 831-656-3093.

NEW COLLEGE OF CALIFORNIA
San Francisco, CA 94102-5206

General application contact: Michael Price, Director of Admissions, 415-437-3400.

NEWSCHOOL OF ARCHITECTURE
San Diego, CA 92101-6634

General application contact: Mitra Kanaani, Adviser, 619-235-4100 Ext. 109.

OCCIDENTAL COLLEGE
Los Angeles, CA 90041-3392

General application contact: Susan Molik, Administrative Assistant, Graduate Office, 213-259-2921.

OTIS COLLEGE OF ART AND DESIGN
Los Angeles, CA 90045-9785

General application contact: Roy Dowell, Chair, College of Fine Arts, 310-665-6891.

PACIFICA GRADUATE INSTITUTE
Carpinteria, CA 93013

General application contact: Diane Huerta, Admissions Office, 805-969-3626 Ext. 128.

PACIFIC COLLEGE OF ORIENTAL MEDICINE
San Diego, CA 92108

General application contact: Jack Miller, President, 619-574-6909.

PACIFIC GRADUATE SCHOOL OF PSYCHOLOGY
Palo Alto, CA 94303-4232

General application contact: Elizabeth M. Hilt, Vice President of Student Services, 650-843-3419.

PACIFIC LUTHERAN THEOLOGICAL SEMINARY
Berkeley, CA 94708-1597

General application contact: Ardelle Hester, Registrar, 510-524-5264.

PACIFIC OAKS COLLEGE
Pasadena, CA 91103

General application contact: Marsha Franker, Director of Admissions, 626-397-1349.

PACIFIC SCHOOL OF RELIGION
Berkeley, CA 94709-1323

General application contact: Dr. Ronald E. Parker, Dean of Admissions, Research, and Planning, 510-849-8231.

PACIFIC STATES UNIVERSITY
Los Angeles, CA 90006

http://www.psuca.edu/

General application contact: Barren Kim, Office Manager, 888-200-2383.

PACIFIC UNION COLLEGE
Angwin, CA 94508

http://www.puc.edu/

General application contact: Dr. Jean Buller, Chair of the Department of Education, 707-965-7265.

PALMER COLLEGE OF CHIROPRACTIC WEST
San Jose, CA 95134-1617

General application contact: Karin Butters, Director of Enrollment Services and Development, 408-944-6024.

PHILLIPS GRADUATE INSTITUTE
Encino, CA 91316-1509

General application contact: Michelle Browning, Registrar and Admissions Officer, 818-386-5638.

RAND GRADUATE SCHOOL OF POLICY STUDIES
Santa Monica, CA 90407-2138

http://www.rand.org/

General application contact: Marcy Agmon, Assistant to the Dean, 310-393-0411.

ST. JOHN'S SEMINARY
Camarillo, CA 93012-2598

General application contact: Rosa Garza Coleman, Registrar, 805-482-2755.

ST. PATRICK'S SEMINARY
Menlo Park, CA 94025-3596

General application contact: Rev. Gerald D. Coleman, SS, President and Rector, 650-325-5621.

SAMRA UNIVERSITY OF ORIENTAL MEDICINE
Los Angeles, CA 90034-2014

General application contact: Dr. Aaron Sui, Admissions Director, 310-202-6444 Ext. 102.

SAMUEL MERRITT COLLEGE
Oakland, CA 94609-3108

http://www.samuelmerritt.edu/

General application contact: John Garten-Schuman, Director of Admissions, 510-869-6576.

SAN FRANCISCO ART INSTITUTE
San Francisco, CA 94133

General application contact: Mark Takiguchi, Director of Admissions, 800-345-7324.

SAN FRANCISCO CONSERVATORY OF MUSIC
San Francisco, CA 94122-4411
http://www.sfcm.edu/
General application contact: Joan Gordon, Admission Officer, 415-759-3431.

SAN FRANCISCO THEOLOGICAL SEMINARY
San Anselmo, CA 94960-2997
General application contact: Gloria Pulido, Dean of Admissions, 415-258-6531.

SAN JOAQUIN COLLEGE OF LAW
Clovis, CA 93612-1312
General application contact: Joyce Morodomi, Registrar/Admissions Officer, 209-323-2100.

SANTA BARBARA COLLEGE OF ORIENTAL MEDICINE
Santa Barbara, CA 93101
General application contact: Allegra Heidelinde, Registrar, 805-898-1180.

SAYBROOK GRADUATE SCHOOL
San Francisco, CA 94133-4640
http://www.saybrook.org/
General application contact: Mindy Myers, Vice President for Recruitment and Admissions, 415-433-9200.

THE SCRIPPS RESEARCH INSTITUTE
La Jolla, CA 92037
http://www.scripps.edu/
General application contact: Marylyn Rinaldi, Graduate Program Administrator, 619-784-8469.

SIMPSON COLLEGE AND GRADUATE SCHOOL
Redding, CA 96003-8606
http://www.simpson.edu/
General application contact: Murry Evans, Vice President for Enrollment Management and Marketing, 530-224-5606.

SOUTH BAYLO UNIVERSITY
Anaheim, CA 92801-1701
http://www.southbaylo.edu/
General application contact: Ron Sokolsky, Director, 714-533-1495.

SOUTHERN CALIFORNIA COLLEGE
Costa Mesa, CA 92626-6597
General application contact: Phyllis Jerssen, Coordinator of Graduate Studies, 714-556-3610 Ext. 248.

SOUTHERN CALIFORNIA COLLEGE OF OPTOMETRY
Fullerton, CA 92831-1615
General application contact: Dr. Lorraine I. Voorhees, Dean of Student Affairs, 714-449-7445.

SOUTHERN CALIFORNIA INSTITUTE OF ARCHITECTURE
Los Angeles, CA 90066-7017
General application contact: Debra Abel, Admissions Coordinator, 310-574-3625.

SOUTHWESTERN UNIVERSITY SCHOOL OF LAW
Los Angeles, CA 90005-3905
http://www.swlaw.edu/
General application contact: Anne Wilson, Director of Admissions, 213-738-6717.

STARR KING SCHOOL FOR THE MINISTRY
Berkeley, CA 94709-1209
General application contact: Patti Lawrence, Registrar, 510-845-6232.

THOMAS JEFFERSON SCHOOL OF LAW
San Diego, CA 92110-2905
General application contact: Jennifer Keller, Assistant Dean of Admissions, Records, and Financial Assistance, 619-297-9700 Ext. 1472.

UNIVERSITY OF CALIFORNIA, HASTINGS COLLEGE OF THE LAW
San Francisco, CA 94102-4978
http://www.uchastings.edu/
General application contact: Cornelius H. Darcy, Director of Admissions, 415-565-4885.

UNIVERSITY OF JUDAISM
Bel Air, CA 90077-1599
http://www.uj.edu/
General application contact: Tamara Greenbaum, Dean of Admissions, 310-476-9777.

UNIVERSITY OF WEST LOS ANGELES
Inglewood, CA 90301-2902
General application contact: Candy Suenaga, Director of Admissions, 310-342-5200 Ext. 209.

WESTERN STATE UNIVERSITY COLLEGE OF LAW
Fullerton, CA 92831-3014
http://www.wsulaw.edu/
General application contact: Joel H. Goodman, Dean of Admissions, 714-738-1000 Ext. 2911.

WESTERN UNIVERSITY OF HEALTH SCIENCES
Pomona, CA 91766-1854
General application contact: Susan M. Hanson, Director of Admissions, 909-469-5335.

WESTMINSTER THEOLOGICAL SEMINARY IN CALIFORNIA
Escondido, CA 92027-4128
General application contact: John Sowell, Director of Admissions, 760-480-8474.

WHITTIER COLLEGE
Whittier, CA 90608-0634

General application contact: David J. Muller, Associate Academic Dean, 562-907-4200.

WRIGHT INSTITUTE
Berkeley, CA 94704-1796

General application contact: Virginia J. Morgan, Registrar, 510-841-9230.

YO SAN UNIVERSITY OF TRADITIONAL CHINESE MEDICINE
Santa Monica, CA 90401

General application contact: Doris Johnson, Admissions Counselor, 310-917-2202 Ext. 13.

COLORADO

COLLEGE FOR FINANCIAL PLANNING
Denver, CO 80237-3403

General application contact: Keith R. Fevurly, Vice President of Education, 303-220-4823.

THE COLORADO COLLEGE
Colorado Springs, CO 80903-3294

General application contact: Charlotte Mendoza, Chair, Department of Education, 719-389-6474.

COLORADO TECHNICAL UNIVERSITY
Colorado Springs, CO 80907-3896

General application contact: Judy Galante, Graduate Admissions, 719-590-6720.

COLORADO TECHNICAL UNIVERSITY DENVER CAMPUS
Greenwood Village, CO 80111

DENVER CONSERVATIVE BAPTIST SEMINARY
Denver, CO 80250-0100

General application contact: Dr. Gary C. Huckabay, Director of Admissions, 303-761-2482 Ext. 234.

DENVER PARALEGAL INSTITUTE
Denver, CO 80202

http://www.paralegal-education.com/

General application contact: Maryanne White, Coordinator, 303-295-0550.

DENVER TECHNICAL COLLEGE
Denver, CO 80224-1658

General application contact: David Phillips, Director of Admissions, 303-329-3000 Ext. 216.

ILIFF SCHOOL OF THEOLOGY
Denver, CO 80210-4798

General application contact: Susan A. Mitchell, Director of Admissions, 303-765-3118.

INTERNATIONAL UNIVERSITY
Englewood, CO 80155-6512

http://www.international.edu/

General application contact: Enrollment and Student Services Manager, 800-777-6463 Ext. 3153.

ISIM UNIVERSITY
Denver, CO 80246

http://www.isimu.edu/

General application contact: Kristine Larson, Registrar, 303-333-4224.

MESA STATE COLLEGE
Grand Junction, CO 81502-2647

http://mesastate.edu/

General application contact: Dr. Tim Hatten, MBA Coordinator, 970-248-1731.

THE NAROPA INSTITUTE
Boulder, CO 80302-6697

http://www.naropa.edu/

General application contact: Susan Kropf, Director of Admissions, 303-546-3572.

NATIONAL TECHNOLOGICAL UNIVERSITY
Fort Collins, CO 80526-1842

http://www.ntu.edu/

General application contact: Dr. Gearold Johnson, Academic Vice President, 970-495-6400.

NATIONAL THEATRE CONSERVATORY
Denver, CO 80204-2157

General application contact: Mark Bridges, Registrar/ Administrator, 303-446-4855.

UNIVERSITY OF COLORADO HEALTH SCIENCES CENTER
Denver, CO 80262

http://www.uchsc.edu/

General application contact: Dr. David Sorenson, Director, Student and Administrative Services and Admissions, 303-315-7676.

UNIVERSITY OF SOUTHERN COLORADO
Pueblo, CO 81001-4901

General application contact: Christie Kangas, Director, 719-549-2461.

YESHIVA TORAS CHAIM TALMUDICAL SEMINARY
Denver, CO 80204-1415

CONNECTICUT

ALBERTUS MAGNUS COLLEGE
New Haven, CT 06511-1189

http://www.albertus.edu/

General application contact: Dr. Charles Marie Brantl, Vice President for Academic Affairs, 203-773-8539.

BETH BENJAMIN ACADEMY OF CONNECTICUT
Stamford, CT 06901-1202
General application contact: Director of Graduate Studies, 203-325-4351.

CONNECTICUT COLLEGE
New London, CT 06320-4196
General application contact: Director of Continuing Education, 860-439-2060.

HARTFORD SEMINARY
Hartford, CT 06105-2279
General application contact: Dr. Kelton Cobb, Director of Degree Programs, 860-509-9513.

HOLY APOSTLES COLLEGE AND SEMINARY
Cromwell, CT 06416-2005
General application contact: Office of Admissions, 860-632-3010.

RENSSELAER AT HARTFORD
Hartford, CT 06120-2991
http://www.hgc.edu/
General application contact: Rebecca Danchak, Admissions Office, 860-548-2420.

TRINITY COLLEGE
Hartford, CT 06106-3100
http://www.trincoll.edu/
General application contact: Dr. Nancy Birch Wagner, Director of Graduate Studies, 860-297-2527.

UNIVERSITY OF CONNECTICUT HEALTH CENTER
Farmington, CT 06030
http://www.uchc.edu/
General application contact: Graduate Course Manager, 860-679-3150.

WESLEYAN UNIVERSITY
Middletown, CT 06459-0260
General application contact: Allison M. Insall, Director of Graduate Office, 860-685-2390.

DELAWARE

GOLDEY–BEACOM COLLEGE
Wilmington, DE 19808-1999
http://goldey.gbc.edu/
General application contact: Bruce D. Marsland, Director of Graduate Programs, 302-998-8814 Ext. 276.

WESLEY COLLEGE
Dover, DE 19901
http://www.wesley.edu/

DISTRICT OF COLUMBIA

DOMINICAN HOUSE OF STUDIES
Washington, DC 20017-1585
General application contact: Fr. Steven C. Boguslawski, OP, Academic Dean, 202-529-5300.

JOINT MILITARY INTELLIGENCE COLLEGE
Washington, DC 20340-5100
General application contact: Director of Admissions, 202-231-3299.

NATIONAL DEFENSE UNIVERSITY
Washington, DC 20319-6000
http://www.ndu.edu/

SOUTHEASTERN UNIVERSITY
Washington, DC 20024-2788
General application contact: Jack Flinter, Director of Admissions, 202-265-5343.

STRAYER UNIVERSITY
Washington, DC 20005-2603
http://www.strayer.edu/
General application contact: Michael Williams, Campus Coordinator, 202-408-2400.

WASHINGTON THEOLOGICAL UNION
Washington, DC 20012
http://www.wtu.edu/
General application contact: Joseph C. Dicine, Admissions Administrator, 202-541-5210.

WESLEY THEOLOGICAL SEMINARY
Washington, DC 20016-5690
General application contact: Rev. Michael W. Armstrong, Director of Admissions, 202-885-8653.

FLORIDA

CARIBBEAN CENTER FOR ADVANCED STUDIES/ MIAMI INSTITUTE OF PSYCHOLOGY
Miami, FL 33166-6653
General application contact: Dr. Kevin Keating, Special Assistant to the Chancellor, 305-593-1223 Ext. 102.

FLORIDA GULF COAST UNIVERSITY
Fort Myers, FL 33965-6565

http://www.fgcu.edu/

General application contact: Michelle Yovanovich, Director of Admissions, 888-889-1015.

FLORIDA METROPOLITAN UNIVERSITY–FORT LAUDERDALE COLLEGE
Fort Lauderdale, FL 33304-2522

General application contact: Tony Wallace, Director of Admissions, 954-568-1600.

FLORIDA METROPOLITAN UNIVERSITY–ORLANDO COLLEGE, NORTH
Orlando, FL 32810-5674

General application contact: Annette Gallina, Director of Admissions, 407-851-2525 Ext. 30.

FLORIDA METROPOLITAN UNIVERSITY–TAMPA COLLEGE
Tampa, FL 33614-5899

General application contact: Foster Thomas, Director of Admissions, 813-879-6000 Ext. 36.

FLORIDA SCHOOL OF PROFESSIONAL PSYCHOLOGY
Tampa, FL 33619

General application contact: Susan Beecroft, Campus Administration Coordinator, 813-246-4419.

FLORIDA SOUTHERN COLLEGE
Lakeland, FL 33801-5698

http://www.flsouthern.edu/

General application contact: Bill Walker, Coordinator of External Programs, 941-680-4205.

GOODING INSTITUTE OF NURSE ANESTHESIA
Panama City, FL 32401

General application contact: David Ely, Director, 850-747-6918.

THE HARID CONSERVATORY
Boca Raton, FL 33431-5518

General application contact: Music Division, 561-997-2677.

 LYNN UNIVERSITY
Boca Raton, FL 33431-5598

http://www.lynn.edu/

General application contact: Pat Sieredzki, Graduate Admissions Coordinator, 800-544-8035.

PALM BEACH ATLANTIC COLLEGE
West Palm Beach, FL 33416-4708

General application contact: Carolanne M. Brown, Director of Graduate Admissions, 800-281-3466.

REFORMED THEOLOGICAL SEMINARY
Maitland, FL 32751-7130

General application contact: David Gordon, Director of Admissions, 800-752-4382.

REGIONAL SEMINARY OF SAINT VINCENT DE PAUL IN FLORIDA, INC.
Boynton Beach, FL 33436-4899

General application contact: Rev. Pablo Navarro, Rector, 561-732-4424.

SAINT LEO COLLEGE
Saint Leo, FL 33574-2008

http://www.saintleo.edu/

General application contact: Gary Bracken, Dean of Admissions and Financial Aid, 352-588-8283.

SCHILLER INTERNATIONAL UNIVERSITY
Dunedin, FL 34698-7532

http://www.schiller.edu/

General application contact: Muriel Jault, Admissions Representative, 813-736-5082.

TALMUDIC COLLEGE OF FLORIDA
Miami Beach, FL 33139

General application contact: Administrator, 305-534-7050.

TRINITY INTERNATIONAL UNIVERSITY, SOUTH FLORIDA CAMPUS
Miami, FL 33101-9674

http://www.tiu.edu/

General application contact: Yvette Grant, Director of Graduate Admissions, 305-577-4600 Ext. 135.

UNIVERSITY OF ST. AUGUSTINE FOR HEALTH SCIENCES
St. Augustine, FL 32084

http://www.usa.edu/

General application contact: Julie T. Cook, Registrar, 904-810-0330.

UNIVERSITY OF SARASOTA
Sarasota, FL 34235-8246

http://www.sarasota.edu/

General application contact: Kathy Ketterer, Admissions Representative, 800-331-5995.

WEBBER COLLEGE
Babson Park, FL 33827-0096

http://www.webber.edu/academ.html

General application contact: Jeanne Sobierajski, MBA Marketing Director, 941-638-2927.

GEORGIA

AGNES SCOTT COLLEGE
Decatur, GA 30030-3797

http://www.agnesscott.edu/

General application contact: Ruth Bettandorff, Associate Dean of the College, 404-471-6228.

AMERICAN INTERCONTINENTAL UNIVERSITY
Atlanta, GA 30326-1019
http://www.aiuniv.edu/

General application contact: Jeff Bostic, Director of Admissions, 404-812-7400.

BERRY COLLEGE
Mount Berry, GA 30149-0159
http://www.berry.edu/

General application contact: Dr. Ouida W. Dickey, Dean of Academic Services, 706-232-5374 Ext. 2229.

COLUMBIA THEOLOGICAL SEMINARY
Decatur, GA 30031-0520

General application contact: Ann Clay Adams, Director of Admissions, 404-378-8821.

COVENANT COLLEGE
Lookout Mountain, GA 30750

General application contact: Rebecca Dodson, Assistant Director, Program in Education, 706-820-1560 Ext. 1406.

GEORGIA SCHOOL OF PROFESSIONAL PSYCHOLOGY
Atlanta, GA 30328-5505

General application contact: Dan Rosenfield, Director of Enrollment Services, 770-671-1200.

INSTITUTE OF PAPER SCIENCE AND TECHNOLOGY
Atlanta, GA 30318-5794
http://www.ipst.edu/

General application contact: Dana Carter, Student Development Counselor, 404-894-5745.

INTERDENOMINATIONAL THEOLOGICAL CENTER
Atlanta, GA 30314-4112

General application contact: Kirk Hatcher, Associate Director of Admissions, 404-527-7709.

LAGRANGE COLLEGE
LaGrange, GA 30240-2999
http://www.lgc.peachnet.edu/

General application contact: Andy Geeter, Director of Admissions, 706-812-7260.

LIFE UNIVERSITY
Marietta, GA 30060-2903
http://www.life.edu/

General application contact: Dr. Ronald Roland, Director of Admission, 800-543-3202.

LUTHER RICE BIBLE COLLEGE AND SEMINARY
Lithonia, GA 30038-2418

General application contact: Dr. Dennis Dieringer, Director of Admissions and Records, 770-484-1204.

MEDICAL COLLEGE OF GEORGIA
Augusta, GA 30912-1003

General application contact: Elizabeth Griffin, Director of Academic Admissions, 706-721-2725.

MOREHOUSE SCHOOL OF MEDICINE
Atlanta, GA 30310-1495
http://www.msm.edu/

General application contact: Karen Lewis, Assistant Director of Admissions, 404-752-1650.

OGLETHORPE UNIVERSITY
Atlanta, GA 30319-2797

General application contact: Bill Price, Graduate Admissions Counselor, 404-364-8307.

PIEDMONT COLLEGE
Demorest, GA 30535-0010
http://www.piedmont.edu/

General application contact: James L. Clement, Associate Dean for Admissions and Financial Aid, 800-277-7020.

SAVANNAH COLLEGE OF ART AND DESIGN
Savannah, GA 31402-3146
http://www.scad.edu/

General application contact: Marie Vea, Dean of International and Graduate Admissions, 912-238-2483.

SAVANNAH STATE UNIVERSITY
Savannah, GA 31404

General application contact: Dr. Roy A. Jackson, Director of Admissions, 912-356-2181.

SOUTHERN POLYTECHNIC STATE UNIVERSITY
Marietta, GA 30060-2896
http://www.spsu.edu/

General application contact: Virginia Head, Director of Admissions, 770-528-7281.

TOCCOA FALLS COLLEGE
Toccoa Falls, GA 30598-1000
http://www.toccoafalls.edu/

General application contact: Allen M. Bañez, Coordinator, 706-886-6831 Ext. 5423.

WESLEYAN COLLEGE
Macon, GA 31210-4462
http://www.wesleyan-college.edu/

General application contact: Patricia R. Hardeman, Assistant Dean and Registrar, 912-477-1110.

HAWAII

AMERICAN SCHOOL OF PROFESSIONAL PSYCHOLOGY, HAWAII CAMPUS
Honolulu, HI 96816

General application contact: Valerie C. Wong, Coordinator of Admissions and Financial Aid, 808-735-0109.

INTERNATIONAL COLLEGE AND GRADUATE SCHOOL
Honolulu, HI 96817

General application contact: Dean, 808-595-4247 Ext. 103.

TAI HSUAN FOUNDATION: COLLEGE OF ACUPUNCTURE AND HERBAL MEDICINE
Honolulu, HI 96826

General application contact: Lili Chen, Vice President of Admissions, 808-947-4788.

IDAHO

NORTHWEST NAZARENE COLLEGE
Nampa, ID 83686-5897

General application contact: Dr. Larry McMillin, Director, Graduate and Continuing Studies, 208-467-8345.

ILLINOIS

ADLER SCHOOL OF PROFESSIONAL PSYCHOLOGY
Chicago, IL 60601-7203

http://www.adler.edu/

General application contact: Suzann Lebda, Director of Admissions and Financial Aid, 312-201-5900.

AMERICAN CONSERVATORY OF MUSIC
Chicago, IL 60603-2901

General application contact: Dr. Marvin Ziporyn, Dean, 312-263-4161.

BARAT COLLEGE
Lake Forest, IL 60045-3297

http://www.barat.edu/

General application contact: Mary Kay Farrell, Associate Director of Admissions, 847-615-5678.

CATHOLIC THEOLOGICAL UNION AT CHICAGO
Chicago, IL 60615-5698

General application contact: Milton Kobus, Director of Admissions, 773-753-5316.

CHICAGO SCHOOL OF PROFESSIONAL PSYCHOLOGY
Chicago, IL 60605-2024

http://www.csopp.edu/cspp.html

General application contact: Anna Endicott, Director of Admissions, 312-786-9443.

CHICAGO THEOLOGICAL SEMINARY
Chicago, IL 60637-1507

http://www.chgosem.edu/

General application contact: Veronica O'Neill Morrison, Director of Admissions, Recruitment and Financial Planning, 773-752-5757 Ext. 221.

DR. WILLIAM M. SCHOLL COLLEGE OF PODIATRIC MEDICINE
Chicago, IL 60610-2856

http://scholl.edu/

General application contact: Cassandra Flambouras, Director, Student Recruitment, 312-280-2995.

FINCH UNIVERSITY OF HEALTH SCIENCES/THE CHICAGO MEDICAL SCHOOL
North Chicago, IL 60064-3095

General application contact: Dana Frederick, Admissions Officer, 847-578-3209.

GARRETT–EVANGELICAL THEOLOGICAL SEMINARY
Evanston, IL 60201-2926

http://www.garrett.nwu.edu/

General application contact: Kelly Dahlman-Oeth, Director of Admissions, 847-866-3926.

ILLINOIS COLLEGE OF OPTOMETRY
Chicago, IL 60616-3816

General application contact: Dr. Mark Colip, Dean for Student Affairs, 312-949-7400.

ILLINOIS SCHOOL OF PROFESSIONAL PSYCHOLOGY, CHICAGO CAMPUS
Chicago, IL 60603

General application contact: Director of Admissions, 312-201-0200 Ext. 531.

ILLINOIS SCHOOL OF PROFESSIONAL PSYCHOLOGY, MEADOWS CAMPUS
Rolling Meadows, IL 60008

General application contact: Todd M. Ricard, Coordinator of Admissions and Financial Aid, 847-290-7400.

INSTITUTE FOR CLINICAL SOCIAL WORK
Chicago, IL 60601

General application contact: Dr. Barbara Berger, Dean of Admissions, 312-726-8480 Ext. 31.

JEWISH UNIVERSITY OF AMERICA
Skokie, IL 60077-3248

General application contact: Dr. Steven Greenspan, Associate Dean of the Graduate School, 773-539-8312.

JOHN MARSHALL LAW SCHOOL
Chicago, IL 60604-3968

General application contact: William B. Powers, Dean of Admission and Student Affairs, 312-987-1403.

KELLER GRADUATE SCHOOL OF MANAGEMENT
Oak Brook Terrace, IL 60181

General application contact: Michael J. Alexander, Director, Central Services, 630-574-1957.

KNOWLEDGE SYSTEMS INSTITUTE
Skokie, IL 60076
http://www.ksi.edu/

General application contact: Judy Pan, Executive Director, 847-679-3135.

LAKE FOREST COLLEGE
Lake Forest, IL 60045-2399
http://www.lfc.edu/

General application contact: Carol Gayle, Associate Director, 847-735-5083.

LAKE FOREST GRADUATE SCHOOL OF MANAGEMENT
Lake Forest, IL 60045-2497
http://www.lfgsm.edu/

General application contact: Carolyn Brune, Admissions Director, 847-234-5080.

LINCOLN CHRISTIAN SEMINARY
Lincoln, IL 62656-2167
http://www.lccs.edu/

General application contact: Lyle Swanson, Director of Admissions, 217-732-3168 Ext. 2275.

LUTHERAN SCHOOL OF THEOLOGY AT CHICAGO
Chicago, IL 60615-5199
http://www.lstc.edu/

General application contact: Marilyn Olson, Director of Admissions, 773-256-0726.

MCCORMICK THEOLOGICAL SEMINARY
Chicago, IL 60637-1693
http://www.mccormick.edu/

General application contact: Genet Soule, Admissions Officer, 773-947-6314.

MEADVILLE/LOMBARD THEOLOGICAL SCHOOL
Chicago, IL 60637-1602

General application contact: Kerry Smith, Admissions Officer, 773-256-3000 Ext. 237.

MENNONITE COLLEGE OF NURSING
Bloomington, IL 61701-3078
http://www.mcon.edu/

General application contact: Mary Ann Watkins, Director of Admissions and Financial Aid, 309-829-0718.

MIDWESTERN UNIVERSITY
Downers Grove, IL 60515-1235
http://www.midwestern.edu/

General application contact: Julie Rosenthall, Director of Admissions, 800-458-6253.

MOODY BIBLE INSTITUTE
Chicago, IL 60610-3284

General application contact: Annette Moy, Associate Dean of Enrollment Management/Admissions, 312-329-4267.

THE NATIONAL COLLEGE OF CHIROPRACTIC
Lombard, IL 60148-4583

General application contact: Julie Talarico, Director of Admissions, 800-826-6285.

NORTHERN BAPTIST THEOLOGICAL SEMINARY
Lombard, IL 60148-5698
http://northern.seminary.edu/

General application contact: Karen Walker-Freeburg, Director of Admissions, 630-620-2128.

NORTH PARK THEOLOGICAL SEMINARY
Chicago, IL 60625-4895
http://www.northpark.edu/sem/

General application contact: Stephen Graham, Dean of Faculty, 773-244-6222.

NORTH PARK UNIVERSITY
Chicago, IL 60625-4895

General application contact: John Baworowsky, Dean of Admissions and Financial Aid, 773-244-5500.

QUINCY UNIVERSITY
Quincy, IL 62301-2699

General application contact: Dr. Gary Carter, Academic Dean, 217-228-5200.

RUSH UNIVERSITY
Chicago, IL 60612-3832

General application contact: Hicela Castruita, Director, College Admissions Services, 312-942-7100.

SCHOOL OF THE ART INSTITUTE OF CHICAGO
Chicago, IL 60603-3103

General application contact: Jennifer Stein, Associate Director of Graduate Admissions, 312-899-5219.

SEABURY–WESTERN THEOLOGICAL SEMINARY
Evanston, IL 60201-2938
http://www.swts.nwu.edu/

General application contact: Jesse Lehman, Coordinator of Admissions, 847-328-9300 Ext. 28.

SPERTUS INSTITUTE OF JEWISH STUDIES
Chicago, IL 60605-1901

General application contact: Lisa Burnstein, Director of Student Services, 312-322-1722.

TELSHE YESHIVA–CHICAGO
Chicago, IL 60625-5598

TRINITY INTERNATIONAL UNIVERSITY
Deerfield, IL 60015-1284
http://www.tiu.edu/
General application contact: Ken Botton, Director of
 Admissions, 800-345-8337.

**UNIVERSITY OF SAINT MARY OF THE LAKE–
MUNDELEIN SEMINARY**
Mundelein, IL 60060
General application contact: Rev. John F. Canary, Rector-
 President, 847-566-6401.

VANDERCOOK COLLEGE OF MUSIC
Chicago, IL 60616-3886
http://www.mcs.com/~vcmusic/
General application contact: George Pierard, Director of
 Admissions, 312-225-6288.

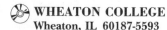 **WHEATON COLLEGE**
  Wheaton, IL 60187-5593
http://www.wheaton.edu/
General application contact: Associate Director of Graduate
 Admissions, 630-752-5195.

INDIANA

ANDERSON UNIVERSITY
Anderson, IN 46012-3495
http://www.anderson.edu/
General application contact: Dr. Christina Accornero,
 Director of Advancement and Recruitment, 765-641-
 3005.

ASSOCIATED MENNONITE BIBLICAL SEMINARY
Elkhart, IN 46517-1947
http://www.ambs.edu/
General application contact: Randall C. Miller, Director of
 Admissions, 219-296-6227.

BETHANY THEOLOGICAL SEMINARY
Richmond, IN 47374-4019
http://www.brethren.org/bethany/
General application contact: David Shetler, Associate for
 Admissions, 800-BTS-8822.

BETHEL COLLEGE
Mishawaka, IN 46545-5591
http://www.bethel-in.edu/
General application contact: Dr. Robert Laurent, Director
 of Graduate Studies, 219-257-3353.

CHRISTIAN THEOLOGICAL SEMINARY
Indianapolis, IN 46208-3301
General application contact: Kathy Talen, Director of
 Admissions, 317-931-2300.

CONCORDIA THEOLOGICAL SEMINARY
Fort Wayne, IN 46825-4996
General application contact: Rev. Scott Klemsz, Admissions
 Officer, 219-452-2100.

EARLHAM SCHOOL OF RELIGION
Richmond, IN 47374-5360
General application contact: Nancy Wood Nelson, Director
 of Admissions, 765-983-1523.

GRACE COLLEGE
Winona Lake, IN 46590-1294
General application contact: Ron Henry, Director of
 Admissions, 219-372-5131.

GRACE THEOLOGICAL SEMINARY
Winona Lake, IN 46590-9907
http://www.grace.edu/
General application contact: Ron Henry, Director of
 Admissions, 219-372-5131.

HUNTINGTON COLLEGE
Huntington, IN 46750-1299
General application contact: Dr. David D. Rahn, Associate
 Dean for the Graduate School, 219-359-4039.

MANCHESTER COLLEGE
North Manchester, IN 46962-1225
http://www.manchester.edu/
General application contact: Dr. Jo Young Switzer, Vice
 President for Academic Affairs, 219-982-5051.

MARTIN UNIVERSITY
Indianapolis, IN 46218-3867
General application contact: Sr. Jane Schilling, Vice
 President of Academic Affairs, 317-543-4890.

OAKLAND CITY UNIVERSITY
Oakland City, IN 47660-1099
General application contact: Rob Allen, Counselor for
 Graduate Admissions, 812-749-1241.

PURDUE UNIVERSITY NORTH CENTRAL
Westville, IN 46391-9528
General application contact: Dr. Edward Hackett, Chair,
 219-785-5485.

ROSE-HULMAN INSTITUTE OF TECHNOLOGY
Terre Haute, IN 47803-3920
http://www.rose-hulman.edu/
General application contact: Dr. Buck F. Brown, Dean for
 Research and Graduate Studies, 812-877-8403.

SAINT JOSEPH'S COLLEGE
Rensselaer, IN 47978
http://www.saintjoe.edu/

General application contact: Rev. James Challancin, Director of the Graduate Program, 219-866-6352.

SAINT MARY-OF-THE-WOODS COLLEGE
Saint Mary-of-the-Woods, IN 47876

General application contact: Sr. Ruth Eileen Dwyer, Director of Graduate Program, 812-535-5206.

SAINT MEINRAD SCHOOL OF THEOLOGY
Saint Meinrad, IN 47577
http://www.saintmeinrad.edu/

General application contact: Rev. Amador Garza, Associate Director of Enrollment, 812-357-6971.

IOWA

BUENA VISTA UNIVERSITY
Storm Lake, IA 50588
http://www.bvu.edu/

General application contact: Jon E. Hixon, Director of Graduate Studies, 712-749-2190.

CLARKE COLLEGE
Dubuque, IA 52001-3198

General application contact: Bobbe Ames, Vice President of Marketing and Enrollment Management, 319-588-6316.

COE COLLEGE
Cedar Rapids, IA 52402-5070

General application contact: Dr. Terry McNabb, Director, Graduate Program, 319-399-8000.

DORDT COLLEGE
Sioux Center, IA 51250-1697
http://www.dordt.edu/

General application contact: Dr. Jack Fennema, Director of Graduate Education, 712-722-6226.

FAITH BAPTIST BIBLE COLLEGE AND THEOLOGICAL SEMINARY
Ankeny, IA 50021-2152
http://www.faith.edu/

General application contact: Tim Nilius, Vice President of Enrollment, 888-FAITH4U.

GRACELAND COLLEGE
Lamoni, IA 50140
http://www.graceland.edu/

General application contact: Lewis Smith, Director, Student Information Service, 800-537-6276.

LORAS COLLEGE
Dubuque, IA 52004-0178

General application contact: Office of Admissions, 319-588-7236.

MORNINGSIDE COLLEGE
Sioux City, IA 51106-1751

General application contact: Dr. Glenna Tevis, Director, Graduate Division, 712-274-5375.

PALMER COLLEGE OF CHIROPRACTIC
Davenport, IA 52803-5287
http://www.palmer.edu/

General application contact: Gary Mohr, Director of Institutional Advancement, 319-326-9626.

UNIVERSITY OF OSTEOPATHIC MEDICINE AND HEALTH SCIENCES
Des Moines, IA 50312-4104

General application contact: Dr. Dennis L. Bates, Director of Admissions, 515-271-1450.

UPPER IOWA UNIVERSITY
Fayette, IA 52142-1857
http://www.uiu.edu/

General application contact: Jerilyn Carlson, Administrative Assistant, 800-773-9298.

WARTBURG THEOLOGICAL SEMINARY
Dubuque, IA 52004-5004

General application contact: Gloria Keiser, Director of Admissions, 319-589-0200.

KANSAS

BENEDICTINE COLLEGE
Atchison, KS 66002-1499
http://www.benedictine.edu/

General application contact: Dr. Jo Ann Fellin, OSB, Director of Graduate Studies, 913-367-5340 Ext. 2435.

CENTRAL BAPTIST THEOLOGICAL SEMINARY
Kansas City, KS 66102-3964

General application contact: Tom Davis, Director of Recruitment, 913-371-5313.

KANSAS WESLEYAN UNIVERSITY
Salina, KS 67401-6196
http://www.kwu.edu/

General application contact: Jeffery Miller, Director of Admissions, 785-827-5541 Ext. 1283.

NEWMAN UNIVERSITY
Wichita, KS 67213-2084

General application contact: Dale Shubert, Coordinator of Graduate Admissions, 316-942-4291 Ext. 355.

OTTAWA UNIVERSITY
Ottawa, KS 66067-3399

General application contact: David Leiter, Admissions Officer, 913-451-1431.

SAINT MARY COLLEGE
Leavenworth, KS 66048-5082

General application contact: Dr. Sandra Van Hoose, Vice President for Academic Affairs and Graduate Dean, 913-798-6115.

SOUTHWESTERN COLLEGE
Winfield, KS 67156-2499

General application contact: William Medley, Director of Graduate Studies, 800-846-1543.

UNITED STATES ARMY COMMAND AND GENERAL STAFF COLLEGE
Fort Leavenworth, KS 66027-1352

General application contact: Helen Davis, Educational Technician, 913-684-2741.

KENTUCKY

ASBURY THEOLOGICAL SEMINARY
Wilmore, KY 40390-1199
http://www.ats.wilmore.ky.us/

General application contact: W. Thomas Pope, Director of Admissions, 606-858-2250.

BRESCIA COLLEGE
Owensboro, KY 42301-3023
http://www.brescia.edu/

General application contact: Rick Eber, Director of Admissions, 502-686-4241.

CAMPBELLSVILLE UNIVERSITY
Campbellsville, KY 42718-2799
http://www.campbellsvil.edu/

General application contact: Trent Argo, Director of Admissions, 502-789-5007.

GEORGETOWN COLLEGE
Georgetown, KY 40324-1696

General application contact: Dr. Ben R. Oldham, Dean of Education, 502-863-8176.

LEXINGTON THEOLOGICAL SEMINARY
Lexington, KY 40508-3218

General application contact: Rachel Childress, Registrar, 606-252-0361.

LINDSEY WILSON COLLEGE
Columbia, KY 42728-1298

General application contact: Dr. John Rigney, Director of Graduate Program, 800-264-0138.

LOUISVILLE PRESBYTERIAN THEOLOGICAL SEMINARY
Louisville, KY 40205-1798

General application contact: James A. Hubert, Director of Admissions, 502-895-3411.

PIKEVILLE COLLEGE
Pikeville, KY 41501
http://www.pc.edu/

General application contact: Stephen M. Payson, Associate Dean for Student Affairs, 606-432-9640.

SOUTHERN BAPTIST THEOLOGICAL SEMINARY
Louisville, KY 40280-0004
http://www.sbts.edu/

General application contact: Robert Cheong, Director of Admissions, 800-626-5525.

SULLIVAN COLLEGE
Louisville, KY 40205

General application contact: Admissions Office, 502-456-6505.

THOMAS MORE COLLEGE
Crestview Hills, KY 41017-3495

General application contact: Dale Myers, Vice President of Graduate and Continuing Education, 606-341-4554.

LOUISIANA

LOUISIANA STATE UNIVERSITY MEDICAL CENTER
New Orleans, LA 70112-2223

General application contact: Nancy W. Rhodes, Director, Student Affairs, 504-568-4804.

NEW ORLEANS BAPTIST THEOLOGICAL SEMINARY
New Orleans, LA 70126-4858

General application contact: Dr. Paul E. Gregoire Jr., Director of Admissions and Registrar, 504-282-4455.

NOTRE DAME SEMINARY
New Orleans, LA 70118-4391

General application contact: Rev. José Lavastida, Dean of the Graduate School of Theology, 504-866-7426 Ext. 3107.

OUR LADY OF HOLY CROSS COLLEGE
New Orleans, LA 70131-7399

General application contact: Dr. Judith G. Miranti, Dean of Education, 504-394-7744.

MAINE

BANGOR THEOLOGICAL SEMINARY
Bangor, ME 04401-4699
http://www.bts.edu/

General application contact: Bill Friederich, Director of Admissions, 207-942-6781.

COLLEGE OF THE ATLANTIC
Bar Harbor, ME 04609-1198

General application contact: Dr. Craig W. Greene, Dean for Advanced Studies, 207-288-5015 Ext. 261.

HUSSON COLLEGE
Bangor, ME 04401-2999

General application contact: Dr. Robert M. Smith, Dean of Graduate Studies, 207-941-7062.

MAINE COLLEGE OF ART
Portland, ME 04101-3987

http://www.meca.edu/

General application contact: Shannon Rose Riley, Assistant to the Director of Graduate Studies, 207-775-3052 Ext. 262.

MAINE MARITIME ACADEMY
Castine, ME 04420

http://www.mainemaritime.edu/

General application contact: Carolyn J. Ulrich, Administrative Assistant, 207-326-2485.

SAINT JOSEPH'S COLLEGE
Standish, ME 04084-5263

General application contact: Admissions Department, 800-752-4723.

THOMAS COLLEGE
Waterville, ME 04901-5097

General application contact: Dr. Nelson Madore, Graduate Adviser, 207-873-0771 Ext. 323.

MARYLAND

BALTIMORE HEBREW UNIVERSITY
Baltimore, MD 21215-3996

http://www.bhu.edu/

General application contact: Dr. Barry M. Gittlen, Dean of Graduate Studies, 410-578-6922.

CAPITAL BIBLE SEMINARY
Lanham, MD 20706-3599

http://www.bible.edu/

General application contact: Bill Walker, Director of Admissions, 800-787-0256.

CAPITOL COLLEGE
Laurel, MD 20708-9759

http://www.capitol-college.edu/

General application contact: Sandy Perriello, Coordinator of Graduate Administration, 703-998-5503.

GOUCHER COLLEGE
Baltimore, MD 21204-2794

http://www.goucher.edu/

General application contact: Robert Welch, Academic Dean and Vice President, 410-337-6044.

HARVEST CHRISTIAN COLLEGE
Camp Springs, MD 20746

MAPLE SPRINGS BAPTIST BIBLE COLLEGE AND SEMINARY
Capitol Heights, MD 20743

MARYLAND INSTITUTE, COLLEGE OF ART
Baltimore, MD 21217-4192

http://www.mica.edu/

General application contact: Dr. Leslie King-Hammond, Dean of Graduate Studies, 410-225-2255.

NER ISRAEL RABBINICAL COLLEGE
Baltimore, MD 21208

ST. JOHN'S COLLEGE
Annapolis, MD 21404

General application contact: Miriam L. Callahan-Hean, Graduate Admissions Counselor, 410-626-2541.

ST. MARY'S SEMINARY AND UNIVERSITY
Baltimore, MD 21210-1994

General application contact: Rev. James J. Conn, SJ, Dean, School of Theology, 410-864-3600.

TRADITIONAL ACUPUNCTURE INSTITUTE
Columbia, MD 21044-3422

General application contact: Vicki Rapoport, Admissions Coordinator, 410-997-4888 Ext. 647.

UNIFORMED SERVICES UNIVERSITY OF THE HEALTH SCIENCES
Bethesda, MD 20814-4799

General application contact: Janet M. Anastasi, Graduate Program Coordinator, 301-295-9474.

UNIVERSITY OF MARYLAND, BALTIMORE
Baltimore, MD 21201-1627

General application contact: Keith T. Brooks, Director, Graduate Admissions and Records, 410-706-7131.

VILLA JULIE COLLEGE
Stevenson, MD 21153

General application contact: Judy Snyder, Registrar, 410-653-6400.

WASHINGTON COLLEGE
Chestertown, MD 21620-1197

General application contact: Dr. Michael Kerchner, Director of the Graduate Program, 410-778-2800 Ext. 7730.

WESTERN MARYLAND COLLEGE
Westminster, MD 21157-4390

General application contact: Dr. Kenneth W. Pool, Dean of Graduate Affairs, 410-857-2500.

MASSACHUSETTS

ANDOVER NEWTON THEOLOGICAL SCHOOL
Newton Centre, MA 02159-2243
http://www.ants.edu/
General application contact: Elaine M. Lapomardo, Director of Enrollment, 800-964-2687 Ext. 272.

ARTHUR D. LITTLE SCHOOL OF MANAGEMENT
Chestnut Hill, MA 02167
http://www.arthurdlittle.com/som/som.html
General application contact: Virginia Leonardos, Registrar, 617-552-2871.

ATLANTIC UNION COLLEGE
South Lancaster, MA 01561-1000
http://www.atlanticuc.edu/
General application contact: Dr. Roger Bothwell, Graduate Coordinator, 978-368-2434.

BABSON COLLEGE
Babson Park, MA 02157-0310
http://www.babson.edu/mba/
General application contact: Rita S. Edmunds, Director of Graduate Admissions, 781-239-5591.

BENTLEY COLLEGE
Waltham, MA 02154-4705
http://www.bentley.edu/
General application contact: Sharon M. Oliver, Director of Graduate Admissions, 781-891-2108.

BOSTON ARCHITECTURAL CENTER
Boston, MA 02115-2795
http://www.the-bac.edu/
General application contact: Jennifer Marshall, Admissions Counselor, 617-262-5000.

BOSTON CONSERVATORY
Boston, MA 02215
http://www.bostonconservatory.edu/
General application contact: Director of Enrollment, 617-536-6340.

BOSTON GRADUATE SCHOOL OF PSYCHOANALYSIS
Brookline, MA 02446-4602
http://www.bgsp.edu/
General application contact: Dr. Dena Reed, Dean of Graduate Studies, 617-277-3915.

CAMBRIDGE COLLEGE
Cambridge, MA 02138-5304
http://www.cambridge.edu/
General application contact: Bruce D. Grigsby, Assistant Vice President for Administration, 617-868-1000 Ext. 142.

COLLEGE OF OUR LADY OF THE ELMS
Chicopee, MA 01013-2839
General application contact: Sr. Kathleen M. Kirley, Dean of Continuing Education and Graduate Studies, 413-594-2761.

CONWAY SCHOOL OF LANDSCAPE DESIGN
Conway, MA 01341-0179
http://www.csld.edu/
General application contact: Mollie Babize, Administrative Director, 413-369-4044.

ENDICOTT COLLEGE
Beverly, MA 01915-2096
http://www.endicott.edu/
General application contact: Dr. Paul Tortolani, Dean of Continuing Education and Graduate Studies, 978-232-2199.

EPISCOPAL DIVINITY SCHOOL
Cambridge, MA 02138-3494
http://www.episdivschool.org/
General application contact: Anne K. Frame, Director of Admissions, Recruitment, and Financial Aid, 617-868-3450.

GORDON COLLEGE
Wenham, MA 01984-1899
General application contact: Dr. Muriel Radtke, Director, 978-927-2300 Ext. 4315.

GORDON-CONWELL THEOLOGICAL SEMINARY
South Hamilton, MA 01982-2395
General application contact: Tim Myrick, Director of Admissions, 800-428-7329.

HEBREW COLLEGE
Brookline, MA 02146-5495
General application contact: Norma Frankel, Registrar, 617-278-4944.

HOLY CROSS GREEK ORTHODOX SCHOOL OF THEOLOGY
Brookline, MA 02146-7415
General application contact: Dr. John Klentos, Director of Admissions and Records, 617-731-3500 Ext. 260.

LONGY SCHOOL OF MUSIC
Cambridge, MA 02138
http://www.longy.edu/
General application contact: Kurt Piemonte, Administrator for Admissions and Financial Aid, 617-876-0956 Ext. 144.

MASSACHUSETTS COLLEGE OF ART
Boston, MA 02115-5882
General application contact: Kay Ransdell, Dean for Admissions and Retention, 617-232-1555 Ext. 235.

MASSACHUSETTS COLLEGE OF LIBERAL ARTS
North Adams, MA 01247-4100

General application contact: Dr. Elaine C. Collins, Dean of Graduate and Academic Affairs, 413-662-5207.

MASSACHUSETTS COLLEGE OF PHARMACY AND ALLIED HEALTH SCIENCES
Boston, MA 02115-5896

http://www.mcp.edu/

General application contact: Lovie Condrick, Coordinator of Graduate Admissions, 617-732-2986.

MASSACHUSETTS SCHOOL OF PROFESSIONAL PSYCHOLOGY
Boston, MA 02132

General application contact: Cathleen Clark Fucillo, Director of Admissions, 617-327-6777.

MERRIMACK COLLEGE
North Andover, MA 01845-5800

http://www.merrimack.edu/

General application contact: George Rogers, Director, Continuing and Professional Education, 978-837-5101.

MGH INSTITUTE OF HEALTH PROFESSIONS
Boston, MA 02114-4719

http://www.mgh.harvard.edu/depts/ihp/mgh.htm

General application contact: Valerie Abrahamsen, Registrar, 617-726-3136.

NEW ENGLAND COLLEGE OF OPTOMETRY
Boston, MA 02115-1100

General application contact: Lawrence Shattuck, Director of Admissions, 617-236-6210.

NEW ENGLAND CONSERVATORY OF MUSIC
Boston, MA 02115-5000

General application contact: Allison Ball, Dean of Enrollment Services, 617-262-1120 Ext. 430.

NEW ENGLAND SCHOOL OF ACUPUNCTURE
Watertown, MA 02472

General application contact: Cindy Rosenbaum, Dean of Students and Admissions, 617-926-1788 Ext. 119.

NEW ENGLAND SCHOOL OF LAW
Boston, MA 02116-5687

http://www.nesl.edu/

General application contact: Pamela Jorgensen, Director of Admissions, 617-422-7210.

NICHOLS COLLEGE
Dudley, MA 01571

General application contact: William F. Keith, Director, MBA Program, 508-213-2207.

PINE MANOR COLLEGE
Chestnut Hill, MA 02167-2332

http://www.pmc.edu/

General application contact: Pat Dunbar, Graduate Admissions, 617-731-7111.

POPE JOHN XXIII NATIONAL SEMINARY
Weston, MA 02193-2699

General application contact: Msgr. Francis D. Kelly, President and Rector, 781-899-5500.

REGIS COLLEGE
Weston, MA 02493

General application contact: Office of Graduate and Continuing Studies, 781-768-7189.

SAINT JOHN'S SEMINARY
Brighton, MA 02135

General application contact: Msgr. Timothy J. Moran, Rector, 617-254-2610.

SCHOOL OF THE MUSEUM OF FINE ARTS
Boston, MA 02115

General application contact: John Williamson, Director of Enrollment and Student Services, 617-369-3626.

SMITH COLLEGE
Northampton, MA 01063

General application contact: Margaret Anderson, Acting Director, 413-585-3051.

SOUTHERN NEW ENGLAND SCHOOL OF LAW
North Dartmouth, MA 02747-1252

General application contact: Nancy Fitzsimmons Hebert, Admissions Coordinator, 508-998-9400.

UNIVERSITY OF MASSACHUSETTS MEDICAL CENTER AT WORCESTER
Worcester, MA 01655-0115

http://www.ummed.edu/

General application contact: Dr. Thomas B. Miller Jr., Dean, School of Biomedical Sciences, 508-856-2256.

WESTON JESUIT SCHOOL OF THEOLOGY
Cambridge, MA 02138-3495

General application contact: Mary Pat St. Jean, Director of Admissions, 617-492-1960.

WHEELOCK COLLEGE
Boston, MA 02215

General application contact: Martha Sheehan, Director of Graduate Admissions, 617-734-5200 Ext. 212.

WILLIAMS COLLEGE
Williamstown, MA 01267

http://www.williams.edu/

General application contact: Dr. Charles W. Haxthausen, Director of Graduate Program, 413-458-2303 Ext. 534.

MICHIGAN

BAKER COLLEGE CENTER FOR GRADUATE STUDIES
Flint, MI 48507
http://www.baker.edu/
General application contact: Chuck Gurden, Director of Admissions, 800-469-3165.

CALVIN THEOLOGICAL SEMINARY
Grand Rapids, MI 49546-4387
http://www.calvin.edu/seminary/
General application contact: John Vander Lugt, Registrar, 616-957-6027.

CENTER FOR HUMANISTIC STUDIES
Detroit, MI 48202-3802
General application contact: Patricia Hagan, Registrar, 313-875-7440.

CRANBROOK ACADEMY OF ART
Bloomfield Hills, MI 48303-0801
General application contact: Katharine E. Willman, Dean of Admissions and Financial Aid, 248-645-3300.

DETROIT COLLEGE OF BUSINESS
Dearborn, MI 48126-3799
http://www.dcb.edu/
General application contact: Ofelia Tabarez, Graduate Admissions Representative, 313-581-4400 Ext. 378.

DETROIT COLLEGE OF LAW AT MICHIGAN STATE UNIVERSITY
Detroit, MI 48201-3454
http://www.dcl.edu/
General application contact: Andrea Heatley, Director of Admissions, 517-432-0222.

ECUMENICAL THEOLOGICAL SEMINARY
Detroit, MI 48201
General application contact: Beverly Schneider, Registrar, Admissions and Financial Aid, 313-831-5200 Ext. 203.

KETTERING UNIVERSITY
Flint, MI 48504-4898
http://www.gmi.edu/
General application contact: Dr. C. David Hurt, Associate Dean, Graduate Studies and Extension Services, 810-762-7953.

LAWRENCE TECHNOLOGICAL UNIVERSITY
Southfield, MI 48075-1058
General application contact: Maryanne Clink, Director, Institutional Research and Academic Planning, 248-204-2403.

MICHIGAN THEOLOGICAL SEMINARY
Plymouth, MI 48170
http://www.mts.edu/
General application contact: Kris Udd, Registrar, 313-207-9581.

NORTHWOOD UNIVERSITY
Midland, MI 48640-2398
http://www.northwood.edu/
General application contact: Lisa Marie Boyd, Director of Graduate Admissions, 517-837-4488.

OLIVET COLLEGE
Olivet, MI 49076-9701
http://www.olivetnet.edu/
General application contact: Norma Curtis, Chairperson, 616-749-7615.

SACRED HEART MAJOR SEMINARY
Detroit, MI 48206-1799
General application contact: Rev. Patrick Halfpenny, Vice Rector, 313-883-8500.

SAINTS CYRIL AND METHODIUS SEMINARY
Orchard Lake, MI 48324
General application contact: Rev. Stanislaw Flis, Director of Recruitment and Admissions, 248-683-0318.

SIENA HEIGHTS UNIVERSITY
Adrian, MI 49221-1796
General application contact: Director, Graduate Studies, 517-264-7665.

SPRING ARBOR COLLEGE
Spring Arbor, MI 49283-9799
General application contact: Denise B. Schonhard, Admissions Representative, 517-750-6536.

THOMAS M. COOLEY LAW SCHOOL
Lansing, MI 48901-3038
General application contact: Stephanie Gregg, Director of Admissions, 517-371-5140.

WALSH COLLEGE OF ACCOUNTANCY AND BUSINESS ADMINISTRATION
Troy, MI 48007-7006
General application contact: Vickie Ming, Coordinator of Enrollment Services, 248-689-8282 Ext. 218.

WESTERN THEOLOGICAL SEMINARY
Holland, MI 49423-3622
General application contact: Timothy Brown, Recruitment, 616-392-8555.

MINNESOTA

ALFRED ADLER INSTITUTE OF MINNESOTA
Hopkins, MN 55305
http://www.alfredadler.edu/
General application contact: Evelyn Haas, Director, 612-988-4170.

AUGSBURG COLLEGE
Minneapolis, MN 55454-1351
http://www.augsburg.edu/
General application contact: Coordinator, 612-330-1787.

BETHEL COLLEGE
St. Paul, MN 55112-6999
http://www.bethel.edu/
General application contact: Dr. Neil McBride, Dean of Continuing Studies, 612-638-8000.

BETHEL THEOLOGICAL SEMINARY
St. Paul, MN 55112-6998
http://www.bethel.edu/seminary/btshome.htm
General application contact: Morris Anderson, Director of Admissions, 612-638-6288.

CONCORDIA UNIVERSITY AT ST. PAUL
St. Paul, MN 55104-5494
http://www.csp.edu/
General application contact: Dr. Robert DeWerff, Dean of Graduate and Continuing Studies, 612-641-8277.

CROWN COLLEGE
St. Bonifacius, MN 55375-9001
http://www.crown.edu/
General application contact: Dr. W. Vernon Caston, Director, 612-446-4109.

THE GRADUATE SCHOOL OF AMERICA
Minneapolis, MN 55401
http://www.tgsa.edu/
General application contact: Associate Director of Admissions, 800-987-1133.

HAMLINE UNIVERSITY
St. Paul, MN 55104-1284
General application contact: Joe Graba, Acting Dean, 651-523-2900.

LUTHER SEMINARY
St. Paul, MN 55108-1445
http://www.luthersem.edu/
General application contact: Ron Olson, Director of Admissions, 612-641-3521.

MAYO GRADUATE SCHOOL
Rochester, MN 55905
General application contact: Catharine J. Chellgren, Registrar and Administrator of Graduate School, 507-284-3163.

MAYO MEDICAL SCHOOL
Rochester, MN 55905
http://www.mayo.edu/education/mms/MMS_Home_Page.html
General application contact: Marion K. Kelly, Assistant Dean, 507-284-2316.

MAYO SCHOOL OF HEALTH-RELATED SCIENCES
Rochester, MN 55905
General application contact: Carol Cooper, Administrative Secretary, 507-284-3293.

MINNEAPOLIS COLLEGE OF ART AND DESIGN
Minneapolis, MN 55404-4347
http://www.mcad.edu/
General application contact: Rebecca Haas, Director of Admissions, 800-874-6223.

MINNESOTA SCHOOL OF PROFESSIONAL PSYCHOLOGY
Minneapolis, MN 55425-1569
http://www.aspp.edu/
General application contact: Linda Berglin, Director of Admissions, 612-858-8800.

NORTHWESTERN COLLEGE OF CHIROPRACTIC
Bloomington, MN 55431-1599
General application contact: Lynn Heieie, Associate Director of Admissions, 612-888-4777.

SAINT JOHN'S UNIVERSITY
Collegeville, MN 56321
http://www.csbsju.edu/sot/
General application contact: Mary Beth Banken, OSB, Director of Enrollment, 320-363-2102.

SOUTHWEST STATE UNIVERSITY
Marshall, MN 56258-1598
General application contact: Rich Shearer, Director of Admissions, 507-537-6286.

UNITED THEOLOGICAL SEMINARY OF THE TWIN CITIES
New Brighton, MN 55112-2598
http://www.unitedseminary-mn.org/
General application contact: Norma Rae Hunt, Dean of Admissions and Student Services, 612-633-4311.

WALDEN UNIVERSITY
Minneapolis, MN 55401
http://www.waldenu.edu/
General application contact: Assistant Vice President of Recruitment and Outreach, 800-444-6795.

WILLIAM MITCHELL COLLEGE OF LAW
St. Paul, MN 55105-3076
http://www.wmitchell.edu/
General application contact: Connie Lawrence, Assistant to Associate Dean of Academic Affairs, 612-290-6467.

MISSISSIPPI

BELHAVEN COLLEGE
Jackson, MS 39202-1789
General application contact: Frank Tamboli, Director of
Marketing, 601-968-5988.

MILLSAPS COLLEGE
Jackson, MS 39210-0001
General application contact: Bart Herridge, Director of
Graduate Business Admissions, 601-974-1253.

MISSISSIPPI UNIVERSITY FOR WOMEN
Columbus, MS 39701-9998
http://www.muw.edu/
General application contact: Dr. Kathleen Martin, Director,
Graduate School, 601-329-7177.

MISSISSIPPI VALLEY STATE UNIVERSITY
Itta Bena, MS 38941-1400
General application contact: Office of Admissions, 601-254-
3344.

REFORMED THEOLOGICAL SEMINARY
Jackson, MS 39209-3099
General application contact: Dr. Allen Curry, Dean,
601-922-4988.

UNIVERSITY OF MISSISSIPPI MEDICAL CENTER
Jackson, MS 39216-4505
General application contact: Dr. Billy M. Bishop, Director,
Student Services and Records, 601-984-1080.

WESLEY BIBLICAL SEMINARY
Jackson, MS 39206
General application contact: Mary Spencer, Assistant to the
Vice President for Institutional Advancement, 800-788-
9571.

MISSOURI

AQUINAS INSTITUTE OF THEOLOGY
St. Louis, MO 63108-3396
http://www.op.org/aquinas/
General application contact: Ron Knapp, Director of
Admissions, 314-977-3869.

ASSEMBLIES OF GOD THEOLOGICAL SEMINARY
Springfield, MO 65802-2191
http://www.agts.edu/
General application contact: Dorothea J. Lotter, Director of
Admissions and Records, 417-268-1000.

BAPTIST BIBLE COLLEGE
Springfield, MO 65803-3498
http://www.seebbc.edu/
General application contact: Martha Barker, Graduate
School Secretary, 417-268-6054.

**BEREAN UNIVERSITY OF THE ASSEMBLIES OF
GOD**
Springfield, MO 65802-1805
http://www.berean.edu/
General application contact: Lattis Campbell, Student
Services Representative, 800-443-1083 Ext. 2318.

**CALVARY BIBLE COLLEGE AND THEOLOGICAL
SEMINARY**
Kansas City, MO 64147-1341
http://www.calvary.edu/index.htm
General application contact: John Bryden, Director of
Admissions, 800-326-3960 Ext. 1320.

CENTRAL METHODIST COLLEGE
Fayette, MO 65248-1198
http://www.cmc.edu/
General application contact: Ann Oberhaus, Coordinator of
Off-Campus Programs, 660-248-6286.

**CLEVELAND CHIROPRACTIC COLLEGE OF
KANSAS CITY**
Kansas City, MO 64131-1181
General application contact: Brenda Holland, Director of
Admissions, 816-333-8230.

COLUMBIA COLLEGE
Columbia, MO 65216-0002
http://www.ccis.edu/
General application contact: Virginia Wilson, Assistant
Director, Admissions, 573-875-7339.

CONCORDIA SEMINARY
St. Louis, MO 63105-3199
General application contact: Rev. Scott C. Sailer, Director,
Ministerial Recruitment, 314-505-7222.

COVENANT THEOLOGICAL SEMINARY
St. Louis, MO 63141-8697
General application contact: Kevin Vanden Brink, Director
of Admissions, 314-434-4044.

EDEN THEOLOGICAL SEMINARY
St. Louis, MO 63119-3192
General application contact: Diane Windler, Admissions
Office, 314-961-3627.

**FOREST INSTITUTE OF PROFESSIONAL
PSYCHOLOGY**
Springfield, MO 65807
General application contact: Dr. Ann Elise Parkhurst,
Director of Admissions, 417-823-3477.

JEWISH HOSPITAL COLLEGE OF NURSING AND ALLIED HEALTH
St. Louis, MO 63110-1091

General application contact: Connie Stohlman, Chief Admissions Officer, 314-454-7538.

KENRICK–GLENNON SEMINARY
St. Louis, MO 63119-4330

General application contact: Rev. Lawrence C. Brennan, CM, Academic Dean, 314-644-0266.

KIRKSVILLE COLLEGE OF OSTEOPATHIC MEDICINE
Kirksville, MO 63501
http://www.kcom.edu/

General application contact: Lori Haxton, Director of Admissions, 816-626-2237.

LOGAN COLLEGE OF CHIROPRACTIC
Chesterfield, MO 63006-1065

General application contact: Melvin Reynolds, Dean of Admissions, 314-227-2100.

MIDWESTERN BAPTIST THEOLOGICAL SEMINARY
Kansas City, MO 64118-4697
http://www.mbts.edu/

General application contact: Office of Student Enlistment, 800-944-6287.

NAZARENE THEOLOGICAL SEMINARY
Kansas City, MO 64131-1263
http://www.nts.edu/

General application contact: Susan Middendorf, Director of Enrollment Services, 816-333-6255 Ext. 233.

RESEARCH COLLEGE OF NURSING
Kansas City, MO 64132

General application contact: Leslie Mendenhall, Director of Transfer and Graduate Admissions, 816-276-4033.

ST. LOUIS COLLEGE OF PHARMACY
St. Louis, MO 63110-1088

General application contact: Lisa Boeschen, Director of Admissions, 314-367-8700 Ext. 1072.

SAINT PAUL SCHOOL OF THEOLOGY
Kansas City, MO 64127-2440
http://www.spst.edu/

General application contact: Jacqueline A. Conley, Director of Admissions, 816-483-9600 Ext. 211.

STEPHENS COLLEGE
Columbia, MO 65215-0002
http://www.stephens.edu/

General application contact: Dr. Joan T. Rines, Director of Graduate Programs, 800-388-7579.

UNIVERSITY OF HEALTH SCIENCES
Kansas City, MO 64106-1453
http://www.uhs.edu/

General application contact: Minnie Marrs, Admissions Director, 816-283-2350.

WILLIAM WOODS UNIVERSITY
Fulton, MO 65251-1098

General application contact: Mary Henley, Director of Recruitment, 800-995-3199.

MONTANA

UNIVERSITY OF GREAT FALLS
Great Falls, MT 59405

General application contact: Dr. Al Johnson, Dean of Graduate Studies Division, 406-791-5337.

NEBRASKA

CLARKSON COLLEGE
Omaha, NE 68131-2739

General application contact: Jeff Beals, Director of Enrollment Management, 402-552-3100.

CONCORDIA UNIVERSITY
Seward, NE 68434-1599
http://www.ccsn.edu/

General application contact: Dr. Judy Preuss, Dean of Graduate Studies, 402-643-7475.

DOANE COLLEGE
Crete, NE 68333-2430
http://www.doane.edu/

General application contact: Wilma Daddario, Director, Office of Graduate Studies, 402-464-1223.

GRACE UNIVERSITY
Omaha, NE 68108

General application contact: Debi Mitchell, Graduate Admissions Counselor, 402-449-2917.

HASTINGS COLLEGE
Hastings, NE 68902-0269
http://www.hastings.edu/

General application contact: Fred Condos, Director of Graduate Education, 402-461-7388.

NEBRASKA METHODIST COLLEGE OF NURSING AND ALLIED HEALTH
Omaha, NE 68114-3426

General application contact: Jeannie Hannan, Coordinator of Health Promotions, 402-354-4933.

NEBRASKA

PERU STATE COLLEGE
Peru, NE 68421
http://www.peru.edu/
General application contact: Dr. Daniel J. Cox, Division
Chair, 402-872-2244.

UNIVERSITY OF NEBRASKA MEDICAL CENTER
Omaha, NE 68198-0001
General application contact: Jo Wagner, Associate Director
of Admissions, 402-559-4206.

NEVADA

SIERRA NEVADA COLLEGE
Incline Village, NV 89450-4269
http://www.sierranevada.edu/
General application contact: Dr. Skip Wenda, Director,
800-332-8666.

NEW HAMPSHIRE

**ANTIOCH NEW ENGLAND GRADUATE
SCHOOL**
Keene, NH 03431-3516
http://www.antiochne.edu/
General application contact: Diane K. Hewitt, Co-Director
of Admissions, 603-357-6265 Ext. 286.

FRANKLIN PIERCE COLLEGE
Rindge, NH 03461-0060
http://www.fpc.edu/
General application contact: Dr. Duncan G. LaBay, MBA
Coordinator, 603-898-1263.

FRANKLIN PIERCE LAW CENTER
Concord, NH 03301-4197
http://www.fplc.edu/
General application contact: Lory Attalla, Acting Director
of Admissions, 603-228-9217.

NEW ENGLAND COLLEGE
Henniker, NH 03242-3293
General application contact: Dr. Patricia Prinz, Director of
Graduate and Continuing Studies, 603-428-2252.

NEW HAMPSHIRE COLLEGE
Manchester, NH 03106-1045
General application contact: Dr. Paul Schneiderman, Acting
Dean, 603-644-3102.

NEW JERSEY

BETH MEDRASH GOVOHA
Lakewood, NJ 08701-2797

CALDWELL COLLEGE
Caldwell, NJ 07006-6195
http://www.caldwell.edu/
General application contact: Dr. Rina Spano, Director of
Graduate Studies, 973-228-4424 Ext. 408.

CENTENARY COLLEGE
Hackettstown, NJ 07840-2100
General application contact: Dr. Thomas A. Brunner,
Director of Graduate Studies, 908-852-1400 Ext. 2299.

COLLEGE OF SAINT ELIZABETH
Morristown, NJ 07960-6989
General application contact: see individual programs,
973-290-4100.

DREW UNIVERSITY
Madison, NJ 07940-1493
General application contact: George B. Soroka, Director of
Graduate Admissions, 973-408-3110.

FELICIAN COLLEGE
Lodi, NJ 07644-2198
General application contact: Office of Admissions, 973-778-
1190 Ext. 6131.

NEW BRUNSWICK THEOLOGICAL SEMINARY
New Brunswick, NJ 08901-1107
General application contact: Dr. David Waanders, Director
of Admissions, 908-246-5614.

PRINCETON THEOLOGICAL SEMINARY
Princeton, NJ 08542-0803
General application contact: Rev. Jeffrey V. O'Grady III,
Director of Vocations and Admissions, 609-497-7805.

RAMAPO COLLEGE OF NEW JERSEY
Mahwah, NJ 07430-1680
General application contact: Dr. Sydney Weinberg, Director,
201-529-7423.

**THE RICHARD STOCKTON COLLEGE OF NEW
JERSEY**
Pomona, NJ 08240-9988
http://www.stockton.edu/
General application contact: Sal Catalfamo, Dean of
Enrollment Management, 609-652-4261.

TALMUDICAL ACADEMY OF NEW JERSEY
Adelphia, NJ 07710

THOMAS EDISON STATE COLLEGE
Trenton, NJ 08608-1176
General application contact: Dr. Esther Taitsman, Director
of Graduate Studies, 609-292-5143.

UNIVERSITY OF MEDICINE AND DENTISTRY OF NEW JERSEY
Newark, NJ 07107-3001
http://www.umdnj.edu/
General application contact: Dean of the appropriate
school, 973-972-4300.

NEW MEXICO

COLLEGE OF SANTA FE
Santa Fe, NM 87505-7634
General application contact: Dolores E. Roybal, Assistant
Dean for Academic Services, 505-473-6177.

COLLEGE OF THE SOUTHWEST
Hobbs, NM 88240-9129
General application contact: Terri Blandin, Secretary, Vice
President of Academic Affairs, 505-392-6561.

INTERNATIONAL INSTITUTE OF CHINESE MEDICINE
Santa Fe, NM 87502
General application contact: Dr. Michael Zeng, Director,
505-473-5233.

NEW MEXICO INSTITUTE OF MINING AND TECHNOLOGY
Socorro, NM 87801
General application contact: Dr. David Johnson, Dean of
Graduate Studies, 505-835-5513.

ST. JOHN'S COLLEGE
Santa Fe, NM 87501-4599
General application contact: Heather Harrell, Graduate
Admissions Counselor, 505-984-6083.

SOUTHWEST ACUPUNCTURE COLLEGE
Santa Fe, NM 87505
http://www.swacupuncture.com/
General application contact: James Ventresca, Academic
Dean, 505-438-8884.

SOUTHWESTERN COLLEGE
Santa Fe, NM 87502-4788
General application contact: Debra Thompson-Morris,
Director of Admissions, 505-471-5756.

NEW YORK

ALBANY COLLEGE OF PHARMACY OF UNION UNIVERSITY
Albany, NY 12208-3425
http://panther.ucp.edu/
General application contact: Jacqueline Harris, Assistant
Registrar, 518-445-7221.

ALBANY LAW SCHOOL OF UNION UNIVERSITY
Albany, NY 12208-3494
http://www.als.edu/
General application contact: Dawn M. Chamberlaine,
Assistant Dean of Admissions and Financial Aid, 518-445-2326.

ALBANY MEDICAL COLLEGE
Albany, NY 12208-3479
http://www.amc.edu/html/medical_college.html
General application contact: Admissions Coordinator,
518-262-5253.

AUDREY COHEN COLLEGE
New York, NY 10013-1919
http://www.audrey-cohen.edu/
General application contact: Steven K. Lenhart, Director of
Admissions, 212-343-1234 Ext. 2700.

BANK STREET COLLEGE OF EDUCATION
New York, NY 10025-1120
http://www.bnkst.edu/
General application contact: Ann Morgan, Director of
Admissions, 212-875-4404.

BARD COLLEGE
Annandale-on-Hudson, NY 12504
http://www.bard.edu/
General application contact: Robert L. Martin, Dean of
Graduate Studies, 914-758-7419.

BARD GRADUATE CENTER FOR STUDIES IN THE DECORATIVE ARTS
New York, NY 10024-3602
http://www.bard.edu/aca_frames.html
General application contact: Judith Maiorana, Assistant
Dean for Student Academic Services, 212-501-3056.

BETH HAMEDRASH SHAAREI YOSHER INSTITUTE
Brooklyn, NY 11204

BETH HATALMUD RABBINICAL COLLEGE
Brooklyn, NY 11214

BORICUA COLLEGE
New York, NY 10032-1560
General application contact: Miriam Pfeiffer, Director of
Student Services, 718-782-2200.

BROOKLYN LAW SCHOOL
Brooklyn, NY 11201-3798
http://www.brooklaw.edu/
General application contact: Henry W. Haverstick III, Dean
  of Admissions and Financial Aid, 718-780-7906.

**CENTRAL YESHIVA TOMCHEI
TMIMIM–LUBAVITCH**
Brooklyn, NY 11230

CHRIST THE KING SEMINARY
East Aurora, NY 14052
General application contact: Sr. Judith M. Kubicki,
  Academic Dean, 716-652-8900.

**CITY UNIVERSITY OF NEW YORK SCHOOL OF
LAW AT QUEENS COLLEGE**
Flushing, NY 11367-1358
General application contact: William D. Perez, Director of
  Admissions, 718-340-4210.

**COLGATE ROCHESTER DIVINITY SCHOOL/
BEXLEY HALL/CROZER THEOLOGICAL
SEMINARY**
Rochester, NY 14620-2530
General application contact: Dale Davis, Director of Church
  Leadership, 716-271-1320.

COLGATE UNIVERSITY
Hamilton, NY 13346-1386
General application contact: Charles E. McClennen,
  Associate Dean of the Faculty and Director of Graduate
  Studies, 315-228-7220.

COLLEGE OF INSURANCE
New York, NY 10007-2165
General application contact: Theresa C. Marro, Director of
  Admissions, 212-815-9232.

COLLEGE OF MOUNT SAINT VINCENT
Riverdale, NY 10471-1093
http://www.cmsv.edu/
General application contact: Francis P. Nash, Director of
  Transfer and Graduate Admissions, 718-405-3267.

CORNELL UNIVERSITY MEDICAL COLLEGE
New York, NY 10021-4896
http://www.med.cornell.edu/
General application contact: Assistant Dean of Admissions,
  212-746-1067.

DAEMEN COLLEGE
Amherst, NY 14226-3592
General application contact: Deborah Fargo, Associate
  Director of Admissions, 716-839-8225.

DARKEI NOAM RABBINICAL COLLEGE
Brooklyn, NY 11219

DOMINICAN COLLEGE OF BLAUVELT
Orangeburg, NY 10962-1210
General application contact: Colleen O'Connor, Director of
  Admissions, 914-359-7800.

FASHION INSTITUTE OF TECHNOLOGY
New York, NY 10001-5992
General application contact: Dr. Bruce W. Chambers, Dean
  of Graduate Studies, 212-760-7714.

FIVE TOWNS COLLEGE
Dix Hills, NY 11746-6055
http://www.fivetowns.edu/
General application contact: Christina Kuhl, Admissions
  Coordinator, 516-424-7000.

GENERAL THEOLOGICAL SEMINARY
New York, NY 10011-4977
General application contact: Antoinette J. Daniels, Director
  of Admissions, 212-243-5150 Ext. 280.

**GRADUATE SCHOOL OF FIGURATIVE ART
OF THE NEW YORK ACADEMY OF ART**
New York, NY 10013-2911
General application contact: David Davidson, Vice
  President, Academic Affairs, 212-966-0300.

**HEBREW UNION COLLEGE–JEWISH INSTITUTE
OF RELIGION**
New York, NY 10012-1186
General application contact: Dean of Students, 212-674-
  5300 Ext. 219.

**JEWISH THEOLOGICAL SEMINARY OF
AMERICA**
New York, NY 10027-4649
General application contact: Dr. Stephen Garfinkel, Dean
  of the Graduate School, 212-678-8022.

**JOHN JAY COLLEGE OF CRIMINAL JUSTICE,
THE CITY UNIVERSITY OF NEW YORK**
New York, NY 10019-1093
General application contact: Shirley Rodriguez, Admissions
  Assistant, 212-237-8863.

THE JUILLIARD SCHOOL
New York, NY 10023-6588
General application contact: Mary Grey, Director of
  Admissions, 212-799-5000 Ext. 223.

KEHILATH YAKOV RABBINICAL SEMINARY
Brooklyn, NY 11211-7207

KOL YAAKOV TORAH CENTER
Monsey, NY 10952-2954
General application contact: Registrar, 914-425-3863.

LE MOYNE COLLEGE
Syracuse, NY 13214-1399

http://www.lemoyne.edu

General application contact: Director of the appropriate program.

MACHZIKEI HADATH RABBINICAL COLLEGE
Brooklyn, NY 11204-1805

General application contact: Boruch Rozmarin, Financial Aid Administrator, 718-854-8777.

MANHATTAN SCHOOL OF MUSIC
New York, NY 10027-4698

http://www.msmnyc.edu

General application contact: Lee Cioppa, Director of Admission, 212-749-2802 Ext. 2.

MANHATTANVILLE COLLEGE
Purchase, NY 10577-2132

General application contact: Barry Ward, Vice President of Enrollment and Student Development, 914-323-5153.

MEDAILLE COLLEGE
Buffalo, NY 14214-2695

http://www.medaille.edu/

General application contact: Jacqueline Matheny, Director of Enrollment Management, 716-884-3281.

MERCY COLLEGE
Dobbs Ferry, NY 10522-1189

http://www.mercynet.edu/

General application contact: Joy Colelli, Dean for Admissions, 914-674-7600.

MESIVTA OF EASTERN PARKWAY RABBINICAL SEMINARY
Brooklyn, NY 11218-5559

MESIVTA TIFERETH JERUSALEM OF AMERICA
New York, NY 10002-6301

MESIVTA TORAH VODAATH SEMINARY
Brooklyn, NY 11218-5209

MID–AMERICA BAPTIST THEOLOGICAL SEMINARY NORTHEAST BRANCH
Schenectady, NY 12303-3463

http://www.mabts.edu/

General application contact: Dr. Jeffery B. Ginn, Director, 518-355-4000.

MIRRER YESHIVA
Brooklyn, NY 11223-2010

MOLLOY COLLEGE
Rockville Centre, NY 11571-5002

General application contact: Dr. Carol A. Clifford, Director, Graduate Program, 516-256-2218.

MOUNT SINAI SCHOOL OF MEDICINE OF THE CITY UNIVERSITY OF NEW YORK
New York, NY 10029-6504

http://www.mssm.edu/

General application contact: Administrative Manager, 212-241-6546.

NEW YORK CHIROPRACTIC COLLEGE
Seneca Falls, NY 13148-0800

http://www.nycc.edu/

General application contact: Barbara Gianneschi, Dean of Enrollment Management, 315-568-3040.

NEW YORK COLLEGE OF PODIATRIC MEDICINE
New York, NY 10035-1815

http://www.nycpm.edu/

General application contact: Steve Broder, Director of Admissions, 800-526-6966.

NEW YORK LAW SCHOOL
New York, NY 10013-2959

http://www.nyls.edu

General application contact: Pamela McKenna, Director of Admissions, 212-431-2888.

NEW YORK MEDICAL COLLEGE
Valhalla, NY 10595-1691

http://www.nymc.edu/

General application contact: Dr. Francis L. Belloni, Dean of the Graduate School of Basic Medical Sciences, 914-594-4110.

NEW YORK SCHOOL OF INTERIOR DESIGN
New York, NY 10021-5110

General application contact: Scott Ageloff, Dean, 212-472-1500 Ext. 301.

NEW YORK THEOLOGICAL SEMINARY
New York, NY 10001

General application contact: Yon Su Kang, Registrar, 212-532-4012.

NYACK COLLEGE
Nyack, NY 10960-3698

General application contact: Director of Admissions, 800-541-6891.

OHR HAMEIR THEOLOGICAL SEMINARY
Peekskill, NY 10566

PICOWER GRADUATE SCHOOL OF MOLECULAR MEDICINE
Manhasset, NY 11030

General application contact: Lydia Moser, Administrative Assistant, 516-562-9442.

PRATT INSTITUTE
Brooklyn, NY 11205-3899

http://www.pratt.edu/

General application contact: Vice President for Enrollment, 718-636-3669.

PURCHASE COLLEGE, STATE UNIVERSITY OF NEW YORK
Purchase, NY 10577-1400

General application contact: Janice Marie Hamm, Assistant Director of Admissions, 914-251-6300.

RABBI ISAAC ELCHANAN THEOLOGICAL SEMINARY
New York, NY 10033-2807

General application contact: Zevulun Charlop, Dean, 212-960-5344.

RABBINICAL ACADEMY MESIVTA RABBI CHAIM BERLIN
Brooklyn, NY 11230-4715

General application contact: Administrator, 718-377-0777.

RABBINICAL COLLEGE BETH SHRAGA
Monsey, NY 10952-3035

RABBINICAL COLLEGE BOBOVER YESHIVA B'NEI ZION
Brooklyn, NY 11219

RABBINICAL COLLEGE CH'SAN SOFER
Brooklyn, NY 11204

RABBINICAL COLLEGE OF LONG ISLAND
Long Beach, NY 11561-3305

RABBINICAL SEMINARY M'KOR CHAIM
Brooklyn, NY 11219

RABBINICAL SEMINARY OF AMERICA
Forest Hills, NY 11375

General application contact: Registrar, 718-268-4700.

ROBERTS WESLEYAN COLLEGE
Rochester, NY 14624-1997

General application contact: Kathy Merz, Admissions Secretary, 716-594-6600.

SAINT BERNARD'S INSTITUTE
Rochester, NY 14620-2545

General application contact: Dr. D. N. Premnath, Registrar, 716-271-3657 Ext. 296.

ST. JOSEPH'S COLLEGE, SUFFOLK CAMPUS
Patchogue, NY 11772-2399

General application contact: Marion E. Salgado, Director of Admissions, 516-447-3219.

ST. JOSEPH'S SEMINARY
Yonkers, NY 10704

General application contact: Rev. Msgr. Francis J. McAree, STD, Rector, 914-968-6200.

ST. LAWRENCE UNIVERSITY
Canton, NY 13617-1455

General application contact: Dr. James Shuman, Chair, Department of Education, 315-229-5847.

ST. THOMAS AQUINAS COLLEGE
Sparkill, NY 10976
http://www.stac.edu/

General application contact: Joseph L. Chillo, Executive Director of Enrollment Services, 914-398-4100.

ST. VLADIMIR'S ORTHODOX THEOLOGICAL SEMINARY
Crestwood, NY 10707-1699
http://www.svots.edu/

General application contact: Ann Sanchez, Student Affairs Administrator, 914-961-8313 Ext. 323.

SARAH LAWRENCE COLLEGE
Bronxville, NY 10708

General application contact: Director of Graduate Studies, 914-395-2373.

SCHOOL OF VISUAL ARTS
New York, NY 10010-3994

General application contact: Brenda Hanegan, Admissions Coordinator, 212-592-2109.

SEMINARY OF THE IMMACULATE CONCEPTION
Huntington, NY 11743-1696

General application contact: Rev. Robert J. Smith, Academic Dean, 516-423-0483.

SH'OR YOSHUV RABBINICAL COLLEGE
Far Rockaway, NY 11691-4002

SIENA COLLEGE
Loudonville, NY 12211-1462
http://www.siena.edu/

General application contact: Leonard Stokes, Director, MBA Program, 518-786-5015.

SKIDMORE COLLEGE
Saratoga Springs, NY 12866-1632
http://www.skidmore.edu/

General application contact: Dr. Lawrence Ries, Director, 518-580-5480.

STATE UNIVERSITY OF NEW YORK COLLEGE OF OPTOMETRY
New York, NY 10010-3610
http://www.sunyopt.edu/

General application contact: Dr. Edward Johnston, Vice President for Student Affairs, 212-780-5100.

STATE UNIVERSITY OF NEW YORK EMPIRE STATE COLLEGE
Saratoga Springs, NY 12866-4391

General application contact: Patricia Ryan, Assistant Director of Student Services for Graduate Studies, 518-587-2100.

STATE UNIVERSITY OF NEW YORK HEALTH SCIENCE CENTER AT BROOKLYN
Brooklyn, NY 11203-2098

General application contact: Dilek Takil, Admissions Officer, 718-270-1155.

STATE UNIVERSITY OF NEW YORK HEALTH SCIENCE CENTER AT SYRACUSE
Syracuse, NY 13210-2334

General application contact: Dr. Maxwell M. Mozell, Dean of the College of Graduate Studies, 315-464-4538.

STATE UNIVERSITY OF NEW YORK MARITIME COLLEGE
Throgs Neck, NY 10465-4198

General application contact: Dr. Shmuel Yahalom, Director, 718-409-7285.

TOURO COLLEGE
New York, NY 10010

General application contact: Dean of the appropriate school, 212-463-0400.

UNIFICATION THEOLOGICAL SEMINARY
Barrytown, NY 12507-5000
http://www.uts.edu/

General application contact: Hong-Yu Kovic, Director of Admissions, 914-752-3015.

UNION COLLEGE
Schenectady, NY 12308-2311
http://gmi.union.edu/

General application contact: Head of the appropriate unit, 518-388-6000.

UNION THEOLOGICAL SEMINARY
New York, NY 10027-5710
http://www.uts.columbia.edu/

General application contact: David McDonagh, Director of Admissions, 212-280-1317.

UNITED TALMUDICAL SEMINARY
Brooklyn, NY 11211-7900

VASSAR COLLEGE
Poughkeepsie, NY 12604

General application contact: Lloyd Peterson, Director, Office of Admissions, 914-437-7300.

WEBB INSTITUTE
Glen Cove, NY 11542-1398
http://www.webb-institute.edu/

General application contact: William G. Murray, Director of Admissions, 516-671-2213.

YESHIVA DERECH CHAIM
Brooklyn, NY 11218

YESHIVA KARLIN STOLIN
Brooklyn, NY 11204

YESHIVA OF NITRA RABBINICAL COLLEGE
Mount Kisco, NY 10549

YESHIVA SHAAR HATORAH TALMUDIC RESEARCH INSTITUTE
Kew Gardens, NY 11418-1469

YESHIVATH VIZNITZ
Monsey, NY 10952

YESHIVATH ZICHRON MOSHE
South Fallsburg, NY 12779

NORTH CAROLINA

BELMONT ABBEY COLLEGE
Belmont, NC 28012-1802
http://www.bac.edu/

General application contact: Dr. Henry Loehr, Director of Graduate Studies in Business, 704-825-6223.

CATAWBA COLLEGE
Salisbury, NC 28144-2488

General application contact: Dr. Shirley Haworth, Chair, Department of Teacher Education, 704-637-4461.

HIGH POINT UNIVERSITY
High Point, NC 27262-3598

General application contact: Dr. Alberta Herron, Dean of Graduate Studies, 336-841-9198.

MONTREAT COLLEGE
Montreat, NC 28757-1267
http://www.montreat.edu/

General application contact: Joe Sharp, Director of Recruitment, 800-436-2777.

NORTH CAROLINA SCHOOL OF THE ARTS
Winston-Salem, NC 27117-2189

General application contact: Carol Palm, Director of Admissions, 336-770-3290.

PIEDMONT BAPTIST COLLEGE
Winston-Salem, NC 27101-5197

General application contact: Gene Haithcox, Director of Admissions, 336-725-8344 Ext. 2326.

SALEM COLLEGE
Winston-Salem, NC 27108-0548

General application contact: Dr. Robin L. Smith, Director of Graduate Studies, 336-721-2656.

SOUTHEASTERN BAPTIST THEOLOGICAL SEMINARY
Wake Forest, NC 27588-1889

General application contact: Anthony Allen, Admissions Director, 919-556-3101.

UNIVERSITY OF NORTH CAROLINA AT ASHEVILLE
Asheville, NC 28804-3299

General application contact: Dr. Ted Uldricks, Director, MLA Program, 704-251-6620.

WARREN WILSON COLLEGE
Asheville, NC 28815-9000

http://www.warren-wilson.edu/

General application contact: Peter Turchi, Director, 704-298-3325 Ext. 380.

WINGATE UNIVERSITY
Wingate, NC 28174

General application contact: Dr. William M. Christie, Provost, 704-233-8123.

OHIO

AIR FORCE INSTITUTE OF TECHNOLOGY
Wright-Patterson AFB, OH 45433-7765

http://www.afit.af.mil/

General application contact: Registrar, 937-255-7168.

ART ACADEMY OF CINCINNATI
Cincinnati, OH 45202-1700

http://www.artacademy.edu/main.html

General application contact: Sarah Colby, Director of Enrollment Services, 513-562-8754.

ATHENAEUM OF OHIO
Cincinnati, OH 45230-5900

General application contact: Michael E. Sweeney, Registrar, 513-231-2223.

BLUFFTON COLLEGE
Bluffton, OH 45817-1196

http://www.bluffton.edu/

General application contact: Diane Neal, Graduate Recruitment and Admissions, 419-358-3328.

CENTRAL STATE UNIVERSITY
Wilberforce, OH 45384

General application contact: Constance Robinson, Coordinator, Graduate Program, 937-376-6536.

CINCINNATI BIBLE COLLEGE AND SEMINARY
Cincinnati, OH 45204-1799

http://www.cincybible.edu/

General application contact: Dr. William C. Weber, Graduate Dean, 513-244-8192.

CLEVELAND COLLEGE OF JEWISH STUDIES
Beachwood, OH 44122-7116

General application contact: Linda L. Rosen, Registrar, 216-464-4050.

CLEVELAND INSTITUTE OF MUSIC
Cleveland, OH 44106-1776

General application contact: E. William Fay, Director of Admissions, 216-795-3107.

DEFIANCE COLLEGE
Defiance, OH 43512-1610

General application contact: Sally Bissell, Director of Continuing Education, 419-784-4010.

FRANKLIN UNIVERSITY
Columbus, OH 43215-5399

http://www.franklin.edu/

General application contact: MBA Associate, 614-341-6387.

HEBREW UNION COLLEGE–JEWISH INSTITUTE OF RELIGION
Cincinnati, OH 45220-2488

General application contact: Rabbi Kenneth E. Ehrlich, Dean of Rabbinic School, 513-221-1875.

HEIDELBERG COLLEGE
Tiffin, OH 44883-2462

http://www.heidelberg.edu/

General application contact: Dr. Charles E. Moon, Dean of Graduate Studies, 419-448-2288.

MALONE COLLEGE
Canton, OH 44709-3897

http://www.malone.edu

General application contact: Dr. Alexandra Gregory, Dean of the Graduate School, 330-471-8210.

MARIETTA COLLEGE
Marietta, OH 45750-4000

General application contact: Mark Bruce, Acting Registrar, 740-376-4728.

THE MCGREGOR SCHOOL OF ANTIOCH UNIVERSITY
Yellow Springs, OH 45387-1609

General application contact: Terri Haney, Director of Admissions, 937-767-6325.

MEDICAL COLLEGE OF OHIO
Toledo, OH 43699-0008

http://www.mco.edu/

General application contact: Dr. Keith K. Schlender, Dean of the Graduate School, 419-383-4112.

METHODIST THEOLOGICAL SCHOOL IN OHIO
Delaware, OH 43015-8004

http://www.mtso.edu/

General application contact: Mary L. Harris, Director of Admissions, 740-362-3370.

MOUNT VERNON NAZARENE COLLEGE
Mount Vernon, OH 43050-9500
http://www.mvnc.edu/

General application contact: Dr. Henry L. Smith, Coordinator of Graduate Program, 740-397-1244.

MUSKINGUM COLLEGE
New Concord, OH 43762

General application contact: Dr. Rolf G. Schmitz, Director of Graduate Studies, 614-826-8037.

NORTHEASTERN OHIO UNIVERSITIES COLLEGE OF MEDICINE
Rootstown, OH 44272-0095
http://www.neoucom.edu/

General application contact: Karen Berger, Associate Director of Admissions, 330-325-6270.

NOTRE DAME COLLEGE OF OHIO
South Euclid, OH 44121-4293

General application contact: Sr. Helene Marie Gregos, SN, Director of Graduate Studies, 216-381-1680 Ext. 337.

OHIO COLLEGE OF PODIATRIC MEDICINE
Cleveland, OH 44106-3082
http://www.ocpm.edu/

General application contact: John E. Andrews, Dean of Student Affairs, 216-231-3300 Ext. 341.

OHIO NORTHERN UNIVERSITY
Ada, OH 45810-1599
http://www.law.onu.edu/

General application contact: Office of Admissions, 419-772-2211.

OTTERBEIN COLLEGE
Westerville, OH 43081

General application contact: Dr. Ann Rottersman, Coordinator of Graduate Studies, 614-823-3209.

PAYNE THEOLOGICAL SEMINARY
Wilberforce, OH 45384-0474

General application contact: Dr. Marcia Foster Boyd, Academic Dean, 937-376-2946 Ext. 201.

PONTIFICAL COLLEGE JOSEPHINUM
Columbus, OH 43235-1498

General application contact: Thomas Olmsted, President/Rector, 614-885-5585.

SAINT MARY SEMINARY AND GRADUATE SCHOOL OF THEOLOGY
Wickliffe, OH 44092-2527

General application contact: Donald B. Cozzens, President-Rector, 440-943-7600.

TIFFIN UNIVERSITY
Tiffin, OH 44883-2161

General application contact: Dr. Ellen S. Jordan, Dean of the Graduate School, 419-448-3401.

TRINITY LUTHERAN SEMINARY
Columbus, OH 43209-2334

General application contact: Ruth C. Fortis, Director of Admissions, 614-235-4136.

UNITED THEOLOGICAL SEMINARY
Dayton, OH 45406-4599

General application contact: Donna J. Wert, Registrar, 937-278-5817.

THE UNIVERSITY OF FINDLAY
Findlay, OH 45840-3653

General application contact: Kenneth E. Zirkle, President, 419-424-4512.

UNIVERSITY OF RIO GRANDE
Rio Grande, OH 45674

General application contact: Dr. Mark Abell, Director of Administration, 740-245-5353.

URSULINE COLLEGE
Pepper Pike, OH 44124-4398

General application contact: Sr. Kathleen Burke, Dean of Graduate Studies, 440-646-8119.

WINEBRENNER THEOLOGICAL SEMINARY
Findlay, OH 45839-0478
http://www.winebrenner.edu/

General application contact: Jennifer J. Cobb, Admissions Counselor, 419-422-4824.

OKLAHOMA

AMERICAN BIBLE COLLEGE AND SEMINARY
Bethany, OK 73008-0099

General application contact: Perry Kepford, Admissions, 405-495-2526.

CAMERON UNIVERSITY
Lawton, OK 73505-6377
http://www.cameron.edu/

General application contact: Dr. David L. Carl, Dean, School of Graduate and Professional Studies, 580-581-2986.

LANGSTON UNIVERSITY
Langston, OK 73050-0838

General application contact: Dr. Alex O. Lewis, Director, 405-466-3379.

OKLAHOMA BAPTIST UNIVERSITY
Shawnee, OK 74801-2558
http://www.okbu.edu/

General application contact: Dr. J. Oscar Jeske, Director of Graduate Studies in Marriage and Family Therapy, 405-878-2225.

OKLAHOMA CHRISTIAN UNIVERSITY OF SCIENCE AND ARTS
Oklahoma City, OK 73136-1100

General application contact: Dr. Lynn A. McMillon, Dean, College of Biblical Studies, 405-425-5370.

OKLAHOMA STATE UNIVERSITY COLLEGE OF OSTEOPATHIC MEDICINE
Tulsa, OK 74107-1898

General application contact: Dr. Daniel Overack, Assistant Dean of Students, 918-582-1972 Ext. 8442.

PHILLIPS THEOLOGICAL SEMINARY
Tulsa, OK 74145

http://www.ptsem.org/

General application contact: Rev. Myrna J. Jones, Director of Admissions, 918-610-8303.

SOUTHWESTERN COLLEGE OF CHRISTIAN MINISTRIES
Bethany, OK 73008-0340

General application contact: Beverly Haug, Graduate Program Secretary, 405-789-7661 Ext. 3447.

UNIVERSITY OF OKLAHOMA HEALTH SCIENCES CENTER
Oklahoma City, OK 73190

General application contact: Dr. O. Ray Kling, Dean of the Graduate College, 405-271-2085.

OREGON

CONCORDIA UNIVERSITY
Portland, OR 97211-6099

General application contact: Dr. Peter Johnson, Director of Admissions, 503-280-8501.

EASTERN OREGON UNIVERSITY
La Grande, OR 97850-2899

General application contact: Dr. R. Doyle Slater, Director of Teacher Education, 541-962-3772.

GEORGE FOX UNIVERSITY
Newberg, OR 97132-2697

http://www.georgefox.edu/

General application contact: Jackie Baysinger, Director of Graduate Admissions, 800-631-0921.

LEWIS & CLARK COLLEGE
Portland, OR 97219-7899

General application contact: Dean, Graduate School of Professional Studies, 503-768-7700.

MOUNT ANGEL SEMINARY
Saint Benedict, OR 97373

General application contact: President-Rector, 503-845-3951.

MULTNOMAH BIBLE COLLEGE AND BIBLICAL SEMINARY
Portland, OR 97220-5898

http://www.multnomah.edu/

General application contact: Joyce L. Kehoe, Director of Admissions and Registrar, 503-255-0332.

NATIONAL COLLEGE OF NATUROPATHIC MEDICINE
Portland, OR 97201

http://www.ncnm.edu/

General application contact: Glenn Young, Assistant Director of Admissions, 503-499-4343.

NORTHWEST CHRISTIAN COLLEGE
Eugene, OR 97401-3727

General application contact: Dr. Anna K. Hultquist, Director of Graduate Studies, 541-684-7246.

OREGON COLLEGE OF ORIENTAL MEDICINE
Portland, OR 97216

http://www.infinite.org/oregon.acupuncture/

General application contact: James Eddy, Dean of Institutional Affairs, 503-253-3443.

OREGON GRADUATE INSTITUTE OF SCIENCE AND TECHNOLOGY
Portland, OR 97291-1000

http://www.ogi.edu/

General application contact: Frances M. Hewitt, Enrollment Manager, 800-685-2423.

OREGON HEALTH SCIENCES UNIVERSITY
Portland, OR 97201-3098

General application contact: Office of Admissions, 503-494-4863.

OREGON INSTITUTE OF TECHNOLOGY
Klamath Falls, OR 97601-8801

General application contact: Saichi Oba, Director of Admissions, 541-885-1152.

REED COLLEGE
Portland, OR 97202-8199

http://web.reed.edu/

General application contact: Barbara Amen, Director of Special Programs, 503-777-7259.

WARNER PACIFIC COLLEGE
Portland, OR 97215-4099

General application contact: Dr. Steve Carver, Director, 503-788-7501.

WESTERN SEMINARY
Portland, OR 97215-3367

General application contact: Dr. Robert W. Wiggins, Registrar/Vice President of Student Services, 503-233-8561.

WESTERN STATES CHIROPRACTIC COLLEGE
Portland, OR 97230-3099

http://www.wschiro.edu/

General application contact: Randall Hand, Dean of Enrollment Management, 800-641-5641.

WILLAMETTE UNIVERSITY
Salem, OR 97301-3931

General application contact: James M. Sumner, Vice President for Enrollment, 503-370-6303.

PENNSYLVANIA

ALLENTOWN COLLEGE OF ST. FRANCIS DE SALES
Center Valley, PA 18034-9568

http://www.allencol.edu/

General application contact: Dr. Karen Doyle Walton, Vice President for Academic Affairs, 610-282-1100 Ext. 1342.

AMERICAN COLLEGE
Bryn Mawr, PA 19010-2105

http://www.amercoll.edu/

General application contact: Joanne F. Patterson, Associate Director of Graduate Administration, 610-526-1366.

BAPTIST BIBLE COLLEGE OF PENNSYLVANIA
Clarks Summit, PA 18411-1297

http://www.bbc.edu/index.htm

General application contact: Dr. Howard Bixby, Vice President/Academic Dean, 717-586-2400.

BIBLICAL THEOLOGICAL SEMINARY
Hatfield, PA 19440-2499

General application contact: B. Scott Camilleri, Director of Admissions, 215-368-5000.

BRYN ATHYN COLLEGE OF THE NEW CHURCH
Bryn Athyn, PA 19009-0717

http://www.newchurch.edu/college/

General application contact: Brian W. Keith, Dean of the Theological School, 215-938-2525.

BRYN MAWR COLLEGE
Bryn Mawr, PA 19010-2899

http://www.brynmawr.edu/

General application contact: Admissions Office of the appropriate school, 610-526-5000.

BUCKNELL UNIVERSITY
Lewisburg, PA 17837

http://www.bucknell.edu/

General application contact: Dr. Marion Lois Huffines, Director of Graduate Studies, 717-524-1304.

CARLOW COLLEGE
Pittsburgh, PA 15213-3165

General application contact: Dr. Mary Catherine Conroy Hayden, Vice President of Day, Continuing Education and Graduate Education, 412-578-8766.

CHATHAM COLLEGE
Pittsburgh, PA 15232-2826

General application contact: Heidi Hemming, Graduate Admissions, 412-365-1290.

THE CURTIS INSTITUTE OF MUSIC
Philadelphia, PA 19103-6107

General application contact: Director of Admissions, 215-893-5262.

THE DICKINSON SCHOOL OF LAW OF THE PENNSYLVANIA STATE UNIVERSITY
Carlisle, PA 17013-2899

http://www.dsl.edu/

General application contact: Barbara W. Guillaume, Director, Law Admissions, 717-240-5207.

EASTERN BAPTIST THEOLOGICAL SEMINARY
Wynnewood, PA 19096-3430

http://www.ebts.edu/

General application contact: Stephen Hutchison, Director of Admissions, 610-896-5000.

EVANGELICAL SCHOOL OF THEOLOGY
Myerstown, PA 17067-1212

General application contact: Tom M. Maiello, Director of Enrollment Services, 800-532-5775.

GENEVA COLLEGE
Beaver Falls, PA 15010-3599

General application contact: Philip Van Bruggen, Chairman, Program in Professional Psychology, 724-847-6547.

GRATZ COLLEGE
Melrose Park, PA 19027

General application contact: Evelyn Klein, Director of Admissions, 215-635-7300.

GROVE CITY COLLEGE
Grove City, PA 16127-2104

General application contact: Admissions Office, 724-458-2000.

HOLY FAMILY COLLEGE
Philadelphia, PA 19114-2094

General application contact: Dr. Antoinette M. Schiavo, Dean, Graduate Studies, 215-637-7700 Ext. 3230.

KING'S COLLEGE
Wilkes-Barre, PA 18711-0801

http://www.kings.edu/

General application contact: Dr. Elizabeth S. Lott, Director of Graduate Programs, 717-208-5991.

LAKE ERIE COLLEGE OF OSTEOPATHIC MEDICINE
Erie, PA 16509

General application contact: Krista Wojtkielewicz, Admissions Coordinator, 814-866-6641.

LANCASTER BIBLE COLLEGE
Lancaster, PA 17601-5036

General application contact: Dr. Miles A. Lewis, Dean of Graduate Studies, 717-560-8297.

LANCASTER THEOLOGICAL SEMINARY
Lancaster, PA 17603-2812

General application contact: Patricia Huffman, Director of Admissions, 717-290-8737.

LEBANON VALLEY COLLEGE
Annville, PA 17003-0501

General application contact: Cheryl L. Batdorf, Academic Adviser, 717-867-6335.

LOCK HAVEN UNIVERSITY OF PENNSYLVANIA
Lock Haven, PA 17745-2390

General application contact: Office of Admission, 717-893-2027.

LUTHERAN THEOLOGICAL SEMINARY AT GETTYSBURG
Gettysburg, PA 17325-1795

General application contact: Dr. Richard L. Thulin, Dean, 717-334-6286.

THE LUTHERAN THEOLOGICAL SEMINARY AT PHILADELPHIA
Philadelphia, PA 19119-1794

General application contact: George E. Keck, Director of Admissions, 800-286-4616.

MERCYHURST COLLEGE
Erie, PA 16546

General application contact: Mary Ellen Dahlkemper, Director, Office of Adult and Graduate Programs, 814-824-2294.

MORAVIAN COLLEGE
Bethlehem, PA 18018-6650

General application contact: Dr. Santo D. Marabella, Director, Program in Business Administration, 610-807-4444.

MORAVIAN THEOLOGICAL SEMINARY
Bethlehem, PA 18018-6614

http://www.moravian.edu/misc/docs/seminary.htm

General application contact: W. Thomas Stapleton, Associate Dean, 610-861-1529.

NEUMANN COLLEGE
Aston, PA 19014-1298

http://www.neumann.edu/

General application contact: Mark Osborn, Director of Admissions and Financial Aid, 610-558-5616.

PENNSYLVANIA ACADEMY OF THE FINE ARTS
Philadelphia, PA 19102

General application contact: Michael S. Smith, Director of Admissions, 215-972-2047.

PENNSYLVANIA COLLEGE OF OPTOMETRY
Philadelphia, PA 19141-3323

General application contact: Robert E. Horne, Director of Admissions, 215-276-6262.

PENNSYLVANIA STATE UNIVERSITY GREAT VALLEY SCHOOL OF GRADUATE PROFESSIONAL STUDIES
Malvern, PA 19355-1488

http://www.gv.psu.edu/

General application contact: Dr. Madlyn L. Hanes, Campus Executive Officer and Associate Dean, 610-648-3200.

PENNSYLVANIA STATE UNIVERSITY MILTON S. HERSHEY MEDICAL CENTER
Hershey, PA 17033-2360

http://www.hmc.psu.edu/

General application contact: Dr. C. McCollister Evarts, Senior Vice President, 717-531-8521.

PHILADELPHIA COLLEGE OF BIBLE
Langhorne, PA 19047-2990

http://www.pcb.edu/

General application contact: Ted McKown, Director of Marketing/Recruiting, 800-572-2472.

PHILADELPHIA COLLEGE OF OSTEOPATHIC MEDICINE
Philadelphia, PA 19131

http://www.pcom.edu/

General application contact: Carol Fox, Associate Dean for Admission and Enrollment Management, 215-871-6700.

PITTSBURGH THEOLOGICAL SEMINARY
Pittsburgh, PA 15206-2596

General application contact: Director of Admissions and Student Relations, 412-362-5610.

POINT PARK COLLEGE
Pittsburgh, PA 15222-1984

http://www.ppc.edu/

General application contact: Michele Lawrence, Office of Admissions, 412-392-3430.

RECONSTRUCTIONIST RABBINICAL COLLEGE
Wyncote, PA 19095-1898

http://www.rrc.edu/

General application contact: Rabbi Reena Spicehandler, Dean of Admissions, 215-576-0800.

ROBERT MORRIS COLLEGE
Moon Township, PA 15108-1189

General application contact: Vincent J. Kane, Recruiting Coordinator, 412-262-8535.

 **ROSEMONT COLLEGE**
Rosemont, PA 19010-1699

General application contact: Stan Rostkowski, Enrollment
Coordinator, 610-527-0200 Ext. 2187.

ST. CHARLES BORROMEO SEMINARY, OVERBROOK
Wynnewood, PA 19096

General application contact: Head of the appropriate
division, 610-667-3394.

SAINT VINCENT SEMINARY
Latrobe, PA 15650-2690
http://www.stvincent.edu/

General application contact: Sr. Cecilia Murphy, RSM,
Academic Dean, 724-539-9761.

SETON HILL COLLEGE
Greensburg, PA 15601
http://www.setonhill.edu/

General application contact: Mary Kay Cooper, Graduate
Adviser, 800-826-6234.

THOMAS JEFFERSON UNIVERSITY
Philadelphia, PA 19107
http://www.tju.edu/

General application contact: Jessie F. Pervall, Director of
Admissions, 215-503-4400.

TRINITY EPISCOPAL SCHOOL FOR MINISTRY
Ambridge, PA 15003-2397
http://www.episcopalian.org/TESM/index.htm

General application contact: Tina L. Lockett, Director of
Admissions, 724-266-3838.

UNIVERSITY OF THE ARTS
Philadelphia, PA 19102-4944

General application contact: Director of Admissions,
215-732-4832 Ext. 108.

UNIVERSITY OF THE SCIENCES IN PHILADELPHIA
Philadelphia, PA 19104-4495

General application contact: Dr. Charles W. Gibley Jr.,
Dean, School of Graduate Studies, 215-596-8937.

WAYNESBURG COLLEGE
Waynesburg, PA 15370-1222

General application contact: Dr. Joseph A. Graff, Director,
MBA Program, 412-854-3600.

WESTMINSTER COLLEGE
New Wilmington, PA 16172-0001

General application contact: Dr. Samuel A. Farmerie,
Graduate Director, 724-946-7181.

WESTMINSTER THEOLOGICAL SEMINARY
Philadelphia, PA 19118
http://www.wts.edu/

General application contact: Steve Casselli, Director of
Admissions, 215-887-5511 Ext. 3810.

YESHIVA BETH MOSHE
Scranton, PA 18505-2124

YORK COLLEGE OF PENNSYLVANIA
York, PA 17405-7199
http://www.ycp.edu/

General application contact: John F. Barbor, MBA
Coordinator, 717-815-1491.

PUERTO RICO

BAYAMÓN CENTRAL UNIVERSITY
Bayamón, PR 00960-1725

CARIBBEAN CENTER FOR ADVANCED STUDIES
San Juan, PR 00902-3711

General application contact: Carlos Rodríguez, Dean of
Students, 787-725-6500.

CENTRO DE ESTUDIOS AVANZADOS DE PUERTO RICO Y EL CARIBE
Old San Juan, PR 00902-3970

General application contact: Executive Director, 787-723-
4481.

EVANGELICAL SEMINARY OF PUERTO RICO
San Juan, PR 00925

General application contact: Rosa E. Rosado, Registrar,
787-763-6700 Ext. 238.

INTER AMERICAN UNIVERSITY OF PUERTO RICO, ARECIBO CAMPUS
Arecibo, PR 00614-4050

POLYTECHNIC UNIVERSITY OF PUERTO RICO
Hato Rey, PR 00919

PONCE SCHOOL OF MEDICINE
Ponce, PR 00732-7004

General application contact: Dean for Admissions, 787-840-
2511.

UNIVERSIDAD CENTRAL DEL CARIBE, ESCUELA DE MEDICINA
Bayamon, PR 00960-6032

General application contact: Dr. Aristides Cruz, Dean for
Admissions and Student Affairs, 787-740-1611.

UNIVERSITY OF PUERTO RICO, MEDICAL SCIENCES CAMPUS
San Juan, PR 00936-5067

General application contact: Admission Office Director, 787-753-2962.

RHODE ISLAND

BRYANT COLLEGE
Smithfield, RI 02917-1284

http:/www.bryant.edu/graduate/index.html

General application contact: Cathy Lalli, Assistant Director of Graduate Programs, 401-232-6230.

JOHNSON & WALES UNIVERSITY
Providence, RI 02903-3703

http://www.jwu.edu/

General application contact: Dr. Allan G. Freedman, Director of Graduate Admissions, 401-598-1015.

NAVAL WAR COLLEGE
Newport, RI 02841-1207

General application contact: Jean Olds, Registrar, 401-841-3373.

RHODE ISLAND SCHOOL OF DESIGN
Providence, RI 02903-2784

General application contact: Director of Admissions, 401-454-6300.

ROGER WILLIAMS UNIVERSITY
Bristol, RI 02809

General application contact: Mary D. Upton, Director of Admissions, 401-254-4555.

SOUTH CAROLINA

COASTAL CAROLINA UNIVERSITY
Conway, SC 29528-6054

General application contact: Timothy McCormick, Director of Admissions, 843-349-2026.

COLUMBIA COLLEGE
Columbia, SC 29203-5998

http://www.colacoll.edu/

General application contact: Laura McElwaine, Director of Graduate Admissions, 803-786-3871.

COLUMBIA INTERNATIONAL UNIVERSITY
Columbia, SC 29230-3122

General application contact: Brian O'Donnell, Director of Admissions, 803-754-4100.

ERSKINE THEOLOGICAL SEMINARY
Due West, SC 29639-0668

http://www.erskine.edu/seminary/index.html

General application contact: Dr. Randall T. Ruble, Associate Director of Admissions, 864-379-8885.

FURMAN UNIVERSITY
Greenville, SC 29613

General application contact: Dr. Hazel W. Harris, Director of Graduate Studies, 864-294-2213.

LUTHERAN THEOLOGICAL SOUTHERN SEMINARY
Columbia, SC 29203-5863

General application contact: Dr. H. Frederick Reisz Jr., President, 803-786-5150.

MEDICAL UNIVERSITY OF SOUTH CAROLINA
Charleston, SC 29425-0002

General application contact: Julie Johnston, Director of Admissions, 843-792-8710.

SHERMAN COLLEGE OF STRAIGHT CHIROPRACTIC
Spartanburg, SC 29304-1452

General application contact: Julie W. Clayton, Registrar, 864-578-8770 Ext. 1255.

SOUTHERN WESLEYAN UNIVERSITY
Central, SC 29630-1020

General application contact: Dr. Jim Rohe, Associate Academic Vice President, 864-639-2453 Ext. 401.

UNIVERSITY OF CHARLESTON, SOUTH CAROLINA
Charleston, SC 29424-0001

http://www.cofc.edu/

General application contact: Laura H. Hines, Graduate School Coordinator, 843-953-5614.

UNIVERSITY OF SOUTH CAROLINA–AIKEN
Aiken, SC 29801-6309

http://www.usca.sc.edu/

General application contact: Karen Morris, Graduate Studies Coordinator, 803-641-3489.

UNIVERSITY OF SOUTH CAROLINA SPARTANBURG
Spartanburg, SC 29303-4999

http://www.uscs.edu/

General application contact: Dr. Linda Randolph, Director of Graduate Programs, 864-503-5573.

SOUTH DAKOTA

AUGUSTANA COLLEGE
Sioux Falls, SD 57107
http://www.augie.edu/
General application contact: Director, 605-336-4611.

BLACK HILLS STATE UNIVERSITY
Spearfish, SD 57799-9502
http://www.bhsu.edu/
General application contact: George Earley, Director of
Graduate Studies, 605-642-6270.

**COLORADO TECHNICAL UNIVERSITY SIOUX
FALLS CAMPUS**
Sioux Falls, SD 57108

HURON UNIVERSITY
Huron, SD 57350-2798
General application contact: Dr. John Zingg, Vice President
of Academic Affairs, 605-352-8721.

MOUNT MARTY COLLEGE
Yankton, SD 57078-3724
General application contact: J. C. Crane, Director of
Admissions, 800-658-4552.

NORTH AMERICAN BAPTIST SEMINARY
Sioux Falls, SD 57105-1599
General application contact: Gordon Stork, Director of
Admissions, 605-336-6588.

OGLALA LAKOTA COLLEGE
Kyle, SD 57752-0490
General application contact: Ed Starr, Director, Graduate
Studies, 605-455-2321.

SINTE GLESKA UNIVERSITY
Rosebud, SD 57570-0490
General application contact: Dr. Archie Beauvais, Chair,
Graduate Education Programs, 605-747-2263.

**SOUTH DAKOTA SCHOOL OF MINES AND
TECHNOLOGY**
Rapid City, SD 57701-3995
General application contact: Dean of the Graduate Division,
605-394-2493.

UNIVERSITY OF SIOUX FALLS
Sioux Falls, SD 57105-1699
General application contact: Dr. Nancy Johnson, Director of
Graduate Studies, 605-331-6710.

TENNESSEE

BETHEL COLLEGE
McKenzie, TN 38201
General application contact: Dr. Ben G. McClure, Director
of Graduate Studies, 901-352-4023.

CARSON-NEWMAN COLLEGE
Jefferson City, TN 37760
General application contact: Jane W. McGill, Graduate
Admissions and Services Adviser, 423-471-3460.

CHURCH OF GOD THEOLOGICAL SEMINARY
Cleveland, TN 37320-3330
General application contact: John Jefferson, Registrar,
423-478-1131.

CUMBERLAND UNIVERSITY
Lebanon, TN 37087-3554
http://www.cumberland.edu/
General application contact: Stephanie Walker, Director of
Admissions, 615-444-2562 Ext. 1120.

DAVID LIPSCOMB UNIVERSITY
Nashville, TN 37204-3951
General application contact: Dr. Gary Holloway, Director of
Graduate Bible Studies, 615-269-1000 Ext. 2451.

EMMANUEL SCHOOL OF RELIGION
Johnson City, TN 37601-9438
General application contact: David Fulks, Director of
Admissions, 423-461-1536.

FISK UNIVERSITY
Nashville, TN 37208-3051
General application contact: Anthony Jones, Director of
Admissions, 615-329-8665.

FREED–HARDEMAN UNIVERSITY
Henderson, TN 38340-2399
General application contact: Dr. W. Stephen Johnson,
Director of Graduate Studies, 901-989-6004.

**HARDING UNIVERSITY GRADUATE SCHOOL OF
RELIGION**
Memphis, TN 38117-5499
General application contact: Donald Kinder, Associate
Dean, 901-761-1353.

JOHNSON BIBLE COLLEGE
Knoxville, TN 37998-0001
http://www.jbc.edu/
General application contact: Richard Beam, Vice President
of Academics, 423-579-2358.

LEE UNIVERSITY
Cleveland, TN 37320-3450
http://www.leeuniversity.edu/
General application contact: Admissions Office, 423-614-
8500.

LEMOYNE–OWEN COLLEGE
Memphis, TN 38126-6595

General application contact: June Jones, Director of
Admissions, 901-942-7302.

MEHARRY MEDICAL COLLEGE
Nashville, TN 37208-9989

http://www.mmc.edu/

General application contact: Allen D. Mosley, Director of
Admissions and Records, 615-327-6223.

MEMPHIS COLLEGE OF ART
Memphis, TN 38104-2764

General application contact: Susan S. Miller, Director of
Admissions, 800-727-1088.

MEMPHIS THEOLOGICAL SEMINARY
Memphis, TN 38104-4395

General application contact: Evelyn McDonald, Registrar,
901-458-8232.

MID–AMERICA BAPTIST THEOLOGICAL SEMINARY
Germantown, TN 38183-1528

General application contact: Louise Burnett, Registrar,
901-751-8453.

MIDDLE TENNESSEE SCHOOL OF ANESTHESIA
Madison, TN 37116

General application contact: Mary E. DeVasher, Vice
President and Dean, 615-868-6503.

MILLIGAN COLLEGE
Milligan College, TN 37682

General application contact: Mike Johnson, Director of
Admissions, 423-461-8730.

RHODES COLLEGE
Memphis, TN 38112-1690

http://www.rhodes.edu/

General application contact: Bill Berg, Director of
Institutional Planning and Analysis, 901-843-3551.

SOUTHERN ADVENTIST UNIVERSITY
Collegedale, TN 37315-0370

General application contact: Victor Czerkasij, Director of
Admissions, 423-238-2843.

SOUTHERN COLLEGE OF OPTOMETRY
Memphis, TN 38104-2222

General application contact: Joseph H. Hauser, Director of
Records and Admissions, 901-722-3228.

TEMPLE BAPTIST SEMINARY
Chattanooga, TN 37404-3530

General application contact: Paulette M. Trachian,
Admissions Secretary, 423-493-4221.

TENNESSEE TEMPLE UNIVERSITY
Chattanooga, TN 37404-3587

General application contact: Dr. Joe Ray, Director, Graduate
Studies in Education, 423-493-4385.

UNION UNIVERSITY
Jackson, TN 38305-3697

http://www.uu.edu/

General application contact: Carroll Griffin, Assistant Vice
President for Admissions, 901-661-5007.

UNIVERSITY OF TENNESSEE, MEMPHIS
Memphis, TN 38163-0002

General application contact: Director of Admissions,
901-448-5560.

UNIVERSITY OF TENNESSEE–OAK RIDGE GRADUATE SCHOOL OF BIOMEDICAL SCIENCES
Oak Ridge, TN 37830-8026

http://www.bio.ornl.gov/htbiomed/biomed_home.html

General application contact: Kay Gardner, Administrative
Secretary, 423-574-1227.

UNIVERSITY OF TENNESSEE SPACE INSTITUTE
Tullahoma, TN 37388-9700

General application contact: Dr. Edwin M. Gleason,
Assistant Dean for Admissions and Student Affairs,
931-393-7432.

UNIVERSITY OF THE SOUTH
Sewanee, TN 37383-1000

http://www.sewanee.edu/

General application contact: The Very Rev. Guy F. Lytle,
Dean, School of Theology, 931-598-1288.

TEXAS

AUSTIN COLLEGE
Sherman, TX 75090-4440

http://www.austinc.edu/

General application contact: Dr. John White, Director of
Teaching Program, 903-813-2459.

AUSTIN PRESBYTERIAN THEOLOGICAL SEMINARY
Austin, TX 78705-5797

General application contact: Rev. E. Quinn Fox, Director of
Vocation and Admissions, 512-472-6736.

BAPTIST MISSIONARY ASSOCIATION THEOLOGICAL SEMINARY
Jacksonville, TX 75766-5407

General application contact: Dr. Wilbur K. Benningfield,
Dean/Registrar, 903-586-2501.

BAYLOR COLLEGE OF DENTISTRY
Dallas, TX 75266-0677
http://www.tambcd.edu/
General application contact: Dr. Jack L. Long, Director of Admissions, 214-828-8230.

BAYLOR COLLEGE OF MEDICINE
Houston, TX 77030-3498
http://www.bcm.tmc.edu/
General application contact: Dr. L. Leighton Hill, Assistant Dean of the Medical School, 713-798-4842.

THE CRISWELL COLLEGE
Dallas, TX 75246-1537
http://www.criswell.edu/
General application contact: Richard A. Grimm, Vice President of Enrollment Services, 214-821-5433.

DALLAS THEOLOGICAL SEMINARY
Dallas, TX 75204-6499
http://www.dts.edu/
General application contact: Eugene W. Pond, Director of Admissions, 800-992-0998.

EAST TEXAS BAPTIST UNIVERSITY
Marshall, TX 75670-1498
General application contact: Caroline Olson, Recruitment Coordinator, 903-935-7963 Ext. 400.

EPISCOPAL THEOLOGICAL SEMINARY OF THE SOUTHWEST
Austin, TX 78768-2247
General application contact: Jan F. Wallace, Executive Secretary to the Dean, 512-472-4133 Ext. 307.

HOUSTON GRADUATE SCHOOL OF THEOLOGY
Houston, TX 77004
General application contact: Dr. Ronald D. Worden, Vice President for Academic Affairs, 713-942-9505.

ICI UNIVERSITY
Irving, TX 75063-2631
General application contact: Dr. George Stotts, Dean, 972-751-1111.

LETOURNEAU UNIVERSITY
Longview, TX 75607-7001
General application contact: Dr. Don Connors, Associate Dean of Graduate, Adult, and Continuing Studies, 903-233-3250.

LUBBOCK CHRISTIAN UNIVERSITY
Lubbock, TX 79407-2099
General application contact: Dr. Charles B. Stephenson, Director, 806-796-8800 Ext. 369.

OBLATE SCHOOL OF THEOLOGY
San Antonio, TX 78216-6693
General application contact: Christiane B. Scheel, Director of Admissions/Registrar, 210-341-1366.

PARKER COLLEGE OF CHIROPRACTIC
Dallas, TX 75229-5668
General application contact: Director of Development and Alumni, 972-438-6932 Ext. 7790.

SCHREINER COLLEGE
Kerrville, TX 78028-5697
General application contact: Dr. Thomas J. Purifoy, Director of Graduate Education Program, 830-792-7377.

SOUTH TEXAS COLLEGE OF LAW AFFILIATED WITH TEXAS A&M UNIVERSITY
Houston, TX 77002-7000
http://www.stcl.edu/
General application contact: Alicia K. Cramer, Director of Admissions, 713-646-1810.

SOUTHWESTERN ADVENTIST UNIVERSITY
Keene, TX 76059
http://www.swau.edu/
General application contact: Danna Burt, Admissions Counselor, 817-645-3921 Ext. 252.

SOUTHWESTERN ASSEMBLIES OF GOD UNIVERSITY
Waxahachie, TX 75165-2397
General application contact: Eddie Davis, Enrollment Services, 972-937-4010 Ext. 1123.

SOUTHWESTERN BAPTIST THEOLOGICAL SEMINARY
Fort Worth, TX 76122-0000
General application contact: Judy Morris, Director of Admissions, 817-923-1921 Ext. 2600.

TEXAS CHIROPRACTIC COLLEGE
Pasadena, TX 77505-1699
General application contact: Dr. Don Ellis, Provost, 281-998-6009.

TEXAS TECH UNIVERSITY HEALTH SCIENCES CENTER
Lubbock, TX 79430-0002
http://www.ttuhsc.edu/
General application contact: Dr. Barbara C. Pence, Associate Dean, 806-743-2556.

UNIVERSITY OF DALLAS
Irving, TX 75062-4799
http://www.udallas.edu/
General application contact: Dr. Glen E. Thurow, Dean, 972-721-5242.

UNIVERSITY OF NORTH TEXAS HEALTH SCIENCE CENTER AT FORT WORTH
Fort Worth, TX 76107-2699
http://www.hsc.unt.edu/
General application contact: Dr. T. John Leppi, Associate Dean of Admissions, 817-735-2204.

THE UNIVERSITY OF TEXAS HEALTH SCIENCE CENTER AT SAN ANTONIO
San Antonio, TX 78284-6200

General application contact: Interim Director of Student Services, 210-567-2628.

THE UNIVERSITY OF TEXAS–HOUSTON HEALTH SCIENCE CENTER
Houston, TX 77225-0036
http://gsbs.gs.uth.tmc.edu/

General application contact: Lois B. Monroe, Registrar, 713-500-3334.

THE UNIVERSITY OF TEXAS MEDICAL BRANCH AT GALVESTON
Galveston, TX 77555

General application contact: Robert C. Bennett, Associate Dean for Administration and Student Affairs, 409-772-2665.

THE UNIVERSITY OF TEXAS SOUTHWESTERN MEDICAL CENTER AT DALLAS
Dallas, TX 75235

General application contact: Dean, Southwestern Graduate School of Biomedical Sciences, 214-648-2174.

WAYLAND BAPTIST UNIVERSITY
Plainview, TX 79072-6998
http://www.wbu.edu/

General application contact: Dr. Bobby Hall, Director of Graduate Studies, 806-296-4574.

VERMONT

 **BENNINGTON COLLEGE**
Bennington, VT 05201-9993

General application contact: Barbara Caron, Associate Director of Admissions, 802-440-4312.

COLLEGE OF ST. JOSEPH
Rutland, VT 05701-3899

General application contact: Steve Soba, Director of Admissions, 802-773-5900 Ext. 206.

LYNDON STATE COLLEGE
Lyndonville, VT 05851

General application contact: Elaine L. Turner, Administrative Secretary, 802-626-6497.

MARLBORO COLLEGE
Marlboro, VT 05344

General application contact: John Hayes, Dean of Faculty, 802-257-4333 Ext. 234.

MIDDLEBURY COLLEGE
Middlebury, VT 05753-6002
http://www.middlebury.edu/

General application contact: appropriate program office, 802-443-5510.

SCHOOL FOR INTERNATIONAL TRAINING
Brattleboro, VT 05302-0676
http://www.sit.edu/

General application contact: Kim Noble, Admissions Assistant, 802-257-7751 Ext. 3267.

TRINITY COLLEGE OF VERMONT
Burlington, VT 05401-1470
http://www.trinityvt.edu/

General application contact: Bruce Bergland, Vice President for Academic Affairs, 802-658-0337.

VERMONT LAW SCHOOL
South Royalton, VT 05068-0096
http://www.vermontlaw.edu/

General application contact: Geoffrey R. Smith, Assistant Dean and Director of Admissions, 888-APPLYVLS.

VIRGINIA

AMERICAN MILITARY UNIVERSITY
Manassas Park, VA 20111
http://www.amunet.edu/

General application contact: Jay R. Avella, Dean, 703-330-5398 Ext. 103.

AMERICAN SCHOOL OF PROFESSIONAL PSYCHOLOGY, VIRGINIA CAMPUS
Arlington, VA 22209
http://www.aspp.edu/

General application contact: Megan M. Rigney, Coordinator of Admissions and Financial Aid, 703-243-5300.

ATLANTIC UNIVERSITY
Virginia Beach, VA 23451

General application contact: Greg Deming, Director of Admissions, 757-631-8101.

THE CATHOLIC DISTANCE UNIVERSITY
Hamilton, VA 20158
http://www.cdu.edu/

General application contact: Carla Overbeck, Graduate Registrar, 540-338-2700.

CHRISTENDOM COLLEGE
Front Royal, VA 22630-5103

General application contact: Luther P. Niehoff, Administrative Director, 703-658-4304.

CHRISTOPHER NEWPORT UNIVERSITY
Newport News, VA 23606-2998
http://www.cnu.edu/
General application contact: Graduate Admissions, 800-333-4268.

EASTERN MENNONITE UNIVERSITY
Harrisonburg, VA 22802-2462
http://www.emu.edu/
General application contact: Don A. Yoder, Director of Seminary and Graduate Programs, 540-432-4257.

EASTERN VIRGINIA MEDICAL SCHOOL
Norfolk, VA 23501-1980
http://www.evms.edu/
General application contact: Dr. Robert McCombs, Associate Dean of Student Affairs, 757-446-5805.

HOLLINS UNIVERSITY
Roanoke, VA 24020-1688
http://www.hollins.edu/
General application contact: Cathy S. Koon, Administrative Assistant, 540-362-6575.

INSTITUTE OF TEXTILE TECHNOLOGY
Charlottesville, VA 22903-4614
General application contact: Tracey Templeton, Registrar, 804-296-5511 Ext. 275.

JUDGE ADVOCATE GENERAL'S SCHOOL, U.S. ARMY
Charlottesville, VA 22903-1781
General application contact: Lt. Col. Wendell Jewell, Admissions Director, 804-972-6310.

MARY BALDWIN COLLEGE
Staunton, VA 24401
General application contact: Dr. Beth Roberts, Director, MAT Program, 540-887-7333.

THE PROTESTANT EPISCOPAL THEOLOGICAL SEMINARY IN VIRGINIA
Alexandria, VA 22304
General application contact: Jan Sienkiewicz, Admissions Secretary, 703-370-6600.

REGENT UNIVERSITY
Virginia Beach, VA 23464-9800
http://www.regent.edu/
General application contact: Admissions Office of the appropriate school, 800-373-5504.

UNION THEOLOGICAL SEMINARY AND PRESBYTERIAN SCHOOL OF CHRISTIAN EDUCATION
Richmond, VA 23227-4597
http://www.utsva.edu/
General application contact: James W. Dale, Director of Admissions, 804-355-0671.

VIRGINIA UNION UNIVERSITY
Richmond, VA 23220-1170
General application contact: Ella N. Grimes, Registrar, 804-257-5715.

WASHINGTON AND LEE UNIVERSITY
Lexington, VA 24150 0303
General application contact: Susan Palmer, Assistant Dean, 540-463-8503.

WASHINGTON

ANTIOCH UNIVERSITY SEATTLE
Seattle, WA 98121-1814
http://www.seattleantioch.edu/
General application contact: Vicki Tolbert, Admissions Officer, 206-441-5352.

BASTYR UNIVERSITY
Bothell, WA 98011
General application contact: Stephen Bangs, Director of Admissions, 425-602-3100.

THE EVERGREEN STATE COLLEGE
Olympia, WA 98505
General application contact: Dr. Masao Saigiyama, Academic Dean, 360-866-6000 Ext. 6512.

THE LEADERSHIP INSTITUTE OF SEATTLE
Bellevue, WA 98004-6934
General application contact: Lynn Morrison, Admissions Director, 425-635-1187 Ext. 253.

NORTHWEST BAPTIST SEMINARY
Tacoma, WA 98407

NORTHWEST GRADUATE SCHOOL OF THE MINISTRY
Kirkland, WA 98033-5932
General application contact: Gail Tuck, Admissions Coordinator, 425-828-9112.

NORTHWEST INSTITUTE OF ACUPUNCTURE AND ORIENTAL MEDICINE
Seattle, WA 98103
General application contact: Frederick O. Lanphear, President, 206-633-2419.

UNIVERSITY OF PUGET SOUND
Tacoma, WA 98416-0005
General application contact: George Mills, Director of Admissions, 253-756-3211.

WEST VIRGINIA

ALDERSON–BROADDUS COLLEGE
Philippi, WV 26416
http://ab.wvnet.edu/
General application contact: Dick Mercer, Director, Master's Degree Program, 304-457-6356.

SALEM–TEIKYO UNIVERSITY
Salem, WV 26426-0500
http://stulib.salem-teikyo.wvnet.edu/
General application contact: Carolyn S. Ritter, Director of Admissions, 304-782-5336.

WEST VIRGINIA SCHOOL OF OSTEOPATHIC MEDICINE
Lewisburg, WV 24901-1128
General application contact: John N. Gorby, Director of Admissions and Registrar, 304-645-6270 Ext. 373.

WEST VIRGINIA UNIVERSITY INSTITUTE OF TECHNOLOGY
Montgomery, WV 25136
General application contact: S. E. Thornton, Associate Dean, 304-442-3162.

WISCONSIN

ALVERNO COLLEGE
Milwaukee, WI 53234-3922
http://www.alverno.edu/
General application contact: Sara Jane Kennedy, Assistant Director of Admissions, 414-382-6100.

CARROLL COLLEGE
Waukesha, WI 53186-5593
http://carroll1.cc.edu/
General application contact: Dr. Mary Hauser, Director, 414-524-7289.

CONCORDIA UNIVERSITY WISCONSIN
Mequon, WI 53097-2402
http://www.cuw.edu/
General application contact: Dr. John F. Walther, Dean of Graduate Studies, 414-243-4285.

LAKELAND COLLEGE
Sheboygan, WI 53082-0359
General application contact: Rebecca Hagan, Graduate Program Coordinator, 414-565-1256.

MARANATHA BAPTIST BIBLE COLLEGE
Watertown, WI 53094
http://www.mbbc.edu/
General application contact: Jeannie Wetzel, Registrar's Secretary, 920-261-9300 Ext. 363.

MEDICAL COLLEGE OF WISCONSIN
Milwaukee, WI 53226-0509
http://www.mcw.edu/
General application contact: Nancy J. Heltemes, Graduate Coordinator, 414-456-8603.

MILWAUKEE SCHOOL OF ENGINEERING
Milwaukee, WI 53202-3109
http://www.msoe.edu/
General application contact: Dan Vande Yacht, Graduate Counselor, 800-321-6763.

MOUNT MARY COLLEGE
Milwaukee, WI 53222-4597
General application contact: Sr. Jane Forni, Associate Academic Dean for Graduate Programs, 414-256-1252.

NASHOTAH HOUSE
Nashotah, WI 53058-9793
General application contact: Chip Swearngan, Director of Admissions, 414-646-3371 Ext. 222.

SACRED HEART SCHOOL OF THEOLOGY
Hales Corners, WI 53130-0429
General application contact: Rev. Thomas L. Knoebel, Director of Admissions, 414-425-8300 Ext. 6984.

SAINT FRANCIS SEMINARY
St. Francis, WI 53235-3795
General application contact: Dr. David A. Stosur, Academic Dean, 414-747-6450.

ST. NORBERT COLLEGE
De Pere, WI 54115-2099
General application contact: see individual programs, 920-403-3181.

SILVER LAKE COLLEGE
Manitowoc, WI 54220-9319
General application contact: Sandra Schwartz, Director of Admissions, 920-684-5955.

WISCONSIN SCHOOL OF PROFESSIONAL PSYCHOLOGY
Milwaukee, WI 53225-4960
General application contact: Dr. Howard J. Haven, Dean, 414-464-9777.

School Index